Copyright © 1983, 1987, 1992

BY

The Michie Company

Library of Congress Card Number: 92-82874

ISBN 1-55834-001-7

# FEDERAL CRIMINAL TRIALS

## Third Edition

## JAMES C. CISSELL

Cincinnati, Ohio

Formerly, United States Attorney,
Southern District of Ohio

THE MICHIE COMPANY
*Law Publishers*
CHARLOTTESVILLE, VIRGINIA

# SUMMARY TABLE OF CONTENTS

*Page*

*Summary Table of Contents* ............................................... iii
*Table of Contents* ........................................................ v
*Preface to Third Edition* ................................................. xxi
*Foreword to First Edition* ............................................... xxiii
*Preface to First Edition* ................................................ xxv

---

## PART I

## CONSTITUTIONAL PROTECTIONS AND PROCEDURES

Chapter

1    Jurisdiction and Venue .................................... 3
2    Search and Seizure ....................................... 13
3    Fifth and Sixth Amendment Protections ............. 77
4    The Grand Jury and Immunity ......................... 111
5    Preliminary Proceedings .............................. 141
6    Arraignment and Plea .................................. 153
7    Pretrial Discovery and Disclosure .................... 167
8    Trial Discovery of Prior Statements ................. 191
9    Joinder and Severance ................................. 207
10   Jeopardy and Mistrial ................................. 223
11   Prosecutorial Misconduct and Vindictiveness ....... 237
12   Trial ................................................... 255
13   Post-Trial Proceedings ................................ 309

## PART II

## THE LAW OF EVIDENCE

14   Judicial Notice ......................................... 345
15   Weight of the Evidence and Relevancy ............... 353
16   Demonstrative Evidence ............................... 377
17   Documentary Evidence ................................ 387
18   Examination of a Witness ............................. 397
19   Privileges ............................................. 425
20   Opinion Evidence ..................................... 463
21   Hearsay and Exceptions .............................. 477

Appendix A. Amendments to the Constitution of the United
            States ........................................... 517

*Page*

Appendix B. Federal Rules of Criminal Procedure ................. 519

Appendix C. Federal Rules of Evidence ............................ 559

---

*Table of Cases* .............................................................. 579
*Table of Statutes, Rules and Sentencing Guidelines* ................. 705
*Index* ....................................................................... 715

# TABLE OF CONTENTS

|                                          | Page   |
|------------------------------------------|--------|
| *Summary Table of Contents*              | iii    |
| *Preface to Third Edition*               | xxi    |
| *Foreword to First Edition*              | xxiii  |
| *Preface to First Edition*               | xxv    |

PART I

CONSTITUTIONAL PROTECTIONS AND PROCEDURES

CHAPTER 1. JURISDICTION AND VENUE ...... 3
§ 101. Jurisdiction ...... 3
§ 102. — Subject Matter Jurisdiction ...... 4
§ 103. — Jurisdiction Over the Person of the Defendant ...... 5
§ 104. Venue ...... 5
§ 105. — State and District of the Crime ...... 6
§ 106. — — Offenses Committed in More Than One District .... 6
§ 107. — — Offenses Not Committed in Any District ...... 7
§ 108. — Proof of Venue ...... 7
§ 109. — Waiver of Venue ...... 8
§ 110. — Transfer of Venue ...... 9
§ 111. — — Transfer Because of Prejudice to Defendant ...... 9
§ 112. — — Transfer for the Convenience of Parties and Witnesses ...... 10
§ 113. — — Transfer for Plea and Sentence ...... 11

CHAPTER 2. SEARCH AND SEIZURE ...... 13
§ 201. Fourth Amendment Protections ...... 14
§ 202. Private Searches ...... 15
§ 203. Foreign Searches of Aliens ...... 16
§ 204. Search Warrants ...... 16
§ 205. Who May Issue a Search Warrant ...... 16
§ 206. — Probable Cause for Search Warrant ...... 17
§ 207. — — Probable Cause Established by Hearsay ...... 18
§ 208. — — Sufficiency Determined by Common Sense Standards ...... 20
§ 209. — — Magistrate Must Be Neutral ...... 20
§ 210. — — False Statements in Affidavit ...... 21
§ 211. — Particularity of Description ...... 22
§ 212. — Execution of Search Warrant ...... 24

*Page*

§ 213. — — Who May Execute Warrant .............................. 24

§ 214. — — When Must Search Warrant Be Executed ............ 25

§ 215. — — Manner of Entry to Search .............................. 26

§ 216. — Telephone Search Warrants .............................. 28

§ 217. Warrantless Searches .......................................... 29

§ 218. — Search Incident to Valid Arrest .......................... 30

§ 219. — — Validity of the Arrest .................................. 30

§ 220. — — When a Person Is Under Arrest ...................... 33

§ 221. — — Arrest Must Be Made in Good Faith and Not as a Pretext to Justify Search .......................................... 34

§ 222. — — Search Must Be Contemporaneous With Arrest .... 34

§ 223. — — Scope of Warrantless Searches Incident to Arrest .. 35

§ 224. — — — Search of the Person .............................. 36

§ 225. — — — Articles Carried by Arrestee ...................... 36

§ 226. — — — Areas Within Arrestee's Immediate Control .... 37

§ 227. — Seizures Without Probable Cause ........................ 38

§ 228. — — "Stop and Frisk" ...................................... 38

§ 229. — — Border and Customs Searches ........................ 42

§ 230. — — Detention of Occupants While Home Is Searched Pursuant to a Warrant .......................................... 44

§ 231. — Exigent Circumstances That Justify a Warrantless Search .............................................................. 44

§ 232. — — Officers Responding to Emergency .................... 45

§ 233. — — Threatened Destruction or Removal of Contraband or Likely Escape of Suspect .................................... 46

§ 234. — — "Hot Pursuit" .......................................... 47

§ 235. — Vehicle Searches .......................................... 48

§ 236. — — Inventory Searches of Vehicles ........................ 49

§ 237. — — Searches of Containers Found in Vehicle ............ 50

§ 238. — Evidence in Plain View .................................... 51

§ 239. — — Abandoned Property .................................... 52

§ 240. — — Curtilage and the Open Fields Doctrine .............. 53

§ 241. — Anti-Skyjacking Searches .................................. 54

§ 242. — Prison Searches ............................................ 55

§ 243. — Consent Searches .......................................... 56

§ 244. — — Use of Deceit to Secure Consent ...................... 58

§ 245. — — Third-Party Consent .................................... 58

§ 246. Evidence Affected by a Search and Seizure ................ 60

§ 247. — Property That May Be Seized .............................. 60

§ 248. — The Exclusionary Rule .................................... 61

§ 249. Motions to Suppress .......................................... 64

*Page*

§ 250. — Timing of Motions to Suppress ............................. 64
§ 251. — Hearing ................................................. 64
§ 252. — — Burden of Proof ..................................... 64
§ 253. — — Evidentiary Rules .................................. 65
§ 254. — — Right to a Hearing ................................. 65
§ 255. — Standing ............................................... 66
§ 256. — Appeal From Suppression Hearing ..................... 67
§ 257. Wiretapping and Other Electronic Surveillance ........... 68
§ 258. — Interception Pursuant to Court Order ................. 68
§ 259. — — Authorization ..................................... 69
§ 260. — — Application and Order ............................. 69
§ 261. — — — Application .................................... 69
§ 262. — — — Order .......................................... 71
§ 263. — — — Surreptitious Entry ............................ 72
§ 264. — — — Minimization ................................... 72
§ 265. — — — Sealing of Applications, Orders, and Intercepted
       Communications ......................................... 73
§ 266. — — — Motion to Suppress ............................. 73
§ 267. — — Scope of Title III ................................. 74
§ 268. — Interception With Consent of One Party ............... 75

CHAPTER 3. FIFTH AND SIXTH AMENDMENT PROTEC-
TIONS ......................................................... 77
§ 301. Confessions .............................................. 77
§ 302. — Form .................................................. 78
§ 303. — Need for Corroboration ............................... 78
§ 304. — Confession After Arrest But Before Initial Appearance
       — "Unnecessary Delay." ................................. 80
§ 305. — Confessions and the Rights to Silence and Counsel ..... 83
§ 306. — — When Miranda Rights Attach ....................... 86
§ 307. — — Scope of Miranda .................................. 89
§ 308. — — Right to Terminate Questioning .................... 90
§ 309. — — Silence of Defendant .............................. 92
§ 310. — — Confessions Obtained After Indictment ............. 92
§ 311. — — Impeachment with Statements Taken in Violation
       of the Fifth and Sixth Amendments ..................... 94
§ 312. — "Fruit of the Poisonous Tree" ........................ 95
§ 313. — Coerced Confessions .................................. 96
§ 314. — Use of Confessions at Joint Trials ................... 98
§ 315. — Inadmissibility of Statements Related to Pleas and Of-
       fers of Pleas ............................................ 100

*Page*

§ 316. Identifications Before Trial ..................................... 100
§ 317. — Sixth Amendment Rights .................................... 101
§ 318. — Fifth Amendment Due Process Rights ................... 104
§ 319. — Evidence of Extrajudicial Identifications ................ 108

CHAPTER 4. THE GRAND JURY AND IMMUNITY ............ 111
§ 400. Introduction .................................................... 111
§ 401. Procedures ..................................................... 112
§ 402. Supervisory Powers of District Court ........................ 114
§ 403. Evidence Before Grand Jury ................................. 115
§ 404. — Calling and Questioning of Witnesses and Warnings .. 117
§ 405. — — Miranda Warnings ..................................... 119
§ 406. — — Exclusionary Rule ..................................... 119
§ 407. — — Questions Based on Illegal Electronic
Surveillance ..................................................... 120
§ 408. — — After Indictment Returned ............................. 121
§ 409. — Subpoenas Duces Tecum ................................. 121
§ 410. Secrecy of Proceedings and Disclosure ...................... 124
§ 411. — Matters Occurring Before Grand Jury ................... 125
§ 412. — Attorney for the Government ............................. 127
§ 413. — Other Government Personnel ............................. 127
§ 414. — Preliminary to or in Connection With Judicial Proceedings ......................................................... 128
§ 415. — Disclosure by or to Witnesses ............................ 129
§ 416. — For Use in Government Civil Actions .................... 130
§ 417. — Sealed Indictments ....................................... 130
§ 418. Motions Challenging Multiple Representation of Witnesses ........................................................... 131
§ 419. Immunity ...................................................... 132
§ 420. — Prosecution for Perjury .................................. 134
§ 421. — Other Sovereigns .......................................... 135
§ 422. — Use in Civil Proceedings ................................. 135
§ 423. — Immunity for Defense Witnesses ......................... 136
§ 424. Procedures for Enforcement of Subpoenas and Orders
Compelling Testimony ......................................... 137
§ 425. — Civil Contempt Proceedings .............................. 137
§ 426. — Criminal Contempt Proceedings ......................... 139
§ 427. Grand Jury Reports ........................................... 140

CHAPTER 5. PRELIMINARY PROCEEDINGS ................... 141
§ 501. Initial Appearance ............................................ 141
§ 502. Removal Hearing ............................................. 142

*Page*

§ 503. Preliminary Examination .................................... 143
§ 504. Bail ................................................................. 144
§ 505. Release or Detention ...................................... 146
§ 506. — Pretrial Release or Detention ...................... 146
§ 507. — — Release on Conditions ............................ 146
§ 508. — — Temporary Detention .............................. 147
§ 509. — — Detention .............................................. 147
§ 510. — — Factors to be Considered ........................ 148
§ 511. — — Release or Detention Order ..................... 149
§ 512. — — Appeal of Release or Detention Order ........ 149
§ 513. — Release During Trial ................................... 150
§ 514. — Release or Detention After Conviction ........... 150
§ 515. — — Pending Sentencing ................................ 150
§ 516. — — Pending Appeal ...................................... 150
§ 517. — — — Substantial Question ........................... 150
§ 518. — — — Likely to Result in Reversal or New Trial ........ 151
§ 519. — — Procedures and Appeal of Denial ............... 151
§ 520. — Release of Material Witness ......................... 151
§ 521. — Penalties for Failure to Appear .................... 152
§ 522. — Penalty for Offense Committed While on Release ...... 152

CHAPTER 6. ARRAIGNMENT AND PLEA ...................... 153
§ 601. Arraignment ................................................. 153
§ 602. Pleas ............................................................ 154
§ 603. — Effect of Guilty Plea ................................... 154
§ 604. — Nolo Contendere Plea ................................. 155
§ 605. — Requirements for Accepting Pleas of Guilty or Nolo Contendere ................................................. 155
§ 606. — — Voluntariness of Plea .............................. 155
§ 607. — — Advice to Defendant ............................... 156
§ 608. — — — Understanding the Nature of the Charge ........ 157
§ 609. — — — Understanding the Penalty ................... 158
§ 610. — — Factual Basis for the Plea ........................ 160
§ 611. — Plea Agreements ........................................ 160
§ 612. — — Participation by Judge in Plea Discussions .......... 162
§ 613. — — Breach of Plea Agreement ....................... 162
§ 614. — Conditional Pleas ....................................... 163
§ 615. — Inadmissibility of Pleas and Plea Discussions .......... 164
§ 616. — Effect of a Technical Violation of Rule 11 ........ 165
§ 617. Withdrawal of Plea of Guilty or Nolo Contendere .......... 165
§ 618. — Withdrawal Before Sentence ........................ 165

*Page*

§ 619. — Withdrawal After Sentence ................................. 166

CHAPTER 7. PRETRIAL DISCOVERY AND DISCLOSURE .. 167
§ 700. Introduction ........................................... 167
§ 701. Bill of Particulars ..................................... 168
§ 702. Notice of Alibi ......................................... 170
§ 703. Notice of Defense Based Upon Mental Condition ........... 171
§ 704. Notice of Defense Based Upon Public Authority ........... 172
§ 705. Discovery and Inspection ............................... 173
§ 706. — Statements of Defendant ............................. 173
§ 707. — Defendant's Prior Record ............................ 175
§ 708. — Documents and Tangible Objects ...................... 175
§ 709. — Reports of Examinations and Tests ................... 177
§ 710. — Disclosure of Evidence by the Defendant .............. 177
§ 711. — Limitations Upon Discovery .......................... 178
§ 712. — — Discovery of Witness Statements and the Identities
      of Witnesses ......................................... 178
§ 713. — — Disclosure of Identities of Informants ............. 180
§ 714. — — Duty to Disclose "Exculpatory" Evidence ........... 181
§ 715. — Protective Orders ................................... 182
§ 716. — Sanctions for Failure to Provide Discovery ........... 182
§ 717. Subpoena for the Production of Documentary Evidence
      and Objects .......................................... 184
§ 718. Rule of *Brady v. Maryland* ........................... 185
§ 719. — Situations Requiring Disclosure ..................... 186
§ 720. — Material That Must Be Disclosed .................... 188
§ 721. — — Exculpatory Material ............................. 188
§ 722. — — Impeachment Material ............................ 189
§ 723. — Time for Disclosure ................................ 190
§ 724. Preservation of Evidence ............................. 190

CHAPTER 8. TRIAL      DISCOVERY      OF      PRIOR
STATEMENTS ................................................. 191
§ 801. Jencks Act: 18 U.S.C. § 3500; and Rule 26.2 ............ 191
§ 802. — Procedure for Obtaining Documents .................. 192
§ 803. — — Request by Defense Counsel ...................... 192
§ 804. — — Time for Production ............................. 193
§ 805. — — The Trial Court's Obligation ..................... 194
§ 806. — — Possession of the United States .................. 195
§ 807. — — Relation to Witness' Direct Testimony ............. 196
§ 808. — Documents Subject to Production .................... 198

*Page*

§ 809. — — Written, Signed, Adopted, or Approved by the Witness ........................................................... 199
§ 810. — — Substantially Verbatim and Contemporaneously Made ........................................................... 200
§ 811. — Consequences of Refusal to Produce ...................... 201
§ 812. — — Destruction of Notes ............................... 201
§ 813. — — Harmless Error Rule ............................... 203
§ 814. Rule 26.2 Material of Defense Witnesses .................... 204

CHAPTER 9. JOINDER AND SEVERANCE ...................... 207
§ 901. Joinder of Offenses and Defendants ...................... 207
§ 902. — Joinder of Offenses ............................... 208
§ 903. — — Multiple Counts ............................... 208
§ 904. — — Multiple Indictments ............................ 209
§ 905. — — Duplicity and Multiplicity ........................ 210
§ 906. — Joinder of Defendants ............................ 211
§ 907. — — Same Indictment ............................... 211
§ 908. — — Consolidation for Trial ......................... 213
§ 909. — — Conspiracy ................................... 213
§ 910. Severance — Relief From Prejudicial Joinder .............. 214
§ 911. — Trial Court's Discretion ........................... 215
§ 912. — Severance of Offenses ............................ 215
§ 913. — Severance of Defendants .......................... 216
§ 914. — — Need for Codefendant's Testimony ................ 217
§ 915. — — Codefendant's Confession ....................... 218
§ 916. — — Conflicting Defenses ........................... 219
§ 917. — — Conspiracy ................................... 220
§ 918. — Waiver ......................................... 220
§ 919. Misjoinder ......................................... 220

CHAPTER 10. JEOPARDY AND MISTRIAL ...................... 223
§ 1001. Jeopardy ......................................... 223
§ 1002. — Same Offense ................................... 224
§ 1003. — Lesser Included Offense .......................... 226
§ 1004. — Dual Sovereigns ................................. 227
§ 1005. — The Petite Policy ................................ 228
§ 1006. — Acquittals and Dismissals ........................ 228
§ 1007. Mistrial ........................................... 229
§ 1008. — Manifest Necessity ............................... 230
§ 1009. — Prosecutorial Manipulation to Abort Trial ............ 231
§ 1010. Appeals ........................................... 231
§ 1011. Collateral Estoppel ................................. 233

Page

§ 1012. Sentencing ........................................................ 234

CHAPTER 11. PROSECUTORIAL MISCONDUCT AND VIN-
DICTIVENESS .......................................................... 237
§ 1100. Introduction ...................................................... 237
§ 1101. Prosecutorial Misconduct ...................................... 237
§ 1102. — Opening Statement Errors .................................. 237
§ 1103. — — Reference to Inadmissible Evidence .................. 238
§ 1104. — — Statements of Personal Opinion ...................... 239
§ 1105. — — Argumentative and Inflammatory Comments ..... 240
§ 1106. — Proof Presentation Problems ............................. 240
§ 1107. — — False or Misleading Testimony ....................... 240
§ 1108. — — Undiscovered and Undisclosed Favorable Defense
Evidence .......................................................... 241
§ 1109. — — Forcing a Claim of Privilege ......................... 243
§ 1110. — Closing Argument Errors ................................. 243
§ 1111. — — Reasonable Inferences and Inflammatory Comments ............................................................. 244
§ 1112. — — Response to Defense Provocations ................... 246
§ 1113. — — Statement of Law — Invading the Province of the
Court .............................................................. 247
§ 1114. — — Statement of Personal Opinion ....................... 247
§ 1115. — — Comment on Post-Arrest and In-Trial Silence ..... 249
§ 1116. — Standard for Review ...................................... 250
§ 1117. — Sanctions .................................................... 251
§ 1118. Prosecutorial Vindictiveness ................................ 252

CHAPTER 12. TRIAL ................................................... 255
§ 1201. Speedy Trial .................................................... 256
§ 1202. — The Right to a Speedy Trial ............................. 256
§ 1203. — Constitutional Speedy Trial Protection ................. 257
§ 1204. — — When the Right to a Speedy Trial Attaches ........ 257
§ 1205. — — The Barker v. Wingo Balancing Test ............... 258
§ 1206. — — — Length of Delay ..................................... 258
§ 1207. — — — Reasons for Delay ................................... 259
§ 1208. — — — Timely Assertion of Speedy Trial Right ......... 260
§ 1209. — — — Prejudice to the Defendant Caused by Delay ... 260
§ 1210. — The Speedy Trial Act ..................................... 261
§ 1211. — — Application ............................................... 262
§ 1212. — — First Interval ............................................ 262
§ 1213. — — Second Interval ......................................... 263
§ 1214. — — Reinstitution of Prosecution .......................... 264

|  |  | *Page* |
|---|---|---|
| § 1215. — — — Dismissed Charges | | 264 |
| § 1216. — — — Charges Reinstated on Appeal | | 264 |
| § 1217. — — — Retrial | | 265 |
| § 1218. — — Excludable Time | | 265 |
| § 1219. — — — Other Proceedings | | 265 |
| § 1220. — — — Examination, Deferral, and Treatment | | 266 |
| § 1221. — — — Trial of Defendant on Other Charges | | 266 |
| § 1222. — — — Interlocutory Appeals | | 267 |
| § 1223. — — — Pretrial Motions | | 267 |
| § 1224. — — — Removal of Defendant or Transfer of Case | | 268 |
| § 1225. — — — Plea Agreement | | 268 |
| § 1226. — — — Proceedings Under Advisement | | 268 |
| § 1227. — — — Pretrial Diversion | | 269 |
| § 1228. — — — Absence or Unavailability of Defendant or Witness | | 269 |
| § 1229. — — — Physical or Mental Incompetency | | 270 |
| § 1230. — — — Joinder and Severance | | 270 |
| § 1231. — — — Continuance Which Furthers Ends of Justice | | 270 |
| § 1232. — — Withdrawn Plea | | 271 |
| § 1233. — — Incarcerated Defendant | | 271 |
| § 1234. — — Sanctions | | 272 |
| § 1235. — — Waiver | | 273 |
| § 1236. — — High Risk Designees and Detainees | | 273 |
| § 1237. — — Dismissal by the Court | | 274 |
| § 1238. — — Appeal | | 274 |
| § 1239. — Pre-Accusation Delay | | 275 |
| § 1240. The Right to Trial by Jury | | 277 |
| § 1241. — Size of Jury | | 278 |
| § 1242. — Unanimous Jury Verdict | | 279 |
| § 1243. — Waiver of Jury Trial | | 279 |
| § 1244. Jury Selection and Control | | 280 |
| § 1245. — Challenge of Array | | 281 |
| § 1246. — Voir Dire | | 282 |
| § 1247. — Challenges for Cause | | 285 |
| § 1248. — Peremptory Challenges | | 286 |
| § 1249. — Contamination by Trial Participants | | 287 |
| § 1250. — Materials in Jury Room | | 289 |
| § 1251. Trial Management | | 290 |
| § 1252. — Limiting and Cautionary Instructions | | 290 |
| § 1253. — Requests for Instructions | | 291 |
| § 1254. — Objections to Instructions and Waiver | | 292 |

Page

§ 1255. — Special Verdicts and Interrogatories ..................... 293
§ 1256. — — Special Verdicts ........................................ 293
§ 1257. — — Criminal Forfeiture Special Verdicts ................ 293
§ 1258. — — Special Interrogatories ................................. 294
§ 1259. — — Post-Verdict Juror Interrogation ..................... 294
§ 1260. — Supplemental Instructions ............................... 295
§ 1261. — Allen Charge ................................................ 296
§ 1262. — Polling Jurors .............................................. 298
§ 1263. Instructions on the Law ..................................... 299
§ 1264. — The Contents of the Charge ............................. 299
§ 1265. — — Lesser Included Offenses ............................. 301
§ 1266. — — Defense Theories ...................................... 302
§ 1267. — Reasonable Doubt and Presumptions ................... 303
§ 1268. — — Reasonable Doubt ..................................... 303
§ 1269. — — Presumptions .......................................... 303
§ 1270. — Credibility Issues ......................................... 304
§ 1271. Motion for Acquittal ......................................... 306
§ 1272. — Grounds for Motion for Acquittal ....................... 306
§ 1273. — Time for Making Motion ................................. 307
§ 1274. — — At Close of Government's Case ...................... 307
§ 1275. — — At Close of All the Evidence ......................... 307
§ 1276. — — After Discharge of Jury ............................... 307

CHAPTER 13. POST-TRIAL PROCEEDINGS ..................... 309
§ 1301. Motion for New Trial ........................................ 310
§ 1302. — Newly Discovered Evidence ............................. 310
§ 1303. — Other Grounds ............................................ 312
§ 1304. — Time for Motion ........................................... 312
§ 1305. Motion for Arrest of Judgment ............................. 313
§ 1306. Sentence ..................................................... 314
§ 1307. — Introduction ............................................... 314
§ 1308. — — Guidelines, Policy Statements and Commentary .. 315
§ 1309. — — Policy Considerations ................................. 315
§ 1310. — Real Offense or Charge Offense Sentencing ........... 316
§ 1311. — — Effective Date of Sentencing Reform Act .......... 316
§ 1312. — — Constitutionality ...................................... 316
§ 1313. — — Plea Agreements ...................................... 317
§ 1314. — Plea Agreement Procedure .............................. 317
§ 1315. — — Standards for Acceptance of Plea Agreements ..... 318
§ 1316. — Presentence Investigation and Report ................. 318

Page

§ 1317. — — Contents of the Report of Presentence Investigation ........................................................................ 319

§ 1318. — — Disclosure of the Report of Presentence Investigation ........................................................................ 320

§ 1319. — Imposition of Sentence ..................................... 321

§ 1320. — — Time for Imposition ..................................... 321

§ 1321. — — Allocution .............................................. 323

§ 1322. — — Factors Which May Not Be Considered .............. 323

§ 1323. — — Application of Sentencing Guidelines ............... 325

§ 1324. — — Departure from Guidelines ........................... 328

§ 1325. — — — Departure to Increase Sentence .................. 329

§ 1326. — — — Departure to Reduce Sentence .................... 330

§ 1327. Appeal where there is Departure .......................... 331

§ 1328. — — Departure for Substantial Assistance to Authorities ....................................................................... 331

§ 1329. — — Probation .............................................. 332

§ 1330. — — Concurrent and Consecutive Sentences ............. 333

§ 1331. — — Term of Supervisory Release after Imprisonment .. 333

§ 1332. — — Imposition of Fine ..................................... 333

§ 1333. — — — Factors to be Considered in Imposing Fines ..... 334

§ 1334. — — — Modification or Remission of Fine ............... 334

§ 1335. — — Assistance for Victims ................................ 335

§ 1336. — — — Special Assessments ................................ 335

§ 1337. — — — Restitution .......................................... 335

§ 1338. — — — Notice to Victims ................................... 336

§ 1339. — — Resolving Disputed Sentencing Facts .............. 336

§ 1340. — — Sentencing of Organizations ......................... 338

§ 1341. — — Juvenile Offenders .................................... 338

§ 1342. — Judgment of Conviction ................................. 339

§ 1343. — Correction of Sentence .................................. 339

§ 1344. — Modification of Sentence after Imposition ............ 339

§ 1345. — Notice to Defendant of Right to Appeal .............. 340

§ 1346. — Review of Sentences .................................... 341

### PART II

### THE LAW OF EVIDENCE

CHAPTER 14. JUDICIAL NOTICE .................................. 345

§ 1400. Introduction ............................................... 345

§ 1401. Adjudicative Facts ........................................ 345

§ 1402. Procedure for Taking Notice .............................. 346

*Page*

§ 1403. Matters to be Noticed .......................................... 347

CHAPTER 15. WEIGHT OF THE EVIDENCE AND RELE-
VANCY ............................................................... 353
§ 1501. Burden of Proof ................................................ 353
§ 1502. — Motion for Judgment of Acquittal ....................... 354
§ 1503. — Specific Items of Proof ................................... 355
§ 1504. Presumptions and Inferences ............................... 356
§ 1505. — Constitutionality of Presumptions in Criminal
Cases ............................................................ 356
§ 1506. — Specific Presumptions and Inferences ................... 357
§ 1507. — — Presumption of Innocence ............................ 357
§ 1508. — — Sanity .................................................. 357
§ 1509. — — Intent .................................................. 357
§ 1510. — — Continuance of Conspiracy ........................... 358
§ 1511. — — Knowledge of the Law ................................ 358
§ 1512. — — Regularity of Proceedings ........................... 358
§ 1513. — — Recent Possession of Fruits of Crime ............... 359
§ 1514. — — Failure to Call a Witness ............................ 360
§ 1515. — — Failure of Defendant to Testify ..................... 361
§ 1516. Circumstantial Evidence ................................... 361
§ 1517. Relevancy ..................................................... 362
§ 1518. — Evidence of the Defendant's Character ................. 364
§ 1519. — — Methods of Proving Character ....................... 365
§ 1520. — — Cross-Examination and Rebuttal of Character
Witnesses ...................................................... 366
§ 1521. — Proof of Other Crimes ................................... 367
§ 1522. — — Prerequisites .......................................... 368
§ 1523. — — Motive .................................................. 370
§ 1524. — — Intent and Knowledge ................................ 371
§ 1525. — — Identity ................................................ 372
§ 1526. — — Plan, Scheme, or Design ............................. 373
§ 1527. — Evidence of a Guilty Mind .............................. 373
§ 1528. — — Flight and Concealment of Identity ................. 373
§ 1529. — — False Exculpatory Statements ....................... 374
§ 1530. — — Suppression, Destruction, or Fabrication of Evidence ........................................................... 374
§ 1531. — Habit and Custom ........................................ 374
§ 1532. — Motive ..................................................... 375

CHAPTER 16. DEMONSTRATIVE EVIDENCE ................. 377
§ 1600. Introduction .................................................. 377

*Page*

§ 1601. Audio and Video Recordings ................................... 377
§ 1602. — Audio Recordings ............................................ 377
§ 1603. — Video Recordings ............................................ 379
§ 1604. Photographs ....................................................... 380
§ 1605. Summary Charts ................................................. 380
§ 1606. Models, Overlays, and Experiments ......................... 383
§ 1607. — Models .......................................................... 383
§ 1608. — Overlays ........................................................ 384
§ 1609. — Experiments ................................................... 384
§ 1610. Computer Records ............................................... 385
§ 1611. Jury View of Premises .......................................... 385

CHAPTER 17. DOCUMENTARY EVIDENCE .................... 387
§ 1701. Authentication and Admissibility ............................ 387
§ 1702. — Official Documents ........................................... 388
§ 1703. — Private or Nonofficial Documents ........................ 389
§ 1704. — Documents Containing Inadmissible Material ........ 391
§ 1705. Best Evidence Rule .............................................. 392
§ 1706. — Exceptions ..................................................... 393
§ 1707. — Admission of Secondary Evidence ........................ 394
§ 1708. Use of Entire Writing or Recorded Statement ............. 396

CHAPTER 18. EXAMINATION OF A WITNESS ................. 397
§ 1801. Leading Questions .............................................. 397
§ 1802. Refreshing Recollection ....................................... 399
§ 1803. — Inspection of an Exhibit .................................... 401
§ 1804. — Use on Cross-Examination ................................. 402
§ 1805. Cross-Examination .............................................. 402
§ 1806. Impeachment and Support .................................... 405
§ 1807. — Impeaching Own Witness .................................. 405
§ 1808. — Character Evidence .......................................... 405
§ 1809. — Prior Misconduct and Other Crimes .................... 406
§ 1810. — — Probative Value Versus Prejudicial Effect ......... 407
§ 1811. — — Evidence Showing Witness Bias ...................... 410
§ 1812. — Prior Inconsistent Statements ........................... 412
§ 1813. — — For Impeachment ........................................ 412
§ 1814. — — Affirmative Evidence .................................... 414
§ 1815. — Insanity and Narcotics Addiction ........................ 414
§ 1816. Rebuttal ........................................................... 415
§ 1817. — Permissible Scope ........................................... 416
§ 1818. — Evidence Inadmissible Under an Exclusionary Rule  417
§ 1819. Exclusion or Separation of Witnesses ....................... 421

*Page*

§ 1820. Use of Interpreters ............................................... 422

CHAPTER 19. PRIVILEGES ........................................ 425
§ 1901. Privilege Against Self-Incrimination ........................ 425
§ 1902. — Applicability of the Privilege ............................. 426
§ 1903. — Scope of the Privilege ..................................... 430
§ 1904. — Exercise of the Privilege .................................. 433
§ 1905. — Registration and Reporting Provisions ................. 435
§ 1906. — Waiver of the Privilege .................................... 437
§ 1907. — Comment on Failure to Testify ........................... 442
§ 1908. Privileged Communications .................................. 443
§ 1909. — Marital Communications Privilege ...................... 443
§ 1910. — — Adverse Testimony Privilege .......................... 444
§ 1911. — — Confidential Communications ......................... 445
§ 1912. — — Existence of Marriage .................................. 446
§ 1913. — — Objection and Waiver .................................. 446
§ 1914. — — Exceptions ............................................... 447
§ 1915. — Attorney-Client Privilege ................................. 448
§ 1916. — — Privilege Holder Must Be Client ...................... 448
§ 1917. — — Communication With Lawyer .......................... 449
§ 1918. — — Communication by Client for Legal Services ....... 451
§ 1919. — — Waiver .................................................... 454
§ 1920. — Work-Product Doctrine ................................... 456
§ 1921. — Physician-Patient Privilege .............................. 457
§ 1922. — Reporter-Source Privilege ............................... 458
§ 1923. Government Privilege — Identities of Informants ........ 458
§ 1924. Other Privileges ............................................. 462

CHAPTER 20. OPINION EVIDENCE ........................... 463
§ 2001. Testimony of Lay Witnesses ................................ 463
§ 2002. Testimony of Expert Witnesses ............................ 466
§ 2003. — Scientific, Technical, or Specialized Knowledge ....... 466
§ 2004. — Basis of Opinion Testimony by Experts ................ 473
§ 2005. — Ultimate Issue Rule ....................................... 474
§ 2006. — Hypothetical Questions ................................... 475
§ 2007. — Court-Appointed Experts ................................ 476

CHAPTER 21. HEARSAY AND EXCEPTIONS .................. 477
§ 2100. Introduction .................................................. 478
§ 2101. Out-of-Court Statements .................................... 479
§ 2102. Non-Hearsay .................................................. 479
§ 2103. — Non-Hearsay by Use ...................................... 480

*Page*

§ 2104. — — Proof That a Statement Was Made .................. 480

§ 2105. — — To Show Effect on Listener's Conduct .............. 480

§ 2106. — — Res Gestae — Spontaneous, Contemporaneous Declarations ........................................................ 481

§ 2107. — Non-Hearsay by Definition ............................... 481

§ 2108. — — Prior Statement of a Witness ......................... 481

§ 2109. — — — Inconsistent Statements ......................... 482

§ 2110. — — — Consistent Statements ............................ 483

§ 2111. — — — Pretrial Identification ............................. 483

§ 2112. — — Admissions .............................................. 484

§ 2113. — — — Admissions by Defendant .......................... 484

§ 2114. — — — Defendant's Adoptive Admissions ............... 485

§ 2115. — — — Vicarious and Representative Admissions ..... 486

§ 2116. — — — Declarations of Coconspirators .................. 487

§ 2117. Hearsay Exceptions — Availability of Declarant Immaterial ............................................................... 490

§ 2118. — Present Sense Impression: Rule 803(1) ................. 490

§ 2119. — Excited Utterances: Rule 803(2) ......................... 491

§ 2120. — Then Existing Mental, Emotional, or Physical Condition: Rule 803(3) ............................................... 491

§ 2121. — Statements for Purposes of Medical Diagnosis or Treatment: Rule 803(4) ....................................... 492

§ 2122. — Recorded Recollection: Rule 803(5) ...................... 493

§ 2123. — Records of Regularly Conducted Activity: Rule 803(6) ............................................................... 494

§ 2124. — Absence of Entries in Records Kept in Regularly Conducted Activity: Rule 803(7) .................................... 497

§ 2125. — Public Records and Reports: Rule 803(8) ............... 497

§ 2126. — Records of Vital Statistics: Rule 803(9) .................. 498

§ 2127. — Absence of Public Record or Entry: Rule 803(10) ...... 499

§ 2128. — Records of Religious Organizations; Marriage, Baptismal, and Similar Certificates; and Family Records: Rule 803(11), (12), and (13) ......................................... 499

§ 2129. — Records of Documents and Statements in Documents Affecting an Interest in Property: Rule 803(14) and (15) 500

§ 2130. — Statements in Ancient Documents: Rule 803(16) ...... 500

§ 2131. — Market Reports, Commercial Publications: Rule 803(17) ............................................................. 501

§ 2132. — Learned Treatises: Rule 803(18) ......................... 501

Page

§ 2133. — Reputation of Personal or Family History, Boundaries or General History, or Character: Rule 803(19), (20), and (21) .................................................... 501

§ 2134. — Judgment of Previous Conviction: Rule 803(22) ....... 502

§ 2135. — Judgment as to Personal, Family or General History, or Boundaries: Rule 803(23) .................................. 503

§ 2136. — Other Exceptions: Rule 803(24) .......................... 503

§ 2137. Hearsay Exceptions — Declarant Unavailable ............ 504

§ 2138. — Limitations ..................................................... 504

§ 2139. — — Sixth Amendment Confrontation Clause ........... 504

§ 2140. — — Unavailability Sufficient to Qualify Under the Rule ................................................................. 506

§ 2141. — Former Testimony: Rule 804(b)(1) ...................... 508

§ 2142. — Statement Under Belief of Impending Death: Rule 804(b)(2) ............................................................ 509

§ 2143. — Statements Against Interest: Rule 804(b)(3) .......... 509

§ 2144. — — Statements Against Interest Generally ............. 509

§ 2145. — — Statements Against Penal Interest Offered to Exculpate .............................................................. 511

§ 2146. — Statement of Personal or Family History: Rule 804(b)(4) ............................................................ 513

§ 2147. — Other Exceptions: Rule 804(b)(5) ........................ 513

§ 2148. Hearsay Within Hearsay ....................................... 514

§ 2149. Attacking and Supporting the Credibility of Declarant .. 515

Appendix A. Amendments to the Constitution of the United States ............................................................... 517

Appendix B. Federal Rules of Criminal Procedure ................. 519

Appendix C. Federal Rules of Evidence ............................. 559

Table of Cases ............................................................ 579
Table of Statutes, Rules and Sentencing Guidelines ................. 705
Index ....................................................................... 715

# PREFACE TO THIRD EDITION

In keeping with the original purpose of *Federal Criminal Trials,* this Third Edition may be used both as a starting point for research and as a speedy in-trial resource. This volume has been updated with simple, straightforward language, citations within the text and no footnotes.

This new edition covers constitutional protections, federal criminal procedure and rules of evidence, taking into account the pertinent statutory and rule changes and all pertinent Supreme Court decisions released through the October 1991 Term. Some sections have been added and others entirely rewritten. The chapter on Post-Trial Proceedings has been greatly expanded and is almost entirely new due to establishing the Sentencing Guidelines.

I would like to particularly thank my wife Jeanette who typed the manuscript in addition to running her own business.

James C. Cissell

# FOREWORD TO FIRST EDITION

Beginning in 1954, the United States Attorney's Office for the Southern District of New York has authored and revised *Proving Federal Crimes.* Since that time, the book has been recognized as an invaluable research tool and ready-reference manual for Federal prosecutors. Defense counsel and others involved in Federal criminal justice system were also quick to recognize its usefulness, and demand for the book has steadily grown.

In 1980, the task of revising this work was undertaken by the United States Attorney's Office for the Southern District of Ohio, under the leadership of then United States Attorney James Cissell. This 1980 edition substantially expanded the coverage of *Proving Federal Crimes* and continued and enhanced the traditions of excellence which had been established by previous editions.

In authoring *Federal Criminal Trials,* the first privately published update of *Proving Federal Crimes,* James Cissell has met the high standards he set for himself in the prior edition. The volume has been completely updated and four new chapters have been added: Jurisdiction and Venue, Preliminary Proceedings, Arraignment and Plea, and Post Trial Proceedings. These chapters deal with pre- and post-trial matters that have become increasingly important as the issues brought to trial and their procedural contexts have become increasingly complex. They are a welcome and needed addition.

As one who has been both a Federal prosecutor and a defense attorney, I know, first hand, the value of this work and the enthusiasm with which it will be received by bench and bar alike. As a co-author of one of the prior Southern District editions, I also know, first hand, the difficulty of producing this comprehensive work.

*Federal Criminal Trials* is a worthy successor to *Proving Federal Crimes.* It will continue to be an indispensable tool for practitioners of Federal criminal law.

*Rudolph W. Giuliani*
*Associate Attorney General*
*U. S. Department of Justice*

# PREFACE TO FIRST EDITION

In the trial of a lawsuit there is often the immediate need for a quick review of a point of law or a citation to support or oppose an objection. Since 1954, *Proving Federal Crimes* has served this function in criminal trials for Department of Justice attorneys and such state prosecutors and private attorneys who were aware of this publication and who were able to secure it. First published and then maintained until 1976 by the staff of the United States Attorney for the Southern District of New York, it was written and revised by the staff of the United States Attorney for the Southern District of Ohio in 1980.

This revised and expanded edition under the title *Federal Criminal Trials* is the first to be published privately. As with previous editions, it is intended to be a starting point and an in-trial resource. Four chapters have been added. All of the existing chapters have been updated and some have been expanded and have had sections added to them. Citations have been added or removed throughout the book. Subtopics within chapters have been expanded for greater and quicker accessibility. The addition of the Bill of Rights, the Federal Rules of Criminal Procedure, the Federal Rules of Evidence and the Table of Cases should greatly increase its use as a trial aid.

Thanks is due to those attorneys from the offices of the United States Attorney for the Southern District of New York and the United States Attorney for the Southern District of Ohio who worked on the previous editions. On a personal note, I would like to again thank my friends, Judge Bernard J. Gilday, for his encouragement and help when I was United States Attorney and requested his assistance with the revision done by the members of my staff and the assistance of Assistant U. S. Attorney, Bob Behlen, which was far beyond his normal duties.

Considerable thanks is also due to Betty Harris who bore the burden of typing and proofreading this manuscript in addition to her normal duties. Finally, I would like to thank my law partners, Howard Gould, Dave Reichert, Steve Strauss, Tom Gould, and Mike Reed for bearing up to the disruption this book caused to the office and to my time.

James Cissell

# PART I
# CONSTITUTIONAL PROTECTIONS AND PROCEDURES

# CHAPTER 1

## JURISDICTION AND VENUE

§ 101. Jurisdiction.
§ 102. — Subject Matter Jurisdiction.
§ 103. — Jurisdiction Over the Person of the Defendant.
§ 104. Venue.
§ 105. — State and District of the Crime.
§ 106. — — Offenses Committed in More Than One District.
§ 107. — — Offenses Not Committed in Any District.
§ 108. — Proof of Venue.
§ 109. — Waiver of Venue.
§ 110. — Transfer of Venue.
§ 111. — — Transfer Because of Prejudice to Defendant.
§ 112. — — Transfer for the Convenience of Parties and Witnesses.
§ 113. — — Transfer for Plea and Sentence.

## § 101. Jurisdiction.

Jurisdiction is the power or authority of a court to hear and decide a case. It refers both to the power over the subject matter and the person being prosecuted. Venue, however, refers to the geographic location where the prosecution and trial will occur.

The judicial power extends to all cases arising under the Constitution and laws of the United States. U.S. Const. art. III, § 2, cl. 1. The district courts "have original jurisdiction, exclusive of the courts of the States, of all offenses against the laws of the United States." 18 U.S.C. § 3231. This includes the district court of the district of Puerto Rico, *Miranda v. U.S.,* 255 F.2d 9, 13 (1st Cir. 1958), and the district courts for the Canal Zone and the Virgin Islands have jurisdiction "under the laws of the United States, not locally inapplicable, committed within the territorial jurisdiction of such courts, and jurisdiction, concurrently with the district courts of the United States committed upon the high seas," 18 U.S.C. § 3241.

The special maritime and territorial jurisdiction of the United States provides for crimes committed upon the high seas, various vessels and aircraft, and the lands used by the United States under exclusive or concurrent jurisdiction with any state. 18 U.S.C. § 7. Various drug violations aboard American vessels on the high seas are covered by 21 U.S.C. § 955a; *U.S. v. Riker,* 670 F.2d 987 (11th Cir. 1982). The place of trial for such offenses is provided for in 18 U.S.C. § 3238.

Under the Assimilative Crimes Act, any act committed within an area subject to federal control which would be a criminal act in the state or territory where the federal reservation is located is also a crime under federal law. 18 U.S.C. § 13. The government bears the burden of proof of the status of the site of an offense, *U.S. v. Gipe,* 672 F.2d 777 (9th Cir. 1982).

In a murder or manslaughter case, the offense is deemed to have been committed at the place where the injury was inflicted or at the place where other means were employed which caused the death, rather than where the death occurs. 18 U.S.C. § 3236. Thus, if a person is injured outside the territorial jurisdiction of the federal government but subsequently dies of that injury on a federal reservation, there is no federal crime. *U.S. v. Parker,* 622 F.2d 298, 302 (8th Cir.), *cert. denied,* 449 U.S. 851 (1980).

Certain prosecutions commenced in state court against federal officers and members of the armed forces arising out of or under color of their office, and certain civil rights cases raising a federal question may be removed to the district court embracing the place where the state action is pending. 28 U.S.C. §§ 1442-1443.

United States district courts may also have concurrent jurisdiction with state courts or courts of military justice over acts that violate the laws of both the United States and a state, 18 U.S.C. § 3231, or both the United States and the Uniform Code of Military Justice. *U.S. v. Walker,* 552 F.2d 566, 567 (4th Cir.), *cert. denied,* 434 U.S. 848 (1977). In the latter instance, however, the double jeopardy clause prohibits prosecutions by both units of the same government. *See* Chapter 10, *infra.*

### § 102. — Subject Matter Jurisdiction.

There are no common-law offenses against the United States; only those offenses which are defined by an act of Congress may be prosecuted. *U.S. v. Eaton,* 144 U.S. 677, 687 (1892). However, resort to the common law may occur for the definition of terms used in the statutes. *Pettibone v. U.S.,* 148 U.S. 197, 203 (1893).

Where an indictment is required for jurisdiction, a waiver of indictment which is not authorized by rule or statute will not give a court jurisdiction to hear a case. *U.S. v. Choate,* 276 F.2d 724, 728 (5th Cir. 1960). An indictment must also allege a federal offense to give a court jurisdiction to try the defendant. *Thor v. U.S.,* 554 F.2d 759, 762 (5th Cir. 1977).

Lack of subject matter jurisdiction may not be waived by the defendant, *U.S. v. Isaacs,* 493 F.2d 1124, 1140 (7th Cir.), *cert. denied,* 417 U.S. 976 (1974); *Evans v. U.S.,* 325 F.2d 596, 602-03 (8th Cir. 1963), *cert. denied,* 377 U.S. 968 (1964); and it may be raised at any time during the proceedings, Rule 12(b)(2), Fed. R. Crim. P.

### § 103. — Jurisdiction Over the Person of the Defendant.

In addition to subject matter jurisdiction, the court must have personal jurisdiction over the defendant. This may be acquired by warrant or summons served pursuant to Rules 4 and 9 of the Federal Rules of Criminal Procedure or by voluntary appearance. A corporation may enter its appearance through its attorney. Rule 43(c)(1), Fed. R. Crim. P.

As a general rule, under the *Ker-Frisbie* doctrine the personal presence of the defendant before the court gives the court complete jurisdiction over him even though he may have been brought into the jurisdiction by abduction, illegal arrest, or improper extradition. *U.S. v. Crews*, 445 U.S. 463, 474 (1980); *Frisbie v. Collins*, 342 U.S. 519, 522 (1952); *Ker v. Illinois*, 119 U.S. 436, 444 (1886); *U.S. v. Cordero*, 668 F.2d 32, 36-38 (1st Cir. 1981); *U.S. v. Lopez*, 542 F.2d 283, 284-85 (5th Cir. 1976); *U.S. v. Lovato*, 520 F.2d 1270, 1271 (9th Cir.), *cert. denied*, 423 U.S. 985 (1975); *U.S. v. Zammiello*, 432 F.2d 72, 73 (9th Cir. 1970). This is true even where there is governmental involvement in the abduction unless an extradition treaty prohibits such an abduction. *U.S. v. Alvarez-Machain*, 112 S. Ct. 2188 (1992).

Unlike subject matter jurisdiction, jurisdiction over the person may be waived, *U.S. v. Kahl*, 583 F.2d 1351, 1356 (5th Cir. 1978), and is waived if not raised before a plea, *Ford v. U.S.*, 273 U.S. 593, 606 (1927); *Pon v. U.S.*, 168 F.2d 373, 374 (1st Cir. 1948).

### § 104. Venue.

Venue refers to the district or geographic area in which a prosecution and trial must be held. The right to be tried in the state where the crime was committed was considered so important that it was provided for twice in the Constitution. Trial shall be held "in the State where the said crimes shall have been committed." U.S. Const. art. II, § 2, cl. 3. Trial shall be by a "jury of the State and district wherein the crime shall have been committed." U.S. Const. amend. VI. Except as otherwise permitted by statute or rule, the prosecution shall be held in the district where the crime was committed and the place of trial within the district shall be fixed with regard to the "convenience of the defendant and the witnesses and the prompt administration of justice." Rule 18, Fed. R. Crim. P.; *U.S. v. Stratton*, 649 F.2d 1066, 1076 (5th Cir. 1981). There is no constitutional right to a trial within a particular division of a district. *U.S. v. Malmay*, 671 F.2d 869, 876 (5th Cir. 1982); *U.S. v. Lawson*, 670 F.2d 923, 926 (10th Cir. 1982), even where the particular division of a district is inconvenient for the defendant, *U.S. v. McRary*, 616 F.2d 181, 185 (5th Cir. 1980).

## § 105. — State and District of the Crime.

Whether venue is correct depends upon a determination of where the crime was committed. This may not be readily apparent, and venue must be determined from an examination of the nature of the crime and the location of the acts constituting the offense. *U.S. v. Anderson,* 328 U.S. 699, 704-06 (1946). Thus, proper venue for an offense of filing a false affidavit was Washington, D.C., where the affidavit was to be filed, not Colorado where it was executed and mailed. *Travis v. U.S.,* 364 U.S. 631, 635 (1961). A number of circuits have held that venue for the prosecution for obstruction of justice was proper in the district where the investigation or trial that was obstructed took place, even though no act of obstruction took place in that district. It is the "impact of the acts, not their location, that controls." *U.S. v. Tedesco,* 635 F.2d 902, 906 (1st Cir. 1980), *cert. denied,* 452 U.S. 902 (1981); *U.S. v. Kibler,* 667 F.2d 452, 454-55 (4th Cir.), *cert. denied,* 50 U.S.L.W. 3881 (1982); *U.S. v. O'Donnell,* 510 F.2d 1190, 1193 (6th Cir.), *cert. denied,* 421 U.S. 1001 (1975). The Seventh Circuit has held to the contrary, that the gravamen of the offense was the act (a beating) and the trial must be held where that act took place. *U.S. v. Nadolny,* 601 F.2d 940, 943 (7th Cir. 1979).

In tax cases, venue has been held to have been proper in either the district of filing or the district where the return was prepared and signed. *U.S. v. King,* 563 F.2d 559, 562 (2d Cir. 1977), *cert. denied,* 435 U.S. 918 (1978); *U.S. v. Lawhon,* 499 F.2d 352, 355 (5th Cir. 1974), *cert. denied,* 419 U.S. 1121 (1975); *U.S. v. Slutsky,* 487 F.2d 832, 839 (2d Cir. 1973), *cert. denied,* 416 U.S. 937 (1974).

## § 106. — — Offenses Committed in More Than One District.

An offense committed in more than one district may be prosecuted in any district in which such offense was begun, continued, or completed. 18 U.S.C. § 3237(a). In the case of any offense involving the use of the mails or transportation in interstate commerce, this includes any district from, through, or into which such commerce or mail moved. *Id.* Thus, conspiracy may be prosecuted in any district in which the agreement was formed or in which there was an act in furtherance of the conspiracy. *U.S. v. Lewis,* 676 F.2d 508, 511 (11th Cir. 1982); *U.S. v. Petersen,* 611 F.2d 1313, 1333 (10th Cir. 1979), *cert. denied,* 447 U.S. 905 (1980); *U.S. v. Lawson,* 507 F.2d 433, 445 (7th Cir. 1974), *cert. denied,* 420 U.S. 1004 (1975). An offense may be prosecuted in any district where commerce was affected in a Hobbs Act prosecution even though neither the agreement nor any act in furtherance of the con-

6

spiracy was committed in that district. *U.S. v. Craig,* 573 F.2d 513, 517 (7th Cir.), *cert. denied,* 439 U.S. 820 (1978).

Venue is not proper in a district where the only acts performed by the defendants were preparatory to the offense and not part of the offense. *U.S. v. Beech-Nut Nutrition Corp.,* 871 F.2d 1181 (2d Cir. 1989).

## § 107. — — Offenses Not Committed in Any District.

Trial of crimes not committed in any state shall be at such place as Congress may direct. U.S. Const. art. III, § 2, cl. 3. Congress has directed that all offenses begun or committed upon the high seas or out of the jurisdiction of a state or district shall be in the district in which the defendant, or any one of two or more joint defendants is arrested or first brought. 18 U.S.C. § 3238. Thus, prosecution of a defendant who had committed a drug violation on an American vessel on the high seas, *U.S. v. Liles,* 670 F.2d 989, 991 (11th Cir. 1982), or who had committed a kidnapping on the high seas was proper in the Southern District of Florida, the district to which he was returned, *U.S. v. McRary,* 616 F.2d 181, 185 (5th Cir. 1980). Likewise, where a defendant committed alleged acts of treason in Japan and was brought from Japan to California, trial was proper in that California district. *D'Aquino v. U.S.,* 192 F.2d 338, 351 (9th Cir. 1951), *cert. denied,* 343 U.S. 935 (1952).

If an offender is not arrested or brought into any district, an indictment or information may be brought in the district of the last known residence of the offender or any one of two or more offenders, or if no residence is known, in the District of Columbia. 18 U.S.C. § 3238. The purpose of this provision is to relieve the prosecution of the burden of proving that a defendant who remained outside the territorial jurisdiction of the United States was a "person fleeing from justice" under 18 U.S.C. § 3290 for purposes of tolling the statute of limitations. *U.S. v. McRary,* 616 F.2d at 185.

## § 108. — Proof of Venue.

The burden of proving proper venue is an essential part of the government's case. *U.S. v. Passodelis,* 615 F.2d 975, 978 (3d Cir. 1980); *U.S. v. White,* 611 F.2d 531, 534 (5th Cir.), *cert. denied,* 446 U.S. 992 (1980); *U.S. v. Black Cloud,* 590 F.2d 270, 272 (8th Cir. 1979); *U.S. v. Branan,* 457 F.2d 1062, 1065 (6th Cir. 1972). Where the government does not prove the offense was committed in the district of trial, the conviction must be reversed. *U.S. v. Passodelis, supra.* Reopening the prosecution's case to prove venue has been permitted. *U.S. v. Hinderman,* 625 F.2d 994 (10th Cir. 1980).

The standard for proving venue is by a preponderance of the evidence not proof beyond a reasonable doubt. *U.S. v. White, supra; U.S. v. John Bernard Industries, Inc.,* 589 F.2d 1353, 1361 (8th Cir. 1979); *U.S. v. Jenkins,* 510 F.2d 495, 498 (2d Cir. 1975). There need not be direct proof of venue where circumstantial evidence supports the inference that the crime was committed in the district where venue was laid. *U.S. v. Turner,* 586 F.2d 395, 397 (5th Cir. 1978), *cert. denied,* 440 U.S. 926 (1979); *U.S. v. Haley,* 500 F.2d 302, 305 (8th Cir. 1974). In determining venue, the court may take judicial notice of a map of an area and geographic location or from such circumstantial evidence as streets, business establishments, and parks. *U.S. v. Trenary,* 473 F.2d 680, 682 (9th Cir. 1973); *U.S. v. Mendell,* 447 F.2d 639, 641 (7th Cir.), *cert. denied,* 404 U.S. 991 (1971).

It has been held that venue is a jury question. *U.S. v. Black Cloud,* 590 F.2d at 272. It is generally not plain error to fail to instruct on the burden of proof of venue, *U.S. v. White,* 611 F.2d at 536; but such failure is reversible error if venue is disputed, *U.S. v. Black Cloud,* 590 F.2d at 273.

### § 109. — Waiver of Venue.

A defendant's right to trial in the state and district where the alleged crime occurred is a personal privilege which may be waived. *Singer v. U.S.,* 380 U.S. 24, 35 (1965); *Yeloushan v. U.S.,* 339 F.2d 533, 536 (5th Cir. 1964); *Hilderbrand v. U.S.,* 304 F.2d 716, 717 (10th Cir. 1962). Waiver occurs when the defendant files a motion to transfer under Rule 20 or Rule 21 of the Federal Rules of Criminal Procedure. *U.S. v. Angiulo,* 497 F.2d 440, 441-42 (1st Cir.), *cert. denied,* 419 U.S. 896 (1974); *Jackson v. U.S.,* 489 F.2d 695, 696 (1st Cir. 1974). This waiver is effective even when the count of an indictment which formed the basis for the transfer is dropped. *U.S. v. Mohney,* 476 F. Supp. 421, 424 (D. Hawaii 1979).

Waiver of proper venue also occurs when the defendant fails to object before trial when the indictment or statements by the prosecutor reveal a venue defect, *U.S. v. Menendez,* 612 F.2d 51, 54-55 (2d Cir. 1979); *U.S. v. Bohle,* 445 F.2d 54, 59 (7th Cir. 1971), fails to object until after the jury returns a guilty verdict, *U.S. v. Powell,* 498 F.2d 890, 891 (9th Cir.), *cert. denied,* 419 U.S. 866 (1974); *U.S. v. Polin,* 323 F.2d 549, 557 (3d Cir. 1963); or when the defendant raises the issue for the first time on appeal, *U.S. v. Boney,* 572 F.2d 397, 400 (2d Cir. 1978); *U.S. v. King,* 563 F.2d 559, 562 (2d Cir. 1977), *cert. denied,* 435 U.S. 918

(1978). If an indictment contains a proper allegation of venue and the defendant has no notice of a defect of venue until the government rests its case, the objection is timely if made at the close of the evidence. *U.S. v. Black Cloud,* 590 F.2d 270, 272 (8th Cir. 1979).

Waiver of venue without a motion to transfer under Rule 20 or 21 does not furnish authority to transfer the proceedings to another district. *U.S. v. Choate,* 276 F.2d 724, 728 (5th Cir. 1960).

### § 110. — Transfer of Venue.

Upon motion of the defendant, trial of a case may be transferred to another district because of prejudice against the defendant or for the convenience of parties and witnesses, Rule 21, Fed. R. Crim. P., or because the defendant (who is being held in a district other than that in which the charges are pending) states in writing that he wishes to plead guilty or nolo contendere in the district in which he is present, Rule 20, Fed. R. Crim. P. A motion for transfer shall be made at or before arraignment or at such time as the court or rules may prescribe. Rule 22, Fed. R. Crim. P. Generally, a request for transfer which is made just before trial will be refused. *U.S. v. Testa,* 458 F.2d 847, 857 (9th Cir. 1977).

### § 111. — — Transfer Because of Prejudice to Defendant.

The district court, upon the motion of the defendant, may transfer the proceeding to another district if the court is satisfied that so great a prejudice against the defendant exists in the district that he cannot obtain a fair trial at any place in the district. Rule 21(a), Fed. R. Crim. P. The prejudice addressed through Rule 21(a) is juror prejudice, not the prejudice of a judge. *U.S. v. Thomas,* 299 F. Supp. 494, 497 (E.D. Mo. 1968).

The burden of proving that venue should be changed lies with the defendant. *U.S. v. Delay,* 500 F.2d 1360, 1365 (8th Cir. 1974). Such a request is addressed to the sound discretion of the trial court. *U.S. v. Tokoph,* 514 F.2d 597, 606 (10th Cir. 1975). It should not be granted merely upon a showing of widespread or even adverse publicity. *Irvin v. Dowd,* 366 U.S. 717, 722-23 (1961); *U.S. v. Brown,* 540 F.2d 364, 378 (8th Cir. 1976); *U.S. v. McNally,* 485 F.2d 398, 403 (8th Cir. 1973), *cert. denied,* 415 U.S. 978 (1974). The issue is whether it is possible to select a fair and impartial jury, *U.S. v. Chapin,* 515 F.2d 1274, 1285-86 (D.C. Cir.), *cert. denied,* 423 U.S. 1015 (1975); and it is not required that the jury be totally ignorant of the facts and issues, but it is sufficient if a juror can lay aside his impressions or opinions and render a verdict

9

based upon the evidence presented in court, *Irvin v. Dowd,* 366 U.S. at 723; *U.S. v. Lamb,* 575 F.2d 1310, 1315 (10th Cir.), *cert. denied,* 439 U.S. 854 (1978); *U.S. v. Haldeman,* 559 F.2d 31, 70 (D.C. Cir. 1976), *cert. denied,* 431 U.S. 933 (1977); *U.S. v. Brown,* 540 F.2d at 378; *Bishop v. Wainwright,* 511 F.2d 664, 666 (5th Cir. 1975), *cert. denied,* 425 U.S. 980 (1976).

In extreme cases it may be that prejudicial pretrial publicity has so infected community sentiment that the selection of a fair and impartial jury is improbable and a venue change should be granted before voir dire. *Rideau v. Louisiana,* 373 U.S. 723 (1963). The usual occasion for such a determination is upon voir dire examination where the trial court may test whether it is possible to select a fair and impartial jury. *U.S. v. McDonald,* 576 F.2d 1350, 1354 (9th Cir.), *cert. denied,* 439 U.S. 830 (1978); *U.S. v. Williams,* 523 F.2d 1203, 1209 n.10 (5th Cir. 1975); *U.S. v. Chapin,* 515 F.2d at 1286.

The fact that a venue change was granted for an indictment which was dismissed by the prosecution under Rule 48(a) of the Federal Rules of Criminal Procedure is not controlling on a superseding indictment. The second trial is an independent prosecution, and the finding on the original indictment was a finding only that at that time a fair trial could not be held in the district. *U.S. v. Crow Dog,* 532 F.2d 1182, 1188 (8th Cir. 1976), *cert. denied,* 430 U.S. 929 (1977); *U.S. v. Holder,* 399 F. Supp. 220, 227 (D.S.D. 1975). *See also U.S. v. Eagle,* 586 F.2d 1193, 1196 (8th Cir. 1978).

## § 112. — — Transfer for the Convenience of Parties and Witnesses.

The court may transfer the proceedings to another district upon the motion of the defendant for the convenience of parties and witnesses and in the interest of justice. Rule 21(b), Fed. R. Crim. P. If there is a transfer, the court may select the district to which transfer is made. Advisory Committee Note (1966 Amendment).

Factors which have been considered in determining whether a requested transfer is in the interest of justice include the locations of the defendant, witnesses, events likely to be in issue, documents, records and property involved, and counsel; the disruption of defendant's business if the case is not transferred; the relative accessability of the place to trial; the docket conditions of each district involved; and the promotion of the goals of the Speedy Trial Act. *Platt v. Minnesota Mining Co.,* 376 U.S. 240 (1964); *U.S. v. Keuylian,* 602 F.2d 1033, 1039 (2d Cir. 1979); *U.S. v. Celaya-Garcia,* 583 F.2d 210, 211 (5th Cir. 1978), *cert. denied,* 440 U.S. 926 (1979). Whether a transfer or change of venue is granted is within the discretion of the trial court, *U.S. v. Hunter,* 672 F.2d 815, 816 (10th Cir. 1982); *U.S. v. Keuylian,* 602 F.2d at 1038; *U.S. v. Cook,* 592 F.2d 877, 881 (5th Cir.), *cert. denied,* 442 U.S. 921 (1979); and a denial of such a request will be reversed only upon a showing of an abuse of that discretion, *U.S. v. Pry,* 625 F.2d 689, 691 (5th Cir. 1980), *cert. denied,* 450 U.S. 925 (1981). It is not an abuse of discretion to refuse to transfer a case to defendant's home district as a defendant has no right to be tried in his or her home district. *U.S. v. Walker,* 559 F.2d 365, 372 (5th Cir. 1977); *U.S. v. McManus,* 535 F.2d 460, 463 (8th Cir. 1976), *cert. denied,* 429 U.S. 1052 (1977).

Transfer can be made only for those defendants who request it, and severance may occur so that an indictment may be transferred for one defendant and not others. *Yeloushan v. U.S.,* 339 F.2d 533, 536-37 (5th Cir. 1964); *U.S. v. Aronoff,* 463 F. Supp. 454, 458 (S.D.N.Y. 1978).

### § 113. — — Transfer for Plea and Sentence.

A defendant who is arrested, held, or present in a district other than the district in which an indictment, information, or complaint is pending against him, may state in writing that he wishes to plead guilty or nolo contendere and consents to disposition in the district in which he was arrested, held, or is present. Rule 20, Fed. R. Crim. P. The approval of the United States Attorneys from both districts is required to avoid forum shopping. Advisory Committee Note (1974 Amendment).

The purpose of the rule is to spare defendants the hardship of removal to the place where the prosecution is pending. Advisory Committee Note; *In re Arvedon,* 523 F.2d 914, 916 (1st Cir. 1975). It applies to violations of the District of Columbia Code, even though the local District of Columbia judiciary has exclusive jurisdiction of such prosecutions. *U.S. v. Ford,* 627 F.2d 807, 811 (7th Cir.), *cert. denied,* 449 U.S. 923 (1980). This rule applies in a multiple-defendant indictment as there is no requirement that all parties defendant be tried in the same district, and transfer at the request of one defendant to plead under Rule 20 may be granted over the objection of codefendants. *Snowden v. Smith,* 413 F.2d 94 (7th Cir. 1969); *Yeloushan v. U.S.,* 339 F.2d 533, 536-37 (5th Cir. 1964).

Transfer is predicated upon the approval of the United States Attorneys from both the transferor and transferee districts. *U.S. v. Herbst,* 565 F.2d 638, 643 (10th Cir. 1977); *U.S. v. Smith,* 515 F.2d 1028, 1030 (5th Cir. 1975), *cert. denied,* 424 U.S. 917 (1976). However, one court has held that as Rule 20 is not jurisdictional, but is a venue waiving provision, the failure to have the written approval of the United States Attorney from the transferor district does not deprive the transferee district of jurisdiction. *Jackson v. U.S.,* 489 F.2d 695, 696 (1st Cir. 1974).

Where an information or indictment is not pending, and the defendant has waived venue and trial under Rule 20(b), charges may be filed in the district of his arrest or presence. Advisory Committee Note (1982 Amendment). Presumably, such a waiver is not voided where the plea agreement is not accepted by the court. *U.S. v. Scavo,* 593 F.2d 837, 843 (8th Cir. 1979).

The transferee court has jurisdiction of the case solely for the purpose of a guilty or nolo contendere plea and sentencing; and if the court refuses to accept a nolo contendere plea under Rule 11, the proceeding must be returned to the original district. Rule 20(c), Fed. R. Crim. P. If a nolo contendere plea is refused, the transferee court still has jurisdiction to receive a guilty plea from the defendant. *Singleton v. Clemmer,* 166 F.2d 963, 965 (D.C. Cir. 1948).

If a defendant should change his mind and decide to plead not guilty after the proceeding has been transferred, it shall be returned to the district in which prosecution was commenced and the defendant's statement that he wished to plead guilty or nolo contendere may not be used against him. Rule 20(c), Fed. R. Crim. P.

# CHAPTER 2

## SEARCH AND SEIZURE

§ 201. Fourth Amendment Protections.
§ 202. Private Searches.
§ 203. Foreign Searches of Aliens.
§ 204. Search Warrants.
§ 205. Who May Issue a Search Warrant.
§ 206. — Probable Cause for Search Warrant.
§ 207. — — Probable Cause Established by Hearsay.
§ 208. — — Sufficiency Determined by Common Sense Standards.
§ 209. — — Magistrate Must Be Neutral.
§ 210. — — False Statements in Affidavit.
§ 211. — Particularity of Description.
§ 212. — Execution of Search Warrant.
§ 213. — — Who May Execute Warrant.
§ 214. — — When Must Search Warrant Be Executed.
§ 215. — — Manner of Entry to Search.
§ 216. — Telephone Search Warrants.
§ 217. Warrantless Searches.
§ 218. — Search Incident to Valid Arrest.
§ 219. — — Validity of the Arrest.
§ 220. — — When a Person Is Under Arrest.
§ 221. — — Arrest Must Be Made in Good Faith and Not as a Pretext to Justify Search.
§ 222. — — Search Must Be Contemporaneous With Arrest.
§ 223. — — Scope of Warrantless Searches Incident to Arrest.
§ 224. — — — Search of the Person.
§ 225. — — — Articles Carried by Arrestee.
§ 226. — — — Areas Within Arrestee's Immediate Control.
§ 227. — Seizures Without Probable Cause.
§ 228. — — "Stop and Frisk."
§ 229. — — Border and Customs Searches.
§ 230. — — Detention of Occupants While Home Is Searched Pursuant to a Warrant.
§ 231. — Exigent Circumstances That Justify a Warrantless Search.
§ 232. — — Officers Responding to Emergency.
§ 233. — — Threatened Destruction or Removal of Contraband or Likely Escape of Suspect.
§ 234. — — "Hot Pursuit."
§ 235. — Vehicle Searches.
§ 236. — — Inventory Searches of Vehicles.
§ 237. — — Searches of Containers Found in Vehicle.
§ 238. — Evidence in Plain View.
§ 239. — — Abandoned Property.
§ 240. — — Curtilage and the Open Fields Doctrine.
§ 241. — Anti-Skyjacking Searches.
§ 242. — Prison Searches.
§ 243. — Consent Searches.
§ 244. — — Use of Deceit to Secure Consent.

§ 245. — — Third-Party Consent.
§ 246. Evidence Affected by a Search and Seizure.
§ 247. — Property That May Be Seized.
§ 248. — The Exclusionary Rule.
§ 249. Motions to Suppress.
§ 250. — Timing of Motions to Suppress.
§ 251. — Hearing.
§ 252. — — Burden of Proof.
§ 253. — — Evidentiary Rules.
§ 254. — — Right to a Hearing.
§ 255. — Standing.
§ 256. — Appeal From Suppression Hearing.
§ 257. Wiretapping and Other Electronic Surveillance.
§ 258. — Interception Pursuant to Court Order.
§ 259. — — Authorization.
§ 260. — — Application and Order.
§ 261. — — — Application.
§ 262. — — — Order.
§ 263. — — — Surreptitious Entry.
§ 264. — — — Minimization.
§ 265. — — — Sealing of Applications, Orders, and Intercepted Communications.
§ 266. — — — Motion to Suppress.
§ 267. — — Scope of Title III.
§ 268. — Interception With Consent of One Party.

> The right of the people to be secure in their persons, houses, papers, and effects, against unreasonable searches and sei-zures, shall not be violated, and no Warrants shall issue, but upon probable cause, supported by Oath or affirmation, and particularly describing the place to be searched, and the per-sons or things to be seized.
>
> U.S. Const. amend IV.

## § 201. Fourth Amendment Protections.

The fourth amendment "protects people, not places." It protects a person's reasonable expectation of privacy against government intru-sion. This includes a person's home, *Steagald v. U.S.*, 451 U.S. 204 (1981), his person against a surgical intrusion to remove a bullet fired by a victim, *Winston v. Lee*, 470 U.S. 753 (1985), and may include places where the public has access such as a public telephone booth, *Katz v. U.S.*, 389 U.S. 347 (1967), a union office, *Mancusi v. DeForte*, 392 U.S. 364 (1968), a public employee's desk or file cabinets in his office, *O'Connor v. Ortega*, 480 U.S. 709 (1987), or areas of a store open to the general public, *Lo-Ji Sales Inc. v. New York*, 442 U.S. 319 (1979). The test of a legitimate expectation of privacy under the fourth amendment is (1) whether the individual has a subjective expectation of privacy, and (2) whether that expectation is one that society is prepared to recognize as "reasonable." *Smith v. Maryland,* 442 U.S. 735 (1979).

It has been held no legitimate expectation of privacy is violated by a warrantless installation of a pen register on a telephone, *Smith, supra;* nor did the mere presence of non-owner passengers in a car bestow upon them a legitimate expectation of privacy in the car's locked glove compartment or the area under the seat, *Rakas v. Illinois,* 439 U.S. 128 (1978); nor is there an expectation of privacy in publicly displayed wares in a bookstore, *Maryland v. Macon,* 472 U.S. 463 (1985); or garbage left for collection outside the curtilage of the home, *California v. Greenwood,* 486 U.S. 35 (1988); nor did motel room occupants have a reasonable expectation of privacy against DEA agents eavesdropping from an adjoining room by pressing their ears against a connecting door, *U.S. v. Agapito,* 620 F.2d 324 (2d Cir.), *cert. denied,* 449 U.S. 834 (1980). Where the owner of contraband shipped it by Federal Express, he put it beyond his control and reduced the scope of privacy he could reasonably expect, particularly where he made no effort to hide the incriminating nature of the pills. *U.S. v. Barry,* 673 F.2d 912, 915 (6th Cir.), *cert. denied,* 459 U.S. 927 (1982). However, the warrantless use of a telescope to observe the interior of a home does violate a legitimate expectation of privacy, *U.S. v. Taborda,* 635 F.2d 131 (2d Cir. 1980); *contra, On Lee v. U.S.,* 343 U.S. 747, 754 (1952) (dicta).

The warrantless monitoring of a "beeper" inside a container did not violate the fourth amendment when it revealed no information that could not have been attained through legitimate visual surveillance. *U.S. v. Knotts,* 460 U.S. 276 (1983). However, the monitoring of a "beeper" within a residence which reveals information that could not have been obtained through visual surveillance violates the fourth amendment rights of those who have a privacy interest in the residence. *U.S. v. Karo,* 468 U.S. 705 (1984).

### § 202. Private Searches.

The fourth amendment is a limitation on the government. It does not require the exclusion of evidence obtained through a search or seizure by a private citizen acting on his own without government suggestion or participation. *Coolidge v. New Hampshire,* 403 U.S. 443 (1971); *Burdeau v. McDowell,* 256 U.S. 465 (1921); *U.S. v. Barry,* 673 F.2d 912, 914-15 (6th Cir. 1982); *U.S. v. Roberts,* 644 F.2d 683 (8th Cir. 1980); *U.S. v. Lamar,* 545 F.2d 488 (5th Cir.), *cert. denied,* 430 U.S. 959 (1977); *U.S. v. Newton,* 510 F.2d 1149 (7th Cir. 1975); *U.S. v. Pryba,* 502 F.2d 391 (D.C. Cir. 1974), *cert. denied,* 419 U.S. 1127 (1975).

As a general rule, a government search may not exceed the scope of a private search, and a warrant may be required for the government to conduct a search that is of the same or lesser scope than a private search. *Walter v. U.S.*, 447 U.S. 649 (1980). It has been held, however, that a DEA field test of a white powdery substance originally discovered in a search by employees of a private freight carrier exceeded the scope of the private search, but no legitimate privacy interests were compromised and the safeguards of a warrant would only minimally advance fourth amendment interests. *U.S. v. Jacobsen,* 466 U.S. 109 (1984).

### § 203. Foreign Searches of Aliens.

While resident aliens who have developed substantial connections with the United States may be invested with the rights guaranteed by the Constitution, the fourth amendment does not apply to a search and seizure by United States agents of property that is owned by a nonresident alien and which took place in a foreign country. *U.S. v. Verdugo-Urquidez,* 110 S. Ct. 1056 (1990).

### § 204. Search Warrants.

Where there is a privacy right protected by the fourth amendment, a search is reasonable if there is a search warrant supported by probable cause. Rule 41 of the Federal Rules of Criminal Procedure provides limitations and procedures for securing a search warrant.

### § 205. Who May Issue a Search Warrant.

Under Rule 41(a)(1) of the Federal Rules of Criminal Procedure, a search warrant may be issued by a federal magistrate or a judge of a state court of record within the federal district, for a search of property or for a person within the district.

Under Rule 41(a)(2), only a federal magistrate may issue a search warrant for property or a person in another district. This is permitted if the property or persons are within the district when the warrant is sought but might move outside the district before the warrant is executed.

Whereas Rule 41(a) previously required that the property or person sought must be "located" in the district at the time the warrant was issued, Rule 41(a) now permits anticipatory warrants where the person or property is expected to be within the district. *See* Advisory Committee's Note.

## § 206. — Probable Cause for Search Warrant.

Rule 41(c) of the Federal Rules of Criminal Procedure states that a warrant may issue upon an affidavit sworn to before a federal magistrate or state judge if the magistrate or judge is satisfied that the affidavit reflects probable cause. The affidavit must be in writing, not tape-recorded, although this failure to comply with the rule is not "fundamental." *U.S. v. Vasser*, 648 F.2d 507 (9th Cir. 1980). The rule further provides that probable cause may be based upon hearsay evidence in whole or in part.

Probable cause exists where "the facts and circumstances within their [the agents'] knowledge, and of which they had reasonably trustworthy information ... [are] sufficient in themselves to warrant a man of reasonable caution in the belief that ..." a crime has been or is being committed, and that seizable property can be found at the place or on the person to be searched. *Carroll v. U.S.*, 267 U.S. 132, 162 (1925); *Brinegar v. U.S.*, 338 U.S. 160 (1949); *U.S. v. Drake*, 673 F.2d 15, 17 (1st Cir. 1982). The word "probable" is less stringent than "more likely than not" or "by a preponderance." "[T]he words 'reasonable cause' are perhaps closer to what is meant." *U.S. v. Melvin*, 596 F.2d 492, 495 (1st Cir.), *cert. denied*, 444 U.S. 837 (1979). "'[R]easonableness' is the overriding test of compliance with the Fourth Amendment...." *Zurcher v. Stanford Daily*, 436 U.S. 547, 559 (1978). Although proof of criminal activity is not required, *U.S. v. Tasto*, 586 F.2d 1068 (5th Cir. 1978), *cert. denied*, 440 U.S. 928 (1979), more than mere good faith and suspicion are required, *Brinegar v. U.S.*, 338 U.S. at 176-77; *U.S. v. Taylor*, 599 F.2d 832 (8th Cir. 1979); *U.S. v. Williams*, 594 F.2d 86 (5th Cir. 1979), *cert. denied*, 101 S. Ct. 946 (1981).

There is no higher standard of probable cause required by the first amendment for the seizure of books or movies than for other objects such as weapons or drugs. *New York v. P.J. Video, Inc.*, 106 S. Ct. 1610 (1986).

The use of a trained dog to sniff airline luggage for drugs has been held not to be a search, *U.S. v. Harvey*, 961 F.2d 1361 (8th Cir. 1992), and when coupled with other facts will support probable cause for a search warrant. *U.S. v. Sullivan*, 625 F.2d 9 (4th Cir. 1980), *cert. denied*, 450 U.S. 923 (1981). *Contra, U.S. v. Beale*, 674 F.2d 1327, 1335 (9th Cir. 1982), holding that use of such a trained dog is a fourth-amendment intrusion, but which may be conducted upon an officer's "founded" or "articulable" suspicion rather than probable cause. The smelling of marijuana in luggage by a DEA agent to supply part of the probable cause for a warrant has been upheld. *U.S. v. Sentovich*, 677 F.2d 834 (11th Cir. 1982).

The probable cause must be present or timely. Timeliness must be determined in the circumstances of each case. Information four-months-old may be timely, *U.S. v. Diecidue,* 603 F.2d 535 (5th Cir. 1979); or information six-months-old may be timely when combined with other information, *U.S. v. Williams,* 603 F.2d 1168 (5th Cir. 1979). If the probable offense is ongoing or a continuing one, the staleness prohibition does not apply. Also, contraband does not have to be currently located at the place described in the warrant if there is probable cause to believe that it will be there when the search warrant is executed. *U.S. v. Lowe,* 575 F.2d 1193 (6th Cir.), *cert. denied,* 439 U.S. 869 (1978).

Search warrants are directed at places, not persons. Once there is probable cause to believe that a federal crime has been committed, a warrant may issue for the search of any place there is probable cause to believe may be the place of concealment of evidence of the crime, even though the owner is not culpable. *Zurcher v. Stanford Daily,* 436 U.S. at 558-559. There must, however, be a substantial basis to conclude that the instrumentalities of the crime will be found on the premises to be searched. *U.S. v. Lockett,* 674 F.2d 843, 846 (11th Cir. 1982).

An affidavit that alleges facts based on the personal observation of the affiant sufficient to establish probable cause will support the issuance of a warrant. *James v. U.S.,* 418 F.2d 1150 (D.C. Cir. 1969); *U.S. v. Clancy,* 276 F.2d 617, 628 (7th Cir. 1960), *rev'd on other grounds,* 365 U.S. 312 (1961); *Overton v. U.S.,* 275 F.2d 897, 898 (D.C. Cir.), *cert. dismissed,* 362 U.S. 957 (1960). But personal knowledge is not essential for the issuance of a search warrant.

### § 207. — — Probable Cause Established by Hearsay.

Under Rule 41(c)(1) of the Federal Rules of Criminal Procedure the affidavit supporting a search warrant may be based upon hearsay.

When an informant was involved, the Supreme Court had established a two-pronged test to establish probable cause, requiring that the judge or magistrate be informed of underlying circumstances or facts sufficient that he could make an independent determination of (1) the credibility of the informant, and (2) the reliability of the information. *Aguilar v. Texas,* 378 U.S. 108 (1964); *Spinelli v. U.S.,* 393 U.S. 410 (1969). This test has been abandoned in favor of a "totality of the circumstances" approach to determine probable cause. The task of the magistrate is to make a practical, common-sense decision whether, given the matters set forth in the affidavit, there is a fair probability that contraband or evidence of a crime will be found in a particular place. An informant's reliability and basis for his knowledge is relevant to the totality of the circumstances test, but police work alone may be sufficient if it corroborates details of an informant's anonymous tip. *Massachusetts v. Upton,* 466 U.S. 727 (1984); *Illinois v. Gates,* 462 U.S. 213 (1983).

Traditionally, the credibility of the informant may be established by a recital of instances of his previous reliability, *U.S. v. Sumpter,* 669 F.2d 1215, 1220 (8th Cir. 1982); *U.S. v. Dudek,* 560 F.2d 1288 (6th Cir. 1977), *cert. denied,* 434 U.S. 1037 (1978), or by corroboration by the affiant's independent investigation of parts of the informant's story, *U.S. v. McGlynn,* 671 F.2d 1140, 1145 (8th Cir. 1982); *U.S. v. Williams,* 605 F.2d 495 (10th Cir.), *cert. denied,* 444 U.S. 932 (1979); *U.S. v. Rasor,* 599 F.2d 1330 (5th Cir. 1979); *U.S. v. Sclamo,* 578 F.2d 888 (1st Cir. 1978). Personal observation by the informant is sufficient to establish the reliability of the information. *U.S. v. McEachin,* 670 F.2d 1139, 1142-43 (D.C. Cir. 1981); *U.S. v. Rollins,* 522 F.2d 160, 164 (2d Cir. 1975), *cert. denied,* 424 U.S. 918 (1976); *U.S. v. Viggiano,* 433 F.2d 716, 719 (2d Cir. 1970), *cert. denied,* 401 U.S. 938 (1971). The fact that the informant was a government agent establishes a presumption of credibility. *U.S. v. Beusch,* 596 F.2d 871 (9th Cir. 1979). Likewise, the statement of the victim of a crime will be presumed credible, *U.S. v. Mahler,* 442 F.2d 1172 (9th Cir.), *cert. denied,* 404 U.S. 993 (1971), as well as that of an eyewitness to a crime, *U.S. v. Bell,* 457 F.2d 1231 (5th Cir. 1972). A statement against an informant's penal interest may provide a basis to credit the reliability of an informant, even if he is unidentified, *U.S. v. Harris,* 403 U.S. 573 (1971). *See also U.S. v. Lace,* 669 F.2d 46, 49 (2d Cir. 1982); *U.S. v. Hunley,* 567 F.2d 822 (8th Cir. 1977).

The credibility of the informer and the reliability of his information is satisfied if he has described criminal activity in sufficient detail. *U.S. v. Fried,* 576 F.2d 787 (9th Cir.), *cert. denied,* 439 U.S. 895 (1978); *U.S. v. Swihart,* 554 F.2d 264 (6th Cir. 1977). The description in an agent's affidavit giving specific facts of the contents of an allegedly obscene magazine was more than a mere conclusion and was held sufficient for the magistrate to make his own determination of probable cause. *U.S. v. Sherwin,* 572 F.2d 196 (9th Cir. 1977), *cert. denied,* 437 U.S. 909 (1978).

Even though the informant's past reliability is sufficiently established, when the underlying circumstances from which the magistrate might have concluded that the informant's information was accurate, were not recorded in any manner, even though testified to under oath, the affidavit did not reveal the underlying circumstances and there was not sufficient probable cause. *U.S. v. Hittle,* 575 F.2d 799 (10th Cir.

1978). An affidavit for a search warrant, with or without an attached transcript of testimony taken under oath by the magistrate, cannot be bolstered. It stands or falls on its own four corners in the face of an attack. *U.S. v. Hittle, supra.*

An evenly divided Supreme Court left standing a lower court holding that a statement taken in violation of *Miranda v. Arizona,* 384 U.S. 436 (1966), could not be used to establish probable cause for a search warrant. *Massachusetts v. White,* 439 U.S. 280 (1978).

## § 208. — — Sufficiency Determined by Common Sense Standards.

To encourage the obtaining of search warrants by law enforcement officials, common sense, not stringent or hypertechnical standards, is to be used in determining probable cause. *U.S. v. Sumpter,* 669 F.2d 1215, 1218 (8th Cir. 1982); *U.S. v. Seta,* 669 F.2d 400, 402 (6th Cir. 1982); *U.S. v. Williams,* 605 F.2d 495 (10th Cir.), *cert. denied,* 444 U.S. 932 (1979); *U.S. v. Middleton,* 599 F.2d 1349 (5th Cir. 1979); *U.S. v. Valenzuela,* 596 F.2d 824 (9th Cir. 1979). As the Supreme Court stated in *U.S. v. Ventresca,* 380 U.S. 102, 108 (1965):

> [A]ffidavits for search warrants, such as the one involved here, must be tested and interpreted by magistrates and courts in a common sense and realistic fashion. They are normally drafted by nonlawyers in the midst and haste of a criminal investigation. Technical requirements of elaborate specificity once exacted under common law pleadings have no proper place in this area. A grudging or negative attitude by reviewing courts toward warrants will tend to discourage police officers from submitting their evidence to a judicial officer before acting.

If a judge or magistrate is provided with sufficient information to enable him to make a considered judicial determination of probable cause, whether such determination is grounded upon the personal observation of the affiant or hearsay information secured by an informant, a reviewing court will pay substantial deference to that determination. *Aguilar v. Texas,* 378 U.S. at 111; *U.S. v. Allen,* 588 F.2d 1100 (5th Cir.), *cert. denied,* 441 U.S. 965 (1979); *U.S. v. Brown,* 584 F.2d 252 (8th Cir. 1978).

## § 209. — — Magistrate Must Be Neutral.

The magistrate must not "serve merely as a rubber stamp for the police." He must be neutral and detached in deciding whether there is sufficient cause to justify issuance of a search warrant. *U.S. v. Ventresca,* 380 U.S. at 109; *U.S. v. Ford,* 553 F.2d 146 (D.C. Cir. 1977).

In *Coolidge v. New Hampshire,* 403 U.S. 443, 449-53 (1971), although applicable state law authorized the attorney general, who was actively in charge of the investigation and later was to be chief prosecutor at the trial, to issue a search warrant, the Court held that the practice violated the fourth amendment. In doing so, the Court refused to consider the state's contentions that the attorney general did, in fact, act as a neutral and detached magistrate and that the state's showing of probable cause was so substantial any magistrate would have issued the warrant in question. The Supreme Court also has held that, when a town justice authorized a search warrant and then accompanied the police in its execution and ordered certain items to be seized, it was "difficult to discern when he was acting as a 'neutral and detached' judicial officer and when he was one with the police and prosecutors." *Lo-Ji Sales, Inc. v. New York,* 442 U.S. 319, 328 (1979). *See also Connally v. Georgia,* 429 U.S. 245 (1977).

### § 210. — — False Statements in Affidavit.

There is a presumption of the validity of the affidavit supporting a search warrant. If a defendant wishes to challenge the probable cause for a search warrant by claiming there were false statements in the affidavit supporting the warrant, he must make a substantial preliminary showing that: (1) the false statement was made knowingly and intentionally, or with reckless disregard for the truth; and (2) the allegedly false statement is necessary to the finding of probable cause. If the defendant establishes these two points, a hearing must be held. To mandate such a hearing, however, the attack must be more than conclusory, and it must be supported by more than a mere desire to cross-examine. The defendant must point out specifically, with supporting reasons, the portion of the affidavit claimed to be false, accompanied by an offer of proof including affidavits or otherwise reliable statements of witnesses or a satisfactory explanation of their absence. Allegations of negligence or innocent mistake are insufficient. The deliberate falsity or reckless disregard can be only that of the affiant, not of any nongovernmental informant. Furthermore, no hearing will be held if the affidavit is still sufficient for probable cause without the false statement.

At the hearing, the defendant must establish by a preponderance of the evidence that a false statement, made knowingly and intentionally or with reckless disregard for the truth, is included in the affidavit. Then, only if the affidavit is insufficient to establish probable cause without the false material, will the search warrant be voided and the fruits of the search excluded. *Franks v. Delaware,* 438 U.S. 154 (1978); *U.S. v. Damon,* 676 F.2d 1060, 1065 (5th Cir. 1982); *U.S. v. Axselle,* 604

F.2d 1330 (10th Cir. 1979); *U.S. v. Licavoli,* 604 F.2d 613 (9th Cir. 1979); *U.S. v. House,* 604 F.2d 1135 (8th Cir. 1979).

Ambiguity of statements does not constitute recklessness or an intent to deceive. *U.S. v. Lyon,* 567 F.2d 777 (8th Cir. 1977), *cert. denied,* 435 U.S. 918 (1978). Erroneous assumptions in an affidavit made by a federal agent from information he had received did not amount to reckless inclusion of false statements in his affidavit. *U.S. v. Smith,* 588 F.2d 737 (9th Cir. 1978), *cert. denied,* 440 U.S. 939 (1979). An informant, whether paid or not, is not a government agent whose perjury would vitiate a search warrant so long as the affiant accurately represented what he was told. *U.S. v. Barnes,* 604 F.2d 121 (2d Cir. 1979); *U.S. v. Abramson,* 553 F.2d 1164 (8th Cir.), *cert. denied,* 433 U.S. 911 (1977).

## § 211. — Particularity of Description.

The fourth amendment requires that a search warrant "particularly" describe (1) "the place to be searched," and (2) "the persons or things to be seized." General exploratory searches are forbidden. *Stanford v. Texas,* 379 U.S. 476 (1965). But the Supreme Court has interpreted this provision to require only that the description be "such that the officer with a search warrant can with reasonable effort ascertain and identify the place intended." *Steele v. U.S.,* 267 U.S. 498, 503 (1925). Thus, in *Steele,* where a building having two different addresses was used as one unit, a warrant listing one address was held sufficient to authorize a search of the entire building.

Where there was a mistake of fact by the police officer who provided the information for the warrant in that he described an apartment as the entire floor when there were actually two apartments does not invalidate the warrant if the officer's failure to realize the overbreath of the warrant was objectively reasonable. *Maryland v. Garrison,* 107 S. Ct. 1013 (1987).

A test for determining the sufficiency of the description of the places to be searched is "whether the place to be searched is described with sufficient particularity to enable the executing officer to locate and identify the premises with reasonable effort, and whether there is any reasonable probability that another premise might be mistakenly searched." *U.S. v. McCain,* 677 F.2d 657, 660 (8th Cir. 1982); *Kenney v. U.S.,* 157 F.2d 442 (D.C. Cir. 1946). Thus, specifying a place by its commonly known name is sufficient even though the exact description may not be correct. *U.S. v. Palmer,* 667 F.2d 1118, 1120 (4th Cir. 1981).

Where the address on the warrant is a building which contains a number of apartments but the name on the warrant enables the officers to determine which apartment is intended, the description has been held sufficient. *U.S. v. Campanile,* 516 F.2d 288 (2d Cir. 1975). Probable cause must be shown to search each specific apartment, however, and a warrant naming an entire building containing four apartments has been struck down. *U.S. v. Hinton,* 219 F.2d 324 (7th Cir. 1955). On the other hand, the search of a two-unit building was upheld where the officers had reason to believe it was a single-family dwelling and upon discovering the separate occupancy ceased searching the second unit. *U.S. v. Davis,* 557 F.2d 1239 (8th Cir.), *cert. denied,* 434 U.S. 971 (1977). Also, a warrant directed to the "entire premises" was upheld even though the building was a rooming house, where there were no separate entrances, doorbells, mailboxes, or other indicia by which the police could reasonably know that the building was a multiple dwelling. *U.S. v. Dorsey,* 591 F.2d 922 (D.C. Cir. 1978). Specifying by mistake the wrong city in the body of a search warrant was not fatal where the correct address and city were listed in the affidavit and the caption of the search warrant. *U.S. v. Avarello,* 592 F.2d 1339 (5th Cir.), *cert. denied,* 444 U.S. 844 (1979).

The degree of specificity required for a warrant may vary depending upon the circumstances. It has been held that a warrant authorizing the search of persons and/or baggage being met at the airport by named person on specific date was sufficiently definite where the agent had probable cause to believe cocaine was being delivered, but could not ascertain the identities of persons arriving or get a description of the baggage. *U.S. v. Muckenthaler,* 584 F.2d 240 (8th Cir. 1978).

Where property to be seized is being moved from place to place and it was reasonable that it would be found at either or both places it was proper to issue warrants to multiple locations. *U.S. v. Hillyard,* 677 F.2d 1336, 1339 (9th Cir. 1982).

The items to be seized must be particularized. "As to what is to be taken, nothing is left to the discretion of the officer executing the warrant." *Marron v. U.S.,* 275 U.S. 192, 196 (1927). *Accord, Stanford v. Texas,* 379 U.S. 476, 486 (1965). Open-ended or general warrants are prohibited. Authorizing the seizure of "material evidence of violation of 28 U.S.C. §§ 841, 846. Manufacture and possession with intent to distribute amphetamine and conspiracy," is too general. *U.S. v. Crozier,* 674 F.2d 1293, 1299 (9th Cir. 1982). Where the warrant specified two allegedly obscene films and also authorized seizure of similar items on the premises, it was held the warrant left it entirely to the officials conducting the search to decide what was obscene. The fact that the local justice participated in the search did not cure the warrant's defect. *Lo-Ji Sales, Inc. v. New York,* 442 U.S. 319 (1979). The particularity requirement was violated where the warrant authorized seizure of all records, including patient files, relating to fraudulent Medicare and Medicaid claims because there was no time limitation or description of the records to be seized and the agents — without guidance to distinguish *bona fide* records from fraudulent records — seized all of the records in the doctor's office. *U.S. v. Abrams,* 615 F.2d 541 (1st Cir. 1980). Warrants were likewise defective where all illegal recordings were to be seized, without differentiating these from the rest of the inventory. *Montilla Records of Puerto Rico, Inc. v. Morales,* 575 F.2d 324 (1st Cir. 1978). *See also U.S. v. Drebin,* 557 F.2d 1316 (9th Cir. 1977), *cert. denied,* 436 U.S. 904 (1978).

The Court upheld the seizure of incriminating documents under a warrant containing a long list of particular items relating to Lot 13T followed by the phrase "together with other fruits, instrumentalities and evidence of crime at this [time] unknown." *Andresen v. Maryland,* 427 U.S. 463 (1976). In that case, the Court said that it was not a general warrant, and in context authorized a search only for evidence relevant to the crime of false pretenses and Lot 13T. The warrant must be "reasonably specific, rather than elaborately detailed, in its description of the objects of the search." *U.S. v. Brock,* 667 F.2d 1311, 1322 (9th Cir. 1982). A warrant authorizing a search for evidence of various crimes "which facts recited in the accompanying [33-page] affidavit make out," has been upheld. *In re Search Warrant Dated July 4, 1977, Etc.,* 572 F.2d 321, 326 (D.C. Cir. 1977), *cert. denied,* 435 U.S. 925 (1978).

A generic description may be used in a warrant where there is reason to believe a large collection of similar contraband is on the premises to be searched, and a method to differentiate contraband from the rest of the inventory is set out, *U.S. v. Cortellesso,* 601 F.2d 28 (1st Cir. 1979), or where more than a general description would be impossible as "white string, brown paper, corregated *(sic)* paper ..." which were materials found in the vicinity of an explosion, *U.S. v. Davis,* 589 F.2d 904, 906 (5th Cir.), *cert. denied,* 441 U.S. 950 (1979).

## § 212. — Execution of Search Warrant.

## § 213. — — Who May Execute Warrant.

Under Rule 41(c) of the Federal Rules of Criminal Procedure a search warrant shall be directed to a law enforcement officer. Pursuant to 18 U.S.C. § 3105, it may be executed by: (1) the person to whom the warrant is directed, (2) any officer authorized by law to execute a search warrant, or (3) some other person aiding a person under (1) or

(2) who is present and acting in execution of the warrant. Execution of a search warrant by an unauthorized person renders the search illegal. *U.S. v. Martin,* 600 F.2d 1175 (5th Cir. 1979).

Under 18 U.S.C. § 3105, unnamed federal agents may aid other federal agents who are named in the warrant, *U.S. v. Hare,* 589 F.2d 1291 (6th Cir. 1979); state officers may participate with federal agents executing a federal warrant, *U.S. v. Wright,* 667 F.2d 793, 797 (9th Cir. 1982); *U.S. v. Lee,* 581 F.2d 1173 (6th Cir.), *cert. denied,* 439 U.S. 1048 (1978); *U.S. v. Echols,* 577 F.2d 308 (5th Cir.), *cert. denied,* 440 U.S. 939 (1979); federal agents may assist state law enforcement officers in executing a state search warrant, *U.S. v. Martin,* 600 F.2d at 1182; and security officers of a telephone company have been permitted to accompany agents executing a warrant to identify any telephone company property on the premises, *U.S. v. Clouston,* 623 F.2d 485 (6th Cir. 1980). However, a federal agent who has the time and probable cause to obtain a search warrant for explosives cannot validate his warrantless search for explosives by assisting a state narcotics officer who is searching for narcotics under a proper search warrant. These are two simultaneous but distinct searches. *U.S. v. Sanchez,* 509 F.2d 886 (6th Cir. 1975).

## § 214. — — When Must Search Warrant Be Executed.

Rule 41(c) of the Federal Rules of Criminal Procedure further directs an officer to serve a warrant within 10 days and "in the daytime, unless the issuing authority, by appropriate provision in the warrant, and for reasonable cause shown, authorizes its execution at times other than daytime." Rule 41(h), defines the term "daytime" as "the hours from 6 a.m. to 10 p.m. according to local time."

Searches which began at 8:12 p.m., *U.S. v. Forsythe,* 560 F.2d 1127 (3d Cir. 1977), and at 9 p.m., *U.S. v. Lustig,* 555 F.2d 737 (9th Cir. 1977), *cert. denied,* 434 U.S. 1045 (1978), have been held to be daytime searches. A case, decided before Rule 41(h) defined "daytime" as 6 a.m. to 10 p.m., held that a search begun in the afternoon which continued after nightfall qualified as a daytime search. *U.S. v. Joseph,* 278 F.2d 504 (3d Cir.), *cert. denied,* 364 U.S. 823 (1960).

Where a state judge did not explicitly authorize a night search, but the warrant was issued at night and the preprinted forms stated and the issuing judge understood that it was to be executed immediately, it was held to be a permitted nighttime search within the requirements of Rule 41(c). *U.S. v. Sturgeon,* 501 F.2d 1270 (8th Cir.), *cert. denied,* 419 U.S. 1071 (1974). In similar circumstances, another circuit has disagreed with this holding, noting that Rule 41 requires an explicit authorization justified by reasonable cause for a night search; but, since this was a procedural matter rather than a constitutional right, in the circumstances of the particular case, that violation of the rule did not require suppression of the evidence. *U.S. v. Searp*, 586 F.2d 1117 (6th Cir. 1978), *cert. denied*, 440 U.S. 921 (1979).

Pursuant to 21 U.S.C. § 879, search warrants involving drug offenses require "no special showing for a nighttime search, other than a showing that the contraband is likely to be on the property or person to be searched at that time." *Gooding v. U.S.*, 416 U.S. 430, 458 (1974).

A search warrant has been sustained which was not served for nine days because the agents were waiting for the defendant to return to his apartment. They had information that he was using the apartment only as a plant to repackage heroin and wished to wait until he was at the apartment so that they could be sure that the alleged contraband was present. *U.S. v. Dunnings*, 425 F.2d 836 (2d Cir. 1969), *cert. denied*, 397 U.S. 1002 (1970).

## § 215. — — Manner of Entry to Search.

An officer serving a search warrant at a house, absent exigent circumstances, must announce: (1) the authority under which he is acting, and (2) the purpose of his call. If he is refused admittance to the premises after such announcement, he may enter forcibly. 18 U.S.C. § 3109; *U.S. v. Woodring*, 444 F.2d 749 (9th Cir. 1971). Merely opening an unlocked door is a forced entry. *Sabbath v. U.S.*, 391 U.S. 585 (1968). In *Miller v. U.S.*, 357 U.S. 301, 304 (1958), because "[t]hey did not expressly demand admission or state their purpose for their presence," an arrest was held unlawful when officers responded "police" in a low voice to the defendant's inquiry, "Who's there?", and then broke into his home when the defendant quickly attempted to close the door. All evidence seized as a result of the unlawful arrest was inadmissible.

Although 18 U.S.C. § 3109 does not apply to warrants executed by state officers only, their conduct must be reasonable within the meaning of the fourth amendment, and "to some extent" the requirements of 18 U.S.C. § 3109 "have been incorporated into the Fourth Amendment." *U.S. v. Bustamante-Gamez*, 488 F.2d 4, 9 (9th Cir. 1973), *cert. denied*, 416 U.S. 970 (1974); *U.S. v. Valenzuela*, 596 F.2d 824 (9th Cir. 1979).

If the agent does announce his authority and purpose, exigent circumstances may justify his breaking-in, even though he has not been refused admittance, when the agent heard someone yell, "It's the cops," and running, where there was concern about destruction of evidence, *U.S. v. Carter*, 566 F.2d 1265, 1267-68 (5th Cir.), *cert. denied*, 436 U.S.

956 (1978); and the same reason may justify an entry simultaneously with the announcement of identity and purpose, *U.S. v. Jackson,* 585 F.2d 653 (4th Cir. 1978). But when the agents turned a door knob and plunged into the living room before they had intended to enter, and there were no exigent circumstances, the evidence was inadmissible. *U.S. v. Pratter,* 465 F.2d 227 (7th Cir. 1972).

Forcible entries without announcement of purpose and a refusal of admittance have been approved where: (1) there would be danger to the officer, (2) there would be danger of flight or destruction of evidence, (3) in situations where a victim or some other person is in peril, or (4) where it would be a "useless gesture" such as when the persons within already knew the officers' authority and purpose. *U.S. v. Wylie,* 462 F.2d 1178 (D.C. Cir. 1972); *Ker v. California,* 374 U.S. 23, 39 (1963); *U.S. v. Artieri,* 491 F.2d 440 (2d Cir.), *cert. denied,* 419 U.S. 878 (1974); *U.S. v. Mapp,* 476 F.2d 67, 75 (2d Cir. 1973); *U.S. v. Manning,* 448 F.2d 992, 1001-02 (2d Cir.), *cert. denied,* 404 U.S. 995 (1971).

In *U.S. v. Nicholas,* 319 F.2d 697, 698 (2d Cir.), *cert. denied,* 375 U.S. 933 (1963), narcotics agents went to the defendant's apartment to arrest the defendant. When they informed his wife of their identity at the door she threw herself at one of the officers and screamed, "Police." The agents then entered the apartment, observed the defendant throw narcotics out of the window, and arrested him. The court held that "the agents had no opportunity to announce their purpose and were justified in believing that [the wife] had jumped to the conclusion that the agents were present for the purpose of making an arrest, thus making an announcement a useless gesture." Notice has been held unnecessary where "arresting officers could be virtually certain that the person denying entrance knew their identity and purpose." *U.S. v. Singleton,* 439 F.2d 381, 385-86 (3d Cir. 1971).

If no one is present, it is not necessary to give notice, and the search can be conducted in the absence of the occupant. *U.S. v. Brown,* 556 F.2d 304 (5th Cir. 1977); *Payne v. U.S.,* 508 F.2d 1391 (5th Cir.), *cert. denied,* 423 U.S. 933 (1975); *U.S. v. Gervato,* 474 F.2d 40 (3d Cir.), *cert. denied,* 414 U.S. 864 (1973).

The requirement of announcement of authority and purpose has also been held inapplicable when the agent's entry was not forcible or was obtained with the consent of the occupant. A ruse may not violate § 3109, *U.S. v. Beale,* 445 F.2d 977 (5th Cir. 1971), *cert. denied,* 404 U.S. 1026 (1972); *U.S. v. Syler,* 430 F.2d 68, 70 (7th Cir. 1970); entry through door opened by occupant may be proper, *Reyes v. U.S.,* 417 F.2d 916, 919 (9th Cir. 1969); *U.S. v. Marson,* 408 F.2d 644, 646-47 (4th Cir. 1968), *cert. denied,* 393 U.S. 1056 (1969). An officer who walked in past unaware defendant who unlocked door for another purpose did not "break" in, *U.S. v. Conti,* 361 F.2d 153, 157 (2d Cir. 1966), *vacated per curiam on other grounds,* 390 U.S. 204 (1968). Bribing the five-year-old son of the defendant to lead police to cache of heroin while executing a search warrant has been permitted. *U.S. v. Penn,* 647 F.2d 876 (9th Cir. 1980) *(en banc).*

In *U.S. v. Hutchinson,* 488 F.2d 484 (8th Cir. 1973), *cert. denied,* 417 U.S. 915 (1974), the court approved entry without announcement of authority or purpose where an undercover agent was first invited into a house to complete a narcotics transaction, subsequently left and returned with a search warrant and other agents. *See also Lewis v. U.S.,* 385 U.S. 206 (1966); *U.S. v. Bradley,* 455 F.2d 1181 (1st Cir.), *aff'd,* 410 U.S. 605 (1972).

In *Jones v. U.S.,* 304 F.2d 381 (D.C. Cir.), *cert. denied,* 371 U.S. 852 (1962), the court held that a search warrant was properly executed by narcotics agents and police officers, although the agents tricked the defendant by having the janitor announce himself at the door of the apartment. Upon the defendant opening the door three or four inches, one of the officers thrust his badge and search warrant through the opening and informed the defendant of the warrant. When the defendant ran, the officer pulled the door open, the night chain slipped off, and the officers entered and placed the defendant under arrest. *But see Wong Sun v. U.S.,* 371 U.S. 471, 482-84 (1963), in which the arrest was held improper since probable cause was partially based on the flight of defendant which occurred after officer first misrepresented his purpose and authority. Although eventually the officer did disclose his identity, it was said he "never adequately dispelled the misimpression engendered by his own use."

There is a split of authority whether the knock and announce requirements of 18 U.S.C. § 3109 apply to businesses as well as dwellings. *U.S. v. Agrusa,* 541 F.2d 690 (8th Cir.), *cert. denied,* 429 U.S. 1045 (1976); and *U.S. v. Jones,* 466 F.2d 1364 (5th Cir. 1972), hold that they do; while *U.S. v. Francis,* 646 F.2d 251 (6th Cir. 1981); *U.S. v. Phillips,* 497 F.2d 1131 (9th Cir. 1974); and *U.S. v. Case,* 435 F.2d 766 (7th Cir. 1970), restrict the requirements of 18 U.S.C. § 3109 to dwellings.

## § 216. — Telephone Search Warrants.

Rule 41(c)(2) of the Federal Rules of Criminal Procedure provides for the issuance of a search warrant only by a federal magistrate based upon sworn oral testimony received from the government affiant, either by telephone or other appropriate means, when it is not reasonably practicable for the person to present a written affidavit. The Advisory Committee's Note suggests such circumstances would include delay that might result in the destruction or disappearance of property, the time of day when a warrant is sought, or the distance from the magistrate of the person seeking the warrant.

The availability of a telephone warrant means that a warrant may now be required where the amount of time necessary to obtain a warrant by traditional means would justify the warrantless entry of a home because of exigent circumstances. *U.S. v. McEachin,* 670 F.2d 1139, 1147 (D.C. Cir. 1981); *U.S. v. Baker,* 520 F. Supp. 1080, 1083-85 (S.D. Iowa 1981).

Rule 41(c)(2) contains a number of special, technical requirements. Although it was held that the failure of the government agent to fill out the "duplicate original warrant" before his call to the magistrate was harmless procedural error; failure to administer the required oath "immediately" or in advance of the testimony given (even though the oath was given later in the telephone proceeding), rendered the search invalid because the Congressional purpose was to impress on the caller the "solemnity of the proceeding in spite of the lack of formal appearance before a court." *U.S. v. Shorter,* 600 F.2d 585, 588 (6th Cir. 1979).

## § 217. Warrantless Searches.

Searches that are not conducted pursuant to a valid warrant "are *per se* unreasonable under the Fourth Amendment — subject only to a few specifically established and well-delineated exceptions. *Katz v. U.S.,* 389 U.S. 347 (1967)." *Mincey v. Arizona,* 437 U.S. 385, 390 (1978). Although the burden is on the defendant to go forward and prove that the search was warrantless, the burden is then on the government to prove by a preponderance of the evidence that the search comes within an exception to the warrant requirement. *Lego v. Twomey,* 404 U.S. 477 (1972); *Coolidge v. New Hampshire,* 403 U.S. 443 (1971).

The fourth amendment applies to public school officials as well as law enforcement officials. However, the restrictions which normally apply are eased. School officials need not obtain a warrant before searching a student, and a search by school officials need not be based on probable cause. The legality of such a search depends upon the reasonableness under all of the circumstances. *New Jersey v. T.L.O.,* 469 U.S. 325 (1985). *See also O'Connor v. Ortega,* 107 S. Ct. 1492 (1987), for a discussion of reasonableness under all of the circumstances for a warrantless search of a government employee's office by his employer, and *Griffin v. Wisconsin,* 107 S. Ct. —, 41 Crim. L. Rep. 3424 (1987), where the "reasonable grounds" standard was permitted

for the search for contraband conducted by a probationer's probation
officer without a search warrant.

## § 218. — Search Incident to Valid Arrest.

A person validly arrested may be searched without a warrant. There
does not need to be any indication that the person arrested possessed
weapons or evidence. Although there must be probable cause for the
arrest, probable cause for the search is not required. The lawful arrest,
standing alone, authorizes a search. *Michigan v. DeFillippo,* 443 U.S.
31 (1979); *U.S. v. Robinson,* 414 U.S. 218 (1973); *Chimel v. California,*
395 U.S. 752 (1969); *U.S. v. Matthews,* 603 F.2d 48 (8th Cir. 1979), *cert.
denied,* 444 U.S. 1019 (1980).

## § 219. — — Validity of the Arrest.

When a search is made incident to an arrest, the validity of the
search depends upon the lawfulness of the arrest. If the arrest is illegal, the search pursuant to it will also be illegal, and any items seized
will be inadmissible. *Henry v. U.S.,* 361 U.S. 98 (1959); *U.S. v. Bonds,*
422 F.2d 660 (8th Cir. 1970); *Riccardi v. Perini,* 417 F.2d 645 (6th Cir.
1969); *Jones v. Peyton,* 411 F.2d 857 (4th Cir.), *cert. denied,* 396 U.S.
942 (1969). Thus, where police had the right to make an investigative
stop of a nervous man who paid cash for his airline tickets, but no
probable cause for an arrest, consent of the defendant to search his
luggage while he was being illegally detained was not effective to
justify the search. *Florida v. Rogers,* 460 U.S. 491 (1983). Likewise,
where there was no probable cause to arrest the defendant, no consent
to a journey to the police station and no prior judicial authorization to
detain him, fingerprints taken at the police station were inadmissible.
*Hayes v. Florida,* 470 U.S. 811 (1985).

An arrest based on assumptions later found to be erroneous may be
valid if at the time of the arrest the officer had probable cause to
believe a crime had been committed and that the person arrested committed it. *U.S. v. Allen,* 629 F.2d 51 (D.C. Cir. 1980).

As entry into the home is the chief evil against which the fourth
amendment is directed, exigent circumstances will rarely justify the
warrantless entry of a home to make an arrest for a minor offense.
*Welsh v. Wisconsin,* 466 U.S. 740 (1984).

If an arrest is lawful under a presumptively valid ordinance, the
search which follows is valid even though the ordinance is later declared unconstitutional. *Michigan v. DeFillippo,* 443 U.S. 31 (1979). If,
however, the statute itself authorizes searches under circumstances

which do not satisfy traditional warrant and probable cause requirements of the fourth amendment, evidence obtained pursuant to such searches will be suppressed. Thus, warrantless entry of a home to effect an arrest under authority of a statute authorizing officers to enter a private residence without a warrant to make a routine felony arrest is unconstitutional. *Payton v. New York,* 445 U.S. 573 (1980). However, if officers had probable cause to arrest a defendant, an arrest in his home in violation of *Payton* does not require either release of the defendant once he is removed from the home or suppression of a statement made by the defendant outside the home. *New York v. Harris,* 495 U.S. 14 (1990). *See also Torres v. Puerto Rico,* 442 U.S. 465 (1979) (Puerto Rico statute authorizing baggage search of anyone arriving from the U.S.); *Almeida-Sanchez v. U.S.,* 413 U.S. 266 (1973) (statute authorized border patrol to search any vehicle within a "reasonable distance" of the border plus a regulation fixing 100 miles as "reasonable distance").

For a search incident to arrest to come within the exception to the warrant requirement, two factors must be present. First, the arresting officer must have the authority to make a valid arrest. Second, the arrest must be based on probable cause. *Sibron v. New York,* 392 U.S. 40, 62-63 (1968); *Aguilar v. Texas,* 378 U.S. 108 (1964); *Henry v. U.S.,* 361 U.S. 98, 100 (1959); *Brinegar v. U.S.,* 338 U.S. 160 (1949); *U.S. v. Garrett,* 627 F.2d 14 (6th Cir. 1980); *U.S. v. Fernandez-Guzman,* 577 F.2d 1093 (7th Cir.), *cert. denied,* 439 U.S. 954 (1978).

Federal statutes that authorize federal officers to make arrests generally, or under limitations, include the following: FBI agents, 18 U.S.C. § 3052; United States Marshals, 18 U.S.C. § 3053; Bureau of Prisons employees, 18 U.S.C. § 3050 and 21 U.S.C. § 878(2) and (3); Secret Service, 18 U.S.C. § 3056; probation officers, 18 U.S.C. § 3653; immigration officers and employees, 8 U.S.C. § 1357; Postal Inspectors, 18 U.S.C. § 3061; Treasury Department officers, 19 U.S.C. § 1581(b); State Department security officers, 22 U.S.C. § 2667; Customs officers, 19 U.S.C. § 1581 and 26 U.S.C. § 7607; Internal Revenue enforcement officers, 26 U.S.C. § 7608; Forest Service employees, 16 U.S.C. § 559; and Drug Enforcement Administration agents, 21 U.S.C. § 878(2)-(3). Procedural requirements that govern arrests for federal offenses are found in Rule 5(a) of the Federal Rules of Criminal Procedure and 18 U.S.C. § 3109.

In the absence of an applicable federal statute, the validity of an arrest for a federal offense without a warrant depends on the law of the state where the arrest takes place. *Ker v. California,* 374 U.S. 23, 34-37 (1963); *U.S. v. Di Re,* 332 U.S. 581, 590 (1948); *Montgomery v. U.S.,* 403 F.2d 605, 608 (8th Cir. 1968), *cert. denied,* 396 U.S. 859 (1969).

State law determines the validity of an arrest without a warrant for violation of state law, subject to minimum standards required by the Constitution. *U.S. ex rel. LaBelle v. LaVallee,* 517 F.2d 750 (2d Cir. 1975), *cert. denied,* 423 U.S. 1062 (1976); *Burks v. U.S.,* 287 F.2d 117 (9th Cir. 1961), *cert. denied,* 369 U.S. 841 (1962). *See Sibron v. New York,* 392 U.S. 40 (1968); *Terry v. Ohio,* 392 U.S. 1 (1968); *U.S. v. Lewis,* 362 F.2d 759, 761 (2d Cir. 1966). A search conducted incident to the valid arrest of a citizen comes within this exception to the warrant requirement. *U.S. v. Rosse,* 418 F.2d 38 (2d Cir. 1969), *cert. denied,* 397 U.S. 998 (1970); *U.S. v. Viale,* 312 F.2d 595, 599-601 (2d Cir.), *cert. denied,* 373 U.S. 903 (1963).

Probable cause exists when a "person of reasonable caution would be justified in believing that the individual to be arrested has committed, is committing, or is about to commit a crime." *U.S. v. Marin,* 669 F.2d 73, 81 (2d Cir. 1982). Probable cause is established by the totality of the circumstance. Suspicion, flight, concealment of a transaction, or presence in a neighborhood notorious for narcotics sales alone did not establish probable cause, but all of these factors together provided a sufficient basis to conclude that the defendant was engaged in criminal activity. *U.S. v. Green,* 670 F.2d 1148, 1151-53 (D.C. Cir. 1981).

The arrest may not be justified by what is disclosed upon a subsequent search. If the arrest is unlawful at its inception, it remains so. If there is no probable cause for the arrest, the search is invalid. *Dunaway v. New York,* 442 U.S. 200 (1979); *Beck v. Ohio,* 379 U.S. 89 (1964); *Wong Sun v. U.S.,* 371 U.S. 471, 484 (1963); *U.S. v. Coker,* 599 F.2d 950 (10th Cir. 1979). Even if the arrest is lawful, there is authority for the proposition that the government cannot rely upon the arrest to seize evidence without a warrant if it long had probable cause to know that the evidence would be there and could easily have obtained a search warrant. *Niro v. U.S.,* 388 F.2d 535 (1st Cir. 1968).

When a search is made incident to an arrest, and the arrest is made inside the defendant's dwelling, the standards of 18 U.S.C. § 3109 apply so as to require an announcement of authority and purpose before breaking and entering. *Sabbath v. U.S.,* 391 U.S. 585 (1968); *Miller v. U.S.,* 357 U.S. 301 (1958). These cases, however, are now limited to situations where exigent circumstances exist, as generally a warrant is required to forcibly enter a person's home to make an arrest. *Payton v. New York,* 445 U.S. 573 (1980). But announcement of purpose is not specifically required if certain exigent circumstances exist. *U.S. v. Artieri,* 491 F.2d 440 (2d Cir.), *cert. denied,* 417 U.S. 949 (1974); *U.S. v. Manning,* 448 F.2d 992, 1000-02 (2d Cir.), *cert. denied,* 404 U.S. 995 (1971). However, an arrest warrant is not sufficient to justify the search of the home of a third party for the subject of the warrant. *Steagald v. U.S.*, 451 U.S. 204 (1981).

### § 220. — — When a Person Is Under Arrest.

An arrest requires either physical force to restrain movement, or where that is absent, submission to the assertion of authority. A policeman yelling "Stop, in the name of the law!" at a fleeing form that continues to flee is not sufficient. *California v. Hodari D.*, 111 S. Ct. 1547 (1991).

Once a suspect is taken into custody or otherwise deprived of his freedom of action in any significant way, he is "under arrest." *Henry v. U.S.*, 361 U.S. 98, 103 (1959). In *Henry*, after twice observing cartons being loaded into a car, FBI agents who were investigating theft of an interstate whiskey shipment stopped the car in which two persons were riding. A subsequent search of the car uncovered cartons of stolen radios, and defendants were then formally placed under arrest. The Court held that the arrest occurred when the agents stopped the car, stating that, when "the officers interrupted the two men and restricted their liberty of movement, the arrest, for purposes of this case, was complete" and, finding that the officers did not have probable cause at that point, held the search illegal. *See also Colorado v. Bannister*, 449 U.S. 1 (1980); *Dunaway v. New York*, 442 U.S. 200 (1979). An "arrest unsupported by probable cause [cannot] be saved by redesignating it an investigative stop." *U.S. v. Beck*, 598 F.2d 497, 501 n.3 (9th Cir. 1979).

An arrest is not determined by the subjective intent of the officers, *Taylor v. Arizona*, 471 F.2d 848 (9th Cir. 1972), *cert. denied*, 409 U.S. 1130 (1973), although the intention of the officers to hold the defendant is a factor, *U.S. v. Morin*, 665 F.2d 765, 769-70 (5th Cir. 1982). More than a restriction of liberty is required, and courts will also consider the degree of force used in the stay and detention. *U.S. v. Beck*, 598 F.2d at 502. Whether there is an arrest depends upon an evaluation of all the circumstances. *U.S. v. Richards*, 500 F.2d 1025 (9th Cir. 1974), *cert. denied*, 420 U.S. 924 (1975). Circumstances to consider include, whether probable cause to arrest has arisen, whether intent of the officer was to hold the defendant, whether the defendant believed his freedom was restricted, whether the investigation had focused upon the defendant, and successive stops of the defendant without additional information. *U.S. v. Morin*, 665 F.2d at 769. Cooperation with agents to allay suspicions does not constitute an arrest. *Oregon v. Mathiason*, 429 U.S. 492 (1977); *U.S. v. Chaffen*, 587 F.2d 920 (8th Cir. 1978); *U.S. v. Canales*, 572 F.2d 1182 (6th Cir. 1978). Where the defendant, "incapacitated by alcohol," was placed under temporary detention which was not an "arrest" under state law, there could be no search incident to an arrest; but police could make a routine inventory of defendant's belongings. *U.S. v. Gallop,* 606 F.2d 836 (9th Cir. 1979).

### § 221. — — Arrest Must Be Made in Good Faith and Not as a Pretext to Justify Search.

Evidence seized in a search incident to an arrest without a warrant was suppressed because the court found that the officers' primary reason for going to the defendant's apartment was to make a search, noting that the manner in which officers were posted at the defendant's apartment was "inconsistent with a primary purpose of arrest." *U.S. v. Harris,* 321 F.2d 739, 742 (6th Cir. 1963). In addition, the court noted that one month earlier officers had made a similar search of the defendant's apartment, but released the defendant when no evidence of narcotics was found. *Id. See also U.S. v. Carriger,* 541 F.2d 545 (6th Cir. 1976). Where the arrest of a defendant on a traffic charge by narcotics officers was a pretext to search his automobile, the heroin seized was inadmissible. *Amador-Gonzalez v. U.S.,* 391 F.2d 308 (5th Cir. 1968). However, arrests which were delayed until defendants were inside a house were not a pretext for making a warrantless search of the premises under the circumstances of the case. *U.S. v. Woods,* 544 F.2d 242 (6th Cir. 1976), *cert. denied,* 429 U.S. 1062 (1977).

### § 222. — — Search Must Be Contemporaneous With Arrest.

A search is incident to an arrest only if it is substantially contemporaneous with the arrest and is confined to the immediate vicinity of the arrest. *Shipley v. California,* 395 U.S. 818, 819 (1969); *Von Cleef v. New Jersey,* 395 U.S. 814 (1969). The permitted purposes of the search are (1) to seize weapons to protect the arresting agents, (2) to prevent destruction of evidence, and (3) to prevent escape. *Chimel v. California,* 395 U.S. 752 (1969); *U.S. v. Chadwick,* 433 U.S. 1 (1977).

A search contemporaneous with an arrest is legal where there is probable cause for the arrest. *U.S. v. Costello,* 604 F.2d 589 (8th Cir. 1979). The warrantless search may be before the actual arrest, so long as there was probable cause for the arrest. *U.S. v. Chatman,* 573 F.2d 565 (9th Cir. 1977); *U.S. v. Jenkins,* 496 F.2d 57, 73 (2d Cir. 1974), *cert. denied,* 420 U.S. 925 (1975); *Busby v. U.S.,* 296 F.2d 328 (9th Cir. 1961), *cert. denied,* 369 U.S. 876 (1962). However, the search may not be remote in time from the arrest. *U.S. v. Wyatt,* 561 F.2d 1388 (4th Cir. 1977). An incident search may not precede an arrest and serve as part of the justification for the arrest. *Smith v. Ohio,* 494 U.S. 541 (1990).

A search "contemporaneous" with an arrest does not necessarily mean "simultaneous." It has been held that a search of a defendant's person and the property in his immediate possession, which could be made on the spot at the time of arrest, may be conducted legally later as a normal incident of incarceration when the accused arrived at the place of detention. *U.S. v. Castro,* 596 F.2d 674 (5th Cir.), *cert. denied,* 444 U.S. 963 (1979). A warrantless seizure of the jailed arrestee's clothing when substitute clothing first became available on the morning after an 11 p.m. arrest was held part of normal administrative process incident to an arrest. *U.S. v. Edwards,* 415 U.S. 800 (1974). Seizure of a jailed defendant's shoes six weeks after arrest was held proper as the defendant and his shoes were in custody from arrest until the shoes were taken for use as evidence. To require a warrant, it was said, "would be to require a useless and meaningless formality." *U.S. v. Oaxaca,* 569 F.2d 518, 524 (9th Cir.), *cert. denied,* 439 U.S. 926 (1978).

Other instances where courts have held that a search was not contemporaneous with an arrest include: a search of defendant's apartment four days after he was arrested, *Mincey v. Arizona,* 437 U.S. 385 (1978); the search of a hotel room in California two days before an arrest in Nevada, *Stoner v. California,* 376 U.S. 483 (1964); the search of an office one hour after an arrest in a nearby elevator, *U.S. ex rel. Nickens v. LaVallee,* 391 F.2d 123 (2d Cir. 1968); a search of living quarters three hours after the related arrest, *U.S. ex rel. Clark v. Maroney,* 339 F.2d 710, 714 (3d Cir. 1965); a search of a car made several days after arrest, *Williams v. U.S.,* 323 F.2d 90, 94 (10th Cir. 1963), *cert. denied,* 376 U.S. 906 (1964); a search of defendant's hotel room to which the officers had taken defendant after he was arrested in the hotel's hallway wearing only a bathing suit, *U.S. v. Anthon,* 648 F.2d 669 (10th Cir.), *cert. denied,* 454 U.S. 1164 (1981).

### § 223. — — Scope of Warrantless Searches Incident to Arrest.

Searches incident to arrest are for the purpose of protecting the arresting officers and preventing the destruction of evidence. As such, the scope of such a search is limited to the arrestee's person and the area within his immediate control, meaning "the area from within which he might gain possession of a weapon or destructible evidence." *Chimel v. California,* 395 U.S. 752, 763 (1969); or closets or other spaces immediately adjoining the place of arrest from which an attack could be immediately launched. *Maryland v. Buie,* 494 U.S. 325 (1990).

## § 224. — — — Search of the Person.

When there is a lawful arrest, the arrestee and everything worn by him may be searched. *U.S. v. Robinson*, 414 U.S. 218 (1973). This includes clothing, removal of which may be required for the search, *U.S. v. Edwards*, 415 U.S. 800 (1974), items in coat pockets, *U.S. v. Campbell*, 575 F.2d 505 (5th Cir. 1978); *U.S. v. Smith*, 565 F.2d 292 (4th Cir. 1977), and in pockets of pants after they have been removed, *U.S. v. Chatman*, 573 F.2d 565 (9th Cir. 1977).

A brief strip search, conducted without abuse and in a professional manner for a visual inspection of body surfaces to detect hidden evidence or objects which could be used to harm, is not unlawful. *U.S. v. Klein*, 522 F.2d 296 (1st Cir. 1975).

Body cavity searches have been found to be lawful, but there must be a "clear indication" that contraband is present in the cavity, *U.S. v. Rodriguez*, 592 F.2d 553 (9th Cir. 1979); *U.S. v. Mastberg*, 503 F.2d 465 (9th Cir. 1974); but a body cavity search, which was performed twice by two policewomen rather than skilled medical technicians on a defendant seven months pregnant, was held to violate due process, *U.S. ex rel. Guy v. McCauley*, 385 F. Supp. 193 (E.D. Wis. 1974). X-ray examination and the use of force to prevent a defendant from swallowing evidence have been held lawful. *U.S. v. Caldera*, 421 F.2d 152 (9th Cir. 1970).

## § 225. — — — Articles Carried by Arrestee.

Articles carried by an arrestee may be searched incident to a lawful arrest. These have included a purse, *U.S. v. Moreno*, 569 F.2d 1049 (9th Cir.), *cert. denied*, 435 U.S. 972 (1978), a wallet, *U.S. v. McEachern*, 675 F.2d 618, 622 (4th Cir. 1982), a camera and money, *U.S. v. Matthews*, 603 F.2d 48 (8th Cir. 1979), *cert. denied*, 444 U.S. 1019 (1980), a zippered leather pouch, *U.S. v. Brown*, 671 F.2d 585, 586-87 (D.C. Cir. 1982), a briefcase, *U.S. v. Hayes*, 553 F.2d 824 (2d Cir.), *cert. denied*, 434 U.S. 867 (1977), and hand-carried luggage, *U.S. v. Garcia*, 605 F.2d 349 (7th Cir. 1979), *cert. denied*, 446 U.S. 984 (1980).

If the control of an article, such as a briefcase or luggage, has passed from the defendant to an arresting officer, a warrant will be required as there is no longer any danger that the arrestee will seize a weapon or destroy evidence therein. *U.S. v. Chadwick*, 433 U.S. 1, 15 (1977); *U.S. v. Benson*, 631 F.2d 1336 (8th Cir. 1980); *U.S. v. Schleis*, 582 F.2d 1166 (8th Cir. 1978); *U.S. v. Stevie*, 582 F.2d 1175 (8th Cir. 1978), *cert. denied*, 443 U.S. 911 (1979).

However, it has been held that the police may search a shoulder bag as a routine procedure incident to incarcerating a person in accordance with established inventory procedures. *Illinois v. Lafayette,* 462 U.S. 640 (1983).

## § 226. — — — Areas Within Arrestee's Immediate Control.

A search incident to a lawful arrest may be made of areas within the arrestee's immediate control. These include the passenger compartment and any containers found in the passenger compartment of an automobile whose occupant is subjected to a lawful custodial arrest, *New York v. Belton,* 453 U.S. 454 (1981), the area under a mattress in a room where defendant was taken to get a shirt, *Watkins v. U.S.,* 564 F.2d 201 (6th Cir. 1977), *cert. denied,* 435 U.S. 976 (1978), the front seat of the car occupied by defendant when arrested, *U.S. v. Regan,* 525 F.2d 1151 (8th Cir. 1975), a cabinet two to four feet from where a codefendant was lying on the floor, *U.S. v. Weaklem,* 517 F.2d 70 (9th Cir. 1975), a table in front of the defendants at the time they were arrested, *U.S. v. Artieri,* 491 F.2d 440 (2d Cir.), *cert. denied,* 419 U.S. 878 (1974), a bed and purse within reach of a companion of defendant who was arrested in a hotel room doorway, *U.S. v. Simmons,* 567 F.2d 314 (7th Cir. 1977), and a motel room, *U.S. v. Savage,* 564 F.2d 728 (5th Cir. 1977).

If an area is not within an arrestee's control or reach, or if he is handicapped or otherwise unable to retrieve weapons or evidence therein, the area may not be searched incident to the arrest without a warrant. *U.S. v. Neumann,* 585 F.2d 355 (8th Cir. 1978). Thus, the fruits of the search of a billfold in defendant's bedroom were suppressed where the defendant was shackled to a bed and the billfold was out of his reach. *U.S. v. Berenguer,* 562 F.2d 206 (2d Cir. 1977). *See also U.S. v. Jackson,* 576 F.2d 749 (8th Cir.), *cert. denied,* 439 U.S. 858 (1978).

Officers cannot allow a defendant to wander about an apartment and then search every room that he enters as a search incident to an arrest. *U.S. v. Erwin,* 507 F.2d 937 (5th Cir. 1975). Arresting officers may not order the accused to dress and then not bring him his clothes, requiring him to move about the room as a pretext for searching beyond the area of defendant's immediate control. *U.S. v. Griffith,* 537 F.2d 900 (7th Cir. 1976). There is no justification for searching any room "other than that in which an arrest occurs," or searching "all the desk drawers" in that room where the threat to the arresting officers was the threat posed by the arrestee. *Chimel v. California,* 395 U.S. 752, 763 (1969). Nor may a search of luggage be justified where the agent places it within the arrestee's reach at arrest. *U.S. v. Wright,* 577 F.2d 378 (6th Cir. 1978).

However, as an incident to an arrest in a home, the officers as a precautionary matter and without probable cause or reasonable suspicion may look in closets and other spaces immediately adjoining the arrest from which an attack could be immediately launched. For a further protective sweep, there must be articulable facts which taken together with the rational inferences from these facts would warrant a reasonably prudent officer in believing that the area to be swept harbors an individual posing a threat to the officers, and this may not be a full search but only a cursory inspection. *Maryland v. Buie,* 110 S. Ct. 1093 (1990).

The testimony of a witness whose existence was discovered as a result of search of a file folder which was not in plain view and was beyond the area of defendant's immediate control was suppressed. *U.S. v. Scios,* 590 F.2d 956 (D.C. Cir. 1978).

### § 227. — Seizures Without Probable Cause.

Three types of seizures covered by the fourth amendment are permitted without probable cause as they "constitute such limited intrusions on the personal security of those detained and are justified by such substantial law enforcement interests that they may be made on less than probable cause, so long as police have an articulable basis for suspecting criminal activity." *Michigan v. Summers,* 452 U.S. 692, 699 (1981). These three types are (1) "stop and frisk" where the police may stop a person to question and pat him down if they have reason to believe he is armed and dangerous, (2) a brief stop near international borders, and (3) a detention of a person while his home is being searched pursuant to a search warrant.

For there to be a seizure there must be either physical force to restrain movement or the submission to an assertion of authority. *California v. Hodari D.,* 111 S. Ct. 1547 (1991).

### § 228. — — "Stop and Frisk."

A person who is stopped by a police officer is not necessarily under arrest even though his right to move at will is restricted for some period. The stop itself may violate constitutional protections, as do certain forcible seizures of possessions from a person so stopped.

In *Terry v. Ohio,* 392 U.S. 1 (1968), the Supreme Court held that the police term "stop and frisk" is within the purview of the fourth amendment. The person, who is accosted by a police officer and who is denied the right to walk away, is a seized person. Such governmental intrusion into an individual's life passes constitutional muster only when the police officer's stop is based on a "reasonable suspicion" that the defendant was engaged in wrongdoing supported by specific, articulable facts. In evaluating the validity of a stop, the totality of the circumstances must be considered. *Florida v. Bostick,* 111 S. Ct. 2382 (1991); *U.S. v. Sokolow,* 109 S. Ct. 1581 (1989); *U.S. v. Cortez,* 449 U.S. 411 (1981); *Reid v. Georgia,* 448 U.S. 438 (1980); *U.S. v. Smith,* 574 F.2d 882 (6th Cir. 1978) (drug courier profile characteristics, standing alone, held not enough to create reasonable suspicion to stop); *U.S. v. Cortez,* 595 F.2d 505 (9th Cir. 1979) (nothing occurring after the stop can be used to justify the stop); *U.S. v. Wylie,* 569 F.2d 62 (D.C. Cir. 1977), *cert. denied,* 435 U.S. 944 (1978) (distinguishing between "contact" and a "stop"); *U.S. v. Barry,* 670 F.2d 583, 590-604 (5th Cir. 1982) (distinguishing three tiers of police citizen encounters: communication between police and citizen with no coercion or detention, brief seizures that must be supported by reasonable suspicion, and arrests that must be supported by probable cause).

An anonymous telephone tip, corroborated by independent police work, may have sufficient indicia of reliability to provide reasonable suspicion under the totality of the circumstances to justify an investigative stop even though it may be insufficient to justify an arrest or search warrant. *Alabama v. White,* 110 S. Ct. 2412 (1990).

A police officer's hunch does not justify even a minimal intrusion on freedom or a brief detention. The propriety of a stop is to be resolved by objective rather than subjective standards. *U.S. v. Constantine,* 567 F.2d 266 (4th Cir. 1977), *cert. denied,* 435 U.S. 926 (1978); *U.S. v. Oates,* 560 F.2d 45 (2d Cir. 1977). If a "wanted flyer" has been issued based on articulable facts that the wanted person has committed an offense, reliance upon that flyer justifies a stop. *U.S. v. Hensley,* 469 U.S. 221 (1985).

To determine whether a particular encounter constitutes a seizure, a court must consider all the circumstances to determine whether the police conduct would have communicated to a reasonable person that the person was not free to decline the officer's requests or otherwise terminate the encounter. *Florida v. Bostick, supra; U.S. v. Mendenhall,* 446 U.S. 544, 554 (1980); *U.S. v. Jefferson,* 650 F.2d 854 (6th Cir. 1981); *U.S. v. Barry, supra.* An initial police pursuit of a running pedestrian, although intimidating, was not "so intimidating" that the pedestrian could not reasonably believe he was not free to disregard the police presence and go about his business. *Michigan v. Chesternut,* 108 S. Ct. 1975 (1988). Even if there is a "show of authority" by the police, it must be successful either by physical force or by submission for there to be a seizure. *California v. Hodari D.,* 111 S. Ct. 1547 (1991).

Seeking and succeeding in stopping a fleeing individual by means of a roadblock is a "seizure," *Brower v. County of Inyo,* 489 U.S. 593 (1989), as is stopping a vehicle at a checkpoint. *Michigan Dept. of State Police v. Sitz,* 110 S. Ct. 2481 (1990).

A statute which requires persons who loiter or wander on streets not only to provide information as permitted by *Terry,* but also requires "credible and reliable" information, gives virtually total discretion to the police and is unconstitutionally vague on its face. *Kolender v. Lawson,* 461 U.S. 352 (1983).

The frisk, or partial search, consisting of a police officer's pat down of a person's outer garments, does not automatically follow a stop. A lawful stop and a frisk are not permissible simply because the right to stop existed. It must appear from the facts known to the officer before he conducts a pat down that there is a reasonable likelihood the restrained individual is armed and the officer's safety, therefore, is in jeopardy. *Terry v. Ohio,* 392 U.S. at 27; *Sibron v. New York,* 392 U.S. 40 (1968).

An anonymous telephone tip, corroborated by independent police work, may have sufficient indicia of reliability to provide reasonable suspicion under the totality of the circumstances to justify an investigative stop even though it may be insufficient to justify an arrest or search warrant. *Alabama v. White,* 110 S. Ct. 2412 (1990). Likewise, a person's mere presence in a tavern being searched under a search warrant gives the police no right to pat down or search him absent a particularized suspicion that the person was armed and dangerous. *Ybarra v. Illinois,* 444 U.S. 85 (1979). An occupant of a house, however, may be detained when the house is being searched under a warrant as a judicial officer has found that there is probable cause to believe "someone in the home is committing a crime." *Michigan v. Summers,* 452 U.S. 692, 703 (1981).

Stop and frisk principles apply with equal force to motorists and pedestrians. *Michigan v. Long,* 463 U.S. 1032 (1983). A tip to a police officer from a reliable informant that a parked motorist was armed was held to justify the officer's seizure of the weapon after the motorist rolled down the vehicle window in response to the officer's request to open the car door. *Adams v. Williams,* 407 U.S. 143 (1972). Vehicle stops and the questioning of occupants at permanent border checkpoints are lawful without any individualized or articulable suspicion, *U.S. v. Martinez-Fuerte,* 428 U.S. 543 (1976); *U.S. v. Carroll,* 591 F.2d 1132 (5th Cir. 1979); and roadblock-type stops for all traffic are lawful, *Delaware v. Prouse,* 440 U.S. 648 (1979); and where all traffic "insofar as was humanly possible" was stopped, *U.S. v. Prichard,* 645 F.2d 854

(10th Cir. 1981). A highway sobriety checkpoint under which all vehicles passing through the checkpoint were stopped and then drivers briefly examined for signs of intoxication has passed constitutional challenge. *Michigan Dept. of State Police v. Sitz, supra.* However, random stops of vehicles, without reasonable suspicion, for the purpose of checking licenses are prohibited. *Delaware v. Prouse, supra.* Even authorized roving border patrols have no right to stop and question auto occupants without facts warranting reasonable suspicion that the vehicle passengers are aliens and then only relevant questions may be asked and, absent consent, no vehicle or occupant search may be conducted. *U.S. v. Brignoni-Ponce,* 422 U.S. 873 (1975).

However, the suspicionless boarding of vessels by government officers under 19 U.S.C. § 1581(a) which provides that any customs officer "may at anytime go on board of any vessel ... at any place in the United States ... and examine the manifest and other documents and papers ..." does not violate the fourth amendment. The ancestor to § 1581(a) was written by the same congress that promulgated the fourth amendment and ready access to the open sea is a situation sufficiently different from that involving an automobile on a highway to permit a different result. *U.S. v. Villamonte-Marquez,* 462 U.S. 579 (1983).

Brevity is important in determining whether an investigative detention is unreasonable. In assessing whether a detention is too long, the court must assess whether the delay was necessary to confirm or dispell the suspicions which led to the investigative stop. Thus, a 20-minute stop was reasonable where the police acted diligently and the suspect's actions contributed to the delay. *U.S. v. Sharpe,* 469 U.S. 809 (1985). Ninety minutes to secure a "sniff test" by a narcotics detection dog, however, has been held to be an unreasonably long detention in violation of the limits of *Terry. U.S. v. Place,* 462 U.S. 696 (1983).

Because of the intrusive nature of the seizure and the severity of its consequences, the Supreme Court has refused to extend the reasonable suspicion standard for a stop and frisk to seizures of suspects for the purpose of subsequent station house interrogation. *Dunaway v. New York,* 442 U.S. 200 (1979). Even an individual in a high drug trafficking area who looked suspicious and who refused to produce identification could not lawfully be stopped and questioned. *Brown v. Texas,* 443 U.S. 47 (1979). If the stop is unlawful, no right to interrogate exists.

Examples of approved and rejected "stop and frisk" type encounters include: a justified stop where defendant volunteered a false statement, his companion constantly looked behind him, and female companion tugged uncomfortably at her slacks, *U.S. v. Rico,* 594 F.2d 320 (2d Cir.

1979); a justified stop and frisk where defendants attempted to avoid observation of their faces, one had panty hose protruding from his hat, and the other was wearing a jacket on a warm night, *U.S. v. Bull,* 565 F.2d 869 (4th Cir. 1977), *cert. denied,* 435 U.S. 946 (1978); an unjustified frisk based on a police officer's observation of two men in an argument, *U.S. v. Hammack,* 604 F.2d 437 (5th Cir. 1979); a justified stop and questioning based on a DEA agent's personal knowledge of the person to whom drugs were supposed to be delivered, combined with defendant's arrival at the airport in conformity with an anonymous tipster's detailed statement that defendant was carrying drugs, *U.S. v. Andrews,* 600 F.2d 563 (6th Cir.), *cert. denied,* 444 U.S. 878 (1979). A police officer was held to have acted illegally in stopping persons at random for the purpose of filling out a "field information report" and soliciting information about neighborhood gang fights. *U.S. v. Palmer,* 603 F.2d 1286 (8th Cir. 1979). Customs patrol officers who stopped a taxi containing three men, who four days earlier were cooperative and consented to an unproductive search, were held to have made an arrest and not a limited investigatory stop. *U.S. v. Beck,* 598 F.2d 497 (9th Cir. 1979). But police officers, who are told by a reliable informant that an escapee was attempting to purchase drugs and was driving an automobile parked nearby, were held to have acted reasonably in stopping the vehicle and making a routine check of the vehicle and the driver. *U.S. v. Pelley,* 572 F.2d 264 (10th Cir. 1978).

### § 229. — — Border and Customs Searches.

Border searches and customs searches are "a long-standing, historically recognized exception to the Fourth Amendment's general principle that a warrant be obtained," and such searches without a warrant and without probable cause are reasonable within the meaning of the fourth amendment. *U.S. v. Ramsey,* 431 U.S. 606, 621 (1977); *U.S. v. Grayson,* 597 F.2d 1225 (9th Cir.), *cert. denied,* 444 U.S. 875 (1979). Border searches are distinct from searches of those lawfully within the country. At the border, one can reasonably be searched so as to exclude illegal aliens and contraband from the country. *U.S. v. Thirty-seven Photographs,* 402 U.S. 363 (1971); *Carroll v. U.S.,* 267 U.S. 132 (1925).

The border-search exception applies to incoming international mail. *U.S. v. Ramsey,* 431 U.S. at 623-25; *U.S. v. Richards,* 638 F.2d 765, 773 (5th Cir.), *cert. denied,* 102 S. Ct. 669 (1981). The exception may also be applied to the functional equivalent of the border, such as a permanent checkpoint some distance from the actual border, *U.S. v. Warren,* 594 F.2d 1046 (5th Cir. 1979), to baggage arriving from outside the country in an airport customs area, *U.S. v. Scheer,* 600 F.2d 5 (3d Cir. 1979), to items about to leave the country located within a customs area, *U.S. v. Ajlouny,* 629 F.2d 830 (2d Cir. 1980), *cert. denied,* 449 U.S. 1111 (1981), to a nonstop flight from a foreign country to an inland city, *Almeida-Sanchez v. U.S.,* 413 U.S. 266, 273 (1973), to an aircraft crossing the border without proof the plane's point of origin was foreign, *U.S. v. Garcia,* 672 F.2d 1349, 1357-58 (11th Cir. 1982), and to a foreign package or camper inspected at an inland city where addressed rather than the original port of entry, *U.S. v. Lowe,* 575 F.2d 1193 (6th Cir.), *cert. denied,* 439 U.S. 869 (1978); *U.S. v. Gallagher,* 557 F.2d 1041 (4th Cir.), *cert. denied,* 434 U.S. 870 (1977). These principles apply also to vessels entering coastal waterways. *U.S. v. Weber,* 668 F.2d 552, 559 (1st Cir. 1981); *U.S. v. Kleinschmidt,* 596 F.2d 133 (5th Cir.), *cert. denied,* 444 U.S. 927 (1979); *U.S. v. Whitmire,* 595 F.2d 1303 (5th Cir. 1979), *cert. denied,* 448 U.S. 906 (1980). But sighting a vessel headed toward the Bahamas three days before it docked in the United States was held to be too remote to establish "articulable facts" to believe reasonably that the vessel came from international waters. *U.S. v. Acosta,* 489 F. Supp. 61 (S.D. Fla. 1980).

The detention of a traveler at a border beyond the scope of a routine customs search is justified if customs agents reasonably suspect that the person is smuggling contraband in her alimentary canal. In *U.S. v. Montoya de Hernandez,* 105 S. Ct. 3304 (1985), the Court permitted a detention in excess of 16 hours at the border as it was the defendant's evasive actions that required the long period to either verify or dispel the suspicion.

Under the authority of a section of the Immigration and Nationality Act, 8 U.S.C. § 1357(a)(3), which provides for such searches a "reasonable distance" from a border, roving border patrols are permitted to stop and search automobiles without a warrant, without probable cause to believe the cars contain aliens, even without probable cause to believe that the cars have crossed the border. The Supreme Court has held, however, that such searches are constitutionally prohibited when the distance is 20 to 25 miles from the border, as that is neither the border nor its functional equivalent. *Almeida-Sanchez v. U.S.,* 413 U.S. at 273. But, one circuit has held *Almeida-Sanchez* does not apply to an "extended border search" that took place four miles from the border and seven hours after the observed border crossing where the delay was to "confirm developing suspicion" and the customs officers had reasonable suspicion that they would find illegally imported materials. *U.S. v. Bilir,* 592 F.2d 735 (4th Cir. 1979). Except at the border, or its functional equivalent, a roving border patrol may stop a vehicle and question its occupants concerning citizenship and immigration

status only if the officer has a "reasonable suspicion" that they may be
aliens, and any further detention or a search must be based on consent
or probable cause. *U.S. v. Brignoni-Ponce*, 422 U.S. 873 (1975). Reasonable suspicion to stop a vehicle means that under the totality of the
circumstances there is a suspicion that the particular individual being
stopped is engaged in wrongdoing. *U.S. v. Cortez*, 449 U.S. 411 (1981);
*U.S. v. Kenney*, 601 F.2d 211 (5th Cir. 1979); *U.S. v. Ballard*, 600 F.2d
1115 (5th Cir. 1979). A pat down search at a border requires "some
level of suspicion," *U.S. v. Dorsey*, 641 F.2d 1213 (7th Cir. 1981), or
"mere suspicion," *U.S. v. Sandler*, 644 F.2d 1163, 1167 (5th Cir. 1981).

Unlike a stop by a roving patrol, a stop at a permanent checkpoint
away from the border for brief questioning upon reasonable suspicion
has been upheld as less arbitrary and intrusive. *U.S. v. Martinez-
Fuerte*, 428 U.S. 543 (1976). However, either probable cause or consent
is needed to search at such a checkpoint. *U.S. v. Ortiz*, 422 U.S. 891
(1975).

### § 230. — — Detention of Occupants While Home Is Searched Pursuant to a Warrant.

A person may be detained without probable cause by the police when
they are searching his home under authority of a search warrant. The
detention of an occupant is less intrusive than the search itself, adds
only minimally to the stigma associated with the search, and it may be
assumed "that most citizens — unless they intend flight to avoid arrest
— would elect to remain in order to observe the search of their possessions." *Michigan v. Summers*, 452 U.S. 692, 701 (1981). Detention is
justified because a judicial officer has determined that there is criminal activity in the home to which the occupant is connected and it
minimizes risk of harm to the officers and prevents flight in the event
incriminating evidence is found. *Michigan v. Summers, supra.* A 45-
minute detention has been held to be reasonable. *U.S. v. Timpani*, 665
F.2d 1 (1st Cir. 1981).

### § 231. — Exigent Circumstances That Justify a Warrantless Search.

A warrantless search based upon probable cause, is permitted when
there is some exigency or a compelling urgency for the protection of the
police or the public, or to prevent the destruction of contraband or
evidence.

## § 232. — — Officers Responding to Emergency.

The Supreme Court has said that warrantless entries and searches are permitted (1) when officers reasonably believe that someone is in immediate need of assistance, (2) to protect or to preserve life, or (3) to avoid serious injury. At such times the police may seize any evidence that is in plain view. *Mincey v. Arizona,* 437 U.S. 385, 392-93 (1978). Thus, in *Mincey,* the police could make a prompt, warrantless search to see if there were other victims or if a killer was on the premises, but were not permitted to make a warrantless, exhaustive four-day search of the premises. *See also Thompson v. Louisiana,* 469 U.S. 17 (1984). In *Michigan v. Tyler,* 436 U.S. 499 (1978), the Court said that an entry to fight a fire required no warrant and once in the building officials could remain for a reasonable time to seize evidence of arson that was in plain view and to investigate the causes of the fire. It was also permissible for the investigation which had been hindered at 4 a.m. by darkness, steam, and smoke, to resume without a warrant at 8 a.m. as a continuation of the original entry. Any additional entries, however, were deemed detached from the initial exigency, and a warrant was required. However, where the search of fire-damaged premises was not a continuation of an earlier search and there were no exigent circumstances, the search violated the fourth amendment, *Michigan v. Clifford,* 464 U.S. 287 (1984).

Entry into a vessel to seek an explanation for, and possible victims of, an apparent nautical mishap, where a chart that led to marijuana cache was in plain view, was permissible under exigent circumstances. *U.S. v. Miller,* 589 F.2d 1117 (1st Cir. 1978), *cert. denied,* 440 U.S. 958 (1979). Entry into a mobile home by an officer, investigating the death of a minor child, who entered to see if any other children were present was also held proper for the same reason. *Sallie v. North Carolina,* 587 F.2d 636 (4th Cir. 1978), *cert. denied,* 441 U.S. 911 (1979).

Police may enter where they actually observe a crime in progress, and waiting 30 to 40 minutes does not dissipate this right when it would have taken about two hours to obtain search warrant. *U.S. v. Johnson,* 561 F.2d 832 (D.C. Cir.), *cert. denied,* 432 U.S. 907 (1977). Also, officers may enter where it was necessary to secure a shotgun that had been used to threaten defendant's wife, *U.S. v. Hendrix,* 595 F.2d 883 (D.C. Cir. 1979); or where the safety of an informant may be in jeopardy, *U.S. v. Williams,* 623 F.2d 535 (8th Cir. 1980); or where it was necessary for a physician to examine object that caused child's injury, even though criminal conduct was suspected, *U.S. v. Mayes,* 670 F.2d 126, 128 (9th Cir. 1982).

However, exigent circumstances must be proved to justify a warrant-less search, and they do not exist where officers have time to secure a warrant, *U.S. v. Houle,* 603 F.2d 1297 (8th Cir. 1979); *U.S. v. Martin,* 562 F.2d 673 (D.C. Cir. 1977); *U.S. v. Pacheco-Ruiz,* 549 F.2d 1204 (9th Cir. 1976). Exigent circumstances may not exist where the officers have time to secure a telephone warrant. *U.S. v. McEachin,* 670 F.2d 1139, 1147-48 (D.C. Cir. 1981), *U.S. v. Baker,* 520 F. Supp. 1080, 1183-85 (S.D. Iowa 1981). Forcibly seizing a sample of pubic hair from an inmate's person is not justified by exigent circumstances. *Bouse v. Bussey,* 573 F.2d 548 (9th Cir. 1977).

### § 233. — — Threatened Destruction or Removal of Contraband or Likely Escape of Suspect.

"The conclusion that evidence was probably being destroyed in the apartment not only contributes to the finding of probable cause to believe that evidence existed in the apartment, but also supplies the exigent circumstances necessary to justify a warrantless entry" to pre-serve evidence. *U.S. v. Delguyd,* 542 F.2d 346, 351 (6th Cir. 1976). For example, warrantless entry and seizure of narcotics were permitted where, after knocking, agents heard the sound of a toilet flushing, *U.S. v. Montiell,* 526 F.2d 1008 (2d Cir. 1975); where there was danger that cocaine would be flushed down a toilet, *U.S. v. Gardner,* 553 F.2d 946 (5th Cir. 1977), *cert. denied,* 434 U.S. 1011 (1978); and where someone in a drug suspect's trailer yelled, "It's the cops," upon officer's ap-proach, and running inside the trailer was heard, *U.S. v. Carter,* 566 F.2d 1265 (5th Cir.), *cert. denied,* 436 U.S. 956 (1978). Where agents located the house from which there was a strong odor of ether used to manufacture methamphetamine, the suspected manufacturer had ar-rived earlier than agents anticipated, and the agents concluded that delay in obtaining warrant would result in possible removal of contra-band and explosion from chemicals, an immediate entry and search were justified. *U.S. v. Erb,* 596 F.2d 412 (10th Cir.), *cert. denied,* 444 U.S. 848 (1979). *See also U.S. v. Edwards,* 602 F.2d 458 (1st Cir. 1979); *U.S. v. Botero,* 589 F.2d 430 (9th Cir.), *cert. denied,* 441 U.S. 944 (1979); *U.S. v. Glasby,* 576 F.2d 734 (7th Cir.), *cert. denied,* 439 U.S. 854 (1978); *U.S. v. James,* 555 F.2d 992 (D.C. Cir. 1977); *U.S. v. Shima,* 545 F.2d 1026 (5th Cir.), *aff'd per curiam en banc,* 560 F.2d 1287, *cert. denied,* 434 U.S. 996 (1977).

Probable cause to believe that contraband is in a hotel room is not sufficient for a warrantless entry where the agents had "little reason to suspect" that any evidence would be destroyed. *U.S. v. Allard,* 600 F.2d 1301 (9th Cir. 1979). A court has also found no exigent circumstances justifying a warrantless opening of a suitcase where four agents had three suspects at bay in a well lighted motel room. *U.S. v. Montano,* 613 F.2d 147 (6th Cir. 1980).

Where there is a risk that occupants of a house may escape absent immediate action, police may enter without a warrant to make an arrest. *U.S. v. Campbell,* 581 F.2d 22 (2d Cir. 1978); *U.S. v. Flickinger,* 573 F.2d 1349 (9th Cir.), *cert. denied,* 439 U.S. 836 (1978). And police may make a "protective sweep" search of a house in front of which defendant was arrested where police had reason to fear that there might be an armed accomplice in the house observing defendant's arrest. *U.S. v. Baker,* 577 F.2d 1147 (4th Cir.), *cert. denied,* 439 U.S. 850 (1978). Likewise, where an accomplice cooperating with the government delivered to the defendant a suitcase containing drugs and a beeper, the defendant was observed leaving his house driving at a high rate of speed, he was stopped, and it was discovered the suitcase was not present and the beeper was not working, it was held proper for the agents to make a "protective sweep" of the house to look for accomplices officers thought might be in the house and who might destroy the evidence. It was also held lawful to secure the premises while a search warrant was obtained, which was based in part on items seen in plain view during the protective sweep. Even though there were no accomplices and no immediate danger of destruction of evidence, securing the premises while obtaining a warrant is a matter of reasonableness to be judged at the time of making the decision to search, not in hindsight. *U.S. v. Korman,* 614 F.2d 541 (6th Cir. 1980). *See also U.S. v. Hackett,* 638 F.2d 1179 (9th Cir. 1980); *U.S. v. Young,* 553 F.2d 1132 (8th Cir.), *cert. denied,* 431 U.S. 959 (1977). A suitcase may be impounded but not searched without a warrant where there is reasonable suspicion to believe it contains contraband. *U.S. v. Benjamin,* 637 F.2d 1297 (7th Cir. 1981).

## § 234. — — "Hot Pursuit."

A warrantless search, where (1) there is probable cause to arrest, (2) there is probable cause to believe the suspect is in particular premises, and (3) there is an urgent need for immediate police action because delay would increase the risk of harm or escape, has been approved under the "hot pursuit" exception to the fourth amendment warrant requirement. *U.S. v. Brightwell,* 563 F.2d 569, 574 (3d Cir.), *cert. denied,* 434 U.S. 998 (1977); *U.S. v. Gaultney,* 581 F.2d 1137 (5th Cir. 1978), *cert. denied,* 446 U.S. 907 (1980); *U.S. v. Oaxaca,* 569 F.2d 518 (9th Cir.), *cert. denied,* 439 U.S. 926 (1978). In *Brightwell, supra,* however, the Court held that the hot pursuit exception did not apply because there was not probable cause to arrest Brightwell before the search or an urgent need when the house was surrounded. In *Walsh v. Wisconsin,* 466 U.S. 740 (1984), the hot pursuit exception did not apply to the arrest of a defendant in his home where there was no immediate or continuous pursuit from the scene of the crime.

In *Warden v. Hayden,* 387 U.S. 294 (1967), the Court held where officers were in pursuit of an armed suspect whom two cab drivers had seen enter a house only minutes before, warrantless entry and search were permitted by the exigencies of the situation. Where a suspect retreated into her house from the doorway where an arrest was initiated, it was held she could not avoid arrest by moving to a private place. That the pursuit ended almost as soon as it began did not make it less a "hot pursuit" sufficient to justify warrantless entry into her house. *U.S. v. Santana,* 427 U.S. 38 (1976). Where a car connected with a robbery occurring 40 minutes earlier was found in an apartment house parking lot, although there was not probable cause to search each apartment, when six of the seven apartments were searched without result, it was held that the officers then had probable cause to believe the fugitives were in the seventh apartment and the exigencies of hot pursuit existed so that a warrantless search was proper. *U.S. v. Scott,* 520 F.2d 697 (9th Cir. 1975), *cert. denied,* 423 U.S. 1056 (1976).

## § 235. — Vehicle Searches.

Where there is (1) probable cause to believe that a vehicle on the highway contains contraband, and (2) when there are exigent circumstances, such as where the car can be moved, a warrantless search of the vehicle is permitted under circumstances that would not be considered reasonable in other contexts. *Colorado v. Bannister,* 449 U.S. 1 (1980); *U.S. v. Chadwick,* 433 U.S. 1 (1977); *Carroll v. U.S.,* 267 U.S. 132 (1925); *U.S. v. Smith,* 595 F.2d 1176 (9th Cir. 1979); *U.S. v. Alden,* 576 F.2d 772 (8th Cir.), *cert. denied,* 439 U.S. 855 (1978); *U.S. v. Moreno,* 569 F.2d 1049 (9th Cir.), *cert. denied,* 435 U.S. 972 (1978). This "moving vehicle" exception includes a mobile motor home, *California v. Carney,* 471 U.S. 386 (1985); aircraft, *U.S. v. Flickinger,* 573 F.2d 1349 (9th Cir.), *cert. denied,* 439 U.S. 836 (1978); and vessels, *U.S. v. Hensler,* 625 F.2d 1141 (4th Cir. 1980); *U.S. v. Miller,* 589 F.2d 1117 (1st Cir. 1978), *cert. denied,* 440 U.S. 958 (1979); *U.S. v. Weinrich,* 586 F.2d 481 (5th Cir. 1978), *cert. denied,* 441 U.S. 927 (1979).

The Supreme Court has stated that there are two reasons for this exception: (1) the "inherent mobility of automobiles creates such exigency that, as a practical necessity, rigorous enforcement of the warrant requirement is impossible"; and (2) the "expectation of privacy with respect to one's automobile is significantly less than that relating to one's home or office" in that automobiles travel public thoroughfares with their occupants in plain view and in the interest of public safety there are extensive regulations and inspections of automobiles, and they are frequently taken into custody. *Arkansas v. Sanders,* 442 U.S. 753 (1979); *South Dakota v. Opperman,* 428 U.S. 364, 367-72 (1976); *Cady v. Dombrowski,* 413 U.S. 433 (1973).

Because there is significantly less expectation of privacy in an automobile than one's home or office, "the Court has also upheld warrantless searches where no immediate danger was presented that the car would be removed from the jurisdiction." *South Dakota v. Opperman,* 428 U.S. at 367, citing *Chambers v. Maroney,* 399 U.S. 42 (1970), and *Cooper v. California,* 386 U.S. 58 (1967), both cases in which the car was moved to a police station where the warrantless search took place (in the *Cooper* case a week after the car was impounded). *See also Texas v. White,* 423 U.S. 67 (1975); *U.S. v. Romo,* 669 F.2d 285, 291 (5th Cir. 1982). Where police "have probable cause to believe there is contraband inside an automobile that has been stopped on the road, the officers may conduct a warrantless search of the vehicle, even after it has been impounded and is in police custody." *Michigan v. Thomas,* 102 S. Ct. 3029 (1982).

The Court has also upheld as a proper search the actions of a police officer who saw a gun when he reached into the passenger compartment of a vehicle to move papers obscuring the VIN after the driver had been stopped for a traffic violation and had exited his car. *New York v. Class,* 471 U.S. 1003 (1986).

However, noting that the "word 'automobile' is not a talisman in whose presence the Fourth Amendment fades away and disappears," the Supreme Court held in *Coolidge v. New Hampshire,* 403 U.S. 443, 461-62 (1971), that where the defendant had known for some time he was a suspect and had time to destroy any evidence and where his car was guarded at the time of arrest and then impounded, there was no right to search his car as incident to an arrest. The Court said that the holdings in *Carroll v. U.S.* and *Chambers v. Maroney* were not applicable.

### § 236. — — Inventory Searches of Vehicles.

The courts have held "inventory" searches of impounded automobiles without probable cause are reasonable where the purpose is not investigative but (1) to protect the police or the public from potential danger, (2) for protection of the police against claims of lost property, or (3) for protection of the owner's property while it is in police custody.

There must be some standardized criteria or established routine with respect to the opening of closed containers during an inventory search so that the police officers do not have so much latitude that inventory searches are turned into general rummaging to discover incriminatory evidence. *Florida v. Wells,* 495 U.S. 1 (1990). A search following standard inventory procedures where marijuana was discovered in a closed glove compartment of a locked car that had been impounded for parking violations has been held proper. *South Dakota v. Opperman,* 428 U.S. 364 (1976); as has the inventory of a van's contents, including the opening of a closed backpack, after arresting the defendant for driving under the influence of alcohol. *Colorado v. Bertine,* 479 U.S. 367 (1987). *See also U.S. v. Bosby,* 675 F.2d 1174, 1179 (11th Cir. 1982), and *U.S. v. Strahan,* 674 F.2d 96, 100 (1st Cir.), *cert. denied,* 456 U.S. 1010 (1982) (the detailed review of documents found in a vehicle to determine ownership and the photocopying of these documents before the originals were returned was approved as part of an inventory search). Likewise, searches of cars held for forfeiture have been approved. *Cooper v. California,* 386 U.S. 58 (1967); *U.S. v. One 1972 Chevrolet Nova,* 560 F.2d 464 (1st Cir. 1977). *See also U.S. v. Cromer,* 598 F.2d 738 (2d Cir. 1979); *U.S. v. Fossler,* 597 F.2d 478 (5th Cir. 1979); *U.S. v. Stocks,* 594 F.2d 113 (5th Cir. 1979); *U.S. v. Piatt,* 576 F.2d 659 (5th Cir. 1978).

An on-the-scene inventory of the interior and trunk of an automobile has been approved where the defendants were arrested in a store and their automobile was legally parked in a shopping mall parking lot, *U.S. v. Staller,* 616 F.2d 1284 (5th Cir. 1980), *cert. denied,* 449 U.S. 869 (1980). It was held that a knapsack discovered during an inventory search of a defendant's automobile should have been inventoried as a unit rather than opening and itemizing the contents where the knapsack was tightly sealed and there was no danger of anything slipping out. *U.S. v. Bloomfield,* 594 F.2d 1200 (8th Cir. 1979).

## § 237. — — Searches of Containers Found in Vehicle.

One rule now governs all automobile searches. "The police may search an automobile and the containers within it where they have probable cause to believe contraband or evidence is contained." *California v. Acevedo,* 111 S. Ct. 1982, 1991 (1991). "If probable cause justifies the search of a lawfully stopped vehicle, it justifies the search of every part of the vehicle and its contents that may conceal the object of the search." *U.S. v. Ross,* 456 U.S. 798, 822 (1982). The scope of the warrantless search of a vehicle is not defined by the nature of the container, but rather by the object of the search and the places in which there is probable cause to believe that it may be found. This is as broad as the magistrate could authorize in a warrant to search a vehicle, and includes any luggage or container in which contraband or evidence may be concealed. *U.S. v. Ross,* 456 U.S. at 822; *Robbins v. California,* 453 U.S. 420 (1981). The suggestion in *Arkansas v. Sanders,* 442 U.S. 753 (1979), that a warrantless search of a container found in an automobile could not be sustained as part of the warrantless search of the automobile was overruled by *U.S. v. Ross, supra,* and *California v. Acevedo, supra.*

Where the lawful seizure of a vehicle permits the search of its contents, the warrantless search conducted three days after the packages from the vehicle were placed in a DEA warehouse was permissible. *U.S. v. Johns,* 469 U.S. 478 (1985). *See also Florida v. Meyers,* 466 U.S. 380 (1984).

While a suspect may limit the scope of a search to which he consents, when he gives a general consent to search a car for narcotics, that consent included the consent to search containers within the car which might contain drugs. *Florida v. Jimeno,* 111 S. Ct. 1801 (1991).

## § 238. — Evidence in Plain View.

Seizable items, including contraband, evidence of a crime, dangerous properties, and stolen objects that inadvertently come into the view of a lawfully searching police officer may be retained and used as evidence of the criminal conduct to which they relate. If a law officer (1) is lawfully located in a place where an object may be plainly seen, and (2) the incriminating character of the object is "immediately apparent," and (3) the officer has a lawful right of access to the object itself, he may seize it even though the evidence is wholly unrelated to the offense which justified the search. *Horton v. California,* 496 U.S. 128 (1990); *Coolidge v. New Hampshire,* 403 U.S. 443 (1971). Thus, where an officer accompanies a student whom he has arrested to the student's room for him to obtain identification, the officer has the right to literally remain at his elbow, and when the officer who is standing in the doorway observes what he recognizes as contraband he may enter and seize the contraband. *Washington v. Chrisman,* 455 U.S. 1 (1982). A container which is lawfully opened by a customs officer and its contents identified as illegal is considered to be in "plain view" and the owner's privacy interest in the item is lost. The resealing of the package for a controlled delivery and reopening of the container did not violate the fourth amendment. *Illinois v. Andreas,* 463 U.S. 765 (1983).

It is not a requirement that evidence in plain view be discovered "inadvertently" as was suggested by a four-justice plurality opinion in *Coolidge v. New Hampshire, supra. Horton v. California, supra.*

The use of sensing aids, such as a flashlight for illumination, a magnifying glass, binoculars, or infrared lamps, does not taint plain view observation. *U.S. v. Lee,* 274 U.S. 559 (1927); *U.S. v. Thomas,* 551 F.2d 347 (D.C. Cir. 1976); *U.S. v. Coplen,* 541 F.2d 211 (9th Cir. 1976), *cert. denied,* 429 U.S. 1073 (1977); *U.S. v. Johnson,* 506 F.2d 674 (8th Cir. 1974), *cert. denied,* 421 U.S. 917 (1975). However, attempts to create a plain view or open view exception to the warrant requirement for initial entry have been rejected. For example, officers, recognizing a strong odor of burning opium, who entered a residence when a door was opened after their knock and then placed the occupant under arrest, were held to have acted unlawfully, *Johnson v. U.S.,* 333 U.S. 10 (1948); recognition of a strong odor of mash did not justify warrantless entry into a residence, *Chapman v. U.S.,* 365 U.S. 610 (1961).

For a search or seizure of objects in plain view, the incriminating nature of the evidence must be immediately apparent. This means probable cause. Thus, an initial warrantless entry which was justified by exigent circumstances did not justify the moving of stereo components in order to record serial numbers and their seizure where the police had only "reasonable suspicion" that the stereo equipment was stolen. *Arizona v. Hicks,* 480 U.S. 321 (1987).

Vehicles are also covered by the plain view exception. A stop at a routine driver's license checkpoint during which the officer saw items he knew were frequently related to narcotics permitted the seizure of the items and the inventory search of the vehicle which revealed other contraband. *Texas v. Brown,* 460 U.S. 730 (1983). A police officer who had stopped a motorist for speeding saw him attempting to stuff cash into the glove compartment and who also noticed a gun case on the vehicle floor, was held justified in seizing the property and thoroughly searching the car, *U.S. v. Finnegan,* 568 F.2d 637 (9th Cir. 1977); warrantless, emergency entry into a mobile home was held to allow seizure of evidence of a crime that was in plain view, *Sallie v. North Carolina,* 587 F.2d 636 (4th Cir. 1978), *cert. denied,* 441 U.S. 911 (1979).

### § 239. — — Abandoned Property.

One cannot successfully challenge the search of a premise and seizure of objects he has voluntarily abandoned. *Abel v. U.S.,* 362 U.S. 217 (1960) (a guest who surrendered a hotel room would not be heard to complain when it was entered with management permission by officers who seized property left behind). *See also U.S. v. Miller,* 589 F.2d 1117 (1st Cir. 1978), *cert. denied,* 440 U.S. 958 (1979); *U.S. v. Savage,* 564 F.2d 728 (5th Cir. 1977), holding that there was nothing unlawful in entering a yacht of unknown origin, abandoned at another's mooring, and seizing a chart in plain view on the floor; and *U.S. v. Edwards,* 644 F.2d 1 (5th Cir.), *cert. denied,* 454 U.S. 855 (1981), where the court held that when the defendant called for and accepted aid from the Coast Guard in a storm, he had voluntarily abandoned his ship and may not claim an expectation of privacy in the ship. A defendant who threw a sack onto the hood of his car when approached by the police did not abandon, but attempted to protect the bag. *Smith v. Ohio,* 494 U.S. 541 (1990). *But see California v. Hodari D.,* 111 S. Ct. 1547 (1991), where it was held that a suspect who tossed away cocaine fleeing from the police abandoned the cocaine as he was not "seized" during the time of the pursuit.

Denying knowledge of or ownership of luggage constitutes abandonment. *U.S. v. Washington,* 677 F.2d 394, 396 (4th Cir.), *cert. denied,* 459 U.S. 854 (1982); *U.S. v. Pirolli,* 673 F.2d 1200, 1204 (11th Cir.), *cert. denied,* 459 U.S. 871 (1982).

Garbage or trash is discarded and exposed to the public sufficiently to defeat the fourth amendment protection when it is set out for collection. *California v. Greenwood,* 486 U.S. 35 (1988). An apartment dweller who mingles his trash with others in the building has been held to have abandoned it before the collection process commenced. *Magda v. Benson,* 536 F.2d 111 (6th Cir. 1976). A partially burned pile of trash a short distance from a residence is also abandoned property, and a piece of cardboard removed therefrom which listed radio scanning channels was held not suppressible. *U.S. v. Alden,* 576 F.2d 772 (8th Cir.), *cert. denied,* 439 U.S. 855 (1978).

## § 240. — — Curtilage and the Open Fields Doctrine.

The curtilage of a residence is an area protected by the fourth amendment. The curtilage is the area to which extends the intimate activity associated with the "sanctity of a man's home and the privacies of life," and as such is considered part of the home itself for fourth amendment purposes. *Boyd v. U.S.,* 116 U.S. 616, 630 (1886).

Whether an area claimed to be curtilage is so intimately tied to the home that it takes on the home's fourth amendment protection "should be resolved with particular reference to four factors: the proximity of the area claimed to be curtilage to the home, whether the area is included within an enclosure surrounding the home, the nature of the uses to which the area is put, and the steps taken by the resident to protect the area from observation by people passing by." *U.S. v. Dunn,* 480 U.S. 294, 301 (1987).

The fourth amendment protection, however, does not extend to open fields. *Hester v. U.S.*, 265 U.S. 57 (1924). This is true even though the government agent may be trespassing on private property which is surrounded with "No Trespassing" signs. *Oliver v. U.S.*, 466 U.S. 170 (1984). The touchstone of the fourth amendment analysis involves two inquiries, whether the individual had a subjective expectation of privacy and whether it was one which society is willing to recognize. *Katz v. U.S.*, 389 U.S. 347 (1967). Thus, police observations from a private airplane which flew over the defendant's house at an altitude of 1,000 feet did not violate the fourth amendment, even though the observed marijuana crop may have been within the curtilage of the defendant's home, because the defendant's expectation of privacy from police observations within public navigable airspace was unreasonable. *California v. Ciraolo*, 472 U.S. 1025 (1986). Likewise, no search warrant is required for observations of the interior of a greenhouse from a helicopter flying in compliance with the law. *Florida v. Riley*, 488 U.S. 445 (1989). Aerial photographs of an industrial plant complex were held not to be analogous to the "curtilage" of a dwelling and, as such, not protected by the fourth amendment. *Dow Chemical Co. v. U.S.*, 472 U.S. 1007 (1986).

## § 241. — Anti-Skyjacking Searches.

Courts have almost universally permitted warrantless searches without probable cause of air passengers and baggage to discover weapons and prevent air piracy. The theories for such holdings have differed widely.

Implied consent has been used by a number of circuits. Generally, there is a sign advising that all passengers and baggage are subject to search. A baggage search and a pat-down search have been approved where the passenger could elect not to be searched by deciding not to board the aircraft. *Singleton v. Commissioner*, 606 F.2d 50 (3d Cir. 1979); *U.S. v. Freeland*, 562 F.2d 383 (6th Cir.), *cert. denied*, 434 U.S. 957 (1977). And, where the defendant had stated he would not take the flight rather than permit physical inspection of his briefcase that could not adequately be inspected by X-ray, and the briefcase was opened, nevertheless, revealing marijuana and hashish, one court has held that, after having consented to the search, the defendant could not then withhold permission, once the first step in the process disclosed he was carrying articles concealed from the X-ray. *U.S. v. DeAngelo*, 584 F.2d 46 (4th Cir. 1978), *cert. denied*, 440 U.S. 935 (1979).

Some cases have held that searches of baggage by airline personnel, even when viewed by an officer, are private searches and therefore not within the scope of the fourth amendment. A factor in these cases is that the search or the particular type of search conducted was not specifically required by federal regulations. *U.S. v. Keuylian,* 602 F.2d 1033 (2d Cir. 1979); *U.S. v. Gumerlock,* 590 F.2d 794 (9th Cir.) *(en banc), cert. denied,* 441 U.S. 948 (1979).

Other cases have held that, when a passenger fits the FAA anti-skyjacking profile, usually followed by an activation of the magnetometer which detects the presence of metal objects, there is a "reasonable belief" that he may have a weapon and therefore a "frisk" within the *Terry v. Ohio* test is permitted. *U.S. v. Bell,* 464 F.2d 667 (2d Cir.), *cert. denied,* 409 U.S. 991 (1972). In *U.S. v. Ruiz-Estrella,* 481 F.2d 723 (2d Cir. 1973), however, the same circuit held, based on the facts of that case, there was not "reasonable suspicion," and the search was illegal. Another circuit has used the *Terry* rationale, even where the magnetometer was not activated but there was other suspicious activity, because the situation "involved a necessarily swift action predicated upon on-the-spot observations of a law enforcement officer which could not be 'subjected to the warrant procedure.'" *U.S. v. Homburg,* 546 F.2d 1350, 1352 (9th Cir. 1976), *cert. denied,* 431 U.S. 940 (1977). *See also U.S. v. Epperson,* 454 F.2d 769 (4th Cir.), *cert. denied,* 406 U.S. 947 (1972).

One circuit has applied the "plain view" test to approve a search which was initially a private search by an airfreight employee who then called the police. The officer looked into the opened box and saw what looked like narcotics. *U.S. v. Rodriguez,* 596 F.2d 169 (6th Cir. 1979).

## § 242. — Prison Searches.

A prisoner has no reasonable expectation of privacy in his prison cell entitling him to fourth amendment protection. *Hudson v. Palmer,* 468 U.S. 517 (1984). The need to maintain prison security and discipline provides the basis for dispensing with the warrant and probable cause requirements when searching a prisoner's cell, *Block v. Rutherford,* 468 U.S. 576 (1984); *Bell v. Wolfish,* 441 U.S. 520 (1979), or when electronically monitoring his conversation with a visitor, *Lanza v. New York,* 370 U.S. 139 (1962), or his telephone conversation, *U.S. v. Paul,* 614 F.2d 115 (6th Cir.), *cert. denied,* 446 U.S. 941 (1980). "[I]t is obvious that a jail shares none of the attributes of privacy of a home, an automobile, an office, or a hotel room." *Lanza v. New York,* 370 U.S. at 143. The warrantless monitoring of a conversation is not permitted, however, if it involves a "special relationship" which the law has tradi-

tionally endowed with confidentiality, such as the attorney-client relationship. *Id.* at 144.

Routine body cavity searches of prisoners following contact visits
have been sustained against a fourth amendment challenge, *Bell v.
Wolfish, supra,* but a body cavity search of a prisoner who left the
prison daily for a school program was prohibited where the "highly
intrusive and humiliating" search was found to be unreasonable under
the circumstances because she had no notice that her voluntary ab-
sences would subject her to such a search. The court said, however, it
was not holding that notice was required in every fact situation. *U.S. v.
Lilly,* 576 F.2d 1240, 1246 (5th Cir. 1978).

Prison visitors may not be strip searched unless there are reasonable, articulable grounds to suspect a particular visitor of smuggling
contraband. *Hunter v. Auger,* 672 F.2d 668, 675 (8th Cir. 1982).

## § 243. — Consent Searches.

Another exception to the fourth amendment warrant requirement is
the consent search. A valid search of premises may be made without a
warrant and without probable cause if the person in control thereof has
given his voluntary consent. *Schneckloth v. Bustamonte,* 412 U.S. 218
(1973); *U.S. v. Petty,* 601 F.2d 883 (5th Cir. 1979), *cert. denied,* 445 U.S.
962 (1980); *U.S. v. Price,* 599 F.2d 494 (2d Cir. 1979); *U.S. v. Stanley,*
597 F.2d 866 (4th Cir. 1979); *U.S. v. Hendrix,* 595 F.2d 883 (D.C. Cir.
1979); *U.S. v. Scott,* 590 F.2d 531 (3d Cir. 1979); *U.S. v. Miller,* 589
F.2d 1117 (1st Cir. 1978), *cert. denied,* 440 U.S. 958 (1979); *U.S. v.
DiGiacomo,* 579 F.2d 1211 (10th Cir. 1978); *U.S. v. Glasby,* 576 F.2d
734 (7th Cir.), *cert. denied,* 439 U.S. 854 (1978); *U.S. v. Sumlin,* 567
F.2d 684 (6th Cir. 1977), *cert. denied,* 435 U.S. 932 (1978); *U.S. v.
Frazier,* 560 F.2d 884 (8th Cir. 1977), *cert. denied,* 435 U.S. 968 (1978);
*U.S. v. Tolias,* 548 F.2d 277 (9th Cir. 1977). Consent, however, is not
lightly inferred. *U.S. v. Patacchia,* 602 F.2d 218 (9th Cir. 1979).
Whether voluntary consent to search has been given is a fact question
for the court, *U.S. v. Scott,* 578 F.2d 1186 (6th Cir.), *cert. denied,* 439
U.S. 870 (1978); and in making that decision the court must examine
the totality of the circumstances, *U.S. v. Mendenhall,* 446 U.S. 544
(1980); *Schneckloth v. Bustamonte,* 412 U.S. at 238; *U.S. v. Rojas,* 671
F.2d 159, 166-67 (5th Cir. 1982); *U.S. v. Lopez,* 581 F.2d 1338 (9th Cir.
1978); *U.S. v. Shields,* 573 F.2d 18 (10th Cir. 1978); *U.S. v. McCaleb,*
552 F.2d 717 (6th Cir. 1977). The burden is on the government to prove
that consent was voluntary. *U.S. v. Price, supra; U.S. v. Scott,* 578 F.2d
1186 (6th Cir.), *cert. denied,* 439 U.S. 870 (1978); *U.S. v. Glasby, supra;
U.S. v. Juarez,* 573 F.2d 267 (5th Cir.), *cert. denied,* 439 U.S. 915

(1978). It has been held that the government's proof of consent must be "'clear and positive.'" *U.S. v. McCaleb,* 552 F.2d at 721.

The Supreme Court has identified factors relevant in assessing the voluntariness of consent: the age of the person, his education and intelligence, his mental and physical condition at the time, whether he is under arrest, the length and nature of other interrogation, and whether he has been advised of his right to refuse to consent. *Schneckloth v. Bustamonte,* 412 U.S. at 226. However, no single factor will determine the voluntariness of consent. The Supreme Court has held that failure to inform the person of his right to refuse consent does not necessarily make consent involuntary. *Schneckloth v. Bustamonte, supra. See also U.S. v. Matthews,* 603 F.2d 48 (8th Cir.), *cert. denied,* 444 U.S. 1019 (1979); *U.S. v. Scott,* 590 F.2d 531 (3d Cir. 1979); *U.S. v. Juarez,* 573 F.2d at 274. Nor is consent obtained after a person has been arrested and placed in custody necessarily involuntary. *U.S. v. Watson,* 423 U.S. 411 (1976); *U.S. v. Vasquez-Santiago,* 602 F.2d 1069 (2d Cir.) *cert. denied,* 447 U.S. 911 (1979); *U.S. v. Frazier, supra; U.S. v. Tolias, supra.* It has been held, however, when trying to establish that there was voluntary consent after an illegal stop, the test is stricter than when consent is given after a permissible stop. *U.S. v. Ballard,* 573 F.2d 913, 916 (5th Cir. 1978).

Consent can be given voluntarily even though *Miranda* warnings have not been given. *U.S. v. Tobin,* 576 F.2d 687 (5th Cir.), *cert. denied,* 439 U.S. 1051 (1978); *U.S. v. Hall,* 565 F.2d 917 (5th Cir. 1978); *U.S. v. Lemon,* 550 F.2d 467 (9th Cir. 1977). Consent also can be voluntary after a person has exercised his *Miranda* right to remain silent. *U.S. v. Busic,* 592 F.2d 13 (2d Cir. 1978). And consent can be voluntary even though the government agent fails to identify himself as such. *U.S. v. Bullock,* 590 F.2d 117 (5th Cir. 1979). Where an FBI agent served a union official with a subpoena for union records and the official mistakenly believed that it gave the agent authority to search the premises, the search was held valid as a consent search under the totality of the circumstance test. *U.S. v. Allison,* 619 F.2d 1254 (8th Cir. 1980).

Consent to search can be express or implied from all the circumstances. Examples of implied consent follow: consent to search airline baggage, *U.S. v. Freeland,* 562 F.2d 383 (6th Cir.), *cert. denied,* 434 U.S. 957 (1977), consent to search of fourth class mail by postal officials, *U.S. v. Riley,* 554 F.2d 1282 (4th Cir. 1977), consent to search person upon entry into a prison facility, *U.S. v. Sihler,* 562 F.2d 349 (5th Cir. 1977), and upon entry into a secured courtroom, *McMorris v. Alioto,* 567 F.2d 897 (9th Cir. 1978). However, the Supreme Court has held that a retail store does not consent to a wholesale search just because it has invited the public to enter. *Lo-Ji Sales, Inc. v. New York*, 442 U.S. 319 (1979).

A person giving consent to search may limit the area to be searched. *U.S. v. Griffin*, 530 F.2d 739 (7th Cir. 1976), but where he has given a general consent to search his car, closed containers within the car may be searched. *Florida v. Jimeno*, 111 S. Ct. 1801 (1991).

### § 244. — — Use of Deceit to Secure Consent.

Where, however, a government agent uses deceit, trickery, or misrepresentation to secure consent to search, the consent has been held to be involuntary. *U.S. v. Tweel*, 550 F.2d 297 (5th Cir. 1977); *U.S. v. Robson*, 477 F.2d 13 (9th Cir. 1973), *cert. denied*, 420 U.S. 927 (1975). Consent is also involuntary where it is the product of coercion or threat, express or implied. *Schneckloth v. Bustamonte*, 412 U.S. at 228. For example, a threat to ransack the house unless consent was given invalidated the consent. *U.S. v. Kampbell*, 574 F.2d 962 (8th Cir. 1978). Consent following the warrantless entry of eight officers with guns drawn was invalidated. *U.S. v. Calhoun*, 542 F.2d 1094 (9th Cir. 1976), *cert. denied*, 429 U.S. 1064 (1977). Consent obtained from a girl after repeated requests, assistance from the girl's mother, and notice that the girl might be a suspect was held involuntary. *U.S. v. Mayes*, 552 F.2d 729 (6th Cir. 1977). However, the statement that a search warrant will be obtained if consent to search is not given does not, in and of itself, render the consent involuntary. *U.S. v. Miller*, 589 F.2d 1117 (1st Cir. 1978), *cert. denied*, 440 U.S. 958 (1979); *U.S. v. Miley*, 513 F.2d 1191 (2d Cir.), *cert. denied*, 423 U.S. 842 (1975).

### § 245. — — Third-Party Consent.

A third party may consent to a search, but only to the extent that he or she exercises authority or control over the area or items to be searched. For example, authority of a third party to consent to a search of a commonly used room does not necessarily extend to a search of a locked box or bag found therein. *U.S. v. Diggs*, 569 F.2d 1264 (3d Cir. 1977). *See also U.S. v. Block*, 590 F.2d 535 (4th Cir. 1978); *U.S. v. Isom*, 588 F.2d 858 (2d Cir. 1978); *U.S. v. Wilson*, 536 F.2d 883 (9th Cir.), *cert. denied*, 429 U.S. 982 (1976).

The Supreme Court has stated that "the consent of one who possesses common authority over premises or effects is valid as against the absent, nonconsenting person with whom that authority is shared." *U.S.*

*v. Matlock,* 415 U.S. 164, 170 (1974). Common authority, it was said, 415 U.S. at 171 n.7, is

> not to be implied from the mere property interest a third party has in the property. The authority which justifies the third-party consent does not rest upon the law of property, ... but rests rather on mutual use of the property by persons generally having joint access or control for most purposes, so that it is reasonable to recognize that any of the co-inhabitants has the right to permit the inspection in his own right and that the others have assumed the risk that one of their number might permit the common area to be searched.

In determining whether there was common authority or mutual use, the court should examine the totality of the circumstances. *U.S. v. Patterson,* 554 F.2d 852 (8th Cir. 1977). If there is reasonable belief that the third person had "the right to permit the inspection in his own right and that the absent target has assumed the risk that the third person may grant this permission to others," there is authority to give consent, *U.S. v. Block,* 590 F.2d 535, 540 (4th Cir. 1978), and this may include the "most private enclosure if the third party has the authority to permit the intrusion," *U.S. v. Buettner-Jamusch,* 646 F.2d 759 (2d Cir. 1981). Mere possession of the keys to the defendant's apartment did not give the possessor of the keys the authority to consent to a search. *Riley v. Gray,* 674 F.2d 522, 528-29 (6th Cir. 1982).

A warrantless entry is likewise valid when based on the consent of a third party whom the police reasonably believe has common authority over the premises, but who in fact does not. The fourth amendment does not assure that no search will occur, only that no search will be "unreasonable." The standard is whether the facts available at the moment would warrant a person of reasonable caution in the belief that the consenting party had authority over the premises. *Illinois v. Rodriguez,* 110 S. Ct. 2793 (1990). It has been held that the police had no basis to believe that a night clerk in a hotel had authority to permit a search of a guest's room. *Stoner v. California,* 376 U.S. 483 (1964). However, an erroneous view of the applicable law, such as an erroneous belief that landladies may generally consent to a search of a tenant's premises, does not validate a search. *U.S. v. Brown,* 961 F.2d 1039 (2d Cir. 1992).

Cases involving third-party consent tend to turn on their separate facts. Courts have examined consent by co-tenants or mutual users of premises. *U.S. v. Bethea,* 598 F.2d 331 (4th Cir.), *cert. denied,* 444 U.S. 860 (1979); *U.S. v. Reeves,* 594 F.2d 536 (6th Cir. 1979), *cert. denied,* 442 U.S. 946 (1979); *U.S. v. Dubrofsky,* 581 F.2d 208 (9th Cir. 1978); *U.S. v. Jones,* 580 F.2d 785 (5th Cir. 1978); *U.S. v. Sumlin,* 567 F.2d

684 (6th Cir. 1977), *cert. denied,* 425 U.S. 932 (1978); *U.S. v. Green,* 523 F.2d 968 (9th Cir. 1975). Courts have also considered consent given by lessors to search leased premises and consent given by building managers. *U.S. v. Cornejo,* 598 F.2d 554 (9th Cir. 1979); *U.S. v. Main,* 598 F.2d 1086 (7th Cir.), *cert. denied,* 444 U.S. 943 (1979); *Marshall v. Western Waterproofing Co., Inc.,* 560 F.2d 947, 950-51 (8th Cir. 1977) (apartment manager); *U.S. v. Kelly,* 551 F.2d 760 (8th Cir.), *cert. denied,* 433 U.S. 912 (1977). Other situations include consent by relatives such as spouses, parents, or children. *U.S. v. Crouthers,* 669 F.2d 635, 642-43 (10th Cir. 1982); *U.S. v. Hendrix,* 595 F.2d 883 (D.C. Cir. 1979); *U.S. v. Wright,* 564 F.2d 785 (8th Cir. 1977); *Wolfel v. Sanborn,* 555 F.2d 583 (6th Cir.), *cert. denied,* 459 U.S. 1115 (1977); *U.S. v. Long,* 524 F.2d 660 (9th Cir. 1975). The government must also show that consent by a third party was given voluntarily. *U.S. v. Block,* 590 F.2d at 539; *U.S. v. Patterson,* 554 F.2d 852 (8th Cir. 1977).

## § 246. Evidence Affected by a Search and Seizure.

### § 247. — Property That May Be Seized.

Rule 41(b) of the Federal Rules of Criminal Procedure provides for issuance of a warrant "to search for and seize any (1) property that constitutes evidence of the commission of a criminal offense, (2) contraband, the fruits of crime, or things otherwise criminally possessed, (3) property designed or intended for use or which is or has been used as a means of committing a criminal offense, or (4) person for whose arrest there is probable cause, or who is unlawfully restrained."

The first of these — property constituting evidence of a criminal offense — was added by Congress to take account of the Supreme Court's holding in *Warden v. Hayden,* 387 U.S. 294 (1967), that "mere evidence" could be seized in a lawful search, thus broadening the prior rule. However, there must still be probable cause and a nexus between the "mere evidence" seized and the crime under investigation. *Warden v. Hayden, supra.*

A sufficient nexus has been found with clothes seized for examination of paint chips possibly matching paint chips found at the scene of the crime, *U.S. v. Edwards,* 415 U.S. 800 (1974); a phone number card seized from the defendant's wallet at the time of arrest to help establish a conspiracy, *U.S. v. Gimelstop,* 475 F.2d 157, 161 (3d Cir.), *cert. denied,* 414 U.S. 828 (1973); a seized scrap of newspaper that matched newspaper found at a bomb site, *U.S. v. Davis,* 589 F.2d 904 (5th Cir.), *cert. denied,* 441 U.S. 950 (1979); seized documents relating to an adjoining lot of land as evidence of intent to defraud with regard to the lot under investigation, *Andresen v. Maryland,* 427 U.S. 463 (1976).

Seized evidence that has been held inadmissible for lack of a sufficient nexus includes a tape cassette seized from the defendant's person where the search warrant authorized only a search of defendant's car, *U.S. v. Rizzo,* 583 F.2d 907 (7th Cir. 1978), *cert. denied,* 440 U.S. 908 (1979), and evidence seized upon a search of an automobile where the warrant authorized a search of a house trailer, *U.S. v. Stanley,* 597 F.2d 866 (4th Cir. 1979).

Although a search warrant must describe with particularity the property to be seized, other evidence not particularly described may sometimes be seized. *U.S. v. Clark,* 531 F.2d 928 (8th Cir. 1976). Where a search is made pursuant to a valid warrant, evidence uncovered which is not specifically the subject of the search may be seized. *U.S. v. Rettig,* 589 F.2d 418 (9th Cir. 1978); *U.S. v. Lee,* 581 F.2d 1173 (6th Cir.), *cert. denied,* 439 U.S. 1048 (1978); *U.S. v. Forsythe,* 560 F.2d 1127 (3d Cir. 1977); *U.S. v. Bills,* 555 F.2d 1250 (5th Cir. 1977). Evidence of other crimes or offenses may also be seized where government agents conducting a search are lawfully searching for property listed in the warrant or for which they had probable cause to search. *Abel v. U.S.,* 362 U.S. 217 (1960); *U.S. v. Cortellesso,* 601 F.2d 28 (1st Cir. 1979) (warrant subsequently obtained for the evidence of other crimes uncovered); *U.S. v. Nedd,* 582 F.2d 965 (5th Cir. 1978); *U.S. v. Lee, supra.*

Rule 41(b)(4) provides for a warrant to search for persons for whose arrest there is probable cause and for persons who are unlawfully restrained, *i.e.,* kidnap victims. Of course, when exigent circumstances exist, a warrantless search for such persons may be made. *U.S. v. Watson,* 423 U.S. 411 (1976). But absent exigent circumstances, a search warrant must be secured from a magistrate. *Steagald v. U.S.,* 451 U.S. 204 (1981); *Payton v. New York,* 445 U.S. 573 (1980); *Virgin Islands v. Gereau,* 502 F.2d 914 (3d Cir. 1974), *cert. denied,* 420 U.S. 909 (1975).

## §248. — The Exclusionary Rule.

As a general rule, illegally obtained evidence, to which there is timely objection, will not be admitted into evidence. This exclusionary rule is not a personal constitutional right of the person aggrieved, but a judicially created remedy designed primarily to deter improper conduct by law enforcement. *U.S. v. Leon,* 468 U.S. 897 (1984); *Michigan v. De Fillippo,* 443 U.S. 31 (1979); *Lego v. Twomey,* 404 U.S. 477 (1972); *Elkins v. U.S.,* 364 U.S. 206 (1960). This rule applies not only to illegally obtained physical evidence, but also to oral testimony about what was seen or found, *Wong Sun v. U.S.,* 371 U.S. 471 (1963); *Gissendanner v. Wainwright,* 482 F.2d 1293 (5th Cir. 1973), and to the fruits of what was illegally obtained, *Alderman v. U.S.,* 394 U.S. 165 (1969); *Wong Sun v. U.S.,* 371 U.S. at 484.

As a general rule, the exclusionary rule does not apply in civil proceedings, including civil tax assessment proceedings, *U.S. v. Janis,* 428 U.S. 433 (1976), and civil deportation proceedings, *Immigration & Naturalization Serv. v. Lopez-Mendoza,* 468 U.S. 1032 (1984).

As the purpose of the exclusionary rule is to deter police misconduct, evidence obtained by police officers acting with objectively reasonable "good faith" reliance on a search warrant issued by a neutral and detached magistrate need not be excluded even though the warrant was not supported by probable cause. This presumes that the magistrate did not abandon his detached and neutral role, the officers were not dishonest or reckless in preparing their affidavit, or could not have harbored an objectively reasonable belief in the lack of existence of probable cause. *U.S. v. Leon, supra; Massachusetts v. Sheppard,* 468 U.S. 981 (1984). The "good faith" exception also applies to warrantless administrative searches pursuant to a subsequently invalidated statute. *Illinois v. Krull,* 480 U.S. 340 (1987).

The exclusionary rule extends to all evidence that is the fruit of an illegal search or arrest. *Wong Sun v. U.S.,* 371 U.S. 471 (1963); *Silverthorne Lumber Co. v. U.S.,* 251 U.S. 385 (1920). For example, in *Wong Sun,* the court excluded a statement given by the defendant after his illegal arrest, and narcotics recovered from a third person who had been identified by the defendant in his post arrest statements. Counterfeit currency seized from a defendant during an inventory search after an illegal arrest was suppressed in *U.S. v. Wynn,* 544 F.2d 786 (5th Cir. 1977).

Not all evidence resulting from an unlawful search or arrest is considered fruit of the unlawful search or arrest. The test is not "but for the illegal actions of the police"; it is whether the evidence has been obtained by "exploitation" of the unlawful conduct or has been obtained by other means "'sufficiently distinguishable to be purged of the primary taint.'" *Wong Sun v. U.S.,* 371 U.S. at 488; *Brown v. Illinois,* 422 U.S. 590 (1975). Where the link between the illegal conduct and the evidence is found to have become sufficiently attenuated to dissipate the taint of the illegal conduct, the evidence will not be excluded. *Nardone v. U.S.,* 308 U.S. 388 (1939); *U.S. v. Scios,* 590 F.2d 956 (D.C. Cir. 1978); *U.S. v. Carsello,* 578 F.2d 199 (7th Cir.), *cert. denied,* 439 U.S. 979 (1978); *U.S. v. Duncan,* 570 F.2d 292 (9th Cir. 1978); *U.S. v. Wilson,* 569 F.2d 392 (5th Cir. 1978); *U.S. v. Moore,* 562 F.2d 106 (1st

Cir. 1977), *cert. denied,* 435 U.S. 926 (1978); *U.S. v. Villano,* 529 F.2d 1046 (10th Cir.), *cert. denied,* 426 U.S. 953 (1976). Further, if the evidence would have been inevitably discovered notwithstanding a constitutional violation, *Nix v. Williams,* 467 U.S. 431 (1984) (sixth amendment violation), or is shown to have been obtained from sources independent of the illegal conduct, it will not be excluded. *New York v. Harris,* 495 U.S. 14 (1990); *Segura v. U.S.,* 468 U.S. 796 (1984); *U.S. v. Crews,* 445 U.S. 463 (1980); *Silverthorne Lumber Co. v. U.S.,* 251 U.S. at 392; *Grimaldi v. U.S.,* 606 F.2d 332 (1st Cir.), *cert. denied,* 444 U.S. 971 (1979); *U.S. v. Allard,* 600 F.2d 1301 (9th Cir. 1979); *U.S. v. Fredericks,* 586 F.2d 470 (5th Cir. 1978), *cert. denied,* 440 U.S. 962 (1979); *U.S. v. Sor-Lokken,* 557 F.2d 755 (10th Cir.), *cert. denied,* 434 U.S. 894 (1977). This "independent source" doctrine applies even where government agents initially discovered evidence during an illegal entry, and then subsequently discovered the same evidence during a search pursuant to a search warrant obtained on the basis of information wholly unconnected with the initial entry. *Murray v. U.S.,* 487 U.S. 533 (1988).

The fruit of the poisonous tree doctrine distinguishes between tangible or documentary evidence and witness testimony. *U.S. v. Ceccolini,* 435 U.S. 268 (1978). Live-witness testimony will not necessarily be excluded even when it was secured through a chain of discovery following illegal conduct. Instead, the court will look at the degree of free will exercised by the witness, the time lapse between the illegal conduct and the live-witness testimony, the status of the witness as either a putative defendant or a third party, and then will balance the benefit of exclusion as a deterrent against the societal cost of permanently disabling a witness from testifying. *U.S. v. Ceccolini,* 435 U.S. at 276-77; *U.S. v. Rubalcava-Montoya,* 597 F.2d 140 (9th Cir. 1978); *U.S. v. Scios,* 590 F.2d at 962-63; *U.S. v. Carsello,* 578 F.2d at 204; *U.S. v. Houltin,* 566 F.2d 1027 (5th Cir.), *cert. denied,* 439 U.S. 826 (1978).

When a defendant establishes that evidence was obtained as a result of unlawful government conduct, the burden is on the government to establish an independent basis for the evidence by a preponderance or to show that the evidence has been purged of its original taint. *U.S. v. Matlock,* 415 U.S. 164 (1974); *Wong Sun v. U.S.,* 371 U.S. at 488.

For a discussion of whether evidence suppressed as the fruit of an unlawful search may be used to impeach a defendant's false trial testimony, see Chapter 18, § 1818, *infra.*

## § 249. Motions to Suppress.

## § 250. — Timing of Motions to Suppress.

Motions to suppress evidence must be filed by the date before trial set by the court. Rule 12(b) and (c), Fed. R. Crim. P. Failure to timely file a motion to suppress constitutes a waiver, "but the court for cause shown may grant relief from the waiver." Rule 12(f), Fed. R. Crim. P. "Cause" has not been found readily by the courts, and appellate courts have regularly upheld trial court decisions denying untimely motions to suppress. *U.S. v. Scavo,* 593 F.2d 837 (8th Cir. 1979); *U.S. v. Hare,* 589 F.2d 242 (5th Cir. 1979); *U.S. v. Bridwell,* 583 F.2d 1135 (10th Cir. 1978); *U.S. v. Echols,* 577 F.2d 308 (5th Cir. 1978), *cert. denied,* 440 U.S. 939 (1979); *U.S. v. Wood,* 550 F.2d 435 (9th Cir. 1976); *U.S. v. Farnkoff,* 535 F.2d 661 (1st Cir. 1976); *U.S. v. Rollins,* 522 F.2d 160 (2d Cir. 1975), *cert. denied,* 424 U.S. 918 (1976). *But see U.S. v. Hall,* 565 F.2d 917 (5th Cir. 1978) (attorney's inadvertence and court's desire to avoid penalizing the defendant constituted "cause").

However, a court may find "cause" where a defendant is not aware of the facts giving rise to the motion to suppress until after the time for the filing of the motion has passed. Thus, it is prudent for the government to notify a defendant as soon as is practicable of the government's intention to use specific evidence that may be subject to a motion to suppress. Rule 12(d)(1), Fed. R. Crim. P.

If a motion to suppress is filed, it must be heard and ruled on by the court before trial, unless "for good cause," the court orders that its ruling on the motion be deferred. However, the court should not defer its ruling where appeal rights of either the defendant or the government would be adversely affected. Rule 12(e), Fed. R. Crim. P.; *U.S. v. Thompson,* 558 F.2d 522 (9th Cir. 1977), *cert. denied,* 435 U.S. 914 (1978). The government can appeal an adverse decision by a court on a motion to suppress heard before trial (18 U.S.C. § 3731), but cannot appeal once jeopardy has attached during trial. *See, e.g., U.S. v. Payner,* 572 F.2d 144 (6th Cir. 1978), *aff'd,* 590 F.2d 206 (1979), *rev'd,* 447 U.S. 727 (1980).

## § 251. — Hearing.

## § 252. — — Burden of Proof.

As a general rule, the burden of proof is on the defendant who seeks to suppress evidence. *U.S. v. Feldman,* 606 F.2d 673 (6th Cir. 1979), *cert. denied,* 445 U.S. 961 (1980); *U.S. v. Evans,* 572 F.2d 455 (5th Cir.), *cert. denied,* 439 U.S. 870 (1978); *U.S. v. Galente,* 547 F.2d 733 (2d Cir.

1976), *cert. denied,* 431 U.S. 969 (1977); *U.S. v. Phillips,* 540 F.2d 319 (8th Cir.), *cert. denied,* 429 U.S. 1000 (1976). Once the defendant has established a basis for his motion, such as an initial showing that the search was conducted without a warrant, or that a statement may not have been voluntary, or that an out-of-court identification may have been improperly suggested, the burden of proof shifts to the government to show that the warrantless search was reasonable, that the statement was voluntary, or that the identification was not suggestive. *U.S. v. Williams,* 604 F.2d 1102 (8th Cir. 1979); *U.S. v. Sacco,* 563 F.2d 552 (2d Cir.), *cert. denied,* 434 U.S. 1039 (1977); *U.S. v. De La Fuente,* 548 F.2d 528 (5th Cir.), *cert. denied,* 434 U.S. 954 (1977); *U.S. v. Ochs,* 461 F. Supp. 1 (S.D.N.Y. 1978), *aff'd,* 636 F.2d 1205 (2d Cir. 1980) (mem.), *cert. denied,* 451 U.S. 1016 (1981). This burden is proof by a preponderance of the evidence. *U.S. v. Matlock,* 415 U.S. 164, 177 (1974); *U.S. v. Finefrock,* 668 F.2d 1168, 1171 (10th Cir. 1982).

### § 253. — — Evidentiary Rules.

The trial court is not bound by the Federal Rules of Evidence except those with respect to privileges in hearing motions to suppress. Rule 104 and Rule 1101(d)(1), Fed. R. Evid.; *U.S. v. Killebrew,* 594 F.2d 1103 (6th Cir.), *cert. denied,* 442 U.S. 933 (1979); *U.S. v. De La Fuente,* 548 F.2d 528 (5th Cir.), *cert. denied,* 434 U.S. 954 (1977); *U.S. v. Ochs,* 461 F. Supp. 1 (S.D.N.Y. 1978), *aff'd,* 636 F.2d 1205 (2d Cir. 1980) *(mem.),* *cert. denied,* 451 U.S. 1016 (1981). Hearsay evidence is admissible on a motion to suppress. *U.S. v. Matlock,* 415 U.S. 164, 172 (1974); *U.S. v. Killebrew,* 594 F.2d at 1105; *U.S. v. Tussell,* 441 F. Supp. 1092 (M.D. Pa. 1977), *aff'd,* 593 F.2d 543 (3d Cir. 1979). Jencks Act material, sought under 18 U.S.C. § 3500, must be disclosed at a pretrial hearing on a motion to suppress evidence, and a law enforcement officer shall be deemed a witness called by the government. Rule 12(i), Fed. R. Crim. P.

The defendant has the right to cross-examine government witnesses at a suppression hearing, but this may be limited by the informant's privilege. *U.S. v. Green,* 670 F.2d 1148, 1154 (D.C. Cir. 1981). *See* Chapters 7, § 713, and 19, § 1923, *infra.*

Suppression hearings involving confessions must be conducted out of the hearing of the jury. Rule 104(c), Fed. R. Evid.

### § 254. — — Right to a Hearing.

The defendant may be entitled to a hearing on his motion to suppress when issues of fact, as opposed to law, are contested and the credibility of witnesses is important, but in reviewing the proposed findings of a magistrate who heard the testimony, the trial court judge is not required to "rehear" the testimony. *U.S. v. Raddatz,* 447 U.S. 667 (1980). Where factual issues are involved, the trial court must state its essential findings on the record. Rule 12(e), Fed. R. Crim. P. However, a condition precedent to a hearing is the allegation which is definite, specific, detailed, and non-conjectural, of facts which, if proved, would require the granting of relief. *Cohen v. U.S.,* 378 F.2d 751 (9th Cir.), *cert. denied,* 389 U.S. 897 (1967).

A suppression hearing may not be closed unless there is an overriding interest likely to be prejudiced. The closure is no broader than necessary to protect that interest, and the court must consider reasonable alternatives to closing the hearing. *Waller v. Georgia,* 467 U.S. 39 (1984).

## § 255. — Standing.

A defendant's right to challenge a search no longer depends upon traditional concepts of standing, but "whether governmental officials violated any legitimate expectation of privacy held by [the defendant]," *Rawlings v. Kentucky,* 448 U.S. 98, 106 (1980), that is, whether the fourth amendment rights of the defendant have in fact been violated. *U.S. v. Salvucci,* 448 U.S. 83 (1980); *Rakas v. Illinois,* 439 U.S. 128 (1978); *U.S. v. Agapito,* 620 F.2d 324 (2d Cir.), *cert. denied,* 449 U.S. 834 (1980). Thus, a defendant may not have evidence suppressed which was seized as a result of a flagrantly illegal search which violated the reasonable expectation of privacy of a third party. *U.S. v. Payner,* 447 U.S. 727 (1980).

Before *Rakas,* a defendant had to establish standing to challenge evidence obtained in an alleged illegal search and seizure. In determining whether standing existed, the courts examined the level and kind of interest the defendant had in the premises searched and the property seized. *Alderman v. U.S.,* 394 U.S. 165 (1969); *Mancusi v. DeForte,* 392 U.S. 364 (1968); *Simmons v. U.S.,* 390 U.S. 377 (1968); *Jones v. U.S.,* 362 U.S. 257 (1960). It had been held that a defendant did not have standing to challenge the admission of items seized from third persons. *Alderman v. U.S.,* 394 U.S. at 174. However, the Supreme Court fashioned two "automatic" exceptions to this rule: (1) where the possession of the seized item was an element of the offense charged, and (2) where the defendant was said to be "legitimately on the premises." *Jones v. U.S.,* 362 U.S. at 263. The "legitimately on the premises" exception was rejected in *Rakas v. Illinois,* 439 U.S. at 143, and the possession of the item as an element of the offense exception was rejected in *U.S. v. Salvucci, supra,* in favor of a fourth amendment analysis of whether the defendant had a reasonable expectation of privacy in the premises searched.

Thus, a defendant can no longer challenge a search merely because it was "directed" at him, because he was "legitimately on the premises," or he had possession of the seized item which was an element of the offense.

Unless a defendant can show that the search and seizure violated his personal fourth amendment rights to a legitimate expectation of privacy, he may not challenge the reasonableness of that search and seizure. Relevant factors include legitimate presence in the area searched, possession or ownership, prior use of the area searched or property seized, the ability to control or exclude other's use of the property and a subjective expectation of privacy. *U.S. v. Lochan,* 674 F.2d 960, 965 (1st Cir. 1982). Thus, a defendant lacks standing to challenge the search of a stolen truck which he was driving, *U.S. v. Hensel,* 672 F.2d 578, 579 (6th Cir.), *cert. denied,* 457 U.S. 1107 (1982), or a hotel room in which he is "merely present," *U.S. v. Irizarry,* 673 F.2d 554, 556-57 (1st Cir. 1982). An overnight guest, however, has a legitimate expectation of privacy in his host's home. *Minnesota v. Olson,* 495 U.S. 91 (1990).

### § 256. — Appeal From Suppression Hearing.

A defendant may not appeal directly from denial of a motion to suppress. He may appeal only on conviction. *DiBella v. U.S.,* 369 U.S. 121 (1962); *U.S. v. Acosta,* 669 F.2d 292, 293 (5th Cir. 1982). However, the government has a right to appeal trial court decisions suppressing evidence where the defendant has not yet been placed in jeopardy. The only additional requirements are that the U.S. Attorney certify to the district court that the appeal is not taken for purposes of delay and that the suppressed evidence is substantial proof of a material fact. 18 U.S.C. § 3731. Such appeals must be made within 30 days after the decision suppressing evidence has been rendered, 18 U.S.C. § 3731; Rule 4(b), Fed. R. App. P. or 30 days from a denial of the government's motion for reconsideration. *U.S. v. Ibarra,* 112 S. Ct. 4 (1991).

A subsequent plea of guilty waives the defendant's right to challenge on appeal a denial of his motion to suppress. *Tollett v. Henderson,* 411 U.S. 258 (1973); *DiBella v. U.S.,* 369 U.S. 121 (1962); *Lott v. U.S.,* 367 U.S. 421 (1961). Rule 11(a)(2) of the Federal Rules of Criminal Procedure provides that a defendant may preserve for appeal the issues raised in a motion to suppress if a "conditional plea" is entered.

The standard of review is "clearly erroneous," *U.S. v. McGlynn,* 671 F.2d 1140, 1143 (8th Cir. 1982); and trial testimony may be used to sustain denial of a motion to suppress, *U.S. v. Sanford,* 673 F.2d 1070, 1072 (9th Cir. 1982).

## § 257. Wiretapping and Other Electronic Surveillance.

Title III of the Omnibus Crime Control and Safe Streets Act of 1968, 18 U.S.C. §§ 2510-2520, contains a comprehensive scheme regulating wiretapping and other forms of electronic surveillance. The principle embodied in this legislation is the one enunciated in *Katz v. U.S.,* 389 U.S. 347 (1967): whether an electronic interception of a conversation is offensive to the fourth amendment depends not on whether the interception resulted from a physical trespass but rather on whether the person whose conversation was intercepted had reasonable expectations of privacy. Because the statutory scheme adheres closely to the fourth amendment constitutional limitations as set forth by the Supreme Court, *Katz v. U.S.,* 389 U.S. at 348-53; *U.S. v. U.S. District Court,* 407 U.S. 297 (1972). Title III's constitutionality has been upheld by numerous courts, *U.S. v. Frederickson,* 581 F.2d 711 (8th Cir. 1978); *U.S. v. Feldman,* 535 F.2d 1175 (9th Cir. 1976), *cert. denied,* 429 U.S. 940 (1976); *U.S. v. Cafero,* 473 F.2d 489 (3d Cir. 1973), *cert. denied,* 417 U.S. 918 (1974).

Evidence obtained in violation of Title III is inadmissible in any state or federal prosecution. Section 2515 of Title 18 provides:

> Whenever any wire or oral communication has been intercepted, no part of the contents of such communication and no evidence derived therefrom may be received in evidence in any trial, hearing, or other proceeding, in or before any court, grand jury, department, officer, agency, regulatory body, legislative committee, or other authority of the United States, a State, or political subdivision thereof if the disclosure of that information would be in violation of this chapter.

There are two broad statutory exceptions to the prohibition of Section 2515: (1) interceptions conducted pursuant to court order as authorized by the statute; and (2) interceptions obtained with the consent of one party.

## § 258. — Interception Pursuant to Court Order.

A two-step procedure must be followed to lawfully intercept an oral or wire communication without consent of one of the parties. First, authorization must be obtained to apply for a court order approving an interception. Second, application must be made to a federal judge and an order obtained.

### § 259. — — Authorization.

Authorization for a wiretap may be given only to obtain evidence of crimes specified in 18 U.S.C. § 2516(1)(a) through (g). Authorization to investigate one crime, however, does not preclude ancillary use of the information obtained to prove a different crime if the new offense was discovered through the surveillance. *U.S. v. Cox,* 567 F.2d 930, 933 (10th Cir. 1977), *cert. denied,* 435 U.S. 927 (1978). Authorization must be granted by the "Attorney General, Deputy Attorney General, Associate Attorney General, any Assistant Attorney General, any acting Assistant Attorney General, or any Deputy Assistant Attorney General in the Criminal Division." 18 U.S.C. § 2516(1); *U.S. v. Giordano,* 416 U.S. 505, 507-08 (1974); *U.S. v. Diadone,* 558 F.2d 775, 778-79 (5th Cir. 1977), *cert. denied,* 434 U.S. 1064 (1978). A designation of an Assistant Attorney General under this section may be made by the Attorney General and relied upon by succeeding Attorney Generals without a new designation. *U.S. v. Wyder,* 674 F.2d 224, 226-27 (4th Cir. 1982). There is no need to authenticate the signature of the Attorney General at trial or hearing where the authorization appears regular on its face. *U.S. v. De La Fuente,* 548 F.2d 528, 531-32 (5th Cir.), *cert. denied,* 434 U.S. 954 (1977); *U.S. v. McCoy,* 539 F.2d 1050, 1055 (5th Cir. 1976), *cert. denied,* 431 U.S. 919 (1977). Further, authorization in writing is not needed where there is other proof that authorization was obtained. *U.S. v. Scully,* 546 F.2d 255, 260-61 (9th Cir. 1976), *vacated,* 430 U.S. 902, *aff'd,* 554 F.2d 363, *cert. denied,* 430 U.S. 970 (1977) (affidavit that proper authorization was given over the telephone).

### § 260. — — Application and Order.

### § 261. — — — Application.

Section 2518(1) requires that application be made to a judge of competent jurisdiction for prior approval of the interception. This includes a federal district judge, court of appeals judge, or a state judge authorized by state statutes. 18 U.S.C. § 2510(9). The application must set forth a full and complete statement of the facts "as to the particular offense that has been, is being, or is about to be committed" and "a particular description of the type of communication sought to be intercepted." A specific crime or series of related crimes must be identified. The nature and type of anticipated conversations must be described.

*U.S. v. Tortorello,* 480 F.2d 764, 778-81 (2d Cir.), *cert. denied,* 414 U.S. 866 (1973). *See also U.S. v. Steinberg,* 525 F.2d 1126 (2d Cir. 1975), *cert. denied,* 425 U.S. 971 (1976). Judicial approval for continuation of the surveillance to obtain evidence of a crime not specified in the original application is required. *U.S. v. Masciarelli,* 558 F.2d 1064, 1068 (2d Cir. 1977) (such approval can be implied and a specific order not needed), and *U.S. v. Cox,* 567 F.2d 931-32. The fruits of one wiretap may be used to set forth the specificity needed in a subsequent application. *U.S. v. Johnson,* 539 F.2d 181, 186-88 (D.C. Cir. 1976), *cert. denied,* 429 U.S. 1061 (1977). Information from a wiretap in one district may be used in another. *U.S. v. Cox,* 567 F.2d 932-33.

The application, as well as the court order, must name those persons law enforcement authorities have probable cause to believe are committing the offense and whose communications are to be intercepted. *U.S. v. Diltz,* 622 F.2d 476 (10th Cir. 1980); *U.S. v. Lee,* 542 F.2d 353 (6th Cir. 1976), *vacated,* 430 U.S. 902, *aff'd,* 557 F.2d 540 (1977). More than just the principal targets must be listed. Failure to name persons whom the government has probable cause to believe are engaged in criminal activity and whose calls the government expects to intercept may lead to suppression. *U.S. v. Donovan,* 429 U.S. 413, 428 (1977). An application need not name persons who are unknown at the time of the application. *U.S. v. Baker,* 589 F.2d 1008 (9th Cir. 1979); *U.S. v. Chiarizio,* 525 F.2d 289 (2d Cir. 1975). *See also U.S. v. Kahn,* 415 U.S. 143, 155 (1974) (application not required to name non-target spouse who was likely to be intercepted and who was only later discovered to be part of gambling conspiracy).

The application must set forth an investigative need, that is, why other techniques have failed or would fail, to justify electronic surveillance. Wiretaps are not to be used routinely as the first step in a criminal investigation. *U.S. v. Martinez,* 588 F.2d 1227, 1231-33 (9th Cir. 1978). However, the government is not required to exhaust all possible investigatory techniques before resorting to a wiretap. *U.S. v. Martin,* 599 F.2d 880, 886-87 (9th Cir. 1979); *U.S. v. McCoy,* 539 F.2d 1050, 1055-56 (5th Cir. 1976), *cert. denied,* 431 U.S. 919 (1977); *U.S. v. Matya,* 541 F.2d 741, 745-46 (8th Cir. 1976), *cert. denied,* 429 U.S. 1091 (1977). More than mere conclusory language is needed to fulfill the investigatory need requirement. *U.S. v. Martinez,* 588 F.2d at 1231; *U.S. v. Gerardi,* 586 F.2d 896, 898 (1st Cir. 1978). For example, unwillingness of informants to testify has been held to be a valid reason to use the electronic surveillance technique. *Id.* at 898; *U.S. v. Feldman,* 535 F.2d 1175 (9th Cir.), *cert. denied,* 429 U.S. 940 (1976); *U.S. v. Vento,* 533 F.2d 838, 850 (3d Cir. 1976). *See also U.S. v. Giordano,* 416

U.S. 505, 515 (1974); *U.S. v. Rotchford,* 575 F.2d 166, 173 (8th Cir. 1978); *U.S. v. Steinberg,* 525 F.2d at 1130; *U.S. v. Kerrigan,* 514 F.2d 35 (9th Cir.), *cert. denied,* 423 U.S. 924 (1975).

As with any other search and seizure, it must be shown there is probable cause to believe that a specific crime has been or is about to be committed before the government may be permitted to invade a constitutionally protected area. 18 U.S.C. § 2518(3)(a). Subparagraph (3) of § 2518 prescribes the necessary elements of probable cause needed for authorization. As to the quantum of probable cause required, *see generally U.S. v. Tortorello,* 480 F.2d at 775-76; *U.S. v. Poeta,* 455 F.2d 117, 121-22 (2d Cir.), *cert. denied,* 406 U.S. 948 (1972). Hearsay may be sufficient if there is a substantial basis for its belief. *U.S. v. Agrusa,* 541 F.2d 690, 694 (8th Cir. 1976), *cert. denied,* 429 U.S. 1045 (1977).

### § 262. — — — Order.

Subparagraph (4) of § 2518 sets forth the required contents of the order. Each order must specify "a particular description of the type of communication sought to be intercepted, and a statement of the particular offense to which it relates." The order must include a statement on how long the interception will last and whether the interception will automatically terminate when the communication sought to be intercepted has been obtained. The order must terminate when the communication sought is first obtained unless the court finds probable cause to intercept additional communications. *See U.S. v. Cafero,* 473 F.2d 489 (3d Cir. 1973), *cert. denied,* 417 U.S. 918 (1974); *U.S. v. Poeta,* 455 F.2d at 120-21. Provisions for minimization should be spelled out in the court order. *See generally U.S. v. Cirillo,* 499 F.2d 872, 879-80 (2d Cir.), *cert. denied,* 419 U.S. 1056 (1974); *U.S. v. Rizzo,* 492 F.2d 443, 446 (2d Cir.), *cert. denied,* 417 U.S. 944 (1974); *U.S. v. Manfredi,* 488 F.2d 588, 598 (2d Cir. 1973), *cert. denied,* 417 U.S. 936 (1974); all holding that, where affidavit and order are read together and construed in a commonsense manner, there was sufficient language to satisfy the statutory requirement that the order contain a minimization provision.

Subparagraph (5) of § 2518 provides that no interception shall be approved for longer than 30 days and provides a procedure for obtaining an extension for a maximum of 30 days. Extension orders require the approval of the Attorney General or the specially designated Assistant Attorney General. *U.S. v. Bynum,* 513 F.2d 533, 535 n.2 (2d Cir.), *cert. denied,* 423 U.S. 952 (1975).

## § 263. — — — Surreptitious Entry.

Whether or not the court order specifically authorizes a surreptitious entry to effect the interception, such authority is implicit in the order to intercept. *Dilia v. U.S.*, 441 U.S. 238 (1979) (order itself acted as a warrant to enter the premises). *See also U.S. v. Licavoli*, 604 F.2d 613, 618-19 (9th Cir. 1979); *U.S. v. Scafidi*, 564 F.2d 633, 638-40 (2d Cir. 1977), *cert. denied*, 436 U.S. 903 (1978).

## § 264. — — — Minimization.

Title 18 U.S.C. § 2518(5) provides that all orders must contain a statement that the interception "shall be conducted in such a way as to minimize the interception of communication not otherwise subject to interception." The court will objectively assess the interceptor's actions in light of the circumstances surrounding him at the time. Good faith is not necessarily enough. *Scott v. U.S.*, 436 U.S. 128 (1978). Specialized jargon or code making criminal conversations harder to decipher will affect attempts at minimization. *U.S. v. Daly*, 535 F.2d 434, 441 (8th Cir. 1976).

Minimization must be judged on a case by case basis; and while interception of a substantial portion of irrelevant calls is suspect, it does not automatically warrant an inference of failure to minimize. For cases upholding the minimization procedures followed, *see U.S. v. Manfredi*, 488 F.2d at 599 (upholding minimization procedures that monitored and recorded all calls in the context of a complex, far-flung narcotics conspiracy); *U.S. v. Capra*, 501 F.2d 267, 275-76 (2d Cir. 1974), *cert. denied*, 420 U.S. 990 (1975) (interception of some personal calls, including those with family and with an attorney, did not automatically vitiate properly conducted minimization); *U.S. v. Rizzo*, 492 F.2d 443, 446 (2d Cir.), *cert. denied*, 417 U.S. 944 (1974); and *U.S. v. Rizzo*, 491 F.2d 215 (2d Cir.), *cert. denied*, 416 U.S. 990 (1974) (minimization held proper where monitoring ceased as soon as a determination could be made that a conversation was not pertinent).

In sustaining surveillance in the face of claims of failure to minimize the overhearing of irrelevant conversations, reviewing courts have emphasized the degree of judicial supervision of the surveillance. *U.S. v. Bynum*, 485 F.2d 490, 501 (2d Cir. 1973), *vacated on other grounds*, 417 U.S. 903 (1974) (logs submitted to the court every four to six days). *See U.S. v. Sklaroff*, 323 F. Supp. 296, 316-17 (S.D. Fla. 1971), *aff'd*, 506 F.2d 837 (5th Cir. 1975).

The government has a statutory duty to inform the issuing judge of the identities of all parties known whose communications have been intercepted. 18 U.S.C. § 2518(8)(d); *U.S. v. Donovan,* 429 U.S. 413 (1977). Unintentional omission does not necessarily require suppression, but naming only the principal targets of the investigation is not enough. *Donovan, supra.* To object to the seizure, one must be an aggrieved party whose primary rights have been violated. *U.S. v. Cruz,* 594 F.2d 268, 273-74 (1st Cir.), *cert. denied,* 444 U.S. 898 (1979) (drug dealer who was caught through surveillance of monitored party held not aggrieved where his name and address not mentioned in intercepted conversation). Standing to complain about illegal entry to implant the surveillance differs from standing to complain as an aggrieved party. *U.S. v. Scafidi,* 564 F.2d at 638.

## § 265. — — — Sealing of Applications, Orders, and Intercepted Communications.

Applications and orders for electronic surveillance shall be sealed by the judge and kept for 10 years. 18 U.S.C. § 2518(8)(b).

Any electronic recordings made pursuant to Title III shall be sealed "immediately" by the judge, and the presence of a seal provided for in the statute or a "satisfactory explanation for the absence thereof, shall be a prerequisite for the use or disclosure of the contents of any wire, oral, or electronic communication or evidence derived therefrom...." 18 U.S.C. § 2518(8)(a); *U.S. v. Rios,* 495 U.S. 257 (1990).

## § 266. — — — Motion to Suppress.

Whether the fruits of an electronic surveillance will be suppressed may depend on whether the defendant has standing to object to the electronic seizure. Defendants with standing may move under 18 U.S.C. § 2518(10)(a) to suppress the contents and fruits of electronic surveillance on the grounds that (1) the interception was unlawful; (2) the court order is insufficient on its face; or (3) the interception was not made in conformance with the court order. *See U.S. v. Chavez,* 416 U.S. 562 (1974). Such a motion must be made before trial or it is waived. 18 U.S.C. § 2518(10)(a); *U.S. v. Wright,* 524 F.2d 1100 (2d Cir. 1975). The government has the right to appeal from a pretrial suppression order. 18 U.S.C. § 2518(10)(b). Suppression hearings are not necessarily required. *U.S. v. Losing,* 539 F.2d 1174 (8th Cir. 1976), *cert. denied,* 434 U.S. 969 (1977); *U.S. v. Steinberg,* 525 F.2d 1126 (2d Cir. 1975), *cert. denied,* 425 U.S. 971 (1976). Likewise, a defendant is not necessarily entitled to an evidentiary hearing on the reasonableness of the surreptitious entry. *U.S. v. Licavoli,* 604 F.2d 613 (9th Cir.), *cert. denied,* 446 U.S. 935 (1979).

Section 2518(8)(a) requires that the recording shall be done in such a way as will protect the recording from editing or other alterations and that "immediately upon the expiration of the period of the order, or extensions thereof," the recording shall be made available to the judge issuing the order and sealed "immediately" under his direction. This section further provides that the presence of a seal or "a satisfactory explanation for the absence, thereof, shall be a prerequisite for the use or disclosure" of the evidence obtained from the recordings. Section 2518(8)(a) applies to a delay in sealing as well as complete failure to seal tapes, and the "satisfactory explanation" exception to immediately sealing requires not only that the government explain why the delay occurred but the government must also demonstrate why the delay is excusable. *U.S. v. Rios,* 495 U.S. 257 (1990).

Technical noncompliance with 18 U.S.C. § 2518(8)(b), requiring that wiretap application and orders be sealed, will not require suppression where there has been no breach of confidentiality and the defendant has not been prejudiced. *U.S. v. Caggiano,* 667 F.2d 1176, 1178-79 (5th Cir. 1982).

### § 267. — — Scope of Title III.

It is clear that only acquisition of aural communications is covered by the statute. Thus, electronic devices such as pen registers, which do not intercept the contents of conversations, are not wiretaps within the meaning of the statute. *Smith v. Maryland,* 442 U.S. 735 (1979). A pen register is a device which, by monitoring the electronic impulses caused by dialing a telephone, can record the number dialed. The Supreme Court in *Smith, supra,* found no expectation of privacy in which numbers were dialed.

Since federal statutes apply only within the territorial jurisdiction of the United States, evidence from wiretaps conducted by foreign governments outside the United States without judicial authorization may still be used in U.S. courts. *U.S. v. Cotroni,* 527 F.2d 708 (2d Cir. 1975), *cert. denied,* 426 U.S. 906 (1976); *U.S. v. Toscanino,* 500 F.2d 267 (2d Cir. 1974).

Evidence obtained under Title III may be used even though it may violate a more restrictive state law concerning the interception of wire communications. *U.S. v. Daniel,* 667 F.2d 783, 784-85 (9th Cir. 1982); *U.S. v. Hall,* 543 F.2d 1229, 1232 (9th Cir. 1976), *cert. denied,* 429 U.S. 1075 (1977).

Evidence legally seized by a wiretap in a criminal case can be used in a subsequent civil proceeding. *Fleming v. U.S.,* 547 F.2d 872 (5th Cir.), *cert. denied,* 434 U.S. 831 (1977).

## § 268. — Interception With Consent of One Party.

Subdivisions (c) and (d) of § 2511(2) provide exceptions to the prohibition against wiretapping or other electronic surveillance if consent is given by one of the parties to a conversation. The consenting party may himself intercept and record the conversation, or may consent to having law enforcement personnel effect the interception. There is no expectation within the meaning of *Katz v. U.S.*, 389 U.S. 347 (1967), that one party to a conversation will not repeat what has been said by the other party, *Hoffa v. U.S.*, 385 U.S. 293, 302 (1966); *U.S. v. Horton*, 601 F.2d 319 (7th Cir.), *cert. denied*, 444 U.S. 937 (1979), or that such party may not himself be a government agent or informant, *Hoffa v. U.S.*, 385 U.S. at 300-04. Nor is the fourth amendment violated because an undisclosed agent simultaneously records a conversation with an electronic device on his person, *Lopez v. U.S.*, 373 U.S. 427 (1963), or because the conversation is electronically transmitted by the undisclosed agent to a remote place where it is overheard by other agents and recorded, *U.S. v. White*, 401 U.S. 745 (1971); *U.S. v. Horton*, 601 F.2d at 320-24. Warrantless recordings with the consent of only one party to a conversation have been consistently admitted into evidence over fourth amendment objections. *U.S. v. Wright*, 573 F.2d 681, 684 (1st Cir.), *cert. denied*, 436 U.S. 949 (1978); *U.S. v. Craig*, 573 F.2d 455, 474 (7th Cir. 1977), *cert. denied*, 439 U.S. 820 (1978); *U.S. v. Hodge*, 539 F.2d 898, 905 (6th Cir. 1976), *cert. denied*, 429 U.S. 1091 (1977); *U.S. v. Bastone*, 526 F.2d 971 (7th Cir. 1975), *cert. denied*, 425 U.S. 973 (1976); *U.S. v. McMillan*, 508 F.2d 101, 104 (8th Cir. 1974), *cert. denied*, 421 U.S. 916 (1975); *U.S. v. Santillo*, 507 F.2d 629 (3d Cir. 1975), *cert. denied*, 421 U.S. 968 (1975); *U.S. v. Bonanno*, 487 F.2d 654, 658-59 (2d Cir. 1973); *U.S. v. Dowdy*, 479 F.2d 213, 229 (4th Cir.), *cert. denied*, 414 U.S. 823 (1973).

The motives of the consenting party in giving his consent are irrelevant unless there is an illegal purpose in making the interception. Thus, the benefit of a plea bargain does not vitiate an otherwise voluntary consent, *U.S. v. Craig*, 573 F.2d at 475-77; nor does a hope for leniency, *U.S. v. Hodge*, 539 F.2d 898, 904-05 (6th Cir.), *cert. denied*, 429 U.S. 1091 (1976); *U.S. v. Franks*, 511 F.2d 25, 30-31 (6th Cir.), *cert. denied*, 422 U.S. 1042 (1975). Likewise, a promise of relocation expenses to be paid by the government did not negate a finding that the informant had voluntarily consented to record the conversation. *U.S. v. Juarez*, 573 F.2d 267, 278 (5th Cir.), *cert. denied*, 439 U.S. 915 (1978). The pressure of potential indictment or promise of future immunity will not render such consent involuntary. *U.S. v. Dowdy*, 479 F.2d at 229. *See also Cooper v. U.S.*, 594 F.2d 12, 14 (4th Cir. 1979). Actual threats of a physical nature, however, or of unfounded prosecution may negate consent. *U.S. v. Horton,* 601 F.2d at 322-23. *Cf., U.S. v. Ryan,* 548 F.2d 782 (9th Cir.), *cert. denied,* 429 U.S. 939 (1976).

The interception of a wire or oral communication is prohibited where the purpose is criminal or tortious. 18 U.S.C. § 2511(2)(d). *See U.S. v. Turk,* 526 F.2d 654 (5th Cir.), *cert. denied,* 429 U.S. 823 (1976); *U.S. v. Jones,* 542 F.2d 661 (6th Cir. 1976) (recording for purposes of extortion). However, a conversation was admitted which was recorded by a private detective at the request of one of the defendants for illegal purposes, where the defendant was unaware that the detective was cooperating with the FBI. *U.S. v. Shields,* 675 F.2d 1152, 1156-57 (11th Cir. 1982).

The consenting party's later unavailability does not prevent proof of consent being shown by other evidence. *U.S. v. White,* 401 U.S. at 746-54; *U.S. v. Gladney,* 563 F.2d 491 (1st Cir. 1977).

# CHAPTER 3

# FIFTH AND SIXTH AMENDMENT PROTECTIONS

§ 301. Confessions.
§ 302. — Form.
§ 303. — Need for Corroboration.
§ 304. — Confession After Arrest But Before Initial Appearance — "Unnecessary Delay."
§ 305. — Confessions and the Rights to Silence and Counsel.
§ 306. — — When Miranda Rights Attach.
§ 307. — — Scope of Miranda.
§ 308. — — Right to Terminate Questioning.
§ 309. — — Silence of Defendant.
§ 310. — — Confessions Obtained After Indictment.
§ 311. — — Impeachment with Statements Taken in Violation of the Fifth and Sixth Amendments.
§ 312. — "Fruit of the Poisonous Tree."
§ 313. — Coerced Confessions.
§ 314. — Use of Confessions at Joint Trials.
§ 315. — Inadmissibility of Statements Related to Pleas and Offers of Pleas.
§ 316. Identifications Before Trial.
§ 317. — Sixth Amendment Rights.
§ 318. — Fifth Amendment Due Process Rights.
§ 319. — Evidence of Extrajudicial Identifications.

## § 301. Confessions.

The fifth amendment protects an individual's right to be free from compelled self-incrimination. Thus, the government may use at trial only those confessions that are voluntarily made. *Malloy v. Hogan,* 378 U.S. 1 (1964). The introduction into evidence of an involuntary confession requires reversal of a subsequent conviction. *Mincey v. Arizona,* 437 U.S. 385, 398 (1978); *Jackson v. Denno,* 378 U.S. 368, 376-77 (1964). Since coerced confessions are not only inherently unreliable but also obtained through unlawful methods, courts are concerned with more than just the truth or falsity of a confession. Because of this, whether or not a confession is the truth is irrelevant to the issue of voluntariness. *U.S. v. Shoemaker,* 542 F.2d 561 (10th Cir.), *cert. denied,* 429 U.S. 1004 (1976).

While the ultimate test of admissibility of a confession is its voluntariness, there are many factors and circumstances that interact in enabling a court to reach that determination. *U.S. v. Brown,* 557 F.2d 541 (6th Cir. 1977). The test is the totality of the circumstances. *Arizona v. Fulminante,* 496 U.S. 903 (1991).

It is the government's burden to prove the voluntariness of a confession, but only by a preponderance of the evidence. *Lego v. Twomey,* 404 U.S. 477, 482-84 (1972). A coerced confession which is admitted is subject to a harmless beyond a reasonable doubt standard. *Arizona v. Fulminante, supra.*

The fifth amendment's protection against compelled self-incrimination includes the right to counsel at custodial interrogations, *Minnick v. Mississippi,* 495 U.S. 903 (1990); *Michigan v. Jackson,* 475 U.S. 625 (1986); *Edwards v. Arizona,* 451 U.S. 477 (1981).

## § 302. — Form.

If it is properly identified as coming from the defendant, the form in which an admissible confession is received has long been held to be immaterial. *Thomas v. U.S.,* 15 F.2d 958 (8th Cir. 1926).

A statement reduced to writing by one other than the accused is admissible where the accused reads it and signs it or orally adopts it. *U.S. v. Johnson,* 529 F.2d 581 (8th Cir.), *cert. denied,* 426 U.S. 909 (1976). *See U.S. v. Evans,* 320 F.2d 482 (6th Cir. 1963). Rule 801(d)(2) of the Federal Rules of Evidence precludes a hearsay objection to a confession in this form.

An oral confession is not subject to suppression on grounds that it has not been recorded, either electronically or stenographically. *U.S. v. Coades,* 549 F.2d 1303 (9th Cir. 1977).

## § 303. — Need for Corroboration.

A confession must be corroborated to sustain a conviction. A defendant may not be convicted solely on the basis of his own admission. *Smith v. U.S.,* 348 U.S. 147 (1954); *U.S. v. Micieli,* 594 F.2d 102 (5th Cir. 1979).

The requirement for corroboration does not affect the admissibility of a confession. It affects the sufficiency of evidence required to sustain a conviction. *U.S. v. Fearn,* 589 F.2d 1316 (7th Cir. 1978). A degree of corroboration may be found in the detailed nature of the confession itself, or in the recital of facts that would be unknown to anyone other than the criminal. *U.S. v. Gresham,* 585 F.2d 103 (5th Cir. 1978). Hearsay may be relevant and admissible for purposes of corroborating confessions. *U.S. v. Trotter,* 538 F.2d 217 (8th Cir.), *cert. denied,* 429 U.S. 943 (1976) (registration documents admissible for purposes of corroboration); *U.S. v. Jacobson,* 536 F.2d 793 (8th Cir.), *cert. denied,* 429 U.S. 864 (1976) (introduction of theft report upheld).

The corroboration required is of the truth or trustworthiness of the confession, not of the fact that the confession was made. *Cash v. U.S.,*

265 F.2d 346, 347 (D.C. Cir.), *cert. denied,* 359 U.S. 973 (1959). The corroborating evidence standing alone need not be sufficient to sustain the conviction, only sufficient to establish the reliability of the confession beyond a reasonable doubt. *U.S. v. Evans,* 572 F.2d 455 (5th Cir.), *cert. denied,* 439 U.S. 870 (1978). In *Opper v. U.S.,* 348 U.S. 84, 93 (1954), the Supreme Court stated:

> [T]he corroborative evidence need not be sufficient, independent of the statements, to establish the *corpus delecti.* It is necessary, therefore, to require the Government to introduce substantial independent evidence which would tend to establish the trustworthiness of the statement.... It is sufficient if the corroboration supports the essential facts admitted sufficiently to justify a jury inference of their truth. Those facts plus the other evidence besides the admission must, of course, be sufficient to find guilt beyond a reasonable doubt.

"All elements of the offense must be established by independent evidence or corroborated admissions, but one available mode of corroboration is for the independent evidence to bolster the confession itself and thereby prove the offense 'through' the statement of the accused." *Smith v. U.S.,* 348 U.S. 147, 156 (1954).

The degree of corroboration required depends on the nature of the case. Tangible crimes involving injury to person or property, may be corroborated solely by proof that the act was committed; no independent link between the injury and the accused is needed. *U.S. v. Daniels,* 528 F.2d 705, 707-08 (6th Cir. 1976); *U.S. v. Fleming,* 504 F.2d 1045 (7th Cir. 1974). Where the crime involves no tangible *corpus delecti, e.g.,* tax evasion, the corroborative evidence must implicate the one making the confession. *Smith v. U.S.,* 348 U.S. at 153-54. Such corroboration may consist of proof of a negative. *U.S. v. Fearn,* 589 F.2d at 1323-26.

Corroboration may not come from statements by the defendant's partners in crime unless such statements would be admissible as direct evidence of the defendant's guilt. *Wong Sun v. U.S.,* 371 U.S. 471, 488-91 (1963). Thus, in a conspiracy case, corroboration may be found in the form of admissions of codefendants. *U.S. v. Harbin,* 601 F.2d 773 (5th Cir.), *cert. denied,* 444 U.S. 954 (1979). *See also Parker v. Randolph,* 442 U.S. 62 (1979).

Judicial confessions made in earlier proceedings require corroboration. *U.S. v. Wilson,* 529 F.2d 913 (10th Cir. 1976). Admissibility is not contingent upon order of proof. Proof of *corpus delecti* may be offered before or after the confession. *U.S. v. Harbin,* 601 F.2d at 780.

Venue need not be corroborated. If otherwise sufficient corroboration is present, venue may be established solely by the confession. *U.S. v. Wolf,* 535 F.2d 476 (8th Cir.), *cert. denied,* 429 U.S. 920 (1976).

## § 304. — Confession After Arrest But Before Initial Appearance — "Unnecessary Delay."

Arrested individuals must be brought before a federal magistrate without "unnecessary delay." Rule 5(a), Fed. R. Crim. P. A confession obtained during a period of unreasonable delay is not admissible over defendant's objection. *Mallory v. U.S.,* 354 U.S. 449 (1957). This is an evidentiary rather than a constitutional rule. *McNabb v. U.S.,* 318 U.S. 332, 341-42 (1943). This exclusionary rule also prevents the use of other evidence obtained during detentions that violate Rule 5(a). *E.g., Adams v. U.S.,* 399 F.2d 574 (D.C. Cir. 1968), *cert. denied,* 393 U.S. 1067 (1969) (testimony on lineup identification excluded).

Delay solely for the purpose of repeated interrogation is unnecessary. *Mallory v. U.S.,* 354 U.S. at 454-56. A confession taken during an unexplained five-hour delay while defendant sat in a police wagon was excluded from evidence in *U.S. v. Hernandez,* 574 F.2d 1362 (5th Cir. 1978).

Delay for ordinary administrative steps is not unnecessary. This includes "booking," or completing a confession begun before arrest. *Mallory v. U.S.,* 354 U.S. at 453-54; *Walton v. U.S.,* 334 F.2d 343 (10th Cir. 1964), *cert. denied,* 379 U.S. 991 (1965). Delay while having an oral confession transcribed is not unnecessary. *U.S. v. Curry,* 358 F.2d 904 (2d Cir. 1965), *cert. denied,* 385 U.S. 873 (1966).

Delays for unusual circumstances have also been allowed. *E.g., U.S. v. Vasquez,* 534 F.2d 1142 (5th Cir.), *cert. denied,* 429 U.S. 979 (1976) (delay caused by defendant's request to speak with a particular detective). Bad weather can excuse delay. *U.S. v. Standing Soldier,* 538 F.2d 196 (8th Cir.), *cert. denied,* 429 U.S. 1025 (1976) (confession taken during one-week delay due to blizzard and remoteness from site of magistrate). Remoteness itself may excuse delay. *U.S. v. Odom,* 526 F.2d 339 (5th Cir. 1976) (confession during five-day delay while on Coast Guard cutter after arrest on high seas 200 miles from shore).

Defendant's own behavior or condition may justify delay. *U.S. v. Isom,* 588 F.2d 858 (2d Cir. 1978) (delay for medical treatment of defendant); *U.S. v. Shoemaker,* 542 F.2d 561 (10th Cir.), *cert. denied,* 429 U.S. 1004 (1976) (defendant's refusal to appear before magistrate until he spoke with his family); *U.S. v. Bear Killer,* 534 F.2d 1253 (8th Cir.), *cert. denied,* 429 U.S. 846 (1976) (12-hour delay including time for defendant to become sober before appearing). Delays for investigatory reasons have been upheld. *U.S. v. O'Looney,* 544 F.2d 385 (9th Cir.), *cert. denied,* 429 U.S. 1023 (1976); *U.S. v. Hall,* 348 F.2d 837 (2d Cir.), *cert. denied,* 382 U.S. 947 (1965) (recovery of stolen goods); *Amsler v. U.S.,* 381 F.2d 37 (9th Cir. 1967) (delay to verify confession); *U.S. v. Price,* 345 F.2d 256 (2d Cir. 1964), *cert. denied,* 382 U.S. 949 (1965) (destruction of contraband); *Evans v. U.S.,* 325 F.2d 596 (8th Cir. 1963) (search of premises).

There must be an arrest made to trigger the rule. *U.S. v. Vita,* 294 F.2d 524 (2d Cir. 1961), *cert. denied,* 369 U.S. 823 (1962). *See Fuller v. U.S.,* 407 F.2d 1199 (D.C. Cir. 1967), *cert. denied,* 393 U.S. 1120 (1969). Arrest for this purpose is dependent upon the impression conveyed to defendant, not on formal authorization by an Assistant U.S. Attorney. *U.S. v. Middleton,* 344 F.2d 78, 81 (2d Cir. 1965). Arrest without a warrant does not obviate the need for a prompt initial appearance. *U.S. v. Duvall,* 537 F.2d 15 (2d Cir.), *cert. denied,* 426 U.S. 950 (1976). Detention short of arrest does not trigger the rule. *U.S. v. Vita,* 294 F.2d at 533.

Where the arrest occurs at a late hour or after the beginning of a weekend or holiday, overnight detention occasioned by the unavailability of a committing magistrate is reasonable. *U.S. v. Ortega,* 471 F.2d 1350 (2d Cir. 1972), *cert. denied,* 411 U.S. 948 (1973). However, if a federal magistrate is not "reasonably available," the initial appearance should take place before a state or local judicial officer. Rule 5(a), Fed. R. Crim. P.; *U.S. v. Burgard,* 551 F.2d 190 (8th Cir. 1977) (magistrate out of town for 24 hours). Where arrest occurs before a period of unavailability and reasonable delay extends into weekend or evening hours, overnight detention may be allowed. The government should be prepared to explain the delay by accounting for time periods involved and the reasons therefor. *U.S. v. Boyer,* 574 F.2d 951 (8th Cir.), *cert. denied,* 439 U.S. 967 (1978). *See also U.S. v. Ortega,* 471 F.2d at 1362.

The Juvenile Delinquency Act, 18 U.S.C. § 5033, imposes a heavier burden on the government to explain any delay since the act requires that a juvenile defendant be taken before a magistrate "forthwith." *See U.S. v. Indian Boy X,* 565 F.2d 585 (9th Cir. 1977), *cert. denied,* 439 U.S. 841 (1978).

The rule suppressing statements made during unnecessary delay in the initial appearance has also been applied to aliens being held for deportation proceedings. *U.S. v. Sotoj-Lopez,* 603 F.2d 789 (9th Cir. 1979).

The critical period in applying the *Mallory* rule is the time between the arrest and the statement. *U.S. v. Davis,* 532 F.2d 22 (7th Cir. 1976). Illegal detention after a statement has been made will not affect its admissibility. *U.S. v. Watson,* 591 F.2d 1058 (5th Cir.), *cert. denied,* 441 U.S. 965 (1979) (four-and-one-half-day delay in bringing defendant before magistrate did not render confession inadmissible where it was made within six hours of arrest); *U.S. v. Burgos,* 579 F.2d 749 (2d Cir. 1978) (15-hour delay); *U.S. v. Cepeda Penes,* 577 F.2d 754 (1st Cir. 1978) (seven-hour delay where no showing that delay was for purpose of obtaining confession). *See also U.S. v. Mitchell,* 322 U.S. 65, 69-71 (1944); *U.S. v. Montes-Zarate,* 552 F.2d 1330 (9th Cir. 1977), *cert. denied,* 435 U.S. 947 (1978); *U.S. v. Seohnlein,* 423 F.2d 1051 (4th Cir.), *cert. denied,* 399 U.S. 913 (1970).

Title 18 U.S.C. § 3501(c) provides that a confession obtained while a person is under arrest or detention shall not be rendered inadmissible solely because of a delay in bringing the prisoner before a magistrate so long as the confession was given within six hours of the arrest or detention. A voluntary confession made within six hours of arrest or detention is admissible without reference to delay. *U.S. v. Halbert,* 436 F.2d 1226 (9th Cir. 1970). *See U.S. v. Cluchette,* 465 F.2d 749, 754 (9th Cir. 1972). Section 3501(c) also provides that statements made in any period beyond six hours may be admissible if the delay is found to be reasonable after giving consideration to the distance and means of transportation. Courts have recognized certain situations where confessions made beyond six hours after arrest are admissible. *U.S. v. Edwards,* 539 F.2d 689 (9th Cir.), *cert. denied,* 429 U.S. 984 (1976); *U.S. v. Ortega,* 471 F.2d at 1362; *U.S. v. Marrero,* 450 F.2d 373 (2d Cir. 1971), *cert. denied,* 405 U.S. 933 (1972). Any delay between arrest and confession, like the delay between arrest and arraignment, is but an additional factor to be used by the trial judge in determining voluntariness and is not determinative by itself. *U.S. v. Gaines,* 555 F.2d 618 (7th Cir. 1977); *U.S. v. Keeble,* 459 F.2d 757 (8th Cir. 1972), *rev'd on other grounds,* 412 U.S. 205 (1973); *U.S. v. Hathorn,* 451 F.2d 1337 (5th Cir. 1971); *U.S. v. Marrero,* 450 F.2d at 378; *U.S. v. Corral-Martinez,* 592 F.2d 263 (5th Cir. 1979). The trial court has a duty to hear evidence concerning cause of initial appearance delay where the delay is lengthy. *U.S. v. Mayes,* 552 F.2d 729 (6th Cir. 1977).

The time parameters are determined by federal detention, not by previous state incarceration, so long as there has been no collusion between state and federal officials. *U.S. v Jensen,* 561 F.2d 1297 (8th Cir. 1977); *U.S. v. Gaines,* 555 F.2d at 625. Thus, if pre-appearance detention is nonfederal, the government is relieved of its obligation to explain or justify the delay. *U.S. v. Torres,* 663 F.2d 1019, 1024 (10th Cir. 1981), *petition for cert. filed,* 50 U.S.L.W. 3717 (U.S. Feb. 23, 1982) (No. 81-1586) (defendant in state custody for six days before federal charges filed). *See also U.S. v. Mayes*, 552 F.2d at 734; *U.S. v. Young*, 527 F.2d 1334 (5th Cir. 1976); *U.S. v. Davis*, 459 F.2d 167 (6th Cir. 1972).

Since the *Mallory* rule is not based on constitutional grounds, it does not apply to the states. *McNabb v. U.S.*, 318 U.S. 332 (1943); *Van Ermen v. Burke*, 398 F.2d 329 (7th Cir.), *cert. denied*, 393 U.S. 1004 (1968); *U.S. ex rel. Glinton v. Denno*, 309 F.2d 543 (2d Cir. 1962), *cert. denied*, 372 U.S. 938 (1963). Therefore, confessions to federal crimes made during a period of illegal detention by state authorities, even if made to federal officers, are admissible unless the state detention is pursuant to a "working agreement" between state and federal officials. *U.S. v. Coppola*, 281 F.2d 340 (2d Cir. 1960), *aff'd per curiam*, 365 U.S. 762 (1961). *See also U.S. v. Ireland*, 456 F.2d 74, 77 (10th Cir. 1972); *Jarrett v. U.S.*, 423 F.2d 966 (8th Cir. 1970); *U.S. v. Hindmarsh*, 389 F.2d 137 (6th Cir.), *cert. denied*, 393 U.S. 866 (1968); *U.S. v. Frazier*, 385 F.2d 901 (6th Cir. 1967); *U.S. v. Gorman*, 355 F.2d 151 (2d Cir. 1965), *cert. denied*, 384 U.S. 1024 (1966).

The Supreme Court's decision in *Miranda v. Arizona*, 384 U.S. 436 (1966), was a direct attack on the problems which are the basis of the *Mallory* rule; consequently, it has been held that where the defendant has waived his *Miranda* rights he also waived his *Mallory* right to be brought before a magistrate as quickly as possible. *U.S. v. Indian Boy X*, 565 F.2d 585 (9th Cir. 1977), *cert. denied*, 439 U.S. 841 (1978); *U.S. v. Cluchette*, 465 F.2d 749 (9th Cir. 1972); *Frazier v. U.S.*, 419 F.2d 1161 (D.C. Cir. 1969); *Pettyjohn v. U.S.*, 419 F.2d 651, 656 (D.C. Cir. 1969), *cert. denied*, 397 U.S. 1058 (1970).

### § 305. — Confessions and the Rights to Silence and Counsel.

A suspect's fifth amendment privilege against self-incrimination comes into play as soon as law enforcement officers take him into custody or otherwise restrict his freedom of action in any significant way. This includes in-custody questioning concerning misdemeanor traffic offenses. *Berkemer v. McCarty*, 468 U.S. 420 (1984). However, *Miranda* warnings are not required at a roadside questioning of a motorist pursuant to a routine traffic stop, *Pennsylvania v. Bruder*, 488 U.S. 9 (1988), *Berkemer v. McCarty, supra;* or where probationer appeared and answered questions of his probation officer; *Minnesota v. Murphy*, 465 U.S. 420 (1984); or where information requested on tax forms is not obtained in a custodial setting. *U.S. v. Amon*, 669 F.2d 1351, 1358 (10th Cir. 1981), *cert. denied*, 459 U.S. 825 (1982).

A suspect's sixth amendment right to the assistance of counsel attaches upon the initiation of formal adversary proceedings. A formal

adversary proceeding can consist of a formal charge, preliminary hearing, indictment, information, or arraignment. *Michigan v. Jackson,*
475 U.S. 625 (1986); *Kirby v. Illinois,* 406 U.S. 682, 689 (1972). An
initial appearance before a magistrate is not an adversary proceeding,
and thus no right to counsel attaches. *U.S. v. Dohm,* 597 F.2d 535 (5th
Cir. 1979), *rev'd on rehearing en banc on other grounds,* 618 F.2d 1169
(1980); nor are prison inmates who are suspected of murder in prison
and held in administrative detention entitled to appointment of counsel before the initiation of adversary judicial proceedings. *U.S. v.
Gouveia,* 467 U.S. 180 (1984). Any statement or admission, formal or
informal, obtained in violation of those rights is inadmissible as substantive evidence against the suspect at trial. *Miranda v. Arizona,* 384
U.S. 436 (1966); *Escobedo v. Illinois,* 378 U.S. 478 (1964). However,
"[a]ny statement given freely and voluntarily without any compelling
influences" is admissible. *Miranda v. Arizona,* 384 U.S. at 478.

An invocation of the sixth amendment right to counsel during a
judicial proceeding does not constitute a *Miranda* right to counsel under the fifth amendment. The sixth amendment right is offense-specific
and does not attach until after initiation of adversary judicial proceedings, while the fifth amendment *Miranda* right to counsel is non-of-
fense-specific, and once asserted prevents further police initiated interrogation outside the presence of counsel. Thus, questioning on a crime
which has not been charged was permitted even though the defendant
was in jail on an offense for which he had counsel. *McNeil v. Wisconsin,*
111 S. Ct. 2204 (1991).

The *Miranda* procedure requires an interrogating officer to give a
suspect the following warnings: (1) that the suspect has a constitutional right to remain silent; (2) that anything he says can and will be
used against him in court; (3) that he has the right to confer with
counsel before answering any questions and to have counsel present
during the questioning itself; (4) that if he is indigent he has a right to
have appointed counsel present, 384 U.S. at 467-73; and (5) that if he
chooses to answer questions or make a statement and thus waive his
rights, he may rescind that waiver at any time and terminate the
interview by stating that he wishes to remain silent or that he wishes
to do so until an attorney is present, 384 U.S. at 473-74; *U.S. v. James,*
493 F.2d 323 (2d Cir.), *cert. denied,* 419 U.S. 849 (1974).

The precise wording of the warnings set forth in *Miranda* does not
constitute a ritualistic formula which must be repeated without varia-
tion. *California v. Prysock,* 453 U.S. 355 (1981) (*per curiam*); *Duckworth v. Eagan,* 109 S. Ct. 2875 (1989); *Rhode Island v. Innis,* 446 U.S.
291, 297 (1980); *U.S. v. Contreras,* 667 F.2d 976, 979 (11th Cir.), *cert.*

*denied*, 459 U.S. 849 (1982); *U.S. v. Floyd*, 496 F.2d 982 (2d Cir.), *cert. denied*, 419 U.S. 1069 (1974). Words that convey the substance of the warnings along with the required information are sufficient. *U.S. v. Olivares-Vega*, 495 F.2d 827 (2d Cir.), *cert. denied*, 419 U.S. 1020 (1974). The right to appointed counsel, however, has been held to be a significant right which may not be excluded. *U.S. v. DiGiacomo*, 579 F.2d 1211 (10th Cir. 1978). *See Sanchez v. Beto*, 467 F.2d 513 (5th Cir. 1972), *cert. denied*, 411 U.S. 921 (1973).

Failure to read the required rights orally is not fatal to a confession. *U.S. v. Sledge*, 546 F.2d 1120 (4th Cir.), *cert. denied*, 430 U.S. 910 (1977) (defendant read form to himself, then signed waiver). Failure of the suspect to sign the form does not by itself preclude waiver, *McDonald v. Lucas*, 677 F.2d 518, 520 (5th Cir. 1982); *U.S. v. DiGiacomo*, 579 F.2d at 1215 (in both cases the government failed to sustain "heavy burden" of waiver after defendant refused to sign waiver form); *U.S. v. Stewart*, 585 F.2d 799 (5th Cir. 1979), *cert. denied*, 441 U.S. 933 (1979); nor does it make further inquiry illegal, *U.S. v. Klein*, 592 F.2d 909 (5th Cir. 1979). An explicit statement of waiver is not invariably necessary to support a finding that waiver occurred. *North Carolina v. Butler*, 441 U.S. 369 (1979). But signature on the standard FBI form above the space where the waiver appeared, accompanied by a refusal to sign below, amounted to a clear signal to the court that the defendant did not wish to waive his rights, and questioning should have ceased at that time. *U.S. v. Christian*, 571 F.2d 64 (1st Cir. 1978).

There is no burden on police beyond the administration of the warnings. No requirement exists that the police explain the rules of evidence or criminal laws or procedures to a suspect. The duty is discharged when the warnings required by *Miranda* are fully and fairly given. *Harris v. Riddle*, 551 F.2d 936 (4th Cir.), *cert. denied*, 434 U.S. 849 (1977).

A threat to public safety, however, may outweigh the requirement that the *Miranda* warnings be given before a defendant's answer may be admitted. Defendant's answer to the police officer's question asking where the defendant's gun was located was admissible where a witness had stated that the defendant had a gun and he was arrested with an empty shoulder holster; it was a "public safety" exception to the *Miranda* requirements. *New York v. Quarles*, 465 U.S. 649 (1984).

There is still some question whether statements taken in violation of *Miranda* may be used to establish probable cause for issuance of a search warrant. *Massachusetts v. White*, 439 U.S. 280 (1978) (*per curiam*) (equally divided Court upheld state decision that such statements may not be so used).

## § 306. — — When Miranda Rights Attach.

The premise of *Miranda* is that custodial interrogation is inherently coercive, 384 U.S. at 467. *See U.S. v. Bottone,* 365 F.2d 389, 395 (2d Cir.), *cert. denied,* 385 U.S. 974 (1966). Whether the rights thereunder attach depends upon whether a suspect is in custody, but formal arrest is not determinative. *Dunaway v. New York,* 442 U.S. 200 (1979). The inquiry focuses upon whether there has been a significant deprivation of the suspect's freedom. *Oregon v. Mathiason,* 429 U.S. 492 (1977); *U.S. v. Blum,* 614 F.2d 537 (6th Cir. 1980). More than just a coercive setting is required; some significant restraint on freedom of movement is necessary. *U.S. v. Jimenez,* 602 F.2d 139 (7th Cir. 1979) (statement made after auto stopped by police but before custody); *Borodine v. Douzanis,* 592 F.2d 1202, 1206 (1st Cir. 1979).

In *Rhode Island v. Innis,* 446 U.S. 291, 300 (1980), the Supreme Court held, "'Interrogation,' as conceptualized in the *Miranda* opinion, must reflect a measure of compulsion above and beyond that inherent in custody itself." The Court, 446 U.S. at 300-02, concluded

> that the *Miranda* safeguards come into play whenever a person in custody is subjected to either express questioning or its functional equivalent. That is to say, the term "interrogation" under *Miranda* refers not only to express questioning, but also to any words or actions on the part of the police (other than those normally attendant to arrest and custody) that the police should know are reasonably likely to elicit an incriminating response from the suspect. The latter portion of this definition focuses primarily upon the perceptions of the suspect, rather than the intent of the police. This focus reflects the fact that the *Miranda* safeguards were designed to vest a suspect in custody with an added measure of protection against coercive police practices, without regard to objective proof of the underlying intent of the police. A practice that the police should know is reasonably likely to evoke an incriminating response from a suspect thus amounts to interrogation. But, since the police surely cannot be held accountable for the unforeseeable results of their words or actions, the definition of interrogation can extend only to words or actions on the part of police officers that they *should have known* were reasonably likely to elicit an incriminating response.

Police are not required to administer the *Miranda* warnings to everyone whom they question, 384 U.S. at 477-78. *U.S. v. Clark,* 525 F.2d 314 (2d Cir. 1975). Nor is there a requirement that the warnings be given merely because the interview takes place at a station house. *California v. Beheler,* 463 U.S. 1121 (1983); *Oregon v. Mathiason,* 429 U.S. at 495. Asking defendant to come to the station house for statement or photographs does not necessarily lead to a custodial situation.

*Starkey v. Wyrick,* 555 F.2d 1352 (8th Cir.), *cert. denied,* 434 U.S. 848 (1977). But if one is unlawfully detained or confined, incriminating or inculpatory statements are not admissible, even where he has been properly informed of his *Miranda* rights. *Brown v. Illinois,* 422 U.S. 590 (1975). *Miranda* warnings are not required before routine questioning even after arrest if such questioning is limited to asking for information needed for processing. *U.S. v. Prewitt,* 553 F.2d 1082 (7th Cir.), *cert. denied,* 434 U.S. 840 (1977) (asking for aliases).

The grand jury room has been held to be non-custodial for purposes of *Miranda. U.S. v. Mandujano,* 425 U.S. 564 (1976) (no constitutional right to warnings before suspect's testimony before grand jury); *U.S. v. Reed,* 631 F.2d 87, 89 (6th Cir. 1980).

Routine border stops and customs inspections do not amount to custodial interrogations, *U.S. v. Martinez,* 588 F.2d 495 (5th Cir. 1979); *U.S. v. Smith,* 557 F.2d 1206 (5th Cir. 1977), *cert. denied,* 434 U.S. 1073 (1978); but when a suspect is taken out of the mainstream of activity and either questioned singly or searched, custody may be found to exist and *Miranda* applied, *U.S. v. Del Soccorro Castro,* 573 F.2d 213 (5th Cir. 1978); *U.S. v. McCain,* 556 F.2d 253 (5th Cir. 1979) (strip search case in which defendant confessed after being told that narcotics in body cavity would be fatal if container ruptured); *U.S. v. Gomez-Londono,* 553 F.2d 805 (2d Cir. 1977) (asking at airport whether defendant was taking more than $5,000 out of the country was non-custodial questioning).

It is clear that *Miranda* rights attach to aliens at our border or in our country, providing the circumstances triggered the requirements of warnings. *See U.S. v. Henry,* 604 F.2d 908 (5th Cir. 1979). Whether or not a significant deprivation of a suspect's freedom has occurred may depend upon four factors: (1) the probable cause existing to arrest; (2) the subjective intent of the interrogators; (3) the subjective impression of the defendant; and (4) whether the investigation has focused on the suspect. *U.S. v. Micieli,* 594 F.2d 102 (5th Cir. 1979); *Hancock v. Estelle,* 558 F.2d 786 (5th Cir. 1977). No one factor is dispositive. *See U.S. v. Stanley,* 597 F.2d 866 (4th Cir. 1979). The totality of circumstances must be considered. *U.S. v. Kennedy,* 573 F.2d 657 (9th Cir. 1978).

A non-custodial interview may change character when, based upon answers received, the interrogator realizes that he is no longer willing to let the suspect go. When this perception changes, the interrogator has a duty to warn. *U.S. v. Curtis,* 568 F.2d 643 (9th Cir. 1978). Other circuits apply an objective test. *See U.S. ex rel. Sanney v. Montanye,* 500 F.2d 411 (2d Cir.), *cert. denied,* 419 U.S. 1027 (1974). All interrogations of suspects already in prison are not necessarily "custodial" for purposes of *Miranda*. In these situations the court must look to whether there were added restraints on the prisoner's freedom or other changes in the prisoner's normal surroundings. *Cervantes v. Walker*, 589 F.2d 424 (9th Cir. 1978).

The mere fact that the suspect may not be aware of all of the possible subjects of questioning or that more than one crime may be the subject of the interrogation does not require rewarning each time the interrogation focuses on a new crime. *Colorado v. Spring*, 479 U.S. 564 (1987); *U.S. ex rel. Henne v. Fike*, 563 F.2d 809 (7th Cir. 1977), *cert. denied*, 434 U.S. 1072 (1978).

The sole fact that a criminal investigation has been commenced does not require *Miranda* warnings in an otherwise non-custodial setting. *Beckwith v. U.S.*, 425 U.S. 341 (1976) (taxpayer's home). *But see Orozco v. Texas*, 394 U.S. 324 (1969). Thus, mere focus on an investigation of an individual, without more, is insufficient to trigger a need for the warnings. *U.S. v. Jackson*, 578 F.2d 1162 (5th Cir. 1978); *U.S. v. Schmoker*, 564 F.2d 289 (9th Cir. 1977); *U.S. v. Mapp*, 561 F.2d 685 (7th Cir. 1977). A postal inspector's office has been held to be a non-custodial setting for a postal employee called in and questioned about a missing check. *U.S. v. Lewis*, 556 F.2d 446 (6th Cir.), *cert. denied*, 434 U.S. 863 (1977). The boarding of a ship by the Coast Guard under an established "right of approach" doctrine on the high seas did not in itself create a custodial situation. *U.S. v. Postal*, 589 F.2d 862, 887 (5th Cir.), *cert. denied*, 444 U.S. 832 (1979). *But see U.S. v. Glen-Archila*, 677 F.2d 809, 814 n.12 (11th Cir.), *cert. denied*, 459 U.S. 874 (1982).

*Miranda* was designed to curb unfair methods of custodial interrogation. Thus *Miranda* rights do not attach to volunteered statements. They attach only to those which are the product of interrogation. *U.S. v. Waloke*, 962 F.2d 824 (8th Cir. 1992); *U.S. v. Cornejo*, 598 F.2d 554 (9th Cir. 1979); *U.S. v. Vigo*, 487 F.2d 295 (2d Cir. 1973); *U.S. v. Purin*, 486 F.2d 1363, 1367-68 (2d Cir. 1973), *cert. denied*, 417 U.S. 930 (1974). Incriminating statements which the defendant, who was in custody, made to his wife, who was permitted to speak to the defendant upon the condition that a police officer be present, were not the product of interrogation and this *Miranda* did not apply. *Arizona v. Mauro*, 481 U.S. 520 (1987). *Miranda* rights do not attach to excited or spontaneous utterances. *Stanley v. Wainwright*, 604 F.2d 379 (5th Cir.), *cert. denied*, 447 U.S. 925 (1979). *See also U.S. v. Roach*, 590 F.2d 181 (5th Cir. 1979) (codefendant asked authorities why he was being arrested, defendant responded, "shut up — you know why").

Even under the most coercive of settings a statement made without questioning can be said to be volunteered. *Pavao v. Cardwell*, 583 F.2d

1075 (9th Cir. 1978) (defendant face down on pavement at gunpoint). In *Stanley v. Wainwright,* 604 F.2d at 380-81, the defendants were placed in the back of a police car. There were no police present so no questioning could have taken place. However, a concealed tape recorder in the car was recording statements made by defendants to each other. The Fifth Circuit found no need for warnings under these circumstances. Likewise taping of undercover conversations in a non-custodial situation does not trigger *Miranda* rights. *U.S. v. Craig,* 573 F.2d 455 (7th Cir. 1977), *cert. denied,* 439 U.S. 820 (1978); *U.S. v. Gray,* 565 F.2d 881 (5th Cir.), *cert. denied,* 435 U.S. 955 (1978).

Statements by a defendant to undercover agents do not require prior warning for admissibility. This is true even when the defendant is incarcerated on charges unrelated to the crime being investigated by an undercover agent placed in his cellblock. Coercion for *Miranda* purposes is determined from the perspective of the defendant. The danger of coercion results from the interaction of custody and official interrogation whereby the suspect may speak for fear of reprisal or in the hope of more lenient treatment. Where the suspect does not know he is speaking to a government agent, the coercive atmosphere is lacking. *Illinois v. Perkins,* 496 U.S. 292 (1990). *See also U.S. v. Marks,* 603 F.2d 582 (5th Cir. 1979), *cert. denied,* 444 U.S. 1018 (1980). *Cf. U.S. v. Barnes,* 431 F.2d 878 (9th Cir. 1970), *cert. denied,* 400 U.S. 1024 (1971) (person not entitled to *Miranda* warning during commission of a crime); *U.S. v. Gentile,* 525 F.2d 252, 259 (2d Cir. 1975), *cert. denied,* 425 U.S. 903 (1976) (IRS agent not required to give *Miranda* warnings in criminal tax investigation). A defendant need not be advised of his right to silence or counsel while engaging in crime. *U.S. v. Haynes,* 398 F.2d 980, 987-88 (2d Cir. 1968), *cert. denied,* 393 U.S. 1120 (1969). However, after indictment, the absence of counsel may cause any statements to be inadmissible. *See* Chapter 3, § 310, *infra.*

Private security guards are not law enforcement officers and need not give *Miranda* warnings before interrogating a suspect. *U.S. v. Bolden,* 461 F.2d 998 (8th Cir. 1972); *U.S. v. Antonelli,* 434 F.2d 335 (2d Cir. 1970).

### § 307. — — Scope of Miranda.

The rights to silence and counsel do not attach to non-testimonial types of evidence. *Schmerber v. California,* 384 U.S. 757 (1966). Thus, the fifth amendment privilege is limited to testimonial compulsion. *Schmerber* involved the non-consensual taking of blood samples from a motorist after he had been arrested for driving while intoxicated.

Likewise, the fifth amendment privilege does not protect identifying characteristics as they are not testimonial. *See, e.g., Pennsylvania v. Muniz,* 496 U.S. 582 (1990) (videotape recording of sobriety test asking routine booking questions and revealing slurring and other evidence of lack of physical coordination); *U.S. v. Dionisio,* 410 U.S. 1 (1973) (permitting voice exemplars); *Gilbert v. California,* 388 U.S. 263 (1967) (handwriting exemplars); *U.S. v. Wade,* 388 U.S. 218 (1967) (voice and display of person); *In re Grand Jury Proceedings,* 558 F.2d 1177 (5th Cir. 1977) (subpoena directing photographs, fingerprints, and handwriting upheld in face of claim of privilege); *U.S. v. Shaw,* 555 F.2d 1295 (5th Cir. 1977) (voice exemplars).

The sixth amendment right to counsel however, may attach to nontestimonial evidentiary procedures held at a critical stage in the criminal proceedings. *See U.S. v. Ash,* 413 U.S. 300 (1973) (dealing with right to counsel at a post-indictment photographic display).

### § 308. — — Right to Terminate Questioning.

A suspect's right to terminate questioning must be scrupulously honored. *Michigan v. Mosley,* 423 U.S. 96 (1975); *U.S. v. Hernandez,* 574 F.2d 1362 (5th Cir. 1978). If an attorney is requested there is a per se rule against later waiver until the attorney is present. *Arizona v. Roberson,* 486 U.S. 675 (1988); *Michigan v. Jackson,* 475 U.S. 625 (1986); *Edwards v. Arizona,* 451 U.S. 477, 484-85 (1981); *Miranda v. Arizona,* 384 U.S. at 474-75; *Michigan v. Mosley, supra* (White J., concurring); *Cahill v. Rusken,* 678 F.2d 791, 795 (9th Cir. 1982); *U.S. v. Hinckley,* 672 F.2d 115, 122 (D.C. Cir. 1982); *U.S. v. Hernandez,* 574 F.2d at 1370; *White v. Finkbeiner,* 570 F.2d 194, 200 n.3 (7th Cir. 1978). However, where a suspect states after acknowledging his *Miranda* rights, that he would not sign a written statement outside the presence of his attorney but orally admitted his involvement in the crime, his invocation of his right to counsel was limited by its terms to written statements and the oral statements were properly admitted. *Connecticut v. Barrett,* 479 U.S. 523 (1987).

Where "an accused has invoked his right to have counsel present during custodial interrogation, a valid waiver of that right cannot be established by showing only that he responded to further police-initiated custodial interrogation even if he has been advised of his rights." *Edwards v. Arizona,* 451 U.S. at 484. An accused's responses to interrogation after he has requested an attorney may not be used to cast doubt on the initial request for any attorney. *Smith v. Illinois,* 469 U.S. 91 (1984). And where an accused has expressed a desire to deal with the police only through counsel, he is not subject to further interrogation until counsel has been made available to him, and counsel is present, *Minnick v. Mississippi,* 495 U.S. 903 (1990), unless the accused himself initiates further discussions with police. *Edwards v. Arizona,* 451 U.S. at 484-85. This is true even when the interrogation concerns a different crime, and the interrogation officer did not know that the defendant had earlier requested counsel. This is because *Edwards* focuses on the state of mind of the suspect and not on the police. *Arizona v. Roberson, supra.* "Initiate further discussions" involves a two-step inquiry. First, did the accused initiate the conversation with the police, and second, did he waive his right to counsel knowingly and intelligently under the totality of the circumstances, *Oregon v. Bradshaw,* 462 U.S. 1039 (1983). However, where the defendant has made a voluntary, knowing, and intelligent waiver of his right to have counsel present at a polygraph test, he need not again be advised of his rights before being questioned at the same interrogation about the results of the polygraph, *Wyrick v. Fields,* 459 U.S. 42 (1982).

Failure to inform a suspect that a third party has retained an attorney to represent him does not violate the suspect's fifth amendment rights. "Events occurring outside of the presence of the suspect and entirely unknown to him surely can have no bearing on the capacity to comprehend and knowingly relinquish a constitutional right." *Moran v. Burbine,* 475 U.S. 412, 422 (1986).

A request for the suspect's probation officer is not a request for an attorney operating to terminate questioning. *Fare v. Michael C.,* 442 U.S. 707 (1979), nor is the request of a street-wise 17-year-old juvenile to speak with his father a request for an attorney operating to terminate questioning. *U.S. ex rel. Riley v. Franzen,* 653 F.2d 1153, 1158-59 (7th Cir.), *cert. denied,* 454 U.S. 1067 (1981).

Volunteering to resume discussions after asking to terminate the interview, however, can operate as an independent waiver of the earlier request. *U.S. v. Bosby,* 675 F.2d 1174, 1181-82 (11th Cir. 1982) (waiting two weeks after defendant invoked right to remain silent approved where defendant did not ask for counsel and signed waiver form); *U.S. v. Boyce,* 594 F.2d 1246 (9th Cir.), *cert. denied,* 444 U.S. 855 (1979) ("Let's talk"); *U.S. v. Messina,* 507 F.2d 73 (2d Cir. 1974), *cert. denied,* 420 U.S. 993 (1975). *See Rhode Island v. Innis,* 446 U.S. 291 (1980). Mere demonstration that a confession came without objection after resumption of questioning is inadequate evidence of waiver. *U.S. v. Charlton,* 565 F.2d 86 (6th Cir. 1977), *cert. denied,* 434 U.S. 1070 (1978). *See also U.S. v. Ford,* 563 F.2d 1366 (9th Cir. 1977), *cert. denied,* 434 U.S. 1021 (1978); *U.S. v. Finch,* 557 F.2d 1234 (8th Cir.), *cert. denied,* 434 U.S. 927 (1977). Under these circumstances the govern-

ment must show an intentional relinquishment or abandonment of a
known right or privilege. *Maglio v. Jago,* 580 F.2d 202 (6th Cir. 1978).
*See also Johnson v. Zerbst,* 304 U.S. 458, 464 (1938).

### § 309. — — Silence of Defendant.

The *Miranda* warnings impliedly assume that silence will carry no
penalty. Thus, cross-examination of a suspect on his postarrest silence,
after *Miranda* warnings are given, is violative of the fifth amendment.
*Doyle v. Ohio,* 426 U.S. 610 (1976). This includes use of post-*Miranda*
warnings silence as evidence of the defendant's sanity where the defendant's defense was insanity. *Wainright v. Greenfield,* 106 S. Ct. 634
(1986). However, when the court immediately sustained an objection
and instructed the jury to ignore the prosecutor's question to the defendant as to why he did not tell the police his exculpatory trial testimony
at the time of his arrest, there was no *Doyle* violation, as the court did
not permit the violation that *Doyle* forbids. *Greer v. Miller,* 107 S. Ct.
—, 41 Crim. L. Rep. 3405 (1987). Asking a witness whether statements
were made by the defendant at the time the warnings were given may
also violate this rule if the answer is "no." *U.S. v. Martinez,* 577 F.2d
960 (5th Cir.), *cert. denied,* 439 U.S. 914 (1978) (where witness answered that defendant said, "no, not at this time," error held to be
harmless). A witness' comment that the defendant was silent because,
at the time the warnings were being given, a codefendant instructed
the defendant to "say nothing" was allowed by the Fifth Circuit in a
conspiracy case. *U.S. v. Warren,* 578 F.2d 1058, 1072-74 (5th Cir.
1978). *See also U.S. v. Bridwell,* 583 F.2d 1135 (10th Cir. 1978) (comment that defendant refused to sign form).

However, as the basis of the *Doyle* decision is that the *Miranda*
warnings themselves implicitly assure the defendant that his silence
will not be used against him, *Anderson v. Charles,* 447 U.S. 404, 407-08
(1980), such governmental action inducing silence is not present in
pre-arrest silence, *Jenkins v. Anderson,* 447 U.S. 231, 238-40 (1980),
post-arrest silence without *Miranda* warnings, *Fletcher v. Weir,* 102 S.
Ct. 1309 (1982), and post-conviction presentencing silence, *Roberts v.
U.S.,* 445 U.S. 552, 559-62 (1980), and as such the defendant's silence
may be used against him.

### § 310. — — Confessions Obtained After Indictment.

A defendant's sixth amendment right to counsel attaches "at or after
the initiation of adversary judicial criminal proceedings — whether by
way of formal charge, preliminary hearing, indictment, information, or

arraignment." *Kirby v. Illinois,* 406 U.S. 682, 688-89 (1972). A "heavy burden" is placed on the government to show a knowing and intelligent waiver of sixth amendment rights under these circumstances. *Brewer v. Williams,* 430 U.S. 387, 403 (1977); *Faretta v. California,* 422 U.S. 806 (1975). Once the right to counsel is knowingly and intelligently waived, however, the defendant may deal with the police directly if he does not exercise his right to have counsel present. *Patterson v. Illinois,* 108 S. Ct. 2389 (1988).

A post-indictment or arraignment confession made in the absence of counsel may be considered inadmissible wholly apart from considerations of voluntariness. *Massiah v. U.S.,* 377 U.S. 201 (1964). Where the government intentionally creates a situation likely to induce a defendant to make incriminating statements to a paid informant concerning charges which had already been filed without the assistance of counsel, the defendant's sixth amendment right to counsel is violated. *U.S. v. Henry,* 447 U.S. 264, 274 (1980). This includes the situation where the police create a situation to investigate other crimes which the defendant has not been charged with and which the police should know will induce incriminating statements concerning the indicted charges. *Maine v. Moulton,* 474 U.S. 159 (1985). However, statements to a police informant who has been placed in the defendant's cell are admissible so long as the informant merely listens and does not deliberately elicit incriminating remarks. *Kuhlmann v. Wilson,* 477 U.S. 436 (1986).

It is clear that the right to counsel attaches upon indictment and before arrest or interrogation. *U.S. v. Satterfield,* 558 F.2d 655 (2d Cir. 1976). But statements made to an undercover officer after complaint and arrest warrant were filed but before an indictment was returned were admitted over objection in *U.S. v. Archbold-Newball,* 554 F.2d 665, 672-75 (5th Cir.), *cert. denied,* 434 U.S. 1000 (1977). A request for an attorney at arraignment may not preclude subsequent station house interrogation where the request is not made in such a way as to preclude subsequent interrogation. *See Blasingame v. Estelle,* 604 F.2d 893, 896 (5th Cir. 1979). Likewise, a defendant's invocation of his sixth amendment right to counsel at a judicial proceeding did not constitute an invocation of this *Miranda* right to counsel under the fifth amendment for an unrelated crime. *McNeil v. Wisconsin,* 111 S. Ct. 2204 (1991).

Use of a post-indictment statement has been permitted where it was made voluntarily and unexpectedly to a representative of the government. *U.S. v. Gaynor,* 472 F.2d 899 (2d Cir. 1973); *U.S. v. Garcia,* 377 F.2d 321 (2d Cir.), *cert. denied,* 389 U.S. 991 (1967). The circuit courts have also permitted the use of post-indictment confessions when made to codefendants and prison inmates who were not acting on behalf of the prosecutor at the time. *U.S. ex rel. Baldwin v. Yeager,* 428 F.2d 182 (3d Cir. 1970), *cert. denied,* 401 U.S. 919 (1971); *U.S. ex rel. Milani v. Pate,* 425 F.2d 6 (7th Cir.), *cert. denied,* 400 U.S. 867 (1970) (fellow inmate was in contact with police, but was not acting under police instructions). Even statements to a fellow prisoner who has been placed with the defendant by the police with instructions to report incriminating statements do not violate the sixth amendment so long as the informant does not deliberately elicit incriminating statements. *Kuhlmann v. Wilson, supra.*

Statements taken in violation of the sixth amendment are inadmissible and cannot be used to prove the charges in the indictment. *U.S. v. Missler,* 414 F.2d 1293 (4th Cir. 1969), *cert. denied,* 397 U.S. 913 (1970). Such statements may still be used by the government in the investigation of other subjects. *U.S. v. Satterfield,* 558 F.2d at 657.

### § 311. — — Impeachment with Statements Taken in Violation of the Fifth and Sixth Amendments.

Statements which are inadmissible in the prosecution's case-in-chief because they were obtained in violation of *Miranda* may, if trustworthy, be used to attack the credibility of the defendant who takes the stand and testifies contrary to such statements, *Oregon v. Hass,* 420 U.S. 714 (1975); *U.S. v. Miller,* 676 F.2d 359, 363-64 (9th Cir.), *cert. denied,* 459 U.S. 856 (1982); *U.S. v. Rooks,* 577 F.2d 33 (8th Cir.), *cert. denied,* 439 U.S. 862 (1978); or on cross-examination of defendant, *U.S. v. Scott,* 592 F.2d 1139 (10th Cir. 1979). In *Harris v. New York,* 401 U.S. 222, 226 (1971), the Court held, "The shield provided by *Miranda* cannot be perverted into a license to use perjury by way of a defense, free from the risk of confrontation with prior inconsistent statements." Irrespective of *Miranda* violations, if the statement is found to have been made involuntarily, it cannot be used for any purpose as the statements must still satisfy standards of truthworthiness. *Mincey v. Arizona,* 437 U.S. 385 (1978). *See also* Chapter 18, § 1818 *infra.*

The same analysis applies to a sixth amendment violation of *Michigan v. Jackson,* 475 U.S. 625 (1986), and statements which may be inadmissible in the prosecution's case-in-chief may be used to impeach defendant's false or inconsistent testimony. *Michigan v. Harvey,* 494 U.S. 344 (1990).

## § 312. — "Fruit of the Poisonous Tree."

If there has been an illegal search and seizure, or an invalid arrest, any statements derived immediately therefrom are the "fruit" of the illegality and are thus inadmissible, even if they were exculpatory when made. *Wong Sun v. U.S.,* 371 U.S. 471, 485-87 (1963). More than a mere casual relationship between illegal police activity and a subsequent confession is required, however, to warrant exclusion of the confession from evidence. In *Wong Sun, id.* at 487-88, the Court said:

> We need not hold that all evidence is "fruit of the poisonous tree" simply because it would not have come to light but for the illegal actions of the police. Rather, the more apt question in such a case is "whether, granting establishment of the primary illegality, the evidence to which instant objection is made has been come at by exploitation of the illegality or instead by means sufficiently distinguishable to be purged of the primary taint."

The government's burden with respect to the admissibility of a statement derived from illegal activity is to show that the statement was not only given voluntarily, but that it was "sufficiently an act of free will to purge the primary taint." *Id.* at 486. In *Brown v. Illinois,* 422 U.S. 590 (1975), the Court held that the giving of *Miranda* warnings after an illegal arrest does not alone purge the taint of an illegal arrest. The Court said, at 603-04:

> The *Miranda* warnings are an important factor, to be sure, in determining whether the confession is obtained by exploitation of an illegal arrest. But they are not the only factors to be considered. The temporal proximity of the arrest and the confession, the presence of intervening circumstances ... and, particularly, the purpose and flagrancy of the official misconduct are all relevant.

*See also Lanier v. South Carolina,* 106 S. Ct. 297 (1985). Thus, taking a person into custody and to the police station for questioning on less than probable cause to arrest violates the fourth amendment. Confessions obtained during such detention are therefore inadmissible, even if the fifth amendment has been complied with, unless there has been a sufficient break in the casual connection between the illegality and the confession. *Taylor v. Alabama,* 102 S. Ct. 2664, 2667 (1982); *Dunaway v. New York,* 442 U.S. 200 (1979). But where *Miranda* warnings were given, there was a short time lapse between defendant's detention and admissions which was outweighed by a congenial atmosphere, the admissions were apparently a spontaneous reaction to the discovery of drugs, and the defendant did not claim his admissions were involuntary, the Court held that the statements were voluntary and therefore admissible, unaffected by the detention even if it was illegal. *Rawlings v. Kentucky*, 448 U.S. 98, 107-10 (1980). Likewise, a suspect who has responded to unwarned and uncoercive questioning may waive his rights and confess after receiving the *Miranda* warnings. *Oregon v. Elstad*, 470 U.S. 298 (1985).

An improper search can operate to taint an otherwise valid confession. *U.S. v. Cruz*, 581 F.2d 535 (5th Cir. 1978); *U.S. v. Lilly*, 576 F.2d 1240, 1247 (5th Cir. 1978) (statement found to be fruit of illegal body cavity search). *See U.S. v. Scios*, 590 F.2d 956 (D.C. Cir. 1978). Unproductive illegal searches, however, do not taint a later legal search. *U.S. v. Haddad*, 558 F.2d 968 (9th Cir. 1977). Indirect use of tainted evidence is illegal, but illegally seized information that merely causes the government to intensify its investigation may not be enough to taint subsequently discovered evidence. *U.S. v. Cella*, 568 F.2d 1266 (9th Cir. 1977).

Likewise, an improperly taken confession may lead to suppression of the product of an otherwise valid search. *U.S. v. Melvin*, 596 F.2d 492 (1st Cir.), *cert. denied*, 444 U.S. 837 (1979) (discovery of firearms was not the result of defendant's statement). But, if the evidence is obtained by means sufficiently distinguishable as to be purged of the primary taint, it will not be suppressed. *Id.* at 500. The use of a statement taken in violation of *Miranda* to establish probable cause for issuance of a search warrant equally divided the Supreme Court in 1978, *Massachusetts v. White*, 439 U.S. 280 (1978), thereby allowing a state supreme court's decision not to allow use of the statement to stand. A tainted confession has also been held to invalidate an indictment if considered and relied upon by the grand jury. *U.S. v. James*, 493 F.2d 323 (2d Cir. 1974).

Evidence which is the fruit of illegally obtained statements may be admitted so long as the evidence would have been discovered even without the constitutional violation. This is the "inevitable discovery" exception to the exclusionary rule. *Nix v. Williams*, 467 U.S. 431 (1984).

## § 313. — Coerced Confessions.

Coercion, as a method of obtaining a confession, is prohibited. Physical force is but one form of coercion. A credible threat of harm is sufficient. *Arizona v. Fulminante*, 111 S. Ct. 1246 (1991). Physical force includes actual torture. *Brown v. Mississippi*, 297 U.S. 278 (1936). Physical force used to subdue a violent suspect can also render statements inadmissible. *U.S. v. Brown*, 557 F.2d 541 (6th Cir. 1977) (physical force used during arrest, and defendant was struck by arresting officer while in patrol car at time incriminating statement was made).

Keeping the suspect in handcuffs while he confessed, however, is not coercive per se. *U.S. v. Ogden,* 572 F.2d 501 (5th Cir.), *cert. denied,* 439 U.S. 979 (1978). The coercion must be governmental coercion. Thus, a defendant's mental condition where he followed the "voice of God" and confessed does not make the confession involuntary. *Colorado v. Connelly,* 479 U.S. 1577 (1986). It has also been held that where a defendant has the choice to take or refuse a blood-alcohol test, the refusal is not coerced by the police and as such the fact of refusal may be admitted into evidence. *South Dakota v. Neville,* 459 U.S. 553 (1983).

Coerced statements are inherently suspect, and the means of coercion are not limited to acts of physical brutality. *U.S. v. Powe,* 591 F.2d 833, 839-40 (D.C. Cir. 1978); *U.S. v. Fritz,* 580 F.2d 370 (10th Cir.) *(en banc), cert. denied,* 439 U.S. 947 (1978). Coercive pressures can exist independently from threats of use of force. *U.S. v. Hernandez,* 574 F.2d 1362 (5th Cir. 1978) (five hours in police wagon said to be a coercive pressure); *Brooks v. Florida,* 389 U.S. 413 (1967) (defendant held in cage for two weeks with little food or drink).

In determining whether the defendant's will has been overborne by coercive pressure, courts examine personal characteristics of the accused as well as details of the interrogation. *Gallegos v. Colorado,* 370 U.S. 49 (1962); *Henry v. Dees,* 658 F.2d 406, 409 (5th Cir. 1981); *U.S. v. Smith,* 574 F.2d 707 (2d Cir.), *cert. denied,* 439 U.S. 986 (1978) (streetwise 17-year-old); *U.S. v. Schmidt,* 573 F.2d 1057, 1064 (9th Cir.), *cert. denied,* 439 U.S. 881 (1978) (defendant with two years of law school). *See also Hall v. Wolff,* 539 F.2d 1146, 1150 (8th Cir. 1976). Special consideration and caution are taken when the confession is one made by a juvenile. *U.S. v. Spruille,* 544 F.2d 303, 306 (7th Cir. 1976).

Special medical problems may affect the existence of coercion. *Elliott v. Morford,* 557 F.2d 1228 (6th Cir. 1977), *cert. denied,* 434 U.S. 1040 (1978) (allegation of denial of insulin to diabetic defendant for four days before confession required voluntariness hearing). A defendant who is high on drugs or alcohol may still give a voluntary confession. *U.S. v. Dorsett,* 544 F.2d 687, 689 (4th Cir. 1976); *U.S. v. Brown,* 535 F.2d 424, 427 (8th Cir. 1976). A hospitalized defendant may be able to give a voluntary statement. *Johnson v. Havener,* 534 F.2d 1232, 1233 (6th Cir.), *cert. denied,* 429 U.S. 889 (1976) (no coercion where interrogation was conducted with doctor's permission although suspect was hospitalized and was being treated with drugs). But the confession of a critically wounded defendant who was in an intensive care unit was held to be inadmissible. *Mincey v. Arizona,* 437 U.S. 385 (1978) (requests to stop interview because of unbearable pain ignored).

Some psychological pressure may be allowed and confessions based on such pressures are not necessarily involuntary. *E.g., U.S. v. Jordan,* 570 F.2d 635, 643 (6th Cir. 1978) (threat of arrest of pregnant wife); *U.S. v. Charlton,* 565 F.2d 86, 89 (6th Cir. 1977), *cert. denied,* 434 U.S. 1070 (1978) (suspect told confession was only way to exculpate son). But psychological coercion can easily exceed permissible limits. In *Brewer v. Williams,* 430 U.S. 387 (1977), a defendant who was known to have deep religious convictions was persuaded by statements of a police detective to lead officers to the location of his victim's body by what has become famous as the "Christian burial speech," and in *U.S. v. Tingle,* 658 F.2d 1332, 1335-36 (9th Cir. 1981), the agent implied to the defendant that if she did not cooperate she would not see her two-year-old child for a long time. *See also Lynumn v. Illinois,* 372 U.S. 528 (1963). *But see Rhode Island v. Innis,* 446 U.S. 291 (1980), where a suspect arrested for armed robbery told officers he would show them where his gun was located, after interrupting the officers' conversation concerning the missing shotgun in which one officer expressed concern that handicapped children might hurt themselves if they found the weapon. The Court held that the defendant was not "interrogated" in violation of his *Miranda* right to remain silent until he had consulted with a lawyer after he had requested one.

While psychological pressure may be allowed in some instances, the use of deception has been viewed more narrowly. Telling a suspect that his accomplices had confessed when they had not was not allowed in *Schmidt v. Hewitt,* 573 F.2d 794, 801 (3d Cir. 1978). *See also Ferguson v. Boyd,* 566 F.2d 873, 878-79 (4th Cir. 1977) (confession exacted by fostering defendant's erroneous belief that his acknowledgement of guilt was necessary to exonerate his girlfriend was held to be involuntary).

A voluntary confession is one which is the product of an essentially free and unconstrained choice by its maker. Whether or not it is voluntary depends on the totality of the circumstances, and if a coerced confession is admitted, it is subject to a harmless beyond a reasonable doubt review. *Arizona v. Fulminante, supra.*

## § 314. — Use of Confessions at Joint Trials.

*Bruton v. U.S.,* 391 U.S. 123 (1968), held that the admission of a codefendant's post-conspiracy confession implicating the defendant constituted reversible error where the codefendant did not testify. The basis for this rule is the sixth amendment right to confrontation and cross-examination. *See also Nelson v. O'Neil,* 402 U.S. 622 (1971). This rule does not apply to statements made during the course of a conspiracy, *U.S. v. Mitchell,* 556 F.2d 371 (6th Cir.), *cert. denied,* 434 U.S. 925 (1977), or to a confession at joint trial of a codefendant which does not inculpate the accused, *U.S. v. Louderman,* 576 F.2d 1383 (9th Cir. 1978) (statement only about intent of one defendant); *U.S. v. Bailleul,* 553 F.2d 731 (1st Cir. 1977); *U.S. v. Gerry,* 515 F.2d 130 (2d Cir. 1975), *cert. denied,* 423 U.S. 832 (1975). But, if the extrajudicial confession clearly implicates another defendant and is vitally important to the government's case, cautionary instructions will not suffice to remove the taint caused by lack of opportunity to confront the witness. *U.S. v. Knuckles,* 581 F.2d 305 (2d Cir.), *cert. denied,* 439 U.S. 986 (1978) (admission did not clearly inculpate complaining defendant); *Smith v. Estelle,* 569 F.2d 944, 950 (5th Cir. 1978) (introduction of principal offender's unredacted confession under confusing jury instructions held not harmless error). *See U.S. v. Wingate,* 520 F.2d 309 (2d Cir. 1975), *cert. denied,* 423 U.S. 1074 (1976). However, the admission into evidence of one defendant's written statement which made it clear that he was assisted by two others though his accomplices remained unnamed and were not identified by race, age, size, or any other means except by sex did not violate the codefendant's sixth amendment rights. *U.S. v. Holleman,* 575 F.2d 139 (7th Cir. 1978).

"Redaction" or "sanitization" is the process of deleting reference to the non-confessing defendant. Redaction may obviate the need for separate trials if it does not clearly implicate the defendant when revised. *Richardson v. Marsh,* 107 S. Ct. 1703 (1987). Methods of redaction have included substituting the letter "A" for the name of the defendant, *Burkhart v. Lane,* 574 F.2d 346 (6th Cir. 1978) (summary dismissal of habeas corpus petition held to be inappropriate; case remanded to determine whether confession sufficiently redacted); use of the words "someone else," *U.S. v. Weinrich,* 586 F.2d 481 (5th Cir. 1978), *cert. denied,* 441 U.S. 927 (1979) (immediate cautionary instruction also given and speaker later testified); and use of "him and some of his buddies," *U.S. v. Stewart,* 579 F.2d 356 (5th Cir.), *cert. denied,* 439 U.S. 936 (1978) (held not to be sufficiently identifiable to defendant and not error in view of instruction by court not to consider the confession as proof of the other defendant's guilt). Simple deletion of names, however, may not be sufficient to avoid a *Bruton* problem. *U.S. v. Cleveland,* 590 F.2d 24 (1st Cir. 1978). The possibility of spill-over must be considered in considering the choice between sanitization and severance, but mere risk of spill-over is not sufficient to require granting of separate trials. The defendant must make a strong showing of prejudice. *U.S. v. Cleveland,* 590 F.2d at 29.

*Bruton* cannot be circumvented by taking codefendants' statements in the presence of each other. It is the opportunity for confrontation at trial that is important. *Hall v. Wainwright*, 559 F.2d 964 (5th Cir. 1977), *cert. denied*, 434 U.S. 1076 (1978). *Bruton* also applies to interlocking confessions, that is a nontestifying codefendant's confession which facially incriminates the defendant who has himself confessed. *Cruz v. New York*, 107 S. Ct. 1714 (1987). However, despite the lack of opportunity for cross-examination, such a confession may be inadmissible against the defendant if it has sufficient "indicia of reliability." *Id.; see* Chapter 21, § 2139 *infra*.

*Bruton* does not apply when the trial is before a judge. *Cockrell v. Oberhauser*, 413 F.2d 256 (9th Cir. 1969), *cert. denied*, 397 U.S. 994 (1970).

### § 315. — Inadmissibility of Statements Related to Pleas and Offers of Pleas.

Under Rule 11(e)(6) of the Federal Rules of Criminal Procedure and Rule 410 of the Federal Rules of Evidence, evidence of a plea of guilty later withdrawn or a plea of nolo contendere to the crime charged or any other crime, and evidence of offers to so plead, as well as statements made in the course of plea discussions with an attorney for the government which do not result in a plea of guilty or which result in a plea of guilty later withdrawn, are not admissible in any criminal proceeding.

The purpose of this rule is to encourage plea bargaining. The importance of plea negotiations to the criminal justice system was emphasized by the Supreme Court in *Blackledge v. Allison*, 431 U.S. 63 (1977). *See also Santobello v. New York*, 404 U.S. 257 (1971).

The only plea negotiation statements covered by the rule are those with an attorney for the government, not those with an agent.

Admissions not made in the course of formal bargaining, however, may still be adduced at trial. *U.S. v. Levy*, 578 F.2d 896, 901-02 (2d Cir. 1978); *U.S. v. Stirling*, 571 F.2d 708, 730-32 (2d Cir.), *cert. denied*, 439 U.S. 824 (1978).

*See generally* Chapter 6, § 6-2, f, *infra*.

### § 316. Identifications Before Trial.

A federal defendant's right to counsel at all critical stages of the criminal process is guaranteed by the sixth amendment ("and to have the Assistance of Counsel for his defence"). Failure to provide counsel to the accused at these critical stages, without a knowing waiver, renders evidence of a lineup or showup inadmissible per se. Under these circumstances, subsequent in-court identifications of the accused may be admitted only if the government demonstrates the witness' in-court identification was independent of the tainted pretrial identification.

The right to counsel does not extend to on-the-scene identifications, photographic displays, voice identifications, or unplanned confrontations, either before or after the initiation of judicial criminal proceedings.

Due process under the fifth amendment requires the exclusion of testimony identifying an accused where impermissibly suggestive pretrial identification proceedings give rise to a very substantial likelihood of irreparable misidentification. The dominant consideration is the "reliability" of the identification as determined by the "totality of the circumstances" in each case. Presuming the constitutional requirements are met, Rule 801(d)(1)(C) of the Federal Rules of Evidence permits a witness to testify concerning a previous extrajudicial identification of the accused so long as the witness is available for cross-examination.

## § 317. — Sixth Amendment Rights.

The "lineup" or the "showup" at which pretrial identification evidence is obtained is deemed a "critical stage" of the prosecution which, under the sixth amendment, entitles the accused to the presence of counsel. *Stovall v. Denno,* 388 U.S. 293 (1967) (suspect in one-on-one confrontation in victim's hospital room); *Gilbert v. California,* 388 U.S. 263 (1967) (post-indictment lineup); *U.S. v. Wade,* 388 U.S. 218, 237 (1967) (post-indictment lineup). Although the accused may not refuse on fifth amendment grounds to participate in a lineup, *id.* at 221, he must, under ordinary circumstances, be offered the opportunity to have counsel present. Substitute counsel may satisfy this requirement. *U.S. v. Smallwood,* 473 F.2d 98 (D.C. Cir. 1972). In the absence of a knowing waiver by the accused of the right to have counsel present, evidence of the lineup or showup identification is inadmissible per se, *U.S. v. Wade,* 388 U.S. at 237; and no subsequent identification, including an in-court identification, is admissible unless the government can demonstrate that it had a source independent of the tainted pretrial identification, *Gilbert v. California,* 388 U.S. at 272. The Second Circuit, noting that precise compliance with the *Wade-Gilbert* rule may be difficult at the pre-arraignment or pre-indictment stage, has said that an in-court identification after a violation of the rule may be permitted if the trial judge is properly satisfied that the in-court identification was affected only "insignificantly or not at all and that no injustice could have occurred." *U.S. v. Edmons,* 432 F.2d 577, 585 (2d Cir. 1970).

In *Kirby v. Illinois,* 406 U.S. 682 (1972), the Court, in a plurality opinion, held that the *Wade-Gilbert* sixth amendment rule is not applicable to confrontations before the commencement of formal criminal proceedings. Citing *Kirby,* the Second Circuit has held that issuance of a warrant of arrest under New York law sufficiently marks the initiation of judicial criminal proceedings to require that counsel be present at a subsequent showup. *U.S. ex rel. Robinson v. Zelker,* 468 F.2d 159, 163 (2d Cir. 1972), *cert. denied,* 411 U.S. 939 (1973).

A defendant without counsel who was confronted on numerous occasions by potential witnesses in the two days following arrest was not deprived of the sixth amendment right to counsel at the time since adversary judicial proceedings had not been initiated. *McGuff v. Alabama,* 566 F.2d 939, 941 (5th Cir.), *cert. denied,* 436 U.S. 949 (1978). *Accord, U.S. v. Taylor,* 530 F.2d 639, 641 (5th Cir.), *cert. denied,* 429 U.S. 845 (1976).

The Supreme Court in *Moore v. Illinois,* 434 U.S. 220, 226 (1977), citing *Kirby,* did not limit the right to counsel to only post-indictment identifications, but to any corporeal identification "conducted 'at or after the initiation of adversary judicial criminal proceedings — whether by way of formal charge, preliminary hearing, indictment, information, or arraignment.'" In *Boyd v. Henderson,* 555 F.2d 56 (2d Cir.), *cert. denied,* 434 U.S. 927 (1977), the court, relying on *Kirby,* 406 U.S. at 682, held that there was no sixth amendment right to counsel before formal charges were filed where identification was made at defendant's arraignment, with counsel, on another charge.

A courtroom "showup" when defendant was being arraigned on another charge did not constitute a sixth amendment violation where prosecution had not been instituted on the subject charge; and since a critical stage of the prosecution had not been reached, it was not necessary to have counsel present. *Jackson v. Jago,* 556 F.2d 807 (6th Cir.), *cert. denied,* 434 U.S. 940 (1977). *Accord, Sanchell v. Parratt,* 530 F.2d 286, 290 n.2 (8th Cir. 1976).

Since adversary proceedings had not been instituted at the time defendant appeared in a police lineup the evening of the robbery, there was no constitutional right to appointment of counsel at the lineup. *Lacoste v. Blackburn,* 592 F.2d 1321 (5th Cir.), *cert. denied,* 444 U.S. 968 (1979). Nor does an arrest on probable cause without a warrant, even though the arrest is for the crime with which defendant is eventually charged, initiate judicial criminal proceedings, and consequently, there is no constitutional right to counsel at the lineup conducted after arrest but before the formal charge is made. *Caver v. Alabama,* 577 F.2d 1188, 1195 (5th Cir. 1978).

In *U.S. v. Tyler,* 592 F.2d 261 (5th Cir. 1979), a defendant in custody for an unrelated offense at the time of a lineup was not deprived of his right to counsel since the government had not "committed itself to prosecute" on the subject offense. *See also McNeil v. Wisconsin,* 111 S. Ct. 2204 (1991). Use of testimony of a witness, who was unable to identify the defendant in a photographic display two weeks after the crime but nearly nine months later made an identification at a staged confrontation during a trial recess, violated the defendant's sixth amendment right to counsel. *Cannon v. Alabama,* 558 F.2d 1211, 1217 (5th Cir.), *cert. denied,* 434 U.S. 1087 (1977).

The defendant's right to counsel was not abridged by a series of informal "aural showups" consisting of brief, matter-of-fact conversations concerning routine matters when no effort at interrogation was made. *U.S. v. Woods,* 544 F.2d 242, 263 (6th Cir. 1976), *cert. denied,* 429 U.S. 1062 (1977).

The defendant's sixth amendment right to counsel had not attached at the time of confrontation with a potential witness in the absence of the initiation of "adversary judicial proceedings." *U.S. v. Derring,* 592 F.2d 1003, 1006 n.4 (8th Cir. 1979).

The Ninth Circuit, citing *U.S. v. Ash,* 413 U.S. 300, 321 (1973) (no right to have counsel present during witness view of post-indictment photographic array), has held that pretrial identifications by government witnesses of voices obtained through lawful electronic surveillance are not, for sixth amendment purposes, critical stages of the criminal proceedings in which the witnesses are to eventually testify. *U.S. v. Kim,* 577 F.2d 473, 480-81 (9th Cir. 1978); *U.S. v. Thomas,* 586 F.2d 123 (9th Cir. 1978). *Accord, U.S. v. Dupree,* 553 F.2d 1189, 1192 (8th Cir.), *cert. denied,* 434 U.S. 986 (1977).

It is well settled that on-the-scene identifications which occur within minutes of the witnessed crime in the absence of counsel are not prohibited by *Wade. U.S. v. Abshire,* 471 F.2d 116 (5th Cir. 1972); *U.S. v. Savage,* 470 F.2d 948 (3d Cir. 1972), *cert. denied,* 412 U.S. 930 (1973); *Spencer v. Turner,* 486 F.2d 599 (10th Cir. 1972), *cert. denied,* 410 U.S. 988 (1973); *U.S. ex rel. Cummings v. Zelker,* 455 F.2d 714 (2d Cir.), *cert. denied,* 406 U.S. 927 (1972); *U.S. v. Sanchez,* 422 F.2d 1198, 1200 (2d Cir. 1970) ("consistent with good police work").

The Second Circuit has held that *Wade* requires notice to defense counsel before a witness walks into a courtroom during a trial in a prearranged effort to identify the defendant. *U.S. v. Roth,* 430 F.2d 1137 (2d Cir. 1970), *cert. denied,* 400 U.S. 1021 (1971). But it is clear that the sixth amendment is not violated if the confrontation between witness and defendant is inadvertent and not deliberately arranged by the government. *See, e.g., U.S. v. Gentile,* 530 F.2d 461, 468 (2d Cir. 1976), *cert. denied,* 426 U.S. 936 (1976); *U.S. v. Kaylor,* 491 F.2d 1127 (2d Cir. 1973), *vacated on other grounds,* 418 U.S. 909 (1974).

The Supreme Court has differentiated between pretrial lineups and pretrial photographic identifications. Unlike post-indictment pretrial lineups, pretrial photographic identifications, whether before or after indictment, have not been held to be a "critical stage" in the criminal proceedings requiring right to counsel. *U.S. v. Ash,* 413 U.S. 300, 321 (1972). *See also Hill v. Wyrick,* 570 F.2d 748 (8th Cir.), *cert. denied,* 436 U.S. 921 (1978); *Anderson v. Maggio,* 555 F.2d 447, 450 n.5 (5th Cir. 1977). If a witness views both a photo spread and a lineup, it is not necessary that those in the lineup be the same as those in the photo spread. *Nettles v. Wainwright,* 677 F.2d 410, 414 (5th Cir. 1982).

### § 318. — Fifth Amendment Due Process Rights.

> No person shall be held to answer for a capital or otherwise infamous crime..., without due process of law....

> U.S. Const., amend. V

The "totality of the circumstances" must be examined in determining whether police identification procedures in a lineup or showup are "unnecessarily suggestive and conducive to irreparable mistaken identification" and thus violative of due process under the fifth and fourteenth amendments. *Stovall v. Denno,* 388 U.S. 293, 302 (1967). *See Coleman v. Alabama,* 399 U.S. 1 (1970); *Foster v. California,* 394 U.S. 440 (1969). Similarly, photographic identifications must not be "so impermissively suggestive as to give rise to a very substantial likelihood of irreparable misidentification." *Simmons v. U.S.,* 390 U.S. 377, 384 (1968). Whether an identification procedure is improper under the fifth amendment depends upon the totality of the circumstances in each case. *Id.* at 383; *Stovall v. Denno,* 388 U.S. at 302. There is no per se rule that the court conduct a hearing outside the jury's presence whenever a defendant contends that a witness' identification of him was arrived at improperly, even though it may be advisable and possibly required in some circumstances. *Watkins v. Sowders,* 449 U.S. 341, 349 (1981).

In *Neil v. Biggers,* 409 U.S. 188 (1972), involving a rape victim's showup identification seven months after the crime, the Court refused to apply a per se rule and concluded that the identification, although suggestive, was reliable under the totality of the circumstances test. "Reliability" is the linchpin in determining the admissibility of identification testimony. *Manson v. Brathwaite,* 432 U.S. 98, 114 (1977). The factors to be weighed in assessing reliability against the corrupting effect of the suggestive procedure include (1) the witness' opportunity to view the criminal at the time of the crime, (2) the witness' degree of attention, (3) the accuracy of his prior description of the criminal, (4) the level of certainty demonstrated at the confrontation, and (5) the time between the crime and the confrontation. *Neil v. Biggers,* 409 U.S. at 199-200; *Joshua v. Maggio,* 674 F.2d 376, 378 (5th Cir. 1982); *U.S. v. Hadley,* 671 F.2d 1112, 1115-16 (8th Cir. 1982); *Allen v. Estelle,* 568 F.2d 1108 (5th Cir. 1978). *See Brown v. Harris,* 666 F.2d 782, 785-87 (2d Cir. 1981), *cert. denied,* 102 S. Ct. 2017 (1982), for a discussion of these principles in the context of a voice identification. An in-court identification not fatally tainted by suggestive procedure was the showing to the witness single photographs of defendant and codefendant the day before trial, six months after the robbery. *Hudson v. Blackburn,* 601 F.2d 785 (5th Cir. 1979), *cert. denied,* 444 U.S. 1086 (1980). However, a pre-lineup confrontation at stationhouse arranged by police was suggestive and trial identifications denied due process. *Jackson v. Fogg,* 589 F.2d 108 (2d Cir. 1978). A difference in height, weight, and facial hair of those in lineup is not necessarily suggestive, *U.S. v. Bierey,* 588 F.2d 620 (8th Cir.), *cert. denied,* 440 U.S. 927 (1979), and an in-court identification was sufficiently reliable even though the photographic spread was suggestive. *Cronnon v. Alabama,* 587 F.2d 246 (5th Cir.), *cert. denied,* 440 U.S. 974 (1979). Where the defendant in a photospread was the only one wearing stolen sweater the photo identification was excluded as unreliable. *U.S. v. Baykowski,* 583 F.2d 1046 (8th Cir. 1978). An in-court identification was not invalid where witness was with defendants for two or three hours, was aware he would be called to identify them, and photos displayed were not suggestive. *U.S. v. Herring,* 582 F.2d 535 (10th Cir. 1978).

In *U.S. v. Sheehan,* 583 F.2d 30 (1st Cir. 1978), two later photo displays, six and one-half months apart, which then included defendant, where witness' selections were not suggested and cross-examination was vigorous and extensive, did not give rise to substantial likelihood of irreparable misidentification.

The Supreme Court in *Simmons v. U.S.,* 390 U.S. at 384, established the standard for judging photographic identification procedures and said that such identification would be set aside only if the "procedure was so impermissibly suggestive as to give rise to a very substantial likelihood of irreparable misidentification." The Fifth Circuit in *U.S. v. Henderson,* 489 F.2d 802, 805 (5th Cir. 1973), *cert. denied,* 417 U.S. 913 (1974), applied a two-step test: "(1) whether the procedures followed were 'impermissibly suggestive,' and then (2) whether, being so, they

created 'a substantial risk of misidentification.'" To make these determinations the district courts conduct *in camera* hearings to inquire
into the circumstances of the challenged identification procedures. *See,
e.g., U.S. v. Baykowski,* 583 F.2d 1046, 1047 (8th Cir. 1978); *U.S. v.
Bubar,* 576 F.2d 192, 197 (2d Cir. 1977); *Williams v. McKenzie,* 576
F.2d 566, 571 (4th Cir. 1978); *U.S. v. Flickinger,* 573 F.2d 1349, 1358
(9th Cir.), *cert. denied,* 439 U.S. 836 (1978).

In *U.S. ex rel. Moore v. Illinois,* 577 F.2d 411 (7th Cir. 1978), *cert.
denied,* 440 U.S. 919 (1979), the court weighed the possibly corrupting
effect of a suggestive confrontation as bearing on the reliability of the
victim's in-court identification and found that the victim's identification was based upon her observation of defendant other than at the
suggestive pretrial confrontation. *See also U.S. v. Alden,* 576 F.2d 772
(8th Cir.), *cert. denied,* 439 U.S. 855 (1978); *U.S. v. Flickinger,* 573 F.2d
at 1358 (voice identification).

In *U.S. v. Bubar,* 567 F.2d at 198, since the government witness, a
participant in the alleged crime, had an independent basis in memory
sufficient to support his in-court identification without reliance on an
intervening single photograph, his in-court identification was deemed
reliable. *See also U.S. v. Bennett,* 675 F.2d 596, 597-98 (4th Cir. 1982),
where an in-court identification was permitted by a witness who had
failed to identify the defendant when shown his photograph three
months before trial.

Applying the "totality of the circumstances" test, the court, in *Boyd
v. Henderson,* 555 F.2d 56 (2d Cir.), *cert. denied,* 434 U.S. 927 (1977),
found a courtroom showup not suggestive where the defendant was one
of six black defendants who appeared for arraignment on other charges
and the witness had no idea when or where he would appear. *See also
U.S. v. Smith,* 602 F.2d 834 (8th Cir.), *cert. denied,* 444 U.S. 902 (1979)
(procedure not so impermissibly suggestive where defendant was only
person wearing bib overalls in photospread in light of fact all but two of
the eyewitnesses failed to identify him); *U.S. v. Coades,* 549 F.2d 1303
(9th Cir. 1977) (suspect returned to the scene of the crime for a showup
shortly after the occurrence); *Sanchell v. Parratt,* 530 F.2d 286 (8th Cir.
1976) (substantial likelihood of irreparable misidentification as defendant repeatedly was presented as a single suspect to victims who initially failed to identify him). *Cf. Williams v. McKenzie,* 576 F.2d 566
(4th Cir. 1978) (photographic identification from only four photos was
not unduly suggestive; no per se rule requiring six photos in spread).

In *Dupuie v. Egeler,* 552 F.2d 704 (6th Cir. 1977), the court declined
to apply a per se rule that federal due process requires rejection of
otherwise admissible identification testimony simply because the wit-

ness to a crime might have seen a newspaper photograph of the accused before the lineup or in-court identification.

Because the possibility of irreparable misidentification is as great when the out-of-court identification is from a tape recording as when it is from a photograph or a lineup, the same due process protection applies to either method. *U.S. v. Pheaster*, 544 F.2d 353 (9th Cir. 1976), *cert. denied*, 429 U.S. 1099 (1977).

In *U.S. v. Milhollan*, 599 F.2d 518, 522 (3d Cir.), *cert. denied*, 444 U.S. 909 (1979), the court held that in-court identifications of defendant were admissible even in view of earlier tainted identification procedures if the prosecution established by "clear and convincing" evidence that the later identifications were based on independent observations at the scene of the crime and not on the tainted procedure. It was held in *U.S. v. Crews*, 445 U.S. 463 (1980), that an in-court identification of defendant was admissible since it was based upon the victim's untainted independent recollection which had no causal relationship with the intervening inadmissible photographic and lineup identifications of defendant following his illegal arrest.

Identifications resulting from unexpected and unplanned encounters with defendants usually do not violate due process. *U.S. v. Massaro*, 544 F.2d 547 (1st Cir. 1976), *cert. denied*, 429 U.S. 1052 (1977) (witness outside courtroom waiting for trial to begin saw defendant walk down the hall with two other men and immediately recognized him); *U.S. v. Colclough*, 549 F.2d 937 (4th Cir. 1977) (robbery victim's unexpected encounter with defendant who was standing in hallway outside courtroom). Although most accidental encounters do not involve any significant degree of suggestiveness requiring a review on constitutional grounds, the Ninth Circuit concluded in *Green v. Loggins*, 614 F.2d 219, 223 (9th Cir. 1980), that a chance holding cell encounter between the state's star witness (who previously identified another as the assailant) and the murder suspect defendant, was unnecessarily and impermissibly suggestive under the totality of the circumstances, where (1) the setting of the encounter made it clear the defendant had been accused of some crime; (2) the defendant was identified as the state's suspect by the booking officer mentioning his name; and (3) the encounter resulted from the state's negligent exercise of its control over the witness and the accused.

When defendant fails to allege the existence of any lineup conditions that would justify the in-court identification tainted in any way, the preindictment lineup does not violate defendant's due process rights. *U.S. v. Taylor*, 530 F.2d 639 (5th Cir.), *cert. denied*, 429 U.S. 845 (1976). *See also Hill v. Wyrick*, 570 F.2d 748 (8th Cir.), *cert. denied*, 436

U.S. 921 (1978) (no factual allegations that pretrial photographic display was in any way impermissibly suggestive); *Johnson v. Riddle,* 562 F.2d 312 (4th Cir. 1977) (general unsupported allegation of due process violation in a showup).

In *U.S. v. Hines,* 455 F.2d 1317 (D.C. Cir. 1971), *cert. denied,* 406 U.S. 975 (1972), the court held that once an eyewitness has made a positive identification at a valid showup or lineup, government counsel's review of that identification with the witness through the use of photographs in preparation for trial does not taint an in-court identification.

One court, without any discussion of the principles that apply to a lineup, has admitted the identification of the defendant by a tracking dog at a lineup. *U.S. v. Gates,* 680 F.2d 1117, 1119 (6th Cir. 1982).

Rights of defendants are not prejudiced by the use of photographs rather than a lineup to obtain eyewitness identifications. *U.S. v. Boston,* 508 F.2d 1171 (2d Cir. 1974), *cert. denied,* 421 U.S. 1001 (1975). Even though a defendant has no constitutional right to a lineup, a court ordered lineup may be granted by the trial judge, in the exercise of his discretion; and if the request is made promptly after the crime or arrest, it may be of value to both sides. *U.S. v. Estremera,* 531 F.2d 1103, 1111 (2d Cir.), *cert. denied,* 425 U.S. 979 (1976).

In a bench trial, it should be noted, the court may exercise more lenient standards with respect to identification evidence. *See Smith v. Paderick,* 519 F.2d 70 (4th Cir.), *cert. denied,* 423 U.S. 935 (1975).

It is important that photographic spreads used by the government be retained for possible use at trial, or at least be subject to reconstruction. Otherwise the court, being unable to make an independent judicial review of their contents, may assume the pretrial identification procedures were impermissibly suggestive. *See, e.g., U.S. v. Sanchez,* 603 F.2d 381 (2d Cir. 1979).

### § 319. — Evidence of Extrajudicial Identifications.

Rule 801(d)(1)(C) of Federal Rules of Evidence provides, "A statement is not hearsay if ... the declarant testifies at the trial or hearing and is subject to cross-examination concerning the statement, and the statement is ... one of identification of a person made after perceiving him." The purpose of the rule is to permit the introduction of identifications made by a witness when his memory was fresher and there was less opportunity for influence to be exerted upon the witness' recollection. Protection against misidentifications is afforded by the requirement that the declarant be available for cross-examination. *U.S. v. Owens,* 484 U.S. 554 (1988). Questions about the probative value of the testimony are for the jury. Consequently, Rule 801(d)(1)(C) governs admissibility, not sufficiency. *See, e.g., U.S. v. Hudson,* 564 F.2d 1377 (9th Cir. 1977). In *U.S. v. Marchand,* 564 F.2d 983, 996 (2d Cir. 1977), *cert. denied,* 434 U.S. 1015 (1978), the court held that "'Rule 801(d)(1)(C) should ... be interpreted as allowing evidence of prior identification by the witness of a photograph of the person whom he had initially perceived,' 4 Weinstein & Berger, Commentary on Rules of Evidence for the United States Courts and Magistrates 801-107 to 108 (1976), and also to descriptions and sketches [photographic identification and sketch made by a witness rather than a police artist]."

The sketch itself need not satisfy the requirements of Rule 801(d)(1)(C), but only the authentication requirements of Rule 901. Statements of witnesses that the sketch looked like the robber met the requirements of Rule 801 in *U.S. v. Moskowitz,* 581 F.2d 14, 21 (2d Cir.), *cert. denied,* 439 U.S. 871 (1978). The testimony of the artist was no more necessary as a condition of admissibility than a photographer's testimony would have been had the witnesses identified a photograph. *Id.* In *U.S. v. Watson,* 587 F.2d 365 (7th Cir. 1978), *cert. denied,* 439 U.S. 1132 (1979), the court permitted out-of-court identification testimony of a witness who was positive and unequivocal about his identification of the defendants at a showup, yet some six months later at trial he was somewhat less certain. The court noted that the application of the criteria set forth in *Neil v. Biggers,* 409 U.S. 188 (1972), established the reliability of the identification and that there were other circumstances (incriminating physical evidence) which showed the reliability of the identification. *U.S. v. Watson,* 587 F.2d at 368 n.3. *See also U.S. v. Lewis,* 565 F.2d 1248 (2d Cir. 1977), *cert. denied,* 435 U.S. 973 (1978) (failure of witness who made pretrial photographic identification of defendant to make corporeal identifications at trial did not render testimony of FBI agent, that witness had previously identified defendant, inadmissible where witness recalled prior identifications and so testified); *Anderson v. Maggio,* 555 F.2d 447 (5th Cir. 1977) (witness at trial could properly testify that he identified a particular photograph, seen by him at an unsuggestive pretrial proceeding, of the defendant as the robber).

The absence of counsel in violation of *U.S. v. Wade,* 388 U.S. 218 (1967), would render the out-of-court identification inadmissible per se. Where counsel was not required, such out-of-court identification is subject to the due process standards of *Stovall v. Denno,* 388 U.S. 293 (1967). If, under *Stovall,* the out-of-court identification is found to have been unnecessarily obtained by impermissibly suggestive means, evidence of it must be excluded from trial. *Manson v. Brathwaite,* 432 U.S. 98 (1977); *Neil v. Biggers,* 409 U.S. 188, 199-200 (1972).

It should be noted that one circuit, citing *Mallory v. U.S.*, 354 U.S. 449 (1957), has held that evidence of lineups, conducted during an investigatory delay in violation of Rule 5(a), should be excluded. *Adams v. U.S.*, 399 F.2d 574 (D.C. Cir. 1968), *cert. denied*, 393 U.S. 1067 (1969). *See U.S. v. Broadhead*, 413 F.2d 1351 (7th Cir. 1969), *cert. denied*, 396 U.S. 1017 (1970) (Rule 5 applies to lineups as well as confessions).

Although mug shots are generally indicative of past criminal conduct and likely to raise inferences of past criminal behavior in the minds of the jury, they may be admitted under certain circumstances, particularly where their probative value outweighs the prejudicial effect. The First and Second Circuits have adopted principles governing the introduction into evidence of "mug shot" photographs which have been used in making out-of-court identifications: (1) the government must have demonstrable need to introduce the photographs; (2) the photographs themselves, if shown to the jury, must not imply that the defendant has a prior criminal record; and (3) the manner of introduction at trial must be such that it does not draw particular attention to the source or implications of the photographs. *U.S. v. Fosher*, 568 F.2d 207, 214 (1st Cir. 1978). In *Fosher*, even though a "demonstrable need" was present for introduction of mug shots, their admission was an abuse of discretion where defendant's guilt was less than overwhelming, when the photographs were clearly mug shots showing inartistic masking of prejudicial features, and colloquy concerning admissibility had taken place in the presence of the jury. *U.S. v. Harrington*, 490 F.2d 487, 494 (2d Cir. 1973) (in spite of "demonstrable need," the introduction of "mug shots" constituted reversible error where the method of masking defendant's criminality and the police source of the photograph had been awkwardly handled before the jury).

# CHAPTER 4

## THE GRAND JURY AND IMMUNITY

§ 400. Introduction.
§ 401. Procedures.
§ 402. Supervisory Powers of District Court.
§ 403. Evidence Before Grand Jury.
§ 404. — Calling and Questioning of Witnesses and Warnings.
§ 405. — — Miranda Warnings.
§ 406. — — Exclusionary Rule.
§ 407. — — Questions Based on Illegal Electronic Surveillance.
§ 408. — — After Indictment Returned.
§ 409. — Subpoenas Duces Tecum.
§ 410. Secrecy of Proceedings and Disclosure.
§ 411. — Matters Occurring Before Grand Jury.
§ 412. — Attorney for the Government.
§ 413. — Other Government Personnel.
§ 414. — Preliminary to or in Connection With Judicial Proceedings.
§ 415. — Disclosure by or to Witnesses.
§ 416. — For Use in Government Civil Actions.
§ 417. — Sealed Indictments.
§ 418. Motions Challenging Multiple Representation of Witnesses.
§ 419. Immunity.
§ 420. — Prosecution for Perjury.
§ 421. — Other Sovereigns.
§ 422. — Use in Civil Proceedings.
§ 423. — Immunity for Defense Witnesses.
§ 424. Procedures for Enforcement of Subpoenas and Orders Compelling Testimony.
§ 425. — Civil Contempt Proceedings.
§ 426. — Criminal Contempt Proceedings.
§ 427. Grand Jury Reports.

## § 400. Introduction.

The Constitution requires that federal felonies be charged by grand jury indictment. U.S. Const. amend. V. The grand jury may use its subpoena powers to determine whether there is probable cause to believe a crime has been committed and that a particular individual or corporation committed it. Information gathered during the course of a grand jury's investigation is also a primary source of evidence that may be offered by the prosecution at trial.

The grand jury can investigate merely on suspicion that the law is being violated, or just because it wants assurance that it is not. *U.S. v. R. Enterprises, Inc.*, 111 S. Ct. 722 (1991).

The powers of the grand jury are not defined in federal statutory law. The statutes authorize district courts to call grand juries, provide for the manner of such calling, define a quorum, and give the court the right to excuse or discharge grand jurors; but, the powers of the grand jury, a common-law institution, have been defined by the courts on a case-by-case basis. However, the Jury Selection and Service Act of 1968, 28 U.S.C. §§ 1861-1875, must be strictly followed, but it has been held that indictments were not to be dismissed where violations of the act did not seriously frustrate the purposes of the act. *U.S. v. Bearden,* 659 F.2d 590, 602 (5th Cir. 1981). Exclusion of minorities or the existence of influences of sex, religion, and race is unconstitutional. *Vasquez v. Hillery,* 474 U.S. 254 (1986); *Castaneda v. Partida,* 430 U.S. 482 (1977).

## § 401. Procedures.

Rule 6 of the Federal Rules of Criminal Procedure and 18 U.S.C. §§ 3331-3334 vest in the district courts the power to summon regular and special grand juries. Special grand juries serve for a term of 18 months, and a district court may extend that term for additional periods of six months, not to exceed a total of 36 months except for the limited reasons specified in 18 U.S.C. § 3333(e). 18 U.S.C. § 3331(a). The term of a regular grand jury is 18 months and may be extended up to an additional six months. Rule 6(g), Fed. R. Crim. P. A grand jury's life begins on the date it is impaneled and sworn; and an indictment returned more than 18 months after that date is not valid. *U.S. v. Armored Transport, Inc.,* 629 F.2d 1313 (9th Cir. 1980), *cert. denied,* 450 U.S. 965 (1981). The day on which the grand jury is impaneled is not counted in computing the 18-month period. Rule 45(a), Fed. R. Crim. P.; *U.S. v. Carver,* 671 F.2d 577 (D.C. Cir. 1982). Extension of a special grand jury's term is not reviewable on appeal, absent a showing of flagrant abuse. *In re Korman,* 486 F.2d 926 (7th Cir. 1973).

Federal grand juries must consist of at least 16 and not more than 23 persons. An indictment may be found upon the concurrence of 12 or more jurors. Rule 6(f), Fed. R. Crim. P. There is neither a fifth amendment nor a Rule 6 requirement that any minimum number of grand jurors who vote to indict must hear all of the evidence presented. *U.S. v. Cronic,* 675 F.2d 1126, 1130 (10th Cir. 1982); *U.S. v. Leverage Funding Systems, Inc.,* 637 F.2d 645 (9th Cir. 1980), *cert. denied,* 452 U.S. 961 (1981); *U.S. v. Colasurdo,* 453 F.2d 585 (2d Cir. 1971), *cert. denied,* 406 U.S. 917 (1972). The Seventh Circuit reached the same result when it refused to dismiss an indictment because only 11 grand jurors heard all of the evidence, and found that nothing in Rule 6 limits the number of substitutions that can be made in the membership of the grand jury. *U.S. v. Lang,* 644 F.2d 1232 (7th Cir. 1981).

The impaneling court appoints one of the jurors to be foreman and another to be deputy foreman. Rule 6(c), Fed. R. Crim. P. Although systematic exclusion of blacks from a grand jury requires the reversal of a conviction, *Vasquez v. Hillery*, 106 S. Ct. 617 (1986), discrimination in the selection of the foreman is not a constitutional violation so long as the composition of the grand jury as a whole satisfies constitutional concerns. *Hobby v. U.S.*, 468 U.S. 317 (1984).

All grand jury proceedings, except deliberations or voting, must be recorded electronically or by a stenographer. Rule 6(e)(1), Fed. R. Crim. P. The attorney for the government is responsible for maintaining the recordings or the reporter's notes.

No federal grand jury can indict without the concurrence of the attorney for the government. He must sign the indictment. Rule 7(c), Fed. R. Crim. P. The practice of presigning proposed indictments by the United States Attorney before they are presented to the grand jury does not alone show undue influence on the grand jury. *U.S. v. Civella*, 666 F.2d 1122, 1127 (8th Cir. 1981). A court cannot compel an attorney for the government to sign an indictment because in signing the indictment the attorney for the government is exercising a power belonging to the executive branch of the government. *See Smith v. U.S.*, 375 F.2d 243 (5th Cir.), *cert. denied*, 389 U.S. 841 (1967); *U.S. v. Cox*, 342 F.2d 167 (5th Cir.), *cert. denied*, 381 U.S. 935 (1965); *In re Grand Jury January 1969*, 315 F. Supp. 662 (D. Md. 1970).

In *U.S. v. Mandujano*, 425 U.S. 564 (1976), the Supreme Court ruled that the sixth amendment right to counsel does not apply to grand jury appearances because criminal proceedings have not yet been instigated. However, a witness may leave the grand jury room to consult with counsel. *In re Taylor*, 567 F.2d 1183 (2d Cir. 1977); *U.S. v. George*, 444 F.2d 310 (6th Cir. 1971). Such departures from the grand jury room to consult with counsel may be subject to reasonable limitations. *See In re Tierney*, 465 F.2d 806, 810 (5th Cir. 1972), *cert. denied*, 410 U.S. 914 (1973). A motion by counsel for a grand jury witness, who had been designated a target, for supplemental instructions by the court on the elements of the offense was denied by a trial court that reasoned that at the pre-indictment stage a court should not intervene unless serious prosecutorial abuse has been demonstrated. *In re Grand Jury 79-01*, 489 F. Supp. 844 (N.D. Ga. 1980).

A witness has the right to object to the presence of unauthorized persons during his testimony. *In re Grand Jury Investigation*, 424 F. Supp. 802 (E.D. Pa.), *appeal dismissed*, 576 F.2d 1071 (1976), *cert. denied*, 439 U.S. 953 (1978); *U.S. v. DiGirlomo*, 393 F. Supp. 997 (W.D. Mo. 1975), *aff'd*, 520 F.2d 372, *cert. denied*, 423 U.S. 1033 (1975). The presence of unauthorized persons may also serve to void the grand jury's indictment. *Latham v. U.S.*, 226 F. 420, 424 (5th Cir. 1915); *U.S. v. Phillips Petroleum Co.*, 435 F. Supp. 610, 618 (N.D. Okla. 1977). *But see U.S. v. Glassman*, 562 F.2d 954 (5th Cir. 1977), where the presence of an agent operating a movie projector did not vitiate an indictment, and *U.S. v. Mechanik*, 106 S. Ct. 938 (1986), holding that where two witnesses testifying in tandem before the grand jury did not affect the substantial rights of the defendant, a conviction will not be reversed.

Defendants have frequently challenged the validity of letters of appointment of Justice Department attorneys appearing before grand juries. These challenges have been uniformly rejected. *U.S. v. Sklaroff*, 552 F.2d 1156, 1160-61 (5th Cir. 1977), *cert. denied*, 434 U.S. 1009 (1978); *U.S. v. Cravero*, 545 F.2d 406 (5th Cir. 1976), *cert. denied*, 429 U.S. 1100 (1977); *Schebergen v. U.S.*, 536 F.2d 674 (6th Cir. 1976); *In re DiBella*, 518 F.2d 955 (2d Cir. 1975). However, courts are increasingly sensitive about potential conflicts created by attorneys from other federal agencies appearing before grand juries by special appointment. *See e.g.*, *U.S. v. Birdman*, 602 F.2d 547 (3d Cir. 1979), *cert. denied*, 444 U.S. 1032 (1980); *In re April 1977 Grand Jury Subpoenas: General Motors Corp. v. U.S.*, 573 F.2d 936 (6th Cir.), *appeal dismissed en banc*, 584 F.2d 1366 (1978), *cert. denied*, 440 U.S. 934 (1979); *U.S. v. Gold*, 470 F. Supp. 1336 (N.D. Ill. 1979).

The initiation of a grand jury investigation before, during, or after the commencement of a civil investigation by government agencies concerning the same allegations is not improper. *SEC v. Dresser Industries, Inc.*, 628 F.2d 1368 (D.C. Cir. 1980), *cert. denied*, 449 U.S. 993 (1981); but parallel investigations can be fraught with peril and should be closely and carefully monitored, *U.S. v. LaSalle National Bank*, 437 U.S. 297 (1978).

## § 402. Supervisory Powers of District Court.

Although the grand jury must turn to the court for enforcement of its orders, it has an independent constitutional identity and is not subject to the courts' directions and orders with respect to the exercise of its essential functions. *U.S. v. Williams*, 112 S. Ct. 1735 (1992); *U.S. v. U.S. District Court*, 238 F.2d 713, 719 (4th Cir. 1956), *cert. denied*, 352 U.S. 981 (1957). The courts of appeals do have authority to issue mandamus to district courts under the All Writs Act, 28 U.S.C. § 1651(a), when the district court exceeds its authority by interfering with the work of a grand jury. *Id.* at 718. A court may not order a grand jury to come to a decision concerning an indictment, *id.* at 722; nor may a court stay a grand jury's investigation pending the outcome of state litigation, *In re Grand Jury Proceedings,* 525 F.2d 151 (3d Cir. 1975). A court may not interfere with the prosecutor's decision of what evidence to present to the grand jury and how to present it. *U.S. v. Chanen,* 549 F.2d 1306 (9th Cir.), *cert. denied,* 434 U.S. 825 (1977); *Bursey v. U.S.,* 466 F.2d 1059 (9th Cir. 1972).

A court may not invoke its supervisory powers to dismiss an indictment for prosecutorial misconduct not prejudicial to the defendant. To do so would circumvent the harmless error requirement of Rule 52(a) of the Federal Rules of Criminal Procedure. The test is whether the violation substantially influenced the grand jury decision to indict or there was "grave doubt" that that decision was free from such substantial influence. *Bank of Nova Scotia v. U.S.,* 487 U.S. 250 (1988).

### § 403. Evidence Before Grand Jury.

If an indictment is valid on its face, it is not subject to challenge on the ground that the grand jury acted on the basis of inadequate or incompetent evidence, or even evidence obtained in violation of the defendant's fifth amendment privilege against self-incrimination. *U.S. v. Calandra,* 414 U.S. 338, 345 (1974); *U.S. v. Blue,* 384 U.S. 251 (1966); *Lawn v. U.S.,* 355 U.S. 339 (1958); *Costello v. U.S.,* 350 U.S. 359 (1956). Other than privileges, the rules of evidence do not apply to grand jury proceedings. Rule 1101(d)(2), Fed. R. Evid.; *U.S. v. McKenzie,* 678 F.2d 629, 632-33 (5th Cir. 1982). A grand jury may return an indictment based partly or solely on hearsay evidence. *U.S. v. Brown,* 573 F.2d 1274 (5th Cir. 1978); *U.S. v. Newcomb,* 488 F.2d 190 (5th Cir.), *cert. denied,* 417 U.S. 931 (1974); *U.S. v. Hickok,* 481 F.2d 377 (9th Cir. 1973); *Doss v. U.S.,* 431 F.2d 601 (9th Cir. 1970). There is a presumption of regularity that attaches to all grand jury proceedings, and irregularity must be proved by a defendant. *U.S. v. Battista,* 646 F.2d 237 (6th Cir. 1981).

Courts have rejected defense arguments that the government's failure to produce key witnesses before the grand jury and its reliance upon hearsay before the grand jury substantially undermined the policy underlying the Jencks Act, 18 U.S.C. § 3500. *U.S. v. Head,* 586 F.2d 508 (5th Cir. 1978); *U.S. v. Short,* 493 F.2d 1170 (9th Cir.), *cert. denied,* 419 U.S. 1000 (1974). However, the grand jury should not be misled into believing that a witness is basing his testimony on firsthand knowledge when he is not. *U.S. v. Harrington,* 490 F.2d 487 (2d Cir. 1973); *U.S. v. Estepa,* 471 F.2d 1132 (2d Cir. 1972). Use of hearsay testimony when non-hearsay testimony is readily available could invalidate an indictment if the court finds that there is a high probability that had the grand jury heard the eyewitnesses it would not have indicted. *U.S. v. Cruz,* 478 F.2d 408, 410 (5th Cir.), *cert. denied,* 414 U.S. 910 (1973). An indictment may not be based solely on the informal unsworn hearsay testimony of the prosecutor. *U.S. v. Hodge,* 496 F.2d 87 (5th Cir. 1974).

Where there is perjury before the grand jury, the Seventh Circuit holds that where it is discovered before trial, the government may withdraw the indictment and seek a new one, or may request an *in camera* inspection of the grand jury transcripts for a determination whether other sufficient evidence supports the indictment. If there is other sufficient evidence the indictment cannot be challenged on the basis of the perjury. *U.S. v. Udziela,* 671 F.2d 995, 1001 (7th Cir. 1982). In *U.S. v. Basurto,* 497 F.2d 781, 785 (9th Cir. 1974), the Ninth Circuit said that an indictment must be dismissed that is based on partially perjured testimony, which is material, and which the government knew, before jeopardy attached, was perjured. *See also U.S. v. Flaherty,* 668 F.2d 566, 583-85 (1st Cir. 1981).

Because the grand jury determines only probable cause, the prosecutor may be selective in deciding what evidence to present to the grand jury. There is no obligation to present all evidence that might be exculpatory or undermine the credibility of the government's witnesses. *U.S. v. Williams,* 112 S. Ct. 1735 (1992).

The presentation of inaccurate and incomplete summaries of testimony presented to an expired grand jury voids an indictment regardless of the prosecutor's motive. *U.S. v. Mahoney,* 508 F. Supp. 263 (E.D. Pa. 1980). However, a grand jury that returned an indictment charging conspiracy to violate the obscenity statute, 18 U.S.C. § 1462, was not required to view the movie "Deep Throat," which had been seen by a prior grand jury, where a witness read a detailed account of the movie including examples of oral and group sex. *U.S. v. Battista,* 646 F.2d 237 (6th Cir. 1981).

Erroneous grand jury instructions on the law by the prosecutor do not automatically invalidate an otherwise proper indictment. *U.S. v. Wright,* 667 F.2d 793, 796 (9th Cir. 1982). Where there is a claim of prosecutorial misconduct, the indictment will be dismissed only upon a showing of actual prejudice to the defendant. This means that the misconduct must be so overbearing to the will of the grand jury that the indictment is in effect that of the prosecutor rather than the grand jury. *U.S. v. McKenzie,* 678 F.2d 629, 631-32 (5th Cir. 1982).

Rule 12(b)(2) of the Federal Rules of Criminal Procedure requires that arguments regarding the propriety of matters occurring before the grand jury must be raised before trial or they will be deemed to be waived. *U.S. v. Daley,* 564 F.2d 645 (2d Cir. 1977), *cert. denied,* 435

U.S. 933 (1978); *U.S. v. Kaplan,* 554 F.2d 958 (9th Cir.), *cert. denied,* 434 U.S. 956 (1977).

### § 404. — Calling and Questioning of Witnesses and Warnings.

The grand jury's broad authority to subpoena witnesses is considered essential to its task and the Supreme Court has declined to make exceptions to the longstanding principle that "the public has a right to every man's evidence." *Branzburg v. Hayes,* 408 U.S. 665, 668 (1972); *U.S. v. Mandujano,* 425 U.S. 564 (1976). A witness may not refuse to answer questions before a grand jury unless he can assert his fifth amendment privilege or establish that some other common-law privilege applies. *U.S. v. Mandujano,* 425 U.S. at 571. *(See* chapter on Privileges, *infra.)* Even when a grand jury witness asserts his fifth amendment right, a prosecutor may continue the examination by pursuing other lines of inquiry. *U.S. v. Cohen,* 444 F. Supp. 1314 (E.D. Pa. 1978). A witness' claim that he cannot remember may lead to civil contempt if the government can prove by clear and convincing evidence that the claim of memory loss is false. *Matter of Battaglia,* 653 F.2d 419, 422 (9th Cir. 1981).

The grand jury's right to inquire into possible offenses is generally "unrestrained by the technical procedural and evidentiary rules governing the conduct of criminal trials." *U.S. v. R. Enterprises, Inc.,* 111 S. Ct. 722 (1991); *U.S. v. Calandra,* 414 U.S. 338, 343 (1974). The only rule in the Federal Rules of Evidence that applies to grand jury proceedings is Rule 501 (privileges). *See* Rules 101 and 1101(c) and (d), Fed. R. Evid.; *In re Sealed Case,* 676 F.2d 793 (D.C. Cir. 1982). The subpoenaed party has the burden of showing that a privilege applies, but in the Fourth Circuit where the attorney for the target is subpoenaed, the government may be required to make a preliminary showing of relevance. *In re Special Grand Jury No. 81-1,* 676 F.2d 1005, 1009 (4th Cir. 1982).

The standards set forth in *U.S. v. Nixon,* 418 U.S. 683 (1974), for trial subpoenas do not apply to grand jury subpoenas. Nevertheless, the grand jury's investigatory powers are not unlimited and it may not engage in arbitrary fishing expeditions, nor select targets out of malice or intent to harass. *U.S. v. R. Enterprises, Inc., supra.*

A witness may not refuse to respond to a subpoena or refuse to answer questions on the grounds of relevance, *Blair v. U.S.,* 250 U.S. 273 (1919); *Matter of Fula,* 672 F.2d 279, 283 (2d Cir. 1982); *U.S. v. Weinberg,* 439 F.2d 743 (9th Cir. 1971), or because he feels that testifying may result in physical harm, *U.S. v. Gomez,* 553 F.2d 958 (5th Cir. 1977); *Dupuy v. U.S.,* 518 F.2d 1295 (9th Cir. 1975); *U.S. v. Doe,* 478

F.2d 194 (1st Cir. 1973); *In re Kilgo,* 484 F.2d 1215 (4th Cir. 1973); *Latona v. U.S.,* 449 F.2d 121 (9th Cir. 1971). A witness must respond to a grand jury subpoena even if his compliance results in hardship or inconvenience. *U.S. v. Calandra,* 414 U.S. at 345.

The first amendment does not protect a reporter from being called by a grand jury to testify concerning his news sources. *Branzburg v. Hayes, supra.* However, post-*Branzburg* departmental policy requires approval of the Attorney General before a reporter is subpoenaed. The first amendment also does not preclude questioning a grand jury witness concerning his past political associations. *U.S. v. Weinberg, supra.*

A potential defendant may properly be subpoenaed to appear before a grand jury that is investigating his activities. "It is in keeping with the grand jury's historic function as a shield against arbitrary accusations to call before it persons suspected of criminal activity, so that the investigation can be complete." *U.S. v. Mandujano,* 425 U.S. 564, 573 (1976). However, a potential defendant does not have the right to appear before the grand jury. *U.S. v. Smith,* 552 F.2d 257 (8th Cir. 1977); *U.S. v. Gardner,* 516 F.2d 334 (7th Cir.), *cert. denied,* 423 U.S. 861 (1975); *U.S. v. Neidelman,* 356 F. Supp. 979 (S.D.N.Y. 1973). There is no duty of the prosecution to tell a grand jury witness what evidence it may have against him. *U.S. v. Del Toro,* 513 F.2d 656, 664 (2d Cir.), *cert. denied,* 423 U.S. 826 (1975). A defendant who falsely testified and is later charged with perjury cannot claim entrapment because the government used taped conversations between the defendant and an informant to frame its questions and did not advise the defendant that such tapes existed. *U.S. v. Edelson,* 581 F.2d 1290 (7th Cir. 1978), *cert. denied,* 440 U.S. 908 (1979).

A grand jury witness should be given fair opportunity to respond fully to questions and, whenever possible, should not be limited to the "yes" and "no" answers that typify responses to leading questions. *U.S. v. Boberg,* 565 F.2d 1059 (8th Cir. 1977). A perjury conviction that rests on a witness' response to leading questions will be strictly scrutinized for fairness. *Id.* at 1063. Unnecessary, repetitious questioning designed to coax a witness into the commission of perjury or contempt of court is an abuse of the grand jury process. *Bursey v. U.S.,* 466 F.2d 1059 (9th Cir. 1972). In *U.S. v. Bruzgo,* the Third Circuit criticized a prosecutor for threatening a reluctant witness with loss of citizenship and calling her a "thief" and a "racketeer." 373 F.2d 383, 384 (3d Cir. 1967). Gratuitous comments by the prosecutor that the defendants were connected with organized crime have also been condemned. *U.S. v. Serubo,* 604 F.2d 807 (3d Cir. 1979); *U.S. v. Riccobene,* 451 F.2d 586 (3d Cir. 1971). And an indictment has been dismissed where a district court found that the prosecutor misled the potential defendant-witness into believing he could be compelled to answer without explaining his fifth amendment rights and the immunity procedure. *U.S. v. Pepe,* 367 F. Supp. 1365 (D. Conn. 1973).

### § 405. — — Miranda Warnings.

The Supreme Court has not decided whether fifth amendment warnings are constitutionally required for grand jury witnesses. *See U.S. v. Washington,* 431 U.S. 181, 186 (1977). The Court has decided that a grand jury witness' incriminating testimony, if not compelled, is admissible against him in a subsequent prosecution even if he was not told that he was a potential defendant, *Washington, supra;* and, the failure of the prosecution to give full *Miranda* warnings or of the witness to understand them does not require suppression of perjured testimony in a subsequent perjury trial, *U.S. v. Mandujano,* 425 U.S. 564 (1976); *U.S. v. Wong,* 431 U.S. 174 (1977); *U.S. v. D'Auria,* 672 F.2d 1085, 1093 (2d Cir. 1982). Nonetheless, the Justice Department has established an internal policy of advising grand jury witnesses of their fifth amendment rights and of their status as "targets," if that is the case. The Second Circuit has affirmed the suppression of perjured grand jury testimony because a Strike Force attorney failed to warn a witness that he was a putative defendant. That court based its ruling on its supervisory powers rather than on constitutional grounds, observing that it was the uniform practice among federal prosecutors in the Second Circuit to give such warnings. *U.S. v. Jacobs,* 547 F.2d 772 (2d Cir. 1976), *cert. dismissed,* 436 U.S. 931 (1978). While other circuits have not followed the Second, such rulings are possible in view of the Justice Department's announced practice of giving warnings. *See U.S. v. Reed,* 647 F.2d 678 (6th Cir. 1980); *U.S. v. Crocker,* 568 F.2d 1049, 1055 (3d Cir. 1977).

### § 406. — — Exclusionary Rule.

The Supreme Court has declined to extend the fourth amendment's exclusionary rule to grand jury proceedings. Questions based on evidence obtained from an illegal search and seizure do not constitute independent violations of a grand jury witness' fourth amendment rights. *U.S. v. Calandra, supra. Costello v. U.S.,* 350 U.S. 359 (1956), prevents the same sort of issues being raised to invalidate the indictment. In a case involving a confession obtained by torture, the Ninth Circuit has extended the *Calandra* analysis to statements given in violation of the fifth amendment. *In re Weir,* 495 F.2d 879 (9th Cir.), *cert. denied,* 419 U.S. 1038 (1974).

### § 407. — — Questions Based on Illegal Electronic Surveillance.

Questions derived from illegal electronic surveillance, however, are not permissible because of the specific statutory prohibition in the Omnibus Crime Control and Safe Streets Act of 1968 against the use of such evidence, 18 U.S.C. §§ 2510-2520. *Gelbard v. U.S.*, 408 U.S. 41 (1972). *Gelbard* left open the issue of whether a witness who refuses to answer a question because he believes that it was derived from illegal electronic surveillance is entitled to a plenary hearing on the issue. In cases where the legality of court-ordered surveillance is challenged, the Second, Fifth, Seventh, and Ninth Circuits have held that a judge's findings of facial validity after an *in camera* review of electronic surveillance documents is sufficient, and no discovery or further hearing is required. *Matter of Special February 1977 Grand Jury*, 570 F.2d 674 (7th Cir. 1978); *In re Grand Jury Proceedings (Worobyst)*, 522 F.2d 196 (5th Cir. 1975); *Droback v. U.S.*, 509 F.2d 625 (9th Cir. 1974), *cert. denied*, 421 U.S. 964 (1975); *In re Persico*, 491 F.2d 1156 (2d Cir.), *cert. denied*, 419 U.S. 924 (1974). In contrast, the First, Eighth, and District of Columbia Circuits have held that the witness is entitled to inspect the application for the wiretap, the supporting affidavits, the court order, and the affidavit stating the length of the surveillance. If the government interposes a secrecy objection, the court should excise the secret information and then release the documents. *In re Grand Jury Proceedings (Katsouros)*, 613 F.2d 1171 (D.C. Cir. 1979); *Melickian v. U.S.*, 547 F.2d 416 (8th Cir.), *cert. denied*, 430 U.S. 986 (1977); *In re Lochiatto*, 497 F.2d 803 (1st Cir. 1974).

In cases where a witness alleges that illegal electronic surveillance occurs and there is no court order, the necessity for and the specificity of the denial that the government must make depend upon the specificity of the witness' claim. *Matter of Archeluta*, 561 F.2d 1059 (2d Cir. 1977); *In re Millow*, 529 F.2d 770 (2d Cir. 1976); *Matter of Grand Jury Impaneled January 21, 1975 (Freedman)*, 529 F.2d 543 (3d Cir.), *cert. denied*, 425 U.S. 992 (1976); *U.S. v. Tucker*, 526 F.2d 279 (5th Cir.), *cert. denied*, 425 U.S. 958 (1976); *In re Quinn*, 525 F.2d 222 (1st Cir. 1975); *Matter of Grand Jury (Vigil)*, 524 F.2d 209 (10th Cir. 1975), *cert. denied*, 425 U.S. 927 (1976) (this opinion has an appendix that discusses all earlier cases by circuit). A general denial by affidavit of the government attorney is sufficient in response to a general unsubstantiated allegation, *U.S. v. Stevens*, 510 F.2d 1101 (5th Cir. 1975), whereas a hearing might be appropriate where there are particularized allegations, *see Vigil, supra*. A person who is not a witness or a defendant has no standing to allege improper use before a grand jury of evidence derived from illegal electronic surveillance. *In re Vigorito,* 499 F.2d 1351 (2d Cir. 1974).

## § 408. — — After Indictment Returned.

Once an indictment has been returned, it is an abuse of process to call a defendant to testify concerning pending charges or to use the grand jury's subpoena power to gather other evidence for trial. *U.S. v. Doss,* 563 F.2d 265 (6th Cir. 1977); *U.S. v. Fahey,* 510 F.2d 302 (2d Cir. 1974) (held to be harmless error and usable for impeachment); *U.S. v. Fisher,* 455 F.2d 1101 (2d Cir. 1972). However, despite the fact that a prosecution is pending, the government may call witnesses before the grand jury if the primary purpose of calling them is to investigate the possible commission of other offenses, even if the evidence received may also relate to the pending indictment. *U.S. v. Gibbons,* 607 F.2d 1320 (10th Cir. 1979); *In re Grand Jury Proceedings (Pressman),* 586 F.2d 724 (9th Cir. 1978); *U.S. v. Zarattini,* 552 F.2d 753 (7th Cir.), *cert. denied,* 431 U.S. 942 (1977); *U.S. v. Beasley,* 550 F.2d 261 (5th Cir.), *cert. denied,* 434 U.S. 863 (1977); *U.S. v. Woods,* 544 F.2d 242 (6th Cir.), *cert. denied,* 429 U.S. 1062 (1976); *U.S. v. Braasch,* 505 F.2d 139 (7th Cir. 1974), *cert. denied,* 421 U.S. 910 (1975). While ordinarily the party alleging abuse must bear the burden of proving that grand jury process is being used to gather evidence for trial, *Woods, supra,* where the underlying facts sought to be established are the same for both investigations, the burden may shift to the government to demonstrate good faith. *U.S. v. Kovaleski,* 406 F. Supp. 267 (E.D. Mich. 1976). A grand jury should never be used to gather evidence for a civil case, *In re Grand Jury Subpoenas April 1978, Etc.,* 581 F.2d 1103 (4th Cir. 1978), *cert. denied,* 440 U.S. 971 (1979); *FTC v. Atlantic Richfield Co.,* 567 F.2d 96, 104 n.19 (D.C. Cir. 1977); *In re Special March 1974 Grand Jury, Etc.,* 541 F.2d 166 (7th Cir. 1976), *cert. denied,* 430 U.S. 929 (1977); but a witness' fear that evidence may improperly find its way into the hands of governmental agencies for use in future civil litigation is no basis for failure to comply with a subpoena, *Coson v. U.S.,* 533 F.2d 1119 (9th Cir. 1976).

## § 409. — Subpoenas Duces Tecum.

The grand jury has the power to subpoena physical evidence in addition to testimony. It can subpoena voice exemplars, *U.S. v. Dionisio,* 410 U.S. 1 (1973), and handwriting samples, *U.S. v. Mara,* 410 U.S. 19 (1973). The grand jury may provide that such identification evidence be provided outside the presence of the grand jury, even where the subpoenas were issued by the United States Attorney without actual prior grand jury authorization. *U.S. v. Santucci,* 674 F.2d 624, 627 (7th Cir. 1982). It can summon a witness to appear in a lineup, *In re Melvin,* 550 F.2d 674, 677 (1st Cir. 1977); and a district court may order reasonable physical force to compel a defiant grand jury witness to appear in a lineup, *Appeal of Maguire,* 571 F.2d 675 (1st Cir.), *cert. denied,* 436 U.S. 911 (1978). The majority of cases concerning subpoenas duces tecum involve requests by grand juries for documents.

Grand jury subpoenas are governed by Rule 17(c) of the Federal Rules of Criminal Procedure, which provides that a court may quash or modify any subpoena duces tecum if compliance therewith would be unreasonable or oppressive. The party opposing enforcement of the subpoena bears the burden of showing that it is unreasonable or oppressive. *In re Lopreato,* 511 F.2d 1150 (1st Cir. 1975); *In re Grand Jury Proceedings (Schofield I),* 507 F.2d 963 (3d Cir. 1975). What is reasonable depends on the context. *U.S. v. R. Enterprises, Inc.,* 111 S. Ct. 722 (1991). The issue can be raised by the witness filing a motion to quash pursuant to Rule 17(c) or by the witness' refusal to comply, thereby forcing the government to move for enforcement. *(See* Procedures for Enforcement of Subpoenas and Compulsion Orders, this chapter, *infra.)* An order denying a motion to quash is not appealable. *U.S. v. Ryan,* 402 U.S. 530 (1971); *In re Grand Jury Subpoenas, April 1978,* 581 F.2d 1103 (4th Cir. 1978), *cert. denied,* 440 U.S. 971 (1979). However, any court order suppressing evidence during a grand jury investigation is appealable by the government pursuant to 18 U.S.C. § 3731. *In re Grand Jury Investigation,* 599 F.2d 1224 (3d Cir. 1979). A contempt order is appealable. *In re Grand Jury Subpoena, May 1978, At Baltimore,* 596 F.2d 630 (4th Cir. 1979); *In re Grand Jury Investigation, Etc.,* 566 F.2d 1293 (5th Cir.), *cert. denied,* 437 U.S. 905 (1978). Where the district court has permitted a non-witness intervenor to be heard, courts will permit appeal by an intervenor without the necessity of a contempt sentence. *In re Grand Jury Proceedings (Cianfrani),* 563 F.2d 577 (3d Cir. 1977).

The Tenth Circuit has adopted a three-pronged test that has been widely used by district courts for evaluating grand jury subpoenas duces tecum for documents: (1) the material sought must be relevant to the investigation being pursued; (2) the documents sought must be described with reasonable particularity; and (3) the subpoena must be limited to a reasonable period of time. *U.S. v. Gurule,* 437 F.2d 239 (10th Cir.), *cert. denied,* 403 U.S. 904 (1970). The requirement of relevance is not the same test of probative value used at trial; rather, the court should determine whether the records sought have some conceivable relation to a legitimate object of grand jury inquiry. *In re Rabbinical Seminary, Etc.*, 450 F. Supp. 1078 (E.D.N.Y. 1978); *In re Special November 1975 Grand Jury, Etc.*, 433 F. Supp. 1094 (N.D. Ill. 1977); *In re Grand Jury Subpoenas Duces Tecum, Etc.*, 391 F. Supp. 991 (D.R.I. 1975). In deciding what constitutes "reasonable particularity," courts are cognizant of the limitations on a grand jury's ability to know precisely how a witness' books and records are kept; thus, a subpoena calling for the entire contents of three file cabinets could meet the requirement of reasonable particularity because the witness knew what was wanted. *In re Horowitz*, 482 F.2d 72 (2d Cir. 1973). Designation of records by general terms used in the accounting and financial fields is sufficiently definite and reasonable. *Matter of Witness Before the Grand Jury*, 546 F.2d 825 (9th Cir. 1976). The statute of limitations may be used as a guide to determine what constitutes a reasonable time period; however, the statute of limitations is not necessarily determinative because time-barred facts might be relevant to issues such as intent. *Coson v. U.S.*, 533 F.2d 1119 (9th Cir. 1976).

Since the cost of compliance normally falls on the party being subpoenaed, it is one of the factors that a court may consider in determining whether a subpoena is unreasonable or oppressive under Rule 17(c). Cost should be measured by what it costs to provide original documents since copying is generally undertaken by the witness for his own convenience. *In re Grand Jury No. 76-3 (MIA) Subpoena Duces Tecum*, 555 F.2d 1306 (5th Cir. 1977). *See also In re Grand Jury Subpoena Duces Tecum, Etc.*, 436 F. Supp. 46 (D. Md. 1977). Financial institutions may be entitled to reimbursement for the costs associated with subpoena compliance under the Right to Financial Privacy Act, 12 U.S.C. § 3415, depending upon the kinds of documents subpoenaed.

The fact that successive grand juries subpoena the same documents does not demonstrate an abuse of process. *Robert Hawthorne, Inc. v. Director of Internal Revenue*, 406 F. Supp. 1098 (E.D. Pa. 1976); *U.S. v. Culver*, 224 F. Supp. 419 (D. Md. 1963). *See U.S. v. Thompson*, 251 U.S. 407 (1920).

Alteration or destruction of records requested by an investigating agency and sought by grand jury subpoena duces tecum served before any tampering occurred constitutes obstruction of justice. *U.S. v. Faudman*, 640 F.2d 20 (6th Cir. 1981).

Motions to quash grand jury subpoenas frequently rely on the case of *Hale v. Henkel*, 201 U.S. 43 (1906), to support the proposition that an overly broad grand jury subpoena constitutes a forbidden search in violation of the fourth amendment. Although not explicitly overruled, that decision has been substantially undermined by a subsequent Supreme Court decision. *In re Horowitz,* 482 F.2d 72 (2d Cir. 1973). In *U.S. v. Dionisio,* 410 U.S. at 9, the Supreme Court held that "a subpoena to appear before a grand jury is not a 'seizure' in the Fourth Amendment sense, even though that summons may be inconvenient or burdensome."

The records of a state are not immune from grand jury process because of any constitutional considerations of state sovereignty. *In re Special April 1977 Grand Jury (Scott),* 581 F.2d 589 (7th Cir. 1978), *cert. denied,* 439 U.S. 1046 (1978). If subpoenaed records do not bear on protected legislative acts, the federal common-law legislative privilege or state constitutional speech and debate clauses do not protect state senators and other legislative officials from subpoenas for their records. *In re Grand Jury Proceedings (Cianfrani),* 563 F.2d 577 (3d Cir. 1977).

Recognizing that direct delivery of a mass of documents to 23 laymen would be "unproductive if not chaotic," courts have upheld the use of subpoenas, provided that they could be satisfied by delivery of the described documents to agents of the IRS or FBI. *Robert Hawthorne, Inc. v. Director of Internal Revenue,* 406 F. Supp. at 1118. Court orders providing that records may be delivered to investigative agents are proper. *U.S. v. Universal Manufacturing Co.,* 525 F.2d 808 (8th Cir. 1975). Such arrangements are not the same as the "forthwith subpoenas" that were severely criticized by the Sixth Circuit in *Consumer Credit Insurance Agency, Inc. v. U.S.,* 599 F.2d 770 (6th Cir. 1979), *cert. denied,* 445 U.S. 903 (1980), and the Third Circuit in *U.S. v. Hilton,* 534 F.2d 556 (3d Cir. 1976), *cert. denied,* 429 U.S. 828 (1976), as improper attempts to circumvent the requirements of the fourth amendment for obtaining search warrants. Subpoenas duces tecum should only direct compliance on dates when the grand jury is sitting. *See U.S. v. Hilton, supra.*

## § 410. Secrecy of Proceedings and Disclosure.

The Supreme Court has consistently held that the proper functioning of the grand jury system depends upon maintaining the secrecy of grand jury proceedings. In *Douglas Oil Company of California v. Petrol Stops, Etc.,* 411 U.S. 211, 219 (1979), the Court reiterated the distinct interests that are served by this policy.

> First, if preindictment proceedings were made public, many prospective witnesses would be hesitant to come forward voluntarily, knowing that those against whom they testify would be aware of that testimony. Moreover, witnesses who appeared before the grand jury would be less likely to testify fully and frankly, as they

would be open to retribution as well as to inducements. There also would be the risk that those about to be indicted would flee, or would try to influence individual grand jurors to vote against indictment. Finally, by preserving the secrecy of the proceedings, we assure that persons who are accused but exonerated by the grand jury will not be held up to public ridicule.

Rule 6(e)(2) of the Federal Rules of Criminal Procedure imposes an obligation to maintain the secrecy of matters occurring before the grand jury upon grand jurors, interpreters, stenographers, operators of recording devices, typists who transcribe testimony, attorneys for the government, and government personnel authorized to assist attorneys for the government. Rule 6(e) further defines six limited exceptions to the secrecy requirement: (1) disclosure to an attorney for the government in the performance of such attorney's duty; (2) disclosure to such government personnel as an attorney for the government deems necessary to assist such attorney in the enforcement of federal criminal law; (3) disclosure by a court preliminary to or in connection with a judicial proceeding; and (4) disclosure to a defendant who can demonstrate that matters occurring before the grand jury may be grounds for dismissing the indictment; (5) disclosure by an attorney for the government to another federal grand jury; and (6) when permitted by the court at the request of an attorney for the government to a state official for the purpose of enforcing a violation of state law.

Hearings affecting a grand jury proceeding shall be closed; and records, orders and subpoenas relating to grand jury proceedings shall be sealed to the extent necessary to prevent disclosure of matters occurring before a grand jury. Rule 6(e)(5) and (6), Fed. R. Crim. P.

However, certain "ministerial" records of the grand jury that relate to the impanelling, extension, and operation of the grand jury may be required to be disclosed where there is no violation of Rule 6(e) or the purposes for secrecy. *In re Special Grand Jury (for Anchorage, Alaska)*, 674 F.2d 778, 781 (9th Cir. 1982).

A denial of a defendant's motion to dismiss an indictment because of a claimed violation of the grand jury secrecy rule is not immediately appealable. *Midland Asphalt v. U.S.*, 489 U.S. 794 (1989).

## §411. — Matters Occurring Before Grand Jury.

The prohibition against disclosure of "matters occurring before the grand jury" was not intended to prohibit disclosure of all information presented to a grand jury. "The aim of the rule is to prevent disclosure of the way in which information was presented to the grand jury, the specific questions and inquiries of the grand jury, the deliberations and

125

vote of the grand jury, the targets upon which the grand jury's suspicion focuses, and specific details of what took place before the grand jury." *In re Grand Jury Investigation of Ven-Fuel*, 441 F. Supp. 1299, 1302-03 (M.D. Fla. 1977).

Transcripts of the testimony of witnesses and statements made before the grand jury are clearly "matters occurring before the grand jury" and thus cannot be released, unless pursuant to one of the exceptions set forth in Rule 6(e)(3) of the Federal Rules of Criminal Procedure. The same is true of internal government memoranda reflecting what transpired before the grand jury. *In re Grand Jury Proceedings*, 613 F.2d 501, 505-06 (5th Cir. 1980); *U.S. Industries, Inc. v. U.S. District Court*, 345 F.2d 18 (9th Cir.), *cert. denied*, 382 U.S. 814 (1965). As a general rule, however, physical evidence, such as a document, does not become secret merely because it has been presented to a grand jury if it was created for purposes other than the grand jury investigation, and its disclosure "does not constitute disclosure of matters occurring before the grand jury," that is, the documents are sought for the information they contain, rather than to reveal the direction or strategy of the grand jury investigation. *SEC v. Dresser Industries, Inc.*, 628 F.2d 1368, 1382-83, (D.C. Cir. 1980), *cert. denied*, 444 U.S. 993 (1981); *U.S. v. Stanford*, 589 F.2d 285, 291 (7th Cir. 1978), *cert. denied*, 440 U.S. 983 (1979). *Stanford* involved the use of subpoenaed documents by FBI agents during interviews of defendants, but courts have similarly interpreted the phrase where private parties sought documents, subpoenaed by a grand jury, for use in civil litigation. *See also U.S. v. Interstate Dress Carriers, Inc.*, 280 F.2d 52 (2d Cir. 1960); *U.S. v. Saks & Co.*, 426 F. Supp. 812 (S.D.N.Y. 1976); *Capital Indemnity Corp. v. First Minnesota Construction Co.*, 405 F. Supp. 929 (D. Mass. 1975); *Davis v. Romney*, 55 F.R.D. 337 (E.D. Pa. 1972); *Commonwealth Edison Co. v. Allis-Chalmers Manufacturing Co.*, 211 F. Supp. 729 (N.D. Ill. 1962). A court order must be obtained to disclose documents or physical evidence subpoenaed by a grand jury if some form of privilege, such as the right of the owner to maintain the confidentiality of his records, would otherwise shield them from inspection. *See U.S. v. RMI Co.*, 599 F.2d 1183 (3d Cir. 1979), that held that third parties from whom documents were subpoenaed have a right to intervene at the stage of a Rule 16 discovery motion. *See also In re Grand Jury Investigation (General Motors Corporation)*, 210 F. Supp. 904 (S.D.N.Y. 1962). Situations may also arise where disclosing documents may in fact reveal what transpired before the grand jury. An example would be a general request for "all documents collected or received in connection with the investigation of antitrust violations." *In re Grand Jury Investigation of Ven-*

*Fuel,* 441 F. Supp. 1299, 1303 (M.D. Fla. 1977). *See also Corona Construction Co. v. Ampress Brick Co.,* 376 F. Supp. 598 (N.D. Ill. 1974).

## § 412. — Attorney for the Government.

The phrase "attorney for the government" in Rule 6(e)(3)(A)(i), Fed. R. Crim. P. is limited by Rule 54(c) to "the Attorney General, an authorized assistant of the Attorney General, a United States Attorney, an authorized assistant of the United States Attorney." It encompasses even Civil Division attorneys of the Justice Department so long as such an attorney has been detailed to conduct a criminal grand jury investigation and disclosure relates to his prosecutorial duties. *U.S. v. Sells Engineering, Inc.,* 463 U.S. 418 (1983). Furthermore, an attorney who has participated in a grand jury investigation may handle a subsequent civil proceeding involving the same matters without a court order authorizing disclosure for the reason that there is no disclosure of facts that he already knows from his grand jury experience. *U.S. v. John Doe, Inc., I,* 481 U.S. 102 (1987); *U.S. v. Archer-Daniels-Midland Co.,* 785 F.2d 206 (8th Cir. 1986), *cert. denied,* 107 S. Ct. 1952 (1987). The Rule does not include attorneys for state and county government. *In re Grand Jury Matter (Catania),* 682 F.2d 61 (3d Cir. 1982); *In re Grand Jury Investigation of Cuisinarts, Inc.,* 665 F.2d 24, 30-36 (2d Cir. 1981); *In re Holvochka,* 317 F.2d 834 (7th Cir. 1963), or attorneys for other federal government agencies, *U.S. v. Bater,* 627 F.2d 349, 351 (D.C. Cir. 1980).

## § 413. — Other Government Personnel.

Attorneys for the government may disclose grand jury material to such government personnel including personnel of a state or state subdivision whom the attorneys for the government deem necessary to assist them in said attorneys' duty to enforce federal criminal law. Rule 6(e)(3)(A)(ii), Fed. R. Crim. P. The attorney must disclose to the court a list of the persons to whom such disclosure has been made. Rule 6(e)(3)(B), Fed. R. Crim. P. There is no requirement that the assistance offered by other government personnel be technical in nature. *In re Perlin,* 589 F.2d 260 (7th Cir. 1978). The disclosure notice need not be filed prior to disclosure, though the legislative history recommends doing so. *In re Grand Jury Proceedings (Larry Smith),* 579 F.2d 836 (3d Cir. 1978). There is no requirement that a witness be given a copy of the government's disclosure notice before he can be required to comply with a subpoena. *Id.* at 840.

A retired IRS agent, even though he is not a permanent civil service employee, may be included within the term "government personnel" to whom disclosure is permitted. *U.S. v. Lartey,* 716 F.2d 955 (2d Cir. 1983).

### § 414. — Preliminary to or in Connection With Judicial Proceedings.

Courts may order disclosure "preliminary to or in connection with judicial proceedings." Rule 6(e)(3)(C)(i), Fed. R. Crim. P. The procedures for petitioning for disclosure under this section are set forth in Rule 6(e)(3)(D), Fed. R. Crim. P. Grand jury proceedings, *U.S. v. Stanford,* 589 F.2d 285 (7th Cir.), *cert. denied,* 440 U.S. 983 (1978), impeachment hearings, *Haldeman v. Sirica,* 501 F.2d 714 (D.C. Cir. 1974), bar association grievance committee hearings, *U.S. v. Sobotka,* 623 F.2d 764 (2d Cir. 1980), and police disciplinary hearings, *Special February Grand Jury v. Conlisk,* 490 F.2d 894 (7th Cir. 1973); *In re Grand Jury Transcripts,* 309 F. Supp. 1050 (S.D. Ohio 1970), have all been held to be "preliminary to or in connection with judicial proceedings." *But see U.S. v. Tager,* 638 F.2d 167 (10th Cir. 1980); *Bradley v. Fairfax,* 634 F.2d 1126 (8th Cir. 1980); *In re April 1977 Grand Jury Proceedings,* 506 F. Supp. 1174 (E.D. Mich. 1981). There is no first amendment right of the press to grand jury testimony not made public at trial. *U.S. v. Gurney,* 558 F.2d 1202 (5th Cir. 1977), *cert. denied,* 435 U.S. 968 (1978). A defendant seeking pretrial disclosure of grand jury transcripts other than those he can obtain under the Jencks Act, 18 U.S.C. § 3500, must demonstrate a particularized need. *Dennis v. U.S.,* 384 U.S. 855, 870 (1966). In *Douglas Oil Co. v. Petrol Stops, Inc.,* 441 U.S. 211, 221 (1979), the Supreme Court restated its earlier holding in *U.S. v. Proctor and Gamble Co.,* 356 U.S. 677 (1958), and held that

> a private party seeking to obtain grand jury transcripts must demonstrate that "without the transcript a defense would be greatly prejudiced or that without reference to it an injustice would be done." 356 U.S. at 682. Moreover, the Court required that the showing of need for the transcripts be made "with particularity" so that "the secrecy of the proceedings [may] be lifted discreetly and limitedly." *Id.,* at 683.

The Supreme Court, in denying disclosure in *Douglas Oil, supra,* held that the party seeking disclosure bears the burden of demonstrating that the public interest in disclosure outweighs the interest in secrecy, and describes the procedure to be followed when private plaintiffs who sue in one district seek to discover transcripts of grand jury proceedings that occurred in another district.

More than a general need for discovery must be shown to tip the balance in favor of lifting the veil of secrecy, and courts also consider such factors as whether the grand jury investigation is ongoing and whether there is a possibility that disclosure might deter future witnesses from freely coming forward to testify. *U.S. v. Sells Engineering, Inc.*, 463 U.S. 418 (1983); *Douglas Oil Co. v. Petrol Stops, Inc., supra; U.S. v. Proctor & Gamble Co.*, 356 U.S. 677 (1958); *Illinois v. Sarbaugh*, 552 F.2d 768 (7th Cir.), *cert. denied*, 424 U.S. 889 (1977); *Texas v. U.S. Steel Corp.*, 546 F.2d 626 (5th Cir.), *cert. denied*, 434 U.S. 889 (1977); *U.S. Industries, Inc. v. U.S. District Court*, 345 F.2d 18 (9th Cir.), *cert. denied*, 382 U.S. 814 (1965); *SEC v. National Student Marketing Corporation*, 430 F. Supp. 639 (D.D.C. 1977). The standard for reviewing orders granting or denying disclosure is abuse of discretion. *Douglas Oil, supra.* Unsubstantiated assertions of impropriety occurring before the grand jury do not establish particularized need. *U.S. v. Migely*, 596 F.2d 511 (1st Cir.), *cert. denied*, 442 U.S. 943 (1979); *U.S. v. Edelson*, 581 F.2d 1290 (7th Cir.), *cert. denied*, 440 U.S. 908 (1978); *U.S. v. Kim*, 577 F.2d 473 (9th Cir. 1978); *U.S. v. Wallace*, 528 F.2d 863 (4th Cir. 1976); *U.S. v. Tucker*, 526 F.2d 279 (5th Cir.), *cert. denied*, 425 U.S. 958 (1976). A general claim that the grand jury transcripts would reveal exculpatory evidence does not establish particularized need. *U.S. v. Short*, 671 F.2d 178, 186 (6th Cir. 1982); nor does the desire to cross-examine effectively. *In re Federal Grand Jury Proceedings*, 760 F.2d 436 (2d Cir. 1985). The Freedom of Information Act, 5 U.S.C. § 552, does not create a right to obtain grand jury transcripts. *Thomas v. U.S.*, 597 F.2d 656 (8th Cir. 1979). However, *in camera* inspection may also be appropriate. *See Star of Wisconsin v. Schaffer*, 565 F.2d 961 (7th Cir. 1977), which held that a grand jury transcript could be released to a state court judge with suitable instructions to release it to counsel for a state defendant if it developed that grand jury minutes might be exculpatory. Disclosure in habeas corpus actions is also governed by the particularized need test. *DeVincent v. U.S.*, 602 F.2d 1006 (1st Cir. 1979), *cert. denied*, 449 U.S. 1038 (1981). The requirement of a showing of particularized need is required in antitrust cases where disclosure requests made under the Clayton Act, 15 U.S.C. § 15f(b), are received. *Illinois v. Abbott & Associates, Inc.*, 460 U.S. 557 (1983).

## §415. — Disclosure by or to Witnesses.

Rule 6(e) does not impose a secrecy obligation on witnesses, *In re Investigation Before April 1975 Grand Jury*, 531 F.2d 600 (D.C. Cir. 1976); and it is improper for a prosecutor to instruct a witness that he must keep his knowledge of the proceedings confidential, *U.S. v. Radetsky*, 535 F.2d 556, 569 nn.15-16 (10th Cir.), *cert. denied*, 429 U.S. 820 (1976). In fact, "(n)o obligation of secrecy may be imposed on any

person except in accordance with this rule." Rule 6(e)(2), Fed. R. Crim.
P.

However, a witness has no general right to a transcript of his testimony. *In re Bianchi,* 542 F.2d 98 (1st Cir. 1976); *Bast v. U.S.,* 542 F.2d 893 (4th Cir. 1976). This rule has been applied even where a witness asserts a need for a transcript to decide whether to recant his testimony to avoid perjury charges, but refuses to verify his petition at the request of the court. *U.S. v. Clavey,* 565 F.2d 111 (7th Cir.), *cert. denied,* 439 U.S. 954 (1978).

Reasoning that a witness is aware of his own testimony, courts have held that permitting a witness to review a transcript of his own testimony before trial is not a prohibited disclosure. *U.S. v. Heinze,* 361 F. Supp. 46, 57 (D. Del. 1973). It is improper, however, to disclose the grand jury testimony of one witness to another witness. *U.S. v. Bazzano,* 570 F.2d 1120, 1124-26 (3d Cir. 1977), *cert. denied,* 436 U.S. 917 (1978). *Bazzano* distinguishes prohibited verbatim disclosure from the acceptable practice in which a prosecutor states in general terms the evidence which other witnesses may give. 570 F.2d at 1125.

### § 416. — For Use in Government Civil Actions.

Disclosure of grand jury material to agency attorneys or other government personnel for use in civil actions requires a court order based upon a showing of particularized need. *U.S. v. Sells Engineering, Inc.,* 463 U.S. 418 (1983). Particularized need for disclosure of grand jury materials to previously uninvolved attorneys for use in possible civil actions include consultation with Civil Division attorneys and the relevant United States attorney in order to secure "efficient, effective and even-handed enforcement of federal statutes...." *U.S. v. John Doe, Inc. I,* 107 S. Ct. 1656, 1663 (1987).

The release to the IRS of grand jury information for the purpose of conducting a civil tax audit is not permitted as a disclosure preliminary to a judicial proceeding. *U.S. v. Baggot,* 463 U.S. 476 (1983).

### § 417. — Sealed Indictments.

Rule 6(e)(4) which provides that an indictment may be sealed until the defendant is in custody or has been released pending trial does not restrict the sealing of indictments for these reasons only. Furthermore, so long as the indictment is returned by the grand jury within the statute of limitations period, the indictment may be unsealed after the statute of limitations has passed. U.S. v. Shell, 961 F.2d 138 (9th Cir. 1992); *U.S. v. Southland Corp.,* 760 F.2d 1366 (2d Cir.), *cert. denied,* 106 S. Ct. 82 (1985).

## §418. Motions Challenging Multiple Representation of Witnesses.

A district court has jurisdiction to discipline an attorney whose unethical conduct relates to a grand jury proceeding within that court's control. *U.S. v. Gopman,* 531 F.2d 262, 266 (5th Cir. 1976). When it appears that a conflict of interest exists on the part of an attorney representing multiple grand jury witnesses, the prosecutor may ask the court to disqualify the attorney from representing more than one witness or category of witnesses. Before making such a motion, the prosecutor should be prepared to demonstrate that an actual conflict (as opposed to a potential conflict) exists and that the actions of witnesses would have been different, but for the conflict. *Matter of Investigative Grand Jury Proceedings,* 480 F. Supp. 162 (N.D. Ohio 1979), *appeal dismissed,* 621 F.2d 813 (6th Cir. 1980), *cert. denied,* 449 U.S. 1124 (1981); *In re Special Grand Jury,* 480 F. Supp. 174 (E.D. Wis. 1979).

An actual conflict exists when an attorney represents an organizational client, such as a labor union, that would have an interest in making full disclosure, and individual witnesses who have an interest in resisting disclosure. *Gopman, supra.* An actual conflict also exists where one attorney represents an immunized witness and a target witness, because it would be in the immunized witness' interest to make full disclosure, *Matter of Grand Jury Proceedings,* 428 F. Supp. 273 (E.D. Mich. 1976), or where the attorney himself is a target of the investigation or a defendant in a related case, *U.S. v. Clarkson,* 567 F.2d 270 (4th Cir. 1977) (contempt proceeding against an attorney who continued representation); *In re Investigation Before February 1977 Lynchburg Grand Jury,* 563 F.2d 652 (4th Cir. 1977). In such situations, a witness cannot waive the right to conflict-free representation because of the competing public interest in the effective functioning of the grand jury. *In re Grand Jury Investigation,* 436 F. Supp. 818 (W.D. Pa. 1977).

Because of the importance attached to the right to counsel of one's choosing, courts are reluctant to disqualify counsel where only a potential for conflict can be shown. Such a situation exists where several witnesses who are jointly represented all claim their fifth amendment privilege or experience a failure of recollection, but where none has been immunized. *In re Taylor,* 567 F.2d 1183 (2d Cir. 1977); *Matter of Grand Jury Empaneled January 21, 1975 (Curran),* 536 F.2d 1009 (3d Cir. 1976); *In re Investigation Before April 1975 Grand Jury,* 531 F.2d 600 (D.C. Cir. 1976); *In re Grand Jury,* 446 F. Supp. 1132 (N.D. Tex. 1978).

The Seventh Circuit has held that the government need not show an actual conflict but only a grave danger of conflict. However, in the same case, the court ruled that the government must do more than show that some jointly represented witnesses have been immunized while others have not, it must further demonstrate that the immunized witnesses could in fact provide information incriminating to the attorney's other clients. *Matter of Special February 1977 Grand Jury,* 581 F.2d 1262 (7th Cir. 1978).

In *Cuyler v. Sullivan,* 446 U.S. 335 (1980), the U.S. Supreme Court considered multiple representation and held that unless and until a convicted defendant established that his attorney actually and actively represented conflicting interests, no constitutional predicate for a claim of ineffective and inefficient assistance of counsel exists. The Court further ruled that, absent special circumstances, trial courts are free to assume that multiple representation entails no conflict of interest and that two or more defendants represented by the same lawyer knowingly accept the risk that a conflict of interest may exist.

### § 419. Immunity.

The Organized Crime Control Act of 1970 added §§ 6001-6005 to Title 18 of the U.S. Code, creating a single comprehensive provision to govern immunity grants in judicial, administrative, and congressional proceedings, and amending or repealing all prior immunity provisions. The immunity granted under this provision is that "no testimony or other information compelled under the order (or any information directly or indirectly derived from such testimony or other information) may be used against the witness in any criminal case...." 18 U.S.C. § 6002.

The act was designed to reflect the "use" and "derivative use" immunity concept of *Murphy v. Waterfront Commission,* 378 U.S. 52 (1964), rather than the "transactional" immunity concept of *Counselman v. Hitchock,* 142 U.S. 547 (1892). This statutory immunity is intended to be as broad as, but no broader than, the privilege against self-incrimination. In *Kastigar v. U.S.,* 406 U.S. 441, 462 (1972), the Supreme Court held that this limited grant of immunity by which testimony is compelled under threat of imprisonment is constitutional:

> We conclude that the immunity provided by 18 U.S.C. § 6002 leaves the witness and the prosecutorial authorities in substantially the same position as if the witness had claimed the Fifth Amendment privilege. The immunity therefore is coextensive with the privilege and suffices to supplant it.

In addition to granting only use and derivative use immunity, these provisions differ from prior immunity statutes in three ways: (1) the immunity may be granted without regard to the particular federal violation at issue; (2) the witness must claim his privilege; and (3) use of the immunity provisions must be approved in advance by the Attorney General or certain other designated persons.

Before application to the court, the United States Attorney must make a judgment that the testimony or information sought may be necessary and in the public interest and that the witness has refused or is likely to refuse to testify. 18 U.S.C. § 6003(b). Within these parameters, the choice of who should receive immunity is extremely broad. Under the act, even the target of an investigation who has been arrested and charged with a crime the grand jury is investigating may be compelled to respond to questions concerning that very crime. *Goldberg v. U.S.*, 472 F.2d 513 (2d Cir. 1973). The decision to grant or not to grant immunity is essentially an executive function.

The court may not withhold the order granting immunity if the factual prerequisites are met. *U.S. v. Lenz*, 616 F.2d 960, 963 (6th Cir. 1980), *cert. denied*, 447 U.S. 129 (1981); *Ryan v. Commissioner*, 568 F.2d 531 (7th Cir. 1977), *cert. denied*, 439 U.S. 820 (1978); *U.S. v. Vancier*, 515 F.2d 1378 (2d Cir. 1975), *cert. denied*, 423 U.S. 857 (1975); 1970 U.S. Code Cong. and Ad. News 4018.

Witnesses who are granted immunity are not entitled, under the due process clause, to notice and hearing on an immunity request. *U.S. v. Berger*, 657 F.2d 88 (6th Cir. 1981); *Ryan v. Commissioner, supra.* The immunity authorized by the statute is not self-executing; the witness may properly invoke his privilege against self-incrimination until there has been an application to a court, a judicial grant of immunity, an accompanying order to testify, and communication of that order to the witness. *U.S. v. DiMauro*, 441 F.2d 428 (8th Cir. 1971). A second immunity order is not required when a witness who was called to testify and held in contempt for his refusal to testify before one grand jury is recalled before a second grand jury. *In re Weir*, 520 F.2d 662 (9th Cir. 1975).

Once the witness has been granted immunity, he may not refuse to testify on the ground of the privilege against self-incrimination. Such refusal may be followed by contempt and a sentence. However, a witness may not be held in contempt if the body or court before which he testified clearly led him to believe he might still claim the privilege. *Raley v. Ohio*, 360 U.S. 423 (1959).

## § 420. — Prosecution for Perjury.

Even after a witness has been granted "derivative use" immunity, he may still be prosecuted for crimes about which he has testified. Such prosecutions, however, face two hurdles. First, because it is the policy of the Department of Justice to avoid future prosecutions of witnesses for offenses disclosed under a grant of immunity, any such prosecution must be authorized in writing and personally signed by the Attorney General. Second, the immunity prohibits the prosecution from using the compelled testimony in any respect. The testimony therefore may not be used either for investigative leads or to focus investigation on the witness. Once the defendant establishes that he has testified under a grant of immunity to matters related to the federal prosecution, the government has an affirmative duty to prove that the evidence it proposes to use is derived from a legitimate source wholly independent of the compelled testimony. *Kastigar v. U.S.*, 406 U.S. 441, 453, 460 (1972). That is, the government cannot satisfy its burden merely by denying that immunized testimony was used; it must affirmatively prove an independent source of evidence. *U.S. v. Nemes*, 555 F.2d 51 (2d Cir. 1977).

Where immunity is conferred on a potential defendant, the government has been strongly advised to make a written certification, before the testimony, stating what evidence it already has. *Goldberg v. U.S.*, 472 F.2d 513, 516 n.5 (2d Cir. 1973). If testimony relevant to the charges is compelled from a witness before a grand jury, and the government then seeks his indictment, it may be appropriate to present the case to a different grand jury. *Id.* at 516.

In the view of some courts that have adopted a highly attenuated notion of "taint" in connection with use immunity statutes even these procedures may be insufficient. *U.S. v. McDaniel*, 482 F.2d 305, 311 (8th Cir. 1973); *U.S. v. Dornau*, 359 F. Supp. 684 (S.D.N.Y. 1973), *rev'd on other grounds*, 491 F.2d 473 (2d Cir.), *cert. denied*, 419 U.S. 872 (1974). *But see U.S. v. Bianco*, 534 F.2d 501, 511 n.14 (2d Cir.), *cert. denied*, 429 U.S. 822 (1976).

The use immunity statute applies only to past offenses. Specifically excepted by the statute are "a prosecution for perjury, giving a false statement, or otherwise failing to comply with the order." 18 U.S.C. § 6002. These exceptions were considered unnecessary by the drafters, *see Glickstein v. U.S.*, 222 U.S. 139 (1911), but were included out of caution, 1970 U.S. Code Cong. & Ad. News 4018. The grant of immunity covers only truthful testimony. It does not protect the witness against the subsequent use by the government of falsehoods or willful evasion in his immunized testimony. *U.S. v. Tramunti*, 500 F.2d 1334

(2d Cir.), *cert. denied,* 419 U.S. 1079 (1974). The fifth amendment clause itself would not protect a witness' refusal to answer questions which would incriminate him in the future on crimes about to be committed. *See U.S. v. Freed,* 401 U.S. 601, 606-07 (1971).

In *New Jersey v. Portash,* 440 U.S. 450 (1979), the Supreme Court ruled that testimony compelled pursuant to a grant of use immunity could not be used to impeach a defendant in a later trial. In *U.S. v. Apfelbaum,* 445 U.S. 115 (1980), the Supreme Court held that the prosecution may use all relevant portions of an immunized witness' testimony in a subsequent perjury prosecution, and that the evidence should not be limited to those portions of the witness' testimony that constitute the *corpus delicti* or core of the false statement offense. *See also U.S. v. Frumento,* 552 F.2d 534 (3d Cir. 1977) *(en banc); U.S. v. Hockenberry,* 474 F.2d 247 (3d Cir. 1973). Truthful immunized testimony cannot be used to prove earlier or later perjury. *U.S. v. Berardelli,* 565 F.2d 24 (2d Cir. 1977); *U.S. v. Housand,* 550 F.2d 818 (2d Cir.), *cert. denied,* 431 U.S. 970 (1977).

### § 421. — Other Sovereigns.

The requirement that every sovereign, state or federal, recognize immunity granted by another sovereign protects a witness from use of immunized testimony in a subsequent state prosecution. *In re Bianchi,* 542 F.2d 98 (1st Cir. 1976); *U.S. v. Watkins,* 505 F.2d 545 (7th Cir. 1974). Because Rule 6(e) strictly limits disclosure of grand jury proceedings, a witness cannot refuse to testify because he fears prosecution by the authorities of foreign countries. *In re Grand Jury Proceedings (Postal),* 559 F.2d 234 (5th Cir. 1977), *cert. denied,* 434 U.S. 1062 (1978); *In re Parker,* 411 F.2d 1067 (10th Cir. 1969), *vacated as moot,* 397 U.S. 96 (1970). However, the Second Circuit has specifically not decided the question of whether, when immunity is granted, the fifth amendment protects the witness against a disclosure that would expose him to a "substantial risk of foreign prosecution." The case involved a witness whose fear of foreign prosecution was "remote and speculative, rather than real, reasonable, or substantial." *In re Grand Jury Subpoena of Flanagan,* 691 F.2d 116, 121-22 (2d Cir. 1982).

### § 422. — Use in Civil Proceedings.

Because the fifth amendment privilege extends only to use in criminal proceedings, compelled testimony can be used in subsequent civil proceedings. *Ryan v. Commissioner,* 568 F.2d 531 (7th Cir. 1977), *cert. denied,* 439 U.S. 820 (1978); *In re Grand Jury Proceedings,* 443 F.

Supp. 1273 (D.S.D. 1978). Immunized testimony may be used in subsequent state bar disciplinary proceedings. *In re Daley,* 549 F.2d 469 (7th Cir.), *cert. denied,* 434 U.S. 829 (1977). It may also be used in license revocation hearings. *Childs v. Schlitz,* 556 F.2d 1178 (4th Cir. 1977).

Although specifically immunized testimony may be used in subsequent civil actions, a civil deposition deponent may not be compelled over a valid assertion of his fifth amendment privilege to repeat verbatim or closely track his prior immunized testimony. Such testimony is from the witness' current independent memory, and as such is a new "source" of information to a prosecutor. If the prior grant of immunity extended to the deposition testimony, it would in effect provide the deponent with transactional immunity on matters about which he had previously testified under use immunity. Furthermore, requiring the testimony would impose risks on the deponent as the court cannot predict at the time of the civil deposition whether the court in a subsequent criminal prosecution will agree that such civil deposition whether the court in a subsequent criminal prosecution will agree that such civil testimony was immunized. *Pillsbury v. Conboy,* 103 S. Ct. 608 (1983).

## § 423. — Immunity for Defense Witnesses.

Neither the courts nor defense counsel have a legal or constitutional right to use the immunity statute to compel the testimony of defense witnesses. *U.S. v. Chagra,* 669 F.2d 241, 261 (5th Cir. 1982); *U.S. v. Heldt,* 668 F.2d 1238, 1281-83 (D.C. Cir. 1981), *cert. denied,* 102 S. Ct. 1971 (1982); *U.S. v. Lenz,* 616 F.2d 960, 962 (6th Cir. 1980), *cert. denied,* 447 U.S. 129 (1981); *U.S. v. Herman,* 589 F.2d 1191, 1200 (3d Cir. 1978), *cert. denied,* 441 U.S. 913 (1979); *U.S. v. Alessio,* 528 F.2d 1079 (9th Cir.), *cert. denied,* 426 U.S. 948 (1976); *U.S. v. Allstate Mortgage Corporation,* 507 F.2d 492 (7th Cir.), *cert. denied,* 421 U.S. 999 (1974); *In re Kilgo,* 484 F.2d 1215 (4th Cir. 1973). Likewise, the compulsion clause of the sixth amendment may not be used as a basis for defense witness immunity. *U.S. v. Chagra, supra.*

A court has no authority to grant nonstatutory use immunity to a witness even where the Assistant U.S. Attorney says that his testimony will not subsequently be used against him. This is not coextensive with the fifth amendment privilege. *U.S. v. D'Apice,* 664 F.2d 75 (5th Cir. 1981).

## § 424. Procedures for Enforcement of Subpoenas and Orders Compelling Testimony.

When a witness refuses to testify or to provide other information to a grand jury without good cause, the attorney for the government can ask the court for an order to show cause why the witness should not be held in contempt. Rule 17(g), Fed. R. Crim. P. The Supreme Court has decided that the district court should first consider the feasibility of effecting compliance through the imposition of civil contempt pursuant to the Recalcitrant Witness Statute, 28 U.S.C. § 1826, before resorting to more drastic criminal contempt powers under 18 U.S.C. § 401 as applied by Rule 42 of the Federal Rules of Criminal Procedure. *Shillitani v. U.S.*, 384 U.S. 36 (1966); *Yates v. U.S.*, 355 U.S. 66, 74-75 (1957). Successive contempts are punishable as separate offenses. *U.S. v. Hawkins*, 501 F.2d 1029 (9th Cir.), *cert. denied*, 419 U.S. 1079 (1974); *U.S. v. Gebhard*, 426 F.2d 965 (9th Cir. 1970). The court may use a combination of civil and criminal contempt to vindicate its authority. *U.S. v. Morales*, 566 F.2d 402 (2d Cir. 1977); *U.S. v. Marra*, 482 F.2d 1196, 1202 (2d Cir. 1973).

## § 425. — Civil Contempt Proceedings.

Civil contempt proceedings brought under 28 U.S.C. § 1826 do not give rise to a constitutional right to trial by jury because a fine or incarceration would be coercive and not punitive. *Shillitani v. U.S., supra; U.S. v. Boe*, 491 F.2d 970 (8th Cir. 1974); *U.S. v. Handler*, 476 F.2d 709 (2d Cir. 1973). However, courts have held that Rule 42(b) does apply to such proceedings, and a recalcitrant witness is entitled to notice and a reasonable opportunity to prepare a defense. *In re Grand Jury Investigation*, 545 F.2d 385 (3d Cir. 1976); *In re DiBella*, 518 F.2d 955 (2d Cir. 1975); *In re Sadin*, 509 F.2d 1252 (2d Cir. 1975); *U.S. v. Alter*, 482 F.2d 1016 (9th Cir. 1973). While five days is generally deemed to be adequate, what constitutes a reasonable time to prepare a defense is committed to the discretion of the district judge. *In re Grand Jury Proceedings*, 550 F.2d 1240 (3d Cir. 1977); *Matter of Grand Jury*, 524 F.2d 209 (10th Cir.), *cert. dismissed*, 425 U.S. 927 (1975); *In re Sadin, supra; U.S. v. Alter, supra*. As little as one day has been held to be sufficient. *U.S. v. Hawkins, supra*. A witness who may be held in contempt is entitled to representation, and an indigent is entitled to court-appointed counsel. *U.S. v. Anderson*, 553 F.2d 1154 (8th Cir. 1977); *In re DiBella*, 518 F.2d 955 (2d Cir. 1975); *In re Kilgo*, 484 F.2d 1215 (4th Cir. 1973); *Henkel v. Bradshaw*, 483 F.2d 1386 (9th Cir. 1973). The contempt proceeding must be held in public except to the degree necessary to protect the secrecy of the grand jury process. *In re Rosahn,* 671 F.2d 690, 696-97 (2d Cir. 1982).

The party seeking to demonstrate that a subpoena is improper bears the burden of proof in a proceeding brought under 28 U.S.C. § 1826. *In re Liberatore,* 574 F.2d 78 (2d Cir. 1978); *In re Horowitz,* 482 F.2d 72 (2d Cir.), *cert. denied,* 414 U.S. 867 (1973). While accepting that the witness has the burden of showing cause for noncompliance, the Third Circuit requires that the United States make a minimum showing by affidavit that the information sought is relevant to an investigation properly within the grand jury's jurisdiction and is not sought primarily for another purpose. *In re Grand Jury Proceedings (Schofield II),* 507 F.2d 963 (3d Cir.), *cert. denied,* 421 U.S. 1015 (1975); *In re Grand Jury Proceedings (Schofield I),* 486 F.2d 85 (3d Cir. 1973). Other circuits have declined to require such affidavits. *In re Liberatore,* 574 F.2d 78 (2d Cir. 1978); *In re Grand Jury Investigation (McLean),* 565 F.2d 318 (5th Cir. 1977); *In re Hergenroeder,* 555 F.2d 686 (9th Cir. 1977). The First Circuit has held that the right is waived unless the witness requests such an affidavit. *In re Lopreato,* 511 F.2d 1150 (1st Cir. 1975). *See also Universal Manufacturing Co. v. U.S.,* 508 F.2d 684 (8th Cir. 1975). An affidavit may be presented *in camera* if disclosure of its contents might result in the destruction of evidence or otherwise disrupt the grand jury proceedings. *Schofield I,* 486 F.2d at 93. Exclusion of the public from civil contempt proceedings does not violate a defendant's sixth amendment right to public trial. *In re DiBella, supra.*

When a witness is found in civil contempt, he may be incarcerated for the term of the grand jury, including extensions, but his confinement cannot exceed 18 months. 28 U.S.C. § 1826(a)(2). Although not explicitly stated in 28 U.S.C. § 1826, a court may impose a fine; however, a fine and incarceration should not be imposed simultaneously absent a finding that such severe action is necessary. *Matter of Grand Jury Impaneled January 21, 1975 (Freedman),* 529 F.2d 543 (3d Cir.), *cert. denied,* 425 U.S. 992 (1976). A district court may increase or decrease a penalty once imposed. *Id.; In re Cueto,* 443 F. Supp. 857 (S.D.N.Y. 1978). A witness already incarcerated is not entitled to credit against his sentence for time spent in civil contempt confinement. *In re Grand Jury Proceedings,* 534 F.2d 41 (5th Cir. 1976); *In re Grand Jury Proceedings,* 532 F.2d 410 (5th Cir.), *cert. denied,* 429 U.S. 924 (1976); *Martin v. U.S.,* 517 F.2d 906 (8th Cir.), *cert. denied,* 423 U.S. 856 (1975).

Appeals taken from civil contempt judgments must be disposed of within 30 days of the filing of the appeal. 28 U.S.C. § 1826; *In re Berry,* 521 F.2d 179 (10th Cir. 1975), *cert. denied,* 423 U.S. 928 (1975). New reasons for the witness' failure to comply with the court's order cannot be raised on appeal, even if they would have constituted justification for the witness' silence. *In re Bianchi,* 542 F.2d 98 (1st Cir. 1976); *In re Grand Jury Investigation,* 542 F.2d 166 (3d Cir. 1976), *cert. denied,* 429 U.S. 1047 (1977). Bail pending appeal is not available if it appears that the appeal is frivolous or taken for delay. 28 U.S.C. § 1826(b). The provisions of 18 U.S.C. § 3148 do not apply to determinations by the district court to grant bail. *In re Visitor,* 400 F. Supp. 446 (D. S.D. 1975). Instead, the considerations governing stays pending appeal in civil proceedings are applicable. Rule 62, Fed. R. Civ. P.; Rule 8, Fed. R. App. P.; *Beverly v. U.S.,* 468 F.2d 732 (5th Cir. 1972).

## § 426. — Criminal Contempt Proceedings.

If it is appropriate to impose punishment upon a recalcitrant witness, a court may invoke the provisions of 18 U.S.C. § 401 by giving oral notice on the record or by directing the United States Attorney to file appropriate criminal charges. Rule 42(b), Fed. R. Crim. P.; *U.S. v. DiMauro,* 441 F.2d 428 (8th Cir. 1971). A grand jury may also charge a violation of 18 U.S.C. § 401. *See U.S. v. Sternman,* 415 F.2d 1165 (6th Cir. 1969), *cert. denied,* 397 U.S. 907 (1970). It is not required that a defendant receive notice that his disobedience of a court order to testify under immunity could result in criminal as well as civil sanctions. *U.S. v. Petito,* 671 F.2d 68, 72-73 (2d Cir.), *cert. denied,* 459 U.S. 824 (1982).

The Supreme Court held in *Harris v. U.S.,* 382 U.S. 162 (1965), that where the contempt consists of a refusal to testify before a grand jury, the court must proceed under Rule 42(b) with its requirements of notice and hearing; the summary contempt provisions of Rule 42(a) may not be brought into play merely by having the witness repeat his refusal in the court's presence. Refusals to testify during a trial by a witness who has been granted immunity, however, may be punished summarily under Rule 42(a). *U.S. v. Wilson, supra.* While case law limits summary punishment under Rule 42(a) to imprisonment for six months, there is no maximum set for punishing criminal contempt after notice and hearing under Rule 42(b). A court may not impose a sentence of more than six months unless a defendant in a criminal contempt action is afforded a right to jury trial. *Frank v. U.S.,* 395 U.S. 147 (1969); *Cheff v. Schnackenberg,* 384 U.S. 373 (1966). Bail for a defendant in a criminal contempt action is controlled by the provisions of Rule 46 of the Federal Rules of Criminal Procedure.

Criminal contempt proceedings require proof beyond a reasonable doubt. *Hicks on Behalf of Feiock v. Feiock,* 485 U.S. 624 (1988).

## § 427. Grand Jury Reports.

In addition to its authority to indict or return a no true bill, a federal grand jury possesses common law authority to issue a report that does not indict for a crime. *In re Johnson,* 484 F.2d 791 (7th Cir. 1973) (and cases cited therein). *See also U.S. v. Cox,* 342 F.2d 167, 185-90 (5th Cir. 1965) (Wisdom, J., concurring), *cert. denied,* 381 U.S. 935. Congress has specifically authorized special grand juries to issue reports and has spelled out the procedures to be followed. 18 U.S.C. § 3333. The subject matter of such reports is limited by that section to matters relating to organized crime conditions in the district or the noncriminal misconduct in office of appointed public officers or employees. The district judge who receives the grand jury's report may expunge portions of such a report and order that it be disseminated. *In re Report of Grand Jury Proceedings,* 479 F.2d 458 (5th Cir. 1973). Decisions to disseminate such reports are appealable by interested parties under the All Writs Act, 28 U.S.C. § 1651; the standard of review is abuse of discretion, *Haldeman v. Sirica,* 501 F.2d 714 (D.C. Cir. 1974).

# CHAPTER 5

## PRELIMINARY PROCEEDINGS

§ 501. Initial Appearance.
§ 502. Removal Hearing.
§ 503. Preliminary Examination.
§ 504. Bail.
§ 505. Release or Detention.
§ 506. — Pretrial Release or Detention.
§ 507. — — Release on Conditions.
§ 508. — — Temporary Detention.
§ 509. — — Detention.
§ 510. — — Factors to be Considered.
§ 511. — — Release or Detention Order.
§ 512. — — Appeal of Release or Detention Order.
§ 513. — Release During Trial.
§ 514. — Release or Detention After Conviction.
§ 515. — — Pending Sentencing.
§ 516. — — Pending Appeal.
§ 517. — — — Substantial Question.
§ 518. — — — Likely to Result in Reversal or New Trial.
§ 519. — — Procedures and Appeal of Denial.
§ 520. — Release of Material Witness.
§ 521. — Penalties for Failure to Appear.
§ 522. — Penalty for Offense Committed While on Release.

## § 501. Initial Appearance.

A person arrested under a warrant issued upon a complaint or without a warrant must be brought before a magistrate without "unnecessary delay." Rule 5(a), Fed. R. Crim. P. The purpose of the rule is to protect the rights of the accused from improper pressures by the policy of having a judicial officer advise the accused of his constitutional rights. *Mallory v. U.S.*, 354 U.S. 449, 453 (1957); *U.S. v. Carignan*, 342 U.S. 36, 44-45 (1951); *U.S. v. Mendoza*, 473 F.2d 697, 702 (5th Cir. 1973). Confessions or other evidence obtained during periods of unreasonable delay may not be admissible at trial. *See* Chapter 3, § 304 *supra.*

The defendant shall not be called upon to plead at his initial appearance. The magistrate shall (1) inform the accused of the charges against him; (2) advise him of his right to retain counsel, or the right to appointed counsel if he is unable to hire counsel; (3) inform him of his right to remain silent and that any statement made may be used against him; (4) detain or conditionally release the defendant; and (5) advise the accused of his right to a preliminary examination. Rule 5(c), Fed. R. Crim. P.

There is no constitutional right to counsel at the initial appearance. *U.S. v. Dohm,* 597 F.2d 535, 543 (5th Cir. 1979), *rev'd en banc on other grounds,* 618 F.2d 1169 (1980). However, a defendant "unable to obtain counsel shall be entitled to have counsel assigned to represent him at every stage of the proceedings from his initial appearance." Rule 44(a), Fed. R. Crim. P.; *Canal Zone v. Peach,* 602 F.2d 101, 104 (5th Cir.), *cert. denied,* 444 U.S. 952 (1979).

Rule 5(a) applies to arrests made pursuant to indictment. *Miller v. U.S.,* 396 F.2d 492, 496 (8th Cir.), *cert. denied,* 393 U.S. 1031 (1968).

## § 502. Removal Hearing.

If a person is arrested in a district other than the district in which the offense is alleged to have occurred, he shall be taken without unnecessary delay to the nearest available magistrate, and preliminary proceedings shall be conducted in accordance with Rules 5 and 5.1 of the Federal Rules of Criminal Procedure. Rule 40(a), Fed. R. Crim. P.

Rule 40 protects against improvident removal and prevents frustration of the prosecution by delay. Advisory Committee Note; *Galloway v. U.S.,* 302 F.2d 457, 458 (10th Cir. 1962).

No preliminary examination shall be held if the person elects to have the preliminary examination in the district where the prosecution is pending, if an indictment has already been returned, or if an information has been filed. Rule 40(a), Fed. R. Crim. P. An indictment is conclusive on the issue of probable cause and once a certified copy of the indictment or information is produced, the only issue left for the removal hearing is identification of the person arrested as the defendant named in the indictment or information. *U.S. v. Green,* 499 F.2d 538, 540-41 (D.C. Cir. 1974); *In re Ellsberg,* 446 F.2d 954, 960 (1st Cir. 1971); *Cox v. U.S.,* 373 F.2d 500, 504 (8th Cir. 1967). The defendant is not entitled to a psychiatric examination as ability to assist counsel and understand the proceedings are of minimal significance when identification is the sole issue. *U.S. v. LaVallee,* 436 F. Supp. 946, 947 (S.D. Tex. 1977). *See also U.S. v. Perkins,* 433 F.2d 1182, 1189 (D.C. Cir. 1970).

The burden of showing that there was unnecessary delay in bringing the accused before the nearest magistrate rests with the accused. *Miller v. U.S.,* 396 F.2d 492, 496 (8th Cir. 1968), *cert. denied,* 393 U.S. 1031 (1969). Delay because of the unavailability of a magistrate, *Granza v. U.S.,* 377 F.2d 746, 749 (5th Cir.), *cert. denied,* 389 U.S. 939 (1967), or for questioning to determine whether the person should be held or released is permitted, *Jones v. U.S.,* 342 F.2d 863, 865 (D.C.

Cir. 1964) (en banc); but the absence of a complaint or warrant does not justify delay, *U.S. v. Schwartz,* 372 F.2d 678, 681 (4th Cir. 1967).

In addition to the requirements of Rule 5, the magistrate shall inform the defendant of the provisions of Rule 20, about disposition of the case in the district where he was arrested. Rule 40(b), Fed. R. Crim. P. Failure to so inform, however, should not invalidate the removal procedure. Advisory Committee Note.

Rule 40 also provides procedures for dealing with the arrest of a probationer or supervised releasee in a district other than the district having jurisdiction, Rule 40(d), Fed. R. Crim. P., and with the arrest in a district, other than that in which the warrant was issued, of a defendant or witness upon a warrant for failure to appear, Rule 40(e), Fed. R. Crim. P.

If a person was previously detained or conditionally released in another district where the warrant, indictment or information was issued, the magistrate shall take into account the previous decision and the reasons set forth, but is not bound by that decision. If he amends the release or detention decision or alters the conditions of release from that previously fixed, he must state the reasons in writing. Rule 40(f), Fed. R. Crim. P.

There is no appeal from an order of removal. *U.S. v. Rivero-Nunez,* 605 F.2d 152 (5th Cir. 1979); *U.S. v. McCray,* 458 F.2d 389 (9th Cir.), *cert. denied,* 409 U.S. 865 (1972); *Galloway v. U.S.,* 302 F.2d at 458.

## § 503. Preliminary Examination.

Before indictment or the filing of an information, a defendant charged with any offense other than a petty offense is entitled to a preliminary examination, Rule 5(c), Fed. R. Crim. P., to determine if there is probable cause that an offense has been committed and that the defendant committed it, Rule 5.1(a), Fed. R. Crim. P. The preliminary examination justifies "holding the defendant in custody or on bail during the period of time it takes to bond the defendant over to the district court for trial." Advisory Committee Note to Rule 5(c) (1972 Amendment).

Unless waived, the preliminary examination is to be held not later than 10 days following the initial appearance if the defendant is in custody or not later than 20 days if he is not in custody. Rule 5(c), Fed. R. Crim. P.; 18 U.S.C. § 3060. These time limits may be extended by a magistrate with the consent of the defendant for good cause, taking into account the public interest in the prompt disposition of criminal cases, or by a judge without the consent of the defendant upon a showing that extraordinary circumstances exist and that delay is indispensable to the interests of justice. Rule 5(c), Fed. R. Crim. P. Once an indictment or information is filed the preliminary examination shall not be held. Rule 5(c), Fed. R. Crim. P.; 18 U.S.C. § 3060(e); *Jaben v. U.S.,* 381 U.S. 214, 220 (1965); *U.S. v. DeRosa,* 670 F.2d 889, 897 n.8 (9th Cir. 1982); *U.S. v. Mase,* 556 F.2d 671, 676 (2d Cir. 1977), *cert. denied,* 435 U.S. 916 (1978). In such an instance probable cause has been determined by the grand jury. *Gerstein v. Pugh,* 420 U.S. 103, 117 n.19 (1975).

The finding of probable cause may be based upon hearsay. Furthermore, unlawfully obtained evidence may not be properly objected to at the preliminary examination. Motions to suppress must be made to the trial court. Rule 5.1(a), Fed. R. Crim. P. Except for privileges (Rule 501), the Federal Rules of Evidence do not apply to preliminary examinations. Rule 1101(d)(3), Fed. R. Evid.

The preliminary examination is a critical state of the criminal process at which the defendant is entitled to be represented by counsel. *Adams v. Illinois,* 405 U.S. 278, 279 (1972); *Coleman v. Alabama,* 399 U.S. 1, 9-10 (1970). *See also* Rule 44(a), Fed. R. Crim. P. A plea of guilty or an identification of the defendant made at a preliminary hearing without counsel is inadmissible at trial. *Moore v. Illinois,* 434 U.S. 220 (1977); *White v. Maryland,* 373 U.S. 59, 60 (1963).

The defendant may cross-examine witnesses against him and may introduce evidence in his own behalf. Rule 5.1(a), Fed. R. Crim. P. Cross-examination may be limited to the scope of direct examination, *Coleman v. Burnett,* 477 F.2d 1187, 1201 (D.C. Cir. 1973); and the disclosure of the identity of a government informant may be properly withheld upon cross-examination, *U.S. v. Hart,* 526 F.2d 344 (5th Cir.), *cert. denied,* 426 U.S. 937 (1976). A defendant is entitled to a transcript of the preliminary examination, Rule 5.1(c)(1), (2), Fed. R. Crim. P.; but access to a tape recording of the preliminary examination may be sufficient, *U.S. v. Vandivere,* 579 F.2d 1240, 1243 (10th Cir. 1978). The unavailability of a transcript because of a recording equipment malfunction without a significant risk of prejudice to the defendant is not a basis to reverse a conviction. *U.S. v. Coleman,* 631 F.2d 908, 915 (D.C. Cir. 1980).

If the magistrate does not find probable cause that an offense has been committed by the defendant, the complaint shall be dismissed. This does not preclude the government from instituting a subsequent prosecution for the same offense. Rule 5.1(b), Fed. R. Crim. P.

### § 504. Bail.

The eighth amendment provides, "Excessive bail shall not be required." The amendment has been interpreted to mean that if bail is set it must not be excessive, but bail is not required in every case. *Carlson v. Landon,* 342 U.S. 524, 545-46 (1952); *U.S. v. Perry,* 788 F.2d 100 (3d Cir. 1986); *U.S. v. Giangrosso,* 763 F.2d 849 (7th Cir. 1985). The rebuttable presumptions in the Bail Reform Act of 1984 which operate against a defendant do not violate the eighth amendment. *U.S. v. Salerno,* 107 S. Ct. 2095 (1987); *U.S. v. Porter,* 786 F.2d 758 (7th Cir. 1985).

The purpose of bail is to allow an accused who has not been tried to be free, yet insure that the defendant will appear for trial and sentencing. *Stack v. Boyle,* 342 U.S. 1, 4 (1952); *U.S. v. Smith,* 444 F.2d 61, 62 (8th Cir. 1971), *cert. denied,* 405 U.S. 977 (1972). Compelling interests other than flight may also be the basis to refuse a defendant bail. *U.S. v. Salerno, supra.*

If bail is set at an amount higher than an amount reasonably calculated to insure the presence of the defendant, it is "excessive" under the eighth amendment. *Stack v. Boyle,* 342 U.S. at 5; *U.S. v. James,* 674 F.2d 886, 891 (11th Cir. 1982); *U.S. v. Beaman,* 631 F.2d 85, 86 (6th Cir. 1980). The test is not the financial status of the defendant, but whether the amount is reasonably calculated to assure his presence. *U.S. v. Wright,* 483 F.2d 1068, 1070 (4th Cir. 1973).

Even though the financial standing of the bail which the court sets is beyond question, the court may nevertheless conduct a *Nebbia* hearing concerning the source of the funds. If the court is not satisfied with the purpose or the ability of the surety to assure the appearance of the defendant, it may refuse to accept the bond. *U.S. v. Nebbia,* 357 F.2d 303, 304 (2d Cir. 1966). If the bond was secured by property of family or close friends, the court could conclude that the defendant will appear so as not to cause financial harm to these people. However, if the source of the funds is an illegitimate source, it may be considered merely a "business" expense to allow the defendant to escape the jurisdiction. *U.S. v. DeMarchena,* 330 F. Supp. 1223, 1226-27 (S.D. Cal. 1971); *U.S. v. Melville,* 309 F. Supp. 822, 824 (S.D.N.Y. 1970). *See also U.S. v. Skipper,* 633 F.2d 1177, 1180 (5th Cir. 1981).

Rule 46 of the Federal Rules of Criminal Procedure and the Bail Reform Act of 1984, 18 U.S.C. §§ 3141-3150, provide the procedures for release and detention. Where a warrant is issued upon an indictment or information, the amount of bail may be fixed by the court and endorsed on the warrant. Rule 9(b)(1), Fed. R. Crim. P.

## § 505. Release or Detention.

## § 506. — Pretrial Release or Detention.

As a general rule, release is favored over pretrial detention. However, the court may consider the danger a defendant may pose to a person or the community as part of his release decision. *U.S. v. Orta,* 760 F.2d 887 (8th Cir. 1985). Pretrial detention on the grounds of danger to the community with the safeguards set forth in the Bail Reform Act of 1984 is a regulatory measure and does not constitute punishment before trial in violation of the due process clause. *U.S. v. Salerno,* 107 S. Ct. 2095 (1987).

Under 18 U.S.C. § 3142, the judicial officer must select from four alternatives, progressing from one alternative to the next:

(1) release of the defendant on personal recognizance or unsecured appearance bond;

(2) release of the defendant on conditions reasonably necessary to assure the appearance of the defendant as required and to assure the safety of any person and the community;

(3) under certain conditions, order the detention of the defendant for a period of not more than 10 days;

(4) pretrial detention if he finds that no condition or combination of conditions will reasonably assure the appearance of the person and the safety of any person or the community.

## § 507. — — Release on Conditions.

If the judicial officer determines that release upon personal recognizance or an unsecured appearance bond will not reasonably assure the appearance of the defendant or will endanger the safety of any person or the community, he shall order the pretrial release of the defendant subject to the condition that he not commit any crime during the period of release and subject to the least restrictive conditions that will reasonably assure the appearance of the person and the safety of any person and the community. Under 18 U.S.C. § 3142(c), such conditions may include release to the custody of a designated person, the maintenance of employment or educational programs, restrictions on personal associations, place of abode or travel, avoiding contact with the alleged victim and pretrial witnesses, reporting requirements, curfew, refraining from possessing dangerous weapons or the excessive use of alcohol or any use of a controlled substance, medical or psychiatric treatment, a bail bond, return to custody for specified hours, and any other condition that is reasonably necessary to assure the defendant's appearance and the safety of any person or the community. These conditions may at any time be amended to impose additional or different conditions.

A financial condition may not be imposed that results in the pretrial detention of the defendant. 18 U.S.C. § 3142(c). However, the mere inability to raise the money does not mean that bond must be lowered as the defendant is not being held because he cannot raise the money, but because "without the money, the risk of flight is too great." *U.S. v. Jessup,* 757 F.2d 378 (1st Cir. 1985).

## § 508. — — Temporary Detention.

Under 18 U.S.C. § 3142(b), the judicial officer may detain the defendant for a period of not more than 10 days if he determines that (1) the person was, at the time of the offense he is charged with, on release pending trial for a felony; or on release pending imposition, execution, appeal of sentence or conviction, or on probation or parole; or not a citizen or lawfully admitted for permanent residence; and (2) the person may flee or pose a danger to any person or the community.

## § 509. — — Detention.

The judicial officer shall order the detention of the defendant before trial if after a hearing he finds that no condition or combination of conditions will reasonably assure the appearance of the person and the safety of any person or the community. 18 U.S.C. § 3142(e). "Reasonably assure" does not mean that release conditions must "guarantee" community safety and the defendant's appearance. *U.S. v. Orta,* 760 F.2d 887 (8th Cir. 1985).

There is a rebuttable presumption that no condition or combination of conditions will reasonably assure the safety of any person or the community if the judge finds that the defendant has been convicted of a crime of violence, a felony with a maximum sentence of life imprisonment or death, or a drug felony which has a maximum term of imprisonment of 10 years or more, if not more than five years has elapsed since the date of conviction or release from imprisonment, whichever is later. 18 U.S.C. § 3142(e).

There is likewise a rebuttal presumption that no condition or combination of conditions will reasonably assure the appearance of the defendant or the safety of the community if the judge finds there is probable cause to believe the defendant committed a 10-year drug felony or used or carried a firearm while committing a federal crime of violence. 18 U.S.C. § 3142(e).

The indictment itself is sufficient to create the probable cause creating the rebuttable presumption of flight. *U.S. v. Hurtado,* 779 F.2d

1467 (11th Cir. 1985). Once the defendant has produced evidence that in his particular circumstances he is not likely to flee or engage in criminal activity while on release, the presumption is rebutted. Economic and social stability and no relevant criminal record may provide such rebutting evidence. *U.S. v. Dominguez,* 783 F.2d 702 (7th Cir. 1986). The presumption, however, does not disappear once the defendant has produced some evidence. The judge should continue to give the presumption "some weight" in light of the Congressional finding that there is a "strong possibility" such offenders will flee. *U.S. v. Martin,* 782 F.2d 1141 (2d Cir. 1986).

The presumption shifts the burden of production, not the burden of persuasion, to the defendant. *U.S. v. Portes,* 786 F.2d 758 (7th Cir. 1985). The government retains the burden of proof by a preponderance where the issue is risk of flight, *U.S. v. Vortis,* 785 F.2d 327 (D.C. Cir. 1986), or by clear and convincing evidence if the issue is danger to a person or the community. 18 U.S.C. § 3142(f).

The detention hearing shall be held immediately upon the defendant's first appearance before the judicial officer, except that the defendant may have a continuance not to exceed five days, and the government a continuance not to exceed three days. The defendant shall be held during the period of continuance. 18 U.S.C. § 3142(f). It is mandatory that the government's motion for pretrial detention be made at the "first appearance," *U.S. v. Holloway,* 781 F.2d 124 (8th Cir. 1986); *U.S. v. Payden,* 759 F.2d 202 (2d Cir. 1985). The "first appearance" for purposes of § 3142(f) is the first appearance in the charging district after the defendant has appeared before a magistrate in another district where he was arrested. *U.S. v. Dominguez, supra.*

If there is failure to comply with the first appearance requirement, the government may ask for a prompt detention hearing and make its case to detain based upon the requirements set forth in the statute. *U.S. v. Montalvo-Murillo,* 493 U.S. 807 (1990).

Preventive detention is a civil and not criminal commitment and, as such, a jury trial is not required. *U.S. v. Perry,* 788 F.2d 100 (3d Cir. 1986).

### § 510. — — Factors to be Considered.

In determining whether there are conditions of release that will reasonably assure the appearance of the defendant and the safety of any person or the community, the judge shall take into consideration the available information concerning:

(1) the nature and circumstances of the offense charged, including whether it is a crime of violence or involves drugs;

(2) the weight of evidence against the defendant;

(3) the history and characteristics of the defendant, including character, physical and mental condition, family ties, employment, financial resources, community ties, past conduct, drug or alcohol abuse history, criminal history and records concerning appearance at court proceedings, whether he was on probation, parole or release pending another trial, sentencing or appeal; and

(4) the nature and seriousness of the danger to any other person or the community that would be posed by the defendant's release. 18 U.S.C. § 3142(g).

## § 511. — — Release or Detention Order.

The judge is required to issue a written release order or detention order. If it is a detention order, the judge must include written findings of fact and a written statement of the reasons for the detention. 18 U.S.C. § 3142(h) and (i).

Although as a condition of release under 18 U.S.C. § 3142(c)(2)(J), the court may order psychiatric treatment, it may not order a psychiatric examination on the question of dangerousness for purposes of detention as § 3142(g) requires that the court make its determination based upon "the available information"; and § 3142(f) requires that the hearing be "immediately upon the person's first appearance...." *U.S. v. Martin-Trigona,* 767 F.2d 35 (2d Cir. 1985).

## § 512. — — Appeal of Release or Detention Order.

A release or detention order issued by the magistrate or a person other than a judge of the court having original jurisdiction over the offense may be considered by the court with original jurisdiction upon motion of the government or the defendant. 18 U.S.C. § 3145.

The standard for appellate review of decisions of the magistrate or district court under the Bail Reform Act of 1984 has been held to be an independent review of the entire record to determine if the detention decision was correct. *U.S. v. Portes,* 786 F.2d 758 (7th Cir. 1985); *U.S. v. Hurtado,* 779 F.2d 1467 (11th Cir. 1985); *U.S. v. Maull,* 773 F.2d 1479 (8th Cir. 1985); *U.S. v. Montamedi,* 767 F.2d 1403 (9th Cir. 1985); *U.S. v. Hazime,* 762 F.2d 34 (6th Cir. 1985); (a clearly erroneous standard) *U.S. v. Chimurenga,* 760 F.2d 400 (2d Cir. 1985); *U.S. v. Williams,* 753 F.2d 329 (4th Cir. 1985); (supported by the proceedings below standard) *U.S. v. Fortna,* 769 F.2d 243 (5th Cir. 1985).

## § 513. — Release During Trial.

Unless the court determines that other conditions of release or termination of release are necessary to assure the defendant's presence during trial or to assure that his conduct will not obstruct the orderly and expeditious progress of the trial, he shall continue on release on the same terms and conditions as previously imposed. Rule 46(b), Fed. R. Crim. P. The court may revoke bail during trial to insure the orderly trial process, *U.S. v. Gilbert,* 425 F.2d 490, 491 (D.C. Cir. 1969), or where defendant attempted to tamper with witnesses, *U.S. v. Cozzetti,* 441 F.2d 344, 350 (9th Cir. 1971), but the bond of a defendant was improperly revoked who was 37 minutes late returning from a recess which had been granted to allow him to go to his office to gather evidence, *Bittner v. U.S.,* 389 U.S. 15, 17 (1967).

## § 514. — Release or Detention After Conviction.

## § 515. — — Pending Sentencing.

A defendant who has been found guilty and is awaiting imposition of sentence shall be detained unless the defendant shows by clear and convincing evidence that he is (1) not likely to flee, and (2) does not pose a danger to any other person or the community if released. 18 U.S.C. § 3143(a); *U.S. v. Strong,* 775 F.2d 504 (3d Cir. 1985).

## § 516. — — Pending Appeal.

A defendant who has been sentenced and who has filed an appeal shall be detained unless the judicial officer finds by clear and convincing evidence that the defendant (1) is not likely to flee; (2) does not pose a danger to any other person or the community; (3) the appeal is not for the purpose of delay; and (4) raises a substantial question of law or fact likely to result in a reversal or an order for a new trial. 18 U.S.C. § 3143(b). The burden is on the convicted defendant to establish these four factors to obtain release pending appeal. *U.S. v. Valera-Elyonda,* 761 F.2d 1020 (5th Cir. 1985).

## § 517. — — — Substantial Question.

The requirement in 18 U.S.C. § 3143(b)(2) that the judicial officer must make a finding that a defendant's appeal must raise "a substantial question of law or fact likely to result in reversal or an order for a new trial," has been interpreted as meaning that the appeal presents "a close question or one that could go either way" or the question is "so integral to the merits of the conviction that it is more probable than not that reversal or a new trial will occur if the question is decided in defendant's favor." *U.S. v. Powell,* 761 F.2d 1277, 1233-34 (8th Cir. 1985); *U.S. v. Pollard,* 788 F.2d 1177 (6th Cir. 1985).

The "substantial question" part of the standard also has been defined as "novel," "not ... decided by controlling precedent," or "fairly doubtful," *U.S. v. Miller,* 753 F.2d 19 (3d Cir. 1985); as "fairly debatable," *U.S. v. Handy,* 753 F.2d 1487 (9th Cir. 1985); and as "one of more substance than would be necessary to a finding that it was not frivolous. It is a 'close' question or one that could well be decided the other way." *U.S. v. Giancola,* 754 F.2d 898, 901 (11th Cir. 1985).

### § 518. — — — Likely to Result in Reversal or New Trial.

"Likely" means that it is more probable than not that reversal or a new trial will be granted. In addition, the defendant must also demonstrate that if he prevails upon the substantial question, a reversal or new trial is likely upon all counts for which imprisonment has been imposed. *Morrison v. U.S.,* 108 S. Ct. 1837 (1988); *U.S. v. Powell,* 788 F.2d 1227 (8th Cir. 1985).

### § 519. — — Procedures and Appeal of Denial.

Application after conviction shall be made in the first instance to the district court which shall state in writing the reasons for its action if it refuses release pending appeal or imposes conditions of release. An appeal for release or modification of conditions of release may be made to the court of appeals or a judge thereof. Rule 9(b), Fed. R. App. P.; *U.S. v. Hart,* 779 F.2d 575 (10th Cir. 1985).

### § 520. — Release of Material Witness.

If it appears by affidavit filed by a party that the testimony of a person is material in a criminal proceeding and that it may become impracticable to secure his presence by subpoena, a judicial officer may order the arrest of the person and impose conditions of release pursuant to § 3142. 18 U.S.C. § 3144. The witness shall not be detained because of inability to comply with a condition of release if his testimony can be secured by deposition. The witness may be detained until after the taking of the deposition. 18 U.S.C. § 3144; Rule 15(a), Fed. R. Crim. P. The attorney for the government shall make a biweekly report to the court for each witness held more than 10 days stating why the witness should not be released with or without taking his deposition. Rule 46(g), Fed. R. Crim. P.

## § 521. — Penalties for Failure to Appear.

Whoever, having been released, willfully fails to appear before a court or fails to surrender for service of sentence as required shall forfeit any security pledged. 18 U.S.C. § 3146. Forfeiture of the security is governed by Rule 46(e) of the Federal Rules of Criminal Procedure.

In addition, a defendant who has been released in connection with a charge, or while awaiting sentence, surrender for service of sentence or appeal or certiorari, shall be fined or imprisoned according to grading levels set forth in 18 U.S.C. § 3146(b). Such imprisonment shall be consecutive to the sentence for any other offense. 18 U.S.C § 3146(b).

Actual notice of a court hearing may not be required where defendant had changed his appearance and his residence without notifying the court, *U.S. v. Phillips*, 625 F.2d 543, 545 (5th Cir. 1980), or had engaged in conduct designed to prevent him from receiving notice, *U.S. v. Bright*, 541 F.2d 471, 479 (5th Cir. 1976), *cert. denied*, 430 U.S. 935 (1977); *U.S. v. DePugh*, 434 F.2d 548, 552 (8th Cir. 1970), *cert. denied*, 401 U.S. 978 (1971), or had failed to advise his attorney of his whereabouts, *Gant v. U.S.*, 506 F.2d 518, 520 (8th Cir. 1974), *cert. denied*, 420 U.S. 1005 (1975).

It is an affirmative defense that uncontrollable circumstances prevented the person from appearing or surrendering, if the person did not contribute to the creation of the circumstances in reckless disregard of the requirement that he appear or surrender, and that he appeared or surrendered as soon as such circumstances ceased to exist. 18 U.S.C. § 3146(c).

The failure of the judicial officer to inform the defendant of the penalties if he violated the conditions of his release was not a prerequisite to prosecution under the former bail act and presumably under § 3146, *U.S. v. Cardello*, 473 F.2d 325, 327 (4th Cir. 1973); *U.S. v. Eskew*, 469 F.2d 278, 279 (9th Cir. 1972); nor is forfeiture of bail a condition precedent to such a prosecution, *U.S. v. Phillips*, 625 F.2d at 544.

Failure to appear because of threats on defendant's life which were unrelated to the trial is not a defense. *U.S. v. Atencio*, 586 F.2d 744, 747 (9th Cir. 1978).

## § 522. — Penalty for Offense Committed While on Release.

A person convicted of a crime while on release shall receive a sentence of imprisonment in addition to that prescribed for the offense, which shall be consecutive to any other sentence of imprisonment. 18 U.S.C. § 3147.

# CHAPTER 6

# ARRAIGNMENT AND PLEA

§ 601. Arraignment.
§ 602. Pleas.
§ 603. — Effect of Guilty Plea.
§ 604. — Nolo Contendere Plea.
§ 605. — Requirements for Accepting Pleas of Guilty or Nolo Contendere.
§ 606. — — Voluntariness of Plea.
§ 607. — — Advice to Defendant.
§ 608. — — — Understanding the Nature of the Charge.
§ 609. — — — Understanding the Penalty.
§ 610. — — Factual Basis for the Plea.
§ 611. — Plea Agreements.
§ 612. — — Participation by Judge in Plea Discussions.
§ 613. — — Breach of Plea Agreement.
§ 614. — Conditional Pleas.
§ 615. — Inadmissibility of Pleas and Plea Discussions.
§ 616. — Effect of a Technical Violation of Rule 11.
§ 617. Withdrawal of Plea of Guilty or Nolo Contendere.
§ 618. — Withdrawal Before Sentence.
§ 619. — Withdrawal After Sentence.

## § 601. Arraignment.

The arraignment is the proceeding where the defendant is brought before the court, is informed of the charges in the information or indictment, and is called upon to answer the charges by his plea. The arraignment is to be conducted in open court, and consists of reading the indictment or information or advising the defendant about the substance of the charge, and calling on him to plead. Before being called upon to plead, the defendant is to be given a copy of the indictment or information. Rule 10, Fed. R. Crim. P. The defendant is required to be present for arraignment and at the time of the plea. Rule 43(a), Fed. R. Crim. P. However, for offenses punishable by fine or imprisonment for not more than one year or both, the court, with the defendant's written consent, may permit arraignment and plea in the defendant's absence. Rule 43 (c)(2), Fed. R. Crim. P.

Although arraignment has been termed a *sine qua non* to the trial, *Hamilton v. Alabama,* 368 U.S. 52, 54 n.4 (1961), failure to comply with technical arraignment requirements does not warrant reversal of a conviction, absent prejudice to the defendant. *Garland v. Washington,* 232 U.S. 642, 645-47 (1914); *U.S. v. Rogers,* 469 F.2d 1317, 1318 (5th Cir. 1972). Thus, there is no error where the indictment was not read at arraignment where the defendant knew of what he was accused. *U.S. v. Romero,* 640 F.2d 1014, 1015 (9th Cir. 1981); *Owensby v. U.S.,* 353 F.2d 412, 416 (10th Cir. 1965), *cert. denied,* 383 U.S. 962 (1966). Receipt of a copy of the indictment by the defendant meets the requirements of Rule 10. *U.S. v. Bey,* 499 F.2d 194, 201 (3d Cir. 1974), *cert. denied,* 419 U.S. 1003 (1974); *U.S. v. Clark,* 407 F.2d 1336 (4th Cir. 1969).

### § 602. Pleas.

Rule 11 of the Federal Rules of Criminal Procedure sets forth the requirements and procedures for pleas in federal criminal cases. A defendant is required to be present at the time of plea, Rule 43(a), Fed. R. Crim. P., but a corporate defendant may appear by counsel, Rule 43(c)(1), Fed. R. Crim. P. A defendant may enter a plea of not guilty, guilty, or nolo contendere, and if he refuses to plead, the court shall enter a plea of not guilty. Rule 11(a), Fed. R. Crim. P. Under certain restrictions, a defendant may enter a conditional plea of guilty or nolo contendere, reserving the right to appeal the adverse determination of a specified pretrial motion. Rule 11(a)(2), Fed. R. Crim. P. A defendant may not plead guilty to a lesser included charge without the consent of the government. *U.S. v. Gray,* 448 F.2d 164, 168 (9th Cir. 1971), *cert. denied,* 405 U.S. 926 (1972).

A defendant is entitled to be represented by counsel. Rule 11(c)(2), Fed. R. Crim. P. A verbatim record of the proceeding must be made. Rule 11(g), Fed. R. Crim. P.

The Rule 11 procedure is used to make the constitutionally required determination that a defendant's guilty plea is truly voluntary, and to produce a complete record at the time the plea is entered of the factors relevant to the voluntariness determination. *Boykin v. Alabama,* 395 U.S. 238, 244 (1969); *McCarthy v. U.S.,* 394 U.S. 459, 465 (1969).

### § 603. — Effect of Guilty Plea.

A knowing and voluntary guilty plea is an admission of all the elements or material facts of the charge, *U.S. v. Broce,* 488 U.S. 563 (1989); *McCarthy v. U.S.,* 394 U.S. 459, 466 (1969); *U.S. v. Bejar-Matrecios,* 618 F.2d 81, 84 (9th Cir. 1980), and waives all nonjurisdictional defects in the proceedings, *U.S. v. Davis,* 900 F.2d 1524 (10th Cir. 1990); *Barrientos v. U.S.,* 668 F.2d 838, 842 (5th Cir. 1982); *U.S. v. Jackson,* 659 F.2d 73, 74 (5th Cir.), *cert. denied,* 455 U.S. 1003 (1981). It is also a waiver of constitutional rights to a trial by jury, to confront and cross-examine witnesses against the defendant, and the privilege against self-incrimination. *Boykin v. Alabama,* 395 U.S. 238, 243

(1969). The guilty plea is itself a conviction, *Boykin v. Alabama,* 395 U.S. at 242, unless state law provides that a defendant is not "convicted" until judgment is actually rendered. Thus, a defendant cannot be federally convicted of receipt of firearms by a convicted felon where he entered a guilty plea in state court, but the state court never entered judgment. *U.S. v. Stober,* 604 F.2d 1274, 1278 (10th Cir. 1979) (en banc).

Jurisdictional issues or the failure of the information or indictment to charge an offense are not waived by a plea of guilty or nolo contendere. These issues may be raised within seven days after the plea by a motion for arrest of judgment. Rule 34, Fed. R. Crim. P.

### § 604. — Nolo Contendere Plea.

A plea of nolo contendere is an admission of the facts in the indictment or information, but it is not an admission of the defendant's guilt and is not a conviction. It is the judgment of the court that determines guilt. *Lott v. U.S.,* 367 U.S. 421, 426 (1961). It has the effect of a guilty plea. *U.S. v. Norris,* 281 U.S. 619, 622 (1930). For purposes of punishment, a plea of nolo contendere is the same as a plea of guilty. *Bell v. Commissioner,* 320 F.2d 953, 956 (8th Cir. 1963). It cannot, however, be used against the defendant in a subsequent civil or criminal proceeding. Rule 11(e)(6)(B), Fed. R. Crim. P.

A nolo contendere plea may be entered only with the consent of the court. It will be accepted by the court only after consideration of the views of the parties and the interest of the public in the effective administration of justice. Rule 11(b), Fed. R. Crim. P. A court has wide discretion in refusing to accept a nolo contendere plea. *U.S. v. Dorman,* 496 F.2d 438, 440 (4th Cir. 1974), *cert. denied,* 419 U.S. 945 (1974); *Mason v. U.S.,* 250 F.2d 704, 706 (10th Cir. 1957). Unlike a guilty plea, a nolo contendere plea does not require that the court satisfy itself that there is a factual basis for the plea. Rule 11(f), Fed. R. Crim. P.; Advisory Committee Note (1966 Amendment).

### § 605. — Requirements for Accepting Pleas of Guilty or Nolo Contendere.

### § 606. — — Voluntariness of Plea.

It is error for a judge to accept a defendant's guilty or nolo contendere plea without an affirmative showing on the record that it was intelligent and voluntary. *Boykin v. Alabama,* 395 U.S. 238, 243-44 (1969); *McCarthy v. U.S.,* 394 U.S. 459, 565 (1969). No plea shall be accepted unless the court addresses the defendant in open court and determines that the plea is voluntary and is not the result of force or threats or promises apart from a plea agreement. Rule 11(d), Fed. R. Crim. P. Compliance with Rule 11 to determine the voluntary nature of the plea depends on a consideration of all the surrounding circumstances in each case. *Brady v. U.S.*, 397 U.S. 742, 749 (1970); *Williams v. Missouri*, 640 F.2d 140, 143 (8th Cir.), *cert. denied*, 451 U.S. 990 (1981); *Harris v. U.S.*, 493 F.2d 1213, 1214 (8th Cir.), *cert. denied*, 417 U.S. 949 (1974).

A plea induced by threats is involuntary, *Waley v. Johnston*, 316 U.S. 101, 104 (1942); *U.S. v. Taylor*, 303 F.2d 165, 168 (4th Cir. 1962), as may be a plea made while defendant is under the influence of drugs, *Manley v. U.S.*, 396 F.2d 699, 701 (5th Cir. 1968). A plea induced by unfulfilled promises is not voluntary, *Brady v. U.S.*, 397 U.S. at 755; *Reed v. Turner*, 444 F.2d 206, 208-09 (10th Cir. 1971); although where the misrepresentation was the unfulfilled promise to impose concurrent sentences, the court may either set aside the plea or grant belated performance of the promise, *Lepera v. U.S.*, 587 F.2d 433, 436 n.4 (9th Cir. 1978). The voluntariness of a plea may be reviewed where the defendant claims that it was induced by his attorney's misrepresentation that he would receive a suspended sentence or probation, *U.S. v. Marzgliano*, 588 F.2d 395, 399 (3d Cir. 1978), or where his attorney misrepresented and withheld information to induce a guilty plea, *U.S. v. Sanderson*, 595 F.2d 1021, 1022 (5th Cir. 1979). Where a defendant stated that he was being pressured into pleading guilty and then answered, "Yes," to the court's inquiry whether the plea was "entirely free and voluntary" requires that the court probe further to resolve the contradiction, and failure to do so requires reversal. *Mack v. U.S.*, 635 F.2d 20, 24 (1st Cir. 1980).

## § 607. — — Advice to Defendant.

Before accepting a plea of guilty or nolo contendere, the court is required to address the defendant personally in open court and advise him about and determine that he understands the nature of the charge; any mandatory minimum penalty and the maximum possible penalty, including the effect of any special parole terms; the fact that the court is required to consider any applicable sentencing guidelines but may depart from those guidelines under some circumstances; that he has the right to be represented by an attorney and that, if necessary, one will be appointed to represent him; that he has the right to plead not guilty or persist in that plea if it has been already made; that he has the right to a jury trial; that at trial he has the right to counsel and the right to confront and cross-examine witnesses against him; the right not to incriminate himself; that if his plea of guilty or nolo contendere is accepted by the court he waives the right to a trial; and that if the court asks him questions about the offense to which he has pleaded and if he answers under oath, on the record, and in the presence of counsel, the answers may be used against him in a prosecution for perjury or false statement. Rule 11(c), Fed. R. Crim. P.; *U.S. v. Carter,* 619 F.2d 293, 299 (3d Cir. 1980).

In accepting guilty pleas the court may address multiple defendants jointly without violating the requirement that this court address each defendant "personally," but failure to inquire of each defendant individually the various questions required under Rule 11 requires that the judgments be vacated. *U.S. v. Fels,* 599 F.2d 142, 146 (7th Cir. 1979).

### §608. — — — Understanding the Nature of the Charge.

Failure of the judge to personally address the defendant and explain the elements or the nature of the charge is per se error. *U.S. v. Carter,* 662 F.2d 274, 276 (4th Cir. 1981). The mere reading of the indictment may not be sufficient to inform the defendant of the charge. *Mack v. U.S.,* 635 F.2d 20, 25 (1st Cir. 1980); *U.S. v. Dayton,* 604 F.2d 931, 937-38 (5th Cir. 1979), *cert. denied,* 445 U.S. 904 (1980); *U.S. v. Wetterlin,* 583 F.2d 346, 350 n.6 (7th Cir. 1978), *cert. denied,* 439 U.S. 1127 (1979). Furthermore, simply advising the defendant of the charge or merely asking if he understands the charge does not insure that he understands the nature of the charge. *Mack v. U.S.,* 635 F.2d at 26; *Woodward v. U.S.,* 426 F.2d 959, 962 (3d Cir. 1970). It is necessary for the court to take the time to determine, and that the record demonstrate, that the defendant does indeed understand the charge. *U.S. v. Syal,* 963 F.2d 900 (6th Cir. 1992); *U.S. v. Adams,* 566 F.2d 962, 967-68 (5th Cir. 1978); *U.S. v. Coronado,* 554 F.2d 166, 173 (5th Cir.), *cert. denied,* 434 U.S. 870 (1977). The exact colloquy may vary from case to case depending upon the complexion of the charges and the personal characteristics of the defendant. *U.S. v. Gray,* 611 F.2d 194, 200 (7th Cir. 1979), *cert. denied,* 446 U.S. 911 (1980).

It is the judge and not the Assistant United States Attorney, *U.S. v. Hart,* 566 F.2d 977, 978 (5th Cir. 1978), or the clerk, *U.S. v. Carter,* 662 F.2d at 276, who must address the defendant and ascertain that he understands the charge. Likewise, neither a written guilty plea, *U.S. v. Adams,* 566 F.2d at 967 n.6, nor private discussions by the defendant with his attorney about the nature of the charge satisfy the Rule 11 requirements, *Horsely v. U.S.,* 583 F.2d 670, 672 (3d Cir. 1978). *But see U.S. v. Gray,* 611 F.2d at 199, where although the preferable practice was for the court to conduct all inquiries, it was held not to be error where the prosecutor handled the inquiry in the presence of the court and the court was satisfied that the information was fully explained and understood by the defendant.

## § 609. — — — Understanding the Penalty.

Under Rule 11(c)(1), the defendant must also understand the minimum penalty, if any, and the maximum possible penalty, including the effect of any special parole terms. Failure to establish this on the record brings into question the voluntariness of the plea and is a due process violation requiring a reversal of the conviction resulting from the guilty plea; *U.S. v. Yazbeck*, 524 F.2d 641, 643 (1st Cir. 1975). Pleas have been vacated even where the defendant was told that maximum penalty was in excess of what he could actually receive. *U.S. v. Herrold*, 635 F.2d 213, 215 (3d Cir. 1980). *Contra Keel v. U.S.*, 585 F.2d 110, 113 (5th Cir. 1978); *U.S. v. Davis*, 544 F.2d 1056, 1058-59 (10th Cir. 1976). The bottom end of an applicable sentencing range under the sentencing guidelines is not a "mandatory minimum sentence" which the defendant must then be advised by the court pursuant to Rule 11(c)(1) when entering a guilty plea. *U.S. v. Salva*, 894 F.2d 225 (7th Cir. 1990).

A defendant need not be advised of the probability of receiving a particular sentence, only that he understand the range of possible sentences. *Lewis v. U.S.*, 601 F.2d 1100, 1101 (9th Cir. 1979); *Hinds v. U.S.*, 429 F.2d 1322, 1323 (9th Cir. 1970).

The defendant must be told that a special parole term is part of the sentence. *Richardson v. U.S.*, 577 F.2d 447, 451 (8th Cir. 1978), *cert. denied*, 442 U.S. 910 (1979). However, accepting a guilty plea without informing the defendant of a mandatory special parole term where the defendant does not allege he was actually unaware of the special parole term and he was not prejudiced because his sentence plus special parole term did not exceed the maximum possible sentence which had been explained to the defendant, is merely a technical violation of Rule 11 and not subject to collateral attack. *U.S. v. Timmreck*, 441 U.S. 780, 784 (1978). However, where the defendant alleges that he would not have pleaded guilty if he had been aware that he could receive a sentence of six years under the Youth Corrections Act rather than the five-year penalty under the criminal statute, collateral relief may be granted. *U.S. v. Scott*, 625 F.2d 623, 625 (5th Cir. 1980). A plea is involuntary where the court refuses to accept the plea of a defendant's codefendant brother unless the defendant also pleads guilty. *U.S. v. Cammisano*, 599 F.2d 851, 856-57 (8th Cir. 1979).

A plea of guilty is not invalid because it was entered to avoid the possibility of the death penalty, *Brady v. U.S.*, 397 U.S. 742, 755 (1970), or a lower possible penalty, *Parker v. North Carolina*, 397 U.S. 790, 794-95 (1970), or because the state prosecutor said he would not bring charges, *Ford v. U.S.*, 418 F.2d 855, 859 (8th Cir. 1969), or would increase the number of counts, *Meyer v. U.S.*, 424 F.2d 1181, 1188 (8th Cir.), *cert. denied*, 400 U.S. 853 (1970), or use an habitual offender statute, *Williams v. Missouri*, 640 F.2d 140, 143 (8th Cir.), *cert. denied*, 451 U.S. 990 (1981), or would reindict under more serious charges, *Bordenkircher v. Hayes*, 434 U.S. 357, 365 (1978). Erroneous prediction by defense counsel concerning sentence will not invalidate a guilty plea, *Stout v. U.S.*, 508 F.2d 951, 953 (6th Cir. 1975); *Villarreal v. U.S.*, 508 F.2d 1132, 1133 (9th Cir. 1974); nor will the failure of the court to give a count-by-count breakdown of the maximum penalties where the court informed the defendant of the total maximum penalty, *U.S. v. Ammirato*, 670 F.2d 552, 555 (5th Cir. 1982).

The court must specifically ask if the plea was induced by force, threats, or promises, and failure to so inquire requires reversal, *U.S. v. Dayton*, 604 F.2d 931, 938 (5th Cir. 1979), *cert. denied*, 445 U.S. 904 (1980); *U.S. v. Cammisano*, 599 F.2d at 855; *U.S. v. Fels*, 599 F.2d 142, 149 (7th Cir. 1979), even where no real prejudice has been shown, *U.S. v. Gray*, 584 F.2d 96, 97 (5th Cir. 1978). Merely asking the defendant if his plea is coerced and receiving a negative answer does not establish voluntariness per se, but it is persuasive evidence of voluntariness, *Camillo v. Wyrick*, 640 F.2d 931, 935 (9th Cir. 1981); *U.S. v. Bambulas*, 571 F.2d 525, 526 (10th Cir. 1978). However, defendant need not be informed of all consequences of a guilty plea, including such matters as the loss of his right to vote, *U.S. v. Washington*, 341 F.2d 277, 288 (3d Cir.), *cert. denied*, 382 U.S. 850 (1965), the possibility of consecutive sentences under a multi-count charge, *Paradiso v. U.S.*, 482 F.2d 409, 415 (3d Cir. 1973), and the possibility of deportation, *Steinsvik v. Vinzant*, 640 F.2d 949, 956 (9th Cir. 1981). The court need not advise the defendant of the court's inability to order concurrent state-federal sentences, *U.S. v. Jackson*, 627 F.2d 883, 885 (8th Cir.), *cert. denied*, 449 U.S. 998 (1980); *U.S. v. Degand*, 614 F.2d 176, 178 (8th Cir. 1980); *Cobb v. U.S.*, 583 F.2d 695, 697 (4th Cir. 1978); *Kincade v. U.S.*, 559 F.2d 906, 908 (3d Cir.), *cert. denied*, 434 U.S. 970 (1977). *But see U.S. v. Myers*, 451 F.2d 402 (9th Cir. 1972), where failure to advise a defendant already in state custody that his federal sentence would not begin until after the state sentence was served may require vacating the sentence.

159

## § 610. — — Factual Basis for the Plea.

A court may not enter a judgment upon a guilty plea unless it is satisfied that there is a factual basis for the plea. Rule 11(f), Fed. R. Crim. P. The judge must determine that the conduct that the defendant admits constitutes the offense charged or an offense included therein so that the defendant does not mistakenly plead guilty. *McCarthy v. U.S.*, 394 U.S. 459, 467 (1969); *U.S. v. Keiswetter*, 866 F.2d 1301 (10th Cir. 1989).

The factual basis developed on the record may come from several sources, including the days of trial before a change of plea, *U.S. v. Ammirato*, 670 F.2d 552, 555 (5th Cir. 1982), an agent's statement of facts, *Tallent v. U.S.*, 604 F.2d 370, 372 (5th Cir. 1979), a prosecutor's statement of facts, *U.S. v. Dayton*, 604 F.2d 931, 943 (5th Cir. 1979), *cert. denied*, 445 U.S. 904 (1980), or by examining the presentence report, Advisory Committee Note (1966 Amendment). The test is whether the judge is subjectively satisfied with the factual basis, *U.S. v. Ammirato*, 670 F.2d at 555.

The court is not required to personally address the defendant for the determination of the factual basis. *U.S. v. Kriz*, 586 F.2d 1178, 1181 (8th Cir. 1978), *cert. denied*, 442 U.S. 945 (1979). If the court determines that there is a factual basis, it may accept a guilty plea even where the defendant claims his innocence. *North Carolina v. Alford*, 400 U.S. 25, 37 (1970); *U.S. v. Hecht*, 638 F.2d 651, 656 (3d Cir. 1981).

Although Rule 11(h) provides a harmless error rule for violations of Rule 11, where the failure of the court to secure a factual basis is not harmless, the remedy is to remand for repleading. *U.S. v. Goldberg*, 862 F.2d 101 (6th Cir. 1988).

Unlike a guilty plea, the court may enter a judgment upon a plea of nolo contendere without inquiry into the factual basis for the plea. Advisory Committee Note (1966 Amendment).

## § 611. — Plea Agreements.

The Supreme Court has held that not only is "plea bargaining" not unconstitutional, *Brady v. U.S.*, 397 U.S. 742, 753 (1970), but, "[p]roperly administered, it is to be encouraged," *Santobello v. New York*, 404 U.S. 257, 260 (1971). A defendant, however, does not have a constitutional right to a plea bargain, *Weatherford v. Bursey*, 429 U.S. 545, 561 (1977); *U.S. v. Herrera*, 640 F.2d 958, 962 (9th Cir. 1981). A defendant who voluntarily and intelligently pled guilty does not have a right to specific performance of an earlier proposed plea bargain which the prosecutor withdrew. *Mabry v. Johnson*, 467 U.S. 504 (1984).

Rule 11(d) of the Federal Rules of Criminal Procedure requires that in determining whether the plea is voluntary, the court inquire whether the defendant's willingness to plead guilty or nolo contendere results from prior discussions between the defense and the prosecution. Rule 11(e) specifically states that the government and defendant may engage in discussions with a view to reaching a plea agreement, and sets forth the procedures to be followed.

If a plea agreement is reached for the defendant to plead guilty or nolo contendere to the charged offense or a lesser offense, the attorney for the government may move for dismissal of other charges; make a recommendation, or agree not to oppose the defendant's request for a particular sentence, with the understanding that such recommendation or request is not binding on the court; or agree that a specific sentence is appropriate. Rule 11(e)(1), Fed. R. Crim. P.

However, plea agreements may not be used to undermine the Sentencing Reform Act of 1984 and its guidelines. *See* Chapter 13, §§ 1313-1315, *infra*.

If a plea agreement has been reached, it must be disclosed in open court, or for good cause, it may be disclosed *in camera*. Rule 11(e)(2), Fed. R. Crim. P.

If the plea agreement is a nonbinding recommendation or request under Rule 11(e)(1)(B), the court must advise the defendant that if the court does not accept the recommendation or request the defendant has no right to withdraw his plea. Rule 11(e)(2), Fed. R. Crim. P.; *Smith v. U.S.*, 670 F.2d 145, 148 n.6 (11th Cir. 1982); *U.S. v. Incrovato*, 611 F.2d 5, 6-7 (1st Cir. 1979). *But see U.S. v. American Bag & Paper Corp.*, 609 F.2d 1066 (3d Cir. 1979); *U.S. v. White*, 583 F.2d 819 (6th Cir. 1978), concerning defendant's right to withdraw plea.

If the plea agreement calls for dismissal of other charges or a specific sentence under Rule 11(e)(1)(A) and (C), then the court may accept or reject the plea agreement or defer its decision until it has reviewed the presentence report. Rule 11(e)(2), Fed. R. Crim. P. If the court accepts the plea agreement, it will embody in the judgment and sentence the disposition called for in the plea agreement. Rule 11(e)(3), Fed. R. Crim. P. Once the court has accepted the plea agreement, it may not order restitution beyond that required in the plea agreement. *U.S. v. Runck*, 601 F.2d 968, 970 (8th Cir. 1979), *cert. denied*, 444 U.S. 1015 (1980). If the court rejects the plea agreement, it must advise the defendant personally of this fact, afford the defendant an opportunity to withdraw his plea, and advise the defendant that if he persists in his plea of guilty or nolo contendere the disposition may be less favorable than contemplated in the plea agreement. Rule 11(e)(4), Fed. R. Crim. P.

The government may withdraw from a plea agreement at any time before the defendant actually pleads guilty. *U.S. v. Papaleo,* 853 F.2d 16 (1st Cir. 1988). Once a plea is accepted by the court, the government is not free to withdraw from the agreement even where the defendant was by mistake charged with a misdemeanor rather than a felony. *U.S. v. Partida-Parra,* 859 F.2d 629 (9th Cir. 1988).

A court may not categorically refuse to accept all plea agreements in which the prosecution chooses to leave standing only one count of a multiple count indictment, *U.S. v. Miller,* 772 F.2d 562 (9th Cir. 1983), but may refuse to accept a guilty plea in its sound discretion, *U.S. v. Crosby,* 739 F.2d 1542 (11th Cir. 1984).

### § 612. — — Participation by Judge in Plea Discussions.

Although participation by the judge in plea discussions may not amount to a constitutional violation, Rule 11(e)(1) specifically forbids such participation by the judge. *Toler v. Wyrick,* 563 F.2d 372 (8th Cir. 1977), *cert. denied,* 435 U.S. 907 (1978). As a judge's role is limited to acceptance or rejection of the plea agreement, it is improper for the court to advise a defendant of a probable sentence before accepting a plea agreement. *Hinds v. U.S.,* 429 F.2d 1322, 1323 (9th Cir. 1970). As a probation officer is an agent of the court, it is likewise improper for him to disclose the sentence recommendations before trial or the acceptance of a plea where it could affect the defendant's decision to plead guilty or go to trial. *U.S. v. Harris,* 635 F.2d 526, 529 (6th Cir. 1980), *cert. denied,* 451 U.S. 989 (1981).

### § 613. — — Breach of Plea Agreement.

If a defendant is induced to plead guilty by a promise or agreement of the prosecutor, the defendant has a constitutional right to the performance of the promise, *Santobello v. New York,* 404 U.S. 257, 263 (1971), but not until such time as the plea is actually entered. *Mabry v. Johnson,* 467 U.S. 504 (1984); *U.S. v. Papaleo,* 853 F.2d 16 (1st Cir. 1988). A plea agreement also has been described as contractual in nature, and that when it is breached, the underlying basis for the plea fails. *Jones v. Estelle,* 584 F.2d 687, 689 (5th Cir. 1978). There is more involved than a contract, however, as the court plays a critical role in that no agreement is effective until the court approves the agreement and accepts the plea. *U.S. v. Ocanas,* 628 F.2d 353, 358 (5th Cir. 1980), *cert. denied,* 451 U.S. 984 (1981); *U.S. v. Bean,* 564 F.2d 700, 702 (5th Cir. 1977).

When a plea agreement with the defendant has been breached, the remedies are to allow the withdrawal of the guilty plea, *U.S. v. Cook,*

668 F.2d 317, 321 (7th Cir. 1982), to order specific performance of the agreement, *Santobello v. New York, supra* at 2631, or resentencing, *Brunelle v. U.S.,* 864 F.2d 64 (8th Cir. 1988); *U.S. v. Wilson,* 669 F.2d 922, 923 (4th Cir. 1982). Generally the choice is within the trial court's discretion. *U.S. v. Bowler,* 585 F.2d 851, 856 (7th Cir. 1978).

The prosecutor does not breach a plea agreement where he merely makes the agreed recommendation without "enthusiasm." *U.S. v. Benchimol,* 471 U.S. 453 (1985).

When, after sentencing, a defendant breaches a plea agreement that calls for him to testify against others, the double jeopardy bar that would otherwise apply is removed, and the original charges may be reinstated. *Ricketts v. Adamson,* 483 U.S. 1 (1987).

Disclosing unfavorable background and character information about the defendant to the probation officer has been held not to violate the plea agreement where the government has promised to make no recommendation and stand mute at sentencing. *U.S. v. Avery,* 621 F.2d 214, 216 (5th Cir. 1980), *cert. denied,* 450 U.S. 933 (1981). However, where the government has promised to offer nothing in aggravation of defendant's sentence, but provides damaging information for the presentence report, the defendant can withdraw his plea. This is true, even though the government may not have the authority to withhold relevant information. *U.S. v. Cook,* 668 F.2d at 321; *U.S. v. Moscahlaidis,* 868 F.2d 1357 (3d Cir. 1989). *But see U.S. v. Williamsburg Check Cashing Corp.,* 905 F.2d 25 (2d Cir. 1990). The Parole Board, in determining whether to grant parole on a related charge, may consider conduct underlying counts which had been dismissed pursuant to a plea agreement. *U.S. ex rel. Goldberg v. Warden,* 622 F.2d 60, 64-65 (3d Cir.), *cert. denied,* 449 U.S. 871 (1980).

## § 614. — Conditional Pleas.

The general rule is that a guilty or nolo contendere plea waives all nonjurisdictional defects in the proceedings. *U.S. v. Jackson,* 659 F.2d 73, 74 (5th Cir.), *cert. denied,* 455 U.S. 1003 (1981). As a result a defendant who has lost a pretrial motion, such as a suppression motion, may go through a trial just to preserve this issue for appeal.

To alleviate the expense and waste of court time of requiring a trial just so that a defendant who has lost a pretrial motion may preserve that issue for appeal, conditional pleas are permitted whereby a defendant may plead guilty or nolo contendere and preserve that issue for appellate review. Rule 11(a)(2), Fed. R. Crim. P. For a conditional plea to be appropriate, however, the issue preserved for appeal must be dispositive of the case, *U.S. v. Wong Ching Hing,* 867 F.2d 754 (2d Cir. 1989).

The rule requires that a conditional plea may be made only with the consent of the court and the government. The court may refuse to accept a conditional plea for any reason or for no reason. *U.S. v. Davis,* 900 F.2d 1524 (10th Cir. 1990). The defendant must also reserve in writing the right to appeal an adverse ruling of any specified pretrial motion. If the defendant prevails on appeal, he may withdraw his guilty plea.

## § 615. — Inadmissibility of Pleas and Plea Discussions.

Evidence of a withdrawn guilty plea, a nolo contendere plea, any statement made in the course of any proceeding regarding either of the foregoing pleas, or any statement made in the course of plea discussions with an attorney for the government, are inadmissible in any civil or criminal proceeding against the defendant who made the plea or who was a participant in the plea discussions. However, such a statement is admissible in a proceeding where another statement made during the course of the same plea or plea discussions is introduced (such as where the statement is not "against" the person who entered the plea and as such is not prohibited by this rule) and the statement should in fairness be considered contemporaneously with it. Pleas or plea discussions may also be introduced in a criminal proceeding for perjury or false statement if the statement was made by the defendant under oath, on the record, and in the presence of counsel. Rule 11(e)(6), Fed. R. Crim. P.; Rule 410, Fed. R. Evid.

The rule permits the unrestrained candor which produces effective plea discussions and even an attempt to open plea bargaining is inadmissible. Advisory Committee Note, Rule 11(e)(6) (1979 Amendment). The note points out that the only discussions which are covered by Rule 11(e)(6) are those with the attorney for the government. Cases where statements were made to law enforcement agents purporting to have authority to bargain are not covered by Rule 11(e)(6), but "must be resolved by that body of law dealing with police interrogations."

If there is a dispute whether a statement by a defendant or his attorney to a government attorney was made in the course of plea discussions, it will presumably be resolved by the test which was applied in the cases decided before the rule was amended. In these instances the defendant would claim that his statement made to an agent was in the course of plea discussions. The courts resolved this claim by a two-tiered test: the defendant must exhibit an actual subjective intent to negotiate a plea at the time of the discussion, and the expectation of negotiating a plea at the time must be reasonable under the totality of the circumstances. *See U.S. v. O'Brien,* 618 F.2d 1234, 1241 (7th Cir.), *cert. denied,* 449 U.S. 858 (1980); *U.S. v. Castillo,* 615 F.2d 878, 885 (9th Cir. 1980); *U.S. v. Posey,* 611 F.2d 1389, 1390 (5th Cir. 1980). Thus under Rule 11(e)(6), as amended, a defendant's mere offer to the prosecutor to cooperate may be a subjective intent to negotiate a plea under all the circumstances.

## § 616. — Effect of a Technical Violation of Rule 11.

*McCarthy v. U.S.,* 394 U.S. 459 (1969), which involved a direct appeal from a plea of guilty, required strict adherence to the provisions of Rule 11. Rule 11(h) now provides that the harmless error rule applies to Rule 11.

The Supreme Court has held that collateral relief is not available to a defendant where the only claim is a technical violation of Rule 11. *U.S. v. Timmreck,* 441 U.S. 780, 785 (1979).

## § 617. Withdrawal of Plea of Guilty or Nolo Contendere.

A motion to withdraw a plea of guilty or nolo contendere may be made only before sentence is imposed or imposition of sentence is suspended. After sentencing, a plea may be set aside only on direct appeal or by motion under 28 U.S.C. § 2255.

## § 618. — Withdrawal Before Sentence.

The standard for permitting withdrawal of the plea is a "fair and just" standard. *Kercheval v. U.S.,* 274 U.S. 220, 224 (1927); *U.S. v. Bryant,* 640 F.2d 170, 172 (8th Cir. 1981); *Virgin Islands v. Berry,* 631 F.2d 214, 219 (3d Cir. 1980). The general rule is that before sentencing such permission should be liberally granted. *U.S. v. Hancock,* 607 F.2d 337 (10th Cir. 1979); *U.S. v. Pressley,* 602 F.2d 709, 711 (5th Cir. 1979).

However, there is no absolute right to withdraw a guilty plea before sentence. This is a matter which is within the discretion of the trial court and will be reversed only for an abuse of that discretion. *U.S. v. Crumbley,* 872 F.2d 975 (11th Cir. 1989); *U.S. v. Rasmussen,* 642 F.2d 165 (5th Cir. 1981); *U.S. v. King,* 618 F.2d 550 (9th Cir. 1980); *U.S. v. Brown,* 617 F.2d 54 (4th Cir. 1980).

Factors to be considered in determining whether to allow a presentence motion to withdraw a plea include: (1) whether a fair and just reason to withdraw the plea is established; (2) whether the defendant asserts his innocence; (3) the length of time between the guilty plea and the motion to withdraw; and (4) whether the government will be prejudiced. *U.S. v. Boone,* 869 F.2d 1089 (8th Cir.), *cert. denied,* 493 U.S. 822 (1989).

### § 619. — Withdrawal After Sentence.

After sentence is imposed, a plea may be set aside only on direct appeal or by motion under 28 U.S.C. § 2255, Rule 32(d), Fed. R. Crim. P. The "applicable standard is that stated in *Hill v. United States,* 368 U.S. 424 (1962): 'a fundamental defect which inherently results in a complete miscarriage of justice' or 'an omission inconsistent with the rudimentary demands of fair procedure.'" Advisory Committee Note, Rule 32(d) (1983 Amendment).

# CHAPTER 7

# PRETRIAL DISCOVERY AND DISCLOSURE

§ 700. Introduction.
§ 701. Bill of Particulars.
§ 702. Notice of Alibi.
§ 703. Notice of Defense Based Upon Mental Condition.
§ 704. Notice of Defense Based Upon Public Authority.
§ 705. Discovery and Inspection.
§ 706. — Statements of Defendant.
§ 707. — Defendant's Prior Record.
§ 708. — Documents and Tangible Objects.
§ 709. — Reports of Examinations and Tests.
§ 710. — Disclosure of Evidence by the Defendant.
§ 711. — Limitations Upon Discovery.
§ 712. — — Discovery of Witness Statements and the Identities of Witnesses.
§ 713. — — Disclosure of Identities of Informants.
§ 714. — — Duty to Disclose "Exculpatory" Evidence.
§ 715. — Protective Orders.
§ 716. — Sanctions for Failure to Provide Discovery.
§ 717. Subpoena for the Production of Documentary Evidence and Objects.
§ 718. Rule of *Brady v. Maryland*.
§ 719. — Situations Requiring Disclosure.
§ 720. — Material That Must Be Disclosed.
§ 721. — — Exculpatory Material.
§ 722. — — Impeachment Material.
§ 723. — Time for Disclosure.
§ 724. — Preservation of Evidence.

## § 700. Introduction.

Pretrial discovery and disclosure of evidence by either the government or the defense in a criminal case are primarily controlled by the Federal Rules of Criminal Procedure and a body of case law dealing with the disclosure by the government of the identity of an informant and evidence potentially favorable to a defendant.

The basic purposes of the Federal Rules of Criminal Procedure concerning discovery are to simplify the discovery procedure by clearly outlining the steps involved, and to avoid surprise and eliminate unfair advantage to either the government or the defendant, by requiring the disclosure of certain evidence in advance of trial. Disclosure was designed to enable both parties to be better informed before trial, thereby resulting in (1) the elimination of numerous pretrial motions based on speculation and misinformation, (2) reducing and narrowing the legal and factual issues on the remaining pretrial motions, (3) more meaningful plea bargain negotiations, (4) the orderly presentation of

167

the evidence at the trial itself, and (5) the elimination of motions for "last minute" trial continuances or mid-trial recesses based upon a claim of surprise to the introduction of certain evidence.

Consequently, Rule 7(f) of the Federal Rules of Criminal Procedure provides that a defendant may obtain a bill of particulars where the charge is not framed with sufficient detail to enable him to prepare his defense, or to enter a plea of former jeopardy. Rule 12.1 mandates that, upon written demand of the government, a defendant must serve written notice of his intention to offer an alibi defense and state the place the defendant claims to have been and the names and addresses of witnesses upon whom he intends to rely to establish the defense. Rule 12.2 requires that a defendant notify the government of his intention to base his defense upon insanity or mental disease or defect or of his intention to introduce expert testimony to establish the inconsistency of the mental condition with the mental state required for the offense charged. Rule 12.3 requires that a defendant notify the government of his intention to base a defense upon the claim of actual or believed exercise of public authority on behalf of a law enforcement or federal intelligence agency at the time of the alleged offense.

Rule 16 of the Federal Rules of Criminal Procedure defines or describes the evidence which a defendant may discover from the government. Generally, a defendant may discover any written or relevant oral statement he has made, his criminal record, documents and tangible objects taken from him or to be used in the government's case-in-chief, and the results of any tests or examinations conducted by the government in relation to the case. Under the rule, the government has a reciprocal but limited right of discovery to certain evidence of the defendant. The rule also balances the rights of the parties to discovery against the potential abuse caused by such disclosure and, in appropriate circumstances, provides for protective orders to deny or restrict discovery. In addition, the rule provides for sanctions against a party for negligent or willful noncompliance with the discovery process.

## § 701. Bill of Particulars.

Rule 7(f) of the Federal Rules of Criminal Procedure provides that the court "may direct the filing of a bill of particulars." The rule further provides that a motion for a bill of particulars may be made before arraignment, within 10 days after arraignment, or at such later time as the court may permit.

A bill of particulars is granted only where necessary to inform the accused of the charge against him with sufficient precision to enable him to prepare his defense, to avoid or minimize the danger of surprise at trial, or to enable him to plead his acquittal or conviction in bar of further prosecution for the same offense. *Wong Tai v. U.S.*, 273 U.S. 77 (1927); *U.S. v. Giese*, 597 F.2d 1170 (9th Cir.), *cert. denied*, 444 U.S. 979 (1979); *U.S. v. Hill*, 589 F.2d 1344 (8th Cir.), *cert. denied*, 442 U.S. 919 (1979); *U.S. v. Haas*, 583 F.2d 216 (5th Cir. 1978), *cert. denied*, 440 U.S. 981 (1979); *U.S. v. Birmley*, 529 F.2d 103 (6th Cir. 1976). In a conspiracy case, a bill of particulars may be granted to compel the government to disclose the names of unindicted coconspirators if the government plans to use them as witnesses. *U.S. v. Barrentine*, 591 F.2d 1069 (5th Cir.), *cert. denied*, 444 U.S. 990 (1979).

A bill of particulars is not an investigative vehicle for the defense and is not available as a tool "to obtain detailed disclosure of the government's evidence prior to trial." *U.S. v. Kilrain*, 566 F.2d 979, 985 (5th Cir.), *cert. denied*, 439 U.S. 819 (1978); *U.S. v. Matlock*, 675 F.2d 981, 986 (8th Cir. 1982). Thus, a defendant may not use a motion for a bill of particulars to compel the disclosure of a government witness list. *U.S. v. Largent*, 545 F.2d 1039 (6th Cir. 1976). As a general rule, an inquiry into the government's legal or evidentiary theory as to the means by which a defendant committed a specific criminal act is not a proper purpose for a bill of particulars. *See, e.g., U.S. v. Leonelli*, 428 F. Supp. 880 (S.D.N.Y. 1977); *U.S. v. Bozza*, 234 F. Supp. 15 (E.D.N.Y. 1964); *U.S. v. Kahaner*, 203 F. Supp. 78 (S.D.N.Y.), *aff'd*, 317 F.2d 459 (2d Cir.), *cert. denied*, 375 U.S. 836 (1963).

The particulars furnished by the government may confine the government's theory of proof, as a defendant is entitled to rely upon the statements contained in the response. As a result, it is reversible error for the government then to introduce other unambiguous statements in the bill of particulars even though it may have been "voluntarily" filed by the government. *U.S. v. Flom*, 558 F.2d 1179 (5th Cir. 1977).

A denial of a bill of particulars is within the discretion of the court and is reviewable only for an abuse of discretion. *U.S. v. Abreu*, 952 F.2d 1458 (1st Cir. 1992); *Wong Tai v. U.S., supra; U.S. v. Diecidue*, 603 F.2d 535 (5th Cir. 1979); *U.S. v. Giese, supra; U.S. v. Cooper*, 577 F.2d 1079 (6th Cir.), *cert. denied*, 439 U.S. 868 (1978); *U.S. v. Cohen*, 518 F.2d 727 (2d Cir.), *cert. denied*, 423 U.S. 926 (1975). A delay in furnishing particulars until a few days before trial does not require reversal, absent a showing the defendant was so burdened by the response that he could not properly assimilate the information before trial. The court may grant a continuance until the material is properly digested. *U.S. v. Salazar*, 485 F.2d 1272 (2d Cir. 1973), *cert. denied*, 415 U.S. 985 (1974).

## § 702. Notice of Alibi.

Rule 12.1 of the Federal Rules of Criminal Procedure enables the government to discover whether a defendant intends to offer an alibi defense. Under the rule, however, the attorney for the government must demand in writing that the defendant declare his intention to use an alibi defense at trial, and the demand by the government must include the time, date, and place of the alleged offense. In a conspiracy, the notice-of-alibi demand of the government may be restricted to a limited period, rather than the entire criminal transaction. *U.S. v. Vela,* 673 F.2d 86, 88-89 (5th Cir. 1982).

Within 10 days, unless the court extends or contracts the time, the defendant must then serve upon the government written notice of his intention to rely upon an alibi defense and must state in the notice the specific time and place or places he claims to have been at the time of the alleged offense and the names and addresses of the witnesses relied upon to establish his alibi. In response, the government must provide the defense with the names and addresses of any witnesses it intends to use to place defendant at the scene of the offense or to rebut defendant's alibi witnesses.

Failure of either party to comply with the requirements of Rule 12.1 may result in exclusion at trial of the undisclosed alibi or rebuttal witnesses. The rule empowers the court to grant exceptions to the requirements of Rule 12.1(a) through (d) upon a showing of "good cause." Factors to be considered include "(1) the amount of prejudice that resulted from the failure to disclose, (2) the reason for nondisclosure, (3) the extent to which the harm caused by nondisclosure was mitigated by subsequent events, (4) the weight of the properly admitted evidence supporting the defendant's guilt, and (5) other relevant factors arising out of the circumstances of the case." *U.S. v. Myers,* 550 F.2d 1036, 1043 (5th Cir.), *cert. denied,* 439 U.S. 847 (1977). *Accord U.S. v. Woodard,* 671 F.2d 1097, 1099 (8th Cir. 1982). The sanction of exclusion of a defendant's alibi witnesses at trial has been imposed when the defendant either failed to provide a response to the government's demand within the time set by the rule or by the court, or made absolutely no response until the time of trial depriving the government of an opportunity to investigate and adequately prepare a rebuttal. *U.S. v. White,* 583 F.2d 899 (6th Cir. 1978); *U.S. v. Fitts,* 576 F.2d 837 (10th Cir. 1978); *U.S. v. Barron,* 575 F.2d 752 (9th Cir. 1978). *See also Williams v. Florida,* 399 U.S. 78 (1970). Similarly, failure of the government to respond with its list of alibi rebuttal witnesses until trial also has triggered the sanction of exclusion where the defendant was deprived of the opportunity to interview those witnesses, and the other evidence of guilt against the defendant was less than overwhelming. *U.S. v. Myers, supra.* However, nondisclosure by the government under the rule has been held not to be reversible error where overwhelming evidence of the defendant's guilt was introduced at trial and the defendant knew the identities of the rebuttal witnesses long before trial. *McClendon v. U.S.,* 587 F.2d 384 (8th Cir. 1978), *cert. denied,* 440 U.S. 983 (1979).

There is no obligation upon the defendant to provide notice of alibi if he is the only witness who will attempt to establish his alibi defense. Rule 12.1(d), Fed. R. Crim. P. Therefore, "good cause" should exist to allow the government to call undisclosed witnesses on rebuttal to refute the "solo" alibi defense. The rule also provides that no evidence of an intention to rely on an alibi defense that is later withdrawn is admissible in any civil or criminal proceeding against the person who gave notice of the intention. Rule 12.1(f), Fed. R. Crim. P.

### § 703. Notice of Defense Based Upon Mental Condition.

Rule 12.2 of the Federal Rules of Criminal Procedure provides that, within the time set by the court for the filing of pretrial motions or within any additional time granted by the court, a defendant must notify the government in writing of his intention to rely upon the defense of insanity or to introduce expert testimony of mental disease bearing upon the issue of his guilt. The rule further requires that defendant file a copy of such notice with the clerk. Also, the rule vests the court with power to allow late filing, "for cause shown," or to grant additional time to prepare for trial.

The basic purpose for requiring the defendant to give notice of his intention to rely upon an insanity defense is to give the government time to prepare to rebut such a defense. *U.S. v. Winn,* 577 F.2d 86 (9th Cir.), *cert. denied,* 435 U.S. 946 (1978); *U.S. v. Hudson,* 566 F.2d 889 (4th Cir. 1977), *cert. denied,* 435 U.S. 946 (1978).

The rule provides that failure by the defendant to give proper and timely notice of an insanity defense may result in the court excluding any evidence on the insanity issue and may properly refuse to instruct the jury on the issue of insanity. *U.S. v. Duggan,* 743 F.2d 59 (2d Cir. 1984); *U.S. v. Veatch,* 674 F.2d 1217, 1224-25 (9th Cir. 1981).

Likewise, Rule 12.2(b) requires a defendant to give timely notice of his intention to use expert testimony to show he suffered from a mental disease or defect sufficient to affect his mental capacity to form specific intent where such intent is an element of the crime charged. *U.S. v. Olson,* 576 F.2d 1267 (8th Cir.), *cert. denied,* 439 U.S. 896 (1978). However, the notice requirement of Rule 12.2(b) applies only to expert testimony; consequently, no notice is necessary where lay testimony is introduced about a defendant's mental state in an attempt to show his lack of specific intent by reason of mental defect or disease. *U.S. v. Winn, supra.*

Rule 12.2(c) gives the court authority, upon motion by the government, to order the defendant to submit to a psychiatric or psychological examination. However, the rule expressly provides that any statements made by the defendant during the course of such examination, no testimony by the expert based upon such statement, nor any fruits of the statement shall be introduced against the defendant in any criminal proceeding except on an issue regarding mental condition on which the defendant has introduced testimony. If a defendant ultimately decides to forego his insanity defense before trial, no such statements made by him during the examination can be used by the government, even for the limited purpose of impeachment. *U.S. v. Leonard,* 609 F.2d 1163 (5th Cir. 1980).

At trial, the defendant has the burden of proving the defense of insanity by clear and convincing evidence. 18 U.S.C. § 20.

## § 704. Notice of Defense Based Upon Public Authority.

Rule 12.3 of the Federal Rules of Criminal Procedure provides that, within the time provided for the filing of pretrial motions or within such additional time granted by the Court, a defendant intending to claim a defense of actual or believed exercise of public authority on behalf of a law enforcement or federal intelligence agency, must serve written notice of his defense on the attorney for the government and with the clerk. The notice shall identify the law enforcement or federal intelligence agency, the member of such agency on behalf of which and the time period in which the defendant claims the actual or believed existence of public authority occurred. If the notice identifies a federal intelligence agency, the copy filed with the clerk shall be filed under seal. Within ten days, or in any event, no less than twenty days before trial, the attorney for the government must admit or deny that the defendant exercised the public authority identified in the defendant's notice.

At the time the government serves its response, but no less than twenty days before trial, the government may serve upon the defendant a written demand for the names and addresses of witnesses, if any, upon whom the defendant intends to rely in establishing the defense identified in the notice. Within seven days of the demand, the defendant shall serve upon the attorney for the government the names and addresses of any such witnesses. Seven days after receiving the defendant's written statement, the government must serve upon the defendant a written statement of names and addresses of any witnesses the government intends to rely on in opposing the defense identified in the defendant's notice.

## § 705. Discovery and Inspection.

Rule 16 of the Federal Rules of Criminal Procedure is the basic and, in most cases, the exclusive discovery tool that can be utilized by a defendant. Generally, recorded and written statements made by the defendant before or after arrest, the substance of any oral statements made by the defendant to any person then known to the defendant to be a government agent, the defendant's prior arrest record, documents and tangible objects to be introduced by the government during its case-in-chief or taken from the possession of the defendant, and reports of scientific tests and medical examinations are all subject to discovery upon request under Rule 16.

In addition, the rule provides that documents and tangible objects that are material to the preparation of the defense, although not intended to be introduced by the government during its case-in-chief, are discoverable under the rule. There is also a continuing duty upon the attorney for the government to exercise due diligence in disclosing additional material which may become known to him before trial. If disclosure is requested by the defense and the government complies, the prosecution has a reciprocal but limited right to discovery under the rule. Request for discovery must be made within the time provided by the trial court for pretrial motions. See Rule 12(b) and (c), Fed. R. Crim. P.

## § 706. — Statements of Defendant.

Effective December 1, 1991, Rule 16(a)(1)(A) provides that upon request of a defendant, the government shall disclose and make available for inspection, copying or photographing any of four types of statements he has made which the government possesses: (1) any relevant written or recorded statements; (2) that portion of any written record containing the substance of any relevant oral statements made by the defendant in response to interrogation by any person then known to the defendant to be a government agent; (3) any testimony of the defendant before a grand jury which relates to the offense charged; and (4) the substance of any other relevant oral statement made by the defendant before or after arrest in response to interrogation by any person then known by the defendant to be a government agent if the government intends to use that statement at trial. Even if the attorney for the government does not know of the existence of any written or recorded statement by the defendant at the time of such request, the rule imposes an affirmative duty on the prosecutor to exercise due diligence in determining whether any such statements exist. This duty requires that the attorney for the government make a demand on the agency responsible for the investigation to search its files to determine if any such statements exist. *U.S. v. Jensen,* 608 F.2d 1349 (10th Cir. 1979); *U.S. v. James,* 495 F.2d 434 (5th Cir.), *cert. denied,* 419 U.S. 899 (1974). And, as with all of the sections of Rule 16 providing for discovery, Rule 16(c) imposes upon both the government and the defense a continuing duty to disclose promptly upon discovery additional evidence previously requested by either side, or ordered by the court to be provided.

Written or recorded statements by the defendant include those made in either a pre-arrest or post-arrest setting. Any written statement, either inculpatory or exculpatory, made by the defendant is obviously included under this rule and should be provided whether given by the defendant in response to pre-arrest investigation questioning or the more usual post-arrest setting.

Written or recorded statements of the defendant are not limited to recitals of past occurrences. Recorded statements made of telephone conversations or face-to-face meetings between a defendant and a government agent (and the transcripts subsequently produced by the government of those statements) made during the course of a commission of a crime are also discoverable. *U.S. v. Walker,* 538 F.2d 266 (9th Cir. 1976); *U.S. v. Crisona,* 416 F.2d 107 (2d Cir. 1969), *cert. denied,* 397 U.S. 961 (1970). For example, a tape recording made of a conversation in which the defendant allegedly offered a government agent a bribe is a "statement" under Rule 16(a)(1)(A) and is discoverable by the defendant. Letters written by a defendant in the possession of the government and tape recordings of conversations between a defendant and a third person not associated with the government are also discoverable. *U.S. v. Pascual,* 606 F.2d 561 (5th Cir. 1979); *U.S. v. Caldwell,* 543 F.2d 1333 (D.C. Cir. 1974), *cert. denied,* 423 U.S. 1087 (1976); *U.S. v. Crisona, supra.* However, under Rule 16(d)(1), a protective order denying defendant's request for tape recordings of her statements was proper where there was concern for the safety of persons cooperating on the case whose identity would be revealed to the defendant if she heard the tape. *U.S. v. Pelton,* 578 F.2d 701 (8th Cir.), *cert. denied,* 439 U.S. 964 (1978). If the government's recorded statement of a defendant was the fruit of electronic surveillance under Title III, disclosure of the defendant's statement is mandatory under 18 U.S.C. § 2518(9).

A defendant's relevant oral statement made to a person then known to the defendant to be a government agent, even though neither recorded nor reduced to writing, is nonetheless required to be produced pursuant to the rule. *U.S. v. Manetta,* 551 F.2d 1352 (5th Cir. 1977); *U.S. v. Lewis,* 511 F.2d 798 (D.C. Cir. 1975). Even summary reports and interview memoranda made by government agents, merely setting forth the substance of the defendant's remarks, are within the scope of the rule. *U.S. v. Johnson,* 525 F.2d 999 (2d Cir. 1975), *cert. denied,* 424 U.S. 920 (1976).

However, production of pre-arrest oral statements made by the defendant to an undercover agent, not then known as such to the defendant, is not required. Rule 16(a)(1)(A) of the Federal Rules of Criminal Procedure provides that only oral statements made by a defendant "in response to interrogation by any person then known to the defendant to be a government agent" are discoverable by the defense. *U.S. v. Johnson,* 562 F.2d 515 (8th Cir. 1977); *U.S. v. Green,* 548 F.2d 1261 (6th Cir. 1977). Likewise, oral statements of the defendant made to a third party, incorporating admissions or acknowledgements of guilt, are not discoverable under the rule. *U.S. v. Zarattini,* 552 F.2d 753 (7th Cir.), *cert. denied,* 431 U.S. 942 (1977). One court has applied the rule when a third-party conversation was overheard by a government agent whose presence was not known to the defendant. *U.S. v. Viserto,* 596 F.2d 531 (2d Cir.), *cert. denied,* 444 U.S. 841 (1979).

The recorded testimony of the defendant before a grand jury must be made available to the defendant. In addition, under Rule 16(a)(1)(A), where the defendant is a corporation, partnership, association, or labor union, it is entitled to discover the grand jury testimony of a witness who was an officer or employee at the time of his testimony and able to legally bind the defendant to acts constituting the offense in question.

## §707. — Defendant's Prior Record.

Rule 16(a)(1)(B) of the Federal Rules of Criminal Procedure provides that, upon request, the government shall furnish the defendant with a copy of his prior criminal record, if any, which is in the possession of the government, known by the government to exist, or becomes known to the government after the exercise of due diligence, *i.e.,* an inquiry made to the agency responsible for the investigation of the case.

## §708. — Documents and Tangible Objects.

Rule 16(a)(1)(C) provides that, upon request, the government shall permit the defendant to inspect and copy "books, papers, documents, photographs, tangible objects, buildings or places..." if any one of the following conditions is met: (1) the defendant shows that disclosure of the document or tangible object is material to the defense; (2) the government intends to introduce the document or tangible object as evidence in its case-in-chief; or (3) the document or tangible object was obtained from or belonged to the defendant. In the latter two instances, the defendant need not specifically designate the items sought, and if a decision is later made to use other evidence in the government's case-in-chief, the defense must be notified immediately or the government faces the risk of having the evidence excluded under Rule 16(c). *U.S. v. Bowers,* 593 F.2d 376 (10th Cir.), *cert. denied,* 444 U.S. 852 (1979).

If the evidence sought by the defendant does not fall into either of the above categories, the government has no obligation to turn over other documents or tangible objects, absent a showing of materiality by the defense. *U.S. v. Jordan,* 399 F.2d 610 (2d Cir.), *cert. denied,* 393 U.S. 1005 (1968). Materiality means more than that the evidence in question bears some abstract or logical relationship to the issues in the case. To obtain documents and tangible objects not originally the property of the accused or evidence to be used in the government's case-in-chief, the defendant must show that the pretrial disclosure of the material would "enable the accused to substantially alter the quantum of proof in his favor." *U.S. v. Marshall,* 532 F.2d 1279, 1285 (9th Cir. 1976); *U.S. v. Buckley,* 586 F.2d 498, 506 (5th Cir. 1978), *cert. denied,* 440 U.S. 982 (1979); *U.S. v. Ross,* 511 F.2d 757 (5th Cir. 1975). In addition, the defendant's request must also be reasonable. Therefore, a request for documents by a defendant must not be unduly burdensome to the government and must be framed in specific terms to show the government what it must produce. Factors to be considered by the court in determining whether the government must produce such material include the extensiveness of the material and its availability from other sources, including the defendant's own knowledge. *U.S. v. Marshall, supra; U.S. v. Ross, supra.*

Rule 16(a)(1)(C) applies only to items "within possession, custody or control of the government." Accordingly, disclosure is not required, for example, where the evidence is in the custody of foreign police authorities or other persons not subject to the control of the government attorney. *U.S. v. Flores,* 540 F.2d 432 (9th Cir. 1976); *U.S. v. Cotroni,* 527 F.2d 708 (2d Cir. 1975), *cert. denied,* 426 U.S. 906 (1976). However, the language of the rule is sufficiently broad to require disclosure by the United States Attorney of evidence in the custody of another federal agency. *U.S. v. Scruggs,* 583 F.2d 238 (5th Cir. 1978); *U.S. v. Bryant,* 439 F.2d 642 (D.C. Cir. 1971). However, even if there is a violation of the rule, "sufficient prejudice" to the defendant must be shown for reversal. *U.S. v. Scruggs,* 583 F.2d at 242.

### §709. — Reports of Examinations and Tests.

Upon request, the government must permit the defendant to inspect and copy results or reports of physical or mental examinations, as well as results or reports of any scientific tests or experiments, which are within the possession, custody, or control of the government and which are (1) material to the preparation of the defense, or (2) to be used by the government during its case-in-chief. Therefore, the government is compelled to produce copies of the reports of fingerprint and handwriting experts who have examined known fingerprint or handwriting exemplars of the defendant and have compared them to questioned specimens. *U.S. v. Buchanan,* 585 F.2d 100 (5th Cir. 1978). Similarly, a defendant has the right to inspect and copy results or reports of examinations made by the government of controlled substances. *U.S. v. Gordon,* 580 F.2d 827 (5th Cir.), *cert. denied,* 439 U.S. 1051 (1978).

Rule 16(a)(1)(D), like Rule 16(a)(1)(C) relating to the production of documents and tangible objects, contains a threshold requirement of materiality. A defendant must meet this burden where the government does not intend to use such tests and examinations as evidence at trial. *U.S. v. Thompson,* 493 F.2d 305 (9th Cir.), *cert. denied,* 419 U.S. 834 (1974). Therefore, the government is not required to provide memoranda related to the tests necessary for determining whether a substance represented is an unlawful isomer of a particular substance if such memoranda were not made in connection with any particular prosecution. *U.S. v. Orzechowski,* 547 F.2d 978 (7th Cir.), *cert. denied,* 431 U.S. 906 (1977).

### §710. — Disclosure of Evidence by the Defendant.

Rule 16(b)(1) is one of the few provisions allowing discovery of a defendant's evidence by the government. The materials potentially discoverable by the government parallel the materials obtainable by the defendant under Rule 16(a)(1)(C) and (D). They are books, papers, documents, photographs, or tangible objects in the possession of the defendant, and results of scientific tests and experiments conducted on behalf of the defendant. Before any evidence may be discovered by the government under the rule, however, there must be a discovery request by the defendant, and the government must comply with the request. *U.S. v. Opager,* 589 F.2d 799 (5th Cir. 1979). Additionally, the court must find that the government's request is material and reasonable and not designed to harass the defendant or probe into defense strategy. *U.S. v. Estremera,* 531 F.2d 1103 (2d Cir.), *cert. denied,* 425 U.S. 979 (1976).

This material is subject to a government discovery request only if the defense intends to introduce the material as evidence in chief, or in the case of the results of a test or examination, the defense intends to call the preparer of such report at trial and the results of such test or examination relate to his testimony. Rule 16(b)(1)(B), Fed. R. Crim. P. Thus, the disclosure obligation of the defense is more limited under the rule than is that of the government under Rule 16(a)(1)(D), since the government must disclose any reports "material to the defense." For example, government psychiatric reports concerning the defendant, including any supporting the contentions of the defense, must be disclosed; but the defendant need not disclose any psychiatric report supporting the government position if the defendant decides not to call the examining psychiatrist who wrote the report. *U.S. v. Alvarez,* 519 F.2d 1036, 1046 (3d Cir. 1975).

## § 711. — Limitations Upon Discovery.

## § 712. — — Discovery of Witness Statements and the Identities of Witnesses.

Rule 16(a)(2) of the Federal Rules of Criminal Procedure specifically excludes from pretrial discovery (1) "reports, memoranda, or other internal government documents made by the attorney for the government or other government agents in connection with the investigation or prosecution of the case," and (2) statements made by government witnesses or potential government witnesses except as provided under the Jencks Act (18 U.S.C. § 3500). Thus, written or oral statements of witnesses, including coconspirators and codefendants, are not discoverable under Rule 16. *U.S. v. Fearn,* 589 F.2d 1316 (7th Cir. 1978); *U.S. v. Cook,* 530 F.2d 145 (7th Cir. 1976), *cert. denied,* 426 U.S. 909 (1977); *U.S. v. Percevault,* 490 F.2d 126 (2d Cir. 1974).

Likewise, Rule 16(b)(2) precludes the discovery of (1) "reports, memoranda or other internal defense documents" made in connection with the case, and (2) statements made by the defendant or by witnesses or prospective witnesses to the defense.

Rule 16(a)(3) states that, "except as provided in Rules 6, 12(i), 26.2 and subdivision (a)(1)(A) of this rule, these rules do not relate to discovery or inspection of the recorded proceedings of a grand jury." Thus, recorded statements of a witness made before a grand jury are generally not subject to pretrial discovery by a defendant.

Likewise, Rule 16 does not mandate disclosure of the names of witnesses. *U.S. v. Dark,* 597 F.2d 1097 (6th Cir.), *cert. denied,* 444 U.S. 927 (1979); *U.S. v. Dreitzler,* 577 F.2d 539, 553 (9th Cir. 1978), *cert. denied,* 440 U.S. 921 (1979); *U.S. v. Little,* 562 F.2d 578 (8th Cir. 1978); *U.S. v. Mitchell,* 540 F.2d 1163, 1166 (3d Cir. 1976); *U.S. v. Cook, supra; U.S. v. Cannone,* 528 F.2d 296, 302 (2d Cir. 1975).

Attempts to amend Rule 16 to compel the disclosure of the names of prospective witnesses by either side have been rejected by Congress. H.R. Conf. Rep. No. 414, 94th Cong., 1st Sess. 12 (1975). The conference report accompanying the 1975 amendments to the Rules of Criminal Procedure notes:

> A majority of the Conferees believe it is not in the interest of the effective administration of criminal justice to require that the government or the defendant be forced to reveal the names and addresses of its witnesses before trial. Discouragement of witnesses and improper contacts directed at influencing their testimony, were deemed paramount concerns in the formation of this policy.

The fact that Rule 16 does not compel disclosure of the names and addresses of government witnesses does not mean that a defendant is necessarily precluded outright from obtaining this information. Generally, the granting of a defendant's request for pretrial disclosure of the identities of the government's witnesses is within the discretion of the trial court. *U.S. v. John Bernard Industries, Inc.,* 589 F.2d 1353 (8th Cir. 1979); *U.S. v. Chaplinski,* 579 F.2d 373 (5th Cir.), *cert. denied,* 439 U.S. 1050 (1978); *U.S. v. Sclamo,* 578 F.2d 888 (1st Cir. 1978); *U.S. v. Dreitzler,* 577 F.2d 539 (9th Cir. 1978); *U.S. v. Harris,* 542 F.2d 1283 (7th Cir. 1976), *cert. denied,* 430 U.S. 934 (1977); *U.S. v. Cannone,* 528 F.2d 296 (2d Cir. 1975). In a capital case under any federal criminal statute, 18 U.S.C. § 3432 requires the government to provide the defense with a list of witnesses at least three days before trial.

Generally, to obtain a government witness list a defendant must make a specific showing that such disclosure is both material to the preparation of his defense and reasonable in light of the circumstances. A defense request for disclosure of a government witness list for the general need to prepare for cross-examination does not constitute a showing of necessity. *U.S. v. Sclamo,* 578 F.2d 888 (1st Cir. 1978). Where the government has made a motion for a protective order under Rule 16(d)(1), representing that disclosure of the names of the witnesses would involve potential physical danger to the witness and supporting its position by materials submitted *in camera,* a trial court does not abuse its discretion by refusing to order the government to provide a defendant with a witness list. *U.S. v. Harris, supra.*

A refusal by the government to obey a court order requiring it to exchange witness lists, witness testimony, and copies of exhibits, not sanctioned by Rule 16, will not necessarily result in reversal upon appeal. Such factors as the defendant's minimal compliance with a reciprocal discovery order, the defendant's failure to call to the court's attention at trial the government's refusal to comply with a previous discovery order, or overwhelming evidence of the defendant's guilt mitigate any such failure of disclosure by the government. *See, e.g., U.S. v. Seymour*, 576 F.2d 1345 (9th Cir. 1978); *U.S. v. Larson*, 555 F.2d 673 (8th Cir. 1977). In addition, interlocutory appeal of a trial court's order requiring pretrial disclosure of the identities of government witnesses, where the government has presented some evidence of potential danger to the witnesses and the defense has presented no specific reason of its need for disclosure, may be proper. It has been held an abuse of discretion for the trial court to allow a defendant to obtain the names and addresses of witnesses under such circumstances. *U.S. v. Cannone, supra.*

Another provision used by defendants attempting to go beyond Rule 16 for discovery of the government's case is the Freedom of Information Act, 5 U.S.C. § 552. However, it has been held that this act does not enlarge the scope of criminal discovery under Rule 16. *U.S. v. Buckley*, 586 F.2d 498 (5th Cir. 1978), *cert. denied*, 440 U.S. 982 (1979); *Fruehauf Corp. v. Thornton*, 507 F.2d 1253 (6th Cir. 1974).

## § 713. — — Disclosure of Identities of Informants.

Disclosure of the identity of a government informant is required only where it would be helpful to the defense or essential to a fair determination of the cause. *Roviaro v. U.S.*, 353 U.S. 53 (1957); *U.S. v. Hernandez-Berceda*, 572 F.2d 680 (9th Cir. 1978). There must be more than a mere request and more than mere speculation that disclosure will be helpful. *U.S. v. Trejo-Zambrano*, 582 F.2d 460 (9th Cir. 1978), *cert. denied*, 439 U.S. 1005 (1978); *In re U.S.*, 565 F.2d 19 (2d Cir. 1977).

Basically, disclosure is required if the court finds "it is reasonably probable that the informer can give relevant testimony" material to the defense. *U.S. v. McManus*, 560 F.2d 747, 751 (6th Cir. 1977), *cert. denied*, 434 U.S. 1047 (1978). *See also U.S. v. Opager*, 589 F.2d 799 (5th Cir. 1979); *U.S. v. Silva*, 580 F.2d 144 (5th Cir. 1978). Where a defendant cannot show with "reasonable probability" that the informant was an active participant in the criminal matter under review, but only a "mere tipster," the government is not required to disclose the identity of the informant. *U.S. v. Lewis*, 671 F.2d 1025, 1027 (7th Cir.

1982); *U.S. v. Suarez,* 582 F.2d 1007, 1011 (5th Cir. 1978); *U.S. v. Sherman,* 576 F.2d 292 (10th Cir.), *cert. denied,* 439 U.S. 913 (1978); *U.S. v. Alonzo,* 571 F.2d 1384 (5th Cir.), *cert. denied,* 439 U.S. 847 (1978). Similarly, disclosure is not required where the informant played only a small or passive role in the offense charged, had no firsthand information, or where his potential disclosures are already known to the defendant. *U.S. v. Moreno,* 588 F.2d 490 (5th Cir. 1978), *cert. denied,* 441 U.S. 936 (1979); *U.S. v. Suarez, supra; U.S. v. Weir,* 575 F.2d 668 (8th Cir. 1978); *U.S. v. Robinson,* 530 F.2d 1076 (D.C. Cir. 1976). Likewise, disclosure will not be ordered where the witness would be in personal danger and the potential testimony of the witness was not of an exculpatory nature. *U.S. v. Pelton,* 578 F.2d 701 (8th Cir. 1978), *cert. denied,* 439 U.S. 964 (1979); *U.S. v. Cannone,* 528 F.2d 296 (2d Cir. 1975). When, before trial, the defendant knows the informant's identity, he may not later claim that the government's refusal to confirm the identity denied him a fair trial. *U.S. v. Brown,* 562 F.2d 1144 (9th Cir. 1977); *U.S. v. Gonzalez,* 555 F.2d 308 (2d Cir. 1977).

Even when the informant is substantially involved in the alleged criminal transaction and disclosure of his identity is required, the government has no duty to physically produce the informant at trial. *U.S. v. Fuentes,* 563 F.2d 527 (2d Cir. 1977), *cert. denied,* 434 U.S. 959 (1977); *U.S. v. Turbide,* 558 F.2d 1053 (2d Cir.), *cert. denied,* 434 U.S. 934 (1977). When disclosure is mandated by the court, however, the government must exercise due diligence in supplying the informant's name and available information about his whereabouts, and reasonably cooperate in securing the informant's appearance at trial. *U.S. v. Turbide, supra.* The government may not take affirmative steps to secrete the informant after such disclosure is made. *Lockett v. Blackburn,* 571 F.2d 309 (5th Cir.), *cert. denied,* 439 U.S. 873 (1978).

*See also* Chapter 19, § 1923, *infra.*

### §714. — — Duty to Disclose "Exculpatory" Evidence.

Apart from its duty to disclose evidence under Rule 16 or as ordered by the court in its discretion, the government may have a duty to disclose when a defendant specifically requests exculpatory evidence material to (1) guilt or innocence, or (2) punishment. *Brady v. Maryland,* 373 U.S. 83 (1963). *Brady* is not a rule of discovery, but a rule of due process fundamental fairness. *U.S. v. Starusko,* 729 F.2d 256 (3d Cir. 1984).

However, failure of the prosecutor to preserve potentially useful evidence is not a violation of due process unless the defendant can show bad faith on the part of the police. *Arizona v. Youngblood,* 488 U.S. 51 (1988).

## § 715. — Protective Orders.

Rule 16(d)(1) of the Federal Rules of Criminal Procedure vests the court with discretion, upon a sufficient showing of necessity by either party, to deny, restrict, or defer discovery or inspection. The rule further allows the party seeking a protective order to submit a written statement for an *in camera* inspection and decision. An FBI file relating to the activities of the defendant as a prior informant is not discoverable when the file contains nothing exculpatory, material, or relevant to the indictment in the case. *Xydas v. U.S.,* 445 F.2d 660 (D.C. Cir. 1971), *cert. denied,* 404 U.S. 826 (1972).

## § 716. — Sanctions for Failure to Provide Discovery.

Rule 16(d)(2) gives the court wide discretion in dealing with the failure of either party to comply with the discovery procedures of Rule 16; the court "may order such party to permit the discovery or inspection, grant a continuance, or prohibit the party from introducing evidence not disclosed, or it may enter such other order as it deems just under the circumstances." *See, e.g., U.S. v. Weatherspoon,* 581 F.2d 595 (7th Cir. 1978); *U.S. v. Jackson,* 508 F.2d 1001 (7th Cir. 1975).

If a party fails to provide evidence required to be produced under Rule 16 until immediately before or during the trial, the opposing party has a duty to move for a continuance or a recess if trial has commenced and to show that additional time is needed to properly consider, investigate, or utilize the new evidence. *U.S. v. Krohn,* 558 F.2d 390 (8th Cir.), *cert. denied,* 434 U.S. 868 (1977); *U.S. v. Bailey,* 550 F.2d 1099 (8th Cir. 1977).

A recess during a trial has been held sufficient to cure any prejudice to a defendant where previous failure to disclose by the government was inadvertent and the recess gave the defense time to investigate the ramifications of the new material or to prepare for cross-examination. *U.S. v. Lambert,* 580 F.2d 740 (5th Cir. 1978); *U.S. v. Fulton,* 549 F.2d 1325 (9th Cir. 1977). Where the defense until trial concealed its intention to assert that a substance seized from the defendant was not a controlled substance and, in response, the government tested the material but failed to inform the defendant of the results, it was held that the granting of a recess to give the defense time to conduct its own test cured any prejudice resulting from the mid-trial disclosure. *U.S. v. Bockius,* 564 F.2d 1193 (5th Cir. 1977). Even withholding evidence until trial will not result in reversal if a recess will enable the defense sufficient time to review and use the material supplied. *U.S. v. Kaplan,* 554 F.2d 577 (3d Cir. 1977). The admission of previously undisclosed evidence that can be classified as merely supplementary to other evidence already made available to the defense is within the discretion of the trial judge and will not be reversed unless there is prejudice to the defendant's substantial rights. *Hansen v. U.S.,* 393 F.2d 763 (5th Cir. 1968).

Even the failure of the government to respond until trial to a request of a defendant for his statements under Rule 16(a)(1)(A) generally does not require reversal where the failure to provide pretrial discovery was inadvertent, the statement contains nothing of a significant exculpatory nature, or the impact of the failure to produce the statement could not have reasonably deprived the defendant of a meritorious defense. Thus, the government's inadvertent failure to produce a defendant's statement containing no exculpatory statements was excused as being non-prejudicial to any reasonable interest of the defendant. *U.S. v. Gladney,* 563 F.2d 491 (1st Cir. 1977); *U.S. v. Smith,* 557 F.2d 1206 (5th Cir.), *cert. denied,* 434 U.S. 1073 (1977); *U.S. v. Eddy,* 549 F.2d 108 (9th Cir. 1976). Likewise, the government's failure to produce one of four of defendant's statements in timely fashion did not require reversal where such failure had no impact on the defense strategy. *U.S. v. Johnson,* 525 F.2d 999 (2d Cir.), *cert. denied,* 424 U.S. 920 (1975). Prejudice does not exist when the contents of the withheld statement are known to the defendant in advance of trial. *U.S. v. Arquelles,* 594 F.2d 109 (5th Cir.), *cert. denied,* 444 U.S. 860 (1979).

Failure to produce a defendant's statement may result in more severe sanctions where more than inadvertence or mere negligence on the part of the government is present. The government's failure to provide a tape recording of a conversation between a government agent and the defendant before trial resulted in the court forbidding the use of the tape and instructions to the jury to ignore previous mention of it by the government. *U.S. v. Gillings,* 568 F.2d 1307, 1310 (9th Cir.), *cert. denied,* 436 U.S. 919 (1978). Reversal has occurred where the government withheld a defendant's post-arrest statement that had substantial bearing on the contested issue of the defendant's mental capacity. *U.S. v. Manetta,* 551 F.2d 1352 (5th Cir. 1977). The prosecutor's use on cross-examination of the defendant's statement, a copy of which the court has ordered furnished to the defense but which was withheld by the prosecution, was highly prejudicial and reversal was ordered in *U.S. v. Pardone,* 406 F.2d 560 (2d Cir. 1969). Even an inadvertent failure by the government to supply a defendant with a document, even though a codefendant had received a copy, resulted in the government being barred from placing the document into evidence. *U.S. v. Kelly,* 569 F.2d 928 (5th Cir.), *cert. denied,* 439 U.S. 829 (1978).

## § 717. Subpoena for the Production of Documentary Evidence and Objects.

Rule 17(c) of the Federal Rules of Criminal Procedure governs the issuance of trial subpoenas duces tecum of documents or objects in criminal cases. *See* Chapter 4, *supra,* for the rule as applied to the issuance of grand jury subpoenas.

Subpoenas duces tecum can be issued for returns before trial by the prosecution or the defense. One of the purposes of Rule 17(c) is to expedite the trial by providing a means for pretrial inspection of subpoenaed materials. *U.S. v. Nixon,* 418 U.S. 683, 698 (1974). Decisions to enforce subpoenas and order pretrial production are discretionary with the trial court "since the necessity for the subpoena most often turns upon a determination of factual issues." *Id.* at 702.

Defendants will sometimes direct pretrial subpoenas to the government requesting production of items that are not discoverable pursuant to Rule 16 of the Federal Rules of Criminal Procedure. In *Bowman Dairy Co. v. U.S.,* 341 U.S. 214, 221 (1951), the Supreme Court stated that "any document or other materials, admissible as evidence, obtained by the Government by solicitation or voluntarily from third persons is subject to subpoena." However, the Court went on to say that pretrial subpoenas are not intended to provide an alternate means of pretrial discovery in criminal cases. *See U.S. v. Nixon,* 418 U.S. at 698; *U.S. v. Zirpolo,* 288 F. Supp. 993 (D.N.J. 1968), *rev'd on other grounds,* 450 F.2d 424 (3d Cir. 1971).

In *U.S. v. Nixon,* 418 U.S. at 699, the Supreme Court approved the criteria outlined in *U.S. v. Iozia,* 13 F.R.D. 335, 338 (S.D.N.Y. 1952), for considering Rule 17(c) subpoenas. They are (1) that the material sought is evidentiary and relevant; (2) that it is not otherwise procurable by the defendant reasonably in advance of trial by the exercise of due diligence; (3) that the defendant cannot properly prepare for trial without such production and inspection in advance and the failure to produce may tend unreasonably to delay the trial; and (4) that the application is made in good faith and is not intended as a general fishing expedition. The Court in *Nixon* further refined the criteria by requiring a minimal showing of (1) relevancy, (2) admissibility, and (3) specificity. *Nixon,* 418 U.S. at 700. Examples of applications of the criteria are found in *U.S. v. Cuthbertson,* 630 F.2d 139 (3d Cir. 1980), *cert. denied,* 449 U.S. 1126 (1980); *U.S. v. Campagnuolo,* 592 F.2d 852

(5th Cir. 1979); *U.S. v. Hill*, 589 F.2d 1344, 1352 (8th Cir.), *cert. denied*, 442 U.S. 919 (1979); *U.S. v. Bailey*, 550 F.2d 1099, 1100 (8th Cir. 1977); *U.S. v. Anderson*, 481 F.2d 685 (4th Cir. 1973), *aff'd*, 417 U.S. 211 (1974); *U.S. v. Purin*, 486 F.2d 1363 (2d Cir. 1973), *cert. denied*, 416 U.S. 987 (1974); *U.S. v. Marchisio*, 344 F.2d 653, 669 (2d Cir. 1965).

Where a defendant's discovery motion is sweeping and broadly phrased in an endeavor to secure a whole array of materials without designating with reasonable particularity the documents sought, the motion fails to comply with the rule. *U.S. v. Haldeman*, 559 F.2d 31 (D.C. Cir. 1976), *cert. denied*, 431 U.S. 933 (1977). In *U.S. v. Murray*, 297 F.2d 812, 821 (2d Cir.), *cert. denied*, 369 U.S. 828 (1962), the court stated that the moving party should intend that the material he seeks be used as evidence.

As under Rule 16, the government has a "continuing duty" under Rule 17(c) for the production of documents subpoenaed before trial. A new trial may be ordered where documents are negligently suppressed. *U.S. v. Consolidated Laundries Corp.*, 291 F.2d 563 (2d Cir. 1961). *See Kyle v. U.S.*, 297 F.2d 507 (2d Cir. 1961).

Subject to applicable privileges, the government may also use Rule 17(c) to subpoena evidence before trial. Like the defendant, however, the government may not utilize the rule as an additional means of discovery inasmuch as the purpose is simply to allow inspection of subpoenaed material by all parties before trial. *U.S. v. Nixon*, 418 U.S. at 698.

## §718. Rule of *Brady v. Maryland*.

In *Brady v. Maryland*, 373 U.S. 83 (1963), the Supreme Court held that, irrespective of good or bad faith, suppression by the prosecution of evidence favorable to a defendant who has requested it violates due process where such evidence is material to either guilt or punishment. The *Brady* holding imposes an affirmative duty on the prosecution to produce at the appropriate time requested evidence that is materially favorable to the accused, either as direct or impeaching evidence. *Brady* is not a rule of discovery; it is a rule of fairness and minimum prosecutorial obligation. *U.S. v. Beasley*, 576 F.2d 626, 630 (5th Cir. 1978), *cert. denied*, 440 U.S. 947 (1979), citing *U.S. v. Agurs*, 427 U.S. 97, 107 (1976). *See also U.S. v. Campagnuolo*, 592 F.2d 852, 859 (5th Cir. 1979). The obligation to disclose is measured by the "character of the evidence, not the character of the prosecutor." *U.S. v. Agurs*, 427 U.S. at 110; *Smith v. Phillips*, 455 U.S. 209, 220 (1982).

Grand jury testimony of a witness may be required to be disclosed under the *Brady* rule. *U.S. v. Campagnuolo*, 592 F.2d 852, 859 (5th Cir.

1979); *U.S. v. Azzarelli Constr. Co.,* 459 F. Supp. 146 (E.D. Ill. 1978), *aff'd,* 612 F.2d 292 (7th Cir.), *cert. denied,* 447 U.S. 920 (1980); *U.S. v. Brighton Building & Maintenance Co.,* 435 F. Supp. 222 (N.D. Ill. 1977), *aff'd,* 598 F.2d 1101 (1979).

### § 719. — Situations Requiring Disclosure.

The *Agurs* decision, following *Brady,* articulated three distinct types of situations in which the *Brady* doctrine applies. 427 U.S. at 103-06. The defense need only demonstrate that the prosecutor suppressed material evidence favorable to the defendant in order to establish a violation of one of the three categories of nondisclosure cases set forth in *Agurs.* Each category requires a separate analysis, however, and has a distinct test for materiality to determine whether the alleged suppression was so fundamentally unfair as to deny the due process right of a fair trial. If the suppressed evidence is then found to be material, the conviction cannot stand.

Under the first category of nondisclosure discussed in *Agurs,* where the prosecution knew or should have known that its case contained perjured testimony (as in *Mooney v. Holohan,* 294 U.S. 103 (1935)), the test of materiality is so applied that the conviction will be set aside if there is "any reasonable likelihood" that the false testimony "could have affected" the jury's judgment. *U.S. v. Agurs,* 427 U.S. at 103; *U.S. v. Anderson,* 574 F.2d 1347, 1352-53 (5th Cir. 1978); *U.S. v. Hedgeman,* 564 F.2d 763, 766 (7th Cir. 1977), *cert. denied,* 434 U.S. 1070 (1978); *U.S. v. Brown,* 562 F.2d 1144, 1150 (9th Cir. 1977).

Under the second category of nondisclosure set forth in *Agurs,* where the prosecution fails to respond to a defendant's specific request for information (as in *Brady v. Maryland,* 373 U.S. 83 (1963)), a new trial must be granted if the suppressed evidence "might have affected the outcome." 427 U.S. at 104; *Monroe v. Blackburn,* 607 F.2d 148, 151-52 (5th Cir. 1979); *U.S. v. Goldberg,* 582 F.2d 483, 489-90 (9th Cir. 1978), *cert. denied,* 440 U.S. 973 (1979); *U.S. v. Sutton,* 542 F.2d 1239, 1242-43 (4th Cir. 1976). The mere possibility that undisclosed information might have helped the defendant is, however, insufficient to establish "materiality." *U.S. v. Jackson,* 579 F.2d 553 (10th Cir.), *cert. denied,* 439 U.S. 981 (1978). Further, for the defense request under this category to be considered sufficiently specific, it must provide the prosecutor with notice of exactly what the defense desires. *U.S. v. Agurs,* 427 U.S. at 106; *U.S. v. DiCarlo,* 575 F.2d 952, 959-60 (1st Cir.), *cert. denied,* 439 U.S. 834 (1978); *Marzeno v. Gengler,* 574 F.2d 730, 736 (3d Cir. 1978); *U.S. v. Mackey,* 571 F.2d 376, 389 (7th Cir. 1978); *U.S. v. McCrane,* 547 F.2d 204, 207-08 (3d Cir. 1976).

In the third category of nondisclosure set out in *Agurs*, where the defendant fails to request, or only generally requests, exculpatory evidence (as in *Agurs* itself), reversal is necessary only if the undisclosed evidence "creates a reasonable doubt that did not otherwise exist." 427 U.S. at 112; *U.S. v. Alberico*, 604 F.2d 1315 (10th Cir.), *cert. denied*, 444 U.S. 992 (1979); *Galtieri v. Wainwright*, 582 F.2d 348 (5th Cir. 1978); *Ostrer v. U.S.*, 577 F.2d 782, 786 (2d Cir. 1978), *cert. denied*, 439 U.S. 1115 (1979); *U.S. v. Di Carlo*, 575 F.2d 952, 960 (1st Cir.), *cert. denied*, 439 U.S. 834 (1978); *U.S. v. Mackey*, 571 F.2d 376, 389 (7th Cir. 1977). Thus, a greater showing of materiality is required when the defense request is absent or is general than when the request is specific.

In *U.S. v. Bagley*, 105 S. Ct. 3375 (1985), the Court stated that in all three instances of prosecutorial failure to disclose evidence favorable to the accused, reversal is required only where, if disclosed, there was a reasonable probability the result of the trial would have been different, that is, failure to disclose created a probability sufficient to undermine the confidence in the outcome of the trial.

Materiality is determined by evaluating all the evidence introduced at trial. 427 U.S. at 112. Reversal is not required where the defendant fails to establish materiality of suppressed evidence. *U.S. v. Parker*, 586 F.2d 422 (5th Cir. 1978), *cert. denied*, 441 U.S. 962 (1979). *See also U.S. v. Friedman*, 593 F.2d 109 (9th Cir. 1979). The duty of disclosure under *Brady* obviously extends to the individual prosecutor and his office. *See U.S. v. Morell*, 524 F.2d 550 (2d Cir. 1975). In general, that duty also extends to persons working as part of the prosecution team or intimately connected with the government's case, even if not employed in the prosecutor's office. *See U.S. v. Morell*, 524 F.2d at 555 (BNDD agent with knowledge of confidential file concerning key government witness). Since the investigative officers are part of the prosecution, the taint on the trial is no less if they, rather than the prosecutor, are guilty of nondisclosure. *U.S. v. Butler*, 567 F.2d 885 (9th Cir. 1978). *See also U.S. v. Deutsch*, 475 F.2d 55 (5th Cir. 1973) (Post Office Department in possession of key personnel folder).

However, the prosecutor is not deemed to have constructive knowledge of material of which he would logically be unaware. *U.S. v. Quinn*, 445 F.2d 940, 944 (2d Cir.), *cert. denied*, 404 U.S. 850 (1971) (sealed indictment against government witness in another district). Nor is the prosecutor required to furnish information available only from public records or from outside the United States and not within the government's control. *U.S. v. Flores*, 540 F.2d 432, 438 (9th Cir. 1976); *U.S. v. Reyes-Padron*, 538 F.2d 33 (2d Cir. 1976), *cert. denied*,

429 U.S. 1046 (1977). Moreover, the prosecutor is generally not held to a duty of disclosure of evidence or witnesses who are already known or are accessible to the defendant. *U.S. v. Shelton,* 588 F.2d 1242 (9th Cir. 1978), *cert. denied,* 442 U.S. 909 (1979); *U.S. v. Craig,* 573 F.2d 455, 492 (7th Cir. 1977), *cert. denied,* 439 U.S. 820 (1978); *U.S. v. Prior,* 546 F.2d 1254, 1259 (5th Cir. 1977); *U.S. v. DiGiovanni,* 544 F.2d 642, 645 (2d Cir. 1976); *U.S. v. Stewart,* 513 F.2d 957 (2d Cir. 1975).

Further, the government cannot be held to have suppressed *Brady* material where material sought is unavailable to either the government or the defendant because of its loss by state officials. *U.S. v. Johnston,* 543 F.2d 55 (8th Cir. 1976) (breath test results; government apprised defense of name of administering officer placing defendant in position of parity with the government); *U.S. v. McDaniel,* 428 F. Supp. 1226 (W.D. Okla. 1977).

Finally, the defense is not entitled under *Brady* to know everything the government investigation has unearthed. *U.S. v. Arroyo-Angulo,* 580 F.2d 1137 (2d Cir.), *cert. denied,* 439 U.S. 913 (1978). Where the government stated that it complied with requirements of *Brady,* the court is not required to order that all evidence in the government's possession be given to defendants. *U.S. v. Azzarelli Constr. Co.,* 459 F. Supp. 146 (E.D. Ill. 1978), *aff'd,* 612 F.2d 292 (7th Cir.), *cert. denied,* 447 U.S. 920 (1980).

## § 720. — Material That Must Be Disclosed.

There are two general categories of material required to be disclosed under the *Brady* rule: (1) material which tends to be exculpatory, and (2) material which may be used to impeach or discredit government witnesses. For purposes of *Brady,* there is no distinction between impeachment evidence and exculpatory evidence. *U.S. v. Bagley,* 105 S. Ct. 3375 (1985).

## § 721. — — Exculpatory Material.

As in the case of *Brady v. Maryland,* 373 U.S. at 86-87, failure to reveal the existence of another person's confession would merit reversal because such evidence obviously tends to exculpate the defendant. Likewise, failure by the prosecution to disclose the existence of an eyewitness whose testimony, developed by skilled counsel, could have induced reasonable doubt was reversible error. *Grant v. Alldredge,* 498 F.2d 376 (2d Cir. 1974) (government's duty was not met by statement merely that eyewitness had failed to select defendant's photograph from spread when actually witness had identified someone else). *But see U.S. v. Stone,* 471 F.2d 170 (7th Cir.), *cert. denied,* 411 U.S. 931 (1973) (no error in failing to give notice that witnesses failed to identify defendant before trial, where witnesses were produced at trial). *See also Jackson v. Wainwright,* 390 F.2d 288 (5th Cir. 1968); *U.S. ex rel. Meers v. Wilkins,* 326 F.2d 135 (2d Cir. 1964).

The prosecution has no duty to disclose the inability of certain eyewitness to positively identify a defendant. *U.S. v. Rhodes,* 569 F.2d 384 (5th Cir.), *cert. denied,* 439 U.S. 844 (1978) (where eyewitnesses did not state that defendant was not involved in the crime, but, rather, testified that they could not state whether he was or was not one of the perpetrators). In *Moore v. Illinois,* 408 U.S. 786, 794 (1972), the Supreme Court restricted the government's obligation so as to require only revelation of exculpatory material that is "material either to guilt or to punishment." The Court there rejected a defense *Brady* claim where the state had not revealed the existence of a witness' prior misidentification of the defendant as one "Slick," when others testified that Moore was not "Slick" but had committed the murder.

Physical evidence or information from police reports favorable to the defense should be disclosed. *Barbee v. Warden, Maryland Penitentiary,* 331 F.2d 842 (4th Cir. 1964), and, the prosecutor has the duty to disclose to the defense favorable results of a physical or mental examination. *Orr v. U.S.,* 386 F.2d 988 (D.C. Cir. 1967) (a finding that the defendant was mentally incompetent when an insanity defense was raised).

## § 722. — — Impeachment Material.

Evidence that may be used to substantially impeach the credibility of a key government witness must also be disclosed to the defense. *U.S. v. Bagley,* 105 S. Ct. 3375 (1985); *Giles v. Maryland,* 386 U.S. 66 (1967); *U.S. v. Crowell,* 586 F.2d 1020 (4th Cir. 1978), *cert. denied,* 440 U.S. 959 (1979); *U.S. v. Butler,* 567 F.2d 885 (9th Cir. 1978); *U.S. v. Sweet,* 548 F.2d 198 (7th Cir.), *cert. denied,* 430 U.S. 969 (1977); *U.S. v. Miller,* 411 F.2d 825 (2d Cir. 1969). Thus, the government must reveal promises of leniency or immunity for its witnesses. *Giglio v. U.S.,* 405 U.S. 150 (1972); *U.S. v. Joseph,* 533 F.2d 282, 286-87 (5th Cir. 1976), *cert. denied,* 431 U.S. 905 (1977); *U.S. v. Pfingst,* 490 F.2d 262 (2d Cir. 1973), *cert. denied,* 417 U.S. 919 (1974); *U.S. v. Harris,* 462 F.2d 1033 (10th Cir. 1972). In *Weatherford v. Bursey,* 429 U.S. 545 (1977), however, the Supreme Court held that the government is not required under *Brady* to reveal its arrangements with undercover agents or other witnesses who will testify, when the informant in question has concealed his identity from the defendant.

189

The government must disclose the prior criminal record or other prior material acts of misconduct of its witnesses. *U.S. v. Seijo,* 514 F.2d 1357 (2d Cir. 1975), *cert. denied,* 429 U.S. 1043 (1977); *U.S. v. Rosner,* 516 F.2d 269 (2d Cir. 1975), *cert. denied,* 427 U.S. 911 (1976); *U.S. v. Fried,* 486 F.2d 201 (2d Cir. 1973), *cert. denied,* 416 U.S. 983 (1974) (indictment pending against witness in neighboring district). Disclosure of a presentence report on a government witness, however, was not required under the *Brady* rule since the reports were unavailable to the prosecutors. *U.S. v. Dingle,* 546 F.2d 1378 (10th Cir. 1976). Letters or information sent to the prosecutor by the witness, showing his understanding of promises or revealing pressure on him to testify, must also be disclosed. *U.S. v. Badalamente,* 507 F.2d 12 (2d Cir. 1974), *cert. denied,* 421 U.S. 911 (1975). In *Moore v. Illinois,* 408 U.S. 786, 797 (1972), however, the Court refused to find that production of a diagram reflecting one prosecution witness' story was inconsistent with that of another was required under *Brady.*

## § 723. — Time for Disclosure.

The appropriate time for disclosure of requested evidence that is materially favorable to the accused is unsettled. Some courts have held that the appropriate time to turn over *Brady* material is before trial. *U.S. v. Pollack,* 534 F.2d 964, 973-74 (D.C. Cir.), *cert. denied,* 429 U.S. 924 (1976); *Grant v. Alldredge,* 498 F.2d 376, 382 (2d Cir. 1974); *U.S. v. Deutsch,* 373 F. Supp. 289, 290-91 (S.D.N.Y. 1974). There is other authority, however, that the prosecutor is not required to turn over *Brady* material until trial. *U.S. v. Allain,* 671 F.2d 248, 255 (7th Cir. 1982); *U.S. v. Campagnuolo,* 592 F.2d 852, 859 (5th Cir. 1979); *U.S. ex rel. Lucas v. Regan,* 503 F.2d 1, 3 n.1 (2d Cir. 1974), *cert. denied,* 420 U.S. 939 (1975). The due process standard is that such evidence must be turned over before it is too late for the defendant to make use of any benefits of the evidence. *U.S. v. Allain,* 671 F.2d at 255.

## § 724. — Preservation of Evidence.

Any duty to preserve evidence is limited to that which might be expected to play a significant role in the defense of the charge. The evidence must possess an exculpatory value that was apparent before it was destroyed, and the defendant must be unable to obtain comparable evidence by other reasonable means. *California v. Trombetta,* 467 U.S. 479 (1984).

# CHAPTER 8

## TRIAL DISCOVERY OF PRIOR STATEMENTS

§ 801. Jencks Act: 18 U.S.C. § 3500; and Rule 26.2.
§ 802. — Procedure for Obtaining Documents.
§ 803. — — Request by Defense Counsel.
§ 804. — — Time for Production.
§ 805. — — The Trial Court's Obligation.
§ 806. — — Possession of the United States.
§ 807. — — Relation to Witness' Direct Testimony.
§ 808. — Documents Subject to Production.
§ 809. — — Written, Signed, Adopted, or Approved by the Witness.
§ 810. — — Substantially Verbatim and Contemporaneously Made.
§ 811. — Consequences of Refusal to Produce.
§ 812. — — Destruction of Notes.
§ 813. — — Harmless Error Rule.
§ 814. Rule 26.2 Material of Defense Witnesses.

## § 801. Jencks Act: 18 U.S.C. § 3500; and Rule 26.2.

The 1957 legislation, 18 U.S.C. § 3500, commonly referred to as the "Jencks Act," was designed to clarify and limit the Supreme Court's holding in *Jencks v. U.S.*, 353 U.S. 657 (1957). Rule 26.2 of the Federal Rules of Criminal Procedure provides for the production of the statements of witnesses of both parties at trial in essentially the same manner as is provided in the Jencks Act for the production of the statements of government witnesses. The Jencks Act permits the government to refuse to disclose pretrial statements of any of its witnesses in federal criminal cases until each such witness has concluded his direct examination at trial. At that time, upon a defendant's motion, the court is required to order the government to produce the witness' prior statements that are in its possession and which relate to his testimony.

The purpose of the Jencks Act and Rule 26.2 is to provide appropriate material to enable the opposing party to cross-examine thoroughly, while giving protection from unwarranted disclosure. *U.S. v. Robinson*, 585 F.2d 274, 280-81 (7th Cir.), *cert. denied*, 441 U.S. 947 (1979); *U.S. v. Nickell*, 552 F.2d 684, 688 (6th Cir. 1977), *cert. denied*, 436 U.S. 904 (1978); *U.S. v. Smaldone*, 544 F.2d 456, 460 (10th Cir. 1976), *cert. denied*, 430 U.S. 967 (1977); *U.S. v. Percevault*, 490 F.2d 126, 129-30 (2d Cir. 1974). Rule 26.2 and 18 U.S.C. § 3500 are the exclusive means for obtaining statements of government witnesses made before trial. *Palermo v. U.S.*, 360 U.S. 343, 351 (1959); *U.S. v. Covello*, 410 F.2d 536 (2d Cir.), *cert. denied*, 396 U.S. 879 (1969). Neither the requirements nor the limitations of the Jencks Act either derive from, or violate, the

191

U.S. Constitution. *Weatherford v. Bursey,* 429 U.S. 545, 559 (1977); *U.S. v. Beasley,* 576 F.2d 626, 629 (5th Cir. 1978), *cert. denied,* 440 U.S. 947 (1979); *U.S. v. Washabaugh,* 442 F.2d 1127, 1129 (9th Cir. 1971).

If Jencks Act statements of a potential government witness also contain exculpatory information, the government is further obligated under the *Brady* doctrine not to suppress that information, just as it is with any other exculpatory information in its hands. *See U.S. v. Agurs,* 427 U.S. 97 (1976); *Brady v. Maryland,* 373 U.S. 83 (1963). It has been held that the Jencks Act does not impair the government's duty to disclose exculpatory information, *U.S. v. Murphy,* 569 F.2d 771, 774 (3d Cir.), *cert. denied,* 435 U.S. 955 (1978), and that, conversely, the duty to provide exculpatory information does not abrogate the requirements of the Jencks Act, *U.S. v. Dotson,* 546 F.2d 1151, 1153 (5th Cir. 1977). *See generally U.S. v. Campagnuolo,* 592 F.2d 852, 858-61 (5th Cir. 1979).

Under Rule 26.2, the statements of a defendant who testifies need not be produced by the defense, and if the government refuses to produce a statement as directed by the court, a mistrial may be declared and the testimony of the witness may be stricken from the record.

Rule 26.2 does not apply to preliminary hearings, *Robbins v. U.S.,* 476 F.2d 26, 32 (10th Cir. 1973); but it does apply to suppression hearings, and a law enforcement officer shall be deemed a witness called by the government whether in fact called by the government or by the defendant. Rule 12(i), Fed. R. Crim. P.

## § 802. — Procedure for Obtaining Documents.

## § 803. — — Request by Defense Counsel.

The requirement of a request for statements of a government witness is set forth at 18 U.S.C. § 3500(b):

> After a witness called by the United States has testified on direct examination, the court shall, *on motion of the defendant,* order the United States to produce any statement (as hereinafter defined) of the witness in the possession of the United States which relates to the subject as to which the witness has testified. [Emphasis supplied.]

When read in conjunction with subsection (a) of the Jencks Act, it is clear that such motion of the defendant applies only to witnesses at trial and not to those called by the government at a pretrial hearing. *U.S. v. Bernard,* 623 F.2d 551 (9th Cir. 1980); *U.S. v. Murphy,* 569 F.2d 771 (3d Cir.), *cert. denied,* 435 U.S. 955 (1978).

No particular language is required for a defendant to trigger the government's responsibilities under the Jencks Act. *Lewis v. U.S.,* 340 F.2d 678, 682 (8th Cir. 1965); *U.S. v. Aviles,* 315 F.2d 186, 191 (2d Cir. 1963). But, the request must be timely. *Wilson v. U.S.,* 554 F.2d 893, 894 (8th Cir.), *cert. denied,* 434 U.S. 849 (1977). For example, although a request for Jencks Act statements made immediately after the conclusion of cross-examination may be timely, *Banks v. U.S.,* 348 F.2d. 231, 234-35 (8th Cir. 1965), such a request presented after the trial, *U.S. v. Petito,* 671 F.2d 68, 73 (2d Cir. 1982), or after the government had rested its case the day before has been held to have been untimely, *U.S. v. Sacasas,* 381 F.2d 451, 454 (2d Cir. 1967). There is no appellate review of Jencks Act questions without a timely request. *Wilson v. U.S.,* 554 F.2d at 894.

Apparently a request for the Jencks Act statements of a particular witness who testifies in the government's case-in-chief may not automatically reapply to that same witness if he testifies in rebuttal. In *U.S. v. Goldberg,* 582 F.2d 483, 487 (9th Cir. 1978), *cert. denied,* 440 U.S. 973 (1979), the defense failed to make a second request for Jencks Act statements after such rebuttal testimony and thereby did not obligate the government to produce statements the witness had made after his initial trial appearance.

### § 804. — — Time for Production.

Although the defendant may present a Jencks Act motion before trial, the court may not compel the government to disclose statements of a witness before the conclusion of his direct testimony. 18 U.S.C. § 3500(a); *U.S. v. Algie,* 667 F.2d 569, 571 (6th Cir. 1982); *U.S. v. Campagnuolo,* 592 F.2d 852, 858 (5th Cir. 1979); *U.S. v. Murphy,* 569 F.2d at 774; *U.S. v. McMillen,* 489 F.2d 229, 230 (7th Cir. 1972), *cert. denied,* 410 U.S. 955 (1973). This is true even when such statements relate to conversations with the defendant, *U.S. v. Harris,* 542 F.2d 1283, 1291 (7th Cir. 1976), *cert. denied,* 430 U.S. 934 (1977), or contain exculpatory evidence otherwise producible under the *Brady* doctrine, *U.S. v. Anderson,* 574 F.2d 1347, 1352 (5th Cir. 1978). However, appellate courts encourage the practice of pretrial disclosure of Jencks Act materials in order to expedite discovery and trials, and to avoid potential *Brady* questions. *U.S. v. Algie,* 667 F.2d at 572; *U.S. v. Campagnuolo,* 592 F.2d at 858; *U.S. v. Murphy,* 569 F.2d at 774 n.10; *U.S. v. Dotson,* 546 F.2d 1151, 1153 (5th Cir. 1977).

## § 805. — — The Trial Court's Obligation.

The government may respond to a defense motion by producing or refusing to produce the statement of the witness. Thereafter, the defendant must specify with reasonable particularity, typically through cross-examination of the witness at trial that material which may be a Jencks Act statement exists which the government failed to provide in its response, to invoke the protection of the court. *U.S. v. Robinson,* 585 F.2d 274, 280-81 (7th Cir.), *cert. denied,* 441 U.S. 947 (1979). Further inquiry about whether such material must be produced under the Jencks Act should then be made in a hearing out of the presence of the jury, *U.S. v. Chitwood,* 457 F.2d 676, 678 (6th Cir.), *cert. denied,* 409 U.S. 858 (1972), or by an *in camera* examination of such material, *U.S. v. Gross,* 961 F.2d 1097 (3rd Cir. 1992); *U.S. v. Rivero,* 532 F.2d 450, 460 (5th Cir. 1976), or both. If the defendant fails to provide a foundation for the government to turn over any materials as Jencks Act statements, or for the court to screen any materials, it is not an abuse of discretion for the court to refuse either to order the government to produce or to screen materials *in camera. U.S. v. Nickell,* 552 F.2d 684, 689-90 (6th Cir. 1977), *cert. denied,* 436 U.S. 904 (1978); *U.S. v. Dingle,* 546 F.2d 1378, 1381 (10th Cir. 1976). If the defendant does provide such a foundation, the court's obligation is to determine "productibility," i.e., if the material is a statement, if it is in the government's possession, and whether it relates to the witness' direct testimony. These questions, to be resolved out of the presence of the jury, must be considered by the court with the aid of the extrinsic evidence which is available and germane. *Lewis v. U.S.,* 340 F.2d 678, 682 (8th Cir. 1965). The examination may be conducted *ex parte* by the court, and the court is not required to disclose the material to defense counsel unless it is determined that it was discoverable under the act. 18 U.S.C. § 3500(c); *U.S. v. Truong Dihn Hung,* 667 F.2d 1105, 1108 (4th Cir. 1981), *cert. denied,* 102 S. Ct. 1004 (1982). Whether, and to what extent, the material must be produced are questions of fact committed to the discretion of the trial judge. 18 U.S.C. § 3500(c); *U.S. v. Cuesta,* 597 F.2d 903, 914 (5th Cir.), *cert. denied,* 444 U.S. 964 (1979). Such determination will not be overturned unless clearly erroneous. *U.S. v. Medel,* 592 F.2d 1305, 1316 (5th Cir. 1979); *U.S. v. Sten,* 342 F.2d 491, 494 (2d Cir. 1965).

Within the Second Circuit the motion of the defendant for Jencks Act statements should be made only after he has sought leave to so move, out of the jury's presence, whereupon a record as to the extent of the government response is to be made. *U.S. v. Gardin,* 382 F.2d 601, 605 (2d Cir. 1967). The purpose for removing the jury is to avoid the implication that any prior statements produced, but not used to impeach, reinforce a witness' testimony. *U.S. v. Frazier,* 479 F.2d 983, 986 (2d Cir. 1973).

### § 806. — — Possession of the United States.

The government is not obligated to produce a requested statement unless it is in the government's possession. 18 U.S.C. § 3500(b). A former additional limitation that only a statement made directly "to an agent of the Government" needed to be produced, was removed by a 1970 amendment to the Jencks Act. Accordingly, almost any statement or report in the government's possession may be encompassed. Although it has been held that a transcript of a witness' testimony in a prior trial was not within the Jencks Act, *U.S. v. Harris,* 542 F.2d 1283, 1293 (7th Cir. 1976), *cert. denied,* 430 U.S. 934 (1977), because that holding was based upon a pre-1970 case wherein a court reporter was found not to be "an agent of the Government" to whom the statement was made, the above-mentioned amendment may bring such prior transcripts within the Jencks Act.

Statements in the possession of the United States may include a letter that a witness wrote to a government attorney who, both at the time he received the letter and at the time of trial, was no longer working on the case. *U.S. v. Sperling,* 506 F.2d 1323, 1333 (2d Cir. 1974), *cert. denied,* 420 U.S. 962 (1975). Grand jury testimony that has never been transcribed is still within the possession of the government and must be produced. *U.S. v. Merlino,* 595 F.2d 1016, 1019 (5th Cir. 1979). However, sworn statements a witness made to state officers who investigated the case, and which were never actually requested or received by the federal attorney prosecuting the case, or by any other federal agent, have been held not to be "in the possession of the United States." *U.S. v. Smith,* 433 F.2d 1266, 1269 (5th Cir. 1970), *cert. denied,* 401 U.S. 977 (1971); *Beavers v. U.S.,* 351 F.2d 507, 509 (9th Cir. 1965); *U.S. v. Harris,* 368 F. Supp. 697, 708-09 (E.D. Pa. 1973), *aff'd,* 498 F.2d 1164 (3d Cir.), *cert. denied,* 419 U.S. 1069 (1974). *Contra, U.S. v. Heath,* 580 F.2d 1011, 1018-19 (10th Cir. 1978), *cert. denied,* 439 U.S. 1075 (1979). Reports in the possession of state authorities where there is a joint state-federal investigation are covered, however. *U.S. v. Heath,* 580 F.2d 1011, 1018-19 (10th Cir. 1978), *cert. denied,* 439 U.S. 1075 (1979). A witness' notes or a personal diary which were not disclosed to government agents and attorneys and which the witness maintained privately, are not within the government's possession. *U.S. v. Escobar,* 674 F.2d 469, 478 (5th Cir. 1982); *U.S. v. Friedman,* 593 F.2d 109, 120

(9th Cir. 1979); *U.S. v. Goldberg,* 582 F.2d 483, 486 (9th Cir. 1978), *cert. denied,* 440 U.S. 973 (1979).

It has been held that the Jencks Act includes only statements in the possession of federal prosecutorial agencies, such as the United States Attorney or the Federal Bureau of Investigation. Accordingly, presentence reports in the possession of the court's probation department which may contain statements of a previously convicted witness are not "in the possession of the United States" for Jencks Act purposes. *U.S. v. Trevino,* 556 F.2d 1265, 1271 (5th Cir. 1977); *U.S. v. Dansker,* 537 F.2d 40, 61 (3d Cir. 1976), *cert. denied,* 429 U.S. 1038 (1977). Furthermore, a statement a witness had given to an NLRB official may not have been in the government's possession, within the meaning of the Jencks Act, since the NLRB is not a prosecutorial agency. *U.S. v. Weidman,* 572 F.2d 1199, 1207 (7th Cir.), *cert. denied,* 439 U.S. 821 (1978).

## § 807. — — Relation to Witness' Direct Testimony.

The statement or report must relate to the subject matter of the witness' direct testimony, or the government is not obligated to produce it. 18 U.S.C. § 3500(b) and (c); *U.S. v. Carter,* 621 F.2d 238 (6th Cir.), *cert. denied,* 449 U.S. 858 (1980). Of course, no such materials can be considered to relate to any direct testimony if the witness is not called to testify by the government. *U.S. v. Medel,* 592 F.2d 1305, 1316 n.12 (5th Cir. 1979); *U.S. v. Warden,* 545 F.2d 32, 37 (7th Cir. 1976); *U.S. v. Snow,* 537 F.2d 1166, 1168 (4th Cir. 1976). If the government does call a witness whose prior statement is generally related to events or activities he testifies to on direct examination, the statement is a Jencks Act statement; but if it is incidental or collateral, it is not. *U.S. v. Birnbaum,* 337 F.2d 490, 497 (2d Cir. 1964). The courts appear to apply pragmatic case-by-case analyses, inquiring as to the relative importance of the witness, the relationship of the prior statement to the critical issues of the trial, and the extent to which such statement exposes the credibility of the witness. For example, letters written by witnesses to government attorneys or agents containing apologies for having been untruthful, complaints about improper government pressure, or displaying an eagerness to tailor testimony to fit the government's theory of the case have been held to be related to the witness' direct testimony when such testimony was critical to the case. *U.S. v. Badalamente,* 507 F.2d 12, 18 (2d Cir. 1974), *cert. denied,* 421 U.S. 911 (1975); *U.S. v. Sperling,* 506 F.2d 1323, 1332-33 (2d Cir. 1974), *cert. denied,* 420 U.S. 962 (1975); *U.S. v. Pacelli,* 491 F.2d 1108, 1119 (2d

Cir.), *cert. denied,* 419 U.S. 826 (1974); *U.S. v. Borelli,* 336 F.2d 376, 393 (2d Cir. 1964), *cert. denied,* 379 U.S. 960 (1965).

In *U.S. v. Ribero,* 532 F.2d 450 (5th Cir. 1976), the defendant was convicted of attempting to distribute eleven pounds of cocaine. A government witness testified about defendant's intent by describing a prior transaction of the defendant involving two ounces of cocaine. The prior transaction had been the subject of the same witness' testimony before a federal grand jury that returned a prior indictment against the defendant, dismissed shortly thereafter. The appellate court held that the trial judge should have examined the transcript of the witness' prior grand jury testimony and required the production of that which related to the witness' testimony at trial.

General debriefing of an informant witness about prior events and his knowledge of particular areas of illegal activity may not relate to trial testimony which is focused upon the particular facts and circumstances involving the defendant and therefore may not be within the Jencks Act. *U.S. v. Smaldone,* 544 F.2d 456, 460 (10th Cir. 1976), *cert. denied,* 430 U.S. 967 (1977); *U.S. v. Covello,* 410 F.2d 536, 546 (2d Cir.), *cert. denied,* 396 U.S. 879 (1969); *U.S. v. Cardillo,* 316 F.2d 606, 615-16 (2d Cir.), *cert. denied,* 375 U.S. 822 (1963). A witness' statement concerning a prior narcotics transfer, wherein the defendant paid money, was held not to relate to the witness' direct testimony which concerned the facts of the defendant's income tax evasion. *U.S. v. Mackey,* 571 F.2d 376, 389 (7th Cir. 1978).

In a Ninth Circuit extortion case and a Second Circuit gambling case, defendants sought, but were denied, the federal income tax returns filed by critical witnesses. In each case the appellate court held that the defendant suffered no prejudice thereby, without actually deciding whether such returns constituted Jencks Act statements related to the witness' direct testimony. *U.S. v. Phillips,* 577 F.2d 495, 503 (9th Cir.), *cert. denied,* 439 U.S. 831 (1978); *U.S. v. Covello,* 410 F.2d 536, 545-46 (2d Cir.), *cert. denied,* 396 U.S. 879 (1969). In another case involving defendants' attempts to procure the tax returns of important witnesses, the court held that "[u]nless the tax returns were substantial verbatim recitals they were not clearly statements within the meaning of the Jencks Act [footnote omitted]." *U.S. v. Carrillo,* 561 F.2d 1125, 1128 (5th Cir. 1977).

If the government claims that a statement the court has ordered it to produce contains material not related to the witness' direct testimony, the statement must then be submitted for *in camera* inspection, whereupon the court must excise those portions which are not so related. 18 U.S.C. § 3500(c). Although the government may suggest that certain

197

portions of a statement do not relate, the task of determining which parts are to be produced is vested in the trial court alone. *Scales v. U.S.,* 367 U.S. 203, 258 (1961); *U.S. v. Conroy,* 589 F.2d 1258, 1273 (5th Cir.), *cert. denied,* 444 U.S. 831 (1979); *U.S. v. Del Valle,* 587 F.2d 699, 705 (5th Cir.), *cert. denied,* 442 U.S. 909 (1979).

If the case agent testifies about part of the case, typically not all of his reports about the case relate to his testimony; and, therefore, not all need be produced. *U.S. v. Nickell,* 552 F.2d 684, 688 (6th Cir. 1977), *cert. denied,* 436 U.S. 904 (1978). Standard agency forms filled out by federal agents, such as booking forms, daily attendance sheets, and expense itemizations have been held not to relate to agents' direct testimony. *U.S. v. Augello,* 451 F.2d 1167, 1170 (2d Cir. 1971), *cert. denied,* 405 U.S. 1070 (1972); *Smith v. U.S.,* 416 F.2d 1255, 1256 (2d Cir. 1969). However, the Seventh Circuit has ruled that, in tax evasion cases using the net worth method of proof, the entire, unredacted special agent's report relates to his testimony if he is called as a witness by the government. *U.S. v. Cleveland,* 507 F.2d 731, 736-37 (7th Cir. 1974).

Since there is no "work product" exception to the Jencks Act, an attorney's notes of an interview with a witness could be within the Jencks Act. *Goldberg v. U.S.,* 425 U.S. 94, 101-02 (1976). However, if a witness should adopt or approve an attorney's notes containing trial strategy or tactics, such notes need not be produced since they would not relate to the witness' direct testimony; "[t]hus, the primary policy underlying the work-product doctrine — *i.e.,* protection of the privacy of an attorney's mental process ... — is adequately safeguarded by the Jencks Act itself." *Id.* at 106. Notwithstanding the absence of a "work product" exception, the Fourth Circuit has apparently recognized a "confidentiality" exception to the Jencks Act. When a defendant sought the presentence report of a previously convicted accomplice-witness, prepared pursuant to Rule 32(c) of the Federal Rules of Criminal Procedure, that court stated that the basic issue is one of "materiality," with confidentiality to be maintained unless disclosure is "required to meet the ends of justice." *U.S. v. Figurski,* 545 F.2d 389, 391-92 (4th Cir. 1976).

## § 808. — Documents Subject to Production.

"Statement" is defined by subsection (e) of the Jencks Act, as amended by the Organized Crime Control Act of 1970, as:

> (1) a written statement made by said witness and signed or otherwise adopted or approved by him;

(2) a stenographic, mechanical, electrical, or other recording, or a transcription thereof, which is a substantially verbatim recital of an oral statement made by said witness and recorded contemporaneously with the making of such oral statement; or

(3) a statement, however taken or recorded, or a transcription thereof, if any, made by said witness to a grand jury.

The primary purpose in limiting the government's obligation to the production of only a witness' own statements is to insure that each witness be impeached only with that which can fairly be said to be his own, and not by the selections or interpretations of another. *U.S. v. Carrasco*, 537 F.2d 372, 376 (9th Cir. 1976). Accordingly, even if a witness signs or approves a writing consisting of trial strategy or an investigator's mental impressions, personal beliefs, or legal conclusions, such a writing cannot fairly be said to be the witness' own statement producible under the Jencks Act. *Goldberg v. U.S.*, 425 U.S. 94, 106 (1976).

Relative to the recorded but untranscribed grand jury testimony of a witness, courts may require the government to transcribe the recording and produce the transcript. *U.S. v. Merlino*, 595 F.2d 1016, 1019 (5th Cir. 1979), *cert. denied*, 444 U.S. 1071 (1980).

### § 809. — — Written, Signed, Adopted, or Approved by the Witness.

The writing must be a statement attributable to the witness to fall within the Jencks Act. *U.S. v. Crumpler*, 536 F.2d 1063 (5th Cir. 1976). Therefore, the notes and reports written by an investigative agent amount to Jencks Act statements of an agent who testifies. *U.S. v. Del Toro Soto*, 676 F.2d 13, 15-16 (1st Cir. 1982); *U.S. v. Sink*, 586 F.2d 1041, 1051 (5th Cir. 1978), *cert. denied*, 443 U.S. 912 (1979). However, if the agent neither wrote the reports nor approved their substantive detail, but, rather, simply signed off on other agents' reports in his administrative or supervisory capacity, said reports are not thereby rendered to be his statements. *Virgin Islands v. Lovell*, 410 F.2d 307, 310 (3d Cir.), *cert. denied*, 396 U.S. 964 (1969).

If a witness approves the notes, taken during an interview of him, or approves a more formal interview report prepared thereafter, such approval renders the notes or report the witness' own statement under the Jencks Act, to the same extent as it would if he had written the notes, or signed them, himself. *Goldberg v. U.S.*, 425 U.S. 94 (1976); *U.S. v. Peterson*, 524 F.2d 167 (4th Cir. 1975), *cert. denied*, 424 U.S. 925 (1976); *U.S. v. Pacheco*, 489 F.2d 554, 566 (5th Cir. 1974), *cert. denied*, 421 U.S. 909 (1975); *U.S. v. Chitwood*, 457 F.2d 676, 678 (6th Cir.), *cert. denied,* 409 U.S. 858 (1972). On the other hand, interview reports not signed or otherwise adopted or approved by the witness at the conclusion of the interview, or sometime thereafter, are not his statements. *U.S. v. Gross,* 961 F.2d 1097 (3d Cir. 1992); *U.S. v. Shannahan,* 605 F.2d 539, 542 (10th Cir. 1979); *U.S. v. Foley,* 598 F.2d 1323 (4th Cir. 1979), *cert. denied,* 444 U.S. 1043 (1980); *U.S. v. Gates,* 557 F.2d 1086, 1089 (5th Cir. 1977), *cert. denied,* 434 U.S. 1017 (1978); *U.S. v. Larson,* 555 F.2d 673, 677 (8th Cir. 1977). This rule may be followed even if an agent's notes are extremely accurate, containing occasional verbatim recitations of the witness. *U.S. v. Cuesta,* 597 F.2d 903, 914 (5th Cir.), *cert. denied,* 444 U.S. 964 (1979). *But see U.S. v. Harris,* 542 F.2d 1283, 1292 (7th Cir. 1976), *cert. denied,* 430 U.S. 934 (1977). When a defendant claimed that the government failed to record interviews with witnesses to avoid producing Jencks materials, the court held that there is no requirement that interview notes of witnesses be reduced to statement form and approved by the witness. *U.S. v. Martino,* 648 F.2d 367, 387 (5th Cir. 1981), *cert. denied,* 102 S. Ct. 2020 (1982).

Pretrial questioning by a government attorney based upon notes or a report of a prior interview with the witness does not, in itself, result in adoption or approval of such notes or report by the witness. *U.S. v. Strahl,* 590 F.2d 10, 15 (1st Cir. 1978), *cert. denied,* 440 U.S. 918 (1979); *U.S. v. Adams,* 581 F.2d 193, 199 (9th Cir.), *cert. denied,* 439 U.S. 1006 (1978). However, if in the course of such a review the witness actually reads them, the notes or report can thereby become his own statements. *U.S. v. Harris,* 542 F.2d at 1292.

In *U.S. v. Scaglione,* 446 F.2d 182, 184 (5th Cir.), *cert. denied,* 404 U.S. 941 (1971), at a pretrial review of a witness' anticipated testimony, the government attorney showed the witness an agent's report of a previous interview whenever the witness' recollection varied from the report. Although it was held there that the witness had not adopted or approved the report, the court recognized that a witness might, in piecemeal fashion, ratify substantially all of a report and thereby make it his statement.

### § 810. — — Substantially Verbatim and Contemporaneously Made.

Under subdivision (e)(2), the statement must be a stenographic, mechanical, electrical, or other recording, or a transcription thereof, which contains a substantially verbatim account of an oral statement made by the witness, and it must have been recorded contemporaneously with the making of the statement.

The government's obligation to produce recorded statements of a witness is not fulfilled through delivery of only the best of two or more tape recordings which were made contemporaneously and simultaneously. Because separately made back-up recordings may help resolve potential questions concerning alleged gaps or inaudible passages on the primary recording, all recordings should be produced. *U.S. v. Bufalino,* 576 F.2d 446, 449 (2d Cir.), *cert. denied,* 439 U.S. 928 (1978). *See also U.S. v. Well,* 572 F.2d 1383, 1384 (9th Cir. 1978).

The government may be required to produce notes of an interview of the witness if the notes are substantially verbatim and made at the time of the interview. *U.S. v. Harris,* 542 F.2d 1283, 1292 (7th Cir. 1976), *cert. denied,* 430 U.S. 934 (1977). However, interview notes that tend to be summaries, even if containing occasional verbatim quotes, do not constitute Jencks Act statements. *U.S. v. Foley,* 598 F.2d 1323 (4th Cir. 1979); *U.S. v. Friedman,* 593 F.2d 109, 120 (9th Cir. 1979); *U.S. v. Medel,* 592 F.2d 1305, 1316 (5th Cir. 1979). Moreover, if the account of the witness' statement was prepared after the interview, and not contemporaneously, it does not constitute a Jencks Act statement, no matter how accurate in may be. *U.S. v. Consolidated Packaging,* 575 F.2d 117, 129 (7th Cir. 1978); *U.S. v. Hodges,* 556 F.2d 366, 368 (5th Cir. 1977), *cert. denied,* 434 U.S. 1016 (1978).

Photographs identified by a witness as part of a statement otherwise producible under the Jencks Act must also be produced. *Simmons v. U.S.,* 390 U.S. 377, 387 (1968). An artist's composite sketch of a criminal derived from the descriptions of witnesses does not, however, comprise a statement of a witness because it does not fully reveal what witnesses actually said and, therefore, is not accurate to the extent required by 18 U.S.C. § 3500(e)(2). *U.S. v. Zurita,* 369 F.2d 474, 477 (7th Cir. 1966).

### § 811. — Consequences of Refusal to Produce.

According to 18 U.S.C. § 3500(d):

> If the United States elects not to comply with an order ... [to produce], the court shall strike from the record the testimony of the witness, and the trial shall proceed unless the court in its discretion shall determine that the interests of justice require that a mistrial be declared.

### § 812. — — Destruction of Notes.

The unequivocal obligation of the court, as set forth in subsection (d), is complicated in cases where Jencks Act statements have been previously destroyed and are, therefore, not "in possession of the United

States" [subsection (b)], and in cases where the government cannot fairly be said to have elected not to comply. *See* the separate opinion of Justice Frankfurter in *Campbell v. U.S.,* 365 U.S. 85, 102 (1961), and *U.S. v. Pope,* 574 F.2d 320, 325 (6th Cir.), *cert. denied,* 436 U.S. 929 (1978). In most of the cases addressing the issue of destruction of notes, an agent had destroyed his investigative rough notes pursuant to administrative policy after they had been incorporated in a more formal report; and if the agent testified, the rough notes might have constituted his Jencks Act statements. In other cases the courts have addressed the question in circumstances where an agent's rough notes of a pretrial interview with a witness might have constituted that witness' Jencks Act statement and, therefore, should not have been destroyed.

The circuit courts are divided on the issue of generally requiring the preservation of agents' rough notes. Most of the circuits that have addressed the issue agree that the routine destruction of rough interview notes, after having been used and incorporated in a more formal report, is an acceptable practice which does not violate the Jencks Act. *U.S. v. Martin,* 565 F.2d 362 (5th Cir. 1978); *U.S. v. Mase,* 556 F.2d 671, 676 (2d Cir. 1977), *cert. denied,* 435 U.S. 916 (1978); *U.S. v. McCallie,* 554 F.2d 770, 773 (6th Cir. 1977); *U.S. v. Dupree,* 533 F.2d 1189, 1191 (8th Cir.), *cert. denied,* 434 U.S. 986 (1977); *U.S. v. Harris,* 542 F.2d 1283, 1292 (7th Cir. 1976), *cert. denied,* 430 U.S. 934 (1977). The Ninth Circuit and the D.C. Circuit, and perhaps the Third Circuit as well, require rough notes to be preserved. *U.S. v. Niederberger,* 580 F.2d 63, 71 (3d Cir.), *cert. denied,* 439 U.S. 980 (1978); *U.S. v. Robinson,* 546 F.2d 309, 314 n.3 (9th Cir. 1976), *cert. denied,* 430 U.S. 918 (1977); *U.S. v. Harris,* 543 F.2d 1247, 1248 (9th Cir. 1976); *U.S. v. Harrison,* 524 F.2d 421, 433 (D.C. Cir. 1975). The reasoning employed by these three circuits is that it is the duty of the judiciary, and not the executive, to determine what is a Jencks Act statement, as well as what may qualify as exculpatory information under the *Brady* doctrine. Accordingly, the raw material necessary for a proper judicial determination must be maintained, and not routinely destroyed. In *U.S. v. Marques,* 600 F.2d 742, 748 (9th Cir.), *cert. denied,* 444 U.S. 858 (1979), an agent destroyed her rough notes after preparation of a typed summary, which was later produced as her Jencks Act statement. The court ruled that it was error to destroy such notes, particularly in light of her testimony on a critical point that did not appear in the summary. In *U.S. v. Walden,* 590 F.2d 85, 86 (3d Cir.), *cert. denied,* 444 U.S. 849 (1979), the court held that any error involved in the destruction of rough notes was cured by the production of typed copies of the same notes, with only minor spelling and grammatical changes.

In *U.S. v. Crowell,* 586 F.2d 1020, 1028 (4th Cir. 1978), the witness read the agent's rough interview notes and approved them immediately after the interview. Thereafter, the agent typed a summary of the interview and destroyed the notes. Although the typed summary was provided for cross-examination of the witness, the court held that it was error to have failed to produce the notes because they, and not the summary, constituted the Jencks Act statement. In *U.S. v. Stulga,* 584 F.2d 142, 147-48 (6th Cir. 1978), the agent destroyed his rough notes of an interview after he had a more formal, typed report prepared. Thereafter, the witness reviewed and signed the typed report which was provided as his Jencks Act statement at trial. The court held that the government's failure to preserve and produce the agent's rough notes did not reflect bad faith and did not prejudice the defendant. Thus, an agent's rough notes of an interview do not constitute the Jencks Act statement of the witness who was interviewed unless that witness has signed or otherwise adopted or approved such notes. Therefore, it should not be a violation to destroy such unadopted notes, or otherwise refuse to provide them upon Jencks Act demand at trial. *U.S. v. Gates,* 557 F.2d 1086, 1089 (5th Cir. 1977), *cert. denied,* 434 U.S. 1017 (1978).

A tape recorded interview of a witness is his Jencks Act statement. The erasure of such a tape, even if summarized in a written report that is produced at trial, violates the Jencks Act and may lead to suppression of the witness' testimony. *U.S. v. Well,* 572 F.2d 1383, 1384 (9th Cir. 1978). It may also be error to destroy an inferior quality back-up tape made simultaneously with a tape recording which is produced. *See U.S. v. Bufalino,* 576 F.2d 446, 449 (2d Cir.), *cert. denied,* 439 U.S. 928 (1978).

## §813. — — Harmless Error Rule.

The harmless error rule must be strictly applied in Jencks Act cases because the courts will not speculate whether materials the government failed to produce could have been used effectively in the cross-examination of its witnesses. *See Goldberg v. U.S.,* 425 U.S. 94, 111 n.21 (1976); *U.S. v. Del Toro Soto,* 676 F.2d 13, 17 (1st Cir. 1982). The D.C. Circuit weighs the following factors: (1) the degree of governmental negligence or bad faith, (2) the importance of the evidence not produced, and (3) the evidence of guilt adduced at trial. *U.S. v. Rippy,* 606 F.2d 1150, 1154 (D.C. Cir. 1979); *U.S. v. Harrison,* 524 F.2d 421, 434-35 (D.C. Cir. 1975). The Second Circuit applies a test based primarily upon perceived governmental motive: (1) if the failure was deliberate, and the material is merely favorable to the defense, the error cannot be harmless; but (2) if the failure is inadvertent it may be harmless error, so long as the potential that the material could have induced reasonable doubt was relatively insignificant. *U.S. v. Hilton,* 521 F.2d 164, 166 (2d Cir. 1975), *cert. denied,* 425 U.S. 939 (1976). For the most part, courts actually appear to apply a pragmatic, case-by-case analysis similar to the test used in the Second Circuit. *See U.S. v. Heath,* 580 F.2d 1011, 1019 (10th Cir. 1978), *cert. denied,* 439 U.S. 1075 (1979); *U.S. v. Pope,* 574 F.2d 320, 325-26 (6th Cir.), *cert. denied,* 436 U.S. 929 (1978); *U.S. v. Carrasco,* 537 F.2d 372, 377-78 (9th Cir. 1976).

When the government has made no conscious choice to withhold the statement from the defendant, the principal focus is upon whether the missing statement has significantly prejudiced the defendant's position. "[V]iolation of the [Jencks] Act should be excused only where it is perfectly clear that the defense was not prejudiced thereby." *U.S. v. Snow,* 537 F.2d 1166, 1168 (4th Cir. 1976). For example, a grand jury transcript, which the government inadvertently failed to provide, reflected lies and inconsistencies in the witness' trial testimony; and, therefore, its omission was held to have been reversible error. *U.S. v. Knowles,* 594 F.2d 753, 755-56 (9th Cir. 1979). On the other hand, where the information contained in the omitted statement was also contained in statements that had been produced, any possible prejudice was neutralized and the error has been held to have been harmless. *U.S. v. Walden,* 590 F.2d 85, 86 (3d Cir.), *cert. denied,* 444 U.S. 849 (1979); *U.S. v. Anthony,* 565 F.2d 533, 537 (8th Cir. 1977), *cert. denied,* 434 U.S. 1079 (1978). If the government's evidence of defendant's guilt is extremely strong, a finding of harmless error is more likely. *U.S. v. Rippy,* 606 F.2d 1150, 1154 (D.C. Cir. 1979); *U.S. v. Niederberger,* 580 F.2d 63, 71 (3d Cir.), *cert. denied,* 439 U.S. 980 (1978); *U.S. v. Kilrain,* 566 F.2d 979, 985 (5th Cir.), *cert. denied,* 439 U.S. 819 (1978). Irrespective of the evidence of guilt, where the witness' credibility has been thoroughly impeached, even without the benefit of a Jencks Act statement, the failure to have produced it has been held harmless error. *U.S. v. Marques,* 600 F.2d 742, 748 (9th Cir.), *cert. denied,* 444 U.S. 858 (1979); *U.S. v. Crowell,* 586 F.2d 1020, 1028 (4th Cir. 1978).

When the initial failure to provide a Jencks Act statement is cured through recall of the witness and cross-examination with the benefit of such statement, any error occasioned by the initial failure has been rendered harmless. *U.S. v. Pope,* 574 F.2d 320, 326 (6th Cir.), *cert. denied,* 436 U.S. 929 (1978); *U.S. v. Gottlieb,* 493 F.2d 987, 993-94 (2d Cir. 1974).

### § 814. Rule 26.2 Material of Defense Witnesses.

In *U.S. v. Nobles,* 422 U.S. 225 (1975), a defendant sought to impeach the credibility of critical government witnesses through the proffered trial testimony of a defense investigator regarding his interviews with those witnesses. The prosecution requested relevant portions of the investigator's report for its use in cross-examining him. The Supreme Court upheld the district court's refusal to permit the investigator to testify until the court had both inspected his report *in camera,* to delete material not related to the interviews, and turned the redacted report over to the government for use in cross-examination. Citing *Jencks v. U.S.,* 353 U.S. 657 (1957), the Supreme Court held that the judiciary's inherent power to require the government to produce prior statements of its witnesses may be employed to require the same from the defense. *U.S. v. Nobles,* 422 U.S. at 231, 232. Consistent with the reasoning in *Nobles,* the Sixth Circuit has upheld a district court order requiring the defendant to deliver to the government certain notes adopted and approved by a defense witness. *U.S. v. Tarnowski,* 583 F.2d 903, 906 (6th Cir. 1978), *cert. denied,* 440 U.S. 918 (1979).

The Supreme Court has incorporated the substance of the Jencks Act into the Federal Rules of Criminal Procedure as Rule 26.2. In this rule, the Court has incorporated its holding in *U.S. v. Nobles, supra,* in that production of prior statements of defense witnesses — except those of the defendant — are required on the same basis that statements of government witnesses are provided to the defense. Advisory Committee's Note. If defense counsel elects not to comply with an order to deliver a statement of a witness to the attorney for the government, the trial court shall order that the testimony of the witness be striken from the record. Rule 26.2(e), Fed. R. Crim. P. Under the Rule, if it is the government attorney who fails to comply with such an order, a mistrial may be declared if required by the "interest of justice."

# CHAPTER 9

## JOINDER AND SEVERANCE

§ 901. Joinder of Offenses and Defendants.
§ 902. — Joinder of Offenses.
§ 903. — — Multiple Counts.
§ 904. — — Multiple Indictments.
§ 905. — — Duplicity and Multiplicity.
§ 906. — Joinder of Defendants.
§ 907. — — Same Indictment.
§ 908. — — Consolidation for Trial.
§ 909. — — Conspiracy.
§ 910. Severance — Relief From Prejudicial Joinder.
§ 911. — Trial Court's Discretion.
§ 912. — Severance of Offenses.
§ 913. — Severance of Defendants.
§ 914. — — Need for Codefendant's Testimony.
§ 915. — — Codefendant's Confession.
§ 916. — — Conflicting Defenses.
§ 917. — — Conspiracy.
§ 918. — Waiver.
§ 919. Misjoinder.

## § 901. Joinder of Offenses and Defendants.

Rule 8 of the Federal Rules of Criminal Procedure authorizes joinder of both offenses and defendants. Rule 8(a) provides that two or more offenses may be charged in the same indictment if the offenses charged "are of the same or similar character or are based on the same act or transaction or on two or more acts or transactions connected together or constituting parts of a common scheme or plan." Rule 8(b) permits two or more defendants to be joined in the same indictment "if they are alleged to have participated in the same act or transaction or in the same series of acts or transactions constituting an offense or offenses." The defendants "may be charged in one or more counts together or separately and all of the defendants need not be charged in each count." *Id.*

The rule is designed to promote judicial economy and efficiency by avoiding multiple trials where that can be done without substantial prejudice to the right of defendants to a fair trial. *Bruton v. U.S.,* 391 U.S. 123, 131 n.6 (1968) (quoting *Daley v. U.S.,* 231 F.2d 123, 125 (1st Cir.), *cert. denied,* 351 U.S. 964 (1956)). Rule 8 is to be interpreted broadly in favor of initial joinder. *U.S. v. Forrest,* 623 F.2d 1107, 1114 (5th Cir. 1980); *U.S. v. Satterfield,* 548 F.2d 1341, 1344 (9th Cir. 1977), *cert. denied,* 439 U.S. 840 (1978); *Haggard v. U.S.,* 369 F.2d 968, 973 (8th Cir. 1966), *cert. denied,* 386 U.S. 1023 (1967).

## § 902. — Joinder of Offenses.

Rule 8(a) of the Federal Rules of Criminal Procedure provides for joinder of offenses; however, it applies only where there is a single defendant. (Where multiple defendants are joined, subsection (b) of the rule provides the test for joinder.) Rule 8(a) authorizes joinder of offenses where the offenses charged (1) are of the same or similar character, (2) are based on the same act or transaction, or (3) are based on two or more acts or transactions constituting parts of a common scheme or plan.

## § 903. — — Multiple Counts.

Rule 8(a) is permissive; it does not require that all offenses against a single defendant be joined in the same indictment. Department of Justice policy, however, directs "'that several offenses arising out of a single transaction should be alleged and tried together and should not be made the basis of multiple prosecutions, a policy dictated by considerations both of fairness to defendants and of efficient and orderly law enforcement.'" *Petite v. U.S.,* 361 U.S. 529, 530 (1960).

Offenses have been found "of the same or similar character" so as to be properly joined where all counts involved interference with the mail, *U.S. v. Harris,* 635 F.2d 526 (6th Cir. 1980), *cert. denied,* 451 U.S. 989 (1981); where all counts involved the same dangerous drug, *U.S. v. Lewis,* 626 F.2d 940, 944 (D.C. Cir. 1980); where counts charged a 1976 theft of foreign currency and a 1978 violation of the Hobbs Act, both involving theft of valuables from the same place and defendant was an insider, *U.S. v. Werner,* 620 F.2d 922, 926 (2d Cir. 1980); where two armed robberies occurred in the same area during a two-week period, *U.S. v. Shearer,* 606 F.2d 819, 820 (8th Cir. 1979); where two counts arose from nearly identical incidents two days apart, *U.S. v. Jordan,* 602 F.2d 171, 172 (8th Cir.), *cert. denied,* 444 U.S. 878 (1979); where three counts charged failure to file federal income tax returns for three consecutive years, *U.S. v. Bowman,* 602 F.2d 160, 163 (8th Cir. 1979); where all three offenses charged were for counterfeiting, *U.S. v. Bronco,* 597 F.2d 1300, 1301 (9th Cir. 1979); where offenses charged arose from a state legislator's scheme to obtain money through the power and authority of his state office, *U.S. v. Rabbitt,* 583 F.2d 1014, 1021 (8th Cir. 1978), *cert. denied,* 439 U.S. 1116 (1979); where counts charged selling heroin and cocaine, *U.S. v. Tillman,* 470 F.2d 142, 143

(3d Cir. 1972), *cert. denied,* 410 U.S. 968 (1973); where counts charged three armed robberies and evidence of each was relevant on issues of common scheme and identity, *U.S. v. Miller,* 449 F.2d 974, 981 (D.C. Cir. 1970); where two counts of burglary involved the same house where defendant was employed and there was evidence of an "inside job," *U.S. v. Leonard,* 445 F.2d 234, 235 (D.C. Cir. 1971).

Offenses have been found to be "based on the same act or transaction" so as to be properly joined where perjury and jury tampering charges arose from the same trial, *U.S. v. Forrest,* 623 F.2d 1107, 1114 (5th Cir. 1980); where perjury count and civil rights violation count were joined and statements on which perjury count was based were made during grand jury investigation of the civil rights violation, *U.S. v. Duzac,* 622 F.2d 911, 913 (5th Cir.), *cert. denied,* 449 U.S. 1012 (1980); where drugs and a gun were found during a search of defendant's home, and charges were for manufacturing a controlled substance and receipt by a convicted felon of guns, *U.S. v. Park,* 531 F.2d 754, 761 (5th Cir. 1976) ("transaction" may comprehend many occurrences based on their logical relationship).

Offenses have been found to be "based on two or more acts or transactions constituting parts of a common scheme or plan" so as to be properly joined where two of three bank robberies were committed the same day and the other a month earlier, *U.S. v. Armstrong,* 621 F.2d 951, 954 (9th Cir. 1980); where defendant committed two assaults in Naval Academy locker rooms and was apprehended in another locker room cutting locks off lockers, *U.S. v. Eades,* 615 F.2d 617, 624 (4th Cir. 1980); where escape and a substantive offense were joined and the escape was to avoid prosecution for the substantive charge, *U.S. v. Ritch,* 583 F.2d 1179, 1181 (1st Cir.), *cert. denied,* 439 U.S. 970 (1978); where charges of causing interstate travel and use of interstate facilities to promote prostitution showed motive for threat and perjury charges, *U.S. v. Raineri,* 670 F.2d 702, 708-09 (7th Cir. 1982).

Venue lies only in the district in which the offense was committed. Rule 18, Fed. R. Crim. P.

### § 904. — — Multiple Indictments.

Rule 13 of the Federal Rules of Criminal Procedure allows the court to "order two or more indictments or informations or both to be tried together if the offenses … could have been joined in a single indictment or information." Where two or more indictments or informations are so consolidated for trial, "[t]he procedure shall be the same as if the prosecution were under such single indictment or information." Rule 13, Fed. R. Crim. P.; *Dunaway v. U.S.,* 205 F.2d 23, 24 n.4 (D.C. Cir. 1953).

Rule 8(a), therefore, provides the standard for consolidation. Indictments may be consolidated for trial together where they charge offenses that (1) are of the same or similar character, (2) are based on the
same act or transaction, or (3) are based on two or more acts or transactions constituting parts of a common scheme or plan.

Consolidation has been held proper where two indictments charged
extortion under color of office, *Williams v. U.S.,* 168 U.S. 382, 390
(1897); where three counts of failure to file federal income tax returns
were joined for trial and evidence of defendant's failure to file each
year was relevant on the issue of willfulness in other years, *U.S. v.
Bowman,* 602 F.2d 160, 163 (8th Cir. 1979); where two indictments for
selling heroin were joined and evidence of each sale would have been
admissible in separate trials, *U.S. v. Burkley,* 591 F.2d 903, 920 (D.C.
Cir. 1978), *cert. denied,* 440 U.S. 966 (1979); where escape and kidnapping charges were joined, *U.S. v. Elliott,* 418 F.2d 219, 221 (9th Cir.
1969); and where counterfeiting and bail jumping charges were joined,
*U.S. v. Bourassa,* 411 F.2d 69, 74 (10th Cir.), *cert. denied,* 396 U.S. 915
(1969).

The question of consolidation is addressed to the sound discretion of
the trial court. *U.S. v. Halper,* 590 F.2d 422, 428 (2d Cir. 1978); *U.S. v.
Haygood,* 502 F.2d 166, 169 n.5 (7th Cir. 1974), *cert. denied,* 419 U.S.
1114 (1975). It has been held an abuse of discretion, however, to allow
consolidation for trial of a medicaid fraud indictment with a later,
personal income tax evasion indictment. *U.S. v. Halper,* 590 F.2d at
433.

### § 905. — — Duplicity and Multiplicity.

"Duplicity is the joining in a single count of two or more distinct and
separate offenses." *U.S. v. Starks,* 515 F.2d 112, 116 (3d Cir. 1975);
*U.S. v. Tanner,* 471 F.2d 128, 138 (7th Cir.), *cert. denied,* 409 U.S. 949
(1972); *U.S. v. Gibson,* 310 F.2d 79, 80 n.1 (2d Cir. 1962). "'Multiplicity'
is the charging of a single offense in separate counts." *U.S. v. Hairrell,*
521 F.2d 1264, 1266 (6th Cir.), *cert. denied,* 423 U.S. 1035 (1975); *U.S.
v. Starks,* 515 F.2d at 116 n.5; *Gerberding v. U.S.,* 471 F.2d 55, 58 (8th
Cir. 1973).

Duplicity is not necessarily fatal to an indictment. *Reno v. U.S.,* 317
F.2d 499, 502 (5th Cir.), *cert. denied,* 375 U.S. 828 (1963). However,
appellate courts have reversed verdicts of guilty on duplicitous counts.
*U.S. v. Stanley,* 597 F.2d 866, 871-72 (4th Cir. 1979); *Bins v. U.S.,* 331
F.2d 390, 393 (5th Cir.), *cert. denied,* 379 U.S. 880 (1964). The government may be required to elect the charge on which it will proceed at
trial. *Thomas v. U.S.,* 418 F.2d 567, 568 (5th Cir. 1969); *Franklin v.*

*U.S.*, 330 F.2d 205, 207 (D.C. Cir. 1964); *U.S. v. Goodman*, 285 F.2d 378, 379 (5th Cir. 1960), *cert. denied*, 366 U.S. 930 (1961).

Dismissal, likewise, is not required where the same offense is charged in more than one count. *U.S. v. DeStafano*, 429 F.2d 344, 348 (2d Cir. 1970), *cert. denied*, 402 U.S. 972 (1971). The defendant may ask the trial court to require the government to elect the count on which proof will be presented. *U.S. v. Universal C.I.T. Credit Corp.*, 344 U.S. 218, 225 (1952).

An indictment is not duplicitous where two or more separate offenses are charged in one count if one crime charged contains as an essential element the other crime charged, *U.S. v. Warner*, 428 F.2d 730, 735 (8th Cir.), *cert. denied*, 400 U.S. 930 (1970); or where several related acts are charged as means of accomplishing the crime, Rule 7(c)(1), Fed. R. Crim. P. (provision intended to eliminate the use of multiple counts to allege commission of an offense by different means or in different ways); *U.S. v. Berardi*, 675 F.2d 894, 897 (7th Cir. 1982); *U.S. v. Droms*, 566 F.2d 361, 363 (2d Cir. 1977); *U.S. v. Outpost Development Co.*, 552 F.2d 868, 869 (9th Cir. 1977); *U.S. v. Tanner*, 471 F.2d 128, 138 (7th Cir.), *cert. denied*, 409 U.S. 949 (1972); *Frankfort Distilleries v. U.S.*, 144 F.2d 824, 832 (10th Cir. 1944), *rev'd on other grounds*, 324 U.S. 293 (1945). An indictment charging conspiracy to commit more than one crime is not duplicitous. *Braverman v. U.S.*, 317 U.S. 49, 54 (1942); *U.S. v. Carson*, 464 F.2d 424, 435 (2d Cir.), *cert. denied*, 409 U.S. 949 (1972).

## § 906. — Joinder of Defendants.

Where two or more defendants are charged, Rule 8(b) of the Federal Rules of Criminal Procedure governs both joinder of offenses and defendants. *U.S. v. Jackson*, 562 F.2d 789, 793 (D.C. Cir. 1977); *U.S. v. Satterfield*, 548 F.2d 1341, 1344 (9th Cir. 1977), *cert. denied*, 439 U.S. 840 (1978); *U.S. v. Park*, 531 F.2d 754, 760 n.4 (5th Cir. 1976); *U.S. v. Eagleston*, 417 F.2d 11, 14 (10th Cir. 1968); *Williams v. U.S.*, 416 F.2d 1064, 1068 (8th Cir. 1969). Whether joinder is proper under Rule 8(b) is to be determined from the face of the indictment. *U.S. v. Grassi*, 616 F.2d 1295, 1302 (5th Cir.), *cert. denied*, 449 U.S. 956 (1980); *U.S. v. Leach*, 613 F.2d 1295, 1299 (5th Cir. 1980).

## § 907. — — Same Indictment.

Rule 8(b) provides that defendants may be joined in a single indictment where they are alleged to have participated (1) in the same act or transaction or (2) in the same series of acts or transactions constituting an offense or offenses. It is not required, however, that each defendant be charged in every count of the indictment. *Id.; U.S. v. Barbosa,* 666 F.2d 704, 707 (1st Cir. 1981); *U.S. v. Weisman,* 624 F.2d 1118, 1129 (2d Cir.), *cert. denied,* 449 U.S. 871 (1980); *U.S. v. Colatriano,* 624 F.2d 686, 688 (5th Cir. 1980); *U.S. v. Santoni,* 585 F.2d 667, 673 (4th Cir. 1978), *cert. denied,* 440 U.S. 910 (1979); *U.S. v. Ross,* 464 F.2d 1278, 1280 (9th Cir. 1972). But, because guilt is both individual and personal, a defendant charged with others has "the right not to be tried *en masse* for the conglomeration of distinct and separate offenses committed by others." *Kotteakos v. U.S.,* 328 U.S. 750, 775 (1946). Similarity of offenses is not sufficient for joinder under Rule 8(b). *U.S. v. Jackson,* 562 F.2d 789, 796 (D.C. Cir. 1977); *U.S. v. Satterfield,* 548 F.2d 1341, 1344 (9th Cir. 1977), *cert. denied,* 439 U.S. 840 (1978); *U.S. v. Whitehead,* 539 F.2d 1023, 1026 (4th Cir. 1976); *King v. U.S.,* 355 F.2d 700, 704 (1st Cir. 1966).

Joinder is proper where the defendants are alleged to have participated in the same act or transaction. *U.S. v. Colatriano,* 624 F.2d at 688; *U.S. v. Corall-Martinez,* 592 F.2d 263, 268 (5th Cir. 1979); *U.S. v. Santoni,* 585 F.2d at 673; *U.S. v. Whitehead,* 539 F.2d at 1025; *Stern v. U.S.,* 409 F.2d 819, 820 (2d Cir. 1969).

Defendants have been held to have been properly joined as having participated in the same act or transaction where various defendants were charged with conspiracy and forcible rescue of seized property and/or forcible assault on federal officials, *U.S. v. Heck,* 499 F.2d 778, 789 (9th Cir.), *cert. denied,* 419 U.S. 1088 (1974).

Joinder is also permitted where the defendants are alleged to have participated in the same series of acts or transactions. *U.S. v. Weisman,* 624 F.2d 1118, 1129 (2d Cir.), *cert. denied,* 449 U.S. 871 (1980); *U.S. v. Zicree,* 605 F.2d 1381, 1387 (5th Cir. 1979), *cert. denied,* 445 U.S. 966 (1980); *U.S. v. Ortiz,* 603 F.2d 76, 78 (9th Cir. 1979), *cert. denied,* 444 U.S. 1020 (1980); *U.S. v. Jackson,* 562 F.2d at 796; *U.S. v. Martinez,* 479 F.2d 824, 827 (1st Cir. 1973). However, the mere showing that the acts occurred at or about the same time or that such acts violated the same statutes is not sufficient to show that the acts constitute a series of acts or transactions within the meaning of the Rule. *U.S. v. Satterfield, supra; U.S. v. Martinez,* 479 F.2d at 827; *King v. U.S.,* 355 F.2d at 703.

Defendants have been held properly joined where they were charged with conspiracy to defraud, wire fraud, mail fraud, and interstate transportation of checks. *U.S. v. Becker,* 569 F.2d at 964, where one defendant was charged only with drug offenses with codefendants who were also charged with weapons violations, *U.S. v. Laca,* 499 F.2d at

925; where the indictment charged both defendants with Hobbs Act violations and each defendant was separately charged with making false material declarations to the grand jury, *U.S. v. Gill,* 490 F.2d 233, 238 (7th Cir. 1973), *cert. denied,* 417 U.S. 968 (1974); where one defendant was charged with forging and cashing travelers' checks and codefendant was charged with aiding and abetting in interstate transportation of forged travelers' checks, *U.S. v. Rickey,* 457 F.2d 1027, 1029 (3d Cir.), *cert. denied,* 409 U.S. 863 (1972).

### § 908. — — Consolidation for Trial.

Rule 13 of the Federal Rules of Criminal Procedure provides that the court may order two or more indictments or informations or both to be tried together if the offenses and the defendants could have been joined initially, and that the standard for consolidation of defendants for trial is Rule 8(b). *Daley v. U.S.,* 231 F.2d 123, 125 (1st Cir.), *cert. denied,* 351 U.S. 964 (1956); *Malatkofski v. U.S.,* 179 F.2d 905, 909 (1st Cir. 1950). Rule 8(b) provides that two or more defendants may be charged in the same indictment where they are alleged to have participated in the same act or transaction or in the same series of acts or transactions constituting an offense or offenses.

Joint trial has been held proper where defendants were charged with contempt for violating a court order against fishing in violation of a treaty. *U.S. v. Olander,* 584 F.2d 876, 885 (9th Cir. 1978), *vacated on other grounds,* 443 U.S. 914 (1979).

### § 909. — — Conspiracy.

A conspiracy count may be joined with a count to commit the substantive offense. *Pinkerton v. U.S.,* 328 U.S. 640, 643 (1946); *U.S. v. Heck,* 499 F.2d 778, 789 (9th Cir.), *cert. denied,* 419 U.S. 1088 (1974); *U.S. v. Sweig,* 441 F.2d 114, 118 (2d Cir.), *cert. denied,* 403 U.S. 932 (1971); *Gordon v. U.S.,* 438 F.2d 858, 878 (5th Cir.), *cert. denied,* 404 U.S. 828 (1971); *Pegram v. U.S.,* 361 F.2d 820, 821 (8th Cir. 1966). All of the conspirators do not need to be charged in every substantive count, *Schaffer v. U.S.,* 362 U.S. 511, 512-13 (1960); *U.S. v. Leach,* 613 F.2d 1295, 1303 (5th Cir. 1980); *U.S. v. Graham,* 548 F.2d 1302, 1310 (8th Cir. 1977); and all of the conspirators do not need to have participated in all phases of the conspiracy, *Blumenthal v. U.S.,* 332 U.S. 539, 556-57 (1947); *U.S. v. Leach,* 613 F.2d at 1299; *U.S. v. Petersen,* 611 F.2d 1313, 1332 (10th Cir. 1979); *U.S. v. Woolridge,* 572 F.2d 1027, 1029 (5th Cir.), *cert. denied,* 439 U.S. 849 (1978); *U.S. v. Hutul,* 416 F.2d 607, 619 (7th Cir. 1969), *cert. denied,* 396 U.S. 1012 (1970); but all of the substantive offenses charged must be within the scope of the conspiracy, *U.S. v. Gentile,* 495 F.2d 626, 632 (5th Cir. 1974); *U.S. v. Donaway,* 447 F.2d 940, 943 (9th Cir. 1971).

Charging multiple and unrelated conspiracies will not justify joinder of defendants in the same indictment. *Kotteakos v. U.S.,* 328 U.S. 750 (1946); *U.S. v. Nettles,* 570 F.2d 547, 551-52 (5th Cir. 1978). Separate conspiracies with different participants may be joined, however, if the conspiracies are part of the same series of transactions. *U.S. v. Grassi,* 616 F.2d 1295, 1303 (5th Cir.), *cert. denied,* 449 U.S. 956 (1980); *U.S. v. McDaniel,* 538 F.2d 408, 411 (D.C. Cir. 1976). And where an indictment charges a single conspiracy but the evidence proves separate conspiracies, joinder is improper. *Kotteakos v. U.S., supra; U.S. v. Gross,* 329 F.2d 180, 183 (4th Cir. 1964).

Joinder of defendants in a conspiracy count that is later dismissed or reversed or on which the defendants are acquitted does not require reversal of convictions on the substantive counts on grounds of misjoinder. Severance need not be ordered because a conspiracy count is dismissed before submission of the substantive counts to the jury if the conspiracy was alleged in good faith and joinder was not prejudicial. *Schaffer v. U.S.,* 362 U.S. 511 (1960); *U.S. v. Woolridge,* 572 F.2d at 1029; *U.S. v. Scafidi,* 564 F.2d 633, 642 (2d Cir. 1977), *cert. denied,* 436 U.S. 903 (1978). However, if prejudice or bad faith is shown, severance is required. *U.S. v. Lane,* 584 F.2d 60, 63-66 (5th Cir. 1978). Reversal of convictions on substantive counts is not required where a conspiracy conviction is reversed on appeal. *U.S. v. Valenzuela,* 596 F.2d 824, 829 (9th Cir.), *cert. denied,* 441 U.S. 965 (1979). Where the jury convicts the defendants on the substantive counts but acquits on the conspiracy count, the convictions on the substantive counts remain valid. *Cacy v. U.S.,* 298 F.2d 227, 228-29 (9th Cir. 1961).

### § 910. Severance — Relief From Prejudicial Joinder.

Rule 14 of the Federal Rules of Criminal Procedure allows the trial court to order separate trials of counts or severance of defendants where it appears that joinder of offenses or defendants prejudices a defendant or the government, even though initial joinder was proper under Rule 8. *U.S. v. Davis,* 623 F.2d 188, 194 (1st Cir. 1980); *U.S. v. Werner,* 620 F.2d 922, 928 (2d Cir. 1980); *U.S. v. Thomas,* 610 F.2d 1166, 1169 (3d Cir. 1979); *U.S. v. Shearer,* 606 F.2d 819 (8th Cir. 1979); *U.S. v. Michel,* 588 F.2d 986, 1001 (5th Cir.), *cert. denied,* 444 U.S. 825 (1979); *U.S. v. Frazier,* 584 F.2d 790, 795 (6th Cir. 1978).

## §911. — Trial Court's Discretion.

Whether there is sufficient prejudice in joinder to warrant separate trials is a question committed to the sound discretion of the trial court. The trial court will not be reversed on appeal absent a showing of abuse of discretion. *U.S. v. Lane,* 106 S. Ct. 725, 732 n.12 (1986).

A showing that a defendant would have a better chance of acquittal in a separate trial does not establish prejudice requiring severance. *U.S. v. Thomas,* 676 F.2d 239, 243 (7th Cir. 1980); *U.S. v. Brim, supra; U.S. v. Petersen, supra; U.S. v. Rucker,* 586 F.2d 899, 902 (2d Cir. 1978); *U.S. v. Santoni, supra; U.S. v. Ritch,* 583 F.2d 1179, 1181 (1st Cir.), *cert. denied,* 439 U.S. 970 (1978). To show enough prejudice to require severance, a defendant must establish "substantial prejudice," *U.S. v. Werner,* 620 F.2d 922, 928 (2d Cir. 1980); "undue prejudice," *U.S. v. McDonald,* 576 F.2d at 1355; *U.S. v. McClintic,* 570 F.2d 685, 689 (8th Cir. 1978); "compelling prejudice," *U.S. v. Staller,* 616 F.2d at 1294; "clear prejudice," *U.S. v. Bridwell,* 583 F.2d 1135, 1142 (10th Cir. 1978); *U.S. v. Mullens,* 583 F.2d 134, 142 (5th Cir. 1978); or must make a "clear showing of prejudice," *U.S. v. Grabiec,* 563 F.2d 313, 318 (7th Cir. 1977); must make a "strong showing of prejudice," *U.S. v. Thomann,* 609 F.2d 560, 564 (1st Cir. 1979); must bear a "heavy burden" of showing prejudice, *U.S. v. Herring,* 602 F.2d 1220, 1225 (5th Cir. 1979), *cert. denied,* 444 U.S. 1046 (1980); *U.S. v. Starr,* 584 F.2d 235, 238 (8th Cir. 1978), *cert. denied,* 439 U.S. 1115 (1979); *U.S. v. Adams,* 581 F.2d 193, 198 (9th Cir.), *cert. denied,* 439 U.S. 1006 (1978); *U.S. v. Niederberger,* 580 F.2d 63, 66 (3d Cir.), *cert. denied,* 439 U.S. 980 (1978); or must "'affirmatively demonstrate that the joint trial prejudiced [his] right to a fair trial,'" *U.S. v. Knife,* 592 F.2d 472, 480 (8th Cir. 1979).

## §912. — Severance of Offenses.

Rule 14 of the Federal Rules of Criminal Procedure provides that, if a defendant or the government is prejudiced by a joinder of offenses, the trial court may order an election or separate trial of counts. A defendant may be prejudiced by joinder of offenses because "(1) he may become embarrassed or confounded in presenting separate defenses; (2) the jury may use the evidence of one of the crimes charged to infer a criminal disposition on the part of the defendant from which is found his guilt of the crime or crimes charged; or (3) the jury may cumulate the evidence of the various crimes charged and find guilt when, if considered separately, it would not do so." *Drew v. U.S.,* 331 F.2d 85, 88 (D.C. Cir. 1964); *U.S. v. Lewis,* 626 F.2d 940, 945 (D.C. Cir. 1980).

Where a defendant wants to testify about one offense but not the other joined offense, prejudice may develop. *Cross v. U.S.*, 335 F.2d 987, 989 (D.C. Cir. 1964). Severance, however, is not mandatory merely because a defendant says he wants and intends to testify on some but not all counts. *Alvarez v. Wainwright*, 607 F.2d 683, 685 (5th Cir. 1979). The defendant must make "a convincing showing that he has both important testimony to give concerning one count and strong need to refrain from testifying on the other." *Baker v. U.S.*, 401 F.2d 958, 977 (D.C. Cir. 1968); *U.S. v. Armstrong*, 621 F.2d 951, 954 (9th Cir. 1980). And, the defendant must present enough information about the nature of his testimony on one count and his reasons for not testifying on the other to show that the claim of prejudice is genuine. *U.S. v. Forrest*, 623 F.2d 1107, 1115 (5th Cir. 1980); *U.S. v. Bronco*, 597 F.2d 1300, 1303 (9th Cir. 1979); *U.S. v. Jamar*, 561 F.2d 1103, 1108 n.9 (4th Cir. 1977); *Baker v. U.S.*, 401 F.2d at 977.

Where evidence that a defendant committed one crime would be admissible at a separate trial for another crime, the defendant does not suffer additional prejudice where the two offenses are tried jointly. *U.S. v. Harris*, 635 F.2d 526 (6th Cir. 1980), *cert. denied*, 451 U.S. 989 (1981); *U.S. v. Dennis*, 625 F.2d 782, 802 (8th Cir. 1980); *U.S. v. Thomas*, 610 F.2d 1166, 1169 (3d Cir. 1979); *U.S. v. Kim*, 595 F.2d 755, 770 (D.C. Cir. 1979); *U.S. v. Ritch*, 583 F.2d 1179, 1181 (1st Cir.), *cert. denied*, 439 U.S. 970 (1978); *U.S. v. Foutz*, 540 F.2d 733, 736 (4th Cir. 1976); *U.S. v. Begun*, 446 F.2d 32, 33 (9th Cir. 1971); *U.S. v. Sweig*, 441 F.2d 114, 118 (2d Cir.), *cert. denied*, 403 U.S. 932 (1971).

Severance is not required merely because evidence on one joined count is "separable and distinct" from evidence on another. *U.S. v. Lewis*, 626 F.2d at 945; *U.S. v. Lewis*, 547 F.2d 1030, 1033 (8th Cir. 1976), *cert. denied*, 429 U.S. 1111 (1977); *U.S. v. Kellerman*, 432 F.2d 371, 374-75 (10th Cir. 1970); *Drew v. U.S.*, 331 F.2d at 91-92.

## § 913. — Severance of Defendants.

Generally, persons indicted together should be tried together. *U.S. v. McCulley*, 673 F.2d 346, 349 (11th Cir. 1982); *U.S. v. Phillips*, 607 F.2d 808 (8th Cir. 1979); *U.S. v. Avarello*, 592 F.2d 1339, 1345 (5th Cir.), *cert. denied*, 444 U.S. 844 (1979); *U.S. v. Mandel*, 591 F.2d 1347, 1371 (4th Cir. 1979), *cert. denied*, 445 U.S. 961 (1980); *U.S. v. Caldwell*, 543 F.2d 1333, 1358 (D.C. Cir. 1974), *cert. denied*, 423 U.S. 1087 (1976); *Parker v. U.S.*, 404 F.2d 1193, 1196 (9th Cir. 1968), *cert. denied*, 394 U.S. 1004 (1969). The substantial public interest in joint trials is that a joint trial expedites "the administration of justice, reduces the congestion of trial dockets, conserves judicial time, lessens the burden upon citizens who must sacrifice both time and money to serve upon juries, and avoids the necessity of recalling witnesses who would otherwise be called upon to testify only once." *Parker v. U.S., supra* (footnote omitted).

Where the same evidence is admissible against all defendants, severance will not be granted. *U.S. v. Ciampaglia,* 628 F.2d 632, 643 (1st Cir.), *cert. denied,* 449 U.S. 956 (1980); *U.S. v. Boyd,* 610 F.2d 521, 525 (8th Cir. 1979), *cert. denied,* 444 U.S. 1089 (1980); *U.S. v. McPartlin,* 595 F.2d 1321, 1333 (7th Cir.), *cert. denied,* 444 U.S. 833 (1979); *U.S. v. Arroyo-Angulo,* 580 F.2d 1137, 1144 (2d Cir.), *cert. denied,* 439 U.S. 913 (1978); *U.S. v. Dye,* 508 F.2d 1226, 1236 (6th Cir. 1974), *cert. denied,* 420 U.S. 974 (1975); *U.S. v. Shuford,* 454 F.2d 772, 775-76 (4th Cir. 1971).

Severance is not required unless the evidence is so complex or confusing that the jury would be unable to make individual determinations about guilt for each of the defendants, *U.S. v. Bright,* 630 F.2d 804, 813 (5th Cir. 1980); but severance must be granted if the jurors cannot determine the guilt of each individual defendant solely on the basis of the evidence presented about each defendant, *U.S. v. Crawford,* 581 F.2d 489, 491 (5th Cir. 1978). However, that evidence may be admissible against one defendant but not others does not alone require severance. *U.S. v. Reeves,* 674 F.2d 739, 746 (8th Cir. 1982); *U.S. v. Lyles,* 593 F.2d 182, 190 (2d Cir.), *cert. denied,* 440 U.S. 972 (1979); *U.S. v. Hoffa,* 349 F.2d 20, 43 (6th Cir. 1965), *aff'd,* 385 U.S. 293 (1966).

A defendant is not entitled to severance because the prosecution's proof is stronger against a codefendant. *U.S. v. Williams,* 604 F.2d 1102, 1119 (8th Cir. 1979); *U.S. v. Anderson,* 626 F.2d 1358, 1373 (8th Cir. 1980); *U.S. v. Dansker,* 537 F.2d 40 (3d Cir. 1976), *cert. denied,* 429 U.S. 1038 (1977), or because of claim that interracial relationship of the defendants would prejudice them in the eyes of the jury, *U.S. v. Sellers,* 667 F.2d 1123, 1125 (4th Cir. 1981). Nor is a defendant entitled to severance because a codefendant has a criminal record. *U.S. v. Dalzotto,* 603 F.2d 642, 646 (7th Cir.), *cert. denied,* 444 U.S. 994 (1979); *U.S. v. Rucker,* 586 F.2d at 903; *U.S. v. Bazinet,* 462 F.2d 982, 992 (8th Cir.), *cert. denied,* 409 U.S. 1010 (1972). The trial court, however, has a continuing duty throughout the trial to grant severance if prejudice develops. *U.S. v. Petersen,* 611 F.2d 1313, 1331 (10th Cir. 1979), *cert. denied,* 447 U.S. 905 (1980); *U.S. v. Boyd,* 610 F.2d at 526.

## §914. — — Need for Codefendant's Testimony.

"The 'great mass' of cases refuse to grant a severance despite the anticipated exculpatory testimony of a codefendant." *U.S. v. Gay,* 567

F.2d 916, 919 (9th Cir.), *cert. denied*, 435 U.S. 999 (1978). The defendant must show that he would call the codefendant at a separate trial, that the codefendant would testify, and that the testimony would be exculpatory. *U.S. v. Haro-Espinosa*, 619 F.2d 789, 793 (9th Cir. 1979); *U.S. v. Vigil*, 561 F.2d 1316 (9th Cir. 1977). Severance is not required where there has not been a showing that the testimony is needed, that it would be available at a separate trial, and that it would be exculpatory. *U.S. v. Butler*, 611 F.2d 1066, 1071 (5th Cir.), *cert. denied*, 449 U.S. 830 (1980); *U.S. v. Smolar*, 557 F.2d 13, 21 (1st Cir.), *cert. denied*, 434 U.S. 971 (1977); *U.S. v. Henderson*, 471 F.2d 204, 206 (7th Cir. 1972). In ruling on such a motion for severance the trial court may consider (1) the sufficiency of the showing that a codefendant would testify at a separate trial and waive his fifth amendment privilege, *U.S. v. Finkelstein*, 526 F.2d 517, 523 (2d Cir. 1975), *cert. denied*, 425 U.S. 960 (1976); *U.S. v. Kahn*, 381 F.2d 824, 841 (7th Cir.), *cert. denied*, 389 U.S. 1015 (1967); *Gorin v. U.S.*, 313 F.2d 641, 646 (1st Cir.), *cert. denied*, 374 U.S. 829 (1963), (2) the degree to which the testimony would be exculpatory, *U.S. v. Boscia*, 573 F.2d 827, 832 (3d Cir.), *cert. denied*, 436 U.S. 911 (1978); *Byrd v. Wainwright*, 428 F.2d 1017, 1020 (5th Cir. 1970), (3) the likelihood that the testimony would be subject to damaging impeachment, *U.S. v. Boscia*, *supra*; *U.S. v. Finkelstein*, 526 F.2d at 524, and (4) judicial economy, *U.S. v. Duzac*, 622 F.2d 911, 912 (5th Cir.), *cert. denied*, 449 U.S. 1012 (1980); *U.S. v. Boscia*, *supra*; *U.S. v. Finkelstein*, *supra*; *Byrd v. Wainwright*, *supra*. A trial court may refuse to grant severance where a codefendant bases his offer to give exculpatory testimony on the condition that he be tried first. *U.S. v. Haro-Espinosa*, *supra*; *U.S. v. Gay*, 567 F.2d at 919-20.

### § 915. — — Codefendant's Confession.

Admission of a codefendant's confession at a joint trial where the codefendant does not testify and therefore cannot be cross-examined, violates a defendant's sixth amendment right of confrontation. *Bruton v. U.S.*, 391 U.S. 123 (1968). However, that the government seeks to introduce a codefendant's confession at trial does not mandate severance. For a discussion of the use of confessions in joint trials, *see* Chapter 3, § 313 *supra*.

If the purpose of admitting an accomplice's confession is not to prove the matter within the statement, but is to prove the nonhearsay aspect of what happened when the defendant confessed, that is, to rebut the account of the defendant regarding defendant's confession, there is no confrontation issue and the accomplice's confession may be admitted. *Tennessee v. Street*, 469 U.S. 929 (1985).

## § 916. — — Conflicting Defenses.

Hostility among defendants or the attempt of one defendant to save himself by inculpating another does not require that defendants be tried separately. *U.S. v. Talavera,* 668 F.2d 625 (1st Cir.), *cert. denied,* 102 S. Ct. 2245 (1982); *U.S. v. Boyd,* 610 F.2d 521, 526 (8th Cir. 1979), *cert. denied,* 444 U.S. 1089 (1980); *U.S. v. Vinson,* 606 F.2d 149, 154 (6th Cir. 1979), *cert. denied,* 444 U.S. 1074 (1980); *U.S. v. McPartlin,* 595 F.2d 1321, 1334 (7th Cir.), *cert. denied,* 444 U.S. 833 (1979); *U.S. v. Ehrlichman,* 546 F.2d 910, 929 (D.C. Cir. 1976), *cert. denied,* 429 U.S. 1120 (1977); *U.S. v. Barber,* 442 F.2d 517, 530 (3d Cir.), *cert. denied,* 404 U.S. 846 (1971); *U.S. v. Hutul,* 416 F.2d 607, 620-21 (7th Cir. 1969), *cert. denied,* 396 U.S. 1012 (1970); *Dauer v. U.S.,* 189 F.2d 343, 344 (10th Cir.), *cert. denied,* 342 U.S. 898 (1951). Neither does a difference in trial strategies require that defendants be tried separately, *U.S. v. Whitehead,* 618 F.2d 523 (4th Cir. 1980); nor inconsistent defense strategies, *U.S. v. Crawford,* 581 F.2d 489, 491 (5th Cir. 1978). To obtain severance because of conflicting defenses, a defendant must show more than antagonistic defense strategies, *U.S. v. Davis,* 623 F.2d 188 (1st Cir. 1980); *U.S. v. Boyd, supra;* a defendant must show that "the conflict is so prejudicial that defenses are irreconcilable, and the jury will unjustifiably infer that this conflict alone demonstrates that both are guilty," *U.S. v. Davis,* 623 F.2d at 194-95; *U.S. v. Boyd, supra; U.S. v. Herring,* 602 F.2d 1220, 1225 (5th Cir. 1979), *cert. denied,* 444 U.S. 1046 (1980); *U.S. v. Haldeman,* 559 F.2d 31, 71 (D.C. Cir. 1976), *cert. denied,* 431 U.S. 933 (1977); *U.S. v. Ehrlichman, supra; U.S. v. Robinson,* 432 F.2d 1348, 1351 (D.C. Cir. 1970); or that antagonism will mislead or confuse the jury, *U.S. v. Kendricks,* 623 F.2d 1165, 1168 (6th Cir. 1980); or that acceptance of one defendant's defense will preclude acquittal of the codefendant, *U.S. v. Ziperstein,* 601 F.2d 281, 285 (7th Cir. 1979), *cert. denied,* 444 U.S. 1031 (1980).

Where defense counsel concludes that effective presentation of his client's case requires that he direct the jury's attention to the in-trial silence of a codefendant, the trial court must order severance. *De Luna v. U.S.,* 308 F.2d 140, 141 (5th Cir. 1962). This rule, however, applies only where the defenses of the codefendants are antagonistic, *Gurleski v. U.S.,* 405 F.2d 253, 265 (5th Cir. 1968), *cert. denied,* 395 U.S. 981 (1969); and denial of severance is not prejudicial unless a defendant can demonstrate that his defense probably would have benefited from commenting on a codefendant's refusal to testify, *U.S. v. De La Cruz Bellinger,* 422 F.2d 723, 727 (9th Cir.), *cert. denied,* 398 U.S. 942 (1970); *Kolod v. U.S.,* 371 F.2d 983, 991 (10th Cir. 1967); *Hayes v. U.S.,* 329 F.2d 209, 221-22 (8th Cir.), *cert. denied,* 377 U.S. 980 (1964). However, in *U.S. v. McKinney,* 379 F.2d 259, 265 (6th Cir. 1967), the court said that a defendant's attorney could not comment on the failure of a codefendant to testify because this would violate a codefendant's fifth amendment right guaranteed by 18 U.S.C. § 3481 not to have his in-trial silence commented upon.

## § 917. — — Conspiracy.

Generally, persons charged in a conspiracy should be tried together. *U.S. v. Boyd,* 610 F.2d 521 (8th Cir. 1979), *cert. denied,* 444 U.S. 1089 (1980); *U.S. v. McGuire,* 608 F.2d 1028, 1031 (5th Cir. 1979), *cert. denied,* 446 U.S. 910 (1980); *U.S. v. Goble,* 512 F.2d 458, 465-66 (6th Cir.), *cert. denied,* 423 U.S. 914 (1975). Courts have consistently re-jected motions for severance filed by individual defendants in conspir-acy cases. *U.S. v. Goble, supra; U.S. v. Mayes,* 512 F.2d 637, 645 (6th Cir.), *cert. denied,* 422 U.S. 1008 (1975). A defendant is not entitled to severance because his role in the conspiracy was minor, *U.S. v. Smolar,* 557 F.2d 13, 21 (1st Cir.), *cert. denied,* 434 U.S. 971 (1977), or because the evidence against a codefendant is more damaging, *U.S. v. Fuel,* 583 F.2d 978, 988 (8th Cir. 1978), *cert. denied,* 439 U.S. 1127 (1979). Where the trial court instructs the jury about the limited admissibility of coconspirator statements and to consider each count and the evidence against each defendant separately, severance is not required. *U.S. v. Cuesta,* 597 F.2d 903 (5th Cir.), *cert. denied,* 444 U.S. 964 (1979).

## § 918. — Waiver.

Rule 12(b)(5) requires that a motion for severance of charges or de-fendants under Rule 14 must be made before trial. Where a party fails to comply with this provision, the objection is deemed to have been waived. Rule 12(f), Fed. R. Crim. P.; *U.S. v. DeRosa,* 670 F.2d 889, 897 n.10 (9th Cir. 1982). Failure to renew a motion for severance at the close of the government's case or at the conclusion of the evidence constitutes a waiver of a demand for separate trials. *U.S. v. Barker,* 675 F.2d 1055, 1058 (9th Cir. 1982); *U.S. v. Brim,* 630 F.2d 1307, 1310 (8th Cir. 1980). But where the trial court indicated that renewal of the motion would be useless, failure to renew the motion at the close of the evidence was not waiver. *U.S. v. Kaplan,* 554 F.2d 958, 966 (9th Cir.), *cert. denied,* 434 U.S. 956 (1977).

## § 919. Misjoinder.

An error involving misjoinder is subject to a harmless error analysis and requires reversal only if the misjoinder had substantial and injurious effect or influence on the jury's verdict. *U.S. v. Lane,* 106 S. Ct. 725 (1986).

# CHAPTER 10

# JEOPARDY AND MISTRIAL

§ 1001. Jeopardy.
§ 1002. — Same Offense.
§ 1003. — Lesser Included Offense.
§ 1004. — Dual Sovereigns.
§ 1005. — The Petite Policy.
§ 1006. — Acquittals and Dismissals.
§ 1007. Mistrial.
§ 1008. — Manifest Necessity.
§ 1009. — Prosecutorial Manipulation to Abort Trial.
§ 1010. Appeals.
§ 1011. Collateral Estoppel.
§ 1012. Sentencing.

## § 1001. Jeopardy.

The fifth amendment states that no person shall "be subject for the same offense to be twice put in jeopardy of life or limb." The double jeopardy clause embodies three protections: it protects against a second prosecution for the same offense after acquittal; it protects against a second prosecution for the same offense after conviction; and it protects against multiple punishments for the same offense. *Grady v. Corbin,* 110 S. Ct. 2084 (1990); *U.S. v. Dinitz,* 424 U.S. 600 (1976); *North Carolina v. Pearce,* 395 U.S. 711 (1969); *U.S. v. Ball,* 163 U.S. 662 (1896); *Ex parte Lange,* 85 U.S. 163 (1873). Corporations as well as individuals are protected by the double jeopardy clause. *U.S. v. Martin Linen Supply Co.,* 430 U.S. 564 (1977).

Jeopardy attaches when, in a jury trial, the jury is empaneled and sworn; and, in a bench trial, when the judge begins to hear evidence. *Crist v. Bretz,* 437 U.S. 28 (1978); *Serfass v. U.S.,* 420 U.S. 377, 388 (1975); *Downum v. U.S.,* 372 U.S. 734 (1963). Jeopardy does not attach after a lawfully withdrawn or vacated plea. *Klobuchir v. Pennsylvania,* 639 F.2d 966 (3d Cir. 1981).

The double jeopardy clause applies "only if there has been some event, such as an acquittal, which terminates the original jeopardy." *Richardson v. U.S.,* 468 U.S. 317, 325 (1984).

The defense of double jeopardy is waived unless raised by the defendant before trial. *U.S. v. Perez,* 565 F.2d 1227, 1232 (2d Cir. 1977). *See* Rule 12(b)(1), Fed. R. Crim. P. Once raised, the trial court should decide the double jeopardy issue before trial. *U.S. v. Stricklin,* 591 F.2d 1112 (5th Cir.), *cert. denied,* 444 U.S. 963 (1979). If the claim is deemed not to be frivolous by the court, the burden is on the government to show by a preponderance of the evidence that there is no double jeopardy. When considering two separate substantive offenses, the test is the "same evidence" test. Where considering two conspiracies the test is the "totality of the circumstances." *U.S. v. Tercero,* 580 F.2d 312 (8th Cir. 1978); *U.S. v. Jabara,* 644 F.2d 574 (6th Cir. 1981).

The defendant has the initial burden of establishing a prima facie nonfrivolous double jeopardy claim. If he does, the government then has the burden to show that separate crimes are charged. *U.S. v. Sargent Elec. Co.,* 785 F.2d 1123 (3d Cir. 1986); *U.S. v. Garcia,* 721 F.2d 721 (11th Cir. 1983).

## § 1002. — Same Offense.

If offenses have identical statutory elements or one is a lesser included offense of the other, a subsequent prosecution is barred. *Blockburger v. U.S.,* 284 U.S. 299 (1932). This test has been improperly called the "same evidence" test but, in fact, has nothing to do with the evidence presented at trial, but is concerned solely with the statutory elements of the offenses charged. *Grady v. Corbin,* 110 S. Ct. 2084 n.12 (1990). Even though a successive prosecution may meet the *Blockburger* test, the double jeopardy clause still bars a subsequent prosecution if, to establish an essential element of an offense charged, the second prosecution requires the relitigation of factual issues already resolved by the first or the government will prove conduct that constitutes an offense for which a defendant has already been prosecuted. *Id.; Brown v. Ohio,* 432 U.S. 161 (1977). As it is the proof of "conduct" that is critical, the presentation of specific "evidence" in one trial does not forever prohibit the government from introducing that same evidence in a subsequent proceeding. *Dowling v. U.S.,* 110 S. Ct. 668 (1990).

A defendant may be prosecuted and punished for the same act under separate federal criminal statutes if each statute requires proof of a fact which the other does not. *Blockburger v. U.S.,* supra. Conviction or acquittal for one offense is not a bar to a second trial unless the government's evidence is the same for both offenses. If either offense requires proof of an additional fact, not part of and not necessary to the other, the double jeopardy prohibition does not apply. *Ciucci v. Illinois,* 356 U.S. 571 (1958); *U.S. v. Frady,* 607 F.2d 383 (D.C. Cir. 1979); *U.S. v. Solano,* 605 F.2d 1141 (9th Cir. 1979), *cert. denied,* 444 U.S. 1020 (1980); *U.S. v. Ford,* 603 F.2d 1043 (2d Cir. 1979); *U.S. v. Stricklin,* 591 F.2d 1112 (5th Cir. 1979), *cert. denied,* 444 U.S. 963 (1980). Nor does it apply to bar consecutive sentences where a defendant has been convicted of separate offenses, though stemming from a single transaction, if each offense required proof of a fact the other did not. *Albernaz v. U.S.,* 450 U.S. 333 (1981); *Whalen v. U.S.,* 445 U.S. 684 (1980). The question is the intent of Congress. If Congress intended to authorize separate offenses and thus separate sentences for acts arising out of a single transaction, the double jeopardy clause is not offended. In construing Congressional intent, the *Blockburger* test will be applied. *Illinois v. Vitale,* 447 U.S. 410 (1980). The assumption underlying *Blockburger* is that the legislature does not intend to punish the same offense under two different statutes unless there is a clear contrary intent. *Whalen v. U.S.,* 445 U.S. at 691-92. Thus, where the legislature specifically authorizes cumulative punishment under two statutes for the "same" conduct under *Blockburger, Blockburger* does not apply and such cumulative punishment may be imposed in a single trial without violating the double jeopardy clause. *Missouri v. Hunter,* 459 U.S. 359 (1983). The double jeopardy clause prohibits punishment in excess of that authorized by the legislature. *Jones v. Thomas,* 491 U.S. 376 (1989). Thus, as Congress has recognized that receipt of a firearm necessarily involves possession, a convicted felon may not be convicted of both receiving and possessing the firearm. *Ball v. U.S.,* 470 U.S. 856 (1985).

Where two conspiracies are charged, five factors will be considered in deciding whether they are the same: "(1) the time during which the activities occurred; (2) the persons involved in the conspiracies; (3) the places involved; (4) whether the same evidence was used to prove the two conspiracies; and (5) whether the same statutory provision was involved in both conspiracies." *U.S. v. Booth,* 673 F.2d 27, 29 (1st Cir.), *cert. denied,* 102 S. Ct. 2245 (1982). The remedy where the defendant is convicted of multiple conspiracies when only one exists is to reverse and dismiss all but one of the counts with the defendant to be resentenced on the remaining count, *U.S. v. Olwares,* 786 F.2d 659 (5th Cir. 1986).

The double jeopardy clause does not apply where there are separate convictions for a substantive crime and for a conspiracy to commit that crime, *U.S. v. Felix,* 112 S. Ct. 1377 (1992), where there are separate convictions for a predicate offense and continuing criminal enterprise, *Garrett v. U.S.,* 471 U.S. 773 (1985); where there are separate convictions for RICO and a substantive offense involving receipt of illegal payments, *U.S. v. Baylan,* 620 F.2d 359 (2d Cir.), *cert. denied,* 449 U.S. 833 (1980); where there are separate convictions of RICO and drug conspiracy, *U.S. v. Solano, supra;* separate convictions of conspiracy to possess drugs and possession of drugs, *U.S. v. Brunk,* 615 F.2d 210 (5th Cir. 1980); separate convictions for conspiracy to import marijuana and conspiracy to distribute marijuana, *Albernaz v. U.S.,* 450 U.S. 333 (1981); separate convictions for conspiracy and conspiracy to violate the RICO statute, *U.S. v. Barton,* 647 F.2d 224 (2d Cir. 1981); and separate convictions for RICO involving a single "enterprise" but separate "patterns of racketeering activities," *U.S. v. Dean,* 647 F.2d 779 (8th Cir. 1981); separate convictions for violating the continuing criminal narcotics enterprise section and a predicate violation, *Jeffers v. U.S.,* 432 U.S. 137 (1977); *U.S. v. Chagra,* 669 F.2d 241, 261-62 (5th Cir. 1982); separate convictions under RICO and the Travel Act, *U.S. v. Watchmaker,* 761 F.2d 1459 (11th Cir. 1985). However, in the Sixth Circuit, cumulative sentences for violation of the Mann Act and Travel Act under the same set of facts run afoul of the double jeopardy clause. *Pandelli v. U.S.,* 635 F.2d 553 (6th Cir. 1980). The Sixth Circuit held that under the particular facts of the case, the elements of the Mann Act and the Travel Act were merged. Thus, even though proof of a Mann Act violation could require facts different from proof of a Travel Act violation, they did not as charged in the indictment. The *Blockburger* test, therefore, was not satisfied.

### § 1003. — Lesser Included Offense.

Greater and lesser offenses are, for jeopardy purposes, the same offense when the greater offense does not require proof of a fact different from that required to prove the lesser offense. *Brown v. Ohio,* 432 U.S. 161 (1977); *U.S. v. Cruz,* 568 F.2d 781 (1st Cir. 1978), *cert. denied,* 444 U.S. 898 (1979); *Virgin Islands v. Smith,* 558 F.2d 691 (3d Cir.), *cert. denied,* 434 U.S. 957 (1977); *U.S. v. Scijo,* 537 F.2d 694 (2d Cir. 1976), *cert. denied,* 429 U.S. 1043 (1977). This rule applies only where separate trials are involved. It has no application where, in the same trial, the accused stands charged with both the greater and lesser offenses, such as felony murder arising from an armed robbery and armed robbery. *Harris v. Oklahoma,* 433 U.S. 682 (1977); *U.S. v. DeVincent,* 632 F.2d 155 (1st Cir. 1980); *U.S. v. Larkin,* 605 F.2d 1360, 1367 (5th Cir. 1979), *cert. denied,* 446 U.S. 939 (1980). However, if a defendant, in a single trial, is convicted of both the greater and lesser offenses, the lesser offense merges into the greater for purposes of sentencing. *Whalen v. U.S.,* 445 U.S. 684 (1980); *U.S. v. Stroman,* 667 F.2d 416, 417 (2d Cir. 1981).

If the defendant moves for and receives separate trials where greater and lesser offenses are charged, or if the defendant agrees to or fails to object to separation of trials without raising the issue that greater and lesser offenses are involved, he cannot successfully complain that the double jeopardy protection has been violated. *Jeffers v. U.S.,* 432 U.S.

137 (1977). Separate trials for a greater and a lesser offense are also permitted where the evidence to support the greater charge did not exist or could not reasonably be discovered when the trial on the lesser charge commenced, or where the first and lesser included conviction was in a court of limited jurisdiction. *Diaz v. U.S.,* 223 U.S. 442 (1912); *U.S. v. Fultz,* 602 F.2d 830 (8th Cir. 1979); *U.S. v. Stavros,* 597 F.2d 108 (7th Cir. 1979); *U.S. v. John,* 587 F.2d 683 (5th Cir.), *cert. denied,* 441 U.S. 925 (1979); *U.S. v. Walking Crow,* 560 F.2d 386 (8th Cir. 1977), *cert. denied,* 435 U.S. 953 (1978); *U.S. v. Shepard,* 515 F.2d 1324 (D.C. Cir. 1975).

A trial court's acceptance of a guilty plea to a lesser included offense over the state's objection does not prohibit the state from continuing the prosecution of the remaining charges. *Ohio v. Johnson,* 467 U.S. 493 (1984).

## § 1004. — Dual Sovereigns.

The federal constitution recognizes multiple sovereigns with separate and distinct rights, responsibilities, and authority. A single act often violates both state and federal laws. The double jeopardy clause does not prohibit prosecution by a state merely because the accused has been convicted or acquitted of the identical offense by a federal court or vice versa. *U.S. v. Wheeler,* 435 U.S. 313 (1978); *Abbate v. U.S.,* 359 U.S. 187 (1959); *Bartkus v. Illinois,* 359 U.S. 121 (1959); *U.S. v. Lanza,* 260 U.S. 377 (1922); *Pope v. Thone,* 671 F.2d 298, 299-300 (8th Cir. 1982); *U.S. v. Solano,* 605 F.2d 1141 (9th Cir. 1979), *cert. denied,* 444 U.S. 1020 (1980); *U.S. v. Mejias,* 552 F.2d 435 (2d Cir.), *cert. denied,* 434 U.S. 847 (1977). Likewise, successive prosecutions by two states for the same conduct are not barred by the double jeopardy clause, *Heath v. Alabama,* 106 S. Ct. 433 (1985); nor by a foreign government and the United States, *Chua Han Mow v. U.S.,* 730 F.2d 1308 (9th Cir. 1984), *cert. denied,* 105 S. Ct. 1403 (1985). However, federal authorities may not "orchestrate" a state charge to form a basis for a subsequent federal charge. *See U.S. v. Aboumoussallem,* 726 F.2d 906 (2d Cir. 1984); *U.S. v. Aleman,* 609 F.2d 298, 309 (7th Cir. 1979). Double jeopardy restrictions prohibit prosecutions by different units of the same government. For example, trial by court-martial precludes trial for the same offense in a federal district court. *Grafton v. U.S.,* 206 U.S. 333 (1907); *U.S. v. Jones,* 527 F.2d 817 (D.C. Cir. 1975). (For a discussion of the same offense prosecuted by different units of the same sovereign, *see Waller v. Florida,* 397 U.S. 387 (1970), and *Douglas v. Nixon,* 459 F.2d 325 (6th Cir.), *cert. denied,* 409 U.S. 1010 (1972).)

## § 1005. — The Petite Policy.

It is a general policy of the Department of Justice, not a prohibition of the double jeopardy clause, that several offenses arising out of a single transaction should not be the basis of successive federal prosecutions, nor should a violation already prosecuted at the state or local level be federally prosecuted without the approval of the Attorney General. *Petite v. U.S.*, 361 U.S. 529 (1960). Such approval is to be predicated only upon a clear showing of a compelling federal interest in a second prosecution, sufficient to override the policy. This is designed to protect the individual from needless multiple prosecutions, to pro- mote fairness, and to provide for orderly and efficient law enforcement. A trial court abuses its discretion if it denies a government motion to dismiss a charge filed in violation of this policy, even where the policy violation results from a U.S. Attorney's misrepresentation to the trial court that approval of the Attorney General had been obtained to pro- ceed with a successive prosecution. *Rinaldi v. U.S.*, 434 U.S. 22 (1977). *See also Thompson v. U.S.*, 444 U.S. 248 (1980). This policy, however, is strictly internal. It is not constitutionally mandated, and it is not enforceable against the government. *U.S. v. Simpkins*, 953 F.2d 443 (8th Cir. 1992); *U.S. v. Mitchell*, 778 F.2d 1271 (7th Cir. 1985); *U.S. v. Booth*, 673 F.2d 27, 30 (1st Cir.), *cert. denied*, 102 S. Ct. 2245 (1982); *U.S. v. Renfro*, 620 F.2d 568 (6th Cir.), *cert. denied*, 449 U.S. 1078 (1980); *U.S. v. Solano*, 605 F.2d 1141 (9th Cir. 1979). The policy does not apply and is not intended to apply where the federal charges are totally different in nature and degree from the state charges. *U.S. v. Fossler*, 597 F.2d 478 (5th Cir. 1979); *U.S. v. Snell*, 592 F.2d 1083 (9th Cir.), *cert. denied*, 442 U.S. 944 (1979); *U.S. v. Howard*, 590 F.2d 564 (4th Cir.), *cert. denied*, 440 U.S. 976 (1979); *U.S. v. Valenzuela*, 584 F.2d 374 (10th Cir. 1978); *U.S. v. Frederick*, 583 F.2d 273 (6th Cir. 1978), *cert. denied*, 444 U.S. 860 (1979); *U.S. v. Wallace*, 578 F.2d 735 (8th Cir.), *cert. denied*, 439 U.S. 898 (1978).

## § 1006. — Acquittals and Dismissals.

While there is no doubt that the jeopardy protection prohibits a second prosecution for the same offense following an acquittal, *U.S. v. Ball*, 163 U.S. 622 (1896), the question remains: What is an acquittal and how does it differ from a dismissal? If the issue of factual guilt is resolved by the trial court in defendant's favor following a hung jury, the result is an acquittal, and the government may not re-try the accused on that charge. *U.S. v. Martin Linen Supply Co.*, 430 U.S. 564 (1977). Or if an appellate court finds that the government's evidence produced at trial was insufficient to sustain a guilty verdict, such is deemed an acquittal and retrial is barred. *Hudson v. Louisiana,* 450 U.S. 40 (1980); *Burks v. U.S.,* 437 U.S. 1, 10-11 (1978). However, where a reversal was due to the incorrect admission of evidence rather than insufficient evidence, *Lockhart v. Nelson,* 488 U.S. 33 (1988), or due to the weight rather than the insufficiency of the evidence, *Tibbs v. Florida,* 457 U.S. 31 (1982), or where the charge is simply dismissed after trial because of indictment defect or other valid reason, the original jeopardy has not terminated and retrial may occur. *Lee v. U.S.,* 432 U.S. 23 (1977).

Jeopardy does not attach when a defense motion to dismiss is granted where the motion is not related to factual guilt or innocence. *Montana v. Hall,* 481 U.S. 400 (1987); *U.S. v. Scott,* 437 U.S. 82 (1978), *overruling U.S. v. Jenkins,* 420 U.S. 358 (1975). *See also U.S. v. Alberti,* 568 F.2d 617 (2d Cir. 1977). Even when erroneous evidentiary rulings during trial lead to an acquittal for insufficient evidence, further prosecution is prohibited. *Sanabria v. U.S.,* 437 U.S. 54 (1978). But, the label affixed to a trial court's ruling is not necessarily determinative. It is the substance of the order that determines whether there was a factual finding for the defendant and a resulting attachment of jeopardy. *Smalis v. Pennsylvania,* 476 U.S. 140 (1986); *U.S. v. Bodey,* 607 F.2d 265 (9th Cir. 1979); *U.S. v. Hospital Monteflores, Inc.,* 575 F.2d 332 (1st Cir. 1978); *U.S. v. Boyd,* 566 F.2d 929 (5th Cir. 1978); *U.S. v. Appawoo,* 553 F.2d 1242 (10th Cir. 1977); *U.S. v. Lasater,* 535 F.2d 1041 (8th Cir. 1976); *U.S. v. Esposito,* 492 F.2d 6 (7th Cir. 1973), *cert. denied,* 414 U.S. 1135 (1974).

## § 1007. Mistrial.

The double jeopardy clause of the fifth amendment does not require that every time a defendant goes on trial before a competent tribunal he is entitled to go free if the trial fails to end in a final judgment. *Wade v. Hunter,* 336 U.S. 684, 688 (1949). A balance has been struck between the public interest in affording the prosecution a full and fair opportunity to convict one accused of crime, *Wade v. Hunter,* 336 U.S. at 688-90; *Downum v. U.S.,* 372 U.S. 734 (1963), and the defendant's right to have his trial completed by a particular jury, *Illinois v. Somerville,* 410 U.S. 458 (1973). Any strict rule which operates only to a defendant's advantage, however, is too high a price to pay for the added assurance of personal security and freedom from government harrassment. *U.S. v. Jorn,* 400 U.S. 470 (1971).

## § 1008. — Manifest Necessity.

Since 1824, trial courts have had discretion to declare a mistrial over the objection of the defendant without barring a second trial whenever there is manifest necessity to do so or where the ends of justice would be defeated if a tainted trial were not terminated before the verdict was reached. *U.S. v. Perez,* 22 U.S. 579 (1824) (hung jury). *"Perez* dealt with the most common form of 'manifest necessity': a mistrial declared by the judge following the jury's declaration that it was unable to reach a verdict." *Oregon v. Kennedy,* 102 S. Ct. 2083, 2087 (1982). This standard provides sufficient protection to the defendant's interests in having his case finally decided by the jury first impaneled while maintaining society's interest in fair trials ending in just judgments. *Id.* at 2087-88. *See also Richardson v. U.S.,* 468 U.S. 317 (1984).

The general rule now is that trial cannot be aborted over a defendant's objection without jeopardy attaching unless the court first considers all available alternatives. If choices exist, including but not limited to a continuance in progress, the choice that most effectively purifies the trial contamination must be selected and used. Manifest necessity to terminate a trial is present only when effective alternatives are absent. *U.S. v. Huang,* 960 F.2d 1128 (2d Cir. 1992); *U.S. v. Jorn,* 400 U.S. 470 (1971); *Harris v. Young,* 607 F.2d 1081 (4th Cir. 1979), *cert. denied,* 444 U.S. 1025 (1980); *U.S. v. Nelson,* 599 F.2d 714 (5th Cir. 1979); *U.S. v. Lynch,* 598 F.2d 132 (D.C. Cir. 1978), *cert. denied,* 440 U.S. 939 (1979); *U.S. v. Love,* 597 F.2d 81 (6th Cir. 1979); *U.S. v. Pierce,* 593 F.2d 415 (1st Cir. 1979); *U.S. v. McKoy,* 591 F.2d 218 (3d Cir. 1979); *U.S. v. Rich,* 589 F.2d 1025 (10th Cir. 1978); *U.S. v. Hooper,* 576 F.2d 1382 (9th Cir. 1978). Manifest necessity existed where the trial court believed that defendant was responsible for murder of essential government witness even though there was no actual showing of the defendant's complicity in the death of the witness. The court did consider the alternatives including reversing its earlier decision not to admit certain evidence because it was unfairly prejudicial to a codefendant. *U.S. v. Mastrangelo,* 662 F.2d 946, 951-52 (2d Cir. 1981).

Where a defendant elects to terminate the proceedings against him by requesting a mistrial which is granted, the manifest necessity standard is not applicable. *Oregon v. Kennedy,* 102 S. Ct. at 2088. If a mistrial is granted with the consent or at the request of a defendant, reprosecution ordinarily is not barred. The defendant has primary control, and it is basically his decision either to surrender his first jury right or to continue the trial tainted by judicial or prosecutorial error. *U.S. v. Dinitz,* 424 U.S. 600 (1976).

## § 1009. — Prosecutorial Manipulation to Abort Trial.

Where the defendant moves for a mistrial, there is a narrow exception to the rule that the double jeopardy clause does not bar retrial. "Only where the governmental conduct in question is intended to 'goad' the defendant into moving for a mistrial may a defendant raise the bar of double jeopardy to a second trial after having succeeded in aborting the first on his own motion." *Oregon v. Kennedy,* 102 S. Ct. at 2089. The standard is the intent of the prosecutor and when he asked a prosecution witness if he had never done business with the defendant because he was "a crook," he did not intend to provoke a mistrial and the defendant may be retried. Prosecutorial conduct that might be viewed as harassment or overreaching, even if sufficient to justify a mistrial on defendant's motion, therefore, does not bar retrial absent intent on the part of the prosecutor to subvert the protections afforded by the double jeopardy clause." *Id.*

Defense counsel error or defendant's bad conduct which denies a fair trial to the government may permit retrial without offending the jeopardy clause. *Arizona v. Washington,* 434 U.S. 497 (1978); *U.S. v. Bobo,* 586 F.2d 355 (5th Cir. 1978), *cert. denied,* 440 U.S. 976 (1979). Where defense tactics make a fair trial virtually impossible, the trial judge has no obligation to consider alternatives to a mistrial order or to make a record finding of the presence of manifest necessity. *Arizona v. Washington,* 434 U.S. at 510-16.

## § 1010. Appeals.

Defendants who successfully appeal convictions because of trial errors are subject to re-prosecution. *Ball v. U.S.,* 163 U.S. 662 (1896). New evidence which supports the indictment can be used at the retrial. *U.S. v. Gallagher,* 602 F.2d 1139 (3d Cir. 1979), *cert. denied,* 444 U.S. 1043 (1980). Retrial of a defendant, *de novo* before a jury of his conviction, at a prior bench trial under a two-tiered system of trial courts where the evidence at the first trial was insufficient to support a finding of guilt does not violate the double jeopardy clause. *Justices of Boston Municipal Court v. Lydon,* 466 U.S. 294 (1984). It is only when an appellate court reverses a conviction because of insufficient evidence that the defendant may not be retried. *U.S. v. DiFrancesco,* 449 U.S. 117, 131 (1980); *Greene v. Massey,* 437 U.S. 19 (1978); *Burks v. U.S.,* 437 U.S. 1 (1978); *U.S. v. Wilkinson,* 601 F.2d 791 (5th Cir. 1979). Retrial may occur when evidence erroneously admitted at trial would have been sufficient to sustain a guilty verdict, *Lockhart v. Nelson,* 488 U.S. 33 (1988), or where the conviction was reversed based upon the weight, rather than the insufficiency of the evidence. *Tibbs v. Florida,* 457 U.S. 31 (1982). Evidentiary insufficiency is different from incorrect receipt or rejection of evidence, *Lockhart v. Nelson, supra.* A conviction for a lesser included offense, which is successfully appealed on grounds other than evidence insufficiency, does not reinstate the greater charge on retrial. Only the lesser charge may be the subject of a second prosecution. *Price v. Georgia,* 398 U.S. 323 (1970); *Green v. U.S.,* 355 U.S. 184 (1957); *U.S. v. Larkin,* 605 F.2d 1360 (5th Cir. 1979), *cert. denied,* 446 U.S. 939 (1980). However, the court may reduce a conviction for a jeopardy-barred offense to one for an unbarred lesser included offense unless the defendant can demonstrate that he would not have been convicted of the lesser offense except for the presence of the jeopardy-barred charge. *Morris v. Matthews,* 475 U.S. 237 (1986).

A defendant has a right to immediately appeal the denial of his pretrial double jeopardy motion as the double jeopardy clause does not merely bar a second conviction, but also protects a person from being put on trial twice for the same offense. *Abney v. U.S.,* 431 U.S. 651 (1977). However, the filing of an appeal does not automatically strip the trial court of jurisdiction to go forward with the trial. The test is whether the double jeopardy motion is frivolous. A trial court finding of nonfrivolousness does preclude further hearing on the merits pending appeal. *U.S. v. Leppo,* 634 F.2d 101 (3d Cir. 1980); *U.S. v. Dunbar,* 611 F.2d 985 (5th Cir.), *cert. denied,* 447 U.S. 926 (1980).

Government appeals are authorized and controlled by 18 U.S.C. § 3731, but only where double jeopardy would not result. *U.S. v. Scott,* 437 U.S. 82, 91 (1978). *See also Smalis v. Pennsylvania,* 476 U.S. 140 (1986). Once a trial court has found for a defendant on the merits of the case the result is not reviewable even when the ruling is clearly and obviously erroneous. *Fong Foo v. U.S.,* 369 U.S. 141 (1962) (directed verdict of acquittal during government's case). But, where the trial court grants judgment of acquittal after a jury verdict of guilty, the government may seek appellate review because if the government prevailed on appeal the guilty verdict would simply be reinstated and the defendant would not be tried twice. *U.S. v. Wilson,* 420 U.S. 332 (1975); *Virgin Islands v. Christensen,* 673 F.2d 713, 717-19 (3d Cir. 1982); *U.S. v. Steed,* 646 F.2d 136 (4th Cir. 1981), *cert. denied,* 459 U.S. 829 (1982); *U.S. v. Mandel,* 591 F.2d 1347 (4th Cir. 1979), *cert. denied,* 445 U.S. 961 (1980); *U.S. v. Blasco,* 581 F.2d 681 (7th Cir.), *cert. denied,* 439 U.S. 966 (1978); *U.S. v. Jones,* 580 F.2d 219 (6th Cir. 1978); *U.S. v. Donahue,* 539 F.2d 1131 (8th Cir. 1976).

Where the trial court granted defendant's Rule 29(a) motion for acquittal noting that there is some evidence which goes to the government's case, and the jury has not been discharged, the government's petition for mandamus asking that the trial court's action be stayed was proper and double jeopardy did not apply as the trial was halted but not completed. *U.S. v. Ellison,* 684 F.2d 664 (10th Cir. 1982).

## § 1011. Collateral Estoppel.

The double jeopardy clause includes the collateral estoppel doctrine under certain limited circumstances. Where an issue of ultimate fact was once determined by a valid final judgment, that issue cannot be relitigated against a defendant in a second trial. *Ashe v. Swenson,* 397 U.S. 436 (1970).

However, later use of evidence relating to alleged criminal conduct for which the defendant has been previously acquitted may be used to relitigate an issue presented in a subsequent action governed by a lower standard of proof such as the issue of identity under Rule 404(b). *Dowling v. U.S.,* 493 U.S. 342 (1990).

A gun owner's acquittal on a charge of dealing firearms without a license did not preclude a subsequent *in rem* forfeiture proceeding. The acquittal did not prove that the defendant was innocent; it proved only the existence of a reasonable doubt as to guilt. *U.S. v. One Assortment of 89 Firearms,* 465 U.S. 354 (1984); *One Lot Emerald Cut Stones and One Ring v. U.S.,* 409 U.S. 232 (1972) (because of the difference of the burden of proof in criminal and civil cases, civil forfeiture proceedings are not affected by an acquittal; *Simpson v. Florida,* 403 U.S. 384 (1971); *Ashe v. Swenson,* 397 U.S. 436 (1970); *Helvering v. Mitchell,* 303 U.S. 391 (1938) (IRS monetary penalty were merely a remedial civil sanction and not affected by acquittal).

Collateral estoppel is available only to a formerly acquitted defendant. *U.S. v. Brunk,* 615 F.2d 210 (5th Cir. 1980). Also, its benefit is denied to a defendant where it is unclear from the first trial record whether the not guilty verdict rested on an issue or issues common to the separate trials. The burden is on the defendant to establish that the issue which he seeks to foreclose in the present prosecution was necessarily decided in his favor by the prior not guilty verdict. *Dowling v. U.S., supra; U.S. v. Clark,* 613 F.2d 391 (2d Cir. 1979), *cert. denied,* 449 U.S. 820 (1980); *U.S. v. Mock,* 604 F.2d 341 (5th Cir. 1979), *cert. denied,* 449 U.S. 820 (1980); *U.S. v. Lasky,* 600 F.2d 765 (9th Cir.), *cert. denied,* 444 U.S. 979 (1979); *U.S. v. Mespoulede,* 597 F.2d 329 (2d Cir. 1979); *U.S. v. Huffman,* 595 F.2d 551 (10th Cir. 1979); *Oliphant v. Koehler,* 594 F.2d 547 (6th Cir.), *cert. denied,* 444 U.S. 877 (1979); *U.S. v. Hatrak,* 588 F.2d 414 (3d Cir. 1978), *cert. denied,* 440 U.S. 974 (1979); *U.S. v. MacDonald,* 585 F.2d 1211 (4th Cir. 1978), *cert. denied,*

440 U.S. 961 (1979); *U.S. v. Brown*, 547 F.2d 438 (8th Cir.), *cert. denied*, 430 U.S. 937 (1977); *U.S. v. Haines*, 485 F.2d 564 (7th Cir. 1973), *cert. denied*, 417 U.S. 977 (1974); *Ottomano v. U.S.*, 468 F.2d 269 (1st Cir. 1972), *cert. denied*, 409 U.S. 1128 (1973).

The collateral estoppel doctrine does not bar the government from retrying a defendant on substantive charges, following a hung jury even though that same jury acquitted the defendant on a conspiracy charge. Nor does this acquittal preclude the introduction of hearsay statements of the defendant's alleged coconspirators. *U.S. v. Clark*, *supra*. Inconsistent verdicts do not violate double jeopardy. *U.S. v. Powell*, 469 U.S. 57 (1984). The acquittal of a principal does not preclude the government from trying and convicting the aider and abettor. The Supreme Court has rejected the rule of non-mutual collateral estoppel in criminal cases. *Standefer v. U.S.*, 447 U.S. 10 (1980). Acquittal of a defendant's coconspirators in a previous trial does not preclude the government from convicting that defendant of conspiracy in a subsequent trial, *U.S. v. Espinosa-Cerpa*, 630 F.2d 328 (5th Cir. 1980); nor does acquittal in a mail fraud trial necessarily decide the issues in a subsequent perjury prosecution. *U.S. v. Baugus*, 761 F.2d 506 (8th Cir. 1985).

## § 1012. Sentencing.

The imposition of a harsher sentence following conviction on retrial does not violate the double jeopardy prohibition where there is no vindictiveness. *Alabama v. Smith*, 493 U.S. 1029 (1989); *Wasman v. U.S.*, 468 U.S. 559 (1984); *Bullington v. Missouri*, 451 U.S. 430 (1981); *Chaffin v. Stynchcombe*, 412 U.S. 17 (1973); *North Carolina v. Pearce*, 395 U.S. 711 (1969); *U.S. v. Hayes*, 676 F.2d 1359, 1364-66 (11th Cir.), *cert. denied*, 459 U.S. 1040 (1982); *U.S. v. Fredenburgh*, 602 F.2d 1143 (3d Cir. 1979); *U.S. v. Denson*, 588 F.2d 1112 (5th Cir. 1979). However, where a capital sentencing procedure is like a trial on the issue of guilt or innocence the jury is required to determine whether the prosecution has proved its case, the sentence of life imprisonment meant that the jury acquitted the defendant of whatever was necessary for the death penalty and he could not receive the death penalty after a second trial. *Bullington v. Missouri*, 451 U.S. 430 (1981). Double jeopardy does not bar increasing an illegal or erroneous sentence. *U.S. v. Wingender*, 711 F.2d 869 (9th Cir. 1983). *See also Poland v. Arizona*, 476 U.S. 147 (1986); *Arizona v. Rumsey*, 467 U.S. 203 (1984).

Double jeopardy does not bar revocation of probation and imposition of a sentence previously suspended. *Sims v. U.S.*, 607 F.2d 757 (6th Cir. 1979). Nor does it prevent the government from seeking an appeal for a more severe sentence than was imposed by the trial court. *U.S. v. DiFrancesco,* 449 U.S. 117 (1980), nor prohibit increasing a sentence before a defendant has begun serving his sentence where the original sentence was based upon a misunderstanding by the court of the factual record. *U.S. v. Smith,* 929 F.2d 1453 (10th Cir. 1991). The Supreme Court said in *DiFrancesco* "that the Double Jeopardy Clause does not require that a sentence be given a degree of finality [such as the finality that attends an acquittal] that prevents its later increase." 449 U.S. at 137. *See also Pennsylvania v. Goldhammer,* 474 U.S. 28 (1985); *McClain v. U.S.,* 676 F.2d 915, 918 (2d Cir.), *cert. denied,* 459 U.S. 879 (1982).

# CHAPTER 11

# PROSECUTORIAL MISCONDUCT AND VINDICTIVENESS

§ 1100. Introduction.
§ 1101. Prosecutorial Misconduct.
§ 1102. — Opening Statement Errors.
§ 1103. — — Reference to Inadmissible Evidence.
§ 1104. — — Statements of Personal Opinion.
§ 1105. — — Argumentative and Inflammatory Comments.
§ 1106. — Proof Presentation Problems.
§ 1107. — — False or Misleading Testimony.
§ 1108. — — Undiscovered and Undisclosed Favorable Defense Evidence.
§ 1109. — — Forcing a Claim of Privilege.
§ 1110. — Closing Argument Errors.
§ 1111. — — Reasonable Inferences and Inflammatory Comments.
§ 1112. — — Response to Defense Provocations.
§ 1113. — — Statement of Law — Invading the Province of the Court.
§ 1114. — — Statement of Personal Opinion.
§ 1115. — — Comment on Post-Arrest and In-Trial Silence.
§ 1116. — Standard for Review.
§ 1117. — Sanctions.
§ 1118. Prosecutorial Vindictiveness.

## § 1100. Introduction.

"The function of the prosecutor under the federal constitution is not to tack as many skins of victims as possible to the wall. His function is to vindicate the right of people as expressed in the laws and give those accused of crime a fair trial." *Donnelly v. DeChristoforo,* 416 U.S. 637 (1974) (Douglas, J., dissenting).

## § 1101. Prosecutorial Misconduct.

## § 1102. — Opening Statement Errors.

The purpose of the prosecution's opening statement is to outline broadly the facts of the case so that the jury will understand the evidence as it unfolds. A clear, concise, prima facie case should be stated, *Chatman v. U.S.,* 557 F.2d 147 (8th Cir.), *cert. denied,* 434 U.S. 863 (1977); *U.S. v. DiGregorio,* 605 F.2d 1184 (1st Cir.), *cert. denied,* 444 U.S. 937 (1979), the evidence supporting each count should be outlined, *U.S. v. D'Alora,* 585 F.2d 16 (1st Cir. 1978), and nothing should be said which is designed to poison the minds of the jury against the defendant or to destroy his credibility before the evidence is offered, *Virgin Islands v. Turner,* 409 F.2d 102 (3d Cir. 1968); *U.S. v. Lynn,* 608 F.2d 132 (5th Cir. 1979).

237

A federal prosecutor "carries a special aura of legitimacy about him." Attempts to take advantage of his position by inferring in his opening statement that he is an impartial truth seeker who would not ask for conviction unless the evidence established guilt beyond a reasonable doubt, may raise serious questions about the fairness of the trial. *U.S. v. Bess*, 593 F.2d 749 (6th Cir. 1979). Generally, anticipation of a defense to a charge in opening remarks risks a mistrial. *U.S. v. Gentile*, 525 F.2d 252 (2d Cir.), *cert. denied*, 425 U.S. 903 (1976). An exception to this rule is found in cases where the defense is obvious, as absence of intent where intent is an essential element to be proved by the government, *U.S. v. Jardan*, 552 F.2d 216 (8th Cir.), *cert. denied*, 433 U.S. 912 (1977), or where there has been a previous trial resulting in a hung jury, *U.S. v. Adderly*, 529 F.2d 1178 (5th Cir. 1976).

### § 1103. — — Reference to Inadmissible Evidence.

Opening statements must be limited to evidence to be offered that the prosecutor in good faith believes is both available and admissible. *U.S. v. Mahone*, 537 F.2d 922 (7th Cir.), *cert. denied*, 429 U.S. 1025 (1976). Statements containing references to irrelevant material amounting to character assassination invite reversal. *U.S. v. Dinitz*, 538 F.2d 1214 (5th Cir.), *cert. denied*, 429 U.S. 1104 (1976). Discussion of unrelated events not affecting the outcome of the trial is reversible error, even though the objectionable statements are struck. *U.S. v. Steinkoetter*, 593 F.2d 747 (6th Cir. 1979). A likening of a defendant's alleged tax violations to a fox in the hen house fable was held to be highly prejudicial. *U.S. v. Signer*, 482 F.2d 394 (6th Cir.), *cert. denied*, 414 U.S. 1092 (1973). A verbatim reading of wiretap transcripts, while not plain error, has been said to abuse the purpose of an opening statement. *U.S. v. DeRosa*, 548 F.2d 464 (3d Cir. 1977). *See also U.S. v. Griffin*, 579 F.2d 1104 (8th Cir.), *cert. denied*, 439 U.S. 981 (1978), where the prosecutor in his opening statement read portions of unsigned statements of defendants.

The circuits agree that, where there is mention of prior offenses and coconspirator convictions in opening statements, the chances of prejudicial error are substantially increased, even when the jury is told of the purpose for which such evidence is offered. *Grimaldi v. U.S.*, 606 F.2d 332 (1st Cir. 1979); *U.S. v. Handly*, 591 F.2d 1125 (5th Cir. 1979); *U.S. v. Watkins*, 600 F.2d 201 (9th Cir.), *cert. denied*, 444 U.S. 871 (1979); *U.S. v. Bailey*, 505 F.2d 417 (D.C. Cir. 1974), *cert. denied*, 420 U.S. 961 (1975).

Other examples of improper, out-of-place opening statement comments which may rise to the plain error level are statements that the government proposes to introduce a representative sample of some 150 conversations and that the balance had been made available to the defendants who could play them for the jury if they wished, *U.S. v. Chong,* 544 F.2d 58 (2d Cir. 1976), *cert. denied,* 429 U.S. 1101 (1977); statements that, instead of calling two or three witnesses who would all testify to the same thing, only one would be called, *U.S. v. Humer,* 542 F.2d 254 (5th Cir. 1976); repeated insinuations that information outside of the record, obtained from unknown witnesses, identified defendant as the robber and by the name "Meatball," *U.S. v. Hilliard,* 569 F.2d 143 (D.C. Cir. 1977); reference to defendant's admissions made in a suppression hearing, *U.S. v. Morrow,* 541 F.2d 1229 (7th Cir. 1976), *cert. denied,* 430 U.S. 933 (1977). *See also U.S. v. Calvert,* 498 F.2d 409 (6th Cir. 1974).

Ordinarily, where evidence is misstated or discussed in the opening statement but rejected by the trial court, both the good faith of the prosecutor and the impact of the statements on the trial determine whether there was prejudicial error. *U.S. v. Akin,* 562 F.2d 459 (7th Cir. 1977), *cert. denied,* 435 U.S. 933 (1978); *U.S. v. Jones,* 592 F.2d 1038 (9th Cir.), *cert. denied,* 441 U.S. 951 (1979).

## § 1104. — — Statements of Personal Opinion.

The prohibition against interjection of personal opinion by a federal prosecutor, at any stage of the case, is strict and is an important part of the Code of Professional Responsibility of the American Bar Association. DR 7-106(C)(4) provides that a lawyer shall not:

> Assert his personal opinion as to the justness of a cause, as to the credibility of a witness, ... or as to the guilt or innocence of an accused; but he may argue, on his analysis of the evidence, for any position or conclusion with respect to the matters stated herein.

And the Standards for Criminal Justice Nos. 5 and 8 of the American Bar Association further provide:

> (b) It is unprofessional conduct for the prosecutor to express his personal belief or opinion as to the truth or falsity of any testimony or evidence or the guilt of the defendant.

Quoted in *U.S. v. Young,* 470 U.S. 1 (1985).

Violations of these principles occur most frequently in closing arguments. Courts have often and forcefully addressed this subject at that stage of the case, but without limiting the "no personal comment" restriction to final argument. The strong position assumed by the Eighth Circuit in *U.S. v. Splain,* 545 F.2d 1131 (8th Cir. 1976), is representative of the general attitude of the courts toward professionalism. *But see U.S. v. Tropeano,* 476 F.2d 586 (1st Cir. 1973), *cert. denied,* 414 U.S. 839 (1973), where the prosecutor stated: "Do you recall that I said in my opening statement[,] perhaps improperly, it is not a very nice story, because I believe that is true, it is not a very nice story. It is a story that happened." The court held that this was not such a positive statement of a prosecutor's personal belief in defendant's guilt as to require reversal. In *U.S. v. Flaherty,* 668 F.2d 566, 596-97 (1st Cir. 1981), the prosecutor's statement that the government did not shrink from its burden of proving defendants guilty, and that the evidence would show the defendants were in fact guilty was found to be troublesome but not a direct statement of the prosecutor's belief. *See also U.S. v. Davis,* 564 F.2d 840 (9th Cir.), *cert. denied,* 434 U.S. 1015 (1978); *U.S. v. Davis,* 548 F.2d 840 (9th Cir. 1977). *Compare U.S. v. Prince,* 515 F.2d 564 (5th Cir.), *cert. denied,* 423 U.S. 1032 (1975), where the prosecutor in his opening statement said that the government's first witness would tell the truth; and *U.S. v. Medel,* 592 F.2d 1305 (5th Cir. 1979), in which the prosecutor stated that she believed a careful appraisal of the evidence would result in a guilty verdict, neither of which is plain error.

### § 1105. — — Argumentative and Inflammatory Comments.

Problems involving improper comment by the prosecutor arise most frequently in closing arguments. In general, however, the same types of comment are as much improper in opening statements as they are in closings and, except that there is more time for curative instructions, such improper statements have the same potential for introducing reversible error. For example, the recognized prejudice resulting from a prosecutor's request of the jury to do him a "favor by being fair to public interest in law enforcement" was cured by admonishment that no favors are granted by the court. *U.S. v. Miller,* 478 F.2d 1315 (2d Cir.), *cert. denied,* 414 U.S. 851 (1973).

### § 1106. — Proof Presentation Problems.

### § 1107. — — False or Misleading Testimony.

The due process guarantee and the fair trial right of the accused are destroyed when a prosecutor obtains a conviction with the aid of evidence which he actually knows, or should know, to be false and allows it to go uncorrected. Deliberate deception of a court and jurors by the presentation of false evidence is reprehensible and incompatible with "rudimentary demands of justice." *Giglio v. U.S.,* 405 U.S. 150 (1972); *Napue v. Illinois,* 360 U.S. 264 (1959); *Mooney v. Holohan,* 294 U.S. 103

(1935). It is immaterial whether the prosecutor consciously solicited the false evidence. It is also immaterial whether the false testimony directly concerns an essential element of the crime charged or it bears only on the credibility of a witness. *U.S. v. Barham,* 595 F.2d 231 (5th Cir. 1979). If there is any reasonable likelihood that the false testimony could have affected the jury's judgment, a new trial must be ordered. *U.S. v. Runge,* 593 F.2d 66 (8th Cir.), *cert. denied,* 444 U.S. 859 (1979); *U.S. v. Antone,* 603 F.2d 566 (5th Cir. 1979). The prosecutor's duty to correct the false testimony arises when the false evidence appears, *U.S. v. Sanfilippo,* 565 F.2d 176 (5th Cir. 1977), or as soon as he becomes aware of inaccuracies, *U.S. v. Glover,* 588 F.2d 876 (2d Cir. 1978). Promises of leniency, plea bargains, payments to informers, and all arrangements with government witnesses must promptly be disclosed where a government witness gives either an evasive answer or denies the existence of any of the arrangements. *U.S. v. Carter,* 566 F.2d 1265 (5th Cir.), *cert. denied,* 436 U.S. 956 (1978); *U.S. v. McClintic,* 570 F.2d 685 (8th Cir. 1978); *U.S. v. Butler,* 567 F.2d 885 (9th Cir. 1978); *U.S. v. Pope,* 529 F.2d 112 (9th Cir. 1976); *Sanders v. U.S.,* 541 F.2d 190 (8th Cir. 1976), *cert. denied,* 429 U.S. 1066 (1977).

Use of misleading evidence, unrelated to the charge, is grounds for reversal. *U.S. v. McFayden-Snider,* 552 F.2d 1178 (6th Cir. 1977), *cert. denied,* 435 U.S. 995 (1978). A federal prosecutor, who knowingly gives a false response to a court's question whether any members of an anti-war organization subpoenaed as grand jury witnesses were government informers, is entitled only to qualified rather than absolute immunity from a civil suit since his role is investigative and is not as an advocate. *Briggs v. Goodwin,* 569 F.2d 10 (D.C. Cir.), *cert. denied,* 437 U.S. 904 (1978).

## § 1108. — — Undiscovered and Undisclosed Favorable Defense Evidence.

Prosecutorial suppression of evidence favorable to an accused which is supportive of a claim of innocence denies a defendant of his right to a fair trial, is a due process violation, and vitiates a conviction. *U.S. v. Agurs,* 427 U.S. 97 (1976). This rule applies in cases where there has been only a general request for information or even no defense request for disclosure. *U.S. v. Jackson,* 579 F.2d 553 (10th Cir.), *cert. denied,* 439 U.S. 981 (1978). However, every nondisclosure to a general defense request, or where there is no request, is not constitutional error. It is where the omitted evidence creates a reasonable doubt that did not otherwise exist that prejudicial error permeates the trial record. A request seeking all evidence of any kind favorable to the defendant is considered general in nature. *U.S. v. DiCarlo,* 575 F.2d 952 (1st Cir.), *cert. denied,* 439 U.S. 834 (1978); *U.S. v. Hearst,* 563 F.2d 1331 (9th Cir. 1977), *cert. denied,* 435 U.S. 1000 (1978).

A specific request points with particularity to the evidence desired and is clear and unambiguous. The prosecution must respond to a specific defense request for purely impeaching evidence which does not concern a substantive issue, provided the evidence sought is relevant. *U.S. v. Anderson,* 574 F.2d 1347 (5th Cir. 1978). Even when faced with a detailed, explicit defense demand, the prosecution has no constitutional duty to make a detailed accounting of all investigative work on the case. *Moore v. Illinois,* 408 U.S. 786 (1972).

For a defendant to force production of evidence, a strict standard of materiality of the evidence as to guilt or punishment applies. *U.S. v. Gaston,* 608 F.2d 607 (5th Cir. 1979). The defendant has the burden of establishing the materiality of any evidence allegedly suppressed by the prosecution, *U.S. v. Parker,* 586 F.2d 422 (5th Cir. 1978), *cert. denied,* 441 U.S. 962 (1979), together with the need for any withheld evidence, *Monroe v. Blackburn,* 607 F.2d 148 (5th Cir. 1979). For a discussion of timely and late disclosure of evidence which might create reasonable doubt, *see U.S. v. McPartlin,* 595 F.2d 1321 (7th Cir.), *cert. denied,* 444 U.S. 833 (1979). The good faith of the prosecutor ordinarily is not in issue. Even where the facts suggest bad faith, a defendant must prove prejudice if he is to overturn a conviction. *U.S. v. Goldberg,* 582 F.2d 483 (9th Cir. 1978), *cert. denied,* 440 U.S. 973 (1979). *But see U.S. v. Disston,* 582 F.2d 1108 (7th Cir. 1978), which held that if the withheld evidence is material, the good faith of the prosecution may well bear on the materiality determination. Materiality means reasonable doubt about defendant's guilt where there has been no specific defense demand to disclose favorable evidence. *U.S. v. Ramirez,* 608 F.2d 1261 (9th Cir. 1979). The standard by which materiality of undisclosed information for which the defendant made a specific request, which assertedly could have been used for impeachment purposes, is whether the materials could have been used to impeach a government witness in a manner which might have affected the outcome of the trial. *U.S. v. DiFrancesco,* 604 F.2d 769 (2d Cir. 1979).

No due process violation or fair trial denial results if the defendant is aware of the favorable evidence, knows of its source, and has access to it. *U.S. v. Weidman,* 572 F.2d 1199 (7th Cir.), *cert. denied,* 439 U.S. 821 (1978); *U.S. v. Haro-Espinosa,* 619 F.2d 789 (9th Cir. 1979). Lack of defense diligence to obtain evidence through an available witness known to defendant, coupled with a good-faith government effort to locate such evidence, satisfy constitutional requirements. *U.S. v. Shel-*

*ton,* 588 F.2d 1242 (9th Cir. 1978), *cert. denied,* 442 U.S. 909 (1979). Information concerning "favors or deals" made with a key government witness need not be disclosed before trial. Since they reach only the issue of witness credibility, they must be disclosed only after the witness testifies. *U.S. v. Rinn,* 586 F.2d 113 (9th Cir. 1978), *cert. denied,* 441 U.S. 931 (1979).

### § 1109. — — Forcing a Claim of Privilege.

Where the prosecution knows that a witness, if called to testify, would assert his fifth amendment privilege against self-incrimination and that such claim of privilege would be proper and lawful, prejudicial error results when the witness is compelled to appear and to invoke the privilege where the government's purpose is to bolster its case upon inferences arising from the use of the constitutional protection. *Namet v. U.S.,* 373 U.S. 179 (1963); *U.S. v. Maloney,* 262 F.2d 535 (2d Cir. 1959). Each case must be decided in light of its own facts and circumstances with consideration given to the motive of the prosecutor and the likelihood that the jury will draw unwarranted inferences against the defendant from the declination to testify. *U.S. v. Quinn,* 543 F.2d 640 (8th Cir. 1976); *U.S. v. Peterson,* 549 F.2d 654 (9th Cir. 1977); *U.S. v. Crouch,* 528 F.2d 625 (7th Cir.), *cert. denied,* 429 U.S. 900 (1976). *Compare U.S. v. Ritz,* 548 F.2d 510 (5th Cir. 1977). Where it is uncertain whether a witness will claim his self-incrimination privilege, it is not error to call him, provided there is termination of questioning after four refusals to answer. *Skinner v. Cardwell,* 564 F.2d 1381 (9th Cir. 1977), *cert. denied,* 435 U.S. 1009 (1978). The Tenth Circuit in *U.S. v. Dingle,* 546 F.2d 1378 (10th Cir. 1976), found that it is preferable to dismiss the jury before calling a witness who is certain to claim his privilege. The court should examine the witness, rule on any privilege assertion, and consider any request for a grant of immunity outside the presence of the jury.

Defense witnesses, who are simply advised by a prosecutor of the penalties for perjury and that immunity does not extend to perjury, are not government-intimidated witnesses when they are called by the defense and invoke the fifth amendment. *U.S. v. Valdes,* 545 F.2d 957 (5th Cir. 1977).

### § 1110. — Closing Argument Errors.

While the singular purpose of final argument is to persuade, prosecutors should refrain from injecting issues broader than the accused's guilt or innocence, or predicting the consequences of a particular verdict. Such tactics divert the jury from its duty to decide the case on the evidence. *U.S. v. Mikka,* 586 F.2d 152 (9th Cir. 1978), *cert. denied,* 440 U.S. 921 (1979); *U.S. v. Bess,* 593 F.2d 749 (6th Cir. 1979). The "prosecutor, as representative of the government, should at all times maintain the dignity and decorum demanded by his office. Our courts are not to provide a stage for theatrical argument, but instead were created as a forum for the service of the interests of justice by assuring the defendant a fair and impartial trial by a jury of his peers, unswayed by prejudicial comment." *U.S. v. Schackelford,* 677 F.2d 422, 426 (5th Cir. 1982).

Although closing argument cannot be used to inflame the jury, it is not restricted to sterile recitation of uncontroverted facts. *U.S. v. Greene,* 497 F.2d 1068, 1085 (7th Cir. 1974), *cert. denied,* 420 U.S. 909 (1975). A prosecutor must be given a certain degree of latitude in summation. *U.S. v. Calandrella,* 605 F.2d 236, 254 (6th Cir.), *cert. denied,* 444 U.S. 991 (1979). "Forensic zeal by prosecutor and defense counsel alike is apt to be displayed in these final moments at trial." *U.S. v. DeAlesandro,* 361 F.2d 694, 697 (2d Cir.), *cert. denied,* 385 U.S. 842 (1966). "To shear him [the prosecutor] of all oratorical emphasis while leaving wide latitude to the defense, is to load the scales of justice...." *Di Carlo v. U.S.,* 6 F.2d 364, 368 (2d Cir. 1925); *U.S. v. Spain,* 536 F.2d 170, 174 (7th Cir.), *cert. denied,* 429 U.S. 833 (1976); *U.S. v. Greene,* 497 F.2d at 1085.

### § 1111. — — Reasonable Inferences and Inflammatory Comments.

Statements by the prosecutor, whether deliberate or otherwise, that tend to incite and inflame the jury or which are likely to cajole a guilty verdict without full consideration of all the evidence may amount to reversible error despite curative instructions. It is beyond the bounds of propriety for the prosecutor to suggest that unless a defendant is convicted it will be impossible to maintain "law and order" in the community. *Brown v. U.S.,* 370 F.2d 242, 246 (D.C. Cir. 1966). *See also U.S. v. Wiley,* 524 F.2d 659, 665 (6th Cir.), *cert. denied,* 425 U.S. 995 (1976) ("if this man goes free you have chalked up one point for the criminal"); *U.S. v. Barker,* 553 F.2d 1013 (6th Cir. 1977) (prosecutor's statement that if the defendants are acquitted, "We might as well open all the banks and say, 'Come on in and get the money, boys,'" was reversible error). *But see U.S. v. Fulton,* 549 F.2d 1325 (9th Cir. 1977) (prosecutor's reference to the Manson murders was not prejudicial error because of immediate admonishment).

The line between merely over-zealous emotional comment and impermissible inflammatory statements is a fine one. The presence or absence of repetition, apparent design, or bad faith frequently determine whether prejudicial error is found. Urging conviction to stamp out the drug problem was held harmless error, *Malley v. Manson,* 547 F.2d 25 (2d Cir. 1976), *cert. denied,* 430 U.S. 918 (1977), as was the statement that a guilty verdict would inform every "dishonest cop" that "we are sick and tired" of those who abuse their office. *Perry v. Mulligan,* 544 F.2d 674 (3d Cir.), *cert. denied,* 430 U.S. 972 (1977). *See also U.S. v. Mattucci,* 502 F.2d 883 (6th Cir. 1974). Also, reference to the jurors' tax dollars in a government overbilling scheme trial was harmless error. *U.S. v. Smyth,* 556 F.2d 1179 (5th Cir.), *cert. denied,* 434 U.S. 862 (1977). *See also U.S. v. Homer,* 545 F.2d 864 (3d Cir. 1976), *cert. denied,* 431 U.S. 954 (1977). Describing the defendant as "a clever, diabolical woman" was approved, while calling her Pontius Pilate and asking how she could, like Judas Iscariot, enjoy refreshments with a lady whose death was being planned was held to be too prejudicial. *U.S. v. Steinkoetter,* 633 F.2d 719, 720-21 (6th Cir. 1980).

Counsel is not free to go outside the evidence to vouch for the credibility of a government witness, or to substitute emotion for evidence, either directly or by innuendo. *U.S. v. Roberts,* 618 F.2d 530 (9th Cir. 1980); *U.S. v. Hawkins,* 595 F.2d 751 (D.C. Cir.), *cert. denied,* 441 U.S. 910 (1979); *U.S. v. McPartlin,* 595 F.2d 1321 (7th Cir.), *cert. denied,* 444 U.S. 833 (1979). Where there is a factual basis in the record, however, use of strong and indecorous terms, including "liar," is not prejudicial. *U.S. v. Craig,* 573 F.2d 455 (7th Cir. 1977), *cert. denied,* 439 U.S. 820 (1978).

Examples of remarks found to be prejudicial in the circumstance of the particular case include: analogizing the crime charged with the offenses involving Sirhan Sirhan, James Earl Ray, Richard Speck, and Jack Ruby, *U.S. v. Phillips,* 476 F.2d 538 (D.C. Cir. 1973); *U.S. v. Marques,* 600 F.2d 742 (9th Cir. 1979), *cert. denied,* 444 U.S. 1019 (1980); telling the jury they either had to find the defendant guilty or conclude that the federal agents were liars, *U.S. v. Vargas,* 583 F.2d 380 (7th Cir. 1978); the prosecutor's suggestion that the defendant is guilty merely because he was indicted and is being prosecuted, *U.S. v. Bess,* 593 F.2d 749 (6th Cir. 1979); commenting that "not one white witness has been produced in this case that contradicts [the victim's] position in this case," *Withers v. U.S.,* 602 F.2d 124 (6th Cir. 1979); stating that "we are trying to convict him because he committed a crime, and we are convinced of that or we wouldn't be trying him," *U.S. v. Splain,* 545 F.2d 1131 (8th Cir. 1976); and telling the jury "you can believe all of it and turn him loose and we'll send him [the defendant] down in the elevator with you with his gun. He'll go out the front door with you," *U.S. v. McRae,* 593 F.2d 700 (5th Cir.), *cert. denied,* 444 U.S. 862 (1979) (held to be harmless error, however). Examples of comments which did not warrant reversal in the context of the case include: characterizing defendant as "Chinatown's chief corrupter for 20 years," *U.S. v. Ong,* 541 F.2d 331 (2d Cir. 1976); referring to a record piracy defendant as a "scavenger," "parasite," "fraud," and "a professional con-man," *U.S. v. Taxe,* 540 F.2d 961 (9th Cir. 1976), *cert. denied,* 429 U.S. 1040 (1977); commenting that defendant presented a "tailored defense" to fit the government's evidence, *U.S. v. Duff,* 551 F.2d 187 (7th Cir. 1977); stating that "there is no difference in these guys [false statements and wire fraud defendants] and people who go out and stick up banks," *U.S. v. Calandrella,* 605 F.2d 236 (6th Cir. 1979); remarking that the verdict would be the jury's verdict and "I wish it was mine," *U.S. v. Juarez,* 566 F.2d 511 (5th Cir. 1978); and stating that even the very best counsel money could buy couldn't disentangle the defendant, *U.S. v. Rapoport,* 545 F.2d 802 (2d Cir. 1976), *cert. denied,* 430 U.S. 931 (1977).

## § 1112. — — Response to Defense Provocations.

Impugning the prosecution's integrity or motivation by the defense may open the door and may justify a reply in kind. *U.S. v. Hoffa,* 349 F.2d 20 (6th Cir. 1965), *aff'd on other grounds,* 385 U.S. 293 (1966). The prosecutor's "invited response," however, may be inappropriate and error. In determining whether the prosecutor's remarks amount to prejudicial error, the court will consider defense counsel's conduct, the prosecutor's response, and the effect the prosecutor's remarks would probably have on the fairness of the trial or the jury's ability to fairly judge the evidence. *U.S. v. Young,* 470 U.S. 1 (1985).

The "invited response" rule in closing argument has been applied in cases where defense counsel attacked the quality of the investigation and the attitude of the investigators, *U.S. v. Hiett,* 581 F.2d 1199 (5th Cir. 1978); or attacked the integrity of the government witnesses, *U.S. v. West,* 670 F.2d 675, 689 (7th Cir.), *cert. denied,* 457 U.S. 1124 (1982) (permitted response was, "I will stand up for everyone in the government, that's who I represent"). Likewise, the government has been permitted to state that a nontestifying defendant "could have taken the stand and explain it to you" where the defense stated that the government did not permit the defendant to explain his side of the story. *U.S. v. Robinson,* 485 U.S 25 (1988).

Other examples of defense accusation which have excused a response include: claiming that "the Witness Protection Program was about to be revealed as a major government scandal," *U.S. v. Ricco,* 549 F.2d 264 (2d Cir.), *cert. denied,* 431 U.S. 905 (1977); the prosecutor's professional integrity, *U.S. v. Alpern,* 564 F.2d 755 (7th Cir. 1977); attacking the government for failure to call certain witnesses, *U.S. v. Sherrif,* 546 F.2d 604 (5th Cir. 1977); repeatedly asserting that the government was participating in or knowingly abetting a frameup, *U.S. v. Stassi,* 544 F.2d 579 (2d Cir. 1976), *cert. denied,* 430 U.S. 907 (1977); arguing that a coconspirator was not given a polygraph test "because government counsel and agents do not believe in them," *U.S. v. Gabriel,* 597 F.2d 95 (7th Cir.), *cert. denied,* 444 U.S. 858 (1979); attempting to shift the blame to an alleged coconspirator thereby giving rise to the justifiable, biblical response, "I'm not my brother's keeper," *U.S. v. Mackey,* 571 F.2d 376 (7th Cir. 1978). In each of the foregoing instances and in other cases of similar character, the prosecutor's disparaging remarks in rebuttal argument, which are not so inflammatory as to deny a fair trial, do not constitute reversible error. *U.S. v. Grabiec,* 563 F.2d 313 (7th Cir. 1977).

### § 1113. — — Statement of Law — Invading the Province of the Court.

It is the duty of the court and not the privilege of the prosecutor to advise the jury as to the law which controls the case. Departure from this principle, however, is not reversible error absent some possibility of prejudice. *U.S. v. Parr-Pla,* 549 F.2d 660 (9th Cir.), *cert. denied,* 431 U.S. 972 (1977); *U.S. v. Rosenfeld,* 545 F.2d 98 (10th Cir. 1976), *cert. denied,* 430 U.S. 941 (1977); *U.S. v. Leon,* 534 F.2d 667 (6th Cir. 1976); *U.S. v. Figurski,* 545 F.2d 389 (4th Cir. 1976). But erroneous and misleading statements of the law by the prosecutor, particularly in a close case, are plain error, notwithstanding the court's instructions which correctly state the law. *U.S. v. Segna,* 555 F.2d 226 (9th Cir. 1977). *But see U.S. v. Whitson,* 587 F.2d 948 (9th Cir. 1978), and *U.S. v. Hollinger,* 553 F.2d 535 (7th Cir. 1977), where the prosecutor stated that the judge decides whether immunity shall be granted to a witness, and *U.S. v. Fullmer,* 457 F.2d 447 (7th Cir. 1972), in which the prosecutor commented on legislative intent, Congressional purpose, and the development of a statute.

### § 1114. — — Statement of Personal Opinion.

While an expression of personal opinion in final argument is not necessarily fatal to the government's case, repeated, pronounced, and persistent assertion of the prosecutor's belief in the honesty, sincerity, and good motives of his witnesses, the guilt of the accused, and the weakness of the defense case is misconduct. The "evil influence" of such misconduct on the jury cannot be removed by "stern, judicial rebuke," and instructions to ignore the comments. *Berger v. U.S.*, 295 U.S. 78, 85 (1935).

Statements of personal belief permit the prosecutor to testify as an expert witness. This use of his personal status is not only improper, it is "pernicious." *U.S. v. Garza*, 608 F.2d 659 (5th Cir. 1979) (where the prosecutor said that in his opinion his witnesses simply wanted to make the community a better place and "if I thought that I had framed an innocent man and sent him to the penitentiary I would quit"). The circuits are in agreement: *U.S. v. Vargas*, 558 F.2d 631 (1st Cir. 1977); *U.S. v. Farnkoff*, 535 F.2d 661 (1st Cir. 1976) (where the prosecutor said, "I suggest to you, I ask you to consider these things, come to the decision which I think you should come to, based upon the evidence, that the defendant is guilty as charged"); *U.S. v. Smith*, 962 F.2d 923 (9th Cir. 1992) (where the prosecutor said that the witness could not say "whatever he wanted to say" because he would be prosecuted for perjury and that "if I [the prosecutor] did anything wrong in this trial, I wouldn't be here."); *U.S. v. Modica*, 663 F.2d 1173, 1178 (2d Cir. 1981), *cert. denied,* 102 S. Ct. 2269 (1982) (prosecutor said, "I'm here to tell you," and vouched for the government's witness); *U.S. v. Rodarte*, 596 F.2d 141 (5th Cir. 1979); *U.S. v. Handly*, 591 F.2d 1125 (5th Cir. 1979); *U.S. v. Bess*, 593 F.2d 749 (6th Cir. 1979); *U.S. v. Creamer*, 555 F.2d 612 (7th Cir.), *cert. denied,* 434 U.S. 833 (1977). The Third Circuit rule, however, as expressed in *U.S. v. Gallagher*, 576 F.2d 1028 (3d Cir. 1978), is that reversal is not warranted, even though the prosecutor makes numerous statements vouching for the varacity of his witnesses unless the statements are based on information not before the court and, therefore, are outside the record. If the statements are based on the evidence, prejudice must be established before a conviction will be overturned. And, where prejudice is shown, it may be cured by instruction or may be disregarded if there is overwhelming evidence to support the conviction. *See also U.S. v. Allain*, 671 F.2d 248, 253-54 (7th Cir. 1982), for a discussion of argument which places the integrity of the government behind a prosecution witness.

The prosecutor may state, "I believe that the evidence has shown defendant's guilt," but not "I believe that defendant is guilty." *U.S. v. Rodriguez*, 585 F.2d 1234 (5th Cir. 1978). Use of the phrase "I submit" is not the equivalent of expressing a personal opinion. *U.S. v. Stulga*, 584 F.2d 142 (6th Cir. 1978). "We know, if we know nothing else in this case, that Agent Lopez is a careful and completely honest, scrupulous man and would not make such an identification if he were not absolutely sure," is not erroneous as vouching for a government witness in the absence of proof that the word "we" was used to suggest personal knowledge of the prosecutor outside the record, *U.S. v. Williams,* 583 F.2d 1194 (2d Cir. 1978), *cert. denied,* 439 U.S. 1117 (1979).

### § 1115. — — Comment on Post-Arrest and In-Trial Silence.

Reference in final argument to a defendant's post-arrest, pretrial, or in-trial silence, while generally condemned, is not always reversible error. The test for determining when a prosecutor's comment is a reference, direct or oblique, to the silence of the accused is whether the language used was manifestly intended, or was of such character, that the jury would naturally and necessarily accept it as a reminder that the defendant did not testify. *U.S. v. Waller,* 607 F.2d 49 (3d Cir. 1979); *U.S. v. Harbin,* 601 F.2d 773 (5th Cir. 1979); *U.S. v. Muscarella,* 585 F.2d 242 (7th Cir. 1978); *Catches v. U.S.,* 582 F.2d 453 (8th Cir. 1978); *U.S. v. Carleo,* 576 F.2d 846 (10th Cir.), *cert. denied,* 439 U.S. 850 (1978). Failure to object is not a bar to review and reversal. *O'Connor v. Ohio,* 385 U.S. 92 (1966). The error, however, may be nonprejudicial if it is harmless beyond a reasonable doubt. *U.S. v. Hastings,* 461 U.S. 499 (1983); *Chapman v. California,* 386 U.S. 18 (1967). It was prosecutor characterizations of evidence, or any parts thereof, as "unrefuted," "uncontradicted," and "unimpeached," which prompted the rule that the use of such words is plain error only where the defendant alone could have contested and contradicted the government testimony. *U.S. v. Hooker,* 541 F.2d 300 (1st Cir. 1976); *U.S. v. Rodriguez,* 556 F.2d 638 (2d Cir. 1977), *cert. denied,* 434 U.S. 1062 (1978); *U.S. v. Jenkins,* 544 F.2d 180 (4th Cir. 1976), *cert. denied,* 431 U.S. 931 (1977); *U.S. v. Sorzano,* 602 F.2d 1201 (5th Cir. 1979). Where defense counsel focuses on the silence of the defendant by announcing near the end of the case that "defendant would be the next witness," then, even though defendant did not testify, the prosecution's argument that the evidence was unrefuted and uncontradicted violated no constitutional right of the accused. *Lockett v. Ohio,* 438 U.S. 586 (1978). Of course, if the defendant takes the stand he may be cross-examined on his pre-arrest silence, *Jenkins v. Anderson,* 447 U.S. 231, 238-40 (1980); post-arrest silence without *Miranda* warnings, *Fletcher v. Weir,* 102 S. Ct. 1309 (1982). *See* Chapter 3, § 309 *supra.*

Carefully planned questions and answers by a prosecutor with a government witness may constitute comment on a defendant's failure to testify, "despite its obliquity." *U.S. v. Helina,* 549 F.2d 713, 718 (9th

Cir. 1977). The test for determining whether an indirect, in-trial remark constitutes improper comment on a defendant's silence is: "Was the language used intended to be or was it of such character that the jury naturally and necessarily would take it to be a comment on the failure of the accused to testify." *U.S. v. Anderson*, 481 F.2d 685, 701 (4th Cir. 1973), *aff'd*, 417 U.S. 211 (1974). Thus, where a prosecution witness who, when asked if he testified in his tax evasion trial responded, "No, if I would have testified to the truth, it would have convicted me and if I would have lied under oath I would have been guilty of perjury — I would not lie under oath," is not a prosecutor's deliberate attempt to establish indirectly that the avoidance of perjury was the reason the defendant failed to testify. *U.S. v. Whitehead*, 618 F.2d 523, 526-28 (4th Cir. 1980).

Examples of remarks which were held not to be comments on a defendant's silence follow: "the evidence is uncontradicted," *Williams v. Wainwright*, 673 F.2d 1182, 1184-85 (11th Cir. 1982); you've got to believe what the defendant "says through his counsel about not being involved in all of this," *U.S. v. Chisem*, 667 F.2d 1192, 1194-95 (5th Cir. 1982); "that stands uncontradicted based on the cross-examination of the testimony," *U.S. v. Goldman*, 563 F.2d 501 (1st Cir. 1977), *cert. denied*, 434 U.S. 1067 (1978); "there is no conflict in the testimony of any of the witnesses in this case," *U.S. v. McDowell*, 539 F.2d 435 (5th Cir. 1976); "one who engages in criminal activity is not going to make it public knowledge," *U.S. v. Cornfeld*, 563 F.2d 967 (9th Cir. 1977), *cert. denied*, 435 U.S. 922 (1978); that there was no evidence by the defense why the defendant hastily left town, *U.S. v. Thurmond*, 541 F.2d 744 (8th Cir. 1976), *cert. denied*, 430 U.S. 933 (1977); that defendant has not told us "when the gold cap was put around one of his teeth," *U.S. v. Parker*, 549 F.2d 1217 (9th Cir.), *cert. denied*, 430 U.S. 971 (1977); that one defendant is "the man in the shadows" in this case, *U.S. v. Hansen*, 583 F.2d 325 (7th Cir.), *cert. denied*, 439 U.S. 912 (1978); where the prosecutor commented upon the body weight of the non-testifying defendant at the time of alleged offense, *U.S. v. Snow*, 552 F.2d 165 (6th Cir.), *cert. denied*, 434 U.S. 970 (1977); where the prosecutor challenged counsel for defendants charged with various narcotic violations to explain the sources of defendant's large income, *U.S. v. Barnes*, 604 F.2d 121 (2d Cir. 1979).

*See also* Chapter 11, § 1112 and Chapter 19, § 1907, *infra*.

### § 1116. — Standard for Review.

The "touchstone of due process analysis in cases of alleged prosecutorial misconduct is the fairness of the trial, not the culpability of the prosecutor." *Smith v. Phillips,* 455 U.S. 209, 220 (1982) (prosecutor failed to reveal that a juror had filed an application with the prosecutor's office during trial for a job as an investigator). *See also U.S. v. Agurs,* 427 U.S. 97 (1976); *Brady v. Maryland,* 373 U.S. 83 (1963); *U.S. v. Corona,* 551 F.2d 1386, 1388 (5th Cir. 1977).

Generally, isolated prosecutor misconduct, if followed by curative instructions upon a defense objection, are not reversible error, unless in the context of the entire record, it appears that the constitutional privileges of the accused have been affected and the misconduct has permeated the entire trial. *U.S. v. Nickerson,* 669 F.2d 1016, 1020 (5th Cir. 1982); *U.S. v. Massey,* 594 F.2d 676 (8th Cir. 1979); *U.S. v. Jones,* 592 F.2d 1038 (9th Cir.), *cert. denied,* 441 U.S. 951 (1979); *U.S. v. Brown,* 541 F.2d 858 (10th Cir.), *cert. denied,* 429 U.S. 1026 (1976).

If the defendant fails to object if the prosecutor misstates the evidence, the issue will not be considered on appeal. If the evidence is misstated there should be an opportunity for correction. *U.S. v. Bizzard,* 674 F.2d 1382, 1389 (11th Cir. 1982); *U.S. v. Barbosa,* 666 F.2d 704, 709 (1st Cir. 1981). Plain error is required for consideration on appeal where there was no objection. *U.S. v. West,* 670 F.2d 675, 688 (7th Cir.), *cert. denied,* 102 S. Ct. 2944 (1982); *U.S. v. Burns,* 668 F.2d 855, 860-61 (5th Cir. 1982). *U.S. v. Librach,* 536 F.2d 1228 (8th Cir.), *cert. denied,* 429 U.S. 939 (1976); *U.S. v. Miranda,* 593 F.2d 590 (5th Cir. 1979); *U.S. v. Cornfeld,* 563 F.2d 967 (9th Cir. 1977), *cert. denied,* 435 U.S. 922 (1978). Where corrective instructions have been given, reversal is required only where the damage conceivably inflicted cannot be removed by the judicial order to disregard the prosecutor's remarks. *U.S. v. Harbin,* 601 F.2d 773 (5th Cir. 1979); *U.S. v. Segna,* 555 F.2d 226 (9th Cir. 1977).

## § 1117. — Sanctions.

One circuit has stated that the solution to persistent prosecutorial misconduct is not reversing valid convictions, but sanctions against the prosecutor, particularly when done on repeated occasions. It has suggested that at the trial court level sanctions might include a reprimand on the spot, contempt, reference to a local grievance committee or suspension from practice before the district court. On the appellate level it could include a reprimand of a named prosecutor in a published opinion, initiate action in the district court, or suspend the individual from practice before the federal courts of the circuit. *U.S. v. Modica,* 663 F.2d 1173, 1182-86 (2d Cir. 1981), *cert. denied,* 102 S. Ct. 2269 (1982). In *U.S. v. Sears Roebuck & Co.,* 518 F. Supp. 179 (C.D. Cal. 1981), the prosecutor was named and chastised for his activities before the grand jury which resulted in the dismissal of the indictment against Sears.

## § 1118. Prosecutorial Vindictiveness.

While the decision to charge rests solely with the prosecutor, the exercise of his discretion is not without constitutional limits since it is subject to abuse. In *North Carolina v. Pearce,* 395 U.S. 711 (1969), the Supreme Court held that a due process violation of the most basic sort results when the government seeks to punish a person through the filing of additional, harsher charges because he has done what the law plainly allows him to do by demanding trial by jury or by appealing a conviction. However, there is generally not a *Pierce* violation when a judge imposes a harsher sentence after a new trial where the judge's reasons for the new sentence affirmatively appear. *Wasman v. U.S.,* 468 U.S. 559 (1984).

In *Blackledge v. Perry,* 417 U.S. 21 (1974) and *Thigpen v. Roberts,* 468 U.S. 27 (1984), the Court spoke in terms of the danger of retaliating against the accused for attacking his conviction. In these cases the court applied a presumption of vindictiveness so that a defendant be freed of retaliation where he exercised a procedural right that caused a complete retrial after he had been once tried and convicted. The due process violation was not the "possibility that a defendant might be deterred from the exercise of a legal right, ... but rather in the danger that the State might be retaliating against the accused for lawfully attacking his conviction." *Bordenkircher v. Hayes,* 434 U.S. 357, 363 (1978). The court held that in these post conviction cases there was a "realistic likelihood of 'vindictiveness.'" *Blackledge v. Perry,* 417 U.S. at 27. *See also Chaffin v. Stynchcombe,* 412 U.S. 17 (1973), which noted that it is "patently unconstitutional" to pursue a course of action, the object of which is to penalize a person's reliance upon his legal rights but which permitted the second sentence which was imposed by a jury which was not aware of the prior sentence, had no motive to engage in self-vindication, and was not sensitive to the institutional bias of a judge desirous of discouraging what he might regard to be meritless appeals.

Where a judge granted the defendant a new trial based upon the prosecutor's misconduct and then imposed a more severe sentence than the jury did at the first trial and stated on the record that in sentencing she relied upon new evidence not present in the first trial, the facts provide no basis for a presumption of vindictiveness. *Texas v. McCullough,* 106 S. Ct. 976 (1986).

A pretrial decision to increase the charges is less likely to be vindictively motivated as there is not present the institutional bias against the retrial of issues that have already been decided. *U.S. v. Goodwin,* 102 S. Ct. 2485 (1982). Even where the state prosecutor carried out his threat made during plea negotiations that he would reindict the accused as a habitual offender if he did not plead guilty to uttering a forged instrument and agree to a five-year committed sentence, there was the absence of any element of punishment in the give-and-take of plea negotiations so long as the accused was free to accept or reject the prosecution's offer. *Bordenkircher v. Hayes, supra. See also U.S. v. Mays,* 738 F.2d 1188 (11th Cir. 1984); *U.S. v. Vaughan,* 565 F.2d 283 (4th Cir. 1977); *U.S. v. Allsup,* 573 F.2d 1141 (9th Cir.), *cert. denied,* 436 U.S. 961 (1978); *Blackmon v. Wainwright,* 608 F.2d 183 (5th Cir. 1979).

Vindictiveness basically occurs in those instances where the prosecutor's motive in filing additional charges is to discourage or preclude an appeal in a particular case or in certain future cases, regardless of any ill will toward a particular defendant. *Jackson v. Walker,* 585 F.2d 139 (5th Cir. 1978). But, when there is strong evidence that a prosecutor or a responsible member of an administrative agency has instituted or recommended prosecution out of personal ill will or on invidious grounds, a charge of discriminatory prosecution will be sustained. *U.S. v. Bourque,* 541 F.2d 290 (1st Cir. 1976).

The Supreme Court has rejected a "mere opportunity for vindictiveness" test in *U.S. v. Goodwin, supra.* Possibly, this is dispositive of the "appearances of vindictiveness test," in favor of an actual or a reasonable likelihood of vindictiveness standard. *See also U.S. v. Andrews,* 612 F.2d 235 (6th Cir. 1979) (mere appearance is insufficient); *Jackson v. Walker,* 585 F.2d 139 (5th Cir. 1978) (whether either actual or reasonable apprehension of vindictiveness should be required, the court should nonetheless balance the prosecutor's freedom to decide what to prosecute with the defendant's freedom to decide whether he should appeal). *But see Miracle v. Estelle,* 592 F.2d 1269 (5th Cir. 1979) (holding that the accused must show actual vindictiveness to establish a due process violation).

The line between prosecutorial zeal and vindictiveness is a narrow one as shown by the following examples. A prosecutor's proposal to a defense contractor to terminate the grand jury investigation into possible fraud in exchange for the contractor's agreement to forego the Armed Services Board of Contract Appeals reconsideration of an award, which offer was rejected and a criminal fraud indictment was then returned, was not vindictive or retaliative. *U.S. v. Litton Systems,*

*Inc.*, 573 F.2d 195 (4th Cir.), *cert. denied,* 439 U.S. 828 (1978). A new charge for relatively distinct criminal conduct following dismissal of an indictment, where the new criminal charge resulted from the "same spree of activity," gives rise to a prima facie case of vindictiveness to which the prosecutor must have an opportunity to respond. *U.S. v. Thomas,* 593 F.2d 615 (5th Cir. 1979). Prosecution of federal drug conspiracy charges following a state court conviction of the same charges is not prosecutorial vindictiveness. *U.S. v. Sellers,* 603 F.2d 53 (8th Cir. 1979). Prosecutorial vindictiveness did not appear where a second indictment is returned following dismissal of the first indictment upon which there had been a conviction upon which defendant had served a period of probation. *U.S. v. Hall,* 559 F.2d 1160 (9th Cir. 1977). The court found a likelihood of vindictiveness where a defendant was indicted for perjury after acquittal of the initial charges where the perjurious nature of the testimony was not manifest. *U.S. v. Eddy,* 737 F.2d 564 (6th Cir. 1984).

Re-indictment for first-degree murder after declaration of a mistrial on second-degree murder charge, which mistrial was provoked by the prosecution, was held vindictive, absent a government showing of justification for the increased degree of the charge. *U.S. v. Jamison,* 505 F.2d 407 (D.C. Cir. 1974). Government concession that efforts by defendant to recover impounded funds were factored into the decision to indict did not describe action designed to foreclose civil remedies and was not vindictive conduct. *U.S. v. Stacey,* 571 F.2d 440 (8th Cir. 1978). Return of an indictment for a felony marijuana charge against one who prevailed on a motion to dismiss a prior cocaine possession charge because of a speedy trial denial, was held vindictive action which the prosecution did not overcome by asserting "failure to cooperate" where the government knew that cooperation would not extend beyond the name and address of the source of supply. *U.S. v. Groves,* 571 F.2d 450 (9th Cir. 1978). Specific acts of misconduct sufficient to require dismissal of an indictment, however, do not bar the government from re-charging through new prosecutors who need not avoid all contact with the dismissed attorney and the evidence he gathered. *In re November 1979 Grand Jury,* 616 F.2d 1021, 1025-27 (7th Cir. 1980).

Denial of a motion to dismiss based upon a claim of prosecutorial vindictiveness is not appealable before trial. *U.S. v. Hollywood Motor Car Co.,* 102 S. Ct. 3081 (1982); *U.S. v. Rosario,* 677 F.2d 614, 617 (7th Cir. 1982).

# CHAPTER 12

# TRIAL

§ 1201. Speedy Trial.
§ 1202. — The Right to a Speedy Trial.
§ 1203. — Constitutional Speedy Trial Protection.
§ 1204. — — When the Right to a Speedy Trial Attaches.
§ 1205. — — The Barker v. Wingo Balancing Test.
§ 1206. — — — Length of Delay.
§ 1207. — — — Reasons for Delay.
§ 1208. — — — Timely Assertion of Speedy Trial Right.
§ 1209. — — — Prejudice to the Defendant Caused by Delay.
§ 1210. — The Speedy Trial Act.
§ 1211. — — Application.
§ 1212. — — First Interval.
§ 1213. — — Second Interval.
§ 1214. — — Reinstitution of Prosecution.
§ 1215. — — — Dismissed Charges.
§ 1216. — — — Charges Reinstated on Appeal.
§ 1217. — — — Retrial.
§ 1218. — — Excludable Time.
§ 1219. — — — Other Proceedings.
§ 1220. — — — Examination, Deferral, and Treatment.
§ 1221. — — — Trial of Defendant on Other Charges.
§ 1222. — — — Interlocutory Appeals.
§ 1223. — — — Pretrial Motions.
§ 1224. — — — Removal of Defendant or Transfer of Case.
§ 1225. — — — Plea Agreement.
§ 1226. — — — Proceedings Under Advisement.
§ 1227. — — — Pretrial Diversion.
§ 1228. — — — Absence or Unavailability of Defendant or Witness.
§ 1229. — — — Physical or Mental Incompetency.
§ 1230. — — — Joinder and Severance.
§ 1231. — — — Continuance Which Furthers Ends of Justice.
§ 1232. — — Withdrawn Plea.
§ 1233. — — Incarcerated Defendant.
§ 1234. — — Sanctions.
§ 1235. — — Waiver.
§ 1236. — — High Risk Designees and Detainees.
§ 1237. — — Dismissal by the Court.
§ 1238. — — Appeal.
§ 1239. — Pre-Accusation Delay.
§ 1240. The Right to Trial by Jury.
§ 1241. — Size of Jury.
§ 1242. — Unanimous Jury Verdict.
§ 1243. — Waiver of Jury Trial.
§ 1244. Jury Selection and Control.
§ 1245. — Challenge of Array.
§ 1246. — Voir Dire.

§ 1247. — Challenges for Cause.
§ 1248. — Peremptory Challenges.
§ 1249. — Contamination by Trial Participants.
§ 1250. — Materials in Jury Room.
§ 1251. Trial Management.
§ 1252. — Limiting and Cautionary Instructions.
§ 1253. — Requests for Instructions.
§ 1254. — Objections to Instructions and Waiver.
§ 1255. — Special Verdicts and Interrogatories.
§ 1256. — — Special Verdicts.
§ 1257. — — Criminal Forfeiture Special Verdicts.
§ 1258. — — Special Interrogatories.
§ 1259. — — Post-Verdict Juror Interrogation.
§ 1260. — Supplemental Instructions.
§ 1261. — Allen Charge.
§ 1262. — Polling Jurors.
§ 1263. Instructions on the Law.
§ 1264. — The Contents of the Charge.
§ 1265. — — Lesser Included Offenses.
§ 1266. — — Defense Theories.
§ 1267. — Reasonable Doubt and Presumptions.
§ 1268. — — Reasonable Doubt.
§ 1269. — — Presumptions.
§ 1270. — Credibility Issues.
§ 1271. Motion for Acquittal.
§ 1272. — Grounds for Motion for Acquittal.
§ 1273. — Time for Making Motion.
§ 1274. — — At Close of Government's Case.
§ 1275. — — At Close of All the Evidence.
§ 1276. — — After Discharge of Jury.

## § 1201. Speedy Trial.

## § 1202. — The Right to a Speedy Trial.

The right to a speedy trial in federal criminal prosecutions is protected by the sixth amendment, which provides, "In all criminal prosecutions, the accused shall enjoy the right to a speedy and public trial...." Additionally, the Speedy Trial Act, 18 U.S.C. §§ 3161-3174, sets specific time limits in which federal criminal cases are to be charged and tried. Rule 48(b) of the Federal Rules of Criminal Procedure permits district courts to dismiss charges where there has been unnecessary delay in filing charges or bringing a defendant to trial. There are also protections against unreasonable pre-accusation delay in cases where the defendant has not been arrested or issued a summons before the filing of charges. While not, strictly speaking, an aspect of the right to a speedy trial, statutes of limitation and fifth amendment due process afford some protection against unreasonable pre-accusation delay.

## § 1203. — Constitutional Speedy Trial Protection.

The sixth amendment right to a speedy trial is a fundamental right and applies to the states through the fourteenth amendment. *Klopfer v. North Carolina,* 386 U.S. 213, 222-23 (1967). The only remedy for deprivation of the constitutional right to a speedy trial is dismissal of the charge. *Strunk v. U.S.,* 412 U.S. 434, 440 (1973). A pretrial order denying a speedy trial claim is not appealable as a collateral order. *U.S. v. McDonald,* 435 U.S. 850, 861 (1978). However, a state court defendant may, by means of a habeas corpus action, obtain a federal court order requiring a prompt state trial. *Atkins v. Michigan,* 644 F.2d 543 (6th Cir. 1981).

## § 1204. — — When the Right to a Speedy Trial Attaches.

The constitutional speedy trial protection does not apply to any period before a defendant is "indicted, arrested, or otherwise officially accused." *U.S. v. MacDonald,* 102 S. Ct. 1497, 1501 (1982); *U.S. v. Lovasco,* 431 U.S. 783, 788-89 (1977); *U.S. v. Marion,* 404 U.S. 307, 313 (1971). Thus, once charges are dismissed, the speedy trial protection no longer applies, even where the defendant may be subsequently indicted for the same act. The purpose of the speedy trial protection is to minimize the possibility of lengthy incarceration before trial and the other lesser, but substantial impairment of liberty and disruption of life caused by arrest and unresolved criminal charges. Other interests such as prejudice to the defense due to the passage of time because of delay by the government in bringing charges is protected by the due process clause. *U.S. v. MacDonald,* 102 S. Ct. at 1502. *See also U.S. v. Loud Hawk,* 106 S. Ct. 648 (1986).

Extensive pre-indictment publicity does not constitute an accusation for purposes of attachment of the speedy trial protection of the sixth amendment. *U.S. v. Elsbery,* 602 F.2d 1054, 1058 (2d Cir. 1979). The issuance of an arrest warrant does not constitute accusation. *U.S. v. Ramos,* 586 F.2d 1078, 1079 (5th Cir. 1978). The sixth amendment speedy trial guarantee does not attach when an individual is required to appear before a grand jury. *U.S. v. Kopel,* 552 F.2d 1265, 1276 (7th Cir. 1977). Neither does it attach when the defendant is the subject of a search, even though he is detained and given *Miranda* warnings. *U.S. v. Costanza,* 549 F.2d 1126, 1131-32 (8th Cir. 1977); *Fagan v. U.S.,* 545 F.2d 1005, 1007-08 (5th Cir. 1977); *U.S. v. Vispi,* 545 F.2d 328, 331 (2d

Cir. 1976). Mere targeting for grand jury investigation without actual restraint on the individual does not trigger the sixth amendment speedy trial guarantee. *U.S. v. Joyce,* 499 F.2d 9, 19-20 (7th Cir.), *cert. denied,* 419 U.S. 1031 (1974); *U.S. v. Ricketson,* 498 F.2d 367, 370 (7th Cir. 1974). The sixth amendment speedy trial provision does not attach from the time government agents may have learned of the crime. *U.S. v. Largent,* 545 F.2d 1039, 1042 (6th Cir. 1976), *cert. denied,* 429 U.S. 1098 (1977). Speedy trial rights for federal charges do not attach upon state arrest even though state and federal officials agree to allow the state to prosecute first. *U.S. v. Tanu,* 589 F.2d 82, 88 (2d Cir. 1978); *U.S. v. Romero,* 585 F.2d 391, 398 (9th Cir. 1978); *U.S. v. Burkhalter,* 583 F.2d 389, 392 (8th Cir. 1978); *U.S. v. Mejias,* 552 F.2d 435, 440-42 (2d Cir.), *cert. denied,* 434 U.S. 847 (1977). Confinement and administrative segregation do not amount to an arrest or accusation for sixth amendment purposes. *U.S. v. Blevins,* 593 F.2d 646, 647 (5th Cir. 1979); *U.S. v. Manetta,* 551 F.2d 1352, 1353-54 (5th Cir. 1977). An administrative segregation of a prisoner for possession of drugs does not render him an accused for purposes of the speedy trial right. *U.S. v. Duke,* 527 F.2d 386, 390 (5th Cir.), *cert. denied,* 426 U.S. 952 (1976). The constitutional speedy trial protection applies when arrestees are out on bail and are bound over to the grand jury for investigation of criminal activity, even though an indictment has not been returned. *U.S. v. Macino,* 486 F.2d 750, 753 (7th Cir. 1973).

### § 1205. — — The Barker v. Wingo Balancing Test.

Determination of whether a particular defendant has been denied a speedy trial is made on a case-by-case basis. The Supreme Court established a test, in *Barker v. Wingo,* 407 U.S. 514 (1972), which balances four factors: (1) the length of delay; (2) the reasons for the delay; (3) the timeliness and vigor of the defendant's assertion of the speedy trial right; and (4) the degree of prejudice which the defendant suffers. 407 U.S. at 530. The *Barker* balancing test applies to delay between arrest and indictment as well as to delay between indictment and trial. *U.S. v. Edwards,* 577 F.2d 883 (5th Cir.), *cert. denied,* 439 U.S. 968 (1978), and delay for government interlocutory appeals. *U.S. v. Loud Hawk,* 106 S. Ct. 648 (1986).

### § 1206. — — — Length of Delay.

Circuit courts generally have considered the other *Barker* factors only if the defendant has made a threshold showing that the length of the delay was presumptively prejudicial to him. *Barker v. Wingo,* 407

U.S. at 530; *U.S. v. Walters,* 591 F.2d 1195, 1201 (5th Cir.), *cert. denied,* 442 U.S. 945 (1979). Postaccusation delay which approaches one year has generally been held to be "presumptively prejudicial." *Doggett v. U.S.,* 112 S. Ct. 2686, 2691 n.1 (1992).

### § 1207. — — — Reasons for Delay.

Courts generally look to the reasons for the delay in commencing the defendant's trial to determine whether those reasons are deliberate, neutral, or valid.

Intentional delays which obtain a strategic advantage for the prosecution are weighed heavily against the government. *Barker v. Wingo,* 407 U.S. at 531; *U.S. v. Henry,* 615 F.2d 1223, 1233 (9th Cir. 1980); *U.S. v. Carter,* 603 F.2d 1204, 1207 (5th Cir. 1979). Delay resulting from government negligence or factors beyond the control of the prosecution are viewed less critically by the courts. A six year failure to seriously pursue a defendant has been held against the government. *Doggett v. U.S.,* 112 S. Ct. 2686 (1992).

The following have been found to be neutral or valid reasons for delay: further investigation, *U.S. v. Roberts,* 548 F.2d 665, 667 (6th Cir.), *cert. denied,* 431 U.S. 931 (1977); negligent delay in reassigning case to prosecutor, *U.S. v. Henry,* 615 F.2d at 1233; crowded docket, *Barker v. Wingo,* 407 U.S. at 531; *U.S. v. Brown,* 600 F.2d 248, 254 (10th Cir. 1979); *U.S. v. Canales,* 573 F.2d 908, 910 (5th Cir. 1978); awaiting decision on controlling point of law, *U.S. v. Canales,* 573 F.2d at 910; valid interlocutory appeal, *U.S. v. Loud Hawk,* 106 S. Ct. 648 (1986); reversal on appeal which requires a retrial, *U.S. v. Bizzard,* 674 F.2d 1382, 1386 (11th Cir. 1982); determination of proper venue, *U.S. v. Noll,* 600 F.2d 1123, 1127 (5th Cir. 1979); complexity of charges, *U.S. v. Enright,* 579 F.2d 980, 990 (6th Cir. 1978); *U.S. v. Dreitzler,* 577 F.2d 539, 549-50 (9th Cir. 1978); unavailability of witnesses, *U.S. v. Askew,* 584 F.2d 960, 962 (10th Cir. 1978), *cert. denied,* 439 U.S. 1132 (1979); unavailability of judge, *U.S. v. Grismore,* 564 F.2d 929, 932 (10th Cir. 1977), *cert. denied,* 435 U.S. 954 (1978); *U.S. v. Lane,* 561 F.2d 1075, 1078-79 (2d Cir.), *cert. denied,* 434 U.S. 969 (1977); weather, *U.S. v. Richman,* 600 F.2d 286, 293 (1st Cir. 1979); and "acts of nature," *U.S. v. Furlow,* 644 F.2d 764, 768 (9th Cir. 1981). The Second Circuit, however, has followed *Barker's* admonition (407 U.S. at 531) that the government bears the "ultimate responsibility" for "institutional delays." It held the government responsible for causes such as crowded docket, delays in ruling on defendant's motions, or delays resulting from plea bargaining. *U.S. v. New Buffalo Amusement Corp.,* 600 F.2d 368, 377-78 (2d Cir. 1979). Delays attributable to the defendant have not been weighed against the government by courts applying the *Barker* test. *U.S. v. DiFrancesco,* 604 F.2d 769, 776-77 (2d Cir. 1979), *rev'd on other grounds,* 449 U.S. 117 (1980) (defense counsel's illness, motions, other trial); *U.S. v. Carter,* 603 F.2d at 1207 (defendant's deliberate absence); *U.S. v. Vila,* 599 F.2d 21, 24 (2d Cir.), *cert. denied,* 444 U.S. 837 (1979) (postponement of first trial date at defense request); *U.S. v. Askew,* 584 F.2d at 962 (refusal to give exemplars); *U.S. v. Herman,* 576 F.2d at 1145 (guilty plea and subsequent withdrawal). There is a split in authority about the government's responsibility for delay resulting from the defendant's foreign incarceration. The Seventh Circuit has held that the government must make a diligent, good faith effort to extradite. *U.S. v. McConahy,* 505 F.2d 770, 773-74 (7th Cir. 1974). The Ninth Circuit rejected the *McConahy* rule in *U.S. v. Hooker,* 607 F.2d 286, 288-89 (9th Cir. 1979), *cert. denied,* 445 U.S. 905 (1980).

### § 1208. — — — Timely Assertion of Speedy Trial Right.

It is not essential in proving a constitutional violation that the defendant made a timely and vigorous assertion of his right to a speedy trial. Failure to assert his right during the delay does not necessarily constitute a waiver, but it probably will weigh heavily against the defendant. *Barker v. Wingo,* 407 U.S. at 522-30. Asserting his speedy trial right after arrest and 8½ years after indictment was timely where the defendant did not know of the indictment until arrest. *Doggett v. U.S.,* 112 S. Ct. 2686 (1992). Belated or *pro forma* assertions of the right are given less weight than timely assertions. *U.S. v. DiFrancesco,* 604 F.2d at 777; *U.S. v. Martin,* 587 F.2d 31, 33 (9th Cir. 1978), *cert. denied,* 440 U.S. 910 (1979); *U.S. ex rel. Barksdale v. Sielaff,* 585 F.2d 288, 291 (7th Cir. 1978), *cert. denied,* 441 U.S. 962 (1979); *U.S. v. Enright,* 579 F.2d at 990; *U.S. v. Greene,* 578 F.2d at 655 (1978). A defendant may expressly waive his constitutional right to a speedy trial if the waiver is knowing and voluntary. *U.S. v. Spaulding,* 588 F.2d 669, 670 (9th Cir. 1978).

### § 1209. — — — Prejudice to the Defendant Caused by Delay.

*Barker* requires the defendant to show actual prejudice to support a claimed speedy trial violation. 407 U.S. at 532. The dangers incident to delay from which the defendant is owed protection are (1) oppressive pretrial incarceration, (2) anxiety and concern, and (3) impairment of defenses. *Id.* If the defendant fails to demonstrate actual prejudice in one of these three areas, there need be no dismissal of the charge. *U.S. v. Greer,* 620 F.2d 1383, 1386 (10th Cir. 1980); *U.S. v. Metz,* 608 F.2d

147, 152 (5th Cir. 1979). In fact, if the other three *Barker* factors favor the defendant, but he admits he suffered no prejudice, his claim based on violation of the constitutional right to a speedy trial must fail. *U.S. v. Henry,* 615 F.2d at 1234.

Allegations of prejudice generally must be particular not general. *U.S. v. Metz,* 608 F.2d at 152. There may be "presumptive prejudice" which is unspecified and which results from prolonged and unjustified delays in prosecution. Excessive delay can compromise a trial's reliability in unidentifiable ways. *Doggett v. U.S.,* 112 S. Ct. 2686 (1992). The most common type of prejudice alleged by defendants is that causing impairment of their defenses, and courts are most concerned with such allegations. *Id. Barker v. Wingo,* 407 U.S. at 532. Impairment is often alleged because witnesses are unavailable. *U.S. v. New Buffalo Amusement Corp.,* 600 F.2d at 379; *Jones v. Morris,* 590 F.2d 684, 687 (7th Cir.), *cert. denied,* 440 U.S. 965 (1979); *U.S. v. Becker,* 585 F.2d 703, 708 (4th Cir. 1978), *cert. denied,* 439 U.S. 1080 (1979) (government witness), or because witnesses' memories have faded, *U.S. v. Wiggins,* 566 F.2d 944, 945-46 (5th Cir.), *cert. denied,* 436 U.S. 950 (1978); *U.S. v. Netterville,* 553 F.2d 903, 915-16 (5th Cir. 1977), *cert. denied,* 434 U.S. 1009 (1978). Loss of records during the delay, *U.S. v. Pitts,* 569 F.2d 343, 347-48 (5th Cir.), *cert. denied,* 436 U.S. 959 (1978), or the onset of financial difficulties, *U.S. v. Romero,* 585 F.2d at 399, has been found not to impair the defense. Courts are especially unimpressed if the defendant is responsible for the loss of evidence during the delay. *U.S. v. Pitts,* 569 F.2d at 347-48; *U.S. v. Netterville,* 553 F.2d at 915-17. A significant change in public opinion during a pretrial delay may be prejudicial in an obscenity case. *U.S. v. New Buffalo Amusement Corp.,* 600 F.2d at 379.

Incarceration during a pretrial delay is generally not prejudicial enough to justify dismissal of the charge. *U.S. v. Traylor,* 578 F.2d 108, 109 (5th Cir. 1978), *cert. denied,* 439 U.S. 1074 (1979); *U.S. v. Harrington,* 543 F.2d 1151, 1153 (5th Cir. 1976). *But see Smith v. Hooey,* 393 U.S. 374, 378 (1969); *U.S. v. Graham,* 538 F.2d 261, 264-65 (9th Cir.), *cert. denied,* 429 U.S. 925 (1976). Courts have been little impressed by allegations of prejudice arising from heightened anxiety during pretrial delay. *U.S. v. Van Dyke,* 605 F.2d 220, 226 (6th Cir.), *cert. denied,* 444 U.S. 994 (1979); *U.S. v. Noll,* 600 F.2d at 1128; *U.S. v. Johnson,* 579 F.2d 122, 124-25 (5th Cir. 1978).

### § 1210. — The Speedy Trial Act.

The Speedy Trial Act, 18 U.S.C. §§ 3161-3174, sets specific time limits in which federal criminal cases are to be charged and tried. The act requires that a defendant be charged by indictment or information within 30 days from arrest or service of summons (the first interval). 18 U.S.C. § 3161(b). Trial in a case where a not guilty plea is entered must commence within 70 days from the filing of the indictment or information, or from the defendant's appearance before a judicial officer of the court in which the charge is pending, whichever occurs last (the second interval). 18 U.S.C. § 3161(c)(1). Both intervals may be expanded by excludable delays. 18 U.S.C. § 3161(h). The act prohibits the commencement of trial earlier than 30 days from the date the defendant first appears through counsel or expressly waives counsel and elects to proceed *pro se,* unless the defendant consents in writing. 18 U.S.C. § 3161(c)(2). In cases commenced by arrest or filing of charges on or after July 1, 1980, a court must dismiss the charge if the time requirements for either interval are violated. 18 U.S.C. § 3162. *See U.S. v. West,* 607 F.2d 300, 305 (9th Cir. 1979). The time limits and dismissal sanction are intended to protect the defendant's right to a speedy trial and the public's right to a prompt disposition of criminal cases. A defendant is not entitled to take an interlocutory appeal of a denial of his Speedy Trial Act claim. *U.S. v. Grabinski,* 674 F.2d 677, 680 (8th Cir.), *cert. denied,* 103 S. Ct. 67 (1982); *U.S. v. Mehrmanesh,* 652 F.2d 766, 769-70 (7th Cir. 1981).

### § 1211. — — Application.

The Speedy Trial Act applies to all federal criminal cases except petty offenses and offenses triable by military tribunals. 18 U.S.C. § 3172. *U.S. v. Baker,* 641 F.2d 1311, 1319 (9th Cir. 1981). The act does not bar a defendant's claim that a violation of his sixth amendment speedy trial rights has occurred. 18 U.S.C. § 3173. Like the sixth amendment, the Speedy Trial Act provides no protection against pre-accusation delay where a defendant is not arrested or served a summons before charges are filed. The Federal Juvenile Delinquency Act, 18 U.S.C. §§ 5031-5042, has its own speedy trial requirements. 18 U.S.C. § 5036.

### § 1212. — — First Interval.

The first interval usually begins with the arrest of the defendant. Arrest of the defendant by state authorities on state charges does not commence the running of the act's first interval for federal offenses. *U.S. v. Iaquinta,* 674 F.2d 260, 267 (4th Cir. 1982); *U.S. v. Leonard,* 639 F.2d 101, 103-105 (2d Cir. 1981); *U.S. v. Tanu,* 589 F.2d at 87-88; *U.S. v. Phillips,* 569 F.2d 1315, 1316-17 (5th Cir. 1978); *U.S. v. Mejias,* 552

F.2d at 440-43. However, when an arrest is made by a state at the request of federal authorities, the first interval will begin to run when custody of the defendant is transferred to a federal agency. *See U.S. v. Tanu, supra.* Also, the first interval begins to run only on the charge for which the defendant is arrested. If the defendant is later charged with a different offense, he has not been arrested for purposes of calculating the first interval regarding that different offense. *U.S. v. Lyon,* 567 F.2d 777, 781 n.3 (8th Cir. 1977), *cert. denied,* 435 U.S. 918 (1978); *U.S. v. Cabral,* 475 F.2d 715, 718 (1st Cir. 1973); *U.S. v. DeTienne,* 468 F.2d 151, 155 (7th Cir. 1972). The 30-day limit does not apply where escapees are recaptured and later indicted for escape. *U.S. v. Wilson,* 666 F.2d 1241, 1248-49 (9th Cir. 1982). If a defendant is arrested based on the non-judicial opinion of a law enforcement officer and is later released without being charged, the first interval is not triggered. *U.S. v. Jones,* 676 F.2d 327, 331 (8th Cir. 1982); *U.S. v. Padro,* 508 F. Supp. 184, 185-86 (D. Del. 1981).

If a grand jury is not in session during the initial 30-day interval, the act permits an additional 30 days in which to indict. 18 U.S.C. § 3161(b). This extension may not be available if the defendant was arrested for a misdemeanor. A superceding indictment need not be filed within the 30-day interval. *U.S. v. Wilks,* 629 F.2d 669, 673 (10th Cir. 1980).

### § 1213. — — Second Interval.

Before the Speedy Trial Act was amended in 1979, arraignment on federal criminal charges had to occur within 10 days and trial had to commence within 60 days from the filing of charges. Effective July 1, 1979, however, the second interval is 70 days between the defendant's first appearance or the filing and making public of charges (whichever occurs later) and trial. 18 U.S.C. § 3161(c)(1). A preindictment initial appearance is considered an appearance before a judicial officer for purposes of determining the later occurring date. *U.S. v. Carrasquillo,* 667 F.2d 382, 384 (3d Cir. 1981).

If an indictment or information is sealed, the second interval begins to run when it is unsealed. *U.S. v. Villa,* 470 F. Supp. 315, 325 (N.D.N.Y. 1979). If the defendant is not arrested or is not issued a summons before the filing of charges, the second interval does not begin to run until the defendant has appeared before a judicial officer in the district where the charges are pending. 18 U.S.C. § 3161(c)(1); *U.S. v. Umbower,* 602 F.2d 754, 758 (5th Cir. 1979); *U.S. v. Taylor,* 569 F.2d 448, 450 (7th Cir.), *cert. denied,* 435 U.S. 952 (1978). Generally, trial is deemed to commence at jury voir dire. *U.S. v. Gonzalez,* 671

F.2d 441, 443 (11th Cir. 1982); *U.S. v. Barboza*, 612 F.2d 999, 1000 (5th Cir. 1980).

### § 1214. — — Reinstitution of Prosecution.

### § 1215. — — — Dismissed Charges.

If the court upon a defendant's motion dismisses an indictment, information, or complaint and charges are refiled, new first and second intervals commence pursuant to 18 U.S.C. § 3161(b) and (c)(1). 18 U.S.C. § 3161(d)(1); *U.S. v. Dennis*, 625 F.2d 782, 793 (8th Cir. 1980). If the government withdraws or obtains the dismissal of a complaint, new first and second intervals commence. 18 U.S.C. § 3161(d)(1); *U.S. v. Belleville*, 505 F. Supp. 1083, 1084 (E.D. Mich. 1981). But if an indictment or information is dismissed upon motion of the government and the same charge or one required to be charged with it is later filed, the original intervals continue to run but the period between the entry of the order of dismissal of the first charge and the filing of the second is excludable. 18 U.S.C. § 3161(d)(1) and (h)(6); *U.S. v. Arkus*, 675 F.2d 245, 247 (9th Cir. 1982); *U.S. v. Hillegas*, 578 F.2d 453, 459 (2d Cir. 1978); *U.S. v. Sebastian*, 428 F. Supp. 967, 973 (W.D.N.Y.), *aff'd*, 562 F.2d 211 (2d Cir. 1977).

The Speedy Trial Act does not require that the 30-day preparation period be restarted upon the filing of a superseding indictment for the same offense. 18 U.S.C. § 3161(c)(2); *U.S. v. Rojas-Contreras*, 106 S. Ct. 555 (1985); *U.S. v. Reynolds*, 781 F.2d 135 (8th Cir. 1986). However, granting only 10 days to prepare a defense to a RICO claim in a superseding indictment has been held to violate the defendant's sixth amendment right to counsel. *U.S. v. Gallo*, 763 F.2d 1504 (6th Cir. 1985). New charges (not the same offense or one required to be joined) in the superceding indictment, complaint, or information cause a new second interval to commence under the act. *U.S. v. Peters*, 587 F.2d 1267, 1270-74 (D.C. Cir. 1978).

### § 1216. — — — Charges Reinstated on Appeal.

Trial on an indictment or information which was dismissed by the trial court and which is subsequently reinstated on appeal, must commence within 70 days of the date on which the mandate of the court of appeals is filed with the district court. The court may expand that interval to 180 days if the 70-day limit proves to be impractical. 18 U.S.C. § 3161(d)(2).

## §1217. — — — Retrial.

A new 70-day interval begins to run from the date on which a trial court declares a mistrial or enters an order granting a new trial. 18 U.S.C. §3161(e); *U.S. v. Gilliss*, 645 F.2d 1269, 1275 (8th Cir. 1981). A new 70-day interval also commences upon the date on which a mandate for retrial is received from a court of appeals by a district court. 18 U.S.C. §3161(e); *U.S. v. Cook*, 592 F.2d 877, 880 (5th Cir.), *cert. denied*, 442 U.S. 921 (1979).

A timely motion requesting reconsideration of an order granting a new trial, tolls the running of the 70-day period. *U.S. v. Spiegel*, 604 F.2d 961, 971-72 (5th Cir. 1979). A court which retries a case following a successful appeal or collateral attack may extend the 70-day period to 180 days if the shorter period is impractical. 18 U.S.C. §3161(e); *U.S. v. Lyon*, 588 F.2d 581, 582 (8th Cir. 1978).

The sanctions of 18 U.S.C. §3162 and exclusions of 18 U.S.C. §3161(h) apply to the intervals associated with reinstatement of charges and retrial (including the extended periods of up to 180 days). 18 U.S.C. §3161(d)(2) and (3).

## §1218. — — Excludable Time.

Section 3161(h)(1) through (7) of the Speedy Trial Act sets forth seven specific events which may cause delay that is excludable in computing first or second intervals. Section 3161(h)(8) is a general provision which permits exclusion of delay resulting from a continuance granted to further the ends of justice.

## §1219. — — — Other Proceedings.

Section 3161(h)(1) of the act enumerates some but not all of the proceedings which may cause excludable delay in computing the intervals. These include proceedings (not just the examinations themselves) about the defendant's physical and mental competency to stand trial. The exclusion applies only to court-ordered examinations pursuant to Rule 12.2 of the Federal Rules of Criminal Procedure and 18 U.S.C. §4244. The excludable time generally runs from the date the motion is filed seeking the examination to the date the matter is taken under advisement after receipt by the court of results and briefs and completion of any hearings. *See U.S. v. McCrary*, 569 F.2d 429, 430 (6th Cir. 1978); *U.S. v. Bigelow*, 544 F.2d 904, 907 (6th Cir. 1976); *Moore v. District Court*, 525 F.2d 328, 329 (9th Cir. 1975). Any time during which the matter is under advisement is more properly excluded under 18 U.S.C. §3161(h)(1)(J). Time devoted to transportation for examination purposes is more properly excluded under 18 U.S.C. § 3161-(h)(1)(H). Any transportation time in excess of 10 days from the order causing the transportation is presumed to be unreasonable under the act. 18 U.S.C. § 3161(h)(1)(H). Delay resulting from a parole or probation revocation proceeding may be excluded. *U.S. v. Lopez-Espindola,* 632 F.2d 107 (9th Cir. 1980). Delay attributable to habeas corpus proceedings is excludable. *U.S. v. Bryant,* 612 F.2d 806, 811 (4th Cir. 1979), *cert. denied,* 446 U.S. 920 (1980). A North Carolina court of appeals, interpreting a state speedy trial statute taken verbatim from the federal act, has held that a defendant's efforts to obtain counsel cause excludable time pursuant to the "other proceedings" provision. *State v. Rogers,* 271 S.E.2d 535 (N.C. 1980).

### § 1220. — — — Examination, Deferral, and Treatment.

The Narcotics Addict Rehabilitation Act (NARA), 28 U.S.C. § 2902, allows voluntary civil commitment for treatment by a narcotics addict. The Speedy Trial Act excludes delay resulting from NARA proceedings, 18 U.S.C. § 3161(h)(1)(B); from deferral of prosecution, 18 U.S.C. § 3161(h)(1)(C); and treatment, § 3161(h)(5). Generally, excludable time resulting from NARA events begins to run when the court advises the defendant that he may participate, and includes time devoted to examination, treatment, transmittal of reports, hearings, and submission of briefs. Transportation for examination and treatment, 18 U.S.C. § 3161(h)(1)(H), and periods when the matter is under advisement, 18 U.S.C. § 3161(h)(1)(J), are also excludable. The period of excludable time ends when the Surgeon General notifies the court that the defendant has completed the program (charges are then dismissed) or that the defendant is not being helped by the program (the interval starts to run again).

### § 1221. — — — Trial of Defendant on Other Charges.

Delay resulting from trial of the defendant on other state or federal charges (including counts severed from the indictment by the trial court) is excludable. *See U.S. v. Bryant,* 612 F.2d at 811. Not only is actual court time excludable, but all delay attributable to the other charges is excludable. *U.S. v. Lopez-Espindola,* 632 F.2d 107-10; *U.S. v. Goodwin,* 612 F.2d 1103, 1105 (8th Cir. 1980); *U.S. v. Allsup,* 573 F.2d 1141, 1144 (9th Cir.), *cert. denied,* 436 U.S. 961 (1978); *U.S. v. Lyon,* 588 F.2d at 582.

## § 1222. — — — Interlocutory Appeals.

Delays attributable to interlocutory appeals by the government pursuant to 18 U.S.C. § 3731 (suppression and exclusion of evidence) and 18 U.S.C. § 2518(10)(b) (wire interception) or by either party pursuant to 28 U.S.C. § 1292 (interlocutory appeals), are excludable. § 3161-(h)(1)(E). It is unclear whether appeals pursuant to 18 U.S.C. § 3174(b) (conditions of release) result in excludable delay. Generally, excludable time stretches from the date of filing the notice of appeal in the district court to the date the mandate of the court of appeals is filed in the district court. *U.S. v. McGrath*, 622 F.2d 36, 40 (2d Cir. 1980).

## § 1223. — — — Pretrial Motions.

The period of time from the date any pretrial motion is filed or made orally through the date of the court's disposition of the motion is excludable under 18 U.S.C. § 3161(h)(1)(F). *U.S. v. Jodoin*, 672 F.2d 232, 238 (1st Cir. 1982); *U.S. v. Regilio*, 669 F.2d 1169, 1171-73 (7th Cir. 1981), *cert. denied*, 102 S. Ct. 2959 (1982); *Furlow v. U.S.*, 644 F.2d at 768. All delay, not just reasonably necessary delays, due to a pretrial motion is excludable, including the time a court waits for additional filings that are needed for the dispostion of the motion. *Henderson v. U.S.*, 106 S. Ct. 1871 (1986).

Section 3161(h)(1)(J) provides an additional basis for excluding that portion of the delay for up to 30 days when any proceeding concerning the defendant is under advisement. *See U.S. v. McGrath*, 622 F.2d at 40. Ordinary pretrial motions, such as those for discovery and disclosure of alibi witnesses, do give rise to excludable time. *U.S. v. Brim*, 630 F.2d 1307, 1312 (8th Cir. 1980). The time devoted to preparation of motions involving complex fact questions or novel legal issues may be excludable under 18 U.S.C. § 3161(h)(8)(B). *U.S. v. Molt*, 631 F.2d 258, 262 (3d Cir. 1980) (suppression motion). Time during the pendency of a motion for dismissal on the basis of a Speedy Trial Act violation is excludable, *U.S. v. Rogers*, 899 F.2d 917 (10th Cir.), *cert. denied*, 111 S. Ct. 113 (1990), as is delay caused by an attempted interlocutory appeal of the court's denial of a speedy trial claim. *U.S. v. New Buffalo Amusement Corp.*, 600 F.2d at 375; *U.S. v. Didier*, 542 F.2d 1182, 1188 (2d Cir. 1970).

Excludable time devoted to pretrial motions may expand the interval between remand for retrial and the trial itself. *U.S. v. Stulga*, 584 F.2d 142, 146 (6th Cir. 1978).

### § 1224. — — — Removal of Defendant or Transfer of Case.

A delay caused by a proceeding relating to the transfer of a case or the removal of a defendant pursuant to the Federal Rules of Criminal Procedure is excludable time under 18 U.S.C. § 3161(h)(1)(G). In a Rule 20 proceeding, excludable time commences on the date the defendant executes his consent to transfer. The period of excludable time ends with the receipt of the papers in the initiating district following failure of the proceedings because the defendant has refused to plead guilty or the court has refused to accept the plea. The excludable time also ends on the date one of the U.S. Attorneys refuses to consent to the transfer.

If a motion for change of venue is filed pursuant to Rule 21 of the Federal Rules of Criminal Procedure, excludable time begins on that date. The excludable period ends when the court has received everything it needs to consider the motion. This time is most properly excluded under 18 U.S.C. § 3161(h)(1)(F). While the motion is under advisement, time is excluded under 18 U.S.C. § 3161(h)(1)(J). After the motion is granted, delay resulting from the actual transfer of the proceedings, up to the defendant's first appearance in the new district, is excludable under 18 U.S.C. § 3161(h)(1)(G).

Ordinarily, delay resulting from proceedings pursuant to Rule 40 of the Federal Rules of Criminal Procedure, is excludable from the defendant's arrest in the non-charging district to his first appearance before a judicial officer in the charging district. 18 U.S.C. § 3161(h)(1)(G). Time attributable to transportation is excludable, but delay beyond 10 days from the order causing the transportation is presumed to be unreasonable. 18 U.S.C. § 3161(h)(1)(H).

### § 1225. — — — Plea Agreement.

Section 3161(h)(1)(I) excludes time during which the court is considering a proposed plea agreement which has been submitted for approval. The exclusion does not apply to the period of negotiation. Section 3161(h)(8) may permit an exclusion during a continuance obtained to pursue plea negotiations. *But see U.S. v. Carini*, 562 F.2d 144, 149 (2d Cir. 1977); *U.S. v. Roberts*, 515 F.2d 642, 646-47 (2d Cir. 1975).

### § 1226. — — — Proceedings Under Advisement.

The excludable period during which a matter is under advisement may not exceed 30 days. 18 U.S.C. § 3161(h)(1)(J). *See U.S. v. Martin*, 587 F.2d 31, 33 (9th Cir. 1978). The period begins on the date the court has received everything it needs to take the matter under advisement and ends when the judge's decision is filed or rendered orally in open court or after 30 days. When two judges are considering separate motions relating to the same case, it is proper to exclude up to 30 days for each motion under advisement. *U.S. v. Molt,* 631 F.2d at 261-62 (motion to suppress and a challenge to the constitutionality of a statute).

### § 1227. — — — Pretrial Diversion.

If, after arrest or indictment, a defendant is placed in pretrial diversion pursuant to a written agreement, the time in the diversion program is exludable. 18 U.S.C. § 3161(h)(2). The time is excluded from the date the court approves the diversion to the date the case is dismissed or the date of the U.S. Attorney's notice to the defendant of his intent to resume prosecution.

### § 1228. — — — Absence or Unavailability of Defendant or Witness.

Section 3161(h)(3) provides that any period during which the defendant or an essential witness is absent or unavailable is excludable. Under 18 U.S.C. § 3161(h)(3)(A), a person is absent when his whereabouts are unknown to the prosecution and, in addition, he is attempting to avoid apprehension or prosecution or his whereabouts cannot be determined by due diligence. Excludable time starts on the date he fails to make an appearance or the date the court receives notice that his whereabouts are unknown. The period ends when the prosecutor receives notice of the person's whereabouts.

A witness or defendant is unavailable when his whereabouts are known but he resists appearing or his presence cannot be obtained by due diligence. 18 U.S.C. § 3161(h)(3)(B); *U.S. v. Fielding,* 645 F.2d 719, 722-23 (9th Cir. 1981). Excludable time begins on the date the witness or defendant fails to appear and ends on the date when the government can produce him in court.

While the defendant bears the burden of proof supporting a motion to dismiss a charge for violation of the second interval time limits under the act, the government has the burden of going forward with evidence of excludable time based on absence or unavailability of the defendant or an essential witness. 18 U.S.C. § 3162(a)(2); *U.S. v. Fielding,* 645 F.2d at 723.

If a defendant is in state custody, but the federal authorities do not attempt to secure his presence by writ or otherwise, 18 U.S.C. § 3161(h)(3)(A) cannot be used as a basis for excludable time. *U.S. v. Lopez-Espindola,* 632 F.2d at 109.

### § 1229. — — — Physical or Mental Incompetency.

Delay attributable to the defendant's physical or mental incompetency is excludable. 18 U.S.C. § 3161(h)(4). The excludable period begins when the court finds the defendant incompetent or unable to stand trial and ends on the date the court finds that the defendant is fit to stand trial.

### § 1230. — — — Joinder and Severance.

Section 3161(h)(7) excludes a reasonable period of delay attributable to the defendant's joinder for trial with a codefendant for whom time for trial has not run and no motion for severance has been granted. *See U.S. v. McGrath,* 613 F.2d 361, 366 (2d Cir. 1979); *U.S. v. Strand,* 566 F.2d 530, 533 (5th Cir. 1978).

### § 1231. — — — Continuance Which Furthers Ends of Justice.

Delay resulting from the court's continuance may be excludable under 18 U.S.C. § 3161(h)(8) if certain requisites are met. The continuance may be granted by the judge on his own motion or that of either party. The court must set forth on the record (orally or in writing) its reasons for finding that the ends of justice served by the granting of the continuance outweigh the interests of the public and the defendant in a speedy trial. *U.S. v. Molt,* 631 F.2d at 262; *U.S. v. Fielding,* 645 F.2d at 722; *U.S. v. Edwards,* 627 F.2d at 461 (reasons can be placed on record at date later than granting of continuance); *U.S. v. New Buffalo Amusement Corp.,* 600 F.2d at 375. The court may grant the continuance for any number of reasons, only four of which are enumerated in 18 U.S.C. § 3161(h)(8)(B): (1) whether failure to grant delay would likely make continuation of the proceeding impossible or would result in a miscarriage of justice, *United States v. Aviles,* 623 F.2d 1192, 1195-96 (7th Cir. 1980); (2) whether the case is so unusual or complex that additional time for preparation is justified; (3) whether arrest occurs at a time or the case is so unusual or complex that it is unreasonable to expect return of the indictment in the 30 days specified, *U.S. v. McGrath,* 613 F.2d at 366; *see also U.S. v. Dennis,* 625 F.2d at 794 (delay to allow government to reassess case after dismissal of principal count of indictment *sua sponte* by the court); (4) whether failure to allow delay in a case not unusual or complex would unreasonably deny continuity of counsel or effective and diligent preparation by counsel.

No continuance under 18 U.S.C. § 3161(h)(8)(A) may be justified by general congestion of the court's calendar, lack of diligent preparation, or failure to obtain witnesses by government counsel. 18 U.S.C.

§ 3161(h)(8)(C); *U.S. v. Nance,* 666 F.2d 353, 359 (9th Cir.), *cert. denied,* 102 S. Ct. 1776 (1982).

Any continuance granted under 18 U.S.C. § 3161(h)(8)(A) must be granted by the judge. Where the deputy clerk grants a continuance to defense counsel to accommodate defense counsel's schedule, this time is not excludable and may result in dismissal of the indictment. *U.S. v. Carrasquillo,* 667 F.2d 382, 385 (3d Cir. 1981). If a continuance is valid when granted, and unforeseen contingencies prevent the government from using the continuance for the reasons it was granted, the court may revoke or shorten the continuance, but it is not required to revoke the continuance with effect back to the original trial date. *U.S. v. Carlone,* 666 F.2d 1112, 1115 (7th Cir. 1981), *cert. denied,* 102 S. Ct. 2272 (1982).

## § 1232. — — Withdrawn Plea.

Where a defendant is permitted to withdraw a plea of guilty or nolo contendere, the act deems him to be indicted on the date the order permitting the withdrawal becomes final. 18 U.S.C. § 3161(i); *U.S. v. Gilliss,* 645 F.2d 1269, 1275 n.14 (8th Cir. 1981). Thus a new second interval begins to run (for all charges even if a plea to less than all is withdrawn) on that date. 18 U.S.C. § 3161(i). When the plea agreement involves dismissal of an entire indictment in exchange for a guilty plea to charges contained in a new indictment and that guilty plea is withdrawn, 18 U.S.C. § 3161(i) may not provide for the commencement of a new interval upon withdrawal of the plea. Section 3161(h)(8) may appropriately be used in such a case.

## § 1233. — — Incarcerated Defendant.

A federal prosecutor is not relieved of the obligation to afford a speedy trial because the defendant is in custody elsewhere. *See Smith v. Hooey,* 393 U.S. 374 (1969). The Speedy Trial Act requires a federal prosecutor to take steps to obtain the presence of a defendant who is serving a term of imprisonment on other charges. This duty under 18 U.S.C. § 3161(j) arises only at the time a federal charge is filed against such a defendant. *U.S. v. Burkhalter,* 583 F.2d 389, 392 n.6 (8th Cir. 1978). The federal prosecutor must either (a) undertake, usually by writ, to obtain the defendant's presence for trial, or (b) cause a detainer to be filed with the person maintaining custody of the defendant, asking that the defendant be advised of his right to demand trial. If counsel for the government is notified that the defendant demands trial, counsel must then take steps to obtain the defendant's presence.

The Interstate Agreement on Detainers "prescribes procedures by which a member State may obtain for trial a prisoner incarcerated in another member jurisdiction and by which the prisoner may demand the speedy disposition of charges pending against him in another jurisdiction." *U.S. v. Mauro,* 436 U.S. 340, 343 (1978). The United States and the District of Columbia are parties to the agreement. Pub. L. No. 91-538; 84 Stat. 1397. The provisions of the agreement attach only at the time a detainer is filed. If the defendant then demands a speedy trial, he is deemed to have waived extradition and the jurisdiction which has filed the detainer must bring the defendant to trial on all untried charges underlying the detainer within 180 days. Art. III(a), (d), and (e). The prosecutor filing the detainer obtains the prisoner from the custodian jurisdiction by written request. Art IV(a). Trial must commence within 120 days from the defendant's arrival in the receiving jurisdiction (Art. IV(c)) or the charges must be dismissed (Art. V(e)). For good cause shown, the time requirements may be expanded by continuance. Thus, where the Speedy Trial Act and the Interstate Agreement on Detainers both apply, requirements of both must be met. (If the requirements conflict, the more stringent apply.) *U.S. v. Mauro,* 436 U.S. at 356-57 n.23.

### § 1234. — — Sanctions.

Failure to observe the time requirements of the act requires dismissal of the charges. 18 U.S.C. §§ 3162(a)(1) (first interval) and 3162(a)(2) (second interval). Dismissal may be with or without prejudice depending on the court's consideration of the seriousness of the offense, the facts and circumstances leading to dismissal, and the impact of re-prosecution on the administration of the Speedy Trial Act and on the administration of justice. 18 U.S.C. § 3162(a)(1) and (2); *U.S. v. Carreon,* 626 F.2d at 533 (1980). Clearly, charges can be dismissed for failure to meet second interval time requirements only if the defendant meets the burden on a motion to dismiss made before trial commences. 18 U.S.C. § 3162(a)(2). The legislative history suggests that a timely motion by a defendant is also required to trigger a dismissal for violation of first interval time limits.

Before dismissing an indictment with prejudice, the court must consider the three factors set forth in 18 U.S.C. § 3162(a)(1) and (2) and must give weight of the presence or absence of prejudice to the defendant. If the court does not consider each of these factors, dismissal with prejudice is an abuse of discretion. *U.S. v. Taylor,* 487 U.S. 326 (1988). Likewise, a dismissal may not be with prejudice where the governmental misconduct cited for the dismissal "with prejudice" was unrelated to the passing of the speedy trial clock. *U.S. v. Hastings,* 847 F.2d 920 (1st Cir.), *cert. denied,* 488 U.S. 925 (1988).

Sanctions for violations of 18 U.S.C. § 3162(b) by government or defense counsel include fines, reduced compensation, suspension from practice before the court, and referral for disciplinary action. Violations which may cause such sanctions are (1) allowing the case to be set for trial without disclosing the unavailability of a necessary witness; (2) filing a frivolous motion solely for purposes of delay; (3) making a false material statement to obtain a continuance; and (4) otherwise willfully failing to proceed to trial without justification.

## § 1235. — — Waiver.

Section 3162(a)(2) states that failure of a defendant to move for dismissal of charges (for a violation of second interval limits) before trial or entry of a guilty or nolo contendere plea constitutes a waiver of his right to dismissal. *U.S. v. Ballard,* 779 F.2d 287 (5th Cir. 1986); *U.S. v. Tenorio-Angel,* 756 F.2d 1505 (11th Cir. 1985); *U.S. v. Tercero,* 640 F.2d 190, 195 (9th Cir. 1980); *Smith v. U.S.,* 635 F.2d 693, 697 (8th Cir. 1980), *cert. denied,* 450 U.S. 934 (1981). There is no comparable express requirement that a motion to dismiss for violation of the first interval time limits be filed before charges are filed. *See* 18 U.S.C. § 3162(a)(1). The Speedy Trial Act does not provide that a defendant may expressly waive his right to speedy trial protections. Some courts have recognized the validity of such express waivers. *Smith v. U.S.,* 635 F.2d at 697; *U.S. v. McGrath,* 613 F.2d at 366-67; *U.S. v. Didier,* 542 F.2d at 1187. The legislative history indicates, however, that such an express waiver is contrary to legislative intent.

## § 1236. — — High Risk Designees and Detainees.

The trial of any defendant designated as a "high risk" (a term not defined by the act) by a U.S. Attorney must commence within 90 days of the high-risk designation. 18 U.S.C. § 3164(a)(2). Trial of a defendant being held in detention solely because he is awaiting trial (detainee) must commence within 90 days of the beginning of continuous detention. 18 U.S.C. § 3164(a)(2). The periods of delay enumerated in 18 U.S.C. § 3161(h) are excluded in computing this time limitation. 18 U.S.C. § 3164(b). The remedy for failure to commence the trial of a detainee is his release, not dismissal of the case. *Lambert v. U.S.,* 600 F.2d 476, 477 (5th Cir. 1979). If a designee intentionally causes delay, the nonfinancial release conditions may be modified to assure his appearance.

273

### § 1237. — — Dismissal by the Court.

Federal criminal cases in which charges were filed before July 1, 1980, are governed by speedy trial plans developed by the district courts pursuant to Rule 50(b) of the Federal Rules of Criminal Procedure. Rule 48(b) of the Federal Rules of Criminal Procedure authorizes a district court to dismiss charges where there has been unnecessary delay in bringing charges against a defendant who has been arrested or summoned or unnecessary delay in commencing trial. Rule 48(b) provides, "If there is unnecessary delay in presenting the charge to a grand jury or in filing an information against a defendant who has been held to answer to the district court, or if there is unnecessary delay in bringing a defendant to trial, the court may dismiss the indictment, information or complaint." Rule 48(b) applies only to post-arrest delay. *U.S. v. Marion,* 404 U.S. at 319. Rule 48(b) implements the sixth amendment. *U.S. v. Pilla,* 550 F.2d 1085, 1093 (8th Cir.), *cert. denied,* 432 U.S. 907 (1977). A district court may also exercise its inherent power to dismiss a case with prejudice pursuant to Rule 48(b) for want of prosecution, even if no sixth amendment violation is present. *U.S. v. Simmons,* 536 F.2d 827, 833-34 (9th Cir.), *cert. denied,* 429 U.S. 854 (1976); *U.S. v. Novelli,* 544 F.2d at 803. *But see U.S. v. Rucker,* 586 F.2d 899, 907 (2d Cir. 1978) (Rule 48(b) claim is coterminous with sixth amendment claim).

Dismissal under Rule 48(b) is committed to the discretion of the trial court and is reviewable on appeal for abuse. *U.S. v. Barney,* 550 F.2d 1251, 1254-55 (10th Cir. 1977); *U.S. v. Simmons,* 536 F.2d at 837-38. The factors which the Supreme Court in *Barker v. Wingo, supra,* utilized to weigh a claimed constitutional violation also apply to a Rule 48(b) claim. *U.S. v. Hill,* 622 F.2d 900, 908 (5th Cir. 1980); *U.S. v. Crow Dog,* 532 F.2d 1182, 1194 (8th Cir. 1976), *cert. denied,* 430 U.S. 929 (1977).

### § 1238. — — Appeal.

The denial of a speedy trial claim is not appealable before trial, *U.S. v. MacDonald,* 435 U.S. 850, 860 (1978), including a claimed violation of the Speedy Trial Act, *U.S. v. Grabinski,* 674 F.2d 677, 680 (8th Cir.), *cert. denied,* 103 S. Ct. 67 (1982); *U.S. v. Bilsky,* 664 F.2d 613, 617-18 (6th Cir. 1981); *U.S. v. Mehrmanesh,* 652 F.2d 766, 769-70 (7th Cir. 1981). The standards of review are "clearly erroneous" and "not normally reversible error." *U.S. v. Guerrero,* 667 F.2d 862, 865 (10th Cir. 1981).

## § 1239. — Pre-Accusation Delay.

The sixth amendment does not afford protection against unreasonable delay before accusation by arrest, the issuance of a summons, or the filing of charges. *U.S. v. MacDonald,* 102 S. Ct. 1497, 1501 (1982); *U.S. v. Marion,* 404 U.S. at 313. The applicable statute of limitations is the primary guarantee that there will be no undue delay between commission of a crime and accusation. *U.S. v. Ewell,* 383 U.S. 116, 122 (1966). *See also U.S. v. Lovasco,* 431 U.S. 783, 789 (1977); *U.S. v. Marion,* 404 U.S. at 322-24 (1971). Nonetheless, even where accusation occurs within the statutory time limit, delay before arrest or indictment may give rise to a due process claim under the fifth amendment. *U.S. v. MacDonald,* 102 S. Ct. at 1501; *U.S. v. Marion,* 404 U.S. at 324. The burden which the defendant bears in establishing that a due process violation has occurred because of pre-accusation delay is an extremely heavy one. The defendant must prove that he suffered actual and substantial prejudice as a result of the delay *and* that the government intentionally caused the delay to harrass or to gain a tactical advantage. *U.S. v. Marion,* 404 U.S. at 324; *U.S. v. Wehling,* 676 F.2d 1053, 1059 (5th Cir. 1982). A showing of prejudice is a necessary but not a sufficient basis in itself for establishing a due process claim. *U.S. v. Lovasco,* 431 U.S. at 790. The defendant must prove specific prejudice; generalized or speculative allegations that pre-accusation delay caused prejudice will not suffice. *U.S. v. Marion,* 404 U.S. at 325-26; *U.S. v. Comosona,* 614 F.2d 695, 697 (10th Cir. 1980); *U.S. v. Taylor,* 603 F.2d 732, 735 (8th Cir. 1977), *cert. denied,* 444 U.S. 982 (1979); *U.S. v. Blevins,* 593 F.2d 646, 647 (5th Cir. 1979).

Allegations of prejudice based upon the following have been rejected by the courts: (1) loss of or impaired memory, *U.S. v. Marion,* 404 U.S. at 326; *U.S. v. Snyder,* 668 F.2d 686, 689 (2d Cir. 1982); *U.S. v. Kail,* 612 F.2d 443, 446 (9th Cir. 1980), *cert. denied,* 446 U.S. 912 (1980); *U.S. v. Lieberman,* 608 F.2d 889, 903 (1st Cir. 1979), *cert. denied,* 444 U.S. 1019 (1980); *U.S. v. Rippy,* 606 F.2d 1150, 1153 (D.C. Cir. 1979); *U.S. v. Taylor,* 603 F.2d at 735; *U.S. v. Elsbery,* 602 F.2d at 1059; *U.S. v. Blevins,* 593 F.2d at 647 (5th Cir. 1979); *U.S. v. Radmall,* 591 F.2d 548, 550 (10th Cir. 1978); *U.S. v. D'Andrea,* 585 F.2d 1351, 1356 (7th Cir. 1978), *cert. denied,* 440 U.S. 983 (1979); *U.S. v. Alred,* 513 F.2d 330, 332-33 (6th Cir.), *cert. denied,* 423 U.S. 828 (1975); (2) death or unavailability of one or more defense witnesses, *U.S. v. Walker,* 601 F.2d at 1057; *U.S. v. Tempesta,* 587 F.2d 931, 933 (8th Cir. 1978), *cert. denied,* 441 U.S. 910 (1979); *U.S. v. Ramos Algarin,* 584 F.2d 562, 567 (1st Cir. 1978); *U.S. v. Swainson,* 548 F.2d 657, 664 (6th Cir.), *cert. denied,* 431 U.S. 937 (1977); (3) loss or destruction of exculpatory evidence, *U.S. v. Lieberman,* 608 F.2d at 902; *U.S. v. Walker,* 601 F.2d at 1057; *U.S. v. Willis,* 583 F.2d 203, 208 (5th Cir. 1978); (4) disruption of personal life, *U.S. v. Marion,* 404 U.S. at 320; *U.S. v. Rowell,* 612 F.2d 1176, 1181 (7th Cir. 1980); and (5) extended duration of the delay, *U.S. v. Comosona,* 614 F.2d at 697; *U.S. v. Watson,* 599 F.2d 1149, 1152-53 (2d Cir. 1979); *U.S. v. Valenzuela,* 596 F.2d 824, 826 (9th Cir. 1979) *(dictum); U.S. v. Hooper,* 596 F.2d 219, 224 (7th Cir. 1979); *U.S. v. Parker,* 586 F.2d 422, 431 (5th Cir. 1978), *cert. denied,* 441 U.S. 962 (1979).

Good faith delays between the commission of the crime and accusation of the defendant do not violate fifth amendment due process. The following reasons have been upheld by courts of appeals as legitimate and good faith reasons for delay: (1) the need to conduct investigation or to have the case reviewed by superiors, *U.S. v. Watson,* 599 F.2d at 1152-53; *U.S. v. Stinson,* 594 F.2d 982, 984 (4th Cir. 1979); *U.S. v. Radmall,* 591 F.2d at 550; *U.S. v. Robertson,* 588 F.2d 575, 577 (8th Cir. 1978), *cert. denied,* 441 U.S. 946 (1979); *U.S. v. Tempesta,* 587 F.2d at 934; *U.S. v. Parker,* 586 F.2d at 431-32; *U.S. v. Ramos Algarin,* 584 F.2d at 567-68; *U.S. v. Kopel,* 552 F.2d 1265, 1276 (7th Cir. 1977); *U.S. v. Ricco,* 549 F.2d 264, 272 (2d Cir.), *cert. denied,* 431 U.S. 905 (1977); (2) government's desire not to expose a larger investigation, *U.S. v. Rippy,* 606 F.2d at 1152 n.7; *U.S. v. Van Cleave,* 599 F.2d 954, 956 (10th Cir. 1979); (3) delays which are primarily the responsibility of the defendant himself, *U.S. v. Rowell,* 612 F.2d at 1181; *U.S. v. Nix,* 601 F.2d 214, 215 (5th Cir.), *cert. denied,* 444 U.S. 937 (1979); *U.S. v. Jones,* 543 F.2d 1171, 1174 (5th Cir. 1976), *cert. denied,* 430 U.S. 957 (1977); *U.S. v. Pollack,* 534 F.2d at 970; *U.S. v. Jones,* 524 F.2d at 843; (4) government desire to avoid wrongful indictment or evaluate strength of case, *U.S. v. Comosona,* 614 F.2d at 697; *U.S. v. Walker,* 601 F.2d at 1057; (5) desire or need to strengthen the case against a particular suspect, *U.S. v. Watson,* 599 F.2d at 1152-53; *U.S. v. Stinson,* 594 F.2d 982, 984 (4th Cir. 1979); *U.S. v. Radmall,* 591 F.2d at 550; *U.S. v. Robertson,* 588 F.2d at 577; *U.S. v. Tempesta,* 587 F.2d at 934; *U.S. v. Parker,* 586 F.2d at 431-32; *U.S. v. Ramos Algarin,* 584 F.2d at 567-68; *U.S. v. Kopel,* 552 F.2d at 1276; *U.S. v. Ricco,* 549 F.2d at 272; *U.S. v. Jones,* 543 F.2d at 1174; *U.S. v. Marion,* 404 U.S. at 325 n.18 (quoting *Hoffa v. U.S.,* 385 U.S. 293, 310 (1966)); *U.S. v. Butts,* 524 F.2d 975, 977 (5th Cir. 1975); (6) review by superiors, *U.S. v. Tempesta,* 587 F.2d at 934; (7) personnel shortages, *U.S. v. Ramos Algarin,* 584 F.2d at 567; *U.S. v. D'Andrea,* 585 F.2d at 1357; (8) fear that the suspect will flee, *U.S. v. Ramos,* 586 F.2d at 1079; (9) the greater urgency to proceed with other cases, *U.S. v. Radmall,* 591 F.2d at 550; and (10) delay to permit restitution to be made, *Jordan v. Beto,* 471 F.2d 779, 781 (5th Cir. 1973).

### § 1240. The Right to Trial by Jury.

The right to trial by jury in criminal prosecutions is specifically recognized and guaranteed in two places in the Constitution. Article III, section 2, clause 3 provides that "[t]he trial of all Crimes, except in Cases of Impeachment, shall be by Jury...." The sixth amendment provides that "in all criminal prosecutions, the accused shall enjoy the right to a speedy and public trial, by an impartial jury of the State and district wherein the crime shall have been committed...." Rule 23 of the Federal Rules of Criminal Procedure provides substance and limitations to the application of these constitutional protections in federal criminal prosecutions. A corporation has the same rights as an individual to a trial by jury. *U.S. v. Troxler Hosiery Co.,* 681 F.2d 934 (4th Cir. 1982).

Further, the Supreme Court has determined that the sixth amendment right to a jury trial is fundamental to the American scheme of justice and hence applicable to the states through the fourteenth amendment. *Duncan v. Louisiana,* 391 U.S. 145, 149 (1968). While noting that this right offers protection from oppressive governmental action and prosecutorial misconduct, the Court recognized and preserved the common law distinction between serious and petty offenses by exempting the latter from the constitutional dictates of a jury trial. *Id.* at 156-58.

The definitional task of separating petty from serious offenses requires judicial reference to objective criteria by which to measure degrees of criminality. The criteria normally considered are the former availability of a jury trial at common law, *District of Columbia v. Clawans,* 300 U.S. 617, 625 (1937), the nature of the offense, *District of Columbia v. Colts,* 282 U.S. 63, 73 (1930); *U.S. v. Sanchez-Meza,* 547 F.2d 461 (9th Cir. 1976), and most importantly, the severity of the maximum authorized penalty, *Baldwin v. New York,* 399 U.S. 66 (1970); *Duncan v. Louisiana,* 391 U.S. at 159. The Court ruled in *Baldwin* that, for purposes of the right to trial by jury, no offense can be deemed petty if the defendant could be imprisoned for more than six months. 399 U.S. at 69. Such a ruling accords with the legislative prescription of a petty offense articulated in 18 U.S.C. § 1(3) that any misdemeanor, the penalty for which does not exceed imprisonment for a period of six months or a fine of $500, or both, is a petty offense.

The presumption is that society views an offense as petty if the maximum authorized period of incarceration is six months or less.

However, "penalty" does not refer solely to the maximum prison term authorized, but may include other penalties to show the legislature's view of the seriousness of the offense. The additional penalties of a $1000 fine and 48 hours of community service with the offender dressed in clothing identifying him as a DUI offender was held insufficient to entitle the defendant to a jury trial for a "serious" offense. *Blanton v. City of North Las Vegas, Nev.,* 489 U.S. 538 (1989).

The fact that the defendant may be eligible to be sentenced under the Youth Corrections Act does not convert a petty offense into a crime requiring a jury trial. Sentencing under the act is distinguishable from an ordinary prison sentence in that the aim is to rehabilitate, not punish, and in any event, the court could not sentence the defendant to a longer term under the Youth Corrections Act than could be normally imposed on an adult for a violation of the charge. *U.S. v. Hunt,* 661 F.2d 72 (6th Cir. 1981).

When the legislature has not expressed a judgment on the seriousness of an offense by fixing a maximum penalty, the court must then look to the penalty actually imposed. *Cheff v. Schnackenberg,* 384 U.S. 373 (1966). This rule has been applied most notably in criminal contempt cases for which no maximum penalty had been authorized. *See Codispoti v. Pennsylvania,* 418 U.S. 506, 511 (1974) (where ruled upon after trial, multiple contempt convictions to be served consecutively and totaling more than six months required jury trial); *Taylor v. Hayes,* 418 U.S. 488, 495 (1974) (multiple contempt citations of six months to be served concurrently did not require jury trial); *Frank v. U.S.,* 395 U.S. 147, 148-49 (1969) (in criminal contempt proceedings where no maximum penalty is authorized, the penalty actually imposed is best indication of the seriousness of an offense).

## § 1241. — Size of Jury.

Although juries historically have been comprised of 12 members, that number is not constitutionally mandated. *Williams v. Florida,* 399 U.S. 78, 89 (1970) (the number 12 is "historical accident"). The ruling in *Williams* was somewhat refined in 1978, however, when the Supreme Court held that a jury of only five members does not comport with the constitutional guarantee of a jury trial. *Ballew v. Georgia,* 435 U.S. 223, 239 (1978) (jury of five raises substantial doubts about the reliability and representative nature of a jury trial). Rule 23(b) of the Federal Rules of Criminal Procedure preserves the 12-member jury in federal prosecutions unless the parties stipulate otherwise with court approval or absent such a stipulation, if after the jury has retired to consider its verdict the court finds it necessary to excuse a juror for just cause, a verdict may be returned by the remaining 11 jurors. "Just cause" includes juror absence due to religious observance. *U.S. v. Stratton,* 779 F.2d 820 (2d Cir. 1985).

If, after deliberations begin, a juror is excused, the jury of 11 members is to proceed to deliberate and an alternate juror may not be substituted for the missing juror. Rule 24(c), Fed. R. Crim. P.; *U.S. v. Gambino,* 788 F.2d 938 (3d Cir. 1986).

### § 1242. — Unanimous Jury Verdict.

The Constitution does not require a unanimous jury verdict, *Apodaca v. Oregon,* 406 U.S. 404 (1972); *Johnson v. Louisiana,* 406 U.S. 356 (1972), except at some point with juries of reduced size, *Burch v. Louisiana,* 441 U.S. 130 (1979). The Court in *Burch* concluded that a conviction for a serious offense by five out of six jurors sufficiently threatens the fairness of the proceedings and the proper role of the jury so as to violate the sixth amendment right to trial by jury. 441 U.S. at 138. *See also Schad v. Arizona,* 111 S. Ct. 2491 n.5 (1991).

In federal court a verdict by a unanimous jury is mandated by Rule 31(a) of the Federal Rules of Criminal Procedure. Historically, the right to a unanimous verdict in a federal criminal trial has been considered an essential element of constitutional due process and one of the few rights a criminal defendant cannot waive under any circumstances. *Andres v. U.S.,* 333 U.S. 740 (1948); *Hibdon v. U.S.,* 204 F.2d 834 (6th Cir. 1953). Although the *Apodaca* decision casts doubt on the constitutional basis for the right, federal courts continue to hold that under the rules the right to a unanimous verdict in federal criminal trials is absolute and is not subject to waiver by any party. *U.S. v. Pachay,* 711 F.2d 488 (2d Cir. 1983); *U.S. v. Lopez,* 581 F.2d 1338 (9th Cir. 1978); *U.S. v. Scalzitti,* 578 F.2d 507 (3d Cir. 1978); *Sincox v. U.S.,* 571 F.2d 876 (5th Cir. 1978). Even with Rule 23(b) permitting an 11-member jury, a jury of 12 which deliberates until it reaches an 11-1 vote does not reach a unanimous verdict by excusing the dissenting juror. *U.S. v. Smedes,* 760 F.2d 109 (6th Cir. 1985).

### § 1243. — Waiver of Jury Trial.

Even though the right to trial by jury is fundamental, it nevertheless may be waived by the express and intelligent consent of the defendant. *Duncan v. Louisiana,* 391 U.S. at 158; *Singer v. U.S.,* 380 U.S. 24, 34 (1965); *Patton v. U.S.,* 281 U.S. 276, 312 (1930); *U.S. v. Helgesen,* 669 F.2d 69, 72-73 (2d Cir.), *cert. denied,* 102 S. Ct. 1978 (1982). In federal court, however, such a waiver is not automatically effective. Under

Rule 23(a) of the Federal Rules of Criminal Procedure, waiver of a jury trial must be made in writing, with the consent of the government and approval of the trial court. When such approval is withheld, only an abuse of discretion will constitute prejudical error and cause for reversal. *U.S. v. Wright,* 491 F.2d 942 (6th Cir.), *cert. denied,* 419 U.S. 862 (1974).

Failure to comply with the writing requirement for waiver of jury trial under Rule 23(a) is reversible error. However, some courts have permitted the defendant's express and intelligent oral waiver if it was part of the record. *U.S. v. Davidson,* 477 F.2d 136 (6th Cir. 1973); *U.S. v. McCurdy,* 450 F.2d 282 (9th Cir. 1971). Failure to comply with the writing requirement of Rule 23(b) for stipulating to a jury of less than 12 has been held to be a procedural error that, under the harmless error rule, does not require reversal of a conviction. *See U.S. v. Roby,* 592 F.2d 406, 408 (8th Cir.), *cert. denied,* 442 U.S. 944 (1979).

Neither the sixth amendment nor the Federal Rules of Criminal Procedure require a federal judge to interrogate a defendant about his waiver of a jury trial. Nevertheless, the Seventh Circuit resorted to its supervisory powers to impose such a requirement, *U.S. v. Scott,* 583 F.2d 362, 363 (7th Cir. 1978), and the Fourth Circuit has endorsed the practice to ensure that a waiver is voluntarily and intelligently given, *Wyatt v. U.S.,* 591 F.2d 260, 264-65 (4th Cir. 1979). *See also U.S. ex rel. Gentry v. Circuit Court, Etc.,* 586 F.2d 1142, 1146 (7th Cir. 1978) (absent supervisory power over state court proceedings, the interrogation rule does not apply).

## § 1244. Jury Selection and Control.

Each United States district court is responsible for devising and putting into operation a written plan for random selection of grand and petit juries. Jury Selection and Service Act of 1968, 28 U.S.C. §§ 1861-1871. Prospective jurors are selected from voter registration lists, lists of actual voters within the district, or from other appropriate sources. 28 U.S.C. § 1863(a). To qualify for jury service in a federal court, a person must be an adult citizen of the United States who is mentally, physically, and legally capable of rendering satisfactory service. 28 U.S.C. § 1865(a) and (b). The act provides that no citizen shall be excluded from jury service on the basis of race, color, religion, sex, national origin, or economic status. 28 U.S.C. § 1862.

A district judge may not delegate jury selection to a magistrate without the defendant's consent. *Peretz v. U.S.,* 111 S. Ct. 2661 (1991); *Gomez v. U.S.,* 490 U.S. 858 (1989).

## § 1245. — Challenge of Array.

The Jury Selection Act requires that juries be drawn from "a fair cross section of the community." 28 U.S.C. § 1861. A jury selection system may not systematically exclude any distinctive groups present in the community. *Taylor v. Louisiana,* 419 U.S. 522 (1975). However, juries actually chosen need not mirror the community. *Id.* at 538. *See U.S. v. Werbrouck,* 589 F.2d 273, 276 (7th Cir. 1978), *cert. denied,* 440 U.S. 962 (1979); *U.S. v. D'Alora,* 585 F.2d 16, 22 (1st Cir. 1978).

Under the sixth amendment a defendant has standing to object to the exclusion of a distinctive group from jury selection even if the defendant is not a member of that group and cannot demonstrate any actual prejudice resulting from the exclusion. *Holland v. Illinois,* 494 U.S. 1050 (1990); *Duren v. Missouri,* 439 U.S. 357, 359 n.1 (1979); *Taylor v. Louisiana,* 419 U.S. at 526; *Peters v. Kiff,* 407 U.S. 493, 504 (1972). To establish a prima facie violation, the defendant must show that a "distinctive" community group is not fairly represented and that this under representation is due to systematic exclusion of the group by the jury selection process. *Duren v. Missouri,* 439 U.S. at 364. Persons between the ages of 18 and 21 are not a cognizable group or class for purposes of the jury venire. *Davis v. Greer,* 675 F.2d 141, 146 (7th Cir.), *cert. denied,* 459 U.S. 975 (1982).

Composition of the jury may also be challenged on fourteenth amendment equal protection grounds, by either the defense or the prosecution, when the prospective jurors are selected in an intentionally discriminatory fashion. *Georgia v. McCollum,* 112 S. Ct. 2348 (1992); *Hernandez v. New York,* 111 S. Ct. 1859 (1991); *Batson v. Kentucky,* 476 U.S. 79 (1986); *Castaneda v. Partida,* 430 U.S. 482, 492 (1977). If a defendant can demonstrate substantial underrepresentation of the class to which he belongs, he has made out a prima facia case of discriminatory purpose. The disparity of representation must be "sufficiently large [that] it is unlikely ... [the disparity] is due solely to chance or accident." *Id.* at 494 n.13, 494-95, 497-98; *Rose v. Mitchell,* 443 U.S. 545 (1979); *U.S. ex rel. Barksdale v. Blackburn,* 610 F.2d 253 (5th Cir. 1980), *cert. denied,* 454 U.S. 1056 (1981) (20 per cent disparity held sufficient to establish prima facie case); *U.S. v. Maskeny,* 609 F.2d 183 (5th Cir.), *cert. denied,* 447 U.S. 921 (1980) (absolute disparity of 10 per cent held insufficient).

If either side makes a prima facie showing of discriminatory intent, the burden then shifts to the other side to prove that neutral, nondiscriminatory procedures produced the disparate result or that the discrimination is justified by a sufficiently important governmental interest. *Rose v. Mitchell,* 443 U.S. at 565; *Duren v. Missouri,* 439 U.S. at

368; *Castaneda v. Partida,* 430 U.S. at 495. In *Reed v. Wainwright,* 587 F.2d 260 (5th Cir. 1979), the court upheld a jury selection statute that imposed durational residency and voter registration requirements and declined to apply the "compelling state interest" test, finding these requirements did have some "rational basis" and were thus justified. *See also* § 1248 *infra.*

The Jury Selection and Service Act provides the exclusive means of challenging the selection and composition of a grand or petit jury. Rule 6(b)(1) and (2), Fed. R. Crim. P.; *U.S. v. D'Alora,* 585 F.2d at 22. Compliance with the act's procedures for challenging jury composition is strictly enforced. *U.S. v. Young,* 570 F.2d 152 (6th Cir. 1978). The procedure for a challenge of the petit jury is a motion for stay of proceedings. 28 U.S.C. § 1867; *U.S. v. Raineri,* 670 F.2d 702, 706-07 (7th Cir.), *cert. denied,* 459 U.S. 1035 (1982). Failure to make timely objections in criminal cases, before the voir dire examination begins or within seven days after the defendant discovers or could have discovered noncompliance with the act, may be fatal. 28 U.S.C. § 1867(a). *See U.S. v. Foxworth,* 599 F.2d 1 (1st Cir. 1979); *U.S. v. Tarnowski,* 583 F.2d 903 (6th Cir. 1978), *cert. denied,* 440 U.S. 918 (1979); *U.S. v. Hawkins,* 566 F.2d 1006 (5th Cir.), *cert. denied,* 439 U.S. 848 (1978); *U.S. v. Rickus,* 351 F. Supp. 1386 (E.D. Pa. 1972), *aff'd mem.,* 480 F.2d 919 (3d Cir.), *cert. denied,* 414 U.S. 1006 (1973); *U.S. v. Noah,* 475 F.2d 688 (9th Cir.), *cert. denied,* 414 U.S. 821 (1973); *U.S. v. Silverman,* 449 F.2d 1341 (2d Cir. 1971), *cert. denied,* 405 U.S. 918 (1972). *But cf. U.S. v. Santos,* 588 F.2d 1300, 1303 (9th Cir.) *(per curiam), cert. denied,* 441 U.S. 906 (1979), in which the court found no error where the defendant filed his motion 25 days after the records were released to him.

To challenge jury selection, the act provides that a defendant has the right to inspect the records of the jury selection process. 28 U.S.C. § 1867(f). Denial of a motion to inspect such records constitutes reversible error. *Test v. U.S.,* 420 U.S. 28 (1975); *Canal Zone v. Davis,* 592 F.2d 887 (5th Cir. 1979). *See also U.S. v. Lawson,* 670 F.2d 923, 926 (10th Cir. 1982).

## § 1246. — Voir Dire.

Both the prosecution and the defense are entitled to a fair and impartial jury. Voir dire examination of prospective jurors permits counsel to make informed use of peremptory challenges and challenges for cause to strike those jurors who reveal bias or prejudice. The right to challenge jurors is meaningless unless it is accompanied by the right to ask relevant questions on voir dire. *Ham v. South Carolina,* 409 U.S. 524, 532-33 (1973) (Marshall, J., concurring and dissenting). The essential function of voir dire is to allow impanelling of a fair and impartial jury through questions that permit intelligent exercise of challenges by counsel. *U.S. v. Barnes,* 604 F.2d 121, 142 (2d Cir. 1979), *cert. denied,* 446 U.S. 907 (1980); *U.S. v. Moss,* 591 F.2d 428, 438 (8th Cir. 1979); *U.S. v. Johnson,* 584 F.2d 148, 155 (6th Cir. 1978), *cert. denied,* 440 U.S. 918 (1979); *U.S. v. Mutchler,* 559 F.2d 955, 958-59 (5th Cir. 1977); *U.S. v. Rucker,* 557 F.2d 1046, 1048-49 (4th Cir. 1977). The purpose of challenges is to assure parties that jurors will decide the case on the evidence before them. *Swain v. Alabama,* 380 U.S. 202, 219-21 (1965).

The trial court has broad discretion to control the scope and manner of voir dire examination, but "the exercise of that discretion is limited by 'the essential demands of fairness.'" *U.S. v. Rucker,* 557 F.2d at 1049 (quoting *Aldridge v. U.S.,* 238 U.S. 308, 310 (1931)); *U.S. v. Duncan,* 598 F.2d 839 (4th Cir.), *cert. denied,* 444 U.S. 871 (1979); *U.S. v. Giese,* 597 F.2d 1170, 1182-83 (9th Cir.), *cert. denied,* 444 U.S. 979 (1979); *U.S. v. Dixon,* 596 F.2d 178, 182 (7th Cir. 1979) (appellate court must rely on judgment of trial court regarding nature and extent of voir dire required); *U.S. v. Corbin,* 590 F.2d 398, 400 (1st Cir. 1979); *U.S. v. Conroy,* 589 F.2d 1258, 1275 (5th Cir.) (Rubin, J., dissenting), *cert. denied,* 444 U.S. 831 (1979); *U.S. v. Clabaugh,* 589 F.2d 1019, 1023 (9th Cir. 1979); *U.S. v. Hall,* 588 F.2d 613, 615 (8th Cir. 1978); *U.S. v. Johnson,* 584 F.2d 148, 155 (6th Cir. 1978), *cert. denied,* 440 U.S. 918 (1979); *U.S. v. Price,* 573 F.2d 356, 363-65 (5th Cir. 1978) (trial court abused discretion in failing to conduct supplemental voir dire after six-week delay between jury selection and trial); *U.S. v. Haldeman,* 559 F.2d 31 (D.C. Cir. 1976), *cert. denied,* 431 U.S. 933 (1977). The court must ask questions about racial prejudice only where "special circumstances" indicate that the defendant's race may be a factor in the trial. *Rosales-Lopez v. U.S.,* 451 U.S. 182, 191 (1981); *Ristaino v. Ross,* 424 U.S. 589 (1976).

The trial court may conduct voir dire itself, *U.S. v. L'Hoste,* 609 F.2d 796, 801-03 (5th Cir.), *cert. denied,* 449 U.S. 833 (1980); *U.S. v. Conroy,* 589 F.2d at 1271, or in its sound discretion may permit counsel to conduct part or all of the voir dire, *U.S. v. Long Elk,* 565 F.2d 1032, 1041-42 (8th Cir. 1977). *See generally* Rule 24(a), Fed. R. Crim. P. A magistrate may not conduct the jury selection unless the defendant consents. *Peretz v. U.S.,* 111 S. Ct. 2661 (1991); *Gomez v. U.S.,* 490 U. S. 858 (1989).

The trial court may refuse to ask voir dire questions in the precise form required by counsel, and may reject questions or areas of inquiry if they are not reasonably calculated to elicit bias or prejudice by jurors. *Mu'min v. Virginia,* 111 S. Ct. 1899 (1991); *U.S. v. Bosby,* 675

F.2d 1174, 1184 (11th Cir. 1982); *U.S. v. Rosales-Lopez,* 617 F.2d 1349, 1353-54 (9th Cir. 1980); *U.S. v. Dixon,* 596 F.2d at 181-82 (when inquiry into possible racial prejudice adequate, it was held that no particular pattern of inquiry required and no error in refusing to ask additional questions requested by defense counsel); *U.S. v. Conroy,* 589 F.2d at 1271 (when voir dire fair and adequate to disclose prejudice, held no abuse of discretion in refusing to ask precise questions requested by defendant); *U.S. v. Clabaugh,* 589 F.2d at 1023 (decision whether to ask certain questions held committed to trial court's discretion; decision to limit questions held not abuse of discretion in absence of substantial possibility of bias); *U.S. v. Caggiano,* 667 F.2d 1176, 1178 (5th Cir. 1982) (coupled with court's cautionary instructions, it was not error for the court to refuse to ask jury panel if it would attach greater credibility to the testimony of employees of the FBI). The trial court may also question jurors as a group rather than individually. *Mu'min v. Virginia, supra; U.S. v. Dixon,* 596 F.2d at 182; *U.S. v. Carroll,* 582 F.2d 942, 947 (5th Cir. 1978).

A defendant accused of an interracial capital crime is entitled to have prospective jurors informed of the victim's race and questioned on the issue of racial bias so long as the defendant has specifically requested such an inquiry. *Turner v. Murray,* 476 U.S. 28 (1986).

A defendant has the right to be present during the voir dire, Rule 43(a), Fed. R. Crim. P.; but voluntary absence from trial can amount to waiver of this right, *U.S. v. Pastor,* 557 F.2d 930, 933-34 (2d Cir. 1977).

Objections to the nature or extent of voir dire must be made before commencement of testimony at trial or such objections are considered to be waived. *U.S. v. Moss,* 591 F.2d at 437-38 (where defense counsel waited until three weeks after trial to inform court that juror had answered voir dire question falsely, held no abuse of discretion in denying motion for new trial); *U.S. v. Conzemius,* 586 F.2d 97, 100 n.6 (8th Cir. 1978), *cert. denied,* 440 U.S. 971 (1979) (counsel's acquiescence in voir dire waived objection).

Jurors have an obligation during voir dire to answer honestly all questions regarding qualifications. *U.S. v. Moss,* 591 F.2d at 438. A defendant is not necessarily entitled to a new trial, however, if a juror's false answer is inadvertent. *Id.* at 437-38; *Taylor v. Mabry,* 593 F.2d 318, 320 (8th Cir. 1979).

The jury voir dire is presumptively open to the press and public, but legitimate privacy interests may be protected by limited closure. *Press-Enterprise Co. v. Superior Court of California,* 464 U.S. 501 (1984).

## § 1247. — Challenges for Cause.

Jurors may be excused for cause for failure to meet statutory requirements, 28 U.S.C. § 1865, for bias, or for other reasons such as undue hardship or threat to the secrecy of the proceedings, 28 U.S.C. § 1866(c)(1) and (5). The trial court has broad discretion in determining whether to dismiss a juror for cause and will be reversed only if the defendant shows a clear abuse of discretion. *U.S. v. Giacalone,* 588 F.2d 1158, 1162-63 (6th Cir. 1978), *cert. denied,* 441 U.S. 944 (1979) (no abuse of discretion found in refusing to strike for cause prospective jurors who associated defendant's name with illegal or improper activities, but who stated, under careful questioning by court, that they could put aside prior opinions); *U.S. v. Gullion,* 575 F.2d 26, 29 (1st Cir. 1978) (no abuse of discretion shown in trial court's denial of challenge for cause based on juror's knowledge of defendant's name from pretrial publicity); *U.S. v. Garza,* 574 F.2d 298, 303 (5th Cir. 1978) (no abuse of discretion found in denying challenges for cause based on prior jury service, when no clear bias or prejudice shown); *Virgin Islands v. Felix,* 569 F.2d 1274 (3d Cir. 1978) (no abuse of discretion found in refusing to ask jurors whether they had come from a geographic area other than defendant's, even though defendant argued such information was necessary to challenge for cause); *U.S. v. Mitchell,* 556 F.2d 371, 379 (6th Cir.), *cert. denied,* 434 U.S. 925 (1977) (trial court's refusal to excuse former member of police department who knew prospective witness held not abuse of discretion warranting reversal).

A juror in a capital case may not be excused for cause because of conscientious scruples against capital punishment if that juror states that he can render an impartial verdict. *Witherspoon v. Illinois,* 391 U.S. 510 (1968). In *Adams v. Texas,* 448 U.S. 38 (1980), the Supreme Court held that a prospective juror may not be excused merely because he could not swear, as required by state law, that the nature of the death penalty would not "affect" his deliberations on factual issues. A juror may, however, be removed for cause if his opposition to the death penalty is so strong that it would substantially impair the performance of his duties at the sentencing phase of a bifurcated trial. *Lockhart v. McCree,* 106 S. Ct. 1758 (1986).

The court may excuse a juror *sua sponte. U.S. v. Richardson,* 582 F.2d 968, 969 (5th Cir. 1978) *(per curiam)* (court acted properly in excusing on its own motion juror who admitted lack of belief in reasonable doubt as philosophical matter); *U.S. v. Redmond,* 546 F.2d 1386, 1389 (10th Cir. 1977), *cert. denied,* 435 U.S. 995 (1978) (in prosecution for using mails in fraudulent sale of securities held no error where court excused prospective jurors with certain stockholdings). Challenges for cause are waived if not made during voir dire, unless it is clear that there has been a manifest injustice. *U.S. v. Cepeda Penes,* 577 F.2d 754, 759 (1st Cir. 1978).

## § 1248. — Peremptory Challenges.

In contrast to challenges for cause, peremptory challenges may be used without explanation or justification to exclude otherwise qualified jurors. *Swain v. Alabama,* 380 U.S. 202, 220-22 (1965), except that either side may be required to justify racially suspect peremptory challenges. *Georgia v. McCollum,* 112 S. Ct. 2348 (1992); *Batson v. Kentucky,* 476 U.S. 79 (1986).

Pursuant to Rule 24(b) of the Federal Rules of Criminal Procedure, the prosecution and the defense are each entitled to 20 peremptory challenges in a capital case and three in a misdemeanor prosecution. In felony cases the defendant is entitled to 10 peremptory challenges and the prosecution is entitled to six. In multiple-defendant trials, the court may grant additional peremptory challenges to the defense and permit those challenges to be exercised separately or jointly. Rule 24(b), Fed. R. Crim. P. If alternate jurors are to be impanelled, each side is entitled to additional peremptory challenges, which may be exercised only against alternate jurors. Rule 24(c), Fed. R. Crim. P.

The trial court has broad discretion to control the manner in which peremptory challenges are used. *U.S. v. Durham,* 587 F.2d 799, 801 (5th Cir. 1979); *U.S. v. Anderson,* 562 F.2d 394, 396 (6th Cir. 1977). The court may require that the government and defense exercise their peremptory challenges simultaneously, *U.S. v. Roe,* 670 F.2d 956, 961 (11th Cir.), *cert. denied,* 459 U.S. 856 (1992), by rounds on an alternating basis without selection of replacements until completion of a round, *U.S. v. Blouin,* 666 F.2d 796 (2d Cir. 1981), or a challenge-and-tender system whereby one side challenges the panel and tenders it back to the other side until both sides had used all of their peremptories or are satisfied with the jury, *U.S. v. Bryant,* 671 F.2d 450, 455 (11th Cir. 1982).

Peremptory challenges are not of constitutional dimension, but only a means to achieve an impartial jury. *Georgia v. McCollum, supra*; *Holland v. Illinois,* 494 U.S. 1050 (1990); *Ross v. Oklahoma,* 108 S. Ct. 2273 (1988).

The sixth amendment's requirement of a fair cross section on the venire is not meant to assure a representative jury, but an impartial jury. Thus, "once a fair hand is dealt," the sixth amendment's requirements of a fair cross section does not extend from the venire stage to the individual petit jury and the sixth amendment does not prohibit the racially motivated use of peremptory challenges. *Holland v. Illinois, supra.*

However, under the equal protection clause of the fourteenth amendment, neither the prosecution nor the defense may use peremptory challenges systematically to exclude minority groups from petit jury service. *Georgia v. McCollum, supra; Swain v. Alabama,* 380 U.S. at 220-22. To prove an improper use of challenges, the defendant need no longer demonstrate a continuing and systematic exclusion of minority groups as held in *Swain v. Alabama, supra.* There is a three-step process for evaluating an objection to peremptory challenges. First, either side must make a prima facie showing of racial discrimination by relying solely on the jury selection process in his case. Second, once either side makes this prima facie showing, the burden shifts to the other side to come forward with a race-neutral explanation for striking the jurors in question. Third, the court must determine whether the side claiming racially discriminatory peremptory challenges has carried its burden of proving purposeful discrimination. *Hernandez v. New York,* 111 S. Ct. 1859 (1991); *Batson v. Kentucky, supra.* A defendant not of the same race as an excluded juror may likewise object to race-based exclusions of jurors effected through peremptory challenges. *Powers v. Ohio,* 494 U.S. 1054 (1991).

The equal protection clause also has been held to prohibit striking venire persons on the basis of gender. *U.S. v. DeGross,* 960 F.2d 1433 (9th Cir. 1992).

## § 1249. — Contamination by Trial Participants.

The defense and prosecution are entitled to an impartial jury free from extrajudicial influence and contact. Any private communication or contact with a juror during a trial about a pending matter is deemed presumptively prejudicial. The presumption is not conclusive, but the government has a heavy burden to establish that such contact was harmless. *Remmer v. U.S.,* 347 U.S. 227, 229 (1954). Due process does not require a new trial every time a juror is placed in a potentially compromising situation. Due process means a jury capable and willing to decide the case on the merits. If there are improper contacts, the effect of such contact can be determined by a hearing as occurred in *Remmer v. U.S., supra. See Smith v. Phillips,* 455 U.S. 209, 219 (1982) (during the trial a juror applied for employment as an investigator in the District Attorney's office). Where a juror appeared to be involved in a bribery attempt, the defendant was entitled to determine whether the jury was prejudiced. *U.S. v. Moten,* 582 F.2d 654, 660 (2d Cir. 1978). *See also U.S. v. Shapiro,* 669 F.2d 593, 599 (9th Cir. 1982), where the court held that the government did not sustain its burden of showing that juror who attempted to extort money from a defendant did not influence other jurors.

Unauthorized communication or contact among jurors or between jurors and trial participants may result in mistrial or reversal, unless such contact is both incidental and not prejudicial. *U.S. v. Almonte,* 594 F.2d 261, 265-66 (1st Cir. 1979) (juror excused after incidental contact with prosecution witness, but court's refusal to excuse foreman who advised court of contact held not reversible error); *U.S. v. Fleming,* 594 F.2d 598 (7th Cir.), *cert. denied,* 442 U.S. 931 (1979) (no abuse of discretion found in denying mistrial where each juror questioned about ex parte contact with two other jurors stated that he was not prejudiced and could render impartial verdict); *U.S. v. Mitchell,* 590 F.2d 816, 817 (6th Cir. 1979) (held unnecessary to excuse juror to whom defendant spoke in elevator, where juror claimed ability to decide case impartially); *U.S. v. Holleman,* 575 F.2d 139, 144 (7th Cir. 1978) (held not error to deny mistrial after two jurors were dismissed because they received anonymous telephone calls concerning trial, where remaining jurors not involved); *U.S. v. Boscia,* 573 F.2d 827, 830-32 (3d Cir.), *cert. denied,* 436 U.S. 911 (1978) (denial of mistrial upheld where several jurors knew of telephone call to dismissed juror, but only one knew that call came from defense investigator); *U.S. v. Wright,* 564 F.2d 785, 789 (8th Cir. 1977) (denial of mistrial upheld despite possibility of jurors seeing defendant handcuffed and in custody, where defense declined to question jury on the matter, court gave cautionary instruction, and no prejudice was shown); *U.S. v. Walker,* 557 F.2d 741, 743-44 (10th Cir. 1977) (mistrial held proper where aura of intimidation established by government witness' repeated refusals to testify because of threats by defendant's associates and accosting of witness in open court).

Unless the defendant demonstrates prejudice, contact between court and jurors out of presence of the defendant is generally held to be harmless despite defendant's right, pursuant to Rule 43 of the Federal Rules of Criminal Procedure, to be present at all phases of trial. *Rushen v. Spain,* 464 U.S. 114 (1983); *Rogers v. U.S.,* 422 U.S. 35, 38 (1975); *U.S. v. Hood,* 593 F.2d 293 (8th Cir. 1979) (absent clear indication of prejudice held no error in court's responding to jury's inquiry, without prior consultation with defense); *U.S. v. Giacalone,* 588 F.2d 1158, 1164-65 (6th Cir. 1978), *cert. denied,* 441 U.S. 944 (1979) (error held harmless where trial court instructed jury in absence of defendant to continue deliberations); *U.S. v. Breedlove,* 576 F.2d 57, 60 (5th Cir. 1978) (*per curiam*) (no prejudice shown where court responded in writing to jury inquiry by stating applicable law). *But see U.S. v. U.S.*

*Gypsum Co.,* 438 U.S. 422, 462 (1978), where, despite counsel's acquiescence in ex parte meeting between court and jury foreman regarding a report on the prospect for a verdict, the discussion developed into supplemental instruction to reach verdict. The Supreme Court, in an alternative holding, found such conduct constituted reversible error.

If a defendant knows that a conference is taking place between the judge and a juror and he fails to invoke his right to be present under Rule 43, he waives his right to be present. *U.S. v. Gagnon,* 470 U.S. 522 (1985).

## § 1250. — Materials in Jury Room.

A jury may consider only evidence established in open court that has been subjected to the adversary process. *Patterson v. Colorado,* 205 U.S. 454, 464 (1907). However, where the jury receives or considers extrinsic materials there will be no reversal unless the defendant demonstrates prejudice. *Llewellyn v. Stynchcombe,* 609 F.2d 194 (5th Cir. 1980) (no reasonable possibility of prejudice found where jury had written jury charges and witness list in jury room); *U.S. v. Brighton Building & Maintenance Co.,* 598 F.2d 1101, 1107-08 (7th Cir.), *cert. denied,* 444 U.S. 840 (1979) (no abuse of discretion found in sending copy of instructions into jury room); *U.S. v. Perez,* 648 F.2d 219, 222 (5th Cir.), *cert. denied,* 102 S. Ct. 516 (1981) (court disapproves the submission of written jury instructions, but reversal not required); *U.S. v. Watson,* 669 F.2d 1374, 1385-86 (11th Cir. 1982) (providing the jury with a taped copy of the instructions was not reversible error); *U.S. v. Vasquez,* 597 F.2d 192 (9th Cir. 1979) (reversal required where official file left in jury room contained motions and instructions that had been denied, as well as certain inadmissible evidence regarding previous prosecutions of defendant); *U.S. v. Cooper,* 577 F.2d 1079 (6th Cir.), *cert. denied,* 439 U.S. 868 (1978) (no prejudicial error found where jury had copy of indictment and subpoena listing materials in evidence, when jury given cautionary instructions); *U.S. v. Dorn,* 561 F.2d 1252 (7th Cir. 1977) (use of transcripts of telephone conversations held not error, even though transcripts not in evidence, where jury instructed that tapes of conversation, which were in evidence, controlled in any conflict between tapes and transcripts).

The trial court has discretion to determine what materials will be permitted in the jury room. *U.S. v. Johnson,* 584 F.2d 148, 157-58 (6th Cir. 1978), *cert. denied,* 440 U.S. 918 (1979); *U.S. v. Peterson,* 548 F.2d 279 (9th Cir. 1977); *U.S. v. Burrell,* 963 F.2d 976 (7th Cir. 1992) (jury's physical examination of weapons allegedly used in a crime is proper); *U.S. v. Scales,* 594 F.2d 558, 563-64 (6th Cir.), *cert. denied,* 441 U.S.

946 (1979) (no prejudicial error found in allowing jury to have summary of evidence where proper limiting instruction given). In complex cases the court may allow the jury to take and use notes where jurors are properly instructed that such notes are only aids to memory and are not conclusive. *See U.S. v. Maclean,* 578 F.2d 64, 65-66 (3d Cir. 1978) (and cases cited therein from the Second, Fifth, Seventh, Eighth, Ninth, Tenth, and District of Columbia circuits); *U.S. v. Johnson,* 584 F.2d at 157-58.

## § 1251. Trial Management.

## § 1252. — Limiting and Cautionary Instructions.

When a jury is exposed to improper comments or evidence that should not be considered or should be considered only for a limited purpose, the court should give a curative instruction. Such an instruction enables the court to guide the jury in its fact-finding function and should be given immediately after the impropriety occurs. Where evidence is admissible for one purpose, but not another, there should be a request by the affected party for a limiting instruction, Rule 105, Fed. R. Evid.; *U.S. v. Regner,* 677 F.2d 754, 757 (9th Cir. 1982).

A prosecutor's potentially prejudicial comments during closing argument may, without consideration of the weight of the evidence, be cured by a timely instruction from the bench. *U.S. v. Martinez,* 616 F.2d 185 (5th Cir. 1980). Where a prosecutor's comments during closing argument inappropriately focus on a defendant's refusal to testify and the defense objects to the comments, the court's failure to instruct the jury to disregard the comments may not be prejudicial error, if there is substantial evidence in the record to support a conviction. *U.S. v. Buege,* 578 F.2d 187 (7th Cir.), *cert. denied,* 439 U.S. 871 (1978).

Out-of-court declarations by coconspirators are often the subject of limiting instructions. The necessity, extent, and character of the additional instruction are generally within the sound discretion of the court. *U.S. v. Staller,* 616 F.2d 1284 (5th Cir.), *cert. denied,* 449 U.S. 869 (1980); *U.S. v. Miller,* 546 F.2d 320, 324 (9th Cir. 1976). Frequently, the failure of defense counsel to request an instruction prohibiting the jury consideration of post-conspiracy statement by one defendant against another defendant will preclude a finding of reversible error. *U.S. v. Washington,* 586 F.2d 1147 (7th Cir. 1978); *U.S. v. Johnson,* 569 F.2d 269 (5th Cir.), *cert. denied,* 437 U.S. 906 (1978). However, if a coconspirator's statement is inadmissible as direct evidence against a codefendant, failure of the ocurt to give a cautionary instruction, *sua sponte,* is reversible error. *U.S. v. Vinson,* 606 F.2d 149 (6th Cir. 1979), *cert. denied,* 444 U.S. 1074 (1980); *U.S. v. Bell,* 573 F.2d 1040 (8th Cir. 1978); *U.S. v. Sisto,* 534 F.2d 616 (5th Cir. 1976); *U.S. v. Geaney,* 417 F.2d 1116 (2d Cir. 1969), *cert. denied,* 397 U.S. 1028 (1970).

Limiting and cautionary instructions may also be necessary where evidence of a defendant's prior acts or criminal activity has been introduced at trial. The limiting instruction may be used to charge the jury that evidence of a prior crime should be considered only on the issue of intent or knowledge to commit the offense charged. *U.S. v. O'Brien,* 601 F.2d 1067 (9th Cir. 1979). And, a cautionary instruction must be given if affirmative evidence of prior criminal conduct is inadmissible under Rule 404(b) of the Federal Rules of Evidence, regardless of whether the instruction is requested. *U.S. v. Ailstock,* 546 F.2d 1285 (6th Cir. 1976). *But see Nutt v. U.S.,* 335 F.2d 817 (10th Cir.), *cert. denied,* 379 U.S. 909 (1964) (no error when limiting instruction not requested). If the evidence of prior acts is admissible for a limited purpose and defense counsel fails to request a cautionary instruction, it is generally held there is no reversible error even though the court could have given an instruction *sua sponte. Grimaldi v. U.S.,* 606 F.2d 332, 339 (1st Cir.), *cert. denied,* 444 U.S. 971 (1979); *U.S. v. Sangrey,* 586 F.2d 1312 (9th Cir. 1978).

At least one circuit has held that where evidence of a defendant's prior criminal conduct has been introduced for impeachment purposes, rather than as affirmative evidence, a limiting instruction is required and the duty to insure such an instruction lies with the prosecutor, as well as with the judge and defense counsel. *U.S. v. Diaz,* 585 F.2d 116, 117 (5th Cir. 1978).

## § 1253. — Requests for Instructions.

Rule 30 of the Federal Rules of Criminal Procedure provides that "[a]t the close of the evidence or at such earlier time during the trial as the court reasonably directs, any party may file written requests that the court instruct the jury on the law as set forth in the requests." Requests for instructions must be timely made; thus, it has been held that such requests filed on the day the judge was scheduled to charge the jury were untimely. *U.S. v. Lustig,* 555 F.2d 737 (9th Cir. 1977), *cert. denied,* 434 U.S. 1045 (1978). A timely request enables the court to review the instructions and to inform the counsel of the proposed action before closing arguments. Thus, fairly advised, counsel may intelligently argue. *U.S. v. Davis,* 583 F.2d 190 (5th Cir. 1978).

### § 1254. — Objections to Instructions and Waiver.

Rule 30 of the Federal Rules of Criminal Procedure provides, that "[n]o party may assign as error any portion of the charge or omission therefrom unless that party objects thereto before the jury retires to consider its verdict, stating distinctly the matter to which that party objects and the grounds of the objection." Under this rule the issue of allegedly erroneous jury instructions cannot be raised on appeal unless the defendant proposed alternate instructions or objected at trial to the instructions that were given. *U.S. v. Bryant,* 612 F.2d 799 (4th Cir. 1979), *cert. denied,* 446 U.S. 919 (1980). If the defendant did not request certain instructions, it is immaterial whether the omission was inadvertent or a matter of trial strategy. *U.S. v. Harbin,* 585 F.2d 904 (8th Cir. 1978).

The requirements of Rule 30, however, are subject to exceptions. An objection by a codefendant is sufficient to preserve any error. *U.S. v. White,* 589 F.2d 1283, 1290 n.14 (5th Cir. 1979). It also has been held that, where the court is aware of an objection, a formal restatement would be "pointless formality" and therefore unnecessary to preserve the record. *U.S. v. Davis,* 583 F.2d 190, 194-95 (5th Cir. 1978) (trial judge was aware of attorneys' objections because they were thoroughly aired in a charge conference before the judge); *Brown v. Avemco Investment Corp.,* 603 F.2d 1367 (9th Cir. 1979). When the defense counsel insists that the court omit a standard or curative instruction, the omission will be deemed harmless error. *U.S. v. Splain,* 545 F.2d 1131, 1133 (8th Cir. 1976); *U.S. v. Gibson,* 536 F.2d 1110 (5th Cir. 1976).

The most common exception to the rule requiring an objection to preserve the record is the "plain error rule." Under Rule 52(b) of the Federal Rules of Criminal Procedure, "[p]lain errors or defects affecting substantial rights may be noticed although they were not brought to the attention of the court." *U.S. v. Bates,* 600 F.2d 505 (5th Cir. 1979); *U.S. v. Denton,* 556 F.2d 811 (6th Cir.), *cert. denied,* 434 U.S. 892 (1977). Failure of a party to make a timely objection to alleged errors waives those objections for purposes of appeal unless the error is so fundamental as to result in a miscarriage of justice. *U.S. v. Faulkner,* 538 F.2d 724 (6th Cir.), *cert. denied,* 429 U.S. 1023 (1976). However, the Supreme Court has stated that "[i]t is the rare case in which an improper instruction will justify reversal of a criminal conviction when no objection has been made in the trial court." *Henderson v. Kibbe,* 431 U.S. 145, 154 (1977). Furthermore, the "plain error" standard is intended only for use on direct appeal, not in a collateral attack. *U.S. v. Frady,* 102 S. Ct. 1584, 1592 (1982).

## § 1255. — Special Verdicts and Interrogatories.

## § 1256. — — Special Verdicts.

Although there is no per se rule against the use of special verdicts in criminal jury cases, *U.S. v. O'Looney,* 544 F.2d 385, 392 (9th Cir.), *cert. denied,* 429 U.S. 1023 (1976), it is established that special verdicts in such trials are generally disfavored, *U.S. v. Frezzo Bros., Inc.,* 602 F.2d 1123, 1129 (3d Cir. 1979), *cert. denied,* 444 U.S. 1074 (1980). While the trial court may submit a special verdict in appropriate cases, there is no authority holding that the refusal to do so in a criminal jury trial is error. *U.S. v. Shelton,* 588 F.2d 1242, 1251 (9th Cir. 1978), *cert. denied,* 442 U.S. 909 (1979).

Courts do not look with favor on special verdicts because such verdicts are not favorable to defendants. "[B]y a progression of questions each of which seems to require an answer unfavorable to the defendant, a reluctant juror may be led to vote for a conviction which, in the large, he would have resisted." *U.S. v. Frezzo Bros., Inc.,* 602 F.2d at 1129 (quoting *U.S. v. Spock,* 416 F.2d 165, 182 (1st Cir. 1969)). In *U.S. v. O'Looney,* 544 F.2d at 392 (quoting *U.S. v. Ogull,* 149 F. Supp. 272, 276 (S.D.N.Y. 1957), *aff'd sub nom. U.S. v. Gernie,* 252 F.2d 664 (2d Cir.), *cert. denied,* 356 U.S. 968 (1958)), the court elaborated on this reasoning and indicated that special verdicts tend to infringe upon certain historic functions of the jury — to temper the law with common sense, to decide whether to follow instructions, and to reach a general verdict without enunciating its reasons.

## § 1257. — — Criminal Forfeiture Special Verdicts.

Rule 31(e) of the Federal Rules of Criminal Procedure provides that "a special verdict shall be returned as to the extent of the interest or property subject to forfeiture, if any," where the indictment or information alleges that an interest or property is subject to criminal forfeiture. This rule and Rule 7(c)(2) procedurally implement the criminal forfeiture provisions of 18 U.S.C. § 1963(a) and 21 U.S.C. § 848(a)(2). Advisory Committee's Note; *U.S. v. Huber,* 603 F.2d 387, 396 (2d Cir. 1979), *cert. denied,* 445 U.S. 927 (1980). "[T]he amount of the interest or property subject to criminal forfeiture is an element of the offense to be alleged and proved." Advisory Committee's Note; Rule 7(c), Fed. R. Crim. P. A special verdict was upheld where the jury was instructed to determine a defendant's interest in an enterprise as well as to identify the membership of the enterprise so that it could determine the extent of the property subject to forfeiture. *U.S. v. Huber,* 603 F.2d at 396.

## § 1258. — — Special Interrogatories.

Courts generally view propounding of special interrogatories to a jury with the same disfavor as they do special verdicts. In *U.S. v. Jackson,* 542 F.2d 403, 412-13 (7th Cir. 1976), it was held that the trial court's refusal to submit defendant's proposed special interrogatory about defendant's sanity to the jury was not error. The defendant in *Jackson* argued that, since in a bench trial the defendant may compel special findings of fact pursuant to Federal Rules of Criminal Procedure 23(c), such right should not be lost by the exercise of the constitutional right to a jury trial. However, the Seventh Circuit held the trial court's refusal of the special interrogatory was proper because it "would have served no useful purpose" in that the "proposed special interrogatory merely tracks much of the language utilized by the trial court in giving the insanity instruction...." *U.S. v. Jackson,* 542 F.2d at 412. In *U.S. v. Wilson,* 629 F.2d 439, 442 (6th Cir. 1980), which involved the use of special interrogatories on the insanity defense, the court stated that "one danger of using special interrogatories [was] the likelihood of confusion and the shifting or weakening of the government's burden of proof." Citing additional criticisms of special verdicts and interrogatories in criminal jury trials, the court held that the use of special interrogatories in this case was error because they "'may in fact be more productive of confusion than of clarity.'" *Id.* at 444. *See also U.S. v. Desmond,* 670 F.2d 414 (3d Cir. 1982), where the use of special interrogatories in an uncomplicated tax trial was upheld; and *U.S. v. Wilson,* 629 F.2d 439 (6th Cir. 1980), where the court held special interrogatories in an insanity defense shifted the burden to the defendant and as such were improper.

## § 1259. — — Post-Verdict Juror Interrogation.

Post-verdict interrogation of jurors to impeach the verdict is looked upon with disfavor by the courts. In upholding a trial court's denial of a request for a post-verdict interrogation, the court in *U.S. v. Eldred,* 588 F.2d 746 (9th Cir. 1978), held that, under the local rules of the court which permitted post-verdict interrogation of jurors, a showing of sufficient reason to do so was still necessary. The *Eldred* court found nothing in the record to indicate or support a suspicion of misconduct. "The fact that the jury once announced a deadlock is not such a reason." 588 F.2d at 752. The court reasoned that the jurors were under oath and faithful performance of their official duties is to be presumed. Therefore, the refusal to allow post-verdict interrogation of the jurors did not amount to a constitutional or statutory deprivation of rights.

Rule 606(b) of the Federal Rules of Evidence also prohibits the testimony of a juror concerning the validity of a verdict or indictment except on the questions of whether extraneous prejudicial information or outside influences were improperly before the jury. *See Rushen v. Spain,* 464 U.S. 114 (1983). "[J]uror intoxication is not an 'outside influence' about which jurors may testify to impeach their verdict." *Tanner v. Conover,* 107 S. Ct. —, 41 Crim. L. Rep. 3340, 3346 (1987).

## § 1260. — Supplemental Instructions.

Supplemental instructions sometimes are given by the trial court in response to a jury's request for additional instructions or a specific question. *U.S. v. Viserto,* 596 F.2d 531 (2d Cir.), *cert. denied,* 444 U.S. 841 (1979); *U.S. v. Sanfilippo,* 581 F.2d 1152 (5th Cir. 1978); *U.S. v. Walker,* 575 F.2d 209 (9th Cir.), *cert. denied,* 439 U.S. 931 (1978); *U.S. v. Castenada,* 555 F.2d 605 (7th Cir.), *cert. denied,* 434 U.S. 847 (1977). Generally, the necessity, extent, and character of any supplemental instructions to the jury are matters within the sound discretion of the trial court. *U.S. v. Castenada,* 555 F.2d at 611; *U.S. v. Fuiman,* 546 F.2d 1155 (5th Cir.), *cert. denied,* 434 U.S. 856 (1977). Thus, failure to give supplemental instructions where there is no conclusion that the jury was confused or had erroneous impressions and where additional instructions could have produced improper results has been held not to be error. *U.S. v. Czarnecki,* 552 F.2d 698 (6th Cir.), *cert. denied,* 431 U.S. 939 (1977) (jury posed question concerning separability of counts and judge declined to give instruction forbidding compromise verdicts.)

The basic reason for giving supplemental instructions is to eliminate any jury confusion arising during deliberations. Thus, where a jury is or appears to be confused, the trial judge must ask whether a supplemental instruction will eliminate the confusion. *U.S. v. Walker,* 575 F.2d at 213; *Powell v. U.S.,* 347 F.2d 156 (9th Cir. 1965). In responding to a request for further instruction, the trial judge must attempt to clarify the confusion of the jury. *U.S. v. Sanfilippo,* 581 F.2d at 1155.

The Supreme Court has noted that "[w]hen a jury makes explicit its difficulties a trial judge should clear them away with concrete accuracy." *Bollenbach v. U.S.,* 326 U.S. 607, 612-13 (1946). In responding to this request, the judge may either supplement the request with more of the original instruction, reread the entire charge, or reread portions of the original instruction if the reinstruction will not mislead or confuse the jury. *U.S. v. Castenada,* 555 F.2d at 612; *U.S. v. Moreno-Nunez,* 595 F.2d 1186 (9th Cir. 1979). However, simply repeating instructions already given after the jury admits the need for further explanation does not satisfy the judge's responsibility to dispel confusion. *U.S. v.*

*Sanfilippo,* 581 F.2d at 1155. Therefore, the supplemental charge is balanced to avoid favoring either side of the case — it need not be a complete reiteration of the court's original instructions. *U.S. v. Fuiman,* 546 F.2d 1160-62.

Where the jury requests instructions in "layman's language," a supplemental charge that accurately states the law may contain hypotheticals. *U.S. v. Hayes,* 553 F.2d 824, 829 (2d Cir.), *cert. denied,* 434 U.S. 867 (1977). These hypotheticals are proper if the trial judge distinguishes the "layman's language" used in the examples from the "language the law lays down," which in effect emphasizes that the hypotheticals are being used for purposes of illustration only. *Id.* at 829.

To determine whether a supplemental charge is prejudicial, both the original and supplemental charge must be reviewed as a whole to insure that it was balanced (that is, that there is no evidence of partiality), and that it was responsive to the jury's request. *U.S. v. Viserto,* 596 F.2d 531 (2d Cir.), *cert. denied,* 444 U.S. 841 (1979); *U.S. v. Sanfilippo,* 581 F.2d at 1154; *U.S. v. Fuiman,* 546 F.2d 1160-62. "It is no answer to say that the supplemental instruction was correct, so far as it went; or that it was to be read in the light of the original instructions and that these fairly presented the issues." The ultimate question is "whether the charge taken as a whole was such as to confuse or leave an erroneous impression in the minds of the jurors." *Powell v. U.S.,* 347 F.2d at 158. A court may properly attempt to avoid intrusion into the deliberations of the jury by framing responses in terms of supplemental instructions rather than following precisely the form of the question asked by the jury. *U.S. v. Walker,* 575 F.2d at 214. However, a supplemental instruction that by implication constitutes an amendment to an indictment, thereby working a prejudice on the defendant, has been held to be reversible error. *Id.* at 214.

In *U.S. v. Spagnolo,* 546 F.2d 1117 (4th Cir. 1976), *cert. denied,* 433 U.S. 909 (1977), it was held not error for a jury to resume deliberations and reach a verdict after being told the trial judge was not available to answer their question. The appellate court reasoned that because the original charge fully covered the matter embraced within the question, it was "readily understandable that the jury could proceed without seeking further elucidation from the court." "[I]t must be assumed that they [the jury] had determined that they did not need an answer to their inquiry in order to reach a verdict." *Id.* at 1119-20.

## § 1261. — Allen Charge.

In *Allen v. U.S.,* 164 U.S. 492 (1896), the Supreme Court held valid an instruction to a deadlocked jury which emphasized that the jury has a duty to decide the case and that each juror should listen to the others with a disposition to be convinced. This instruction has been criticized as inherently coercive, and a limit beyond which the trial court should not venture in urging a jury to reach a verdict. *U.S. v. Seawell*, 583 F.2d 416, 418 (9th Cir.), *cert. denied*, 439 U.S. 991 (1978); *U.S. v. Scruggs*, 583 F.2d 238 (5th Cir. 1978); *U.S. v. Scott*, 547 F.2d 334 (6th Cir. 1977). If the *Allen* charge is considered to have a potentially coercive effect upon the members of the jury holding the minority position at the time of instruction, it has been held to be reversible error. *U.S. v. Robinson*, 953 F.2d 433 (8th Cir. 1992). One circuit has indicated a preference for giving the charge as a part of the original instructions and before a deadlock has occurred, although not prohibiting it as a supplemental instruction. *U.S. v. Wiebold*, 507 F.2d 932, 934 (8th Cir. 1974).

Giving the *Allen* charge *sua sponte* and without any indication from the jury that it is deadlocked was not error where it appeared the jury properly deliberated thereafter. *U.S. v. Beattie*, 613 F.2d 762 (9th Cir.), *cert. denied*, 446 U.S. 982 (1980); *U.S. v. Scruggs*, 583 F.2d at 241. However, repeating the *Allen* charge, except at the jury's request, has been held to be more an admonishment than an instruction and is impermissible. *U.S. v. Seawell*, 550 F.2d 1159, 1163 (9th Cir. 1977), *cert. denied*, 439 U.S. 991 (1978).

Although there is disagreement over whether modified versions of the *Allen* charge are permissible, generally they are accepted today. *Ellis v. Reed*, 596 F.2d 1195 (4th Cir.), *cert. denied*, 444 U.S. 973 (1979); *U.S. v. Bright*, 588 F.2d 504 (5th Cir.), *cert. denied*, 440 U.S. 972 (1979); *Salemme v. Ristaino*, 587 F.2d 81 (1st Cir. 1978); *U.S. v. Seawell*, 583 F.2d 416 (9th Cir.), *cert. denied*, 439 U.S. 991 (1978); *U.S. v. Brown*, 582 F.2d 197 (2d Cir.), *cert. denied*, 439 U.S. 915 (1978). The Ninth Circuit has expressed a preference for the American Bar Association's suggested formulation of the charge. *U.S. v. Beattie*, 613 F.2d at 766-67.

In determining whether an *Allen*-type instruction is coercive, the court must consider all circumstances of the case. *Jenkins v. U.S.*, 380 U.S. 445, 446 (1965); *U.S. v. Peterson*, 549 F.2d 654 (9th Cir. 1977). A defendant attacking the use of the *Allen* charge must establish that, even if the instruction may be inherently coercive, it had a coercive effect upon the jury in the particular circumstances. *U.S. v. Guglielmini*, 598 F.2d 1149 (9th Cir.), *cert. denied*, 444 U.S. 943 (1979); *U.S. v. Gabriel*, 597 F.2d 95 (7th Cir.), *cert. denied*, 444 U.S. 858 (1979); *U.S. v. Irwin*, 593 F.2d 138 (1st Cir. 1979); *U.S. v. Bright*, 588 F.2d at 510; *U.S. v. Giacalone*, 588 F.2d 1158 (6th Cir. 1978), *cert. denied*, 441 U.S. 944 (1979).

Other actions that may be coercive upon jury deliberations include
(1) inquiry into the numerical division of a jury as to the merits.
*Brasfield v. U.S.*, 272 U.S. 448 (1926); (2) statements to a deliberating
jury that they must reach a verdict, *Jenkins v. U.S., supra;* (3) allu-
sions to the undesirability of a retrial; and (4) setting a time limit upon
further deliberations. *U.S. ex rel. Anthony v. Sielaff*, 552 F.2d 588, 590
(7th Cir. 1977). However, polling a deliberating jury to determine the
prospect of agreement on a verdict and asking how the jurors stood on
the question of further deliberations has held to be proper, where no
inquiry has been made into the numerical division of the jury as to the
merits. *Lowenfield v. Phelps*, 484 U.S. 231 (1988).

## § 1262. — Polling Jurors.

The right to poll a jury is established by Rule 31(d) of the Federal
Rules of Criminal Procedure. Although of ancient origin, this right is
not of constitutional dimensions; yet it has been described as substantial, and, where timely requested, its denial is reversible error. *U.S. v.
Shepherd*, 576 F.2d 719, 724 (7th Cir.), *cert. denied*, 439 U.S. 852
(1978). A request to poll the jury is "seasonably asserted" if it occurs
between the return of the verdict and the time the verdict is recorded,
and the trial judge must allow adequate time for the request. *U.S. v.
Morris*, 612 F.2d 483 (10th Cir. 1979); *U.S. v. Shepherd*, 576 F.2d at
724 n.3. Therefore, Rule 31(d) compels the conclusion that a verdict is
not final when announced since a party may request a poll wherein a
juror may register his dissent or the court on its own motion may
require a poll to determine unanimity. *U.S. v. Love*, 597 F.2d 81, 84-86
(6th Cir. 1979); *U.S. v. Taylor*, 507 F.2d 166, 168-69 (5th Cir. 1975).

The primary purpose of a jury poll is to make certain that one of the
prerequisites of a valid verdict, unanimity, has been achieved. *U.S. v.
Morris*, 612 F.2d at 490; *U.S. v. Love*, 597 F.2d at 85. In *U.S. v. Shepherd*, 576 F.2d at 725 (quoting *U.S. v. Mathis*, 535 F.2d 1303, 1307
(D.C. Cir. 1976)), the court held that the poll's purpose "'is to test the
uncoerced unanimity of the verdict by requiring each juror to answer
for himself, thus creating individual responsibility, eliminating any
uncertainty as to the verdict announced by the foreman.'" Likewise,
Rule 31(d) erves the need to determine clarity and certainty as to the
meaning of the verdict. *U.S. v. Rastelli*, 870 F.2d 822 (2d Cir. 1989).

A jury poll serves an additional purpose. Under Rule 31(d) of the
Federal Rules of Criminal Procedure, a juror is entitled to change his
mind about a verdict that he had agreed to in the jury room. *U.S. v.
Shepherd*, 576 F.2d at 725; *Sincox v. U.S.*, 571 F.2d 876 (5th Cir. 1978).
The object of a poll is to give each juror an opportunity, before the

verdict is recorded, to declare in open court his assent to or dissent from the announced verdict. *U.S. v. Love,* 597 F.2d at 84. Thus, the question "was this and is this now your verdict," suggests that a juror has a right to change his or her mind about a verdict to which he or she has agreed in the jury room. *U.S. v. Shepherd,* 576 F.2d at 724.

If, upon the poll of a jury, there is not unanimous concurrence, the trial court is vested with the remedial discretion to discharge the jury or to send it back for further deliberation. *Sincox v. U.S.,* 571 F.2d at 878; *U.S. v. Smith,* 562 F.2d 619, 621-22 (10th Cir. 1977); *U.S. v. Edwards,* 469 F.2d 1362, 1367 n.5 (5th Cir. 1972) (subject to limited exceptions). A trial court does not abuse its discretion in denying a motion for a mistrial and directing further deliberation when a poll of the jurors reveals that the jury had not yet reached a unanimous decision as the foreman had announced. *U.S. v. Warren,* 594 F.2d 1046, 1049-50 (5th Cir. 1979). It is, however, an abuse of discretion if a trial court fails to take any remedial measures, such as requiring further deliberations, declaring a mistrial, or repolling the jury, where there is uncertainty about a verdict. *U.S. v. Morris,* 612 F.2d at 491.

Although Rule 31(d) provides for the poll of a jury, it does not provide guidance on how the poll is to be conducted. This is a matter left to the sound discretion of the trial court. *U.S. v. Shepherd,* 576 F.2d at 724. Where a jury announces a verdict as to some counts, but continues to deliberate as to other counts, the court may wait until the jury has concluded deliberations on all counts before conducting a poll. *U.S. v. Portac, Inc.,* 869 F.2d 1288 (9th Cir. 1989), *cert. denied,* 111 S. Ct. 129 (1990).

### § 1263. Instructions on the Law.

### § 1264. — The Contents of the Charge.

Rule 30 of the Federal Rules of Criminal Procedure provides that "The court may instruct the jury before or after the arguments are completed or at both times." While no rule specifically addresses itself to what such instructions must or may include, it is clear the law of the case must be given orally by the judge, *U.S. v. Noble,* 155 F.2d 315 (3d Cir. 1946), and not read to the jury by counsel, *Medley v. U.S.,* 155 F.2d 857 (D.C. Cir.), *cert. denied,* 328 U.S. 873 (1946). Although not always prejudicial, error is committed if instructions on the law are given outside the presence of the defendant and counsel, *U.S. v. Schor,* 418 F.2d 26 (2d Cir. 1969); *Callahan v. U.S.,* 371 F.2d 658 (9th Cir. 1967); *U.S. v. Grosso,* 358 F.2d 154 (3d Cir. 1966), *rev'd on other grounds,* 390 U.S. 62 (1968); *Jones v. U.S.,* 308 F.2d 307 (D.C. Cir. 1962); *But see*

*Rogers v. U.S.*, 422 U.S. 35 (1975), where the Court held that giving instructions in response to a jury question, in the absence of counsel and the defendant, is error. Written copies of the court's charge may be furnished to the jurors, *Haupt v. U.S.*, 330 U.S. 631 (1947); *U.S. v. Blane*, 375 F.2d 249 (6th Cir.), *cert. denied*, 389 U.S. 835 (1967); and such practice is considered "desirable," *Copeland v. U.S.*, 152 F.2d 769, 770 (D.C. Cir. 1945), *cert. denied*, 328 U.S. 841 (1946), particularly in complex cases, *U.S. v. Standard Oil Co.*, 316 F.2d 884 (7th Cir. 1963).

Repetitious and unnecessarily long charges produce confusion and interfere with a proper resolution of questions of fact. *U.S. v. Salliey*, 360 F.2d 699 (4th Cir. 1966). Whether requested or not, however, the jury is to be instructed on each and every essential element of the offense charged, *Screws v. U.S.*, 325 U.S. 91 (1945), and failure to do so constitutes reversible error, *Morissette v. U.S.*, 342 U.S. 246 (1952). *See also U.S. v. King*, 521 F.2d 61 (10th Cir. 1975), where a court was reversed because it omitted an element of the crime of conspiracy, and *U.S. v. Bryant*, 461 F.2d 912 (6th Cir. 1972), which resulted in reversal because specific intent was ignored in the instructions.

Accuracy of definition is essential, *U.S. v. Hiscott*, 586 F.2d 1271 (8th Cir. 1978); and the clarity of the evidence establishing an element of the crime does not relieve the court of its duty to define that element, *United Brotherhood of Carpenters and Joiners of America v. U.S.*, 330 U.S. 395 (1947). However, words of ordinary meaning which are commonly understood need not be defined, *U.S. v. Beasley*, 519 F.2d 233 (5th Cir. 1975), *vacated on other grounds*, 425 U.S. 956 (1976), and use of statutory language is sufficient if the words are free from uncertainty, *Batsell v. U.S.*, 403 F.2d 395 (8th Cir. 1968), *cert. denied*, 393 U.S. 1094 (1969); *Lumetta v. U.S.*, 362 F.2d 644 (8th Cir. 1966). *But see Gagliardo v. U.S.*, 366 F.2d 720 (9th Cir. 1966), which held that failure to define the word "indecent" was reversible error. Instructions must be restricted to the issues and the facts which the proof tends to establish. *U.S. v. Hill*, 417 F.2d 279 (5th Cir. 1969); *U.S. v. Gosser*, 339 F.2d 102 (6th Cir. 1964), *cert. denied*, 382 U.S. 819 (1965).

Federal judges also have the power to comment on the evidence, *Quercia v. U.S.*, 289 U.S. 466 (1933), provided that the jury is also informed that it is not bound by the court's comments, *U.S. v. Musgrave*, 444 F.2d 755 (5th Cir. 1971), *cert. denied*, 414 U.S. 1023 (1973), and the judge "studiously avoids onesidedness," *U.S. v. Dunmore*, 446 F.2d 1214, 1218 (8th Cir. 1971), *cert. denied*, 404 U.S. 1041 (1972); *U.S. v. Lombardi*, 550 F.2d 827 (2d Cir. 1977); *U.S. v. Fischer*, 531 F.2d 783 (5th Cir. 1976).

## § 1265. — — Lesser Included Offenses.

Rule 31(c) of the Federal Rules of Criminal Procedure provides that a defendant "may be found guilty of an offense necessarily included in the offense charged...."

A lesser included offense instruction should be given only where "there are disputed issues of fact which would enable the jury rationally to find" that all elements of the lesser offense had been proved. *Sansone v. U.S.*, 380 U.S. 343, 351 (1965); *U.S. v. Seijo*, 537 F.2d 694 (2d Cir. 1976), *cert. denied*, 429 U.S. 1043 (1977); *U.S. v. Madden*, 525 F.2d 972 (5th Cir. 1976); *U.S. v. Thompson*, 490 F.2d 1218 (8th Cir. 1974). Thus, it was proper to refuse to give an involuntary manslaughter instruction where the defendant claimed the use of excessive force in self-defense, as self-defense is an intentional killing and as such a rational jury could not find him guilty of involuntary manslaughter. *U.S. v. Skinner*, 667 F.2d 1306, 1309-10 (9th Cir. 1982).

Instructions on a lesser included offense are improper where the lesser offense requires an element not required for the greater offense. This is the "elements test" whereby one offense is necessarily included within another only when the elements of the lesser offense form a subset of the elements of the offense charged. *Schmuck v. U.S.*, 489 U.S. 705 (1989).

In every instance where the evidence is sufficient to allow the jury to return a verdict of guilty of the lesser included offense, the defendant as a matter of right is entitled to an instruction thereon when he so requests. *Keeble v. U.S.*, 412 U.S. 205 (1973); *Berra v. U.S.*, 351 U.S. 131 (1956). Absent such a defense request, however, it is not error to omit a lesser included offense instruction from the charge. *U.S. v. Carey*, 475 F.2d 1019 (9th Cir. 1973); *Walker v. U.S.*, 418 F.2d 1116 (D.C. Cir. 1969). It also has been held that the government is entitled, upon timely request, to a lesser included offense instruction unless the element distinguishing the greater and lesser offense is not disputed. *U.S. v. Harary*, 457 F.2d 471 (2d Cir. 1972). And, it has been held that, even absent a request, the trial court may, upon notice to the parties, instruct on lesser included offenses. *U.S. v. Singleton*, 447 F. Supp. 852 (S.D.N.Y. 1978). The Second Circuit in *U.S. v. Tsanas*, 572 F.2d 340 (2d Cir.), *cert. denied*, 435 U.S. 995 (1978), further held that, in determining whether to request a lesser included offense charge, a defendant may rely upon the trial court's obligation to inform the jury that it must unanimously find he is not guilty of the crime charged before it may consider the lesser included offense. *See also Fuller v. U.S.*, 407 F.2d 1199 (D.C. Cir. 1967), *cert. denied*, 393 U.S. 1120 (1969).

301

The District of Columbia Circuit has held that a defendant is not entitled to a lesser included offense instruction if his evidence is completely exculpatory. *U.S. v. Sinclair,* 444 F.2d 888 (D.C. Cir. 1971). *Compare Driscoll v. U.S.,* 356 F.2d 324, 327 (1st Cir. 1966), which held that "when the Government has made out a compelling case, uncontroverted on the evidence, on an element required for the charged offense but not for the lesser-included offense, there is a duty on defendant to come forward with some evidence on that issue if he wishes to have the benefit of a lesser-included offense charge."

### § 1266. — — Defense Theories.

Whether a defendant is entitled to jury instructions on the theory of his defense depends upon the production of evidence which supports such a theory under recognized legal principles. If the defense theory is legally sufficient and if there is evidence before the jury to support it, a court that fails to instruct on such defense theory commits reversible error. *U.S. v. Wright,* 593 F.2d 105 (9th Cir. 1979). *But see U.S. v. Hall,* 536 F.2d 313 (10th Cir.), *cert. denied,* 429 U.S. 919 (1976). Respecting this rule, the Fifth Circuit said in a somewhat different tone that "it is reversible error to refuse a charge on a defense theory for which there is an evidentiary foundation and *which if believed by the jury,* would be legally sufficient to render the accused innocent." *U.S. v. Lewis,* 592 F.2d 1282, 1285 (5th Cir. 1979) (emphasis added). Where the evidence fails to reflect the presence of a legally accepted defense, there is neither reason nor justification for defining and discussing the defense for the jury. *U.S. v. Hammons,* 566 F.2d 1301 (5th Cir. 1978), *vacated on other grounds,* 439 U.S. 810 (1978). Thus, a requested alibi instruction is properly refused in a prosecution for conspiracy, *U.S. v. Dye,* 508 F.2d 1226 (6th Cir. 1974), *cert. denied,* 420 U.S. 974 (1975), as are instructions on issues not in dispute at trial, *U.S. v. White,* 671 F.2d 1126, 1131 (8th Cir. 1982); but a good faith instruction in a mail fraud trial is necessary where there is some evidence to support this defense, *U.S. v. Westbo,* 576 F.2d 285 (10th Cir. 1978). Finally, even though evidence forming the foundation for the defense to the charge is wobbly, weak, insufficient, inconsistent, of doubtful credibility, and consists solely of defendant's own testimony, the accused, nonetheless, is entitled to instructions about his theory of the case. *U.S. v. Young,* 464 F.2d 160 (5th Cir. 1972). Likewise, a good-faith belief by the defendant that he is not violating the law, even if that belief is not objectively reasonable (belief that federal tax system is unconstitutional) negates willfulness and it is error to instruct the jury to disregard evidence of this issue, *Cheek v. U.S.,* 111 S. Ct. 604 (1991).

The court has the discretion to frame instructions in a manner and style it deems appropriate and is not bound by the wording of defense-authored charges even though they correctly state the law and are in proper form. *U.S. v. Thetford,* 676 F.2d 170, 178 (5th Cir.), *cert. denied,* 459 U.S. 1148 (1982); *U.S. v. Czeck,* 671 F.2d 1195, 1197 (8th Cir. 1982); *U.S. v. Davis,* 597 F.2d 1237 (9th Cir. 1979).

## § 1267. — Reasonable Doubt and Presumptions.

## § 1268. — — Reasonable Doubt.

A court commits reversible error if it fails to define adequately the prosecution's burden of proving guilt beyond a reasonable doubt. *Holland v. U.S.,* 348 U.S. 121, 139-41 (1954); *Dunn v. Perrin,* 570 F.2d 21 (1st Cir.), *cert. denied,* 437 U.S. 910 (1978). There is no standard, model definition of this burden. Circuit cases giving approval to various particular formulations of the reasonable doubt burden include *U.S. v. Reeves,* 594 F.2d 536 (6th Cir.), *cert. denied,* 442 U.S. 946 (1979); *U.S. v. Zimeri-Safie,* 585 F.2d 1318 (5th Cir. 1978); *U.S. v. Collins,* 552 F.2d 243, 248 (8th Cir.), *cert. denied,* 434 U.S. 870 (1977); *U.S. v. Wright,* 365 F.2d 135 (7th Cir. 1966), *cert. denied,* 386 U.S. 918 (1967). *Compare U.S. v. Cummings,* 468 F.2d 274 (9th Cir. 1972). When challenged, the adequacy of the language selected by the trial court to define this term is to be evaluated in light of the content of the overall charge. *Cupp v. Naughten,* 414 U.S. 141 (1973). *See also U.S. v. Pinkney,* 551 F.2d 1241 (D.C. Cir. 1976). In *U.S. v. Regilio,* 669 F.2d 1169, 1178 (7th Cir. 1981), *cert. denied,* 102 S. Ct. 2959 (1982), the court stated that the "better practice is not to define 'reasonable doubt.'"

The due process clause is the constitutional basis for the reasonable doubt standard. *In re Winship,* 397 U.S. 358 (1970).

*See also* Chapter 15, § 1501, *infra.*

## § 1269. — — Presumptions.

Juries are to be concerned only with permissive (that is, rebuttable as opposed to conclusive) presumptions. *U.S. v. U.S. Gypsum Co.,* 438 U.S. 422 (1978). Juries must be instructed that a presumption created by statute does not shift the burden of persuasion to a defendant. *Mullaney v. Wilbur,* 421 U.S. 684 (1975). *See also Cupp v. Naughten,* 414 U.S. 141 (1973). If a statute defines the elements of a crime so that it creates a presumption of the existence of a fact essential to guilt, due process is violated as the defendant has a burden of proof and the government is not called upon to prove every element of the crime. *Patterson v. New York,* 432 U.S. 197 (1977); *Carter v. Jago,* 637 F.2d

449, 455 (6th Cir. 1980), *cert. denied,* 456 U.S. 980 (1981). Instructions on presumptions that a jury could consider to be mandatory or conclusive do place a burden on the accused and must be avoided. *Carella v. California,* 489 U.S. 1075 (1989); *Francis v. Franklin,* 471 U.S. 307 (1985); *Sandstrom v. Montana,* 442 U.S. 510 (1979).

Once an evidentiary presumption operating in favor of the government is met and overcome, the court should make no reference to it. *U.S. v. Johnson,* 476 F.2d 1251 (5th Cir.), *cert. denied,* 414 U.S. 852 (1973). *But see U.S. v. Rodriguez-Sandoval,* 475 F.2d 542 (1st Cir.), *cert. denied,* 414 U.S. 869 (1973), where the court stated that explicit reference to a presumption instructions where the jury was carefully charged that it did not have to be rebutted by the defendant's own testimony was not error. The Fifth Circuit also has expressed its preference for instructions in terms of inferences rather than presumptions. *U.S. v. Marshall,* 431 F.2d 944 (5th Cir. 1970). *Accord, U.S. v. Wharton,* 433 F.2d 451 (D.C. Cir. 1970).

The presumption of innocence has been accorded a singular position, with the Supreme Court describing it as "a basic component of a fair trial under our system of criminal justice." *Estelle v. Williams,* 425 U.S. 501, 503 (1976). But even here, a failure to so instruct does not necessarily violate the Constitution. *Kentucky v. Whorton,* 441 U.S. 786 (1979). Any such failure or refusal to charge on the presumed innocence of a defendant is to be "evaluated in light of the totality of the circumstances — including all the instructions to the jury, the arguments of counsel, whether the weight of the evidence was overwhelming and other relevant factors." *Id.* at 789; *Payne v. Smith,* 667 F.2d 541, 545-46 (6th Cir. 1981), *cert. denied,* 456 U.S. 932 (1982). Failure to give the charge on the presumption of innocence on the facts of the particular case may be a due process violation. *Taylor v. Kentucky,* 436 U.S. 478 (1978).

*See also* Chapter 15, § 1504 *infra.*

### § 1270. — Credibility Issues.

Jury instructions that fail to point specifically to a juror's right to accept or reject, wholly or in part, the testimony of any particular witness are erroneous. *U.S. v. Partin,* 493 F.2d 750 (5th Cir. 1974); *U.S. v. Bilotti,* 380 F.2d 649 (2d Cir.), *cert. denied,* 389 U.S. 944 (1967). A charge that it is presumed a witness speaks the truth is disfavored and invites reversal. *U.S. v. Johnson,* 371 F.2d 800 (3d Cir. 1967); *U.S. v. Persico,* 349 F.2d 6 (2d Cir. 1965). Although such an instruction is not plain error, *Knapp v. U.S.,* 316 F.2d 794 (5th Cir. 1963), it is reversible error in the Sixth Circuit, *U.S. v. Maselli,* 534 F.2d 1197 (6th Cir. 1976).

In ruling on a state case, the Supreme Court has held a trial court may give the "protective instruction" that a defendant's in-trial silence is to be disregarded and may not be used to infer guilt, despite a defense objection, without infringing upon any fifth amendment privilege. *Lakeside v. Oregon,* 435 U.S. 333 (1978).

Juries are to be instructed that the testimony of both an accomplice and an immunized witness is to be scrutinized with caution, considered with care, and accorded what weight, if any, the jury finds it deserves. *U.S. v. Jones,* 612 F.2d 453 (9th Cir. 1979), *cert. denied,* 445 U.S. 966 (1980); *U.S. v. Partin,* 552 F.2d 621 (5th Cir.), *cert. denied,* 434 U.S. 903 (1977); *U.S. v. DeVincent,* 546 F.2d 452 (1st Cir. 1976), *cert. denied,* 431 U.S. 903 (1977); *U.S. v. Goble,* 512 F.2d 458 (6th Cir.), *cert. denied,* 423 U.S. 914 (1975). No defense request is required before an accomplice instruction may be given. *U.S. v. Marzano,* 537 F.2d 257 (7th Cir. 1976), *cert. denied,* 429 U.S. 1038 (1977). Instructions that the jury is not duty bound to accept the uncontradicted and uncontroverted testimony of a witness and that conviction may be had on the uncorroborated testimony of an accomplice are proper. *U.S. v. Miller,* 529 F.2d 1125 (9th Cir.), *cert. denied,* 426 U.S. 924 (1976).

An aider and abetter instruction directing the jury first to find that a principal committed the offense charged before it comes to consider the culpability of those defendants who assisted or cooperated is not erroneous. *U.S. v. McCoy,* 539 F.2d 1050 (5th Cir. 1976), *cert. denied,* 431 U.S. 919 (1977). A joint venture, common scheme charge in a case where the crime of conspiracy is not charged and where the court clearly describes the acts of one as the acts of all members of the unlawful combine is not error. *U.S. v. Wilkinson,* 513 F.2d 227, 233 (7th Cir. 1975). An instruction that one intends the natural and probable consequences of his voluntary acts, which a jury could construe as binding, is prejudicial because it shifts the burden of proof. *Francis v. Franklin,* 471 U.S. 307 (1985); *Sandstrom v. Montana,* 442 U.S. 510 (1979).

"Guarding instructions" that charts and summaries are not evidence but are only aids in evaluating the evidence are required. *U.S. v. Scales,* 594 F.2d 558, 564 (6th Cir.), *cert. denied,* 441 U.S. 946 (1979).

The weighing of an expert's testimony is also for the jury, *U.S. v. Barker,* 553 F.2d 1013 (6th Cir. 1977); but it is not plain error to omit telling the jury that it need not accept expert testimony, *Chatman v. U.S.,* 557 F.2d 147 (8th Cir.), *cert. denied,* 434 U.S. 863 (1977).

Giving instructions on the voluntariness of a confession is always safe practice. *U.S. v. Sauls,* 520 F.2d 568 (5th Cir.), *cert. denied,* 423

U.S. 1021 (1975). But such instruction is not required if the evidence is overwhelming, where the defendant offers no defense, and where the defendant denies ever having made the admission or confession, *U.S. v. Lewis,* 565 F.2d 1248 (2d Cir. 1977), *cert. denied,* 435 U.S. 973 (1978).

### § 1271. Motion for Acquittal.

There is no directed verdict in a federal criminal case, but a motion for a judgment of acquittal may be used in its place. Rule 29(a), Fed. R. Crim. P. A motion for a "directed verdict of acquittal" will be treated as a motion for a judgment of acquittal. *U.S. v. Luman,* 622 F.2d 490, 492 (10th Cir. 1980).

### § 1272. — Grounds for Motion for Acquittal.

The motion may be made by the court or the defendant, and the only proper basis for the motion is that the evidence is insufficient to sustain a conviction. Rule 29(a), Fed. R. Crim. P.; *U.S. v. Lopez,* 625 F.2d 889, 897 (9th Cir. 1980); *U.S. v. Cox,* 593 F.2d 46, 48 (6th Cir. 1979). If the government's case has passed the test of legal sufficiency, a motion for acquittal may not be granted in the interests of justice, *U.S. v. Brown,* 602 F.2d 1073, 1076 (2d Cir.), *cert. denied,* 444 U.S. 952 (1979); *U.S. v. Brown,* 587 F.2d 187, 190 (5th Cir. 1979), even where the judge does not believe the prosecution's witness, *U.S. v. Weinstein,* 452 F.2d 704, 713 (2d Cir. 1971), *cert. denied,* 406 U.S. 917 (1972). It may be, however, that a new trial might be granted under Rule 33 of the Federal Rules of Criminal Procedure in the interests of justice.

The test for reviewing the sufficiency of the evidence is whether a reasonable mind could fairly find the defendant guilty beyond a reasonable doubt, viewing the evidence in the light most favorable to the government. *U.S. v. Gibson,* 675 F.2d 825, 829 (6th Cir. 1982); *U.S. v. Brandon,* 633 F.2d 773, 780 (9th Cir. 1980); *U.S. v. Artuso,* 618 F.2d 192, 195 (2d Cir.), *cert. denied,* 449 U.S. 861 (1980); *U.S. v. De Jean,* 613 F.2d 1356, 1358-59 (5th Cir.), *cert. denied,* 446 U.S. 945 (1980); *U.S. v. Dreitzler,* 577 F.2d 539, 545 (9th Cir. 1978), *cert. denied,* 440 U.S. 921 (1979). If a defendant does not stand on his motion for acquittal offered at the close of the government's case, but introduces evidence in defense, all of the evidence, including that offered by the defendant may be used to determine the sufficiency of the evidence. *U.S. v. Lopez,* 625 F.2d at 897; *U.S. v. Fearn,* 589 F.2d 1316, 1321 (7th Cir. 1978).

## § 1273. — Time for Making Motion.

A motion for acquittal may be made at the close of the government's case, at the close of all the evidence, or within seven days after the jury is discharged. Rule 29, Fed. R. Crim. P.

## § 1274. — — At Close of Government's Case.

The court must rule on a motion made at the close of the government's case before the defense is required to go forward with its evidence, if any. *U.S. v. Dreitzler,* 577 F.2d 539, 552 (9th Cir. 1978), *cert. denied,* 440 U.S. 921 (1979); *Jackson v. U.S.,* 250 F.2d 897, 901 (5th Cir. 1958). If a defendant presents evidence after his motion for acquittal has been denied he is deemed to have waived any objection to such denial. *U.S. v. Douglas,* 668 F.2d 459, 461 (10th Cir. 1982); *U.S. v. Siegel,* 587 F.2d 721, 725 (5th Cir. 1979). The fact that a codefendant puts on evidence after the denial of a motion for acquittal is not a waiver by the defendant to his objections to the sufficiency of the evidence, *U.S. v. Evans,* 572 F.2d 455, 475 (5th Cir.), *cert. denied,* 439 U.S. 870 (1978); nor is there a waiver where the defendant limits himself to cross-examination of a codefendant, *U.S. v. Belt,* 574 F.2d 1234, 1236 (5th Cir. 1978).

## § 1275. — — At Close of All the Evidence.

A motion made at the close of all the evidence will be determined by a review of the evidence offered by both sides. *U.S. v. Fearn,* 589 F.2d 1316, 1321 (7th Cir. 1978). The court may reserve a decision on the motion and may decide it either before the jury returns a verdict, after it returns a verdict of guilty, or after it is discharged without having returned a verdict. Rule 29(b), Fed. R. Crim. P.

Failure of the defendant to make or renew his motion for acquittal at the close of all the evidence is a waiver and operates to foreclose appellate review of the issue. *U.S. v. Sherod,* 960 F.2d 1075 (D.C. Cir. 1992); *U.S. v. Rone,* 598 F.2d 564, 572 (9th Cir. 1979), *cert. denied,* 445 U.S. 946 (1980); *U.S. v. Phipps,* 543 F.2d 576, 577 (5th Cir. 1976), *cert. denied,* 429 U.S. 1110 (1977).

## § 1276. — — After Discharge of Jury.

If the jury returns a verdict of guilty or is discharged without returning a verdict, a motion for acquittal may be made within seven days after the jury is discharged or within such further time as the court may fix within the seven-day period. Rule 29(c), Fed. R. Crim. P. Any extension of time must be within the seven-day period. Rule 45(b), Fed.

R. Crim. P. The court may then enter a judgment of acquittal after a verdict of guilty or where no verdict has been returned. It is not required that a motion for acquittal be made before submission of the case to the jury, Rule 29(c), Fed. R. Crim. P., and making the motion for the first time within seven days of a guilty verdict preserves the issue for appeal, *U.S. v. Allison,* 616 F.2d 779, 784 (5th Cir.), *cert. denied,* 449 U.S. 857 (1980); *Virgin Islands v. Carr,* 451 F.2d 652, 655 (3d Cir. 1971).

# CHAPTER 13

## POST-TRIAL PROCEEDINGS

§ 1301. Motion for New Trial.
§ 1302. — Newly Discovered Evidence.
§ 1303. — Other Grounds.
§ 1304. — Time for Motion.
§ 1305. Motion for Arrest of Judgment.
§ 1306. Sentencing.
§ 1307. — Introduction.
§ 1308. Guidelines, Policy Statements and Commentary.
§ 1309. — Policy Considerations.
§ 1310. — Real Offense or Charge Offense Sentencing.
§ 1311. — Effective Date of the Sentencing Reform Act.
§ 1312. — Constitutionality.
§ 1313. — Plea Agreements.
§ 1314. — Plea Agreement Procedure.
§ 1315. — — Standards for Acceptance of Plea Agreements.
§ 1316. — Presentence Investigation and Report.
§ 1317. — — Contents of the Report of Presentence Investigation.
§ 1318. — — Disclosure of the Report of Presentence Investigation.
§ 1319. — Imposition of Sentence.
§ 1320. — — Time for Imposition.
§ 1321. — — Allocution.
§ 1322. — — Factors Which May Not Be Considered.
§ 1323. — — Application of Sentencing Guidelines.
§ 1324. — — Departure from Guidelines.
§ 1325. — — — Departure to Increase Sentence.
§ 1326. — — — Departure to Reduce Sentence.
§ 1327. — — — Appeal where there is Departure.
§ 1328. — — Departure for Substantial Assistance to Authorities.
§ 1329. — — Probation.
§ 1330. — — Concurrent and Consecutive Sentences.
§ 1331. — — Term of Supervisory Release after Imprisonment.
§ 1332. — — Imposition of Fine.
§ 1333. — — — Factors to be Considered in Imposing Fines.
§ 1334. — — — Modification or Remission of Fine.
§ 1335. — — Assistance for Victims.
§ 1336. — — — Special Assessments.
§ 1337. — — — Restitution.
§ 1338. — — — Notice to Victims.
§ 1339. — — Resolving Disputed Sentencing Facts.
§ 1340. — — Sentencing of Organizations.
§ 1341. — — Juvenile Offenders.
§ 1342. — Judgment of Conviction.
§ 1343. — Correction of Sentence.
§ 1344. — Modification of Sentence after Imposition.
§ 1345. — Notice to Defendant of Right to Appeal.
§ 1346. — Review of Sentences.

309

## § 1301. Motion for New Trial.

On the motion of a defendant, the court may grant a new trial if required in the "interest of justice." Rule 33, Fed. R. Crim. P. A motion for a new trial and a motion for acquittal may be combined. *U.S. v. Rojas,* 574 F.2d 476 (9th Cir. 1978); *U.S. v. Beran,* 546 F.2d 1316, 1319 n.1 (8th Cir. 1976), *cert. denied,* 430 U.S. 916 (1977).

The court may not order a new trial on its own motion. Advisory Committee Note to Rule 33 (1966 Amendment); *U.S. v. Brown,* 587 F.2d 187, 189 (5th Cir. 1979). (However, if because of a disability the trial judge is unable to perform the duties to be performed after a verdict or finding of guilty and the judge assigned to do these duties is satisfied that he cannot perform such duties because he did not preside or for any other reason, he may in his discretion grant a new trial. Rule 25(b), Fed. R. Crim. P.)

The burden of justifying a new trial rests with the defendant. *U.S. v. Geders,* 625 F.2d 31, 33 (5th Cir. 1980). The decision to grant a new trial falls within the sound discretion of the trial court and will be reversed only for an abuse of that discretion. *U.S. v. Webster,* 960 F.2d 1301 (5th Cir. 1992); *U.S. v. Barlow,* 693 F.2d 954, 966 (6th Cir.), *cert. denied,* 461 U.S. 945 (1982); *U.S. v. Oliver,* 683 F.2d 224, 228 (7th Cir. 1982); *U.S. v. Kenny,* 645 F.2d 1323, 1343 (9th Cir.), *cert. denied,* 452 U.S. 920 (1981); *U.S. v. Williams,* 613 F.2d 573, 575 (5th Cir.), *cert. denied,* 449 U.S. 849 (1980); *U.S. v. Conzemius,* 611 F.2d 695, 696 (8th Cir. 1979).

The government may appeal a district court order granting a new trial. 18 U.S.C. § 3731. This may be applied retroactively to new trials ordered before the enactment of the Comprehensive Crime Control Act of 1984. *Nilson Van & Storage Co. v. Marsh,* 755 F.2d 362, 365-66 (4th Cir.), *cert. denied,* 474 U.S. 818 (1985).

Rule 33 applies only to cases in which there has been a trial, and a defendant may not challenge his guilty plea by a motion for a new trial. *U.S. v. Lambert,* 603 F.2d 808, 809 (10th Cir. 1979).

## § 1302. — Newly Discovered Evidence.

Five requirements must be met for a court to grant a new trial on the grounds of newly discovered evidence: (1) the evidence must in fact be newly discovered, that is, it was unknown to the defendant at the time of the trial; (2) facts must be alleged from which the court may infer diligence on the part of the defendant; (3) the newly discovered evidence must not be merely cumulative or impeaching; (4) the evidence must be material to the issues involved; and (5) the newly discovered evidence must be of such a nature that it would probably produce an acquittal at a new trial. *U.S. v. Johnson,* 713 F.2d 654, 661-62 (11th Cir.), *cert. denied,* 465 U.S. 1030 (1983); *Bentley v. U.S.,* 701 F.2d 897, 898 (11th Cir. 1983); *U.S. v. Widgery,* 674 F.2d 710, 712 (8th Cir.), *cert. denied,* 459 U.S. 894 (1982); *U.S. v. Herman,* 614 F.2d 369, 371 (3d Cir. 1980); *U.S. v. Williams,* 613 F.2d 573, 575 (5th Cir. 1980), *cert. denied,* 449 U.S. 849 (1980); *U.S. v. Pappas,* 602 F.2d 131, 133 (7th Cir.), *cert. denied,* 444 U.S. 949 (1979).

The granting of a new trial must be based upon newly discovered evidence, not a new legal theory. *U.S. v. Hoffa,* 247 F. Supp. 692, 696 (E.D. Tenn. 1965). Evidence questioning the existence of probable cause for search may be considered in a motion for a new trial. *U.S. v. Bascaro,* 742 F.2d 1335, 1344 (11th Cir.), *cert. denied,* 472 U.S. 1017 (1984). Testimony of a witness who was not called at trial because of trial strategy is not newly discovered. *U.S. v. Pordum,* 451 F.2d 1015, 1017 (2d Cir. 1971), *cert. denied,* 405 U.S. 998 (1972); nor are the results of a polygraph examination of defendant taken after trial newly discovered evidence where the defendant was present at all times to assist in his defense, *McCroskey v. U.S.,* 339 F.2d 895, 897 (8th Cir. 1965). Likewise, a new trial will not be granted where the movant makes no showing why he could not have discovered the new evidence before or during trial, *U.S. v. Alessi,* 638 F.2d 466, 479 (2d Cir. 1980); *U.S. v. DiCarlo,* 575 F.2d 952, 961 (1st Cir.), *cert. denied,* 439 U.S. 834 (1978), or where the movant presents no evidence demonstrating his lack of knowledge of the evidence before the end of trial, *U.S. v. Jones,* 597 F.2d 485, 489 (5th Cir. 1979), *cert. denied,* 444 U.S. 1043 (1980). Failure of the defense to pursue matters brought to its attention before trial is lack of due diligence. *U.S. v. Pappas,* 602 F.2d at 133-34.

Evidence further impeaching the credibility of a trial witness is not sufficient for awarding a new trial, *U.S. v. Scherer,* 673 F.2d 176, 179 (7th Cir. 1982); *U.S. v. Hirst,* 668 F.2d 1180, 1185 (11th Cir. 1982); *U.S. v. Gilbert,* 668 F.2d 94, 96 (2d Cir.), *cert. denied,* 456 U.S. 946 (1981), nor is the recantation of the testimony of a minor witness on a minor issue, *U.S. v. Krasny,* 607 F.2d 840, 845 (9th Cir. 1979), *cert. denied,* 445 U.S. 942 (1980).

A defendant was not entitled to a new trial where state convictions were reversed which had been entered against him at his federal trial and which precluded him from testifying. It was not shown that the alleged new evidence would probably produce an acquittal since the defendant did not show what his trial testimony would be. *U.S. v. Perno,* 605 F.2d 432, 433 (9th Cir. 1979).

Where it is shown that the government's case includes false testimony and the government knew or should have known of the false-

311

hood, a new trial must be held if there is any reasonable likelihood that
the false testimony would have affected the jury. *U.S. v. Agurs,* 427
U.S. 97, 103 (1976). If, however, there is no misconduct by the prosecution, the standard is that the new evidence would probably produce an
acquittal. *U.S. v. Street,* 570 F.2d 1, 3-4 (1st Cir. 1977). Where the
defendant alleges that the government made a witness whom he intended to call unavailable, a new trial was properly denied where the
testimony would have been cumulative, or irrelevant, and there was no
showing of obstruction of justice by the government. *U.S. v. Marvin,*
720 F.2d 12, 14 (8th Cir. 1983).

### § 1303. — Other Grounds.

Prosecutorial misconduct, including prejudicial remarks before the
jury, *U.S. v. Woodring,* 446 F.2d 733, 737 (10th Cir. 1971), or the
knowing use of false testimony, *U.S. v. Butler,* 567 F.2d 885, 891 (9th
Cir. 1978), may be the basis for a new trial. Failure of the government
to disclose the pretrial hypnosis of its principal witness also has been
held to be a basis for a new trial. *U.S. v. Miller,* 411 F.2d 825, 832-33
(2d Cir. 1969).

Prejudicial exposure of the jurors to news accounts during the trial
may be grounds for a new trial. *Marshall v. U.S.,* 360 U.S. 310, 313
(1959); *U.S. v. Rhodes,* 556 F.2d 599, 602 (1st Cir. 1977); *U.S. v.
Concepcion Cueto,* 515 F.2d 160, 163 (1st Cir. 1975).

An incorrect charge to the jury, *U.S. v. Wilson,* 629 F.2d 439 (6th Cir.
1980), improper introduction of evidence, *U.S. v. Renaldi,* 301 F.2d
576, 578 (2d Cir. 1962), the misconduct of the court, *U.S. v. Nazzaro,*
472 F.2d 302 (2d Cir. 1973), or the jury, *Mattox v. U.S.,* 146 U.S. 140
(1892), may also require the granting of a new trial. A party seeking a
new trial because of nondisclosure by a juror during voir dire must
show actual bias. *U.S. v. Perkins,* 748 F.2d 1519, 1532 (11th Cir. 1984);
*U.S. v. Tutt,* 704 F.2d 1567, 1569 (11th Cir.), *cert. denied,* 464 U.S. 855
(1983).

### § 1304. — Time for Motion.

A motion for a new trial on the ground of newly discovered evidence
must be filed within two years after final judgment, *U.S. v. Cook,* 705
F.2d 350, 351 (9th Cir. 1983), but where an appeal is pending the court
may grant the motion only on remand of the case. Rule 33, Fed. R.
Crim. P. The words "final judgment" mean the last date for taking an
appeal, if no appeal is taken, or if an appeal is taken, the date when the
appellate process is terminated. *Casias v. U.S.,* 337 F.2d 354, 356 (10th

Cir. 1964). Although the court may not grant a motion for a new trial while an appeal is pending, *U.S. v. Blanton,* 697 F.2d 146, 148 (6th Cir. 1983), it may deny such a motion, *U.S. v. Coleman,* 688 F.2d 663, 664 (9th Cir. 1982); *U.S. v. Burns,* 668 F.2d 855, 858 (5th Cir. 1982).

A motion for new trial on any other grounds must be made within seven days of the verdict or finding of guilty or within such further time as the court may fix within the seven-day period. Rule 33, Fed. R. Crim. P. Any extension of time must be requested within the seven-day time period. Rule 45(b), Fed. R. Crim. P. The seven-day time period is jurisdictional, and no motion for new trial beyond seven days may be entertained unless it is based on newly discovered evidence. *U.S. v. Brown,* 742 F.2d 363, 368 (7th Cir. 1984); *U.S. v. Hazeem,* 679 F.2d 770, 774 (9th Cir.), *cert. denied,* 459 U.S. 848 (1982); *U.S. v. Fontanez,* 628 F.2d 687, 691 (1st Cir. 1980), *cert. denied,* 450 U.S. 935 (1981).

A timely motion for a new trial, on grounds other than newly discovered evidence or based upon newly discovered evidence, if made within 10 days after entry of the judgment, extends the time within which a notice of appeal must be filed to 10 days after the entry of an order denying the motion. Rule 4(b), Fed. R. App. P. *See also U.S. v. Dukes,* 727 F.2d 34, 40 (2d Cir. 1984). The filing of a motion for reconsideration of an order denying a new trial does not toll the time for filing an appeal. *U.S. v. March,* 700 F.2d 1322, 1328 (10th Cir. 1983); *U.S. v. Janovich,* 688 F.2d 1227, 1228 (9th Cir. 1982). If a defendant files his notice of appeal before the court rules on his motion for new trial, the motion is premature and should be dismissed with the right to refile the notice of appeal within 10 days after the entry denying the motion for new trial. *U.S. v. Jones,* 669 F.2d 559, 561 (8th Cir. 1982). *Contra U.S. v. Moore,* 616 F.2d 1030, 1031 (7th Cir.), *cert. denied,* 446 U.S. 987 (1980) (holding that the prematurely filed notice of appeal becomes effective if and when the court denies the motion).

## § 1305. Motion for Arrest of Judgment.

After a verdict or finding of guilty or after a plea of guilty or nolo contendere a court may grant a motion for arrest of judgment. The only grounds for such a motion are that the indictment or information does not charge an offense, or the court was without jurisdiction of the offense charged. Rule 34, Fed. R. Crim. P. Granting of such a motion renders the judgment void. In granting such a motion, the court may not look beyond the face of the record, *U.S. v. Sisson,* 399 U.S. 267, 281 (1970); and the evidence is not part of the record, *Sutton v. U.S.,* 157 F.2d 661, 663 (5th Cir. 1946).

The motion must be made within seven days after verdict or finding of guilty, or after plea of guilty or nolo contendere, or within such further period as may be fixed within the seven-day period. Rule 34, Fed. R. Crim. P.

## § 1306. Sentencing.

## § 1307. — Introduction.

The Comprehensive Crime Control Act of 1984, 28 U.S.C. § 991, established the United States Sentencing Commission to establish sentencing policies and practices that "provide certainty and fairness in meeting the purpose of sentencing, avoiding unwarranted sentencing disparities among defendants with similar records who have been found guilty of similar criminal conduct while maintaining sufficient flexibility to permit individualized sentences when warranted by mitigating or aggravating factors not taken into account in the establishment of general sentencing practices." 28 U.S.C. § 991(b)(1)(B). The Sentencing Guidelines are to "further the basic purposes of criminal punishment, *i.e.,* deterring crime, incapacitating the offender, providing just punishment, and rehabilitating the offender." U.S.S.G. Ch. 1, Pt. A2. Rehabilitation is rejected as a reason for imposing a term of imprisonment. 28 U.S.C. § 994(k).

The statute contained many detailed instructions to meet the purposes of the Act but, in particular, instructed the Commission to create categories of offense behavior and offender characteristics. In doing this the Commission was required to prescribe guideline ranges, coordinating the offense behavior categories with the offender characteristic categories. Where imprisonment was called for, the range cannot exceed the minimum by more than a greater of 25% or six months. 28 U.S.C. § 994(b). The Commission established forty-three ranges.

The sentencing judge must select a sentence from within a guideline range. If there are atypical features, the judge may depart from the guideline and sentence outside the range, but he must state the reasons for his departure. 18 U.S.C. § 3553(b) and (c).

If the defendant is sentenced within a guideline range, an appellate court may review the sentence to see if the guideline was correctly applied. If the sentencing judge departs from the guideline range, then the appellate court may review the reasonableness of the departure. 18 U.S.C. § 3742. Parole is abolished. Credit for good behavior is limited to a maximum of fifty-four days per year after the first year for which no credit is permitted. 18 U.S.C. § 3624(b). As such, the offender will serve virtually all of any prison sentence imposed.

For the sake of judicial economy, the Sentencing Commission has exempted all Class B or C misdemeanors and infractions (offenses for which the statutory maximum sentence may not exceed six months' imprisonment) from the Sentencing Guidelines. U.S.S.G. § 1B1.9.

As an organization cannot be imprisoned and because the primary purpose for organizational crimes is generally monetary, the Sentencing Reform Act provides a schedule of fines greater than those which may be imposed on individuals as sentences for organizations. 18 U.S.C. § 3571. An organization is "a person other than an individual." 18 U.S.C. § 18.

## § 1308. Guidelines, Policy Statements and Commentary.

The duties of the Sentencing Commission include promulgating "guidelines" for the use of a sentencing court determining the sentence to be imposed in a criminal case and promulgating "general policy statements" regarding the application of the Guidelines. 28 U.S.C. § 994(a). Accompanying the Guidelines is "commentary," which interprets and explains the application of the Guidelines, and which along with policy statements may provide guidance in assessing the reasonableness of departure from the Guidelines. U.S.S.G. § 1B1.7.

Both the Guidelines and the general policy statements are binding on the court and error in interpreting a policy statement could result in a sentence that was imposed as a result of an incorrect application of the Sentencing Guidelines. *Williams v. U.S.*, 112 S. Ct. 1112 (1992). Commentary, however, is not binding and "the courts will treat the commentary much like legislative history or other legal material that helps determine the intent of a drafter." U.S.S.G. § 1B1.7, comment; *U.S. v. Stinson*, 957 F.2d 813 (11th Cir. 1992).

## § 1309. — Policy Considerations.

The objectives which Congress sought to achieve in the new sentencing law were honesty, uniformity, and proportionality in sentencing. U.S.S.G. Ch. 1, Pt. A3, p.s.

Honesty occurs through imposing definite sentences that will actually be served rather than the previous system where the defendant often served only about one-third of the Court's sentence. Thus, parole is abolished.

Uniformity was to be achieved by narrowing the wide disparities in sentences imposed by different courts for similar criminal conduct by similar offenders, and proportionality was to be achieved by appropriately different sentences for criminal conduct of different severity. The

Guidelines recognize that the tension between the mandate of uniformity and the mandate of proportionality is difficult to achieve simultaneously. The Commission states that there is "no completely satisfying solution" to the stalemate, and it sought to balance the virtues and vices of overbroad, simple categorization and a detailed, complex sub-categorization "and within the constraints established by that balance, minimize the discretionary powers of the sentencing court." U.S.S.G. Ch. 1, Pt. A3, p.s.

### § 1310. — Real Offense or Charge Offense Sentencing.

The Commission originally sought to develop a real offense system, meaning that the defendant would be sentenced for the conduct in which he or she engaged whether or not the defendant was actually indicted or convicted upon all of that activity.

This was ultimately changed to a "charge offense" system in which the defendant is to be sentenced for the actual conduct which the prosecutor proved in court or to which the defendant pleaded guilty. U.S.S.G. Ch. 1, Pt. A4(a), p.s.

This is not, however, a pure system as it has a number of "real" elements. For example, the Guidelines are descriptive of generic conduct, rather than specific statutory language, and through adjustments take into account a number of real offense elements such as the role in the offense, the presence of a gun, or the amount of money actually taken. *Id.*

### § 1311. — Effective Date of the Sentencing Reform Act.

The Sentencing Reform Act applies only to crimes committed on or after November 1, 1987. 18 U.S.C. § 235(a)(1). Further, the Sentencing Reform Act of 1984 may not be used to seek modification of a sentence imposed before November 1, 1987. *U.S. v. Charleus,* 871 F.2d 265 (2d Cir. 1989); *U.S. v. Argitakos,* 862 F.2d 423 (2d Cir. 1988); *U.S. v. Rewald,* 835 F.2d 215, 216 (9th Cir. 1988).

The Sentencing Reform Act applies to crimes which began before, but were completed after, the date of the Act. *U.S. v. Story,* 891 F.2d 988 (2d Cir. 1990).

### § 1312. — Constitutionality.

Constitutional challenges to the 1984 Sentencing Reform Act and its Guidelines claiming that: (1) the Sentencing Reform Act improperly delegated legislative authority to the Sentencing Commission, and (2) the Guidelines issued by the Sentencing Commission are invalid because the Commission was constituted in violation of the separation of powers doctrine, have been rejected by the Supreme Court. *Mistretta v. U.S.*, 488 U.S. 361 (1989).

A challenge to the Sentencing Guidelines claiming that they unconstitutionally violate the due process clause because they curtail the judge's discretion, limiting "individualized" sentencing, also has been rejected, with the courts holding that the constitution does not guarantee individualized sentencing. *U.S. v. Brady,* 895 F.2d 538 (9th Cir. 1990); *U.S. v. Pinto,* 875 F.2d 143 (7th Cir. 1989); *U.S. v. Allen,* 873 F.2d 963 (6th Cir. 1989); *U.S. v. Seluk,* 873 F.2d 15 (1st Cir. 1989); *U.S. v. Brittman,* 872 F.2d 827 (8th Cir.), *cert. denied,* 110 S. Ct. 184 (1989); *U.S. v. White,* 869 F.2d 822 (5th Cir. 1989); *U.S. v. Frank,* 864 F.2d 992 (3d Cir. 1988), *cert. denied,* 490 U.S. 1095 (1989).

Likewise rejected has been a challenge that under the Sentencing Guidelines the probation officer investigates the offense instead of the offender and thus he acts as an arm of the executive branch in violation of the separation of powers doctrine. *U.S. v. Belgrad,* 894 F.2d 1092 (9th Cir.), *cert. denied,* 111 S. Ct. 164 (1990).

### § 1313. — Plea Agreements.

The Sentencing Commission was directed to promulgate general policy statements regarding the application of the Guidelines to the authority granted to the courts to accept or reject plea agreements entered into pursuant to Rule 11(e) of the Federal Rules of Criminal Procedure. 28 U.S.C. § 994 (a)(2)(E). The reason for this is that Congress expects judges "to examine plea agreements to make certain the prosecutors have not used plea bargaining to undermine the sentencing guidelines." S. Rep. No. 98-225, 98th Cong., 1st Sess. 63 (1983), quoted in Introductory Commentary to Part B of Chapter 6 of the Sentencing Guidelines Manual.

### § 1314. — Plea Agreement Procedure.

The procedure for accepting a plea agreement under the Sentencing Reform Act parallels Rule 11(e) of the Federal Rules of Criminal Procedure. In sum, this means that the plea agreement shall be on the record in open court (or *in camera* upon a showing of good cause); that if there is a nonbinding recommendation as to sentence, the court must advise the defendant that the court is not bound by the recommendation, and the defendant has no right to withdraw the guilty plea if the court decides not to accept the recommendation in the plea agreement; and that the court will defer its decision to accept or reject any non-

binding recommendation until it has the opportunity to consider the
presentence report, unless a presentence report is not required pursuant to § 6A1.1 of the Sentencing Guidelines.

*See also* Chapter 6, § 611, *infra.*

### § 1315. — — Standards for Acceptance of Plea Agreements.

Any plea agreement that includes a dismissal of any charges or an
agreement not to pursue potential charges may be accepted by the
court if the court determines, for reasons stated on the record, that the
remaining charges adequately reflect the seriousness of the actual offense behavior, and that the agreement will not undermine the statutory purposes of sentencing. U.S.S.G. § 6B1.2.

If there is either a nonbinding recommendation of sentence or a
specific sentence specified as part of the agreement, the court may
accept the agreement if the court is satisfied that: (1) the recommended
sentence is within applicable guideline range; or, (2) it departs from
the applicable guideline range for justifiable reasons. U.S.S.G. § 6B1.2.

If any plea agreement pursuant to Rule 11(e)(1)(A) or Rule
11(e)(1)(C) is rejected, the defendant may withdraw his or her guilty
plea. Rule 11(e)(4), Fed. R. Crim. P.; U.S.S.G. § 6B1.3.

The Sentencing Guidelines state that any plea agreement may be
accompanied by a written stipulation of facts relevant to sentencing.
The stipulation shall: (1) set forth relevant facts and circumstances of
the offense conduct and offender characteristics; (2) not contain misleading facts; and (3) set forth with specificity why the sentencing
range resulting from the proposed agreement is appropriate. The court
is not bound by this stipulation, but with the aid of the presentence
report may determine the facts relevant to sentencing. U.S.S.G.
§ 6B1.4.

The sections of the Sentencing Guidelines regarding plea agreements are in the form of policy statements rather than Guidelines.
Title 18 U.S.C. § 3742 relating to appeal of a sentence specifies that "an
incorrect application of the sentencing guidelines" may be appealed.

Section 6B1.2(b)(c) of the policy statements appears to permit an
agreed sentence which is at variance with the Guidelines. This varies
from the more restricted language of 18 U.S.C. § 3553(b) and may be
contrary to the purposes of the Sentencing Reform Act to reduce disparity in sentencing.

### § 1316. — Presentence Investigation and Report.

Before the imposition of sentence or the granting of probation, the
probation officer shall make a presentence investigation and report,

unless the court finds that there is sufficient information in the record for the meaningful exercise of sentencing authority. In the latter instance, the court must explain its finding on the record. Rule 32(c)(1), Fed. R. Crim. P. The defendant may not waive preparation of the presentencing report. U.S.S.G § 6A1.1(a).

Except with the written consent of the defendant, the report shall not be submitted to the court or its contents disclosed to anyone until the defendant has pleaded guilty or nolo contendere or has been found guilty. Rule 32(c)(1), Fed. R. Crim. P. The report may be prepared before entry of a plea or conviction, even though the court may not be permitted to review it until after plea or conviction. Advisory Committee Note (1974 Amendment); *Gregg v. U.S.*, 394 U.S. 489, 491-92 (1968). A judge who rejects a plea agreement after reading a presentence report may preside at the defendant's trial. *U.S. v. Bunch,* 730 F.2d 517, 519 (7th Cir. 1984); *U.S. v. Sonderup,* 639 F.2d 294, 296-97 (5th Cir.), *cert. denied,* 452 U.S. 920 (1981).

### § 1317. — — Contents of the Report of Presentence Investigation.

The report of the presentence investigation must contain: (1) information about the history and characteristics of the defendant including his prior criminal record, if any, his financial condition, and any circumstances affecting his behavior that may be helpful imposing sentence or in the correctional treatment of the defendant; (2) the classification of the offense and of the defendant under the Sentencing Commission categories that the probation officer believes to be applicable, the kinds of sentence and the sentencing range suggested for such a category of offense committed by such a category of defendant, any explanation by the probation officer of any factors that may indicate that a sentence of different kind or of a different length from one within the applicable guideline would be more appropriate under all the circumstances; (3) any pertinent policy statement issued by the Sentencing Commission; (4) information stated in a "nonargumentative style" containing an assessment of the financial, social, psychological, and medical impact upon, and cost to, any individual against whom the offense has been committed; (5) information concerning the nature and extent of nonprison programs and resources available for the defendant, unless the court orders otherwise; and (6) such other information as may be required by the court. Rule 32(c)(2), Fed. R. Crim. P.

**§ 1318. — — Disclosure of the Report of Presentence Investigation.**

The court shall provide the defendant and his counsel a copy of the presentence report, including the information required by Rule 32(c)(2), exclusive of any final recommendations as to sentence and any information in the report which the court finds should not be disclosed. Rule 32(c)(3)(A) and (B), Fed. R. Crim. P.; *U.S. v. Ainesworth,* 716 F.2d 769, 772 (10th Cir. 1983). Providing the report must be made at least ten days prior to sentencing, unless this minimum period is waived by the defendant. 18 U.S.C. § 3552(d); U.S.S.G. § 6A1.1(b).

The parties are required to respond in writing to the presentence report and identify their respective positions on the report, including any issues in dispute. U.S.S.G. § 6A1.2.

When the report or part of it is not disclosed, the court must state orally or in writing a summary of any such information to be relied on in sentencing and give the defendant or his counsel an opportunity to comment thereon. *U.S. v. Scalzo,* 716 F.2d 463, 467 (7th Cir. 1983). The statement may be made to the parties *in camera.* Rule 32(c)(3)(B), Fed. R. Crim. P. Failure to do so will cause the sentence to be vacated. *U.S. v. Aguero-Segovia,* 622 F.2d 131, 132 (5th Cir. 1980). If the court states it does not rely on the undisclosed portion of the report, that portion does not need to be summarized. *U.S. v. Dubrofsky,* 581 F.2d 208, 215 (9th Cir. 1978).

The purpose of this rule is to insure that sentencing is based upon accurate information, *U.S. v. Missio,* 597 F.2d 60, 61 (5th Cir. 1979), and to avoid belated attacks upon the accuracy of the report, *U.S. v. Leonard,* 589 F.2d 470, 472 (9th Cir. 1970). At the discretion of the judge, the defendant may introduce testimony or other information relating to an alleged factual inaccuracy in the presentence report. Rule 32(c)(3)(A), Fed. R. Crim. P.; *U.S. v. LoRusso,* 695 F.2d 45, 51 n.2 (2d Cir. 1982), *cert. denied,* 460 U.S. 1070 (1983). If any factual inaccuracy in the presentence investigation report is alleged, the court is required to make a finding for each allegation or to determine that no such finding is necessary because the controverted matter will not be taken into account in sentencing. Rule 32(c)(3)(D), Fed. R. Crim. P.; *U.S. v. Fernandez-Angulo,* 897 F.2d 1514 (9th Cir. 1990); *U.S. v. Eschweiler,* 782 F.2d 1385, 1388-91 (7th Cir. 1986); *U.S. v. O'Neill,* 767 F.2d 780, 787 (11th Cir. 1985). A written record of the findings and determinations shall be attached to and accompany any copy of the presentence report made available to the Bureau of Prisons. Rule 32(c)(3)(D), Fed. R. Crim. P. In imposing sentence the court will not be presumed to have considered a matter in the presentence report which it states it disregarded, *U.S. v. Fay,* 668 F.2d 375, 380 (8th Cir. 1981); but if the court relies on materially false or unreliable information there is a violation of defendant's due process rights, *U.S. v. Williams,* 668 F.2d 1064, 1072 (9th Cir. 1981).

Information which the court may determine should not be disclosed are diagnostic opinions which might disrupt a program of rehabilitation, sources of information which were obtained upon a promise of confidentiality, or other information which might result in harm, physical or otherwise, to the defendant or others. Rule 32(c)(3)(A), Fed. R. Crim. P. Reports of studies and recommendations made by the Director of the Bureau of Prisons pursuant to 18 U.S.C. § 3552(b) are considered a presentence investigation, the disclosure of which is controlled by Rule 32(c)(3). Rule 32(c)(3)(E), Fed. R. Crim. P. Under this rule, information relating to ongoing investigations need not be disclosed, *U.S. v. Dubrofsky,* 581 F.2d 208, 215 (9th Cir. 1978); nor must certain medical opinions or confidential sources be revealed, *U.S. v. Perri,* 513 F.2d 572, 575 (9th Cir. 1975).

Any material disclosed to the defense must also be disclosed to the attorney for the government. Rule 32(c)(3)(C), Fed. R. Crim. P. The rule is silent on disclosure to third parties, but such disclosure has been held to be contrary to public interest, *U.S. v. Evans,* 454 F.2d 813, 820 (8th Cir.), *cert. denied,* 406 U.S. 969 (1972), and has been refused to codefendants, *U.S. v. Martinello,* 556 F.2d 1215, 1216 (5th Cir. 1977) and to the news media, *U.S. v. Corbitt (Pulitzer Community Newspapers, Inc.),* 879 F.2d 224 (7th Cir. 1989). There is language in *U.S. v. Figurski,* 545 F.2d 389, 391 (4th Cir. 1976), that disclosure to third parties may be made "to meet the ends of justice," meaning that disclosure is permitted if there is evidence in the report that would create a reasonable doubt to the trier of the fact which did not otherwise exist from evidence presented at trial. However, the court refused to order disclosure of the presentence report of a government witness. *See also U.S. v. Anderson,* 724 F.2d 596 (7th Cir. 1984).

Under the Freedom of Information Act, a prisoner is entitled to disclosure of his or her presentence report except for matters relating to confidential sources, diagnostic opinions, and possibly harmful information. *U.S. Department of Justice v. Julian,* 486 U.S. 1 (1987).

## § 1319. — Imposition of Sentence.

## § 1320. — — Time for Imposition.

Sentence shall be imposed without unnecessary delay. Rule 32(a)(1), Fed. R. Crim. P. Before imposing sentence, the court shall determine that the defendant and his attorney have had an opportunity to read and to discuss the presentence report or a summary thereof. Rule 32(a)(1), Fed. R. Crim. P.; *U.S. v. Rone,* 743 F.2d 1169, 1173 (7th Cir. 1984).

Whether delay in sentencing amounts to a violation of either due process, sixth amendment speedy trial rights, or Rule 32(a), depends upon circumstances. Where delay was accidental and not oppressive, and was promptly remedied when discovered, there is no such violation. *Pollard v. U.S.,* 352 U.S. 354, 361-62 (1957). There was a violation where the defendant was sentenced two years and seven months after a guilty plea where events after the plea caused the court to impose the maximum sentence. *Juarez-Casares v. U.S.,* 496 F.2d 190, 192-93 (5th Cir. 1974).

Where there is a factor important to the sentencing determination which is not then capable of being resolved, the court may postpone imposition of sentence for a reasonable time until the factor is capable of being resolved. Rule 32(a)(1), Fed. R. Crim. P.

Under the law previous to the Sentencing Reform Act, and presumably after the Act, sentencing may be delayed until after the defendant has testified in another case or at a codefendant's trial, *U.S. v. Scheffer,* 463 F.2d 567, 572 (5th Cir.), *cert. denied,* 409 U.S. 984 (1972); *Welsh v. U.S.,* 348 F.2d 885, 887 (6th Cir. 1965), or has been tried on another pending indictment, *U.S. v. Pruitt,* 341 F.2d 700, 702 (4th Cir. 1965). The right to imposition of sentence without unreasonable delay is a personal right of the defendant being sentenced and may not be asserted by third parties. Thus, a defendant against whom codefendants had testified did not have standing to assert that codefendants should have been sentenced immediately. *U.S. v. Sherwood,* 435 F.2d 867, 868 (10th Cir. 1970), *cert. denied,* 402 U.S. 909 (1971); *U.S. v. Scheffer,* 463 F.2d at 572.

Sentencing may also be delayed until the presentence report is completed, *U.S. v. Campisi,* 583 F.2d 692, 693 (3d Cir. 1978), to give the defendant the opportunity to cooperate with authorities, *White v. Henderson,* 467 F. Supp. 96, 98-99 (S.D.N.Y. 1979), or where the whereabouts of the defendant are not known, *Whaley v. U.S.,* 394 F.2d 399, 401-02 (10th Cir. 1968).

Where the defendant has not yet begun to serve his sentence, the court may recall the defendant and increase the sentence. *U.S. v. DiFrancesco,* 449 U.S. 117, 134 (1980); *U.S. v. Lawson,* 670 F.2d 923, 929 (10th Cir. 1982); *Neidinger v. U.S.,* 647 F.2d 408, 410 (4th Cir.), *cert. denied,* 454 U.S. 859 (1981).

The court may permit a defendant to withdraw a plea of guilty or nolo contendere before sentence is imposed for any fair and just reason, or where disposition of sentence is suspended, or disposition is made under 18 U.S.C. § 4205(c). However, after sentencing a plea may be set aside only on direct appeal or by a motion under 28 U.S.C. § 2255. Rule 32(d), Fed. R. Crim. P.

### § 1321. — — Allocution.

Before imposing sentence, the court must provide counsel for the defendant and the attorney for the government with the probation officer's determination of the sentencing classifications and guideline range believed to be applicable and provide both attorneys the opportunity to comment upon the probation officer's determination and other matters relating to the appropriate sentence. Rule 32(a)(1), Fed. R. Crim. P. The court must also address the defendant personally and give him and his attorney the right to make any statement on the defendant's behalf and present information in mitigation of the sentence. Rule 32(a)(1)(B) and (C), Fed. R. Crim. P.; *Hill v. U.S.,* 368 U.S. 424, 426 (1962); *Green v. U.S.,* 365 U.S. 301 (1961); *U.S. v. Sparrow,* 673 F.2d 862, 864-65 (5th Cir. 1982); *U.S. v. Meyers,* 646 F.2d 1142, 1146 (6th Cir. 1981). The rule is not complied with when only counsel is given the right to speak, *U.S. v. Navarro-Flores,* 628 F.2d 1178, 1184 (9th Cir. 1980).

Failure to afford the defendant his right of allocution is not a jurisdictional or constitutional error and unless there are exceptional circumstances habeas corpus relief will not be granted even though relief may have been granted upon direct appeal. *Hill v. U.S.,* 368 U.S. at 426. Allocution is not required at a resentencing due to a probation violation. *U.S. v. Coffey,* 871 F.2d 39 (6th Cir. 1989). *Contra U.S. v. Turner,* 741 F.2d 696 (5th Cir. 1984).

The prosecutor has an "equivalent opportunity to speak to the court." Rule 32(a)(1), Fed. R. Crim. P.

If there is a joint motion by the defendant and the government, the court may hear *in camera* such statement by the defendant, his counsel, or the attorney for the government. Rule 32(a)(1), Fed. R. Crim. P.

### § 1322. — — Factors Which May Not Be Considered.

Congress has required that the Sentencing Guidelines be "entirely neutral as to the race, sex, national origin, creed and socioeconomic status of offenders," 28 U.S.C. § 994(d)(11), and must "reflect the general inappropriateness of considering the education, vocational skills, employment record, family ties and responsibilities, and community ties of the defendant," 28 U.S.C. § 994(e). *See also* U.S.S.G. §§ 5H1.1 —

5H1.10. Sentencing is to be based upon the crime committed, not the offender. *U.S. v. Jimenez-Lopez,* 873 F.2d 769 (5th Cir. 1989). Departing from a sentencing range based upon a person's education and socioeconomic status is not permitted. *U.S. v. Burch,* 873 F.2d 765 (5th Cir. 1989). Considering a person's national origin as a sentencing consideration may likewise violate due process. *U.S. v. Borrero-Isaza,* 887 F.2d 1349 (9th Cir. 1989).

The defendant's refusal to assist authorities in the investigation of other persons may not be considered as an aggravating sentencing factor. U.S.S.G. § 5K1.2.

Where a defendant in a plea agreement agrees to cooperate and provide information about others to the government, such information may not be used to increase the sentencing range unless the plea agreement specifically states that the court may consider the defendant's disclosures in calculating the sentencing range. U.S.S.G. § 1B1.8(a); *U.S. v. Shorteeth,* 887 F.2d 253 (10th Cir. 1989).

A court may not consider previous uncounseled felony convictions in determining sentence. *U.S. v. Tucker,* 404 U.S. 443, 449 (1972); *Walker v. U.S.,* 636 F.2d 1138, 1139 (6th Cir. 1980). Nor may it consider a previous uncounseled misdemeanor conviction which converts a subsequent misdemeanor into a felony with a prison term. *Baldasar v. Illinois,* 446 U.S. 222 (1980). It has been held that a sentencing judge may not consider evidence obtained through an illegal search and seizure, *Verdugo v. U.S.,* 402 F.2d 599, 613 (9th Cir. 1968), *cert. denied,* 397 U.S. 925 (1970), while the same circuit has permitted the use of such evidence in sentencing where the illegal search was caused by a "technical error," *U.S. v. Larios,* 640 F.2d 938, 942 (9th Cir. 1981). The court is also prohibited from considering information received *ex parte* from the prosecutor, *U.S. v. Wolfson,* 634 F.2d 1217 (9th Cir. 1980); *U.S. v. Rosner,* 485 F.2d 1213, 1221 (2d Cir. 1973), *cert. denied,* 417 U.S. 950 (1974), or that the defendant refused a plea bargain, *U.S. v. Derrich,* 519 F.2d 1, 3-5 (6th Cir. 1975).

The court may not consider or impose a greater sentence because a defendant exercised any of his rights, such as the right to trial, *U.S. v. Hutchings,* 757 F.2d 11, 14 (2d Cir.), *cert. denied,* 472 U.S. 1031 (1984); *U.S. v. Wiley,* 278 F.2d 500, 504 (7th Cir. 1960), or the right to appeal, *North Carolina v. Pearce,* 395 U.S. 711, 723-24 (1969). The punishment imposed after a conviction on a retrial which occurs after a reversal may not be increased without justification. *North Carolina v. Pearce,* 395 U.S. at 723. When, however, a defendant is sentenced to a harsher sentence after a trial which took place following a first sentence based upon a guilty plea which was set aside, there is no presumption of vindictiveness as in *Pearce,* because the evidence at trial will provide more information to the court for sentencing. *Alabama v. Smith,* 490 U.S. 794 (1989).

### § 1323. — — Application of Sentencing Guidelines.

Each federal offense is assigned an offense level ranging from one to forty-three. Each offense level is a potential imprisonment range. Instructions for applying the Guidelines and determining the offense level and the criminal history category may be found at § 1B1.1 of the Sentencing Guidelines. Applying the Guidelines to the offense is basically a mechanical exercise. The steps which should be followed in establishing the sentence are as follows:

1. Determine the guideline section in Chapter 2 of the Sentencing Guidelines most applicable to the statute of conviction. This is determined by correlating the statute with the guideline in the statutory index which is found at Appendix "A" of the Sentencing Guidelines. For example, if the defendant is convicted under 18 U.S.C. § 495, the statutory index will refer to U.S.S.G. § 2F1.1(a).

If, however, there is a conviction by a plea of guilty or *nolo contendere* containing a stipulation that specifically establishes a more serious offense than the offense of conviction, determine the offense guideline section in Chapter Two which is most applicable to the more serious offense. U.S.S.G. § 1B1.2(a). If a stipulation in a statement of facts given at a plea hearing supports two reasonable readings, one being simply that of the conviction and another reading which would encompass a more serious offense, a sentence based upon the guideline for the more serious offense cannot stand. *Braxton v. U.S.,* 111 S. Ct. 1854 (1991).

Conduct that is relevant in determining the applicable guideline range may include acts or quantities involved in an overall scheme rather than just the act or quantity specified in the count or counts involved in the guilty finding. For example, in a drug distribution case, quantities and types of drugs not specified in the count of conviction are to be included in determining the offense level if they were "part of the same course of conduct or a common scheme or plan as the offense of conviction." U.S.S.G. § 1B1.3(a)(2); *U.S. v. Salva,* 894 F.2d 225 (7th Cir. 1990); *U.S. v. Guerrero,* 863 F.2d 245 (2d Cir. 1988).

2. Refer to the particular guideline which has been referenced through the statutory index to determine the base level for the offense. In the example above, the defendant will have been convicted under 18 U.S.C. § 495 for an offense involving fraud, and his or her base offense

level is "6." The offense level may then be increased depending upon how much loss in terms of dollars was caused by the offense.

For offenses involving drugs, § 2D1.1 of the Sentencing Guidelines provides a drug quantity table which may apply to determine the base offense level. In determining weights for the purpose of this table for an LSD conviction, the blotter-paper medium is to be included. *Chapman v. U.S.,* 111 S. Ct. 1919 (1991).

3. Adjustments to the base offense level are then made upward depending upon the appropriate considerations of the victim, the role of the defendant, and obstruction of justice by the defendant as set forth in Parts A, B, and C of Chapter 3 of the Sentencing Guidelines.

Throwing bags of marijuana out of the window of a fleeing automobile while being pursued by Border Patrol agents constitutes willfully obstructing the administration of justice permitting the increase of the defendant's offense level pursuant to § 3C1.1 of the Sentencing Guidelines. *U.S. v. Galvan-Garcia,* 872 F.2d 638 (5th Cir.), *cert. denied,* 110 S. Ct. 164 (1989). Likewise, lying to the probation officer preparing a presentence report, *U.S. v. Christman,* 894 F.2d 339 (9th Cir. 1990); *U.S. v. Velasquez-Mercado,* 872 F.2d 632 (5th Cir.), *cert. denied,* 110 S. Ct. 187 (1989), and threatening a prospective witness, *U.S. v. Shoulberg,* 895 F.2d 882 (2d Cir. 1990), may be used to adjust the base offense level.

If the defendant was a minimal or minor participant, the offense level may be reduced. A minimal participant is entitled to a four-level reduction and a minor participant to a two-level reduction. Whether the defendant is a minimal participant is a factual determination turning upon culpability. A minor participant is one who was less culpable than others, but whose role was not minimal. The standard of review is "clearly erroneous." U.S.S.G. § 3B1.2.; *U.S. v. Franco-Torres,* 869 F.2d 797 (5th Cir. 1989).

4. If the defendant has been convicted of multiple counts, the counts are combined pursuant to the application of Part D of Chapter 3 of the Sentencing Guidelines, and the offense level is adjusted accordingly.

5. The offense level may be reduced by two levels under § 3E1.1(a) of the Sentencing Guidelines if the defendant "clearly demonstrates acceptance of responsibility for his offense." A defendant who, of course, maintains her innocence at trial, and then purports to accept responsibility after conviction, "may have a difficult time persuading the trial judge that her later position is sincere rather than merely convenient." *U.S. v. Thomas,* 870 F.2d 174, 177 (5th Cir. 1989). *See also U.S. v. Henry,* 883 F.2d 1010 (11th Cir. 1989), which discusses and rejects fifth and sixth amendment challenges to the acceptance of responsibility

guidelines. A guilty plea does not entitle the defendant to a reduction as a matter of right U.S.S.G. § 3E1.1, comment; *U.S. v. Carroll*, 893 F.2d 1502 (6th Cir. 1990). A guilty plea without additional affirmative facts may, however, be sufficient to justify the reduction. *U.S. v. Knight*, 905 F.2d 189 (8th Cir. 1990). Likewise, an agreement signed by the defendant and the assistant U.S. attorney that the defendant accepts responsibility for her conduct does not require the judge to agree and reduce the offense level. *U.S. v. Nunley*, 873 F.2d 182 (8th Cir. 1989).

In the context of a plea agreement, "acceptance of personal responsibility" means responsibility for the conduct to which the defendant pleads guilty, not all counts in the indictment. *U.S. v. Oliveras*, 905 F.2d 623 (2d Cir. 1990); *U.S. v. Perez-Franco*, 873 F.2d 455 (1st Cir. 1989).

It has been held that the entrapment defense is not necessarily inconsistent with the notion of acceptance of responsibility. *U.S. v. Fleener*, 900 F.2d 914 (6th Cir. 1990).

Once the court finds that the defendant has in fact accepted responsibility, the downward adjustment must be made. Before November 1, 1989, a career offender was not eligible for the downward adjustment for acceptance of responsibility. *U.S. v. Alves*, 873 F.2d 495 (1st Cir. 1989); *U.S. v. Huff*, 873 F.2d 709 (3rd Cir. 1989). Since November 1, 1989, a career offender qualifies for the acceptance of responsibility adjustment. U.S.S.G. § 4B1.1.

A defendant may receive a reduction of one additional level for acceptance of responsibility, if he is at level sixteen or greater and if the defendant has assisted authorities in the investigation or prosecution of the offense by: (1) timely providing complete information concerning his involvement, or (2) timely notifying authorities of his intention to enter a plea of guilty, thereby permitting the government to avoid preparing for trial and permitting the court to allocate its resources efficiently. U.S.S.G. § 3E1.1.(b).

These first five steps establish the offense level to be used with the sentencing table. Now:

6. Determine the criminal history of the defendant by applying Part A of Chapter 4 of the Sentencing Guidelines. This determines the criminal history category for use with the sentencing table.

Where the criminal history category seriously underrepresents the seriousness of the defendant's criminal history or the likelihood that he will commit other crimes, the court may depart from the otherwise applicable guideline range. U.S.S.G. § 4A1.3; *U.S. v. Spraggins*, 868 F.2d 1541 (11th Cir. 1989); *U.S. v. De Luna-Trujillo*, 868 F.2d 122 (5th Cir. 1989).

7. From Part B of Chapter 4 of the Sentencing Guidelines, determine if the defendant is a career offender or committed the offense as part of a criminal livelihood. If the defendant is found to be a career offender, apply the imprisonment section listed there if that table provides for a greater offense level than the offense level otherwise applicable.

8. Refer to the table in Part A of Chapter 5 to determine the specific guideline range that corresponds to the total offense level and criminal history category.

9. For the particular guideline range, refer to Parts B through G of Chapter 5 to determine any sentencing requirements and options related to probation, imprisonment, supervision conditions, fines and restitution.

10. Refer to Parts H and K of Chapter 5 of the Sentencing Guidelines, Specific Offender Characteristics and Departures, and to any other policy statements or commentary in the guidelines that might warrant consideration in imposing sentence.

Prior sentences in "related" cases shall be treated as one sentence. U.S.S.G. § 4A1.2(a)(2). Although Application Note 3 states that cases are related if they are "consolidated for trial or sentencing," a defendant may receive an upward departure so as not to take advantage of the situation where he previously pled guilty to a number of crimes in a Rule 20 proceeding and then claims he should be treated as a defendant with only one prior conviction. *U.S. v. Dorsey,* 888 F.2d 79 (11th Cir. 1989), *cert. denied,* 110 S. Ct. 756 (1990).

### § 1324. — — Departure from Guidelines.

If there is any aggravating or mitigating circumstance of a kind or to a degree that was not adequately taken into consideration by the Sentencing Commission in formulating the Guidelines, the court may depart from the Guidelines. 18 U.S.C. § 3553(b). The court must state the "specific reason" for a sentence different from that required by the Guidelines. 18 U.S.C. § 3553(c)(2); *U.S. v. White,* 893 F.2d 276 (10th Cir. 1990). However, any factors adequately taken into account by the Sentencing Commission in establishing the guidelines or factors that the Commission has expressly rejected as an appropriate ground for departure may not be used for a departure from the Guidelines. *Williams v. U.S.,* 112 S. Ct. 1112 (1992).

If a court is considering an upward departure from the Guidelines on a ground that is not identified either in the presentence report or in a prehearing submission by the government, Rule 32 requires that the court give the parties reasonable notice that it is contemplating such a ruling, specifically identifying the ground on which it is considering an upward departure. *Burns v. U.S.,* 111 S. Ct. 2182 (1991).

The courts have adopted a three-step analysis to determine whether there are such aggravating or mitigating circumstances not taken into account by the Sentencing Commission to justify departure from the Guidelines. First, plenary review of the circumstances relied on by the district court in determining that the case was sufficiently "unusual" to warrant departure. This is a question of law. Second, determine whether the circumstances actually exist in the particular case. Third, if the factors the court considered were appropriate for departure, and these factors are supported by the record, the measure of the departure is a standard of reasonableness. 18 U.S.C. § 3742(e)(2); *U.S. v. Brewer,* 899 F.2d 503 (6th Cir.), *cert. denied,* 111 S. Ct. 127 (1990); *U.S. v. White, supra; U.S. v. Diaz-Villafane,* 874 F.2d 43 (1st Cir. 1989), *cert. denied,* 493 U.S. 862 (1990).

A court may not, however, make an upward departure based on a factual matter which was necessarily rejected by the jury. *U.S. v. Brady,* 928 F.2d 844 (9th Cir. 1991). *Contra U.S. v. Ryan,* 866 F.2d 604 (3d Cir. 1989).

### § 1325. — — — Departure to Increase Sentence.

Factors identified in the Guidelines which may serve as a possible basis for departure to increase the sentence above the authorized guidelines include: death, § 5K2.1; significant physical injury, § 5K2.2; extreme psychological injury to a victim, § 5K2.3; abduction or unlawful restraint of a person, § 5K2.4; property damage or loss not taken into account within the guidelines, § 5K2.5; use or possession of a weapon or dangerous instrument, § 5K2.6; significant disruption of a governmental function, § 5K2.7; conduct which was unusually heinous, cruel, brutal, or degrading to the victim, § 5K2.8; committing an offense in order to facilitate or conceal the commission of another offense, § 5K2.9; and significantly endangering the national security, public health, or safety, § 5K2.14.

Cases where the courts have found aggravating or mitigating circumstances not adequately taken into consideration by the Sentencing Commission to justify an upward departure include: acquittals by reason of insanity which is past dangerous conduct not computed as part of a defendant's criminal history, *U.S. v. McKenley,* 895 F.2d 184 (4th Cir. 1990); great risk of recidivism, *U.S. v. Coe,* 891 F.2d 405 (2d Cir. 1989).

Upward departures which have been rejected because the circumstances have been adequately considered in formulating the guidelines include: prior arrest record alone, *Williams v. U.S.,* 112 S. Ct. 1112

(1992); use of a weapon when in fact there was no weapon, *U.S. v. Hawkins,* 901 F.2d 863 (10th Cir. 1990); *U.S. v. Coe, supra;* special circumstances in the district of the offense and particular local antipathy toward the crime, *U.S. v. Aguilar-Pena,* 887 F.2d 347 (1st Cir. 1989); drug dependency, *U.S. v. Hawkins, supra.*

### § 1326. — — — Departure to Reduce Sentence.

Factors identified in the Guidelines which may serve as a possible basis for departure from the Guidelines by reducing the sentence below the guideline range are: wrongful conduct by the victim which contributed significantly to provoking the offense, § 5K2.10; committing a crime in order to avoid a perceived greater harm, § 5K2.11; committing an offense because of serious coercion, blackmail, or duress, under circumstances not amounting to a complete defense, § 5K2.12; and commission of a nonviolent offense while suffering from significantly reduced mental capacity not resulting from voluntary use of drugs or other intoxicants, § 5K2.13. The Sentencing Commission also did not deal with "single acts of aberrant behavior" that may justify departure. U.S.S.G. § 1A.4(d).

Cases where the courts have found aggravating or mitigating circumstances not adequately taken into consideration by the Sentencing Commission to justify a downward departure include: a bisexual who was delicate looking and peculiarily vulnerable to being victimized in prison, *U.S. v. Lara,* 905 F.2d 599 (2d Cir. 1990); mitigating employment, family and community factors of such a "magnitude" that they were not adequately taken into consideration in formulating the guidelines, *U.S. v. Big Crow,* 898 F.2d 1326 (8th Cir. 1990); duress rejected as a defense by the jury, *U.S. v. Cheape (Appeal of Klinefelter),* 889 F.2d 477 (3d Cir. 1989).

A career offender's situation may be so "atypical" that downward departure may be appropriate. *U.S. v. Brown,* 903 F.2d 540 (8th Cir. 1990). Letters describing a defendant's good character and background may be considered for certain limited purposes including where within an applicable sentencing range a sentence should fall. *U.S. v. Duarte,* 901 F.2d 1498 (9th Cir. 1990).

Downward departures which have been rejected because the circumstances have been adequately considered in formulating the guidelines include: restitution, age, and physical condition, *U.S. v. Carey,* 895 F.2d 318 (7th Cir. 1990); pregnancy and coercion by a husband without threat of physical injury, *U.S. v. Pozzy,* 902 F.2d 133 (1st Cir.), *cert. denied,* 111 S.Ct. 353 (1990); restitution, first-time offender, mother of small children and clemency recommendation by the victim, *U.S. v.*

*Brewer,* 899 F.2d 503 (6th Cir.), *cert. denied,* 111 S. Ct. 127 (1990); drug dependency, minimal prior record, reform, ineffective as a robber, *U.S. v. Williams,* 891 F.2d 212 (1st Cir.), *cert. denied,* 110 S. Ct. 1496 (1989); disparity between the sentences of individual co-defendants, *U.S. v. Minicone,* 960 F.2d 1099 (2d Cir. 1992); post-offense conduct such as entering a drug treatment program, *U.S. v. Van Dyke,* 895 F.2d 984 (4th Cir.), *cert. denied,* 111 S. Ct. 112 (1990).

### § 1327. — — — Appeal where there is Departure.

An appellate court lacks jurisdiction to hear an appeal of a court's denial of a defendant's request for a downward departure of a legal sentence within the applicable guideline range, but appeal is proper for an upward departure. 18 U.S.C. § 3742(a); *U.S. v. Franz,* 886 F.2d 973 (7th Cir. 1989). The government may appeal a sentence that is less than that specified in the applicable guideline range. 18 U.S.C. § 3742(b).

Findings of fact on issues of departure from the Guidelines are reviewed under a "clearly erroneous" standard and departure will be affirmed if the court gives "acceptable reasons" for the departure. 18 U.S.C. § 3742(d); *U.S. v. Velasquez-Mercado,* 872 F.2d 632 (5th Cir. 1989), *cert. denied,* 110 S. Ct. 187 (1990).

A departure from the guideline range based on both valid and invalid factors does not necessarily require a remand. A two-step analysis is necessary: first, was the sentence imposed as a result of an incorrect application of the Guidelines — requiring remand — or would the court have imposed the same sentence absent the erroneous factor — not requiring remand; second, was the departure reasonable under 18 U.S.C. § 3742(f)(2). *Williams v. U.S.,* 112 S. Ct. 1112 (1992).

### § 1328. — — Departure for Substantial Assistance to Authorities.

Upon the motion of the government, the court may depart from the Guidelines and give a lesser sentence than required by the Guidelines if the defendant has made a good-faith effort to provide substantial assistance in the investigation or prosecution of another person who has committed an offense. This court may depart even from a statutorily required minimum sentence. 18 U.S.C. § 3553(e); 28 U.S.C. § 994(n). This reduction is independent of any reduction for acceptance of responsibility. U.S.S.G. §5K1.1, comment.

A court lacks authority to impose a sentence below the statutory minimum where the defendant claims such a departure is justified due

331

to cooperation with the government where the government refuses to move for a departure. A motion by the government is a prerequisite before the court may consider such cooperation. *U.S. v. Alamin,* 895 F.2d 1335 (11th Cir. 1990); *U.S. v. La Guardia,* 902 F.2d 1010 (1st Cir. 1990); *U.S. v. Francois,* 889 F.2d 1341 (4th Cir. 1989), *cert. denied,* 494 U.S. 1085 (1990); *U.S. v. Huerta,* 878 F.2d 89 (2d Cir. 1989), *cert. denied,* 493 U.S. 1046 (1990). A government refusal to move for a departure is not reviewable for arbitrariness. *U.S. v. Burrell,* 963 F.2d 976 (7th Cir. 1992). However, the government's refusal to file such a motion may be reviewed for constitutional violations, such as failure to file the motion because of the defendant's race or religion. *Wade v. U.S.,* 112 S. Ct. 1840 (1992).

In setting the reduction, the court may consider, but is not limited to, these considerations: (1) the court's evaluation of the significance and usefulness of the defendant's assistance, considering also the government's evaluation of the assistance; (2) the truthfulness, completeness, and reliability of the information or testimony provided by the defendant; (3) the nature and extent of the defendant's assistance; (4) any injury suffered or risk of injury to the defendant or his family resulting from his assistance; (5) the timeliness of the defendant's assistance. U.S.S.G. § 5K1.1.

In reducing a sentence under § 3553(e), there is no lower limit placed on the court's authority. Probation may be the sentence. Should the government be dissatisfied with the extent of the downward departure, it may appeal and the issue is whether the sentence imposed was reasonable. *U.S. v. Snelling,* 961 F.2d 93 (6th Cir. 1991); *U.S. v. Wilson,* 896 F.2d 856 (4th Cir. 1990).

If a sentence is reduced, a sentencing judge must state the reasons for the reduction under this section. 18 U.S.C. § 3553(c).

## § 1329. — — Probation.

The court may sentence a defendant to a term of probation unless: (1) the offense is a class A or class B felony (a class A felony is one calling for life imprisonment or death, a class B felony is one calling for imprisonment for twenty-five years or more) 18 U.S.C. § 3559(a)(1); (2) the offense is an offense for which probation has been expressly precluded; or (3) the defendant is sentenced at the same time to imprisonment for the same or a different offense. 18 U.S.C. § 3561.

If the offense is a felony or misdemeanor, there is a mandatory condition that the defendant not commit another federal, state, or local crime during the term of probation. If the conviction was for a felony, the defendant must also as a mandatory condition of probation either pay a fine, make restitution to a victim, or work in community service as directed by the court. The statute also sets forth discretionary conditions of probation which the court may impose including "such other conditions as the court may impose." 18 U.S.C. § 3563. The Sentencing Guidelines provisions for probation are found at §§ 5B1.1 — 5B1.4.

If the defendant violates a condition of probation, the court may revoke the sentence of probation and impose any other sentence that was available at the time of the initial sentencing. 18 U.S.C. § 3565.

## § 1330. — — Concurrent and Consecutive Sentences.

When multiple terms of imprisonment are imposed at the same time, or if imprisonment is imposed upon a defendant who is already subject to an undischarged term of imprisonment, the terms may run concurrently or consecutively, except that the terms may not run consecutively for an attempt and for another offense that was the sole object of the attempt. 18 U.S.C. § 3584.

Multiple terms of imprisonment imposed at the same time run concurrently unless the court orders or the statute mandates that the terms are to run consecutively. Multiple terms of imprisonment imposed at different times run consecutively unless the court orders that they are to run concurrently. *Id.*

## § 1331. — — Term of Supervisory Release after Imprisonment.

In addition to imposing a sentence of imprisonment for a felony or Class A misdemeanor, the court may include as part of the sentence a requirement that the defendant be placed upon a term of supervised release after imprisonment. 18 U.S.C. § 3583. The Sentencing Guidelines provisions regarding supervised release are found at U.S.S.G. §§ 5D3.1 — 5D3.3.

## § 1332. — — Imposition of Fine.

Any individual who is convicted of a felony or a misdemeanor resulting in the loss of human life may be fined up to $250,000; up to $100,000 for a Class A misdemeanor that does not result in death; and up to $5000 for a Class B or C misdemeanor that does not result in death and for an infraction. In the alternative, an individual may be fined up to twice the gross gain to the defendant or twice the gross loss from the offense to any other person. 18 U.S.C. § 3571.

· The guidelines mandate a fine according to a schedule for all individual defendants, except where a defendant is not able, even with the use of a reasonable installment schedule, to pay all or part of a fine, or, if a

fine would unduly burden the defendant's dependents. U.S.S.G.
§ 5E1.2(f). In addition, an additional fine amount shall be imposed "at
least sufficient to pay the costs to the government of any imprisonment, probation, or supervised release order." U.S.S.G. § 5E1.2(i).

An organization is fined according to a special schedule for organizations. 18 U.S.C. § 3571. *See* § 1340, *infra*.

## § 1333. — — — Factors to be Considered in Imposing Fines.

In determining whether to impose a fine and the amount, time and
method of payment, the court shall consider in addition to the factors
set forth in 18 U.S.C. § 3553(a): (1) the defendant's income, earning
capacity and financial resources; (2) the burden the fine will impose
upon the defendant and any person who is financially dependent upon
the defendant, or any person (including a government) that would be
responsible for the welfare of any person financially dependent upon
the defendant, relative to the burden that alternate punishments
would impose; (3) any pecuniary loss inflicted upon others as a result of
the offense; (4) whether restitution is ordered or made and the amount
of restitution; (5) the need to deprive the defendant of illegally obtained gains from the offense; (6) whether the defendant can pass on to
consumers or others the expenses of the fine; and (7) if the defendant is
an organization, the size of the organization and any measure taken by
the organization to discipline any officer, director, employee or agent
in the organization responsible for the offense and to prevent a recur-
rence. 18 U.S.C. § 3572(a).

The payment of a fine is due immediately unless the court either
requires payment by a certain date or establishes an installment
schedule. 18 U.S.C. § 3572(d). The court may not impose an alternative
sentence to be served in the event that the fine is not paid. 18 U.S.C.
§ 3572(e).

If a fine is imposed on an agent or shareholder of an organization,
the fine shall not be paid directly or indirectly out of the assets of the
organization unless the court finds that such payment is expressly
permitted under state law. 18 U.S.C. § 3572(f).

## § 1334. — — — Modification or Remission of Fine.

Upon petition of the government showing that reasonable efforts to
collect a fine are not likely to be effective, the court may: (1) remit all
or part of the unpaid portion of the fine; (2) defer payment of the fine,
or (3) extend a date certain or an installment schedule previously ordered. 18 U.S.C. § 3573.

## § 1335. — — Assistance for Victims.

## § 1336. — — — Special Assessments.

A convicted defendant must pay a special assessment for the purpose of funding the Crime Victims Fund. If the defendant is an individual, the assessment is $50 if the conviction is a felony. If the defendant is an organization, the assessment is $200 for a felony conviction. 18 U.S.C. § 3013; U.S.S.G. § 5E1.3.

It has been held that the special assessment statute is not a revenue bill for purposes of the "Origination Clause," Art. I, § 7, which requires revenue bills to start in the House of Representatives. *U.S. v. Munoz-Flores*, 110 S. Ct. 1964 (1990).

## § 1337. — — — Restitution.

A defendant shall be ordered to make restitution. A fine shall not impair the ability of the defendant to make restitution, 18 U.S.C. § 3572(b), and any payments shall first be applied to satisfy restitution and then any fine imposed. U.S.S.G. § 5E1.1(c).

A victim impact statement is part of the report of a presentence investigation, Rule 32(c)(2)(D), Fed. R. Crim. P., and the procedures for issuing an order of restitution are set out at 18 U.S.C. §§ 3663 and 3664.

A court may order restitution to any identifiable victim of the offense limited by the victim's actual losses, 18 U.S.C. § 3663. Restitution may also be made to any person who has compensated the victim for such loss, 18 U.S.C. § 3663(e)(1), including any insurance company. *U.S. v. Cloud*, 872 F.2d 846 (9th Cir. 1989); *U.S. v. Cannizzaro*, 871 F.2d 809 (9th Cir.), *cert. denied*, 110 S. Ct. 245 (1989). A court is limited in ordering restitution to only those acts for which the defendant was convicted, *Hughey v. U.S.*, 110 S. Ct. 1979 (1990). When a juror causes a trial to be aborted because she had impermissible contact with a defendant, the government is a "victim," and the defendant-juror may be required to pay the cost of the aborted criminal trial. *U.S. v. Hand*, 863 F.2d 1100 (3d Cir. 1988).

In determining whether to order restitution, the court "shall consider" the amount of loss to the victim, the financial resources of the defendant, the financial needs and earning ability of the defendant and the defendant's dependents, and such other factors as the court deems appropriate. 18 U.S.C. § 3664(a). Although they do not need to be explicitly stated, nevertheless, if the court fails to consider these mandatory factors, the restitution order will be reversed on appeal. *U.S. v.*

*Gomer,* 764 F.2d 1221 (7th Cir. 1985); *U.S. v. McClellan,* 868 F.2d 210 (7th Cir. 1989). It was held that the court failed to consider the defendant's ability to pay and needs of his family when it ordered restitution of an amount that was nine times his annual salary to be paid in five years. *U.S. v. Mahoney,* 859 F.2d 47 (7th Cir. 1988). However, the court is not required to consider defendant's relative culpability in the crime in determining the amount of restitution, as this is not a mandatory factor to consider. *U.S. v. Cloud, supra.* Restitution may be ordered even when the defendant is indigent. *U.S. v. Schwarck,* 961 F.2d 121 (8th Cir. 1992).

Any dispute as to the proper amount or type of restitution is determined by a preponderance of the evidence. The burden of demonstrating the amount of loss to the victim is on the government. The burden of demonstrating the financial resources of the defendant and the needs of the defendant and his dependents is on the defendant. 18 U.S.C. § 3664(d).

### § 1338. — — — Notice to Victims.

If a defendant has been found guilty of an offense involving fraud or other intentionally deceptive practices, he or she may be required to give reasonable notice and explanation of the conviction, in such form as the court may approve, to the victims of the offense. The notice may be ordered to be given by mail, through the media, or other appropriate means, and the court shall not require the defendant to bear the costs of notice in the excess of $20,000. 18 U.S.C. § 3555.

Victims may be permitted to participate in the sentencing so that their losses may be accurately determined. *U.S. v. Weir,* 861 F.2d 542 (9th Cir. 1988), *cert. denied,* 489 U.S. 1089 (1989).

### § 1339. — — Resolving Disputed Sentencing Facts.

If the defendant disputes any factual inaccuracy in the report of the presentence investigation, the court shall permit the defendant and his counsel an opportunity to comment on the report and, in the court's discretion, introduce testimony or other information relating to any alleged factual inaccuracy. Rule 32(c)(3)(A), Fed. R. Crim. P.

Concerning any controverted matter in the report, the court may: (1) make a finding as to the allegation of factual inaccuracy; or (2) make a determination that no such finding is necessary because the matter will not be taken into account in sentencing. Rule 32(c)(3)(D), Fed. R. Crim. P. However, if the disputed fact is one that would have a material effect upon the sentence as established through the guidelines, it appears that the court's options to permit or not permit a hearing or to find that the controverted matter will not be taken into account in sentencing may not be permitted. The Sentencing Commission has stated that: "The court's resolution of disputed sentencing factors will usually have a measurable effect on the applicable punishment. More formality is therefore unavoidable if the sentencing process is to be accurate and fair." U.S.S.G. § 6A1.3, comment. The Commentary also states that, "[a]n evidentiary hearing may sometimes be the only reliable way to resolve disputed issues.... The sentencing court must determine the appropriate procedure in light of the nature of the dispute, its relevance to the sentencing determination, and applicable case law." *Id.*

Under Rule 32(c)(3)(A) of the Federal Rules of Criminal Procedure, the court has complete discretion to permit the defendant to introduce testimony or other information relating to any claimed factual inaccuracy in the presentence investigation report. The Rules of Evidence do not apply to sentencing proceedings. Rule 1101(d)(3), Fed. R. Evid.; U.S.S.G. § 6A1.3. Likewise, there is still no limitation on the information which the court may consider in imposing a sentence. 18 U.S.C. § 3661. *But see* U.S.S.G. § 1B1.4 and § 1322, *infra*.

Unresolved are the issues of who has the burden of going forward regarding controverted facts and who has the burden of persuasion. Is the burden of going forward on the party challenging the facts? Who has the burden of persuasion? Is it on the government if the disputed fact would enhance the sentence? Is it on the defendant if it would reduce the sentence? In *U.S. v. Lee,* 818 F.2d 1052 (2d Cir.), *cert. denied,* 484 U.S. 956 (1987), the government conceded that it had the burden of persuasion concerning disputed factors which were offered to enhance the defendant's sentence.

The standard approved for the resolution of a disputed fact is the preponderance of evidence standard. U.S.S.G. § 6A1.3, comment; *McMillin v. Pennsylvania,* 477 U.S. 79 (1986); *U.S. v. Carroll,* 893 F.2d 1502 (6th Cir. 1990); *U.S. v. Lee, supra; U.S. v. Wilson,* 900 F.2d 1350 (9th Cir. 1990). Likewise, 18 U.S.C. § 3664(d) states that a dispute regarding restitution is resolved by the "preponderance" test.

If a court fails to make the required findings of fact or determine that such findings are unnecessary, the sentence will be vacated and remanded to the district court for resentencing. *U.S. v. Fernandez-Angula,* 897 F.2d 1514 (9th Cir. 1990); *U.S. v. Burch,* 873 F.2d 765 (5th Cir. 1989); *U.S. v. Garbett,* 867 F.2d 1132 (8th Cir. 1989); but failure to dispute matters in a presentence report until after sentencing relieves the court of the requirement that it make findings concerning alleged factual inaccuracies. *U.S. v. Brown,* 870 F.2d 1354 (7th Cir. 1989).

If the court makes a determination that it will not take a controverted matter into account in imposing sentence, this determination must be clearly reduced to writing and accompany any presentence report made available to the Bureau of Prisons or Parole Commission. Rule 32(c)(3)(D), Fed. R. Crim. P.; *U.S. v. Miller,* 871 F.2d 488 (4th Cir. 1989).

### § 1340. — — Sentencing of Organizations.

An organization that is convicted of a felony or a misdemeanor resulting in the loss of human life may be fined up to $500,000; up to $200,000 for a Class A misdemeanor that does not result in death; and up to $10,000 for either a Class B or Class C misdemeanor that does not result in death, or for an infraction. In the alternative, an organization may be fined up to twice the gross gain to the organization or twice the gross loss from the offense to any other person. 18 U.S.C. § 3571.

"Organization" means "a person other than an individual." 18 U.S.C. § 18. The term includes "corporations, partnerships, associations, joint-stock companies, unions, trusts, pension funds, unincorporated organizations, governments and political subdivisions thereof, and non-profit organizations." U.S.S.G. § 8A1.1, comment.

The sentencing of organizations chapter reflects four general principles. First, whenever practicable, order the organization to remedy any harm caused by the offense. Second, if the organization operated primarily for a criminal purpose or primarily by criminal means, the fine should be set sufficiently high to divest the organization of all its assets. Third, the fine range should be based on the seriousness of the offense and the culpability of the organization. Fourth, probation is appropriate when needed to ensure that another sanction will be fully implemented, or to ensure that steps will be taken within the organization to reduce the likelihood of future criminal conduct. U.S.S.G. Ch. 8, intro. comment.

### § 1341. — — Juvenile Offenders.

The provisions of 18 U.S.C. § 5037(c)(1)(B) limiting the detention of a juvenile to "the maximum term of imprisonment that would be authorized if the juvenile had been tried and convicted as an adult" refers to the maximum sentence to which a similarly situated adult would be subject if convicted including application of the Sentencing Guidelines. Plenary application of the Guidelines to juveniles is not required. The sentencing court's concern goes only to the upper limit of the proper guideline range as setting the maximum term for which a juvenile may be committed, absent circumstances that would warrant departure. *U.S. v. R.L.C.*, 112 S. Ct. 1329 (1992).

### §1342. — Judgment of Conviction.

The judgment of conviction shall set forth the defendant's plea, the verdict or finding, and the adjudication and sentence imposed by the court. The judgment is to be signed by the judge and entered by the clerk. If the defendant is found not guilty, judgment shall be entered accordingly. Rule 32(b)(1), Fed. R. Crim. P. When a verdict contains a finding of property subject to criminal forfeiture, the judgment of forfeiture shall authorize the Attorney General to seize the interest or property subject to forfeiture upon such terms as the court determines to be proper. Rule 32(b)(2), Fed. R. Crim. P.

### §1343. — Correction of Sentence.

The court shall correct a sentence that is determined on appeal under 18 U.S.C. § 3742 to have been imposed in violation of law, to have been imposed as a result of an incorrect application of the Sentencing Guidelines, or to be unreasonable upon remand of the case to the court (1) for imposition of a sentence in accordance with the findings of the court of appeals; or (2) for further sentencing proceedings if, after such proceedings, the court determines that the original sentence was incorrect. Rule 35(a), Fed. R. Crim. P.

Within seven days after the imposition of sentence, the court may correct a sentence that was imposed as a result of arithmetical, technical, or other clear error. Rule 35(c), Fed. R. Crim. P. Corrections under this section are intended to be very narrow and to extend only to those matters where there is obvious error or mistake. It is not intended to afford an opportunity to reconsider the application or interpretation of the Sentencing Guidelines. *See* Advisory Committee's note.

### §1344. — Modification of Sentence after Imposition.

Rule 35(b) of the Federal Rules of Criminal Procedure, as it existed prior to the Sentencing Reform Act of 1984, has been repealed. That rule permitted the court virtually unlimited power to reduce a sentence for crimes committed before November 1, 1987, within certain time limits.

The Sentencing Reform Act provides for three instances in which a sentence may be reduced after imposition. 18 U.S.C. § 3582(c).

The first instance for which a sentence may be lowered is upon the motion of the director of the bureau of prisons. The court may reduce the term of imprisonment if the court finds that extraordinary and compelling reasons warrant such a reduction and that the reduction is consistent with applicable policy statements issued by the Sentencing Commission. 18 U.S.C. § 3582(c)(1)(A).

The second instance is where, upon the motion of the government made within one year after the imposition of sentence, the court may reduce the sentence to reflect the defendant's subsequent, substantial assistance in the investigation of or prosecution of another person who has committed an offense. Further, the court may consider a government motion to reduce the sentence made more than one year after imposition of sentence where the defendant's substantial assistance involves information or evidence not known by the defendant until one year or more after the imposition of sentence. In accordance with the Guidelines and policy statements issued by the Sentencing Commission, pursuant to 28 U.S.C. § 994, the court's authority includes that of lowering the sentence to a level below that established by statute as a minimum sentence. 18 U.S.C. § 3553(e); 18 U.S.C. § 3582(c)(1)(B); Rule 35(b), Fed. R. Crim. P. The policy statement of the Sentencing Commissioners relating to substantial assistance to the authorities is found at U.S.S.G. § 5K1.1. *See also* § 1328, *infra*.

The third instance is when the Sentencing Commission subsequently lowers the sentencing range upon which the defendant had previously been sentenced, the court may reduce the term of imprisonment upon its own motion or upon the motion of the defendant or the director of bureau of prisons. 18 U.S.C. § 3582(c)(2).

This section does not apply to permit the reduction of sentences for offenses committed prior to November 1, 1987. *U.S. v. Watson*, 868 F.2d 157 (5th Cir. 1989); *U.S. v. Argitakos*, 862 F.2d 423 (2d Cir. 1988).

## § 1345. — Notice to Defendant of Right to Appeal.

After sentence has been imposed in a case which has gone to trial upon a plea of not guilty, the court must advise the defendant of his right to appeal, including any right to appeal the sentence, and his right to appeal in forma pauperis if he is unable to pay the cost of his appeal. The court is not required to advise a defendant of any right to appeal after sentence is imposed upon a defendant who was convicted upon a plea of guilty or nolo contendere, except that the court shall advise the defendant of any right to appeal his sentence. Upon defendant's request, the clerk of the court shall prepare and file forthwith a notice of appeal on behalf of a defendant. Rule 32(a)(2), Fed. R. Crim. P.

## § 1346. — Review of Sentences.

A sentence may be appealed by either the defendant or the government if it is claimed that the sentence: (1) was imposed in violation of the law; (2) was imposed in violation of the Guidelines issued by the Sentencing Commission; (3) was greater than the sentence specified in the applicable guideline, and the defendant claims it is unreasonable; or by the government if the sentence includes a lesser fine or term of imprisonment than the minimum established in the guideline, and the government claims that this is unreasonable; or (4) was imposed for an offense for which no sentencing guideline has been issued by the Sentencing Commission and as imposed was greater or lesser than the sentence specified in a plea agreement under Rule 11(e)(1)(B) or (C). 18 U.S.C. § 3742.

The Attorney General or the Solicitor General must personally approve the filing of a notice of appeal by the government. 18 U.S.C. § 3742(b)(4). A government appeal must be filed within thirty days. Rule 4(b), Fed. R. App. P. The constitutionality of a government appeal of a sentence is settled. *Pennsylvania v. Goldhammer,* 474 U.S. 28 (1985); *U.S. v. Di Fransesco,* 449 U.S. 117 (1980).

A reviewing court will uphold a sentence, unless it is in violation of law, imposed as a result of an incorrect application of the Guidelines, or is outside the range of the applicable guidelines and is unreasonable. The reviewing court will accept the findings of fact of the district court unless they are "clearly erroneous." 18 U.S.C. § 3742(e); *Williams v. U.S.,* 112 S. Ct. 1112 (1992); *U.S. v. Wright,* 873 F.2d 437 (1st Cir. 1989); *U.S. v. Buenrostro,* 868 F.2d 135 (5th Cir.), *cert. denied,* 110 S. Ct. 1957 (1989). The extent of a court's permitted downward departure may not be reviewed on appeal. *U.S. v. Hazel,* 928 F.2d 420 (D.C. Cir. 1991).

# PART II
# THE LAW OF EVIDENCE

# CHAPTER 14

# JUDICIAL NOTICE

§ 1400. Introduction.
§ 1401. Adjudicative Facts.
§ 1402. Procedure for Taking Notice.
§ 1403. Matters to be Noticed.

## § 1400. Introduction.

Judicial notice is that process by which a court may declare certain propositions to be proven, on the basis of general policy considerations, without requiring evidence of the same. This relieves a part of the burden of offering evidence of a particular fact since judicial notice of that fact is the same as proof of it and is of equal force. *Ohio Bell Telephone Co. v. Public Utilities Commission*, 301 U.S. 292 (1937); *Ricaud v. American Metal Co.*, 246 U.S. 304 (1918); *Wilson v. Shaw*, 204 U.S. 24 (1907); *Deshotels v. Liberty Mut. Ins. Co.*, 116 F. Supp. 55 (W.D. La. 1953), *aff'd*, 219 F.2d 271 (5th Cir. 1955).

It has been suggested that it is improper for the trial court to allow the introduction of evidence in support of matters of which the court is taking judicial notice. *See Public Ser. Ry. v. Wursthorn*, 278 F. 408 (3d Cir.), *cert. denied*, 259 U.S. 585 (1922). Judicial notice is to be distinguished from a judge's actual knowledge. *Williams v. U.S.*, 218 F.2d 473, 475 (5th Cir. 1955). Even if a judge has personal knowledge of facts, unless they are appropriate for judicial notice, such facts must be proved. *Brown v. Piper*, 91 U.S. 37 (1875); *Virgin Islands v. Gereau*, 523 F.2d 140, 147-48 (3d Cir. 1975), *cert. denied*, 424 U.S. 917 (1976). Similarly, it is not essential that a judge be personally acquainted with matters proper for judicial notice, since the court may inform itself in any manner it sees fit. *Brown v. Piper, supra.*

## § 1401. Adjudicative Facts.

The Federal Rules of Evidence regarding judicial notice apply only to "adjudicative facts." Rule 201(a), Fed. R. Evid. They are the facts of the particular case which normally go to the jury after having been established through the introduction of evidence. This process is dispensed with if the facts are beyond reasonable dispute. They are specifically distinguished from "legislative" facts which are not dealt with in the Federal Rules of Evidence. "Legislative facts, on the other hand, do not relate specifically to the activities or characteristics of the litigants." *U.S. v. Gould*, 536 F.2d 216, 219-20 (8th Cir. 1976). Legislative facts "are those which have relevance to legal reasoning and the lawmaking process, whether in the formulation of a legal principle or ruling by a judge or court or in the enactment of a legislative body .... [They deal with] 'judicial thinking about the factual ingredients of problems of what the law ought to be....'" Advisory Committee's Note. *See, e.g., Roe v. Wade,* 410 U.S. 113 (1973), for the use of social, scientific and medical data in review of statutes regulating abortion. While "[t]he precise line of demarcation between adjudicative facts and legislative facts is not always easily identified," it is to be noted that judicial access to "legislative" facts is unrestricted. *U.S. v. Gould,* 536 F.2d at 219. *See also* Advisory Committee's Note. No rule deals with judicial notice of "legislative facts."

Rule 201(b) of the Federal Rules of Evidence provides that a judicially noticed adjudicative fact "must be one not subject to reasonable dispute in that it is either (1) generally known within the territorial jurisdiction of the trial court, or (2) capable of accurate and ready determination by resort to sources whose accuracy cannot reasonably be questioned." *See Werk v. Parker,* 249 U.S. 130 (1919); *Brown v. Piper, supra; St. Louis Baptist Temple, Inc. v. F.D.I.C.,* 605 F.2d 1169, 1172 (10th Cir. 1979) (court's own files and records); *U.S. v. Gould,* 536 F.2d at 219; *U.S. ex rel. Fong Foo v. Shaughnessy,* 234 F.2d 715 (2d Cir. 1955); *Nice v. Chesapeake & O. Ry.,* 305 F. Supp. 1167, 1181 (W.D. Mich. 1969) (HEW mortality tables). Courts may take judicial notice of adjudicative facts which are obvious and indisputable. *U.S. v. Ricciardi,* 357 F.2d 91, 95 (2d Cir.), *cert. denied,* 384 U.S. 942 (1966) (general knowledge of jurors). Similarly, adjudicative facts which are "capable of certain, easily accessible, and indisputably accurate verification" may be noticed. *U.S. v. Gould,* 536 F.2d at 219. Absent a showing that the facts are unreliable for some good reason, courts may take judicial notice of them. *Mitchell v. Rose,* 570 F.2d 129, 132 n.2 (6th Cir. 1978) (census figures).

## § 1402. Procedure for Taking Notice.

A court may take judicial notice, whether requested or not, but shall take judicial notice if requested by a party and supplied with the necessary information. Rule 201(d), Fed. R. Evid. "For a court to notice facts judicially, if they are matters of general knowledge, the sources of those facts must be placed before the court." *Clark v. South Central Bell Telephone Co.,* 419 F. Supp. 697, 704 (W.D. La. 1976). However, in the absence of a request, failure of the court to notice such fact is not error. *U.S. v. Sorenson,* 504 F.2d 406, 410 (7th Cir. 1974); *O'Neill v. U.S.,* 411 F.2d 139, 144 (3d Cir. 1969); *Pellerin Laundry Mach. Sales Co. v. Reed,* 300 F.2d 305, 309-10 (8th Cir. 1962) (one relying on the law of a foreign state must call it to the attention of the trial court); *Prudential Ins. Co. v. Carlson,* 126 F.2d 607, 611-12 (10th Cir. 1942).

Judicial notice may be taken at any stage of proceedings whether in the trial court or on appeal. Rule 201(f), Fed. R. Evid.; *U.S. v. Salzmann,* 417 F. Supp. 1139, 1159-62 (E.D.N.Y.), *aff'd,* 548 F.2d 395 (2d Cir. 1976) (on motion to dismiss under speedy trial rules court noticed practice in the jurisdiction); *Fox v. Kane-Miller Corp.,* 398 F. Supp. 609, 651 (D. Md. 1975), *aff'd,* 542 F.2d 915 (4th Cir. 1976) (on motion for judgment n.o.v.). In keeping with the rule, it has also been held that judicial notice may be taken by the appellate court even though not taken by the trial court. *Massachusetts v. Westcott,* 431 U.S. 322, 323 n.2 (1977); *Canal Zone v. Burjan,* 596 F.2d 690, 693-94 (5th Cir. 1979); *U.S. v. Garcia,* 555 F.2d 708 (9th Cir. 1977); *U.S. v. Rivero,* 532 F.2d 450, 458 (5th Cir. 1976). *But see Garner v. Louisiana,* 368 U.S. 157, 173 (1961); *U.S. v. Jones,* 580 F.2d 219, 223-24 (6th Cir. 1978) (which limits the rule to civil cases).

A party is entitled to be heard on the propriety of taking judicial notice. Rule 201(e), Fed. R. Evid. Opposing counsel should be informed before trial of the facts of which the government will request the court to take judicial notice, thereby providing an opportunity to prepare objections. Facts judicially noticed may be subject to rebuttal. *Virgin Islands v. Gereau,* 523 F.2d 140, 147 (3d Cir. 1975), *cert. denied,* 424 U.S. 917 (1976).

Judicial notice of an adjudicative fact does not offend the sixth amendment's guarantee of the right to confront witnesses where the facts are indisputable. *Canal Zone v. Burjan,* 596 F.2d at 690; *U.S. v. Alvarado,* 519 F.2d 1133, 1135 (5th Cir. 1975). *But see U.S. v. Jones, supra.*

Once judicial notice has been taken, the jury must be properly instructed that in a criminal case the judicially noticed fact is not conclusive. "In a criminal case the court shall instruct the jury that it may, but is not required to, accept as conclusive any fact judicially noticed." Rule 201(g), Fed. R. Evid. It is not reversible error, however, when an instruction varies slightly from the language set out in the rule. *U.S. v. Anderson,* 528 F.2d 590, 592 (5th Cir. 1976), *cert. denied,* 439 U.S. 898 (1977).

## § 1403. Matters to be Noticed.

All federal courts of original jurisdiction are bound to take judicial notice of the constitution and public laws of each state, whether statutory or based on judicial opinion. *Laman v. Micou,* 114 U.S. 218 (1885); *McDermott v. John Hancock Mut. Life Ins. Co.,* 255 F.2d 562 (3d Cir.

1958), *cert. denied,* 358 U.S. 935 (1959); *Leis v. Opportunity Consultants,* 441 F. Supp. 1314, 1315 n.1 (S.D. Ohio 1977); *McGee v. Schmidt,* 411 F. Supp. 43, 44 (W.D. Wis. 1976).

The federal courts must also take notice of the U.S. Constitution, *Marbury v. Madison,* 5 U.S. (1 Cranch) 137 (1803), treaties entered into by the United States with other nations, *U.S. v. Rauscher,* 119 U.S. 407 (1886), and public acts of Congress, *Hurley v. Crawley,* 50 F.2d 1010 (D.C. Cir. 1931). An act is public, although it may pertain solely to a particular locale, if it affects the public at large. If private laws have a clause declaring them to be public, then the courts must take cognizance of them. *Case v. Kelly,* 133 U.S. 21 (1890).

Federal courts will take notice of executive orders, proclamations which are legally effective, and administrative regulations having the force of law. *NLRB v. E. C. Atkins & Co.,* 331 U.S. 398, 406 n.2 (1947); *Colonial Airlines, Inc. v. Janas,* 202 F.2d 914, 919 n.1 (2d Cir. 1953) (action of federal agencies); *Stasiukevich v. Nicolls,* 168 F.2d 474 (1st Cir. 1948) (official reports of legislative committees); *U.S. v. Lucas,* 6 F.2d 327 (W.D. Wash. 1925) (rules and regulations of the executive department). Judicial notice has been taken of presidential proclamations, *Green v. U.S.,* 67 F.2d 846 (9th Cir. 1933), and official acts of the United States government, *Underhill v. Hernandez,* 168 U.S. 250, 253 (1897); *Jones v. U.S.,* 137 U.S. 202 (1890) (recognition of a foreign government). *See Oetjen v. Central Leather Co.,* 246 U.S. 297, 301 (1918); *U.S. v. Bank of New York & Trust Co.,* 77 F.2d 866 (2d Cir. 1935), *aff'd,* 296 U.S. 463 (1936).

The courts will also notice rules and regulations prescribed by the principal departments of the federal government under express authority of Congress. *Caha v. U.S.,* 152 U.S. 211 (1894). *See Tucker v. Texas,* 326 U.S. 517 (1946) (Federal Housing Authority regulations); *Bowles v. U.S.,* 319 U.S. 33 (1943) (regulations of Director of Selective Service); *Foster v. Biddle,* 14 F.2d 280 (8th Cir. 1926) (postal regulations); *U.S. v. Holmes,* 414 F. Supp. 831, 839 (D. Md. 1976) (lawfully issued army regulations); *U.S. v. Gibbs,* 233 F. Supp. 934 (W.D. Pa. 1964) (records of United States Weather Bureau); *U.S. ex rel. Ormento v. Warden,* 216 F. Supp. 609 (D. Kan. 1963) (regulations of Bureau of Prisons). In this connection, *see* 44 U.S.C. § 1507 (contents of Federal Register shall be judicially noticed). One court, however, has held that state regulations are beyond the scope of judicial notice provided for in the Federal Rules of Evidence. *Campbell v. Mincey,* 413 F. Supp. 16, 19 (N.D. Miss. 1975), *aff'd,* 542 F.2d 573 (5th Cir. 1976) (mem). A domestic statute or rule prescribed by an agency acting under legislative authority must be judicially noticed whether it is pleaded or proved, and failure to bring it to the trial court's attention will not prevent reliance upon it on appeal. *Lilly v. Grand Trunk W. Ry.,* 317 U.S. 481 (1943); *Schultz v. Tecumseh Prods.,* 310 F.2d 426, 432-34 (6th Cir. 1962). Municipal ordinances, however, will not be judicially noticed. *Ruhs v. Pacific Power & Light,* 671 F.2d 1268, 1273 (10th Cir. 1982).

The principles and traditions of "international law" will be noticed in federal courts. *Skiriotes v. Florida,* 313 U.S. 69, 72 (1941); *Brown v. Piper,* 91 U.S. 37, 42 (1875). With respect to judicial notice of foreign law, Rule 26.1 of the Federal Rules of Criminal Procedure provides:

> A party who intends to raise an issue concerning the law of a foreign country shall give reasonable written notice. The court, in determining foreign law, may consider any relevant material or source, including testimony, whether or not submitted by a party or admissible under the Federal Rules of Evidence. The court's determination shall be treated as a ruling on a question of law.

A full analysis of the purpose and operation of this rule is contained in the Advisory Committee's Note to Rule 26.1. *See also* Rule 44.1, Fed. R. Civ. P.

Courts will generally take notice of records and matters within the files of the court. *Rothenberg v. Security Management Co.,* 667 F.2d 958, 961 n.8 (11th Cir. 1982); *St. Louis Baptist Temple, Inc. v. F.D.I.C.,* 605 F.2d 1169, 1172 (10th Cir. 1979) (judicial notice taken of court's own records of prior litigation closely related to the case before it); *U.S. v. Doss,* 563 F.2d 265, 269 n.2 (6th Cir. 1977); *U.S. v. Haldeman,* 559 F.2d 31, 107 (D.C. Cir. 1976), *cert. denied,* 431 U.S. 933 (1977) (judicial notice of testimony presented at a hearing at which trial judge had presided on a related matter); *U.S. v. Lucchetti,* 533 F.2d 28 (2d Cir. 1976), *cert. denied,* 429 U.S. 849 (1976) (conditions of a jail based on records from a previous case); *Virgin Islands v. Testamark,* 528 F.2d 742 (3d Cir. 1976) (prior conviction for impeachment purposes); *U.S. v. Gorham,* 523 F.2d 1088, 1096 (D.C. Cir. 1975); *U.S. v. Alvarado,* 519 F.2d 1133, 1135 (5th Cir. 1975), *cert. denied,* 424 U.S. 911 (1976) (judicial notice of previous criminal proceeding regarding location and physical aspects of border checkpoint); *People ex rel. Snead v. Kirkland,* 462 F. Supp. 914, 919 (E.D. Pa. 1978); *U.S. v. Salzmann,* 417 F. Supp. 1139 (E.D.N.Y.), *aff'd,* 548 F.2d 395 (2d Cir. 1976) (extradition practice and treatment in previous cases); *Oburn v. Shapp,* 393 F. Supp. 561 (E.D. Pa.), *aff'd,* 521 F.2d 142 (3d Cir. 1975). Judicial notice has been taken of a state court pleading referred to in a state court judgment entry. *Matter of Phillips,* 593 F.2d 356, 358 (8th Cir. 1979).

Courts are more willing to notice a general than a specific fact. For example, "[a] court takes judicial notice of the fact that Confederate money depreciated in value during the war between the states ... but not of the extent of the depreciation at a given time and place." *Ohio Bell Telephone Co. v. Public Utilities Commission,* 301 U.S. 292, 301 (1937). Similarly, courts are usually more willing to notice facts judicially when they are collaterally involved in the case, rather than the central point in issue. *Id.*

In seeking to inform itself, the trial court is free to consult any source that it considers reliable, but it is error for it to notice textbooks not a part of the record unless the facts are matters of common knowledge or are capable of certain verification. *Alvary v. U.S.,* 302 F.2d 790, 794 (2d Cir. 1962). A fact enters the realm of "common knowledge" when sufficient notoriety attaches to it so as to make it proper to assume its existence without proof. *Waters-Pierce Oil Co. v. Deselms,* 212 U.S. 159 (1909); *Jacobson v. Massachusetts,* 197 U.S. 11 (1905). A medical treatise has been cited as a basis for taking judicial notice, as has the dictionary. *U.S. v. Umentum,* 401 F. Supp. 746, 748-49 (E.D. Wis. 1975), *aff'd,* 547 F.2d 987, 992 (7th Cir. 1976), *cert. denied,* 430 U.S. 983 (1977).

The wide variety of facts that may properly be noticed is indicated by the following criminal cases: *Canal Zone v. Burjan,* 596 F.2d 690, 693-94 (5th Cir. 1979) (governmental boundaries); *U.S. v. Foster,* 580 F.2d 388 (10th Cir. 1978) (reliability and general acceptance of equipment used by telephone company); *U.S. v. Hughes,* 542 F.2d 246, 248 n.1 (5th Cir. 1976) (certain named streets and intersections being located on a federal enclave); *U.S. v. Berrojo,* 628 F.2d 368, 370 (5th Cir. 1980) (cocaine hydrochloride derived from coca leaves and therefore a controlled substance); *U.S. v. Harris,* 530 F.2d 576 (4th Cir. 1976) ("national bank" established by name on charter); *U.S. v. Anderson,* 528 F.2d 590 (5th Cir. 1976), *cert. denied,* 439 U.S. 898 (1977) (federal correctional institution within the special territorial jurisdiction of the United States); *Brathwaite v. Manson,* 527 F.2d 363 (2d Cir.), *rev'd on other grounds,* 432 U.S. 98 (1977) (time of sunset); *U.S. v. Alvarado,* 519 F.2d at 1135 (immutable geographical and physical facts); *U.S. v. Quinones,* 516 F.2d 1309 (1st Cir. 1975), *cert. denied,* 423 U.S. 852 (1976) (Fort Buchanan is a military base); *U.S. v. H. B. Gregory Co.,* 502 F.2d 700 (7th Cir. 1974), *cert. denied,* 422 U.S. 1007 (1975) (cornmeal, poppy seed, caraway seed, and corn grits are "foods" within meaning of the Federal Food, Drug, and Cosmetic Act); *U.S. v. Mauro,* 501 F.2d 45 (2d Cir.), *cert. denied,* 419 U.S. 969 (1974) ("national bank" is established where the bank employed "national" in name); *U.S. v. Daniels,* 429 F.2d 1273 (6th Cir. 1970) (Jehovah's Witnesses were responding to court orders to perform identical conscientious objector work that they would not perform in response to Selective Service Board orders); *U.S. v. Tucker*, 380 F.2d 206, 212 (2d Cir. 1967) (outright perjury by federal agents not a common occurrence); *U.S. v. Armone*, 363 F.2d 385, 406 (2d Cir.), *cert. denied*, 385 U.S. 957 (1966) ("Many who would touch pen to paper will not stand up to be counted in person under oath and in Court"); *U.S. v. Ricciardi*, 357 F.2d 91, 97 (2d Cir.), *cert. denied*, 384 U.S. 942 (1966) (a labor dispute involving apartment buildings would have a palpable effect on interstate commerce); *Hansford v. U.S.*, 353 F.2d 858, 859 n.1 (D.C. Cir. 1965) (most "street peddlers" of narcotics are themselves addicts whose habit is exploited by others); *U.S. v. Kelly*, 349 F.2d 720, 779 (2d Cir. 1965), *cert. denied*, 384 U.S. 947 (1966) (population of the various counties in the Southern District of New York); *U.S. v. Fatico*, 441 F. Supp. 1285 (E.D.N.Y. 1977), *rev'd on other grounds*, 579 F.2d 707 (2d Cir. 1978) (major hijacking gangs have preyed on Kennedy Airport); *U.S. v. Umentum, supra* (cocaine is derived from coca leaves, a controlled substance); *U.S. v. Bell*, 335 F. Supp. 797, 800-01 n.2 (E.D.N.Y. 1971), *aff'd*, 464 F.2d 667 (2d Cir. 1972) (finding made by a brother judge that the FAA "profile" used in aid of the preflight apprehension of air pirates did not rely on characteristics the use of which might be constitutionally impermissible); *U.S. v. Garcia*, 672 F.2d 1349, 1356-57 (11th Cir. 1982) (particular geographic point was beyond the three-mile territorial limit recognized as border of U.S.).

Further examples of proper judicial notice may be found in the following civil cases: *Massachusetts v. Westcott*, 431 U.S. 322, 323 n.2 (1977) (Coast Guard records); *Mitchell v. Rose*, 570 F.2d 129, 132 n.2 (6th Cir. 1978) (census figures); *United Klans of America v. McGovern*, 453 F. Supp. 836, 838 (N.D. Ala. 1978), *aff'd*, 621 F.2d 15 (5th Cir. 1980) (United Klans of America is a "white hate group"); *Harris v. U.S.*, 431 F. Supp. 1173, 1177 (E.D. Va.), *aff'd without opinion*, 565 F.2d 156 (4th Cir. 1977) (pyramid plan). *Kessler Institute for Rehabilitation v. N.L.R.B.*, 669 F.2d 138, 141 (3d Cir. 1982) (delays in the postal system have been increasing over the years); *U.S. v. Dykema*, 666 F.2d 1096, 1104 (7th Cir. 1981), *cert. denied*, 102 S. Ct. 2257 (1982) (vows of poverty have been known in the Catholic tradition for many years); *Eden Toys, Inc. v. Marshall Field & Co.*, 675 F.2d 498, 500 n.1 (2d Cir. 1982) (the traditional features of snowmen are generally known).

# CHAPTER 15

## WEIGHT OF THE EVIDENCE AND RELEVANCY

§ 1501. Burden of Proof.
§ 1502. — Motion for Judgment of Acquittal.
§ 1503. — Specific Items of Proof.
§ 1504. Presumptions and Inferences.
§ 1505. — Constitutionality of Presumptions in Criminal Cases.
§ 1506. — Specific Presumptions and Inferences.
§ 1507. — — Presumption of Innocence.
§ 1508. — — Sanity.
§ 1509. — — Intent.
§ 1510. — — Continuance of Conspiracy.
§ 1511. — — Knowledge of the Law.
§ 1512. — — Regularity of Proceedings.
§ 1513. — — Recent Possession of Fruits of Crime.
§ 1514. — — Failure to Call a Witness.
§ 1515. — — Failure of Defendant to Testify.
§ 1516. Circumstantial Evidence.
§ 1517. Relevancy.
§ 1518. — Evidence of the Defendant's Character.
§ 1519. — — Methods of Proving Character.
§ 1520. — — Cross-Examination and Rebuttal of Character Witnesses.
§ 1521. — Proof of Other Crimes.
§ 1522. — — Prerequisites.
§ 1523. — — Motive.
§ 1524. — — Intent and Knowledge.
§ 1525. — — Identity.
§ 1526. — — Plan, Scheme, or Design.
§ 1527. — Evidence of a Guilty Mind.
§ 1528. — — Flight and Concealment of Identity.
§ 1529. — — False Exculpatory Statements.
§ 1530. — — Suppression, Destruction, or Fabrication of Evidence.
§ 1531. — Habit and Custom.
§ 1532. — Motive.

## § 1501. Burden of Proof.

In criminal cases, the burden is on the government to establish each and every element of the crime charged beyond a reasonable doubt. *Jackson v. Virginia*, 443 U.S. 307, 324 (1979); *In re Winship*, 397 U.S. 358, 364 (1970); *Davis v. U.S.*, 160 U.S. 469 (1895). This burden never shifts to the defendant. The defendant maintains his presumption of innocence throughout the trial. *Wilbur v. Mullaney*, 496 F.2d 1303, 1307 (1st Cir. 1974), *aff'd*, 421 U.S. 684 (1975).

At common law, the burden of defenses was generally on the defendant. This was the rule when both the fifth and fourteenth amend-

353

ments were adopted. Thus it has been held that requiring the defendant to prove an affirmative defense does not relieve the state of proving all of the elements beyond a reasonable doubt nor does such a requirement violate the Constitution. *Martin v. Ohio,* 107 S. Ct. 1098 (1987); *Patterson v. New York,* 432 U.S. 197 (1977).

However, the general federal rule for some defenses has been that the burden of proof is that the defendant is only required to produce sufficient evidence to place a matter of defense in issue; the government then has the burden of negating the defense beyond a reasonable doubt. This rule has been applied to entrapment, *Jacobson v. U.S.,* 112 S. Ct. 1535 (1992); *U.S. v. Jannotti,* 673 F.2d 578, 597 (3d Cir.), *cert. denied,* 102 S. Ct. 906 (1982); self-defense, *Berrier v. Egler,* 428 F. Supp. 750 (E.D. Mich. 1976), *aff'd,* 583 F.2d 515 (6th Cir.), *cert. denied,* 439 U.S. 955 (1978); and alibi, *U.S. v. Burse,* 531 F.2d 1151 (2d Cir. 1976); *U.S. v. Booz,* 451 F.2d 719 (3d Cir. 1971), *cert. denied,* 414 U.S. 820 (1973); *U.S. v. Carter,* 433 F.2d 874 (10th Cir. 1970).

By statute, the defendant has the burden of proof for the affirmative defense of insanity by "clear and convincing evidence." 18 U.S.C. § 20. If the defendant is charged with solicitation to commit a crime of violence, the defendant may raise the affirmative defense that he completely renounced his criminal intent and prevented the commission of the crime solicited, but must prove the defense by a preponderance. 18 U.S.C. § 373. Likewise, an affirmative defense to a charge of trafficking in counterfeit goods or services must be proved by the defendant by a preponderance of the evidence. 18 U.S.C. § 2320.

## § 1502. — Motion for Judgment of Acquittal.

If the government fails to present evidence sufficient "to sustain a conviction" the trial court, on motion, must acquit the defendant. Rule 29(a), Fed. R. Crim. P. Evidence sufficient to sustain a conviction and to overcome a Rule 29 motion is that evidence which would warrant a jury finding the defendant guilty beyond a reasonable doubt. *Burks v. U.S.,* 437 U.S. 1, 16 (1978). In considering such a motion, the trial court should not weigh the evidence or assess the credibility of the witnesses, but must view the evidence and the inferences to be drawn therefrom in the light most favorable to the government. *U.S. v. Gibson,* 675 F.2d 825, 829 (6th Cir. 1982); *U.S. v. Brandon,* 633 F.2d 773, 780 (9th Cir. 1980); *U.S. v. DeJean,* 613 F.2d 1356, 1358 (5th Cir.), *cert. denied,* 444 U.S. 945 (1980); *Burks v. U.S.,* 437 U.S. at 16-17; *U.S. v. Walton,* 552 F.2d 1354 (10th Cir.), *cert. denied,* 431 U.S. 959 (1977). Where the facts equally support inferences of guilt beyond a reasonable doubt or of innocence, the motion for acquittal must be denied.

*U.S. v. Bohle*, 475 F.2d 872 (2d Cir. 1973). *But see U.S. v. Kelton*, 446 F.2d 669 (8th Cir. 1971).

The test for considering the sufficiency of the evidence under Rule 29 is the same whether made at the close of the government's case, at the close of all the evidence, after the jury verdict, or on appeal. *U.S. v. Austin*, 585 F.2d 1271 (5th Cir. 1978); *U.S. v. Anderson*, 532 F.2d 1218 (9th Cir.), *cert. denied*, 429 U.S. 839 (1976). If the defendant introduces evidence on his own behalf, he waives any objection to the sufficiency of the government's case alone. *McGautha v. California*, 402 U.S. 183, 215-16 (1971), *vacated on other grounds*, 408 U.S. 941 (1972); *U.S. v. Douglas*, 668 F.2d 459, 461 (10th Cir. 1982); *U.S. v. Evans*, 572 F.2d 455 (5th Cir.), *cert. denied*, 439 U.S. 870 (1978); *U.S. v. Black*, 525 F.2d 668 (6th Cir. 1975). However, if a Rule 29 motion is made at the close of the government's case, the trial court must rule on it then. It cannot reserve decision until after the defendant rests. *U.S. v. Wyant*, 576 F.2d 1312 (5th Cir. 1978); *U.S. v. House*, 551 F.2d 756 (8th Cir.), *cert. denied*, 434 U.S. 850 (1977); *U.S. v. Brown*, 456 F.2d 293 (2d Cir.), *cert. denied*, 407 U.S. 910 (1972).

Although it is now clear that an appellate court must order an acquittal where the government failed to present evidence sufficient to sustain a conviction for the offense charged, *Burks v. U.S.*, 437 U.S. at 17, an appellate court may still, in its discretion, modify a judgment by reducing the conviction to that of a lesser included offense which is supported by the evidence. *U.S. v. Industrial Laboratories Co.*, 456 F.2d 908 (10th Cir. 1972); *U.S. v. Berkowitz*, 429 F.2d 921, 928 (1st Cir. 1970).

## §1503. — Specific Items of Proof.

*Time:* The government is generally not required to prove the exact time or date of the offense. It is only required to prove that the offense occurred "during a period of time reasonably related to the date alleged in the indictment." *U.S. v. Henderson*, 434 F.2d 84, 86 (6th Cir. 1970); *U.S. v. Francisco*, 575 F.2d 815 (10th Cir. 1978).

*Amount:* The government need not prove the exact amount or quantity of an item charged in an indictment where there is proof of a substantial amount, and, if applicable, proof of the jurisdictional minimum. *U.S. v. Shafer*, 445 F.2d 579 (7th Cir.), *cert. denied*, 404 U.S. 986 (1971); *Ramsey v. U.S.*, 245 F.2d 295, 297 (9th Cir. 1957), *rev'd on other grounds*, 263 F.2d 805 (9th Cir. 1959).

*Multispecification counts:* Where, as in a perjury or mail fraud indictment, a single count alleges more than one specification of falsity or misrepresentation, the government is not required to prove each and every specification alleged. *U.S. v. Stirling*, 571 F.2d 708 (2d Cir.), *cert. denied*, 439 U.S. 824 (1978); *U.S. v. Bonacorsa*, 528 F.2d 1218 (2d Cir.), *cert. denied*, 426 U.S. 935 (1976); *U.S. v. Joyce*, 499 F.2d 9, 22-23 (7th Cir.), *cert. denied*, 419 U.S. 1031 (1974).

*Charges made in the conjunctive:* The government need only prove one of the several means the commission alleged where they are set forth in the conjunctive. *U.S. v. UCO Oil Co.*, 546 F.2d 833 (9th Cir. 1976), *cert. denied*, 430 U.S. 966 (1977); *Fields v. U.S.*, 408 F.2d 885 (5th Cir. 1969).

### § 1504. Presumptions and Inferences.

Traditionally, a "presumption" was defined as a conclusion that the law directs the jury to find from other established facts, and an "inference" was defined as a conclusion that the law permits the jury to find from other established facts. *U.S. v. Burns*, 597 F.2d 939, 943 n.7 (5th Cir. 1979). In recent cases, however, the Supreme Court has spoken not of presumption versus inference but of differing degrees of presumptions. *Ulster County Court v. Allen*, 442 U.S. 140 (1979); *Sandstrom v. Montana*, 442 U.S. 510 (1979). *See also Pigee v. Israel*, 670 F.2d 690, 692-693 (7th Cir. 1982).

### § 1505. — Constitutionality of Presumptions in Criminal Cases.

A mandatory or conclusive presumption, *i.e.*, a presumption that the trier of fact must accept as opposed to being merely permissive, is unconstitutional as it conflicts with the presumption of innocence and invades the fact-finding function. *Carella v. California*, 491 U.S. 263 (1989); *U.S. v. U.S. Gypsum Co.*, 438 U.S. 422 (1978); *Morissette v. U.S.*, 342 U.S. 246 (1952). A presumption, though not conclusive, that has the effect of shifting the burden of proof to the defendant, is also unconstitutional for like reasons. *Yates v. Evatt*, 111 S. Ct. 1884 (1991); *Francis v. Franklin*, 471 U.S. 307 (1985); *Connecticut v. Johnson*, 460 U.S. 73 (1983); *Sandstrom v. Montana*, 442 U.S. 510, 524 (1979); *Patterson v. New York*, 432 U.S. 197 (1977); *Mullaney v. Wilbur*, 421 U.S. 684 (1975).

A presumption, not conclusive, but which shifts to the defendant the burden of production, may be constitutional on the facts if (1) there is a rational connection between the fact proved and the ultimate fact presumed, *Tot v. U.S.*, 319 U.S. 463, 467-72 (1943), and (2) the "fact proved is sufficient to support the inference of guilt beyond a reasonable doubt," *Ulster County Court v. Allen*, 442 U.S. 140, 167 (1979).

A permissive presumption is constitutional and may be applied if there is a rational connection between the fact proved and the ultimate fact presumed to the extent that the "presumed fact is more likely than not to flow from the proved fact on which it is made to depend." *Leary v. U.S.*, 395 U.S. 6, 32-36 (1969); *Ulster County Court v. Allen*, 442 U.S. at 165-67. A permissive presumption is one on which the jury may rely, but only in concert with all of the evidence, and one which the jury may also reject. There is no burden of proof of any kind on the defendant.

## § 1506. — Specific Presumptions and Inferences.

## § 1507. — — Presumption of Innocence.

The presumption of innocence is a mandatory presumption in favor of the defendant which can only be overcome by proof of guilt beyond a reasonable doubt. Although there is no constitutional requirement to give a specific instruction on presumption of innocence, the trial court must make it clear to the jury that it cannot convict unless and until the government has proved its case beyond a reasonable doubt. *Kentucky v. Whorton*, 441 U.S. 786 (1979); *Taylor v. Kentucky*, 436 U.S. 478 (1978).

## § 1508. — — Sanity.

A defendant is presumed to be sane. Severe mental disease or defect which caused the defendant to be unable to appreciate the nature and quality of the wrongfulness of his acts is an affirmative defense which the defendant has the burden of proving by clear and convincing evidence. 18 U.S.C. § 20.

## § 1509. — — Intent.

The Supreme Court has held a jury instruction that a defendant is presumed to intend the natural and probable consequences of his acts, or that a jury may so infer, in a case where intent is an element, violates the constitutional requirement that the prosecution prove every element of the offense charged beyond a reasonable doubt. *Yates v. Evatt*, 111 S. Ct. 1884 (1991); *Francis v. Franklin*, 471 U.S. 307 (1985); *Connecticut v. Johnson*, 460 U.S. 73 (1983); *Sandstrom v. Montana*, 442 U.S. 510 (1979). Likewise, unconstitutional is an instruction that "the intent to commit theft by fraud is presumed" if the person fails to return leased personal property after the owner makes a 20-day written demand for return of the property. *Carella v. California*, 489 U.S. 1075 (1989). However, a defendant's intent, although not presumed as a matter of law, can be inferred from all the evidence presented, including direct and circumstantial evidence. *U.S. v.*

*McCracken,* 581 F.2d 719 (8th Cir. 1978); *U.S. v. Flickinger,* 573 F.2d 1349 (9th Cir.), *cert. denied,* 439 U.S. 836 (1978); *U.S. v. Haldeman,* 559 F.2d 31, 115-16 (D.C. Cir. 1976), *cert. denied,* 431 U.S. 933 (1977).

### § 1510. — — Continuance of Conspiracy.

Once a conspiracy has been established involving a defendant, it is presumed to continue unless and until the defendant proves, by showing affirmative acts, that the conspiracy was terminated or that he had withdrawn from it. *Hyde v. U.S.,* 225 U.S. 347, 369-70 (1912); *U.S. v. Panebianco,* 543 F.2d 447 (2d Cir. 1976), *cert. denied,* 429 U.S. 1103 (1977). The burden is on the defendant to show that he has withdrawn. *U.S. v. Gillen,* 599 F.2d 541 (3d Cir.), *cert. denied,* 444 U.S. 866 (1979); *U.S. v. Wentland,* 582 F.2d 1022 (5th Cir. 1978), *cert. denied,* 439 U.S. 1133 (1979); *U.S. v. Parnell,* 581 F.2d 1374, 1384 (10th Cir. 1978), *cert. denied,* 439 U.S. 1076 (1979); *U.S. v. Dorn,* 561 F.2d 1252 (7th Cir. 1977). Mere cessation of activity is not enough. *U.S. v. Goldberg,* 401 F.2d 644, 648 (2d Cir. 1968), *cert. denied,* 393 U.S. 1099 (1969). There must be "[a]ffirmative acts inconsistent with the object of the conspiracy and communicated in a manner reasonably calculated to reach co-conspirators...." *U.S. v. U.S. Gypsum Co.,* 438 U.S. 422, 464 (1978).

### § 1511. — — Knowledge of the Law.

Generally, a defendant is presumed to know the law. *U.S. v. Bryza,* 522 F.2d 414, 423 (7th Cir. 1975), *cert. denied,* 426 U.S. 912 (1976). However, in cases involving specific intent as an essential element, there is no such presumption. *U.S. v. Davis,* 583 F.2d 190 (5th Cir. 1978); *U.S. v. Ehrlichman,* 546 F.2d 910, 919 (D.C. Cir. 1976), *cert. denied,* 429 U.S. 1120 (1977); *U.S. v. San Juan,* 545 F.2d 314 (2d Cir. 1976).

### § 1512. — — Regularity of Proceedings.

There is a presumption that proceedings before a legally constituted and unbiased grand jury are in all respects regular and adequate. *Costello v. U.S.,* 350 U.S. 359, 363 (1956); *U.S. v. Helstoski,* 576 F.2d 511 (3d Cir. 1978), *aff'd,* 442 U.S. 477 (1979); *U.S. v. Dzialak,* 441 F.2d 212 (2d Cir.), *cert. denied,* 404 U.S. 883 (1971). A heavy burden is placed on one who seeks to overcome this presumption. *U.S. v. West,* 549 F.2d 545 (8th Cir.), *cert. denied,* 430 U.S. 956 (1977). There is also a presumption that grand jurors have properly performed their duties and that a grand juror who votes to indict an individual has heard sufficient evidence. *U.S. v. Barker,* 675 F.2d 1055, 1058 (9th Cir. 1982).

There is a presumption that trial jurors properly followed the court's instructions of law. *U.S. v. Eldred*, 588 F.2d 746 (9th Cir. 1978); *U.S. v. Cosby*, 529 F.2d 143 (8th Cir.), *cert. denied*, 426 U.S. 935 (1976). Upon a showing of improper extrinsic influence on a jury, the presumption is rebutted, and the burden shifts to the government to establish that the influence was harmless. *U.S. v. Winkle*, 587 F.2d 705 (5th Cir.), *cert. denied*, 444 U.S. 827 (1979).

There is a presumption that executive officials act pursuant to the authority conferred upon them. *Wilson v. U.S.*, 369 F.2d 198, 200 (D.C. Cir. 1966); *Maresca v. U.S.*, 277 F. 727, 735-36 (2d Cir. 1921), *cert. denied*, 257 U.S. 657 (1922). There is a presumption that official acts of public officers are in all respects regular, until evidence to the contrary can be shown. *Lewis v. U.S.*, 279 U.S. 63, 73 (1929); *U.S. v. Hulphers*, 421 F.2d 1291, 1292 (9th Cir. 1969). And there is a presumption of regularity attached to official proceedings of administrative bodies. *U.S. v. Burnett*, 476 F.2d 726, 728 (5th Cir. 1973); *U.S. v. Roberts*, 466 F.2d 193, 196 (7th Cir.), *cert. denied*, 409 U.S. 1026 (1972).

## § 1513. — — Recent Possession of Fruits of Crime.

Possession of the fruits of crime, recently after its commission, may, if not satisfactorily explained, create a permissible inference, in light of all the circumstances of the case, that the possessor was concerned in the crime or knew that the items in question were wrongfully acquired. *Barnes v. U.S.*, 412 U.S. 837, 843-46 (1973); *U.S. v. Cowden*, 545 F.2d 257 (1st Cir. 1976), *cert. denied*, 430 U.S. 909 (1977); *U.S. v. Jacobson*, 536 F.2d 793 (8th Cir.), *cert. denied*, 429 U.S. 864 (1976); *U.S. v. Ortiz*, 507 F.2d 1224 (6th Cir. 1974). It has been held that this inference may extend to guilty participation in the crime. *McNamara v. Henkel*, 226 U.S. 520, 524-25 (1913); *U.S. v. Jennewein*, 590 F.2d 191 (6th Cir. 1978). And possession in one state of property recently stolen in another state may create an inference that the defendant transported the stolen property in interstate commerce. *U.S. v. Allen*, 497 F.2d 160 (5th Cir.), *cert. denied*, 419 U.S. 1035 (1974); *U.S. v. Coppola*, 424 F.2d 991, 993 (2d Cir.), *cert. denied*, 399 U.S. 928 (1970).

Based on all of the evidence, a jury is not bound to accept this inference, however, even though the defendant offers no satisfactory explanation. *U.S. v. Coppola*, 424 F.2d at 994. And conversely, a jury may convict upon such an inference, regardless of the defendant's explanation. The court may therefore give a charge on the inference even though the defendant has offered evidence to explain his possession of recently stolen property. *U.S. v. Fairchild*, 505 F.2d 1378 (5th Cir.

1975); *U.S. v. Carneglia,* 468 F.2d 1084, 1087-88 (2d Cir. 1972), *cert. denied,* 410 U.S. 945 (1973).

### § 1514. — — Failure to Call a Witness.

"[I]f a party has it peculiarly within his power to produce witnesses whose testimony would elucidate the transaction, the fact that he does not do it creates the presumption [or inference] that the testimony, if produced, would be unfavorable." *Graves v. U.S.,* 150 U.S. 118, 121 (1893). *Accord, U.S. v. Di Re,* 332 U.S. 581, 593 (1948). As with other inferences, the jury need not draw the inference if it does not wish to. *U.S. v. Comulada,* 340 F.2d 449, 452 (2d Cir.), *cert. denied,* 380 U.S. 978 (1965). Before arguing the inference to a jury, an advance ruling should be sought from the court. *U.S. v. Beeler,* 587 F.2d 340, 343 (6th Cir. 1978); *U.S. v. Blakemore,* 489 F.2d 193 (6th Cir. 1973).

Whether to charge on the "missing witness" inference is largely within the sound discretion of the trial court. *U.S. v. Williams,* 604 F.2d 1102 (8th Cir. 1979); *U.S. v. Johnson,* 562 F.2d 515 (8th Cir. 1977). Defendant requests for instructions on the missing witness inference have been denied where the witness' testimony would not have been favorable to the defendant, *U.S. v. Long,* 533 F.2d 505 (9th Cir.), *cert. denied,* 429 U.S. 829 (1976), where it would be cumulative or unnecessary, *U.S. v. Mahone,* 537 F.2d 922 (7th Cir.), *cert. denied,* 429 U.S. 1025 (1976), and where it was found that the party was not in full control of the witness, *U.S. v. Williams,* 604 F.2d at 1119-20; *U.S. v. Johnson,* 562 F.2d at 517; *U.S. v. Wilson,* 534 F.2d 375 (D.C. Cir. 1976).

When a witness is equally available to both parties and neither party calls the witness, the jury may draw such inferences as it chooses: that the testimony would have been unfavorable to either party, to neither party, or to both. *U.S. v. Ploof,* 464 F.2d 116, 119 (2d Cir.), *cert. denied,* 409 U.S. 952 (1972). But, when a witness is unavailable to both parties, no inferences, favorable or unfavorable, may be drawn from a party's failure to call the witness, absent a showing that he was under the control of either party or that his absence resulted from conduct of either party. *U.S. v. Secondino,* 347 F.2d 725, 726 (2d Cir.), *cert. denied,* 382 U.S. 931 (1965).

A codefendant is regarded as being equally available to both parties. *U.S. v. Deutsch,* 451 F.2d 98, 117 (2d Cir. 1971), *cert. denied,* 404 U.S. 1019 (1972). Although in some cases the government may have the power to free a codefendant from fifth amendment claims by a grant of use or transactional immunity, this is not a situation that is recognized as leaving the codefendant within the government's power. *U.S. v. Stofsky,* 527 F.2d 237, 249 (2d Cir. 1975), *cert. denied,* 429 U.S. 819

(1976); *Morrison v. U.S.*, 365 F.2d 521, 524 (D.C. Cir. 1966). Similarly, the government is under no duty to grant a prospective witness any kind of immunity in order to permit him to testify. *U.S. v. Bautista*, 509 F.2d 675, 677-78 (9th Cir.), *cert. denied*, 421 U.S. 976 (1975). Therefore, a defendant is not entitled to an instruction that the jury is entitled to draw an inference adverse to the government from its failure to grant immunity to a witness whose testimony, had he not invoked the fifth amendment, would arguably have favored the defendant. *U.S. v. Stulga*, 584 F.2d 142 (6th Cir. 1978); *U.S. v. Sircovich*, 555 F.2d 1301 (5th Cir. 1977); *Bowles v. U.S.*, 439 F.2d 536 (D.C. Cir. 1970), *cert. denied*, 401 U.S. 995 (1971); *Morrison v. U.S.*, 365 F.2d 521 (D.C. Cir. 1966).

## § 1515. — — Failure of Defendant to Testify.

No unfavorable inference may be drawn from a defendant's failure to testify, 18 U.S.C. § 3481; *Carter v. Kentucky*, 450 U.S. 288, 300 (1981); and no comment on a defendant's failure to testify may be made by a prosecutor, *Griffin v. California*, 380 U.S. 609, 613 (1965); subject, however, to a harmless error review. *U.S. v. Hastings*, 461 U.S. 499 (1983). In instances where a presumption arises in the government's favor, however, an instruction to the jury that the defendant must offer evidence to rebut the presumption is not a commentary on the defendant's failure to testify. *U.S. v. Gainey*, 380 U.S. 63, 70-71 (1965); *U.S. v. Gulley*, 374 F.2d 55, 60 (6th Cir. 1967).

If the defendant does not request an instruction on his right not to testify, it is not reversible error if the judge does give such an instruction that no inference of guilt arises from the silence of the accused. *Lakeside v. Oregon*, 435 U.S. 333 (1978); *U.S. v. Ballard*, 418 F.2d 325, 326-27 (9th Cir. 1969); *U.S. ex rel. Miller v. Follette*, 397 F.2d 363, 367 n.6 (2d Cir. 1968), *cert. denied*, 393 U.S. 1039 (1969).

## § 1516. Circumstantial Evidence.

"Circumstantial evidence is that evidence which tends to prove a disputed fact, by proof of other facts...." *Rumely v. U.S.*, 293 F. 532, 551 (2d Cir. 1923). Circumstantial evidence may be accorded the same weight and probative value as direct evidence and may be sufficient by itself to sustain a conviction. *U.S. v. Richards*, 638 F.2d 765, 768 (5th Cir.), *cert. denied*, 102 S. Ct. 669 (1981); *U.S. v. Bycer*, 593 F.2d 549 (3d Cir. 1979); *U.S. v. Brown*, 584 F.2d 252 (8th Cir. 1978), *cert. denied*, 440 U.S. 910 (1979); *U.S. v. Harper*, 579 F.2d 1235 (10th Cir.), *cert. denied*, 439 U.S. 968 (1978); *U.S. v. Brady*, 579 F.2d 1121 (9th Cir.

1978), *cert. denied,* 439 U.S. 1074 (1979); *Durns v. U.S.,* 562 F.2d 542 (8th Cir.), *cert. denied,* 434 U.S. 959 (1977); *U.S. v. Colclough,* 549 F.2d 937 (4th Cir. 1977).

There is no requirement that circumstantial evidence exclude every reasonable hypothesis except that of guilt. *Holland v. U.S.,* 348 U.S. 121, 139-40 (1954); *U.S. v. Kirk,* 584 F.2d 773 (6th Cir.), *cert. denied,* 439 U.S. 1048 (1978); *U.S. v. Parnell,* 581 F.2d 1374 (10th Cir. 1978), *cert. denied,* 439 U.S. 1076 (1979); *U.S. v. Pelton,* 578 F.2d 701 (8th Cir.), *cert. denied,* 430 U.S. 964 (1978); *U.S. v. Gabriner,* 571 F.2d 48 (1st Cir. 1978); *U.S. v. George,* 568 F.2d 1064 (4th Cir. 1978); *U.S. v. Cooper,* 567 F.2d 252 (3d Cir. 1977); *U.S. v. Davis,* 562 F.2d 681 (D.C. Cir. 1977); *U.S. v. Daniels,* 549 F.2d 665 (9th Cir. 1977); *U.S. v. Warren,* 453 F.2d 738, 745 (2d Cir.), *cert. denied,* 406 U.S. 944 (1972). Although a conviction may rest solely on circumstantial evidence, there must be a logical and convincing connection between the facts established and the conclusions inferred. *U.S. v. Bycer,* 593 F.2d 549 (3d Cir. 1979). A conviction may not rest on mere conjecture or speculation. *U.S. v. Knife,* 592 F.2d 472 (8th Cir. 1979); *U.S. v. Thomas,* 453 F.2d 141 (9th Cir. 1971), *cert. denied,* 405 U.S. 1069 (1972). In the Fifth Circuit, circumstantial evidence must be such as to exclude every reasonable hypothesis except that of guilt. *U.S. v. Sink,* 586 F.2d 1041 (5th Cir. 1978), *cert. denied,* 443 U.S. 913 (1979); *U.S. v. Marshall,* 557 F.2d 527 (5th Cir. 1977); *U.S. v. Brown,* 547 F.2d 1264 (5th Cir. 1977).

## § 1517. Relevancy.

Rule 401 of the Federal Rules of Evidence defines "relevant evidence" as "evidence having any tendency to make the existence of any fact that is of consequence to the determination of the action more probable or less probable than it would be without the evidence." There are two requirements in the rule: (1) the evidence must tend to prove the matter sought to be proved, and (2) the matter sought to be proved must be one that is of consequence to the determination of the action. *U.S. v. Hall,* 653 F.2d 1002, 1005 (5th Cir. 1981). Evidence which is not relevant is not admissible. Rule 402, Fed. R. Evid. Testimony of a general and hypothetical nature about the difficulties of obtaining evidence against the "higher echelons" of a narcotics conspiracy lacked substantial relevance to the case, and caused reversal, *U.S. v. Hall,* 653 F.2d at 1007.

Rule 403 of the Federal Rules of Evidence provides that "relevant" evidence may be inadmissible "if its probative value is substantially outweighed by the danger of undue prejudice, confusion of the issues, or misleading the jury, or by considerations of undue delay, waste of time, or needless presentation of cumulative evidence."

Where evidence is admissible about one party or for one purpose, but not admissible about another party or purpose, the judge must upon request restrict the evidence and instruct the jury accordingly. Rule 105, Fed. R. Evid. Failure to give such an instruction may result in reversal of a conviction. *U.S. v. Eckmann*, 656 F.2d 308, 311-14 (8th Cir. 1981). Likewise, where a party has introduced a part of a writing, an adverse party may require the introduction of the remainder of the writing which, in fairness, should be considered contemporaneously. When the second portion is required for completeness and to avoid misunderstanding, it is *ipso facto* relevant. Rule 106, Fed. R. Evid.; *Beech Aircraft Corp. v. Rainey*, 488 U.S. 153 (1988).

The trial judge has broad discretion in ruling on questions of "relevancy" and in balancing the probative value of relevant evidence against any undue prejudice. *Hamling v. U.S.*, 418 U.S. 87, 124-25 (1974); *U.S. v. Guerrero*, 650 F.2d 728, 734 (5th Cir. 1981); *U.S. v. Brady*, 595 F.2d 359 (6th Cir.), *cert. denied*, 444 U.S. 862 (1979); *U.S. v. Hernandez*, 588 F.2d 346 (2d Cir. 1978); *U.S. v. Cassasa*, 588 F.2d 282 (9th Cir. 1978), *cert. denied*, 441 U.S. 909 (1979); *U.S. v. Johnson*, 585 F.2d 119 (5th Cir. 1978); *U.S. v. Long*, 574 F.2d 761 (3d Cir.), *cert. denied*, 439 U.S. 985 (1978); *U.S. v. Williams*, 545 F.2d 47 (8th Cir. 1976). Only an abuse of discretion will result in the reversal of a trial court's ruling on this point. *U.S. v. Williams*, 545 F.2d at 50. It has been held that, in reviewing a trial court's decision on an issue of relevancy, the appellate court should look at the evidence in the light most favorable to its proponent, maximizing its probative value and minimizing its prejudicial effect. *U.S. v. Brady*, 595 F.2d at 361.

Each case, of course, turns on its own set of facts. Circuit cases have dealt with photographs of dead victims, *U.S. v. Brady*, 595 F.2d at 361-62; *U.S. v. Shoemaker*, 542 F.2d 561, 564 (10th Cir.), *cert. denied*, 429 U.S. 1004 (1976), mug shots, *U.S. v. Fosher*, 568 F.2d 207 (1st Cir. 1978), computer information, *U.S. v. Scholle*, 553 F.2d 1109 (8th Cir.), *cert. denied*, 434 U.S. 940 (1977), reports of government agents, *U.S. v. Juarez*, 549 F.2d 1113 (7th Cir. 1977), possession of a shotgun in a drug case, *U.S. v. Daniels*, 572 F.2d 535 (5th Cir. 1978), informer's compensation from government, *U.S. v. Leja*, 568 F.2d 493 (6th Cir. 1977), possession of a .38-caliber revolver 10 weeks after a bank robbery, *U.S. v. Robinson*, 560 F.2d 507 (2d Cir. 1977), *cert. denied*, 435 U.S. 905 (1978), and alleged threats by defendant against informant and FBI agent, *U.S. v. Weir*, 575 F.2d 668 (8th Cir. 1978).

## § 1518. — Evidence of the Defendant's Character.

Under Rule 404(a)(1) of the Federal Rules of Evidence, the defendant may offer evidence of a pertinent trait of his character for the purpose of proving that he acted in conformity therewith on a particular occasion. That is, the defendant may present evidence of pertinent good character traits to suggest to the jury that a person of his good character would not commit the offense with which he is charged. *Michelson v. U.S.*, 335 U.S. 469 (1948); *U.S. v. Cylkouski,* 556 F.2d 799 (6th Cir. 1977); *U.S. v. Lechoco,* 542 F.2d 84 (D.C. Cir. 1976); *U.S. v. Lewin,* 467 F.2d 1132 (7th Cir. 1972); *U.S. v. Sedillo,* 496 F.2d 151 (9th Cir.), *cert. denied,* 419 U.S. 947 (1974). The defendant need not take the stand to offer evidence of his reputation for integrity, as a law-abiding citizen, and for peacefulness, and failure to admit such evidence is error. *Darland v. U.S.,* 626 F.2d 1235, 1237 (5th Cir. 1980), *cert. denied,* 454 U.S. 1157 (1982). Intelligence is not a character trait within this rule. *U.S. v. West,* 670 F.2d 675, 682 (7th Cir.), *cert. denied,* 457 U.S. 1124 (1982).

On the other hand, the government may offer evidence of a pertinent trait of the defendant's bad character, but only in limited circumstances: (1) in rebuttal of defendant's character evidence where the defendant has put his good character "in issue"; (2) where the defendant's character trait is an element of the charge, as in a perjury case, *U.S. v. Ridling,* 350 F. Supp. 90, 98 (E.D. Mich. 1972), or a Hobbs Act prosecution, *U.S. v. Billingsley,* 474 F.2d 63, 66 (6th Cir.), *cert. denied,* 414 U.S. 819 (1973); *see also* Rule 405(b), Fed. R. Evid.; and (3) where the purpose is to show motive, opportunity, intent, preparation, plan, knowledge, identity, absence of mistake, or accident under Rule 404(b). Beyond these limited circumstances, however, the government may not offer evidence of a defendant's bad character or character trait to circumstantially show the defendant's propensity to commit the crime with which he is charged. *Michelson v. U.S.,* 335 U.S. 469 (1948). By merely taking the stand, the defendant does not put his general character in issue. General character evidence under Rule 404(a) relates to the witness' reputation for honesty, and being a law-abiding citizen in contrast to opinion and reputation evidence under Rule 608(a) which is used for impeachment and which may refer only to character for truthfulness or untruthfulness. *U.S. v. Thomas,* 676 F.2d 531, 537 (11th Cir. 1982).

Character testimony is admissible only when relevant to a particular issue, and witnesses may testify only about the character trait relevant to that issue. Usually, this issue is the state of mind necessary to the commission of the offense charged. *U.S. v. Lechoco,* 542 F.2d at 88. For example, the character traits of honesty and dishonesty relate to theft and fraud offenses and the character trait of peacefulness relates to assault and homicide cases. But the character trait of truthfulness has been held not pertinent to a controlled substance case. *U.S. v. Jackson,* 588 F.2d 1046 (5th Cir.), *cert. denied,* 442 U.S. 941 (1979).

Character evidence must be considered with all other evidence in determining if the defendant is guilty beyond a reasonable doubt. *U.S. v. Callahan,* 588 F.2d 1078 (5th Cir.), *cert. denied,* 444 U.S. 826 (1979); *U.S. v. Crosby,* 294 F.2d 928, 948 (2d Cir. 1961), *cert. denied,* 368 U.S. 984 (1962); *Poliafico v. U.S.,* 237 F.2d 97 (6th Cir. 1956), *cert. denied,* 352 U.S. 1025 (1957). In *U.S. v. Haller,* 543 F.2d 62, 64 (9th Cir. 1976), and *U.S. v. Lewis,* 482 F.2d 632 (D.C. Cir. 1973), it was held that character evidence, standing alone, may be enough to create reasonable doubt. And, in *Michelson v. U.S.,* 335 U.S. at 476, the Supreme Court also held that character evidence alone, in some circumstances, may be enough to create reasonable doubt. But no defendant may be convicted upon his bad reputation or character alone. *U.S. v. Tropiano,* 418 F.2d 1069, 1081 (2d Cir. 1969), *cert. denied,* 397 U.S. 1021 (1970). (Character of a victim is dealt with in Rule 404(a)(2), but it has limited application in federal criminal prosecutions as, generally, such evidence is only offered in homicide or rape cases. Evidence of the character of a sex offense victim is further regulated by Rule 412 of the Federal Rules of Evidence. Character of a witness, Rule 404(a)(3), is considered in Chapter 18, § 18-4, under "Impeachment and Support.")

## § 1519. — — Methods of Proving Character.

Rule 405 deals with the methods of proving character, once it has been determined that character evidence, good or bad, is relevant and admissible. Rule 405 provides that the methods of proving character are (1) testimony as to reputation, (2) testimony in the form of an opinion, and (3) where character or a trait of character is an essential element of a charge, claim, or defense, testimony as to specific instances of conduct.

Reputation is the community's opinion of the defendant. When a character witness testifies as to a defendant's "reputation," he is summarizing what he has heard in the community. Such testimony is, indeed must be, hearsay in nature. It may not properly include personal observations or knowledge about the defendant (opinion testimony), nor testimony as to the defendant's specific acts or courses of conduct. *Michelson v. U.S.,* 335 U.S. 469, 477 (1948); *U.S. v. Lewis,* 482 F.2d 632, 637 (D.C. Cir. 1973). The reputation or character witness must first be qualified "by showing such acquaintance with the defendant, the community in which he has lived, and the circles in which he has moved as to speak with authority of the terms in which generally he is regarded." *Michelson v. U.S.,* 335 U.S. at 478.

Opinion testimony, not admissible prior to the Federal Rules of Evidence, is specifically authorized in Rule 405 as a means by which the defendant may introduce evidence of his good character. Thus, a defense character witness can give his personal opinion of the defendant's character, based on personal contacts with the defendant. But such a witness may only give an opinion; he may not testify about the specific acts or conduct of the defendant upon which his opinion is based.

The trial court may, in its discretion, limit the number of character witnesses. *Michelson v. U.S.,* 335 U.S. at 480; *U.S. v. Gibson,* 675 F.2d 825, 834 (6th Cir. 1982); *U.S. v. Henry,* 560 F.2d 963 (9th Cir. 1977).

### § 1520. — — Cross-Examination and Rebuttal of Character Witnesses.

Rule 405(a) permits cross-examination of defendant's character witnesses, including inquiry into the witnesses' knowledge of relevant specific instances of the defendant's past conduct. This includes inquiry about the defendant's past crimes or wrongful acts and even the defendant's arrests. *Michelson v. U.S.,* 335 U.S. 469, 482-87 (1948); *U.S. v. Watson,* 587 F.2d 365 (7th Cir. 1978), *cert. denied,* 439 U.S. 1132 (1979); *U.S. v. Evans,* 569 F.2d 209 (4th Cir.), *cert. denied,* 435 U.S. 975 (1978); *U.S. v. Morgan,* 554 F.2d 31 (2d Cir.), *cert. denied,* 434 U.S. 965 (1977); *U.S. v. Edwards,* 549 F.2d 362 (5th Cir.), *cert. denied,* 434 U.S. 828 (1977); *U.S. v. Lewis,* 482 F.2d 632, 638 (D.C. Cir. 1973). The two preconditions to such cross-examination are that there be a good faith basis for belief in the incident inquired about, and that the incidents inquired about are relevant to the character trait involved. *U.S. v. Bright,* 588 F.2d 504 (5th Cir.), *cert. denied,* 440 U.S. 972 (1979); *U.S. v. Crippen,* 570 F.2d 535, 539 (5th Cir. 1978), *cert. denied,* 439 U.S. 1069 (1979). This form of cross-examination should not be confused with the impeachment of a witness under Rules 608 and 609. *Kilgore v. U.S.,* 467 F.2d 22 (5th Cir. 1972). For example, inquiry into knowledge of prior convictions of the defendant is not necessarily limited to convictions within the past 10 years. *U.S. v. Edwards,* 549 F.2d at 366-68.

The trial court has wide discretion in allowing or disallowing this form of cross-examination. *Michelson v. U.S.,* 335 U.S. at 480. The trial court should apply the balancing test set forth in Rule 403, *U.S. v. Lewis,* 482 F.2d at 639, and in this regard may consider the remoteness of the prior incident, *Michelson v. U.S.,* 335 U.S. at 484; *U.S. v. DeVincent,* 546 F.2d 452 (1st Cir. 1976), *cert. denied,* 431 U.S. 903

(1977), *rev'd on other grounds*, 602 F.2d 1006 (1979); *U.S. v. Null*, 415 F.2d 1178 (4th Cir. 1969), and whether the incident is similar or dissimilar to the offense charged, *Michelson v. U.S.*, 335 U.S. at 483; *McCowan v. U.S.*, 376 F.2d 122, 124 (9th Cir. 1967). Inquiry about a defendant's juvenile record has been questioned. *U.S. v. Canniff*, 521 F.2d 565, 573 n.8 (2d Cir. 1975), *cert. denied*, 423 U.S. 1059 (1976). *See* Rule 609(d), Fed. R. Evid. But inquiry about the facts of the case for which the defendant is on trial has been held to be proper. *U.S. v. Morgan*, 554 F.2d at 33. However, error occurred where character witnesses who had testified only about community reputation were asked if their opinions would change if the defendant were convicted of the acts he was charged with. Not only had the witnesses not expressed their personal opinions, but the question assumed as a fact the very issue which the jury had been impaneled to decide and an opinion based upon an assumption of guilt cannot have probative value on that issue. *U.S. v. Polsinelli*, 649 F.2d 793, 795 (10th Cir. 1981). If, on cross-examination, a defense character witness denies knowledge of an alleged prior incident of misconduct committed by the defendant, or a prior arrest of the defendant, the government may not thereafter prove such prior act of misconduct or prior arrest by extrinsic evidence. *U.S. v. Herman*, 589 F.2d 1191 (3d Cir. 1978), *cert. denied*, 441 U.S. 913 (1979).

In addition to cross-examining defendant's character witnesses, the government may rebut defendant's evidence of good character by calling its own witnesses to testify to the defendant's bad character. *U.S. v. Reece*, 568 F.2d 1246 (6th Cir. 1977). But such evidence must conform to all the requirements of Rules 403, 404, and 405. Thus, it is limited to statements of reputation or opinion about the relevant character trait involved and may not include testimony about the defendant's specific instances of misconduct. *U.S. v. Reece*, 568 F.2d at 1251-52.

### § 1521. — Proof of Other Crimes.

Rule 404(b) of the Federal Rules of Evidence provides:

> Evidence of other crimes, wrongs, or acts is not admissible to prove the character of a person in order to show that he acted in conformity therewith. It may, however, be admissible for other purposes, such as proof of motive, opportunity, intent, preparation, plan, knowledge, identity, or absence of mistake or accident provided that upon request by the accused, the prosecution in a criminal case shall provide reasonable notice in advance of trial, or during trial if the court excuses pretrial notice on good cause shown, of the general nature of any such evidence it intends to introduce at trial.

## § 1522. — — Prerequisites.

Before such evidence of other crimes is admissible, (1) it must be relevant to an issue other than the character of the defendant, such as identity, knowledge, plan, or scheme, and (2) the probative value must not be substantially outweighed by the dangers of unfair prejudice, confusion of the issues, or misleading material. *U.S. v. Mitchell,* 666 F.2d 1385, 1389 (11th Cir.), *cert. denied,* 457 U.S. 1124 (1982); *U.S. v. McPartlin,* 595 F.2d 1321 (7th Cir.), *cert. denied,* 444 U.S. 833 (1979); *U.S. v. Beechum,* 582 F.2d 898 (5th Cir.), *cert. denied,* 440 U.S. 920 (1978); *U.S. v. Young,* 573 F.2d 1137 (9th Cir. 1978); *U.S. v. Gubelman,* 571 F.2d 1252 (2d Cir.), *cert. denied,* 436 U.S. 948 (1978); *U.S. v. Benedetto,* 571 F.2d 1246 (2d Cir. 1978); *U.S. v. James,* 555 F.2d 992 (D.C. Cir. 1977); *U.S. v. Scholle,* 553 F.2d 1109 (8th Cir.), *cert. denied,* 434 U.S. 940 (1977); *U.S. v. Largent,* 545 F.2d 1039 (6th Cir. 1976), *cert. denied,* 429 U.S. 1098 (1977). The trial court has broad discretion in this area. *U.S. v. Cooper,* 577 F.2d 1079 (6th Cir.), *cert. denied,* 439 U.S. 868 (1978); *U.S. v. Corey,* 566 F.2d 429 (2d Cir. 1977); *U.S. v. Juarez,* 561 F.2d 65 (7th Cir. 1977); *U.S. v. Scholle,* 553 F.2d at 1121; *U.S. v. Myers,* 550 F.2d 1036 (5th Cir.), *cert. denied,* 439 U.S. 847 (1977).

A proposed amendment to Rule 404(b) of the Federal Rules of Evidence scheduled to take effect on December 1, 1991, provides that when there is a request by the accused, a condition precedent to admissibility of Rule 404(b) evidence is that the prosecution shall provide reasonable notice in advance of trial, or during trial if the court excuses pretrial notice, of the general nature of any such evidence the prosecution intends to introduce at trial. The Advisory Committee's Note states the purpose of the Rule is to "reduce surprise and promote early resolution on the issue of admissibility." There are no specific time limits stated as to what constitutes a reasonable request and no specific form of notice is required.

There is no requirement that the court make a preliminary finding, under Rule 104(a) of the Federal Rules of Evidence, that the defendant in fact committed the similar act, but need only decide whether the jury could reasonably find by a preponderance of the evidence that the similar act was committed. *Huddleston v. U.S.,* 485 U.S. 681 (1988).

The Advisory Committee's Note for Rule 404(b) states that, in determining whether evidence of other crimes, wrongs, or acts is admissible, "no mechanical solution is offered." The rule has been described liberally as a rule of inclusion rather than a rule of exclusion. *U.S. v. Halper,* 590 F.2d 422 (2d Cir. 1978); *U.S. v. Long,* 574 F.2d 761 (3d Cir.), *cert. denied,* 439 U.S. 985 (1978); *U.S. v. James,* 555 F.2d 992

(D.C. Cir. 1977). Although there is no "rigid checklist" to follow, *U.S. v. Czarnecki*, 552 F.2d 698, 702 (6th Cir.), *cert. denied*, 431 U.S. 939 (1977), the courts have identified various appropriate considerations: (1) Similarity between the offense charged and the other crime, wrong, or act may be the key factor when it is offered to prove identity, *U.S. v. Powell*, 587 F.2d 443 (9th Cir. 1978); *U.S. v. Beechum*, 582 F.2d 898, 912 n.15 (5th Cir. 1978), *cert. denied*, 440 U.S. 920 (1979); *U.S. v. Myers, supra,* but not necessarily a key factor when it is offered to prove motive, intent, plan, or design, *U.S. v. McPartlin, supra; U.S. v. Beechum,* 582 F.2d at 912 n.15. (2) Remoteness or closeness in time of a prior crime, wrong, or act is also a factor. *U.S. v. Roe,* 670 F.2d 956, 967 (11th Cir.), *cert. denied,* 459 U.S. 856 (1982); *U.S. v. Myers,* 550 F.2d at 1044; *U.S. v. Taglione,* 546 F.2d 194, 199 (5th Cir. 1977); *U.S. v. Largent,* 545 F.2d 1039, 1043 (6th Cir. 1976), *cert. denied,* 429 U.S. 1098 (1977). (3) Whether the other crime, wrong, or act is before or after the offense charged is generally not a factor. *U.S. v. Beechum,* 582 F.2d at 903 n.1; *U.S. v. Espinoza,* 578 F.2d 224 (9th Cir.), *cert. denied,* 439 U.S. 849 (1978). But, where the relevant issue is the defendant's intent or predisposition at the time of the offense, subsequent acts may not be admissible. *U.S. v. Boyd,* 595 F.2d 120 (3d Cir. 1978); *U.S. v. Daniels,* 572 F.2d 535 (5th Cir. 1978).

The evidence is also to be weighed against the requirements of Rule 403, Fed. R. Evid. which requires relevant evidence to be excluded if its probative value is substantially outweighed by unfair prejudice, confusion of the issues, misleading the jury, undue delay, or needless cumulative evidence. Potential prejudice from death threats may be great, but may survive the balancing test. *U.S. v. Qamar,* 671 F.2d 732, 734-37 (2d Cir. 1982). However, a reversal was ordered where a government witness was shot the day the trial began, testified from a wheelchair, and the jury knew from news reports the reason she was confined to a wheelchair. *U.S. v. Richardson,* 651 F.2d 1251, 1253 (8th Cir. 1981).

The trial judge should give the jury a cautionary instruction under Rule 105 at the time such evidence is offered, limiting its purpose. *Huddleston v. U.S., supra.* In one case, failure by the trial judge to give such a cautionary instruction requested by defense counsel was considered "plain error." *U.S. v. Yopp,* 577 F.2d 362 (6th Cir. 1978).

Acts or wrongs, as well as crimes for which the defendant was convicted, come within Rule 404(b). *U.S. v. Cooper,* 577 F.2d 1079 (6th Cir.), *cert. denied,* 439 U.S. 868 (1978); *U.S. v. Miller,* 573 F.2d 388 (7th Cir. 1978). There is no requirement to prove that the defendant was convicted for the prior or subsequent crime. *U.S. v. Hunter,* 672 F.2d

815, 817 (10th Cir. 1982). Evidence of prior arrests has been admissible, *U.S. v. Black,* 595 F.2d 1116 (5th Cir. 1979), and charges of crimes that were later dismissed, *U.S. v. Juarez,* 561 F.2d 65 (7th Cir. 1977). Evidence of foreign convictions may also be admitted. *U.S. v. Rodarte,* 596 F.2d 141 (5th Cir. 1979); *U.S. v. Nolan,* 551 F.2d at 270 (1977).

As evidence of other crimes, wrongs, or acts is admissible to show motive, intent, identity, knowledge, plan, or design — issues which may be material to proving the government's case-in-chief — the government is not required to wait for the defendant to put those matters in issue. *U.S. v. Danzey,* 594 F.2d at 913-14; *U.S. v. Juarez,* 561 F.2d at 73; *U.S. v. Adcock,* 558 F.2d 397 (8th Cir.), *cert. denied,* 434 U.S. 921 (1977). However, some courts have held that, where possible, such evidence should await the conclusion of the defendant's case. This enables the trial court to better evaluate the need for such evidence. *U.S. v. Figueroa,* 618 F.2d 934, 939 (2d Cir. 1980); *U.S. v. Brunson,* 549 F.2d 348 (5th Cir.), *cert. denied,* 434 U.S. 842 (1977).

### § 1523. — — Motive.

Although motive is never an element itself, evidence of it is often relevant to show the defendant's state of mind and purpose for committing the crime charged. If the motive can be proved by prior or subsequent crimes, wrongs, or acts, Rule 404(b) permits their admission in evidence. *U.S. v. Cook,* 592 F.2d 877 (5th Cir.), *cert. denied,* 442 U.S. 921 (1979). The other crimes, wrongs, or acts offered to prove motive may be totally dissimilar to the acts giving rise to the offense charged. For example, evidence of an offer to purchase heroin for $1,000 was admitted to prove defendant's motive for bank robbery. *U.S. v. Cyphers,* 553 F.2d 1064 (7th Cir.), *cert. denied,* 434 U.S. 843 (1977). Evidence of defendant's homosexual relationship with the victim was properly admitted to prove defendant's motive for killing him. *U.S. v. Free,* 574 F.2d 1221 (5th Cir.), *cert. denied,* 439 U.S. 873 (1978). Evidence of the break-in of Daniel Ellsberg's office was admissible to prove the defendant's motivation in making "Watergate" cover-up payments and concealing the identities of higher-ups. *U.S. v. Haldeman,* 559 F.2d 31, 88-91 (D.C. Cir. 1976), *cert. denied,* 431 U.S. 933 (1977). Evidence of a defendant's escape was admitted to show motive for his subsequent theft of a car. *U.S. v. Stover,* 565 F.2d 1010 (8th Cir. 1977). Thus, when the issue is motive, similarity of the physical elements of the crime charged with the extrinsic act need not be established. *U.S. v. Beechum,* 582 F.2d 898 (5th Cir. 1978).

## § 1524. — — Intent and Knowledge.

Intent and knowledge, or the lack thereof, are often contested issues in criminal cases. A defendant may agree that he did the physical acts which form the basis for the charge, but assert that he lacked the intent or criminal knowledge necessary to find him guilty. In such a case, evidence of other crimes, wrongs, or acts is admissible under Rule 404(b) to prove that the defendant did, in fact, have the requisite intent and knowledge. *U.S. v. Taglione*, 546 F.2d 194 (5th Cir. 1977). Where intent or knowledge is not a material issue, as where the defendant has denied committing the underlying acts, "other crimes" evidence to prove intent has been held inadmissible. *U.S. v. Gubelman*, 571 F.2d 1252 (2d Cir.), *cert. denied*, 436 U.S. 948 (1978). Or, where by the nature of the offense, the defendant's intent is not in issue, "other crimes" evidence to prove intent is not admissible. *U.S. v. Coades*, 549 F.2d 1303, 1306 (9th Cir. 1977) (prior bank robbery to prove intent in committing charged bank robbery).

Not only must intent or knowledge be material to the government's proof, the proffered evidence of the other crimes, wrongs, or acts must be probative. It has been held that previous possession of stolen paintings is not probative of criminal intent with respect to charges of extortion of oil companies for return of credit card vouchers, *U.S. v. Taglione*, 546 F.2d at 199-200, and that possession of a sawed-off shotgun is not probative of predisposition to violate the drug laws. *U.S. v. Daniels*, 572 F.2d 535 (5th Cir. 1978). But where intent or knowledge is in any way contested and the probative value of the other crime, wrong, or act to the issue of intent or knowledge outweighs its dangers of unfair prejudice, etc., the proof is admissible. *U.S. v. Moreno-Nunez*, 595 F.2d 1186 (9th Cir. 1979); *U.S. v. DeFillipo*, 590 F.2d 1228 (2d Cir.), *cert. denied*, 442 U.S. 920 (1979); *U.S. v. Weidman*, 572 F.2d 1199 (7th Cir.), *cert. denied*, 439 U.S. 821 (1978); *U.S. v. Johnson*, 562 F.2d 515 (8th Cir. 1977); *U.S. v. Sparks*, 560 F.2d 1173 (4th Cir. 1977).

It has been held that the government need not wait for the defendant to deny wrongful intent before offering evidence of other acts that are relevant to intent. *U.S. v. Adcock*, 558 F.2d 397, 402 (8th Cir.), *cert. denied*, 434 U.S. 921 (1977). However, if the government has other ample evidence to prove wrongful intent, the probative value of other acts is greatly reduced. *U.S. v. Dolliole*, 597 F.2d 102 (7th Cir.), *cert. denied*, 442 U.S. 946 (1979).

Evidence of other crimes, wrongs, or acts to prove a defendant's criminal intent or knowledge has been held properly admitted in drug cases, *U.S. v. Rentaria*, 625 F.2d 1279, 1281 (5th Cir. 1980); *U.S. v. Moreno-Nunez*, 595 F.2d at 1186; *U.S. v. Sigal*, 572 F.2d 1320 (9th Cir.

1978); *U.S. v. Smith,* 552 F.2d 257 (8th Cir. 1977); *U.S. v. Nolan,* 551 F.2d 266 (10th Cir.), *cert. denied,* 434 U.S. 904 (1977), in mail fraud cases, *U.S. v. Weidman,* 572 F.2d at 1201, in firearms cases, *U.S. v. Johnson,* 562 F.2d at 516; *U.S. v. Dudek,* 560 F.2d 1288 (6th Cir. 1977), *cert. denied,* 434 U.S. 1037 (1978), theft and receiving cases, *U.S. v. DeFillipo,* 590 F.2d at 1230; *U.S. v. Whetzel,* 589 F.2d 707 (D.C. Cir. 1978); *U.S. v. Reese,* 568 F.2d 1246 (6th Cir. 1977); *U.S. v. Nichols,* 534 F.2d 202 (9th Cir. 1976), false statement cases, *U.S. v. Miller,* 573 F.2d 388 (7th Cir. 1978); *U.S. v. Matlock,* 558 F.2d 1328 (8th Cir.), *cert. denied,* 434 U.S. 872 (1977), tax cases, *U.S. v. Pry,* 625 F.2d 689, 692 (5th Cir. 1980), *cert. denied,* 450 U.S. 925 (1981); and where entrapment was raised as a defense, *U.S. v. Henciar,* 568 F.2d 489 (6th Cir. 1977), *cert. denied,* 435 U.S. 953 (1978).

Guns were held to be admissible to show defendant's intent to engage in conspiracy to import cocaine; *U.S. v. Marino,* 658 F.2d 1120, 1123 (6th Cir. 1981); and activities as a tax protestor were relevant on the issue of intent in a failure to file case, *U.S. v. Reed,* 670 F.2d 622, 623 (5th Cir.), *cert. denied,* 102 S. Ct. 2945 (1982).

### § 1525. — — Identity.

When the identity of the defendant is in issue, proof of other crimes, wrongs, or acts is generally limited to such crimes, wrongs, or acts as are substantially similar to the acts that make up the charged offense. *U.S. v. Powell,* 587 F.2d 443 (9th Cir. 1978); *U.S. v. Beechum,* 582 F.2d 898 (5th Cir. 1978). Such evidence has been held properly admitted in a drug case, *U.S. v. Baldarrama,* 566 F.2d 560 (5th Cir.), *cert. denied,* 439 U.S. 844 (1978), a kidnapping case, *Durns v. U.S.,* 562 F.2d 542 (8th Cir.), *cert. denied,* 434 U.S. 959 (1977), a check case, *U.S. v. Maestas,* 546 F.2d 1177 (5th Cir. 1977), and a bank robbery case, *U.S. v. Danzey,* 594 F.2d 905 (2d Cir.), *cert. denied,* 441 U.S. 951 (1979).

In some circumstances, however, other crimes or acts that are not unique signature crimes or the handiwork of the defendant may be probative of the defendant's identity. *U.S. v. Gubelman,* 571 F.2d 1252 (2d Cir.), *cert. denied,* 436 U.S. 948 (1978). For example, death threats have been permitted to show identity, *U.S. v. Qamar,* 671 F.2d 732, 736-37 (2d Cir. 1982), and evidence that the defendant had stolen weapons and retained them was held relevant to the issue of identity in a bank robbery charge where one of the weapons stolen was found in the getaway car. *U.S. v. Waldron,* 568 F.2d 185 (10th Cir. 1977), *cert. denied,* 434 U.S. 1080 (1978).

## § 1526. — — Plan, Scheme, or Design.

Evidence of other crimes, wrongs, or acts is admissible where the other crime, wrong, or act is inextricably tied in with the offense charged. *U.S. v. Derring,* 592 F.2d 1003 (8th Cir. 1979); *U.S. v. Lamb,* 575 F.2d 1310 (10th Cir. 1978); *U.S. v. Carrillo,* 561 F.2d 1125 (5th Cir. 1977); *U.S. v. Dudek,* 560 F.2d 1288 (6th Cir. 1977), *cert. denied,* 434 U.S. 1037 (1978); *U.S. v. Roberts,* 548 F.2d 665 (6th Cir.), *cert. denied,* 432 U.S. 931 (1977); *U.S. v. Blewitt,* 538 F.2d 1099 (5th Cir.), *cert. denied,* 429 U.S. 1026 (1976); *U.S. v. Bloom,* 538 F.2d 704 (5th Cir. 1976), *cert. denied,* 429 U.S. 1074 (1977). This is sometimes referred to as the *res gestae* exception. *U.S. v. Blewitt,* 538 F.2d at 1101.

Evidence of other crimes, wrongs, or acts is also admissible to prove an ongoing or continuing plan or scheme, or the development of a course of conduct leading up to the offense charged. *U.S. v. Weidman,* 572 F.2d 1199 (7th Cir.), *cert. denied,* 439 U.S. 821 (1978); *U.S. v. Adcock,* 558 F.2d 397, 401 (8th Cir.), *cert. denied,* 434 U.S. 921 (1977); *U.S. v. Serlin,* 538 F.2d 737, 747 (7th Cir. 1976). *But see U.S. v. O'Connor,* 580 F.2d 38 (2d Cir. 1978), where evidence that defendant took three other bribes in the six-month to one-year period before he took the bribe for which he was charged was held insufficient to show a plan or scheme.

## § 1527. — Evidence of a Guilty Mind.

## § 1528. — — Flight and Concealment of Identity.

Evidence of flight is admissible to prove a consciousness of guilt. *Sibron v. New York,* 392 U.S. 40, 66 (1968); *U.S. v. Lyon,* 588 F.2d 581 (8th Cir. 1978), *cert. denied,* 441 U.S. 910 (1979); *U.S. v. Peltier,* 585 F.2d 314, 322-25 (8th Cir. 1978), *cert. denied,* 440 U.S. 945 (1979); *U.S. v. Myers,* 550 F.2d 1036, 1048-51 (5th Cir. 1977); *U.S. v. Craig,* 522 F.2d 29 (6th Cir. 1975). Immediacy between the flight and the crime charged is important, and where the time lag is substantial, the "court must be certain there is evidence that a defendant knows he is being sought for the specific crime charged and not for some other crime or event." *U.S. v. Howze,* 668 F.2d 322, 324-25 (7th Cir. 1982).

Similarly, evidence that the defendant concealed his identity or used a false name to avoid apprehension is admissible to prove consciousness of guilt. *U.S. v. Boyle,* 675 F.2d 430, 432 (1st Cir. 1982); *U.S. v. James,* 576 F.2d 1121 (5th Cir. 1978); *U.S. v. Thompson,* 261 F.2d 809, 812 (2d Cir. 1958), *cert. denied,* 359 U.S. 967 (1959).

## § 1529. — — False Exculpatory Statements.

False exculpatory statements made by a defendant are admissible to prove consciousness of guilt. *U.S. v. Rajewski,* 526 F.2d 149 (7th Cir. 1975), *cert. denied,* 426 U.S. 908 (1976); *U.S. v. Parness,* 503 F.2d 430 (2d Cir. 1974), *cert. denied,* 419 U.S. 1105 (1975); *DeVore v. U.S.,* 368 F.2d 396 (9th Cir. 1966).

## § 1530. — — Suppression, Destruction, or Fabrication of Evidence.

In *U.S. v. Graham,* 102 F.2d 436, 442 (2d Cir.), *cert. denied,* 307 U.S. 643 (1939), the court stated, "The manufacture, destruction, or suppression of evidence in defense of a criminal charge is in the nature of an admission of guilt and, though not conclusive, is to be given consideration as such by the jury." *See also U.S. v. Brashier,* 548 F.2d 1315 (9th Cir. 1976), *cert. denied,* 429 U.S. 1111 (1977); *U.S. v. Wilkins,* 385 F.2d 465 (4th Cir. 1967), *cert. denied,* 390 U.S. 951 (1968); *Harney v. U.S.,* 306 F.2d 523 (1st Cir.), *cert. denied,* 371 U.S. 911 (1962).

Evidence that a defendant attempted to influence the testimony of a witness or attempted to impede or prevent a witness from testifying is also admissible to show consciousness of guilt. *U.S. v. Ochs,* 595 F.2d 1247 (2d Cir.), *cert. denied,* 444 U.S. 955 (1979); *U.S. v. Reamer,* 589 F.2d 769 (4th Cir. 1978), *cert. denied,* 440 U.S. 980 (1979); *U.S. v. Hall,* 565 F.2d 1052 (8th Cir. 1977); *U.S. v. Lord,* 565 F.2d 831 (2d Cir. 1977); *U.S. v. Papia,* 560 F.2d 827 (7th Cir. 1977).

## § 1531. — Habit and Custom.

Rule 406 of the Federal Rules of Evidence provides that evidence of habit or custom is relevant to prove that the specific conduct of a person or organization was in conformity with the habit or routine custom. But, habit or custom must be distinguished from character. Character is a trait of an individual unrelated to specific conduct in specific circumstances. Character deals with general qualities such as honesty, peacefulness, and care. Habit or custom, on the other hand, deals with an individual's or organization's specific conduct in specific circumstances. As the Advisory Committee's Note states: "A habit ... is the person's regular practice of meeting a particular kind of situation with a specific type of conduct, such as the habit of going down a particular stairway two stairs at a time, or of giving the hand-signal for a left turn, or of alighting from railway cars while they are moving."

The admissibility of habit and custom has been considered by the federal courts primarily in civil cases. There are, however, a few criminal cases that have considered habit and custom evidence. *U.S. v. Callahan,* 551 F.2d 733 (6th Cir. 1977); *U.S. v. Riley,* 550 F.2d 233 (5th Cir. 1977).

### § 1532. — Motive.

Motive is the state of feeling impelled toward an act and is distinguishable from intent, which is the mental state accompanying the act. Intent is an essential element of most crimes. Proof of motive, while always relevant, is never essential. *Pointer v. U.S.,* 151 U.S. 396, 414 (1894); *U.S. v. Simon,* 425 F.2d 796, 808 (2d Cir. 1969), *cert. denied,* 397 U.S. 1006 (1970). Trial courts are given broad discretion to admit evidence of a fact tending to suggest a motive for the act charged. *U.S. v. King,* 560 F.2d 122 (2d Cir.), *cert. denied,* 434 U.S. 925 (1977); *U.S. v. Adcock,* 558 F.2d 397 (8th Cir.), *cert. denied,* 434 U.S. 921 (1977); *U.S. v. Fernandez,* 497 F.2d 730 (9th Cir. 1974), *cert. denied,* 420 U.S. 990 (1975); *U.S. v. Cifarelli,* 401 F.2d 512 (2d Cir.), *cert. denied,* 393 U.S. 987 (1968).

Evidence of defendant's need for money has been properly admitted in theft and robbery cases. *U.S. v. Seastrunk,* 580 F.2d 800 (5th Cir. 1978), *cert. denied,* 439 U.S. 1080 (1979); *U.S. v. Parker,* 549 F.2d 1217 (9th Cir.), *cert. denied,* 430 U.S. 971 (1977). Evidence of defendant's involvement in a grand jury investigation was held properly admitted to prove his motive to intimidate a grand jury witness. *U.S. v. Bradwell,* 388 F.2d 619 (2d Cir.), *cert. denied,* 393 U.S. 867 (1968). And motive evidence has been held properly admitted in false statement cases. *U.S. v. Sackett,* 598 F.2d 739 (2d Cir. 1979); *U.S. v. Stephen,* 569 F.2d 860 (5th Cir. 1978).

Since evidence of motive may rebut as well as support the prosecution's case, a defendant may offer proof of his good motive to contradict suggestions that his motives were bad. *May v. U.S.,* 175 F.2d 994, 1009 (D.C. Cir.), *cert. denied,* 338 U.S. 830 (1949). He may offer both his own statements and evidence of facts and circumstances tending to show the nonexistence of the motive alleged. *U.S. v. Brown,* 411 F.2d 1134 (10th Cir. 1969); *May v. U.S.,* 175 F.2d at 1009; *Haigler v. U.S.,* 172 F.2d 986, 987 (10th Cir. 1949).

# CHAPTER 16

## DEMONSTRATIVE EVIDENCE

§ 1600. Introduction.
§ 1601. Audio and Video Recordings.
§ 1602. — Audio Recordings.
§ 1603. — Video Recordings.
§ 1604. Photographs.
§ 1605. Summary Charts.
§ 1606. Models, Overlays, and Experiments.
§ 1607. — Models.
§ 1608. — Overlays.
§ 1609. — Experiments.
§ 1610. Computer Records.
§ 1611. Jury View of Premises.

## § 1600. Introduction.

Demonstrative evidence is that class of proof requiring authentication before it may be admitted. It includes documents, records, recordings, photographs, and duplicates, as well as many items, not evidence in themselves, but used to illustrate, clarify, simplify, or emphasize testimony, such as charts, graphs, and summaries.

## § 1601. Audio and Video Recordings.

## § 1602. — Audio Recordings.

Admission of evidence of recordings of conversations between a defendant and a government informant, electronically monitored with the consent of the informant, violates no fourth amendment right of an accused, *U.S. v. White,* 401 U.S. 745 (1971); *U.S. v. Hodge,* 594 F.2d 1163 (7th Cir. 1979); nor is the use of such evidence limited to corroboration of the informant's testimony, *U.S. v. Bonanno,* 487 F.2d 654 (2d Cir. 1973). However, a proper foundation must be laid for the introduction of relevant, recorded conversations. The Eighth Circuit has held that this foundation should include a showing:

(1) That the recording device was capable of taping the conversation now offered in evidence.
(2) That the operator of the device was competent to operate the device.
(3) That the recording is authentic and correct.
(4) That changes, additions or deletions have not been made on the recording.
(5) That the recording has been preserved in a manner that is shown to the court.

(6) That the speakers are identified.
(7) That the conversation elicited was made voluntarily and in good faith, without any kind of inducement.

*U.S. v. McMillan,* 508 F.2d 101, 104 (8th Cir. 1974), *cert. denied,* 421 U.S. 916 (1975); *U.S. v. Brown,* 604 F.2d 557 (8th Cir. 1979).

The burden is on the offering party to produce clear and convincing evidence of the accuracy, authenticity, and trustworthiness of sound recordings. *U.S. v. Blakey,* 607 F.2d 779 (7th Cir. 1979); *U.S. v. King,* 587 F.2d 956 (9th Cir. 1978). A complaint of inaudibility is addressed to the sound discretion of the court. Tapes that are partially unintelligible are admissible unless those portions are so substantial as to render the recording as a whole untrustworthy. *U.S. v. Llinas,* 603 F.2d 506 (5th Cir. 1979).

A composite tape of selected conversations made from accurate duplicate copies may be played at trial. *U.S. v. Denton,* 556 F.2d 811 (6th Cir. 1977). Tapes of recorded conversations containing references to extraneous subjects may be carefully constructed from the master tape. *U.S. v. Anderson,* 577 F.2d 258 (5th Cir. 1978). Irrelevant matter should be deleted, and the method of trial tape construction preserved as a foundation for the admissibility of the trial tapes. Composite tapes of representative conversations fall within the same principle. Trial courts may order the deletion of obscene language. *U.S. v. DiMuro,* 540 F.2d 503 (1st Cir. 1976). Evidence of the accuracy and authenticity of all tapes that the government proposes to use in trial must be offered along with a showing that the defendant was afforded a reasonable pretrial opportunity to examine and compare the master and the trial tapes. *U.S. v. Denton, supra.* Sufficient copies of any transcripts should be available and provided for each juror and defendant, and all counsel and concerned court personnel.

Verbatim transcripts of tape recorded conversations are prepared either from the original tape or an exact copy, made to protect the integrity of the master tape. While the circuits generally agree that a defendant may submit a transcript of his version of a recorded conversation and that trial courts are not obligated to conduct *in camera* hearings to determine the accuracy of transcripts (although the Tenth Circuit does recommend such a hearing absent a stipulation as to accuracy, *U.S. v. Watson,* 594 F.2d 1330 (10th Cir. 1979)), there is disagreement as to the admissibility of the transcript in evidence. The Fifth Circuit's position is that a transcript is more than an aid to the jury in understanding the recorded conversations; and transcripts offered by the government or the defendant are to be received for the limited purpose of identifying the speakers. *U.S. v. Onori,* 535 F.2d 938 (5th

Cir. 1976). The Second and Sixth Circuits, however, agree that, although they may be read by the jury while the tapes are played in open court, transcripts are not admissible unless there is a stipulation that they are accurate. *U.S. v. Crane,* 632 F.2d 663, 664 (6th Cir. 1980); *U.S. v. Chiarizio,* 525 F.2d 289 (2d Cir. 1975); *U.S. v. Smith,* 537 F.2d 862 (6th Cir. 1976). *But see U.S. v. Smith,* 584 F.2d 759 (6th Cir. 1978), *cert. denied,* 441 U.S. 922 (1979). The First and Ninth Circuits agree that only the tapes are admissible and that transcripts considered accurate by the trial court simply aid the jury in understanding the recordings. *U.S. v. Richman,* 600 F.2d 286 (1st Cir. 1979), *U.S. v. Rinn,* 586 F.2d 113 (9th Cir. 1978), *cert. denied,* 441 U.S. 931 (1979).

## § 1603. — Video Recordings.

The investigative technique of videotaping the conduct of one who subsequently becomes a defendant presents only a proper foundation question. Once an adequate foundation has been laid through the testimony of agents who observed the activity, videotapes may be received in evidence and played for the jury. *U.S. v. Medina-Herrera,* 606 F.2d 770 (7th Cir. 1979). There is no requirement, however, that the admitted video recordings be played, unless the defense demands that the jury see and hear what the tapes contain. A defendant cannot complain successfully if he fails to request a viewing. *U.S. v. Taylor,* 612 F.2d 1272, 1276 (10th Cir. 1980). Videotapes containing references to other, prior crimes are subject to editing because of the prejudicial impact of such comments, unless such crimes are relevant to the issue of intent. *U.S. v. Childs,* 598 F.2d 169 (D.C. Cir. 1979). In a prosecution for failing to file income tax returns, use of a videotape of a television "talk show" on which defendant appeared was held to be prejudicial error where other show participants emphasized defendant's own lack of belief in his arguments about the unlawfulness of income taxes and predicted his conviction and confinement. *U.S. v. Schiff,* 612 F.2d 73 (2d Cir. 1979).

Videotapes that are made from a position which prevents the recording of voices or the substance of a defendant's conversation with an agent need not be made available to the defense before trial if there is no factual dispute about what was or was not recorded. *U.S. v. Underwood,* 577 F.2d 157 (1st Cir. 1978). Release to news media of copies of videotaped encounters between a defendant and an undercover agent, while disapproved, was not reversible error where the tapes had been shown to the jury and the defense was entrapment. *U.S. v. Alberico,* 604 F.2d 1315 (10th Cir.), *cert. denied,* 444 U.S. 992 (1979).

A videotaped deposition "supplies an environment substantially comparable to a trial, but where the defendant was not permitted to be an active participant in the video deposition, this procedural substitute is constitutionally infirm." *U.S. v. Benfield*, 593 F.2d 815, 821 (8th Cir. 1979) (defendant monitored the deposition of an alleged kidnapped victim who was kept unaware of defendant's presence in the building; the victim deponent was cross-examined by defense counsel).

Motion pictures are admissible in evidence if they are based upon evidence of accuracy and fairness. *Sanchez v. Denver & Rio Grande Western Railroad*, 538 F.2d 304 (10th Cir.), *cert. denied*, 429 U.S. 1042 (1976). Movies purporting to represent the reenactment of an event are cautiously scrutinized for detail and may be accepted or rejected in the sole and sound discretion of the court. *Wagner v. International Harvester Co.*, 611 F.2d 224 (8th Cir. 1979); *Johnson v. William C. Ellis & Sons, Iron Works, Inc.*, 604 F.2d 950 (5th Cir. 1979).

## § 1604. Photographs.

Photographs are admissible as graphic portrayals of oral testimony. Typically, a witness must testify that the photograph or moving picture correctly and accurately represents facts observed by the witness. *Mikus v. U.S.*, 433 F.2d 719 (2d Cir. 1970). However, if direct testimony as to foundation matters is absent, the contents of the photographs themselves, together with other circumstantial or indirect evidence, may serve to explain and authenticate a photograph sufficiently to justify its admission. *U.S. v. Stearns*, 550 F.2d 1167 (9th Cir. 1977); *U.S. v. Taylor*, 530 F.2d 639 (5th Cir. 1976). A photograph may be enlarged without affecting its admissibility. *U.S. v. Parhms*, 424 F.2d 152 (9th Cir.), *cert. denied*, 400 U.S. 846 (1970); *U.S. v. Nolan*, 416 F.2d 588 (10th Cir.), *cert. denied*, 396 U.S. 912 (1969).

## § 1605. Summary Charts.

Summary charts used to illustrate testimonial and documentary evidence may be essential to jury understanding in cases involving numerous items of evidence. Rule 1006 of the Federal Rules of Evidence provides for their use when a case involves "voluminous writings, recordings, or photographs which cannot conveniently be examined in court ...."

A summary chart may be based on testimony of witnesses or on documents which have been admitted into evidence or which are admissible. *U.S. v. Johnson*, 594 F.2d 1253 (9th Cir. 1979), *cert. denied*, 444 U.S. 964 (1980); *U.S. v. Moody*, 339 F.2d 161 (6th Cir. 1964). Before adoption of Rule 1006, summarized documents had to have been already admitted into evidence; and juries were instructed that the documents, not the summary chart, constituted the evidence. The summary chart was only an aid to jury understanding of the documents. *Holland v. U.S.*, 348 U.S. 121 (1954); *Gordon v. U.S.*, 438 F.2d 858, 876-77 (5th Cir. 1971). However, Rule 1006 implies that the summary chart may be admitted into evidence in lieu of voluminous documents. *See U.S. v. Smyth*, 556 F.2d 1179 (5th Cir. 1977). *But see U.S. v. Foshee*, 606 F.2d 111, 113 (5th Cir. 1979), *cert. denied*, 444 U.S. 1082 (1980). Thus, under the rule, the summary chart is the evidence which the trier of the fact may consider. *U.S. v. Skalicky*, 615 F.2d 1117, 1121 n.5 (5th Cir.), *cert. denied*, 449 U.S. 832 (1980); *U.S. v. Gardner*, 611 F.2d 770, 776 (9th Cir. 1980). While there is no requirement that all of the voluminous evidence supporting a chart be introduced into evidence as a precondition to the introduction of that chart, the court may require the production of the underlying documents in court. Rule 1006, Fed. R. Evid.; *U.S. v. Strissel*, 920 F.2d 1162 (4th Cir. 1990).

Rule 1006 requires only that the summary chart be based on admissible documents that have previously been made available to the defendant at a reasonable time and place. *U.S. v. Foley*, 598 F.2d 1323, 1338 (4th Cir. 1979), *cert. denied*, 444 U.S. 1043 (1980); *U.S. v. Clements*, 588 F.2d 1030, 1039 (5th Cir.), *cert. denied*, 440 U.S. 982 (1979). If the underlying records are not otherwise admissible, it is not sufficient that the other party was given notice they would be used. *U.S. v. Johnson*, 594 F.2d 1253, 1254-57 (9th Cir. 1979). A foundation for the admission of a chart or summary can be laid through the testimony of the witness who supervised the preparation of the exhibit. *U.S. v. Scales*, 594 F.2d 558 (6th Cir.), *cert. denied*, 441 U.S. 946 (1979); *U.S. v. Mortimer*, 118 F.2d 266, 269 (2d Cir. 1941).

A summary under Rule 1006 may be presented in the form of testimony as where a doctor testified about the contents of investigative reports contained in a 94,000-page "new drug application." *Nichols v. Upjohn Co.*, 610 F.2d 293, 294 (5th Cir. 1980).

Summary charts must, of course, be accurate. They must fairly and accurately reflect the contents of the documents or testimony upon which they are based. *Holland v. U.S., supra; U.S. v. Conlin*, 551 F.2d 534 (2d Cir. 1977). There is, however, no requirement that a prosecution summary chart include the defendant's version of the facts. *U.S. v. Ambrosiani*, 610 F.2d 65 (1st Cir. 1979); *Myers v. U.S.*, 356 F.2d 469 (5th Cir.), *cert. denied*, 384 U.S. 952 (1966). However, they may not go beyond an objective summarization of the evidence. *See U.S. v. Kiamie*, 258 F.2d 924 (2d Cir.), *cert. denied*, 358 U.S. 909 (1958); *Elder v. U.S.*, 213 F.2d 876 (5th Cir.), *cert. denied*, 348 U.S. 901 (1954).

Rule 1008(c) of the Federal Rules of Evidence suggests that it is the function of the trier of the fact, rather than the court, to pass upon the accuracy of summary charts. However, it has been held that the use and admissibility of summary charts is a matter within the sound discretion of the trial court. *U.S. v. Johnson,* 319 U.S. 503 (1943); *U.S. v. Collins,* 596 F.2d 166 (6th Cir. 1979); *U.S. v. Honea,* 556 F.2d 906 (8th Cir. 1977); *U.S. v. Diez,* 515 F.2d 892 (5th Cir. 1975) (summaries themselves do not constitute the evidence on the case). The trial court should carefully examine summary charts and their underlying documents, out of the presence of the jury, to determine that everything contained therein is supported by admissible evidence. *U.S. v. Bartone,* 400 F.2d 459, 461 (6th Cir. 1968). But a voir dire by a defendant on the accuracy of a summary chart is not required where the chart is straight forward and its basis in the evidence is clear. *U.S. v. Collins, supra.*

Rule 16 of the Federal Rules of Criminal Procedure requires that the government show the defense any documents it plans to use at trial, and this includes summary charts. Rule 1006 of the Federal Rules of Evidence also requires the government to show the defense all documents upon which a summary chart is based. This disclosure must be made far enough in advance of trial to allow the defense to prepare cross-examination and/or its own summary chart.

If a defendant fails to object at trial to the use of a summary chart, any error is waived for purposes of appeal. *U.S. v. Miller,* 600 F.2d 498 (5th Cir.), *cert. denied,* 444 U.S. 955 (1979); *U.S. v. Brickley,* 426 F.2d 680 (8th Cir. 1970). Objections must be set forth with particularity. *U.S. v. O'Brien,* 601 F.2d 1067, 1071 (9th Cir. 1979); *U.S. v. Jalbert,* 504 F.2d 892, 894 (1st Cir. 1974).

The headings and captions of a summary chart must not contain conclusions or assumptions that may take on independent significance. *Holland v. U.S., supra; Watkins v. U.S.,* 287 F.2d 932 (1st Cir. 1961); *Lloyd v. U.S.,* 226 F.2d 9, 17 (5th Cir. 1955). This does not mean, however, that a summary chart must be devoid of assumptions. As the Fifth Circuit held in *U.S. v. Diez,* 515 F.2d 892, 905 (5th Cir. 1975), "the essential requirement is not that the charts be free from reliance on any assumptions, but rather that these assumptions be supported by evidence in the record." Some captions or headings which have been upheld include "Total Net Unreported Income," *U.S. v. Lacob,* 416 F.2d 756 (7th Cir. 1969); "Schedule of Sales, Net Taxable Gains to Peter A. Palori and Amounts Not Reported or Taxable Gain Reported by Others," *U.S. v. Diez,* 515 F.2d 892, 905 (5th Cir. 1975); "falsified data" and "difference between original/false." *U.S. v. Smyth,* 556 F.2d 1179 (5th Cir. 1977).

The trial court should instruct the jury on the nature and use of a summary chart. *Holland v. U.S.,* 348 U.S. 121, 128 (1954); *U.S. v. Foshee,* 606 F.2d 111 (5th Cir. 1979), *cert. denied,* 444 U.S. 1082 (1980); *U.S. v. Scales,* 594 F.2d 558 (6th Cir.), *cert. denied,* 441 U.S. 946 (1979); *U.S. v. Diez, supra.* Where the chart is admitted in lieu of voluminous documents, under Rule 1006, the court may instruct the jury that the chart is "evidence." *U.S. v. Smyth,* 556 F.2d 1179, 1184 (5th Cir. 1977). Where the chart is used to summarize documents and testimony in evidence, it has been held that the jury should be instructed that the summary "chart is not itself evidence but only an aid in evaluating the evidence." *U.S. v. Scales,* 594 F.2d at 564. This charge may be more than is required since the adoption of Rule 1006, but may be prudent in some circuits. *See U.S. v. Skalicky,* 615 F.2d 1117, 1120-21 (5th Cir.), *cert. denied,* 449 U.S. 832 (1980). Even where the jury has been instructed that the summary charts were not the actual evidence, but only aids, they have been permitted to go to the jury during deliberations. *U.S. v. Scales,* 594 F.2d at 563.

Summary charts are not limited to summarizing documents. Testimonial evidence may be summarized. *Epstein v. U.S.,* 246 F.2d 563, 570 (6th Cir. 1957), *cert. denied,* 355 U.S. 868. A chart has been permitted to summarize government witness' review of 3,000 intercepted phone calls concluding that the gross revenue of a gambling operation exceeded $2,000 a day. *U.S. v. Clements,* 588 F.2d 1030 (5th Cir.), *cert. denied,* 440 U.S. 982 (1979). A chart has been used to summarize computer printouts, *U.S. v. Smyth,* 556 F.2d 1179 (5th Cir. 1977), and as a chronology of significant events occurring over a number of days, compiled from records, surveillances and tape recordings of conversations. *U.S. v. Williams,* 952 F.2d 1504 (6th Cir. 1991). Even the absence of records may be summarized. *U.S. v. Scales,* 594 F.2d at 562.

## § 1606. Models, Overlays, and Experiments.

## § 1607. — Models.

Considerations applicable to the admission of photographs, motion pictures, charts, and other forms of demonstrative evidence are equally applicable to scale models. A proper foundation must be laid and the substantial exactness of the model must be established before it may be used to complement the testimony of a witness. Display and use in trial of models of homemade time bombs and Molotov cocktails, constructed and explained by the government's principal investigator, are proper. *U.S. v. Curtis,* 520 F.2d 1300 (1st Cir. 1975). The trial court may, at its discretion, receive a model in evidence. The standard of review is abuse of discretion. *Gaspard v. Diamond M. Drilling Co.,* 593 F.2d 605 (5th Cir. 1979) (refusal to admit into evidence a model of the crew boat stairway on which a fall occurred).

## § 1608. — Overlays.

Photographic or transparent, individual colored overlays affixed to diagrams or charts, designed to illustrate differences and used for comparison purposes, are acceptable demonstrative evidence techniques. *U.S. v. Saniti,* 604 F.2d 603 (9th Cir.), *cert. denied,* 444 U.S. 969 (1979); *Baker v. Elcona Homes Corp.,* 588 F.2d 551 (6th Cir. 1978), *cert. denied,* 441 U.S. 933 (1979). Only considerations of confusion or misleading the jury properly prevent the use of such materials. Rule 403, Fed. R. Evid.

## § 1609. — Experiments.

Experimental evidence is an attempt to replicate some part of an incident in issue. Both testimony about out-of-court experiments and scientific tests conducted in court, if relevant, are admissible to illustrate and clarify opinions of expert witnesses. *Midwestern Wholesale Drug, Inc. v. Gas Service Co.,* 442 F.2d 663 (10th Cir. 1971). Perfect identity between test and actual conditions is not required. Dissimilarities affect the weight of the evidence, not its admissibility. *Ramseyer v. General Motors Corp.,* 417 F.2d 859 (8th Cir. 1969). Since an experiment is staged, it is subject to manipulation. Thus, even though the experimental evidence is relevant, it may be excluded if its probative worth is overborne by dangers of confusing the issues, lack of reliability, unnecessary delay, or undue prejudice. Rules 401 and 403, Fed. R. Evid. *See Randall v. Warnaco, Inc., Hirsch-Weis Div.,* 677 F.2d 1226, 1234 (8th Cir. 1982).

The Sixth Circuit has fashioned a rule limiting a prosecutor's right to require in-court experiments of a testifying defendant. While a criminal defendant may be required in the presence of the jury to write a specific message, his fair trial right is violated if he is required "to perform acts which would unjustly prejudice him. This would be true in a case in which the requested performance or demonstration would unjustly humiliate or degrade the defendant or in a case in which such performance would be damaging to the defendant's image and irrelevant to the issue on trial." *U.S. v. Doremus,* 414 F.2d 252, 253-54 (6th Cir. 1969). The Fifth Circuit approved denying defense counsel the opportunity to test a law enforcement officer's ability to detect the smell of marijuana by offering to him packets of marjoram, tarragon, basil, oregano, and moloheia, some of which were mixed with marijuana. *U.S. v. Cantu,* 555 F.2d 1327 (5th Cir. 1977). The Fourth Circuit follows a "substantially same" rule and approved refusal to permit courtroom reenactment of a fire on a model of a railroad yard where tubing used to represent drainage pipes was not to scale. *Burriss v. Texaco, Inc.,* 361 F.2d 169 (4th Cir. 1966).

## § 1610. Computer Records.

A sufficient showing of reliability of computer recording procedures generally assures the admissibility of printouts when they are relevant and not subject to a hearsay objection. The Second Circuit, however, cautions that a defendant is entitled to know "what operations the computer has been instructed to perform and to have the precise instruction that had been given ... a reasonable time before trial." *U.S. v. Dioguardi,* 428 F.2d 1033, 1038 (2d Cir.), *cert. denied,* 400 U.S. 825 (1970). The Seventh Circuit has approved the following showings as a means of establishing the reliability of computer printouts:

> (1) what the input procedures were, (2) that the input and printouts were accurate within two percent, (3) that the computer was tested for internal programming errors on a monthly basis, and (4) that the printouts were made, maintained and relied on by the agency in the ordinary course of its business activities.

*U.S. v. Weatherspoon,* 581 F.2d 595, 598 (7th Cir. 1978).

Computer printouts may be used as summaries of original and forged billings under such headings as "original data," "falsified data," "falsified data summarized," and "difference between original/false." *U.S. v. Smyth,* 556 F.2d 1179 (5th Cir. 1977). Computer records maintained by customs officials of license plate numbers of vehicles passing through a border station are within the public records hearsay exception (Rule 803(8), Fed. R. Evid.) and were admissible in a narcotics prosecution as they are not of an adversarial, confrontational nature. *U.S. v. Orozco,* 590 F.2d 789 (9th Cir. 1979); *U.S. v. Cepeda Penes,* 577 F.2d 754 (1st Cir. 1978) (computer records showing that taxes had not been paid for four years were admissible to impeach a testifying defendant). *But see U.S. v. Ruffin,* 575 F.2d 346, 356 (2d Cir. 1978) (computer data compilations, otherwise admissible as a business or public record, could not be used against an accused).

## § 1611. Jury View of Premises.

Whether considered as evidence, a jury view of the premises is not a right, and a trial court's decision to grant or deny a view will not be disturbed on appeal in the absence of abuse of discretion. *U.S. v. Bry-*

*ant,* 563 F.2d 1227, 1230 (5th Cir. 1977); *U.S. v. Lopez,* 475 F.2d 537, 541 (7th Cir.), *cert. denied,* 414 U.S. 839 (1973); *Hughes v. U.S.,* 377 F.2d 515, 516 (9th Cir. 1967); *Virgin Islands v. Taylor,* 375 F.2d 771 (3d Cir. 1967). Considerations in determining whether such a view should be granted are (1) relevance to issues in the trial, (2) time required for a view, (3) territorial limitations, (4) supervision and conduct of the jury, and (5) changes in surrounding physical appearance of premises since the event in issue. Uncertainty in such factors has been held to diminish the value of inspecting premises. *U.S. v. Lopez,* 475 F.2d at 541; *Hughes v. U.S.,* 377 F.2d at 516; *U.S. v. Pinna,* 229 F.2d 216, 219 (7th Cir. 1956); *U.S. v. Pagano,* 207 F.2d 884, 885 (2d Cir. 1953). Photographs may be substituted should the jury need to know how a location appears. *U.S. v. Pagano, supra.*

The Supreme Court has held that the absence of the defendant from a view of the premises is not a denial of due process. *Snyder v. Massachusetts,* 291 U.S. 97 (1934). In *Burke v. U.S.,* 247 F. Supp. 418, 420 (D. Mass. 1965), *aff'd,* 358 F.2d 307 (1st Cir.), *cert. denied,* 384 U.S. 981 (1966), the court held that the trip to and from a view is not a "stage of the trial" for purposes of Rule 43 of the Federal Rules of Criminal Procedure.

# CHAPTER 17

## DOCUMENTARY EVIDENCE

§ 1701. Authentication and Admissibility.
§ 1702. — Official Documents.
§ 1703. — Private or Nonofficial Documents.
§ 1704. — Documents Containing Inadmissible Material.
§ 1705. Best Evidence Rule.
§ 1706. — Exceptions.
§ 1707. — Admission of Secondary Evidence.
§ 1708. Use of Entire Writing or Recorded Statement.

### § 1701. Authentication and Admissibility.

Authentication, or identification, is a precondition to establishing the relevancy of documentary evidence. The proponent must lay the proper foundation for admission of such evidence — he must offer evidence to show that the document in question is what he claims it is. Without such a foundation, the relevancy of the document cannot be established and it is, therefore, inadmissible. *See* Rule 402, Fed. R. Evid.

The procedure for authenticating or identifying documentary evidence is specifically addressed in Rules 901 and 902. Rule 901(a) requires that, for authentication, there must be "evidence sufficient to support a finding that the matter in question is what its proponent claims." This standard is identical to and is based upon that contained in Rule 104(b), the general rule for admission of evidence whose relevancy is conditioned on the fulfillment of a condition of fact. "[T]he traditional justifications for erecting a preliminary condition of fact for admission of writings — possibility of fraud, mistaken attribution, and jury credulity — still militate in favor of explicitly recognizing the special problems of authentication and identification." 5 J. Weinstein and M. Berger, *Commentary on Rules of Evidence,* para. 901(a) [02] at 901-19 (1978). Rule 901(b) enumerates, by way of illustration, examples of authentication or identification which conform to this general rule. Rule 901(b) does not purport to set forth the exclusive means of authenticating documentary evidence. Rule 902 sets out the specific instances where documentary evidence is self-authenticating, *i.e.,* where the evidence is admissible without any extrinsic evidence to show that the writing is what the proponent claims it to be.

Rule 901(a) only requires that the proponent offer evidence sufficient to support a finding of genuineness. Once this prima facie showing is made the document in question is admitted; however, the fact finder then is free, after considering all the evidence offered on the issue, either to rely on or disregard the document. If the evidence offered on authentication or identification does not rise to a prima facie level, the court will not admit the document in question. *See U.S. v. Carriger*, 592 F.2d 312, 316 (6th Cir. 1979); *In re James E. Long Construction Co.*, 557 F.2d 1039 (4th Cir. 1977); *U.S. v. Goichman*, 547 F.2d 778, 784 (3d Cir. 1976).

Proponents should recognize that some courts may apply Rule 403 more rigorously when real evidence, as opposed to testimonial evidence, is involved since real evidence has more potential impact on a jury. Moreover, compliance with the requirement of authentication does not assure admission of an item into evidence. Hearsay, best evidence, and other rules must also be satisfied.

From a practical standpoint, it should always be remembered that the problems of authentication or identification can often be avoided by stipulation or admission.

### § 1702. — Official Documents.

Subparagraphs (1) through (5) of Rule 902 provide for the admissibility of a whole range of public or official documents and records without extrinsic evidence to establish authenticity. The rule sets forth the requirements for admission of domestic public documents under seal, domestic public documents not under seal, foreign public documents, certified copies of public records, and official publications.

While Rule 902 permits the authentication of numerous public documents or records without the use of extrinsic evidence, there may still be instances where resort to another statute or rule will be necessary or helpful to authenticate a specific official document: Rule 27, Fed. R. Crim. P. (incorporates by reference Rule 44, Fed. R. Civ. P. (proof of official record)); 28 U.S.C. § 753(b) (authentication of records or proceedings by court reporters); 28 U.S.C. § 1736 (authentication of Congressional journals); 28 U.S.C. § 1738 (authentication of state and territorial statutes and judicial proceedings); 28 U.S.C. § 1739 (authentication of state and territorial nonjudicial records kept in public offices); 28 U.S.C. § 1740 (authentication of consular papers); 28 U.S.C. § 1741 and 18 U.S.C. §§ 3491-3496 (authentication of foreign documents); and 42 U.S.C. § 3505 (Social Security records). These and other statutes and rules covering authentication of various writings are still in force. The Federal Rules of Evidence are not intended to abrogate them.

Subparagraphs (1) and (2) of Rule 902 provide that domestic public documents, bearing either a public seal and a signature purporting to be an attestation or execution or an official signature certified by an officer who has a seal, are self-authenticating. *See U.S. v. Trotter*, 538

F.2d 217 (8th Cir.), *cert. denied,* 429 U.S. 943 (1976) (motor vehicle records). In addition, Rule 902(3) provides that copies of public records are self-authenticating when they bear a certificate complying with paragraphs (1) or (2). *See also* Rule 44, Fed. R. Civ. P.

Rule 803(10) of the Federal Rules of Evidence and Rule 44(b) of the Federal Rules of Civil Procedure provide an equally convenient way to prove the absence of a specified record or entry. A written statement to the effect that no record or entry has been found to exist after diligent search of designated records will suffice. The statement, however, must itself be authenticated in the same manner as is required for the record or entry if it had been found. *See U.S. v. Lee,* 589 F.2d 980, 987 (9th Cir. 1979), *cert. denied,* 444 U.S. 969 (1979) (affidavits of CIA officials reciting that search of CIA records failed to reveal defendant's employment); *U.S. v. Harris,* 551 F.2d 621 (5th Cir.), *cert. denied,* 434 U.S. 836 (1977) (authenticated certificate stating that defendant had not been granted a license to engage in the business as firearms dealer, despite fact that such certificate did not state diligent search of records had been made); *Hollingsworth v. U.S.,* 321 F.2d 342, 352 (10th Cir. 1963) (statement thus authenticated held admissible to prove the defendant did not file a declaration of intent to make a firearm); *U.S. v. Farris,* 517 F.2d 226, 227 (7th Cir.), *cert. denied,* 423 U.S. 892 (1975) (computer printout showing tax return not filed).

If an official document is not self-authenticating under Rule 902 and cannot be authenticated by employing one of the other methods mentioned in the preceding paragraph, resort to Rule 901(b)(7) should be considered. Under this rule, one means of authenticating a writing to meet the requirements of Rule 901(a) is to show evidence that the writing is authorized by law to be recorded or filed and in fact is recorded or filed in a public office, or the writing is a purported public record, report, statement, or data compilation, in any form, and is from the public office where items of this nature are kept. *See U.S. v. Davis,* 571 F.2d 1354, 1356-57 (5th Cir. 1978), where certain documents were found not to have been properly authenticated as public records or reports.

Certified copies of income tax returns and computer printouts of tax information are admissible when properly introduced in compliance with Rule 902(4). *U.S. v. Farris,* 517 F.2d at 227-28; *Stillman v. U.S.,* 177 F.2d 607, 617 (9th Cir. 1949).

## § 1703. — Private or Nonofficial Documents.

Before private or nonofficial documents may be admitted into evidence, they must be properly authenticated or identified. Rule

901(b)(1) provides that this can be accomplished through the testimony of a witness with knowledge that the matter in question is what it is claimed to be. This rule has been the subject of broad interpretation as was intended. *See* Advisory Committee's Note. Witnesses with knowledge include those who actually write the document in question. *In re Taylor,* 7 F. Supp. 592 (W.D.N.Y. 1934), observed its execution or use in a transaction or otherwise, or acquired familiarity with it in general, *U.S. v. Helberg,* 565 F.2d 993 (8th Cir. 1977); *U.S. v. Levine,* 546 F.2d 658 (5th Cir. 1977); *Jennings v. U.S.,* 73 F.2d 470 (5th Cir. 1934), or were exposed to the document in connection with their work, *U.S. v. Rosenstein,* 474 F.2d 705 (2d Cir. 1973). The possible applications of this rule are almost limitless. *See U.S. v. Gallagher,* 576 F.2d 1028 (3d Cir. 1978); *U.S. v. Rochan,* 563 F.2d 1246 (5th Cir. 1977); *U.S. v. Richardson,* 562 F.2d 476 (7th Cir. 1977), *cert. denied,* 434 U.S. 1072 (1978).

However, even substantial contact with certain documents does not necessarily mean that a witness has the requisite knowledge required for authentication. In *Lipscomb v. U.S.,* 33 F.2d 33 (8th Cir. 1929), the defendant sought to introduce, upon his own testimony, a sheet of paper bearing his signature, allegedly taken from a hotel register, to prove that he was in a different city on the day of the crime. The court held the sheet inadmissible, *id.* at 36, saying:

> [I]t is first necessary to have the register identified by one who had it in custody and knew something about the entries made thereon. After it has been so identified as the register regularly kept in the hotel at the time it purports to cover, then the signature thereon can be identified.

When no one can directly identify the document, it may be satisfactorily identified by circumstantial evidence. *U.S. v. Natale,* 526 F.2d 1160, 1172-73 (2d Cir. 1975); *U.S. v. King,* 472 F.2d 1 (9th Cir.), *cert. denied,* 414 U.S. 864 (1973). Proof of private custody together with other circumstances is strong circumstantial evidence of authenticity. Thousands of prescriptions were properly authenticated which came from a physician coconspirator's office when a state official testified that these prescriptions matched the numbers of the prescriptions which had been issued to the physician. *U.S. v. Bruner,* 657 F.2d 1278, 1284 (D.C. Cir. 1981). In *U.S. v. Imperial Chemical Industries, Ltd.,* 100 F. Supp. 504, 513 (S.D.N.Y. 1951), the court admitted unsigned declarations from the files of defendants. *See Morgan v. U.S.,* 149 F.2d 185 (5th Cir.), *cert. denied,* 326 U.S. 731 (1945) (fact that document was a memorandum sent by defendant to rationing board shown by circumstantial evidence). *See also U.S. v. Stearns,* 550 F.2d 1167 (9th Cir. 1977).

Where a document is alleged to be of a particular origin, authorship must be proved. Thus, the mere fact that a letter is signed in the name of the defendant is not enough to prove that the defendant signed it. *Summers v. McDermott,* 138 F.2d 338 (3d Cir. 1943) (unauthenticated checks rightly excluded where drawer of checks not produced and signatures not identified); *Nicola v. U.S.,* 72 F.2d 780, 783 (3d Cir. 1934).

Even if documents are unsigned, however, their admissibility as documents executed by the defendant may still be shown. *See U.S. v. Wolfish,* 525 F.2d 457 (2d Cir. 1975), *cert. denied,* 423 U.S. 1059 (1976); *U.S. v. Sutton,* 426 F.2d 1202 (D.C. Cir. 1969) (defendant's authorship of unsigned notes held sufficiently proved by circumstantial evidence; lengthy discussion of the point).

Rule 901(b)(2) and Rule 901(b)(3) provide that a document may be authenticated by nonexpert opinions as to the genuineness of handwriting, based upon familiarity not acquired for purposes of the litigation, *U.S. v. Mauchlin,* 670 F.2d 746, 749 (7th Cir. 1982), or by comparison by the trier of fact or by expert witnesses with authenticated specimens. Thus, in the latter situation, the trier of fact is faced with deciding the authenticity of both the document in question and the specimen. The jury may make a handwriting comparison without the aid of expert testimony, and may even reach a conclusion contrary to that of an expert. *Stokes v. U.S.,* 157 U.S. 187, 193-94 (1895); *Strauss v. U.S.,* 311 F.2d 926, 932 (5th Cir.), *cert. denied,* 373 U.S. 910 (1963); *In re Goldberg,* 91 F.2d 996, 997 (2d Cir. 1937). *Cf. U.S. v. Mota,* 598 F.2d 995, 999 (5th Cir. 1979).

When a witness is identifying a document, he should not testify concerning the contents of the document before it is admitted into evidence.

## §1704. — Documents Containing Inadmissible Material.

Generally, an admissible document is not rendered inadmissible because it contains some incompetent matter, *Miller v. New York Produce Exchange,* 550 F.2d 762 (2d Cir.), *cert. denied,* 434 U.S. 823 (1977); *Baltimore & O. R. Co. v. Felgenhauer,* 168 F.2d 12, 17 (8th Cir. 1948); unless that matter constitutes most of the document, *England v. U.S.,* 174 F.2d 466, 469 (5th Cir. 1949); *Olson v. Kilstofte & Vosejpka,*

*Inc.*, 327 F. Supp. 583 (D. Minn. 1971), *aff'd*, 456 F.2d 1299 (8th Cir. 1972).

In handling such problems, consider Rule 106:

> When a writing or recorded statement or part thereof is introduced by a party, an adverse party may require him at that time to introduce any other part or any other writing or recorded statement which ought in fairness to be considered contemporaneously with it.

*See U.S. v. Walker*, 652 F.2d 708, 710 (7th Cir. 1981); *Worden v. Tri State Ins. Co.*, 347 F.2d 336, 341 (10th Cir. 1965); *U.S. v. Corrigan*, 168 F.2d 641, 645 (2d Cir. 1948). But only so much of the balance as is relevant and sheds light on the part already in evidence may be introduced. *U.S. v. Dennis*, 183 F.2d 201, 229-30 (2d Cir. 1950), *aff'd*, 341 U.S. 494 (1951). There is no rule that, once any part is admitted, the entire document must be received. *Camps v. N.Y.C. Transit Authority*, 261 F.2d 320, 322 (2d Cir. 1958). A limiting instruction may be necessary with respect to portions of the document received for background and not for the truth of the matter stated. *See U.S. v. Bohle*, 445 F.2d 54, 66 (7th Cir. 1971).

### § 1705. Best Evidence Rule.

Where the contents of a writing are in issue, secondary evidence of the contents is inadmissible under the "best evidence rule" which requires production of the original document in the absence of a satisfactory explanation for nonproduction. The rule seeks to protect against the inherent risk of inaccurate proof of a writing's contents through erroneous reproduction of the original or erroneous testimony of a witness who purports to recollect its contents. The "best evidence rule" is now codified in Rule 1002 which provides: "To prove the content of a writing, recording, or photograph, the original writing, recording, or photograph is required, except as otherwise provided in these rules or by Act of Congress." *See U.S. v. Rose*, 590 F.2d 232 (7th Cir. 1978), *cert. denied*, 442 U.S. 929 (1979); *U.S. v. Winkle*, 587 F.2d 705, 712 (5th Cir.), *cert. denied*, 444 U.S. 827 (1979).

Pursuant to Rule 1003, a duplicate as defined by Rule 1001(4) is admissible to the same extent as an original unless a genuine question is raised as to the authenticity of the original or in the circumstances it would be unfair to admit the duplicate in lieu of the original. Rule 1001(3) specifies that an original includes "any counterpart intended to have the same effect by a person executing or issuing it." The Advisory Committee's Note states that a "carbon copy of a contract executed in duplicate becomes an original, as does a sales ticket carbon copy given to a customer." *See U.S. v. Morgan,* 555 F.2d 238, 243 (9th Cir. 1977) (photocopy admitted); *U.S. v. Gerhart,* 538 F.2d 807, 809 (8th Cir. 1976) (duplicate of check admitted). The note also states that what is an original for some purposes may be a duplicate for others: "Thus a bank's microfilm record of checks cleared is the original as a record. However, a print offered as a copy of a check whose contents are in controversy is a duplicate." *See U.S. v. Rangel,* 585 F.2d 344 (8th Cir. 1978); *U.S. v. Morgan,* 555 F.2d at 243. A uniform act making regularly kept photographic copies of business and public records admissible without accounting for the original records has been incorporated as an amendment to the Federal Business Records Act, 28 U.S.C. § 1732. Section 1732 provides for the admission of copies made in the ordinary course of business. *See U.S. v. Parker,* 491 F.2d 517 (8th Cir. 1973), *cert. denied,* 416 U.S. 989 (1974); *U.S. v. Jones,* 392 F.2d 567 (4th Cir.), *cert. denied,* 393 U.S. 882 (1968).

## § 1706. — Exceptions.

The best evidence rule, as applied generally in federal courts, is limited to cases where the contents of a writing are to be proved. The rule is not applicable in those cases where the recorded transaction is not regarded by the law as essentially a written transaction. *U.S. v. Gonzales-Benitez,* 537 F.2d 1051 (9th Cir. 1976), *cert. denied,* 429 U.S. 923 (1976) (content of tape recordings was not a factual issue and recordings should have been introduced); *U.S. v. Duffy,* 454 F.2d 809, 811-12 (5th Cir. 1972) (testimony that a shirt bore a certain laundry mark was admissible without producing the shirt); *Rice v. U.S.,* 411 F.2d 485, 486-87 (8th Cir. 1969); *Burney v. U.S.,* 339 F.2d 91, 94 (5th Cir. 1964); *Meyers v. U.S.,* 171 F.2d 800, 812-13 (D.C. Cir. 1948), *cert. denied,* 336 U.S. 912 (1949) (oral evidence of former testimony before a congressional committee was received, even though it had been taken down and embodied in a formal transcript); *Herzig v. Swift & Co.,* 146 F.2d 444, 445-46 (2d Cir. 1945), *cert. denied,* 328 U.S. 849 (1946) (amount of earnings was provable without producing books of account); *U.S. v. Kushner,* 135 F.2d 668, 674 (2d Cir.), *cert. denied,* 320 U.S. 212 (1943) (not necessary to show written bank record of withdrawal to prove that witness withdrew money from bank).

Also, it is possible, without producing the books or records, to introduce testimonial evidence that the books or records do not contain any entry of a particular character. Such negative evidence is ordinarily deemed not to be testifying to the contents of the records and not to require their production. *U.S. v. Scales,* 594 F.2d 558 (6th Cir.), *cert. denied,* 441 U.S. 946 (1979); *U.S. v. Prevatt,* 526 F.2d 400 (5th Cir.

1976); *U.S. v. Allen,* 522 F.2d 1229 (6th Cir. 1975), *cert. denied,* 423 U.S. 1072 (1976); *Christoffel v. U.S.,* 200 F.2d 734, 740-41 (D.C. Cir. 1952), *vacated on other grounds,* 345 U.S. 947 (1953) (written statement by custodian of public records, that search of his office disclosed no particular entry in the record books, was admitted as evidence that no such record was ever made); *Darby v. U.S.,* 132 F.2d 928, 929 (5th Cir. 1943) (summary of records permitted even though records were required to be kept by the Fair Labor Standards Act, where originals were inaccessible under fourth amendment); *Paschen v. U.S.,* 70 F.2d 491, 501 (7th Cir. 1934).

### § 1707. — Admission of Secondary Evidence.

Apart from Rule 1003, concerning the admissibility of duplicates, the rule governing admissibility of secondary evidence concerning content of a writing, recording, or photograph is Rule 1004, which allows admissions where the original is not available for any of several reasons or where only collateral matters are involved. Even though the fact of loss or destruction may excuse production of the original, however, authentication is still required under Rules 901 and 902. *U.S. v. Gerhart,* 538 F.2d 807 (8th Cir. 1976); *U.S. v. Savage,* 482 F.2d 1371 (9th Cir.), *cert. denied,* 415 U.S. 932 (1973); *Hass v. U.S.,* 93 F.2d 427, 437 (8th Cir. 1937); *Carey v. Williams,* 79 F. 906 (2d Cir. 1897). Moreover, when "other evidence" is proferred, its competency must be considered in light of the requirements contained in Rules 1003 and 1004. *Klein v. Frank,* 534 F.2d 1104 (5th Cir. 1976) (testimony concerning the contents of a lost letter was insufficient to authenticate the letter).

Under Rule 1008, preliminary questions related to the admissibility of "other evidence" about the contents of a writing, such as those presented by Rule 1004, are for the court, except where those fact questions are not merely preliminary but are themselves in issue, in which case the question or questions are for the jury, subject to general control by the court.

Loss or destruction may sometimes be provable by direct evidence. More often, however, the only available method is circumstantial, usually by proof of search for the document and inability to locate it, the only requirement being that all reasonable avenues of search should be explored to the extent that reasonable diligence under the circumstances would dictate. *U.S. v. Standing Soldier,* 538 F.2d 196 (8th Cir.), *cert. denied,* 429 U.S. 1025 (1976); *U.S. v. Covello,* 410 F.2d 536 (2d Cir.), *cert. denied,* 396 U.S. 879 (1969); *Robertson v. M/S Sanyo Maru,* 374 F.2d 463 (5th Cir. 1967) (secondary evidence was inadmissible without showing why the original was not introduced). *See also U.S. v.*

*Winkle,* 587 F.2d 705, 712 (5th Cir.), *cert. denied,* 444 U.S. 827 (1979); *Merrill v. U.S.,* 365 F.2d 281 (5th Cir. 1966), *cert. denied,* 386 U.S. 994 (1967) (in Dyer Act prosecution, testimony of witness that defendant's written contract for rental of automobile had been lost was insufficient proof to permit introduction of parole evidence on terms of contract); *Simpson v. U.S.,* 195 F.2d 721 (9th Cir. 1952).

If the original document has been destroyed by the person who offers evidence of its contents, the evidence is not admissible unless such person, by showing that such destruction was accidental or was done in good faith without intention to prevent its use as evidence, rebuts to the satisfaction of the trial judge any inference of fraud. *Reynolds v. Denver & Rio Grande Western R. Co.,* 174 F.2d 673 (10th Cir. 1949); *McDonald v. U.S.,* 89 F.2d 128 (8th Cir.), *cert. denied,* 301 U.S. 697 (1937) (in kidnapping prosecution, government not precluded from giving evidence of the serial numbers on bills after improvidently having them destroyed). *See U.S. v. Patterson,* 446 F.2d 1358 (5th Cir. 1971) (testimony concerning existence of letter was inadmissible where proponent-defendant had not attempted to locate custodian of letter); *U.S. v. Knohl,* 379 F.2d 427 (2d Cir.), *cert. denied,* 389 U.S. 973 (1967) (where witness recorded conversation with defendant and allowed government to make dubbed copy of the tape but retained and ultimately lost the original, government was not at fault and copy was admissible).

Where the originals are unobtainable because they are beyond the jurisdiction of the court, secondary evidence of the nature of their contents is admissible without more. *Burton v. Driggs,* 87 U.S. 125 (1873). *See U.S. v. Marcantoni,* 590 F.2d 1324 (5th Cir.), *cert. denied,* 441 U.S. 937 (1979); *U.S. v. Kaibney,* 155 F.2d 795 (2d Cir. 1946). However, where specific books and records are required by statute for the purpose of proving the matter in issue, testimony thereon in lieu of records themselves is inadmissible. *Bergdoll v. Pollock,* 95 U.S. 337 (1877); *Allen v. W.H.O. Alfalfa Milling Co.,* 272 F.2d 98 (10th Cir. 1959).

There are no clearly defined rules on the types of secondary evidence that may be offered. Copies of the original are better evidence than the recollection of witnesses, but when there are no copies, the recollection of witnesses may be the best secondary evidence. *U.S. v. Marcantoni,* 590 F.2d at 1329 (testimony of police officer concerning serial numbers on money was admissible when bills could not be found); *Kenner v. Commissioner,* 445 F.2d 19 (7th Cir. 1971); *U.S. v. Ross,* 321 F.2d 61 (2d Cir.), *cert. denied,* 375 U.S. 894 (1963) (testimony of contents of written list admitted without proof of search where list was of little significance and could reasonably have been supposed lost); *U.S. v.*

*Bernard*, 287 F.2d 715 (7th Cir.), *cert. denied*, 366 U.S. 961 (1961); *Wiley v. U.S.*, 257 F.2d 900 (8th Cir. 1958); *Corbett v. U.S.*, 238 F.2d 557 (9th Cir. 1956), *cert. denied*, 352 U.S. 990 (1957) (oral testimony of expert accountants permitted on contents of bank records which had been destroyed in the ordinary course of the bank's business); *Darby v. U.S.*, 132 F.2d 928 (5th Cir. 1943).

### § 1708. Use of Entire Writing or Recorded Statement.

Under Rule 106, Federal Rules of Evidence, "When a writing or recorded statement or part thereof is introduced by a party, an adverse party may require the introduction at that time of any other part or any other writing or recorded statement which ought in fairness to be considered contemporaneously with it."

The "rule of completeness" underlies this rule, and when one party has made use of a portion of a document, and the presentation of another portion is required for completeness, the other portion is *ipso facto* relevant and, therefore, admissible. *Beech Aircraft Corp. v. Rainey*, 488 U.S. 153 (1988) .

# CHAPTER 18

# EXAMINATION OF A WITNESS

§ 1801. Leading Questions.
§ 1802. Refreshing Recollection.
§ 1803. — Inspection of an Exhibit.
§ 1804. — Use on Cross-Examination.
§ 1805. Cross-Examination.
§ 1806. Impeachment and Support.
§ 1807. — Impeaching Own Witness.
§ 1808. — Character Evidence.
§ 1809. — Prior Misconduct and Other Crimes.
§ 1810. — — Probative Value Versus Prejudicial Effect.
§ 1811. — — Evidence Showing Witness Bias.
§ 1812. — Prior Inconsistent Statements.
§ 1813. — — For Impeachment.
§ 1814. — — Affirmative Evidence.
§ 1815. — Insanity and Narcotics Addiction.
§ 1816. Rebuttal.
§ 1817. — Permissible Scope.
§ 1818. — Evidence Inadmissible Under an Exclusionary Rule.
§ 1819. Exclusion or Separation of Witnesses.
§ 1820. Use of Interpreters.

## § 1801. Leading Questions.

The test of a leading question is whether it so suggests or indicates the particular answer desired "that such a reply is likely to be given irrespective of an actual memory." *U.S. v. McGovern,* 499 F.2d 1140, 1142 (1st Cir. 1974); *U.S. v. Johnson,* 495 F.2d 1097, 1101 (5th Cir. 1974); *U.S. v. Durham,* 319 F.2d 590, 592 (4th Cir. 1963).

Rule 611(c) of the Federal Rules of Evidence provides that leading questions should not be used on the direct examination of a witness except as may be necessary to develop his testimony, but should be permitted on cross-examination, or with a hostile witness, an adverse party, or a witness identified with an adverse party.

Whether a question is leading depends on the circumstances under which the examination of the witness has been conducted, and the fact that it is a leading question does not necessarily make it objectionable. *See U.S. v. Durham,* 319 F.2d 590 (4th Cir. 1963). Under no circumstances, however, may a material fact in issue properly be assumed in a question asked. But, the mere fact that a question can be answered "yes" or "no" does not necessarily make it leading. *DeWitt v. Skinner,* 232 F. 443 (9th Cir. 1916).

Rule 611(c) states that, ordinarily, leading questions should be permitted on cross-examination. The purpose for which the testimony is offered may also determine the propriety of leading questions. In *U.S. v. Montgomery,* 126 F.2d 151, 153 (3d Cir.), *cert. denied,* 316 U.S. 681 (1942), a rebuttal witness was properly permitted to answer leading questions on direct examination for the purpose of proving a prior contradictory statement of a previous witness. Where new matter has been introduced on cross-examination, there is authority that the witness may be led on redirect with respect to that new matter. In *U.S. v. Stirone,* 168 F. Supp. 490, 500 (W.D. Pa. 1957), *aff'd,* 262 F.2d 571 (3d Cir. 1958), *rev'd on other grounds,* 361 U.S. 212 (1960), the court permitted leading questions where cross-examination had elicited new matter in the form of evidence of the defendant's character. *See also* Rule 404(a)(1), Fed. R. Evid. However, if the witness undergoing cross-examination proves to be biased in favor of the cross-examiner, the court may again limit the leading questions put to the witness. *Mitchell v. U.S.,* 213 F.2d 951, 956 (9th Cir. 1954), *cert. denied,* 348 U.S. 912 (1955).

There are four exceptions to the general proposition that leading questions are undesirable on direct examination: (1) the witness is hostile, unwilling, or biased; (2) the witness is a child or an adult with communication problems; (3) the witness' recollection is exhausted; (4) or the questions relate to undisputed preliminary matters. *See* Advisory Committee's Note. And, Rule 611(c) includes a specific provision authorizing leading questions when a party calls a "hostile witness, an adverse party, or a witness identified with an adverse party."

Whether leading questions will be permitted is generally within the trial court's discretion. *See, e.g., U.S. v. Brown,* 603 F.2d 1022, 1026 (1st Cir. 1979). However, persistence by the prosecutor in asking impermissible, leading questions may be held to be reversible error, and perhaps contempt, *see Locken v. U.S.,* 383 F.2d 340, 341 (9th Cir. 1967), and, excessive use of leading questions to recite to a recalcitrant witness his unsworn oral statements was held to be reversible error in *U.S. v. Shoupe,* 548 F.2d 636 (6th Cir. 1977).

As to children and adults with communication problems, *see Rotolo v. U.S.,* 404 F.2d 316, 317 (5th Cir. 1968) (leading questions were permitted to be asked of a 15-year-old witness who was also nervous and upset), and *U.S. v. Littlewind,* 551 F.2d 244, 245 (8th Cir. 1977).

Where the witness' recollection is exhausted by non-leading questions and he has further information, leading questions may be permitted. *See Thomas v. U.S.,* 227 F.2d 667, 671 (9th Cir.), *cert. denied,* 350 U.S. 911 (1955). *See also* the discussion in *U.S. v. Braunstein,* 474 F. Supp. 1 (D.N.J. 1979). (For other techniques to overcome the problem of the witness with faulty memory, *see* Refreshing Recollection, Rule

612; Recorded Recollection, Rule 803(5); and Impeachment, Rule 607, *infra.*)

There is no requirement that the direct examiner of a witness actually be surprised by the witness' recalcitrance or lack of memory before the use of leading questions may be permitted. *See U.S. v. Long Soldier,* 562 F.2d 601 (9th Cir. 1977).

Finally, where an attorney may lead the witness on preliminary, undisputed matters, he must discontinue such leading when approaching the crucial issues in the case. *U.S. v. Bryant,* 461 F.2d 912, 918 (6th Cir. 1972); *U.S. v. Lewis,* 406 F.2d 486, 493 (7th Cir.), *cert. denied,* 394 U.S. 1013 (1969).

## § 1802. Refreshing Recollection.

Rule 612 of the Federal Rules of Evidence provides that a witness may use a writing, either while testifying or before testifying, to refresh his memory. If used while testifying or, at the court's discretion, before testifying, the adverse party may have the writing produced, inspected, and may cross-examine from it, and introduce into evidence portions which relate to the witness' testimony. The rule also provides for *in camera* inspection and excision of unrelated portions, as well as sanctions for failure to comply with the rule. The Jencks Act, 18 U.S.C. § 3500, may supersede certain applications of Rule 612.

If a witness states in response to a question that he is unable to recall the information requested, he may use any writing or other object, to refresh his memory while testifying on the stand, even if the document or object itself would be inadmissible. *U.S. v. Schwartzbaum,* 527 F.2d 249, 253 (2d Cir. 1975), *cert. denied,* 424 U.S. 942 (1976) (summary of a previous interview used to refresh a witness' recollection on redirect after he had retreated on cross from his direct testimony); *U.S. v. Smith,* 521 F.2d 957, 968 (D.C. Cir. 1975); *U.S. v. Rappy,* 157 F.2d 964, 967 (2d Cir. 1946), *cert. denied,* 329 U.S. 806 (1947). *But see NLRB v. Federal Dairy Co.,* 297 F.2d 487, 489 (1st Cir. 1962) (witness was not permitted to use specially prepared testimonial notes to refresh his memory). The forgetful witness may examine the writing and then, if he says that his recollection is thereby refreshed, testify on the basis of refreshed recollection. *Id.* at 488. But, before the witness may testify, it must be apparent that his memory actually is refreshed by the writing shown to him. *U.S. v. Cheyenne,* 558 F.2d 902 (8th Cir.), *cert. denied,* 434 U.S. 957 (1977); *U.S. v. Riccardi,* 174 F.2d 883, 889 (3d Cir.), *cert. denied,* 337 U.S. 941 (1949).

The initial determination that a witness' need for refreshing material justifies its use and the determination that a witness' recollection actually has been refreshed by the document, are within the discretion of the trial judge. *U.S. v. Conley,* 503 F.2d 520 (8th Cir. 1974). However, the document may not be used to put words into the mouth of the witness. *U.S. v. Faulkner,* 538 F.2d 724, 727 (6th Cir.), *cert. denied,* 429 U.S. 1023 (1976). The witness' recollection must be in need of refreshing, else the use of the prior statement may be considered a pretext for the improper use of inadmissible evidence and constitute reversible error. *U.S. v. Jimenez,* 613 F.2d 1373, 1378 (5th Cir. 1980); *U.S. v. Morlang,* 531 F.2d 183, 191 (4th Cir. 1975).

In the following cases documents were successfully used to refresh the recollection of witnesses: *U.S. v. Socony Vacum Oil Co.,* 310 U.S. 150, 233 (1940) (grand jury minutes properly used to refresh the recollection of a recalcitrant witness); *U.S. v. Landof,* 591 F.2d 36, 39 (9th Cir. 1978); *U.S. v. Cheyenne,* 558 F.2d 902, 904 (8th Cir. 1977), *cert. denied,* 434 U.S. 957 (1977) (FBI agent permitted to testify at trial after previously refreshing his recollection at suppression hearing with memorandum transcribed from notes, where notes had been destroyed pursuant to standard FBI procedure); *U.S. v. Godwin,* 522 F.2d 1135, 1136 (4th Cir. 1975) (FBI agent permitted to refresh his recollection of a stolen vehicle's serial number from an NCIC report); *O'Quinn v. U.S.,* 411 F.2d 78, 79 (10th Cir. 1969) (summaries prepared by government investigators were proper aids to refresh their recollection); *U.S. v. Harris,* 409 F.2d 77, 82 (4th Cir.), *cert. denied,* 396 U.S. 965 (1969) (government witnesses in conspiracy case properly permitted to refer to statements previously given to government and to notes made from witnesses' own records).

A tape recording of telephone conversations, instead of a transcript, has been allowed to refresh a witness' recollection where it was not played within the hearing of the jury, but only listened to by the witness on earphones. *U.S. v. American Radiator & Standard Sanitary Corp.,* 433 F.2d 174, 191 (3d Cir. 1970), *cert. denied,* 401 U.S. 948 (1971); *U.S. v. McKeever,* 271 F.2d 669 (2d Cir. 1959). *See also U.S. v. Faulkner,* 538 F.2d 724, 727 (6th Cir.), *cert. denied,* 429 U.S. 1023 (1976). Hypnotically refreshed recollections may also be used in an appropriate case, *U.S. v. Awkard,* 597 F.2d 667 (9th Cir.), *cert. denied,* 444 U.S. 885 (1979). *Contra Greenfield v. Robinson,* 413 F. Supp. 1113, 1120-21 (W.D. Va. 1976), and a *per se* rule excluding all hypnotically refreshed testimony infringes impermissibly on a criminal defendant's right to testify on his or her own behalf. *Rock v. Arkansas,* 483 U.S. 44 (1987).

The reliability of the memorandum used to refresh recollection need not be established before the witness is permitted to say whether his recollection is refreshed. *U.S. v. Riccardi,* 174 F.2d 883 (3d Cir.), *cert. denied,* 337 U.S. 941 (1949). The reliability or truthfulness of the memorandum is relevant only to a determination of the weight and credibility to be accorded the witness' testimony. *U.S. v. Jackson,* 451 F.2d 259, 261 (5th Cir. 1971). The memorandum used need not be a contemporaneous account of the events it describes, *U.S. v. Horton,* 526 F.2d 884, 888 (5th Cir.), *cert. denied,* 429 U.S. 820 (1976); *Fanelli v. U.S. Gypsum Co.,* 141 F.2d 216 (2d Cir. 1944); and for the purpose of refreshing the witness' recollection, the document itself need not be admitted or even admissible as evidence, *U.S. v. Faulkner, supra.*

It has been held reversible error, however to read aloud in its entirety the prior disavowed, unsworn statement of a witness in order to refresh his recollection. *U.S. v. Shoupe,* 548 F.2d 636, 643 (6th Cir. 1977). *See U.S. v. Davis,* 551 F.2d 233, 235 (8th Cir.), *cert. denied,* 431 U.S. 923 (1977); *U.S. v. Morlang,* 531 F.2d 183, 190 (4th Cir. 1975); *Goings v. U.S.,* 377 F.2d 753, 759-60 (8th Cir. 1967).

The concept of refreshing a witness' recollection should not be confused with that of "past recollection recorded."

### § 1803. — Inspection of an Exhibit.

When exhibits are used at trial to refresh present recollection of past events, the only evidence is the recollection of the witness; but the exhibit which the witness uses to refresh his recollection at the time of testifying may be seen by opposing counsel and shown to the jury so that they may determine what weight is to be given the testimony of the witness whose memory has been thereby refreshed. *See U.S. v. Smith,* 521 F.2d 957, 968 (D.C. Cir. 1975); *U.S. v. Caserta,* 199 F.2d 905, 909 (3d Cir. 1952); *U.S. v. Rappy,* 157 F.2d 964 (2d Cir. 1946), *cert. denied,* 329 U.S. 806 (1947). Material used to refresh a witness' recollection is not admissible by the questioner, but only by the adverse party. Rule 612, Fed. R. Evid.; *U.S. v. Davis,* 551 F.2d 233, 235 (8th Cir.), *cert. denied,* 431 U.S. 923 (1977).

Rule 612 permits the trial judge to order disclosure of documents used by a witness to refresh his recollection either during or prior to taking the stand. This is a significant departure from the preexisting case law, which held that opposing counsel had no right of access to documents consulted by a witness prior to his taking the witness stand. *See Goldman v. U.S.,* 316 U.S. 129, 132 (1942). The rule states, however, that such writings must have been consulted "for the purpose of testifying," if they are to be subject to inspection by opposing counsel. The party seeking the disclosure under Rule 612(2) must, therefore, make some showing that inspection of the writings is "necessary in the interests of justice." *See U.S. v. Nobles,* 422 U.S. 225, 230 (1975), *rev'g U.S. v. Brown,* 501 F.2d 146, 155 (9th Cir. 1974). A court may "enforce a preclusion sanction against a defendant who insists on offering testimony of a witness while resisting disclosure of his prior (and possibly inconsistent) statements and reports." *U.S. v. Smith,* 524 F.2d 1288, 1290 (D.C. Cir. 1975) (citing *Nobles, supra*).

This rule is also explicitly made subject to the provisions of 18 U.S.C. § 3500. To the extent that any such writings used to refresh recollection are discoverable pursuant to § 3500, therefore, they need not be turned over to the defense until the conclusion of the witness' direct examination. However, the Advisory Committee's Note makes clear that Rule 612, unlike § 3500, applies both to writings used by prosecution and defense witnesses.

### § 1804. — Use on Cross-Examination.

Once a witness has had his recollection refreshed, opposing counsel may impeach his recollection on cross-examination. A witness may be confronted with a document and asked whether such document refreshes his recollection. *U.S. v. Baratta,* 397 F.2d 215, 221-22 (2d Cir.), *cert. denied,* 393 U.S. 939 (1968). The document, however, may not be referred to or displayed to the jury or to the witness in the presence of the jury under the guise of refreshing his recollection when in fact it is being used for purposes of impeachment or as substantive evidence. *Eisenberg v. U.S.,* 273 F.2d 127, 131 (5th Cir. 1959).

### § 1805. Cross-Examination.

The purpose of cross-examination is to test the witness' propensity to perceive, remember, and communicate the substance of his direct testimony truthfully. To this end, cross-examination may be used to break down the testimony of the direct examination, to affect the credibility of the witness, or to show bias or motive to lie. *See Olden v. Kentucky,* 488 U.S. 227 (1988); *Davis v. Alaska,* 415 U.S. 308 (1974); *Alford v. U.S.,* 282 U.S. 687 (1931); *U.S. v. Bleckner,* 601 F.2d 382, 385 (9th Cir. 1979); *U.S. v. Vasilios,* 598 F.2d 387, 389 (5th Cir.), *cert. denied,* 444 U.S. 967 (1979); *U.S. v. Palmer,* 536 F.2d 1278, 1282 (9th Cir. 1976). If the court calls a witness, the witness is subject to impeachment upon cross-examination by either party. *U.S. v. Browne,* 313 F.2d 197, 199 (2d Cir.), *cert. denied,* 374 U.S. 814 (1963).

Rule 611(b) of the Federal Rules of Evidence provides that cross-examination should be limited to the subject matter of the direct examination, matters affecting the credibility of the witness, and, in the discretion of the court, additional matters as if on direct examination. As the rule indicates, in federal courts it is within the trial judge's discretion to confine the scope of cross-examination to the subject matter of the direct examination. *U.S. v. Jackson,* 576 F.2d 46, 48 (5th Cir. 1978); *U.S. v. Ellison,* 557 F.2d 128, 135 (7th Cir.), *cert. denied,* 434 U.S. 965 (1977); *U.S. v. Ong,* 541 F.2d 331, 341 (2d Cir. 1976), *cert. denied,* 429 U.S. 1075 (1977). And matters affecting the credibility of witnesses may also be limited by the trial court. *U.S. v. Franklin,* 598 F.2d 954, 958 (5th Cir.), *cert. denied,* 444 U.S. 870 (1979); *Skinner v. Cardwell,* 564 F.2d 1381, 1388 (9th Cir. 1977), *cert. denied,* 435 U.S. 1009 (1978); *U.S. v. Turcotte,* 515 F.2d 145, 151 (2d Cir.), *cert. denied,* 423 U.S. 1032 (1975).

However, the government is not limited on cross-examination of the defendant to those portions of an event which are favorable to a defendant. If the defendant takes the stand the scope of his cross-examination is very broad. *U.S. v. Roper,* 676 F.2d 841, 846-47 (D.C. Cir. 1982).

The scope of cross-examination may also be affected by the witness' assertion of a fifth amendment privilege against self-incrimination. *U.S. v. LaRiche,* 549 F.2d 1088, 1096 (6th Cir.), *cert. denied,* 430 U.S. 987 (1977). It is improper to call a witness simply for the purpose of having him invoke the privilege. *U.S. v. Beechum,* 582 F.2d 898, 908 (5th Cir.), *cert. denied,* 440 U.S. 920 (1978); *Skinner v. Cardwell,* 564 F.2d at 1389. Assertion of the privilege may require that the direct testimony be stricken or a curative charge be given to the jury, *U.S. v. Stephens,* 492 F.2d 1367, 1374-75 (6th Cir.), *cert. denied,* 419 U.S. 852 (1974), or, in some circumstances, the declaration of a mistrial, *U.S. v. Demchak,* 545 F.2d 1029, 1031-32 (5th Cir. 1977).

The court has broad discretion in limiting the scope of cross-examination. *U.S. v. Lavallie,* 666 F.2d 1217, 1220 (8th Cir. 1981), and the court's exercise of discretion will not be readily set aside, *U.S. v. Pacelli,* 521 F.2d 135 (2d Cir.), *cert. denied,* 424 U.S. 911 (1975); *U.S. v. Jenkins,* 510 F.2d 495, 500 (2d Cir. 1975). However, restrictions on a defendant's right of cross-examination may, in certain instances, be deemed violative of his sixth amendment right to confront the witnesses against him. *Delaware v. Van Arsdall,* 475 U.S. 673 (1986); *Davis v. Alaska,* 415 U.S. 308 (1974); *Pointer v. Texas,* 380 U.S. 400 (1965); *U.S. v. Wolfson,* 573 F.2d 216, 223 (5th Cir. 1978); *U.S. v. Callahan,* 551 F.2d 733, 737 (6th Cir. 1977); *U.S. v. Miranda,* 510 F.2d 385, 387 (9th Cir. 1975). Undue restriction of cross-examination, even on matters affecting the witness' credibility, has been deemed violative of the sixth amendment in some cases. *Olden v. Kentucky, supra; U.S. v. Croucher,* 532 F.2d 1042, 1044-45 (5th Cir. 1976); *Snyder v. Coiner,* 510 F.2d 224, 225 (4th Cir. 1975).

The rule must not be so strictly applied as to deprive a defendant of the opportunity to present to the jury a vital element of his defense. *U.S. v. Callahan,* 551 F.2d at 737; *U.S. v. Lewis,* 447 F.2d 134, 139 (2d Cir. 1971); *U.S. v. Fitzpatrick,* 437 F.2d 19, 23 (2d Cir. 1970) (necessity for full cross-examination held particularly acute when its purpose is to demonstrate lack of credibility of an identification by attempting to determine whether the witness had a recollection of specific characteristics of the defendant).

It has been held reversible error to deny wide latitude in cross-examination when the testimony of an accomplice is involved. *U.S. v. Wolfson,* 437 F.2d 862, 874 (2d Cir. 1970). *But see U.S. v. Bagsby,* 489 F.2d 725, 727 (9th Cir. 1973); *U.S. v. Cole,* 449 F.2d 194, 199 (8th Cir. 1971), *cert. denied,* 405 U.S. 931 (1972) (exercise of discretion in limiting cross-examination will not be reversed unless there has been a clear abuse and a showing of prejudice to the defendant). In *U.S. v. Demchak,* 545 F.2d at 1031, a new trial was granted where it became necessary for the trial court to limit cross-examination for fifth amendment reasons and the trial court attempted to remedy the damage by striking the direct testimony.

In *U.S. v. Rudolph,* 403 F.2d 805, 806 (6th Cir. 1968), the court held that a defendant may not be cross-examined about whether he participated in unrelated specific acts of criminal conduct not resulting in a conviction, as there is "no relevancy to the issue of defendant's guilt or innocence of the crime charged, and such evidence is likely to be extremely prejudicial."

Where a witness testifies about a matter on direct, he may "open the door" to cross-examination on a topic not otherwise subject to cross-examination. *See U.S. v. Turquitt,* 557 F.2d 464, 468 (5th Cir. 1977), where the admission into evidence of an unrelated phony lease prejudiced a defendant on trial for possession of stolen mail. In *U.S. v. Parr-Pla,* 549 F.2d 660, 663 (9th Cir.), *cert. denied,* 431 U.S. 972 (1977), after defendant's girlfriend testified as to his probationary status, the government was permitted to disclose the defendant's murder conviction.

In *U.S. v. Fowler,* 465 F.2d 664 (D.C. Cir. 1972), the court held that for impeachment purposes defense counsel had a right to cross-examine the principal government witness, a former narcotics agent, as to the reasons for his dismissal and whether he was using narcotics at the time he observed defendant committing the alleged offense, when counsel had a reasonable basis, however slight, for pursuing the inquiry. Such questions should be non-accusatory or should be asked outside the presence of the jury. *U.S. v. Knight,* 509 F.2d 354, 357 (D.C. Cir. 1974). *See U.S. v. Finkelstein,* 526 F.2d 517, 527, 529 (2d Cir.

1975), *cert. denied,* 425 U.S. 960 (1976); *U.S. v. Harvey,* 526 F.2d 529, 536 (2d Cir. 1975), *cert. denied,* 424 U.S. 956 (1976).

Where there are multiple defendants, what is probative as to one may be prejudicial to another. *U.S. v. Dansker,* 537 F.2d 40, 59-60 (3d Cir. 1976), *cert. denied,* 429 U.S. 1038 (1977).

## § 1806. Impeachment and Support.

## § 1807. — Impeaching Own Witness.

Rule 607 of the Federal Rules of Evidence provides that "[t]he credibility of a witness may be attacked by any party, including the party calling him." The rule thereby removes the previous requirement that a party be "surprised" by the testimony of his own witness before impeachment was permitted. *See U.S. v. Benedetto,* 571 F.2d 1246, 1250 (2d Cir. 1978); *U.S. v. Long Soldier,* 562 F.2d 601, 605 (8th Cir. 1977); *U.S. v. Dixon,* 547 F.2d 1079, 1081-82 (9th Cir. 1976). *But see U.S. v. Shoupe,* 548 F.2d 636 (6th Cir. 1977). However, a party may not impeach its own witness for the primary purpose of placing before the jury evidence which is otherwise inadmissible. *U.S. v. Miller,* 664 F.2d 94, 97 (5th Cir. 1981).

## § 1808. — Character Evidence.

Rule 608(a) of the Federal Rules of Evidence is the general provision governing opinion and reputation evidence of the character of a witness. It provides that the credibility of a witness may be attacked by reputation or opinion evidence as to the witness' character for truthfulness, provided that evidence of truthfulness, used to support the witness' credibility, is only admissible after his credibility has been attacked. *See U.S. v. Benedetto,* 571 F.2d 1246, 1250 (2d Cir. 1978); *U.S. v. Petsas,* 592 F.2d 525, 527-28 (9th Cir.), *cert. denied,* 442 U.S. 910 (1979). The community in which the witness has established a reputation need not be the community in which he lives; it may be the community in which he works, etc. *U.S. v. Mandel,* 591 F.2d 1347, 1370 (4th Cir. 1979), *cert. denied,* 445 U.S. 961 (1980).

Subjecting the witness' credibility to impeachment by opinion or reputation evidence about his truthfulness or untruthfulness is to be distinguished from character evidence under Rule 404(a) of the Federal Rules of Evidence which relates to the witness' reputation for integrity, peacefulness, and for being a law-abiding citizen. *U.S. v. Thomas,* 676 F.2d 531, 536 (11th Cir. 1982); *U.S. v. Walker,* 313 F.2d 236 (6th Cir.), *cert. denied,* 374 U.S. 807 (1963). Reputation evidence requires a foundation that the witness is familiar with the person and his community to insure that his testimony reflects the community sentiment. This foundation is not required for opinion testimony which is the witness' personal impression of the individual's character for truthfulness. *U.S. v. Watson,* 669 F.2d 1374, 1382 (11th Cir. 1982).

## § 1809. — Prior Misconduct and Other Crimes.

Rule 608(b) prohibits the use of extrinsic evidence of misconduct, except Rule 609 convictions, for the purpose of attacking the credibility of the witness, and it permits only cross-examination as to specific instances of conduct concerning the truthfulness or untruthfulness of the witness, subject to the discretion of the court. Rule 609 of the Federal Rules of Evidence establishes ground rules for the introduction of evidence of prior convictions and misconduct. It must be read with Rule 608(b), which provides in general that a witness' credibility may be the subject of cross-examination, but may not be attacked through the introduction of extrinsic evidence. Specific instances of conduct are not generally admissible, except as to prior convictions of a felony or a lesser crime involving dishonesty or false statements, or in the discretion of the court, specific acts of misconduct which did not result in such a conviction if probative of truthfulness or untruthfulness. *U.S. v. Werbrouck,* 589 F.2d 273, 277 (7th Cir. 1978), *cert. denied,* 440 U.S. 962 (1979); *U.S. v. Cluck,* 544 F.2d 195 (5th Cir. 1976); *U.S. v. Kahn,* 472 F.2d 272, 279-80 (2d Cir.), *cert. denied,* 411 U.S. 982 (1973); *U.S. v. Provoo,* 215 F.2d 531, 536 (2d Cir. 1954), *aff'd,* 350 U.S. 857 (1955).

Rule 609(a) strikes a balance between the traditional view that any prior felony conviction could be used to impeach and the more recent view that only convictions for crimes involving dishonesty or false statements could be so used. *U.S. v. Fearwell,* 595 F.2d 771, 777 (D.C. Cir. 1978); *U.S. v. Vannelli,* 595 F.2d 402, 407 (8th Cir. 1979); *U.S. v. Cavender,* 578 F.2d 528, 534 (4th Cir. 1978) (dictum); *U.S. v. Ashley,* 569 F.2d 975, 978 (5th Cir.), *cert. denied,* 439 U.S. 853 (1978); *U.S. v. Seamster,* 568 F.2d 188, 190 (10th Cir. 1978); *U.S. v. Ortega,* 561 F.2d 803, 806 (9th Cir. 1977); *U.S. v. Papia,* 560 F.2d 827, 847-48 (7th Cir. 1977); *U.S. v. Hayes,* 553 F.2d 824, 827 (2d Cir.), *cert. denied,* 434 U.S. 867 (1977); *Virgin Islands v. Toto,* 529 F.2d 278, 281 (3d Cir. 1976).

A criminal record may be elicited during direct or cross-examination, Rule 609(a), and the government may elicit the full criminal record of its own witness, including a plea of guilty to the very indictment on which the defendant is standing trial. *U.S. v. Medical Therapy Sciences, Inc.,* 583 F.2d 36, 39-40 (2d Cir. 1978), *cert. denied,* 439 U.S. 1130 (1979); *U.S. v. Rothman,* 463 F.2d 488, 490 (2d Cir.), *cert. denied,* 409 U.S. 956 (1972); *U.S. v. Panetta,* 436 F. Supp. 114, 128 (E.D. Pa.), *aff'd,* 568 F.2d 771 (3d Cir. 1977) (government witness properly permitted to testify as to unrelated crime committed by defendant to clarify the witness' role in the crime and her motive for testifying).

## § 1810. — — Probative Value Versus Prejudicial Effect.

Rule 609(a)(1) requires that evidence of a conviction of a witness other than the defendant is subject to a Rule 403 analysis, and if the witness is the defendant, is subject to the court determining that the probative value of admitting the conviction outweighs its prejudicial effect to the defendant.

Neither the rule itself nor the accompanying Advisory Committee's Note offers any guidance as to the manner in which the trial court is to weigh the probative value of a conviction against its prejudicial effect on the defendant as required by Rule 609(a)(1). (Under Rule 609(a)(2), which allows impeachment by crimes involving dishonesty or false statement, the judge has no discretion in admitting prior convictions. *U.S. v. Bay,* 748 F.2d 1344 (9th Cir. 1984); *U.S. v. Kiendra,* 663 F.2d 349, 354-55 (1st Cir. 1981).) Likewise, the judge has no discretion to weigh the prejudice to a civil defendant of prior convictions under Rule 609(a)(1). *Green v. Boch Laundry Mach. Co.,* 490 U.S. 504 (1989). A hearing on the record, as well as a specific finding by the court that the probative value outweighs the prejudicial effect to the defendant, was a recommended prerequisite to the admission of such evidence in *U.S. v. Mahone,* 537 F.2d 922 (7th Cir.), *cert. denied,* 429 U.S. 1025 (1976). Quoting *Gordon v. U.S.,* 383 F.2d 936, 940 (D.C. Cir.), *cert. denied,* 390 U.S. 1029 (1967), the *Mahone* court listed the following factors to be considered in the probative/prejudicial assessment:

(1) The impeachment value of the prior crime.
(2) The point in time of the conviction and the witness' subsequent history.
(3) The similarity between the past crime and the charged crime.
(4) The importance of the defendant's testimony.
(5) The centrality of the credibility issue.

*U.S. v. Mahone,* 537 F.2d at 929. *See also U.S. v. Sims,* 588 F.2d 1145 (6th Cir. 1978); *U.S. v. Johnson,* 588 F.2d 961, 962-63 (5th Cir.), *cert. denied,* 440 U.S. 985 (1979); *U.S. v. Mahler,* 579 F.2d 730 (2d Cir.), *cert. denied,* 439 U.S. 991 (1978); *U.S. v. Lamb,* 575 F.2d 1310, 1314-15 (10th Cir.), *cert. denied,* 439 U.S. 854 (1978). The government bears the burden of persuading the court that the probative value of the prior crimes evidence outweighs its prejudicial effect. *Virgin Islands v. Bedford,* 671 F.2d 758, 761 (3d Cir. 1982).

The conviction should not be excluded where such ruling "may allow an accused to appear as one entitled to full belief when that is not the fact." *U.S. v. Palumbo,* 401 F.2d 270, 273 (2d Cir. 1968), *cert. denied,* 394 U.S. 947 (1969); *U.S. v. Hayes,* 553 F.2d 824, 828 (2d Cir.), *cert. denied,* 434 U.S. 867 (1977). *But see U.S. v. Martinez,* 555 F.2d 1273 (5th Cir. 1977), where the use of prior convictions was deemed improper. In *U.S. v. Langston,* 576 F.2d 1138, 1139 (5th Cir. 1978), the defendant's prior conviction was used to impeach credibility in his assertion that he lacked the requisite mental state to commit bank robbery.

It is discretionary with the court whether to give an advance ruling on the admissibility of a prior conviction. *U.S. v. Key,* 717 F.2d 1206 (8th Cir. 1983); *U.S. v. Oakes,* 565 F.2d 170 (1st Cir. 1977). In some circumstances, the desirability of a pretrial ruling should be considered. *U.S. v. Apuzzo,* 555 F.2d 306, 307 (2d Cir. 1977), *cert. denied,* 435 U.S. 916 (1978); *U.S. v. Smith,* 551 F.2d 348, 356-61 (D.C. Cir. 1976). The defendant may request an advance ruling on prior convictions. *U.S. v. Cavender,* 578 F.2d 528, 530 (4th Cir. 1978). Such an advance ruling may be dependent upon the defendant stating that he will take the stand if the convictions are ruled out. *U.S. v. Halbert,* 668 F.2d 489, 494 (10th Cir.), *cert. denied,* 456 U.S. 934 (1982).

To raise and preserve for appeal a claim of improper impeachment with a prior conviction, the defendant must testify. *Luce v. U.S.,* 469 U.S. 38 (1984).

It is clear that any prior conviction involving perjury or false statement may be used to impeach. Other forms of dishonesty such as theft, *U.S. v. Yeo,* 739 F.2d 385 (8th Cir. 1984), shoplifting, *U.S. v. Dorsey,* 591 F.2d 922, 934-35 (D.C. Cir. 1979), attempted robbery, *U.S. v. Hawley,* 554 F.2d 50, 53 n.7 (2d Cir. 1977), and the sale of marijuana, *U.S. v. Williams,* 587 F.2d 1 (6th Cir. 1978), have been held inadmissible as crimes not bearing on the propensity to testify untruthfully.

Rule 609(b) provides that convictions more than 10 years old may not be used to impeach unless the court determines that their probative value "substantially" outweighs their prejudicial effect. *U.S. v. Cathey,* 591 F.2d 268, 274 (5th Cir. 1979); *U.S. v. Sims,* 588 F.2d 1145, 1150 (6th Cir. 1978); *U.S. v. Little,* 567 F.2d 346, 349-50 (8th Cir. 1977), *cert. denied,* 435 U.S. 969 (1978). The burden of demonstrating the relevance of such convictions clearly lies with the government. *U.S. v. Shapiro,* 565 F.2d 479, 480-81 (7th Cir. 1977). The government must give advance written notice of its intent to use such a conviction, and the defense must be given the opportunity to contest its use. *U.S. v. Cathey,* 591 F.2d at 274 n.9 (5th Cir. 1979); *U.S. v. Sims,* 588 F.2d at

1150. *(See* 43 A.L.R. Fed. 390 for a discussion of the time limit on admissibility under Rule 609(b).)

Under Rule 609(c) a conviction that is the subject of a pardon, annulment, or certificate of rehabilitation is not generally admissible for impeachment purposes. *U.S. v. Thorne,* 547 F.2d 56, 58-59 (8th Cir. 1976). Where the conviction is not a federal offense, the pardon, annulment, or rehabilitation provisions of the local jurisdiction are relevant as to the effect of pardon, etc., on the conviction and its admissibility. *U.S. v. Wiggins,* 566 F.2d 944, 946 (5th Cir.), *cert. denied,* 436 U.S. 950 (1978); *U.S. v. Dinapoli,* 557 F.2d 962, 965-66 (2d Cir.), *cert. denied,* 434 U.S. 858 (1977); *U.S. v. Moore,* 556 F.2d 479, 484 (10th Cir. 1977).

Rule 609(d) generally bars admission of a juvenile adjudication unless conviction for the offense would be admissible to impeach an adult and the court finds admission necessary for a fair determination of guilt or innocence. *U.S. v. Jones,* 557 F.2d 1237, 1238-39 (8th Cir. 1977); *U.S. v. Decker,* 543 F.2d 1102, 1104 (5th Cir. 1976), *cert. denied,* 431 U.S. 906 (1977); *U.S. v. Lind,* 542 F.2d 598, 599 (2d Cir. 1976), *cert. denied,* 430 U.S. 947 (1977).

Rule 609(e) codifies the preexisting majority rule that a witness may be cross-examined on prior convictions even when they are pending on appeal. *U.S. v. Soles,* 482 F.2d 105, 107-08 (2d Cir.), *cert. denied,* 414 U.S. 1027 (1973); *U.S. v. Franicevich,* 471 F.2d 427, 428-29 (5th Cir. 1973); *U.S. v. Allen,* 457 F.2d 1361, 1363 (9th Cir.), *cert. denied,* 409 U.S. 869 (1972); *U.S. v. Empire Packing Co.,* 174 F.2d 16, 20 (7th Cir.), *cert. denied,* 337 U.S. 959 (1949). A prior conviction, obtained where the defendant was not represented by counsel, however, may not be used for the purpose of proving guilt, *Burgett v. Texas,* 389 U.S. 109, 114-16 (1967), enhancing punishment, *U.S. v. Tucker,* 404 U.S. 443 (1972), escalating the degree of the crime, *Baldasar v. Illinois,* 446 U.S. 222 (1980), or impeaching credibility, *Loper v. Beto,* 405 U.S. 473 (1972); *Zilka v. Estelle,* 529 F.2d 388 (5th Cir.), *cert. denied,* 429 U.S. 981 (1976) (held to be harmless error in light of other evidence of guilt). *See also U.S. ex rel. Walker v. Follette,* 443 F.2d 167 (2d Cir. 1971), where prior uncounseled convictions were used on cross-examination to refute defendant's direct testimony that he had never been convicted of a crime.

Rule 608(b) slightly broadens the preexisting doctrine that a witness ordinarily may not be cross-examined on acts of misconduct not resulting in a felony conviction. Under the current rule, particular instances of misconduct, even though not the subject of a conviction, may be inquired into if they bear upon the truthfulness of the witness. Inquiry may be made either of the witness himself or of character witnesses called on behalf of the witness. Acts of misconduct may not, however, be proved by extrinsic evidence. *U.S. v. Werbrouck,* 589 F.2d at 277-78; *U.S. v. Ling,* 581 F.2d 1118, 1121 (4th Cir. 1978); *U.S. v. Wood,* 550 F.2d 435, 441 (9th Cir. 1976); *U.S. v. Cluck,* 544 F.2d at 196.

Under some circumstances, where the defendant has "opened the door," the prosecution may be permitted to cross-examine concerning further acts of misconduct. *U.S. v. Hykel,* 461 F.2d 721, 728-29 (3d Cir. 1972); *Carpenter v. U.S.,* 264 F.2d 565, 569 (4th Cir.), *cert. denied,* 360 U.S. 936 (1959). It is well established that questions about prior criminal activities are proper to contradict a specific false factual assertion elicited on a defendant's direct examination. *U.S. v. Opager,* 589 F.2d 799, 801-03 (5th Cir. 1979); *U.S. v. Colletti,* 245 F.2d 781, 782 (2d Cir.), *cert. denied,* 355 U.S. 874 (1957) (defendant put his good conduct in issue by testifying on direct examination that he had never been convicted of any "crime or offense"). *But see U.S. v. Forsythe,* 594 F.2d 947, 948-51 (3d Cir. 1979). Inquiries concerning a defendant's youthful offender status may be justified where he has created an erroneous impression on the uninformed jury that he is "lily-white." *U.S. v. Canniff,* 521 F.2d 565, 570 (2d Cir. 1975), *cert. denied,* 423 U.S. 1059 (1976).

If the defendant does not seek a limiting instruction as to the proper purpose of the evidence of prior misconduct, the prosecutor or the court itself should require one. *U.S. v. Diaz,* 585 F.2d 116, 118 (5th Cir. 1978). The court may also question the jurors on their ability to put the evidence to proper use. *U.S. v. Hall,* 588 F.2d 613, 615 (8th Cir. 1978).

A defendant may not be cross-examined about the convictions of relatives and associates as this is a prejudicial attempt to show "guilt by association." *U.S. v. Romo,* 669 F.2d 285, 288 (5th Cir. 1982).

### § 1811. — — Evidence Showing Witness Bias.

Evidence not normally admissible to impair the credibility of a witness may be permissible to show bias. A denial of a defendant's right to impeach a witness for bias violates the Confrontation Clause, subject to a harmless error analysis. *Olden v. Kentucky,* 109 S. Ct. 480 (1988); *Delaware v. Van Arsdall,* 475 U.S. 673 (1986). An inquiry into an arrest is permissible for the legitimate purpose of showing bias. Such inquiry is subject to limitation only where the jury already has "sufficient other information" to measure the witness' bias. *U.S. v. Hart,* 565 F.2d 360, 362 (5th Cir. 1978); *U.S. v. Baker,* 494 F.2d 1262, 1267 (6th Cir. 1974). If a government witness is the subject of a pending indictment or arrest, that fact may be established, since it constitutes the predicate of an arguable motive to please the prosecution by giving testimony favorable to the government. *U.S. v. Bonanno,* 430 F.2d 1060, 1062 (2d Cir.), *cert. denied,* 400 U.S. 964 (1970).

It is rarely proper to curtail cross-examination relating to a witness' bias or motive to testify falsely. *U.S. v. Brown,* 546 F.2d 166, 169 (5th Cir. 1977). Thus, a defendant is entitled to establish a possible predicate for bias resulting from favorable treatment given the witness by a government agency. A defense witness may be cross examined concerning his and the defendant's membership in a secret prison gang pledged to lie, cheat, steal and kill to protect each other to show the witness' bias toward defendant. *U.S. v. Abel,* 469 U.S. 45 (1984). *See U.S. v. Wolfson,* 437 F.2d 862, 871, 874 (2d Cir. 1970) (SEC gave witness a "no action" letter allowing him to sell certain stock). Where the witness is an accomplice or coconspirator who has struck a plea bargain, courts generally permit rigorous cross-examination to ascertain possible grounds for bias. *U.S. v. Brown,* 546 F.2d at 170; *Boone v. Paderick,* 541 F.2d 447, 451 (4th Cir. 1976), *cert. denied,* 430 U.S. 959 (1977) (failure to inform defense of promise of leniency made by police officer, undisclosed on cross-examination, held improper and warranted reversal); *U.S. v. Verdoon,* 528 F.2d 103, 107 (8th Cir. 1976) (unsuccessful plea negotiations are confidential and not subject to cross-examination); *U.S. v. Harris,* 462 F.2d 1033, 1035 (10th Cir. 1972). The same considerations apply when the witness is an informant, *U.S. v. Alvarez-Lopez,* 559 F.2d 1155, 1160 (9th Cir. 1977), or where immunity has been granted to the witness, *U.S. v. Scharf,* 558 F.2d 498, 501 (8th Cir. 1977); *U.S. v. Smolar,* 557 F.2d 13, 21 (1st Cir.), *cert. denied,* 434 U.S. 971 (1977).

The court is not required to permit cross-examination into all possible grounds for bias and, in its discretion, may limit such inquiry. *U.S. v. Garza,* 574 F.2d 298, 300-02 (5th Cir. 1978); *Skinner v. Cardwell,* 564 F.2d 1381, 1388 (9th Cir. 1977), *cert. denied,* 435 U.S. 1009 (1978); *U.S. v. Poulack,* 556 F.2d 83, 89 (1st Cir.), *cert. denied,* 434 U.S. 986 (1977); *U.S. v. Pfeiffer,* 539 F.2d 668, 671-72 (8th Cir. 1976); *U.S. v. Bastone,* 526 F.2d 971, 981 (7th Cir. 1975), *cert. denied,* 425 U.S. 973 (1976); *U.S. v. Padgent,* 432 F.2d 701 (2d Cir. 1970). *See also U.S. v. Campbell,* 426 F.2d 547, 549 (2d Cir. 1970) (defendant held not entitled to prove IRS made numerous beneficial decisions respecting witness' tax liability in absence of showing that witness knew he was being thus benefited); *U.S. v. DeLeon,* 498 F.2d 1327, 1332-33 (7th Cir. 1974) (court properly limited cross-examination as to prior wrongdoing about which the government had no knowledge).

The line between showing bias and improperly impeaching a witness on the basis of prior bad acts is narrow. For example, the defense in

*U.S. v. Edelman,* 414 F.2d 539, 541 (2d Cir. 1969), *cert. denied,* 396 U.S. 1053 (1970), sought to subpoena customs and postal records to show that the witness was under investigation. Defendant's theory was that since he knew about these cases, the government witness was testifying against him to silence him. The court found no abuse of discretion in the trial judge's decision to exclude this testimony since it bore only slightly on bias but would more likely constitute an improper impeachment of the witness for conduct not resulting in a conviction. *See U.S. v. Harris,* 542 F.2d 1283, 1302 (7th Cir. 1976); *Johnson v. Brewer,* 521 F.2d 556 (8th Cir. 1975).

**§ 1812. — Prior Inconsistent Statements.**

**§ 1813. — — For Impeachment.**

Rule 613 of the Federal Rules of Evidence provides that prior inconsistent statements of a witness are admissible for impeachment of the witness' credibility with respect to both material and collateral issues of fact. The statement need not be shown nor its contents disclosed to the witness at that time, but on request it must be disclosed to opposing counsel. However, a witness may be impeached by extrinsic proof of a prior inconsistent statement only on non-collateral matters, *i.e.,* those matters that are relevant to the issues in the case and could be proved independently. *U.S. v. Nace,* 561 F.2d 763, 771 (9th Cir. 1977); *U.S. v. Shoupe,* 548 F.2d 636, 642-43 (6th Cir. 1977) (discussing the problems of the merely forgetful and the hostile forgetful witness); *U.S. v. Harvey,* 547 F.2d 720, 722 (2d Cir. 1976); *U.S. v. Dinitz,* 538 F.2d 1214, 1224 (5th Cir. 1976), *cert. denied,* 429 U.S. 1104 (1977); *U.S. v. Mendell,* 538 F.2d 1238 (6th Cir. 1976).

In *U.S. v. Barash,* 365 F.2d 395 (2d Cir. 1966), *cert. denied,* 396 U.S. 832 (1969), a bribery prosecution, a government witness denied on cross-examination that he had threatened the defendant into giving him money. Defense counsel then attempted to impeach the witness by questioning him on the basis of tape recordings in which the witness had expressed such threats. The trial court's refusal to permit this examination on the ground that the tapes were not being used for impeachment was held reversible error because "[i]mpeachment was the precise enterprise in which the defense counsel had been properly engaging...." *Id.* at 401; *U.S. v. Benedetto,* 571 F.2d 1246 (2d Cir. 1978); *U.S. v. Marzano,* 537 F.2d 257, 264-69 (7th Cir. 1976), *cert. denied,* 429 U.S. 1038 (1977). *See U.S. v. Borelli,* 336 F.2d 376, 392 (2d Cir. 1964), *cert. denied,* 379 U.S. 960 (1965), where it was held that the trial court erroneously excluded an inconsistent prior written state-

412

ment of a witness that he acknowledged to have been false. The defense should not have been limited in its impeachment evidence to the fleeting oral admission of a previous lie.

The government may use prior inconsistent statements to its own advantage in cases where its witness gives unexpected testimony exculpating the accused. The witness' credibility may then be impeached by examining him with respect to prior statements inconsistent with his trial testimony. In *U.S. v. Kahaner,* 317 F.2d 459, 474 (2d Cir.), *cert. denied,* 375 U.S. 836 (1963), a government witness on cross-examination "completely exculpated" the defendant. The trial court was upheld in permitting the prosecution, on redirect, to examine the witness respecting inconsistent answers previously given before the grand jury.

A witness who has "forgotten" a prior inconsistent statement may be impeached by extrinsic evidence of his statement. Rule 613(b), Fed. R. Evid.; *U.S. v. Rogers,* 549 F.2d 490 (8th Cir. 1976), *cert. denied,* 431 U.S. 918 (1977); 40 A.L.R. Fed. 605 (provides a thorough analysis). But there are limits. *See U.S. v. Shoupe,* 548 F.2d 636, 643 (6th Cir. 1977). *See also U.S. v. Rivera,* 513 F.2d 519, 528 (2d Cir.), *cert. denied,* 423 U.S. 948 (1975). In *U.S. v. Cunningham,* 446 F.2d 194 (2d Cir.), *cert. denied,* 404 U.S. 950 (1971), the government witness testified that he had seen the defendant and the witness' brother, who was identified as a participant in the robbery, together only two or three times. The prosecutor, who was surprised by such testimony, was then allowed to ask the witness whether he had previously made statements concerning more frequent meetings and to confront him with reports of contrary statements to an agent. However, the prosecutor was criticized for overreaching in calling still another agent to testify as to unsworn inconsistent statements made to him by the now recalcitrant witness. Since the effect of the adverse answers had already been cancelled by impeachment, it was said that the testimony of the additional agent could not be offered for impeachment purposes. *See also U.S. v. Long Soldier,* 562 F.2d 601 (8th Cir. 1977); *U.S. v. Joyner,* 547 F.2d 1199, 1201-02 (4th Cir. 1977); *U.S. v. Torres,* 503 F.2d 1120, 1125 (2d Cir. 1974).

When a witness has been impeached on the basis of a prior inconsistent statement, the witness may be rehabilitated by permitting him to explain away the effect of the supposed inconsistency. *U.S. v. Perry,* 550 F.2d 524, 532 (9th Cir.), *cert. denied,* 434 U.S. 827 (1977). Thus, the government may show that the inconsistency was due to the witness' fear for the safety of himself and his family. *U.S. v. Rivera,* 513 F.2d at 526-28; *U.S. v. Franzese,* 392 F.2d 954, 959-61 (2d Cir. 1968), *vacated per curiam on other grounds,* 394 U.S. 310 (1969).

## § 1814. — — Affirmative Evidence.

Rule 801(d)(1)(A) of the Federal Rules of Evidence provides that a statement is not hearsay if the declarant testifies at the trial or hearing and is subject to cross-examination concerning the statement, and the statement is "inconsistent with his testimony, and was given under oath subject to the penalty of perjury at a trial, hearing, or other proceeding, or in a deposition." *See U.S. v. Champion International Corp.,* 557 F.2d 1270, 1274 (9th Cir.), *cert. denied,* 434 U.S. 938 (1977); *U.S. v. Blitz,* 533 F.2d 1329, 1345 (2d Cir.), *cert. denied,* 429 U.S. 819 (1976); *U.S. v. Rivera,* 513 F.2d 519, 525-28 (2d Cir.), *cert. denied,* 423 U.S. 948 (1975); *U.S. v. De Sisto,* 329 F.2d 929, 932-34 (2d Cir.), *cert. denied,* 377 U.S. 979 (1964).

## § 1815. — Insanity and Narcotics Addiction.

Mental derangement may also serve as a ground for impeachment. A ruling on the competency of a witness to testify is within the trial court's discretion. *U.S. v. Heath,* 528 F.2d 191, 192 (9th Cir. 1975). In *U.S. v. Haro,* 573 F.2d 661, 666-67 (10th Cir.), *cert. denied,* 439 U.S. 851 (1978), the court considered the witness' competency in light of the relevant rules of evidence and permitted him to testify in the absence of evidence of demonstrated incapacity. In *Sinclair v. Turner,* 447 F.2d 1158, 1162 (10th Cir. 1971), *cert. denied,* 405 U.S. 1048 (1972), the court noted that "[t]he capacity of a person offered as a witness is presumed, and in order to exclude a witness on the ground of mental or moral incapacity, the existence of the incapacity must be made to appear." This may be shown at the time of testifying, on cross-examination, or by extrinsic evidence. *See U.S. v. Roach,* 590 F.2d 181, 185-86 (5th Cir. 1979) (discussing Rule 601 and its intent); *U.S. v. Glover,* 588 F.2d 876, 878 (2d Cir. 1978); *U.S. v. Honneus,* 508 F.2d 566, 573 (1st Cir. 1974). In *U.S. v. Jackson,* 576 F.2d 46, 48-49 (5th Cir. 1978), it was noted that court-ordered psychiatric examinations of witnesses would not only invade their privacy, but opinion evidence of the results would also invade the jury's province to determine credibility. *See also U.S. v. Moten,* 564 F.2d 620, 629 (2d Cir.), *cert. denied,* 434 U.S. 942 (1977); *U.S. v. Wertis,* 505 F.2d 683, 685 (5th Cir. 1974), *cert. denied,* 422 U.S. 1045 (1975).

In *U.S. v. Green,* 523 F.2d 229 (2d Cir. 1975), *cert. denied,* 423 U.S. 1074 (1976), the district court ruled that a government witness could not be cross-examined about his consultations with a psychiatrist, where the only reason offered by the defense for this questioning was that it might "help to question his credibility." The ruling was affirmed by the Second Circuit, which noted that the witness' credibility had already been extensively and sufficiently attacked by other means on cross-examination. *Id.* at 237.

A witness' use of narcotics at the time of the reported events or at the trial also may serve to impeach his credibility. *U.S. v. Killian,* 524 F.2d 1268, 1275 (5th Cir. 1975), *cert. denied,* 425 U.S. 935 (1976). In *Wilson v. U.S.,* 232 U.S. 563, 568 (1914), where the defendant testified and was asked on cross-examination whether she was addicted to the use of morphine and had used it before coming to court, the Supreme Court ruled that, although the defendant's character had not been put in issue, the examination was proper as bearing on her reliability as a witness. *See U.S. v. Fowler,* 465 F.2d 664 (D.C. Cir. 1972), where limited non-accusatory or *voir dire* examination of the witness was suggested.

In *U.S. v. Leonard,* 494 F.2d 955, 971 (D.C. Cir. 1974), it was held that, before defense counsel could cross-examine a government witness about his narcotics habit, a foundation was required "consisting of evidence that [the witness] had used narcotics on the day he observed the events." This foundation could be established through a *voir dire* of the witness conducted outside the presence of the jury, but if defense counsel was unable to establish the requisite foundation, he would be precluded from cross-examining the witness about his addiction. The court further held that the district court properly excluded defense counsel's proffer of extrinsic evidence to establish the witness' addiction, ruling that the addiction "was plainly a collateral issue." *Id.* at 972. But the court also pointed out the importance of judicial appreciation of the effects of drugs on perception and memory. *See U.S. v. Kearney,* 420 F.2d 170 (D.C. Cir. 1969). For purposes of charging the jury as to the effect of a witness' addiction on his credibility, however, a court is not warranted in taking judicial notice that narcotics addiction lessens the reliability of a witness' testimony. *Weaver v. U.S.,* 111 F.2d 603, 606 (8th Cir. 1940). As a result, to obtain such an instruction, it is necessary to introduce expert medical testimony on the effect of narcotics addiction on the witness' capacities. A proper foundation regarding current drug usage may be required to overcome the court's resistance to extrinsic evidence of specific instances of conduct. There may also be privilege problems if the expert is treating or relying on treatment records of the witness. *U.S. v. Banks,* 520 F.2d 627, 630-31 (7th Cir. 1975).

## § 1816. Rebuttal.

Generally, in the trial judge's discretion, all facts having rational probative value are admissible in rebuttal unless some specific rule of evidence forbids their admission. *U.S. v. Wallace,* 468 F.2d 571, 572 (4th Cir. 1972); *U.S. v. Glaziou,* 402 F.2d 8, 16 (2d Cir.), *cert. denied,* 393 U.S. 1121 (1968); *U.S. v. Coleman,* 340 F. Supp. 451, 454 (E.D. Pa.), *aff'd,* 474 F.2d 1337 (3d Cir. 1972). The trial court is vested with discretion to admit or exclude evidence introduced by the government in rebuttal which might have been introduced in its case-in-chief. *Goldsby v. U.S.,* 160 U.S. 70, 74 (1895); *U.S. v. Fench,* 470 F.2d 1234, 1239 (D.C. Cir. 1972), *cert. denied,* 410 U.S. 909 (1973); *U.S. v. Armstrong,* 462 F.2d 408, 411 (8th Cir. 1972); *U.S. v. Lieblich,* 246 F.2d 890, 895 (2d Cir.), *cert. denied,* 355 U.S. 896 (1957); *Lelles v. U.S.,* 241 F.2d 21, 25 (9th Cir.), *cert. denied,* 353 U.S. 974 (1957).

### § 1817. — Permissible Scope.

Rebuttal evidence may be introduced to refute evidence on material issues of fact, whether elicited on direct or cross-examination, as well as to refute evidence on collateral issues of fact elicited on direct examination. *See U.S. v. Papia,* 560 F.2d 827, 848-49 (7th Cir. 1977); *Sullivan v. U.S.,* 411 F.2d 556, 558 (10th Cir. 1969). *See also U.S. v. Newman,* 481 F.2d 222, 224 (2d Cir.), *cert. denied,* 414 U.S. 1007 (1973); *U.S. v. Hykel,* 461 F.2d 721, 729 (3d Cir. 1972). Rebuttal evidence is, however, inadmissible to refute evidence on collateral issues of fact first elicited on cross-examination. *U.S. v. Schennault,* 429 F.2d 852, 855 (7th Cir. 1970).

On the other hand, rebuttal evidence has been held properly introduced by the government to refute additional elements of a defendant's testimony further elicited on cross-examination. In *Scott v. U.S.,* 172 U.S. 343, 347-48 (1899), a mail carrier charged with theft of a letter stated on direct examination that "somebody had done him a dirty trick," and on cross stated that the money contents of the allegedly stolen letter had been placed on his person by two fellow employees. In rebuttal, the government introduced the testimony of the two employees who refuted the defendant's testimony implicating them in the crime. Although the names of the employees had not been elicited until cross-examination, the court held that the rebuttal evidence was properly received: "The evidence was not collateral to the main issue of guilt or innocence, nor was the subject first drawn out by the Government." *Id.* at 348. Similar cases to the same effect are *U.S. v. Boatner,* 478 F.2d 737, 743 (2d Cir.), *cert. denied,* 414 U.S. 848 (1973), and *Black v. U.S.,* 294 F. 828 (5th Cir. 1923), *cert. denied,* 264 U.S. 580 (1924). *See U.S. v. Perry,* 550 F.2d 524, 531-32 (9th Cir.), *cert. denied,* 434 U.S. 827 (1977): *U.S. v. Hykel,* 461 F.2d at 729; *U.S. v. Perea,* 413 F.2d 65, 68 (10th Cir.), *cert. denied,* 397 U.S. 945 (1969).

It should be noted, however, that, so far as rebuttal evidence is concerned, a party is bound by the answer of a witness on cross-examination with respect to a collateral issue. *U.S. v. Robinson*, 530 F.2d 1076, 1079 (D.C. Cir. 1976). Evidence that a witness has lied in refusing to implicate an unrelated person not indicted is inadmissible even under a liberal test of "collateralness." *Tinker v. U.S.*, 417 F.2d 542, 545 n.16 (D.C. Cir.), *cert. denied*, 396 U.S. 864 (1969); *U.S. v. Franzese*, 392 F.2d 954, 962 (2d Cir. 1968), *vacated per curiam on other grounds*, 394 U.S. 310 (1969).

Because the issue of the bias of a witness is always deemed to be material, rebuttal evidence is permitted to refute assertions related to bias even where first elicited on cross. *U.S. v. Blackwood*, 456 F.2d 526, 530 (2d Cir.), *cert. denied*, 409 U.S. 863 (1972). In *U.S. v. Briggs*, 457 F.2d 908 (2d Cir.), *cert. denied*, 409 U.S. 986 (1972), the court allowed the testimony of a government agent to rebut the denial by a defense witness on cross-examination that the defendant had threatened the witness' life unless he testified in an exculpatory manner. The agent was permitted to testify that the witness had said on two previous occasions that the defendant had attempted to get favorable testimony by such threats on his life. The court observed that, where the relevance of the bias evidence is so apparent, it need not be limited to cross-examination. *Id.* at 910-11. *See also U.S. v. DeFillipo*, 590 F.2d 1228, 1235 n.10 (2d Cir. 1979), *cert. denied*, 442 U.S. 920 (1979); *U.S. v. Brown*, 547 F.2d 438, 445-46 (8th Cir.), *cert. denied*, 430 U.S. 937 (1977); *U.S. v. Kinnard*, 465 F.2d 566, 573-74 (D.C. Cir. 1972); *U.S. v. Blackwood*, 456 F.2d at 530; *U.S. v. Schennault*, 429 F.2d at 855; *U.S. v. Lester*, 248 F.2d 329, 334 (2d Cir. 1957).

## § 1818. — Evidence Inadmissible Under an Exclusionary Rule.

Evidence inadmissible in the government's case-in-chief under an exclusionary rule may be admissible on cross of defendant's witnesses or on rebuttal, solely to impeach the credibility of a defendant on an issue of fact first elicited by the defendant on direct. *See Harris v. New York*, 401 U.S. 222 (1971), relying on *Walder v. U.S.*, 347 U.S. 62 (1954). *See also U.S. v. Bowers*, 593 F.2d 376, 378-79 (10th Cir.), *cert. denied*, 444 U.S. 852 (1979); *U.S. v. Nussen*, 531 F.2d 15, 20-21 (2d Cir.), *cert. denied*, 429 U.S. 839 (1976). In *Walder*, the defendant had been indicted in May 1950, for purchasing and possessing one grain of heroin, but defendant's motion to suppress the heroin capsule as the product of an illegal search and seizure was granted and the case was dismissed. In January 1952, he was again indicted in connection with four other drug transactions, and on direct, the defendant stated that he had never possessed or acted as a conduit for any narcotics in his life. In rebuttal, the government called the agent and chemist who had respectively seized and analyzed the heroin capsule in 1950, and their testimony about the capsule was admitted with a caution by the trial court that the jury should consider the evidence solely with respect to the defendant's credibility as a witness. The Supreme Court affirmed, stating that the Constitution guarantees the defendant the opportunity to deny the charges and put the government to its proof, but it does not shield him from exposure when he perjures himself. *Id.* at 65. *See U.S. v. Kenny,* 462 F.2d 1205, 1225 (3d Cir.), *cert. denied,* 409 U.S. 914 (1972). In *U.S. v. Nathan,* 476 F.2d 456, 460 (2d Cir.), *cert. denied,* 414 U.S. 823 (1973), a defendant charged with conspiracy to import narcotics testified that he did not use cocaine or heroin and had never engaged in the transportation or distribution of narcotic drugs. On cross-examination, however, he admitted to two arrests on drug charges but denied possession of drugs at the time of one arrest or knowledge of the presence of drugs in his apartment at the time of the other arrest. The court held that it was not error to permit the arresting officer to testify as to the circumstances surrounding defendant's post-conspiracy arrests on drug charges.

The Supreme Court held in *Harris v. New York,* 401 U.S. 222 (1971), that statements made by defendants to law enforcement agents in circumstances rendering such statements inadmissible to establish the prosecution's case-in-chief under *Miranda v. Arizona,* 384 U.S. 436 (1966), may, nevertheless, be used to impeach that defendant's credibility. The petitioner in *Harris v. New York* was convicted of the illegal sale of heroin. Statements made by the petitioner were not introduced by the prosecution in its case-in-chief because the statements were concededly inadmissible under *Miranda v. Arizona.* On cross-examination, however, in an attempt to impeach the defendant's testimony that he did not make one sale in issue and that a second transaction involved baking soda rather than heroin, petitioner was asked whether he had made the statements that had been improperly obtained. In this case, the statements used to impeach, unlike those used in *Walder, supra,* specifically dealt with matters directly related to the crime for which petitioner was on trial. The Court, however, was "not persuaded that there is a difference in principle that warrants a result different from that reached by the Court in *Walder.*" *Harris v. New York,* 401 U.S. at 225. In summary, under the *Harris* decision, "The shield provided by *Miranda* cannot be perverted into a license to use perjury by way of a defense, free from the risk of confrontation with prior inconsistent utterances." *Id.* at 226. *Accord, U.S. v. Scott,* 592 F.2d 1139,

1141-42 (10th Cir. 1979); *U.S. v. Johnson,* 525 F.2d 999, 1004-06 (2d Cir. 1975), *cert. denied,* 424 U.S. 920 (1976).

To invoke the rationale of *Harris,* however, care should be exercised to avoid exceeding its bounds. *Harris* does not apply if the defendant does not testify. Thus, the illegally obtained statement of a defendant, may not be used to impeach the testimony of a witness offered by the defense. *James v. Illinois,* 493 U.S. 307 (1990). Nor does *Harris* apply if, in addition to a *Miranda* violation, the statements are involuntary, since the evidence offered for impeachment must still satisfy legal standards of trustworthiness. *Harris v. New York,* 401 U.S. at 224. *Accord, U.S. v. Scott,* 592 F.2d at 1142 (a hearing on voluntariness should be held when there is an allegation or indication of coercion); *U.S. v. Canniff,* 521 F.2d 565, 570-71 (2d Cir. 1975), *cert. denied,* 423 U.S. 1059 (1976). And, of course, *Harris* will not apply if the defendant's statements are not relevant to the credibility of his testimony. If, on the other hand, a defendant takes the stand and gives testimony that conflicts with a prior voluntary statement, the prior inconsistent statement may be used for impeachment. In such cases, however, the court must instruct the jury that the prior inconsistent statement is admissible only on the issue of the defendant's credibility as a witness and not as evidence of guilt or innocence.

The use of prearrest silence to impeach a defendant's credibility does not violate the fifth amendment, *Jenkins v. Anderson,* 447 U.S. 231, 238 (1980), or the sixth amendment, *Michigan v. Harvey,* 494 U.S. 344 (1990). However, in *Doyle v. Ohio,* 426 U.S. 610 (1976), the Court held that a defendant's postarrest silence following *Miranda* warnings may not be used to impeach his exculpatory trial testimony through cross-examination inquiry of why he did not give the arresting officer the exculpatory explanation. But *Doyle* does not apply to cross-examination about prior inconsistent statements as a defendant who voluntarily speaks after receiving *Miranda* warnings has not been induced to remain silent. *Anderson v. Charles,* 447 U.S. 404 (1980) *(per curiam); U.S. v. Ochoa-Sanchez,* 676 F.2d 1283 (9th Cir.), *cert. denied,* 459 U.S. 911 (1982). Postarrest silence without *Miranda* warnings may be used for impeaching the defendant's exculpatory trial testimony or testimony that he cooperated with the police. *Fletcher v. Weir,* 102 S. Ct. 1309 (1982); *U.S. v. Vega,* 589 F.2d 1147, 1150 (2d Cir. 1978). Where the Court immediately sustained an objection and instructed the jury to ignore a question of the defendant concerning exculpatory trial testimony which had not been given to the police at the time of his arrest, there was no *Doyle* violation as the court did not permit the violation that *Doyle* forbids. *Greer v. Miller,* 483 U.S. 756 (1987).

In *U.S. v. Schipani*, 435 F.2d 26, 28 (2d Cir. 1970), *cert. denied*, 401 U.S. 983 (1971), the court held that statements by the defendant, over-heard through unlawful wiretaps, could properly be considered by the sentencing judge in determining that defendant was a professional criminal who deserved an unusually severe sentence. *See U.S. v. Holmes*, 594 F.2d 1167, 1171 (8th Cir.), *cert. denied*, 444 U.S. 873 (1979), where defendant's probation officer testified as to statements made to him by the defendant prior to commission of the crime and in the absence of *Miranda* warnings. *See also U.S. v. Blackwood*, 456 F.2d 526, 529 (2d Cir.), *cert. denied*, 409 U.S. 863 (1972). Tape recordings made in violation of Title III of the Omnibus Crime Control and Safe Street Act of 1968, 18 U.S.C. §§ 2510-2520, have been permitted on rebuttal on the issue of the defendant's sanity and his and his mother's credibility. *Jacks v. Duckworth*, 651 F.2d 480, 484 (7th Cir. 1981), *cert. denied*, 454 U.S. 1147 (1982).

In *U.S. ex rel. Walker v. Follette*, 443 F.2d 167 (2d Cir. 1971), the defendant testified on direct examination that he had never been con-victed of a crime. The court there held that it was proper on cross-examination to elicit the fact that he had been convicted earlier, even though the prior convictions had been obtained without the assistance of counsel in violation of *Gideon v. Wainwright*, 372 U.S. 335 (1963). *But see Loper v. Beto*, 405 U.S. 473, 480-83 (1972), where the Court distinguished *Follette* as being a case in which the record of a prior conviction had been used for the purpose of directly rebutting a specific false statement made by the defendant on direct examination, and not for the purpose of impeaching of his character.

In *U.S. v. Havens*, 446 U.S. 620, 627-28 (1980), the Court held that a defendant's statements made in response to proper cross-examination reasonably suggested by the direct examination of the defendant are subject to otherwise proper impeachment by the government with ille-gally obtained evidence which is inadmissible in the government's case-in-chief. Where the defendant during cross-examination denied any connection with a T-shirt which was inadmissible in the govern-ment's case-in-chief as it was illegally obtained, its admission during the government's rebuttal was proper. *Id.* In *Agnello v. U.S.*, 269 U.S. 20, 35 (1925), the government sought to introduce a suppressed can of cocaine as rebuttal evidence to impeach the defendant's statement on cross that he had never seen narcotics. Since the defendant did not testify on direct concerning prior possession of narcotics, the Court held that he "did nothing to waive his constitutional protection or to justify cross-examination in respect of the evidence claimed to have been obtained by the search." The Court in *Walder v. U.S.*, 347 U.S. at

66, distinguished *Agnello* by pointing out that there the government endeavored to "smuggle" the tainted evidence into the record by introducing the subject on cross-examination. "The implication of *Walder* is that *Agnello* was a case of cross-examination having too tenuous a connection with any subject opened upon direct examination to permit impeachment by tainted evidence." *U.S. v. Havens,* 446 U.S. at 625. *See also U.S. v. Seta,* 669 F.2d 400 (6th Cir. 1982). In *U.S. v. Whitson,* 587 F.2d 948, 952-53 (9th Cir. 1978), the court held that the prosecutor may not use tainted evidence to impeach statements which it elicited on cross-examination and were not raised on direct.

## § 1819. Exclusion or Separation of Witnesses.

Rule 615 of the Federal Rules of Evidence provides for the exclusion or separation of witnesses and provides exceptions for parties, officers of parties, or persons shown to be essential to the presentation of his cause. Whereas previously the decision to exclude witnesses lay in the sound discretion of the trial court, *see e.g., Holder v. U.S.,* 150 U.S. 91 (1893), Rule 615 now makes exclusion mandatory upon the motion of a party. The rule preserves the recognized exception for government agents who participate in the investigation of the case. The agent is permitted to sit at counsel table to consult with the prosecutor, even though he may subsequently testify as a witness. *See U.S. v. Butera,* 677 F.2d 1376, 1381 (11th Cir. 1982); *U.S. v. Holmes,* 594 F.2d 1167, 1172-73 (8th Cir. 1979); *U.S. v. Auton,* 570 F.2d 1284, 1285 (5th Cir.), *cert. denied,* 439 U.S. 899 (1978). The exception for permitting government agents to remain in the courtroom has been held to include non-federal police officers. *U.S. v. Simpkins,* 953 F.2d 443 (8th Cir. 1992).

If a witness disobeys an order excluding him from the courtroom, the trial judge may nevertheless permit the witness to testify, and the decision of a trial court on this point will not be reversed absent an abuse of discretion. *See Holder v. U.S.,* 150 U.S. at 92; *U.S. v. Bizzard,* 674 F.2d 1382, 1388-89 (11th Cir. 1982); *U.S. v. McClain,* 469 F.2d 68, 69 (3d Cir. 1972); *U.S. v. Leftwich,* 461 F.2d 586, 589-90 (3d Cir.), *cert. denied,* 409 U.S. 915 (1972); *Taylor v. U.S.,* 388 F.2d 786, 788 (9th Cir. 1967).

In *Braswell v. Wainwright,* 463 F.2d 1148 (5th Cir. 1972), the court stated that, while defendant's counsel had invoked the rule, the witness had violated it without the knowledge, procurement, or consent of the defendant or his counsel. Since defendant's *pro forma* act of invoking the rule does not rise to waiver under *Johnson v. Zerbst,* 304 U.S. 458 (1938), exclusion by the trial court of a witness who was vital to the defense violated defendant's right to call witnesses in his behalf.

The court observed that "perhaps the consent, procurement, or knowledge on the part of defendant or his counsel might rise to the level of a waiver." *Braswell v. Wainwright,* 463 F.2d at 1155. In this case, however, the court concluded that the trial court had arbitrarily excluded the witness upon no other basis than that he had violated the rule and that such discretion "cannot be permitted when it denies a defendant a fundamental constitutional right." *Id.* at 1156. *See U.S. v. Robbins,* 579 F.2d 1151, 1154 (9th Cir. 1978); *U.S. v. Berdick,* 555 F.2d 1329, 1331 (5th Cir. 1977), *cert. denied,* 434 U.S. 1010 (1978). The defendant must be substantially prejudiced by a violation of a sequestration order before the error gives rise to a reversal. *U.S. v. Bobo,* 586 F.2d 355, 366 (5th Cir. 1978), *cert. denied,* 440 U.S. 976 (1979).

The advisability of keeping witnesses separated before trial is discussed in *U.S. ex rel. Clark v. Fine,* 538 F.2d 750, 758 (7th Cir. 1976), *cert. denied,* 429 U.S. 1064 (1977). The court may also require sequestration during opening statements, *U.S. v. Brown,* 547 F.2d 36, 37 (3d Cir. 1976), *cert. denied,* 431 U.S. 905 (1977), and argument, *U.S. v. Juarez,* 573 F.2d 267, 281 (5th Cir.), *cert. denied,* 439 U.S. 915 (1978).

An expert witness may out of necessity be exempted from the exclusion order where he is to base his testimony on what he has heard in the courtroom. *Morvant v. Construction Aggregates Corp.,* 570 F.2d 626, 629 (6th Cir.), *cert. denied,* 439 U.S. 801 (1978). *See also U.S. v. Rollins,* 522 F.2d 160, 167 (2d Cir. 1975), *cert. denied,* 424 U.S. 918 (1976); *U.S. v. Phillips,* 515 F. Supp. 758, 761 (E.D. Ky. 1981) (psychiatrist allowed to assist prosecutor during testimony of defense experts).

Among those cases where a violation of the separation order resulted in a refusal to permit the disobeying witness to testify are *U.S. v. Gibson,* 675 F.2d 825, 836 (6th Cir. 1982) (witness remained in court with defendant's knowledge and consent); *Stone v. Wingo,* 416 F.2d 857, 867 (6th Cir. 1969); *Nick v. U.S.,* 531 F.2d 936, 937 (8th Cir. 1976); and *U.S. v. Torbert,* 496 F.2d 154, 157-58 (9th Cir.), *cert. denied,* 419 U.S. 857 (1974), where the defendant himself violated the court's sequestration order by speaking with the witnesses in the courthouse.

## § 1820. Use of Interpreters.

Witnesses who do not speak English or who are deaf or dumb may testify through interpreters. *Cf.* Rule 28, Fed. R. Crim. P.; Rule 604, Fed. R. Evid. The appointment of an interpreter lies within the sound discretion of the court, and the exercise of that discretion will be reversed on appeal only where it has been abused. *U.S. v. Salsedo,* 607 F.2d 318, 320 (9th Cir. 1979). Separate interpreters are not required for each defendant in multi-defendant cases. *U.S. v. Yee Soon Shin,* 953 F.2d 559 (9th Cir. 1992).

The right to interpretation may be waived. *Gonzales v. Virgin Islands,* 109 F.2d 215, 217 (3d Cir. 1940). In *Wilcoxon v. U.S.,* 231 F.2d 384, 387 (10th Cir.), *cert. denied,* 351 U.S. 943 (1956), the interpreter failed to translate the oath to two witnesses, and the court observed that the oath itself can be waived and held that the defendant waived this defect by failing to make timely objection.

The determination of the competence, impartiality, and fitness of an interpreter is left to the discretion of the trial judge. *Thiede v. Utah,* 159 U.S. 510, 519-20 (1895) (use of a juror as interpreter was held not prejudicial); *U.S. v. Guerra,* 334 F.2d 138, 142-43 (2d Cir.), *cert. denied,* 379 U.S. 936 (1964) (slight errors in translation held not significant); *U.S. ex rel. Marino v. Holton,* 227 F.2d 886, 897-98 (7th Cir. 1955), *cert. denied,* 350 U.S. 1006 (1956) (where interpreter was alleged to have been biased). The use of a government employee as an interpreter does not deny the effective assistance of counsel, absent specific instances of prejudice resulting from this relationship. *Chee v. U.S.,* 449 F.2d 747, 748 (9th Cir. 1971). Use of a witness' wife as an interpreter for the witness was within the discretion of the court where the court examined the wife as to her ability to translate and any motive to distort the testimony. *U.S. v. Addonizio,* 451 F.2d 49, 68 (3d Cir. 1971), *cert. denied,* 405 U.S. 936 (1972). In a prosecution for burglary with intent to commit rape, however, the appointment of the husband of the deaf mute victim as an interpreter for the victim violated due process since the husband was not an impartial interpreter. *Prince v. Beto,* 426 F.2d 875 (5th Cir. 1970).

# CHAPTER 19

# PRIVILEGES

§ 1901. Privilege Against Self-Incrimination.
§ 1902. — Applicability of the Privilege.
§ 1903. — Scope of the Privilege.
§ 1904. — Exercise of the Privilege.
§ 1905. — Registration and Reporting Provisions.
§ 1906. — Waiver of the Privilege.
§ 1907. — Comment on Failure to Testify.
§ 1908. Privileged Communications.
§ 1909. — Marital Communications Privilege.
§ 1910. — — Adverse Testimony Privilege.
§ 1911. — — Confidential Communications.
§ 1912. — — Existence of Marriage.
§ 1913. — — Objection and Waiver.
§ 1914. — — Exceptions.
§ 1915. — Attorney-Client Privilege.
§ 1916. — — Privilege Holder Must Be Client.
§ 1917. — — Communication With Lawyer.
§ 1918. — — Communication by Client for Legal Services.
§ 1919. — — Waiver.
§ 1920. — Work-Product Doctrine.
§ 1921. — Physician-Patient Privilege.
§ 1922. — Reporter-Source Privilege.
§ 1923. Government Privilege — Identities of Informants.
§ 1924. Other Privileges.

## § 1901. Privilege Against Self-Incrimination.

Every citizen has a duty to testify and aid in enforcement of the law. *Brown v. Walker,* 161 U.S. 591 (1896). *See U.S. v. Dionisio,* 410 U.S. 1, 9-11 (1973). On the other hand, this principle may conflict with the privilege against self-incrimination as stated in the fifth amendment: no person "shall be compelled in any criminal case to be a witness against himself." A witness, whether or not he is the defendant, cannot be compelled to answer any question which may incriminate him or the reply to which would supply evidence by which he could be convicted of a criminal offense. *Ullmann v. U.S.,* 350 U.S. 422 (1956); *Counselman v. Hitchcock,* 142 U.S. 547 (1892). As the Supreme Court emphasized in *Miranda v. Arizona,* 384 U.S. 436, 460 (1966), citing its opinion in *Malloy v. Hogan,* 378 U.S. 1, 8 (1964), "In sum, the privilege is fulfilled only when the person is guaranteed the right 'to remain silent unless he chooses to speak in the unfettered exercise of his own will.'"

Factors determinative of whether the privilege applies in a particular situation are who is asserting the privilege, whether compulsion exists, and the nature and impact of the evidence involved.

## § 1902. — Applicability of the Privilege.

The privilege against self-incrimination applies only to natural persons. *U.S. v. White*, 322 U.S. 694 (1944). It applies to juveniles. *In re Gault*, 387 U.S. 1, 55 (1967); *U.S. v. White Bear*, 668 F.2d 409, 411-12 (8th Cir. 1982). A corporation or other institutional or collective entity as such may not assert the privilege. *Braswell v. U.S.*, 108 S. Ct. 2284 (1988); *Bellis v. U.S.*, 417 U.S. 85 (1974).

Generally, the privilege cannot be asserted on behalf of another. One may not refuse to answer because of a desire to protect others from punishment. *Rogers v. U.S.*, 340 U.S. 367, 371 (1951); *U.S. v. Seavers*, 472 F.2d 607, 611 (6th Cir. 1973); *U.S. v. Seewald*, 450 F.2d 1159, 1161-62 (2d Cir. 1971), *cert. denied*, 405 U.S. 978 (1972); nor may a defendant assert an accomplice's or a coconspirator's privilege against self-incrimination, *U.S. v. Le Pera*, 443 F.2d 810, 812 (9th Cir.), *cert. denied*, 404 U.S. 958 (1971). An employer possessing depositions and interrogatories of employees may not assert the fourth and fifth amendment rights of his employees in reponse to a grand jury subpoena for those documents. *Flavorland Industries, Inc. v. U.S.*, 591 F.2d 524 (9th Cir. 1979).

In certain cases an attorney may assert his client's fifth amendment privilege as a basis for refusing to turn over documents. *Fisher v. U.S.*, 425 U.S. 391 (1976); *U.S. v. Judson*, 322 F.2d 460 (9th Cir. 1963); *Colton v. U.S.*, 306 F.2d 633 (2d Cir.), *cert. denied*, 371 U.S. 951 (1962). *But see U.S. v. White*, 477 F.2d 757, *aff'd per curiam on rehearing en banc*, 497 F.2d 1335 (5th Cir. 1973), *cert. denied*, 419 U.S. 872 (1974). Documents in the hands of an attorney supplied by a client in order to obtain legal assistance are protected from compulsory disclosure by the attorney-client privilege if the documents, in the hands of the client, would have been privileged by reason of the fifth amendment. *Fisher v. U.S.*, *supra*. But the enforcement of a subpoena against a taxpayer's lawyer does not "compel" the taxpayer to be a witness against himself, and thus does not violate the privilege. *Id. See also Andresen v. Maryland*, 427 U.S. 463 (1976), where the Court held no compulsion exists when private business records are seized under a search warrant and the individual claiming the privilege is not asked to identify the documents. In *U.S. v. Helina*, 549 F.2d 713 (9th Cir. 1977), the court concluded that under *Fisher* the subpoena against the taxpayer's attorney did not "compel" the taxpayer to do anything; the court thus ignored

*Fisher's* premise, 425 U.S. at 405, that an attorney may refuse to produce only if the taxpayer could properly do so. Circuits have distinguished *Fisher*. In *U.S. v. Beattie,* 541 F.2d 329 (2d Cir. 1976), the court noted that, because the taxpayer prepared and could authenticate the papers, the privilege did apply. Similarly, in *In re Grand Jury Proceedings (Martinez),* 626 F.2d 1051 (1st Cir. 1980), the court found within the fifth amendment privilege business documents personally held and kept by a doctor, on the ground that his production of them pursuant to a subpoena sufficiently authenticated them such that they could be used against him.

While the privilege prevents compulsory production of an individual's private documents that are incriminating, *see, e.g., In re Grand Jury Proceedings (Johanson),* 632 F.2d 1033 (3d Cir. 1980); *In re Grand Jury Proceedings (Rodriguez),* 627 F.2d 110 (7th Cir. 1980), it exists only if the production is testimonial in nature and incriminatory, *U.S. v. Doe,* 465 U.S. 605 (1984) (compelled production of business records of a sole proprietor was testimonial whereby producing the records would contain implicit statement of facts such as the respondent by the act of production would admit the records were in his possession and authentic); *Fisher v. U.S.,* 425 U.S. at 408. Consequently, mere compliance with a documentary summons, when there is no issue about the existence and location of the papers, does not fall within the scope of the privilege. *Id.* at 411-12. *See also U.S. v. Davis,* 636 F.2d 1028, 1041 (5th Cir. 1981). Likewise, the target of a grand jury may be compelled to execute a consent form directing the disclosure of foreign bank records where the form as written does not acknowledge the existence of a foreign bank account or even identify a relevant bank. The only statement would be that of the bank, that the bank believes the records produced in response to a subpoena are those of the target. *Doe v. U.S.,* 487 U.S. 201 (1988).

The privilege may not be claimed based upon incrimination that may result from the contents or the nature of the thing demanded. *Baltimore City Dept. of Social Services v. Bouknight,* 493 U.S. 549 (1990).

Where the individual holds papers or documents in a representative capacity, rather than personally, he may not claim the personal privilege against self-incrimination for them. *Braswell v. U.S., supra.* However, an agent retains a personal privilege against self-incrimination, *U.S. v. O'Henry's Film Works, Inc.,* 598 F.2d 313 (2d Cir. 1979).

The act of production is the act of the corporation and the government may make no evidentiary use of the "individual act" against the custodian. *Braswell v. U.S., supra.*

An officer, agent or custodian of a corporation or unincorporated association, such as a labor union, may not refuse to produce books of the organization on the ground that they may incriminate the organization. *U.S. v. White,* 322 U.S. 694, 698, 700 (1944); *U.S. v. Peter,* 479 F.2d 147, 149 (6th Cir. 1973). This rule applies even if the records or items sought may incriminate the custodian. *Rogers v. U.S.,* 340 U.S. 367, 371-72 (1951). *Cf. Perial Amusement Corp. v. Morse,* 482 F.2d 515, 519 n.5 (2d Cir. 1973). Moreover, corporate records, which would tend to incriminate a corporate officer, can be subpoenaed even where the corporation is a mere alter ego of its owner. *Braswell v. U.S., supra.* Whether pocket diaries and desk calendars are personal and privileged or corporate documents depends upon an evaluation of factors such as who prepared the documents, the nature of their contents, their purpose, who had possession and access, whether the corporation required their preparation and whether they were necessary to the corporation's business. *In re Grand Jury Subpoena Dated April 23, 1981,* 657 F.2d 5, 8 (2d Cir. 1981). The privilege may properly be invoked, however, in response to oral inquiries designed to locate corporate or association records, *Curcio v. U.S.,* 354 U.S. 118 (1957), but not to the act of producing corporate records. *U.S. v. Rylander,* 460 U.S. 572 (1983).

Once books are produced, an officer may be required to testify to their identity. *U.S. v. Austin-Bagley Corp.,* 31 F.2d 229, 233 (2d Cir.), *cert. denied,* 279 U.S. 863 (1929). *But see U.S. v. Beattie,* 541 F.2d 329 (2d Cir. 1976). It has been held, however, that partnership records, under certain circumstances, may be subject to the privilege because of their personal nature. *Cf. U.S. v. Slutsky,* 352 F. Supp. 1105 (S.D.N.Y. 1972). In *U.S. v. White,* 322 U.S. 694, 701 (1944), the Court said:

> The test, rather, is whether one can fairly say under all the circumstances that a particular type of organization has a character so impersonal in the scope of its membership and activities that it cannot be said to embody or represent the purely private or personal interests of its constituents, but rather to embody their common or group interests only. If so, the privilege cannot be invoked on behalf of the organization or its representatives in their official capacity. Labor unions — national or local, incorporated — clearly meet that test.

This privilege has been held inapplicable to records: of a dissolved law firm of three partners, *Bellis v. U.S.,* 417 U.S. 85 (1974); of an "association" of lawyers, not a partnership, *U.S. v. Schoendorf,* 454 F.2d 349 (7th Cir. 1971); of an impersonal partnership with all the aspects of a corporate enterprise, *In re Mal Bros. Contracting Co.,* 444 F.2d 615 (3d Cir.), *cert. denied,* 404 U.S. 857 (1971); of a general partner of five limited partnerships, *U.S. v. Silverstein,* 314 F.2d 789, 791 (2d Cir.), *cert. denied,* 374 U.S. 807 (1963); of a two-man partnership, after the death of one, regarding papers not the private property of the surviving partner, *U.S. v. Hankins,* 565 F.2d 1344 (5th Cir. 1978), *cert. denied,* 440 U.S. 909 (1979).

A witness may not create a privilege as to his accountant's work papers by taking possession of, or title to them, or by transferring custody of those papers to his attorney. Where records in a safe in corporate custody are individually owned, the individual owner may claim the privilege so long as the corporation has no access to the safe. *U.S. v. Guterma,* 272 F.2d 344 (2d Cir. 1959). That the entries in private documents were actually written by another person does not vitiate the privilege. *Wilson v. U.S.,* 221 U.S. 361, 378 (1911).

The privilege is usually inapplicable when the witness does not have possession of the documents or papers. *Johnson v. U.S.,* 228 U.S. 457 (1913); *U.S. v. Silvestain,* 668 F.2d 1161, 1164 (10th Cir. 1982); *U.S. v. Cohen,* 388 F.2d 464 (9th Cir. 1967). When records have been surrendered to an independent accountant to prepare tax returns, the taxpayer has relinquished any claim to the privilege; the element of compulsion is lacking. *U.S. v. Arthur Young & Co.,* 465 U.S. 805 (1984); *Couch v. U.S.,* 409 U.S. 322 (1973); *In re Horowitz,* 482 F.2d 72, 82-87 (2d Cir.), *cert. denied,* 414 U.S. 867 (1973); *U.S. v. Rosenstein,* 474 F.2d 705, 715 (2d Cir. 1973). *See U.S. v. Falley,* 489 F.2d 33 (2d Cir. 1973) (document must be owned, possessed, and self-incriminating before fifth amendment privilege attaches, and ownership is lacking in regard to a passport); *U.S. v. Cleveland Trust Co.,* 474 F.2d 1234 (6th Cir.), *cert. denied,* 414 U.S. 866 (1973) (financial record submitted to a trust company with application for a loan).

Records required to be kept as part of a regulatory scheme with public purposes are not "private" and thus are not subject to a claim of privilege. *Shapiro v. U.S.,* 335 U.S. 1 (1948) (records required by OPA); *U.S. v. Turner,* 480 F.2d 272, 276 (7th Cir. 1973) (records of a tax preparer); *U.S. v. Kaufman,* 429 F.2d 240, 247 (2d Cir.), *cert. denied,* 400 U.S. 925 (1970); *U.S. v. Stirling,* 571 F.2d 708 (2d Cir.), *cert. denied,* 439 U.S. 824 (1978) (SEC records of a broker-dealer); *In re Grand Jury Subpoena to Custodian of Records, Mid-City Realty Co.,* 497 F.2d 218 (6th Cir. 1974) (real estate broker records); *In re Grand Jury Proceedings,* 601 F.2d 162, 168 (5th Cir. 1979) (customs house records). A doctor's records of acquisition and distribution of amphetamines, made and kept pursuant to regulation, are not protected by the privilege. *U.S. v. Warren,* 453 F.2d 738 (2d Cir.), *cert. denied,* 406 U.S. 944 (1972). The requirement of the Jenkins Act, 15 U.S.C. §§ 375-378, that a seller or shipper of cigarettes in interstate commerce file a monthly statement of such shipments with the state tobacco tax administration does not violate the fifth amendment privilege. *U.S. v. E.A. Goodyear, Inc.*, 334 F. Supp. 1096 (S.D.N.Y. 1971). Nor does the privilege protect against the use of records filed by an attorney as required with a state court which show, *inter alia*, amounts received on a contingent fee basis. *U.S. v. Silverman*, 449 F.2d 1341, 1345 (2d Cir. 1971), *cert. denied*, 405 U.S. 918 (1972). Required reports in bankruptcy proceedings were properly admitted against the defendant in a subsequent trial for concealing assets. *U.S. v. Falcone*, 544 F.2d 607 (2d Cir. 1976), *cert. denied*, 430 U.S. 916 (1977). However, a claim of the privilege may be a complete defense to a charge of failure to pay a tax or keep a record if the court finds that the statute requires information which has no public aspect, is of a kind not customarily kept by the defendant, is not required in an essentially noncriminal and regulatory area, and compliance would subject petitioner to a real and appreciable risk of incrimination. *Leary v. U.S.*, 395 U.S. 6, 16-18 (1969) (marijuana transfer tax); *Haynes v. U.S.*, 390 U.S. 85, 95-100 (1968) (possession of unregistered firearm); *Grosso v. U.S.*, 390 U.S. 62, 67-69 (1968) (excise tax on wagering proceeds). *See Marchetti v. U.S.*, 390 U.S. 39, 44-57 (1968) (registration and payment of occupational tax on wagers). But if the statement made in attempted compliance with such a statute is false, the privilege is neither a defense to a perjury prosecution, *U.S. v. Knox*, 396 U.S. 77 (1969), nor a proper objection to the admissibility of the statement at a trial, *U.S. v. Willoz*, 449 F.2d 1321, 1324-25 (5th Cir. 1971).

### § 1903. — Scope of the Privilege.

The privilege against self-incrimination extends not only to "answers that would in themselves support a conviction under a federal criminal statute," but also to answers that furnish a link in the chain of evidence necessary for prosecution. *Hoffman v. U.S.*, 341 U.S. 479, 486 (1951). This is so even though the crime that would be revealed is only collateral to the matter under inquiry. *See Malloy v. Hogan*, 378 U.S. 1, 11 (1964); *U.S. v. Doto*, 205 F.2d 416 (2d Cir. 1953). The privilege also has been held to apply where the information compelled would supply an investigatory lead or focus investigation on a witness. *Kastigar v. U.S.*, 406 U.S. 441, 460 (1972). *See also U.S. v. Powe*, 591 F.2d 833 (D.C. Cir. 1978).

The original rule in *Hoffman v. U.S.*, *supra*, pertaining to federal prosecutions, was extended by the Supreme Court in *Murphy v. Waterfront Commission*, 378 U.S. 52 (1964), to protect both state and federal witnesses against incrimination in either system. *Id.* at 77-78. *See also*

*U.S. v. Domenech,* 476 F.2d 1229, 1231 (2d Cir.), *cert. denied,* 414 U.S. 840 (1973). The law currently is unsettled on whether a witness may present possible foreign prosecution as the basis for his claim of privilege. It has been held, however, that a witness may not make such a claim if he has been granted immunity against the use of his testimony in federal and state prosecutions. *In re Federal Grand Jury Witness,* 597 F.2d 1166 (9th Cir. 1979); *U.S. v. Yanagita,* 552 F.2d 940 (2d Cir. 1977). In any event, the witness claiming the privilege must demonstrate a real and substantial fear of foreign prosecution, *Zicarelli v. New Jersey Investigation Commission,* 406 U.S. 472, 478 (1972) (fifth amendment issue not reached), but the witness cannot make this showing where his testimony is given before a federal grand jury and is subject to the secrecy rules, *In re Grand Jury Subpoena of Flanagan,* 691 F.2d 116 (2d Cir. 1982); *In re Tierney,* 465 F.2d 806 (5th Cir. 1972), or if the questions objected to would not elicit facts that occurred in the foreign country, *U.S. v. Doe,* 361 F. Supp. 226 (E.D. Pa.), *aff'd mem.,* 485 F.2d 682 (3d Cir. 1973), *cert. denied,* 415 U.S. 689 (1974).

A witness may not refuse to answer on the ground that his answers might tend to disgrace him or bring him into disrepute; the fifth amendment applies solely to incrimination. *U.S. v. Frascone,* 299 F.2d 824, 827 (2d Cir.), *cert. denied,* 370 U.S. 910 (1962); *Brown v. Walker,* 161 U.S. 591, 598 (1896) (the latter case also discusses inapplicability of privilege where incrimination is not possible by reason of prior conviction or acquittal, statute of limitations, pardon, or immunity). *See U.S. v. Stewart,* 445 F.2d 897, 900 (8th Cir. 1971), regarding the statute of limitations. Upon a grant of derivative and use immunity there is no danger of incrimination, and testimony may be compelled. *Kastigar v. U.S.,* 406 U.S. 441 (1972). *See also U.S. v. Frumento,* 552 F.2d 534 (3d Cir. 1977); *U.S. v. Silkman,* 543 F.2d 1218 (8th Cir. 1976), *cert. denied,* 431 U.S. 919 (1977); *Block v. Consino,* 535 F.2d 1165 (9th Cir.), *cert. denied,* 429 U.S. 861 (1976).

Conviction of a crime may result in limitation or termination of the privilege against self-incrimination as to that crime. *U.S. v. Heldt,* 668 F.2d 1238, 1253 (D.C. Cir. 1981). A convicted defendant, serving a period of probation as all or part of his sentence, may not rely on the privilege in refusing to answer questions asked by a probation officer. Such a refusal may result in revocation of the probation and the imposition of a jail sentence. *U.S. v. Manfredonia,* 341 F. Supp. 790, 794-95 (S.D.N.Y.), *aff'd per curiam on opinion below,* 459 F.2d 1392 (2d Cir.), *cert. denied,* 490 U.S. 851 (1972).

One may not use the fifth amendment as a license to lie. *U.S. v. Wong,* 431 U.S. 174 (1974). Consequently, in *Wong,* the Supreme Court held that perjured, although immunized, testimony could be used against the declarant in a subsequent prosecution for perjury, pursuant to 18 U.S.C. § 6002. This section prevents the use of immunized testimony against the declarant in a criminal case, but exempts from this restriction a prosecution for perjury or false statement. The Supreme Court extended the doctrine in *Wong* to allow the use of all immunized testimony in a subsequent trial for perjury or false statements, and not just purportedly perjured statements. *U.S. v. Apfelbaum,* 445 U.S. 115 (1980).

Exercise of the privilege is not restricted to criminal matters; it may be claimed in any proceeding where persons are called upon to give testimony. *In re Gault,* 387 U.S. 1, 47 (1967); *Murphy v. Waterfront Commission,* 378 U.S. 52, 94 (1964) (White, J., concurring). *See U.S. v. Sharp,* 920 F.2d 1167 (4th Cir. 1990) (IRS civil liability investigation); *De Vita v. Sills,* 422 F.2d 1172, 1177 (3d Cir. 1970) (disciplinary proceedings against an attorney); *Yiu Fong Cheung v. Immigration & Naturalization Service,* 418 F.2d 460, 464 (D.C. Cir. 1969) (alien deportation proceedings). The witness must, however, have reasonable cause to apprehend danger of incrimination from a direct answer. *NLRB v. Trans Ocean Export Packing, Inc.,* 473 F.2d 612, 617 (9th Cir. 1973); *U.S. v. Seewald,* 450 F.2d 1159, 1163 (2d Cir. 1971), *cert. denied,* 405 U.S. 978 (1972).

The fifth amendment protects only evidence that is testimonial or communicative in nature from compelled disclosure. *Schmerber v. California,* 384 U.S. 757 (1966). The privilege does not prohibit the introduction in evidence of information obtained through an examination or display of physical characteristics. Thus, a piece of clothing may be put on a defendant to ascertain if it fits. *See, e.g., Holt v. U.S.,* 218 U.S. 215, 252 (1910) (blouse); *U.S. v. Roberts,* 481 F.2d 892, 895 (5th Cir. 1973) (stocking mask). A defendant may be compelled to yield his shoes to police. *Jones v. U.S.,* 405 U.S. 957 (1972); *U.S. v. De Larosa,* 450 F.2d 1057, 1067 (3d Cir. 1971), *cert. denied,* 405 U.S. 927 (1972). A passport is admissible on a cocaine importation charge to show presence in a country, as entries thereon are neither testimonial nor violative of the fifth amendment. *U.S. v. Friedman,* 593 F.2d 109 (9th Cir. 1979). Standardized medical tests, such as the extraction of blood samples, may be made. *Schmerber v. California,* 384 U.S. 757 (1966). Police may take sample scrapings from a suspect's fingernails, *cf. Cupp v. Murphy,* 412 U.S. 291 (1973) (fifth amendment issues not raised), or swab a suspect's hands with a solution to discover traces of nitrate, *U.S. v. Love,* 482 F.2d 213 (5th Cir.), *cert. denied,* 414 U.S. 1026 (1973). A suspect may be required to furnish handwriting or voice exemplars and submit to fingerprinting. *U.S. v. Dionisio,* 410 U.S. 1 (1973); *Gilbert v. California,* 388 U.S. 263 (1967); *U.S. v. Doe,* 457 F.2d 895 (2d Cir. 1972), *cert. denied,* 410 U.S. 941 (1973); *U.S. v. Gibson,* 444 F.2d 275, 277 (5th Cir. 1971); *U.S. v. Izzi,* 427 F.2d 293, 295-96 (2d Cir.), *cert. denied,* 399 U.S. 928 (1970); *U.S. v. Doe,* 405 F.2d 436 (2d Cir. 1968). Slurring and other evidence of lack of physical coordination in a videotaped sobriety test is admissible. *Pennsylvania v. Muniz,* 110 S. Ct. 2638 (1990). Hair and semen samples also may be obtained. *Payne v. Thompson,* 622 F.2d 254 (6th Cir. 1980). However, the method of obtaining the specimen may be violative of the defendant's due process rights if it "shocks the conscience." *Rochin v. California,* 342 U.S. 165, 172 (1952) (administration of an emetic to induce vomiting violative of due process); *Yanes v. Romero,* 619 F.2d 851 (10th Cir. 1980) (obtaining of specimen through threat of use of catheter not a constitutional violation). An individual may be required to appear in a lineup, perform movements, speak certain phrases, or exhibit identifying marks on his body. *U.S. v. Wade,* 388 U.S. 218, 221-23 (1967). *See Stovall v. Denno,* 388 U.S. 293 (1967); *U.S. v. McCarthy,* 473 F.2d 300, 304 n.3 (2d Cir. 1972) (tattoo marks).

The trial court may order a mental examination of the accused under 18 U.S.C. § 4244. *U.S. v. Baird,* 414 F.2d 700 (2d Cir. 1969), *cert. denied,* 396 U.S. 1005 (1970). *But see U.S. v. Driscoll,* 399 F.2d 135 (2d Cir. 1968). The statements of the defendant to a psychiatrist examining him pursuant to Rule 12.2(c) of the Federal Rules of Criminal Procedure may be introduced on the issue of sanity. *U.S. v. Madrid,* 673 F.2d 1114, 1121 (10th Cir. 1982). However, where sanity was the sole issue, compelling the defendant to exercise his own peremptory challenges, necessarily revealing information such as his thought process, was held to produce unreliable information and also to violate his privilege against self-incrimination. *Walker v. Butterworth,* 599 F.2d 1074 (1st Cir. 1979), *cert. denied,* 444 U.S. 937 (1980). A videotape of the defendant's confession is, in itself, not violative of the fifth amendment protection. *Hendricks v. Swenson,* 456 F.2d 503 (8th Cir. 1972).

## § 1904. — Exercise of the Privilege.

The government may call a witness even though it is aware he may claim the fifth amendment privilege. *Namet v. U.S.,* 373 U.S. 179, 188 (1963); *U.S. v. Leighton,* 265 F. Supp. 27, 37 (S.D.N.Y.), *aff'd,* 386 F.2d 822 (2d Cir. 1967), *cert. denied,* 390 U.S. 1025 (1968). A witness may not avoid appearing by submitting an affidavit stating that he will claim the privilege and refuse to testify, *U.S. v. Pilnick,* 267 F. Supp. 791, 798-99 (S.D.N.Y. 1967), or refuse to be sworn, *U.S. v. Romero,* 249 F.2d 371, 375 (2d Cir. 1957). The reluctance of a witness to testify at trial can be adequately established only by compelling his presence and questioning him before the court, but his testing need not take place before the jury. *U.S. v. Sanchez*, 459 F.2d 100 (2d Cir.), *cert. denied*, 409 U.S. 864 (1972). A blanket assertion is unacceptable. *U.S. v. Goodwin*, 625 F.2d 693, 700-01 (5th Cir. 1980). Usually, the privilege must be claimed separately for each question which the witness refuses to answer, and, in general, the claim may not be asserted before the stating of the question. *U.S. v. Harmon*, 339 F.2d 354 (6th Cir. 1964), *cert. denied*, 380 U.S. 944 (1965). But where the position of the witness at a hearing is virtually that of an accused on trial, his blanket refusal to answer may be justified. *Mafie v. U.S.*, 209 F.2d 225 (1st Cir. 1954); *Marcello v. U.S.*, 196 F.2d 437 (5th Cir. 1952). While the prosecutor cannot repeatedly elicit assertions of the fifth amendment privilege without a reasonable relation to the direct testimony, if the defendant makes an issue of his credibility such a line of questioning is not improper. *U.S. v. Hearst*, 563 F.2d 1331 (9th Cir. 1977), *cert. denied*, 435 U.S. 1000 (1978). However, in these circumstances, impeachment of the credibility of an accomplice, who testifies in the trial of the defendant, cannot be the basis for introduction of the accomplice's confession which implicates the defendant. *Douglas v. Alabama*, 380 U.S. 415 (1965).

The witness must exercise the privilege; the court cannot do so when the witness is not reluctant to answer a question. *U.S. v. Colyer*, 571 F.2d 941, 946 (5th Cir.), *cert. denied*, 439 U.S. 933 (1978). Once the privilege is asserted, the court must use discretion and "personal perceptions of the peculiarities of the case" to determine if the claim is valid. In *Hoffman v. U.S.*, 341 U.S. 479, 486-87 (1951), the Supreme Court delineated the test:

> The witness is not exonerated from answering merely because he declares that in so doing he would incriminate himself — his say-so does not of itself establish the hazard of incrimination. It is for the court to say whether his silence is justified ... and to require him to answer if it clearly appears to the court that he is mistaken. To sustain the privilege, it need only be evident from the implications of the question, in the setting in which it is asked, that a responsive answer to the question or an explanation of why it cannot be answered might be dangerous because injurious disclosure could result. The trial judge in appraising the claim must be governed as much by his personal perception of the peculiarities of the case as by the facts actually in evidence.

*See In re Brogna*, 589 F.2d 24 (1st Cir. 1978); *In re U.S. Hoffman Can Corp.*, 373 F.2d 622 (3d Cir. 1967); *U.S. v. Frascone*, 299 F.2d 824 (2d Cir.), *cert. denied*, 370 U.S. 910 (1962).

When it is not readily evident from the question itself or the setting in which it is asked that an injurious disclosure might result from either a response or an explanation why no response could be given, as, for example, when large numbers of documents are subpoenaed by the grand jury, the witness may not be free to rest on a blanket claim of the privilege but may be required to make an *in camera* showing to the court of how each response may tend to incriminate him. *In re Horowitz*, 482 F.2d 72, 82 n.11 (2d Cir.), *cert. denied*, 414 U.S. 867 (1973). *See U.S. v. Reynolds*, 345 U.S. 1, 8-9 (1958); *Brown v. U.S.*, 276 U.S. 134 (1928). This is the procedure currently followed when an Internal Revenue Service summons in a civil investigation is resisted on a fifth amendment claim of privilege. *U.S. v. Ponder*, 475 F.2d 37, 39 (5th Cir. 1973); *U.S. v. Roundtree*, 420 F.2d 845, 852 (5th Cir. 1969). *See Donaldson v. U.S.*, 400 U.S. 517, 531-36 (1971), holding that the summons must be issued in good faith before any recommendation for prosecution.

A witness may refuse to testify upon a showing that the privilege could be asserted properly regarding all relevant questions. *See, e.g., U.S. v. Harris*, 542 F.2d 1283 (7th Cir. 1976), *cert. denied*, 430 U.S. 934 (1977); *U.S. v. Melchor Moreno*, 536 F.2d 1042 (5th Cir. 1976). Before excusing a witness from testifying, the court must determine that the witness will assert the privilege as to essentially all questions which may be asked of him, *U.S. v. Reese*, 561 F.2d 894 (D.C. Cir. 1977), and whether reasonable grounds exist to fear incrimination, *U.S. v. Melchor Moreno, supra.* A refusal to testify must not be permitted where a narrower application of the privilege adequately protects the witness' rights. *Id.*

## § 1905. — Registration and Reporting Provisions.

The government may not prosecute someone for failing to register or report activities or possessions when the registration or filing of the report would subject the individual to substantial hazards of self-incrimination. Thus, for example, the government may not prosecute for failure to pay wagering taxes or failure to register as someone liable to pay wagering taxes because wagering activity subjects a participant to possible state and federal prosecution. *Marchetti v. U.S.*, 390 U.S. 39 (1968). *See also Haynes v. U.S.*, 390 U.S. 85 (1968) (registration of sawed-off shotgun); *Grosso v. U.S.*, 390 U.S. 62 (1968) (wagering tax and registration statement); *U.S. v. Lewis*, 475 F.2d 571 (5th Cir. 1972); *Communist Party v. U.S.*, 384 F.2d 957 (D.C. Cir. 1967) (party registration violated fundamental fifth amendment rights of its members).

A forfeiture proceeding for failure to pay wagering taxes, although civil in form, is criminal in nature, and the privilege against self-incrimination is therefore a defense. *U.S. v. U.S. Coin & Currency,* 401 U.S. 715 (1971). However, the privilege is not a bar to a civil action to recover either the wagering tax or the tax on the transfer of marijuana. *Simmons v. U.S.,* 476 F.2d 715 (10th Cir. 1973); *Cancino v. U.S.,* 451 F.2d 1028 (Ct. Cl. 1971), *cert. denied,* 408 U.S. 925 (1972).

A reporting requirement under the Federal Water Pollution Control Act, coupled with a prohibition against the discharge of oil, does not violate the fifth amendment when a civil penalty is imposed, although the conduct involved is also punishable criminally. *U.S. v. Ward,* 448 U.S. 242 (1980).

The fifth amendment privilege is not a defense where there is no "real and substantial possibility" that the registration provisions will be utilized. *Minor v. U.S.,* 396 U.S. 87, 93 (1969) (marijuana and heroin order forms); *McCutcheon v. Estelle,* 483 F.2d 256 (5th Cir. 1973); *U.S. v. Castanon,* 453 F.2d 932 (9th Cir.), *cert. denied,* 406 U.S. 922 (1972). *See also U.S. v. Whitehead,* 424 F.2d 446 (6th Cir. 1970) (alcohol tax law). In *California v. Byers,* 402 U.S. 424 (1971), the Supreme Court looked to the essentially regulatory nature of a statute requiring a driver involved in a car accident to stop and give his name and address and the slight likelihood of incrimination this entailed, in holding the statute did not violate the privilege. Similarly, a court order requiring a defendant, found in violation of the antifraud provisions of the securities laws, to report all future transactions, was not violative of the privilege. *SEC v. Radio Hill Mines Col, Ltd.,* 479 F.2d 4, 7 (2d Cir. 1973). Nor is the National Firearms Act, 26 U.S.C. §§ 5801-5803, a violation of the privilege. *U.S. v. Freed,* 401 U.S. 601 (1971); *U.S. v. Blac,* 472 F.2d 130 (6th Cir. 1972), *cert. denied,* 411 U.S. 969 (1973).

Similarly, the Comprehensive Drug Abuse Prevention and Control Act of 1970, 21 U.S.C. §§ 801-904, has eliminated the fifth amendment problems dealt with in *Leary v. U.S.,* 395 U.S. 6 (1969), and *U.S. v. Covington,* 395 U.S. 57 (1969), concerning the marijuana transfer tax, for crimes committed after that date. The provisions of Title III of the Omnibus Crime Control and Safe Streets Act of 1968 (18 U.S.C. §§ 2510-2520, as amended by the Organized Crime Control Act of 1970) permitting electronic surveillance of oral and wire conversations, do not violate the fifth amendment. *U.S. v. Tortorello,* 480 F.2d 764, 774 n.6 (2d Cir.), *cert. denied,* 414 U.S. 866 (1973) (cases collected); *U.S. v. Bobo,* 477 F.2d 974, 981 (4th Cir. 1973), *cert. denied,* 421 U.S. 909 (1975); *U.S. v. Cafero,* 473 F.2d 489, 501 (3d Cir. 1973), *cert. denied,* 417 U.S. 918 (1974).

A taxpayer is required to report his income from an illegal source, even though it may increase his risk of prosecution. *U.S. v. Sullivan,* 274 U.S. 259 (1927) (bootlegger's failure to file a return). Similarly, the privilege does not authorize false answers on a filed return. *U.S. v. Knox,* 396 U.S. 77 (1969). The privilege against self-incrimination also is not violated by introduction of a defendant's tax returns into evidence as proof of a federal gambling conspiracy, because disclosures made without claiming the privilege remove the element of compulsion. *Garner v. U.S.,* 424 U.S. 648 (1976).

Inspection of packages and briefcases of persons entering a United States courthouse does not violate the privilege. *Barrett v. Kunzig,* 331 F. Supp. 266, 274 (M.D. Tenn. 1971), *cert. denied,* 409 U.S. 914 (1972).

Statements obtained under threat of removal from office are "compelled" or "coerced" and may not be used in a subsequent criminal proceeding. *Garrity v. New Jersey,* 385 U.S. 493 (1967). A statute providing for removal from office for refusal to testify or waive immunity against subsequent criminal prosecution is unconstitutional in that it compels self-incrimination by imposing sanctions. *Lefkowitz v. Cunningham,* 431 U.S. 801 (1977). A witness has no fifth amendment right to refuse to answer questions directly related to the performance of his official duties. However, the witness may not be fired from his post for refusing to waive the privilege; he may not be made to suffer penalties on account of his insistence upon his constitutional right. *Uniformed Sanitation Men Association v. Commissioner of Sanitation,* 392 U.S. 280 (1968); *Gardner v. Broderick,* 392 U.S. 273 (1968). *See Spevack v. Klein,* 385 U.S. 511 (1967) (disbarment); *Turley v. Lefkowitz,* 342 F. Supp. 544 (W.D.N.Y. 1972), *aff'd,* 414 U.S. 70 (1973).

## § 1906. — Waiver of the Privilege.

Waiver of the privilege against self-incrimination may take many forms and may be made at any time, even after immunity has been secured. *Smith v. U.S.,* 337 U.S. 137, 150 (1949).

One who volunteers information at any time does not meet the fifth amendment's requirement of "compulsion." Thus voluntary disclosure of an incriminating fact waives the privilege for that and all other relevant facts where no further incrimination would result. *Garner v. U.S.,* 424 U.S. 648 (1976) (tax returns). Otherwise, permitting a witness to testify selectively may result in a distortion of the facts. *Rogers v. U.S.,* 340 U.S. 367, 371 (1951). *See Malloy v. Hogan,* 378 U.S. 1, 14 (1964); *U.S. v. Courtney,* 236 F.2d 921 (2d Cir. 1956). *But see Shendal v. U.S.,* 312 F.2d 564 (9th Cir. 1963).

The Constitution does not forbid the imposition of any burden upon the defendant's exercise of constitutional rights. *Chaffin v. Stynchcombe,* 412 U.S. 17, 30 (1973). *See also Jenkins v. Anderson,* 447 U.S. 231 (1980). Consequently, a valid waiver can occur without violation of the defendant's fifth amendment rights, even though some burden may attach. *Crampton v. Ohio,* 402 U.S. 183 (1971) (cross-examination on questions of guilt was permissible where the defendant claimed compulsion to testify on the issue of punishment in a capital case); *U.S. v. Washington,* 431 U.S. 181 (1977) (testimony before a grand jury may be used against the declarant at trial); *U.S. v. Dohm,* 618 F.2d 1169 (5th Cir. 1980) (testimony at bail bond hearing may be used). A balancing of interests may be necessary. *See U.S. v. U.S. Currency,* 626 F.2d 11 (6th Cir.), *cert. denied,* 449 U.S. 993 (1980) (forfeiture proceedings). However, the declarant must be properly advised of his rights in keeping with the applicable law. Waiver does not occur if the decision to waive places an impermissible burden on the defendant. Thus, testimony required at a fourth amendment suppression hearing may not be used against the defendant at trial on the issue of guilt. *Simmons v. U.S.,* 390 U.S. 377 (1968). *See also U.S. v. Doe,* 628 F.2d 694 (1st Cir. 1980) (affidavit in motion to quash grand jury subpoena not a waiver).

For a waiver to be effective, it must be knowing and voluntary, with sufficient awareness of relevant circumstances and likely consequences. *Brady v. U.S.,* 397 U.S. 742, 748 (1970); *U.S. v. Larry,* 536 F.2d 1149 (6th Cir. 1976), *cert. denied,* 429 U.S. 984 (1976). Failure to establish a knowing waiver of the fifth amendment privilege prevents the admission of any statements made while in a custodial atmosphere. *Miranda v. Arizona,* 384 U.S. 436, 476 (1966). *See also Harryman v. Estelle,* 616 F.2d 870 (5th Cir.) *(en banc), cert. denied,* 449 U.S. 860 (1980).

The fifth amendment privilege must be safeguarded by advising a person in custody of his constitutional rights. He must be informed that he has a right to remain silent, that anything he says will be used against him in court, that he may consult with a lawyer who may be present during interrogation, and that if he is indigent an attorney will be appointed to represent him. *Miranda v. Arizona,* 384 U.S. 436 (1966). Absent these warnings, a defendant's statement may not be used against him on the issue of guilt. *Id.* However, rigid and precise compliance with the language of Miranda is not required. *California v. Prysock,* 453 U.S. 355 (1981).

The Supreme Court has held that the fifth amendment requires that *Miranda* warnings be given to a defendant faced with a custodial court-ordered psychiatric examination he neither initiates nor attempts to use in his own behalf. Absent any such warnings, statements made by the defendant cannot be used. *Estelle v. Smith,* 451 U.S. 454 (1981). If, however, the defendant presents psychiatric evidence, the prosecutor may rebut the defendant's presentation with evidence from the reports of the examination that the defendant requested. *Buchanan v. Kentucky,* 107 S. Ct. —, 41 Crim. L. Rep. 3377 (1987).

Where incriminatory statements are given by an uncounseled person who is ignorant of fifth amendment rights in a civil trial, the statements are not thereby inadmissible in a subsequent criminal case. *U.S. v. White,* 589 F.2d 1283 (5th Cir. 1979). But if a witness is not advised of his privilege against self-incrimination at his first criminal trial, his testimony there cannot be considered a waiver for purposes of his second trial. *U.S. v. Larry, supra.*

Waiver must be clear and unequivocal. In *Emspak v. U.S.,* 349 U.S. 190 (1955), the witness was interrogated as follows: "This is a voluntary statement. You do not claim immunity with respect to that statement?" He answered, "No." *Id.* at 196. The Court held that there was sufficient ambiguity to prevent finding a waiver. "To conclude otherwise would be to violate this Court's own oft-repeated admonition that courts 'must indulge every reasonable presumption against waiver of fundamental constitutional rights.'" *Id.* at 198. Defendant's statement that he would not answer "any" of the prosecutor's questions constituted a proper invocation of the privilege. *U.S. v. Yurasovich,* 580 F.2d 1212 (3d Cir. 1978).

Waiver does not automatically occur as a result of a contractual obligation. *See, e.g., Gardner v. Broderick,* 392 U.S. 273 (1968) (police officer); *Curcio v. U.S.,* 354 U.S. 118 (1957) (secretary-treasurer of a union); *Morgan v. Thomas,* 448 F.2d 1356 (5th Cir. 1971), *cert. denied,* 405 U.S. 920 (1972) (surety on a bond).

Waiver occurs by the accused's plea of guilty only in respect to the crime for which he is charged. *See U.S. v. Damiano,* 579 F.2d 1001 (6th Cir. 1978). When the witness has admitted all the elements of the crime, he cannot withhold mere details such as the name of the person to whom embezzled monies were delivered, *U.S. v. St. Pierre,* 132 F.2d 837 (2d Cir. 1942), *cert. dismissed,* 319 U.S. 41 (1943), unless such details could supply leads which might result in his conviction of another crime, *U.S. v. Yurasovich,* 580 F.2d 1212 (3d Cir. 1978); *U.S. v. Damiano, supra; U.S. v. Courtney,* 236 F.2d 921 (2d Cir. 1956). *Cf. Rogers v. U.S.,* 340 U.S. 367 (1951). A witness convicted on a conspiracy charge may claim the privilege on the theory he could be prosecuted on the underlying substantive crimes even though no charges are outstanding. *U.S. v. Miranti,* 253 F.2d 135 (2d Cir. 1958) (also holding that a waiver is not effective at a second appearance before the same grand jury after a lapse of time; a witness may claim the privilege before the grand jury even though he has previously made the incriminating statement to an FBI agent). *See U.S. v. Domenech,* 476 F.2d 1229 (2d Cir.), *cert. denied,* 414 U.S. 840 (1973), in which a codefendant who had pleaded guilty to one charge, but had a remaining charge yet to be dismissed, was permitted to claim his privilege when called as a witness by the defense. However, a defendant who testifies concerning one charge waives the privilege for cross-examination on matters reasonably related to the subject matter and direct examination. *U.S. v. Lamb,* 575 F.2d 1310 (10th Cir.), *cert. denied,* 439 U.S. 854 (1978). *See, e.g., U.S. v. Hood,* 593 F.2d 293 (8th Cir. 1979), where the defendant testified he had offered to talk to the FBI, and the court upheld cross-examination on his refusal to make statements to other law enforcement authorities. *See also U.S. v. Brannon,* 546 F.2d 1242 (5th Cir. 1977); *U.S. v. Palmer,* 536 F.2d 1278 (9th Cir. 1976). Similarly, failure to claim the privilege as to certain questions is a waiver regarding all questions on the same subject matter. *U.S. v. O'Henry's Film Works, Inc.,* 598 F.2d 313 (2d Cir. 1979).

In *Brown v. U.S.,* 356 U.S. 148 (1958), the Court held that the privilege had been waived as to questions asked on cross-examination relevant to the witness' direct examination. *See Jenkins v. Anderson,* 447 U.S. 231 (1980); *U.S. v. Hearst,* 563 F.2d 1331 (9th Cir. 1977), *cert. denied,* 435 U.S. 1000 (1978). *But see U.S. v. Rogers,* 475 F.2d 821, 827 (7th Cir. 1973); *U.S. v. Lipton,* 467 F.2d 1161, 1167 n.13 (2d Cir. 1972), *cert. denied,* 410 U.S. 927 (1973); *U.S. v. Kravitz,* 281 F.2d 581, 588 (3d Cir. 1960), *cert. denied,* 364 U.S. 941 (1961); *Hamer v. U.S.,* 259 F.2d 274, 281 (9th Cir. 1958), *cert. denied,* 359 U.S. 916 (1959) (government witness permitted to raise privilege on cross-examination).

The effect of a waiver is limited to the particular proceeding in which the waiver occurs. *U.S. v. Yurasovich, supra; U.S. v. Cain,* 544 F.2d 1113 (1st Cir. 1976). A witness who testifies before a grand jury may still invoke the privilege at trial. *But see U.S. v. Davis,* 617 F.2d 677 (D.C. Cir. 1979), *cert. denied,* 445 U.S. 967 (1980), where the court held that statements before a grand jury pursuant to a plea agreement could be used against the defendant at trial when necessary after the plea was withdrawn. *U.S. v. Licavoli,* 604 F.2d 613 (9th Cir. 1979), *cert. denied,* 446 U.S. 935 (1980). Similarly, statements made by a defendant during a suppression hearing are not admissible at trial on the issue of guilt, *Simmons v. U.S.,* 390 U.S. 377 (1968); *U.S. v. Frazier,* 476 F.2d 891, 897, 903 (D.C. Cir. 1973), but may be admissible for impeachment purposes. *See, e.g., Woody v. U.S.,* 379 F.2d 130 (D.C. Cir.), *cert. denied,* 389 U.S. 961 (1967), and *Gordon v. U.S.,* 383 F.2d 936 (D.C. Cir. 1967), *cert. denied,* 390 U.S. 1029 (1967). A witness does not waive his fifth amendment privilege when examined on matters which relate only to credibility, even though the witness is also the accused. Rule 608(b), Fed. R. Evid. However, when a defendant asks a magistrate for appointed counsel and lies about his assets, the government may use his false statements in its direct case at his trial without violating fifth or sixth amendment rights. *U.S. v. Kahan,* 415 U.S. 239 (1974).

Taking the stand does not constitute a waiver of earlier exercises of the fifth amendment privilege. In *Grunewald v. U.S.,* 353 U.S. 391 (1957), the Court held it was prejudicial error to permit revelation, on cross-examination of the petitioner, of petitioner's claim of the fifth amendment privilege before the grand jury, to impeach credibility. Similarly, in *Charles v. Anderson,* 610 F.2d 417 (6th Cir. 1979), *vacated,* 629 F.2d 1182 (6th Cir.), *rev'd,* 447 U.S. 404 (1980), the court distinguished between cross-examination of a defendant about a prior inconsistent statement and cross-examination about a previous failure to give his present statement concerning the events, the latter being deemed unconstitutional. The court acknowledged that "the line of demarcation between permissible and impermissible cross-examination may be too difficult to discern." *Id.* at 422. In *Travis v. U.S.,* 247 F.2d 130, 133 (10th Cir. 1957), this reasoning was extended to a case where a character witness was asked whether he had ever heard that the defendant invoked the fifth amendment before a congressional investigating committee. In *U.S. v. Gross,* 276 F.2d 816, 821 (2d Cir.), *cert. denied,* 363 U.S. 831 (1960), the court held it was error for the prosecutor to ask the defendant on cross-examination whether he had told the same story to a congressional committee, on the ground that the witness' "no" answer could have given rise to an inference in the jurors' minds that he had invoked the fifth amendment before the committee. However, in *U.S. v. Sing Kee,* 250 F.2d 236, 240-41 (2d Cir. 1957), *cert. denied,* 355 U.S. 954 (1958), the court upheld questions to a defense witness concerning invocation of the privilege before a grand jury, where on direct examination defense counsel had sought to bolster the witness' credibility by indicating that the witness had been entirely cooperative and candid before the grand jury, and where, under the specific circumstances, the jury would not have been likely to infer the defendant's guilt from the witness' refusals to answer. *See U.S. v. Glasser,* 443 F.2d 994, 1006 (2d Cir.), *cert. denied,* 404 U.S. 854 (1971).

A defendant who takes the stand to testify subjects himself to the same scope of cross-examination as any other witness. *McGautha v. California,* 402 U.S. 183, 215 (1971); *Reagan v. U.S.,* 157 U.S. 301, 305 (1895); *U.S. v. Walker,* 313 F.2d 236, 239 (6th Cir.), *cert. denied,* 374 U.S. 807 (1963).

Use of a defendant's pre-arrest silence to impeach his testimony at trial violates neither the fifth nor fourteenth amendment and is permissible. *Jenkins v. Anderson,* 447 U.S. 231 (1980). Impeachment is permitted even if the pre-arrest silence is held to be an invocation of the fifth amendment right to remain silent. *Id.* The controlling factor is whether "compelling the election impairs to any appreciable extent any of the policies behind the rights involved." 447 U.S. at 236; *Chaffin v. Stynchcombe,* 412 U.S. 17, 32 (1973). *See also Raffel v. U.S.,* 271 U.S. 494 (1926), where the defendant's silence at the first trial was used to impeach his testimony in the second trial. The rule of *Raffel* was reiterated by the Supreme Court in *Jenkins. But see Stewart v. U.S.,* 366 U.S. 1 (1961). The fourteenth amendment's due process provisions, however, prevent the use of post-arrest silence after the giving of *Miranda* warnings to impeach trial testimony; *Doyle v. Ohio,* 426 U.S. 610 (1976); but not the use of post-arrest silence without *Miranda* warnings. *Fletcher v. Weir,* 102 S. Ct. 1309, 1311 (1982). *See Greer v. Miller,* 107 S. Ct. —, 41 Crim. L. Rep. 3405 (1987), where an attempt to impeach with a post-arrest, post-*Miranda* failure to disclose to police at the time of arrest the defendant's exculpatory trial testimony did not violate *Doyle* where the court immediately sustained an objection and instructed the jury to ignore the questions. Proof that a defendant remained silent in the face of questioning upon arrest may constitute harmless error when there is overwhelming evidence of guilt. *Rothschild v. New York,* 525 F.2d 686 (2d Cir. 1975); *U.S. v. Williams,* 523 F.2d 407 (2d Cir. 1975). *Cf. U.S. v. Sobell,* 314 F.2d 314 (2d Cir.), *cert. denied,* 374 U.S. 857 (1963). *But see U.S. v. Tomaiolo,* 249 F.2d 683, 690-93 (2d Cir. 1957), where it was held error to ask defense witness if he refused to testify before grand jury.

## § 1907. — Comment on Failure to Testify.

A defendant in a criminal trial has the right either to take the stand or not, as he chooses, and his failure to take the stand may not be commented upon by the prosecution. 18 U.S.C. § 3481; *Griffin v. California,* 380 U.S. 609 (1965). No adverse inferences may be drawn from the exercise of the fifth amendment privilege. *Carter v. Kentucky,* 450 U.S. 288 (1981). However, a harmless error test must be applied to a violation before a conviction is reversed. *U.S. v. Hastings,* 461 U.S. 499

(1983). Likewise, the defense may open the door to permit the prosecution to mention the defendant's failure to testify. Where the defense in final argument claimed that the government did not permit the defendant to explain his side of the story, it was "fair response" for the prosecution to state that the defendant "could have taken the stand and explain[ed] it to you." *U.S. v. Robinson,* 485 U.S. 25 (1988).

The trial court must, upon request of the defendant, instruct the jury about the defendant's right not to testify and that no inferences of guilt or prejudice can be drawn from the exercise of that right. *James v. Kentucky,* 466 U.S. 341 (1984); *Carter v. Kentucky, supra. See also Bruno v. U.S.,* 308 U.S. 287 (1939).

## § 1908. Privileged Communications.

Privileged communications, even if highly probative and trustworthy, are protected from disclosure because "their disclosure is inimical to a principle or relationship ... that society deems worthy of preserving and fastening." Graham C. Lilly, *An Introduction to the Law of Evidence* (1978) at 317.

As a general rule, privileges and exclusionary rules can be asserted only by persons whose privacy is affected. Privileges usually can be claimed only by the owner of the privilege, that is, by the person vested with the relationship protected by that particular privilege, whether he be a party or a witness. *U.S. v. Hoffa,* 349 F.2d 20 (6th Cir. 1965), *aff'd,* 385 U.S. 293 (1966).

Privileges of witnesses in criminal cases are governed by the "principles of common law as they may be interpreted by courts of the United States in the light of reason and experience." Rule 501, Fed. R. Evid.; Rule 26, Fed. R. Crim. P. Unlike civil cases where reference to state law is mandatory, in criminal cases courts are merely permitted to refer to state law for guidelines, if appropriate, under Rule 501 and Rule 26. *See U.S. v. Allery,* 526 F.2d 1362 (8th Cir. 1975). However, the Supreme Court recently reiterated that "the admissibility of evidence in criminal trials in the federal court 'is to be controlled by common-law principles, not by local statute,'" and held that an evidentiary privilege for a state legislator under that state's constitution did not compel application of the privilege in a federal criminal prosecution. *U.S. v. Gillock,* 445 U.S. 360 (1980).

## § 1909. — Marital Communications Privilege.

Two distinct privileges arising from the marital relationship are recognized by federal courts. The first is the "adverse testimony" or "anti-marital facts" privilege, which permits one spouse to refrain from testifying adversely against the other. *See e.g., Hawkins v. U.S.,* 358 U.S. 74, 75-76 (1958); *U.S. v. Lustig,* 555 F.2d 737 (9th Cir.), *cert. denied,* 434 U.S. 926 (1977); *U.S. v. Smith,* 533 F.2d 1077, 1079 (8th Cir. 1976). The second and more traditional type of privilege protects confidential communications arising from the marital relationship. *Blare v. U.S.,* 340 U.S. 332, 333 (1954); *U.S. v. Lilley,* 581 F.2d 182 (8th Cir. 1978); *U.S. v. Lustig, supra; U.S. v. Fisher,* 518 F.2d 836 (2d Cir. 1975), *cert. denied,* 423 U.S. 1072 (1976).

### § 1910. — — Adverse Testimony Privilege.

The adverse testimony privilege stems from two principles of medieval jurisprudence: that an accused could not testify on his own behalf because of his interest in the proceedings, and that one spouse was incompetent to testify against the other because they were considered to be one person. With the evolution of this rule into one of privilege and not disqualification, its modern justification is "its perceived role in fostering the harmony and sanctity of the marriage relationship." *See* discussion in *Trammel v. U.S.,* 445 U.S. 40 (1980).

The Supreme Court in *Trammel* adopted for the federal system the state law trend of erosion of an accused's privilege to bar adverse spousal testimony. With all justices concurring in the judgment, the Supreme Court modified its earlier ruling in *Hawkins v. U.S., supra,* and held that the witness-spouse alone has the privilege of refusing to testify adversely. Consequently, in federal criminal proceedings a spouse can be neither compelled to testify nor precluded from testifying.

For the privilege to be available, the testimony in question must be adverse to the spouse's interest in the case at hand. *U.S. v. Burks,* 470 F.2d 432 (D.C. Cir. 1972). This privilege differs from that arising from confidential communications in two respects. First, it prohibits adverse testimony regardless of the source of knowledge, while the communications privilege covers only knowledge obtained through confidential communications. Second, the privilege exists only when the accused and the prospective witness are married at the time of trial; the privilege ends at the termination of the marriage. *Pereira v. U.S.,* 347 U.S. 1 (1954); *U.S. v. Bolzer,* 556 F.2d 948 (9th Cir. 1977); *U.S. v. Lustig,* 555 F.2d 737 (9th Cir.), *cert. denied,* 434 U.S. 926 (1977); *U.S. v. Crockett,* 534 F.2d 589 (5th Cir. 1976).

A witness-spouse was permitted to claim the adverse spousal testimony privilege where any testimony by her directed to the activity of a third party would indirectly implicate her husband who was also a target of the investigation. *In re Grand Jury Matter,* 673 F.2d 688, 692 (3d Cir. 1982).

## § 1911. — — Confidential Communications.

The spousal "confidential communications" privilege applies only to utterances or expressions by one spouse to convey a message to another. *Pereira v. U.S.,* 347 U.S. 1 (1954). For the privilege to extend to gestures, they must be communicative in nature or intended as such. *Id.; U.S. v. Lewis,* 433 F.2d 1146 (D.C. Cir. 1970). A husband's practice of secreting heroin on his wife was not such a communication in *U.S. v. Smith,* 533 F.2d 1077 (8th Cir. 1976); nor were spousal observations of a drug transaction in *U.S. v. Lustig,* 555 F.2d 737 (9th Cir.), *cert. denied,* 434 U.S. 926 (1977). Some courts have extended the privilege to cover expressive acts, *Fraser v. U.S.,* 145 F.2d 139 (6th Cir. 1944), *cert. denied,* 324 U.S. 849 (1945) (recognizing a Tennessee statute extending the privilege to acts, but holding it does not necessarily extend to such "communication" in furtherance of a fraud), while others have declined to do so, *Pool v. U.S.,* 260 F.2d 57 (9th Cir. 1958) (regarding the manner in which a statement was made).

One is protected from indirect as well as direct exposure of a marital communication. *See, e.g., Blau v. U.S.,* 340 U.S. 332 (1951) (husband was asked for his wife's whereabouts, which he learned only from her secret communications). Only those communications which are confidential are privileged, *see, e.g., U.S. v. Cotton,* 567 F.2d 958 (10th Cir. 1977), *cert. denied,* 436 U.S. 959 (1978); but all communications in private between a husband and wife are presumed to be confidential, *Wolfle v. U.S.,* 291 U.S. 7, 14 (1934), unless the subject of the message or the circumstances of the communication show otherwise, *Blau v. U.S.,* 340 U.S. at 333-34. Circumstances surrounding a communication may remove the presumption of confidentiality. For example, the presence of a third party will automatically remove the presumption, *U.S. v. Burks,* 470 F.2d 432, 436-37 (D.C. Cir. 1972); *U.S. v. Lustig,* 555 F.2d 737 (9th Cir.), *cert. denied,* 434 U.S. 926 (1977), even if the third party is eavesdropping and the spouses are not aware of his presence, *Hopkins v. Grimshaw,* 165 U.S. 342, 351 (1897); *Narten v. Eyman,* 460 F.2d 184, 191 (9th Cir. 1969). However, where the husband did not know that in return for immunity his wife permitted FBI agents to monitor and record confidential communications, the "presence-of-a-third-party" exception to the privilege was held inapplicable and neither the recordings nor the wife's nor the agent's testimony was admissible. *U.S. v. Neal,* 532 F. Supp. 942, 947 (D. Colo. 1982).

A spouse may testify to circumstances which would remove the presumption and thereby open the door to testimony regarding the communication. *Picciurro v. U.S.*, 250 F.2d 585, 589 (8th Cir. 1958). If the subject of the communication indicates that it was intended to be published, no privilege will attach. *Dobbins v. U.S.*, 157 F.2d 257, 260 (D.C. Cir.), *cert. denied*, 329 U.S. 734 (1946) (business).

Designed to encourage marital communications, the privilege is limited to communications occurring during the marriage. *See Lutwak v. U.S.*, 344 U.S. 604 (1953). This minimizes the possibility of suppressing testimony by marrying the witness. *U.S. v. Van Drunen*, 501 F.2d 1393 (7th Cir. 1974), *cert. denied*, 419 U.S. 1091 (1975). Communications which occur before the marriage, *U.S. v. Pensinger*, 549 F.2d 1150 (8th Cir. 1977); *U.S. v. Van Drunen, supra; U.S. v. Mitchell*, 137 F.2d 1006 (2d Cir. 1943), *cert. denied*, 321 U.S. 794 (1944), or after divorce, *Volianitis v. Immigration & Naturalization Service*, 352 F.2d 766 (9th Cir. 1965); *Yoder v. U.S.*, 80 F.2d 665 (10th Cir. 1935), are not privileged. However, unlike the adverse testimony privilege, the termination of a marriage does not invalidate the privileged nature of a confidential communication made during a valid marriage. *Pereira v. U.S.*, 347 U.S. 1 (1954); *U.S. v. Termini*, 267 F.2d 18 (2d Cir.), *cert. denied*, 361 U.S. 822 (1959).

## § 1912. — — Existence of Marriage.

Both the adverse testimony and confidential communications privileges depend on there being a valid marriage under state law. *U.S. v. Lustig*, 555 F.2d 737 (9th Cir.), *cert. denied*, 434 U.S. 926 (1977); *U.S. v. Apodaca*, 522 F.2d 568 (10th Cir. 1975). This is a question of law for the court. *U.S. v. Barnes*, 368 F.2d 567 (4th Cir. 1966). Voidable and common law marriages, if recognized by state law, qualify for the privilege.

## § 1913. — — Objection and Waiver.

The marital communications privilege can be claimed only by a holder of the privilege; third parties may not assert the privilege even if they may be incriminated by the disclosure. *U.S. v. Crockett*, 534 F.2d 589, 604 (5th Cir. 1976). There is a split in the authorities on which spouse holds the privilege regarding confidential communications. Some courts assert that the privilege belongs only to the communicating spouse, *Fraser v. U.S.*, 145 F.2d 139, 144 (6th Cir. 1944), *cert. denied*, 324 U.S. 849 (1945); while other courts hold that the privilege belongs to both spouses and can be asserted by either, *U.S. v. Mitchell*,

137 F.2d 1006, 1008 (2d Cir. 1943), *cert. denied,* 321 U.S. 794 (1944), and must be waived by both, *Wyatt v. U.S.,* 362 U.S. 525, 528-29 (1960). Either spouse may now waive the privilege against testifying adversely in federal criminal proceedings. *Trammel v. U.S.,* 445 U.S. 40 (1980); *U.S. v. Crouthers,* 669 F.2d 635, 641-42 (10th Cir. 1982).

Waiver occurs several ways. For confidential communications, the privilege is waived when the subject of the communication is disclosed by the spouse claiming the privilege. *U.S. v. Lilley,* 581 F.2d 182 (8th Cir. 1978). Waiver may also occur through failure to make timely objection. *Benson v. U.S.,* 146 U.S. 325 (1892); *U.S. v. Fisher,* 518 F.2d 836 (2d Cir.), *cert. denied,* 423 U.S. 1033 (1975); *U.S. v. Figueroa-Paz,* 468 F.2d 1055, 1057 (9th Cir. 1972); *Canaday v. U.S.,* 354 F.2d 849, 857 (8th Cir. 1966).

Failure to object to a spouse's testimony in the first trial, ending in a hung jury, is a waiver of the privilege for the second trial. *U.S. v. Fisher, supra.* Admission into evidence of a spouse's testimony after a timely objection by the defendant-spouse constitutes reversible error. *Hawkins v. U.S.,* 358 U.S. 74 (1958). It is generally considered prejudicial to require a defendant to claim the privilege in the presence of the jury. *Tallo v. U.S.,* 344 F.2d 467, 469 (1st Cir. 1967); *U.S. v. Tomaiolo,* 249 F.2d 683, 690 (2d Cir. 1957). *But see Grulkey v. U.S.,* 394 F.2d 244 (8th Cir. 1968). Comment may be made on a defendant's failure to call his spouse if the circumstances indicate that her testimony would be material and relevant. *Bisno v. U.S.,* 299 F.2d 711, 721 (9th Cir. 1961), *cert. denied,* 370 U.S. 952 (1962). However, such comment may be reversible error where the privilege has been exercised timely. *Courtney v. U.S.,* 390 F.2d 521, 527 (9th Cir.), *cert. denied,* 393 U.S. 857 (1968).

## § 1914. — — Exceptions.

Communications in furtherance of crime or fraud are not privileged. *U.S. v. Cotroni,* 527 F.2d 708 (2d Cir. 1975), *cert. denied,* 426 U.S. 906 (1976); *U.S. v. Kahn,* 471 F.2d 191, 195 (7th Cir. 1972), *cert. denied,* 411 U.S. 986 (1973); *Fraser v. U.S.,* 145 F.2d 139, 143 (6th Cir. 1944), *cert. denied,* 324 U.S. 849 (1945); *Federal Deposit Ins. Co. v. Alter,* 106 F. Supp. 316 (W.D. Pa. 1952). Similarly, there can be no privilege if the marriage was entered into solely for the purpose of perpetrating a crime. *Lutwak v. U.S.,* 334 U.S. 604 (1953). Furthermore, where both spouses participated in the unlawful enterprise, exclusion of testimony based on the privilege is not required. *U.S. v. Van Drunen,* 501 F.2d 1393 (7th Cir.), *cert. denied,* 419 U.S. 1091 (1974). *But see In re Grand*

*Jury Empanelled October 18, 1979 (Malfitano)*, 633 F.2d 276 (3d Cir. 1980).

The general exception to the privilege, where the spouse is the current victim of the crime with which the defendant is charged, *see, e.g., Wyatt v. U.S.*, 362 U.S. 525 (1960), is largely unnecessary with the Supreme Court's decision in *Trammel;* the substance of most offenses falls within the scope of the adverse testimony privilege, which the victim-spouse can now waive, and not the confidential communications privilege. The exception has been extended in some states and by some courts to include testimony regarding offenses by a spouse against offenses done to a child of either spouse. *See U.S. v. Allery*, 526 F.2d 1362 (8th Cir. 1975).

## § 1915. — Attorney-Client Privilege.

"The attorney-client privilege rests on the need for the advocate and counselor to know all that relates to the client's reasons for seeking representation if the professional mission is to be carried out." *Trammel v. U.S.*, 445 U.S. 40, 51 (1980). Because its effect is to withhold information from the fact-finder, however, the privilege is strictly construed. *In re Grand Jury Investigation*, 599 F.2d 1224 (3d Cir. 1979); *Diversified Industries, Inc. v. Meredith*, 572 F.2d 596 (8th Cir. 1977) (*en banc*).

In the case of *U.S. v. U.S. Machinery Corp.*, 89 F. Supp. 357 (D. Mass. 1950), Judge Wyzanski set out in detail the rule of law relating to the attorney-client privilege. He states at 358-59:

> The privilege applies only if (1) the asserted holder of the privilege is or sought to become a client; (2) the person to whom the communication was made (a) is a member of the bar of a court, or his subordinate and (b) in connection with this communication is acting as a lawyer; (3) the communication relates to a fact of which the attorney was informed (a) by his client (b) without the presence of strangers (c) for the purpose of securing primarily either (i) an opinion on law or (ii) legal services of (iii) assistance in some legal proceeding, and not (d) for the purpose of committing a crime or tort; and (4) the privilege has been (a) claimed and (b) not waived by the client.

*See In re Grand Jury Investigation*, 599 F.2d at 1233, citing *U.S. v. Machinery Corp., supra.*

## § 1916. — — Privilege Holder Must Be Client.

The privilege applies only if "the asserted holder of the privilege is or sought to become a client." A person becomes a client by consulting with a lawyer even though a retainer is refused, although no privilege can be asserted about communications occurring after the attorney refuses the case. *See In re Auclair,* 961 F.2d 65 (5th Cir. 1992); *Sawyer v. Barczak,* 129 F. Supp. 687, 696-97 (E.D. Wis. 1955), *aff'd,* 229 F.2d 805 (7th Cir.), *cert. denied,* 351 U.S. 966 (1956) (no privilege where attorney was consulted in bribery attempt). The existence of a retainer agreement, the payment of a fee, and the placement of the purported client's name before a firm's new business committee are factors for determining if an attorney-client relationship exists. *See In re Grand Jury Subpoena Dated November 9, 1979,* 484 F. Supp. 1099 (S.D.N.Y. 1980).

Corporations as well as individuals can be clients for the purpose of the privilege. *Commodity Futures Trading Comm'n v. Weintraub,* 471 U.S. 343 (1985). The scope of the attorney-client privilege in the corporate context was previously subject to different tests among the circuits. However, in *Upjohn Co. v. U.S.,* 449 U.S. 383 (1981), the Supreme Court explicitly rejected the "control group test" applied by the Second, Third, Sixth, and Tenth circuits. Under this test the privilege only covered communications between the attorney and a top management member or person with actual authority to speak for the corporation. Noting that legal advice frequently involves actions of middle and lower level employees, the Court said that the control group test "frustrates the very purpose of the privilege by discouraging the communication of relevant information by employees of the client to attorneys seeking to render legal advice to the client corporation," as well as "threatens to limit the valuable efforts of corporate counsel to ensure their client's compliance with the law." *Id.* at 392. The Court emphasized, however, two principles still controlled. First, the privilege only applies to communications and not the underlying facts; secondly, the recognition of the privilege must be determined on a case by case basis. The Court explicitly did not undertake "to draft a set of rules which should govern challenges to investigatory subpoenas." 449 U.S. at 396.

## § 1917. — — Communication With Lawyer.

The privilege applies only if "the person to whom the communication was made (a) is a member of the bar of a court, or his subordinate, and (b) in connection with this communication is acting as a lawyer." Communication to a member of the bar, while a prerequisite to assertion of the privilege, does not alone bring it into operation. *Modern Woodmen v. Watkins,* 132 F.2d 352 (5th Cir. 1942); *Underwater Storage, Inc. v. U.S. Rubber Co.,* 314 F. Supp. 546 (D.D.C. 1970). While the lawyer must be admitted to practice before a court, he need not be a member of the bar of the court in which the privilege is asserted. *Garrison v. General Motors Corp.,* 213 F. Supp. 515 (S.D. Cal. 1963).

Most problems in this area arise when a client seeks advice of a legal nature from a non-lawyer, such as a banker-accountant. There is no banker-client, *Rosenblatt v. Northwest Airlines, Inc.,* 54 F.R.D. 21, 22 (S.D.N.Y. 1971), or accountant-client, *U.S. v. Arthur Young & Co.,* 465 U.S. 805 (1984); *Couch v. U.S.,* 409 U.S. 322, 335 (1973); *U.S. v. Wainwright,* 413 F.2d 796, 803 (10th Cir. 1969), *cert. denied,* 396 U.S. 1009 (1970), privilege in federal law. But one court has held that, where an accountant is relied upon for legal advice as in a tax investigation, he must be treated as a lawyer for due process purposes and the privilege does attach. *U.S. v. Tarlowski,* 305 F. Supp. 112, 123-24, (E.D.N.Y. 1969). It is also clear that, when information sought to be withheld by an accountant was given to him at the direction of an attorney for the purpose of obtaining legal advice, the accountant may claim the privilege as an agent or subordinate of the attorney. *U.S. v. Kovel,* 296 F.2d 918, 920-21 (2d Cir. 1961). *But see In re Horowitz,* 482 F.2d 72, 80-81 (2d Cir.), *cert. denied,* 414 U.S. 867 (1973); *U.S. v. Brown,* 478 F.2d 1038 (7th Cir. 1973); *U.S. v. Gurtner,* 474 F.2d 297, 299 (9th Cir. 1973).

Further, for a communication to qualify for the privilege, the client must be consulting with the lawyer as a lawyer, *U.S. v. Stern,* 511 F.2d 1364 (2d Cir. 1975), *cert. denied,* 423 U.S. 829 (1975); *In re Bonanno,* 344 F.2d 830, 833 (2d Cir. 1965); *U.S. v. Brown,* 349 F. Supp. 420, 427 (N.D. Ill. 1972), *modified,* 478 F.2d 1038 (7th Cir. 1973), and not in the capacity as a participant in a business transaction, *U.S. v. Rosenstein,* 474 F.2d 705, 714 (2d Cir. 1973), or accountant, *Colton v. U.S.,* 306 F.2d 633, 638 (2d Cir.), *cert. denied,* 371 U.S. 951 (1962), or engineering adviser, *Paper Converting Mach. Co. v. F.M.C. Corp.,* 215 F. Supp. 249, 252 (E.D. Wis. 1963), or personal advisor, *Young v. Taylor,* 466 F.2d 1329, 1332 (10th Cir. 1972); *Radiant Burners, Inc. v. American Gas Ass'n,* 320 F.2d 314, 324 (7th Cir.), *cert. denied,* 375 U.S. 929 (1963); *Lowry v. Commissioner,* 262 F.2d 809, 812 (2d Cir. 1959), or scrivener, *Canaday v. U.S.,* 354 F.2d 849, 857 (8th Cir. 1966), or go-between in the transfer of a deed or money in a real estate transaction, *U.S. v. DeVasto,* 52 F.2d 26, 30 (2d Cir.), *cert. denied,* 284 U.S. 678 (1931), or messenger, *McFee v. U.S.,* 206 F.2d 872, 876 (9th Cir. 1953), *vacated,* 348 U.S. 905, *aff'd,* 221 F.2d 807 (9th Cir. 1955), or one who merely deposits money for another, *Pollock v. U.S.,* 202 F.2d 281, 286 (5th Cir.), *cert. denied,* 345 U.S. 993 (1953), or parent, *In re Kinoy,* 326 F. Supp. 400, 405-06 (S.D.N.Y. 1970). The privilege fails if the client attempts to secure other than legal services or advice from the attorney. *Colton v. U.S.,* 306 F.2d 633 (2d Cir.), *cert. denied,* 371 U.S. 951 (1962).

## § 1918. — — Communication by Client for Legal Services.

The privilege applies only if the communication relates to a fact of which the attorney was informed "(a) by his client (b) without the presence of strangers (c) for the purpose of securing primarily either (i) an opinion on law or (ii) legal services or (iii) assistance in some legal proceeding, and not (d) for the purpose of committing a crime or tort."

The privilege belongs to the client, and applies only to communications made by the client, or in some cases, by his agent. *U.S. v. Goldfarb,* 328 F.2d 280 (6th Cir.), *cert. denied,* 377 U.S. 976 (1964). It is not violated by recording a conversation between the client and his attorney when the client gives his consent. *U.S. v. Kahn,* 251 F. Supp. 702, 709 (S.D.N.Y.), *aff'd,* 366 F.2d 259 (2d Cir.), *cert. denied,* 385 U.S. 948 (1966). A communication from the attorney to the client is protected insofar as it has the effect of revealing a confidential communication from the client. *See Colton v. U.S.,* 306 F.2d 633, 639 (2d Cir. 1962), *cert. denied,* 371 U.S. 951 (1963). *Cf. U.S. v. Silverman,* 430 F.2d 106, 122 (2d Cir.), *modified,* 439 F.2d 1198 (2d Cir. 1970), *cert. denied,* 402 U.S. 953 (1971).

There can be no privilege if the communication is made to an attorney to aid someone other than the person who made the communication. *City of Philadelphia v. Westinghouse Electric Co.,* 210 F. Supp. 483 (E.D. Pa. 1962). Neither the client nor the attorney may assert the privilege for communications with third parties, *Rucker v. Wabash R.R.,* 418 F.2d 146, 154 (7th Cir. 1969); and communications received from third parties cannot be made privileged by conveyance to an attorney, *Hickman v. Taylor,* 329 U.S. 495, 508 (1947). Further, a third party may not assert the privilege or complain on appeal that the client's claim of privilege was erroneously rejected. *Cf. U.S. v. Silverman,* 430 F.2d 106, 120-22 (2d Cir.), *modified,* 439 F.2d 1198 (2d Cir. 1970), *cert. denied,* 402 U.S. 953 (1971).

It is not enough that the subject of the communication is the product of the attorney-client relationship. *Mead Data Central, Inc. v. U.S. Dept. of Air Force,* 566 F.2d 242 (D.C. Cir. 1977). *See U.S. v. Pipkins,* 528 F.2d 559, 562-63 (5th Cir.), *cert. denied,* 426 U.S. 952 (1976). To be protected, the communication must be confidential. *U.S. v. Merrell,* 303 F. Supp. 490, 492 (N.D.N.Y. 1969). *See U.S. v. Friedman,* 445 F.2d 1076, 1085 (9th Cir.), *cert. denied,* 404 U.S. 958 (1971). It is not privileged if it is made in the presence of a third party. *U.S. v. Blackburn,* 446 F.2d 1089, 1091 (5th Cir. 1971), *cert. denied,* 404 U.S. 1017 (1972). *See also U.S. v. Lechoco,* 542 F.2d 84 (D.C. Cir. 1976); *U.S. v. Gordon-Nikkar,* 518 F.2d 972 (5th Cir. 1975). Furthermore, a communication is not privileged if the communication was made with the intent or understanding that it be imparted to third parties. *U.S. v. Merrell*, 303 F. Supp. at 493. A specific concern for confidentiality, however, is not necessary for invocation of the privilege. *U.S. v. Buckley*, 586 F.2d 498 (5th Cir. 1978), *cert. denied*, 440 U.S. 982 (1979).

Communication to, or the presence of, certain third parties, such as a clerk, agent, or secretary of either the lawyer or the client, who are necessary to provide the legal service or to make the communication, does not destroy the privilege. *Himmelfarb v. U.S.*, 175 F.2d 924, 939 (9th Cir.), *cert. denied*, 338 U.S. 860 (1949). *See Young v. Taylor*, 466 F.2d 1329, 1332 (10th Cir. 1972); *U.S. v. Kovel*, 296 F.2d 918, 920-21 (2d Cir. 1961). The privilege extends to communications to, or in the presence of, an accountant if made in confidence for the purpose of obtaining legal advice from the attorney. *U.S. v. Kovel*, 296 F.2d at 922.

The privilege does not protect an accountant's papers prepared while employed by the taxpayer even though that accountant is subsequently employed by the taxpayer's attorney. *U.S. v. Brown*, 349 F. Supp. 420, 426 (N.D. Ill. 1972), *aff'd*, 478 F.2d 1038 (7th Cir. 1973). There is no privilege where, after advice is received from the attorney, the client makes the communications available to the accountant for purposes unrelated to seeking legal advice. *In re Horowitz*, 482 F.2d 72, 81 (2d Cir.), *cert. denied*, 414 U.S. 867 (1973).

A document that is not confidential to begin with does not become so merely because it is communicated in private to an attorney. *Fisher v. U.S., supra* (documents used to prepare tax returns and transferred to attorneys subject to subpoena). However, documents in the hands of an attorney supplied by a client to obtain legal assistance are protected by the attorney-client privilege from compulsory disclosure, if in the hands of the client the documents would be privileged under the fifth amendment. *See, e.g., In re Grand Jury Proceedings*, 632 F.2d 1033 (3d Cir. 1980). In *U.S. v. Silverman*, 430 F.2d 106, 120-22 (2d Cir.), *modified*, 439 F.2d 1198 (2d Cir. 1970), *cert. denied*, 402 U.S. 953 (1971), the court held the privilege inapplicable to an attorney's report describing the minutes of a labor union, the minute book itself being a public record.

The privilege applies in any legal proceeding, whether judicial, *Continental Oil Co. v. U.S.*, 330 F.2d 347, 349-50 (9th Cir. 1964), or administrative, *CAB v. Air Transport Ass'n of America*, 201 F. Supp. 318 (D.D.C. 1961). One need not be a party to invoke the privilege, and the privilege is not destroyed by a grant of immunity. *U.S. v. Pappadio*, 346 F.2d 5, 9 (2d Cir. 1965), *vacated on other grounds*, 384 U.S. 364 (1966). An attorney may claim the privilege in a grand jury proceeding. However, to do so an attorney must establish the elements of the privilege for each question asked. *Matter of Walsh,* 623 F.2d 489 (7th Cir. 1980), *cert. denied,* 449 U.S. 994 (1981).

The privilege applies only to statements made and advice given concerning legal services. *In re Bonanno, supra.* Some courts have not deemed work by an attorney in preparation of tax returns to be legal in nature. *See, e.g., U.S. v. Davis, supra; Canaday v. U.S.,* 354 F.2d 849 (8th Cir. 1966); *Olender v. U.S.,* 210 F.2d 795 (9th Cir. 1965). However, others have deemed such work sufficiently legal to fall within the scope of the attorney-client privilege. *See Colton v. U.S.,* 306 F.2d 633 (2d Cir. 1962), *cert. denied,* 371 U.S. 951 (1963).

There is no privilege for the identity or physical characteristics and mental condition of a client. *U.S. v. Ponder,* 475 F.2d 37, 39 (5th Cir. 1973); *In re Semel,* 411 F.2d 195 (3d Cir.), *cert. denied,* 396 U.S. 905 (1969); *U.S. v. Kendrick,* 331 F.2d 110 (4th Cir. 1964). Likewise, there is no privilege for the fact and conditions of the attorney-client employment relationship, including the existence of a retainer and the amount of the fee, *In re January 1976 Grand Jury,* 534 F.2d 719 (7th Cir. 1976); *In re Semel, supra,* or whether the attorney has advised a client or provided services for him on a certain matter, *Colton v. U.S., supra. But see In re Special Grand Jury No. 81-1,* 676 F.2d 1005 (4th Cir. 1982), for a discussion of preliminary showing which must be made before attorney for target of investigation may be subpoenaed before the grand jury. The privilege will attach, however, to a client's identity where its revelation would amount to a disclosure of a confidential communication, as where the substance of a communication has already been revealed but not its source. *Colton v. U.S., supra. See also In re Grand Jury Proceedings (Pavlick),* 663 F.2d 1057 (5th Cir. 1981), where court approved assertion of the privilege where a lawyer refused to divulge the name of a person who consulted him regarding prior criminal acts and who paid fees for others involved in the same matter. Even if the disclosure is not within the attorney-client privilege, an attorney may claim the fifth amendment privilege regarding an answer that would be compelled self-incriminating testimony. *Matter of Grand Jury Empanelled Feb. 14, 1978,* 603 F.2d 469 (3d Cir. 1979); *In re Grand Jury Proceedings (Berkley and Co., Inc.),* 629 F.2d 548 (8th Cir. 1980).

Communications between an attorney and his client about a crime or fraud to be committed sometime in the future are not privileged. *U.S. v. Zolin,* 109 S. Ct. 2619 (1989); *In re Grand Jury Proceedings,* 674 F.2d 309, 310 (4th Cir. 1982); *U.S. v. Hoffa,* 349 F.2d 20, 37 (6th Cir. 1965), *aff'd,* 385 U.S. 293 (1966). The crime-fraud exception need not necessarily be established by independent evidence, i.e., without reference to the contested statements themselves. An *in camera* examination of the statements may occur where there is a showing of a factual basis adequate to support a good faith belief by a reasonable person that an *in camera* review of the materials would reveal evidence to establish the crime-fraud exception to the privilege. Privileged materials may not be used to establish the preliminary determination. *U.S. v. Zolin, supra.*

### § 1919. — — Waiver.

The privilege must be "(a) claimed and (b) not waived by the client." The privilege belongs to the client. *U.S. v. Kahn,* 251 F. Supp. 702, 709 (S.D.N.Y.), *aff'd,* 366 F.2d 259, 265 (2d Cir.), *cert. denied,* 385 U.S. 948 (1966). *See Garner v. Wolfinbarger,* 430 F.2d 1093, 1096 (5th Cir. 1970), *cert. denied,* 401 U.S. 974 (1971). It can be claimed by him alone, although a lawyer is "duty-bound" to claim the privilege on behalf of a client, even when the client is not a part of the proceeding in which disclosure is sought. *Republic Gear Co. v. Borg Warner,* 381 F.2d 551, 556 (2d Cir. 1967). An attorney can neither invoke the privilege for his own benefit when his client desires to waive it, nor waive the privilege without his client's consent. *Id. See also U.S. v. Juarez,* 573 F.2d 267 (5th Cir.), *cert. denied,* 439 U.S. 915 (1978). In a bankruptcy proceeding, authority to waive the bankrupt corporation's attorney-client privilege may be exercised exclusively by the trustee. *Commodity Futures Trading Comm'n v. Weintraub,* 471 U.S. 343 (1985); *In re Citibank v. Andros,* 666 F.2d 1192 (8th Cir. 1981). One of jointly interviewed prospective clients cannot waive the privilege as to all participants in the interview. *In re Auclair,* 961 F.2d 65 (5th Cir. 1992).

The general rule on waiver is that, once there has been disclosure to a third party of a confidential communication by the client or by the attorney with the client's permission, such communication is no longer privileged. *In re John Doe Corp.,* 675 F.2d 482, 488-89 (2d Cir. 1982); *In re Horowitz,* 482 F.2d 72 (2d Cir.), *cert. denied,* 414 U.S. 867 (1973); *U.S. v. Aronoff,* 466 F. Supp. 855 (S.D.N.Y. 1979). But disclosure of only a slight amount of privileged information may be insufficient to constitute a waiver. *See, e.g., Champion Intern. Corp. v. International Paper Co.,* 486 F. Supp. 1328 (N.D. Ga. 1980).

Where the disclosure is partial, courts have held that the privilege is waived for the yet unrevealed communications only to the extent that they are relevant to that part of the communication already disclosed. *See Hearn v. Rhay,* 68 F.R.D. 574 (E.D. Wash. 1975); *Magida v. Continental Can Co.,* 12 F.R.D. 74, 77 (S.D.N.Y. 1951); *U.S. v. Monti,* 100 F. Supp. 209, 212 (E.D.N.Y. 1951). The mere failure to invoke the privilege without a disclosure of confidential information is not a waiver. *U.S. v. Jacobs,* 322 F. Supp. 1299, 1303 (C.D. Cal. 1971).

Fairness may dictate waiver of the privilege, as when the confidential communications are a material issue in the judicial proceedings. *See U.S. v. Mierzwicki,* 500 F. Supp. 1331 (D. Md. 1980). Similarly, a claim of reliance on advice of counsel may waive the privilege regarding that advice. *Id.* In *U.S. v. Miller,* 600 F.2d 498 (5th Cir.), *cert. denied,* 444 U.S. 955 (1979), when the defendant asserted a defense of good faith reliance on advice of counsel, the government was permitted to cross-examine the defendant on that point and about the contents of a letter to him from his attorney, notwithstanding a claim that the letter was privileged.

Generally, a waiver occurs when the attorney and client become adverse parties, as where a breach of duty is alleged. *See* Graham C. Lilly, *An Introduction to the Law of Evidence* (1978) at 334; *U.S. v. McCambridge,* 551 F.2d 865, 873-74 (1st Cir. 1977); *Johnson v. U.S.,* 542 F.2d 941, 942 (5th Cir. 1976), *cert. denied,* 430 U.S. 934 (1977). A habeas corpus petition based on communications between the petitioner and his trial attorney constituted a waiver of the client's privilege against disclosure, and the attorney was free to disclose all relevant facts at a hearing. *U.S. ex rel. Richardson v. McMann,* 408 F.2d 48, 53 (2d Cir. 1969), *vacated on other grounds,* 397 U.S. 759 (1970). *See U.S. v. Bostic,* 206 F. Supp. 855, 857 (D.D.C. 1962), *aff'd,* 317 F.2d 143 (D.C. Cir. 1953).

In balancing the privilege against social policy, courts have found no waiver when the disclosure was made inadvertently while complying with a court discovery order in a civil suit, *IBM v. U.S.,* 471 F.2d 507 (2d Cir. 1972), *appeal and petition for mandamus dismissed,* 480 F.2d 293 (2d Cir.), *cert. denied,* 416 U.S. 979 (1973), or when disclosure was made pursuant to settlement negotiations, *IBM v. Sperry Rand Corp.,* 44 F.R.D. 10, 13 (D. Del. 1968). The court in *Diversified Industries, Inc. v. Meredith, supra,* held that only a limited waiver occurred in relation to a separate civil case upon voluntary disclosure of privileged material pursuant to an SEC subpoena in a different and nonpublic proceeding. However, in *Byrnes v. IDS Realty Trust,* 85 F.R.D. 679 (S.D.N.Y. 1980), the court distinguished *Meredith, supra,* and held that the privilege had not been waived for purposes of a private securities fraud suit brought by individuals who were not parties to an SEC investigation in which voluntary disclosures were made. However, where disclosure was made for use by a third party in a United States Patent Office interference proceeding, it was held to be a waiver of the privilege for all third persons. *In re Natta,* 48 F.R.D. 319, 322 (D. Del.), *aff'd on other grounds,* 410 F.2d 187 (3d Cir. 1969). Not protected within the privilege were letters between the corporation's president and its lawyer which were recovered from a trash dumpster located in the parking lot because the client did not take sufficient precautions against disclosure, such as using a paper shredder. *Suburban Sew 'N Sweep, Inc. v. Swiss-Bernina, Inc.,* 91 F.R.D. 254, 257 (N.D. Ill. 1981).

## § 1920. — Work-Product Doctrine.

Materials not within the attorney-client privilege may be covered by the work product doctrine, which applies to both criminal and civil litigation. The doctrine reflects the strong "public policy underlying the orderly prosecution and defense of legal claims" and protects materials prepared by an attorney acting for a client in anticipation of litigation. *Hickman v. Taylor,* 329 U.S. 495, 514-15 (1947). *See also U.S. v. Nobles,* 422 U.S. 225 (1975) (information gathered by an agent at the direction of the attorney can fall within the scope of the attorney's work product). Under Rule 16 of the Federal Rules of Criminal Procedure, the work product of both the prosecution and defense are exempt from disclosure in discovery, except as provided in the Jencks Act (18 U.S.C. § 3500). Unlike the attorney-client privilege, the work-product doctrine may be asserted by either the client or the attorney. *In re Special September Grand Jury II,* 640 F.2d 49 (7th Cir. 1980); *In re Grand Jury Proceedings,* 604 F.2d 798 (3d Cir. 1979).

The work product doctrine privilege can be waived, as when an attorney attempts to make testimonial use of work product materials. *See* discussion in *U.S. v. Nobles,* 422 U.S. at 239. It is also waived where the corporate client submitted its investigative counsel's report and notes to the SEC under a voluntary disclosure program. *In re Sealed Case,* 676 F.2d 793, 809 (D.C. Cir. 1982). *See also* Rule 26(b)(3), Fed. R. Civ. P., which permits disclosure of work product upon a showing of undue hardship. While this rule applies to civil cases, federal courts have extended it to criminal cases.

The attorney work-product doctrine as the attorney-client privilege, is not available to protect on-going fraud by an attorney or his agent, *Matter of Grand Jury Empanelled October 18, 1979, supra,* or by a client, *In re Special September 1978 Grand Jury II,* 640 F.2d 49 (7th Cir. 1980). However, even when fraud by the client is alleged, the doctrine may still protect the attorney's mental impressions, opinions, and legal theories. *Id. See also In re Grand Jury Proceedings (FCM Corp.),* 599 F.2d 1224 (3d Cir. 1979).

## § 1921. — Physician-Patient Privilege.

The physician-patient privilege, unlike the attorney-client privilege, did not exist at common law. It later was established in about half the states as a statutory innovation. Under Rule 501 of the Federal Rules of Evidence, however, the privileges of witnesses are governed by the rules of common law except where a federal statute otherwise provides. Therefore, in the absence of such a statute, the physician-patient privilege has been held inapplicable in the federal courts. *U.S. v. Mullings,* 364 F.2d 173, 176 n.2 (2d Cir. 1966). *See U.S. v. Harper,* 450 F.2d 1032, 1035 (5th Cir. 1971); *U.S. v. Kovel,* 296 F.2d 918, 921 (2d Cir. 1961). *But see Ramer v. U.S.,* 411 F.2d 30, 39 (9th Cir.), *cert. denied,* 396 U.S. 965 (1969).

Although the *Mullings* and *Harper* cases appear to have resolved the question of the general inapplicability of the privilege, at least in the Second and Fifth Circuits, that does not mean all physician-patient communications will be admissible. There may be circumstances where, because of the need for medical treatment, such communications are involuntary and thus inadmissible under traditional concepts. *Haynes v. Washington,* 373 U.S. 503 (1963); *Culombe v. Connecticut,* 367 U.S. 568 (1961); *U.S. v. Mullings,* 364 F.2d 173 (2d Cir. 1966). Furthermore, in the case of *Hawaii Psychiatric Society v. Ariyoshi,* 481 F. Supp. 1028 (D. Hawaii 1979), a district court applied the concepts of confidentiality and the privacy-based right to seek treatment in enjoining the enforcement of a Hawaii statute authorizing administrative warrants to search psychiatrists' confidential Medicaid patient files.

Incriminating statements made during the course of a compulsory psychiatric exam cannot be used on the issue of guilt. 18 U.S.C. § 4244. Such use is permissible on the issue of competency to stand trial or sanity at the time of the offense, however. Generally, the basis for this proscription is the fifth amendment privilege against self-incrimination, and not the physician-patient privilege. *See Estelle v. Smith,* 451 U.S. 454 (1981); *Gibson v. Zahradnick,* 581 F.2d 75 (4th Cir.), *cert. denied,* 439 U.S. 996 (1978); *U.S. v. Reifsteck,* 535 F.2d 1030 (8th Cir. 1976); *U.S. v. Alvarez,* 519 F.2d 1036 (3d Cir. 1975); *U.S. v. Julian,* 469 F.2d 371 (10th Cir. 1972); *U.S. v. Harper,* 450 F.2d 1032 (5th Cir. 1971); *U.S. v. Bohle,* 445 F.2d 54 (7th Cir. 1971); *U.S. v. Driscoll,* 399 F.2d 135 (2d Cir. 1968). Furthermore, notice of a court-ordered examination by a psychiatrist regarding competency does not give adequate notice to the defendant that he is being examined for criminal responsibility, such that the psychiatrist could testify as to the latter at trial. *U.S. v. Driscoll, supra.*

## § 1922. — Reporter-Source Privilege.

The Supreme Court has declined to recognize a broad testimonial privilege for reporters. *Branzburg v. Hayes,* 408 U.S. 665 (1972). However, a qualified privilege may exist in certain situations pursuant to federal common law as recognized in Rule 501 of the Federal Rules of Evidence, and may be more readily available where the public interest in effective criminal law enforcement is not a factor. *See Carey v. Hume,* 492 F.2d 631 (D.C. Cir. 1974). In *Riley v. City of Chester,* 612 F.2d 708 (3d Cir. 1979), the court recognized a reporter's qualified common-law privilege to refuse to divulge a confidential source. This privilege may extend to unpublished materials in the hands of the reporter. *U.S. v. Cuthbertson,* 630 F.2d 139 (3d Cir. 1980). The privilege must be balanced with the obligations of the citizenry and the defendant's rights. *See Branzburg v. Hayes,* 408 U.S. at 710. This privilege can be overcome by a showing that the material sought (1) is evidentiary and relevant, (2) is not reasonably procurable through due diligence and is necessary for preparation in advance of trial, and (3) is the subject of a good faith request and not a "fishing expedition." *U.S. v. Nixon,* 418 U.S. 683, 699-700 (1974); *U.S. v. Cuthbertson,* 630 F.2d at 145. *See also Zerelli v. Bell,* 458 F. Supp. 26 (D.D.C. 1978), *aff'd sub nom Zerelli v. Smith,* 656 F.2d 705 (D.C. Cir. 1981).

The trial court may require the reporter to submit the subpoenaed documents for an *in camera* inspection so the court can determine if the qualified privilege applies. *See U.S. v. Cuthbertson, supra.* Similar guidelines have been adopted by the Department of Justice for subpoenas to reporters or for their telephone records. The keystone of the policy is "to strike the proper balance between the public's interest in the free dissemination of ideas and information and the public's interest in effective law enforcement and the fair administration of justice." 28 C.F.R. § 50.10(a)(1981).

## § 1923. Government Privilege — Identities of Informants.

The law is settled that the government may refuse to disclose the identities of its informants at trial. *McCray v. Illinois,* 386 U.S. 300 (1967); *Roviaro v. U.S.,* 353 U.S. 53 (1957); *U.S. v. Van Orsdell,* 521 F.2d 1323 (2d Cir. 1975), *cert. denied,* 423 U.S. 1059 (1976). The rationale underlying this privilege was expressed in *Roviaro,* 353 U.S. at 59:

> The purpose of the privilege is the furtherance and protection of the public interest in effective law enforcement. The privilege recognizes the obligation of citizens to communicate their knowledge of the commission of crimes to law-enforcement officials and, by

preserving their anonymity, encourages them to perform that obligation.

The privilege, however, is not absolute. Where the defendant can show that disclosure is necessary to insure a "fair trial," the informant's identity must be revealed. *See U.S. v. Hanna,* 341 F.2d 906, 907 (6th Cir. 1965); *U.S. v. Coke,* 339 F.2d 183, 184-85 (2d Cir. 1964). *See also U.S. v. Silva,* 580 F.2d 144 (5th Cir. 1978); *U.S. v. McManus,* 560 F.2d 747 (6th Cir. 1977), *cert. denied,* 434 U.S. 1047 (1978); *U.S. v. Tucker,* 552 F.2d 202 (7th Cir. 1972). Furthermore, when the underlying purpose for the informant privilege is gone, "the privilege no longer applies." *Roviaro v. U.S.,* 353 U.S. at 60.

In *Roviaro,* the court stated that where the "disclosure of an informer's identity ... is relevant and helpful to the defense of an accused, or is essential to a fair determination of a cause, the privilege must give way." 353 U.S. at 60-61. The Court, however, recognized that there was "no fixed rule" and that disclosure of the informant's identity "must depend on the particular circumstances of each case, taking into consideration the crime charged, the possible defenses, the possible significance of the informant's testimony and other relevant factors." *Id.* at 62. The determination on disclosure is within the discretion of the trial court. *U.S. v. Soles,* 482 F.2d 105 (2d Cir.), *cert. denied,* 414 U.S. 1027 (1973). The government's intention to assert the privilege and resist defense demand for disclosure should be made clear promptly to prevent any misunderstanding and prejudice. *U.S. v. Truesdale,* 400 F.2d 620, 623 (2d Cir. 1968). A mere request for disclosure of the informant's identity is generally held to be insufficient. *U.S. v. Mainello,* 345 F. Supp. 863, 881-82 (E.D.N.Y. 1972). Speculation of helpfulness will not compel disclosure, *U.S. v. Trejo-Zambrano,* 582 F.2d 460 (9th Cir.), *cert. denied,* 439 U.S. 1005 (1978); nor will the mere possibility of obtaining relevant testimony, *U.S. v. Moreno,* 588 F.2d 490 (5th Cir.), *cert. denied,* 441 U.S. 936 (1979). *See also U.S. v. Ortega,* 471 F.2d 1350, 1357-59 (2d Cir. 1972), *cert. denied,* 411 U.S. 948 (1973). Rather, disclosure is only required upon the trial court's determination that the need for information by the person seeking disclosure outweighs the government's claim of privilege. *In re U.S.,* 565 F.2d 19 (2d Cir. 1977), *cert. denied,* 436 U.S. 962 (1978).

The extent of the informant's participation in the crime charged is a significant factor in deciding whether his identity should be disclosed. A mere witness or tipster is not necessarily an "informant" whose identity must be disclosed. *U.S. v. Lewis,* 671 F.2d 1025, 1026-27 (7th Cir. 1982); *U.S. v. Alonzo,* 571 F.2d 1384 (5th Cir.), *cert. denied,* 439 U.S. 847 (1978); *U.S. v. Oliver,* 570 F.2d 397 (1st Cir. 1978). Absent a

showing the informant was present on the occasions cited in the indictment, disclosure is not required. *U.S. v. Robinson,* 530 F.2d 1076 (D.C.
Cir. 1976). In *Roviaro v. U.S., supra,* disclosure was required because
the informant was an essential participant in the offense, having actually purchased the narcotics from the defendant. *Accord, U.S. v. Lloyd,*
400 F.2d 414, 415-16 (6th Cir. 1968); *Portomene v. U.S.,* 221 F.2d 582,
583-84 (5th Cir. 1955). But mere presence of the informant during a
transaction may not require disclosure of the identity. *U.S. v. Alonzo,*
571 F.2d 1384 (5th Cir.), *cert. denied,* 439 U.S. 847 (1978). The same is
true when the informant has played only a small role, or is unlikely to
make any material contribution. *See U.S. v. Morris,* 568 F.2d 396 (5th
Cir. 1978); *Simpson v. Kreiger,* 565 F.2d 390 (6th Cir.), *cert. denied,* 435
U.S. 946 (1978).

Where the informant merely introduces the defendant to an undercover agent and thereafter plays no other significant role, disclosure
will not be required without some special showing of prejudice; nor will
disclosure be ordered where the testimony of the informant would only
be cumulative. *U.S. v. Diaz,* 655 F.2d 580, 588 (5th Cir. 1981), *cert.
denied,* 102 S. Ct. 1257 (1982); *U.S. v. Russ,* 362 F.2d 843 (2d Cir.), *cert.
denied,* 385 U.S. 923 (1966). *See U.S. v. Pelley,* 572 F.2d 264 (10th Cir.
1978); *U.S. v. Estrella,* 567 F.2d 1151 (1st Cir. 1977); *U.S. v. McManus,*
560 F.2d 747 (6th Cir. 1977), *cert. denied,* 434 U.S. 1047 (1978).

Denial of a request for disclosure of the informant in a search warrant affidavit was not error where there was no evidence that disclosure would help the defense, facts furnished by this source were cumulative, and the informant's knowledge was not essential to the presentation of the government's case. *U.S. v. Sherman,* 576 F.2d 292 (10th
Cir.), *cert. denied,* 439 U.S. 913 (1978). *See also U.S. v. Alexander,* 559
F.2d 1339 (5th Cir. 1977), *cert. denied,* 434 U.S. 1078 (1978). Similarly,
where the information provided was too attenuated to be essential to
the defense, disclosure of the informant's identity was not mandatory.
*U.S. v. Hare,* 589 F.2d 242 (5th Cir. 1979). However, where the informant was the only witness in a position to buttress or contradict the
agent's testimony and the defendant alleged the informant might have
a revenge motive, disclosure of the informant's identity was required.
*U.S. v. Silva, supra.*

Upon a showing that the defendant's participation in the crime was
the result of entrapment by the informant, disclosure is required. *Cf.
U.S. v. Simonetti,* 326 F.2d 614 (2d Cir. 1964); *U.S. v. White,* 324 F.2d
814, 816 (2d Cir. 1963). But, where the government's proof at trial
indicates a predisposition to commit the crime as a matter of law, error,
if any, in failing to disclose the informer's identity may be harmless.

*U.S. v. Eddings,* 478 F.2d 67, 70-72 (6th Cir. 1973). *See also U.S. v. Fredia,* 319 F.2d 853, 854 (2d Cir. 1963).

Where hearsay evidence derived from an informant is the basis for the issuance of a search warrant, but there is a substantial basis for crediting the hearsay, the court will not require disclosure of the informant's identity. *Jones v. U.S.,* 362 U.S. 257, 271-72 (1960).

Independent verification of an informant's information lessens the necessity of disclosure of the informant's identity to safeguard against fabrication. *See U.S. v. Comissiong,* 429 F.2d 834, 837-39 (2d Cir. 1970). *See also U.S. v. Allen,* 566 F.2d 1193 (3d Cir. 1977), *cert. denied,* 435 U.S. 926 (1978); *U.S. v. Carneglia,* 468 F.2d 1084, 1088-89 (2d Cir. 1972), *cert. denied,* 410 U.S. 945 (1973).

To compel disclosure, a defendant must show that the informant's testimony would probably be material to a substantial issue in the case. *See Encinas-Sierras v. U.S.,* 401 F.2d 228 (9th Cir. 1968); *U.S. v. Franzese,* 392 F.2d 954 (2d Cir. 1968), *vacated per curiam on other grounds,* 394 U.S. 310 (1969). *See also U.S. v. Willis,* 473 F.2d 450 (6th Cir.), *cert. denied,* 412 U.S. 908 (1973).

The timing of disclosure and the particular circumstances of each case, as well as the state of the proceedings at which the issue arises, for example, at a suppression hearing rather than a trial, are also significant factors. *See, e.g., McCray v. Illinois,* 386 U.S. 300 (1967). Disclosure must be timely enough to provide the benefits intended, such as an opportunity to adequately interview the witness. *See U.S. v. Opager,* 589 F.2d 799 (5th Cir. 1979). *But see U.S. v. Hyatt,* 565 F.2d 229 (2d Cir. 1977), in which any error was held to have been cured by disclosure of the informant's identity at the close of defendant's direct testimony and where the identity, and perhaps the whereabouts, of the informant were known to the defendant. Where it appears that the defendant may benefit from disclosure, but the government claims a compelling need to protect the informant, an *in camera* hearing may be necessary for a determination of whether disclosure is required. *Suarez v. U.S.,* 582 F.2d 1007 (5th Cir. 1978).

The government is not the guarantor of the informant's presence at trial, *U.S. v. Montoya,* 676 F.2d 428, 431 (10th Cir. 1982); *U.S. v. Prada,* 451 F.2d 1319 (2d Cir. 1971); although it may be required to give reasonable assistance to the defense in locating the witness and securing his appearance, *U.S. v. Turbide,* 558 F.2d 1053, 1060 (2d Cir.), *cert. denied,* 434 U.S. 934 (1977). The defense cannot rely on the government's calling all witnesses on a witness list, and, absent evidence the informant was crucial to the defense of entrapment, cannot rely on the inclusion of the informant's name on a witness list. *U.S. v. Fuentes,* 563 F.2d 527 (2d Cir.), *cert. denied,* 434 U.S. 959 (1977).

*See also* Chapter 7, § 713, *supra.*

### § 1924. Other Privileges.

The Rules as originally submitted to Congress provided for nine specific nonconstitutional privileges. This approach was rejected, and Rule 501, Fed. R. Evid. provides that privileges "shall be governed by the principles of the common law as they may be interpreted by the courts of the United States in the light of reason and experience." The Senate Report stated that judicial "recognition of a privilege based on a confidential relationship and other privileges should be determined on a case-by-case basis." S. Rep. No. 1277, 93d Cong. 2d Sess. 13 (1974).

In interpreting this provision it has been held that there is no accountant-client privilege, *U.S. v. Arthur Young & Co.,* 465 U.S. 805 (1984); *Couch v. U.S.,* 409 U.S. 322 (1973); no emancipated child-parent privilege, *U.S. v. Ismail,* 756 F.2d 1253 (6th Cir. 1985); and no in-law privilege, *In re Matthews,* 714 F.2d 223 (2d Cir. 1983); and no sibling privilege, *In re Grand Jury Proceedings, Sealed,* 607 F. Supp 1002 (S.D.N.Y. 1985).

A psychotherapist-patient privilege has been both recognized, *In re Zuniga,* 714 F.2d 632 (6th Cir.), *cert. denied,* 104 S. Ct. 426 (1983), and rejected, *U.S. v. Lindstrom,* 698 F.2d 1154 (11th Cir. 1982). One court left open the issue of whether a scholar's privilege exists. *In re Grand Jury Subpoena Dated January 4, 1984,* 750 F.2d 223 (2d Cir. 1984).

# CHAPTER 20

## OPINION EVIDENCE

§ 2001. Testimony of Lay Witnesses.
§ 2002. Testimony of Expert Witnesses.
§ 2003. — Scientific, Technical, or Specialized Knowledge.
§ 2004. — Basis of Opinion Testimony by Experts.
§ 2005. — Ultimate Issue Rule.
§ 2006. — Hypothetical Questions.
§ 2007. — Court-Appointed Experts.

## § 2001. Testimony of Lay Witnesses.

Rule 701 of the Federal Rules of Evidence provides that opinion testimony by lay witnesses is limited to those opinions or inferences that are "(a) rationally based on the perception of the witness and (b) helpful to a clear understanding of his testimony or the determination of a fact in issue." The primary purpose of this rule is to allow nonexpert witnesses to give opinion testimony when, as a matter of practical necessity, events which they have personally observed cannot otherwise be fully presented to the court or jury. However, this rule does not permit a lay witness to express an opinion on matters that are beyond the realm of common experience and which require the special skill and knowledge of an expert witness. *Randolph v. Collectramatic, Inc.,* 590 F.2d 844 (10th Cir. 1979).

The limitation contained in Rule 701(a) "is the familiar requirement of first-hand knowledge or observation." Advisory Committee's Note; *U.S. v. McClintic,* 570 F.2d 685 (8th Cir. 1978); *U.S. v. Jackson,* 569 F.2d 1003 (7th Cir.), *cert. denied,* 437 U.S. 907 (1978). Consequently, testimony of lay witnesses is admissible if predicated on concrete facts within their own observation and recollection, *i.e.,* perceived from their own senses, as distinguished from opinions and conclusions drawn from such perceptions. *Randolph v. Collectramatic, Inc.,* 590 F.2d at 847-48. The brevity of observation does not affect the admission of the opinion, but only the weight of the evidence. *U.S. v. Lawson,* 653 F.2d 299, 303 (7th Cir. 1981), *cert. denied,* 102 S. Ct. 1017 (1982) (three FBI agents who observed defendant on only one occasion were permitted to give their opinions that he was sane).

The limitation of Rule 701(b) "is phrased in terms of requiring testimony to be helpful in resolving issues." Advisory Committee's Note. This differs from the practical necessity test used in many common-law jurisdictions. *U.S. v. Smith,* 550 F.2d 277, 281 (5th Cir.), *cert. denied,* 434 U.S. 841 (1977).

Whether a lay witness will be permitted to testify about any matter of opinion is a preliminary determination within the sound discretion of the trial court. *Bohannon v. Pegelow,* 652 F.2d 729, 732 (7th Cir. 1981); *Randolph v. Collectramatic, Inc.,* 590 F.2d at 847; *John Hancock Mutual Life Insurance Co. v. Dutton,* 585 F.2d 1289, 1294 (5th Cir. 1978); *Cardwell v. Chesapeake & Ohio Railway Co.,* 504 F.2d 444, 448 (6th Cir. 1974). It rarely is held to be reversible error to admit such testimony. *See U.S. v. Trenton Potteries Co.,* 273 U.S. 392 (1927); *Randolph v. Collectramatic, Inc.,* 590 F.2d at 847-48; *U.S. v. Butcher,* 557 F.2d 666 (9th Cir. 1977); *U.S. v. Pierson,* 503 F.2d 173 (D.C. Cir. 1974); *SEC v. Texas Gulf Sulphur Co.,* 446 F.2d 1301 (2d Cir.), *cert. denied,* 404 U.S. 1005 (1971); *Stone v. U.S.,* 385 F.2d 713 (10th Cir. 1967), *cert. denied,* 391 U.S. 966 (1968). *But see U.S. v. Calhoun,* 544 F.2d 291 (6th Cir. 1976), where a trial court did abuse its discretion in admitting lay opinion testimony.

Rule 704 states that "testimony in the form of an opinion or inference otherwise admissible is not objectionable because it embraces an ultimate issue to be decided by the trier of fact." The Advisory Committee's Note states that the "ultimate issue" rule (prohibiting witnesses from giving opinions on the ultimate issue of the case) is specifically abolished by Rule 704 as applied to qualified lay and expert opinions. *U.S. v. Arrasmith,* 557 F.2d 1093 (5th Cir. 1977) (border patrol officer was permitted to testify as to odor of marijuana); *Arcement v. Southern Pacific Transportation Co.,* 517 F.2d 729 (5th Cir. 1975) (nonexpert may testify to what a reasonable person would do); *Panger v. Duluth, Winnipeg & Pacific Railroad Co.,* 490 F.2d 1112 (8th Cir. 1974) (nonexpert employee permitted to testify whether accident could have been avoided). This rule is subject to the requirements of Rules 701 and 702 that the opinion be helpful to the trier of fact and to Rule 403 considerations, however.

The opinions or conclusions of lay witnesses have been admitted into evidence on various matters:

(1) The apparent physical condition of a person, *U.S. v. Mastberg,* 503 F.2d 465, 469-70 (9th Cir. 1974); *Niagara Fire Ins. Co. v. Muhle,* 208 F.2d 191, 196 (8th Cir. 1953); *Cox v. U.S.,* 103 F.2d 133, 135 (7th Cir. 1939);

(2) The apparent mental capacity or condition of a person, *Queenan v. Oklahoma,* 190 U.S. 548 (1903); *Verzosa v. Merrill Lynch, Pierce, Fenner, and Smith, Inc.,* 589 F.2d 974 (9th Cir. 1978); *John Hancock Mutual Life Insurance Co. v. Dutton,* 585 F.2d at 1294; *U.S. v. Smith,* 550 F.2d 277 (5th Cir.), *cert. denied,* 434 U.S. 841 (1977); *Evalt v. U.S.,* 359 F.2d 534 (9th Cir. 1966); *Smith v. U.S.,* 353 F.2d 838 (D.C. Cir.

1965), *cert. denied,* 384 U.S. 910 (1966); however, the witness must have had a reasonable opportunity to observe and form an opinion for his testimony to be admissible, *U.S. v. Kossa,* 562 F.2d 959 (5th Cir. 1977), *cert. denied,* 434 U.S. 1075 (1978); *Kaufman v. U.S.,* 350 F.2d 408, 414-15 (8th Cir. 1965), *cert. denied,* 383 U.S. 951 (1966); the brevity of the observation goes to weight, not admissibility, *U.S. v. Lawson,* 653 F.2d at 303; *U.S. v. Greene,* 497 F.2d 1068, 1084 (7th Cir. 1974), *cert. denied,* 420 U.S. 909 (1975); *U.S. v. Minor,* 459 F.2d 103 (5th Cir. 1972); *Mason v. U.S.,* 402 F.2d 732 (8th Cir. 1968), *cert. denied,* 394 U.S. 950 (1969); a witness cannot testify about his own mental condition, *Frisone v. U.S.,* 270 F.2d 401 (9th Cir. 1959);

(3) The unexpressed state of mind of an accused, *U.S. v. Phillips,* 593 F.2d 553, 558 (4th Cir. 1978), *cert. denied,* 441 U.S. 947 (1979); *U.S. v. McClintic,* 570 F.2d 685 (8th Cir. 1978) (accomplice-witness permitted to give opinion that the defendant knew goods were fraudulently obtained when such opinion was based on the witness' perceptions); *U.S. v. Smith,* 550 F.2d 277 (5th Cir.), *cert. denied,* 434 U.S. 841 (1977) (witness in CETA fraud prosecution permitted to give opinion that defendant knew and understood requirements of CETA); *Bohannon v. Pegelow,* 652 F.2d at 733 (witness gave opinion that arrest was motivated by racial prejudice);

(4) The meaning of words spoken to the witness by one whom he knew well, *U.S. v. Fayer,* 573 F.2d 741 (2d Cir.), *cert. denied,* 439 U.S. 831 (1978) (witness in perjury prosecution allowed to testify what defendant's words meant to him); *U.S. v. Cioffi,* 493 F.2d 1111 (2d Cir.), *cert. denied,* 419 U.S. 917 (1974); *Wiley v. U.S.,* 257 F.2d 900 (8th Cir. 1958);

(5) The handwriting of another, *Rogers v. Ritter,* 79 U.S. 317 (1870); *U.S. v. Gomez,* 603 F.2d 147 (10th Cir.), *cert. denied,* 444 U.S. 969 (1979) (and cases cited therein); *cf. Ryan v. U.S.,* 384 F.2d 379 (1st Cir. 1967) (witness may testify that a piece of writing was written by a specified individual only if that opinion is based on experience in handwriting analysis or on familiarity with the handwriting of the individual in question); Rule 901(b)(2) of the Federal Rules of Evidence requires that familiarity must not have been acquired for purposes of the litigation; 28 U.S.C. § 1731 makes admissible the admitted or proved handwriting of any person for comparison to determine the genuineness of other handwriting attributed to such person; Rule 901(b)(3) provides that the trier of fact may make its own determination without any opinion testimony at all; *see U.S. v. Ranta,* 482 F.2d 1344 (8th Cir. 1973); *Strauss v. U.S.,* 311 F.2d 926 (5th Cir.), *cert. denied,* 373 U.S. 910 (1963); *Brandon v. Collins,* 267 F.2d 731 (2d Cir. 1959); *Desimone v. U.S.,* 227 F.2d 864 (9th Cir. 1955);

(6) The value of the owner's property, or his employer's property, and the value of the damage inflicted on it, *J. & H. Auto Trim Co. v. Bellefonte Ins. Co.*, 677 F.2d 1365, 1371 n.8 (11th Cir. 1982); *Justice v. Pennzoil Co.*, 598 F.2d 1339 (4th Cir.), *cert. denied*, 444 U.S. 967 (1979); *Rich v. Eastman Kodak Co.*, 583 F.2d 435 (8th Cir. 1978); *Meredith v. Hardy*, 554 F.2d 764 (5th Cir. 1977) (owner always competent to value his own property); *Baldwin Cooke Co. v. Keith Clarke, Inc.*, 420 F. Supp. 404 (N.D. Ill. 1976);

(7) The speed of moving objects or vehicles, *Leadbetter v. Glaisyer*, 44 F.2d 350 (9th Cir. 1930); *Attal v. Pennsylvania Railroad Co.*, 212 F. Supp. 306 (W.D. Pa.), *aff'd per curiam*, 323 F.2d 363 (3d Cir. 1963); however, the witness must indicate the basis for his estimate of speed, *Ho v. U.S.*, 331 F.2d 144 (9th Cir. 1964); *Gilliand v. Ruke*, 280 F.2d 544 (4th Cir. 1960); *Carpino v. Kuehnle*, 54 F.R.D. 28 (W.D. Pa. 1971), *aff'd*, 474 F.2d 1339 (3d Cir. 1973) (witness could not testify where he observed for only a split second);

(8) The "irregularity" of the conduct of a business, *U.S. v. Cotter*, 60 F.2d 689 (2d Cir.), *cert. denied*, 287 U.S. 666 (1932);

(9) The identification of a person in a photograph, *U.S. v. Young Buffalo*, 591 F.2d 506 (9th Cir. 1979), *cert. denied*, 441 U.S. 950 (1979); *U.S. v. Butcher*, 557 F.2d 666 (9th Cir. 1977); *U.S. v. Robinson*, 544 F.2d 110 (2d Cir. 1976), *cert. denied*, 434 U.S. 1050 (1978);

(10) The fact that defendant knew that merchandise had been fraudulently obtained, *U.S. v. McClintic*, 570 F.2d 685 (8th Cir. 1978); *see also U.S. v. Freeman*, 514 F.2d 1184 (10th Cir. 1975);

(11) General identification, *U.S. v. Brown*, 540 F.2d 1048 (10th Cir. 1976), *cert. denied*, 429 U.S. 1100 (1977) (if there is an opportunity for personal observation, then testimony is allowed by lay person for personal identification);

(12) Comparison of marijuana, *U.S. v. Honneus*, 508 F.2d 566 (1st Cir. 1974), *cert. denied*, 421 U.S. 948 (1975);

(13) Impact on another's personality because of disfigurement, *Drayton v. Jiffee Chemical Corp.*, 591 F.2d 352 (6th Cir. 1978);

(14) Conduct, *i.e.*, what a person appeared to be doing, based on personal observation and common experience as to physical condition or actions of such person, *U.S. v. Alexander*, 415 F.2d 1352 (7th Cir. 1969), *cert. denied*, 397 U.S. 1014 (1970).

## § 2002. Testimony of Expert Witnesses.

## § 2003. — Scientific, Technical, or Specialized Knowledge.

An intelligent evaluation of facts is often difficult or impossible without the application of some scientific, technical, or other specialized knowledge. The most common source of this knowledge is the expert witness. *Kline v. Ford Motor Co.*, 523 F.2d 1067 (9th Cir. 1975); *U.S. v. R. J. Reynolds Tobacco Co.*, 416 F. Supp. 313 (D.N.J. 1976). As distinguished from a lay witness, who, except under Rule 701, may not give opinion testimony, an expert witness possesses knowledge and skill not possessed by the ordinary witnesses. The expert is in a superior position, because of his training and experience, to draw inferences and conclusions from underlying evidentiary facts.

There is no fixed or general rule that dictates when and if expert testimony on a particular topic is required. However, if that topic requires special experience then only the testimony of one having such special experience should be received. *Randolph v. Collectramatic, Inc.*, 590 F.2d 844, 848 (10th Cir. 1979).

Under Rule 702 a witness may be qualified as an expert "by knowledge, skill, experience, training, or education." Fields of knowledge for which experts may be used include not only scientific and technical but also specialized knowledge. An expert is not viewed in a narrow sense, *e.g.*, architects or physicians, but as a person qualified by knowledge, skill, experience, training, or education, *Soo Line R.R. Co. v. Fruehauf Corp.*, 547 F.2d 1365 (8th Cir. 1977); *U.S. v. Brown*, 540 F.2d 1048 (10th Cir. 1976), *cert. denied*, 429 U.S. 1100 (1977); and there is no requirement that the expert witness be outstanding in his field or have certificates of training, or memberships in professional organizations, *U.S. v. Barker*, 553 F.2d 1013, 1024 (6th Cir. 1977). The rule is to be broadly interpreted in qualifying a person as an expert. *Mannino v. Intern., Mfg. Co.*, 650 F.2d 846 (6th Cir. 1981). Rule 702 is not limited to experts in the strictest sense of the word but also encompasses a large group called "skilled" witnesses such as owners, bankers, and landowners testifying on the value of property. *U.S. v. Johnson*, 575 F.2d 1347, 1360 (5th Cir. 1978), *cert. denied*, 440 U.S. 907 (1979) (coconspirator who testified at conspiracy-to-import-marijuana trial held properly permitted to give expert opinion as to the origin of marijuana he smoked during conspiracy, even though he had no special training or education, where his qualifications came entirely from "the experience of being around a great deal and smoking it"); *Soo Line R. R. Co. v. Fruehauf Corp.*, 547 F.2d at 1377; *U.S. v. Bermudez*, 526 F.2d 89, 97-98 (2d Cir. 1975), *cert. denied*, 425 U.S. 970 (1976) (DEA agent held qualified as expert to testify that white powder was cocaine); *U.S. v. Atkins*, 473 F.2d 308 (8th Cir.), *cert. denied*, 412 U.S. 931 (1973) (heroin addict qualified as expert in identification of heroin).

Although Rule 702 broadens the range of admissible expert testimony, *U.S. v. Barker*, 553 F.2d at 1024, the rule does not alter the well-established principle that the assessment of the expert's qualifications is a matter within the discretion of the trial court which should not be disturbed on appeal unless manifestly erroneous. *Perkins v. Volkswagen of America, Inc.,* 596 F.2d 681 (5th Cir. 1979); *N.V. Maatschappij, Etc. v. A. O. Smith Corp.,* 590 F.2d 415, 418 (2d Cir. 1978); *U.S. v. Viglia,* 549 F.2d 335 (5th Cir.), *cert. denied,* 434 U.S. 834 (1977) (physician who had degrees in medicine and pharmacy, but no experience in treating obesity, could properly provide expert opinion in prosecution for issuance of prescriptions for controlled substances without legitimate medical reason). (A common tactical manuever, sometimes encouraged by the court, is the practice of stipulating to the opposing expert's qualifications to eliminate an impressive litany of such from the jury's hearing. This tactic may be improper in some instances. "[A] jury can better assess the weight to be accorded an expert's opinion if the witness is permitted to explain his qualifications." *Murphy v. National R.R. Passenger Corp.,* 547 F.2d 816, 817 (4th Cir. 1977).)

Under Rule 702, factors to be considered by a trial court in deciding whether to admit expert testimony are (1) whether expert testimony will assist the trier of fact, (2) whether the witness is qualified as an expert, and (3) whether the expert has a sufficient acquaintance with the basic facts, either through personal observation or on the basis of a proper hypothetical question, to express an opinion. *See generally U.S. v. Scavo,* 593 F.2d 837 (8th Cir. 1979); *U.S. v. Watson,* 587 F.2d 365 (7th Cir. 1978), *cert. denied,* 439 U.S. 1132 (1979); *U.S. v. Johnson,* 575 F.2d 1347 (5th Cir. 1978), *cert. denied,* 440 U.S. 907 (1979).

Whether a witness is shown to be qualified as an expert is a preliminary question to be determined by the trial court. *U.S. v. Thomas,* 676 F.2d 531, 538 (11th Cir. 1982). If the expert testimony is admitted, then it is for the trier of fact to decide what weight, if any, is to be given to the testimony. *U.S. v. Stifel,* 433 F.2d 431, 438-39 (6th Cir. 1970), *cert. denied,* 401 U.S. 994 (1971) (expert testimony concerning neutron activation analysis properly permitted). Whether such evidence will be admitted lies within the sound discretion of the trial judge, and his decision will not be reversed unless he abuses that discretion, *Hamling v. U.S.,* 418 U.S. 87, 108 (1974); *Perkins v. Volkswagen of America, Inc.,* 596 F.2d at 682; *U.S. v. Watson,* 587 F.2d at 369; *U.S. v. Moten,* 564 F.2d 620, 629 (2d Cir.), *cert. denied,* 434 U.S. 959 (1977); *U.S. v. Stifel,* 433 F.2d at 441; *Wolford v. U.S.,* 401 F.2d 331 (10th Cir. 1968); *White v. U.S.,* 399 F.2d 813 (8th Cir. 1968); *Harris v. Afran Transport Co.,* 252 F.2d 536 (3d Cir. 1958), or there is a showing that the trial court's decision is "manifestly erroneous," *U.S. v. Brown,* 557 F.2d 541 (6th Cir. 1977); *U.S. v. Viglia,* 549 F.2d at 336-37.

A necessary predicate to the admission of expert testimony is that the principle upon which the expert opinion is based must be nonspeculative, and the principles and procedures that underlie it must be sufficiently established to have gained general acceptance in the particular field or scientific community to which it belongs. *U.S. v. Distler,* 671 F.2d 954, 962 (6th Cir. 1982) (gas chromatograph analysis); *U.S. v. Cyphers,* 553 F.2d 1064 (7th Cir.), *cert. denied,* 434 U.S. 843 (1977) (microscopic comparison of hair samples proper); *U.S. v. Franks,* 511 F.2d 25 (6th Cir.), *cert. denied,* 422 U.S. 1042 (1975) (voiceprint analysis properly admitted); *Frye v. U.S.,* 293 F. 1013 (D.C. Cir. 1923). The decision as to the state of the technology in the field is a decision for the trial court, and neither "newness nor lack of absolute certainty in a test suffices to render it inadmissible in court. Every useful new development must have its first day in court." *U.S. v. Stifel,* 433 F.2d at 438. In cases where the trial court finds the state of the technology too speculative, it should disallow the proffered expert opinion. *U.S. v. Tranowski,* 659 F.2d 750, 755-56 (7th Cir. 1981) (dating a photograph by measuring the lengths of shadows on the photo and the use of a sun chart too untrustworthy); *U.S. v. Fosher,* 590 F.2d 381 (1st Cir. 1979) (expert opinion evidence relating to perception and memory of eyewitnesses and effects on eyewitnesses' identification held not reliable and not generally accepted in scientific community); *U.S. v. Watson,* 587 F.2d at 369 (exclusion of expert testimony regarding unreliability of cross-racial and cross-ethnic eyewitnesses' identification was proper); *U.S. v. Benveniste,* 564 F.2d 335 (9th Cir. 1977) (trial court affirmed in not permitting defendant to introduce expert psychiatric testimony concerning psychological susceptibility to inducement and lack of predisposition, proffered to establish entrapment defense); *U.S. v. Brown,* 557 F.2d at 557 (ion microprobic analysis not generally accepted in scientific community — too experimental to provide acceptable basis for expert testimony). Although the testimony must not be speculative, there is no requirement that the expert's opinion be expressed in terms of absolute certainty. *U.S. v. Cyphers,* 553 F.2d at 1072 (opinion that, after microscopic comparison, hair samples could have come from defendant, not too speculative and admissible under Rule 702).

Notwithstanding the expanded use of expert testimony under Rule 702, an additional factor to be taken into consideration by the trial court in determining its application in criminal cases, over and above those set forth in Rule 702, is the potentially unfair prejudicial impact of the expert's testimony upon the substantial rights of the accused. Where the probative value of the expert testimony is outweighed by the prejudicial effect upon substantial rights, the expert testimony may be excluded under Rule 403. *U.S. v. Green,* 548 F.2d 1261 (6th Cir. 1977) (improperly admitted prejudicial expert testimony concerning distribution of drug DMT). *See also U.S. v. Amaral,* 488 F.2d 1148, 1152 (9th Cir. 1973).

The credibility to be accorded conflicting expert opinions is up to the jury. The trial court only considers whether the expert will aid the trier of fact in arriving at the truth. *U.S. v. Brown,* 557 F.2d at 556; *U.S. v. Barker,* 553 F.2d 1013, 1024 (6th Cir. 1977); *U.S. v. Makris,* 535 F.2d 899 (5th Cir. 1976), *cert. denied,* 430 U.S. 954 (1977). Conflicting conclusions drawn by experts, where they are based on generally accepted and reliable scientific principles, go to the weight of the testimony, not its admissibility. *U.S. v. Brown,* 557 F.2d at 556; *U.S. v. Franks,* 511 F.2d at 33. Generally, properly admitted expert testimony may be given such weight as the fact finder thinks circumstances dictate. *Skar v. City of Lincoln, Nebraska,* 599 F.2d 253 (8th Cir. 1979).

The fact that one party may offer more experts on a particular subject than the other party is not controlling. The issue is to be determined, not by the number of expert witnesses who may testify on behalf of either side, but by the quality of their testimony. *U.S. v. Shepard,* 538 F.2d 107, 110 (6th Cir. 1976); *U.S. v. Handy,* 454 F.2d 885, 888 (9th Cir. 1971), *cert. denied,* 409 U.S. 846 (1972).

Expert testimony introduced by one party may be rejected by the trier of fact even when the opposing party has introduced no expert testimony to contradict it. *U.S. v. Mota,* 598 F.2d 995 (5th Cir. 1979) (jury may find testimony on issue of defendant's sanity rebutted by observations of laymen); *U.S. v. Dube,* 520 F.2d 250 (1st Cir. 1975); *U.S. v. Lutz,* 420 F.2d 414 (3d Cir.), *cert. denied,* 398 U.S. 911 (1970). *But see U.S. v. Smith,* 437 F.2d 538 (6th Cir. 1970) (brief observation by two lay witnesses does not raise a question of fact sufficient to counter defendant's prima facie case of insanity); *Brock v. U.S.,* 387 F.2d 254 (5th Cir. 1967) (testimony of three witnesses, only one of whom had recently seen the defendant, was not sufficient for the jury to reject the testimony of the psychiatric expert).

An expert can be compelled to testify in his area of expertise, as there is no constitutional or statutory privilege not to do so, and there is no need to show the unavailability of other experts. *Kaufman v. Edelstein,* 539 F.2d 811 (2d Cir. 1976).

Opinions of expert witnesses have been admitted into evidence on a wide variety of matters:

(1) The mental capacity or condition of a person, *U.S. v. Davis,* 523 F.2d 1265 (5th Cir. 1975) (except that under Rule 704(b) the expert may not testify concerning the ultimate issue whether the defendant

had the mental state or condition constituting an element of the crime or defense thereto); the results of compulsory psychiatric examinations are admissible on the issue of sanity, but the use of an incriminating statement made during a compulsory examination is impermissible on the issue of guilt; *Gibson v. Zahradnick,* 581 F.2d 75 (4th Cir.), *cert. denied,* 439 U.S. 996 (1978) (and cases cited therein); *but see U.S. v. Reason,* 549 F.2d 309 (4th Cir. 1977); *U.S. v. Reifsteck,* 535 F.2d 1030 (8th Cir. 1976); *U.S. v. Matos,* 409 F.2d 1245 (2d Cir. 1969), *cert. denied,* 397 U.S. 927 (1970); that experts may differ in their opinions concerning the mental condition of a defendant does not mean, in and of itself, that there is a reasonable doubt as to sanity, *U.S. v. Urbanis,* 490 F.2d 384, 386 (9th Cir.), *cert. denied,* 416 U.S. 944 (1974); *U.S. v. Ortiz,* 488 F.2d 175 (9th Cir. 1973). The issue of a defendant's mental condition should be determined from all the evidence rather than from the opinions of experts alone, *U.S. v. Fortune,* 513 F.2d 883, 890-91 (5th Cir.), *cert. denied,* 423 U.S. 1020 (1975); *Mims v. U.S.,* 375 F.2d 135, 143 (5th Cir. 1967);

(2) The teachings and purposes of the Communist Party, *Frankfeld v. U.S.,* 198 F.2d 679 (4th Cir. 1952), *cert. denied,* 344 U.S. 922 (1953);

(3) Current propaganda themes, *U.S. v. German-American Vocational League, Inc.,* 153 F.2d 860 (3d Cir.), *cert. denied,* 328 U.S. 833 (1946);

(4) Value of particular property, *Sartor v. Arkansas Natural Gas Corp.,* 321 U.S. 620, 627 (1944);

(5) Cause of death, *Clay County Cotton Co. v. Home Life Insurance Co.,* 113 F.2d 856 (8th Cir. 1940);

(6) Bookkeeping and income tax returns, *U.S. v. Gray,* 507 F.2d 1013 (5th Cir.), *cert. denied,* 423 U.S. 824 (1975); *U.S. v. Augustine,* 189 F.2d 587 (3d Cir. 1951);

(7) Retail value of consumer goods, *Cave v. U.S.,* 390 F.2d 58 (8th Cir.), *cert. denied,* 392 U.S. 906 (1968);

(8) Markings and stamps on bank checks, *U.S. v. Mustin,* 369 F.2d 626 (7th Cir. 1966);

(9) Mechanics of how the numbers game or bookmaking organizations operate, *U.S. v. Barletta,* 565 F.2d 985 (8th Cir. 1977) (testimony of an FBI agent who had done considerable investigative work in the area); *Moore v. U.S.,* 394 F.2d 818 (5th Cir. 1968), *cert. denied,* 393 U.S. 1030 (1969); *see U.S. v. Scavo,* 593 F.2d 837 (8th Cir. 1979) (agent allowed to testify as to defendant's role in bookmaking operation);

(10) The modus operandi of criminal schemes, *U.S. v. Stull,* 521 F.2d 687 (6th Cir. 1975), *cert. denied,* 423 U.S. 1059 (1976) (testimony of postal inspector describing a mail fraud scheme); *U.S. v. Jackson,* 425

F.2d 574 (D.C. Cir. 1970) (testimony of operation of pickpocket scheme);

(11) Handwriting, *U.S. v. Reece,* 547 F.2d 432 (8th Cir. 1977); *U.S. v. Green,* 523 F.2d 229 (2d Cir. 1975), *cert. denied,* 423 U.S. 1074 (1976); *U.S. v. Galvin,* 394 F.2d 228 (3d Cir. 1968); *U.S. v. Acosta,* 369 F.2d 41 (4th Cir. 1966), *cert. denied,* 386 U.S. 921 (1967); *Wood v. U.S.,* 357 F.2d 425 (10th Cir.), *cert. denied,* 385 U.S. 866 (1966);

(12) The technical operation of the United States Mint, *U.S. v. Sheiner,* 410 F.2d 337 (2d Cir.), *cert. denied,* 396 U.S. 825 (1969);

(13) The ineffectiveness of a weight-reducing drug, *U.S. v. Andreadis,* 366 F.2d 423 (2d Cir. 1966), *cert. denied,* 385 U.S. 1001 (1967);

(14) Spectrograms or "voiceprints," *U.S. v. Williams,* 583 F.2d 1194 (2d Cir. 1978), *cert. denied,* 439 U.S. 1117 (1979); *U.S. v. Baller,* 519 F.2d 463 (4th Cir.), *cert. denied,* 423 U.S. 1019 (1975); *U.S. v. Franks,* 511 F.2d 25 (6th Cir.), *cert. denied,* 422 U.S. 1042 (1975); *but see U.S. v. Addison,* 498 F.2d 741 (D.C. Cir. 1974) (spectrographic identification not then sufficiently accepted in scientific community);

(15) The operation of equipment for the purpose of producing counterfeit currency, *U.S. v. Wilson,* 451 F.2d 209 (5th Cir. 1971), *cert. denied,* 405 U.S. 1032 (1972);

(16) The genuineness of government bonds, *U.S. v. Martin,* 459 F.2d 1009 (9th Cir.), *cert. denied,* 409 U.S. 864 (1972);

(17) The source of marijuana, *U.S. v. Johnson,* 575 F.2d 1347 (5th Cir. 1978), *cert. denied,* 440 U.S. 907 (1979);

(18) Firearms and ballistics, *Davis v. Freels,* 583 F.2d 337 (7th Cir. 1978); *U.S. v. Bowers,* 534 F.2d 186 (9th Cir.), *cert. denied,* 429 U.S. 942 (1976);

(19) Architecture, *Scholz Homes, Inc. v. Wallace,* 590 F.2d 860 (10th Cir. 1979);

(20) Valuation of pecuniary loss, *Driscoll v. U.S.,* 456 F. Supp. 143 (D. Del. 1978), *aff'd,* 605 F.2d 1195 (1979); *D'Angelo v. U.S.,* 456 F. Supp. 127 (D. Del. 1978), *aff'd,* 605 F.2d 1194 (3d Cir. 1979);

(21) Aircraft, *Dychalo v. Copperloy Corp.,* 78 F.R.D. 146 (E.D. Pa.), *aff'd,* 588 F.2d 820 (3d Cir. 1978) (safety of loading ramp);

(22) Defective products, *Nanda v. Ford Motor Co.,* 509 F.2d 213 (7th Cir. 1974);

(23) Design, *Soo Line R.R. Co. v. Fruehauf Corp.,* 547 F.2d 1365, 1375-76 (8th Cir. 1977) (design of railroad cars); *Holmgren v. Massey-Ferguson, Inc.,* 516 F.2d 856 (8th Cir. 1975) (defective design of corn picker);

(24) Law, *U.S. v. Sturgis,* 578 F.2d 1296 (9th Cir.), *cert. denied,* 439 U.S. 970 (1978) (sentences customarily imposed by state courts);

(25) Narcotics, *U.S. v. Wolk,* 398 F. Supp. 405, 414-15 (E.D. Pa. 1975);

(26) Photographs, *U.S. v. Sellers,* 566 F.2d 884 (4th Cir. 1977) (expert on photographs allowed to assist the jury by explaining light, shadowy reflections);

(27) A defendant's susceptibility to influence where an entrapment defense has been raised, *U.S. v. Hill,* 655 F.2d 512, 516 (3d Cir. 1981).

An expert witness may identify and explain charts summarizing his own testimony or the testimony of other witnesses. *U.S. v. Gray,* 507 F.2d 1013 (5th Cir.), *cert. denied,* 423 U.S. 824 (1975); *U.S. v. Rath,* 406 F.2d 757 (6th Cir.), *cert. denied,* 394 U.S. 920 (1969). *See also U.S. v. Scales,* 594 F.2d 558 (6th Cir.), *cert. denied,* 441 U.S. 946 (1979) (expert not needed; agent who catalogued exhibit and who had knowledge of analysis of materials was permitted to summarize).

## § 2004. — Basis of Opinion Testimony by Experts.

Before the codification of the Federal Rules of Evidence, the traditional rule was that expert opinion testimony was inadmissible if based upon information obtained out of court from third parties. "The rationale behind this rule is that the trier of fact should not be presented with evidence grounded on otherwise inadmissible hearsay statements not subject to cross-examination and other forms of verification." *U.S. v. Sims,* 514 F.2d 147, 149 (9th Cir.), *cert. denied,* 423 U.S. 845 (1975); *Elgi Holding, Inc. v. Insurance Company of North America,* 511 F.2d 957, 959-60 (2d Cir. 1975). Under Rule 703, however, and in accord with the strong pre-Rule 703 trend, an expert is no longer tied to the restrictive limitations on the use of facts or data which, technically, may be hearsay. Whether the facts or data relied on by the experts are in evidence, or even could be in evidence, is not controlling where the facts or data relied upon are of the type reasonably relied upon by experts in this particular field. *Bauman v. Centex Corp.,* 611 F.2d 1115, 1120 (5th Cir. 1980). *See U.S. v. Genser,* 582 F.2d 292, 298 (3d Cir. 1978), *cert. denied,* 444 U.S. 928 (1979) (IRS expert properly permitted to rely on facts and data not admitted into evidence which fell within permissible standards of Rule 703); *U.S. v. Shields,* 573 F.2d 18 (10th Cir. 1978) (handwriting expert could properly rely on known exemplars of defendant's handwriting excluded from evidence on grounds that they contained impermissible references to defendant's prior criminal record); *Higgins v. Kinnebrew Motors, Inc.,* 547 F.2d 1223, 1226 (5th Cir. 1977) (expert was properly permitted to use figures taken from U.S. Department of Labor Bureau of Labor Statistics tables); *U.S. v. Golden,* 532 F.2d 1244 (9th Cir.), *cert. denied,* 429

U.S. 842 (1976) (DEA expert's opinion on market value of heroin was not rendered inadmissible due to its basis in part on information obtained from other undercover narcotics agents familiar with the markets involved); *U.S. v. Morrison,* 531 F.2d 1089 (1st Cir.), *cert. denied,* 429 U.S. 837 (1976) (FBI gambling expert was properly permitted to rely on notes and reports of others in arriving at opinion).

Generally, the facts or data upon which an expert bases his opinion can be derived from three possible sources: (1) the firsthand observations of the expert witness, such as a treating physician, *U.S. v. Reece,* 547 F.2d 432 (8th Cir. 1977); *Elgi Holding, Inc. v. Insurance Co. of North America,* 511 F.2d at 959-60; (2) presentation at the trial through hypothetical questions or having the expert attend the trial and hear testimony establishing the facts (thus, one expert can predicate his opinion on another expert's, if he normally relies on such in his profession); and (3) presentation of pertinent data to the expert outside of court other than by his own perception, *U.S. v. Genser,* 582 F.2d at 298-99; *U.S. v. Golden,* 532 F.2d at 1247-48; *U.S. v. Sims,* 514 F.2d at 149-50.

## § 2005. — Ultimate Issue Rule.

With the enactment of Rule 704 of the Federal Rules of Evidence, the ultimate issue rule, previously limiting expert testimony that would "invade the province of the jury" by touching upon ultimate issue, was formally abolished. With the exception of expert testimony concerning an opinion whether the defendant had the mental state or condition constituting an element of the crime or defense thereto, "[t]he approach to admission adopted by the Rules is simply whether an expert opinion will be helpful to the jury in understanding the evidence or determining a fact in issue." *Bauman v. Centex Corp.,* 611 F.2d 1115, 1120-21 (5th Cir. 1980); *U.S. v. Scavo,* 593 F.2d 837, 844 (8th Cir. 1979). If expert testimony is appropriately helpful, Rule 704 provides that the opinion given is not objectionable as an invasion of the province of the jury, notwithstanding that it may be on the very issue that the jury must decide. *U.S. v. Johnson,* 319 U.S. 503 (1943); *U.S. v. Webster,* 960 F.2d 1301 (5th Cir. 1992); *U.S. v. Scavo,* 593 F.2d at 843-44; *U.S. v. Davis,* 564 F.2d 840, 845 (9th Cir. 1977), *cert. denied,* 434 U.S. 1015 (1978).

This rule is subject both to the qualification of helpfulness to the trier of fact and to a Rule 403 weighing of probative value versus prejudicial effect. *U.S. v. Scavo,* 593 F.2d at 844; *Nielson v. Armstrong Rubber Co.,* 570 F.2d 272 (8th Cir. 1978); *U.S. v. Taylor,* 562 F.2d 1345 (2d Cir.), *cert. denied,* 432 U.S. 909 (1977); *U.S. v. Milton,* 555 F.2d

1198 (5th Cir. 1977); *U.S. v. McCoy*, 539 F.2d 1050 (5th Cir. 1976), *cert. denied*, 431 U.S. 919 (1977). The trial court has wide discretion in admitting such ultimate issue opinions. *Stoler v. Penn Central Transp. Co.*, 583 F.2d 896 (6th Cir. 1978); *United Telecommunications, Inc. v. American Television & Communications Corp.*, 536 F.2d 1310 (10th Cir. 1976). Thus, in a federal firearms prosecution, the testimony of a government expert that the defendant's weapon was a machine gun required to be registered under the law was held proper. *U.S. v. McCauley*, 601 F.2d 336, 339 (8th Cir. 1979). *See also U.S. v. Miller*, 600 F.2d at 500 (government expert accounting witness properly permitted to express opinion on ultimate issue that securities were obtained by fraud); *U.S. v. Masson*, 582 F.2d 961 (5th Cir. 1978) (FBI gambling expert permitted to testify that defendant was bookmaker rather than mere player); *U.S. v. Davis*, 564 F.2d 845 (in a prosecution of physician for unlawful prescription and distribution of controlled substances, expert was properly permitted to express opinion that the prescriptions were neither in usual course of professional practice nor for a legitimate medical purpose).

In one area, however, the expert may not testify as to the ultimate issue. Under Rule 704(b), an expert may not testify concerning whether the defendant had the mental state or condition constituting an element of the crime or defense thereto. Expert psychiatric testimony is "limited to presenting and explaining their diagnoses, such as whether the defendant had a severe mental disease or defect and what the characteristics of such a disease or defect, if any, may have been." S.R. No. 225, 98th Cong., 1st Sess. 230 *reprinted in* 1984 U.S. Code Cong. & Ad News 3182, 3412. The rule reaches "all such 'ultimate' issues, *e.g.*, premeditation in a homicide case, or lack of predisposition in entrapment." *Id*. at 231.

Notwithstanding the abolition of the ultimate issue rule, however, some courts are cautious not to permit expert testimony on legal conclusions as opposed to factual conclusions. An expert should not be permitted to testify whether a person's acts are a violation of law. That is a legal conclusion best left to the trial court's instructions and the verdict of the trier of fact. An expert's testimony may not properly act as a substitute for the court's instructions on applicable law. *U.S. v. Milton*, 555 F.2d 1198, 1204-05 (5th Cir. 1977).

### § 2006. — Hypothetical Questions.

The chief objective of Rule 705 is to eliminate the need for the lengthy hypothetical question; such questions are no longer mandatory. *U.S. v. Mangan*, 575 F.2d 32, 47 (2d Cir.), *cert. denied*, 439 U.S.

931 (1978). In any event, the expert may be required to disclose the underlying facts or data on cross-examination. Rule 705, Fed. R. Evid. If the expert had only seen, but did not rely on a certain report it may not be used for cross-examination if it was not admissible, *Bobb v. Modern Products, Inc.*, 648 F.2d 1051, 1055-56 (5th Cir. 1981). If, however, hypothetical questions are used, they should include all material facts necessary for the expert to draw rational conclusions. The question properly must be based upon facts already in the record. *Mears v. Olin*, 527 F.2d 1100 (8th Cir. 1975).

Whether a hypothetical question is a fair statement of all facts in the case is largely a determination within the discretion of the trial judge. *Shapiro, Bernstein & Co. v. Remington Records, Inc.*, 265 F.2d 263, 266-67 (2d Cir. 1959). *Alman Bros. Farms and Feed Mill, Inc. v. Diamond Laboratories, Inc.*, 437 F.2d 1295 (5th Cir. 1971).

### § 2007. — Court-Appointed Experts.

Before the enactment of Rule 706, the inherent power of a trial judge to appoint an independent expert was widely recognized. *Danville Tobacco Ass'n v. Bryant-Buckner Associates, Inc.*, 333 F.2d 202 (4th Cir. 1964), *cert. denied*, 387 U.S. 907 (1967); *Scott v. Spanjer Bros.*, 298 F.2d 928 (2d Cir. 1962). Rule 706 codifies this power and sets up the implementing details. Under Rule 706, the trial court has discretionary power to appoint an expert on its own motion or on the motion of any party. *Fugitt v. Jones*, 549 F.2d 1001 (5th Cir. 1977). The court is not required to appoint an expert when requested to do so by a party. *Georgia-Pacific Corp. v. U.S.*, 640 F.2d 328, 334 (Ct. Cl. 1980).

An expert witness must consent to the appointment, shall be informed of his duties by the court and may be called to testify by either party or the court. Rule 706(a), Fed. R. Evid. The expert shall receive reasonable compensation, Rule 706(b), Fed. R. Evid. and the court has the power to assess the fees of that expert to the parties in the litigation, *U.S. v. R. J. Reynolds Tobacco Co.*, 416 F. Supp. 313 (D.N.J. 1976). In its discretion the court may advise the jury that the court appointed the expert witness. Rule 706(c), Fed. R. Evid.

# CHAPTER 21

# HEARSAY AND EXCEPTIONS

§ 2100. Introduction.

§ 2101. Out-of-Court Statements.

§ 2102. Non-Hearsay.

§ 2103. — Non-Hearsay by Use.

§ 2104. — — Proof That a Statement Was Made.

§ 2105. — — To Show Effect on Listener's Conduct.

§ 2106. — — Res Gestae — Spontaneous, Contemporaneous Declarations.

§ 2107. — Non-Hearsay by Definition.

§ 2108. — — Prior Statement of a Witness.

§ 2109. — — — Inconsistent Statements.

§ 2110. — — — Consistent Statements.

§ 2111. — — — Pretrial Identification.

§ 2112. — — Admissions.

§ 2113. — — — Admissions by Defendant.

§ 2114. — — — Defendant's Adoptive Admissions.

§ 2115. — — — Vicarious and Representative Admissions.

§ 2116. — — — Declarations of Coconspirators.

§ 2117. Hearsay Exceptions — Availability of Declarant Immaterial.

§ 2118. — Present Sense Impression: Rule 803(1).

§ 2119. — Excited Utterances: Rule 803(2).

§ 2120. — Then Existing Mental, Emotional, or Physical Condition: Rule 803(3).

§ 2121. — Statements for Purposes of Medical Diagnosis or Treatment: Rule 803(4).

§ 2122. — Recorded Recollection: Rule 803(5).

§ 2123. — Records of Regularly Conducted Activity: Rule 803(6).

§ 2124. — Absence of Entries in Records Kept in Regularly Conducted Activity: Rule 803(7).

§ 2125. — Public Records and Reports: Rule 803(8).

§ 2126. — Records of Vital Statistics: Rule 803(9).

§ 2127. — Absence of Public Record or Entry: Rule 803(10).

§ 2128. — Records of Religious Organizations; Marriage, Baptismal, and Similar Certificates; and Family Records: Rule 803(11), (12), and (13).

§ 2129. — Records of Documents and Statements in Documents Affecting an Interest in Property: Rule 803(14) and (15).

§ 2130. — Statements in Ancient Documents: Rule 803(16).

§ 2131. — Market Reports, Commercial Publications: Rule 803(17).

§ 2132. — Learned Treatises: Rule 803(18).

§ 2133. — Reputation of Personal or Family History, Boundaries or General History, or Character: Rule 803(19), (20), and (21).

§ 2134. — Judgment of Previous Conviction: Rule 803(22).

§ 2135. — Judgment as to Personal, Family or General History, or Boundaries: Rule 803(23).

§ 2136. — Other Exceptions: Rule 803(24).

§ 2137. Hearsay Exceptions — Declarant Unavailable.

§ 2138. — Limitations.

§ 2139. — — Sixth Amendment Confrontation Clause.

§ 2140. — — Unavailability Sufficient to Qualify Under the Rule.

§ 2141. — Former Testimony: Rule 804(b)(1).
§ 2142. — Statement Under Belief of Impending Death: Rule 804(b)(2).
§ 2143. — Statements Against Interest: Rule 804(b)(3).
§ 2144. — — Statements Against Interest Generally.
§ 2145. — — Statements Against Penal Interest Offered to Exculpate.
§ 2146. — Statement of Personal or Family History: Rule 804(b)(4).
§ 2147. — Other Exceptions: Rule 804(b)(5).
§ 2148. Hearsay Within Hearsay.
§ 2149. Attacking and Supporting the Credibility of Declarant.

## § 2100. Introduction.

Rule 801(c) of the Federal Rules of Evidence defines hearsay in the following terms:

> "Hearsay" is a statement, other than one made by the declarant while testifying at the trial or hearing, offered in evidence to prove the truth of the matter asserted.

Further, Rule 802 provides that hearsay "is not admissible except as provided by these rules or by other rules prescribed by the Supreme Court pursuant to statutory authority or by Act of Congress." This limitation, therefore, bars admissibility of out-of-court statements only when they are offered to "prove the truth of the matter asserted" and when they do not fit an established exception to the rule of exclusion.

The form and content of the rules have the effect of presenting three basic questions where possible hearsay is involved. First, it must be determined if the evidence in question amounts to a statement, because only an out-of-court "statement" can be hearsay. Rule 801(a) defines "statement" as "(1) an oral or written assertion or (2) nonverbal conduct of a person, if it is intended by him as an assertion." Second, it must be determined if the statement is being offered to prove the truth of matter asserted in it and, if so, whether it may nevertheless be non-hearsay by definition. Rule 801(d) makes certain prior statements by a witness who testifies and is subject to cross-examination, certain statements deemed to be by a party-opponent, and certain out-of-court identifications all "not hearsay" by definition. Third, it must be determined if the hearsay is still admissible under one of the 29 exceptions provided in Rules 803 and 804 or for the limited purposes permitted under Rules 806 and 405.

Government use of hearsay in criminal cases may also be limited in certain situations by the confrontation clause of the sixth amendment. *See, e.g., Idaho v. Wright,* 110 S. Ct. 3139 (1990); *Bruton v. U.S.,* 391 U.S. 123 (1968). Ordinarily, however, the introduction of evidence which is permitted by a firmly rooted exception to the hearsay rule violates no constitutional guarantee. *White v. Illinois,* 112 S. Ct. 736

(1992); *Ohio v. Roberts,* 448 U.S. 56, 66 (1980); *California v. Green,* 399 U.S. 149, 155 (1970); *Salinger v. U.S.,* 272 U.S. 542 (1926).

## §2101. Out-of-Court Statements.

The hearsay rule is primarily applicable to statements that are assertions in words, either oral or written. Rule 801(a)(1), Fed. R. Evid. However, Rule 801(a)(2) provides that nonverbal conduct by a person may be a statement "if it is intended by him as an assertion." This provision significantly expands the admissibility of conduct or silence that might otherwise be excludable as hearsay. *See Donnelly v. U.S.,* 228 U.S. 243, 273 (1913). Under prior law, if conduct was offered to show the actor's belief and hence the truth of that belief, such conduct was inadmissible hearsay. *U.S. v. Pacelli,* 491 F.2d 1108 (2d Cir.), *cert. denied,* 419 U.S. 826 (1974). That is no longer true under the rules, unless it can be shown that the conduct was intended as an assertion. Examples of conduct intended to be an assertion are pointing out the location of a heroin source, *U.S. v. Caro,* 569 F.2d 411 (5th Cir. 1978), and selection of a name from a list, *U.S. v. Ross,* 321 F.2d 61 (2d Cir.), *cert. denied,* 375 U.S. 894 (1963).

The Advisory Committee's Note to Rule 801 makes clear, however, that "the rule is so worded as to place the burden upon the party claiming that the intention [to assert] existed" and that "ambiguous and doubtful cases will be resolved ... in favor of admissibility." The admissibility of conduct that may be viewed as assertive now requires a judicial determination whether the conduct was intended to be assertive. Rule 104(a), Fed. R. Evid.; *U.S. v. Mandel,* 591 F.2d 1347 (4th Cir. 1979).

## §2102. Non-Hearsay.

The general hearsay prohibition is applicable only when the out-of-court statement is offered to prove the truth of the assertion it contains. When the statement is offered to prove something other than the truth of what it contains, it is not hearsay and is not inadmissible for that reason. On this, the evidence rules and prior case law are in agreement. *U.S. v. Anderson,* 417 U.S. 211 (1974); *U.S. v. Bernes,* 602 F.2d 716 (5th Cir. 1979). There are several well-recognized non-hearsay, and therefore permissible, uses of extrajudicial statements, and a number of others are, in effect, created by definition in Rule 801.

## § 2103. — Non-Hearsay by Use.

## § 2104. — — Proof That a Statement Was Made.

Overheard threats by the victim against the defendant were admissible to show that they were made, and that ill-feelings existed. *U.S. v. Cline*, 570 F.2d 731 (8th Cir. 1978). Taped conversations of wagers and line information are admissible to show that the conversations took place, but not to prove that bets were made or the truth of the line information. *U.S. v. Boyd*, 566 F.2d 929 (5th Cir. 1978). In a mail fraud prosecution, evidence of untrue statements was received for the purpose of establishing that they were made. *U.S. v. Krohn*, 573 F.2d 1382 (10th Cir.), *cert. denied*, 436 U.S. 949 (1978). Evidence that a witness offered to give perjured testimony is admissible to prove making the offer. *Sawyer v. Barczak*, 229 F.2d 805 (7th Cir.), *cert. denied*, 351 U.S. 966 (1956). *See also Hicks v. U.S.*, 173 F.2d 570 (4th Cir.), *cert. denied*, 337 U.S. 945 (1949) (reports of conversations in which defendant's agent sought to influence a juror). In *U.S. v. Harvey*, 526 F.2d 529 (2d Cir. 1975), *cert. denied*, 424 U.S. 956 (1976), a prosecution charging a civil rights violation for the murder of a potential witness, statements made by the victim indicating his awareness of federal crimes committed by defendant were held admissible as tending to show that the defendant killed the victim because of that knowledge. The hearsay rule was inapplicable to testimony by defrauded investors regarding defendant's representations because they were offered merely to show the statements were made. *U.S. v. McDonnel*, 550 F.2d 1010 (5th Cir.), *cert. denied*, 434 U.S. 835 (1977). A government witness' testimony of threats made by defendant was held not hearsay because it was used to show consciousness of guilt and not the truth of the matter asserted. *U.S. v. Pate*, 543 F.2d 1148 (5th Cir. 1976). Testimony relating to the existence of an automobile theft report was admissible to prove that the car was reported stolen. *U.S. v. Jacobson*, 536 F.2d 793 (8th Cir.), *cert. denied*, 429 U.S. 864 (1976). (For a discussion of the purposes for the introduction of out-of-court declarations, *see U.S. v. Davis*, 551 F.2d 233 (8th Cir.), *cert. denied*, 431 U.S. 923 (1977).)

## § 2105. — — To Show Effect on Listener's Conduct.

A defendant union officer's testimony that former union presidents had told him constitutions were flexible and could be interpreted to fit local needs was not objectionable hearsay, because it was not offered to prove the truth of what past union presidents said but to show the effect such statements had on defendant's actions. *U.S. v. Rubin*, 591

F.2d 278 (5th Cir.), *cert. denied,* 444 U.S. 864 (1979). *See also U.S. v. Roberts,* 676 F.2d 1185, 1187-88 (8th Cir. 1982); *U.S. v. Abascal,* 564 F.2d 821 (9th Cir. 1977), *cert. denied,* 435 U.S. 953 (1978). In a bank robbery prosecution, a police officer's description of a vehicle, as transmitted to him, was admissible to prove why the officer stopped the car and was not objectionable hearsay. *U.S. v. Stout,* 599 F.2d 866 (8th Cir.), *cert. denied,* 444 U.S. 877 (1979).

### § 2106. — — Res Gestae — Spontaneous, Contemporaneous Declarations.

A statement is sometimes said to be admissible, irrespective of the hearsay rule, if it is a declaration that constitutes a part of the *res gestae* or "the thing done." Such a declaration is not really hearsay, however, simply because it is not offered to prove the truth of what was said. When the words spoken only explain the acts done, or when the declarations have an independent legal significance, hearsay is not involved. In *U.S. v. Annunziato,* 293 F.2d 373 (2d Cir.), *cert. denied,* 368 U.S. 919 (1961), a union business agent was prosecuted for receiving moneys from an employer. The court held that the hearsay rule did not prevent the admission of testimony by one witness that the deceased employer had told the witness to draw money for a second witness "to pay somebody," and testimony by the second witness that, upon handing him an envelope, the deceased employer asked him to take money to the defendant. In each instance, the circumstances of the declarations gave legal significance to otherwise ambiguous acts and completed the description of a material transaction.

A declaration of gift accompanying delivery of property is admissible when offered, not for its truth, but as part of the donative act. *U.S. v. White,* 377 F.2d 908 (4th Cir.), *cert. denied,* 389 U.S. 884 (1967) (testimony that a bank janitor had told defendant he had "dropped something" was held admissible to characterize defendant's subsequent conduct); *Shapiro v. U.S.,* 166 F.2d 240 (2d Cir.), *cert. denied,* 334 U.S. 859 (1948) (oral statements of deceased insured were admissible to remove ambiguity in policy).

### § 2107. — Non-Hearsay by Definition.

### § 2108. — — Prior Statement of a Witness.

Rule 801(d)(1) establishes as "not hearsay" certain prior statements of a witness who testifies and is subject to cross-examination.

## § 2109. — — — Inconsistent Statements.

Rule 801(d)(1) excludes from the hearsay definition such prior statements of a testifying witness if "the statement is (A) inconsistent with his testimony, and was given under oath subject to the penalty of perjury at a trial, hearing, or other proceeding, or in a deposition, or (B) consistent with his testimony and is offered to rebut an express or implied charge against him of recent fabrication or improper influence or motive ...." For purposes of the rule, a "partial or vague recollection is inconsistent with total or definite recollection." *U.S. v. Distler,* 671 F.2d 954, 958 (6th Cir. 1981).

Pretrial inconsistent statements of a witness have frequently raised the issue of whether they may be received in evidence as substantive proof of guilt or may be used only for the purpose of impeachment. Rule 801(d)(1)(A) substantially settles this issue by providing that, when the statement is "given under oath subject to the penalty of perjury at a trial, hearing, or other proceeding, or in a deposition," it is not hearsay and the inconsistent statement may be received as proof of guilt of the accused. Prior unsworn inconsistent statements of a witness remain hearsay and may not be considered as direct evidence of guilt. *U.S. v. Palacios,* 556 F.2d 1359 (5th Cir. 1977). A special agent's rebuttal testimony as to a contradictory statement made to him by a defense alibi witness was hearsay, and instructions were necessary to limit its use to impeachment and to avoid it being considered as substantive proof. *U.S. v. Ragghianti,* 560 F.2d 1376 (9th Cir. 1977). *See also U.S. v. Eddy,* 597 F.2d 430 (5th Cir. 1979), holding where there were inconsistencies between a witness' trial testimony and his preliminary hearing testimony, such inconsistent statements were admissible as substantive evidence and not merely for impeachment. *See also U.S. v. Plum,* 558 F.2d 568 (10th Cir. 1977). Prior inconsistent statements before a grand jury implicating defendant in an armed robbery were properly admitted as substantive evidence where the declarant testified at trial, was subject to cross-examination, and his testimony was inconsistent with his earlier statements. *U.S. v. Mosley,* 555 F.2d 191 (8th Cir.), *cert. denied,* 434 U.S. 851 (1977). *See also U.S. v. Morgan,* 555 F.2d 238 (9th Cir. 1977), which acknowledges that trial judges have a high degree of flexibility in deciding the exact point at which a prior statement is sufficiently inconsistent with a witness' trial testimony to permit its use in evidence; there was no abuse of discretion by the trial court in allowing two pages of a grand jury transcript to be received as an exhibit, the written form of the prior inconsistent statement providing no undue importance or improper emphasis to this substantive proof which is admitted for the truth of its contents.

"Other proceeding" includes interrogation under oath at a border station. Statements which are inconsistent with the trial testimony of illegal aliens are admissible for both impeachment value and evidence of guilt. *U.S. v. Coran,* 589 F.2d 70 (1st Cir. 1978); *U.S. v. Castro-Ayon,* 537 F.2d 1055 (9th Cir.), *cert. denied,* 429 U.S. 983 (1976).

## § 2110. — — — Consistent Statements.

Rule 801(d)(1)(B) provides that prior consistent statements are not hearsay and are admissible if offered to rebut an express or implied charge of recent fabrication, improper influence, or motive. The strict condition precedent to the reception of pretrial consistent declarations, therefore, is the presence of at least an attempt to show recent fabrication, improper influence or motive. There are four requirements for admissibility: "(1) the out-of-court declarant must testify at trial; (2) the declarant must be subject to cross-examination concerning the out-of-court declaration; (3) the out-of-court declaration must be consistent with the declarant's trial testimony; and (4) the evidence must be offered to rebut a charge of recent fabrication." *U.S. v. West,* 670 F.2d 675, 686 (7th Cir. 1982). In *U.S. v. Parry,* 649 F.2d 292 (5th Cir. 1981), testimony of defendant's mother (who was not the declarant) that the defendant had told her that the person on the phone was a narcotics agent was admissible not to show that the caller was a narcotics agent, but to establish that the defendant had knowledge of the agent's identity when the government's testimony was that he did not know that he knew the agent's identity. *U.S. v. Quinto,* 582 F.2d 224 (2d Cir. 1978), held that the proponent of the prior consistent statement has the burden of establishing that the statement is being offered to rebut charges of recent fabrication or that the prior consistent statement was made before any supposed motive to falsify arose. *See also U.S. v. Williams,* 573 F.2d 284 (5th Cir. 1978); *U.S. v. Weil,* 561 F.2d 1109 (4th Cir. 1977); *U.S. v. Lombardi,* 550 F.2d 827 (2d Cir. 1977); *U.S. v. Rinn,* 586 F.2d 113 (9th Cir. 1978).

## § 2111. — — — Pretrial Identification.

Rule 801(d)(1)(C) makes admissible as non-hearsay the out-of-court "identification of a person after perceiving him." This rule is conditioned upon the declarant testifying at trial and being subject to cross-examination concerning his out-of-court identification made while or after viewing the accused in non-suggestive photographic or corporeal lineup identification. *U.S. v. Owens,* 484 U.S. 554 (1988); *U.S. v. Lewis,* 565 F.2d 1248 (2d Cir. 1977), *cert. denied,* 435 U.S. 973 (1978); *U.S. v.*

*Marchand,* 564 F.2d 983 (2d Cir. 1977), *cert. denied,* 434 U.S. 1015 (1977). *But see U.S. v. Oaxaca,* 569 F.2d 518 (9th Cir.), *cert. denied,* 439 U.S. 926 (1978). Witnesses' testimony that they had previously said that a sketch made by a police artist on the day after the robbery looked like the robber was properly admitted, even though a prior identification was equivocal; the jury is entitled to give it such weight as it will after direct examination and cross-examination. *U.S. v. Moskowitz,* 581 F.2d 14 (2d Cir.), *cert. denied,* 439 U.S. 871 (1978); *U.S. v. Hudson,* 564 F.2d 1377 (9th Cir. 1977). Voice identification of one allegedly making ransom calls is included in the rule, with weight, not admissibility, being the issue. *U.S. v. Moore,* 571 F.2d 76 (2d Cir. 1978). A trial witness' prior identification may be introduced into evidence by a third party who was present at the original identification. *U.S. v. Elemy,* 656 F.2d 507, 508 (9th Cir. 1981).

Impermissibly suggestive identification procedures will, regardless of the evidence rule, render the evidence inadmissible. *Moore v. Illinois,* 434 U.S. 220 (1977); *Manson v. Brathwaite,* 432 U.S. 98 (1977); *Neil v. Biggers,* 409 U.S. 188 (1972); *Foster v. California,* 394 U.S. 440 (1969); *Stovall v. Denno,* 388 U.S. 293 (1967); *Gilbert v. California,* 388 U.S. 263 (1967).

### § 2112. — — Admissions.

Rule 801(d)(2) provides that an admission by a party-opponent is not hearsay if the statement is offered against him and is (1) his statement, (2) a statement that he has adopted, (3) a statement by a person authorized to make the statement, (4) a statement by this agent concerning a matter within the scope of his agency, or (5) a statement by a coconspirator during the course and in furtherance of the conspiracy. The statement need not have been against the party's interest at the time it was made so long as it is contrary to his interest at trial. *Auto-Owners Ins. Co. v. Jensen,* 667 F.2d 714, 722 (8th Cir. 1981). By denominating admissions "not hearsay," the Federal Rules of Evidence resolve for the federal courts the academic controversy whether admissions are "exceptions" to the hearsay rule or simply not hearsay at all. *See U.S. v. Puco,* 476 F.2d 1099 (2d Cir.), *cert. denied,* 414 U.S. 844 (1973).

### § 2113. — — — Admissions by Defendant.

Judicial admissions, including stipulations and guilty pleas, are included in Rule 801(d)(2)(A). Where neither is withdrawn with the consent of the court, each is binding and conclusive against the accused. However, if a guilty plea is withdrawn and a not guilty pleas is substituted, the former guilty plea is not admissible in a trial held on the substituted plea, nor may the judge or prosecutor comment on it. Rule 11(e)(6), Fed. R. Crim. P.; Rule 410, Fed. R. Evid. *See Kercheval v. U.S.,* 274 U.S. 220 (1927). The pertinent provisions of the Federal Rules of Criminal Procedure and the Federal Rules of Evidence also preclude use of "offers" to plead guilty or of "any statements made in connection with" such plea or offer.

Provided that statements attributed to the accused pass constitutional muster, *i.e.,* they are freely, voluntarily, and intelligently given with full knowledge and understanding of rights, such extrajudicial declarations are not hearsay and are admissible as part of the government's rebuttal evidence even though they could have been produced during the case-in-chief. *U.S. v. Evans,* 572 F.2d 455 (5th Cir.), *cert. denied,* 439 U.S. 870 (1978); *U.S. v. Cline,* 570 F.2d 731 (8th Cir. 1978); *U.S. v. Porter,* 544 F.2d 936 (8th Cir. 1976). Statements to non-law enforcement persons are included in the rule. *U.S. v. Franklin,* 586 F.2d 560 (5th Cir. 1978), *cert. denied,* 440 U.S. 972 (1979); *U.S. v. Buttorff,* 572 F.2d 619 (8th Cir.), *cert. denied,* 437 U.S. 906 (1978). *See also U.S. v. Weinrich,* 586 F.2d 481 (5th Cir. 1978), *cert. denied,* 441 U.S. 927 (1979), for avoidance of *Bruton* problems (*Bruton v. U.S.,* 391 U.S. 123 (1968)) in a joint trial.

Allegations in an indictment contrary to the proof brought out at trial are not admissions of the United States since an indictment is not a pleading of one of the parties but is an instrument of the grand jury. *Falter v. U.S.,* 23 F.2d 420 (2d Cir.), *cert. denied,* 277 U.S. 590 (1928).

## §2114. — — — Defendant's Adoptive Admissions.

Rule 801(d)(2)(B) restates the prior rule that an out-of-court statement acquiesced in or accepted by an accused may be received against him, by providing that such a statement is not hearsay. Where such adoption is manifested by words or actions of the accused that tend to explain or give meaning to the words of the declarant, courts have had little trouble in finding such statements admissible against the accused. *U.S. v. Crockett,* 534 F.2d 589 (5th Cir. 1976). The difficult cases are those involving silence in the face of accusation, comment, or directives about criminal activity. Whether silence may constitute adoptive admission in criminal cases now depends upon the status and position of the defendant at the time of the silence.

Where the defendant is under arrest and has been advised of his *Miranda* rights, his silence in the face of accusation cannot be used against him because he is not expected to speak or offer any exculpatory explanation. *Doyle v. Ohio,* 426 U.S. 610 (1976). *See also U.S. v.*

*Hale,* 422 U.S. 171 (1975), where the Court ruled that failure to speak at the time of arrest is of insufficient probative value to be admissible, though this decision is not binding on the states as it was an exercise of the Court's supervisory power. In *Baxter v. Palmigiano,* 425 U.S. 308 (1976), adverse inferences could be drawn from the silence of inmates at a disciplinary hearing, but not at a criminal prosecution.

However, where one is not in custody prior to indictment, due process, fundamental fairness, and other explicit constitutional rights are not violated by evidence of the silence of the defendant in the face of accusations of criminal behavior. *U.S. v. Giese,* 597 F.2d 1170 (9th Cir.), *cert. denied,* 444 U.S. 979 (1979); *U.S. v. Kilbourne,* 559 F.2d 1263 (4th Cir.), *cert. denied,* 434 U.S. 873 (1977); *U.S. v. Ojala,* 544 F.2d 940 (8th Cir. 1976); *U.S. v. Hoosier,* 542 F.2d 687 (6th Cir. 1976); *U.S. v. Flecha,* 539 F.2d 874 (2d Cir. 1976). To constitute an admission by silence, the statement must be in the presence and hearing of the defendant, he must have understood what was said, and he must have an opportunity to deny it. *U.S. v. Sears,* 663 F.2d 896, 904 (9th Cir. 1981), *cert. denied,* 102 S. Ct. 1731 (1982). The court must make an initial determination whether, under the circumstances, an innocent person would normally be induced to respond. *U.S. v. Sears,* 663 F.2d at 904; *U.S. v. Moore,* 522 F.2d 1068 (9th Cir. 1975), *cert. denied,* 423 U.S. 1049 (1976).

When the government files an affidavit for a search warrant, it may not later object on hearsay grounds to use of the contents of the affidavit during cross-examination. *U.S. v. Morgan,* 581 F.2d 933 (D.C. Cir. 1978).

### § 2115. — — — Vicarious and Representative Admissions.

Subdivisions (C) and (D) of Rule 801(d)(2) exclude from the definition of hearsay a "statement by a person authorized by [a party-opponent] to make a statement concerning the subject" or "a statement by [a party-opponent's] agent or servant concerning a matter within the scope of his agency or employment, made during the existence of the relationship." This provision has been used effectively in criminal cases. In *U.S. v. Ojala,* 544 F.2d 940 (8th Cir. 1976), an IRS agent's testimony that defendant's attorney said the failure of his client to file returns was not the result of political beliefs, where the statements were unequivocal and were made in the presence of the client who registered no objection or complaint, was admissible as non-hearsay because the declarations were made in the scope of the attorney's authority. *See also Mahlandt v. Wild Canid Survival & Research Center, Inc.,* 588 F.2d 626 (8th Cir. 1978). Statements of legislative aides of former Maryland Governor Marvin Mandel, concerning his views on legislative attempts to override his veto, were not hearsay and were properly admitted in his mail fraud trial, since the views expressed were within the scope of and made during the agency relationship. *U.S. v. Mandel,* 591 F.2d 1347 (4th Cir. 1979). *See also U.S. v. Summers,* 598 F.2d 450 (5th Cir. 1979).

## §2116. — — — Declarations of Coconspirators.

Rule 801(d)(2)(E) provides that a statement is not hearsay if made "by a coconspirator of a party during the course and in furtherance of the conspiracy." Under this rule an out-of-court declaration of a coconspirator is admissible against each conspirator even if the indictment fails to include a conspiracy count. *U.S. v. Smith,* 596 F.2d 319 (8th Cir. 1979); *U.S. v. Scavo,* 593 F.2d 837 (8th Cir. 1979); *U.S. v. Durland,* 575 F.2d 1306 (10th Cir. 1978); *U.S. v. Doulin,* 538 F.2d 466 (2d Cir.), *cert. denied,* 429 U.S. 895 (1976); *U.S. v. Wright,* 491 F.2d 942 (6th Cir.), *cert. denied,* 419 U.S. 862 (1974); *U.S. v. Johnson,* 463 F.2d 216 (9th Cir.), *cert. denied,* 409 U.S. 1028 (1972); *U.S. v. Jones,* 438 F.2d 461 (7th Cir. 1971); *Davis v. U.S.,* 409 F.2d 1095 (5th Cir. 1969), *aff'd on other grounds,* 411 U.S. 233 (1973); *U.S. v. Rinaldi,* 393 F.2d 97 (2d Cir.), *cert. denied,* 393 U.S. 913 (1968). A coconspirator's statement is admissible without a showing that the declarant is unavailable. *U.S. v. Inadi,* 475 U.S. 387 (1986).

Proof of the existence of a joint venture determines the admissibility of the coconspirator's declaration. This is so even where the coconspirator to whom the extrajudicial statement is attributed does not testify. *Dutton v. Evans,* 400 U.S. 74 (1970). *See U.S. v. Schwanke,* 598 F.2d 575 (10th Cir. 1979); *U.S. v. Dawson,* 576 F.2d 656 (5th Cir. 1978), *cert. denied,* 439 U.S. 1127 (1979); *U.S. v. Green,* 548 F.2d 1261 (6th Cir. 1977). When a conspiracy count is included and a defendant is acquitted on that count, the coconspirator's statements may still be used because acquittal implies only a failure to prove the conspiracy beyond a reasonable doubt. *U.S. v. Durland,* 575 F.2d at 1308-10; *U.S. v. Stanchich,* 550 F.2d 1294 (2d Cir. 1977); *U.S. v. Beasley,* 545 F.2d 403, *remanded on other grounds,* 563 F.2d 1225 (5th Cir. 1977); *U.S. v. Cravero,* 545 F.2d 406 (5th Cir. 1976), *cert. denied,* 429 U.S. 1100 (1977); *U.S. v. Suchy,* 540 F.2d 254 (6th Cir. 1976) (rejecting a per se rule requiring reversal on the substantive count where it is based on hearsay statements of an acquitted coconspirator). Moreover, the declaring coconspirator need not be indicted, nor identified in the charge as a conspirator, for the admission rule to apply. *U.S. v. Ziperstein,* 601 F.2d 281 (7th Cir. 1979).

Under the rule, coconspirator declarations are not admissible unless it is established that a conspiracy existed at the time and that the defendant participated therein, and the statement was made in furtherance of the conspiracy. *Arnott v. U.S.*, 464 U.S. 948 (1983). The trial court must make an initial determination of when a coconspirator declaration may be received; and this involves a balancing of the government's right to present its case with the defendant's right to be protected from inadmissible evidence. The trial court must decide whether proof of the conspiracy must precede, and be independent of, the coconspirator statement, what quantum of proof the government must furnish before the jury may consider the extrajudicial coconspirator statement as substantive proof of guilt, and whether the coconspirator declaration was made during and in furtherance of the conspiracy. In deciding these questions, the trial court may require the government to establish the conspiracy and the defendant's connection therewith before the coconspirator's declarations are admitted; admit the coconspirator's declarations subject to subsequent proof of the existence of the conspiracy and defendant's role therein; or hear what the government's proof of conspiracy will be and, if found to be sufficient, admit the coconspirator's statements at any stage of the trial. *U.S. v. Vinson,* 606 F.2d 149 (6th Cir. 1979); *U.S. v. Eubanks,* 591 F.2d 513 (9th Cir. 1979); *U.S. v. James,* 590 F.2d 575 (5th Cir.), *cert. denied,* 442 U.S. 917 (1979); *U.S. v. Macklin,* 573 F.2d 1046 (8th Cir.), *cert. denied,* 439 U.S. 852 (1978); *U.S. v. Martorano,* 557 F.2d 1 (1st Cir. 1977), *cert. denied,* 435 U.S. 922 (1978). A defendant's own statements may be used as independent evidence in determining whether a conspiracy existed. *U.S. v. Roe,* 670 F.2d 956, 963 (11th Cir. 1982).

The order of receiving evidence is a matter for the discretion of the trial court. However, evidence erroneously admitted cannot be retroactively justified on appeal on the ground that it fell under this exception, where the trial judge chose not to adopt that ground as a basis for admission. *U.S. v. Kaplan,* 510 F.2d 606, 611-12 (2d Cir. 1974). *Cf. U.S. v. Green,* 523 F.2d 229 (2d Cir. 1975), *cert. denied,* 423 U.S. 1074 (1976).

The circuits have not agreed whether initial establishment of the conspiracy must be proved by (1) non-hearsay evidence independent of the coconspirator's statements, (2) a combination of evidence of the defendant's acts and conduct and the coconspirator declaration, or (3) by the hearsay statement standing alone. *U.S. v. James, supra; U.S. v. Fredericks,* 586 F.2d 470 (5th Cir. 1978), *cert. denied,* 440 U.S. 962 (1979); *U.S. v. Di Rodio,* 565 F.2d 573 (9th Cir. 1977). The Supreme Court has held that under Rules 104(a) and 1101(d)(1) of the Federal

Rules of Evidence, the Court may consider hearsay, including the co-conspirators' statements, for the preliminary factual determination under Rule 801(d)(2)(E). *Bourjaily v. U.S.*, 107 S. Ct. 268 (1987). Whether the hearsay statement alone is sufficient was left unresolved.

The quantum of evidence needed to establish the existence of the conspiracy, defendant's connection and whether the offered statement was made in the course of and in furtherance of the conspiracy so as to make admissible the statements of coconspirators as substantive proof of guilt is the preponderance standard. *Bourjaily v. U.S., supra.*

Whether the conspiracy continues or has expired is determined as a matter of law by the court. A robbery has been held to be in progress until the money is divided. *U.S. v. Hickey*, 596 F.2d 1082 (1st Cir.), *cert. denied*, 444 U.S. 853 (1979). A conspiracy is not completed until the spoils are divided. *U.S. v. Knuckles*, 581 F.2d 305 (2d Cir.), *cert. denied*, 439 U.S. 986 (1978). A conspiracy is completed when its object is achieved and there is no evidence it is continuing, *U.S. v. DeVaugn*, 579 P.2d 225 (2d Cir. 1978); agreement to burn car after bank robbery was not admissible as the conspiracy was completed, *U.S. v. Floyd*, 555 F.2d 45 (2d Cir.), *cert. denied*, 434 U.S. 851 (1977). However, a statement made after arrest may be admissible, *U.S. v. Lam Lek Chong*, 544 F.2d 58 (2d Cir. 1976), *cert. denied*, 429 U.S. 1101 (1977), or not admissible, *U.S. v. Barnes*, 586 F.2d 1052 (5th Cir. 1978). Pointing out the location of a heroin source after arrest was held not admissible in *U.S. v. Caro*, 569 F.2d 411 (5th Cir. 1978).

The last overt act charged and proved does not necessarily mark the duration of the conspiracy, *U.S. v. Mackey*, 571 F.2d 376 (7th Cir. 1978), and conversations with prospective conspirators for membership purposes may be admissible, *U.S. v. Dorn*, 561 F.2d 1252 (7th Cir. 1977), but casual comments between conspirators may not be admissible, *U.S. v. Green*, 600 F.2d 154 (8th Cir. 1979). A post-arrest statement was not admissible in *U.S. v. Di Rodio*, 565 F.2d 573 (9th Cir. 1977); and a letter written after the conspiracy ended, offered by a codefendant, was not admissible in *U.S. v. Montgomery*, 582 F.2d 514 (10th Cir. 1978), *cert. denied*, 439 U.S. 1075 (1979). Tape recordings of past events are admissible if they constitute activity which is plainly in furtherance of the conspiracy. *U.S. v. Haldeman*, 559 F.2d 31 (D.C. Cir. 1976), *cert. denied*, 431 U.S. 933 (1977). In a prosecution for mail fraud to collect life insurance proceeds, statements after the murder by a coconspirator that the defendant had driven the car the day of the killing were admissible as they were made to further the ultimate objective of the conspiracy — the collection of the insurance proceeds. *U.S. v. Handy*, 668 F.2d 407, 408 (8th Cir. 1982).

Statements made after the termination of the conspiracy are not admissible. *Krulewitch v. U.S.,* 336 U.S. 440 (1949); *Wong Sun v. U.S.,* 371 U.S. 471 (1963). The burden of establishing withdrawal from the conspiracy lies on defendant who must demonstrate some type of affirmative action of disavowal either by communicating with law enforcement or informing his coconspirators. *U.S. v. Dorn,* 561 F.2d at 1256.

The fact that an assertion of a coconspirator is an "admission" does not make it a "statement of the defendant" and thus discoverable under Rule 16(a) of the Federal Rules of Criminal Procedure. *U.S. v. Percevault,* 490 F.2d 126, 130 (2d Cir. 1974).

### § 2117. Hearsay Exceptions — Availability of Declarant Immaterial.

Rule 803 provides that certain statements, otherwise inadmissible under the hearsay rule, are not excluded even though the declarant is available as a witness, because there are circumstantial guarantees of trustworthiness or reliability to justify the nonproduction of the declarant. "Trustworthiness" is the key to whether hearsay will be admitted. Rule 803 sets out 23 specific exceptions plus a catchall or general exception that allows other hearsay to be admitted where there are "circumstantial guarantees of trustworthiness." Both Rule 803 and Rule 804 are phrased in the negative ("The following are not excluded ..."), rather than in positive terms of admissibility, meaning that even though the hearsay rule does not exclude a statement, there may be other grounds that would keep the statement from being admitted. The exceptions set out in Rule 803 follow.

### § 2118. — Present Sense Impression: Rule 803(1).

This provision excepts from the hearsay rule statements "describing or explaining an event or condition" where the statement was "made while the declarant was perceiving the event or condition, or immediately thereafter." The Advisory Committee's Note says that the subject matter under this exception is limited to a description or explanation of the event or condition so contemporaneous as to "negate the likelihood of deliberate or conscious misrepresentation." There is no precise definition of "immediately thereafter," but one court held admissible hearsay statements made 15 to 45 minutes after the observation and absent a state of excitement. *Hilyer v. Howat Concrete Co.,* 578 F.2d 422, 426 n.7 (D.C. Cir. 1978). *See also U.S. v. Cain,* 587 F.2d 678 (5th Cir.), *cert. denied,* 440 U.S. 975 (1979); *U.S. v. Medico,* 557 F.2d 309 (2d Cir.), *cert. denied,* 434 U.S. 986 (1977) (double hearsay identification of the license plate of a bank robber meeting all of the specific requirements of admission under Rule 803(1) was admitted under Rule 804(b)(5) because of the Advisory Committee's hesitancy to admit statements without more when a bystander's identity is unknown).

In *U.S. v. Peacock*, 654 F.2d 339, 350 (5th Cir. 1981), a witness testified about comments made by her deceased husband immediately after he talked to the defendant on the phone. Her husband's statements that the defendant told him that the investigation was stopped due to insufficient evidence and that he (the husband) should get out of town were admitted because they were made immediately after talking to the defendant on the phone and there was no time to consciously manipulate the truth.

## § 2119. — Excited Utterances: Rule 803(2).

This provision permits admission of statements "relating to a startling event or condition made while the declarant was under the stress of excitement caused by the event or condition." The theory is that the spontaneous statement in the stress of excitement is not the product of reflective thought and as such is free of conscious fabrication. *See* Advisory Committee's Note; *U.S. v. Knife*, 592 F.2d 472, 481 n.10 (8th Cir. 1979).

This exception is broader than the "present sense impression" exception both as to subject matter and as to the time of the utterance. The statement need only "relate" to a startling event or condition, and actually might be made some time later, as where a person waking from a coma was still under the stress of excitement caused by the event or condition. Thus, the statement of a child to his mother identifying the person who sexually assaulted him was admitted because the child was "suffering distress from the assault." *U.S. v. Nick*, 604 F.2d 1199 (9th Cir. 1979). *See also White v. Illinois*, 112 S. Ct. 736 (1992). Also admitted was the statement of the victim within 15 minutes of the event and after a high-speed flight from the scene of the assault. *U.S. v. Golden*, 671 F.2d 369, 371 (10th Cir.), *cert. denied*, 102 S. Ct. 1777 (1982).

## § 2120. — Then Existing Mental, Emotional, or Physical Condition: Rule 803(3).

This provision excepts from the hearsay rule a "statement of the declarant's then existing state of mind, emotion, sensation, or physical condition (such as intent, plan, motive, design, mental feeling, pain, and bodily health) ...." Testimony by the former attorney of a defendant (who was charged with extortion) that defendant had asked if it would be legal to negotiate for a reward was admissible as a statement of defendant's then existing state of mind. *U.S. v. Taglione,* 546 F.2d 194 (5th Cir. 1977). In a Hobbs Act prosecution, the court allowed testimony by the one liquor representative that another liquor representative had said he paid money to the defendant to show the state of mind of the witness-victim. *U.S. v. Adcock,* 558 F.2d 397 (8th Cir.), *cert. denied,* 434 U.S. 921 (1977).

This rule specifically excludes from the exception a "statement of memory or belief to prove the fact remembered or believed" except in relation to a declarant's will. "He told me that he 'met Smith in the parking lot yesterday'" is not permitted. Thus, testimony of witnesses about what the plaintiff told them concerning his contract with the defendant must be excluded. *Prather v. Prather,* 650 F.2d 88, 90-91 (5th Cir. 1981). Evidence of intention through hearsay statements, such as "He told me that he was 'going to meet Smith in the parking lot,'" is permitted as tending to prove the doing of the act intended. The Supreme Court permits such "[d]eclarations of intention, casting light upon the future, [which] have been sharply distinguished from declarations of memory, pointing backwards to the past. There would be an end, or nearly that, to the rule against hearsay if the distinction were ignored." *Shepard v. U.S.,* 290 U.S. 96, 105-06 (1933). *See also Marshall v. Commonwealth Aquarium,* 611 F.2d 1 (1st Cir. 1979). The statement of a missing person that he intended to meet a person with the same name by which one of the defendants was known could be introduced. From that evidence the jury might infer that the person carried out his stated intention to meet that defendant. *U.S. v. Pheaster,* 544 F.2d 353 (9th Cir. 1976), *cert. denied,* 429 U.S. 1099 (1977).

### § 2121. — Statements for Purposes of Medical Diagnosis or Treatment: Rule 803(4).

This rule allows the admission of statements relating to medical diagnosis or treatment, including medical history, past or present symptoms, pain or sensations, and statements of causation where they are "reasonably pertinent to diagnosis or treatment." The Advisory Committee's Note points out that statements as to causation for the purpose of diagnosis or treatment would ordinarily qualify under the language but that statements about fault would not. Thus, a "patient's statement that he was struck by an automobile will qualify but not a statement that the car was driven through a red light." The statement need not have been made to a physician, and it need not refer to the declarant's physical condition.

The guarantee of the statement's trustworthiness is considered the declarant's need to give information for aid in diagnosis and treatment. One court has said that the test for applicability of the exception is whether a doctor would rely on the facts contained in the utterance solely for the treatment of the patient's specific condition. *U.S. v. Narciso*, 446 F. Supp. 252 (E.D. Mich. 1977). Another court has ruled that the exception applies to statements made to a physician consulted only for the purpose of enabling him to testify where the statement was relied on by the doctor in formulating his opinion. *O'Gee v. Dobbs Houses, Inc.*, 570 F.2d 1084 (2d Cir. 1978).

The statement of a four-year-old girl to an emergency room nurse and doctor, four hours after a sexual assault, was admitted both under the spontaneous declaration exemption and the exception for statements made in the course of securing medical treatment. *White v. Illinois*, 112 S. Ct. 736 (1992).

## § 2122. — Recorded Recollection: Rule 803(5).

When a witness once had knowledge about a matter but now has insufficient recollection to testify fully and accurately, counsel may attempt under Rule 612 to revive his memory through a writing. If the writing is sufficient to cause the witness to recall the matter there is no hearsay problem as the witness is then testifying from his present memory which has been revived by the writing. This is "present recollection revived." But where a witness, after reviewing the writing, is still unable to remember what is in the writing, a memorandum or record concerning the matter may be read into evidence under certain circumstances as "past recollection recorded," according to Rule 803(5).

The rule provides for the admission of recorded recollection if: (1) the "witness once had knowledge but now has insufficient recollection to enable him to testify fully and accurately," (2) the witness can testify that the memorandum of record was "made or adopted by the witness when the matter was fresh in his memory," and (3) the witness can testify that the recorded recollection reflected his then existing knowledge correctly. The memorandum or record may then be read into evidence, but may not itself be received as an exhibit unless offered by an adverse party. *U.S. v. Judon*, 567 F.2d 1289 (5th Cir. 1978). *See also U.S. v. Felix-Jerez*, 667 F.2d 1297, 1300-02 (9th Cir. 1982).

A signed statement of a witness in the words of a Secret Service agent was properly read into evidence because the witness adopted the statement by signing and swearing to it while the matter was fresh in his mind and was generally correct. *U.S. v. Williams,* 571 F.2d 344 (6th Cir.), *cert. denied,* 439 U.S. 841 (1978). A statement given by a witness to an agent was admitted notwithstanding the fact that he was inebriated at the time he made the statement. *U.S. v. Edwards,* 539 F.2d 689 (9th Cir.), *cert. denied,* 429 U.S. 984 (1976). Prior trial testimony may be read into evidence as past recollection recorded in a perjury trial if there is a proper foundation. *U.S. v. Arias,* 575 F.2d 253 (9th Cir.), *cert. denied,* 429 U.S. 868 (1978).

### § 2123. — Records of Regularly Conducted Activity: Rule 803(6).

This rule permits the admission of hearsay contained in a "memorandum, report, record, or data compilation, in any form, of acts, events, conditions, opinions, or diagnoses" where the following conditions are met: (1) it must be "made at or near the time," (2) it must be "by, or from information transmitted by, a person with knowledge," (3) it must be "kept in the course of a regularly conducted business activity," and (4) it must have been "the regular practice of that business activity to make the memorandum, report, record, or data compilation." These conditions must be shown by the testimony of (1) the custodian or (2) some other qualified witness. The evidence will not be admitted, however, if the "source of information or the method or circumstances of preparation indicate lack of trustworthiness." The term "business" includes "business, institution, association, profession, occupation, and calling of every kind, whether or not conducted for profit."

A sampling of the types of records which have been admitted under this rule includes: appointment calendars kept by unindicted coconspirators, *U.S. v. McPartlin,* 595 F.2d 1321 (7th Cir.), *cert. denied,* 444 U.S. 833 (1979); invoice which owner received at the time of purchase of her automobile, *U.S. v. Hines,* 564 F.2d 925 (10th Cir. 1977), *cert. denied,* 434 U.S. 1022 (1978); credit card receipt signed by defendant and maintained by issuing company, *U.S. v. Peden,* 556 F.2d 278 (5th Cir.), *cert. denied,* 434 U.S. 871 (1977); motel registrations, car rentals, and airline shipments, *U.S. v. Wigerman,* 549 F.2d 1192 (8th Cir. 1977); bank's bait money list, *U.S. v. Davis,* 542 F.2d 743 (8th Cir.), *cert. denied,* 429 U.S. 1004 (1976); delivery invoices in possession of manufacturer but prepared by common carrier, *U.S. v. Pfeiffer,* 539 F.2d 668 (8th Cir. 1976); notebooks of taxpayer's employee showing services performed and payments made, *U.S. v. Prevatt,* 526 F.2d 400 (5th Cir. 1976); photocopies of records proving out-of-state manufacture of firearms, *U.S. v. Powers,* 572 F.2d 146 (8th Cir. 1978); scrapbook of press clippings compiled by public relations department of hospital admitted to prove hospital visiting hours, *U.S. v. Reese*, 568 F.2d 1246 (6th Cir. 1977).

Included also as records under this rule is "data compilation" which the Advisory Committee's Note states "includes, but is by no means limited to, electronic computer storage." A computer printout of drug records was admitted, but the court stated that complex nature of computer storage calls for a more comprehensive foundation for the admission of computer printouts. *U.S. v. Scholle*, 553 F.2d 1109 (8th Cir.), *cert. denied*, 434 U.S. 940 (1977); *U.S. v. Vela*, 673 F.2d 86, 89-90 (5th Cir. 1982) (computerized telephone records).

The rule also includes statements of "opinions or diagnoses" as a business records exception. A physician's diagnosis and treatment were admitted as part of the hospital record under Ohio's business records exception. *Stengel v. Belcher*, 522 F.2d 438 (6th Cir. 1975). The statement of defendant that his mother was "preterminal," contained in a hospital record, was admitted to show defendant's state of mind when he provided information on a loan application allegedly for his mother. *U.S. v. Sackett*, 598 F.2d 739 (2d Cir. 1979).

A business record does not necessarily have to be a written document. A fire department sound recording of emergency calls made by a defendant was held admissible in *U.S. v. Verlin*, 466 F. Supp. at 160.

A bank's loan procedure manual, however, was not admissible, as it was not a memorandum or record of any action, occurrence, or event, nor was it made at or near the time of the transaction. *Seattle-First National Bank v. Randall*, 532 F.2d 1291 (9th Cir. 1976).

Before a record may be introduced under this rule, a proper foundation must be laid showing that the requirements of the rule have been met. The phrase "person with knowledge" does not mean that a specific individual must be identified, but that the usual practice of the business was to get the information from a person with knowledge. *See* Senate Judiciary Committee's Note on Rule 803(6); *U.S. v. Ahrens*, 530 F.2d 781 (8th Cir. 1976); *U.S. v. Evans*, 572 F.2d 455 (5th Cir.), *cert. denied*, 439 U.S. 870 (1978). Thus, the "custodian or other qualified witness" testifying at the trial need not have been the declarant or recorder of the items being offered, *U.S. v. Bland*, 961 F.2d 123 (9th Cir. 1992); *U.S. v. Pfieffer*, 539 F.2d at 671; *U.S. v. Jones*, 554 F.2d 251 (5th Cir. 1977), nor employed at the time the records were prepared, *U.S. v. Evans*, 572 F.2d at 490, nor have personal knowledge of the particular evidence on the record, *U.S. v. Reese*, 568 F.2d 1246 (6th Cir. 1977), nor must the report have been prepared by the custodian of records, *U.S. v. Bowers*, 593 F.2d 376 (10th Cir.), *cert. denied*, 444 U.S. 852 (1979). One court also has admitted a record where the witness "only surmised" that the procedures used when the record was prepared were the same as when he thereafter became the custodian, *U.S. v. Rose,* 562 F.2d 409 (7th Cir. 1977). But where the only information was that the document was found in the corporation's records without a signature and the witness said, "I don't know who prepared it" and knew nothing else about its source, it was held to have been properly excluded for insufficient authentication. *Coughlin v. Capitol Cement Co.,* 571 F.2d 290 (5th Cir. 1978).

A letter from bank employees to bank management concerning a bank robbery with a postscript stating that the FBI had notified them that the robber was in custody was held inadmissible, as those statements were "made by a third party outside the scope of the business." *U.S. v. Yates,* 553 F.2d 518 (6th Cir. 1977). A claim form with a buyer's statement that stolen silver was worth $7,690 was not a record of regularly conducted activity, and thus was inadmissible. *U.S. v. Plum,* 558 F.2d 568 (10th Cir. 1977). *See also U.S. v. Powers,* 572 F.2d 146 (8th Cir. 1978); *U.S. v. Davis,* 571 F.2d 1354 (5th Cir. 1978).

Although otherwise admissible under Rule 803(6), a record may be excluded if "the source of information or the method or circumstances of preparation indicates lack of trustworthiness." One indicator may be the motivation in preparing a record. Was the purpose primarily for business purposes or was it prepared primarily for litigation? *Palmer v. Hoffman,* 318 U.S. 109 (1943). A telex providing a summary of the defendant's subpoenaed Korean bank records was held inadmissible for lack of trustworthiness. *U.S. v. Kim,* 595 F.2d 755 (D.C. Cir. 1979). However, inaccurate and incomplete records may be admitted, these deficiencies going to the weight of the evidence not to its admissibility. *Crompton-Richmond Co., Factors v. Briggs,* 560 F.2d 1195 (5th Cir. 1977).

The term "business" is used broadly in the rule and has been interpreted to include a prison. *Stone v. Morris,* 546 F.2d 730 (7th Cir. 1976).

The trial court has broad discretion in determining admissibility under this rule, and its ruling will not be overturned except for an abuse of discretion. *U.S. v. Vela,* 673 F.2d at 90; *U.S. v. Evans,* 572 F.2d at 490; *U.S. v. Reese,* 561 F.2d 894 (D.C. Cir. 1977); *U.S. v. Carranco,* 551 F.2d 1197 (10th Cir. 1977); *U.S. v. Page,* 544 F.2d 982 (8th Cir. 1976).

Rule 803(8) provides for the admission of public records and reports, but it is more restrictive than Rule 803(6) and it is controlling. If the public record or report does not meet the requirements of Rule 803(8), it generally will not be admitted under Rule 803(6) even though it may meet all of the requirements of the latter section. *See U.S. v. Oates,* 560 F.2d 45 (2d Cir. 1977); *U.S. v. American Cyanamid Co.,* 427 F. Supp. 859 (S.D.N.Y. 1977).

## § 2124. — Absence of Entries in Records Kept in Regularly Conducted Activity: Rule 803(7).

This rule provides that failure of a record to include an entry of matter which would ordinarily be included in a record regularly made and preserved, within the meaning of Rule 803(6), is admissible to "prove the nonoccurrence or nonexistence of the matter, ... unless the sources of information or the circumstances indicate lack of trustworthiness." A U.S. Department of Agriculture auditor was permitted to testify, for example, about his search for, and failure to find, deposits by defendant in the Federal Reserve Bank, *U.S. v. Lanier,* 578 F.2d 1246 (8th Cir.), *cert. denied,* 439 U.S. 856 (1978). *See also U.S. v. Zeidman,* 540 F.2d 314 (7th Cir. 1976).

The absence of records to prove the nonoccurrence of relevant matters under Rule 803(7) also may be included as part of summary charts introduced under Rule 1006. *U.S. v. Scales,* 594 F.2d 558 (6th Cir.), *cert. denied,* 441 U.S. 946 (1979).

## § 2125. — Public Records and Reports: Rule 803(8).

This rule provides a hearsay exception for records, reports, statements, or data compilations of public offices or agencies in any form setting forth: (1) "the activities of the office or agency"; (2) "matters observed pursuant to duty imposed by law to which matters there was a duty to report, excluding, however, in criminal cases matters observed by police officers and other law enforcement personnel"; (3) "factual findings resulting from an investigation made pursuant to authority granted by law," but such findings are admissible in a criminal case only when used against the government. Factually based conclusions or opinions may be included as "factual findings" under the Rule. *Beech Aircraft Corp. v. Rainey,* 488 U.S. 153 (1988). The Advisory Committee's Note states that the justification for this exception "is the assumption that a public official will perform his duty properly and the unlikelihood that he will remember details independently of the record." The rule makes no distinction between federal and nonfederal offices and agencies.

Examples of admission permitted under this rule include: a U.S. Marshal's return stating that he had served an injunction on a union and the union officers, *U.S. v. Union Nacional de Trabajadores,* 576

F.2d 388 (1st Cir. 1978); dates on certificates of copyright on record albums in record piracy prosecutions, *U.S. v. Taxe,* 540 F.2d 961 (9th Cir. 1976), *cert. denied,* 429 U.S. 1040 (1977); records of the Ulster Constabulary showing routine recording of serial numbers and receipt of weapons, *U.S. v. Grady,* 544 F.2d 598 (2d Cir. 1976); routine, nonadversarial matters such as a simple recording by a customs inspector of license numbers of vehicles passing his station, *U.S. v. Orozco,* 590 F.2d 789 (9th Cir.), *cert. denied,* 442 U.S. 920 (1979); records of department of revenue showing car ownership, *U.S. v. King,* 590 F.2d 253 (8th Cir. 1978), *cert. denied,* 440 U.S. 973 (1979). A report of the National Highway Safety Bureau containing maximum stopping distances was found to be admissible as a data compilation of a public agency under Rule 803(8)(C). Although the public officials who compiled the report neither produced the figures nor verified their accuracy, they did have firsthand knowledge of the investigation by which it accumulated the published findings. *Robbins v. Whelan,* 653 F.2d 47, 50-52 (1st Cir.), *cert. denied,* 454 U.S. 1123 (1981).

Examples where public records were found to be inadmissible include: reports and worksheets of U.S. Customs Service chemists analyzing a white powdery substance claimed by the prosecution to be heroin were found to be "matters observed" by "law enforcement personnel" and as such not admissible under 803(8)(B), *U.S. v. Oates,* 560 F.2d 45 (2d Cir. 1977); IRS computer printout setting forth matters observed by law enforcement personnel and as such inadmissible, *U.S. v. Ruffin,* 575 F.2d 346 (2d Cir. 1978); SEC release was held not a "determination of facts obtained after administrative proceedings" and as such was inadmissible, *U.S. v. Corr,* 543 F.2d 1042 (2d Cir. 1976). As any judgment from their orders would result in a fine and not a criminal conviction, building inspectors were held not to be law enforcement officers and so records of building code violations were admissible. *U.S. v. Hansen,* 583 F.2d 325 (7th Cir.), *cert. denied,* 439 U.S. 912 (1978).

The Seventh Circuit distinguished *U.S. v. Oates, supra,* and held that Rule 803(8)(B) does not exclude the referral report of an agent that satisfies the criteria of recorded recollection under Rule 803(5) where the agent is testifying. *U.S. v. Sawyer,* 607 F.2d 1190 (7th Cir. 1979), *cert. denied,* 445 U.S. 943 (1980).

### § 2126. — Records of Vital Statistics: Rule 803(9).

This rule allows "[r]ecords or data compilations, in any form, of births, fetal deaths, deaths, or marriages, if the report thereof was made to a public office pursuant to the requirements of law."

## §2127. — Absence of Public Record or Entry: Rule 803(10).

This rule, similar to Rule 803(7), permits proof of the nonoccurrence or nonexistence of a matter or an event by evidence of the absence of a record regularly made and preserved by a public office or agency. The absence of such record may be proven in accordance with Rule 902 or by testimony that a diligent search failed to disclose the record, report, statement, or data compilation or entry.

In failure to file cases, certified statements that a search of the master files indicated that no returns were filed are admitted. *U.S. v. Johnson,* 577 F.2d 1304, 1312 (5th Cir. 1978); *U.S. v. Farris,* 517 F.2d 226, 228 (7th Cir.), *cert. denied,* 423 U.S. 892 (1975).

In a prosecution for dealing in firearms without a license, a certificate from an ATF agent stating that the defendant had not been granted a license to engage in the business of a firearm dealer was held properly admitted even though the certificate did not state that a diligent search of the records had been made. *U.S. v. Harris,* 551 F.2d 621 (5th Cir.), *cert. denied,* 434 U.S. 836 (1977). Affidavits of CIA officials stating that CIA records failed to reveal that the defendant had ever been employed by that agency were held properly admitted in an espionage prosecution where defendant claimed he was a CIA agent. *U.S. v. Lee,* 589 F.2d 980 (9th Cir. 1979). To refute the defendant's statements that he had filed tax returns, a government employee was permitted to testify that a computer check showed the defendant had not filed tax returns. Although there was no error found in this case because the computer program was uncomplicated, "the government is well advised" to give notice in advance of the trial if computer data is to be used. The court also noted that the prohibition in Rule 803(8)(B) and (C) precluding the use of certain public records against an accused is not present in Rule 803(10). *U.S. v. Cepeda Penes,* 577 F.2d 754 (1st Cir. 1978). Although it may be proper for the government to impeach a defense witness by showing the absence of a record indicating his receipt of an unemployment check on the day claimed, where the search has been less than diligent, reliability cannot be assured and admission to prove absence of a record was held to be reversible error. *U.S. v. Robinson,* 544 F.2d 110 (2d Cir. 1976), *cert. denied,* 439 U.S. 1050 (1978).

## §2128. — Records of Religious Organizations; Marriage, Baptismal, and Similar Certificates; and Family Records: Rule 803(11), (12), and (13).

Rule 803(11) provides for the admission of "[s]tatements of births, marriages, divorces, deaths, legitimacy, ancestry, relationship by blood or marriage, or other similar facts of personal or family history, contained in a regularly kept record of a religious organization."

The principle of proof by certification which is recognized in Rule 803(8) for public officials is extended in Rule 803(12) to clergyman and others who perform marriages and other ceremonies or administer sacraments. When the person executing the certificate is not a public official, however, the document is not self-authenticating, and proof is required that the person was authorized to perform the act and did make the certificate.

Rule 803(13) allows admission of "[s]tatements of fact concerning personal or family history contained in family Bibles, genealogies, charts, engravings on rings, inscriptions on family portraits, engravings on urns, crypts, or tombstones, or the like."

## § 2129. — Records of Documents and Statements in Documents Affecting an Interest in Property: Rule 803(14) and (15).

Rule 803(14) permits the introduction of documents affecting an interest in property. Although these records might be offered as exceptions to the hearsay rule as public records, under Rule 803(14) they can be offered for the further purpose of proving execution and delivery, which is information outside the contents of the documents and information which the recorder could not testify to with firsthand knowledge. To be admissible the record must be a record of a public office and must be filed in that office pursuant to an applicable statute authorizing such recording.

Under Rule 803(15) statements and documents establishing or affecting an interest in property are exempt from the hearsay rule "if the matter stated was relevant to the purpose of the document," unless later dealings were inconsistent with the truth of the statement or the purport of the document. For example, a statement in a deed that the grantors are all of the heirs of the last record owner is admissible.

## § 2130. — Statements in Ancient Documents: Rule 803(16).

This rule admits "[s]tatements in a document in existence twenty years or more ..." whose authenticity is established pursuant to Rule 901(b)(8). The Advisory Committee's Note states that "age affords assurance that the writing antedates the present controversy." The exception applies to all sorts of documents. *See Bell v. Combined Registry Co.*, 397 F. Supp. 1241 (N.D. Ill. 1975), *aff'd*, 536 F.2d 164 (7th Cir.), *cert. denied*, 429 U.S. 1001 (1976).

### §2131. — Market Reports, Commercial Publications: Rule 803(17).

This rule allows admission of "market quotations, tabulations, lists, directories, or other published compilations generally used and relied upon by the public or by persons in particular occupations," such as stock market reports, phone directories, life expectancy tables, and city directories.

### §2132. — Learned Treatises: Rule 803(18).

This rule provides that "statements contained in published treatises, periodicals, or pamphlets on a subject of history, medicine, or other science or art ..." are admissible. For example, the National Electrical Safety Code, *Gordy v. City of Canton, Mississippi*, 543 F.2d 558 (5th Cir. 1976); and handwriting charts. *U.S. v. Mangan*, 575 F.2d 32 (2d Cir.), *cert. denied*, 439 U.S. 931 (1978).

The conditions that must be met are: (1) the treatise can be admitted only if it is (a) "called to the attention" of an expert witness upon cross-examination or (b) is "relied upon by him" in direct examination. This requirement assures that an expert witness will be available to interpret or apply the learned treatises, but does away with a requirement, adopted in many jurisdictions, that the expert witness acknowledge the authority of the learned treatises; (2) the learned treatise must be "established as a reliable authority" (a) by the testimony or admission of the witness, (b) by other expert testimony, or (c) by judicial notice. Rather than requiring the witness to state his express reliance upon the treatise, this adopts the liberal position taken by the Supreme Court in *Reilly v. Pinkus*, 338 U.S. 269 (1949); and (3) if admitted, "the statements may be read into evidence but may not be received as exhibits." However, the Advisory Committee's Note emphasizes that, when received into evidence, learned treatises may be considered as substantive proof and not merely as impeaching material.

### §2133. — Reputation of Personal or Family History, Boundaries or General History, or Character: Rule 803(19), (20), and (21).

Rule 803(19) permits the admission of out-of-court statements or reputation as to facts of personal or family history, such as birth, adoption, marriage, legitimacy, and relationship by blood. This reputation may be among members of the family or associates, or in the community.

The first portion of Rule 803(20) allows evidence of reputation about land boundaries or customs affecting land as the reputation developed before the controversy. The second portion of the rule allows reputation testimony about events of general history important to the community, state, or nation.

Rule 803(21) allows evidence of the reputation of the person's character, even though it may be hearsay. But the Advisory Committee's Note emphasizes that this exception must be read together with the provisions of Rules 404, 405(a), and 608 dealing with other specific limitations on such character evidence. In *U.S. v. Prevatt,* 526 F.2d 400 (5th Cir. 1976), the prosecutor was permitted to ask the defendant's character witnesses if they had heard that the defendant while a county commissioner had accepted money from applicants for zoning changes or if the witnesses knew that the defendant had used county employees to make improvements on land he owned.

### § 2134. — Judgment of Previous Conviction: Rule 803(22).

This section removes from the hearsay rule judgments of previous convictions introduced "to prove any fact essential to sustain the judgment" if the following requirements are met: (1) the judgment must have been entered after a trial or upon a plea of guilty, but not upon a plea of nolo contendere; (2) the crime underlying the conviction must have been punishable by death or imprisonment in excess of one year; and (3) the judgment cannot be used by the government in a criminal prosecution against any person other than the accused except for impeachment purposes. The pendency of an appeal may be shown, but does not affect admissibility.

The admission of a judgment of conviction is not conclusive, however. The person against whom the judgment was introduced may offer an explanation or show mitigating circumstances with respect to it. *See* Advisory Committee's Note; *Lloyd v. American Export Lines, Inc.,* 580 F.2d 1179 (3d Cir.), *cert. denied,* 439 U.S. 969 (1978). This rule has been interpreted to include foreign judgments. *Id.* at 1189. Admission of a judgment of acquittal was not permitted in *U.S. v. Viserto,* 596 F.2d 531 (2d Cir.), *cert. denied,* 444 U.S. 841 (1979). A judgment otherwise admissible under Rule 803(22) may be inadmissible for other reasons, such as unfair prejudice under Rule 403. *See Rozier v. Ford Motor Co.,* 573 F.2d 1332 (5th Cir. 1978).

## § 2135. — Judgment as to Personal, Family or General History, or Boundaries: Rule 803(23).

Evidence of a judgment as to proof of (1) personal or family history, (2) general history, or (3) boundaries is admissible to prove a fact which was essential to sustain the judgment if this same matter would be provable by evidence of reputation under Rule 803(19), (20), or (22).

## § 2136. — Other Exceptions: Rule 803(24).

This rule provides that a statement, not specifically covered by one of the other 23 subdivisions of Rule 803, may still be excepted from the hearsay restriction if five conditions are found by the court:

(1) It must have "equivalent circumstantial guarantees of trustworthiness" as the other 23 specific exceptions listed in Rule 803. For example, a written summary of official Chilean records showing dates of defendant's entry into and exit from Chile was admitted in *U.S. v. Friedman,* 593 F.2d 109 (9th Cir. 1979). An affidavit of a witness contradicting his trial testimony was admitted as substantive evidence as it was made closer to the events than his trial testimony, had many handwritten alterations by the witness, and the jury could observe his demeanor when cross-examined about it in *U.S. v. Williams,* 573 F.2d 284 (5th Cir. 1978). Statements made by accomplices introduced for substance when in conflict with their trial testimony were admitted in *U.S. v. Leslie,* 542 F.2d 285 (5th Cir. 1976). However, a telex summary of defendant's subpoenaed Korean bank records did not have sufficient circumstantial guarantees of trustworthiness in *U.S. v. Kim,* 595 F.2d 755 (D.C. Cir. 1979). And, statements made by enemies of defendant in the heat of political battle, based on rumors and general discussions, especially from unidentified declarants, were held not to possess the requisite guarantees of trustworthiness in *U.S. v. Mandel,* 591 F.2d 1347 (4th Cir. 1979).

(2) The "statement is offered as evidence of a material fact."

(3) The statement must be "more probative on the point for which it is offered than any other evidence which the proponent can procure through reasonable efforts." Testimony of witness within the courthouse was held to have more probative value in establishing the truth than the statements transcribed by government agents. *U.S. v. Mathis,* 559 F.2d 294 (5th Cir. 1977).

(4) The general "purposes of these rules and the interests of justice" will best be served by admission of the statement into evidence. *U.S. v. Mathis,* 559 F.2d at 299.

(5) The proponent of the evidence must make known to the adverse party, sufficiently in advance of trial to allow for preparation, the

intention to offer the statement and the particulars of it, including the name and address of the declarant. *U.S. v. Ruffin,* 575 F.2d 346 (2d Cir. 1978); *U.S. v. Davis,* 571 F.2d 1354 (5th Cir. 1978); *U.S. v. Guevara,* 598 F.2d 1094 (7th Cir. 1979). Where the declarant was unidentified, the notice requirements for offering the hearsay evidence were not met. *U.S. v. Mandel,* 591 F.2d at 1369. Notice, however, does not mean that the defendant must be provided with copies of exhibits prior to trial. *U.S. v. Evans,* 572 F.2d 455 (5th Cir.), *cert. denied,* 439 U.S. 870 (1978). In at least one case where the government did not comply with notice requirements, it was nevertheless held that the defendant had "fair opportunity to meet the statements." *U.S. v. Leslie,* 542 F.2d 285 (5th Cir. 1976). Where the government failed to give notice prior to trial of its intention to offer a statement on rebuttal, but the need for rebuttal testimony was not apparent until after trial had commenced and the defendant did not claim he was unable to adequately prepare to meet rebuttal testimony, the defendant was considered to have been given sufficient notice. *U.S. v. Iaconetti,* 540 F.2d 574 (2d Cir. 1976), *cert. denied,* 429 U.S. 1041 (1977).

The trial court's determination as to admissibility of evidence under Rule 803(24) will not be overturned except for an abuse of discretion. *U.S. v. Friedman,* 593 F.2d at 118.

### § 2137. Hearsay Exceptions — Declarant Unavailable.

While Rule 803 provides for certain exceptions to the hearsay rule whether or not the declarant is available as a witness, the exceptions in Rule 804 apply only if the declarant is unavailable. As with the exceptions under Rule 803, the Advisory Committee's Notes emphasize that neither Rule 803 nor Rule 804 dispenses with the requirement of firsthand knowledge of the declarant as stated in Rule 602.

### § 2138. — Limitations.

### § 2139. — — Sixth Amendment Confrontation Clause.

The confrontation clause of the sixth amendment provides two types of protection for the criminal defendant: the right to conduct a cross-examination, *Pennsylvania v. Ritchie,* 487 U.S. 1012 (1987), and the right to physically face those who testify against him, *Coy v. Iowa,* 480 U.S. 39 (1988). The clause's central purpose is to ensure the reliability of the evidence by subjecting it to testing in the adversary proceeding at trial. This is served by the elements of confrontation, physical presence, oath, cross-examination, and observation of the witnesses' demeanor by the trier of fact.

The confrontation clause, however, does not give a defendant an absolute right to physically face all witnesses at trial. If it did, it would abrogate virtually every hearsay exception. The right to a face-to-face confrontation at trial may be satisfied on a case-specific basis where denial of confrontation is necessary to further important public policy and where the reliability of the testimony is satisfied. These conditions were found to be present in *Maryland v. Craig,* 110 S. Ct. 3157 (1990). In this sexual abuse case of a six-year-old child, the judge, jury and defendant remained in the courtroom where the testimony of the child was displayed while he was examined in another room by the prosecutor and defense attorney.

The confrontation clause may prevent use of hearsay testimony that would otherwise be admissible under some exception provided by the hearsay rules. To be admissible the confrontation clause normally requires a showing that the witness is unavailable (if the challenged out-of-court statements were made in the course of a prior judicial proceeding) and that the out-of-court statement bears adequate indicia of reliability.

As the confrontation clause and hearsay rules are "generally designed to protect similar values," *California v. Green,* 399 U.S. 149, 155 (1970), one of the indicia of reliability is that "the evidence falls within a firmly rooted hearsay exception," *Ohio v. Roberts,* 448 U.S. 56, 66 (1980). *See also Bourjaily v. U.S.,* 483 U.S. 171 (1987). For example, spontaneous declarations and statements made for purposes of medical diagnosis or treatment are such "firmly rooted" exceptions as to satisfy the reliability requirement of the confrontation clause, *White v. Illinois,* 112 S. Ct. 736 (1992).

Not all codified hearsay exceptions have passed constitutional review. Residual hearsay exceptions do not share the same tradition of reliability supporting the admissibility of statements under a "firmly rooted" hearsay exception. To determine that a given statement is sufficiently trustworthy for confrontation clause purposes, such trustworthiness guarantees must be shown from the totality of the circumstances that surround the statement and make it particularly worthy of belief. The statement must be so trustworthy that adversarial testing would add little to its reliability. *Idaho v. Wright,* 110 S. Ct. 3139 (1990). Accomplices' confessions are presumptively unreliable and must have sufficient indicia of reliability to rebut this presumption of unreliability. *Lee v. Illinois,* 476 U.S. 530 (1986). The corollary is that the prosecution is entitled to overcome the presumption of unreliability. *New Mexico v. Earnest,* 477 U.S. 648 (1986).

The Supreme Court has held that a coconspirator's statement, offered under Rule 801(d)(2)(E), Fed. Rules. Evid., is admissible without a showing that the declarant is unavailable for the reason that the nature of such coconspirator's statement contains within itself and the circumstances sufficient indicia of reliability. *U.S. v. Inadi,* 475 U.S. 387 (1986). The Court also has held that when an expert witness on cross examination claimed loss of memory as to the basis of his opinion, said loss of memory went to the weight of his testimony and did not deprive the defendant of his right to confrontation. *Delaware v. Fensterer,* 474 U.S. 15 (1985).

Violations of the confrontation clause are subject to a harmless error test. *Coy v. Iowa, supra.*

## § 2140. — — Unavailability Sufficient to Qualify Under the Rule.

"Unavailability as a witness" as defined in Rule 804(a) includes five situations:

(1) Where a declarant "is exempted by ruling of the court on the ground of privilege from testifying concerning the subject matter of his statement." As the Advisory Committee's Note makes clear, a ruling by the judge is required, and thus an actual claim of privilege must be made. *U.S. v. Toney,* 599 F.2d 787, 789-90 (6th Cir. 1979); *Witham v. Mabry,* 596 F.2d 293, 297 (8th Cir. 1979); *U.S. v. Lilley,* 581 F.2d 182, 187 (8th Cir. 1978); *U.S. v. Mangan,* 575 F.2d 32, 44 (2d Cir.), *cert. denied,* 439 U.S. 931 (1978); *U.S. v. Thomas,* 571 F.2d 285, 288 (5th Cir. 1978); *U.S. v. Mathis,* 559 F.2d 294, 298 (5th Cir. 1977); *U.S. v. Wood,* 550 F.2d 435, 439 (9th Cir. 1976).

(2) Where the declarant "persists in refusing to testify ... despite an order of the court to do so." *U.S. v. Carlson,* 547 F.2d 1346, 1354 (8th Cir. 1976), *cert. denied,* 431 U.S. 914 (1977) (coconspirator-declarant's refusal to testify for fear of reprisals despite court order and grant of use of immunity rendered him unavailable).

(3) Where the declarant testifies "to a lack of memory of the subject matter of his statement." *U.S. v. Lyon,* 567 F.2d 777, 784 (8th Cir. 1977), *cert. denied,* 435 U.S. 918 (1978) (FBI agent, allowed to read transcribed interviews of defendant's landlady, gave detailed testimony about how he took and transcribed statement); *California v. Green,* 399 U.S. 149 (1970) (the preliminary hearing testimony of a witness who was present at trial but claimed forgetfulness was admitted); *U.S. v. Davis,* 551 F.2d 233, 235 (8th Cir.), *cert. denied,* 431 U.S. 923 (1977) (witness was ruled unavailable because he couldn't recall previous testimony at related trial); *U.S. v. Amaya,* 533 F.2d 188, 190-92 (5th Cir. 1976), *cert. denied,* 429 U.S. 1101 (1977) (loss of memory after automobile accident satisfied unavailability requirement for admission of prior testimony). *See also U.S. v. Collins,* 478 F.2d 837

(5th Cir.), *cert. denied,* 414 U.S. 1010 (1973), in which a witness' prior testimony against defendants in a first trial was held admissible to impeach his claim of lack of memory and as implicit affirmation of the truth of prior testimony where witness was fully aware of prior testimony but claimed inability to recall virtually all matters testified to in great detail at former trial.

(4) Where the declarant "is unable to be present or to testify at the hearing because of death or then existing physical or mental illness or infirmity." *U.S. v. Bell,* 500 F.2d 1287, 1290 (2d Cir. 1974) (permitting use of bank robbery witness' prior testimony at suppression hearing where witness not present at trial due to illness); *U.S. v. Ricketson,* 498 F.2d 367, 374 (7th Cir.), *cert. denied,* 419 U.S. 965 (1974) (deposition of very ill burglary victim allowed at trial where defense had adequate prior opportunity to cross-examine); *U.S. v. Diehl,* 460 F. Supp. 1282, 1289 (S.D. Tex.), *aff'd per curiam,* 586 F.2d 1080 (5th Cir. 1978). *See also* Rule 32(a)(3), Fed. R. Civ. P., and Rule 15(e), Fed. R. Crim. P., concerning the use of depositions.

(5) Where the declarant is "absent from the hearing and the proponent of his statement has been unable to procure his attendance." In a criminal case, the government must make a good faith effort before trial to locate and present the witness. The prosecution bears the burden of establishing this predicate. *Ohio v. Roberts,* 448 U.S. 56, 74-75 (1980). *See Barber v. Page,* 390 U.S. 719, 724 (1968) (use by the state of prior testimony of a witness then in federal custody in another state was held to deny the defendant his sixth amendment right). *Canal Zone v. P. (Pinto),* 590 F.2d 1344, 1352-54 (5th Cir. 1979) (where prosecution made no showing that it was unable to procure attendance of victims at trial, use of victims' deposition testimony was held not to be plain error); *U.S. v. Mann,* 590 F.2d 361, 367-68 (1st Cir. 1978) (government must show diligent effort to secure voluntary return of witnesses beyond jurisdiction before use of deposition at trial permitted). *But see U.S. v. Seijo,* 595 F.2d 116, 120 (2d Cir. 1979) (where government had done everything in its power to hold witnesses for trial and, failing that, witnesses' prior depositions held admissible); *U.S. v. Mathis,* 550 F.2d 180, 181-82 (4th Cir. 1976), *cert. denied,* 429 U.S. 1107 (1977) (testimony in previous trial which ended in mistrial admissible after prosecution unsuccessfully attempted to locate witness inadvertently released from penal institution); *U.S. v. Hayes,* 535 F.2d 479, 482 (8th Cir. 1976) (testimony in prior trial of defendant's wife whom the government was subsequently unable to locate admissible against defendant in later trial); *U.S. v. Amaya,* 533 F.2d 188, 191 (5th Cir. 1976), *cert. denied,* 429 U.S. 1101 (1977) (establishment of the

permanence of an illness not an absolute requirement; government
need only establish that duration beyond time within which trial can
reasonably be postponed).

### § 2141. — Former Testimony: Rule 804(b)(1).

This exception applies to testimony "given as a witness at another
hearing of the same or a different proceeding, or in a deposition taken
in compliance with law in the course of the same or another proceeding, if the party against whom the testimony is now offered ... had an
opportunity and similar motive to develop the testimony by direct,
cross or redirect examination."

Although the rule does not expressly state that the prior testimony
must have been given under oath or affirmation, such a setting no
doubt is contemplated. *See* J. Weinstein & M. Berger, *Weinstein's Evidence,* § 804(b)(1)[02], at 804-51-52. The requirement that the party
harmed by the testimony has had an opportunity and a similar motive
to cross-examine the witness in the prior case is designed to safeguard
a defendant's sixth amendment right to confrontation. The general
constitutionality of such use of prior testimony has been upheld. *California v. Green,* 399 U.S. 149 (1970); *Mattox v. U.S.,* 156 U.S. 237
(1895).

Where a witness testified to an inability to remember prior statements, his testimony against defendant at prior trial was held admissible in *U.S. v. Davis,* 551 F.2d 233, 235 (8th Cir.), *cert. denied,* 431 U.S.
923 (1977). Testimony from a previous mistrial has likewise been held
admissible. *U.S. v. Bowman,* 609 F.2d 12, 19 (D.C. Cir. 1979); *U.S. v.
Mathis,* 550 F.2d 180, 182 (4th Cir. 1976), *cert. denied,* 429 U.S. 1107
(1977); *U.S. v. Brasco,* 516 F.2d 816, 818-19 (2d Cir.), *cert. denied,* 423
U.S. 860 (1975). The opportunity for cross-examination must have been
full, substantial, and meaningful. *U.S. v. Fiore,* 443 F.2d 112 (2d Cir.
1971), *cert. denied,* 410 U.S. 984 (1973) (introduction of grand jury
testimony of witness who refused to be sworn was held in violation of
both the hearsay rule and the confrontation clause). *See also U.S. v.
Marks,* 585 F.2d 164, 168-69 (6th Cir. 1978). Sufficient opportunity is
available for cross-examination by defense at the preliminary hearing.
*Phillips v. Wyrick,* 558 F.2d 489, 493-95 (8th Cir. 1977), *cert. denied,*
434 U.S. 1088 (1978). Each of the Rule's elements must be satisfied to
admit former testimony. For example, the "similar motive" requirement may not be waived to permit the introduction of exculpatory
grand jury testimony in the interest of adversarial fairness. *U.S. v.
Salerno,* 112 S. Ct. 2503 (1992). (Upon remand the Court found that a
"similar motive" was present in *Salerno. U.S. v. Salerno,* 974 F.2d 231

(2d Cir. 1992)). Testimony of a codefendant given at a pretrial hearing was held inadmissible in favor of a defendant at trial since the government did not have the same motive to cross-examine at the hearing. *U.S. v. Wingate,* 520 F.2d 309, 316 (2d Cir. 1975), *cert. denied,* 423 U.S. 1074 (1976).

In an appropriate case, the pretrial deposition procedure set forth in Rule 15 of the Federal Rules of Criminal Procedure might be used. That rule provides for the taking of a witness' deposition under "exceptional circumstances" on motion by either side and the preservation of his testimony for use at trial. Thereafter, the witness' deposition may be used as substantive evidence at trial if the witness is "unavailable" as that term is defined in Rule 804(a). A videotaped deposition supplies a substantially comparable situation to a trial, but adherence to the procedural prerequisites of Rule 15 is mandatory. *U.S. v. Benfield,* 593 F.2d 815, 821 (8th Cir. 1979) (where defendant was not permitted to be active participant, use of videotaped deposition violated his right to confrontation).

### § 2142. — Statement Under Belief of Impending Death: Rule 804(b)(2).

A "statement made by a declarant while believing that his death was imminent, concerning the cause of circumstances of what he believed to be his impending death" is excepted from the hearsay rule. This exception reflects traditional common law. It is available only in homicide cases to show the cause of death. *See U.S. v. Martinez,* 536 F.2d 886, 889 (9th Cir.), *cert. denied,* 429 U.S. 907 (1976) (declaration was admissible because declarant believed death imminent).

### § 2143. — Statements Against Interest: Rule 804(b)(3).

### § 2144. — — Statements Against Interest Generally.

If the declarant is unavailable, his statement is not barred by the hearsay rule, providing that, at the time of its making, the statement was so far contrary to the declarant's "pecuniary or proprietary interest, or so far tended to subject him to civil or criminal liability, or to render invalid a claim by him against another," that "a reasonable man in his position would not have made the statement unless he believed it to be true." *See U.S. v. Santarpio,* 560 F.2d 448, 453 (1st Cir.), *cert. denied,* 434 U.S. 984 (1977) (statements made by confessed bookmakers concerning gambling operation were held admissible as against penal interest).

Rule 403 requires the judge to evaluate the probative value of proffered statements prior to admission. Other evidence bearing on reliability of the evidence is also relevant to the evaluation. *See U.S. v. Metz,* 608 F.2d 147, 157 (5th Cir. 1979) (statement of codefendant exculpatory of defendant was held inadmissible where declarant stated he did not know defendant, and other guarantees of trustworthiness were lacking); *Witham v. Mabry,* 596 F.2d 293, 297-98 (8th Cir. 1979); *U.S. v. White,* 553 F.2d 310, 313 (2d Cir.), *cert. denied,* 431 U.S. 972 (1977). *But see U.S. v. Toney,* 599 F.2d 787, 790 (6th Cir. 1979) (error for court not to admit alleged robber's statement against his penal interest to FBI following his arrest where sufficient corroborative factors were present). Statements against the penal interest of the declarant must be sufficiently inculpatory to be found admissible. *U.S. v. Hoyos,* 573 F.2d 1111, 1115 (9th Cir. 1978). *See U.S. v. Oropeza,* 564 F.2d 316, 325 (9th Cir. 1977), *cert. denied,* 434 U.S. 1080 (1978). *But see U.S. v. Barrett,* 539 F.2d 244, 251-53 (1st Cir. 1976); *U.S. v. Alvarez,* 584 F.2d 694, 699-700 (5th Cir. 1978) (cases where disserving portions of statements against interest were fortified by a showing of insiders' knowledge).

The courts have also been willing to assume that a reasonable man would be aware of disserving nature of his remarks even when made to a supposed friend. *U.S. v. Goins,* 593 F.2d 88, 90-91 (8th Cir.), *cert. denied,* 444 U.S. 828 (1979), *U.S. v. Barrett,* 539 F.2d at 251; *U.S. v. Bagley,* 537 F.2d 162, 165 (5th Cir. 1976), *cert. denied,* 429 U.S. 1075 (1977). *See also U.S. v. Lang,* 589 F.2d 92 (2d Cir. 1978). Courts have had more difficulty, however, with statements which, although against interest on their face, may have been made to gain an advantage, especially where a person in custody makes a confession as part of a plea bargain. *U.S. v. Mackin,* 561 F.2d 958, 961-62 (D.C. Cir.), *cert. denied,* 434 U.S. 959 (1977); *U.S. v. Gonzalez,* 559 F.2d 1271 (5th Cir. 1977); *U.S. v. Rogers,* 549 F.2d 490, 498 n.8 (8th Cir. 1976), *cert. denied,* 431 U.S. 918 (1977). *Compare U.S. v. Thomas,* 571 F.2d 285, 290 (5th Cir. 1978). *See also U.S. v. White,* 553 F.2d at 313. *Cf. U.S. v. Trejo-Zambrano,* 582 F.2d 460 (9th Cir. 1978), *cert. denied,* 439 U.S. 1005 (1979). Personal motives of a declarant are also considered by the court. *U.S. v. Pena,* 527 F.2d 1356, 1361 (5th Cir.), *cert. denied,* 426 U.S. 949 (1976).

Rule 804(b)(1), of course, does not do away with the Rule 602 requirement of firsthand knowledge. *U.S. v. Lang,* 589 F.2d at 97-98 (statement against penal interest was not admitted because of declarant's admitted lack of knowledge of defendant's criminal involvement).

Inculpatory statements against the penal interest of the defendant offered against him may create confrontation clause problems. The inculpatory confession has been analogized to a statement having both self-serving and disserving aspects. Inculpatory statements, which on their face are against declarant's interest, are admitted only after analysis of reliability in the setting of the particular facts of each case. *See U.S. v. Alvarez,* 584 F.2d 694, 701 (5th Cir. 1978).

Aside from constitutional considerations, unreliable statements are excluded as a matter of evidentiary law. *See U.S. v. Lilley,* 581 F.2d 182, 188 (8th Cir. 1978) (portions of statements not against penal interest should have been excluded because of lack of indicia of truthfulness); *U.S. v. White,* 553 F.2d 310, 314 (2d Cir. 1977), *cert. denied,* 431 U.S. 972 (1977) (trial court redacted bulk of inculpatory statements).

In assessing reliability of declarant and probative value of inculpatory statements, the courts examine several factors, such as the role of the declarant, *see U.S. v. Harris,* 403 U.S. 573, 595 (1971); whether he was in custody; whether appropriate *Miranda* warnings were given before the making of the statement; the present status of the charges and their resolution, *see U.S. v. Love,* 592 F.2d 1022, 1025 (8th Cir. 1979); *U.S. v. Bailey,* 581 F.2d 341, 345-50 (3d Cir. 1978); whether declarant is being tried jointly, *see Bruton v. U.S.,* 391 U.S. 123 (1968). All the above factors are considered by the courts. *See U.S. v. Boyce,* 594 F.2d 1246, 1249-51 (9th Cir.), *cert. denied,* 444 U.S. 855 (1979). *But see U.S. v. Alvarez,* 584 F.2d at 702 n.10, where the court noted several indicia of trustworthiness, including the apparent motive of declarant to misrepresent the matter, his general character, lack of other witnesses, and lack of statement's spontaneity.

Rule 403 provides that evidence must be excluded if its probative value is substantially outweighed by the danger of prejudice, and trial courts will often find that probative value is outweighed by the danger of unfair prejudice. *See U.S. v. White,* 553 F.2d at 314. *But cf. U.S. v. Lang,* 589 F.2d 92, 98 (2d Cir. 1978), in which the court excluded an inculpatory statement because it failed to meet personal knowledge test, but the court never mentioned the prejudice or confrontation problems.

### §2145. — — Statements Against Penal Interest Offered to Exculpate.

The second sentence of Rule 804(b)(3) imposes a further specific requirement for statements "tending to expose the declarant to criminal liability and offered to exculpate the accused" that "corroborating circumstances must clearly indicate the trustworthiness of the statement." Before the exculpating statement is admitted or can be made in the presence of the jury, the court must make a preliminary finding pursuant to Rule 104(a) that sufficient corroborating evidence has been offered. *See U.S. v. Barrett*, 539 F.2d 244, 251 (1st Cir. 1976). This should be done at a hearing immediately before trial. *See* Rule 17.1, Fed. R. Crim. P.

Courts look for sufficient corroboration to satisfy a "reasonable man" standard, requiring that the statement be made in good faith and likely be true. *U.S. v. Satterfield*, 572 F.2d 687, 692 (9th Cir.), *cert. denied*, 439 U.S. 840 (1978) (declarant's statement was not admitted because corroborating circumstances did not "clearly" indicate trustworthiness of the statement); *U.S. v. Hoyos*, 573 F.2d 1111, 1115 (9th Cir. 1978) (the court applied factors in *Satterfield* in refusing to admit the statement offered).

Courts have admitted statements, however, where there is evidence that the declarant was near the scene and criminal motive or other factors connected him with the crime, thus insuring sufficient reliability. *U.S. v. Thomas*, 571 F.2d 285, 290 (5th Cir. 1978); *U.S. v. Benveniste*, 564 F.2d 335, 341-42 (9th Cir. 1977); *U.S. v. Atkins*, 558 F.2d 133, 135 (3d Cir. 1977), *cert. denied*, 434 U.S. 1071 (1978); *U.S. v. Barrett*, 539 F.2d at 253. Courts do not make the burden of corroboration on the part of defendants very high. *See U.S. v. Benveniste*, 564 F.2d at 341-42 (citing *Chambers v. Mississippi*, 410 U.S. 284 (1973)); *U.S. v. Barrett*, 539 F.2d at 253. *But cf. U.S. v. Brandenfels*, 522 F.2d 1259, 1264 (9th Cir.), *cert. denied*, 423 U.S. 1033 (1975).

The four considerations for admission, enunciated by the Supreme Court in *Chambers v. Mississippi*, 410 U.S. at 300-01, are: (1) the time of the declaration and the party to whom the declaration was made; (2) the existence of corroborating evidence in the case; (3) the extent to which the declaration is really against the declarant's penal interest; and (4) the availability of the declarant as a witness. Since Rule 804(b)(3) presupposes unavailability, it is the first three considerations that will normally be determinative as to admission. *See U.S. v. Guillette*, 547 F.2d 743, 753-55 (2d Cir. 1976), *cert. denied*, 434 U.S. 839 (1977) (testimony of government informant excluded because there was lack of requisite corroborative evidence).

Under Rule 804(b)(3), trustworthiness is determined primarily by analysis of two elements: (1) the probable veracity of the in-court witness, and (2) the reliability of the out-of-court declarant. *See U.S. v. Alvarez*, 584 F.2d 694, 701 (5th Cir. 1978). *See also U.S. v. Bagley*, 537 F.2d 162, 165-68 (5th Cir. 1976), *cert. denied*, 429 U.S. 1075 (1977). Credibility of the witness may be considered as an aspect of probativeness. *U.S. v. Satterfield*, 572 F.2d at 691-92 (out-of-court statement was excluded where potential for fabrication and other elements were present suggesting it was untrustworthy).

The defendant must be told of any exculpatory statements in the hands of the government and can compel their production. *See U.S. v. Toney,* 599 F.2d 787, 790 (6th Cir. 1979) (alleged robber's statement to FBI following his arrest was against penal interest and corroborated defendant's story).

### § 2146. — Statement of Personal or Family History: Rule 804(b)(4).

This exception, which applies to statements concerning the declarant's own family history or the family history of someone related by blood or marriage, generally codifies the hearsay exception as it existed in common law. Many decisions previously held that the statement must be made prior to the existence of a lawsuit, but this requirement was dropped by the rule.

### § 2147. — Other Exceptions: Rule 804(b)(5).

This subsection, providing exceptions for statements not specifically covered by the other exceptions, parallels the provisions of Rule 803(24), discussed in this chapter, § 2136, *supra.* Because of the unavailability of the witness, the need for admission of the evidence is self-evident. Where probative value is high, courts have admitted hearsay statements pursuant to this rule when the requisite circumstantial guarantees of trustworthiness have been demonstrated. *U.S. v. Lyon,* 567 F.2d 777, 784 (8th Cir. 1977), *cert. denied,* 435 U.S. 918 (1978) (FBI agent's detailed testimony about how he took and transcribed an unavailable witness' testimony 10 years earlier was permitted); *U.S. v. Ward,* 552 F.2d 1080, 1082-83 (5th Cir.), *cert. denied,* 434 U.S. 850 (1977) (FBI agent's testimony concerning interview of driver of stolen truck, then unavailable, was permitted where content of hearsay was corroborated by other testimony). *But see U.S. v. Bailey,* 581 F.2d 341, 349 n.12 (3d Cir. 1978) (corroborating evidence was found to have sufficient degree of reliability); *U.S. v. Hoyos,* 573 F.2d 1111, 1116 (9th Cir. 1978); *U.S. v. Medico,* 557 F.2d 309, 316 (2d Cir.), *cert. denied,* 434 U.S. 986 (1977) (residual hearsay exception was properly relied upon to admit prosecution testimony concerning the license plate number of the getaway car in a bank robbery).

Grand jury testimony of unavailable witnesses might be admissible as evidence under Rule 804(b)(1) or (5). A conflict has arisen among the circuits concerning the effect of the sixth amendment confrontation clause. This issue has been resolved narrowly in every instance, with each case turning on its peculiar facts. *U.S. v. Carlson,* 547 F.2d 1346,

1354 (8th Cir. 1976), *cert. denied,* 431 U.S. 914 (1977) (government informant who testified before grand jury and refused to testify at trial, but reaffirmed grand jury testimony, was rendered "unavailable" because of threats by defendant). *Accord, U.S. v. Boulahanis,* 677 F.2d 586, 588-89 (7th Cir. 1982); *U.S. v. Balano,* 618 F.2d 624, 628-30 (10th Cir. 1979), *cert. denied,* 449 U.S. 840 (1980). The Fifth Circuit has held that where a defendant murders the chief witness against him, the defendant has waived confrontation and hearsay objections to the witness' previous Grand Jury testimony even though the Court holds there is lacking the requirements of admissibility under Rule 804(b)(5). *U.S. v. Thevis,* 665 F.2d 616, 630 (5th Cir.), *cert. denied,* 103 S. Ct. 57 (1982). Grand jury testimony has been admitted where there was sufficient corroboration at trial. *U.S. v. West,* 574 F.2d 1131, 1135-36, 1138 (4th Cir. 1978); *U.S. v. Garner,* 574 F.2d 1141, 1146 (4th Cir.), *cert. denied,* 439 U.S. 936 (1978). *But see U.S. v. Gonzalez,* 559 F.2d 1271, 1273 (5th Cir. 1977) (grand jury testimony of an unavailable declarant held inadmissible); *U.S. v. Fiore,* 443 F.2d 112, 115 (2d Cir. 1971), *cert. denied,* 410 U.S. 984 (1973) (introduction of grand jury testimony of witness who refused to be sworn was found to be in violation of hearsay rule and the confrontation clause). *See also U.S. v. Marks,* 585 F.2d 164, 168-69 (6th Cir. 1978). A videotaped deposition was ruled inadmissible for insufficient compliance with the confrontation clause in *U.S. v. Benfield,* 593 F.2d 815, 821 (8th Cir. 1979). Where indicia of reliability of declarant's out-of-court statement are found weak, confrontation clause restrictions are not easily overcome. *U.S. v. Love,* 592 F.2d 1022, 1026-27 (8th Cir. 1979).

## § 2148. Hearsay Within Hearsay.

Rule 805 provides that hearsay included within hearsay is not excluded if each part of the out-of-court declaration qualifies for admission under some exception provided in these rules. In other words, multiple hearsay is not excluded so long as each link in the chain of transmission of the statement is covered by a recognized exception to the hearsay rule. *See U.S. v. Diez,* 515 F.2d 892, 895-96 n.2 (5th Cir. 1975), *cert. denied,* 423 U.S. 1052 (1976); *U.S. v. Gerry,* 515 F.2d 130, 141-42 (2d Cir.), *cert. denied,* 423 U.S. 832 (1975); *U.S. v. Maddox,* 444 F.2d 148, 150-51 (2d Cir. 1971). Courts, however, will look for the necessary indicia of reliability for each link in the chain. *See U.S. v. Lang,* 589 F.2d 92, 99 (2d Cir. 1978).

## §2149. Attacking and Supporting the Credibility of Declarant.

Rule 806 provides that, if a hearsay statement is admitted in evidence, the opposing party may attack the credibility of the out-of-court declarant. The proponent of the statement may then introduce evidence to support the declarant's credibility. Credibility may be demonstrated "by any evidence which would be admissible for those purposes if declarant had testified as a witness." Where defense cross-examination of government witness brought out defendant's denial of involvement in crime, defendant's prior felony convictions were held admissible, even though defendant never testified. *U.S. v. Lawson,* 608 F.2d 1129 (6th Cir. 1979). *But see U.S. v. Lechoco,* 542 F.2d 84, 88-89 (D.C. Cir. 1976) (defendant was entitled to present supporting credibility evidence, even though he exercised fifth amendment privilege not to testify, when his credibility was open to attack).

## AMENDMENTS TO THE CONSTITUTION OF
## THE UNITED STATES

### AMENDMENT I

Congress shall make no law respecting an establishment of religion, or prohibiting the free exercise thereof; or abridging the freedom of speech, or of the press; or the right of the people peaceably to assemble, and to petition the Government for a redress of grievances.

### AMENDMENT II

A well regulated Militia, being necessary to the security of a free State, the right of the people to keep and bear Arms, shall not be infringed.

### AMENDMENT III

No Soldier shall, in time of peace be quartered in any house, without the consent of the Owner, nor in time of war, but in a manner to be prescribed by law.

### AMENDMENT IV

The right of the people to be secure in their persons, houses, papers, and effects, against unreasonable searches and seizures, shall not be violated, and no Warrants shall issue, but upon probable cause, supported by Oath or affirmation, and particularly describing the place to be searched, and the persons or things to be seized.

### AMENDMENT V

No person shall be held to answer for a capital, or otherwise infamous crime, unless on a presentment or indictment of a Grand Jury, except in cases arising in the land or naval forces, or in the Militia, when in actual service in time of War or public danger; nor shall any person be subject for the same offence to be twice put in jeopardy of life or limb; nor shall be compelled in any criminal case to be a witness against himself, nor be deprived of life, liberty, or property, without due process of law; nor shall private property be taken for public use, without just compensation.

### AMENDMENT VI

In all criminal prosecutions, the accused shall enjoy the right to a speedy and public trial, by an impartial jury of the State and district wherein the crime shall have been committed, which district shall have been previously ascertained by law, and to be informed of the nature and cause of the accusation; to be confronted with the witnesses against him; to have compulsory process for obtaining witnesses in his favor, and to have the Assistance of Counsel for his defense.

### AMENDMENT VII

In suits at common law, where the value in controversy shall exceed twenty dollars, the right of trial by jury shall be preserved, and no fact tried by a jury, shall be otherwise reexamined in any Court of the United States, than according to the rules of the common law.

## AMENDMENT VIII

Excessive bail shall not be required, nor excessive fines imposed, nor cruel and unusual punishments inflicted.

## AMENDMENT IX

The enumeration in the Constitution, of certain rights, shall not be construed to deny or disparage others retained by the people.

## AMENDMENT X

The powers not delegated to the United States by the Constitution, nor prohibited by it to the States, are reserved to the States respectively, or to the people.

## AMENDMENT XIV

### (Section 1)

All persons born or naturalized in the United States, and subject to the jurisdiction thereof, are citizens of the United States and of the State wherein they reside. No State shall make or enforce any law which shall abridge the privileges or immunities of citizens of the United States; nor shall any State deprive any person of life, liberty, or property, without due process of law; nor deny to any person within its jurisdiction the equal protection of the laws.

# APPENDIX B

## FEDERAL RULES OF CRIMINAL PROCEDURE

### I. SCOPE, PURPOSE, AND CONSTRUCTION.

**Rule 1. Scope.** These rules govern the procedure in all criminal proceedings in the courts of the United States, as provided in Rule 54(a); and, whenever specifically provided in one of the rules, to preliminary, supplementary, and special proceedings before United States magistrates and at proceedings before state and local judicial officers.

**Rule 2. Purpose and Construction.** These rules are intended to provide for the just determination of every criminal proceeding. They shall be construed to secure simplicity in procedure, fairness in administration and the elimination of unjustifiable expense and delay.

### PRELIMINARY PROCEEDINGS.

**Rule 3. The Complaint.** The complaint is a written statement of the essential facts constituting the offense charged. It shall be made upon oath before a magistrate.

**Rule 4. Arrest Warrant or Summons upon Complaint.** (a) *Issuance*. If it appears from the complaint, or from an affidavit or affidavits filed with the complaint, that there is probable cause to believe that an offense has been committed and that the defendant has committed it, a warrant for the arrest of the defendant shall issue to any officer authorized by law to execute it. Upon the request of the attorney for the government a summons instead of a warrant shall issue. More than one warrant or summons may issue on the same complaint. If a defendant fails to appear in response to the summons, a warrant shall issue.

(b) *Probable Cause*. The finding of probable cause may be based upon hearsay evidence in whole or in part.

(c) *Form*.

(1) Warrant. — The warrant shall be signed by the magistrate and shall contain the name of the defendant or, if the defendant's name is unknown, any name or description by which the defendant can be identified with reasonable certainty. It shall describe the offense charged in the complaint. It shall command that the defendant be arrested and brought before the nearest available magistrate.

(2) Summons. — The summons shall be in the same form as the warrant except that it shall summon the defendant to appear before a magistrate at a stated time and place.

(d) *Execution or Service; and Return*.

(1) By Whom. — The warrant shall be executed by a marshal or by some other officer authorized by law. The summons may be served by any person authorized to serve a summons in a civil action.

(2) Territorial Limits. — The warrant may be executed or the summons may be served at any place within the jurisdiction of the United States.

(3) Manner. — The warrant shall be executed by the arrest of the defendant. The officer need not have the warrant at the time of the arrest but upon request shall show the warrant to the defendant as soon as possible. If the officer does not have the

warrant at the time of the arrest, the officer shall then inform the defendant of the offense charged and of the fact that a warrant has been issued. The summons shall be served upon a defendant by delivering a copy to the defendant personally, or by leaving it at the defendant's dwelling house or usual place of abode with some person of suitable age and discretion then residing therein and by mailing a copy of the summons to the defendant's last known address.

(4) Return. — The officer executing a warrant shall make return thereof to the magistrate or other officer before whom the defendant is brought pursuant to Rule 5. At the request of the attorney for the government any unexecuted warrant shall be returned to and canceled by the magistrate by whom it was issued. On or before the return day the person to whom a summons was delivered for service shall make return thereof to the magistrate before whom the summons is returnable. At the request of the attorney for the government made at any time while the complaint is pending, a warrant returned unexecuted and not cancelled or a summons returned unserved or a duplicate thereof may be delivered by the magistrate to the marshal or other authorized person for execution or service.

**Rule 5. Initial Appearance Before the Magistrate.** (a) *In General.* An officer making an arrest under a warrant issued upon a complaint or any person making an arrest without a warrant shall take the arrested person without unnecessary delay before the nearest available federal magistrate or, in the event that a federal magistrate is not reasonably available, before a state or local judicial officer authorized by 18 U.S.C. § 3041. If a person arrested without a warrant is brought before a magistrate, a complaint shall be filed forthwith which shall comply with the requirements of Rule 4(a) with respect to the showing of probable cause. When a person, arrested with or without a warrant or given a summons, appears initially before the magistrate, the magistrate shall proceed in accordance with the applicable subdivisions of this rule.

(b) *Misdemeanors and Other Petty Offenses.* If the charge against the defendant is a misdemeanor or other petty offense triable by a United States magistrate under 18 U.S.C. § 3401, the magistrate shall proceed in accordance with Rule 58.

(c) *Offenses not Triable by the United States Magistrate.* If the charge against the defendant is not triable by the United States magistrate, the defendant shall not be called upon to plead. The magistrate shall inform the defendant of the complaint against the defendant and of any affidavit filed therewith, of the defendant's right to retain counsel or to request the assignment of counsel if the defendant is unable to obtain counsel, and of the general circumstances under which the defendant may secure pretrial release. The magistrate shall inform the defendant that the defendant is not required to make a statement and that any statement made by the defendant may be used against the defendant. The magistrate shall also inform the defendant of the right to a preliminary examination. The magistrate shall allow the defendant reasonable time and opportunity to consult counsel and shall detain or conditionally release the defendant as provided by statute or in these rules.

A defendant is entitled to a preliminary examination, unless waived, when charged with any offense, other than a petty offense, which is to be tried by a judge of the district court. If the defendant waives preliminary examination, the magistrate shall forthwith hold the defendant to answer in the district court. If the defendant does not waive the preliminary examination, the magistrate shall schedule a preliminary examination. Such examination shall be held within a reasonable time but in any event not later than 10 days following the initial appearance if the defendant is in custody and no later than 20 days if the defendant is not in custody, provided, however, that the preliminary examination shall not be held if the defendant is indicted or if an information against the defendant is filed in district court before the date set for the preliminary examination. With the consent of the defendant and upon a showing of good cause, taking into account the public interest in the prompt disposition of criminal cases, time limits specified in this subdivision may be extended one or more times by a federal magistrate. In the absence of such consent by the defendant, time limits may be extended by a judge of the United States only upon a showing that extraordinary circumstances exist and that delay is indispensable to the interests of justice.

(As amended Mar. 9, 1987, eff. Aug. 1, 1987; May 1, 1990, eff. Dec. 1, 1990.)

**Rule 5.1. Preliminary Examination.** (a) *Probable Cause Finding*. If from the evidence it appears that there is probable cause to believe that an offense has been committed and that the defendant committed it, the federal magistrate shall forthwith hold the defendant to answer in district court. The finding of probable cause may be based upon hearsay evidence in whole or in part. The defendant may cross-examine adverse witnesses and may introduce evidence. Objections to evidence on the ground that it was acquired by unlawful means are not properly made at the preliminary examination. Motions to suppress must be made to the trial court as provided in Rule 12.

(b) *Discharge of Defendant*. If from the evidence it appears that there is no probable cause to believe that an offense has been committed or that the defendant committed it, the federal magistrate shall dismiss the complaint and discharge the defendant. The discharge of the defendant shall not preclude the government from instituting a subsequent prosecution for the same offense.

(c) *Records*. After concluding the proceeding the federal magistrate shall transmit forthwith to the clerk of the district court all papers in the proceeding. The magistrate shall promptly make or cause to be made a record or summary of such proceeding.

(1) On timely application to a federal magistrate, the attorney for a defendant in a criminal case may be given the opportunity to have the recording of the hearing on preliminary examination made available to that attorney in connection with any further hearing or preparation for trial. The court may, by local rule, appoint the place for and define the conditions under which such opportunity may be afforded counsel.

(2) On application of a defendant addressed to the court or any judge thereof, an order may issue that the federal magistrate make available a copy of the transcript, or of a portion thereof, to defense counsel. Such order shall provide for prepayment of costs of such transcript by the defendant unless the defendant makes a sufficient affidavit that the defendant is unable to pay or to give security therefor, in which case the expense shall be paid by the Director of the Administrative Office of the United States Courts from available appropriated funds. Counsel for the government may move also that a copy of the transcript, in whole or in part, be made available to it, for good cause shown, and an order may be entered granting such motion in whole or in part, on appropriate terms, except that the government need not prepay costs nor furnish security therefor.

## III. INDICTMENT AND INFORMATION.

**Rule 6. The Grand Jury.** (a) *Summoning Grand Juries*. (1) Generally. — The court shall order one or more grand juries to be summoned at such time as the public interest requires. The grand jury shall consist of not less than 16 nor more than 23 members. The court shall direct that a sufficient number of legally qualified persons be summoned to meet this requirement.

(2) Alternate Jurors. — The court may direct that alternate jurors may be designated at the time a grand jury is selected. Alternate jurors in the order in which they were designated may thereafter be impanelled as provided in subdivision (g) of this rule. Alternate jurors shall be drawn in the same manner and shall have the same qualifications as the regular jurors, and if impanelled shall be subject to the same challenges, shall take the same oath and shall have the same functions, powers, facilities and privileges as the regular jurors.

(b) *Objections to Grand Jury and to Grand Jurors.*

(1) Challenges. — The attorney for the government or a defendant who has been held to answer in the district court may challenge the array of jurors on the ground that the grand jury was not selected, drawn or summoned in accordance with law, and may challenge an individual juror on the ground that the juror is not legally qualified. Challenges shall be made before the administration of the oath to the jurors and shall be tried by the court.

(2) Motion to Dismiss. — A motion to dismiss the indictment may be based on objections to the array or on the lack of legal qualification of an individual juror, if not previously determined upon challenge. It shall be made in the manner prescribed in 28 U.S.C. § 1867(e) and shall be granted under the conditions prescribed in that statute. An indictment shall not be dismissed on the ground that one or more members of the grand jury were not legally qualified if it appears from the record kept pursuant to subdivision (c) of this rule that 12 or more jurors, after deducting the number not legally qualified, concurred in finding the indictment.

(c) *Foreperson and Deputy Foreperson.* The court shall appoint one of the jurors to be foreperson and another to be deputy foreperson. The foreperson shall have power to administer oaths and affirmations and shall sign all indictments. The foreperson or another juror designated by the foreperson shall keep a record of the number of jurors concurring in the finding of every indictment and shall file the record with the clerk of the court, but the record shall not be made public except on order of the court. During the absence of the foreperson, the deputy foreperson shall act as foreperson.

(d) *Who May Be Present.* Attorneys for the government, the witness under examination, interpreters when needed and, for the purpose of taking the evidence, a stenographer or operator of a recording device may be present while the grand jury is in session, but no person other than the jurors may be present while the grand jury is deliberating or voting.

(e) *Recording and Disclosure of Proceedings.*

(1) Recording of Proceedings. — All proceedings, except when the grand jury is deliberating or voting, shall be recorded stenographically or by an electronic recording device. An unintentional failure of any recording to reproduce all or any portion of a proceeding shall not affect the validity of the prosecution. The recording or reporter's notes or any transcript prepared therefrom shall remain in the custody or control of the attorney for the government unless otherwise ordered by the court in a particular case.

(2) General Rule of Secrecy. — A grand juror, an interpreter, a stenographer, an operator of a recording device, a typist who transcribes recorded testimony, an attorney for the government, or any person to whom disclosure is made under paragraph (3)(A)(ii) of this subdivision shall not disclose matters occurring before the grand jury, except as otherwise provided for in these rules. No obligation of secrecy may be imposed on any person except in accordance with this rule. A knowing violation of Rule 6 may be punished as a contempt of court.

(3) Exceptions. —

(A) Disclosure otherwise prohibited by this rule of matters occurring before the grand jury, other than its deliberations and the vote of any grand juror, may be made to:

    (i) an attorney for the government for use in the performance of such attorney's duty; and

    (ii) such government personnel (including personnel of a state or subdivision of a state) as are deemed necessary by an attorney for the government to assist an attorney for the government in the performance of such attorney's duty to enforce federal criminal law.

(B) Any person to whom matters are disclosed under subparagraph (A)(ii) of this paragraph shall not utilize that grand jury material for any purpose other than assisting the attorney for the government in the performance of such attorney's duty to enforce federal criminal law. An attorney for the government shall promptly provide the district court, before which was impaneled the grand jury whose material has been so disclosed, with the names of the persons to whom such disclosure has been made, and shall certify that the attorney has advised such persons of their obligation of secrecy under this rule.

(C) Disclosure otherwise prohibited by this rule of matters occurring before the grand jury may also be made:

    (i) when so directed by a court preliminarily to or in connection with a judicial proceeding;

    (ii) when permitted by a court at the request of the defendant, upon a showing that grounds may exist for a motion to dismiss the indictment because of matters occurring before the grand jury;

    (iii) when the disclosure is made by an attorney for the government to another federal grand jury; or

    (iv) when permitted by a court at the request of an attorney for the government, upon a showing that such matters may disclose a violation of state criminal law, to an appropriate official of a state or subdivision of a state for the purpose of enforcing such law.

If the court orders disclosure of matters occurring before the grand jury, the disclosure shall be made in such manner, at such time, and under such conditions as the court may direct.

(D) A petition for disclosure pursuant to subdivision (e)(3)(C)(i) shall be filed in the district where the grand jury convened. Unless the hearing is ex parte, which it may be when the petitioner is the government, the petitioner shall serve written notice of the petition upon (i) the attorney for the government, (ii) the parties to the judicial proceeding if disclosure is sought in connection with such a proceeding, and (iii) such other persons as the court may direct. The court shall afford those persons a reasonable opportunity to appear and be heard.

(E) If the judicial proceeding giving rise to the petition is in a federal district court in another district, the court shall transfer the matter to that court unless it can reasonably obtain sufficient knowledge of the proceeding to determine whether disclosure is proper. The court shall order transmitted to the court to which the matter is transferred the material sought to be disclosed, if feasible, and a written evaluation of the need for continued grand jury secrecy. The court to which the matter is transferred shall afford the aforementioned persons a reasonable opportunity to appear and be heard.

(4) Sealed Indictments. — The federal magistrate to whom an indictment is returned may direct that the indictment be kept secret until the defendant is in custody or has been released pending trial. Thereupon the clerk shall seal the indictment and no person shall disclose the return of the indictment except when necessary for the issuance and execution of a warrant or summons.

(5) Closed Hearing. — Subject to any right to an open hearing in contempt proceedings, the court shall order a hearing on matters affecting a grand jury proceeding to be closed to the extent necessary to prevent disclosure of matters occurring before a grand jury.

(6) Sealed Records. — Records, orders and subpoenas relating to grand jury proceedings shall be kept under seal to the extent and for such time as is necessary to prevent disclosure of matters occurring before a grand jury.

(f) *Finding and Return of Indictment.* An indictment may be found only upon the concurrence of 12 or more jurors. The indictment shall be returned by the grand jury to a federal magistrate in open court. If a complaint or information is pending against the defendant and 12 jurors do not concur in finding an indictment, the foreperson shall so report to a federal magistrate in writing forthwith.

(g) *Discharge and Excuse.* A grand jury shall serve until discharged by the court, but no grand jury may serve more than 18 months unless the court extends the service of the grand jury for a period of six months or less upon a determination that such extension is in the public interest. At any time for cause shown the court may excuse a juror either temporarily or permanently, and in the latter event the court may impanel another person in place of the juror excused.

**Rule 7. The Indictment and the Information.** (a) *Use of Indictment or Information.* An offense which may be punished by death shall be prosecuted by indictment. An offense which may be punished by imprisonment for a term exceeding one year or at hard labor shall be prosecuted by indictment or, if indictment is waived, it may be prosecuted by information. Any other offense may be prosecuted by indictment or by information. An information may be filed without leave of court.

(b) *Waiver of Indictment.* An offense which may be punished by imprisonment for a term exceeding one year or at hard labor may be prosecuted by information if the defendant, after having been advised of the nature of the charge and of the rights of the defendant, waives in open court prosecution by indictment.

(c) *Nature and Contents.*

(1) In General. — The indictment or the information shall be a plain, concise and definite written statement of the essential facts constituting the offense charged. It shall be signed by the attorney for the government. It need not contain a formal commencement, a formal conclusion or any other matter not necessary to such statement. Allegations made in one count may be incorporated by reference in another count. It may be alleged in a single count that the means by which the defendant committed the offense are unknown or that the defendant committed it by one or more specified means. The indictment or information shall state for each count the official or customary citation of the statute, rule, regulation or other provision of law which the defendant is alleged therein to have violated.

(2) Criminal Forfeiture. — No judgment of forfeiture may be entered in a criminal proceeding unless the indictment or the information shall allege the extent of the interest or property subject to forfeiture.

(3) Harmless Error. — Error in the citation or its omission shall not be ground for dismissal of the indictment or information or for reversal of a conviction if the error or omission did not mislead the defendant to the defendant's prejudice.

(d) *Surplusage.* The court on motion of the defendant may strike surplusage from the indictment or information.

(e) *Amendment of Information.* The court may permit an information to be amended at any time before verdict or finding if no additional or different offense is charged and if substantial rights of the defendant are not prejudiced.

(f) *Bill of Particulars.* The court may direct the filing of a bill of particulars. A motion for a bill of particulars may be made before arraignment or within ten days after arraignment or at such later time as the court may permit. A bill of particulars may be amended at any time subject to such conditions as justice requires.

**Rule 8. Joinder of Offenses and of Defendants.** (a) *Joinder of Offenses.* Two or more offenses may be charged in the same indictment or information in a separate count for each offense if the offenses charged, whether felonies or misdemeanors or both, are of the same or similar character or are based on the same act or transaction or on two or more acts or transactions connected together or constituting parts of a common scheme or plan.

(b) *Joinder of Defendants.* Two or more defendants may be charged in the same indictment or information if they are alleged to have participated in the same act or transaction or in the same series of acts or transactions constituting an offense or offenses. Such defendants may be charged in one or more counts together or separately and all of the defendants need not be charged in each count.

**Rule 9. Warrant or Summons Upon Indictment or Information.** (a) *Issuance.* Upon the request of the attorney for the government the court shall issue a warrant for each defendant named in an information supported by a showing of probable cause under oath as is required by Rule 4(a), or in an indictment. Upon the request of the attorney for the government a summons instead of a warrant shall issue. If no request is made, the court may issue either a warrant or a summons in its discretion. More than one warrant or summons may issue for the same defendant. The clerk shall deliver the warrant or summons to the marshal or other person authorized by law to execute or serve it. If a defendant fails to appear in response to the summons, a warrant shall issue. When a defendant arrested with a warrant or given a summons appears initially before a magistrate, the magistrate shall proceed in accordance with the applicable subdivisions of Rule 5.

(b) *Form.*

(1) Warrant. The form of the warrant shall be as provided in Rule 4(c)(1) except that it shall be signed by the clerk, it shall describe the offense charged in the indictment or information and it shall command that the defendant be arrested and brought before the nearest available magistrate. The amount of bail may be fixed by the court and endorsed on the warrant.

(2) Summons. The summons shall be in the same form as the warrant except that it shall summon the defendant to appear before a magistrate at a stated time and place.

(c) *Execution or Service; and Return.*

(1) Execution or Service. The warrant shall be executed or the summons served as provided in Rule 4(d)(1), (2) and (3). A summons to a corporation shall be served by delivering a copy to an officer or to a managing or general agent or to any other agent authorized by appointment or by law to receive service of process and, if the agent is one authorized by statute to receive service and the statute so requires, by also mailing a copy to the corporation's last known address within the district or at its principal place of business elsewhere in the United States. The officer executing the warrant

shall bring the arrested person without unnecessary delay before the nearest available federal magistrate or, in the event that a federal magistrate is not reasonably available, before a state or local judicial officer authorized by 18 U.S.C. § 3041.

(2) Return. The officer executing a warrant shall make return thereof to the magistrate or other officer before whom the defendant is brought. At the request of the attorney for the government any unexecuted warrant shall be returned and cancelled. On or before the return day the person to whom a summons was delivered for service shall make return thereof. At the request of the attorney for the government made at any time while the indictment or information is pending, a warrant returned unexecuted and not cancelled or a summons returned unserved or a duplicate thereof may be delivered by the clerk to the marshal or other authorized person for execution or service.

(d) *Remand to United States Magistrate for Trial of Minor Offenses. (Abrogated by order adopted April 28, 1982, effective August 1, 1982.)*

## IV. ARRAIGNMENT, AND PREPARATION FOR TRIAL.

**Rule 10. Arraignment.** Arraignment shall be conducted in open court and shall consist of reading the indictment or information to the defendant or stating to the defendant the substance of the charge and calling on the defendant to plead thereto. The defendant shall be given a copy of the indictment or information before being called upon to plead.

**Rule 11. Pleas.** (a) *Alternatives.*

(1) In General. A defendant may plead not guilty, guilty, or nolo contendere. If a defendant refuses to plead or if a defendant corporation fails to appear, the court shall enter a plea of not guilty.

(2) Conditional Pleas. With the approval of the court and the consent of the government, a defendant may enter a conditional plea of guilty or nolo contendere, reserving in writing the right, on appeal from the judgment, to review of the adverse determination of any specified pretrial motion. A defendant who prevails on appeal shall be allowed to withdraw the plea.

(b) *Nolo Contendere.* A defendant may plead nolo contendere only with the consent of the court. Such a plea shall be accepted by the court only after due consideration of the views of the parties and the interest of the public in the effective administration of justice.

(c) *Advice to Defendant.* Before accepting a plea of guilty or nolo contendere, the court must address the defendant personally in open court and inform the defendant of, and determine that the defendant understands, the following:

(1) the nature of the charge to which the plea is offered, the mandatory minimum penalty provided by law, if any, and the maximum possible penalty provided by law, including the effect of any special parole term and, when applicable, that the court may also order the defendant to make restitution to any victim of the offense; and

(2) if the defendant is not represented by an attorney, that the defendant has the right to be represented by an attorney at every stage of the proceeding and, if necessary, one will be appointed to represent the defendant; and

(3) that the defendant has the right to plead not guilty or to persist in that plea if it has already been made, the right to be tried by a jury and at that trial has the right to the assistance of counsel, the right to confront and cross-examine adverse witnesses, and the right against compelled self-incrimination; and

(4) that if a plea of guilty or nolo contendere is accepted by the court there will not be a further trial of any kind, so that by pleading guilty or nolo contendere the defendant waives the right to a trial; and

(5) if the court intends to question the defendant under oath, on the record, and in the presence of counsel about the offense to which the defendant has pleaded, that the defendant's answers may later be used against the defendant in a prosecution for perjury or false statement.

(d) *Insuring That the Plea Is Voluntary.* The court shall not accept a plea of guilty or nolo contendere without first, by addressing the defendant personally in open court, determining that the plea is voluntary and not the result of force or threats or of promises apart from a plea agreement. The court shall also inquire as to whether the defendant's willingness to plead guilty or nolo contendere results from prior discussions between the attorney for the government and the defendant or the defendant's attorney.

(e) *Plea Agreement Procedure.*

(1) In General. — The attorney for the government and the attorney for the defendant or the defendant when acting pro se may engage in discussions with a view toward reaching an agreement that, upon the entering of a plea of guilty or nolo contendere to a charged offense or to a lesser or related offense, the attorney for the government will do any of the following:

(A) Move for dismissal of other charges; or

(B) Make a recommendation, or agree not to oppose the defendant's request, for a particular sentence, with the understanding that such recommendation or request shall not be binding upon the court; or

(C) Agree that a specific sentence is the appropriate disposition of the case. The court shall not participate in any such discussions.

(2) Notice of Such Agreement. — If a plea agreement has been reached by the parties, the court shall, on the record, require the disclosure of the agreement in open court or, on a showing of good cause, in camera, at the time the plea is offered. If the agreement is of the type specified in subdivision (e)(1)(A) or (C), the court may accept or reject the agreement, or may defer its decision as to the acceptance or rejection until there has been an opportunity to consider the presentence report. If the agreement is of the type specified in subdivision (e)(1)(B), the court shall advise the defendant that if the court does not accept the recommendation or request the defendant nevertheless has no right to withdraw the plea.

(3) Acceptance of a Plea Agreement. — If the court accepts the plea agreement, the court shall inform the defendant that it will embody in the judgment and sentence the disposition provided for in the plea agreement.

(4) Rejection of a Plea Agreement. — If the court rejects the plea agreement, the court shall, on the record, inform the parties of this fact, advise the defendant personally in open court or, on a showing of good cause, in camera, that the court is not bound by the plea agreement, afford the defendant the opportunity to then withdraw the plea, and advise the defendant that if the defendant persists in a guilty plea or plea of nolo contendere the disposition of the case may be less favorable to the defendant than that contemplated by the plea agreement.

(5) Time of Plea Agreement Procedure. — Except for good cause shown, notification to the court of the existence of a plea agreement shall be given at the arraignment or at such other time, prior to trial, as may be fixed by the court.

(6) Inadmissibility of Pleas, Plea Discussions, and Related Statements. — Except as otherwise provided in this paragraph, evidence of the following is not, in any civil or

criminal proceeding, admissible against the defendant who made the plea or was a participant in the plea discussions:

(A) a plea of guilty which was later withdrawn;

(B) a plea of nolo contendere;

(C) any statement made in the course of any proceedings under this rule regarding either of the foregoing pleas; or

(D) any statement made in the course of plea discussions with an attorney for the government which do not result in a plea of guilty or which result in a plea of guilty later withdrawn.

However, such a statement is admissible (i) in any proceeding wherein another statement made in the course of the same plea or plea discussions has been introduced and the statement ought in fairness be considered contemporaneously with it, or (ii) in a criminal proceeding for perjury or false statement if the statement was made by the defendant under oath, on the record, and in the presence of counsel.

(f) *Determining Accuracy of Plea.* Notwithstanding the acceptance of a plea of guilty, the court should not enter a judgment upon such plea without making such inquiry as shall satisfy it that there is a factual basis for the plea.

(g) *Record of Proceedings.* A verbatim record of the proceedings at which the defendant enters a plea shall be made and, if there is a plea of guilty or nolo contendere, the record shall include, without limitation, the court's advice to the defendant, the inquiry into the voluntariness of the plea including any plea agreement, and the inquiry into the accuracy of a guilty plea.

(h) *Harmless Error.* Any variance from the procedures required by this rule which does not affect substantial rights shall be disregarded.

**Rule 12. Pleadings and Motions Before Trial; Defenses and Objections.** (a) *Pleadings and Motions.* Pleadings in criminal proceedings shall be the indictment and the information, and the pleas of not guilty, guilty and nolo contendere. All other pleas, and demurrers and motions to quash are abolished, and defenses and objections raised before trial which heretofore could have been raised by one or more of them shall be raised only by motion to dismiss or to grant appropriate relief, as provided in these rules.

(b) *Pretrial Motions.* Any defense, objection, or request which is capable of determination without the trial of the general issue may be raised before trial by motion. Motions may be written or oral at the discretion of the judge. The following must be raised prior to trial:

(1) Defenses and objections based on defects in the institution of the prosecution; or

(2) Defenses and objections based on defects in the indictment or information (other than that it fails to show jurisdiction in the court or to charge an offense which objections shall be noticed by the court at any time during the pendency of the proceedings); or

(3) Motions to suppress evidence; or

(4) Requests for discovery under Rule 16; or

(5) Requests for a severance of charges or defendants under Rule 14.

(c) *Motion Date.* Unless otherwise provided by local rule, the court may, at the time of the arraignment or as soon thereafter as practicable, set a time for the making of pretrial motions or requests and, if required, a later date of hearing.

(d) *Notice by the Government of the Intention to Use Evidence.*

(1) At the Discretion of the Government. — At the arraignment or as soon thereafter as is practicable, the government may give notice to the defendant of its intention to

use specified evidence at trial in order to afford the defendant an opportunity to raise objections to such evidence prior to trial under subdivision (b)(3) of this rule.

(2) At the Request of the Defendant. — At the arraignment or as soon thereafter as is practicable the defendant may, in order to afford an opportunity to move to suppress evidence under subdivision (b)(3) of this rule, request notice of the government's intention to use (in its evidence in chief at trial) any evidence which the defendant may be entitled to discover under Rule 16 subject to any relevant limitations prescribed in Rule 16.

(e) *Ruling on Motion.* A motion made before trial shall be determined before trial unless the court, for good cause, orders that it be deferred for determination at the trial of the general issue or until after verdict, but no such determination shall be deferred if a party's right to appeal is adversely affected. Where factual issues are involved in determining a motion, the court shall state its essential findings on the record.

(f) *Effect of Failure to Raise Defenses or Objections.* Failure by a party to raise defenses or objections or to make requests which must be made prior to trial, at the time set by the court pursuant to subdivision (c), or prior to any extension thereof made by the court, shall constitute waiver thereof, but the court for cause shown may grant relief from the waiver.

(g) *Records.* A verbatim record shall be made of all proceedings at the hearing, including such findings of fact and conclusions of law as are made orally.

(h) *Effect of Determination.* If the court grants a motion based on a defect in the institution of the prosecution or in the indictment or information, it may also order that the defendant be continued in custody or that bail be continued for a specified time pending the filing of a new indictment or information. Nothing in this rule shall be deemed to affect the provisions of any act of Congress relating to periods of limitations.

(i) *Production of Statements at Suppression Hearing.* Except as herein provided, rule 26.2 shall apply at a hearing on a motion to suppress evidence under subdivision (b)(3) of this rule. For purposes of this subdivision, a law enforcement officer shall be deemed a witness called by the government, and upon a claim of privilege the court shall excise the portions of the statement containing privileged matter.

**Rule 12.1. Notice of Alibi.** (a) *Notice by Defendant.* Upon written demand of the attorney for the government stating the time, date, and place at which the alleged offense was committed, the defendant shall serve within ten days, or at such different time as the court may direct, upon the attorney for the government a written notice of the defendant's intention to offer a defense of alibi. Such notice by the defendant shall state the specific place or places at which the defendant claims to have been at the time of the alleged offense and the names and addresses of the witnesses upon whom the defendant intends to rely to establish such alibi.

(b) *Disclosure of Information and Witness.* Within ten days thereafter, but in no event less than ten days before trial, unless the court otherwise directs, the attorney for the government shall serve upon the defendant or the defendant's attorney a written notice stating the names and addresses of the witnesses upon whom the government intends to rely to establish the defendant's presence at the scene of the alleged offense and any other witnesses to be relied on to rebut testimony of any of the defendant's alibi witnesses.

(c) *Continuing Duty to Disclose.* If prior to or during trial, a party learns of an additional witness whose identity, if known, should have been included in the information furnished under subdivision (a) or (b), the party shall promptly notify the other party or the other party's attorney of the existence and identity of such additional witness.

(d) *Failure to Comply*. Upon the failure of either party to comply with the requirements of this rule, the court may exclude the testimony of any undisclosed witness offered by such party as to the defendant's absence from or presence at, the scene of the alleged offense. This rule shall not limit the right of the defendant to testify.

(e) *Exceptions*. For good cause shown, the court may grant an exception to any of the requirements of subdivisions (a) through (d) of this rule.

(f) *Inadmissibility of Withdrawn Alibi*. Evidence of an intention to rely upon an alibi defense, later withdrawn, or of statements made in connection with such intention, is not, in any civil or criminal proceeding, admissible against the person who gave notice of the intention.

**Rule 12.2. Notice of Defense Based upon Mental Condition.** (a) *Defense of Insanity*. If a defendant intends to rely upon the defense of insanity at the time of the alleged offense, the defendant shall, within the time provided for the filing of pretrial motions or at such later time as the court may direct, notify the attorney for the government in writing of such intention and file a copy of such notice with the clerk. If there is a failure to comply with the requirements of this subdivision, insanity may not be raised as a defense. The court may for cause shown allow late filing of the notice or grant additional time to the parties to prepare for trial or make such other order as may be appropriate.

(b) *Expert Testimony of Defendant's Mental Condition*. If a defendant intends to introduce expert testimony relating to a mental disease or defect or any other mental condition of the defendant bearing upon the issue of guilt, the defendant shall, within the time provided for the filing of pretrial motions or at such later time as the court may direct, notify the attorney for the government in writing of such intention and file a copy of such notice with the clerk. The court may for cause shown allow late filing of the notice or grant additional time to the parties to prepare for trial or make such other order as may be appropriate.

(c) *Mental Examination of Defendant*. In an appropriate case the court may, upon motion of the attorney for the government, order the defendant to submit to an examination pursuant to 18 U.S.C. 4241 or 4242. No statement made by the defendant in the course of any examination provided for by this rule, whether the examination be with or without the consent of the defendant, no testimony by the expert based upon such statement, and no other fruits of the statement shall be admitted in evidence against the defendant in any criminal proceeding except on an issue respecting mental condition on which the defendant has introduced testimony.

(d) *Failure to Comply*. If there is a failure to give notice when required by subdivision (b) of this rule or to submit to an examination when ordered under subdivision (c) of this rule, the court may exclude the testimony of any expert witness offered by the defendant on the issue of the defendant's guilt.

(e) *Inadmissibility of Withdrawn Intention*. Evidence of an intention as to which notice was given under subdivision (a) or (b), later withdrawn, is not, in any civil or criminal proceeding, admissible against the person who gave notice of the intention.

**Rule 13. Trial Together of Indictments or Informations.** The court may order two or more indictments or informations or both to be tried together if the offenses, and the defendants if there is more than one, could have been joined in a single indictment or information. The procedure shall be the same as if the prosecution were under such single indictment or information.

**Rule 14. Relief from Prejudicial Joinder.** If it appears that a defendant or the government is prejudiced by a joinder of offenses or of defendants in an indictment or information or by such joinder for trial together, the court may order an election or separate trials of counts, grant a severance of defendants or provide whatever other relief justice requires. In ruling on a motion by a defendant for severance the court may order the attorney for the government to deliver to the court for inspection *in camera* any statements or confessions made by the defendants which the government intends to introduce in evidence at the trial.

**Rule 15. Depositions.** (a) *When Taken.* Whenever due to exceptional circumstances of the case it is in the interest of justice that the testimony of a prospective witness of a party be taken and preserved for use at trial, the court may upon motion of such party and notice to the parties order that testimony of such witness be taken by deposition and that any designated book, paper, document, record, recording, or other material not privileged, be produced at the same time and place. If a witness is detained pursuant to section 3144 of title 18, United States Code, the court on written motion of the witness and upon notice to the parties may direct that the witness' deposition be taken. After the deposition has been subscribed the court may discharge the witness.

(b) *Notice of Taking.* The party at whose instance a deposition is to be taken shall give to every party reasonable written notice of the time and place for taking the deposition. The notice shall state the name and address of each person to be examined. On motion of a party upon whom the notice is served, the court for cause shown may extend or shorten the time or change the place for taking the deposition. The officer having custody of a defendant shall be notified of the time and place set for the examination and shall, unless the defendant waives in writing the right to be present, produce the defendant at the examination and keep the defendant in the presence of the witness during the examination, unless, after being warned by the court that disruptive conduct will cause the defendant's removal from the place of the taking of the deposition, the defendant persists in conduct which is such as to justify exclusion from that place. A defendant not in custody shall have the right to be present at the examination upon request subject to such terms as may be fixed by the court, but a failure, absent good cause shown, to appear after notice and tender of expenses in accordance with subdivision (c) of this rule shall constitute a waiver of that right and of any objection to the taking and use of the deposition based upon that right.

(c) *Payment of Expenses.* Whenever a deposition is taken at the instance of the government, or whenever a deposition is taken at the instance of a defendant who is unable to bear the expenses of the taking of the deposition, the court may direct that the expense of travel and subsistence of the defendant and the defendant's attorney for attendance at the examination and the cost of the transcript of the deposition shall be paid by the government.

(d) *How Taken.* Subject to such additional conditions as the court shall provide, a deposition shall be taken and filed in the manner provided in civil actions except as otherwise provided in these rules, provided that (1) in no event shall a deposition be taken of a party defendant without that defendant's consent, and (2) the scope and manner of examination and cross-examination shall be such as would be allowed in the trial itself. The government shall make available to the defendant or the defendant's

531

counsel for examination and use at the taking of the deposition any statement of the witness being deposed which is in the possession of the government and to which the defendant would be entitled at the trial.

(e) *Use.* At the trial or upon any hearing, a part or all of a deposition, so far as otherwise admissible under the rules of evidence, may be used as substantive evidence if the witness is unavailable, as unavailability is defined in Rule 804(a) of the Federal Rules of Evidence, or the witness gives testimony at the trial or hearing inconsistent with that witness' deposition. Any deposition may also be used by any party for the purpose of contradicting or impeaching the testimony of the deponent as a witness. If only a part of a deposition is offered in evidence by a party, an adverse party may require the offering of all of it which is relevant to the part offered and any party may offer other parts.

(f) *Objections to Deposition Testimony.* Objections to deposition testimony or evidence or parts thereof and the grounds for the objection shall be stated at the time of the taking of the deposition.

(g) *Deposition by Agreement Not Precluded.* Nothing in this rule shall preclude the taking of a deposition, orally or upon written questions, or the use of a deposition, by agreement of the parties with the consent of the court.

**Rule 16. Discovery and Inspection.** (a) *Disclosure of Evidence by the Government.*
(1) Information Subject to Disclosure. —

(A) Statement of Defendant. — Upon request of a defendant the government shall disclose to the defendant and make available for inspection, copying, or photocopying: any relevant written or recorded statements made by the defendant, or copies thereof, within the possession, custody or control of the government, the existence of which is known, or by the exercise of due diligence may become known, to the attorney of the government; that portion of any written record containing the substance of any relevant oral statement made by the defendant whether before or after arrest in response to interrogation by any person then known to the defendant to be a government agent; and recorded testimony of the defendant before a grand jury which relates to the offense charged. The government shall also disclose to the defendant the substance of any other relevant oral statement made by the defendant whether before or after arrest in response to interrogation by any person then known by the defendant to be a government agent if the government intends to use that statement at trial. Where the defendant is a corporation, partnership, association, or labor union, the court may grant the defendant, upon its motion, discovery of relevant recorded testimony of any witness before a grand jury who (1) was, at the time of the testimony, so situated as an officer or employee as to have been able legally to bind the defendant in respect to conduct constituting the offense, or (2) was, at the time of the offense, personally involved in the alleged conduct constituting the offense and so situated as an officer or employee as to have been able legally to bind the defendant in respect to that alleged conduct in which the witness was involved.

(B) Defendant's Prior Record. — Upon request of the defendant, the government shall furnish to the defendant such copy of the defendant's prior criminal record, if any, as is within the possession, custody, or control of the government, the existence of which is known, or by the exercise of due diligence may become known, to the attorney for the government.

(C) Documents and Tangible Objects. — Upon request of the defendant the government shall permit the defendant to inspect and copy or photograph books, papers, documents, photographs, tangible objects, buildings or places, or copies or portions thereof, which are within the possession, custody or control of the government, and which are material to the preparation of the defendant's defense or are intended for use by the government as evidence in chief at the trial, or were obtained from or belong to the defendant.

(D) Reports of Examinations and Tests. — Upon request of a defendant the government shall permit the defendant to inspect and copy or photograph any results or reports of physical or mental examinations, and of scientific tests or experiments, or copies thereof, which are within the possession, custody, or control of the government, the existence of which is known, or by the exercise of due diligence may become known, to the attorney for the government, and which are material to the preparation of the defense or are intended for use by the government as evidence in chief at the trial.

(2) Information Not Subject to Disclosure. — Except as provided in paragraphs (A), (B), and (D) of subdivision (a)(1), this rule does not authorize the discovery or inspection of reports, memoranda, or other internal government documents made by the attorney for the government or other government agents in connection with the investigation or prosecution of the case, or of statements made by government witnesses or prospective government witnesses except as provided in 18 U.S.C. § 3500.

(3) Grand Jury Transcripts. — Except as provided in Rules 6, 12(i) and 26.2, and subdivision (a)(1)(A) of this rule, these rules do not relate to discovery or inspection of recorded proceedings of a grand jury.

[(4) Failure to Call Witness.] (Deleted Dec. 12, 1975)

(b) *Disclosure of Evidence by the Defendant.*

(1) Information Subject to Disclosure. —

(A) Documents and Tangible Objects. — If the defendant requests disclosure under subdivision (a)(1)(C) or (D) of this rule, upon compliance with such request by the government, the defendant, on request of the government, shall permit the government to inspect and copy or photograph books, papers, documents, photographs, tangible objects, or copies or portions thereof, which are within the possession, custody, or control of the defendant and which the defendant intends to introduce as evidence in chief at the trial.

(B) Reports of Examinations and Tests. — If the defendant requests disclosure under subdivision (a)(1)(C) or (D) of this rule, upon compliance with such request by the government, the defendant, on request of the government, shall permit the government to inspect and copy or photograph any results or reports of physical or mental examinations and of scientific tests or experiments made in connection with the particular case, or copies thereof, within the possession or control of the defendant, which the defendant intends to introduce as evidence in chief at the trial or which were prepared by a witness whom the defendant intends to call at the trial when the results or reports relate to that witness' testimony.

(2) Information Not Subject to Disclosure. — Except as to scientific or medical reports, this subdivision does not authorize the discovery or inspection of reports, memoranda, or other internal defense documents made by the defendant, or the defendant's attorneys or agents in connection with the investigation or defense of the case, or of statements made by the defendant, or by government or defense witnesses, or by prospective government or defense witnesses, to the defendant, the defendant's agents or attorneys.

[(3) Failure to Call Witness.] (Deleted Dec. 13, 1975)

(c) Continuing Duty to Disclose. If, prior to or during trial, a party discovers additional evidence or material previously requested or ordered, which is subject to discovery or inspection under this rule, such party shall promptly notify the other party or that other party's attorney or the court of the existence of the additional evidence or material.

(d) *Regulation of Discovery.*

(1) Protective and Modifying Orders. — Upon a sufficient showing the court may at any time order that the discovery or inspection be denied, restricted, or deferred, or make such other order as is appropriate. Upon motion by a party, the court may permit the party to make such showing, in whole or in part, in the form of a written statement to be inspected by the judge alone. If the court enters an order granting relief following such an ex parte showing, the entire text of the party's statement shall be sealed and preserved in the records of the court to be made available to the appellate court in the event of an appeal.

(2) Failure To Comply With a Request. — If at any time during the course of the proceedings it is brought to the attention of the court that a party has failed to comply with this rule, the court may order such party to permit the discovery or inspection, grant an continuance, or prohibit the party from introducing evidence not disclosed, or it may enter such other order as it deems just under the circumstances. The court may specify the time, place and manner of making the discovery and inspection and may prescribe such terms and conditions as are just.

(e) *Alibi Witnesses.* Discovery of alibi witnesses is governed by Rule 12.1.

(As amended, eff. Dec. 1, 1991.)

**Rule 17. Subpoena.** (a) *For Attendance of Witnesses; Form; Issuance.* A subpoena shall be issued by the clerk under the seal of the court. It shall state the name of the court and the title, if any, of the proceeding, and shall command each person to whom it is directed to attend and give testimony at the time and place specified therein. The clerk shall issue a subpoena, signed and sealed but otherwise in blank to a party requesting it, who shall fill in the blanks before it is served. A subpoena shall be issued by a United States magistrate in a proceeding before that magistrate, but it need not be under the seal of the court.

(b) *Defendants Unable to Pay.* The court shall order at any time that a subpoena be issued for service on a named witness upon an *ex parte* application of a defendant upon a satisfactory showing that the defendant is financially unable to pay the fees of the witness and that the presence of the witness is necessary to an adequate defense. If the court orders the subpoena to be issued the costs incurred by the process and the fees of the witness so subpoenaed shall be paid in the same manner in which similar costs and fees are paid in case of a witness subpoenaed in behalf of the government.

(c) *For Production of Documentary Evidence and of Objects.* A subpoena may also command the person to whom it is directed to produce the books, papers, documents or other objects designated therein. The court on motion made promptly may quash or modify the subpoena if compliance would be unreasonable or oppressive. The court may direct that books, papers, documents or objects designated in the subpoena be produced before the court at a time prior to the trial or prior to the time when they are to be offered in evidence and may upon their production permit the books, papers, documents or objects or portions thereof to be inspected by the parties and their attorneys.

(d) *Service.* A subpoena may be served by the marshal, a deputy marshal or by any other person who is not a party and who is not less than 18 years of age. Service of a subpoena shall be made by delivering a copy thereof to the person named and by tendering to that person the fee for 1 day's attendance and the mileage allowed by law. Fees and mileage need not be tendered to the witness upon service of a subpoena issued in behalf of the United States or an officer or agency thereof.

(e) *Place of Service.*

(1) In United States. — A subpoena requiring the attendance of a witness at a hearing or trial may be served at any place within the United States.

(2) Abroad. — A subpoena directed to a witness in a foreign country shall issue under the circumstances and in the manner and be served as provided in Title 28, U.S.C., § 1783.

(f) *For Taking Deposition; Place of Examination.*

(1) Issuance. — An order to take a deposition authorizes the issuance by the clerk of the court for the district in which the deposition is to be taken of subpoenas for the persons named or described therein.

(2) Place. — The witness whose deposition is to be taken may be required by subpoena to attend at any place designated by the trial court, taking into account the convenience of the witness and the parties.

(g) *Contempt.* Failure by any person without adequate excuse to obey a subpoena served upon that person may be deemed a contempt of the court from which the subpoena issued or of the court for the district in which it issued if it was issued by a United States magistrate.

(h) *Information Not Subject to Subpoena.* Statements made by witnesses or prospective witnesses may not be subpoenaed from the government or the defendant under this rule, but shall be subject to production only in accordance with the provisions of Rule 26.2.

**Rule 17.1. Pretrial Conference.** At any time after the filing of the indictment or information the court upon motion of any party or upon its own motion may order one or more conferences to consider such matters as will promote a fair and expeditious trial. At the conclusion of a conference the court shall prepare and file a memorandum of the matters agreed upon. No admissions made by the defendant or the defendant's attorney at the conference shall be used against the defendant unless the admissions are reduced to writing and signed by the defendant and the defendant's attorney. This rule shall not be invoked in the case of a defendant who is not represented by counsel.

## V. VENUE.

**Rule 18. Place of Prosecution and Trial.** Except as otherwise permitted by statute or by these rules, the prosecution shall be had in a district in which the offense was committed. The court shall fix the place of trial within the district with due regard to the convenience of the defendant and the witnesses and the prompt administration of justice.

**Rule 19.** *(Rescinded by order adopted February 28, 1966, effective July 1, 1966.)*

**Rule 20. Transfer From the District for Plea and Sentence.** (a) *Indictment or Information Pending.* A defendant arrested, held, or present in a district other than that in which an indictment or information is pending against that defendant may state in writing a wish to plead guilty or nolo contendere, to waive trial in the district in which the indictment or information is pending, and to consent to disposition of the case in the district in which that defendant was arrested, held, or present, subject to the approval of the United States Attorney for each district. Upon receipt of the defendant's statement and of the written approval of the United States Attorneys, the clerk of the court in which the indictment or information is pending shall transmit the papers in the proceeding or certified copies thereof to the clerk of the court for the district in which the defendant is arrested, held, or present, and the prosecution shall continue in that district.

(b) *Indictment Or Information Not Pending.* A defendant arrested, held, or present, in a district other than the district in which a complaint is pending against that defendant may state in writing a wish to plead guilty or nolo contendere, to waive venue and trial in the district in which the warrant was issued, and to consent to disposition of the case in the district in which that defendant was arrested, held, or present, subject to the approval of the United States Attorney for each district. Upon filing the written waiver of venue in the district in which the defendant is present, the prosecution may proceed as if venue were in such district.

(c) *Effect of Not Guilty Plea.* If after the proceeding has been transferred pursuant to subdivision (a) or (b) of this rule the defendant pleads not guilty, the clerk shall return the papers to the court in which the prosecution was commenced, and the proceeding shall be restored to the docket of that court. The defendant's statement that the defendant wishes to plead guilty or nolo contendere shall not be used against that defendant.

(d) *Juveniles.* A juvenile (as defined in 18 U.S.C. § 5031) who is arrested, held, or present in a district other than that in which the juvenile is alleged to have committed an act in violation of a law of the United States not punishable by death or life imprisonment may, after having advised by counsel and with the approval of the court and the United States Attorney for each district, consent to be proceeded against as a juvenile delinquent in the district in which the juvenile is arrested, held, or present. The consent shall be given in writing before the court but only after the court has apprised the juvenile of the juvenile rights, including the right to be returned to the district in which the juvenile is alleged to have committed the act, and of the consequences of such consent.

**Rule 21. Transfer from the District for Trial.** (a) *For Prejudice in the District.* The court upon motion of the defendant shall transfer the proceeding as to that defendant to another district whether or not such district is specified in the defendant's motion if the court is satisfied that there exists in the district where the prosecution is pending so great a prejudice against the defendant that the defendant cannot obtain a fair and impartial trial at any place fixed by law for holding court in that district.

(b) *Transfer in Other Cases.* For the convenience of parties and witnesses, and in the interest of justice, the court upon motion of the defendant may transfer the proceeding as to that defendant or any one or more of the counts thereof to another district.

(c) *Proceedings on Transfer.* When a transfer is ordered the clerk shall transmit to the clerk of the court to which the proceeding is transferred all papers in the proceeding or duplicates thereof and any bail taken, and the prosecution shall continue in that district.

**Rule 22. Time of Motion to Transfer.** A motion to transfer under these rules may be made at or before arraignment or at such other time as the court or these rules may prescribe.

## VI. TRIAL.

**Rule 23. Trial by Jury or by the Court.** (a) *Trial by Jury.* Cases required to be tried by jury shall be so tried unless the defendant waives a jury trial in writing with the approval of the court and the consent of the government.

(b) *Jury of Less than Twelve.* Juries shall be of 12 but at any time before verdict the parties may stipulate in writing with the approval of the court that the jury shall consist of any number less than 12 or that a valid verdict may be returned by a jury of less than 12 should the court find it necessary to excuse one or more jurors for any just cause after trial commences. Even absent such stipulation, if the court finds it necessary to excuse a juror for just cause after the jury has retired to consider its verdict, in the discretion of the court a valid verdict may be returned by the remaining 11 jurors.

(c) *Trial Without a Jury.* In a case tried without a jury the court shall make a general finding and shall in addition, on request made before the general finding, find the facts specially. Such findings may be oral. If an opinion or memorandum of decision is filed, it will be sufficient if the findings of fact appear therein.

**Rule 24. Trial Jurors.** (a) *Examination.* The court may permit the defendant or the defendant's attorney and the attorney for the government to conduct the examination of prospective jurors or may itself conduct the examination. In the latter event the court shall permit the defendant or the defendant's attorney and the attorney for the government to supplement the examination by such further inquiry as it deems proper or shall itself submit to the prospective jurors such additional questions by the parties or their attorneys as it deems proper.

(b) *Peremptory Challenges.* If the offense charged is punishable by death, each side is entitled to 20 peremptory challenges. If the offense charged is punishable by imprisonment for more than one year, the government is entitled to 6 peremptory challenges and the defendant or defendants jointly to 10 peremptory challenges. If the offense charged is punishable by imprisonment for not more than one year or by fine or both, each side is entitled to 3 peremptory challenges. If there is more than one defendant, the court may allow the defendants additional peremptory challenges and permit them to be exercised separately or jointly.

(c) *Alternate Jurors.* The court may direct that not more than 6 jurors in addition to the regular jury be called and impanelled to sit as alternate jurors. Alternate jurors in the order in which they are called shall replace jurors who, prior to the time the jury retires to consider its verdict, become or are found to be unable or disqualified to perform their duties. Alternate jurors shall be drawn in the same manner, shall have the same qualifications, shall be subject to the same examination and challenges, shall take the same oath and shall have the same functions, powers, facilities and privileges as the regular jurors. An alternate juror who does not replace a regular juror shall be discharged after the jury retires to consider its verdict. Each side is entitled to 1 peremptory challenge in addition to those otherwise allowed by law if 1 or 2 alternate jurors are to be impanelled, 2 peremptory challenges if 3 or 4 alternate jurors are to be impanelled, and 3 peremptory challenges if 5 or 6 alternate jurors are to be impanelled. The additional peremptory challenges may be used against an alternate juror only, and the other peremptory challenges allowed by these rules may not be used against an alternate juror.

**Rule 25. Judge; Disability.** (a) *During Trial.* If by reason of death, sickness or other disability the judge before whom a jury trial has commenced is unable to proceed

537

with the trial, any other judge regularly sitting in or assigned to the court, upon certifying familiarity with the record of the trial, may proceed with and finish the trial.

(b) *After Verdict or Finding of Guilt.* If by reason of absence, death, sickness or other disability the judge before whom the defendant has been tried is unable to perform the duties to be performed by the court after a verdict or finding of guilt, any other judge regularly sitting in or assigned to the court may perform those duties; but if that judge is satisfied that a judge who did not preside at the trial cannot perform those duties or that it is appropriate for any other reason, that judge may grant a new trial.

**Rule 26. Taking of Testimony.** In all trials the testimony of witnesses shall be taken orally in open court, unless otherwise provided by an Act of Congress or by these rules, the Federal Rules of Evidence, or other rules adopted by the Supreme Court.

**Rule 26.1. Determination of Foreign Law.** A party who intends to raise an issue concerning the law of a foreign country shall give reasonable written notice. The court, in determining foreign law, may consider any relevant material or source, including testimony, whether or not submitted by a party or admissible under the Federal Rules of Evidence. The court's determination shall be treated as a ruling on a question of law.

**Rule 26.2. Production of Statements of Witnesses.** (a) *Motion for Production.* After a witness other than the defendant has testified on direct examination, the court, on motion of a party who did not call the witness, shall order the attorney for the government or the defendant and the defendant's attorney, as the case may be, to produce, for the examination and use of the moving party, any statement of the witness that is in their possession and that relates to the subject matter concerning which the witness has testified.

(b) *Production of Entire Statement.* If the entire contents of the statement relate to the subject matter concerning which the witness has testified, the court shall order that the statement be delivered to the moving party.

(c) *Production of Excised Statement.* If the other party claims that the statement contains matter that does not relate to the subject matter concerning which the witness has testified, the court shall order that it be delivered to the court in camera. Upon inspection, the court shall excise the portions of the statement that do not relate to the subject matter concerning which the witness has testified, and shall order that the statement, with such material excised, be delivered to the moving party. Any portion of the statement that is withheld from the defendant over the defendant's objection shall be preserved by the attorney for the government, and, in the event of a conviction and an appeal by the defendant, shall be made available to the appellate court for the purpose of determining the correctness of the decision to excise the portion of the statement.

(d) *Recess for Examination of Statement.* Upon delivery of the statement to the moving party, the court, upon application of that party, may recess proceedings in the trial for the examination of such statement and for preparation for its use in the trial.

(e) *Sanction for Failure to Produce Statement.* If the other party elects not to comply with an order to deliver a statement to the moving party, the court shall order that the testimony of the witness be stricken from the record and that the trial proceed, or, if it is the attorney for the government who elects not to comply, shall declare a mistrial if required by the interest of justice.

(f) *Definition.* As used in this rule, a "statement" of a witness means:

(1) a written statement made by the witness that is signed or otherwise adopted or approved by the witness;

(2) a substantially verbatim recital of an oral statement made by the witness that is recorded contemporaneously with the making of the oral statement and that is contained in a stenographic, mechanical, electrical, or other recording or a transcription thereof; or

(3) a statement, however taken or recorded, or a transcription thereof, made by the witness to a grand jury.

**Rule 27. Proof of Official Record.** An official record or an entry therein or the lack of such a record or entry may be proved in the same manner as in civil actions.

**Rule 28. Interpreters.** The court may appoint an interpreter of its own selection and may fix the reasonable compensation of such interpreter. Such compensation shall be paid out of funds provided by law or by the government, as the court may direct.

**Rule 29. Motion for Judgment of Acquittal.** (a) *Motion Before Submission to Jury.* Motions for directed verdict are abolished and motions for judgment of acquittal shall be used in their place. The court on motion of a defendant or of its own motion shall order the entry of judgment of acquittal of one or more offenses charged in the indictment or information after the evidence on either side is closed if the evidence is insufficient to sustain a conviction of such offense or offenses. If a defendant's motion for judgment of acquittal at the close of the evidence offered by the government is not granted, the defendant may offer evidence without having reserved the right.

(b) *Reservation of Decision on Motion.* If a motion for judgment of acquittal is made at the close of all the evidence, the court may reserve decision on the motion, submit the case to the jury and decide the motion either before the jury returns a verdict or after it returns a verdict of guilty or is discharged without having returned a verdict.

(c) *Motion After Discharge of Jury.* If the jury returns a verdict of guilty or is discharged without having returned a verdict, a motion for judgment of acquittal may be made or renewed within 7 days after the jury is discharged or within such further time as the court may fix during the 7-day period. If a verdict of guilty is returned the court may on such motion set aside the verdict and enter judgment of acquittal. If no verdict is returned the court may enter judgment of acquittal. It shall not be necessary to the making of such a motion that a similar motion has been made prior to the submission of the case to the jury.

(d) *Same: conditional ruling on grant of motion.* If a motion for judgment of acquittal after verdict of guilty under this Rule is granted, the court shall also determine whether any motion for a new trial should be granted if the judgment of acquittal is thereafter vacated or reversed, specifying the grounds for such determination. If the motion for a new trial is granted conditionally, the order thereon does not affect the finality of the judgment. If the motion for a new trial has been granted conditionally and the judgment is reversed on appeal, the new trial shall proceed unless the appellate court has otherwise ordered. If such motion has been denied conditionally, the appellee on appeal may assert error in that denial, and if the judgment is reversed on appeal, subsequent proceedings shall be in accordance with the order of the appellate court.

**Rule 29.1. Closing Argument.** After the closing of evidence the prosecution shall open the argument. The defense shall be permitted to reply. The prosecution shall then be permitted to reply in rebuttal.

**Rule 30. Instructions.** At the close of the evidence or at such earlier time during the trial as the court reasonably directs, any party may file written requests that the court instruct the jury on the law as set forth in the requests. At the same time copies of such requests shall be furnished to all parties. The court shall inform counsel of its proposed action upon the requests prior to their arguments to the jury. The court may instruct the jury before or after the arguments are completed or at both times. No party may assign as error any portion of the charge or omission therefrom unless that party objects thereto before the jury retires to consider its verdict, stating distinctly the matter to which that party objects and the grounds of the objection. Opportunity shall be given to make the objection out of the hearing of the jury and, on request of any party, out of the presence of the jury.

**Rule 31. Verdict.** (a) *Return.* The verdict shall be unanimous. It shall be returned by the jury to the judge in open court.

(b) *Several Defendants.* If there were two or more defendants, the jury at any time during its deliberations may return a verdict or verdicts with respect to a defendant or defendants as to whom it has agreed; if the jury cannot agree with respect to all, the defendant or defendants as to whom it does not agree may be tried again.

(c) *Conviction of Less Offense.* The defendant may be found guilty of an offense necessarily included in the offense charged or of an attempt to commit either the offense charged or an offense necessarily included therein if the attempt is an offense.

(d) *Poll of Jury.* When a verdict is returned and before it is recorded the jury shall be polled at the request of any party or upon the court's own motion. If upon the poll there is not unanimous concurrence, the jury may be directed to retire for further deliberations or may be discharged.

(e) *Criminal Forfeiture.* If the indictment or the information alleges that an interest or property is subject to criminal forfeiture, a special verdict shall be returned as to the extent of the interest or property subject to forfeiture, if any.

## VII. JUDGMENT.

**Rule 32. Sentence and Judgment.** (a) *Sentence.*

(1) Imposition of Sentence. — Sentence shall be imposed without unnecessary delay, but the court may, when there is a factor important to the sentencing determination that is not then capable of being resolved, postpone the imposition of sentence for a reasonable time until the factor is capable of being resolved. Prior to the sentencing hearing, the court shall provide the counsel for the defendant and the attorney for the Government with notice of the probation officer's determination, pursuant to the provisions of subdivision (c)(2)(B), of the sentencing classifications and sentencing guidelines range believed to be applicable to the case. At the sentencing hearing, the court shall afford the counsel for the defendant and the attorney for the Government an opportunity to comment upon the probation officer's determination and on other matters relating to the appropriate sentence. Before imposing sentence, the court shall also—

(A) determine that the defendant and defendant's counsel have had the opportunity to read and discuss the presentence investigation report made available pursuant to subdivision (c)(3)(A) or summary thereof made available pursuant to subdivision (c)(3)(B);

(B) afford counsel for the defendant an opportunity to speak on behalf of the defendant; and

(C) address the defendant personally and determine if the defendant wishes to make a statement and to present any information in mitigation of the sentence.

The attorney for the Government shall have an equivalent opportunity to speak to the court. Upon a motion that is jointly filed by the defendant and by the attorney for the Government, the court may hear in camera such a statement by the defendant, counsel for the defendant, or the attorney for the Government.

(2) Notification of Right to Appeal. — After imposing sentence in a case which has gone to trial on a plea of not guilty, the court shall advise the defendant of the defendant's right to appeal, including any right to appeal the sentence, and of the right of a person who is unable to pay the cost of an appeal to apply for leave to appeal in forma pauperis. There shall be no duty on the court to advise the defendant of any right of appeal after sentence is imposed following a plea of guilty or nolo contendere, except that the court shall advise the defendant of any right to appeal the sentence. If the defendant so requests, the clerk of the court shall prepare and file forthwith a notice of appeal on behalf of the defendant.

(b) *Judgment.*

(1) In General. — A judgment of conviction shall set forth the plea, the verdict or findings, and the adjudication and sentence. If the defendant is found not guilty or for any other reason is entitled to be discharged, judgment shall be entered accordingly. The judgment shall be signed by the judge and entered by the clerk.

(2) *Criminal Forfeiture.* — When a verdict contains a finding of property subject to a criminal forfeiture, the judgment of criminal forfeiture shall authorize the Attorney General to seize the interest or property subject to forfeiture, fixing such terms and conditions as the court shall deem proper.

(c) *Presentence Investigation.*

(1) When Made. — A probation officer shall make a presentence investigation and report to the court before the imposition of sentence unless the court finds that there is in the record information sufficient to enable the meaningful exercise of sentencing authority pursuant to 18 U.S.C. 3553, and the court explains this finding on the record.

Except with the written consent of the defendant, the report shall not be submitted to the court or its contents disclosed to anyone unless the defendant has pleaded guilty or nolo contendere or has been found guilty.

(2) Report. — The report of the presentence investigation shall contain—

(A) information about the history, and characteristics of the defendant, including prior criminal record, if any, financial condition, and any circumstances affecting the defendant's behavior that may be helpful in imposing sentence or in the correctional treatment of the defendant;

(B) the classification of the offense and of the defendant under the categories established by the Sentencing Commission pursuant to section 994(a) of title 28, that the probation officer believes to be applicable to the defendant's case; the kinds of sentence and the sentencing range suggested for such a category of offense committed by such a category of defendant as set forth in the guidelines issued by the Sentencing Commission pursuant to 28 U.S.C. 994(a)(1); and an explanation by the probation officer of any factors that may indicate that a sentence of a different kind or of a different length from one within the applicable guideline would be more appropriate under all the circumstances;

(C) any pertinent policy statement issued by the Sentencing Commission pursuant to 28 U.S.C. 994(a)(2);

(D) verified information stated in a non-argumentative style containing an assessment of the financial, social, psychological, and medical impact upon, and cost to, any individual against whom the offense has been committed;

(E) unless the court orders otherwise, information concerning the nature and extent of nonprison programs and resources available for the defendant; and

(F) such other information as may be required by the court.

(3) Disclosure. —

(A) At least 10 days before imposing sentence, unless this minimum period is waived by the defendant, the court shall provide the defendant and the defendant's counsel with a copy of the report of the presentence investigation, including the information required by subdivision (c)(2) but not including any final recommendation as to sentence, and not to the extent that in the opinion of the court the report contains diagnostic opinions which, if disclosed, might seriously disrupt a program of rehabilitation; or sources of information obtained upon a promise of confidentiality; or any other information which, if disclosed, might result in harm, physical or otherwise, to the defendant or other persons. The court shall afford the defendant and the defendant's counsel an opportunity to comment on the report and, in the discretion of the court, to introduce testimony or other information relating to any alleged factual inaccuracy contained in it.

(B) If the court is of the view that there is information in the presentence report which should not be disclosed under subdivision (c)(3)(A) of this rule, the court in lieu of making the report or part thereof available shall state orally or in writing a summary of the factual information contained therein to be relied on in determining sentence, and shall give the defendant and the defendant's counsel an opportunity to comment thereon. The statement may be made to the parties in camera.

(C) Any material which may be disclosed to the defendant and the defendant's counsel shall be disclosed to the attorney for the government.

(D) If the comments of the defendant and the defendant's counsel or testimony or other information introduced by them allege any factual inaccuracy in the presentence investigation report or the summary of the report or part thereof, the court shall, as to each matter controverted, make (i) a finding as to the allegation, or (ii) a determination that no such finding is necessary because the matter controverted will not be taken into account in sentencing. A written record of such findings and determinations shall be appended to and accompany any copy of the presentence investigation report thereafter made available to the Bureau of Prisons.

(E) The reports of studies and recommendations contained therein made by the Director of the Bureau of Prisons pursuant to 18 U.S.C. § 3552(b) shall be considered a presentence investigation within the meaning of subdivision (c)(3) of this rule.

(F) The reports of studies and recommendations contained therein made by the Director of the Bureau of Prisons pursuant to 18 U.S.C. § 3552(b) shall be considered a presentence investigation within the meaning of subdivision (c)(3) of this rule.

(d) *Plea Withdrawal.* If a motion for withdrawal of a plea of guilty or nolo contendere is made before sentence is imposed, the court may permit withdrawal of the plea upon a showing by the defendant of any fair and just reason. Any later time, a plea may be set aside only on direct appeal or by motion under 28 U.S.C. § 2255.

(e) *Probation.* After conviction of an offense not punishable by death or by life imprisonment, the defendant may be placed on probation if permitted by law.

(f) *[Revocation of Probation.]* (Abrogated Apr. 30, 1979, eff. Dec. 1, 1980)

(As amended, eff. Dec. 1, 1991.)

Rule 32.1. Revocation or Modification of Probation or Supervised Release. (a) *Revocation of Probation or Supervised Release.*

(1) *Preliminary Hearing.* — Whenever a person is held in custody on the ground that the person has violated a condition of probation or supervised release, the person shall be afforded a prompt hearing before any judge, or a United States magistrate who has been given authority pursuant to 28 U.S.C. § 636 to conduct such hearings, in order to determine whether there is probable cause to hold the person for a revocation hearing. The person shall be given

(A) notice of the preliminary hearing and its purpose and of the alleged violation;

(B) an opportunity to appear at the hearing and present evidence in the person's own behalf;

(C) upon request, the opportunity to question witnesses against the person unless, for good cause, the federal magistrate decides that justice does not require the appearance of the witness; and

(D) notice of the person's right to be represented by counsel.

The proceedings shall be recorded stenographically or by an electronic recording device. If probable cause is found to exist, the person shall be held for a revocation hearing. The person may be released pursuant to Rule 46(c) pending the revocation hearing. If probable cause is not found to exist, the proceeding shall be dismissed.

(2) *Revocation Hearing.* — The revocation hearing, unless waived by the person, shall be held within a reasonable time in the district of jurisdiction. The person shall be given

(A) written notice of the alleged violation;

(B) disclosure of the evidence against the person;

(C) an opportunity to appear and to present evidence in the person's own behalf;

(D) the opportunity to question adverse witnesses; and

(E) notice of the person's right to be represented by counsel.

(b) *Modification of Probation or Supervised Release.* A hearing and assistance of counsel are required before the terms or conditions of probation or supervised release can be modified, unless the relief to be granted to the person on probation or supervised release upon the person's request or the court's own motion is favorable to the person, and the attorney for the government, after having been given notice of the proposed relief and a reasonable opportunity to object, has not objected. An extension of the term of probation or supervised release is not favorable to the person for the purposes of this rule.

(As amended, eff. Dec. 1, 1991.)

**Rule 33. New Trial.** The court on motion of a defendant may grant a new trial to the defendant if required in the interest of justice. If trial was by the court without a jury the court on motion of a defendant for a new trial may vacate the judgment if entered, take additional testimony and direct the entry of a new judgment. A motion for a new trial based on the ground of newly discovered evidence may be made only before or within two years after final judgment, but if an appeal is pending the court may grant the motion only on remand of the case. A motion for a new trial based on any other grounds shall be made within 7 days after verdict or finding of guilty or within such further time as the court may fix during the 7-day period.

**Rule 34. Arrest of Judgment.** The court on motion of a defendant shall arrest judgment if the indictment or information does not charge an offense or if the court was without jurisdiction of the offense charged. The motion in arrest of judgment shall be made within 7 days after verdict or finding of guilty, or after plea of guilty or *nolo contendere,* or within such further time as the court may fix during the 7-day period.

**Rule 35. Correction or Reduction of Sentence.** (a) *Correction of a Sentence on Remand.* The court shall correct a sentence that is determined on appeal under 18 U.S.C. 3742 to have been imposed in violation of law, to have been imposed as a result of an incorrect application of the sentencing guidelines, or to be unreasonable, upon remand of the case to the court—

(1) for imposition of a sentence in accord with the findings of the court of appeals; or

(2) for further sentencing proceedings if, after such proceedings, the court determines that the original sentence was incorrect.

(b) *Reduction of Sentence for Changed Circumstances.* The court, on motion of the Government made within one year after the imposition of a sentence, may reduce a sentence to reflect a defendant's subsequent, substantial assistance in the investigation or prosecution of another person who has committed an offense, in accordance with the guidelines and policy statements issued by the Sentencing Commission pursuant to section 994 of title 28, United States Code. The court may consider a government motion to reduce a sentence made one year or more after imposition of the sentence where the defendant's substantial assistance involves information or evidence not known by the defendant until one year or more after imposition of sentence. The court's authority to reduce a sentence under this subdivision includes the authority to reduce such sentence to a level below that established by statute as a minimum sentence.

(c) *Correction of Sentence By Sentencing Court.* — The Court, acting within 7 days after the imposition of sentence, may correct a sentence that was imposed as a result of arithmetical, technical, or other clear error.

(As amended, eff. Dec. 1, 1991.)

**Rule 36. Clerical Mistakes.** Clerical mistakes in judgments, orders or other parts of the record and errors in the record arising from oversight or omission may be corrected by the court at any time and after such notice, if any, as the court orders.

## VIII. APPEAL.

**Rule 37.** *(Abrogated December 4, 1967, effective July 1, 1968.)*

**Rule 38. Stay of Execution.** (a) *Death.* A sentence of death shall be stayed if an appeal is taken from the conviction or sentence.

(b) *Imprisonment.* A sentence of imprisonment shall be stayed if an appeal is taken from the conviction or sentence and the defendant is released pending disposition of appeal pursuant to Rule 9(b) of the Federal Rules of Appellate Procedure. If not stayed, the court may recommend to the Attorney General that the defendant be retained at, or transferred to, a place of confinement near the place of trial or the place where an appeal is to be heard, for a period reasonably necessary to permit the defendant to assist in the preparation of an appeal to the court of appeals.

(c) *Fine.* A sentence to pay a fine or a fine and costs, if an appeal is taken, may be stayed by the district court or by the court of appeals upon such terms as the court deems proper. The court may require the defendant pending appeal to deposit the whole or any part of the fine and costs in the registry of the district court, or to give bond for the payment thereof, or to submit to an examination of assets, and it may make any appropriate order to restrain the defendant from dissipating such defendant's assets.

(d) *Probation.* A sentence of probation may be stayed if an appeal from the conviction or sentence is taken. If the sentence is stayed, the court shall fix the terms of the stay.

(e) *Criminal Forfeiture, Notice to Victims, and Restitution.* A sanction imposed as part of the sentence pursuant to 18 U.S.C. 3554, 3555, or 3556 may, if an appeal of the conviction or sentence is taken, be stayed by the district court or by the court of appeals upon such terms as the court finds appropriate. The court may issue such orders as may be reasonably necessary to ensure compliance with the sanction upon disposition of the appeal, including the entering of a restraining order or an injunction or requiring a deposit in whole or in part of the monetary amount involved into the registry of the district court or execution of a performance bond.

(f) *Disabilities.* A civil or employment disability arising under a Federal statute by reason of the defendant's conviction or sentence, may, if an appeal is taken, be stayed by the district court or by the court of appeals upon such terms as the court finds appropriate. The court may enter a restraining order or an injunction, or take any other action that may be reasonably necessary to protect the interest represented by the disability pending disposition of the appeal.

**Rule 39.** *(Abrogated December 4, 1967, effective July 1, 1968.)*

## IX. SUPPLEMENTARY AND SPECIAL PROCEEDINGS.

**Rule 40. Commitment to Another District.** (a) *Appearance Before Federal Magistrate.* If a person is arrested in a district other than that in which the offense is alleged to have been committed, that person shall be taken without unnecessary delay before the nearest available federal magistrate. Preliminary proceedings concerning the defendant shall be conducted in accordance with Rules 5 and 5.1, except that if no preliminary examination is held because an indictment has been returned or an information filed or because the defendant elects to have the preliminary examination conducted in the district in which the prosecution is pending, the person shall be held to answer upon a finding that such person is the person named in the indictment, information or warrant. If held to answer, the defendant shall be held to answer in the district court in which the prosecution is pending, provided that a warrant is issued in that district if the arrest was made without a warrant, upon production of the warrant or a certified copy thereof.

(b) *Statement by Federal Magistrate.* In addition to the statements required by Rule 5, the federal magistrate shall inform the defendant of the provisions of Rule 20.

(c) *Papers.* If a defendant is held or discharged, the papers in the proceeding and any bail taken shall be transmitted to the clerk of the district court in which the prosecution is pending.

(d) *Arrest of Probationer or Supervised Releasee.* If a person is arrested for a violation of probation or supervised release in a district other than the district having jurisdiction, such person shall be taken without unnecessary delay before the nearest available federal magistrate. The federal magistrate shall:

(1) Proceed under Rule 32.1 if jurisdiction over the person is transferred to that district;

(2) Hold a prompt preliminary hearing if the alleged violation occurred in that district, and either (i) hold the person to answer in the district court of the district having jurisdiction or (ii) dismiss the proceedings and so notify that court; or

(3) Otherwise order the person held to answer in the district court of the district having jurisdiction upon production of certified copies of the judgment, the warrant, and the application for the warrant, and upon a finding that the person before the magistrate is the person named in the warrant.

(e) *Arrest for Failure to Appear.* If a person is arrested on a warrant in a district other than that in which the warrant was issued, and the warrant was issued because of the failure of the person named therein to appear as required pursuant to a subpoena or the terms of that person's release, the person arrested shall be taken without unnecessary delay before the nearest available federal magistrate. Upon production of the warrant or a certified copy thereof and upon a finding that the person before the magistrate is the person named in the warrant, the federal magistrate shall hold the person to answer in the district in which the warrant was issued.

(f) *Release or Detention.* If a person was previously detained or conditionally released, pursuant to chapter 207 of title 18, United States Code, in another district where a warrant, information, or indictment issued, the federal magistrate shall take into account the decision previously made and the reasons set forth therefor, if any, but will not be bound by that decision. If the federal magistrate amends the release or detention decision or alters the conditions of release, the magistrate shall set forth the reasons therefor in writing.

**Rule 41. Search and Seizure.** (a) *Authority to Issue Warrant.* Upon the request of a federal law enforcement officer or any attorney for the government, a search warrant authorized by this rule may be issued (1) by a federal magistrate, or a state court of record within the federal district, for a search of property or for a person within the district and (2) by a federal magistrate for a search of property or for a person either within or outside the district if the property or person is within the district when the warrant is sought but might move outside the district before the warrant is executed.

(b) *Property or Persons Which May Be Seized with a Warrant.* — A warrant may be issued under this rule to search for and seize any (1) property that constitutes evidence of the commission of a criminal offense; or (2) contraband, the fruits of crime, or things otherwise criminally possessed; or (3) property designed or intended for use or which is or has been used as the means of committing a criminal offense; or (4) person for whose arrest there is probable cause, or who is unlawfully restrained.

(c) *Issuance and Contents.*

(1) Warrant Upon Affidavit. — A warrant other than a warrant upon oral testimony under paragraph (2) of this subdivision shall issue only on an affidavit or affidavits sworn to before the federal magistrate or state judge and establishing the grounds for issuing the warrant. If the federal magistrate or state judge is satisfied that grounds for the application exist or that there is probable cause to believe that they exist, that magistrate or state judge shall issue a warrant identifying the property or person to be seized and naming or describing the person or place to be searched. The finding of probable cause may be based upon hearsay evidence in whole or in part. Before ruling on a request for a warrant the federal magistrate or state judge may require the affiant to appear personally and may examine under oath the affiant and any witnesses the affiant may produce, provided that such proceeding shall be taken down by a court reporter or recording equipment and made part of the affidavit. The warrant shall be directed to a civil officer of the United States authorized to enforce or assist in enforcing any law thereof or to a person so authorized by the President of the United States. It shall command the officer to search, within a specified period of time not to exceed 10 days, the person or place named for the property or person specified. The warrant shall

be served in the daytime, unless the issuing authority, by appropriate provision in the warrant, and for reasonable cause shown, authorizes its execution at times other than daytime. It shall designate a federal magistrate to whom it shall be returned.

(2) Warrant upon oral testimony. —

(A) General Rule. — If the circumstances make it reasonable to dispense with a written affidavit, a Federal Magistrate may issue a warrant based upon sworn oral testimony communicated by telephone or other appropriate means.

(B) Application. — The person who is requesting the warrant shall prepare a document to be known as a duplicate original warrant and shall read such duplicate original warrant, verbatim, to the Federal magistrate. The Federal magistrate shall enter, verbatim, what is so read to such magistrate on a document to be known as the original warrant. The Federal magistrate may direct that the warrant be modified.

(C) Issuance. — If the Federal magistrate is satisfied that the circumstances are such as to make it reasonable to dispense with a written affidavit and that grounds for the application exist or that there is probable cause to believe that they exist, the Federal magistrate shall order the issuance of a warrant by directing the person requesting the warrant to sign the Federal magistrate's name on the duplicate original warrant. The Federal magistrate shall immediately sign the original warrant and enter on the face of the original warrant the exact time when the warrant was ordered to be issued. The finding of probable cause for a warrant upon oral testimony may be based on the same kind of evidence as is sufficient for a warrant upon affidavit.

(D) Recording and certification of testimony. — When a caller informs the Federal magistrate that the purpose of the call is to request a warrant, the Federal magistrate shall immediately place under oath each person whose testimony forms a basis of the application and each person applying for that warrant. If a voice recording device is available, the Federal magistrate shall record by means of such device all of the call after the caller informs the Federal magistrate that the purpose of the call is to request a warrant. Otherwise a stenographic or longhand verbatim record shall be made. If a voice recording device is used or a stenographic record made, the Federal magistrate shall have the record transcribed, shall certify the accuracy of the transcription, and shall file a copy of the original record and the transcription with the court. If a longhand verbatim record is made, the Federal magistrate shall file a signed copy with the court.

(E) Contents. — The contents of a warrant upon oral testimony shall be the same as the contents of a warrant upon affidavit.

(F) Additional rule for execution. — The person who executes the warrant shall enter the exact time of execution on the face of the duplicate original warrant.

(G) Motion to suppress precluded. — Absent a finding of bad faith, evidence obtained pursuant to a warrant issued under this paragraph is not subject to a motion to suppress on the ground that the circumstances were not such as to make it reasonable to dispense with a written affidavit.

(d) *Execution and Return with Inventory.* The officer taking property under the warrant shall give to the person from whom or from whose premises the property was taken a copy of the warrant and a receipt for the property taken or shall leave the copy and receipt at the place from which the property was taken. The return shall be made promptly and shall be accompanied by a written inventory of any property taken. The inventory shall be made in the presence of the applicant for the warrant and the person from whose possession or premises the property was taken, if they are present, or in the presence of at least one credible person other than the applicant for the warrant or the person from whose possession or premises the property was taken, and shall be verified by the officer. The federal magistrate shall upon request deliver a copy of the inventory to the person from whom or from whose premises the property was taken and to the applicant for the warrant.

(e) *Motion for Return of Property.* A person aggrieved by an unlawful search and seizure or by the deprivation of property may move the district court for the district in which the property was seized for the return of the property on the ground that such person is entitled to lawful possession of the property. The court shall receive evidence on any issue of fact necessary to the decision of the motion. If the motion is granted, the property shall be returned to the movant, although reasonable conditions may be imposed to protect access and use of the property in subsequent proceedings. If a motion for return of property is made or comes on for hearing in the district of trial after an indictment or information is filed, it shall be treated also as a motion to suppress under Rule 12.

(f) *Motion to Suppress.* A motion to suppress evidence may be made in the court of the district of trial as provided in Rule 12.

(g) *Return of Papers to Clerk.* The federal magistrate before whom the warrant is returned shall attach to the warrant a copy of the return, inventory and all other papers in connection therewith and shall file them with the clerk of the district court for the district in which the property was seized.

(h) *Scope and Definition.* This rule does not modify any act, inconsistent with it, regulating search, seizure and the issuance and execution of search warrants in circumstances for which special provision is made. The term "property" is used in this rule to include documents, books, papers and any other tangible objects. The term "daytime" is used in this rule to mean the hours from 6:00 a. m. to 10:00 p. m. according to local time. The phrase "federal law enforcement officer" is used in this rule to mean any government agent, other than an attorney for the government as defined in Rule 54(c), who is engaged in the enforcement of the criminal laws and is within any category of officers authorized by the Attorney General to request the issuance of a search warrant.

(As amended Apr. 26, 1976, eff. Aug. 1, 1976; July 30, 1977, Pub.L. 95-78, § 2(e), 91 Stat. 320; Apr. 30, 1979, eff. Aug. 1, 1979; Mar. 9, 1987, eff. Aug. 1, 1987; Apr. 25, 1989, eff. Dec. 1, 1989; May 1, 1990, eff. Dec. 1, 1990.)

**Rule 42. Criminal Contempt.** (a) *Summary Disposition.* A criminal contempt may be punished summarily if the judge certifies that the judge saw or heard the conduct constituting the contempt and that it was committed in the actual presence of the court. The order of contempt shall recite the facts and shall be signed by the judge and entered of record.

(b) *Disposition upon Notice and Hearing.* A criminal contempt except as provided in subdivision (a) of this rule shall be prosecuted on notice. The notice shall state the time and place of hearing, allowing a reasonable time for the preparation of the defense, and shall state the essential facts constituting the criminal contempt charged and describe it as such. The notice shall be given orally by the judge in open court in the presence of the defendant or, on application of the United States attorney or of an attorney appointed by the court for that purpose, by an order to show cause or an order of arrest. The defendant is entitled to a trial by jury in any case in which an act of Congress so provides. The defendant is entitled to admission to bail as provided in these rules. If the contempt charged involves disrespect to or criticism of a judge, that judge is disqualified from presiding at the trial or hearing except with the defendant's consent. Upon a verdict or finding of guilt the court shall enter an order fixing the punishment.

## X. GENERAL PROVISIONS.

**Rule 43. Presence of the Defendant.** (a) *Presence Required.* The defendant shall be present at the arraignment, at the time of the plea, at every stage of the trial including the impaneling of the jury and the return of the verdict, and at the imposition of sentence, except as otherwise provided by this rule.

(b) *Continued Presence Not Required.* The further progress of the trial to and including the return of the verdict shall not be prevented and the defendant shall be considered to have waived the right to be present whenever a defendant, initially present,

(1) is voluntarily absent after the trial has commenced (whether or not the defendant has been informed by the court of the obligation to remain during the trial), or

(2) after being warned by the court that disruptive conduct will cause the removal of the defendant from the courtroom, persists in conduct which is such as to justify exclusion from the courtroom.

(c) *Presence Not Required.* A defendant need not be present in the following situations:

(1) A corporation may appear by counsel for all purposes.

(2) In prosecutions for offenses punishable by fine or by imprisonment for not more than one year or both, the court, with the written consent of the defendant, may permit arraignment, plea, trial, and imposition of sentence in the defendant's absence.

(3) At a conference or argument upon a question of law.

(4) At a reduction of sentence under Rule 35.

**Rule 44. Right to and Assignment of Counsel.** (a) *Right to Assigned Counsel.* Every defendant who is unable to obtain counsel shall be entitled to have counsel assigned to represent that defendant at every stage of the proceedings from initial appearance before the federal magistrate or the court through appeal, unless that defendant waives such appointment.

(b) *Assignment Procedure.* The procedures for implementing the right set out in subdivision (a) shall be those provided by law and by local rules of court established pursuant thereto.

(c) *Joint Representation.* Whenever two or more defendants have been jointly charged pursuant to Rule 8(b) or have been joined for trial pursuant to Rule 13, and are represented by the same retained or assigned counsel or by retained or assigned counsel who are associated in the practice of law, the court shall promptly inquire with respect to such joint representation and shall personally advise each defendant of the right to the effective assistance of counsel, including separate representation. Unless it appears that there is good cause to believe no conflict of interest is likely to arise, the court shall take such measures as may be appropriate to protect each defendant's right to counsel.

**Rule 45. Time.** (a) *Computation.* In computing any period of time the day of the act or event from which the designated period of time begins to run shall not be included. The last day of the period so computed shall be included, unless it is a Saturday, a Sunday, or a legal holiday, or, when the act to be done is the filing of some paper in court, a day on which weather or other conditions have made the office of the clerk of the district court inaccessible, in which event the period runs until the end of the next day which is not one of the aforementioned days. When a period of time prescribed or allowed is less than 11 days, intermediate Saturdays, Sundays and legal holidays shall be excluded in the computation. As used in these rules, "legal holiday" includes New Year's Day, Birthday of Martin Luther King, Jr., Washington's Birthday, Memorial Day, Independence Day, Labor Day, Columbus Day, Veterans' Day, Thanksgiving Day, Christmas Day, and any other day appointed as a holiday by the President or the Congress of the United States, or by the state in which the district court is held.

(b) *Enlargement.* When an act is required or allowed to be done at or within a specified time, the court for cause shown may at any time in its discretion (1) with or without motion or notice, order the period enlarged if request therefor is made before the expiration of the period originally prescribed or as extended by a previous order or (2) upon motion made after the expiration of the specified period permit the act to be done if the failure to act was the result of excusable neglect; but the court may not extend the time for taking any action under Rules 29, 33, 34 and 35, except to the extent and under the conditions stated in them.

(c) *(Rescinded February 28, 1966, effective July 1, 1966.)*

(d) *For Motions; Affidavits.* A written motion, other than one which may be heard *ex parte,* and notice of the hearing thereof shall be served not later than 5 days before the time specified for the hearing unless a different period is fixed by rule or order of the court. For cause shown such an order may be made on *ex parte* application. When a motion is supported by affidavit, the affidavit shall be served with the motion; and opposing affidavits may be served not less than 1 day before the hearing unless the court permits them to be served at a later time.

(e) *Additional Time After Service by Mail.* Whenever a party has the right or is required to do an act within a prescribed period after the service of a notice or other paper upon that party and the notice or other paper is served by mail, 3 days shall be added to the prescribed period.

**Rule 46. Release from Custody.** (a) *Release Prior to Trial.* Eligibility for release prior to trial shall be in accordance with 18 U.S.C. §§ 3142 and 3144.

(b) *Release During Trial.* A person released before trial shall continue on release during trial under the same terms and conditions as were previously imposed unless the court determines that other terms and conditions or termination of release are necessary to assure such person's presence during the trial or to assure that such person's conduct will not obstruct the orderly and expeditious progress of the trial.

(c) *Pending Sentence and Notice of Appeal.* Eligibility for release pending sentence or pending notice of appeal or expiration of the time allowed for filing notice of appeal, shall be in accordance with 18 U.S.C. § 3143. The burden of establishing that the defendant will not flee or pose a danger to any other person or to the community rests with the defendant.

(d) *Justification of Sureties.* Every surety, except a corporate surety which is approved as provided by law, shall justify by affidavit and may be required to describe in the affidavit the property by which the surety proposes to justify and the encumbrances thereon, the number and amount of other bonds and undertakings for bail entered into by the surety and remaining undischarged and all the other liabilities of the surety. No bond shall be approved unless the surety thereon appears to be qualified.

(e) *Forfeiture.*

(1) Declaration. — If there is a breach of condition of a bond, the district court shall declare a forfeiture of the bail.

(2) *Setting aside.* — The court may direct that a forfeiture be set aside, in whole or in part, upon such conditions as the court may impose, if a person released upon execution of an appearance bond with a surety is subsequently surrendered by the surety into custody or if it otherwise appears that justice does not require the forfeiture.

(3) *Enforcement.* — When a forfeiture has not been set aside, the court shall on motion enter a judgment of default and execution may issue thereon. By entering into a bond the obligors submit to the jurisdiction of the district court and irrevocably appoint the clerk of the court as their agent upon whom any papers affecting their liability may be served. Their liability may be enforced on motion without the necessity of an independent action. The motion and such notice of the motion as the court prescribes may be served on the clerk of the court, who shall forthwith mail copies to the obligors to their last known addresses.

(4) *Remission.* — After entry of such judgment, the court may remit it in whole or in part under the conditions applying to the setting aside of forfeiture in paragraph (2) of this subdivision.

(f) *Exoneration.* When the condition of the bond has been satisfied or the forfeiture thereof has been set aside or remitted, the court shall exonerate the obligors and release any bail. A surety may be exonerated by a deposit of cash in the amount of the bond or by a timely surrender of the defendant into custody.

(g) *Supervision of Detention Pending Trial.* The court shall exercise supervision over the detention of defendants and witnesses within the district pending trial for the purpose of eliminating all unnecessary detention. The attorney for the government shall make a biweekly report to the court listing each defendant and witness who has been held in custody pending indictment, arraignment or trial for a period in excess of ten days. As to each witness so listed the attorney for the government shall make a statement of the reasons why such witness should not be released with or without the taking of a deposition pursuant to Rule 15(a). As to each defendant so listed the attorney for the government shall make a statement of the reasons why the defendant is still held in custody.

(h) *Forfeiture of Property.* — Nothing in this rule or in chapter 207 of title 18, United States Code, shall prevent the court from disposing of any charge by entering an order directing forfeiture of property pursuant to 18 U.S.C. 3142(c)(1)(B)(xi) if the value of the property is an amount that would be an appropriate sentence after conviction of the offense charged and if such forfeiture is authorized by statute or regulation.

(As amended, eff. Dec. 1, 1991.)


**Rule 47. Motions.** An application to the court for an order shall be by motion. A motion other than one made during a trial or hearing shall be in writing unless the court permits it to be made orally. It shall state the grounds upon which it is made and shall set forth the relief or order sought. It may be supported by affidavit.


**Rule 48. Dismissal.** (a) *By Attorney for Government.* The Attorney General or the United States Attorney may by leave of court file a dismissal of an indictment, information or complaint and the prosecution shall thereupon terminate. Such a dismissal may not be filed during the trial without the consent of the defendant.

(b) *By Court.* If there is unnecessary delay in presenting the charge to a grand jury or in filing an information against a defendant who has been held to answer to the district court, or if there is unnecessary delay in bringing a defendant to trial, the court may dismiss the indictment, information or complaint.

**Rule 49. Service and Filing of Papers.** (a) *Service: When Required.* Written motions other than those which are heard *ex parte,* written notices, designations of record on appeal and similar papers shall be served upon each of the parties.

(b) *Service: How Made.* Whenever under these rules or by an order of the court service is required or permitted to be made upon a party represented by an attorney, the service shall be made upon the attorney unless service upon the party personally is ordered by the court. Service upon the attorney or upon a party shall be made in the manner provided in civil actions.

(c) *Notice of Orders.* Immediately upon the entry of an order made on a written motion subsequent to arraignment the clerk shall mail to each party a notice thereof and shall make a note in the docket of the mailing. Lack of notice of the entry by the clerk does not affect the time to appeal or relieve or authorize the court to relieve a party for failure to appeal within the time allowed, except as permitted by Rule 4(b) of the Federal Rules of Appellate Procedure.

(d) *Filing.* Papers required to be served shall be filed with the court. Papers shall be filed in the manner provided in civil actions.

(e) *Filing of Dangerous Offender Notice.* A filing with the court pursuant to 18 U.S.C. § 3575(a) or 21 U.S.C. § 849(a) shall be made by filing the notice with the clerk of the court. The clerk shall transmit the notice to the chief judge or, if the chief judge is the presiding judge in the case, to another judge or United States magistrate in the district, except that in a district having a single judge and no United States magistrate, the clerk shall transmit the notice to the court only after the time for disclosure specified in the aforementioned statutes and shall seal the notice as permitted by local rule.

**Rule 50. Calendars; Plan for Prompt Disposition.** (a) *Calendars.* The district courts may provide for placing criminal proceedings upon appropriate calendars. Preference shall be given to criminal proceedings as far as practicable.

(b) *Plans for Achieving Prompt Disposition of Criminal Cases.* To minimize undue delay and to further the prompt disposition of criminal cases, each district court shall conduct a continuing study of the administration of criminal justice in the district court and before United States magistrates of the district and shall prepare plans for the prompt disposition of criminal cases in accordance with the provisions of Chapter 208 of Title 18, United States Code.

**Rule 51. Exceptions Unnecessary.** Exceptions to rulings or orders of the court are unnecessary and for all purposes for which an exception has heretofore been necessary it is sufficient that a party, at the time the ruling or order of the court is made or sought, makes known to the court the action which that party desires the court to take or that party's objection to the action of the court and the grounds therefor; but if a party has no opportunity to object to a ruling or order, the absence of an objection does not thereafter prejudice that party.

**Rule 52. Harmless Error and Plain Error.** (a) *Harmless Error.* Any error, defect, irregularity or variance which does not affect substantial rights shall be disregarded.

(b) *Plain Error.* Plain errors or defects affecting substantial rights may be noticed although they were not brought to the attention of the court.

**Rule 53. Regulation of Conduct in the Courtroom.** The taking of photographs in the courtroom during the progress of judicial proceedings or radio broadcasting of judicial proceedings from the courtroom shall not be permitted by the court.

**Rule 54. Application and Exception.** (a) *Courts.* These rules apply to all criminal proceedings in the United States District Courts; in the District Court of Guam; in the District Court for the Northern Mariana Islands, except as otherwise provided in articles IV and V of the covenant provided by the Act of March 24, 1976 (90 Stat. 263); in the District Court of the Virgin Islands; and (except as otherwise provided in the Canal Zone Code) in the United States District Court for the District of the Canal Zone; in the United States Courts of Appeals; and in the Supreme Court of the United States; except that the prosecution of offenses in the District Court of the Virgin Islands shall be by indictment or information as otherwise provided by law.

(b) *Proceedings.*

(1) Removed Proceedings. — These rules apply to criminal prosecutions removed to the United States District Courts from state courts and govern all procedure after removal, except that dismissal by the attorney for the prosecution shall be governed by state law.

(2) Offenses Outside a District or State. — These rules apply to proceedings for offenses committed upon the high seas or elsewhere out of the jurisdiction of any particular state or district, except that such proceedings may be had in any district authorized by 18 U.S.C. § 3238.

(3) Peace Bonds. — These rules do not alter the power of judges of the United States or of United States magistrates to hold to security of the peace and for good behavior under Revised Statutes, § 4069, 50 U.S.C. § 23, but in such cases the procedure shall conform to these rules so far as they are applicable.

(4) Proceedings Before United States Magistrates. — Proceedings involving misdemeanors and other petty offenses are governed by Rule 58.

(5) Other Proceedings. — These rules are not applicable to extradition and rendition of fugitives; civil forfeiture of property for violation of a statute of the United States; or the collection of fines and penalties. Except as provided in Rule 20(d) they do not apply to proceedings under 18 U.S.C. Chapter 403 — Juvenile Delinquency — so far as they are inconsistent with that chapter. They do not apply to summary trials for offenses against the navigation laws under Revised Statutes §§ 4300-4305, 33 U.S.C. §§ 391-396, or to proceedings involving disputes between seamen under Revised Statutes §§ 4079-4081, as amended, 22 U.S.C. §§ 256-258, or to proceedings for fishery offenses under the Act of June 28, 1937, c. 392, 50 Stat. 325-327, 16 U.S.C. §§ 772-772i, or to proceedings against a witness in a foreign country under 28 U.S.C. § 1784.

(c) *Application of Terms.* As used in these rules the following terms have the designated meanings.

"Act of Congress" includes any act of Congress locally applicable to and in force in the District of Columbia, in Puerto Rico, in a territory or in an insular possession.

"Attorney for the government" means the Attorney General, an authorized assistant of the Attorney General, a United States Attorney, an authorized assistant of a United States Attorney, when applicable to cases arising under the laws of Guam the Attorney General of Guam or such other person or persons as may be authorized by the laws of Guam to act therein, and when applicable to cases arising under the laws of the Northern Mariana Islands the Attorney General of the Northern Mariana Islands or any other person or persons as may be authorized by the laws of the Northern Marianas to act therein.

"Civil action" refers to a civil action in a district court.

The words "demurrer," "motion to quash," "plea in abatement," "plea in bar" and "special plea in bar," or words to the same effect, in any act of Congress shall be construed to mean the motion raising a defense or objection provided in Rule 12.

"District court" includes all district courts named in subdivision (a) of this rule.

"Federal magistrate" means a United States magistrate as defined in 28 U.S.C. §§ 631-639, a judge of the United States or another judge or judicial officer specifically empowered by statute in force in any territory or possession, the Commonwealth of Puerto Rico, or the District of Columbia, to perform a function to which a particular rule relates.

"Judge of the United States" includes a judge of a district court, court of appeals, or the Supreme Court.

"Law" includes statutes and judicial decisions.

"Magistrate" includes a United States magistrate as defined in 28 U.S.C. §§ 631-639, a judge of the United States, another judge or judicial officer specifically empowered by statute in force in any territory or possession, the Commonwealth of Puerto Rico, or the District of Columbia, to perform a function to which a particular rule relates, and a state or local judicial officer, authorized by 18 U.S.C. § 3041 to perform the functions prescribed in Rules 3, 4, and 5.

"Oath" includes affirmations.

"Petty offense" is defined in 18 U.S.C. § 19.

"State" includes District of Columbia, Puerto Rico, territory and insular possession.

"United States magistrate" means the officer authorized by 28 U.S.C. §§ 631-639.

(As amended, eff. Dec. 1, 1991.)

**Rule 55. Records.** The clerk of the district court and each United States magistrate shall keep records in criminal proceedings in such form as the Director of the Administrative Office of the United States Courts may prescribe. The clerk shall enter in the records each order or judgment of the court and the date such entry is made.

**Rule 56. Courts and Clerks.** The district court shall be deemed always open for the purpose of filing any proper paper, of issuing and returning process and of making motions and orders. The clerk's office with the clerk or a deputy in attendance shall be open during business hours on all days except Saturdays, Sundays, and legal holidays, but a court may provide by local rule or order that its clerk's office shall be open for specified hours on Saturdays or particular legal holidays other than New Year's Day, Washington's Birthday, Memorial Day, Independence Day, Labor Day, Columbus Day, Veterans' Day, Thanksgiving Day, and Christmas Day.

**Rule 57. Rules of Court.** Each district court by action of a majority of the judges thereof may from time to time, after giving appropriate public notice and an opportunity to comment, make and amend rules governing its practice not inconsistent with these rules. A local rule so adopted shall take effect upon the date specified by the district court and shall remain in effect unless amended by the district court or abrogated by the judicial council of the circuit in which the district is located. Copies of the rules and amendments so made by any district court shall upon their promulgation be furnished to the judicial council and the Administrative Office of the United States Courts and be made available to the public. In all cases not provided for by rule, the district judges and magistrates may regulate their practice in any manner not inconsistent with these rules or those of the district in which they act.

## Rule 58. Procedure for Misdemeanors and Other Petty Offenses. (a) *Scope.*

(1) In General. — This rule governs the procedure and practice for the conduct of proceedings involving misdemeanors and other petty offenses, and for appeals to judges of the district courts in such cases tried by magistrates.

(2) Applicability of Other Federal Rules of Criminal Procedure. — In proceedings concerning petty offenses for which no sentence of imprisonment will be imposed the court may follow such provisions of these rules as it deems appropriate, to the extent not inconsistent with this rule. In all other proceedings the other rules govern except as specifically provided in this rule.

(3) Definition. — The term "petty offenses for which no sentence of imprisonment will be imposed" as used in this rule, means any petty offenses as defined in 18 U.S.C. § 19 as to which the court determines, that, in the event of conviction, no sentence of imprisonment will actually be imposed.

(b) *Pretrial Procedures.*

(1) Trial Document. — The trial of a misdemeanor may proceed on an indictment, information, or complaint or, in the case of a petty offense, on a citation or violation notice.

(2) Initial Appearance. — At the defendant's initial appearance on a misdemeanor or other petty offense charge, the court shall inform the defendant of:

(A) the charge, and the maximum possible penalties provided by law, including payment of a special assessment under 18 U.S.C. § 3013, and restitution under 18 U.S.C. § 3663;

(B) the right to retain counsel;

(C) unless the charge is a petty offense for which appointment of counsel is not required, the right to request the assignment of counsel if the defendant is unable to obtain counsel;

(D) the right to remain silent and that any statement made by the defendant may be used against the defendant;

(E) the right to trial, judgment, and sentencing before a judge of the district court, unless the defendant consents to trial, judgment, and sentencing before a magistrate;

(F) unless the charge is a petty offense, the right to trial by jury before either a magistrate or a judge of the district court; and

(G) if the defendant is held in custody and charged with a misdemeanor other than a petty offense, the right to a preliminary examination in accordance with 18 U.S.C. § 3060, and the general circumstances under which the defendant may secure pretrial release.

(3) Consent and Arraignment. —

(A) Trial Before a Magistrate. If the defendant signs a written consent to be tried before the magistrate which specifically waives trial before a judge of the district court, the magistrate shall take the defendant's plea. The defendant may plead not guilty, guilty, or with the consent of the magistrate, nolo contendere.

(B) Failure to Consent. If the defendant does not consent to trial before the magistrate, the defendant shall be ordered to appear before a judge of the district court for further proceedings on notice.

(c) *Additional Procedures Applicable Only to Petty Offenses for Which No Sentence of Imprisonment Will be Imposed.* With respect to petty offenses for which no sentence of imprisonment will be imposed, the following additional procedures are applicable:

(1) Plea of Guilty or Nolo Contendere. — No plea of guilty or nolo contendere shall be accepted unless the court is satisfied that the defendant understands the nature of the charge and the maximum possible penalties provided by law.

(2) Waiver of Venue for Plea and Sentence. — A defendant who is arrested, held, or present in a district other than that in which the indictment, information, complaint, citation or violation notice is pending against that defendant may state in writing a wish to plead guilty or nolo contendere, to waive venue and trial in the district in which the proceeding is pending, and to consent to disposition of the case in the district in which that defendant was arrested, is held, or is present. Unless the defendant thereafter pleads not guilty, the prosecution shall be had as if venue were in such district, and notice of the same shall be given to the magistrate in the district where the proceeding was originally commenced. The defendant's statement of a desire to plead guilty or nolo contendere is not admissible against the defendant.

(3) Sentence. — The court shall afford the defendant an opportunity to be heard in mitigation. The court shall then immediately proceed to sentence the defendant, except that in the discretion of the court, sentencing may be continued to allow an investigation by the probation service or submission of additional information by either party.

(4) Notification of Right to Appeal. — After imposing sentence in a case which has gone to trial on a plea of not guilty, the court shall advise the defendant of the defendant's right to appeal including any right to appeal the sentence. There shall be no duty on the court to advise the defendant of any right of appeal after sentence is imposed following a plea of guilty or nolo contendere, except that the court shall advise the defendant of any right to appeal the sentence.

(d) *Securing the Defendant's Appearance; Payment in Lieu of Appearance.*

(1) Forfeiture of Collateral. — When authorized by local rules of the district court, payment of a fixed sum may be accepted in suitable cases in lieu of appearance and as authorizing the termination of the proceedings. Local rules may make provision for increases in fixed sums not to exceed the maximum fine which could be imposed.

(2) Notice to Appear. — If a defendant fails to pay a fixed sum, request a hearing, or appear in response to a citation or violation notice, the clerk or a magistrate may issue a notice for the defendant to appear before the court on a date certain. The notice may also afford the defendant an additional opportunity to pay a fixed sum in lieu of appearance, and shall be served upon the defendant by mailing a copy to the defendant's last known address.

(3) Summons or Warrant. — Upon an indictment or a showing by one of the other documents specified in subdivision (b)(1) of probable cause to believe that an offense has been committed and that the defendant has committed it, the court may issue an arrest warrant or, if no warrant is requested by the attorney for the prosecution, a summons. The showing of probable cause shall be made in writing upon oath or under penalty for perjury, but the affiant need not appear before the court. If the defendant fails to appear before the court in response to a summons, the court may summarily issue a warrant for the defendant's immediate arrest and appearance before the court.

(e) *Record.* Proceedings under this rule shall be taken down by a reporter or recorded by suitable sound equipment.

(f) *New Trial.* The provisions of Rule 33 shall apply.

(g) *Appeal.*

(1) Decision, Order, Judgment or Sentence by a District Judge. — An appeal from a decision, order, judgment or conviction or sentence by a judge of the district court shall be taken in accordance with the Federal Rules of Appellate Procedure.

(2) Decision, Order, Judgment or Sentence by a Magistrate. —

(A) Interlocutory Appeal. A decision or order by a magistrate which, if made by a judge of the district court, could be appealed by the government or defendant under any provision of law, shall be subject to an appeal to a judge of the district court provided such appeal is taken within 10 days of the entry of the decision or order. An appeal shall be taken by filing with the clerk of court a statement specifying the decision or order from which an appeal is taken and by serving a copy of the statement upon the adverse party, personally or by mail, and by filing a copy with the magistrate.

(B) Appeal from Conviction or Sentence. An appeal from a judgment of conviction or sentence by a magistrate to a judge of the district court shall be taken within 10 days after entry of the judgment. An appeal shall be taken by filing with the clerk of court a statement specifying the judgment from which an appeal is taken, and by serving a copy of the statement upon the United States Attorney, personally or by mail, and by filing a copy with the magistrate.

(C) Record. The record shall consist of the original papers and exhibits in the case together with any transcript, tape, or other recording of the proceedings and a certified copy of the docket entries which shall be transmitted promptly to the clerk of court. For purposes of the appeal, a copy of the record of such proceedings shall be made available at the expense of the United States to a person who establishes by affidavit the inability to pay or give security therefor, and the expense of such copy shall be paid by the Director of the Administrative Office of the United States Courts.

(D) Scope of Appeal. The defendant shall not be entitled to a trial de novo by a judge of the district court. The scope of the appeal shall be the same as an appeal from a judgment of a district court to a court of appeals.

(3) Stay of Execution; Release Pending Appeal. — The provisions of Rule 38 relating to stay of execution shall be applicable to a judgment of conviction or sentence. The defendant may be released pending appeal in accordance with the provisions of law relating to release pending appeal from a judgment of a district court to a court of appeals.

(As amended, eff. Dec. 1, 1991.)

**Rule 59. Effective Date.** These rules take effect on the day which is 3 months subsequent to the adjournment of the first regular session of the 79th Congress, but if that day is prior to September 1, 1945, then they take effect on September 1, 1945. They govern all criminal proceedings thereafter commenced and so far as just and practicable all proceedings then pending.

**Rule 60. Title.** These rules may be known and cited as the Federal Rules of Criminal Procedure.

# APPENDIX C

# FEDERAL RULES OF EVIDENCE

## I. GENERAL PROVISIONS.

**Rule 101. Scope.** These rules govern proceedings in the courts of the United States and before United States bankruptcy judges and United States magistrates, to the extent and with the exceptions stated in Rule 1101.

**Rule 102. Purpose and Construction.** These rules shall be construed to secure fairness in administration, elimination of unjustifiable expense and delay, and promotion of growth and development of the law of evidence to the end that the truth may be ascertained and proceedings justly determined.

**Rule 103. Rulings on Evidence.** (a) *Effect of Erroneous ruling.* Error may not be predicated upon a ruling which admits or excludes evidence unless a substantial right of the party is affected, and

(1) Objection. — In case the ruling is one admitting evidence, a timely objection or motion to strike appears of record, stating the specific ground of objection, if the specific ground was not apparent from the context; or

(2) Offer of proof. — In case the ruling is one excluding evidence, the substance of the evidence was made known to the court by offer or was apparent from the context within which questions were asked.

(b) *Record of Offer and Ruling.* The court may add any other or further statement which shows the character of the evidence, the form in which it was offered, the objection made, and the ruling thereon. It may direct the making of an offer in question and answer form.

(c) *Hearing of jury.* In jury cases, proceedings shall be conducted, to the extent practicable, so as to prevent inadmissible evidence from being suggested to the jury by any means, such as making statements or offers of proof or asking questions in the hearing of the jury.

(d) *Plain error.* Nothing in this rule precludes taking notice of plain errors affecting substantial rights although they were not brought to the attention of the court.

**Rule 104. Preliminary Questions.** (a) *Questions of admissibility generally.* Preliminary questions concerning the qualification of a person to be a witness, the existence of a privilege, or the admissibility of evidence shall be determined by the court, subject to the provisions of subdivision (b). In making its determination it is not bound by the rules of evidence except those with respect to privileges.

(b) *Relevancy conditioned on fact.* When the relevancy of evidence depends upon the fulfillment of a condition of fact, the court shall admit it upon, or subject to, the introduction of evidence sufficient to support a finding of the fulfillment of the condition.

(c) *Hearing of jury.* Hearings on the admissibility of confessions shall in all cases be conducted out of the hearing of the jury. Hearings on other preliminary matters shall be so conducted when the interests of justice require, or when an accused is a witness and so requests.

(d) *Testimony by accused.* The accused does not, by testifying upon a preliminary matter, become subject to cross-examination as to other issues in the case.

(e) *Weight and credibility.* This rule does not limit the right of a party to introduce before the jury evidence relevant to weight or credibility.

**Rule 105. Limited Admissibility.** When evidence which is admissible as to one party or for one purpose but not admissible as to another party or for another purpose is admitted, the court, upon request, shall restrict the evidence to its proper scope and instruct the jury accordingly.

**Rule 106. Remainder of or Related Writings or Recorded Statements.** When a writing or recorded statement or part thereof is introduced by a party, an adverse party may require the introduction at that time of any other part or any other writing or recorded statement which ought in fairness to be considered contemporaneously with it.

## II. JUDICIAL NOTICE.

**Rule 201. Judicial Notice of Adjudicative Facts.** (a) *Scope of rule.* This rule governs only judicial notice of adjudicative facts.

(b) *Kinds of facts.* A judicially noticed fact must be one not subject to reasonable dispute in that it is either (1) generally known within the territorial jurisdiction of the trial court or (2) capable of accurate and ready determination by resort to sources whose accuracy cannot reasonably be questioned.

(c) *When discretionary.* A court may take judicial notice, whether requested or not.

(d) *When mandatory.* A court shall take judicial notice if requested by a party and supplied with the necessary information.

(e) *Opportunity to be heard.* A party is entitled upon timely request to an opportunity to be heard as to the propriety of taking judicial notice and the tenor of the matter noticed. In the absence of prior notification, the request may be made after judicial notice has been taken.

(f) *Time of taking notice.* Judicial notice may be taken at any stage of the proceeding.

(g) *Instructing jury.* In a civil action or proceeding, the court shall instruct the jury to accept as conclusive any fact judicially noticed. In a criminal case, the court shall instruct the jury that it may, but is not required to, accept as conclusive any fact judicially noticed.

## III. PRESUMPTIONS IN CIVIL ACTIONS AND PROCEEDINGS.

**Rule 301. Presumptions in General in Civil Actions and Proceedings.** In all civil actions and proceedings not otherwise provided for by Act of Congress or by these rules, a presumption imposes on the party against whom it is directed the burden of going forward with evidence to rebut or meet the presumption, but does not shift to such party the burden of proof in the sense of the risk of nonpersuasion, which remains throughout the trial upon the party on whom it was originally cast.

**Rule 302. Applicability of State Law in Civil Actions and Proceedings.** In civil actions and proceedings, the effect of a presumption respecting a fact which is an element of a claim or defense as to which State law supplies the rule of decision is determined in accordance with State law.

## IV. RELEVANCY AND ITS LIMITS.

**Rule 401. Definition of "Relevant Evidence."** "Relevant evidence" means evidence having any tendency to make the existence of any fact that is of consequence to the determination of the action more probable or less probable than it would be without the evidence.

**Rule 402. Relevant Evidence Generally Admissible; Irrelevant Evidence Inadmissible.** All relevant evidence is admissible, except as otherwise provided by the Constitution of the United States, by Act of Congress, by these rules, or by other rules prescribed by the Supreme Court pursuant to statutory authority. Evidence which is not relevant is not admissible.

**Rule 403. Exclusion of Relevant Evidence on Grounds of Prejudice, Confusion, or Waste of Time.** Although relevant, evidence may be excluded if its probative value is substantially outweighed by the danger of unfair prejudice, confusion of the issues, or misleading the jury, or by considerations of undue delay, waste of time, or needless presentation of cumulative evidence.

**Rule 404. Character Evidence Not Admissible to Prove Conduct; Exceptions; Other Crimes.** (a) *Character evidence generally.* — Evidence of a person's character or a trait of his character is not admissible for the purpose of proving action in conformity therewith on a particular occasion, except:

(1) Character of accused. — Evidence of a pertinent trait of character offered by an accused, or by the prosecution to rebut the same;

(2) Character of victim. — Evidence of a pertinent trait of character of the victim of the crime offered by an accused, or by the prosecution to rebut the same, or evidence of a character trait of peacefulness of the victim offered by the prosecution in a homicide case to rebut evidence that the victim was the first aggressor;

(3) Character of witness. — Evidence of the character of a witness, as provided in rules 607, 608, and 609.

(b) *Other crimes, wrongs, or acts.* — Evidence of other crimes, wrongs, or acts is not admissible to prove the character of a person in order to show action in conformity therewith. It may, however, be admissible for other purposes, such as proof of motive, opportunity, intent, preparation, plan, knowledge, identity, or absence of mistake or accident, provided that upon request by the accused, the prosecution in a criminal case shall provide reasonable notice in advance of trial, or during trial if the court excuses pretrial notice on good cause shown, of the general nature of any such evidence it intends to introduce at trial.

(As amended, eff. Dec. 1, 1991.)

**Rule 405. Methods of Proving Character.** (a) *Reputation or opinion.* In all cases in which evidence of character or a trait of character of a person is admissible, proof may be made by testimony as to reputation or by testimony in the form of an opinion. On cross-examination, inquiry is allowable into relevant specific instances of conduct.

(b) *Specific instances of conduct.* In cases in which character or a trait of character of a person is an essential element of a charge, claim, or defense, proof may also be made of specific instances of that person's conduct.

561

**Rule 406. Habit; Routine Practice.** Evidence of the habit of a person or of the routine practice of an organization, whether corroborated or not and regardless of the presence of eyewitnesses, is relevant to prove that the conduct of the person or organization on a particular occasion was in conformity with the habit or routine practice.

**Rule 407. Subsequent Remedial Measures.** When, after an event, measures are taken which, if taken previously, would have made the event less likely to occur, evidence of the subsequent measures is not admissible to prove negligence or culpable conduct in connection with the event. This rule does not require the exclusion of evidence of subsequent measures when offered for another purpose, such as proving ownership, control, or feasibility of precautionary measures, if controverted, or impeachment.

**Rule 408. Compromise and Offers to Compromise.** Evidence of (1) furnishing or offering or promising to furnish, or (2) accepting or offering or promising to accept, a valuable consideration in compromising or attempting to compromise a claim which was disputed as to either validity or amount, is not admissible to prove liability for or invalidity of the claim or its amount. Evidence of conduct or statements made in compromise negotiations is likewise not admissible. This rule does not require the exclusion of any evidence otherwise discoverable merely because it is presented in the course of compromise negotiations. This rule also does not require exclusion when the evidence is offered for another purpose, such as proving bias or prejudice of a witness, negativing a contention of undue delay, or proving an effort to obstruct a criminal investigation or prosecution.

**Rule 409. Payment of Medical and Similar Expenses.** Evidence of furnishing or offering or promising to pay medical, hospital, or similar expenses occasioned by an injury is not admissible to prove liability for the injury.

**Rule 410. Inadmissibility of Pleas, Plea Discussions and Related Statements.** Except as otherwise provided in this rule, evidence of the following is not, in any civil or criminal proceeding, admissible against the defendant who made the plea or was a participant in the plea discussions:
 (1) a plea of guilty which was later withdrawn;
 (2) a plea of nolo contendere;
 (3) any statement made in the course of any proceedings under Rule 11 of the Federal Rules of Criminal Procedure or comparable state procedure regarding either of the foregoing pleas; or
 (4) any statement made in the course of plea discussions with an attorney for the prosecuting authority which do not result in a plea of guilty or which result in a plea of guilty later withdrawn.
However, such a statement is admissible (i) in any proceeding wherein another statement made in the course of the same plea or plea discussions has been introduced and the statement ought in fairness be considered contemporaneously with it, or (ii) in a criminal proceeding for perjury or false statement if the statement was made by the defendant under oath, on the record and in the presence of counsel.

**Rule 411. Liability Insurance.** Evidence that a person was or was not insured against liability is not admissible upon the issue whether the person acted negligently or otherwise wrongfully. This rule does not require the exclusion of evidence of insurance against liability when offered for another purpose, such as proof of agency, owner-ship, or control, or bias or prejudice of a witness.

**Rule 412. Rape Cases; Relevance of Victim's Past Behavior.** (a) Notwithstand-ing any other provision of law, in a criminal case in which a person is accused of rape or of assault with intent to commit rape, reputation or opinion evidence of the past sexual behavior of an alleged victim of such rape or assault is not admissible.

(b) Notwithstanding any other provision of law, in a criminal case in which a person is accused of rape or of assault with intent to commit rape, evidence of a victim's past sexual behavior other than reputation or opinion evidence is also not admissible, unless such evidence other than reputation or opinion evidence is —

(1) admitted in accordance with subdivisions (c)(1) and (c)(2) and is constitution-ally required to be admitted; or

(2) admitted in accordance with subdivision (c) and is evidence of —

(A) past sexual behavior with persons other than the accused, offered by the accused upon the issue of whether the accused was or was not, with respect to the alleged victim, the source of semen or injury; or

(B) past sexual behavior with the accused and is offered by the accused upon the issue of whether the alleged victim consented to the sexual behavior with respect to which rape or assault is alleged.

(c)(1) If the person accused of committing rape or assault with intent to commit rape intends to offer under subdivision (b) evidence of specific instances of the alleged victim's past sexual behavior, the accused shall make a written motion to offer such evidence not later than fifteen days before the date on which the trial in which such evidence is to be offered is scheduled to begin, except that the court may allow the motion to be made at a later date, including during trial, if the court determines either that the evidence is newly discovered and could not have been obtained earlier through the exercise of due diligence or that the issue to which such evidence relates has newly arisen in the case. Any motion made under this paragraph shall be served on all other parties and on the alleged victim.

(2) The motion described in paragraph (1) shall be accompanied by a written offer of proof. If the court determines that the offer of proof contains evidence described in subdivision (b), the court shall order a hearing in chambers to determine if such evidence is admissible. At such hearing the parties may call witnesses, including the alleged victim, and offer relevant evidence. Notwithstanding subdivision (b) of Rule 104, if the relevancy of the evidence which the accused seeks to offer in the trial depends upon the fulfillment of a condition of fact, the court, at the hearing in cham-bers or at a subsequent hearing in chambers scheduled for such purpose, shall accept evidence on the issue of whether such condition of fact is fulfilled and shall determine such issue.

(3) If the court determines on the basis of the hearing described in paragraph (2) that the evidence which the accused seeks to offer is relevant and that the probative value of such evidence outweighs the danger of unfair prejudice, such evidence shall be admissible in the trial to the extent an order made by the court specifies evidence which may be offered and areas with respect to which the alleged victim may be examined or cross-examined.

(d) For purposes of this rule, the term "past sexual behavior" means sexual behavior other than the sexual behavior with respect to which rape or assault with intent to commit rape is alleged.

563

## V. PRIVILEGES.

**Rule 501. General Rule.** Except as otherwise required by the Constitution of the United States or provided by Act of Congress or in rules prescribed by the Supreme Court pursuant to statutory authority, the privilege of a witness, person, government, State, or political subdivision thereof shall be governed by the principles of the common law as they may be interpreted by the courts of the United States in the light of reason and experience. However, in civil actions and proceedings, with respect to an element of a claim or defense as to which State law supplies the rule of decision, the privilege of a witness, person, government, State, or political subdivision thereof shall be determined in accordance with State law.

## VI. WITNESSES.

**Rule 601. General Rule of Competency.** Every person is competent to be a witness except as otherwise provided in these rules. However, in civil actions and proceedings, with respect to an element of a claim or defense as to which State law supplies the rule of decision, the competency of a witness shall be determined in accordance with State law.

**Rule 602. Lack of Personal Knowledge.** A witness may not testify to a matter unless evidence is introduced sufficient to support a finding that the witness has personal knowledge of the matter. Evidence to prove personal knowledge may, but need not, consist of the witness' own testimony. This rule is subject to the provisions of Rule 703, relating to opinion testimony by expert witnesses.

**Rule 603. Oath or Affirmation.** Before testifying, every witness shall be required to declare that the witness will testify truthfully, by oath or affirmation administered in a form calculated to awaken the witness' conscience and impress the witness' mind with the duty to do so.

**Rule 604. Interpreters.** An interpreter is subject to the provisions of these rules relating to qualification as an expert and the administration of an oath or affirmation to make a true translation.

**Rule 605. Competency of Judge as Witness.** The judge presiding at the trial may not testify in that trial as a witness. No objection need be made in order to preserve the point.

**Rule 606. Competency of Juror as Witness.** (a) *At the trial.* A member of the jury may not testify as a witness before that jury in the trial of the case in which the juror is sitting. If the juror is called so to testify, the opposing party shall be afforded an opportunity to object out of the presence of the jury.

(b) *Inquiry into validity of verdict or indictment.* Upon an inquiry into the validity of a verdict or indictment, a juror may not testify as to any matter or statement occurring during the course of the jury's deliberations or to the effect of anything upon that or any other juror's mind or emotions as influencing the juror to assent to or dissent from the verdict or indictment or concerning the juror's mental processes in connection therewith, except that a juror may testify on the question whether extraneous prejudicial information was improperly brought to the jury's attention or whether any outside influence was improperly brought to bear upon any juror. Nor may a juror's affidavit or evidence of any statement by the juror concerning a matter about which the juror would be precluded from testifying be received for these purposes.

**Rule 607. Who May Impeach.** The credibility of a witness may be attacked by any party, including the party calling the witness.

**Rule 608. Evidence of Character and Conduct of Witness.** (a) *Opinion and reputation evidence of character.* The credibility of a witness may be attacked or supported by evidence in the form of opinion or reputation, but subject to these limitations: (1) The evidence may refer only to character for truthfulness or untruthfulness, and (2) evidence of truthful character is admissible only after the character of the witness for truthfulness has been attacked by opinion or reputation evidence or otherwise.

(b) *Specific instances of conduct.* Specific instances of the conduct of a witness, for the purpose of attacking or supporting the witness' credibility, other than conviction of crime as provided in Rule 609, may not be proved by extrinsic evidence. They may, however, in the discretion of the court, if probative of truthfulness or untruthfulness, be inquired into on cross-examination of the witness (1) concerning the witness' character for truthfulness or untruthfulness, or (2) concerning the character for truthfulness or untruthfulness of another witness as to which character the witness being cross-examined has testified.

The giving of testimony, whether by an accused or by any other witness, does not operate as a waiver of the accused's or the witness' privilege against self-incrimination when examined with respect to matters which relate only to credibility.

**Rule 609. Impeachment by Evidence of Conviction of Crime.** (a) *General rule.* — For the purpose of attacking the credibility of a witness,

(1) evidence that the witness has been convicted of a crime shall be admitted subject to Rule 403, if the crime was punishable by death or imprisonment in excess of one year under the law under which the witness was convicted, and the court determines that the probative value of admitting this evidence outweighs its prejudicial effect to the accused; and

(2) evidence that any witness has been convicted of a crime shall be admitted if it involved dishonesty or false statement, regardless of the punishment.

(b) *Time limit.* — Evidence of a conviction under this rule is not admissible if a period of more than ten years has elapsed since the date of the conviction or of the release of the witness from the confinement imposed for that conviction, whichever is the later date, unless the court determines, in the interests of justice, that the probative value of the conviction supported by specific facts and circumstances substantially outweighs its prejudicial effect. However, evidence of a conviction more than ten years old as calculated herein, is not admissible unless the proponent gives to the adverse party sufficient advance written notice of intent to use such evidence to provide the adverse party with a fair opportunity to contest the use of such evidence.

(c) *Effect of pardon, annulment, or certificate of rehabilitation.* — Evidence of a conviction is not admissible under this rule if (1) the conviction has been the subject of a pardon, annulment, certification of rehabilitation, or other equivalent procedure based on a finding of the rehabilitation of the person convicted, and that person has not been convicted of a subsequent crime which was punishable by death or imprisonment in excess of one year, or (2) the conviction has been the subject of a pardon, annulment, or other equivalent procedure based on a finding of innocence.

(d) *Juvenile adjudications.* — Evidence of juvenile adjudications is generally not admissible under this rule. The court may, however, in a criminal case allow evidence of a juvenile adjudication of a witness other than the accused if conviction of the offense would be admissible to attack the credibility of an adult and the court is satisfied that admission in evidence is necessary for a fair determination of the issue of guilt or innocence.

(e) *Pendency of appeal.* — The pendency of an appeal therefrom does not render evidence of a conviction inadmissible. Evidence of the pendency of an appeal is admissible.

(As amended, eff. Dec. 1, 1991.)

**Rule 610. Religious Beliefs or Opinions.** Evidence of the beliefs or opinions of a witness on matters of religion is not admissible for the purpose of showing that by reason of their nature the witness' credibility is impaired or enhanced.

**Rule 611. Mode and Order of Interrogation and Presentation.** (a) *Control by court.* The court shall exercise reasonable control over the mode and order of interrogating witnesses and presenting evidence so as to (1) make the interrogation and presentation effective for the ascertainment of the truth, (2) avoid needless consumption of time, and (3) protect witnesses from harassment or undue embarrassment.

(b) *Scope of cross-examination.* Cross-examination should be limited to the subject matter of the direct examination and matters affecting the credibility of the witness. The court may, in the exercise of discretion, permit inquiry into additional matters as if on direct examination.

(c) *Leading questions.* Leading questions should not be used on the direct examination of a witness except as may be necessary to develop the witness' testimony. Ordinarily leading questions should be permitted on cross-examination. When a party calls a hostile witness, an adverse party, or a witness identified with an adverse party, interrogation may be by leading questions.

**Rule 612. Writing Used to Refresh Memory.** Except as otherwise provided in criminal proceedings by section 3500 of title 18, United States Code, if a witness uses a writing to refresh memory for the purpose of testifying, either —

(1) While testifying, or

(2) Before testifying, if the court in its discretion determines it is necessary in the interests of justice,

an adverse party is entitled to have the writing produced at the hearing, to inspect it, to cross-examine the witness thereon, and to introduce in evidence those portions which relate to the testimony of the witness. If it is claimed that the writing contains matters not related to the subject matter of the testimony the court shall examine the writing in camera, excise any portions not so related, and order delivery of the remainder to the party entitled thereto. Any portion withheld over objections shall be preserved and made available to the appellate court in the event of an appeal. If a writing is not produced or delivered pursuant to order under this rule, the court shall make any order justice requires, except that in criminal cases when the prosecution elects not to comply, the order shall be one striking the testimony or, if the court in its discretion determines that the interests of justice so require, declaring a mistrial.

**Rule 613. Prior Statements of Witnesses.** (a) *Examining witness concerning prior statement.* In examining a witness concerning a prior statement made by the witness, whether written or not, the statement need not be shown nor its contents disclosed to the witness at that time, but on request the same shall be shown or disclosed to opposing counsel.

(b) *Extrinsic evidence of prior inconsistent statement of witness.* Extrinsic evidence of a prior inconsistent statement by a witness is not admissible unless the witness is afforded an opportunity to explain or deny the same and the opposite party is afforded an opportunity to interrogate the witness thereon, or the interests of justice otherwise require. This provision does not apply to admissions of a party-opponent as defined in Rule 801(d) (2).

**Rule 614. Calling and Interrogation of Witnesses by Court.** (a) *Calling by court.* The court may, on its own motion or at the suggestion of a party, call witnesses, and all parties are entitled to cross-examine witnesses thus called.

(b) *Interrogation by court.* The court may interrogate witnesses, whether called by itself or by a party.

(c) *Objections.* Objections to the calling of witnesses by the court or to interrogation by it may be made at the time or at the next available opportunity when the jury is not present.

**Rule 615. Exclusion of Witnesses.** At the request of a party the court shall order witnesses excluded so that they cannot hear the testimony of other witnesses, and it may make the order of its own motion. This rule does not authorize exclusion of (1) a party who is a natural person, or (2) an officer or employee of a party which is not a natural person designated as its representative by its attorney, or (3) a person whose presence is shown by a party to be essential to the presentation of the party's cause.

## VII. OPINIONS AND EXPERT TESTIMONY.

**Rule 701. Opinion Testimony by Lay Witnesses.** If the witness is not testifying as an expert, the witness' testimony in the form of opinions or inferences is limited to those opinions or inferences which are (a) rationally based on the perception of the witness and (b) helpful to a clear understanding of the witness' testimony or the determination of a fact in issue.

**Rule 702. Testimony by Experts.** If scientific, technical, or other specialized knowledge will assist the trier of fact to understand the evidence or to determine a fact in issue, a witness qualified as an expert by knowledge, skill, experience, training, or education, may testify thereto in the form of an opinion or otherwise.

**Rule 703. Bases of Opinion Testimony by Experts.** The facts or data in the particular case upon which an expert bases an opinion or inference may be those perceived by or made known to the expert at or before the hearing. If of a type reasonably relied upon by experts in the particular field in forming opinions or inferences upon the subject, the facts or data need not be admissible in evidence.

**Rule 704. Opinion on Ultimate Issue.** (a) Except as provided in subdivision (b), testimony in the form of an opinion or inference otherwise admissible is not objectionable because it embraces an ultimate issue to be decided by the trier of fact.

(b) No expert witness testifying with respect to the mental state or condition of a defendant in a criminal case may state an opinion or inference as to whether the defendant did or did not have the mental state or condition constituting an element of the crime charged or of a defense thereto. Such ultimate issues are matters for the trier of fact alone.

**Rule 705. Disclosure of Facts or Data Underlying Expert Opinion.** The expert may testify in terms of opinion or inference and give reasons therefor without prior disclosure of the underlying facts or data, unless the court requires otherwise. The expert may in any event be required to disclose the underlying facts or data on cross-examination.

**Rule 706. Court-Appointed Experts.** (a) *Appointment*. The court may on its own motion or on the motion of any party enter an order to show cause why expert witnesses should not be appointed, and may request the parties to submit nominations. The court may appoint any expert witnesses agreed upon by the parties, and may appoint expert witnesses of its own selection. An expert witness shall not be appointed by the court unless the witness consents to act. A witness so appointed shall be informed of the witness' duties by the court in writing, a copy of which shall be filed with the clerk, or at a conference in which the parties shall have opportunity to participate. A witness so appointed shall advise the parties of the witness' findings, if any; the witness' deposition may be taken by any party; and the witness may be called to testify by the court or any party. The witness shall be subject to cross-examination by each party, including a party calling the witness.

(b) *Compensation*. Expert witnesses so appointed are entitled to reasonable compensation in whatever sum the court may allow. The compensation thus fixed is payable from funds which may be provided by law in criminal cases and civil actions and proceedings involving just compensation under the fifth amendment. In other civil actions and proceedings the compensation shall be paid by the parties in such proportion and at such time as the court directs, and thereafter charged in like manner as other costs.

(c) *Disclosure of appointment*. In the exercise of its discretion, the court may authorize disclosure to the jury of the fact that the court appointed the expert witness.

(d) *Parties' experts of own selection*. Nothing in this rule limits the parties in calling expert witnesses of their own selection.

## VIII. HEARSAY.

**Rule 801. Definitions.** The following definitions apply under this article:

(a) *Statement*. A "statement" is (1) an oral or written assertion or (2) nonverbal conduct of a person, if it is intended by the person as an assertion.

(b) *Declarant*. A "declarant" is a person who makes a statement.

(c) *Hearsay*. "Hearsay" is a statement, other than one made by the declarant while testifying at the trial or hearing, offered in evidence to prove the truth of the matter asserted.

(d) *Statements which are not hearsay*. A statement is not hearsay if —

(1) Prior Statement by Witness. — The declarant testifies at the trial or hearing and is subject to cross-examination concerning the statement, and the statement is (A) inconsistent with the declarant's testimony, and was given under oath subject to the penalty of perjury at a trial, hearing, or other proceeding, or in a deposition, or (B) consistent with the declarant's testimony and is offered to rebut an express or

implied charge against the declarant of recent fabrication or improper influence or motive, or (C) one of identification of a person made after perceiving the person; or

(2) Admission by party-opponent. — The statement is offered against a party and is (A) the party's own statement, in either an individual or a representative capacity or (B) a statement of which the party has manifested an adoption or belief in its truth, or (C) a statement by a person authorized by the party to make a statement concerning the subject, or (D) a statement by the party's agent or servant concerning a matter within the scope of the agency or employment, made during the existence of the relationship, or (E) a statement by a coconspirator of a party during the course and in furtherance of the conspiracy.

**Rule 802. Hearsay Rule.** Hearsay is not admissible except as provided by these rules or by other rules prescribed by the Supreme Court pursuant to statutory authority or by Act of Congress.

**Rule 803. Hearsay Exceptions; Availability of Declarant Immaterial.** The following are not excluded by the hearsay rule, even though the declarant is available as a witness:

(1) *Present sense impression.* A statement describing or explaining an event or condition made while the declarant was perceiving the event or condition, or immediately thereafter.

(2) *Excited utterance.* A statement relating to a startling event or condition made while the declarant was under the stress of excitement caused by the event or condition.

(3) *Then existing mental, emotional, or physical condition.* A statement of the declarant's then existing state of mind, emotion, sensation, or physical condition (such as intent, plan, motive, design, mental feeling, pain, and bodily health), but not including a statement of memory or belief to prove the fact remembered or believed unless it relates to the execution, revocation, identification, or terms of declarant's will.

(4) *Statements for purposes of medical diagnosis or treatment.* Statements made for purposes of medical diagnosis or treatment and describing medical history, or past or present symptoms, pain, or sensations, or the inception or general character of the cause or external source thereof insofar as reasonably pertinent to diagnosis or treatment.

(5) *Recorded recollection.* A memorandum or record concerning a matter about which a witness once had knowledge but now has insufficient recollection to enable the witness to testify fully and accurately, shown to have been made or adopted by the witness when the matter was fresh in the witness' memory and to reflect that knowledge correctly. If admitted, the memorandum or record may be read into evidence but may not itself be received as an exhibit unless offered by an adverse party.

(6) *Records of regularly conducted activity.* A memorandum, report, record, or data compilation, in any form, of acts, events, conditions, opinions, or diagnoses, made at or near the time by or from information transmitted by, a person with knowledge, if kept in the course of a regularly conducted business activity, and if it was the regular practice of that business activity to make the memorandum, report, record, or data compilation, all as shown by the testimony of the custodian or other qualified witness, unless the source of information or the method or circumstances of preparation indicate lack of trustworthiness. The term "business" as used in this paragraph includes business, institution, association, profession, occupation, and calling of every kind, whether or not conducted for profit.

(7) *Absence of entry in records kept in accordance with the provisions of paragraph (6).* Evidence that a matter is not included in the memoranda reports, records, or data compilations, in any form, kept in accordance with the provisions of paragraph (6), to prove the nonoccurrence or nonexistence of the matter, if the matter was of a kind of which a memorandum, report, record, or data compilation was regularly made and preserved, unless the sources of information or other circumstances indicate lack of trustworthiness.

(8) *Public records and reports.* Records, reports, statements, or data compilations, in any form, of public offices or agencies, setting forth (A) the activities of the office or agency, or (B) matters observed pursuant to duty imposed by law as to which matters there was a duty to report, excluding, however, in criminal cases matters observed by police officers and other law enforcement personnel, or (C) in civil actions and proceedings and against the Government in criminal cases, factual findings resulting from an investigation made pursuant to authority granted by law, unless the sources of information or other circumstances indicate lack of trustworthiness.

(9) *Records of vital statistics.* Records or data compilations, in any form, of births, fetal deaths, deaths, or marriages, if the report thereof was made to a public office pursuant to requirements of law.

(10) *Absence of public record or entry.* To prove the absence of a record, report, statement, or data compilation, in any form, or the nonoccurrence or nonexistence of a matter of which a record, report, statement, or data compilation, in any form, was regularly made and preserved by a public office or agency, evidence in the form of a certification in accordance with Rule 902, or testimony, that diligent search failed to disclose the record, report, statement, or data compilation, or entry.

(11) *Records of religious organizations.* Statements of births, marriages, divorces, deaths, legitimacy, ancestry, relationship by blood or marriage, or other similar facts of personal or family history, contained in a regularly kept record of a religious organization.

(12) *Marriage, baptismal, and similar certificates.* Statements of fact contained in a certificate that the maker performed a marriage or other ceremony or administered a sacrament, made by a clergyman, public official, or other person authorized by the rules or practices of a religious organization or by law to perform the act certified, and purporting to have been issued at the time of the act or within a reasonable time thereafter.

(13) *Family records.* Statements of fact concerning personal or family history contained in family Bibles, genealogies, charts, engravings on rings, inscriptions on family portraits, engravings on urns, crypts, or tombstones, or the like.

(14) *Records of documents affecting an interest in property.* The record of a document purporting to establish or affect an interest in property, as proof of the content of the original recorded document and its execution and delivery by each person by whom it purports to have been executed, if the record is a record of a public office and an applicable statute authorizes the recording of documents of that kind in that office.

(15) *Statements in documents affecting an interest in property.* A statement contained in a document purporting to establish or affect an interest in property if the matter stated was relevant to the purpose of the document, unless dealings with the property since the document was made have been inconsistent with the truth of the statement or the purport of the document.

(16) *Statements in ancient documents.* Statements in a document in existence 20 years or more the authenticity of which is established.

(17) *Market reports, commercial publications.* Market quotations, tabulations, lists, directories, or other published compilations, generally used and relied upon by the public or by persons in particular occupations.

(18) *Learned treatises.* To the extent called to the attention of an expert witness upon cross-examination or relied upon by the expert witness in direct examination, statements contained in published treatises, periodicals, or pamphlets on a subject of history, medicine, or other science or art, established as a reliable authority by the testimony or admission of the witness or by other expert testimony or by judicial notice. If admitted, the statements may be read into evidence but may not be received as exhibits.

(19) *Reputation concerning personal or family history.* Reputation among members of a person's family by blood, adoption, or marriage, or among a person's associates, or in the community, concerning a person's birth, adoption, marriage, divorce, death, legitimacy, relationship by blood, adoption, or marriage, ancestry, or other similar fact of personal or family history.

(20) *Reputation concerning boundaries or general history.* Reputation in a community, arising before the controversy, as to boundaries of or customs affecting lands in the community, and reputation as to events of general history important to the community or State or nation in which located.

(21) *Reputation as to character.* Reputation of a person's character among associates or in the community.

(22) *Judgment of previous conviction.* Evidence of a final judgment, entered after a trial or upon a plea of guilty (but not upon a plea of nolo contendere), adjudging a person guilty of a crime punishable by death or imprisonment in excess of one year, to prove any fact essential to sustain the judgment, but not including, when offered by the Government in a criminal prosecution for purposes other than impeachment, judgments against persons other than the accused. The pendency of an appeal may be shown but does not affect admissibility.

(23) *Judgment as to personal, family, or general history, or boundaries.* Judgments as proof of matters of personal, family or general history, or boundaries, essential to the judgment, if the same would be provable by evidence of reputation.

(24) *Other exceptions.* A statement not specifically covered by any of the foregoing exceptions but having equivalent circumstantial guarantees of trustworthiness, if the court determines that (A) the statement is offered as evidence of a material fact; (B) the statement is more probative on the point for which it is offered than any other evidence which the proponent can procure through reasonable efforts; and (C) the general purposes of these rules and the interests of justice will best be served by admission of the statement into evidence. However, a statement may not be admitted under this exception unless the proponent of it makes known to the adverse party sufficiently in advance of the trial or hearing to provide the adverse party with a fair opportunity to prepare to meet it, the proponent's intention to offer the statement and the particulars of it, including the name and address of the declarant.

**Rule 804. Hearsay Exceptions; Declarant Unavailable.** (a) *Definition of unavailability.* "Unavailability as a witness" includes situations in which the declarant —

(1) is exempted by ruling of the court on the ground of privilege from testifying concerning the subject matter of the declarant's statement; or

(2) persists in refusing to testify concerning the subject matter of the declarant's statement despite an order of the court to do so; or

(3) testifies to a lack of memory of the subject matter of the declarant's statement; or

(4) is unable to be present or to testify at the hearing because of death or then existing physical or mental illness or infirmity; or

(5) is absent from the hearing and the proponent of a statement has been unable to procure the declarant's attendance (or in the case of a hearsay exception under subdivision (b)(2), (3), or (4), the declarant's attendance or testimony) by process or other reasonable means.

A declarant is not unavailable as a witness if exemption, refusal, claim of lack of memory, inability, or absence is due to the procurement or wrongdoing of the proponent of a statement for the purpose of preventing the witness from attending or testifying.

(b) *Hearsay exceptions.* The following are not excluded by the hearsay rule if the declarant is unavailable as a witness:

(1) Former testimony. — Testimony given as a witness at another hearing of the same or a different proceeding, or in a deposition taken in compliance with law in the course of the same or another proceeding, if the party against whom the testimony is now offered, or, in a civil action or proceeding, a predecessor in interest, had an opportunity and similar motive to develop the testimony by direct, cross, or redirect examination.

(2) Statement under belief of impending death. — In a prosecution for homicide or in a civil action or proceeding, a statement made by a declarant while believing that the declarant's death was imminent, concerning the cause or circumstances of what the declarant believed to be impending death.

(3) Statement against interest. — A statement which was at the time of its making so far contrary to the declarant's pecuniary or proprietary interest, or so far tended to subject the declarant to civil or criminal liability, or to render invalid a claim by the declarant against another, that a reasonable person in the declarant's position would not have made the statement unless believing it to be true. A statement tending to expose the declarant to criminal liability and offered to exculpate the accused is not admissible unless corroborating circumstances clearly indicate the trustworthiness of the statement.

(4) Statement of personal or family history. — (A) A statement concerning the declarant's own birth, adoption, marriage, divorce, legitimacy, relationship by blood, adoption, or marriage, ancestry, or other similar fact of personal or family history, even though declarant had no means of acquiring personal knowledge of the matter stated; or (B) a statement concerning the foregoing matters, and death also, of another person, if the declarant was related to the other by blood, adoption, or marriage or was so intimately associated with the other's family as to be likely to have accurate information concerning the matter declared.

(5) Other exceptions. — A statement not specifically covered by any of the foregoing exceptions but having equivalent circumstantial guarantees of trustworthiness, if the court determines that (A) the statement is offered as evidence of a material fact; (B) the statement is more probative on the point for which it is offered than any other evidence which the proponent can procure through reasonable efforts; and (C) the general purposes of these rules and the interests of justice will best be served by admission of the statement into evidence. However, a statement may not be admitted under this exception unless the proponent of it makes known to the adverse party sufficiently in advance of the trial or hearing to provide the adverse party with a fair

opportunity to prepare to meet it, the proponent's intention to offer the statement and the particulars of it, including the name and address of the declarant.

**Rule 805. Hearsay Within Hearsay.** Hearsay included within hearsay is not excluded under the hearsay rule if each part of the combined statements conforms with an exception to the hearsay rule provided in these rules.

**Rule 806. Attacking and Supporting Credibility of Declarant.** When a hearsay statement, or a statement defined in Rule 801(d) (2), (C), (D), or (E), has been admitted in evidence, the credibility of the declarant may be attacked, and if attacked may be supported, by any evidence which would be admissible for those purposes if declarant had testified as a witness. Evidence of a statement or conduct by the declarant at any time, inconsistent with the declarant's hearsay statement, is not subject to any requirement that the declarant may have been afforded an opportunity to deny or explain. If the party against whom a hearsay statement has been admitted calls the declarant as a witness, the party is entitled to examine the declarant on the statement as if under cross-examination.

## IX. AUTHENTICATION AND IDENTIFICATION.

**Rule 901. Requirement of Authentication or Identification.** (a) *General provision.* The requirement of authentication or identification as a condition precedent to admissibility is satisfied by evidence sufficient to support a finding that the matter in question is what its proponent claims.

(b) *Illustrations.* By way of illustration only, and not by way of limitation, the following are examples of authentication or identification conforming with the requirements of this rule:

(1) Testimony of witness with knowledge. — Testimony that a matter is what it is claimed to be.

(2) Nonexpert opinion on handwriting. — Nonexpert opinion as to the genuineness of handwriting, based upon familiarity not acquired for purposes of the litigation.

(3) Comparison by trier or expert witness. — Comparison by the trier of fact or by expert witnesses with specimens which have been authenticated.

(4) Distinctive characteristics and the like. — Appearance, contents, substance, internal patterns, or other distinctive characteristics, taken in conjunction with circumstances.

(5) Voice identification. — Identification of a voice, whether heard firsthand or through mechanical or electronic transmission or recording, by opinion based upon hearing the voice at any time under circumstances connecting it with the alleged speaker.

(6) Telephone conversations. — Telephone conversations, by evidence that a call was made to the number assigned at the time by the telephone company to a particular person or business, if (A) in the case of a person, circumstances, including self-identification, show the person answering to be the one called, or (B) in the case of a business, the call was made to a place of business and the conversation related to business reasonably transacted over the telephone.

(7) Public records or reports. — Evidence that a writing authorized by law to be recorded or filed and in fact recorded or filed in a public office, or a purported public

record, report, statement, or data compilation, in any form, is from the public office where items of this nature are kept.

(8) Ancient documents or data compilation. — Evidence that a document or data compilation, in any form, (A) is in such condition as to create no suspicion concerning its authenticity, (B) was in a place where it, if authentic, would likely be, and (C) has been in existence 20 years or more at the time it is offered.

(9) Process or system. — Evidence describing a process or system used to produce a result and showing that the process or system produces an accurate result.

(10) Methods provided by statute or rule. — Any method of authentication or identification provided by Act of Congress or by other rules prescribed by the Supreme Court pursuant to statutory authority.

**Rule 902. Self-Authentication.** Extrinsic evidence of authenticity as a condition precedent to admissibility is not required with respect to the following:

(1) *Domestic public documents under seal.* A document bearing a seal purporting to be that of the United States, or of any State, district, Commonwealth, territory, or insular possession thereof, or the Panama Canal Zone, or the Trust Territory of the Pacific Islands, or of a political subdivision, department, officer, or agency thereof, and a signature purporting to be an attestation or execution.

(2) *Domestic public documents not under seal.* A document purporting to bear the signature in the official capacity of an officer or employee of any entity included in paragraph (1) hereof, having no seal, if a public officer having a seal and having official duties in the district or political subdivision of the officer or employee certifies under seal that the signer has the official capacity and that the signature is genuine.

(3) *Foreign public documents.* A document purporting to be executed or attested in an official capacity by a person authorized by the laws of a foreign country to make the execution or attestation, and accompanied by a final certification as to the genuineness of the signature and official position (A) of the executing or attesting person, or (B) of any foreign official whose certificate of genuineness of signature and official position relates to the execution or attestation or is in a chain of certificates of genuineness of signature and official position relating to the execution or attestation. A final certification may be made by a secretary of embassy or legation, consul general, consul, vice-consul, or consular agent of the United States, or a diplomatic or consular official of the foreign country assigned or accredited to the United States. If reasonable opportunity has been given to all parties to investigate the authenticity and accuracy of official documents, the court may, for good cause shown, order that they be treated as presumptively authentic without final certification or permit them to be evidenced by an attested summary with or without final certification.

(4) *Certified copies of public records.* A copy of an official record or report or entry therein, or of a document authorized by law to be recorded or filed and actually recorded or filed in a public office, including data compilations in any form, certified as correct by the custodian or other person authorized to make the certification, by certificate complying with paragraph (1), (2), or (3) of this rule or complying with any Act of Congress or rule prescribed by the Supreme Court pursuant to statutory authority.

(5) *Official publications.* Books, pamphlets, or other publications purporting to be issued by public authority.

(6) *Newspapers and periodicals.* Printed materials purporting to be newspapers or periodicals.

(7) *Trade inscriptions and the like.* Inscriptions, signs, tags, or labels purporting to have been affixed in the course of business and indicating ownership, control, or origin.

(8) *Acknowledged documents.* Documents accompanied by a certificate of acknowledgment executed in the manner provided by law by a notary public or other officer authorized by law to take acknowledgments.

(9) *Commercial paper and related documents.* Commercial paper, signatures thereon, and documents relating thereto to the extent provided by general commercial law.

(10) *Presumptions under Acts of Congress.* Any signature, document, or other matter declared by Act of Congress to be presumptively or prima facie genuine or authentic.

**Rule 903. Subscribing Witness' Testimony Unnecessary.** The testimony of a subscribing witness is not necessary to authenticate a writing unless required by the laws of the jurisdiction whose laws govern the validity of the writing.

## X. CONTENTS OF WRITINGS, RECORDINGS, AND PHOTOGRAPHS.

**Rule 1001. Definitions.** For purposes of this article the following definitions are applicable:

(1) *Writings and recordings.* "Writings" and "recordings" consist of letters, words, or numbers, or their equivalent, set down by handwriting, typewriting, printing, photostating, photographing, magnetic impulse, mechanical or electronic recording, or other form of data compilation.

(2) *Photographs.* "Photographs" include still photographs, X-ray films, video tapes, and motion pictures.

(3) *Original.* An "original" of a writing or recording is the writing or recording itself or any counterpart intended to have the same effect by a person executing or issuing it. An "original" of a photograph includes the negative or any print therefrom. If data are stored in a computer or similar device, any printout or other output readable by sight, shown to reflect the data accurately, is an "original."

(4) *Duplicate.* A "duplicate" is a counterpart produced by the same impression as the original, or from the same matrix, or by means of photography, including enlargements and miniatures, or by mechanical or electronic rerecording, or by chemical reproduction, or by other equivalent techniques which accurately reproduces the original.

**Rule 1002. Requirement of Original.** To prove the content of a writing, recording, or photograph, the original writing, recording, or photograph is required, except as otherwise provided in these rules or by Act of Congress.

**Rule 1003. Admissibility of Duplicates.** A duplicate is admissible to the same extent as an original unless (1) a genuine question is raised as to the authenticity of the original or (2) in the circumstances it would be unfair to admit the duplicate in lieu of the original.

**Rule 1004. Admissibility of Other Evidence of Contents.** The original is not required, and other evidence of the contents of a writing, recording, or photograph is admissible if:

575

(1) *Originals lost or destroyed.* All originals are lost or have been destroyed, unless the proponent lost or destroyed them in bad faith; or

(2) *Original not obtainable.* No original can be obtained by any available judicial process or procedure; or

(3) *Original in possession of opponent.* At a time when an original was under the control of the party against whom offered, that party was put on notice, by the pleadings or otherwise, that the contents would be a subject of proof at the hearing, and that party does not produce the original at the hearing; or

(4) *Collateral matters.* The writing, recording, or photograph is not closely related to a controlling issue.

**Rule 1005. Public Records.** The contents of an official record, or of a document authorized to be recorded or filed and actually recorded or filed, including data compilations in any form, if otherwise admissible, may be proved by copy, certified as correct in accordance with Rule 902 or testified to be correct by a witness who has compared it with the original. If a copy which complies with the foregoing cannot be obtained by the exercise of reasonable diligence, then other evidence of the contents may be given.

**Rule 1006. Summaries.** The contents of voluminous writings, recordings, or photographs which cannot conveniently be examined in court may be presented in the form of a chart, summary, or calculation. The originals, or duplicates, shall be made available for examination or copying, or both, by other parties at reasonable time and place. The court may order that they be produced in court.

**Rule 1007. Testimony or Written Admission of Party.** Contents of writings, recordings, or photographs may be proved by the testimony or deposition of the party against whom offered or by that party's written admission, without accounting for the nonproduction of the original.

**Rule 1008. Functions of Court and Jury.** When the admissibility of other evidence of contents of writings, recordings, or photographs under these rules depends upon the fulfillment of a condition of fact, the question whether the condition has been fulfilled is ordinarily for the court to determine in accordance with the provisions of Rule 104. However, when an issue is raised (a) whether the asserted writing ever existed, or (b) whether another writing, recording, or photograph produced at the trial is the original, or (c) whether other evidence of contents correctly reflects the contents, the issue is for the trier of fact to determine as in the case of other issues of fact.

## XI. MISCELLANEOUS RULES.

**Rule 1101. Applicability of Rules.** (a) *Courts and magistrates.* These rules apply to the United States district courts, the District Court of Guam, the District Court of the Virgin Islands, the District Court for the Northern Mariana Islands, the United States courts of appeals, the United States Claims Court, and to United States bankruptcy judges and United States magistrates, in the actions, cases, and proceedings and to the extent hereinafter set forth. The terms "judge" and "court" in these rules include United States bankruptcy judges and United States magistrates.

(b) *Proceedings generally.* These rules apply generally to civil actions and proceedings, including admiralty and maritime cases, to criminal cases and proceedings, to contempt proceedings except those in which the court may act summarily, and to proceedings and cases under title 11, United States Code.

(c) *Rule of privilege.* The rule with respect to privileges applies at all stages of all actions, cases, and proceedings.

(d) *Rules inapplicable.* The rules (other than with respect to privileges) do not apply in the following situations:

(1) Preliminary questions of fact. — The determination of questions of fact preliminary to admissibility of evidence when the issue is to be determined by the court under Rule 104.

(2) Grand jury. — Proceedings before grand juries.

(3) Miscellaneous proceedings. — Proceedings for extradition or rendition; preliminary examinations in criminal cases; sentencing, or granting or revoking probation; issuance of warrants for arrest, criminal summonses, and search warrants; and proceedings with respect to release on bail or otherwise.

(e) *Rules applicable in part.* In the following proceedings these rules apply to the extent that matters of evidence are not provided for in the statutes which govern procedure therein or in other rules prescribed by the Supreme Court pursuant to statutory authority: the trial of minor and petty offenses by United States magistrates; review of agency actions when the facts are subject to trial de novo under section 706(2)(F) of title 5, United States Code; review of orders of the Secretary of Agriculture under § 2 of the Act entitled "An Act to authorize association of producers of agricultural products" approved February 18, 1922 (7 U.S.C. 292), and under sections 6 and 7(c) of the Perishable Agricultural Commodities Act, 1930 (7 U.S.C. sections 499f, 499g(c)); naturalization and revocation of naturalization under sections 310-318 of the Immigration and Nationality Act (8 U.S.C. 1421-1429); prize proceedings in admiralty under sections 7651-7681 of title 10, United States Code; review of orders of the Secretary of the Interior under section 2 of the Act entitled "An Act authorizing associations of producers of aquatic products" approved June 25, 1934 (15 U.S.C. 522); review of orders of petroleum control boards under section 5 of the Act entitled "An Act to regulate interstate and foreign commerce in petroleum and its products by prohibiting the shipment in such commerce of petroleum and its products produced in violation of State law, and for other purposes," approved February 22, 1935 (15 U.S.C. 715d); actions for fines, penalties, or forfeitures under Part V of title IV of the Tariff Act of 1930 (19 U.S.C. 1581-1624), or under the Anti-Smuggling Act (19 U.S.C. 1701-1711); criminal libel for condemnation, exclusion of imports, or other proceedings under the Federal Food, Drug, and Cosmetic Act (21 U.S.C. 301-392); disputes between seamen under sections 4079, 4080, and 4081 of the Revised Statutes (22 U.S.C. 256-258); habeas corpus under sections 2241-2254 of title 28, United States Code; motions to vacate, set aside or correct sentence under section 2255 of title 28, United States Code; actions for penalties for refusal to transport destitute seamen under section 4578 of the Revised Statutes (46 U.S.C. 679); actions against the United States under the Act entitled "An Act authorizing suits against the United States in admiralty for damage caused by and salvage service rendered to public vessels belonging to the United States, and for other purposes," approved March 3, 1925 (46 U.S.C. 781-790), as implemented by section 7730 of title 10, United States Code.

**Rule 1102. Amendments.** Amendments to the Federal Rules of Evidence may be made as provided in section 2072 of title 28 of the United States Code.

(As amended, eff. Dec. 1, 1991.)

**Rule 1103. Title.** These rules may be known and cited as the Federal Rules of Evidence.

# TABLE OF CASES

## A

Abascal, U.S. v.

Abbate v. U.S., 359 U.S. 187 (1959) — § 1004

Abbott & Associates, Inc., Illinois v.

Abel, U.S. v.

Abel v. U.S., 362 U.S. 217 (1960) — § 239; § 247

Abney v. U.S., 431 U.S. 651 (1977) — § 1010

Aboumoussallem, U.S. v.

Abrams, U.S. v.

Abramson, U.S. v.

Abshire, U.S. v.

Acevedo, California v.

Acosta, U.S. v.

Adams v. Illinois, 405 U.S. 278 (1972) — § 503

Adams v. Texas, 448 U.S. 38 (1980) — § 1247

Adams, U.S. v.

Adams v. U.S., 399 F.2d 574 (D.C. Cir. 1968) — § 304; § 319

Adams v. Williams, 407 U.S. 143 (1972) — § 228

Adamson, Ricketts v.

Adcock, U.S. v.

Adderly, U.S. v.

Addison, U.S. v.

Afran Transport Co., Harris v.

Agapito, U.S. v.

Agnello v. U.S., 269 U.S. 20 (1925) — § 1818

Agrusa, U.S. v.

Aguero-Segovia, U.S. v.

Aguilar v. Texas, 378 U.S. 108 (1964) — § 207; § 208; § 219

Aguilar-Pena, U.S. v.

Agurs, U.S. v.

Ahrens, U.S. v.

Ailstock, U.S. v.

Ainesworth, U.S. v.

Air Transport Ass'n of America, CAB v.

Ajlouny, U.S. v.

Akin, U.S. v.

Alabama, Boykin v.

Alabama, Cannon v.

Alabama, Caver v.

Alabama, Coleman v.

Alabama, Cronnon v.

Alabama, Douglas v.

Alabama, Hamilton v.

Alabama, Heath v.

Alabama, McGuff v.

Alabama v. Smith, 490 U.S. 794 (1989) — § 1322

Alabama v. Smith, 493 U.S. 1029 (1989) — § 1012

Alabama, Swain v.

Alabama, Taylor v.

Alabama v. White, 110 S. Ct. 2412 (1990) — § 228

Alamin, U.S. v.

Alaska, Davis v.

Alberico, U.S. v.

Albernaz v. U.S., 450 U.S. 333 (1981) — § 1002

Alberti, U.S. v.

Alden, U.S. v.

Alderman v. U.S., 394 U.S. 165 (1969) — § 248; § 255

Aldridge v. U.S., 238 U.S. 308 (1931)— § 1246.

Aleman, U.S. v.

Alessi, U.S. v.

Alessio, U.S. v.

Alexander, U.S. v.

Alford, North Carolina v.

Alford v. U.S., 282 U.S. 687 (1931) — § 1805

Algie, U.S. v.

Alioto, McMorris v.

Allain, U.S. v.

Allard, U.S. v.

Alldredge, Grant v.

Allen v. Estelle, 568 F.2d 1108 (5th Cir. 1978) — § 318

Allen, U.S. v.

Allen v. U.S., 164 U.S. 492 (1896) — § 1261

Allen, Ulster County Court v.

579

Allen v. W.H.O. Alfalfa Milling Co., 272 F.2d 98 (10th Cir. 1959) — § 1707

Allery, U.S. v.

Allis-Chalmers Manufacturing Co., Commonwealth Edison Co. v.

Allison, Blackledge v.

Allison, U.S. v.

Allstate Mortgage Corporation, U.S. v.

Allsup, U.S. v.

Alman Bros. Farms and Feed Mill, Inc. v. Diamond Laboratories, Inc., 437 F.2d 1295 (5th Cir. 1971) — § 2006

Almeida-Sanchez v. U.S., 413 U.S. 266 (1973) — § 219; § 229

Almonte, U.S. v.

Alonzo, U.S. v.

Alpern, U.S. v.

Alred, U.S. v.

Alter, Federal Deposit Ins. Co. v.

Alter, U.S. v.

Alvarado, U.S. v.

Alvarez, U.S. v.

Alvarez v. Wainwright, 607 F.2d 683 (5th Cir. 1979) — § 912

Alvarez-Lopez, U.S. v.

Alvarez-Machain, U.S. v.

Alvary v. U.S., 302 F.2d 790 (2d Cir. 1962) — § 1403

Alves, U.S. v.

Amador-Gonzalez v. U.S., 391 F.2d 308 (5th Cir. 1968) — § 221

Amaral, U.S. v.

Amaya, U.S. v.

Ambrosiani, U.S. v.

American Bag & Paper Corp., U.S. v.

American Cyanamid Co., U.S. v.

American Export Lines, Inc., Lloyd v.

American Gas Ass'n, Radiant Burners, Inc. v.

American Metal Co., Ricaud v.

American Radiator & Standard Sanitary Corp., U.S. v.

American Television & Communications Corp., United Telecommunications, Inc. v.

Ammirato, U.S. v.

Amon, U.S. v.

Ampress Brick Co., Corona Construction Co. v.

Amsler v. U.S., 381 F.2d 37 (9th Cir. 1967) — § 304

Anderson, Charles v.

Anderson v. Charles, 447 U.S. 404 (1980) — § 309; § 1818

Anderson, Jenkins v.

Anderson v. Maggio, 555 F.2d 447 (5th Cir. 1977) — § 317; § 319

Anderson, U.S. v.

Andreadis, U.S. v.

Andreas, Illinois v.

Andres v. U.S., 333 U.S. 740 (1948) — § 1242

Andresen v. Maryland, 427 U.S. 463 (1976) — § 211; § 247; § 1902

Andrews, U.S. v.

Andros, In re Citibank v.

Angiulo, U.S. v.

Annunziato, U.S. v.

Anthon, U.S. v.

Anthony, U.S. v.

Antone, U.S. v.

Antonelli, U.S. v.

A. O. Smith Corp., N. V. Maatschappij, Etc. v.

Apfelbaum, U.S. v.

Apodaca v. Oregon, 406 U.S. 404 (1972) — § 1242

Apodaca, U.S. v.

Appawoo, U.S. v.

Appeal of Maguire, 571 F.2d 675 (1st Cir. 1978) — § 409

April 1977 Grand Jury Proceedings, In re

April 1977 Grand Jury Subpoenas, In re

Apuzzo, U.S. v.

Arcement v. Southern Pacific Transportation Co., 517 F.2d 729 (5th Cir. 1975) — § 2001

Archbold-Newball, U.S. v.

Archer-Daniels-Midland Co., U.S. v.

Argitakos, U.S. v.

Arias, U.S. v.

Ariyoshi, Hawaii Psychiatric Society v.

Arizona, Edwards v.

Arizona v. Fulminante, 496 U.S. 903 (1991) — § 301; 313

Arizona v. Hicks, 480 U.S. 321 (1987) — § 238

Arizona v. Mauro, 481 U.S. 520 (1987) — § 306

Arizona, Mincey v.

Arizona, Miranda v.

Arizona, Poland v.

Arizona v. Roberson, 486 U.S. 675 (1988) — § 308

Arizona v. Rumsey, 467 U.S. 203 (1984) — § 1012

Arizona, Schad v.

Arizona, Taylor v.

Arizona v. Washington, 434 U.S. 497 (1978) — § 1009

Arizona v. Youngblood, 488 U.S. 51 (1988) — § 714

Arkansas, Rock v.

Arkansas v. Sanders, 442 U.S. 753 (1979) — § 233; § 235; § 237

Arkansas Natural Gas Corp., Sartor v.

Armone, U.S. v.

Armored Transport, Inc., U.S. v.

Armstrong, U.S. v.

Armstrong Rubber Co., Nielson v.

Arnott v. U.S., 464 U.S. 948 (1983) — § 2116

Aronoff, U.S. v.

Arquelles, U.S. v.

Arrasmith, U.S. v.

Arroyo-Angulo, U.S. v.

Arthur Young & Co., U.S. v.

Artieri, U.S. v.

Artuso, U.S. v.

Arvedon, In re

Ash, U.S. v.

Ashe v. Swenson, 397 U.S. 436 (1970) — § 1011

Ashley, U.S. v.

Askew, U.S. v.

Atencio, U.S. v.

Atkins v. Michigan, 644 F.2d 543 (6th Cir. 1981) — § 1203

Atkins, U.S. v.

Atlantic Richfield Co., FTC v.

Attal v. Pennsylvania Railroad Co., 212 F. Supp. 306 (W.D. Pa. 1963) — § 2001

Auclair, In re

Augello, U.S. v.

Auger, Hunter v.

Augustine, U.S. v.

Austin, U.S. v.

Austin-Bagley Corp., U.S. v.

Auton, U.S. v.

Auto-Owners Ins. Co. v. Jensen, 667 F.2d 714 (8th Cir. 1981) — § 2112

Avarello, U.S. v.

Avemco Investment Corp., Brown v.

Avery, U.S. v.

Aviles, U.S. v.

Awkard, U.S. v.

Axselle, U.S. v.

Azzarelli Constr. Co., U.S. v.

## B

Badalamente, U.S. v.

Baggot, U.S. v.

Bagley, U.S. v.

Bagsby, U.S. v.

Bailey, U.S. v.

Bailleul, U.S. v.

Baird, U.S. v.

Baker v. Elcona Homes Corp., 588 F.2d 551 (6th Cir. 1978) — § 1608

Baker, U.S. v.

Baker v. U.S., 401 F.2d 958 (D.C. Cir. 1968) — § 912

Balana, U.S. v.

Baldarrama, U.S. v.

Baldasar v. Illinois, 446 U.S. 222 (1980) — § 1322; § 1810

Baldwin v. New York, 399 U.S. 66 (1970) — § 1240

Baldwin Cooke Co. v. Keith Clarke, Inc., 420 F. Supp. 404 (N.D. Ill. 1976) — § 2001

Ball, U.S. v.

Ball v. U.S., 163 U.S. 662 (1896) — § 1010

Ball v. U.S., 470 U.S. 856 (1985) — § 1002

Ballard, U.S. v.

Baller, U.S. v.

Ballew v. Georgia, 435 U.S. 223 (1978) — § 1241

Baltimore & O.R. Co. v. Felgenhauer, 168 F.2d 12 (8th Cir. 1948) — § 1704

Bambulas, U.S. v.

Bank of New York & Trust Co., U.S. v.

Bank of Nova Scotia v. U.S., 487 U.S. 250 (1988) — § 402

Banks, U.S. v.

Banks v. U.S., 348 F.2d 231 (8th Cir. 1965) — § 803

Bannister, Colorado v.

Barash, U.S. v.

Baratta, U.S. v.

Barbee v. Warden, Maryland Penitentiary, 331 F.2d 842 (4th Cir. 1964) — § 721

Barber v. Page, 390 U.S. 719 (1968) — § 2140

Barber, U.S. v.

Barbosa, U.S. v.

Barboza, U.S. v.

Barczak, Sawyer v.

Barham, U.S. v.

Barker, U.S. v.

Barker v. Wingo, 407 U.S. 514 (1972) — § 1205; § 1206; § 1207; § 1208; § 1209; § 1237

Barletta, U.S. v.

Barlow, U.S. v.

Barnes, U.S. v.

Barnes v. U.S., 412 U.S. 837 (1973) — § 1513

Barney, U.S. v.

Barrentine, U.S. v.

Barrett, Connecticut v.

Barrett v. Kunzig, 331 F. Supp. 266 (M.D. Tenn. 1971) — § 1905

Barrett, U.S. v.

Barrientos v. U.S., 668 F.2d 838 (5th Cir. 1982) — § 603

Barron, U.S. v.

Barry, U.S. v.

Bartkus v. Illinois, 359 U.S. 121 (1959) — § 1004

Barton, U.S. v.

Bartone, U.S. v.

Bascaro, U.S. v.

Bast v. U.S., 542 F.2d 893 (4th Cir. 1976) — § 415

Bastone, U.S. v.

Basurto, U.S. v.

Bater, U.S. v.

Bates, U.S. v.

Batsell v. U.S., 403 F.2d 395 (8th Cir. 1968) — § 1264

Batson v. Kentucky, 476 U.S. 79 (1986) — § 1245; § 1248

Battista, U.S. v.

Batts, U.S. v.

Baugus, U.S. v.

Bauman v. Centex Corp., 611 F.2d 1115 (5th Cir. 1980) — § 2004; § 2005

Bautista, U.S. v.

Baxter v. Palmigiano, 425 U.S. 308 (1976) — § 2114

Bay, U.S. v.

Baykowski, U.S. v.

Baylan, U.S. v.

Bazinet, U.S. v.

Bazzano, U.S. v.

Beale, U.S. v.

Beaman, U.S. v.

Bean, U.S. v.

Bearden, U.S. v.

Bear Killer, U.S. v.

Beasley, U.S. v.

Beattie, U.S. v.

Beavers v. U.S., 351 F.2d 507 (9th Cir. 1965) — § 806

Beck v. Ohio, 379 U.S. 89 (1964) — § 219

Beck, U.S. v.

Becker, U.S. v.

Beckwith v. U.S., 425 U.S. 341 (1976) — § 306

Bedford, Virgin Islands v.

Beech Aircraft Corp. v. Rainey, 488 U.S. 153 (1988) — § 1517; § 1708; § 2125

Beech-Nut Nutrition Corp., U.S. v.

Beechum, U.S. v.

Beeler, U.S. v.

Begun, U.S. v.

Beheler, California v.

Bejar-Matrecios, U.S. v.

Belcher, Stengel v.

Belgrad, U.S. v.

Bell v. Combined Registry Co., 397 F. Supp. 1241 (N.D. Ill. 1975) — § 2130

Bell v. Commissioner, 320 F.2d 953 (8th Cir. 1963) — § 604

Bell, U.S. v.

Bell v. Wolfish, 441 U.S. 520 (1979) — § 240

Bell, Zerelli v.

Bellefonte Ins. Co., J. & H. Auto Trim Co. v.

Belleville, U.S. v.

Bellis v. U.S., 417 U.S. 85 (1974) — § 1902

Belt, U.S. v.

Belton, New York v.

Benchimol, U.S. v.
Benedetto, U.S. v.
Benfield, U.S. v.
Benjamin, U.S. v.
Bennett, U.S. v.
Benson, Magda v.
Benson, U.S. v.
Benson v. U.S., 146 U.S. 325 (1982) —
    § 1913
Bentley v. U.S., 701 F.2d 897 (11th Cir.
    1983) — § 1302
Benveniste, U.S. v.
Beran, U.S. v.
Berardelli, U.S. v.
Berardi, U.S. v.
Berdick, U.S. v.
Berenguer, U.S. v.
Bergdoll v. Pollock, 95 U.S. 337 (1877) —
    § 1707
Berger, U.S. v.
Berger v. U.S., 295 U.S. 78 (1935) —
    § 1114
Berkemer v. McCarty, 468 U.S. 420
    (1984) — § 305
Berkowitz, U.S. v.
Bermudez, U.S. v.
Bernard, U.S. v.
Bernes, U.S. v.
Berra v. U.S., 351 U.S. 131 (1956) —
    § 1265
Berrier v. Egler, 428 F. Supp. 750 (E.D.
    Mich. 1976) — § 1501
Berrojo, U.S. v.
Berry, In re
Berry, Virgins Islands v.
Bertine, Colorado v.
Bess, U.S. v.
Bethea, U.S. v.
Beto, Jordan v.
Beto, Loper v.
Beto, Prince v.
Beto, Sanchez v.
Beusch, U.S. v.
Beverly v. U.S., 468 F.2d 732 (5th Cir.
    1972) — § 425
Bey, U.S. v.
Bianchi, In re
Bianco, U.S. v.
Biddle, Foster v.
Bierey, U.S. v.

Big Crow, U.S. v.
Bigelow, U.S. v.
Biggers, Neil v.
Bilir, U.S. v.
Billingsley, U.S. v.
Bills, U.S. v.
Bilotti, U.S. v.
Bilsky, U.S. v.
Bins v. U.S., 331 F.2d 390 (5th Cir. 1964)
    — § 905
Birdman, U.S. v.
Birmley, U.S. v.
Birnbaum, U.S. v.
Bishop v. Wainwright, 511 F.2d 664 (5th
    Cir. 1975) — § 111
Bisno v. U.S., 299 F.2d 711 (9th Cir. 1961)
    — § 1913
Bittner v. U.S., 389 U.S. 15 (1967) —
    § 513
Bizzard, U.S. v.
Blac, U.S. v.
Black, U.S. v.
Black v. U.S., 294 F. 828 (5th Cir. 1923)
    — § 1817
Blackburn, Hudson v.
Blackburn, Lacoste v.
Blackburn, Lockett v.
Blackburn, Monroe v.
Blackburn, U.S. v.
Black Cloud, U.S. v.
Blackledge v. Allison, 431 U.S. 63 (1977)
    — § 315
Blackledge v. Perry, 417 U.S. 21 (1974) —
    § 1118
Blackmon v. Wainwright, 608 F.2d 183
    (5th Cir. 1979) — § 1118
Blackwood, U.S. v.
Blair v. U.S., 250 U.S. 273 (1919) — § 404
Blakemore, U.S. v.
Blakey, U.S. v.
Bland, U.S. v.
Blane, U.S. v.
Blanton v. City of North Las Vegas, Nev.,
    489 U.S. 538 (1989) — § 1240
Blanton, U.S. v.
Blare v. U.S., 340 U.S. 332 (1954) —
    § 1909
Blasco, U.S. v.
Blasingame v. Estelle, 604 F.2d 893 (5th
    Cir. 1979) — § 310

Blau v. U.S., 340 U.S. 332 (1951) — § 1911

Bleckner, U.S. v.

Blevins, U.S. v.

Blewitt, U.S. v.

Blitz, U.S. v.

Block v. Consino, 535 F.2d 1165 (9th Cir. 1976) — § 1903

Block v. Rutherford, 468 U.S. 576 (1984) — § 240

Block, U.S. v.

Blockburger v. U.S., 284 U.S. 299 (1932) — § 1002

Bloom, U.S. v.

Bloomfield, U.S. v.

Blouin, U.S. v.

Blue, U.S. v.

Blum, U.S. v.

Blumenthal v. U.S., 332 U.S. 539 (1947) — § 909

Boatner, U.S. v.

Bobb v. Modern Products, Inc., 648 F.2d 1051 (5th Cir. 1981) — § 2006

Boberg, U.S. v.

Bobo, U.S. v.

Boch Laundry Mach. Co., Green v.

Bockius, U.S. v.

Bodey, U.S. v.

Boe, U.S. v.

Bohannon v. Pegelow, 652 F.2d 729 (7th Cir. 1981) — § 2001

Bohle, U.S. v.

Bolden, U.S. v.

Bollenbach v. U.S., 326 U.S. 607 (1946) — § 1260

Bolzer, U.S. v.

Bonanno, In re

Bonanno, U.S. v.

Bonds, U.S. v.

Boney, U.S. v.

Boone v. Paderick, 541 F.2d 447 (4th Cir. 1976) — § 1811

Boone, U.S. v.

Booth, U.S. v.

Booz, U.S. v.

Bordenkircher v. Hayes, 434 U.S. 357 (1978) — § 609; § 1118

Borelli, U.S. v.

Borg Warner, Republic Gear Co. v.

Borodine v. Douzanis, 592 F.2d 1202 (1st Cir. 1979) — § 306

Borrero-Isaza, U.S. v.

Bosby, U.S. v.

Boscia, U.S. v.

Bostic, U.S. v.

Bostick, Florida v.

Boston, U.S. v.

Botero, U.S. v.

Bottone, U.S. v.

Boulahanis, U.S. v.

Bourassa, U.S. v.

Bourjaily v. U.S., 107 S. Ct. 268 (1986) — § 2116

Bourjaily v. U.S., 483 U.S. 171 (1987) — § 2139

Bourque, U.S. v.

Bouse v. Bussey, 573 F.2d 548 (9th Cir. 1977) — § 230

Bowers, U.S. v.

Bowler, U.S. v.

Bowles v. U.S., 319 U.S. 33 (1943) — § 1403

Bowles v. U.S., 439 U.S. 536 (D.C. Cir. 1970) — § 1514

Bowman, U.S. v.

Bowman Dairy Co. v. U.S., 341 U.S. 214 (1951) — § 717

Boyce, U.S. v.

Boyd, Ferguson v.

Boyd v. Henderson, 555 F.2d 56 (2d Cir. 1977) — § 317; § 318

Boyd, U.S. v.

Boyd v. U.S., 116 U.S. 616 (1886) — § 240

Boyer, U.S. v.

Boykin v. Alabama, 395 U.S. 238 (1969) — § 602; § 603; § 606

Boyle, Stack v.

Boyle, U.S. v.

Bozza, U.S. v.

Braasch, U.S. v.

Bradley v. Fairfax, 634 F.2d 1126 (8th Cir. 1980) — § 414

Bradley, U.S. v.

Bradshaw, Henkel v.

Bradshaw, Oregon v.

Bradwell, U.S. v.

Brady v. Maryland, 373 U.S. 83 (1963) — § 714; § 718; § 719; § 721; § 801; § 1116

Brady, U.S. v.

Brady v. U.S., 397 U.S. 742 (1970) — § 606; § 609; § 611; § 1906

Branan, U.S. v.

Brandenfels, U.S. v.

Brandon v. Collins, 267 F.2d 731 (2d Cir. 1959) — § 2001

Brandon, U.S. v.

Brannon, U.S. v.

Branzburg v. Hayes, 408 U.S. 665 (1972) — § 404; § 1922

Brasco, U.S. v.

Brasfield v. U.S., 272 U.S. 448 (1926) — § 1261

Brashier, U.S. v.

Braswell v. U.S., 108 S. Ct. 2284 (1988) — § 1902

Braswell v. Wainwright, 463 F.2d 1148 (5th Cir. 1972) — § 1819

Brathwaite, Manson v.

Brathwaite v. Manson, 527 F.2d 363 (2d Cir.1977) — § 1403

Braunstein, U.S. v.

Braverman v. U.S., 317 U.S. 49 (1942) — § 905

Braxton v. U.S., 111 S. Ct. 1854 (1991) — § 1323

Breedlove, U.S. v.

Bretz, Crist v.

Brewer, Johnson v.

Brewer, U.S. v.

Brewer v. Williams, 430 U.S. 387 (1977) — § 310; § 313

Brickley, U.S. v.

Bridwell, U.S. v.

Briggs, Crompton-Richmond Co., Factors v.

Briggs v. Goodwin, 569 F.2d 10 (D.C. Cir. 1978) — § 1107

Briggs, U.S. v.

Bright, U.S. v.

Brighton Building & Maintenance Co., U.S. v.

Brightwell, U.S. v.

Brignoni-Ponce, U.S. v.

Brim, U.S. v.

Brinegar v. U.S., 338 U.S. 160 (1949) — § 206; § 219

Brittman, U.S. v.

Broadhead, U.S. v.

Broce, U.S. v.

Brock, U.S. v.

Brock v. U.S., 387 F.2d 254 (5th Cir. 1967) — § 2003

Broderick, Gardner v.

Brogna, In re

Bronco, U.S. v.

Brooks v. Florida, 389 U.S. 413 (1967) — § 313

Brower v. County of Inyo, 489 U.S. 593 (1989) — § 228

Brown v. Avemco Investment Corp., 603 F.2d 1367 (9th Cir. 1979) — § 1254

Brown v. Harris, 666 F.2d 782 (2d Cir. 1981) — § 318

Brown v. Illinois, 422 U.S. 590 (1975) — § 248; § 306; § 312

Brown v. Mississippi, 297 U.S. 278 (1936) — § 313

Brown v. Ohio, 432 U.S. 161 (1977) — § 1002; § 1003

Brown v. Piper, 91 U.S. 37 (1875) — § 1400; § 1401; § 1403

Brown, Texas v.

Brown v. Texas, 443 U.S. 47 (1979) — § 228

Brown, U.S. v.

Brown v. U.S., 276 U.S. 134 (1928) — § 1904

Brown v. U.S., 356 U.S. 148 (1958) — § 1906

Brown v. U.S., 370 F.2d 242 (D.C. Cir. 1966) — § 1111

Brown v. Walker, 161 U.S. 591 (1896) — § 1901; § 1903

Browne, U.S. v.

Bruder, Pennsylvania v.

Brunelle v. U.S., 864 F.2d 64 (8th Cir. 1988) — § 613

Bruner, U.S. v.

Brunk, U.S. v.

Bruno v. U.S., 308 U.S. 287 (1939) — § 1907

Brunson, U.S. v.

Bruton v. U.S., 391 U.S. 123 (1968) — § 314; § 901; § 915; § 2100; § 2113; § 2144

Bruzgo, U.S. v.

Bryant, U.S. v.

Bryant-Buckner Associates, Inc., Danville Tobacco Ass'n v.

Bryza, U.S. v.

Buchanan v. Kentucky, 107 S. Ct. —, 41 Crim. L. Rep. 3377 (1987) — § 1906

Buchanan, U.S. v.

Buckley, U.S. v.

Buege, U.S. v.

Buenrostro, U.S. v.

Buettner-Jamusch, U.S. v.

Bufalino, U.S. v.

Buie, Maryland v.

Bull, U.S. v.

Bullington v. Missouri, 451 U.S. 430 (1981) — § 1012

Bullock, U.S. v.

Bunch, U.S. v.

Burbine, Moran v.

Burch v. Louisiana, 441 U.S. 130 (1979) — § 1242

Burch, U.S. v.

Burdeau v. McDowell, 256 U.S. 465 (1921) — § 202

Burgard, U.S. v.

Burgett v. Texas, 389 U.S. 109 (1967) — § 1810

Burgos, U.S. v.

Burjan, Canal Zone v.

Burke v. U.S., 247 F. Supp. 418 (D. Mass. 1965) — § 1611

Burke, Van Ermen v.

Burkhalter, U.S. v.

Burkhart v. Lane, 574 F.2d 346 (6th Cir. 1978) — § 314

Burkley, U.S. v.

Burks, U.S. v.

Burks v. U.S., 287 F.2d 117 (9th Cir. 1961) — § 219

Burks v. U.S., 437 U.S. 1 (1978) — § 1006; § 1010; § 1502

Burnett, Coleman v.

Burnett, U.S. v.

Burney v. U.S., 339 F.2d 91 (5th Cir. 1964) — § 1706

Burns, U.S. v.

Burns v. U.S., 111 S. Ct. 2182 (1991) — § 1324

Burrell, U.S. v.

Burriss v. Texaco, Inc., 361 F.2d 169 (4th Cir. 1966) — § 1609

Burse, U.S. v.

Bursey v. U.S., 466 F.2d 1059 (9th Cir. 1972) — § 402; § 404

Bursey, Weatherford v.

Burton v. Driggs, 87 U.S. 125 (1873) — § 1707

Busby v. U.S., 296 F.2d 328 (9th Cir. 1961) — § 222

Busic, U.S. v.

Bussey, Bouse v.

Bustamante-Gamez, U.S. v.

Bustamonte, Schneckloth v.

Butcher, U.S. v.

Butera, U.S. v.

Butler, North Carolina v.

Butler, U.S. v.

Butterworth, Walker v.

Buttorff, U.S. v.

Butts, U.S. v.

Bycer, U.S. v.

Byers, California v.

Bynum, U.S. v.

Byrd v. Wainwright, 428 F.2d 1017 (5th Cir. 1970) — § 914

Byrnes v. IDS Realty Trust, 88 F.R.D. 679 (S.D.N.Y. 1980) — § 1919

C

CAB v. Air Transport Ass'n of America, 201 F. Supp. 318 (D.D.C. Cir. 1961) — § 1918

Cabral, U.S. v.

Cacy v. U.S., 298 F.2d 227 (9th Cir. 1961) — § 909

Cady v. Dombrowski, 413 U.S. 433 (1973) — § 235

Cafero, U.S. v.

Caggiano, U.S. v.

Caha v. U.S., 152 U.S. 211 (1894) — § 1403

Cahill v. Rusken, 678 F.2d 791 (9th Cir. 1982) — § 308

Cain, U.S. v.

Calandra, U.S. v.

Calandrella, U.S. v.

Caldera, U.S. v.

Caldwell, U.S. v.

Calhoun, U.S. v.

California v. Acevedo, 111 S. Ct. 1982 (1991) — § 237

California v. Beheler, 463 U.S. 1121 (1983) — § 306

California v. Byers, 402 U.S. 424 (1971) — § 1905

California, Carella v.

California v. Carney, 471 U.S. 386 (1985) — § 235

California, Chapman v.

California, Chimel v.

California v. Ciraolo, 472 U.S. 1025 (1986) — § 240

California, Cooper v.

California, Faretta v.

California, Foster v.

California, Gilbert v.

California v. Green, 399 U.S. 149 (1970) — § 2100; § 2139; § 2140; § 2141

California v. Greenwood, 486 U.S. 35 (1988) — § 201; § 239

California, Griffin v.

California v. Hodari D., 111 S. Ct. 1547 (1991) — § 220; § 227; § 228; § 239

California, Horton v.

California, Ker v.

California, McGautha v.

California v. Prysock, 453 U.S. 355 (1981) — § 305; § 1906

California, Robbins v.

California, Rochin v.

California, Schmerber v.

California, Shipley v.

California, Stoner v.

California v. Trombetta, 467 U.S. 479 (1984) — § 724

Callahan, U.S. v.

Callahan v. U.S., 371 F.2d 658 (9th Cir. 1967) — § 1264

Calvert, U.S. v.

Camillo v. Wyrick, 640 F.2d 931 (9th Cir. 1981) — § 609

Cammisano, U.S. v.

Campagnuolo, U.S. v.

Campanile, U.S. v.

Campbell v. Mincey, 413 F. Supp. 16 (N.D. Miss. 1975) — § 1403

Campbell, U.S. v.

Campbell v. U.S., 365 U.S. 85 (1961) — § 812

Campisi, U.S. v.

Camps v. N.Y.C. Transit Authority, 261 F.2d 320 (2d Cir. 1958) — § 1704

Canaday v. U.S., 354 F.2d 849 (8th Cir. 1966) — § 1913; § 1917; § 1918

Canales, U.S. v.

Canal Zone v. Burjan, 596 F.2d 690 (5th Cir. 1979) — § 1402; § 1403

Canal Zone v. Davis, 592 F.2d 887 (5th Cir. 1979) — § 1245

Canal Zone v. P. (Pinto), 590 F.2d 1344 (5th Cir. 1979) — § 2140

Canal Zone v. Peach, 602 F.2d 101 (5th Cir. 1979) — § 501

Cancino v. U.S., 451 F.2d 1028 (Ct. Cl. 1971) — § 1905

Canniff, U.S. v.

Cannizzaro, U.S. v.

Cannon v. Alabama, 558 F.2d 1211 (5th Cir. 1977) — § 317

Cannone, U.S. v.

Cantu, U.S. v.

Capital Indemnity Corp. v. First Minnesota Construction Co., 405 F. Supp. 929 (D. Mass. 1975) — § 411

Capitol Cement Co., Coughlin v.

Capra, U.S. v.

Cardello, U.S. v.

Cardillo, U.S. v.

Cardwell v. Chesapeake & Ohio Railway Co., 504 F.2d 444 (6th Cir. 1974) — § 2001

Cardwell, Pavao v.

Cardwell, Skinner v.

Carella v. California, 489 U.S. 1075 (1989) — § 1269; § 1509

Carella v. California, 491 U.S. 263 (1989) — § 1505

Carey v. Hume, 492 F.2d 631 (D.C. Cir. 1974) — § 1922

Carey, U.S. v.

Carey v. Williams, 79 F. 906 (2d Cir. 1897) — § 1707

Carignan, U.S. v.

Carini, U.S. v.

Carleo, U.S. v.

Carlone, U.S. v.

Carlson v. Landon, 342 U.S. 524 (1952) — § 504

Carlson, Prudential Ins. Co. v.

Carlson, U.S. v.

Carneglia, U.S. v.

Carney, California v.

Caro, U.S. v.

Carpenter v. U.S., 264 F.2d 565 (4th Cir. 1959) — § 1810

Carpino v. Kuehnle, 54 F.R.D. 28 (W.D. Pa. 1971) — § 2001

Carr, Virgins Islands v.

Carranco, U.S. v.

Carrasco, U.S. v.

Carrasquillo, U.S. v.

Carreon, U.S. v.

Carriger, U.S. v.

Carrillo, U.S. v.

Carroll, U.S. v.

Carroll v. U.S., 267 U.S. 132 (1925) — § 206; § 229; § 233

Carsello, U.S. v.

Carson, U.S. v.

Carter v. Jago, 637 F.2d 449 (6th Cir. 1980) — § 1269

Carter v. Kentucky, 450 U.S. 288 (1981) — § 1515; § 1907

Carter, U.S. v.

Carver, U.S. v.

Case v. Kelly, 133 U.S. 21 (1890) — § 1403

Case, U.S. v.

Caserta, U.S. v.

Cash v. U.S., 265 F.2d 346 (D.C. Cir. 1959) — § 303

Casias v. U.S., 337 F.2d 354 (10th Cir. 1964) — § 1304

Cassasa, U.S. v.

Castaneda v. Partida, 430 U.S. 482 (1977) — § 400; § 1245

Castanon, U.S. v.

Castenada, U.S. v.

Castillo, U.S. v.

Castro, U.S. v.

Castro-Ayon, U.S. v.

Catches v. U.S., 582 F.2d 453 (8th Cir. 1978) — § 1115

Cathey, U.S. v.

Cave v. U.S., 390 F.2d 58 (8th Cir. 1968) — § 2003

Cavender, U.S. v.

Caver v. Alabama, 577 F.2d 1188 (5th Cir. 1978) — § 317

Ceccolini, U.S. v.

Celaya-Garcia, U.S. v.

Cella, U.S. v.

Centex Corp., Bauman v.

Central Leather Co., Oetjen v.

Cepeda Penes, U.S. v.

Cervantes v. Walker, 589 F.2d 424 (9th Cir. 1978) — § 306

Chadwick, U.S. v.

Chaffen, U.S. v.

Chaffin v. Stynchcombe, 412 U.S. 17 (1973) — § 1012; § 1118; § 1906

Chagra, U.S. v.

Chambers v. Maroney, 399 U.S. 42 (1970) — § 235

Chambers v. Mississippi, 410 U.S. 284 (1973) — § 2145

Champion Intern. Corp. v. International Paper Co., 486 F. Supp. 1328 (N.D. Ga. 1980) — § 1919

Champion Intern. Corp., U.S. v.

Chanen, U.S. v.

Chapin, U.S. v.

Chaplinski, U.S. v.

Chapman v. California, 386 U.S. 18 (1967) — § 1115

Chapman v. U.S., 365 U.S. 610 (1961) — § 238

Chapman v. U.S., 111 S. Ct. 1919 (1991) — § 1323

Charles, Anderson v.

Charles v. Anderson, 610 F.2d 417 (6th Cir. 1979) — § 1906

Charleus, U.S. v.

Charlton, U.S. v.

Chatman, U.S. v.

Chatman v. U.S., 557 F.2d 147 (8th Cir. 1977) — § 1102; § 1270

Chavez, U.S. v.

Cheape (Appeal of Klinefelter), U.S. v.

Chee v. U.S., 449 F.2d 747 (9th Cir. 1971) — § 1820

Cheek v. U.S., 111 S. Ct. 604 (1991) — § 1266

Cheff v. Schnackenberg, 384 U.S. 373 (1966) — § 426; § 1240

Chesapeake & O. Ry., Nice v.

Chesapeake & Ohio Railway Co., Cardwell v.

Chestnut, Michigan v.

Cheyenne, U.S. v.

Chiarizio, U.S. v.

Childs v. Schlitz, 556 F.2d 1178 (4th Cir. 1977) — § 422

Childs, U.S. v.

Chimel v. California, 395 U.S. 752 (1969) — § 218; § 222; § 223; § 226

Chimurenga, U.S. v.

Chisem, U.S. v.

Chitwood, U.S. v.

Choate, U.S. v.

Chong, U.S. v.

Chrisman, Washington v.

Christensen, Virgin Islands v.

Christian, U.S. v.

Christman, U.S. v.

Christoffel v. U.S., 200 F.2d 734 (D.C. Cir. 1952) — § 1706

Chua Han Mow v. U.S., 730 F.2d 1308 (9th Cir. 1984) — § 1004

Ciampaglia, U.S. v.

Cifarelli, U.S. v.

Cioffi, U.S. v.

Ciraolo, California v.

Circuit Court, etc., U.S. ex rel. Gentry v.

Cirillo, U.S. v.

City of Canton, Mississippi, Gordy v.

City of Chester, Riley v.

City of Lincoln, Nebraska, Skar v.

City of North Las Vegas, Nev., Blanton v.

City of Philadelphia v. Westinghouse Electric Co., 210 F. Supp. 483 (E.D. Pa. 1962) — § 1918

Ciucci v. Illinois, 356 U.S. 571 (1958) — § 1002

Civella, U.S. v.

Clabaugh, U.S. v.

Clancy, U.S. v.

Clark v. South Central Bell Telephone Co., 419 F. Supp. 697 (W.D. La. 1976) — § 1402

Clark, U.S. v.

Clarkson, U.S. v.

Class, New York v.

Clavey, U.S. v.

Clawans, District of Columbia v.

Clay County Cotton Co. v. Home Life Insurance Co., 113 F.2d 856 (8th Cir. 1940) — § 2003

Clements, U.S. v.

Clemmer, Singleton v.

Cleveland Trust Co., U.S. v.

Cleveland, U.S. v.

Clifford, Michigan v.

Cline, U.S. v.

Cloud, U.S. v.

Clouston, U.S. v.

Cluchette, U.S. v.

Cluck, U.S. v.

Coades, U.S. v.

Cobb v. U.S., 583 F.2d 695 (4th Cir. 1978) — § 609

Cockrell v. Oberhauser, 413 F.2d 256 (9th Cir. 1969) — § 314

Codispoti v. Pennsylvania, 418 U.S. 506 (1974) — § 1240

Coe, U.S. v.

Coffey, U.S. v.

Cohen, U.S. v.

Cohen v. U.S., 378 F.2d 751 (9th Cir. 1967) — § 254

Coiner, Snyder v.

Coke, U.S. v.

Coker, U.S. v.

Colasurdo, U.S. v.

Colatriano, U.S. v.

Colclough, U.S. v.

Cole, U.S. v.

Coleman v. Alabama, 399 U.S. 1 (1970) — § 318; § 503

Coleman v. Burnett, 477 F.2d 1187 (D.C. Cir. 1973) — § 503

Coleman, U.S. v.

Collectramatic, Inc., Randolph v.

Colletti, U.S. v.

Collins, Brandon v.

Collins, Frisbie v.

Collins, U.S. v.

Colonial Airlines, Inc. v. Janas, 202 F.2d 914 (2d Cir. 1953) — § 1403

Colorado v. Bannister, 449 U.S. 1 (1980) — § 220; § 235

Colorado v. Bertine, 479 U.S. 367 (1987) — § 236

Colorado v. Connelly, 479 U.S. 1577 (1986) — § 313

Colorado, Gallegos v.

Colorado, Patterson v.

Colorado v. Spring, 479 U.S. 564 (1987) — § 306

Colton v. U.S., 306 F.2d 633 (2d Cir. 1962) — § 1902; § 1917; § 1918
Colts, District of Columbia v.
Colyer, U.S. v.
Combined Registry Co., Bell v.
Comissiong, U.S. v.
Commissioner, Bell v.
Commissioner, Kenner v.
Commissioner, Lowry v.
Commissioner, Ryan v.
Commissioner, Singleton v.
Commissioner of Sanitation, Uniformed Sanitation Men Association v.
Commodity Futures Trading Comm'n v. Weintraub, 471 U.S. 343 (1985) — § 1916; § 1919
Commonwealth Aquarium, Marshall v.
Commonwealth Edison Co. v. Allis-Chalmers Manufacturing Co., 211 F. Supp. 729 (N.D. Ill. 1962) — § 411
Communist Party v. U.S., 384 F.2d 957 (D.C. Cir. 1967) — § 1905
Comosona, U.S. v.
Comulada, U.S. v.
Conboy, Pillsbury v.
Concepcion Cueto, U.S. v.
Conley, U.S. v.
Conlin, U.S. v.
Conlisk, Special February Grand Jury v.
Connally v. Georgia, 429 U.S. 245 (1977) — § 209
Connecticut v. Barrett, 479 U.S. 523 (1987) — § 308
Connecticut, Culombe v.
Connecticut v. Johnson, 460 U.S. 73 (1983) — § 1505; § 1509
Connelly, Colorado v.
Conover, Tanner v.
Conroy, U.S. v.
Consino, Block v.
Consolidated Laundries Corp., U.S. v.
Consolidated Packaging, U.S. v.
Constantine, U.S. v.
Construction Aggregates Corp., Morvant v.
Consumer Credit Insurance Agency, Inc. v. U.S., 599 F.2d 770 (6th Cir. 1979) — § 409
Conti, U.S. v.
Continental Can Co., Magida v.

Continental Oil Co. v. U.S., 330 F.2d 347 (9th Cir. 1964) — § 1918
Contreras, U.S. v.
Conzemius, U.S. v.
Cook, U.S. v.
Coolidge v. New Hampshire, 403 U.S. 443 (1971) — § 202; § 209; § 217; § 235; § 238
Cooper v. California, 386 U.S. 58 (1967) — § 235; § 236
Cooper, U.S. v.
Cooper v. U.S., 594 F.2d 12 (4th Cir. 1979) — § 265
Copeland v. U.S., 152 F.2d 769 (D.C. Cir. 1945) — § 1264
Coplen, U.S. v.
Copperloy Corp., Dychalo v.
Coppola, U.S. v.
Corall-Martinez, U.S. v.
Coran, U.S. v.
Corbett v. U.S., 238 F.2d 557 (9th Cir. 1956) — § 1707
Corbin, Grady v.
Corbin, U.S. v.
Corbitt (Pulitzer Community Newspapers, Inc.), U.S. v.
Cordero, U.S. v.
Corey, U.S. v.
Cornejo, U.S. v.
Cornfield, U.S. v.
Corona, U.S. v.
Corona Construction Co. v. Ampress Brick Co., 376 F. Supp. 598 (N.D. Ill. 1974) — § 411
Coronado, U.S. v.
Corr, U.S. v.
Corral-Martinez, U.S. v.
Corrigan, U.S. v.
Corrugated Container Antitrust Litigation (Conboy), In re
Corrugated Container Antitrust Litigation (Fleischacker), In re
Corrugated Container Antitrust Litigation (Franey), In re
Cortellesso, U.S. v.
Cortez, U.S. v.
Cosby, U.S. v.
Coson v. U.S., 533 F.2d 1119 (9th Cir. 1976) — § 408; § 409
Costanza, U.S. v.

Costello, U.S. v.

Costello v. U.S., 350 U.S. 359 (1956) — § 403; § 406; § 1512

Cotroni, U.S. v.

Cotter, U.S. v.

Cotton, U.S. v.

Couch v. U.S., 409 U.S. 322 (1973) — § 1902; § 1917; § 1924

Coughlin v. Capitol Cement Co., 571 F.2d 290 (5th Cir. 1978) — § 2123

Counselman v. Hitchcock, 142 U.S. 547 (1892) — § 419; § 1901

County of Inyo, Brower v.

Courtney, U.S. v.

Courtney v. U.S., 390 F.2d 521 (9th Cir. 1968) — § 1913

Covello, U.S. v.

Covington, U.S. v.

Cowden, U.S. v.

Cox, U.S. v.

Cox v. U.S., 103 F.2d 133 (7th Cir. 1939) — § 2001

Cox v. U.S., 373 F.2d 500 (8th Cir. 1967) — § 502

Coy v. Iowa, 480 U.S. 39 (1988) — § 2139

Cozzetti, U.S. v.

Craig, Maryland v.

Craig, U.S. v.

Crampton v. Ohio, 402 U.S. 183 (1971) — § 1906

Crane, U.S. v.

Cravero, U.S. v.

Crawford, U.S. v.

Crawley, Hurley v.

Creamer, U.S. v.

Crews, U.S. v.

Crippen, U.S. v.

Crisona, U.S. v.

Crist v. Bretz, 437 U.S. 28 (1978) — § 1001

Crocker, U.S. v.

Crockett, U.S. v.

Cromer, U.S. v.

Crompton-Richmond Co., Factors v. Briggs, 560 F.2d 1195 (5th Cir. 1977) — § 2123

Cronic, U.S. v.

Cronnon v. Alabama, 587 F.2d 246 (5th Cir. 1979) — § 318

Crosby, U.S. v.

Cross v. U.S., 335 F.2d 987 (D.C. Cir. 1964) — § 912

Crouch, U.S. v.

Croucher, U.S. v.

Crouthers, U.S. v.

Crow Dog, U.S. v.

Crowell, U.S. v.

Crozier, U.S. v.

Crumbley, U.S. v.

Crumpler, U.S. v.

Cruz v. New York, 107 S. Ct. 1714 (1987) — § 314

Cruz, U.S. v.

Cuesta, U.S. v.

Cueto, In re

Culombe v. Connecticut, 367 U.S. 568 (1961) — § 1921

Culver, U.S. v.

Cummings, U.S. v.

Cunningham, Lefkowitz v.

Cunningham, U.S. v.

Cupp v. Murphy, 412 U.S. 291 (1973) — § 1903

Cupp v. Naughten, 414 U.S. 141 (1973) — § 1268; § 1269

Curcio v. U.S., 354 U.S. 118 (1957) — § 1902; § 1906

Curry, U.S. v.

Curtis, U.S. v.

Cuthbertson, U.S. v.

Cuyler v. Sullivan, 446 U.S. 335 (1980) — § 418

Cylkouski, U.S. v.

Cyphers, U.S. v.

Czarnecki, U.S. v.

Czeck, U.S. v.

**D**

Daley, In re

Daley, U.S. v.

Daley v. U.S., 231 F.2d 123 (1st Cir. 1956) — § 901; § 908

D'Alora, U.S. v.

Daly, U.S. v.

Dalzotto, U.S. v.

Damiano, U.S. v.

Damon, U.S. v.

D'Andrea, U.S. v.

D'Angelo v. U.S., 456 F. Supp. 127 (D. Del. 1978) — § 2003

Daniel, U.S. v.

Daniels, U.S. v.

Danville Tobacco Ass'n v. Bryant-Buckner Associates, Inc., 333 F.2d 202 (4th Cir. 1964) — § 2007

Danzey, U.S. v.

D'Apice, U.S. v.

D'Aquino v. U.S., 192 F.2d 338 (9th Cir. 1951) — § 107

Darby v. U.S., 132 F.2d 928 (5th Cir. 1943) — § 1706; § 1707

Dark, U.S. v.

Darland v. U.S., 626 F.2d 1235 (5th Cir. 1980) — § 1518

Dauer v. U.S., 189 F.2d 343 (10th Cir. 1951) — § 916

D'Auria, U.S. v.

Davidson, U.S. v.

Davis v. Alaska, 415 U.S. 308 (1974) — § 1805

Davis, Canal Zone v.

Davis v. Freels, 583 F.2d 337 (7th Cir. 1978) — § 2003

Davis v. Greer, 675 F.2d 141 (7th Cir. 1982) — § 1245

Davis v. Romney, 55 F.R.D. 337 (E.D. Pa. 1972) — § 411

Davis, U.S. v.

Davis v. U.S., 409 F.2d 1095 (5th Cir. 1969) — § 2116

Davis v. U.S., 160 U.S. 469 (1895) — § 1501

Dawson, U.S. v.

Dayton, U.S. v.

DeAlesandro, U.S. v.

De Christoforo, Donnelly v.

Dees, Henry v.

DeFillipo, U.S. v.

De Fillippo, Michigan v.

DeForte, Mancusi v.

Degand, U.S. v.

DeGross, U.S. v.

DeJean, U.S. v.

De La Fuente, U.S. v.

De Larosa, U.S. v.

Delaware v. Fensterer, 474 U.S. 15 (1985) — § 2139

Delaware, Franks v.

Delaware v. Prouse, 440 U.S. 648 (1979) — § 228

Delaware v. Van Arsdall, 475 U.S. 673 (1986) — § 1805; § 1811

Delay, U.S. v.

DeLeon, U.S. v.

Delguyd, U.S. v.

Del Soccorro Castro, U.S. v.

Del Toro, U.S. v.

Del Toro Soto, U.S. v.

De Luna v. U.S., 308 F.2d 140 (5th Cir. 1962) — § 916

De Luna-Trujillo, U.S. v.

Del Valle, U.S. v.

DeMarchena, U.S. v.

Demchak, U.S. v.

Dennis, U.S. v.

Dennis v. U.S., 384 U.S. 855 (1966) — § 414

Denno, Jackson v.

Denno, Stovall v.

Denno, U.S. ex rel. Glinton v.

Denson, U.S. v.

Denton, U.S. v.

Denver & Rio Grande Western R. Co., Reynolds v.

Denver & Rio Grande Western Railroad, Sanchez v.

DePugh, U.S. v.

DeRosa, U.S. v.

Derrich, U.S. v.

Derring, U.S. v.

Deselms, Waters-Pierce Oil Co. v.

Deshotels v. Liberty Mut. Ins. Co., 116 F. Supp. 55 (W.D. La. 1953) — § 1400

Desimone v. U.S., 227 F.2d 864 (9th Cir. 1955) — § 2001

De Sisto, U.S. v.

Desmond, U.S. v.

DeStafano, U.S. v.

DeTienne, U.S. v.

Deutsch, U.S. v.

DeVasto, U.S. v.

DeVaugn, U.S. v.

DeVincent, U.S. v.

DeVincent v. U.S., 602 F.2d 1006 (1st Cir. 1979) — § 414

De Vita v. Sills, 422 F.2d 1172 (3d Cir. 1970) — § 1903

De Vore v. U.S., 368 F.2d 396 (9th Cir. 1966) — § 1529

DeWitt v. Skinner, 232 F. 443 (9th Cir. 1916) — § 1801

Diadone, U.S. v.

Diamond Laboratories, Inc., Alman Bros. Farms and Feed Mill, Inc. v.

Diamond M. Drilling Co., Gaspard v.

Diaz, U.S. v.

Diaz v. U.S., 223 U.S. 442 (1912) — § 1003

Diaz-Alvarado, U.S. v.

Diaz-Villafane, U.S. v.

DiBella, In re

DiBella v. U.S., 369 U.S. 121 (1962) — § 256

DiCarlo, U.S. v.

Di Carlo v. U.S., 6 F.2d 364 (2d Cir. 1925) — § 1110

Didier, U.S. v.

Diecidue, U.S. v.

Diehl, U.S. v.

Diez, U.S. v.

DiFrancesco, U.S. v.

Diggs, U.S. v.

DiGiacomo, U.S. v.

DiGiovanni, U.S. v.

DiGirlomo, U.S. v.

DiGregorio, U.S. v.

Dilia v. U.S., 441 U.S. 238 (1979) — § 261

Diltz, U.S. v.

DiMauro, U.S. v.

DiMuro, U.S. v.

Dinapoli, U.S. v.

Dingle, U.S. v.

Dinitz, U.S. v.

Dioguardi, U.S. v.

Dionisio, U.S. v.

Di Re, U.S. v.

Director of Internal Revenue, Robert Hawthorne, Inc. v.

Di Rodio, U.S. v.

Disston, U.S. v.

Distler, U.S. v.

District Court, Moore v.

District of Columbia v. Clawans, 300 U.S. 617 (1937) — § 1240

District of Columbia v. Colts, 282 U.S. 63 (1930) — § 1240

Diversified Industries, Inc. v. Meredith,

572 F.2d 596 (8th Cir. 1977) — § 1915; § 1919

Dixon, U.S. v.

Dobbins v. U.S., 157 F.2d 257 (D.C. Cir. 1946) — § 1911

Dobbs Houses, Inc., O'Gee v.

Doe, U.S. v.

Doe v. U.S., 108 S. Ct. — (1988) — § 1902

Doggett v. U.S., 112 S. Ct. 2686 (1992) — § 1206; § 1207; § 1208; § 1209

Dohm, U.S. v.

Dolliole, U.S. v.

Dombrowski, Cady v.

Domenech, U.S. v.

Dominguez, U.S. v.

Donahue, U.S. v.

Donaldson v. U.S., 400 U.S. 517 (1971) — § 1904

Donaway, U.S. v.

Donnelly v. De Christoforo, 416 U.S. 637 (1974) — § 1100

Donnelly v. U.S., 228 U.S. 243 (1913) — § 2101

Donovan, U.S. v.

Doremus, U.S. v.

Dorman, U.S. v.

Dorn, U.S. v.

Dornau, U.S. v.

Dorsett, U.S. v.

Dorsey, U.S. v.

Doss, U.S. v.

Doss v. U.S., 431 F.2d 601 (9th Cir. 1970) — § 403

Doto, U.S. v.

Dotson, U.S. v.

Douglas v. Alabama, 380 U.S. 415 (1965) — § 1904

Douglas v. Nixon, 459 F.2d 325 (6th Cir. 1972) — § 1004

Douglas, U.S. v.

Douglas Oil Company of California v. Petrol Stops, Etc., 411 U.S. 211 (1979) — § 410; § 414

Doulin, U.S. v.

Douzanis, Borodine v.

Dow Chemical Co. v. U.S., 472 U.S. 1007 (1986) — § 240

Dowd, Irvin v.

Dowdy, U.S. v.

Dowling v. U.S., 493 U.S. 342 (1990) — § 1002; § 1011

Downum v. U.S., 372 U.S. 734 (1963) — § 1001; § 1007

Doyle v. Ohio, 426 U.S. 610 (1976) — § 309; § 1818; § 1906; § 2114

Drake, U.S. v.

Drayton v. Jiffee Chemical Corp., 591 F.2d 352 (6th Cir. 1978) — § 2001

Drebin, U.S. v.

Dreitzler, U.S. v.

Dresser Industries, Inc., SEC v.

Drew v. U.S., 331 F.2d 85 (D.C. Cir. 1964) — § 912

Driggs, Burton v.

Driscoll, U.S. v.

Driscoll v. U.S., 356 F.2d 324 (1st Cir. 1966) — § 1265

Driscoll v. U.S., 456 F. Supp. 143 (D. Del. 1978) — § 2003

Droback v. U.S., 509 F.2d 625 (9th Cir. 1974) — § 407

Droms, U.S. v.

Duarte, U.S. v.

Dube, U.S. v.

Dubrofsky, U.S. v.

Ducksworth, Jacks v.

Duckworth v. Eagan, 109 S. Ct. 2875 (1989) — § 305

Duckworth, Jacks v.

Dudek, U.S. v.

Duff, U.S. v.

Duffy, U.S. v.

Duggan, U.S. v.

Duke, U.S. v.

Dukes, U.S. v.

Duluth, Winnipeg & Pacific Railroad Co., Panger v.

Dunaway v. New York, 442 U.S. 200 (1979) — § 219; § 220; § 228; § 306; § 312

Dunaway v. U.S., 205 F.2d 23 (D.C. Cir. 1953) — § 904

Dunbar, U.S. v.

Duncan v. Louisiana, 391 U.S. 145 (1968) — § 1240; § 1243

Duncan, U.S. v.

Dunmore, U.S. v.

Dunn v. Perrin, 570 F.2d 21 (1st Cir. 1978) — § 1268

Dunn, U.S. v.

Dunnings, U.S. v.

Dupree, U.S. v.

Dupuie v. Egeler, 552 F.2d 704 (6th Cir. 1977) — § 318

Dupuy v. U.S., 518 F.2d 1295 (9th Cir. 1975) — § 404

Duren v. Missouri, 439 U.S. 357 (1979) — § 1245

Durham, U.S. v.

Durland, U.S. v.

Durns v. U.S., 562 F.2d 542 (8th Cir. 1977) — § 1516; § 1525

Dutton v. Evans, 400 U.S. 74 (1970) — § 2116

Dutton, John Hancock Mutual Life Insurance Co. v.

Duvall, U.S. v.

Duzac, U.S. v.

Dye, U.S. v.

Dykema, U.S. v.

Dzialak, U.S. v.

## E

Eades, U.S. v.

Eagan, Duckworth v.

Eagle, U.S. v.

Eagleston, U.S. v.

E. A. Goodyear, Inc., U.S. v.

Earnest, New Mexico v.

Eastman Kodak Co., Rich v.

Eaton, U.S. v.

E. C. Atkins & Co., NLRB v.

Echols, U.S. v.

Eckmann, U.S. v.

Eddings, U.S. v.

Eddy, U.S. v.

Edelman, U.S. v.

Edelson, U.S. v.

Edelstein, Kaufman v.

Eden Toys, Inc. v. Marshall Field & Co., 675 F.2d 498 (2d Cir. 1982) — § 1403

Edmons, U.S. v.

Edwards v. Arizona, 451 U.S. 477 (1981) — § 301; § 308

Edwards, U.S. v.

Egeler, Dupuie v.

Egler, Berrier v.

Ehrlichman, U.S. v.

Eisenberg, U.S. v.

Eisenberg v. U.S., 273 F.2d 127 (5th Cir. 1959) — § 1804

Elcona Homes Corp., Baker v.

Elder v. U.S., 213 F.2d 876 (5th Cir. 1954) — § 1605

Eldred, U.S. v.

Elemy, U.S. v.

Elgi Holding, Inc. v. Insurance Company of North America, 511 F.2d 957 (2d Cir. 1975) — § 2004

Elkins v. U.S., 364 U.S. 206 (1960) — § 248

Elliott v. Morford, 557 F.2d 1228 (6th Cir. 1977) — § 313

Elliott, U.S. v.

Ellis v. Reed, 596 F.2d 1195 (4th Cir. 1979) — § 1261

Ellison, U.S. v.

Ellsberg, In re

Elsbery, U.S. v.

Elstad, Oregon v.

Empire Packing Co., U.S. v.

Emspak v. U.S., 349 U.S. 190 (1955) — § 1906

Encinas-Sierras v. U.S., 401 F.2d 228 (9th Cir. 1968) — § 1923

England v. U.S., 174 F.2d 466 (5th Cir. 1949) — § 1704

Enright, U.S. v.

Epperson, U.S. v.

Epstein v. U.S., 246 F.2d 563 (6th Cir. 1957) — § 1605

Erb, U.S. v.

Erwin, U.S. v.

Eschweiler, U.S. v.

Escobar, U.S. v.

Escobedo v. Illinois, 378 U.S. 478 (1964) — § 305

Eskew, U.S. v.

Espinosa-Cerpa, U.S. v.

Espinoza, U.S. v.

Esposito, U.S. v.

Estelle, Allen v.

Estelle, Blasingame v.

Estelle, Hancock v.

Estelle, Harryman v.

Estelle, Jones v.

Estelle, McCutcheon v.

Estelle, Miracle v.

Estelle, Smith v.

Estelle v. Smith, 451 U.S. 454 (1981) — § 1906; § 1921

Estelle v. Williams, 425 U.S. 501 (1976) — § 1269

Estelle, Zilka v.

Estepa, U.S. v.

Estrella, U.S. v.

Estremera, U.S. v.

Eubanks, U.S. v.

Evalt v. U.S., 359 F.2d 534 (9th Cir. 1966) — § 2001

Evans, Dutton v.

Evans, U.S. v.

Evans v. U.S., 325 F.2d 596 (8th Cir. 1963) — § 102; § 304

Evatt, Yates v.

Ewell, U.S. v.

Ex Parte Lange, 85 U.S. 163 (1873) — § 1001

Eyman, Narten v.

**F**

Fagan v. U.S., 545 F.2d 1005 (5th Cir. 1977) — § 1204

Fahey, U.S. v.

Fairchild, U.S. v.

Fairfax, Bradley v.

Falcone, U.S. v.

Falley, U.S. v.

Falter v. U.S., 23 F.2d 420 (2d Cir. 1928) — § 2113

Fanelli v. U.S. Gypsum Co., 141 F.2d 216 (2d Cir. 1944) — § 1802

Fare v. Michael C., 442 U.S. 707 (1979) — § 308

Faretta v. California, 422 U.S. 806 (1975) — § 310

Farnkoff, U.S. v.

Farris, U.S. v.

Fatico, U.S. v.

Faudman, U.S. v.

Faulkner, U.S. v.

Fay, U.S. v.

Fayer, U.S. v.

F.D.I.C., St. Louis Baptist Temple, Inc. v.

Fearn, U.S. v.

Fearwell, U.S. v.

Federal Dairy Co., NLRB v.

Federal Deposit Ins. Co. v. Alter, 106 F. Supp. 316 (W.D. Pa. 1952) — § 1914

Federal Grand Jury Proceedings, In re

Federal Grand Jury Witness, In re

Feiock, Hicks on Behalf of Feiock v.

Feldman, U.S. v.

Felgenhauer, Baltimore & O.R. Co. v.

Felix, U.S. v.

Felix, Virgin Islands v.

Felix-Jerez, U.S. v.

Fels, U.S. v.

Fench, U.S. v.

Fensterer, Delaware v.

Ferguson v. Boyd, 566 F.2d 873 (4th Cir. 1977) — § 313

Fernandez, U.S. v.

Fernandez-Angula, U.S. v.

Fernandez-Angulo, U.S. v.

Fernandez-Guzman, U.S. v.

Fielding, U.S. v.

Fields v. U.S., 408 F.2d 885 (5th Cir. 1969) — § 1503

Fields, Wyrick v.

Figueroa, U.S. v.

Figueroa-Paz, U.S. v.

Figurski, U.S. v.

Finch, U.S. v.

Fine, U.S. ex rel. Clark v.

Finefrock, U.S. v.

Finkbeiner, White v.

Finkelstein, U.S. v.

Finnegan, U.S. v.

Fiore, U.S. v.

First Minnesota Construction Co., Capital Indemnity Corp. v.

Fischer, U.S. v.

Fisher, U.S. v.

Fisher v. U.S., 425 U.S. 391 (1976) — § 1902; § 1918

Fitspatrick, U.S. v.

Fitts, U.S. v.

Flaherty, U.S. v.

Flavorland Industries, Inc. v. U.S., 591 F.2d 524 (9th Cir. 1979) — § 1902

Flecha, U.S. v.

Fleener, U.S. v.

Fleming, U.S. v.

Fleming v. U.S., 547 F.2d 872 (5th Cir. 1977) — § 267

Fletcher v. Weir, 102 S. Ct. 1309 (1982) — § 309; § 1115; § 1818; § 1906

Flickinger, U.S. v.

Flom, U.S. v.

Flores, U.S. v.

Florida v. Bostick, 111 S. Ct. 2382 (1991) — § 228

Florida, Brooks v.

Florida, Hayes v.

Florida v. Jimeno, 111 S. Ct. 1801 (1991) — § 237; § 243

Florida v. Meyers, 466 U.S. 380 (1984) — § 235

Florida v. Riley, 488 U.S. 445 (1989) — § 240

Florida v. Rogers, 460 U.S. 491 (1983) — § 219

Florida, Simpson v.

Florida, Skiriotes v.

Florida, Tibbs v.

Florida, Waller v.

Florida v. Wells, 495 U.S. 1 (1990) — § 236

Florida, Williams v.

Floyd, U.S. v.

F.M.C. Corp., Paper Converting Mach. Co. v.

Fogg, Jackson v.

Foley, U.S. v.

Follette, U.S. ex rel. Miller v.

Follette, U.S. ex rel. Walker v.

Fong Foo v. U.S., 369 U.S. 141 (1962) — § 1010

Fontanez, U.S. v.

Ford Motor Co., Kline v.

Ford Motor Co., Nanda v.

Ford Motor Co., Rozier v.

Ford v. U.S., 273 U.S. 593 (1927) — § 103

Ford v. U.S., 418 F.2d 855 (8th Cir. 1969) — § 609

Forrest, U.S. v.

Forsythe, U.S. v.

Fortna, U.S. v.

Fortune, U.S. v.

Foshee, U.S. v.

Fosher, U.S. v.

Fossler, U.S. v.

Foster v. Biddle, 14 F.2d 280 (8th Cir. 1926) — § 1403

Foster v. California, 394 U.S. 440 (1969) — § 318; § 2111

Foster, U.S. v.

Foutz, U.S. v.

Fowler, U.S. v.

Fox v. Kane-Miller Corp., 398 F. Supp. 609 (D. Md. 1975) — § 1402

Foxworth, U.S. v.

Frady, U.S. v.

Francis v. Franklin, 471 U.S. 307 (1985) — § 1269; § 1270; § 1505; § 1509

Francis, U.S. v.

Francisco, U.S. v.

Francois, U.S. v.

Franco-Torres, U.S. v.

Franicevich, U.S. v.

Frank, Klein v.

Frank v. U.S., 395 U.S. 147 (1969) — § 426; § 1240

Frank, — F. Supp. —, U.S. v.

Frankfeld v. U.S., 198 F.2d 679 (4th Cir. 1952) — § 2003

Frankfort Distilleries v. U.S., 144 F.2d 824 (10th Cir. 1944) — § 905

Franklin, Francis v.

Franklin, U.S. v.

Franklin v. U.S., 330 F.2d 205 (D.C. Cir. 1964) — § 905

Franks v. Delaware, 438 U.S. 154 (1978) — § 210

Franks, U.S. v.

Franz, U.S. v.

Franzen, U.S. ex rel. Riley v.

Franzese, U.S. v.

Frascone, U.S. v.

Fraser v. U.S., 145 F.2d 139 (6th Cir. 1944) — § 1911; § 1913; § 1914

Frazier, U.S. v.

Frazier v. U.S., 419 F.2d 1161 (D.C. Cir. 1969) — § 304

Fredenburgh, U.S. v.

Frederick, U.S. v.

Fredericks, U.S. v.

Frederickson, U.S. v.

Fredia, U.S. v.

Free, U.S. v.

Freed, U.S. v.

Freeland, U.S. v.

Freels, Davis v.

Freeman, U.S. v.

Frezzo Bros. Inc., U.S. v.

Fried, U.S. v.

Friedman, U.S. v.

Frisbie v. Collins, 342 U.S. 519 (1952) — § 103

Frisone v. U.S., 270 F.2d 401 (9th Cir. 1959) — § 2001

Fritz, U.S. v.

Fruehauf Corp., Soo Line R.R. Co. v.

Fruehauf Corp. v. Thornton, 507 F.2d 1253 (6th Cir. 1974) — § 711

Frumento, U.S. v.

Frye v. U.S., 293 F. 1013 (D.C. Cir. 1923) — § 2003

FTC v. Atlantic Richfield Co., 567 F.2d 96 (D.C. Cir. 1977) — § 408

Fuel, U.S. v.

Fuentes, U.S. v.

Fugitt v. Jones, 549 F.2d 1001 (5th Cir. 1977) — § 2007

Fuiman, U.S. v.

Fuller v. U.S., 407 F.2d 1199 (D.C. Cir. 1967) — § 304; § 1265

Fullmer, U.S. v.

Fulminante, Arizona v.

Fulton, U.S. v.

Fultz, U.S. v.

Furlow, U.S. v.

Furlow v. U.S., 644 F.2d 764 (9th Cir. 1981) — § 1223

G

Gabriel, U.S. v.

Gabriner, U.S. v.

Gagliardo v. U.S., 366 F.2d 720 (9th Cir. 1966) — § 1264

Gagnon, U.S. v.

Gaines, U.S. v.

Gainey, U.S. v.

Galente, U.S. v.

Gallagher, U.S. v.

Gallegos v. Colorado, 370 U.S. 49 (1962) — § 313

Gallo, U.S. v.

Gallop, U.S. v.

Galloway v. U.S., 302 F.2d 457 (10th Cir. 1962) — § 502

Galtieri v. Wainwright, 582 F.2d 348 (5th Cir. 1978) — § 719

Galvan-Garcia, U.S. v.

Galvin, U.S. v.

Gambino, U.S. v.

Gant v. U.S., 506 F.2d 518 (8th Cir. 1974) — § 521

Garbett, U.S. v.

Garcia, U.S. v.

Gardin, U.S. v.

Gardner v. Broderick, 392 U.S. 273 (1968) — § 1905; § 1906

Gardner, U.S. v.

Garland v. Washington, 232 U.S. 642 (1914) — § 601

Garner v. Louisiana, 368 U.S. 157 (1961) — § 1402

Garner, U.S. v.

Garner v. U.S., 424 U.S. 648 (1976) — § 1905; § 1906

Garner v. Wolfinbarger, 430 F.2d 1093 (5th Cir. 1970) — § 1919

Garrett v. U.S., 471 U.S. 773 (1985) — § 1002

Garrison v. General Motors Corp., 213 F. Supp. 515 (S.D. Cal. 1963) — § 1917

Garrison, Maryland v.

Garrity v. New Jersey, 385 U.S. 493 (1967) — § 1905

Garza, U.S. v.

Gaspard v. Diamond M. Drilling Co., 593 F.2d 605 (5th Cir. 1979) — § 1607

Gas Service Co., Midwestern Wholesale Drug, Inc. v.

Gaston, U.S. v.

Gates, Illinois v.

Gates, U.S. v.

Gault, In re

Gaultney, U.S. v.

Gay, U.S. v.

Gaynor, U.S. v.

Geaney, U.S. v.

Gebhard, U.S. v.

Geders, U.S. v.

Gelbard v. U.S., 408 U.S. 41 (1972) — § 407

General Motors Corp., Garrison v.

General Motors Corp., Ramseyer v.

Gengler, Marzeno v.

Genser, U.S. v.

Gentile, U.S. v.

George, U.S. v.

Georgia, Ballew v.

Georgia, Connally v.

Georgia v. McCollum, 112 S. Ct. 2348 (1992) — § 1245; § 1248

Georgia-Pacific Corp. v. U.S., 640 F.2d 328 (Ct. Cl. 1980) — § 2007

Georgia, Price v.

Georgia, Reid v.

Georgia, Waller v.

Gerardi, U.S. v.

Gerberding v. U.S., 471 F.2d 55 (8th Cir. 1973) — § 905

Gereau, Virgin Islands v.

Gerhart, U.S. v.

German-American Vocational League, Inc., U.S. v.

Gernie, U.S. v.

Gerry, U.S. v.

Gerstein v. Pugh, 420 U.S. 103 (1975) — § 503

Gervato, U.S. v.

Giacalone, U.S. v.

Giancola, U.S. v.

Giangrosso, U.S. v.

Gibbons, U.S. v.

Gibbs, U.S. v.

Gibson, U.S. v.

Gibson v. Zahradnick, 581 F.2d 75 (4th Cir. 1978) — § 1921; § 2003

Gideon v. Wainwright, 372 U.S. 335 (1963) — § 1818

Giese, U.S. v.

Giglio v. U.S., 405 U.S. 150 (1972) — § 722; § 1107

Gilbert v. California, 388 U.S. 263 (1967) — § 307; § 317; § 1903; § 2111

Gilbert, U.S. v.

Giles v. Maryland, 386 U.S. 66 (1967) — § 722

Gill, U.S. v.

Gillen, U.S. v.

Gilliand v. Ruke, 280 F.2d 544 (4th Cir. 1960) — § 2001

Gillings, U.S. v.

Gilliss, U.S. v.

Gillock, U.S. v.

Gimelstop, U.S. v.

Giordano, U.S. v.

Gipe, U.S. v.

Gissendanner v. Wainwright, 482 F.2d 1293 (5th Cir. 1973) — § 248

Gladney, U.S. v.

Glaisyer, Leadbetter v.

Glasby, U.S. v.

Glasser, U.S. v.

Glassman, U.S. v.

Glaziou, U.S. v.

Glen-Archila, U.S. v.

Glickstein v. U.S., 222 U.S. 139 (1911) — § 420

Glover, U.S. v.

Goble, U.S. v.

Godwin, U.S. v.

Goichman, U.S. v.

Goings v. U.S., 377 F.2d 753 (8th Cir. 1967) — § 1802

Goins, U.S. v.

Gold, U.S. v.

Goldberg, In re

Goldberg, U.S. v.

Goldberg v. U.S., 472 F.2d 513 (2d Cir. 1973) — § 418; § 419

Goldberg v. U.S., 425 U.S. 94 (1976) — § 807; § 808; § 809; § 813

Golden, U.S. v.

Goldfarb, U.S. v.

Goldhammer, Pennsylvania v.

Goldman, U.S. v.

Goldman v. U.S., 316 U.S. 129 (1942) — § 1803

Goldsby v. U.S., 160 U.S. 70 (1895) — § 1816

Gomer, U.S. v.

Gomez-Londono, U.S. v.

Gomez, U.S. v.

Gomez v. U.S., 490 U.S. 858 (1989) — § 1244; § 1246

Gonzales v. Virgin Islands, 109 F.2d 215 (3d Cir. 1940) — § 1820

Gonzales-Benitez, U.S. v.

Gonzalez, U.S. v.

Gooding v. U.S., 416 U.S. 430 (1974) — § 214

Goodman, U.S. v.

Goodwin, Briggs v.

Goodwin, U.S. v.

Gopman, U.S. v.

Gordon, U.S. v.

Gordon v. U.S., 383 F.2d 936 (D.C. Cir. 1967) — § 1810; § 1906

Gordon v. U.S., 438 F.2d 858 (5th Cir. 1971) — § 909; § 1605

Gordon-Nikkar, U.S. v.

Gordy v. City of Canton, Mississippi, 543 F.2d 558 (5th Cir. 1976) — § 2132

Gorham, U.S. v.

Gorin v. U.S., 313 F.2d 641 (1st Cir. 1963) — § 914

Gorman, U.S. v.

Gosser, U.S. v.

Gottlieb, U.S. v.

Gould, U.S. v.

Gouveia, U.S. v.

Grabiec, U.S. v.

Grabinski, U.S. v.

Grady v. Corbin, 110 S. Ct. 2084 (1990) — § 1001; § 1002

Grady, U.S. v.

Grafton v. U.S., 206 U.S. 333 (1907) — § 1004

Graham, U.S. v.

Grand Jury, In re

Grand Jury 79-01, In re

Grand Jury Empanelled October 18, In re

Grand Jury Investigation, In re

Grand Jury Investigation (General Motors Corporation), In re

Grand Jury Investigation (McLean), In re

Grand Jury Investigation, Etc., In re

Grand Jury Investigation of Cuisinarts, Inc., In re

Grand Jury Investigation of Ven-Fuel, In re

Grand Jury January 1969, In re

Grand Jury Matter, In re

Grand Jury Matter (Catania), In re

Grand Jury No. 76-3 (MIA) Subpoena Duces Tecum, In re

Grand Jury Proceedings, In re

Grand Jury Proceedings (Berkley & Co.), In re

Grand Jury Proceedings (Cianfrani), In re

Grand Jury Proceedings (FCM Corp.), In re

Grand Jury Proceedings (Johanson), In re

Grand Jury Proceedings (Katsouros), In re

Grand Jury Proceedings (Larry Smith), In re

Grand Jury Proceedings (Martinez), In re

Grand Jury Proceedings (Pavlick), In re

Grand Jury Proceedings (Postal), In re

Grand Jury Proceedings (Pressman), In re

Grand Jury Proceedings (Rodriquez), In re

Grand Jury Proceedings (Schofield I), In re

Grand Jury Proceedings, Sealed, In re

Grand Jury Proceedings (Worobyst), In re

Grand Jury Subpoena, May 1978, In re

Grand Jury Subpoena Dated April 23, In re

Grand Jury Subpoena Dated January 4, In re

Grand Jury Subpoena Dated November 9, In re

Grand Jury Subpoena of Flanagan, In re

Grand Jury Subpoenas, April 1978, In re

Grand Jury Subpoenas Duces Tecum, Etc., In re

Grand Jury Subpoena to Custodian of Records, Mid-City Realty Co., In re

Grand Jury Transcripts, In re

Grand Trunk W. Ry., Lilly v.

Grant v. Alldredge, 498 F.2d 376 (2d Cir. 1974) — § 721; § 723

Granza v. U.S., 377 F.2d 746 (5th Cir. 1967) — § 502

Grassi, U.S. v.

Graves, U.S. v.

Graves v. U.S., 150 U.S. 118 (1893) — § 1514

Gray, Riley v.

Gray, U.S. v.

Grayson, U.S. v.

Green v. Boch Laundry Mach. Co., 490 U.S. 504 (1989) — § 1810

Green, California v.

Green v. Loggins, 614 F.2d 219 (9th Cir. 1980) — § 318

Green, U.S. v.

Green v. U.S., 67 F.2d 846 (9th Cir. 1933) — § 1403

Green v. U.S., 355 U.S. 184 (1957) — § 1010

Green v. U.S., 365 U.S. 301 (1961) — § 1321

Greene v. Massey, 437 U.S. 19 (1978) — § 1010

Greene, U.S. v.

Greenfield v. Robinson, 413 F. Supp. 1113 (W.D. Va. 1976) — § 1802

Greenfield, Wainwright v.

Greenwood, California v.

Greer, Davis v.

Greer v. Miller, 483 U.S. 756 (1987) — § 309; § 1818; § 1906

Greer, U.S. v.

Gregg v. U.S., 394 U.S. 489 (1969) — § 1316

Gresham, U.S. v.

Griffin v. California, 380 U.S. 609 (1965) — § 1515; § 1907

Griffin, U.S. v.

Griffin v. Wisconsin, 107 S. Ct. —, 41 Crim. L. Rep. 3424 (1987) — § 217

Griffith, U.S. v.

Grimaldi v. U.S., 606 F.2d 332 (1st Cir. 1979) — § 248; § 1103; § 1252

Grimshaw, Hopkins v.

Grismore, U.S. v.

Gross, U.S. v.

Grosso, U.S. v.

Grosso v. U.S., 390 U.S. 62 (1968) — § 1902; § 1905

Groves, U.S. v.

Grulkey v. U.S., 394 F.2d 244 (8th Cir. 1968) — § 1913

Grunewald v. U.S., 353 U.S. 391 (1957) — § 1906

Gubelman, U.S. v.

Guerra, U.S. v.

Guerrero, U.S. v.

Guevara, U.S. v.

Guglielmini, U.S. v.

Guillette, U.S. v.

Gulley, U.S. v.

Gullion, U.S. v.

Gumerlock, U.S. v.

Gurleski v. U.S., 405 F.2d 253 (5th Cir. 1968) — § 916

Gurney, U.S. v.

Gurtner, U.S. v.

Gurule, U.S. v.

Guterma, U.S. v.

## H

Haas, U.S. v.

Hackett, U.S. v.

Haddad, U.S. v.

Hadley, U.S. v.

Haggard v. U.S., 369 F.2d 968 (8th Cir. 1966) — § 901

Haigler v. U.S., 172 F.2d 986 (10th Cir. 1949) — § 1532

Haines, U.S. v.

Hairrell, U.S. v.

Halbert, U.S. v.

Haldeman v. Sirica, 501 F.2d 714 (D.C. Cir. 1974) — § 414; § 427

Haldeman, U.S. v.

Hale v. Henkel, 201 U.S. 43 (1906) — § 409

Hale, U.S. v.

Haley, U.S. v.

Hall, Montana v.

Hall, U.S. v.

Hall v. Wainwright, 559 F.2d 964 (5th Cir. 1977) — § 314

Hall v. Wolff, 539 F.2d 1146 (8th Cir. 1976) — § 313

Haller, U.S. v.

Halper, U.S. v.

Ham v. South Carolina, 409 U.S. 524 (1973) — § 1246

Hamer v. U.S., 259 F.2d 274 (9th Cir. 1958) — § 1906

Hamilton v. Alabama, 368 U.S. 52 (1961) — § 601

Hamling v. U.S., 418 U.S. 87 (1974) — § 1517; § 2003

Hammack, U.S. v.

Hammons, U.S. v.

Hancock v. Estelle, 558 F.2d 786 (5th Cir. 1977) — § 306

Hancock, U.S. v.

Hand, U.S. v.

Handler, U.S. v.

Handly, U.S. v.

Handy, U.S. v.

Hankins, U.S. v.

Hanna, U.S. v.

Hansen, U.S. v.

Hansen v. U.S., 393 F.2d 763 (5th Cir. 1968) — § 716

Hansford v. U.S., 353 F.2d 858 (D.C. Cir. 1965) — § 1403

Harary, U.S. v.

Harbin, U.S. v.

Hardy, Meredith v.

Hare, U.S. v.

Harmon, U.S. v.

Harney v. U.S., 306 F.2d 523 (1st Cir. 1962) — § 1530

Haro, U.S. v.

Haro-Espinosa, U.S. v.

Harper, U.S. v.

Harrington, U.S. v.

Harris v. Afran Transport Co., 252 F.2d 536 (3d Cir. 1958) — § 2003

Harris, Brown v.

Harris, New York v.

Harris v. New York, 401 U.S. 222 (1971) — § 311; § 1818

Harris v. Oklahoma, 433 U.S. 682 (1977) — § 1003

Harris v. Riddle, 551 F.2d 936 (4th Cir. 1977) — § 305

Harris, U.S. v.

Harris v. U.S., 382 U.S. 162 (1965) — § 426

Harris v. U.S., 493 F.2d 1213 (8th Cir. 1974) — § 606

Harris v. U.S., 431 F. Supp. 1173 (E.D. Va. 1977) — § 1403

Harris v. Young, 607 F.2d 1081 (4th Cir. 1979) — § 1008

Harrison, U.S. v.

Harryman v. Estelle, 616 F.2d 870 (5th Cir. 1980) — § 1906

Hart, U.S. v.

Harvey, Michigan v.

Harvey, U.S. v.

Hass, Oregon v.

Hass v. U.S., 93 F.2d 427 (8th Cir. 1937) — § 1707

Hastings, U.S. v.

Hastings, — F.2d —, U.S. v.

Hathorn, U.S. v.

Hatrak, U.S. v.

Haupt v. U.S., 330 U.S. 631 (1947) — § 1264

Havener, Johnson v.

Havens, U.S. v.

Hawaii Psychiatric Society v. Ariyoshi,

601

481 F. Supp. 1028 (D. Hawaii 1979) —
§ 1921

Hawkins, U.S. v.

Hawkins v. U.S., 358 U.S. 74 (1958) —
§ 1909; § 1913

Hawley, U.S. v.

Hayden, Warden v.

Hayes, Bordenkircher v.

Hayes, Branzburg v.

Hayes v. Florida, 470 U.S. 811 (1985) —
§ 219

Hayes, Taylor v.

Hayes, U.S. v.

Hayes v. U.S., 329 F.2d 209 (8th Cir.
1964) — § 916

Haygood, U.S. v.

Haynes, U.S. v.

Haynes v. U.S., 390 U.S. 85 (1968) —
§ 1902; § 1905

Haynes v. Washington, 373 U.S. 503
(1963) — § 1921

Hazeem, U.S. v.

Hazel, U.S. v.

Hazime, U.S. v.

H. B. Gregory Co., U.S. v.

Head, U.S. v.

Hearn v. Rhay, 68 F.R.D. 574 (E.D. Wash.
1975) — § 1919

Hearst, U.S. v.

Heath v. Alabama, 106 S. Ct. 433 (1985)
— § 1004

Heath, U.S. v.

Hecht, U.S. v.

Heck, U.S. v.

Hedgeman, U.S. v.

Heinze, U.S. v.

Helberg, U.S. v.

Heldt, U.S. v.

Helgesen, U.S. v.

Helina, U.S. v.

Helstoski, U.S. v.

Helvering v. Mitchell, 303 U.S. 391
(1938) — § 1011

Henciar, U.S. v.

Henderson, Boyd v.

Henderson v. Kibbe, 431 U.S. 145 (1977)
— § 1254

Henderson, Tollett v.

Henderson, U.S. v.

Henderson, White v.

Hendricks v. Swenson, 456 F.2d 503 (8th
Cir. 1972) — § 1903

Hendrix, U.S. v.

Henkel v. Bradshaw, 483 F.2d 1386 (9th
Cir. 1973) — § 424

Henkel, Hale v.

Henkel, McNamara v.

Henry v. Dees, 658 F.2d 406 (5th Cir.
1981) — § 312

Henry, See also U.S. v.

Henry, U.S. v.

Henry v. U.S., 361 U.S. 98 (1959) —
§ 219; § 220

Hensel, U.S. v.

Hensler, U.S. v.

Hensley, U.S. v.

Herbst, U.S. v.

Hergenroeder, In re

Herman, U.S. v.

Hernandez v. New York, 111 S. Ct. 1859
(1991) — § 1245; § 1248

Hernandez, U.S. v.

Hernandez-Berceda, U.S. v.

Hernandez, Underhill v.

Herrera, U.S. v.

Herring, U.S. v.

Herrold, U.S. v.

Herzig v. Swift & Co., 146 F.2d 444 (2d
Cir. 1945) — § 1706

Hester v. U.S., 265 U.S. 57 (1924) — § 240

Hewitt, Schmidt v.

Hibdon v. U.S., 204 F.2d 834 (6th Cir.
1953) — § 1242

Hickey, U.S. v.

Hickman v. Taylor, 329 U.S. 495 (1947)
— § 1918; § 1920

Hickok, U.S. v.

Hicks, Arizona v.

Hicks v. U.S., 173 F.2d 570 (4th Cir.
1949) — § 2104

Hicks on Behalf of Feiock v. Feiock, 485
U.S. 624 (1988) — § 426

Hiett, U.S. v.

Higgins v. Kinnebrew Motors, Inc., 547
F.2d 1223 (5th Cir. 1977) — § 2004

Hilderbrand v. U.S., 304 F.2d 716 (10th
Cir. 1962) — § 109

Hill, U.S. v.

Hill v. U.S., 368 U.S. 424 (1962) — § 619;
§ 1321

Hill v. Wyrick, 570 F.2d 748 (8th Cir. 1978) — § 317; § 318

Hillegas, U.S. v.

Hillery, Vasquez v.

Hilliard, U.S. v.

Hillyard, U.S. v.

Hilton, U.S. v.

Hilyer v. Howat Concrete Co., 578 F.2d 422 (D.C. Cir. 1978) — § 2118

Himmelfarb v. U.S., 175 F.2d 924 (9th Cir. 1949) — § 1918

Hinckley, U.S. v.

Hinderman, U.S. v.

Hindmarsh, U.S. v.

Hinds v. U.S., 429 F.2d 1322 (9th Cir. 1970) — § 609; § 612

Hines, U.S. v.

Hinton, U.S. v.

Hirst, U.S. v.

Hiscott, U.S. v.

Hitchcock, Counselman v.

Hittle, U.S. v.

Ho v. U.S., 331 F.2d 144 (9th Cir. 1964) — § 2001

Hobby v. U.S., 468 U.S. 317 (1984) — § 401

Hockenberry, U.S. v.

Hodari D., California v.

Hodge, U.S. v.

Hodges, U.S. v.

Hoffa, U.S. v.

Hoffa v. U.S., 385 U.S. 293 (1966) — § 265

Hoffman, Palmer v.

Hoffman v. U.S., 341 U.S. 479 (1951) — § 1903; § 1904

Hogan, Malloy v.

Holder, U.S. v.

Holder v. U.S., 150 U.S. 91 (1893) — § 1819

Holland v. Illinois, 494 U.S. 1050 (1990) — § 1245; § 1248

Holland v. U.S., 348 U.S. 121 (1954) — § 1268; § 1516; § 1605

Holleman, U.S. v.

Hollinger, U.S. v.

Hollingsworth v. U.S., 321 F.2d 342 (10th Cir. 1963) — § 1702

Holloway, U.S. v.

Hollywood Motor Car Co., U.S. v.

Holmes, U.S. v.

Holmgren v. Massey-Ferguson, Inc., 516 F.2d 856 (8th Cir. 1975) — § 2003

Holohan, Mooney v.

Holt v. U.S., 218 U.S. 215 (1910) — § 1903

Holton, U.S. ex rel. Marino v.

Holvochka, In re

Homburg, U.S. v.

Home Life Insurance Co., Clay County Cotton Co. v.

Homer, U.S. v.

Honea, U.S. v.

Honneus, U.S. v.

Hood, U.S. v.

Hooey, Smith v.

Hooker, U.S. v.

Hooper, U.S. v.

Hoosier, U.S. v.

Hopkins v. Grimshaw, 165 U.S. 342 (1897) — § 1911

Horowitz, In re

Horsley v. U.S., 583 F.2d 670 (3d Cir. 1978) — § 608

Horton v. California, 496 U.S. 128 (1990) — § 238

Horton, U.S. v.

Hospital Monteflores, Inc., U.S. v.

Houle, U.S. v.

Houltin, U.S. v.

Housand, U.S. v.

House, U.S. v.

Howard, U.S. v.

Howat Concrete Co., Hilyer v.

Howze, U.S. v.

Hoyos, U.S. v.

Huang, U.S. v.

Huber, U.S. v.

Huddleston v. U.S., 485 U.S. 681 (1988) — § 1522

Hudson v. Blackburn, 601 F.2d 785 (5th Cir. 1979) — § 318

Hudson v. Louisiana, 450 U.S. 40 (1980) — § 1006

Hudson v. Palmer, 468 U.S. 517 (1984) — § 242

Hudson, U.S. v.

Huerta, U.S. v.

Huffman, U.S. v.

Hughes, U.S. v.

Hughes v. U.S., 377 F.2d 515 (9th Cir. 1967) — § 1611

Hughey v. U.S., 110 S. Ct. 1979 (1990) —
§ 1337
Hulphers, U.S. v.
Hume, Carey v.
Humer, U.S. v.
Hunley, U.S. v.
Hunt, U.S. v.
Hunter v. Auger, 672 F.2d 668 (8th Cir.
1982) — § 242
Hunter, Missouri v.
Hunter, U.S. v.
Hunter, Wade v.
Hurley v. Crawley, 50 F.2d 1010 (D.C.
Cir. 1931) — § 1403
Hurtado, U.S. v.
Hutchings, U.S. v.
Hutchinson, U.S. v.
Hutul, U.S. v.
Hyatt, U.S. v.
Hyde v. U.S., 225 U.S. 347 (1912) —
§ 1510
Hykel, U.S. v.

I

Iaconetti, U.S. v.
Iaquinta, U.S. v.
Ibarra, U.S. v.
IBM v. Sperry Rand Corp., 44 F.R.D. 10
(D. Del. 1968) — § 1919
IBM v. U.S., 471 F.2d 507 (2d Cir. 1972)
— § 1919
Idaho v. Wright, 110 S. Ct. 3139 (1990) —
§ 2100; § 2139
IDS Realty Trust, Byrnes v.
Illinois v. Abbott & Associates, Inc., 460
U.S. 557 (1983) — § 414
Illinois, Adams v.
Illinois v. Andreas, 463 U.S. 765 (1983) —
§ 238
Illinois, Baldasar v.
Illinois, Bartkus v.
Illinois, Brown v.
Illinois, Ciucci v.
Illinois, Escobedo v.
Illinois v. Gates, 462 U.S. 213 (1983) —
§ 207
Illinois, Holland v.
Illinois, James v.
Illinois, Ker v.

Illinois, Kirby v.
Illinois v. Krull, 480 U.S. 340 (1987) —
§ 246; § 248
Illinois v. Lafayette, 462 U.S. 640 (1983)
— § 223
Illinois, Lee v.
Illinois, Lynumn v.
Illinois, McCray v.
Illinois, Moore v.
Illinois, Napue v.
Illinois, Patterson v.
Illinois v. Perkins, 496 U.S. 292 (1990) —
§ 306
Illinois, Rakas v.
Illinois v. Rodriguez, 110 S. Ct. 2793
(1990) — § 245
Illinois v. Sarbaugh, 552 F.2d 768 (7th
Cir. 1977) — § 414
Illinois, Smith v.
Illinois v. Summerville, 410 U.S. 458
(1973) — § 1007
Illinois, U.S. ex rel. Moore v.
Illinois v. Vitale, 447 U.S. 410 (1980) —
§ 1002
Illinois, White v.
Illinois, Witherspoon v.
Illinois, Ybarra v.
Immigration & Naturalization Serv. v.
Lopez-Mendoza, 468 U.S. 1032 (1984)
— § 248
Immigration & Naturalization Service,
Volianitis v.
Immigration & Naturalization Service,
Yiu Fong Cheung v.
Imperial Chemical Industries, Ltd., U.S.
v.
Inadi, U.S. v.
Incrovato, U.S. v.
Indian Boy X, U.S. v.
Industrial Laboratories Co., U.S. v.
Innis, Rhode Island v.
In re April 1977 Grand Jury Proceedings,
506 F. Supp. 1174 (E.D. Mich. 1981) —
§ 414
In re April 1977 Grand Jury Subpoenas,
573 F.2d 936 (6th Cir. 1978) — § 401
In re Arvedon, 523 F.2d 914 (1st Cir.
1975) — § 113
In re Auclair, 961 F.2d 65 (5th Cir. 1992)
— § 1916; § 1919

In re Berry, 521 F.2d 179 (10th Cir. 1975) — § 425

In re Bianchi, 542 F.2d 98 (1st Cir. 1976) — § 415; § 421; § 425

In re Bonanno, 344 F.2d 830 (2d Cir. 1965) — § 1917; § 1918

In re Brogna, 589 F.2d 24 (1st Cir. 1978) — § 1904

In re Cueto, 443 F. Supp. 857 (S.D.N.Y. 1978) — § 425

In re Daley, 549 F.2d 469 (7th Cir. 1977) — § 422

In re DiBella, 518 F.2d 955 (2d Cir. 1975) — § 401; § 425

In re Ellsberg, 446 F.2d 954 (1st Cir. 1971) — § 502

In re Federal Grand Jury Proceedings, 760 F.2d 436 (2d Cir. 1985) — § 414

In re Federal Grand Jury Witness, 597 F.2d 1166 (9th Cir. 1979) — § 1903

In re Gault, 387 U.S. 1 (1967) — § 1902; § 1903

In re Goldberg, 91 F.2d 996 (2d Cir. 1937) — § 1703

In re Grand Jury, 446 F. Supp. 1132 (N.D. Tex. 1978) — § 418

In re Grand Jury 79-01, 489 F. Supp. 844 (N.D. Ga. 1980) — § 401

In re Grand Jury Empanelled October 18, 1979 (Malfitano), 633 F.2d 276 (3d Cir. 1980) — § 1914

In re Grand Jury Investigation, 542 F.2d 166 (3d Cir. 1976) — § 425

In re Grand Jury Investigation, 545 F.2d 385 (3d Cir. 1976) — § 424

In re Grand Jury Investigation, 424 F. Supp. 802 (E.D. Pa. 1976) — § 401

In re Grand Jury Investigation, 436 F. Supp. 818 (W.D. Pa. 1977) — § 418

In re Grand Jury Investigation, 599 F.2d 1224 (3d Cir. 1979) — § 409; § 1915

In re Grand Jury Investigation (General Motors Corporation), 210 F. Supp. 904 (S.D.N.Y. 1962) — § 411

In re Grand Jury Investigation (McLean), 565 F.2d 318 (5th Cir. 1977) — § 425

In re Grand Jury Investigation, etc., 566 F.2d 1293 (5th Cir. 1978) — § 409

In re Grand Jury Investigation of

Cuisinarts, Inc., 665 F.2d 24 (2d Cir. 1981) — § 412

In re Grand Jury Investigation of Ven-Fuel, 441 F. Supp. 1299 (M.D. Fla. 1977) — § 411

In re Grand Jury January 1969, 315 F. Supp. 662 (D. Md. 1970) — § 401

In re Grand Jury Matter, 673 F.2d 688 (3d Cir. 1982) — § 1910

In re Grand Jury Matter (Catania), 682 F.2d 61 (3d Cir. 1982) — § 412

In re Grand Jury No. 76-3 (MIA) Subpoena Duces Tecum, 555 F.2d 1306 (5th Cir. 1977) — § 409

In re Grand Jury Proceedings, 525 F.2d 151 (3d Cir. 1975) — § 402

In re Grand Jury Proceedings, 532 F.2d 410 (5th Cir. 1976) — § 425

In re Grand Jury Proceedings, 534 F.2d 41 (5th Cir. 1976) — § 425

In re Grand Jury Proceedings, 550 F.2d 1240 (3d Cir. 1977) — § 425

In re Grand Jury Proceedings, 558 F.2d 1177 (5th Cir. 1977) — § 307

In re Grand Jury Proceedings, 443 F. Supp. 1273 (D.S.D. 1978) — § 422

In re Grand Jury Proceedings, 601 F.2d 162 (5th Cir. 1979) — § 1902

In re Grand Jury Proceedings, 604 F.2d 798 (3d Cir. 1979) — § 1920

In re Grand Jury Proceedings, 613 F.2d 501 (5th Cir. 1980) — § 411

In re Grand Jury Proceedings, 632 F.2d 1033 (3d Cir. 1980) — § 1918

In re Grand Jury Proceedings, 674 F.2d 309 (4th Cir. 1982) — § 1918

In re Grand Jury Proceedings (Berkley & Co.), 629 F.2d 548 (8th Cir. 1980) — § 1918

In re Grand Jury Proceedings (Cianfrani), 563 F.2d 577 (3d Cir. 1977) — § 409

In re Grand Jury Proceedings (FCM Corp.), 599 F.2d 1224 (3d Cir. 1979) — § 1920

In re Grand Jury Proceedings (Johanson), 632 F.2d 1033 (3d Cir. 1980) — § 1902

In re Grand Jury Proceedings (Katsouros) — § 407

In re Grand Jury Proceedings (Larry

Smith), 579 F.2d 386 (3d Cir. 1978) — § 413

In re Grand Jury Proceedings (Martinez), 626 F.2d 1051 (1st Cir. 1980) — § 1902

In re Grand Jury Proceedings (Pavlick), 663 F.2d 1057 (5th Cir. 1981) — § 1918

In re Grand Jury Proceedings (Postal), 559 F.2d 234 (5th Cir. 1977) — § 421

In re Grand Jury Proceedings (Pressman), 586 F.2d 724 (9th Cir. 1978) — § 408

In re Grand Jury Proceedings (Rodriquez), 627 F.2d 110 (7th Cir. 1980) — § 1902

In re Grand Jury Proceedings (Schofield I), 486 F.2d 85 (3d Cir. 1973) — § 425

In re Grand Jury Proceedings (Schofield II), 507 F.2d 963 (3d Cir. 1975) — § 409; § 425

In re Grand Jury Proceedings (Smith), 579 F.2d 836 (3d Cir. 1978) — § 413

In re Grand Jury Proceedings (Worobyst) — § 407

In re Grand Jury Proceedings, Sealed, 607 F. Supp. 1002 (S.D.N.Y. 1985) — § 1924

In re Grand Jury Subpoena, At Baltimore, May 1978, 596 F.2d 630 (4th Cir. 1979) — § 409

In re Grand Jury Subpoena Dated April 23, 1981, 657 F.2d 5 (2d Cir. 1981) — § 1902

In re Grand Jury Subpoena Dated January 4, 1984, 750 F.2d 223 (2d Cir. 1984) — § 1924

In re Grand Jury Subpoena Dated November 9, 1979, 484 F. Supp. 1099 (S.D.N.Y. 1980) — § 1916

In re Grand Jury Subpoena of Flanagan, 691 F.2d 116 (2d Cir. 1982) — § 421

In re Grand Jury Subpoena of Flanagan, 30 Cr. L. 2471 (E.D.N.Y. 1982) — § 1903

In re Grand Jury Subpoenas, April 1978, 581 F.2d 1103 (4th Cir. 1978) — § 408; § 409

In re Grand Jury Subpoenas Duces Tecum, etc., 391 F. Supp. 991 (D.R.I. 1975) — § 409

In re Grand Jury Subpoenas Duces Tecum, etc., 436 F. Supp. 46 (D. Md. 1977) — § 409

In re Grand Jury Subpoena to Custodian of Records, Mid-City Realty Co., 497 F.2d 218 (6th Cir. 1974) — § 1902

In re Grand Jury Transcripts, 309 F. Supp. 1050 (S.D. Ohio 1970) — § 414

In re Hergenroeder, 555 F.2d 686 (9th Cir. 1977) — § 425

In re Holvochka, 317 F.2d 834 (7th Cir. 1963) — § 412

In re Horowitz, 482 F.2d 72 (2d Cir. 1973) — § 409; § 425; § 1902; § 1904; § 1917; § 1918; § 1919

In re Investigation Before April 1975 Grand Jury, 531 F.2d 600 (D.C. Cir. 1976) — § 415; § 418

In re Investigation Before February 1977 Lynchburg Grand Jury, 563 F.2d 652 (4th Cir. 1977) — § 418

In re James E. Long Construction Co., 557 F.2d 1039 (4th Cir. 1979) — § 1701

In re January 1976 Grand Jury, 534 F.2d 719 (7th Cir. 1976) — § 1918

In re John Doe Corp., 675 F.2d 482 (2d Cir. 1982) — § 1913, 1919

In re Johnson, 484 F.2d 791 (7th Cir. 1973) — § 427

In re Kilgo, 484 F.2d 1215 (4th Cir. 1973) — § 404; § 423; § 425

In re Kinoy, 326 F. Supp. 400 (S.D.N.Y. 1970) — § 1917

In re Korman, 486 F.2d 926 (7th Cir. 1973) — § 401

In re Liberatore, 574 F.2d 78 (2d Cir. 1978) — § 425

In re Lochiatto, 497 F.2d 803 (1st Cir. 1974) — § 407

In re Lopreato, 511 F.2d 1150 (1st Cir. 1975) — § 409; § 425

In re Mal Bros. Contracting Co., 444 F.2d 615 (3d Cir. 1971) — § 1902

In re Matthews, 714 F.2d 223 (2d Cir. 1983) — § 1924

In re Melvin, 550 F.2d 674 (1st Cir. 1977) — § 409

In re Millow, 529 F.2d 770 (2d Cir. 1976) — § 407

In re Natta, 48 F.R.D. 319 (D. Del. 1969) — § 1919

In re November 1979 Grand Jury, 616 F.2d 1021 (7th Cir. 1980) — § 1118

In re Parker, 411 F.2d 1067 (10th Cir. 1969) — § 421

In re Perlin, 589 F.2d 260 (7th Cir. 1978) — § 413

In re Persico, 491 F.2d 1156 (2d Cir. 1974) — § 407

In re Quinn, 525 F.2d 222 (1st Cir. 1975) — § 407

In re Rabbinical Seminary, etc., 450 F. Supp. 1078 (E.D.N.Y. 1978) — § 409

In re Report of Grand Jury Proceedings, 479 F.2d 458 (5th Cir. 1973) — § 427

In re Rosahn, 671 F.2d 690 (2d Cir. 1982) — § 425

In re Sadin, 509 F.2d 1252 (2d Cir. 1975) — § 425

In re Sealed Case, 676 F.2d 793 (D.C. Cir. 1982) — § 404; § 1920

In re Search Warrant Dated July 4, 1977, etc., 572 F.2d 321 (D.C. Cir. 1977) — § 211

In re Semel, 411 F.2d 195 (3rd Cir.), cert. denied, 396 U.S. 905 (1969)— § 1918

In re Special April 1977 Grand Jury (Scott), 581 F.2d 589 (7th Cir. 1978) — § 409

In re Special Grand Jury, 480 F. Supp. 174 (E.D. Wis. 1979) — § 418

In re Special Grand Jury (for Anchorage, Alaska), 674 F.2d 778 (9th Cir. 1982) — § 410

In re Special Grand Jury No. 81-1, 676 F.2d 1005 (4th Cir. 1982) — § 404; § 1918

In re Special March 1974 Grand Jury, 541 F.2d 166 (7th Cir. 1976) — § 408

In re Special November 1975 Grand Jury, etc., 433 F. Supp. 1094 (N.D. Ill. 1977) — § 409

In re Special September Grand Jury II, 640 F.2d 49 (7th Cir. 1980) — § 1920

In re Taylor, 7 F. Supp. 592 (W.D.N.Y. 1934) — § 1703

In re Taylor, 567 F.2d 1183 (2d Cir. 1977) — § 401; § 418

In re Tierney, 465 F.2d 806 (5th Cir. 1972) — § 401; § 1903

In re U.S., 565 F.2d 19 (2d Cir. 1977) — § 713; § 1923

In re U.S. Hoffman Can Corp., 373 F.2d 622 (3d Cir. 1967) — § 1904

In re Vigorito, 499 F.2d 1351 (2d Cir. 1974) — § 407

In re Visitor, 400 F. Supp. 446 (D.S.D. 1975) — § 425

In re Weir, 495 F.2d 879 (9th Cir. 1974) — § 406

In re Weir, 520 F.2d 662 (9th Cir. 1975) — § 419

In re Winship, 397 U.S. 358 (1970) — § 1268; § 1501

In re Zuniga, 714 F.2d 632 (6th Cir. 1983) — § 1924

In re Citibank v. Andros, 666 F.2d 1192 (8th Cir. 1981) — § 1919

Insurance Company of North America, Elgi Holding, Inc. v.

International Harvester Co., Wagner v.

International Mfg. Co., Mannino v.

International Paper Co., Champion Intern. Corp. v.

Interstate Dress Carriers, Inc., U.S. v.

Investigation Before April 1975 Grand Jury, In re

Investigation Before February 1977 Lynchburg Grand Jury, In re

Iowa, Coy v.

Iozia, U.S. v.

Ireland, U.S. v.

Irizarry, U.S. v.

Irvin v. Dowd, 366 U.S. 717 (1961) — § 111

Irwin, U.S. v.

Isaacs, U.S. v.

Ismail, U.S. v.

Isom, U.S. v.

Israel, Pigee v.

Izzi, U.S. v.

## J

J. & H. Auto Trim Co. v. Bellefonte Ins. Co., 677 F.2d 1365 (11th Cir. 1982) — § 2001

Jabara, U.S. v.

Jaben v. U.S., 381 U.S. 214 (1965) — § 503

Jacks v. Duckworth, 651 F.2d 480 (7th Cir. 1981) — § 1818

Jackson v. Denno, 378 U.S. 368 (1964) — § 301

Jackson v. Fogg, 589 F.2d 108 (2d Cir. 1978) — § 318

Jackson v. Jago, 556 F.2d 807 (6th Cir. 1977) — § 317

Jackson, Michigan v.

Jackson, U.S. v.

Jackson v. U.S., 250 F.2d 897 (5th Cir. 1958) — § 1274

Jackson v. U.S., 489 F.2d 695 (1st Cir. 1974) — § 109; § 113

Jackson v. Virginia, 443 U.S. 307 (1979) — § 1501

Jackson v. Wainwright, 390 F.2d 288 (5th Cir. 1968) — § 721

Jackson v. Walker, 585 F.2d 139 (5th Cir. 1978) — § 1118

Jacobs, U.S. v.

Jacobsen, U.S. v.

Jacobson v. Massachusetts, 197 U.S. 11 (1905) — § 1403

Jacobson, U.S. v.

Jacobson v. U.S., 112 S. Ct. 1535 (1992) — § 1501

Jago, Carter v.

Jago, Jackson v.

Jago, Maglio v.

Jalbert, U.S. v.

Jamar, U.S. v.

James v. Illinois, 493 U.S. 307 (1990) — § 1818

James v. Kentucky, 466 U.S. 341 (1984) — § 1907

James, U.S. v.

James v. U.S., 418 F.2d 1150 (D.C. Cir. 1969) — § 206

James E. Long Construction Co., In re

Jamison, U.S. v.

Janas, Colonial Airlines, Inc. v.

Janis, U.S. v.

Jannotti, U.S. v.

Janovich, U.S. v.

January 1976 Grand Jury, In re, 534 F.2d 719 (7th Cir. 1976) — § 1918

Jardan, U.S. v.

Jarrett v. U.S., 423 F.2d 966 (8th Cir. 1970) — § 304

Jeffers v. U.S., 432 U.S. 137 (1977) — § 1002; § 1003

Jefferson, U.S. v.

Jencks v. U.S., 353 U.S. 657 (1957) — § 801; § 814

Jenkins v. Anderson, 447 U.S. 231 (1980) — § 309; § 1115; § 1818; § 1906

Jenkins, U.S. v.

Jenkins v. U.S., 380 U.S. 445 (1965) — § 1261

Jennewein, U.S. v.

Jennings v. U.S., 73 F.2d 470 (5th Cir. 1934) — § 1703

Jensen, Auto-Owners Ins. Co. v.

Jensen, U.S. v.

Jessup, U.S. v.

Jiffee Chemical Corp., Drayton v.

Jimenez, U.S. v.

Jimenez-Lopez, U.S. v.

Jimeno, Florida v.

Jodoin, U.S. v.

John, U.S. v.

John Bernard Industries, Inc., U.S. v.

John Doe, Inc. I, U.S. v.

John Doe Corp., In re

John Hancock Mut. Life Ins. Co., McDermott v.

John Hancock Mutual Life Insurance Co. v. Dutton, 585 F.2d 1289 (5th Cir. 1978) — § 2001

Johns, U.S. v.

Johnson v. Brewer, 521 F.2d 556 (8th Cir. 1975) — § 1811

Johnson, Connecticut v.

Johnson v. Havener, 534 F.2d 1232 (6th Cir. 1976) — § 313

Johnson, In re

Johnson v. Louisiana, 406 U.S. 356 (1972) — § 1242

Johnson, Mabry v.

Johnson, Ohio v.

Johnson v. Riddle, 562 F.2d 312 (4th Cir. 1977) — § 318

Johnson, U.S. v.

Johnson v. U.S., 228 U.S. 457 (1913) — § 1902

Johnson v. U.S., 333 U.S. 10 (1948) — § 236

Johnson v. U.S., 542 F.2d 941 (5th Cir. 1976) — § 1919

Johnson v. William C. Ellis & Sons, Iron Works, Inc., 604 F.2d 950 (5th Cir. 1979) — § 1603

Johnson v. Zerbst, 304 U.S. 458 (1938) — § 308; § 1819

Johnston, U.S. v.

Johnston, Waley v.

Jones v. Estelle, 584 F.2d 687 (5th Cir. 1978) — § 613

Jones, Fugitt v.

Jones v. Morris, 590 F.2d 684 (7th Cir. 1979) — § 1209

Jones v. Peyton, 411 F.2d 857 (4th Cir. 1969) — § 219

Jones v. Thomas, 491 U.S. 376 (1989) — § 1002

Jones, U.S. v.

Jones v. U.S., 137 U.S. 202 (1890) — § 1403

Jones v. U.S., 362 U.S. 257 (1960) — § 255; § 1923

Jones v. U.S., 304 F.2d 381 (D.C. Cir. 1962) — § 215

Jones v. U.S., 308 F.2d 307 (D.C. Cir. 1962) — § 1264

Jones v. U.S., 342 F.2d 863 (D.C. Cir. 1964) — § 502

Jones v. U.S., 405 F.2d 957 (1972) — § 1903

Jordan v. Beto, 471 F.2d 779 (5th Cir. 1973) — § 1239

Jordan, U.S. v.

Jorn, U.S. v.

Joseph, U.S. v.

Joshua v. Maggio, 674 F.2d 376 (5th Cir. 1982) — § 318

Joyce, U.S. v.

Joyner, U.S. v.

Juarez, U.S. v.

Juarez-Casares v. U.S., 496 F.2d 190 (5th Cir. 1974) — § 1320

Judge Elmo B. Hunter's Special Grand Jury, In re

Judon, U.S. v.

Judson, U.S. v.

Julian, U.S. v.

Julian, U.S Department of Justice v.

Justice v. Pennzoil Co., 598 F.2d 1339 (4th Cir. 1979) — § 2001

Justices of Boston Municipal Court v. Lydon, 466 U.S. 294 (1984) — § 1010

**K**

Kahan, U.S. v.

Kahaner, U.S. v.

Kahl, U.S. v.

Kahn, U.S. v.

Kaibney, U.S. v.

Kail, U.S. v.

Kampbell, U.S. v.

Kane-Miller Corp., Fox v.

Kaplan, U.S. v.

Karo, U.S. v.

Kastigar v. U.S., 406 U.S. 441 (1972) — § 419; § 420; § 1903

Katz v. U.S., 389 U.S. 347 (1967) — § 201; § 217; § 240; § 257; § 268

Kaufman v. Edelstein, 539 F.2d 811 (2d Cir. 1976) — § 2003

Kaufman, U.S. v.

Kaufman v. U.S., 350 F.2d 408 (8th Cir. 1965) — § 2001

Kaylor, U.S. v.

Kearney, U.S. v.

Keeble, U.S. v.

Keeble v. U.S., 412 U.S. 205 (1973) — § 1265

Keel v. U.S., 585 F.2d 110 (5th Cir. 1978) — § 609

Keiswetter, U.S. v.

Keith Clarke, Inc., Baldwin Cooke Co. v.

Kellerman, U.S. v.

Kelly, Case v.

Kelly, U.S. v.

Kelton, U.S. v.

Kendrick, U.S. v.

Kendricks, U.S. v.

Kennedy, Oregon v.

Kennedy, U.S. v.

Kenner v. Commissioner, 445 F.2d 19 (7th Cir. 1971) — § 1707

Kenney, U.S. v.

Kenney v. U.S., 157 F.2d 442 (D.C. Cir. 1946) — § 211

Kenny, U.S. v.

Kentucky, Batson v.

Kentucky, Buchanan v.

Kentucky, Carter v.

Kentucky, James v.

Kentucky, Olden v.

Kentucky, Rawlings v.

Kentucky, Taylor v.

Kentucky v. Whorton, 441 U.S. 786 (1979) — § 1269

Ker v. California, 374 U.S. 23 (1963) — § 215; § 219

Ker v. Illinois, 119 U.S. 436 (1886) — § 103

Kercheval v. U.S., 274 U.S. 220 (1927) — § 618; § 2113

Kerrigan, U.S. v.

Kessler Institute for Rehabilitation v. N.L.R.B., 669 F.2d 138 (3d Cir. 1982) — § 1403

Keuylian, U.S. v.

Key, U.S. v.

Kiamie, U.S. v.

Kibbe, Henderson v.

Kibler, U.S. v.

Kiendra, U.S. v.

Kiff, Peters v.

Kilbourne, U.S. v.

Kilgo, In re

Kilgore v. U.S., 467 F.2d 22 (5th Cir. 1972) — § 1520

Killebrew, U.S. v.

Killian, U.S. v.

Kilrain, U.S. v.

Kilstofte & Vosejpka, Inc., Olson v.

Kim, U.S. v.

Kincade v. U.S., 559 F.2d 906 (3d Cir. 1977) — § 609

King, U.S. v.

King v. U.S., 355 F.2d 700 (1st Cir. 1966) — § 907

Kinnard, U.S. v.

Kinnebrew Motors, Inc., Higgins v.

Kinoy, In re

Kirby v. Illinois, 406 U.S. 682 (1972) — § 305; § 310; § 317

Kirk, U.S. v.

Kirkland, People ex rel. Snead v.

Klein v. Frank, 534 F.2d 1104 (5th Cir. 1976) — § 1707

Klein, Spevack v.

Klein, U.S. v.

Kleinschmidt, U.S. v.

Kline v. Ford Motor Co., 523 F.2d 1067 (9th Cir. 1975) — § 2003

Klobuchir v. Pennsylvania, 639 F.2d 966 (3d Cir. 1981) — § 1001

Klopfer v. North Carolina, 386 U.S. 213 (1967) — § 1203

Knapp v. U.S., 316 F.2d 794 (5th Cir. 1963) — § 1270

Knife, U.S. v.

Knight, U.S. v.

Knohl, U.S. v.

Knotts, U.S. v.

Knowles, U.S. v.

Knox, U.S. v.

Knuckles, U.S. v.

Koehler, Oliphant v.

Kolender v. Lawson, 461 U.S. 352 (1983) — § 228

Kolod v. U.S., 371 F.2d 983 (10th Cir. 1967) — § 916

Kopel, U.S. v.

Korman, In re

Korman, U.S. v.

Kossa, U.S. v.

Kotteakos v. U.S., 328 U.S. 750 (1946) — § 907; § 909

Kovaleski, U.S. v.

Kovel, U.S. v.

Krasny, U.S. v.

Kravitz, U.S. v.

Kreiger, Simpson v.

Kriz, U.S. v.

Krohn, U.S. v.

Krulewitch v. U.S., 336 U.S. 440 (1949) — § 2116

Krull, Illinois v.

Kuehnle, Carpino v.

Kuhlmann v. Wilson, 106 S. Ct. 2616 (1986) — § 310

Kunzig, Barrett v.

Kushner, U.S. v.

Kyle v. U.S., 297 F.2d 507 (2d Cir. 1961) — § 716

**L**

Laca, U.S. v.

Lace, U.S. v.

Lacob, U.S. v.

Lacoste v. Blackburn, 592 F.2d 1321 (5th Cir. 1979) — § 317

Lafayette, Illinois v.

La Guardia, U.S. v.

Lakeside v. Oregon, 435 U.S. 333 (1978) — § 1270; § 1515

Lam Lek Chong, U.S. v.

Laman v. Micou, 114 U.S. 218 (1885) — § 1403

Lamar, U.S. v.

Lamb, U.S. v.

Lambert, U.S. v.

Lambert v. U.S., 600 F.2d 476 (5th Cir. 1979) — § 1236

Landof, U.S. v.

Landon, Carlson v.

Lane, Burkhart v.

Lane, U.S. v.

Lang, U.S. v.

Langston, U.S. v.

Lanier v. South Carolina, 106 S. Ct. 297 (1985) — § 312

Lanier, U.S. v.

Lanza v. New York, 370 U.S. 139 (1962) — § 242

Lanza, U.S. v.

Lara, U.S. v.

Largent, U.S. v.

LaRiche, U.S. v.

Larios, U.S. v.

Larkin, U.S. v.

Larry, U.S. v.

Larson, U.S. v.

Lartey, U.S. v.

LaSalle National Bank, U.S. v.

Lasater, U.S. v.

Lasky, U.S. v.

Latham v. U.S., 226 F. 420 (5th Cir. 1915) — § 401

Latona v. U.S., 449 F.2d 121 (9th Cir. 1971) — § 404

LaVallee, U.S. v.

LaVallee, U.S. ex rel. LaBelle v.

LaVallee, U.S. ex rel. Nickens v.

Lavallie, U.S. v.

Lawhon, U.S. v.

Lawn v. U.S., 355 U.S. 339 (1958) — § 403

Lawson, Kolender v.

Lawson, U.S. v.

Leach, U.S. v.

Leadbetter v. Glaisyer, 44 F.2d 350 (9th Cir. 1930) — § 2001

Leary v. U.S., 395 U.S. 6 (1969) — § 1505; § 1902; § 1905

Lechoco, U.S. v.

Lee v. Illinois, 476 U.S. 530 (1986) — § 2139

Lee, U.S. v.

Lee v. U.S., 343 U.S. 747 (1952) — § 201

Lee v. U.S., 432 U.S. 23 (1977) — § 1006

Lee, Winston v.

Lefkowitz v. Cunningham, 431 U.S. 801 (1977) — § 1905

Lefkowitz, Turley v.

Leftwich, U.S. v.

Lego v. Twomey, 404 U.S. 477 (1972) — § 217; § 248; § 301

Leighton, U.S. v.

Leis v. Opportunity Consultants, 441 F. Supp. 1314 (S.D. Ohio 1977) — § 1403

Leja, U.S. v.

Lelles v. U.S., 241 F.2d 21 (9th Cir. 1957) — § 1816

Lemon, U.S. v.

Lenz, U.S. v.

Leon, U.S. v.

Leonard, U.S. v.

Leonelli, U.S. v.

Le Pera, U.S. v.

Lepera v. U.S., 587 F.2d 433 (9th Cir. 1978) — § 606

Leppo, U.S. v.

Leslie, U.S. v.

Lester, U.S. v.

Leverage Funding Systems, Inc., U.S. v.

Levine, U.S. v.

Levy, U.S. v.

Lewin, U.S. v.

Lewis, U.S. v.

Lewis v. U.S., 279 U.S. 63 (1929) — § 1512

Lewis v. U.S., 340 F.2d 678 (8th Cir. 1965) — § 803; § 805

Lewis v. U.S., 385 U.S. 206 (1966) — § 215

Lewis v. U.S., 601 F.2d 1100 (9th Cir. 1979) — § 609

L'Hoste, U.S. v.

Liberatore, In re

Liberty Mut. Ins. Co., Deshotels v.

Librach, U.S. v.

Licavoli, U.S. v.

Lieberman, U.S. v.

Lieblich, U.S. v.

Liles, U.S. v.

Lilley, U.S. v.

Lilly v. Grand Trunk W. Ry., 317 U.S. 481 (1943) — § 1403

Lilly, U.S. v.

Lind, U.S. v.

Lindstrom, U.S. v.

Ling, U.S. v.

Lipscomb v. U.S., 33 F.2d 33 (8th Cir. 1929) — § 1703

Lipton, U.S. v.

Little, U.S. v.

Littlewind, U.S. v.

Litton Systems, Inc., U.S. v.

Llewellyn v. Stynchcombe, 609 F.2d 194 (5th Cir. 1980) — § 1250

Llinas, U.S. v.

Lloyd v. American Export Lines, Inc., 580 F.2d 1179 (3d Cir. 1978) — § 2134

Lloyd, U.S. v.

Lloyd v. U.S., 226 F.2d 9 (5th Cir. 1955) — § 1605

Lo-Ji Sales, Inc. v. New York, 442 U.S. 319 (1979) — § 201; § 209; § 211; § 243

Lochan, U.S. v.

Lochiatto, In re

Locken v. U.S., 383 F.2d 340 (9th Cir. 1967) — § 1801

Lockett v. Blackburn, 571 F.2d 309 (5th Cir. 1978) — § 713

Lockett v. Ohio, 438 U.S. 586 (1978) — § 1115

Lockett, U.S. v.

Lockhart v. McCree, 106 S. Ct. 1758 (1986) — § 1247

Lockhart v. Nelson, 488 U.S. 33 (1988) — § 1006; § 1010

Loggins, Green v.

Lombardi, U.S. v.

Long, Michigan v.

Long, U.S. v.

Long Elk, U.S. v.

Long Soldier, U.S. v.

Loper v. Beto, 405 U.S. 473 (1972) — § 1810; § 1818

Lopez, U.S. v.

Lopez v. U.S., 373 U.S. 427 (1963) — § 268

Lopez-Espindola, U.S. v.

Lopez-Mendoza, Immigration & Naturalization Serv. v.

Lopreato, In re

Lord, U.S. v.

LoRusso, U.S. v.

Losing, U.S. v.

Lott v. U.S., 367 U.S. 421 (1961) — § 254; § 604

Louderman, U.S. v.

Loud Hawk, U.S. v.

Louisiana, Burch v.

Louisiana, Duncan v.

Louisiana, Garner v.

Louisiana, Hudson v.

Louisiana, Johnson v.

Louisiana, Rideau v.

Louisiana, Taylor v.

Louisiana, Thompson v.

Lovasco, U.S. v.

Lovato, U.S. v.

Love, U.S. v.

Lovell, Virgin Islands v.

Lowe, U.S. v.

Lowenfield v. Phelps, 484 U.S. 231 (1988) — § 1261

Lowry v. Commissioner, 262 F.2d 809 (2d Cir. 1959) — § 1917

Lucas, McDonald v.

Lucas, U.S. v.

Lucchetti, U.S. v.

Luce v. U.S., 469 U.S. 38 (1984) — § 1810

Luman, U.S. v.

Lumetta v. U.S., 362 F.2d 644 (8th Cir. 1966) — § 1264

Lustig, U.S. v.

Lutwak v. U.S., 344 U.S. 604 (1953) — § 1911; § 1914

Lutz, U.S. v.

Lydon, Justices of Boston Municipal Court v.

Lyles, U.S. v.

Lynch, U.S. v.

Lynn, U.S. v.

Lynumn v. Illinois, 372 U.S. 528 (1963) — § 313

Lyon, U.S. v.

## M

Mabry v. Johnson, 467 U.S. 504 (1984) — § 611; § 613

Mabry, Taylor v.

Mabry, William v.

Mabry, Witham v.

MacDonald, U.S. v.

Macino, U.S. v.

Mack v. U.S., 635 F.2d 20 (1st Cir. 1980) — § 606; § 608

Mackey, U.S. v.

Mackin, U.S. v.

Macklin, U.S. v.

Maclean, U.S. v.

Macon, Maryland v.

Madden, U.S. v.

Maddox, U.S. v.

Madison, Marbury v.

Madrid, U.S. v.

Maestas, U.S. v.

Mafie v. U.S., 209 F.2d 225 (1st Cir. 1954) — § 1904

Magda v. Benson, 536 F.2d 111 (6th Cir. 1976) — § 239

Maggio, Anderson v.

Maggio, Joshua v.

Magida v. Continental Can Co., 12 F.R.D. 74 (S.D.N.Y. 1951) — § 1919

Maglio v. Jago, 580 F.2d 202 (6th Cir. 1978) — § 308

Mahlandt v. Wild Canid Survival & Research Center, Inc., 588 F.2d 626 (8th Cir. 1978) — § 2115

Mahler, U.S. v.

Mahone, U.S. v.

Mahoney, U.S. v.

Main, U.S. v.

Maine v. Moulton, 474 U.S. 159 (1985) — § 310

Mainello, U.S. v.

Makris, U.S. v.

Malatkofski v. U.S., 179 F.2d 905 (1st Cir. 1950) — § 908

Mal Bros. Contracting Co., In re

Malley v. Manson, 547 F.2d 25 (2d Cir. 1976) — § 1111

Mallory v. U.S., 354 U.S. 449 (1957) — § 304; § 319; § 501

Malloy v. Hogan, 378 U.S. 1 (1964) — § 301; § 1901; § 1903; § 1906

Malmay, U.S. v.

Maloney, U.S. v.

Mancusi v. DeForte, 392 U.S. 364 (1968) — § 201; § 255

Mandel, U.S. v.

Mandujano, U.S. v.

Manetta, U.S. v.

Manfredi, U.S. v.

Manfredonia, U.S. v.

Mangan, U.S. v.

Manley v. U.S., 396 F.2d 699 (5th Cir. 1968) — § 606

Mann, U.S. v.

Manning, U.S. v.

Mannino v. International Mfg. Co., 650 F.2d 846 (6th Cir. 1981) — § 2003

Manson, Brathwaite v.

Manson v. Brathwaite, 432 U.S. 98 (1977) — § 319; § 318; § 2111

Manson, Malley v.

Mapp, U.S. v.

Mara, U.S. v.

Marbury v. Madison, 5 U.S. (1 Cranch) 137 (1803) — § 1403

Marcantoni, U.S. v.

Marcello v. U.S., 196 F.2d 437 (5th Cir. 1952) — § 1904

March, U.S. v.

Marchand, U.S. v.

Marchetti v. U.S., 390 U.S. 39 (1968) — § 1902; § 1905

Marchisio, U.S. v.

Maresca v. U.S., 277 F.2d 727 (2d Cir. 1921) — § 1512

Marin, U.S. v.

Marino, U.S. v.

Marion, U.S. v.

Marks, U.S. v.

Maroney, Chambers v.

Maroney, U.S. ex rel. Clark v.

Marques, U.S. v.

Marra, U.S. v.

Marrero, U.S. v.

Marron v. U.S., 275 U.S. 192 (1927) — § 211

Marsh, Nilson Van & Storage Co. v.

Marsh, Richardson v.

Marshall v. Commonwealth Aquarium, 611 F.2d 1 (1st Cir. 1979) — § 2120

Marshall, U.S. v.

Marshall v. U.S., 360 U.S. 310 (1959) — § 1303

Marshall v. Western Waterproofing Co., Inc., 560 F.2d 947 (8th Cir. 1977) — § 245

Marshall Field & Co., Eden Toys, Inc. v.

Marson, U.S. v.

Martin v. Ohio, 107 S. Ct. 1098 (1987) — § 1501

Martin, U.S. v.

Martin v. U.S., 517 F.2d 906 (8th Cir. 1975) — § 425

Martin Linen Supply Co., U.S. v.

Martin-Trigona, U.S. v.

Martinello, U.S. v.

Martinez, U.S. v.

Martinez-Fuerte, U.S. v.

Martino, U.S. v.

Martorano, U.S. v.

Marvin, U.S. v.

Maryland, Andresen v.

Maryland, Brady v.

Maryland v. Buie, 494 U.S. 325 (1990) — § 223; § 226

Maryland v. Craig, 110 S. Ct. 3157 (1990) — § 2139

Maryland v. Garrison, 107 S. Ct. 1013 (1987) — § 211

Maryland, Giles v.

Maryland v. Macon, 472 U.S. 463 (1985) — § 201

Maryland, Smith v.

Maryland, White v.

Marzano, U.S. v.

Marzeno v. Gengler, 574 F.2d 730 (3d Cir. 1978) — § 719

Marzgliano, U.S. v.

Masciarelli, U.S. v.

Mase, U.S. v.

Maselli, U.S. v.

Maskeny, U.S. v.

Mason v. U.S., 250 F.2d 704 (10th Cir. 1957) — § 604

Mason v. U.S., 402 F.2d 732 (8th Cir. 1968) — § 2001

Massachusetts, Jacobson v.

Massachusetts v. Sheppard, 468 U.S. 981 (1984) — § 248

Massachusetts, Snyder v.

Massachusetts v. Upton, 466 U.S. 727 (1984) — § 207

Massachusetts v. Westcott, 431 U.S. 322 (1977) — § 1402; § 1403

Massachusetts v. White, 439 U.S. 280 (1978) — § 207 § 305; § 312

Massaro, U.S. v.

Massey, Greene v.

Massey, U.S. v.

Massey-Ferguson, Inc., Holmgren v.

Massiah v. U.S., 377 U.S. 201 (1964) — § 310

Masson, U.S. v.

Mastberg, U.S. v.

Mastrangelo, U.S. v.

Mathiason, Oregon v.

Mathis, U.S. v.

Matlock, U.S. v.

Matos, U.S. v.

Matter of Archeluta, 561 F.2d 1059 (2d Cir. 1977) — § 407

Matter of Battaglia, 653 F.2d 419 (9th Cir. 1981) — § 404

Matter of Fula, 672 F.2d 279 (2d Cir. 1982) — § 404

Matter of Grand Jury (Vigil), 524 F.2d 209 (10th Cir. 1975) — § 407; § 425

Matter of Grand Jury Empanelled January 21, 1975 (Curran), 536 F.2d 1009 (3d Cir. 1976) — § 418

Matter of Grand Jury Empanelled Feb. 14, 1978, 603 F.2d 469 (3d Cir. 1979) — § 1918

Matter of Grand Jury Impanelled January 21, 1975 (Freedman), 529 F.2d 543 (3d Cir. 1976) — § 407; § 425

Matter of Grand Jury Proceedings, 428 F. Supp. 273 (E.D. Mich. 1976) — § 418

Matter of Investigative Grand Jury Proceedings, 480 F. Supp. 162 (N.D. Ohio 1979) — § 418

Matter of Phillips, 593 F.2d 356 (8th Cir. 1979) — § 1403

Matter of Special February 1977 Grand Jury, 570 F.2d 674 (7th Cir. 1978) — § 407

Matter of Special February 1977 Grand

Jury, 581 F.2d 1262 (7th Cir. 1978) — § 417

Matter of Walsh, 623 F.2d 489 (7th Cir. 1980) — § 1918

Matter of Witness Before the Grand Jury, 546 F.2d 825 (9th Cir. 1976) — § 409

Matthews, In re

Matthews, Morris v.

Matthews, U.S. v.

Mattox v. U.S., 146 U.S. 140 (1892) — § 1303; § 2141

Mattox v. U.S., 156 U.S. 237 (1895) — § 2141

Mattucci, U.S. v.

Matya, U.S. v.

Mauchlin, U.S. v.

Maull, U.S. v.

Mauro, Arizona v.

Mauro, U.S. v.

May v. U.S., 175 F.2d 994 (D.C. Cir. 1949) — § 1532

Mayes, U.S. v.

Mays, U.S. v.

McCain, U.S. v.

McCaleb, U.S. v.

McCallie, U.S. v.

McCambridge, U.S. v.

McCarthy, U.S. v.

McCarthy v. U.S., 394 U.S. 459 (1969) — § 602; § 603; § 606; § 610; § 616

McCarty, Berkemer v.

McCauley, U.S. v.

McCauley, U.S. ex rel. Guy v.

McClain, U.S. v.

McClain v. U.S., 676 F.2d 915 (2d Cir. 1982) — § 1012

McClellan, U.S. v.

McClendon v. U.S., 587 F.2d 384 (8th Cir. 1978) — § 702

McClintic, U.S. v.

McCollum, Georgia v.

McConahy, U.S. v.

McCowan v. U.S., 376 F.2d 122 (9th Cir. 1967) — § 1520

McCoy, U.S. v.

McCracken, U.S. v.

McCrane, U.S. v.

McCrary, U.S. v.

McCray v. Illinois, 386 U.S. 300 (1967) — § 1923

McCray, U.S. v.

McCree, Lockhart v.

McCroskey v. U.S., 339 F.2d 895 (8th Cir. 1965) — § 1302

McCulley, U.S. v.

McCullough, Texas v.

McCurdy, U.S. v.

McCutcheon v. Estelle, 483 F.2d 256 (5th Cir. 1973) — § 1905

McDaniel, U.S. v.

McDermott v. John Hancock Mut. Life Ins. Co., 255 F.2d 562 (3d Cir. 1958) — § 1403

McDermott, Summers v.

McDonald v. Lucas, 677 F.2d 518 (5th Cir. 1982) — § 305

McDonald, U.S. v.

McDonald v. U.S., 89 F.2d 128 (8th Cir. 1937) — § 1707

McDonnel, U.S. v.

McDowell, Burdeau v.

McDowell, U.S. v.

McEachern, U.S. v.

McEachin, U.S. v.

McFayden-Snider, U.S. v.

McFee v. U.S., 206 F.2d 872 (9th Cir. 1953) — § 1917

McGautha v. California, 402 U.S. 183 (1971) — § 1502; § 1906

McGee v. Schmidt, 411 F. Supp. 43 (W.D. Wis. 1976) — § 1403

McGlynn, U.S. v.

McGovern, U.S. v.

McGovern, United Klans of America v.

McGrath, U.S. v.

McGuff v. Alabama, 566 F.2d 939 (5th Cir. 1978) — § 317

McGuire, U.S. v.

McKeever, U.S. v.

McKenley, U.S. v.

McKenzie, U.S. v.

McKenzie, Williams v.

McKinney, U.S. v.

McKoy, U.S. v.

McMann, U.S. ex rel. Richardson v.

McManus, U.S. v.

McMillan, U.S. v.

McMillen, U.S. v.

McMillin v. Pennsylvania, 477 U.S. 79 (1986) — § 1339

McMorris v. Alioto, 567 F.2d 897 (9th Cir. 1978) — § 243

McNabb v. U.S., 318 U.S. 332 (1943) — § 304

McNally, U.S. v.

McNamara v. Henkel, 226 U.S. 520 (1913) — § 1513

McNeil v. Wisconsin, 111 S. Ct. 2204 (1991) — § 305; § 310; § 317

McPartlin, U.S. v.

McRae, U.S. v.

McRary, U.S. v.

Mead Data Central, Inc. v. U.S. Dept. of Air Force, 566 F.2d 242 (D.C. Cir. 1977) — § 1918

Mears v. Olin, 527 F.2d 1100 (8th Cir. 1975) — § 2006

Mechanik, U.S. v.

Medel, U.S. v.

Medical Therapy Sciences, Inc., U.S. v.

Medico, U.S. v.

Medina-Herrera, U.S. v.

Medley v. U.S., 155 F.2d 857 (D.C. Cir. 1946) — § 1264

Mehrmanesh, U.S. v.

Mejias, U.S. v.

Melchor Moreno, U.S. v.

Melickian v. U.S., 547 F.2d 416 (8th Cir. 1977) — § 407

Melville, U.S. v.

Melvin, In re

Melvin, U.S. v.

Mendell, U.S. v.

Mendenhall, U.S. v.

Mendoza, U.S. v.

Menendez, U.S. v.

Meredith, Diversified Industries, Inc. v.

Meredith v. Hardy, 554 F.2d 764 (5th Cir. 1977) — § 2001

Merlino, U.S. v.

Merrell, U.S. v.

Merrill v. U.S., 365 F.2d 281 (5th Cir. 1966) — § 1707

Merrill Lynch, Pierce, Fenner, and Smith, Inc., Verzosa v.

Mespoulede, U.S. v.

Messina, U.S. v.

Metz, U.S. v.

Meyer v. U.S., 424 F.2d 1181 (8th Cir. 1970) — § 609

Meyers, Florida v.

Meyers, U.S. v.

Meyers v. U.S., 171 F.2d 800 (D.C. Cir. 1948) — § 1706

Michael C., Fare v.

Michel, U.S. v.

Michelson v. U.S., 335 U.S. 469 (1948) — § 1518; § 1519; § 1520

Michigan, Atkins v.

Michigan v. Chestnut, 108 S. Ct. — (1988) — § 228

Michigan v. Clifford, 464 U.S. 287 (1984) — § 232

Michigan v. De Fillippo, 443 U.S. 31 (1979) — § 218; § 219; § 248

Michigan v. Harvey, 494 U.S. 344 (1990) — § 311; § 1818

Michigan v. Jackson, 475 U.S. 625 (1986) — § 301; § 305; § 308

Michigan v. Long, 463 U.S. 1032 (1983) — § 228

Michigan v. Mosley, 423 U.S. 96 (1975) — § 308

Michigan v. Summers, 452 U.S. 692 (1981) — § 227; § 228; § 230

Michigan v. Thomas, 102 S. Ct. 3029 (1982) — § 235

Michigan v. Tyler, 436 U.S. 499 (1978) — § 232

Michigan Dept. of State Police v. Sitz, 110 S. Ct. 2481 (1990) — § 228

Micieli, U.S. v.

Micou, Laman v.

Middleton, U.S. v.

Midland Asphalt v. U.S., 489 U.S. 794 (1989) — § 410

Midwestern Wholesale Drug, Inc. v. Gas Service Co., 442 F.2d 663 (10th Cir. 1971) — § 1609

Mierzwicki, U.S. v.

Migely, U.S. v.

Mikka, U.S. v.

Mikus v. U.S., 433 F.2d 719 (2d Cir. 1970) — § 1604

Miley, U.S. v.

Milhollan, U.S. v.

Miller, Greer v.

Miller v. New York Produce Exchange, 550 F.2d 762 (2d Cir. 1977) — § 1704

Miller, U.S. v.

Miller v. U.S., 357 U.S. 301 (1958) — § 215; § 219

Miller v. U.S., 396 F.2d 492 (8th Cir. 1968) — § 501; § 502

Millow, In re

Milton, U.S. v.

Mims v. U.S., 375 F.2d 135 (5th Cir. 1967) — § 2003

Mincey v. Arizona, 437 U.S. 385 (1978) — § 217; § 222; § 232; § 301; § 311; § 313

Mincey, Campbell v.

Minicone, U.S. v.

Minnesota v. Murphy, 465 U.S. 420 (1984) — § 305

Minnesota v. Olson, 495 U.S. 91 (1990) — § 255

Minnesota Mining Co., Platt v.

Minnick v. Mississippi, 495 U.S. 903 (1990) — § 301; § 308

Minor, U.S. v.

Minor v. U.S., 396 U.S. 87 (1969) — § 1905

Miracle v. Estelle, 592 F.2d 1269 (5th Cir. 1979) — § 1118

Miranda v. Arizona, 384 U.S. 436 (1966) — § 207; § 304; § 305; § 308; § 1818; § 1901; § 1906

Miranda, U.S. v.

Miranda v. U.S., 255 F.2d 9 (1st Cir. 1958) — § 101

Miranti, U.S. v.

Missio, U.S. v.

Mississippi, Brown v.

Mississippi, Chambers v.

Mississippi, Minnick v.

Missler, U.S. v.

Missouri, Bullington v.

Missouri, Duren v.

Missouri v. Hunter, 459 U.S. 359 (1983) — § 1002

Missouri, Williams v.

Mistretta v. U.S., 488 U.S. 361 (1989) — § 1312

Mitchell, Helvering v.

Mitchell, Rose v.

Mitchell v. Rose, 570 F.2d 129 (6th Cir. 1978) — § 1401; § 1403

Mitchell, U.S. v.

Mitchell v. U.S., 213 F.2d 951 (9th Cir. 1954) — § 1801

Mock, U.S. v.

Modern Products, Inc., Bobb v.

Modern Woodmen v. Watkins, 132 F.2d 352 (5th Cir. 1942) — § 1917

Modica, U.S. v.

Mohney, U.S. v.

Molt, U.S. v.

Monroe v. Blackburn, 607 F.2d 148 (5th Cir. 1979) — § 719; § 1108

Montalvo-Murillo, U.S. v.

Montamedi, U.S. v.

Montana v. Hall, 481 U.S. 400 (1987) — § 1006

Montana, Sandstrom v.

Montano, U.S. v.

Montanye, U.S. ex rel. Sanney v.

Montes-Zarate, U.S. v.

Montgomery, U.S. v.

Montgomery v. U.S., 403 F.2d 605 (8th Cir. 1968) — § 219

Monti, U.S. v.

Montiell, U.S. v.

Montilla Records of Puerto Rico v. Morales, 575 F.2d 324 (1st Cir. 1978) — § 211

Montoya, U.S. v.

Montoya de Hernandez, U.S. v.

Moody, U.S. v.

Mooney v. Holohan, 294 U.S. 103 (1935) — § 719; § 1107

Moore v. District Court, 525 F.2d 328 (9th Cir. 1975) — § 1219

Moore v. Illinois, 408 U.S. 786 (1972) — § 721; § 722; § 1108

Moore v. Illinois, 434 U.S. 220 (1977) — § 317; § 503; § 2111

Moore, U.S. v.

Moore v. U.S., 394 F.2d 818 (5th Cir. 1968) — § 2003

Morales, Montilla Records of Puerto Rico v.

Morales, U.S. v.

Moran v. Burbine, 475 U.S. 412 (1986) — § 308

Morell, U.S. v.

Moreno, U.S. v.

Moreno-Nunez, U.S. v.

Morford, Elliott v.

Morgan v. Thomas, 448 F.2d 1356 (5th Cir. 1971) — § 1906

Morgan, U.S. v.

Morgan v. U.S., 149 F.2d 185 (5th Cir. 1945) — § 1703

Morin, U.S. v.

Morissette v. U.S., 342 U.S. 246 (1952) — § 1264; § 1505

Morlang, U.S. v.

Morris, Jones v.

Morris v. Matthews, 106 S. Ct. 1032 (1986) — § 1010

Morris v. Matthews, 475 U.S. 237 (1986) — § 1010

Morris, Stone v.

Morris, U.S. v.

Morrison, U.S. v.

Morrison v. U.S., 365 F.2d 521 (D.C. Cir. 1966) — § 1514

Morrison v. U.S., 108 S. Ct. 1837 (1988) — § 518

Morrow, U.S. v.

Morse, Perial Amusement Corp. v.

Mortimer, U.S. v.

Morvant v. Construction Aggregates Corp., 570 F.2d 626 (6th Cir. 1978) — § 1819

Moscahlaidis, U.S. v.

Moskowitz, U.S. v.

Mosley, Michigan v.

Mosley, U.S. v.

Moss, U.S. v.

Mota, U.S. v.

Moten, U.S. v.

Moulton, Maine v.

M/S Sanyo Maru, Robertson v.

Muckenthaler, U.S. v.

Muhle, Niagara Fire Ins. Co. v.

Mullaney, Wilbur v.

Mullaney v. Wilbur, 421 U.S. 684 (1975) — § 1269; § 1505

Mullens, U.S. v.

Mulligan, Perry v.

Mullings, U.S. v.

Mu'min v. Virginia, 111 S. Ct. 1899 (1991) — § 1246

Muniz, Pennsylvania v.

Munoz-Flores, U.S. v.

Murphy, Cupp v.

Murphy, Minnesota v.

Murphy v. National R.R. Passenger

Corp., 547 F.2d 816 (4th Cir. 1977) — § 2003

Murphy, U.S. v.

Murphy v. Waterfront Commission, 378 U.S. 52 (1964) — § 419; § 1903

Murray, Turner v.

Murray, U.S. v.

Murray v. U.S., 487 U.S. 533 (1988) — § 248

Muscarella, U.S. v.

Musgrave, U.S. v.

Mustin, U.S. v.

Mutchler, U.S. v.

Myers, U.S. v.

Myers v. U.S., 356 F.2d 469 (5th Cir. 1966) — § 1605

## N

Nace, U.S. v.

Nadolney, U.S. v.

Namet v. U.S., 373 U.S. 179 (1963) — § 1109; § 1904

Nance, U.S. v.

Nanda v. Ford Motor Co., 509 F.2d 213 (7th Cir. 1974) — § 2003

Napue v. Illinois, 360 U.S. 264 (1959) — § 1107

Narciso, U.S. v.

Nardone v. U.S., 308 U.S. 388 (1939) — § 248

Narten v. Eyman, 460 F.2d 184 (9th Cir. 1969) — § 1911

Natale, U.S. v.

Nathan, U.S. v.

National R.R. Passenger Corp., Murphy v.

National Student Marketing Corporation, SEC v.

Natta, In re

Natta v. Zletz, 418 F.2d 633 (7th Cir. 1969) — § 1919

Naughten, Cupp v.

Navarro-Flores, U.S. v.

Nazzaro, U.S. v.

Neal, U.S. v.

Nebbia, U.S. v.

Nedd, U.S. v.

Neidelman, U.S. v.

Neidinger v. U.S., 647 F.2d 408 (4th Cir. 1981) — § 1320

Neil v. Biggers, 409 U.S. 188 (1972) — § 318; § 319; § 2111

Nelson, Lockhart v.

Nelson v. O'Neil, 402 U.S. 622 (1971) — § 314

Nelson, U.S. v.

Nemes, U.S. v.

Netterville, U.S. v.

Nettles, U.S. v.

Nettles v. Wainwright, 677 F.2d 410 (5th Cir. 1982) — § 317

Neumann, U.S. v.

Neville, South Dakota v.

New Buffalo Amusement Corp., U.S. v.

Newcomb, U.S. v.

New Hampshire, Coolidge v.

New Jersey, Garrity v.

New Jersey v. Portash, 440 U.S. 450 (1979) — § 420

New Jersey v. T.L.O., 469 U.S. 325 (1985) — § 217

New Jersey, Von Cleef v.

New Jersey Investigation Commission, Zicarelli v.

Newman, U.S. v.

New Mexico v. Earnest, 477 U.S. 648 (1986) — § 2139

New Mexico, Fugate v.

Newton, U.S. v.

New York, Baldwin v.

New York v. Belton, 453 U.S. 454 (1981) — § 226

New York v. Class, 471 U.S. 1003 (1986) — § 235

New York, Cruz v.

New York, Dunaway v.

New York, Harris v.

New York v. Harris, 495 U.S. 14 (1990) — § 219; § 248

New York, Hernandez v.

New York, Lanza v.

New York, Lo-Ji Sales Inc. v.

New York, Patterson v.

New York, Payton v.

New York v. P.J. Video, Inc., 106 S. Ct. 1610 (1986) — § 206

New York v. Quarles, 465 U.S. 649 (1984) — § 305

New York, Rothschild v.

New York, Santobello v.

New York, Sibron v.

New York Produce Exchange, Miller v.

Niagara Fire Ins. Co. v. Muhle, 208 F.2d 191 (8th Cir. 1953) — § 2001

Nice v. Chesapeake & O. Ry., 305 F. Supp. 1167 (W.D. Mich. 1969) — § 1401

Nicholas, U.S. v.

Nichols, U.S. v.

Nichols v. Upjohn Co., 610 F.2d 293 (5th Cir. 1980) — § 1605

Nick, U.S. v.

Nick v. U.S., 531 F.2d 936 (8th Cir. 1976) — § 1819

Nickell, U.S. v.

Nickerson, U.S. v.

Nicola v. U.S., 72 F.2d 780 (3d Cir. 1934) — § 1703

Nicolls, Stasiukevich v.

Niederberger, U.S. v.

Nielson v. Armstrong Rubber Co., 570 F.2d 272 (8th Cir. 1978) — § 2005

Nilson Van & Storage Co. v. Marsh, 755 F.2d 362 (4th Cir. 1985) — § 1301

Niro v. U.S., 388 F.2d 535 (1st Cir. 1968) — § 219

Nix, U.S. v.

Nix v. Williams, 467 U.S. 431 (1984) — § 248; § 312

Nixon, Douglas v.

Nixon, U.S. v.

NLRB v. E. C. Atkins & Co., 331 U.S. 398 (1947) — § 1403

NLRB v. Federal Dairy Co., 297 F.2d 487 (1st Cir. 1962) — § 1802

NLRB, Kessler Institute for Rehabilitation v.

NLRB v. Trans Ocean Export Packing, Inc., 473 F.2d 612 (9th Cir. 1973) — § 1903

Noah, U.S. v.

Noble, U.S. v.

Nobles, U.S. v.

Nolan, U.S. v.

Noll, U.S. v.

Norris, U.S. v.

North Carolina v. Alford, 400 U.S. 25 (1970) — § 610

North Carolina v. Butler, 441 U.S. 369 (1979) — § 305

North Carolina, Klopfer v.

North Carolina, Parker v.
North Carolina v. Pearce, 395 U.S. 711
(1969) — § 1001; § 1012; § 1118; § 1322
North Carolina, Sallie v.
Northwest Airlines, Inc., Rosenblatt v.
Novelli, U.S. v.
November 1979 Grand Jury, In re
Null, U.S. v.
Nunley, U.S. v.
Nussen, U.S. v.
Nutt v. U.S., 335 F.2d 817 (10th Cir.
1964) — § 1252
N. V. Maatschappij, etc. v. A. O. Smith
Corp., 590 F.2d 415 (2d Cir. 1978) —
§ 2003
N.Y.C. Transit Authority, Camps v.

O

Oakes, U.S. v.
Oates, U.S. v.
Oaxaca, U.S. v.
Oberhauser, Cockrell v.
O'Brien, U.S. v.
Oburn v. Shapp, 393 F. Supp. 561 (E.D.
Pa. 1975) — § 1403
Ocanas, U.S. v.
Ochoa-Sanchez, U.S. v.
Ochs, U.S. v.
O'Conner, U.S. v.
O'Connor v. Ohio, 385 U.S. 92 (1966) —
§ 1115
O'Connor v. Ortega, 480 U.S. 709 (1987)
— § 201; § 217
Odom, U.S. v.
O'Donnell, U.S. v.
Oetjen v. Central Leather Co., 246 U.S.
297 (1918) — § 1403
Ogden, U.S. v.
O'Gee v. Dobbs Houses, Inc., 570 F.2d
1084 (2d Cir. 1978) — § 2121
Ogull, U.S. v.
O'Henry's Film Works, Inc., U.S. v.
Ohio, Beck v.
Ohio, Brown v.
Ohio, Crampton v.
Ohio, Doyle v.
Ohio v. Johnson, 467 U.S. 493 (1984) —
§ 1003
Ohio, Lockett v.

Ohio, Martin v.
Ohio, O'Connor v.
Ohio, Powers v.
Ohio, Raley v.
Ohio v. Roberts, 448 U.S. 56 (1980) —
§ 2100; § 2139; § 2140
Ohio, Smith v.
Ohio, Terry v.
Ohio Bell Telephone Co. v. Public Utili-
ties Commission, 301 U.S. 292 (1937) —
§ 1400; § 1403
Ojala, U.S. v.
Oklahoma, Harris v.
Oklahoma, Queenan v.
Oklahoma, Ross v.
Olander, U.S. v.
Olden v. Kentucky, 488 U.S. 227 (1988)
— § 1805; § 1811
Olender v. U.S., 210 F.2d 795 (9th Cir.
1965) — § 1918
Olin, Mears v.
Oliphant v. Koehler, 594 F.2d 547 (6th
Cir. 1979) — § 1011
Olivares-Vega, U.S. v.
Oliver, U.S. v.
Oliver v. U.S., 466 U.S. 170 (1984) —
§ 240
Oliveras, U.S. v.
O'Looney, U.S. v.
Olson v. Kilstofte & Vosejpka, Inc., 327 F.
Supp. 583 (D. Minn. 1971) — § 1704
Olson, Minnesota v.
Olson, U.S. v.
Olwares, U.S. v.
One Assortment of 89 Firearms, U.S. v.
O'Neil, Nelson v.
O'Neill, U.S. v.
O'Neill v. U.S., 411 F.2d 139 (3d Cir.
1969) — § 1402
One Lot Emerald Cut Stones and One
Ring v. U.S., 409 U.S. 232 (1972) —
§ 1011
One 1972 Chevrolet Nova, U.S. v.
Ong, U.S. v.
Onori, U.S. v.
Opager, U.S. v.
Opper v. U.S., 348 U.S. 84 (1954) — § 303
Opperman, South Dakota v.
O'Quinn v. U.S., 411 F.2d 78 (10th Cir.
1969) — § 1802

Opportunity Consultants, Leis v.

Oregon, Apodaca v.

Oregon v. Bradshaw, 462 U.S. 1039 (1983) — § 308

Oregon v. Elstad, 470 U.S. 298 (1985) — § 312

Oregon v. Hass, 420 U.S. 714 (1975) — § 311

Oregon v. Kennedy, 102 S. Ct. 2083 (1982) — § 1008

Oregon, Lakeside v.

Oregon v. Mathiason, 429 U.S. 492 (1977) — § 220; § 306

Oropeza, U.S. v.

Orozco v. Texas, 394 U.S. 324 (1969) — § 306

Orozco, U.S. v.

Orr v. U.S., 386 F.2d 988 (D.C. Cir. 1967) — § 720

Orta, U.S. v.

Ortega, O'Connor v.

Ortega, U.S. v.

Ortiz, U.S. v.

Orzechowski, U.S. v.

Ottomano v. U.S., 468 F.2d 269 (1st Cir. 1972) — § 1011

Outpost Development Co., U.S. v.

Overton v. U.S., 275 F.2d 897 (D.C. Cir. 1960) — § 206

Owens, U.S. v.

Owensby v. U.S., 353 F.2d 412 (10th Cir. 1965) — § 601

## P

P. (Pinto), Canal Zone v.

Pacelli, U.S. v.

Pachay, U.S. v.

Pacheco, U.S. v.

Pacheco-Ruiz, U.S. v.

Pacific Power & Light, Ruhs v.

Paderick, Boone v.

Paderick, Smith v.

Padgent, U.S. v.

Padro, U.S. v.

Pagano, U.S. v.

Page, Barber v.

Page, U.S. v.

Palacios, U.S. v.

Palermo v. U.S., 360 U.S. 343 (1959) — § 801

Palmer v. Hoffman, 318 U.S. 109 (1943) — § 2123

Palmer, Hudson v.

Palmer, U.S. v.

Palmigiano, Baxter v.

Palumbo, U.S. v.

Pandelli v. U.S., 635 F.2d 553 (6th Cir. 1980) — § 1002

Panebianco, U.S. v.

Panetta, U.S. v.

Panger v. Duluth, Winnipeg & Pacific Railroad Co., 490 F.2d 1112 (8th Cir. 1974) — § 2001

Papaleo, U.S. v.

Paper Converting Mach. Co. v. F.M.C. Corp., 215 F. Supp. 249 (E.D. Wis. 1963) — § 1917

Papia, U.S. v.

Pappadio, U.S. v.

Pappas, U.S. v.

Paradiso v. U.S., 482 F.2d 409 (3d Cir. 1973) — § 609

Pardone, U.S. v.

Parhms, U.S. v.

Park, U.S. v.

Parker, In re

Parker v. North Carolina, 397 U.S. 790 (1970) — § 609

Parker v. Randolph, 442 U.S. 62 (1979) — § 303

Parker, U.S. v.

Parker v. U.S., 404 F.2d 1193 (9th Cir. 1968) — § 913

Parker, Werk v.

Parnell, U.S. v.

Parness, U.S. v.

Parratt, Sanchell v.

Parr-Pla, U.S. v.

Parry, U.S. v.

Partida, Castaneda v.

Partida-Parra, U.S. v.

Partin, U.S. v.

Paschen v. U.S., 70 F.2d 491 (7th Cir. 1934) — § 1706

Pascual, U.S. v.

Passodelis, U.S. v.

Pastor, U.S. v.

Patacchia, U.S. v.

Pate, U.S. v.

Pate, U.S. ex rel. Milani v.

Patterson v. Colorado, 205 U.S. 454 (1907) — § 1250

Patterson v. Illinois, 108 S. Ct. — (1988) — § 310

Patterson v. New York, 432 U.S. 197 (1977) — § 1269; § 1501; § 1505

Patterson, U.S. v.

Patton v. U.S., 281 U.S. 276 (1930) — § 1243

Paul, U.S. v.

Pavao v. Cardwell, 583 F.2d 1075 (9th Cir. 1978) — § 306

Payden, U.S. v.

Payne v. Smith, 667 F.2d 541 (6th Cir. 1981) — § 1269

Payne v. Thompson, 622 F.2d 254 (6th Cir. 1980) — § 1903

Payne v. U.S., 508 F.2d 1391 (5th Cir. 1975) — § 215

Payner, U.S. v.

Payton v. New York, 445 U.S. 573 (1980) — § 219; § 247

Peach, Canal Zone v.

Peacock, U.S. v.

Pearce, North Carolina v.

Pebton, Jones v.

Peden, U.S. v.

Pegelow, Bohannon v.

Pegram v. U.S., 361 F.2d 820 (8th Cir. 1966) — § 909

Pellerin Laundry Mach. Sales Co. v. Reed, 300 F.2d 305 (8th Cir. 1962) — § 1402

Pelley, U.S. v.

Peltier, U.S. v.

Pelton, U.S. v.

Pena, U.S. v.

Penn, U.S. v.

Penn Central Transp. Co., Stoler v.

Pennsylvania v. Bruder, 488 U.S. 9 (1988) — § 305

Pennsylvania, Codispoti v.

Pennsylvania v. Goldhammer, 474 U.S. 28 (1985) — § 1012; § 1346

Pennsylvania, Klobuchir v.

Pennsylvania, McMillin v.

Pennsylvania v. Muniz, 110 S. Ct. 2638 (1990) — § 1903

Pennsylvania v. Muniz, 496 U.S. 582 (1990) — § 307

Pennsylvania v. Ritchie, 107 S. Ct. 989 (1987) — § 2139

Pennsylvania v. Ritchie, 487 U.S. 1012 (1987) — § 2139

Pennsylvania, Smalis v.

Pennsylvania Railroad Co., Attal v.

Pennzoil Co., Justice v.

Pensinger, U.S. v.

People ex rel. Snead v. Kirkland, 462 F. Supp. 914 (E.D. Pa. 1978) — § 1403

Pepe, U.S. v.

Percevault, U.S. v.

Perea, U.S. v.

Pereira v. U.S., 347 U.S. 1 (1954) — § 1910; § 1911

Peretz v. U.S., 111 S. Ct. 2661 (1991) — § 1244; § 1246

Perez, U.S. v.

Perez-Franco, U.S. v.

Perial Amusement Corp. v. Morse, 482 F.2d 515 (2d Cir. 1973) — § 1902

Perini, Riccardi v.

Perkins, Illinois v.

Perkins, U.S. v.

Perkins v. Volkswagen of America, Inc., 596 F.2d 681 (5th Cir. 1979) — § 2003

Perlin, In re

Perno, U.S. v.

Perri, U.S. v.

Perrin, Dunn v.

Perry, Blackledge v.

Perry v. Mulligan, 544 F.2d 674 (3d Cir. 1977) — § 1111

Perry, U.S. v.

Persico, In re

Persico, U.S. v.

Peter, U.S. v.

Peters v. Kiff, 407 U.S. 493 (1972) — § 1245

Peters, U.S. v.

Petersen, U.S. v.

Peterson, U.S. v.

Petite v. U.S., 361 U.S. 529 (1960) — § 903; § 1005

Petito, U.S. v.

Petrol Stops, etc., Douglas Oil Company of California v.

Petsas, U.S. v.

Pettibone v. U.S., 148 U.S. 197 (1893) — § 102

Petty, U.S. v.

Pettyjohn v. U.S., 419 F.2d 651 (D.C. Cir. 1969) — § 304

Pfeiffer, U.S. v.

Pfingst, U.S. v.

Pheaster, U.S. v.

Phelps, Lowenfield v.

Phillips, Smith v.

Phillips, U.S. v.

Phillips v. Wyrick, 558 F.2d 489 (8th Cir. 1977) — § 2141

Phillips Petroleum Co., U.S. v.

Phipps, U.S. v.

Piatt, U.S. v.

Picciurro v. U.S., 250 F.2d 585 (8th Cir. 1958) — § 1911

Pickney, U.S. v.

Pierce, U.S. v.

Pierson, U.S. v.

Pigee v. Israel, 670 F.2d 690 (7th Cir. 1982) — § 1504

Pilla, U.S. v.

Pillsbury v. Conboy, — U.S. —, 32 Cr. L. 3007 (1983) — § 422

Pilnick, U.S. v.

Pinkerton v. U.S., 328 U.S. 640 (1946) — § 909

Pinkney, U.S. v.

Pinkus, Reilly v.

Pinna, U.S. v.

Pinto, U.S. v.

Piper, Brown v.

Pipkins, U.S. v.

Pirolli, U.S. v.

Pitts, U.S. v.

P.J. Video, Inc., New York v.

Place, U.S. v.

Platt v. Minnesota Mining Co., 376 U.S. 240 (1964) — § 112

Ploof, U.S. v.

Plum, U.S. v.

Poeta, U.S. v.

Pointer v. Texas, 380 U.S. 400 (1965) — § 1805

Pointer v. U.S., 151 U.S. 396 (1894) — § 1532

Poland v. Arizona, 476 U.S. 147 (1986) — § 1012

Poliafico v. U.S., 237 F.2d 97 (6th Cir. 1956) — § 1518

Polin, U.S. v.

Pollack, U.S. v.

Pollard, U.S. v.

Pollard v. U.S., 352 U.S. 354 (1957) — § 1319

Pollock, Bergdoll v.

Pollock v. U.S., 202 F.2d 281 (5th Cir. 1953) — § 1917

Polsinelli, U.S. v.

Pon v. U.S., 168 F.2d 373 (1st Cir. 1948) — § 103

Ponder, U.S. v.

Pool v. U.S., 260 F.2d 57 (9th Cir. 1958) — § 1911

Pope v. Thone, 671 F.2d 298 (8th Cir. 1982) — § 1004

Pope, U.S. v.

Pordum, U.S. v.

Portac, Inc., U.S. v.

Portash, New Jersey v.

Porter, U.S. v.

Portes, U.S. v.

Portomene v. U.S., 221 F.2d 582 (5th Cir. 1955) — § 1923

Posey, U.S. v.

Postal, U.S. v.

Poulack, U.S. v.

Powe, U.S. v.

Powell, U.S. v.

Powell v. U.S., 347 F.2d 156 (9th Cir. 1965) — § 1260

Powers v. Ohio, 494 U.S. 1054 (1991) — § 1248

Powers, U.S. v.

Pozzy, U.S. v.

Prada, U.S. v.

Prather v. Prather, 650 F.2d 88 (5th Cir. 1981) — § 2120

Pratter, U.S. v.

Press-Enterprise Co. v. Superior Court of California, 464 U.S. 501 (1984) — § 1246

Pressley, U.S. v.

Prevatt, U.S. v.

Prewitt, U.S. v.

Price v. Georgia, 398 U.S. 323 (1970) —
§ 1010

Price, U.S. v.

Prichard, U.S. v.

Prince v. Beto, 426 F.2d 875 (5th Cir.
1970) — § 1820

Prince, U.S. v.

Prior, U.S. v.

Proctor and Gamble Co., U.S. v.

Prouse, Delaware v.

Provoo, U.S. v.

Prudential Ins. Co. v. Carlson, 126 F.2d
607 (10th Cir. 1942) — § 1402

Pruitt, U.S. v.

Pry, U.S. v.

Pryba, U.S. v.

Prysock, California v.

Public Ser. Ry. v. Wursthorn, 278 F. 408
(3d Cir. 1922) — § 1400

Public Utilities Commission, Ohio Bell
Telephone Co. v.

Puco, U.S. v.

Puerto Rico, Torres v.

Pugh, Gerstein v.

Purin, U.S. v.

## Q

Qamar, U.S. v.

Quarles, New York v.

Queenan v. Oklahoma, 190 U.S. 548
(1903) — § 2001

Quercia v. U.S., 289 U.S. 466 (1933) —
§ 1264

Quinn, In re

Quinn, U.S. v.

Quinones, U.S. v.

Quinto, U.S. v.

## R

Rabbinical Seminary, etc., In re

Rabbitt, U.S. v.

Raddatz, U.S. v.

Radetsky, U.S. v.

Radiant Burners, Inc. v. American Gas
Ass'n, 320 F.2d 314 (7th Cir. 1963) —
§ 1917

Radio Hill Mines Col., Ltd., SEC v.

Radmall, U.S. v.

Raffel v. U.S., 271 U.S. 494 (1926) —
§ 1906

Ragghianti, U.S. v.

Raineri, U.S. v.

Rainey, Beech Aircraft Corp. v.

Rajewski, U.S. v.

Rakas v. Illinois, 439 U.S. 128 (1978) —
§ 201; § 255

Raley v. Ohio, 360 U.S. 423 (1959) —
§ 419

Ramer v. U.S., 411 F.2d 30 (9th Cir. 1969)
— § 1921

Ramirez, U.S. v.

Ramos, U.S. v.

Ramos Algarin, U.S. v.

Ramsey, U.S. v.

Ramsey v. U.S., 245 F.2d 295 (9th Cir.
1957) — § 1503

Ramseyer v. General Motors Corp., 417
F.2d 859 (8th Cir. 1969) — § 1609

Randall, Seattle First National Bank v.

Randall v. Warnaco, Inc., Hirsch-Weis
Div., 677 F.2d 1226 (8th Cir. 1982) —
§ 1609

Randolph v. Collectramatic, Inc., 590 F.2d
844 (10th Cir. 1979) — § 2001; § 2003

Randolph, Parker v.

Rangel, U.S. v.

Ranta, U.S. v.

Rapoport, U.S. v.

Rappy, U.S. v.

Rasmussen, U.S. v.

Rasor, U.S. v.

Rastelli, U.S. v.

Rath, U.S. v.

Rauscher, U.S. v.

Rawlings v. Kentucky, 448 U.S. 98 (1980)
— § 255; § 312

Reagan v. U.S., 157 U.S. 301 (1895) —
§ 1906

Reamer, U.S. v.

Reason, U.S. v.

Redmond, U.S. v.

Reece, U.S. v.

Reed, Ellis v.

Reed, Pellerin Laundry Mach. Sales Co.
v.

Reed v. Turner, 444 F.2d 206 (10th Cir.
1971) — § 606

Reed, U.S. v.

Reed v. Wainwright, 587 F.2d 260 (5th Cir. 1979) — § 1245

Reese, U.S. v.

Reeves, U.S. v.

Regan, U.S. v.

Regan, U.S. ex rel. Lucas v.

Regilio, U.S. v.

Regner, U.S. v.

Reid v. Georgia, 448 U.S. 438 (1980) — § 228

Reifsteck, U.S. v.

Reilly v. Pinkus, 338 U.S. 269 (1949) — § 2132

Remington Records, Inc., Shapiro, Bernstein & Co. v.

Remmer v. U.S., 347 U.S. 227 (1954) — § 1249

Renaldi, U.S. v.

Renfro, U.S. v.

Reno v. U.S., 317 F.2d 499 (5th Cir. 1963) — § 905

Rentaria, U.S. v.

R. Enterprises, Inc., U.S. v.

Report of Grand Jury Proceedings, In re

Republic Gear Co. v. Borg Warner, 381 F.2d 551 (2d Cir. 1967) — § 1919

Rettig, U.S. v.

Rewald, U.S. v.

Reyes v. U.S., 417 F.2d 916 (9th Cir. 1969) — § 215

Reyes-Padron, U.S. v.

Reynolds v. Denver & Rio Grande Western R. Co., 174 F.2d 673 (10th Cir. 1949) — § 1707

Reynolds, U.S. v.

Rhay, Hearn v.

Rhode Island v. Innis, 446 U.S. 291 (1980) — § 305; § 306; § 308; § 313

Rhodes, U.S. v.

Ribero, U.S. v.

Ricaud v. American Metal Co., 246 U.S. 304 (1918) — § 1400

Riccardi v. Perini, 417 F.2d 645 (6th Cir. 1969) — § 219

Riccardi, U.S. v.

Ricciardi, U.S. v.

Ricco, U.S. v.

Riccobene, U.S. v.

Rice v. U.S., 411 F.2d 485 (8th Cir. 1969) — § 1706

Rich v. Eastman Kodak Co., 583 F.2d 435 (8th Cir. 1978) — § 2001

Rich, U.S. v.

Richards, U.S. v.

Richardson v. Marsh, 107 S. Ct. 1703 (1987) — § 314

Richardson, U.S. v.

Richardson v. U.S., 468 U.S. 317 (1984) — § 1001; § 1008

Richardson v. U.S., 577 F.2d 447 (8th Cir. 1978) — § 609

Richman, U.S. v.

Ricketson, U.S. v.

Ricketts v. Adamson, 483 U.S. 1 (1987) — § 613

Rickey, U.S. v.

Rickus, U.S. v.

Rico, U.S. v.

Riddle, Harris v.

Riddle, Johnson v.

Rideau v. Louisiana, 373 U.S. 723 (1963) — § 111

Ridling, U.S. v.

Riker, U.S. v.

Riley v. City of Chester, 612 F.2d 708 (3d Cir. 1979) — § 1922

Riley, Florida v.

Riley v. Gray, 674 F.2d 522 (6th Cir. 1982) — § 245

Riley, U.S. v.

Rinaldi, U.S. v.

Rinaldi v. U.S., 434 U.S. 22 (1977) — § 1005

Rinn, U.S. v.

Rios, U.S. v.

Rippy, U.S. v.

Ristaino v. Ross, 424 U.S. 589 (1976) — § 1246

Ristaino, Salemme v.

Ritch, U.S. v.

Ritchie, Pennsylvania v.

Ritter, Rogers v.

Ritz, U.S. v.

Rivera, U.S. v.

Rivero, U.S. v.

Rivero-Nunez, U.S. v.

Rizzo, U.S. v.

R.J. Reynolds Tobacco Co., U.S. v.

R.L.C., U.S. v.

RMI Co., U.S. v.

Roach, U.S. v.

Robbins v. California, 453 U.S. 420 (1981) — § 237

Robbins, U.S. v.

Robbins v. U.S., 476 F.2d 26 (10th Cir. 1973) — § 801

Robbins v. Whelan, 653 F.2d 47 (1st Cir. 1981) — § 2125

Roberson, Arizona v.

Robert Hawthorne, Inc. v. Director of Internal Revenue, 406 F. Supp. 1098 (E.D. Pa. 1976) — § 409

Roberts, Ohio v.

Roberts, Thigpen v.

Roberts, U.S. v.

Roberts v. U.S., 445 U.S. 552 (1980) — § 309

Robertson v. M/S Sanyo Maru, 374 F.2d 463 (5th Cir. 1967) — § 1707

Robertson, U.S. v.

Robinson, Greenfield v.

Robinson, U.S. v.

Robson, U.S. v.

Roby, U.S. v.

Rochan, U.S. v.

Rochin v. California, 342 U.S. 165 (1952) — § 1903

Rock v. Arkansas, 483 U.S. 44 (1987) — § 1802

Rodarte, U.S. v.

Rodriguez, Illinois v.

Rodriguez, U.S. v.

Rodriguez-Sandoval, U.S. v.

Roe, U.S. v.

Roe v. Wade, 410 U.S. 113 (1973) — § 1401

Rogers, Florida v.

Rogers v. Ritter, 79 U.S. 317 (1870) — § 2001

Rogers, State v.

Rogers, U.S. v.

Rogers v. U.S., 340 U.S. 367 (1951) — § 1902; § 1906

Rogers v. U.S., 422 U.S. 35 (1975) — § 1249; § 1264

Rojas, U.S. v.

Rojas-Contreras, U.S. v.

Rollins, U.S. v.

Romero, U.S. v.

Romero, Yanes v.

Romney, Davis v.

Romo, U.S. v.

Rone, U.S. v.

Rooks, U.S. v.

Roper, U.S. v.

Rosahn, In re

Rosales-Lopez, U.S. v.

Rosales-Lopez v. U.S., 451 U.S. 182 (1981) — § 1246

Rosario, U.S. v.

Rose, Mitchell v.

Rose v. Mitchell, 443 U.S. 545 (1979) — § 1245

Rose, U.S. v.

Rosenblatt v. Northwest Airlines, Inc., 54 F.R.D. 21 (S.D.N.Y. 1971) — § 1917

Rosenfeld, U.S. v.

Rosenstein, U.S. v.

Rosner, U.S. v.

Ross v. Oklahoma, 108 S. Ct. 2273 — (1988) — § 1248

Ross, Ristaino v.

Ross, U.S. v.

Rosse, U.S. v.

Rotchford, U.S. v.

Roth, U.S. v.

Rothenberg v. Security Management Co., 667 F.2d 958 (11th Cir. 1982) — § 1403

Rothman, U.S. v.

Rothschild v. New York, 525 F.2d 686 (2d Cir. 1975) — § 1906

Rotolo v. U.S., 404 F.2d 316 (5th Cir. 1968) — § 1801

Roundtree, U.S. v.

Roviaro v. U.S., 353 U.S. 53 (1957) — § 713; § 1923

Rowell, U.S. v.

Rozier v. Ford Motor Co., 573 F.2d 1332 (5th Cir. 1978) — § 2134

Rubalcava-Montoya, U.S. v.

Rubin, U.S. v.

Rucker, U.S. v.

Rucker v. Wabash R.R., 418 F.2d 146 (7th Cir. 1969) — § 1918

Rudolph, U.S. v.

Ruffin, U.S. v.

Ruhs v. Pacific Power & Light, 671 F.2d 1268 (10th Cir. 1982) — § 1403

Ruiz-Estrella, U.S. v.

Ruke, Gilliand v.

Rumely v. U.S., 293 F. 532 (2d Cir. 1923) — § 1516

Rumsey, Arizona v.

Runck, U.S. v.

Runge, U.S. v.

Rushen v. Spain, 464 U.S. 114 (1983) — § 1249; § 1259

Rusken, Cahill v.

Russ, U.S. v.

Rutherford, Block v.

Ryan v. Commissioner, 568 F.2d 531 (7th Cir. 1977) — § 419; § 422

Ryan, U.S. v.

Ryan v. U.S., 384 F.2d 379 (1st Cir. 1967) — § 2001

Rylander, U.S. v.

## S

Sabatka, U.S. v.

Sabbath v. U.S., 391 U.S. 585 (1968) — § 215; § 219

Sacasas, U.S. v.

Sacco, U.S. v.

Sackett, U.S. v.

Sadin, In re

St. Louis Baptist Temple, Inc. v. F.D.I.C., 605 F.2d 1169 (10th Cir. 1979) — § 1401; § 1403

St. Pierre, U.S. v.

Saks & Co., U.S. v.

Salazar, U.S. v.

Salemme v. Ristaino, 587 F.2d 81 (1st Cir. 1978) — § 1261

Salerno, U.S. v.

Salinger v. U.S., 272 U.S. 542 (1926) — § 2100

Sallie v. North Carolina, 587 F.2d 636 (4th Cir. 1978) — § 232; § 238

Salliey, U.S. v.

Salsedo, U.S. v.

Salva, U.S. v.

Salvucci, U.S. v.

Salzmann, U.S. v.

Sanabria v. U.S., 437 U.S. 54 (1978) — § 1006

Sanborn, Wolfel v.

Sanchell v. Parratt, 530 F.2d 286 (8th Cir. 1976) — § 317; § 318

Sanchez v. Beto, 467 F.2d 513 (5th Cir. 1972) — § 305

Sanchez v. Denver & Rio Grande Western Railroad, 538 F.2d 304 (10th Cir. 1976) — § 1603

Sanchez, U.S. v.

Sanchez-Meza, U.S. v.

Sanders, Arkansas v.

Sanders v. U.S., 541 F.2d 190 (8th Cir. 1976) — § 1107

Sanderson, U.S. v.

Sandler, U.S. v.

Sandstrom v. Montana, 442 U.S. 510 (1979) — § 1269; § 1270; § 1504; § 1505; § 1509

Sanfilippo, U.S. v.

Sanford, U.S. v.

Sangrey, U.S. v.

Saniti, U.S. v.

San Juan, U.S. v.

Sansone v. U.S., 380 U.S. 343 (1965) — § 1265

Santana, U.S. v.

Santarpio, U.S. v.

Santillo, U.S. v.

Santobello v. New York, 404 U.S. 257 (1971) — § 315; § 611; § 613

Santoni, U.S. v.

Santos, U.S. v.

Santucci, U.S. v.

Sarbaugh, Illinois v.

Sargent Elec. Co., U.S. v.

Sartor v. Arkansas Natural Gas Corp., 321 U.S. 620 (1944) — § 2003

Satterfield, U.S. v.

Sauls, U.S. v.

Savage, U.S. v.

Sawyer v. Barczak, 129 F. Supp. 687 (E.D. Wis. 1955) — § 1916

Sawyer v. Barczak, 229 F.2d 805 (7th Cir. 1956) — § 2104

Sawyer, U.S. v.

Scafidi, U.S. v.

Scaglione, U.S. v.

Scales, U.S. v.

Scales v. U.S., 367 U.S. 203 (1961) — § 807

Scalzitti, U.S. v.

Scalzo, U.S. v.

Scavo, U.S. v.

Schackelford, U.S. v.

Schad v. Arizona, 111 S. Ct. 2491 (1991) — § 1242

Schaffer, Star of Wisconsin v.

Schaffer v. U.S., 362 U.S. 511 (1960) — § 909

Scharf, U.S. v.

Schebergen v. U.S., 536 F.2d 674 (6th Cir. 1976) — § 401

Scheer, U.S. v.

Scheffer, U.S. v.

Schennault, U.S. v.

Scherer, U.S. v.

Schiff, U.S. v.

Schipani, U.S. v.

Schleis, U.S. v.

Schlitz, Childs v.

Schmerber v. California, 384 U.S. 757 (1966) — § 307; § 1903

Schmidt v. Hewitt, 573 F.2d 794 (3d Cir. 1978) — § 313

Schmidt, McGee v.

Schmidt, U.S. v.

Schmoker, U.S. v.

Schmuck v. U.S., 489 U.S. 705 (1989) — § 1265

Schnackenberg, Cheff v.

Schneckloth v. Bustamonte, 412 U.S. 218 (1973) — § 243; § 244

Schoendorf, U.S. v.

Scholle, U.S. v.

Scholz Homes, Inc. v. Wallace, 590 F.2d 860 (10th Cir. 1979) — § 2003

Schor, U.S. v.

Schultz v. Tecumseh Prods., 310 F.2d 426 (6th Cir. 1962) — § 1403

Schwanke, U.S. v.

Schwarck, U.S. v.

Schwartz, U.S. v.

Schwartzbaum, U.S. v.

Scios, U.S. v.

Scijo, U.S. v.

Sclamo, U.S. v.

Scott v. Spanjer Bros., 298 F.2d 928 (2d Cir. 1962) — § 2007

Scott, U.S. v.

Scott v. U.S., 172 U.S. 343 (1899) — § 1817

Scott v. U.S., 436 U.S. 128 (1978) — § 264

Screws v. U.S., 325 U.S. 91 (1945) — § 1264

Scruggs, U.S. v.

Scully, U.S. v.

Sealed Case, In re

Seamster, U.S. v.

Search Warrant Dated July 4, In re

Searp, U.S. v.

Sears, U.S. v.

Sears, Roebuck & Co., U.S. v.

Seastrunk, U.S. v.

Seattle First Nat'l Bank v. Randall, 532 F.2d 1291 (9th Cir. 1976) — § 2123

Seavers, U.S. v.

Seawald, U.S. v.

Seawell, U.S. v.

Sebastian, U.S. v.

SEC v. Dresser Industries, Inc., 628 F.2d 1368 (D.C. Cir. 1980) — § 401

SEC v. National Student Mktg. Corp., 430 F. Supp. 639 (D.D.C. 1977) — § 414

SEC v. Radio Hill Mines Col., Ltd., 479 F.2d 4 (2d Cir. 1973) — § 1905

SEC v. Texas Gulf Sulphur Co., 446 F.2d 1301 (2d Cir. 1971) — § 2001

Secondino, U.S. v.

Security Mgt. Co., Rothenberg v.

Sedillo, U.S. v.

Segna, U.S. v.

Segura v. U.S., 468 U.S. 796 (1984) — § 248

Seijo, U.S. v.

Sellers, U.S. v.

Sells Engineering, Inc., U.S. v.

Seluk, U.S. v.

Sentovich, U.S. v.

Seohnlein, U.S. v.

Serfass v. U.S., 420 U.S. 377 (1975) — § 1001

Serlin, U.S. v.

Serubo, U.S. v.

Seta, U.S. v.

Seymour, U.S. v.

Shafer, U.S. v.

Shannahan, U.S. v.

Shapiro, U.S. v.

Shapiro, Bernstein & Co. v. Remington Records, Inc., 265 F.2d 263 (2d Cir. 1959) — § 2006

Shapiro v. U.S., 166 F.2d 240 (2d Cir. 1948) — § 2106

Shapiro v. U.S., 335 U.S. 1 (1948) — § 1902

Shapp, Oburn v.

Sharp, U.S. v.

Sharpe, U.S. v.

Shaughnessy, U.S. ex rel. Fong Foo v.

Shaw, U.S. v.

Shaw, Wilson v.

Shearer, U.S. v.

Sheehan, U.S. v.

Sheiner, U.S. v.

Shelton, U.S. v.

Shendal v. U.S., 312 F.2d 564 (9th Cir. 1963) — § 1906

Shepard, U.S. v.

Shepard v. U.S., 290 U.S. 96 (1933) — § 2120

Shepherd, U.S. v.

Sheppard, Massachusetts v.

Sherman, U.S. v.

Sherod, U.S. v.

Sherrif, U.S. v.

Sherwin, U.S. v.

Sherwood, U.S. v.

Shields, U.S. v.

Shillitani v. U.S., 384 U.S. 36 (1966) — § 424; § 425

Shima, U.S. v.

Shipley v. California, 395 U.S. 818 (1969) — § 222

Shoemaker, U.S. v.

Short, U.S. v.

Shorteeth, U.S. v.

Shorter, U.S. v.

Shoulberg, U.S. v.

Shoupe, U.S. v.

Shuford, U.S. v.

Sibron v. New York, 392 U.S. 40 (1968) — § 219; § 228; § 1528

Siegel, U.S. v.

Sielaff, U.S. ex rel. Anthony v.

Sielaff, U.S. ex rel. Barksdale v.

Sigal, U.S. v.

Signer, U.S. v.

Sihler, U.S. v.

Silkman, U.S. v.

Sills, De Vita v.

Silva, U.S. v.

Silverman, U.S. v.

Silverstein, U.S. v.

Silverthorne Lumber Co. v. U.S., 251 U.S. 385 (1920) — § 248

Silvestain, U.S. v.

Simmons, U.S. v.

Simmons v. U.S., 390 U.S. 377 (1968) — § 255; § 318; § 810; § 1906

Simmons v. U.S., 476 F.2d 715 (10th Cir. 1973) — § 1905

Simon, U.S. v.

Simonetti, U.S. v.

Simpkins, U.S. v.

Simpson v. Florida, 403 U.S. 384 (1971) — § 1011

Simpson v. Kreiger, 565 F.2d 390 (6th Cir. 1978) — § 1923

Simpson v. U.S., 195 F.2d 721 (9th Cir. 1952) — § 1707

Simpson v. U.S., 435 U.S. 6 (1978) — § 1012

Sims, U.S. v.

Sims v. U.S., 607 F.2d 757 (6th Cir. 1979) — § 1012

Sinclair v. Turner, 447 F.2d 1158 (10th Cir. 1971) — § 1815

Sinclair, U.S. v.

Sincox v. U.S., 571 F.2d 876 (5th Cir. 1978) — § 1242; § 1262

Sing Kee, U.S. v.

Singer v. U.S., 380 U.S. 24 (1965) — § 109; § 1243

Singleton v. Clemmer, 166 F.2d 963 (D.C. Cir. 1948) — § 113

Singleton v. Commissioner, 606 F.2d 50 (3d Cir. 1979) — § 241

Singleton, U.S. v.

Sink, U.S. v.

Sircovich, U.S. v.

Sirica, Haldeman v.

Sisson, U.S. v.

Sisto, U.S. v.

Sitz, Michigan Dept. of State Police v.

Skalicky, U.S. v.

Skar v. City of Lincoln, Nebraska, 599 F.2d 253 (8th Cir. 1979) — § 2003

Skinner v. Cardwell, 564 F.2d 1381 (9th Cir. 1977) — § 1109; § 1805; § 1811

Skinner, DeWitt v.

Skinner, U.S. v.

Skipper, U.S. v.

Skiriotes v. Florida, 313 U.S. 69 (1941) — § 1403

Sklaroff, U.S. v.

Sledge, U.S. v.

Slutsky, U.S. v.

Smaldone, U.S. v.

Smalis v. Pennsylvania, 476 U.S. 140 (1986) — § 1006; § 1010

Smallwood, U.S. v.

Smedes, U.S. v.

Smith, Alabama v.

Smith, Estelle v.

Smith v. Estelle, 569 F.2d 944 (5th Cir. 1978) — § 314

Smith v. Hooey, 393 U.S. 374 (1969) — § 1209; § 1233

Smith v. Illinois, 469 U.S. 91 (1984) — § 308

Smith v. Maryland, 442 U.S. 735 (1979) — § 201; § 267

Smith v. Ohio, 494 U.S. 541 (1990) — § 222; § 239

Smith v. Paderick, 519 F.2d 70 (4th Cir. 1975) — § 318

Smith, Payne v.

Smith v. Phillips, 455 U.S. 209 (1982) — § 718; § 1116; § 1249

Smith, Snowden v.

Smith, U.S. v.

Smith v. U.S., 337 U.S. 137 (1949) — § 1906

Smith v. U.S., 348 U.S. 147 (1954) — § 303

Smith v. U.S., 353 F.2d 838 (D.C. Cir. 1965) — § 2001

Smith v. U.S., 375 F.2d 243 (5th Cir. 1967) — § 401

Smith v. U.S., 416 F.2d 1255 (2d Cir. 1969) — § 807

Smith v. U.S., 635 F.2d 693 (8th Cir. 1980) — § 1235

Smith v. U.S., 670 F.2d 145 (11th Cir. 1982) — § 611

Smith, Virgin Islands v.

Smolar, U.S. v.

Smyth, U.S. v.

Snell, U.S. v.

Snelling, U.S. v.

Snow, U.S. v.

Snowden v. Smith, 413 F.2d 94 (7th Cir. 1969) — § 113

Snyder v. Coiner, 510 F.2d 224 (4th Cir. 1975) — § 1805

Snyder v. Massachusetts, 291 U.S. 97 (1934) — § 1611

Snyder, U.S. v.

Sobell, U.S. v.

Socony Vacuum Oil Co., U.S. v.

Sokolow, U.S. v.

Solano, U.S. v.

Soles, U.S. v.

Sonderup, U.S. v.

Soo Line R.R. Co. v. Fruehauf Corp., 547 F.2d 1365 (8th Cir. 1977) — § 2003

Sorenson, U.S. v.

Sor-Lokken, U.S. v.

Sorzano, U.S. v.

Sotoj-Lopez, U.S. v.

South Carolina, Ham v.

South Carolina, Lanier v.

South Central Bell Telephone Co., Clark v.

South Dakota v. Neville, 459 U.S. 553 (1983) — § 313

South Dakota v. Opperman, 428 U.S. 364 (1976) — § 235; § 236

Southern Pacific Transportation Co., Arcement v.

Southland Corp., U.S. v.

Sowders, Watkins v.

Spagnolo, U.S. v.

Spain, Rushen v.

Spain, U.S. v.

Spanjer Bros., Scott v.

Sparks, U.S. v.

Sparrow, U.S. v.

Spaulding, U.S. v.

Special April 1977 Grand Jury (Scott), In re

Special February Grand Jury v. Conlisk, 490 F.2d 894 (7th Cir. 1973) — § 414

Special Grand Jury, In re

Special Grand Jury (for Anchorage, Alaska), In re

Special Grand Jury No. 81-1, In re

Special March 1974 Grand Jury, In re

Special November 1975 Grand Jury, etc., In re

Special September Grand Jury II, In re

Spencer v. Turner, 486 F.2d 599 (10th Cir. 1972) — § 317

Sperling, U.S. v.

Sperry Rand Corp., IBM v.

Spevack v. Klein, 385 U.S. 511 (1967) — § 1905

Spiegel, U.S. v.

Spinelli v. U.S., 393 U.S. 410 (1969) — § 207

Splain, U.S. v.

Spraggins, U.S. v.

Spring, Colorado v.

Spruille, U.S. v.

Stacey, U.S. v.

Stack v. Boyle, 342 U.S. 1 (1952) — § 504

Staller, U.S. v.

Stanchich, U.S. v.

Standard Oil Co., U.S. v.

Standefer v. U.S., 447 U.S. 10 (1980) — § 1011

Standing Soldier, U.S. v.

Stanford Daily, Zurcher v.

Stanford v. Texas, 379 U.S. 476 (1965) — § 211

Stanford, U.S. v.

Stanley, U.S. v.

Stanley v. Wainwright, 604 F.2d 379 (5th Cir. 1979) — § 306

Star of Wisconsin v. Schaffer, 565 F.2d 961 (7th Cir. 1971) — § 414

Starkey v. Wyrick, 555 F.2d 1352 (8th Cir. 1977) — § 306

Starks, U.S. v.

Starr, U.S. v.

Starusko, U.S. v.

Stasiukevich v. Nicolls, 168 F.2d 474 (1st Cir. 1948) — § 1403

Stassi, U.S. v.

State v. Rogers, 271 S.E.2d 535 (N.C. 1980) — § 1219

Stavros, U.S. v.

Steagald v. U.S., 451 U.S. 204 (1981) — § 201; § 219; § 247

Stearns, U.S. v.

Steed, U.S. v.

Steele v. U.S., 267 U.S. 498 (1925) — § 211

Steinberg, U.S. v.

Steinkoetter, U.S. v.

Steinsvik v. Vinzant, 640 F.2d 949 (9th Cir. 1981) — § 609

Sten, U.S. v.

Stengel v. Belcher, 522 F.2d 438 (6th Cir. 1975) — § 2123

Stephen, U.S. v.

Stephens, U.S. v.

Stern, U.S. v.

Stern v. U.S., 409 F.2d 819 (2d Cir. 1969) — § 907

Sternman, U.S. v.

Stevens, U.S. v.

Stevie, U.S. v.

Stewart, U.S. v.

Stewart v. U.S., 366 U.S. 1 (1961) — § 1906

Stifel, U.S. v.

Stillman v. U.S., 177 F.2d 607 (9th Cir. 1949) — § 1702

Stinson, U.S. v.

Stirling, U.S. v.

Stirone, U.S. v.

Stober, U.S. v.

Stocks, U.S. v.

Stofsky, U.S. v.

Stokes v. U.S., 157 U.S. 187 (1895) — § 1703

Stoler v. Penn Central Transp. Co., 583 F.2d 896 (6th Cir. 1978) — § 2005

Stone v. Morris, 546 F.2d 730 (7th Cir. 1976) — § 2123

Stone, U.S. v.

Stone v. U.S., 385 F.2d 713 (10th Cir. 1967) — § 2001

Stone v. Wingo, 416 F.2d 857 (6th Cir. 1969) — § 1819

Stoner v. California, 376 U.S. 483 (1964) — § 222; § 245

Story, U.S. v.

Stout, U.S. v.

Stout v. U.S., 508 F.2d 951 (6th Cir. 1975) — § 609

Stovall v. Denno, 388 U.S. 293 (1967) — § 317; § 318; § 319; § 1903; § 2111

Stover, U.S. v.

Strahan, U.S. v.

Strahl, U.S. v.

Strand, U.S. v.

Stratton, U.S. v.

Strauss v. U.S., 311 F.2d 926 (5th Cir. 1963) — § 1703; § 2001
Street, Tennessee v.
Street, U.S. v.
Stricklin, U.S. v.
Strissel, U.S. v.
Stroman, U.S. v.
Strong, U.S. v.
Stulga, U.S. v.
Stull, U.S. v.
Sturgeon, U.S. v.
Sturgis, U.S. v.
Stynchcombe, Chaffin v.
Stynchcombe, Llewellyn v.
Suarez, U.S. v.
Suarez v. U.S., 582 F.2d 1007 (5th Cir. 1978) — § 1923
Suburban Sew 'N Sweep, Inc. v. Swiss-Bernina, Inc., 91 F.R.D. 254 (N.D. Ill. 1981) — § 1919
Suchy, U.S. v.
Sullivan, Cuyler v.
Sullivan, U.S. v.
Sullivan v. U.S., 411 F.2d 556 (10th Cir. 1969) — § 1817
Sumlin, U.S. v.
Summers v. McDermott, 138 F.2d 338 (3d Cir. 1943) — § 1703
Summers, Michigan v.
Summers, U.S. v.
Summerville, Illinois v.
Sumpter, U.S. v.
Superior Court of California, Press-Enterprise Co. v.
Sutton, U.S. v.
Sutton v. U.S., 157 F.2d 661 (5th Cir. 1946) — § 1305
Swain v. Alabama, 380 U.S. 202 (1965) — § 1246; § 1248
Swainson, U.S. v.
Sweet, U.S. v.
Sweig, U.S. v.
Swenson, Ashe v.
Swenson, Hendricks v.
Swift & Co., Herzig v.
Swihart, U.S. v.
Swiss-Bernina, Inc., Suburban Sew 'N Sweep, Inc. v.
Syal, U.S. v.
Syler, U.S. v.

T

Taborda, U.S. v.
Tager, U.S. v.
Taglione, U.S. v.
Talavera, U.S. v.
Tallent v. U.S., 604 F.2d 370 (5th Cir. 1979) — § 610
Tallo v. U.S., 344 F.2d 467 (1st Cir. 1967) — § 1913
Tanner v. Conover, 107 S. Ct. —, 41 Crim. L. Rep. 3340 (1987) — § 1259
Tanner, U.S. v.
Tanu, U.S. v.
Tarlowski, U.S. v.
Tarnowski, U.S. v.
Tasto, U.S. v.
Taxe, U.S. v.
Taylor v. Alabama, 102 S. Ct. 2664 (1982) — § 312
Taylor v. Arizona, 471 F.2d 848 (9th Cir. 1972) — § 220
Taylor v. Hayes, 418 U.S. 488 (1974) — § 1240
Taylor, Hickman v.
Taylor, In re
Taylor v. Kentucky, 436 U.S. 478 (1978) — § 1269
Taylor v. Louisiana, 419 U.S. 522 (1975) — § 1245
Taylor v. Mabry, 593 F.2d 318 (8th Cir. 1979) — § 1246
Taylor, U.S. v.
Taylor v. U.S., 388 F.2d 786 (9th Cir. 1967) — § 1819
Taylor, Virgin Islands v.
Taylor, Young v.
Tecumseh Prods., Schultz v.
Tedesco, U.S. v.
Tempesta, U.S. v.
Tennessee v. Street, 469 U.S. 929 (1985) — § 915
Tenorio-Angel, U.S. v.
Tercero, U.S. v.
Termini, U.S. v.
Terry v. Ohio, 392 U.S. 1 (1968) — § 219; § 228; § 241
Test v. U.S., 420 U.S. 28 (1975) — § 1245
Testa, U.S. v.
Testamark, Virgin Islands v.

Texaco, Inc., Burriss v.

Texas, Adams v.

Texas, Aguilar v.

Texas, Brown v.

Texas v. Brown, 460 U.S. 730 (1983) — § 238

Texas, Burgett v.

Texas v. McCullough, 106 S. Ct. 976 (1986) — § 1118

Texas, Orozco v.

Texas, Pointer v.

Texas, Stanford v.

Texas, Tucker v.

Texas v. U.S. Steel Corp., 546 F.2d 626 (5th Cir. 1977) — § 414

Texas v. White, 423 U.S. 67 (1975) — § 235

Texas Gulf Sulphur Co., SEC v.

Thetford, U.S. v.

Thevis, U.S. v.

Thiede v. Utah, 159 U.S. 510 (1895) — § 1820

Thigpen v. Roberts, 468 U.S. 27 (1984) — § 1118

Thirty-seven Photographs, U.S. v.

Thomann, U.S. v.

Thomas, Jones v.

Thomas, Michigan v.

Thomas, Morgan v.

Thomas, U.S. v.

Thomas v. U.S., 15 F.2d 958 (8th Cir. 1926) — § 302

Thomas v. U.S., 227 F.2d 667 (9th Cir. 1955) — § 1801

Thomas v. U.S., 418 F.2d 567 (5th Cir. 1969) — § 905

Thomas v. U.S., 597 F.2d 656 (8th Cir. 1979) — § 414

Thompson v. Louisiana, 469 U.S. 17 (1984) — § 232

Thompson, Payne v.

Thompson, U.S. v.

Thompson v. U.S., 444 U.S. 248 (1980) — § 1005

Thone, Pope v.

Thor v. U.S., 554 F.2d 759 (5th Cir. 1977) — § 102

Thorne, U.S. v.

Thornton, Fruehauf Corp. v.

Thurmond, U.S. v.

Tibbs v. Florida, 457 U.S. 31 (1982) — § 1006; § 1010

Tierney, In re

Tillman, U.S. v.

Timmreck, U.S. v.

Timpani, U.S. v.

Tingle, U.S. v.

Tinker v. U.S., 417 F.2d 542 (D.C. Cir. 1969) — § 1817

T.L.O., New Jersey v.

Tobin, U.S. v.

Tokoph, U.S. v.

Toler v. Wyrick, 563 F.2d 372 (8th Cir. 1977) — § 612

Tolias, U.S. v.

Tollett v. Henderson, 411 U.S. 258 (1973) — § 256

Tomaiolo, U.S. v.

Toney, U.S. v.

Torbert, U.S. v.

Torres v. Puerto Rico, 442 U.S. 465 (1979) — § 219

Torres, U.S. v.

Tortorello, U.S. v.

Toscanino, U.S. v.

Tot v. U.S., 319 U.S. 463 (1943) — § 1505

Toto, Virgin Islands v.

Trammel v. U.S., 445 U.S. 40 (1980) — § 1910; § 1913; § 1915

Tramunti, U.S. v.

Tranowski, U.S. v.

Trans Ocean Export Packing, Inc., NLRB v.

Travis v. U.S., 247 F.2d 130 (10th Cir. 1957) — § 1906

Travis v. U.S., 364 U.S. 631 (1961) — § 105

Traylor, U.S. v.

Trejo-Zambrano, U.S. v.

Trenary, U.S. v.

Trenton Potteries, Co., U.S. v.

Trevino, U.S. v.

Tri State Ins. Co., Worden v.

Trombetta, California v.

Tropeano, U.S. v.

Tropiano, U.S. v.

Trotter, U.S. v.

Troxler Hosiery Co., U.S. v.

Truesdale, U.S. v.

Truong Dihn Hung, U.S. v.

Tsanas, U.S. v.

Tucker v. Texas, 326 U.S. 517 (1946) —
§ 1403

Tucker, U.S. v.

Turbide, U.S. v.

Turcotte, U.S. v.

Turk, U.S. v.

Turley v. Lefkowitz, 342 F. Supp. 544
(W.D.N.Y. 1972) — § 1905

Turner v. Murray, 476 U.S. 28 (1986) —
§ 1246

Turner, Reed v.

Turner, Sinclair v.

Turner, Spencer v.

Turner, U.S. v.

Turner, Virgin Islands v.

Turquitt, U.S. v.

Tussell, U.S. v.

Tutt, U.S. v.

Tweel, U.S. v.

Twomey, Lego v.

Tyler, Michigan v.

Tyler, U.S. v.

# U

UCO Oil Co., U.S. v.

Udziela, U.S. v.

Ullmann v. U.S., 350 U.S. 422 (1956) —
§ 1901

Ulster County Court v. Allen, 442 U.S.
140 (1979) — § 1504; § 1505

Umbower, U.S. v.

Umentum, U.S. v.

Underhill v. Hernandez, 168 U.S. 250
(1897) — § 1403

Underwater Storage, Inc. v. U.S. Rubber
Co., 314 F. Supp. 546 (D.D.C. 1970) —
§ 1917

Underwood, U.S. v.

Uniformed Sanitation Men Association v.
Commissioner of Sanitation, 392 U.S.
280 (1968) — § 1905

Union Nacional De Trabajadores, U.S. v.

United Brotherhood of Carpenters and
Joiners of America v. U.S., 330 U.S. 395
(1947) — § 1264

United Klans of America v. McGovern,
453 F. Supp. 836 (N.D. Ala. 1978) —
§ 1403

U.S. v. Abascal, 564 F.2d 821 (9th Cir.
1977) — § 2105

U.S., Abbate v.

U.S., Abel v.

U.S. v. Abel, 469 U.S. 45 (1984) — § 1811

U.S., Abney v.

U.S. v. Aboumoussallem, 726 F.2d 906
(2d Cir. 1984) — § 1004

U.S. v. Abrams, 615 F.2d 541 (1st Cir.
1980) — § 211

U.S. v. Abramson, 553 F.2d 1164 (8th Cir.
1977) — § 210

U.S. v. Abshire, 471 F.2d 116 (5th Cir.
1972) — § 317

U.S. v. Acosta, 369 F.2d 41 (4th Cir. 1966)
— § 2003

U.S. v. Acosta, 669 F.2d 292 (5th Cir.
1982) — § 256

U.S., Adams v.

U.S. v. Adams, 566 F.2d 962 (5th Cir.
1978) — § 608

U.S. v. Adams, 581 F.2d 193 (9th Cir.
1978) — § 809; § 911

U.S. v. Adcock, 558 F.2d 397 (8th Cir.
1977) — § 1522; § 1524; § 1526; § 1532;
§ 2120

U.S. v. Adderly, 529 F.2d 1178 (5th Cir.
1976) — § 1102

U.S. v. Addison, 498 F.2d 741 (D.C. Cir.
1974) — § 2003

U.S. v. Agapito, 620 F.2d 324 (2d Cir.
1980) — § 201; § 255

U.S., Agnello v.

U.S. v. Agrusa, 541 F.2d 690 (8th Cir.
1976) — § 215; § 261

U.S. v. Aguero-Segovia, 622 F.2d 131 (5th
Cir. 1980) — § 1318

U.S. v. Aguilar-Pena, 887 F.2d 347 (1st
Cir. 1989) — § 1325

U.S. v. Agurs, 427 U.S. 97 (1976) — § 718;
§ 719; § 801; § 1108; § 1116; § 1302

U.S. v. Ahrens, 530 F.2d 781 (8th Cir.
1976) — § 2123

U.S. v. Ailstock, 546 F.2d 1285 (6th Cir.
1976) — § 1252

U.S. v. Ainesworth, 716 F.2d 769 (10th
Cir. 1983) — § 1317

U.S. v. Ajlouny, 629 F.2d 830 (2d Cir.
1980) — § 229

U.S. v. Akin, 562 F.2d 459 (7th Cir. 1977) — § 1103

U.S. v. Alamin, 895 F.2d 1335 (11th Cir. 1990) — § 1328

U.S. v. Alberico, 604 F.2d 1315 (10th Cir. 1979) — § 719; § 1603

U.S., Albernaz v.

U.S. v. Alberti, 568 F.2d 617 (2d Cir. 1977) — § 1006

U.S. v. Alden, 576 F.2d 772 (8th Cir. 1978) — § 235; § 239; § 317

U.S., Alderman v.

U.S. v. Aleman, 609 F.2d 298 (7th Cir. 1979) — § 1004

U.S. v. Alessi, 638 F.2d 466 (2d Cir. 1980) — § 1302

U.S. v. Alessio, 528 F.2d 1079 (9th Cir. 1976) — § 423

U.S. v. Alexander, 415 F.2d 1352 (7th Cir. 1969) — § 2001

U.S. v. Alexander, 559 F.2d 1339 (5th Cir. 1977) — § 1923

U.S., Alford v.

U.S. v. Algie, 667 F.2d 569 (6th Cir. 1982) — § 804

U.S. v. Allain, 671 F.2d 248 (7th Cir. 1982) — § 723; § 1114

U.S. v. Allard, 600 F.2d 1301 (9th Cir. 1979) — § 233; § 248

U.S., Allen v.

U.S. v. Allen, 457 F.2d 1361 (9th Cir. 1972) — § 1810

U.S. v. Allen, 497 F.2d 160 (5th Cir. 1974) — § 1513

U.S. v. Allen, 522 F.2d 1229 (6th Cir. 1975) — § 1706

U.S. v. Allen, 566 F.2d 1193 (3d Cir. 1977) — § 1923

U.S. v. Allen, 588 F.2d 1100 (5th Cir. 1979) — § 208

U.S. v. Allen, 629 F.2d 51 (D.C. Cir. 1980) — § 219

U.S. v. Allen, 873 F.2d 963 (6th Cir. 1989) — § 1312

U.S. v. Allery, 526 F.2d 1362 (8th Cir. 1975) — § 1908; § 1914

U.S. v. Allison, 616 F.2d 779 (5th Cir. 1980) — § 1276

U.S. v. Allison, 619 F.2d 1254 (8th Cir. 1980) — § 243

U.S. v. Allstate Mortgage Corporation, 507 F.2d 492 (7th Cir. 1974) — § 423

U.S. v. Allsup, 573 F.2d 1141 (9th Cir. 1978) — § 1118; § 1221

U.S., Almeida-Sanchez v.

U.S. v. Almonte, 594 F.2d 261 (1st Cir. 1979) — § 1249

U.S. v. Alonzo, 571 F.2d 1384 (5th Cir. 1978) — § 713; § 1923

U.S. v. Alpern, 564 F.2d 755 (7th Cir. 1977) — § 1112

U.S. v. Alred, 513 F.2d 330 (6th Cir. 1975) — § 1239

U.S. v. Alter, 482 F.2d 1016 (9th Cir. 1973) — § 425

U.S. v. Alvarado, 519 F.2d 1133 (5th Cir. 1975) — § 1402; § 1403

U.S. v. Alvarez, 519 F.2d 1036 (3d Cir. 1975) — § 710; § 1921

U.S. v. Alvarez, 584 F.2d 694 (5th Cir. 1978) — § 2144; § 2145

U.S. v. Alvarez-Lopez, 559 F.2d 1155 (9th Cir. 1977) — § 1811

U.S. v. Alvarez-Machain, 112 S. Ct. 2188 (1992) — § 103

U.S., Alvary v.

U.S. v. Alves, 873 F.2d 495 (1st Cir. 1989) — § 1323

U.S., Amador-Gonzalez v.

U.S. v. Amaral, 488 F.2d 1148 (9th Cir. 1973) — § 2003

U.S. v. Amaya, 533 F.2d 188 (5th Cir. 1976) — § 2140

U.S. v. Ambrosiani, 610 F.2d 65 (1st Cir. 1979) — § 1605

U.S. v. American Bag & Paper Corp., 609 F.2d 1066 (3d Cir. 1979) — § 611

U.S. v. American Cyanamid Co., 427 F. Supp. 859 (S.D.N.Y. 1977) — § 2123

U.S. v. American Radiator & Standard Sanitary Corp., 433 F.2d 174 (3d Cir. 1970) — § 1802

U.S. v. Ammirato, 670 F.2d 552 (5th Cir. 1982) — § 609; § 610

U.S. v. Amon, 669 F.2d 1351 (10th Cir. 1981) — § 305

U.S., Amsler v.

U.S. v. Anderson, 328 U.S. 699 (1946) — § 105

U.S. v. Anderson, 417 U.S. 211 (1974) —
§ 2102

U.S. v. Anderson, 481 F.2d 685 (4th Cir.
1973) —§ 717; § 1115

U.S. v. Anderson, 528 F.2d 590 (5th Cir.
1976) — § 1402; § 1403

U.S. v. Anderson, 532 F.2d 1218 (9th Cir.
1976) — § 1502

U.S. v. Anderson, 553 F.2d 1154 (8th Cir.
1977) — § 425

U.S. v. Anderson, 562 F.2d 394 (6th Cir.
1977) — § 1248

U.S. v. Anderson, 574 F.2d 1347 (5th Cir.
1978) — § 719; § 804; § 1108

U.S. v. Anderson, 577 F.2d 258 (5th Cir.
1978) — § 1602

U.S. v. Anderson, 626 F.2d 1358 (8th Cir.
1980) — § 913

U.S. v. Anderson, 724 F.2d 596 (7th Cir.
1984) — § 1318

U.S. v. Andreadis, 366 F.2d 423 (2d Cir.
1966) — § 2003

U.S., Andres v.

U.S. v. Andrews, 600 F.2d 563 (6th Cir.
1979) — § 228

U.S. v. Andrews, 612 F.2d 235 (6th Cir.
1979) — § 1118

U.S. v. Angiulo, 497 F.2d 440 (1st Cir.
1974) — § 109

U.S. v. Annunziato, 293 F.2d 373 (2d Cir.
1961) — § 2106

U.S. v. Anthon, 648 F.2d 669 (10th Cir.
1981) — § 222

U.S. v. Anthony, 565 F.2d 533 (8th Cir.
1977) — § 813

U.S. v. Antone, 603 F.2d 566 (5th Cir.
1979) — § 1107

U.S. v. Antonelli, 434 F.2d 335 (2d Cir.
1970) — § 306

U.S. v. Apfelbaum, 445 U.S. 115 (1980) —
§ 419; § 1903

U.S. v. Apodaca, 522 F.2d 568 (10th Cir.
1975) — § 1912

U.S. v. Appawoo, 553 F.2d 1242 (10th Cir.
1977) — § 1006

U.S. v. Apuzzo, 555 F.2d 306 (2d Cir.
1977) — § 1810

U.S. v. Archbold-Newball, 554 F.2d 665
(5th Cir. 1977) — § 310

U.S. v. Archer-Daniels-Midland Co., 785
F.2d 206 (8th Cir. 1986) — § 412

U.S. v. Argitakos, 862 F.2d 423 (2d Cir.
1988)— § 1311; § 1344

U.S. v. Arias, 575 F.2d 253 (9th Cir. 1978)
— § 2122

U.S. v. Armone, 363 F.2d 385 (2d Cir.
1966) — § 1403

U.S. v. Armored Transport, Inc., 629 F.2d
1313 (9th Cir. 1980) — § 401

U.S. v. Armstrong, 462 F.2d 408 (8th Cir.
1972) — § 1816

U.S. v. Armstrong, 621 F.2d 951 (9th Cir.
1980) — § 903; § 912

U.S., Arnott v.

U.S. v. Aronoff, 463 F. Supp. 454
(S.D.N.Y. 1978) — § 112

U.S. v. Aronoff, 466 F. Supp. 855
(S.D.N.Y. 1979) — § 1919

U.S. v. Arquelles, 594 F.2d 109 (5th Cir.
1979) — § 716

U.S. v. Arrasmith, 557 F.2d 1093 (5th Cir.
1977) — § 2001

U.S. v. Arroyo-Angulo, 580 F.2d 1137 (2d
Cir. 1978) — § 719; § 913

U.S. v. Arthur Young & Co., 465 U.S. 805
(1984) — § 1902; § 1917; § 1924

U.S. v. Artieri, 491 F.2d 440 (2d Cir.
1974) — § 215; § 219; § 226

U.S. v. Artuso, 618 F.2d 192 (2d Cir.
1980) — § 1272

U.S. v. Ash, 413 U.S. 300 (1973) — § 307;
§ 316

U.S. v. Ashley, 569 F.2d 975 (5th Cir.
1978) — § 1809

U.S. v. Askew, 584 F.2d 960 (10th Cir.
1978) — § 1207

U.S. v. Atencio, 586 F.2d 744 (9th Cir.
1978) — § 521

U.S. v. Atkins, 473 F.2d 308 (8th Cir.
1973) — § 2003

U.S. v. Atkins, 558 F.2d 133 (3d Cir.
1977) — § 2145

U.S. v. Augello, 451 F.2d 1167 (2d Cir.
1971) — § 807

U.S. v. Augustine, 189 F.2d 587 (3d Cir.
1951) — § 2003

U.S. v. Austin, 585 F.2d 1271 (5th Cir.
1978) — § 1502

U.S. v. Austin-Bagley Corp., 31 F.2d 229 (2d Cir. 1929) — § 1902

U.S. v. Auton, 570 F.2d 1284 (5th Cir. 1978) — § 1819

U.S. v. Avarello, 592 F.2d 1339 (5th Cir. 1979) — § 211; § 913

U.S. v. Avery, 621 F.2d 214 (5th Cir. 1980) — § 613

U.S. v. Aviles, 315 F.2d 186 (2d Cir. 1963) — § 803

U.S. v. Aviles, 623 F.2d 1192 (7th Cir. 1980) — § 1231

U.S. v. Awkard, 597 F.2d 667 (9th Cir. 1979) — § 1802

U.S. v. Axselle, 604 F.2d 1330 (10th Cir. 1979) — § 210

U.S. v. Azzarelli Constr. Co., 459 F. Supp. 146 (E.D. Ill. 1978) — § 718; § 719

U.S. v. Badalamente, 507 F.2d 12 (2d Cir. 1974) — § 722; § 807

U.S. v. Baggot, 463 U.S. 476 (1983) — § 416

U.S. v. Bagley, 105 S. Ct. 3375 (1985) — § 719; § 720; § 722

U.S. v. Bagley, 537 F.2d 162 (5th Cir. 1976) — § 2144; § 2145

U.S. v. Bagsby, 489 F.2d 725 (9th Cir. 1973) — § 1805

U.S. v. Bailey, 505 F.2d 417 (D.C. Cir. 1974) — § 1103

U.S. v. Bailey, 550 F.2d 1099 (8th Cir. 1977) — § 716; § 717

U.S. v. Bailey, 581 F.2d 341 (3d Cir. 1978) — § 2144; § 2147

U.S. v. Bailleul, 553 F.2d 731 (1st Cir. 1977) — § 314

U.S. v. Baird, 414 F.2d 700 (2d Cir. 1969) — § 1903

U.S., Baker v.

U.S. v. Baker, 494 F.2d 1262 (6th Cir. 1974) — § 1811

U.S. v. Baker, 520 F. Supp. 1080 (S.D. Iowa 1981) — § 216; § 232

U.S. v. Baker, 577 F.2d 1147 (4th Cir. 1978) — § 233

U.S. v. Baker, 589 F.2d 1008 (9th Cir. 1979) — § 261

U.S. v. Baker, 641 F.2d 1311 (9th Cir. 1981) — § 1211

U.S. v. Balana, 618 F.2d 624 (10th Cir. 1979) — § 2147

U.S. v. Baldarrama, 566 F.2d 560 (5th Cir. 1978) — § 1525

U.S., Ball v.

U.S. v. Ball, 163 U.S. 662 (1896) — § 1001; § 1006

U.S. v. Ballard, 418 F.2d 325 (9th Cir. 1969) — § 1515

U.S. v. Ballard, 573 F.2d 913 (5th Cir. 1978) — § 243

U.S. v. Ballard, 600 F.2d 1115 (5th Cir. 1979) — § 229

U.S. v. Ballard, 779 F.2d 287 (5th Cir. 1986) — § 1235

U.S. v. Baller, 519 F.2d 463 (4th Cir. 1975) — § 2003

U.S. v. Bambulas, 571 F.2d 525 (10th Cir. 1978) — § 609

U.S. v. Bank of New York & Trust Co., 77 F.2d 866 (2d Cir. 1935) — § 1403

U.S., Bank of Nova Scotia v.

U.S., Banks v.

U.S. v. Banks, 520 F.2d 627 (7th Cir. 1975) — § 1815

U.S. v. Barash, 365 F.2d 395 (2d Cir. 1966) — § 1813

U.S. v. Baratta, 397 F.2d 215 (2d Cir. 1968) — § 1804

U.S. v. Barber, 442 F.2d 517 (3d Cir. 1971) — § 916

U.S. v. Barboza, 612 F.2d 999 (5th Cir. 1980) — § 1213

U.S. v. Barbosa, 666 F.2d 704 (1st Cir. 1981) — § 907; § 1116

U.S. v. Barham, 595 F.2d 231 (5th Cir. 1979) — § 1107

U.S. v. Barker, 553 F.2d 1013 (6th Cir. 1977) — § 1111; § 1270; § 2003

U.S. v. Barker, 675 F.2d 1055 (9th Cir. 1982) — § 918; § 1512

U.S. v. Barletta, 565 F.2d 985 (8th Cir. 1977) — § 2003

U.S. v. Barlow, 693 F.2d 954 (6th Cir. 1982) — § 1301

U.S., Barnes v.

U.S. v. Barnes, 368 F.2d 567 (4th Cir. 1966) — § 1912

U.S. v. Barnes, 431 F.2d 878 (9th Cir. 1970) — § 306

U.S. v. Barnes, 586 F.2d 1052 (5th Cir. 1978) — § 2116

U.S. v. Barnes, 604 F.2d 121 (2d Cir. 1979) — § 210; § 1115; § 1246

U.S. v. Barney, 550 F.2d 1251 (10th Cir. 1977) — § 1237

U.S. v. Barrentine, 591 F.2d 1069 (5th Cir. 1979) — § 701

U.S. v. Barrett, 539 F.2d 244 (1st Cir. 1976) — § 2144; § 2145

U.S., Barrientos v.

U.S. v. Barron, 575 F.2d 752 (9th Cir. 1978) — § 702

U.S. v. Barry, 670 F.2d 583 (5th Cir. 1982) — § 228

U.S. v. Barry, 673 F.2d 912 (6th Cir. 1982) — § 201; § 202

U.S. v. Barton, 647 F.2d 224 (2d Cir. 1981) — § 1002

U.S. v. Bartone, 400 F.2d 459 (6th Cir. 1968) — § 1605

U.S. v. Bascaro, 742 F.2d 1335 (11th Cir. 1984) — § 1302

U.S., Bast v.

U.S. v. Bastone, 526 F.2d 971 (7th Cir. 1975) — § 268; § 1811

U.S. v. Basurto, 497 F.2d 781 (9th Cir. 1974) — § 403

U.S. v. Bater, 627 F.2d 349 (D.C. Cir. 1980) — § 412

U.S. v. Bates, 600 F.2d 505 (5th Cir. 1979) — § 1254

U.S., Batsell v.

U.S. v. Battista, 646 F.2d 237 (6th Cir. 1981) — § 403

U.S. v. Batts, 558 F.2d 513 (9th Cir. 1977) — § 1810

U.S. v. Baugus, 761 F.2d 506 (8th Cir. 1985) — § 1011

U.S. v. Bautista, 509 F.2d 675 (9th Cir. 1975) — § 1514

U.S. v. Bay, 748 F.2d 1344 (9th Cir. 1984) — § 1810

U.S. v. Baykowski, 583 F.2d 1046 (8th Cir. 1978) — § 318

U.S. v. Baylan, 620 F.2d 359 (2d Cir. 1980) — § 1002

U.S. v. Bazinet, 462 F.2d 982 (8th Cir. 1972) — § 913

U.S. v. Bazzano, 570 F.2d 1120 (3d Cir. 1977) — § 415

U.S. v. Beale, 445 F.2d 977 (5th Cir. 1971) — § 215

U.S. v. Beale, 674 F.2d 1327 (9th Cir. 1982) — § 206

U.S. v. Beaman, 631 F.2d 85 (6th Cir. 1980) — § 504

U.S. v. Bean, 564 F.2d 700 (5th Cir. 1977) — § 613

U.S. v. Bearden, 659 F.2d 590 (5th Cir. 1981) — § 400

U.S. v. Bear Killer, 534 F.2d 1253 (8th Cir. 1976) — § 304

U.S. v. Beasley, 519 F.2d 233 (5th Cir. 1975) — § 1264

U.S. v. Beasley, 550 F.2d 261 (5th Cir. 1977) — § 408

U.S. v. Beasley, 576 F.2d 626 (5th Cir. 1978) — § 718; § 801

U.S. v. Beattie, 541 F.2d 329 (2d Cir. 1976) — § 1902

U.S. v. Beattie, 613 F.2d 762 (9th Cir. 1980) — § 1261

U.S., Beavers v.

U.S. v. Beck, 598 F.2d 497 (9th Cir. 1979) — § 220; § 228

U.S. v. Becker, 569 F.2d 951 (5th Cir. 1978) — § 907

U.S. v. Becker, 585 F.2d 703 (4th Cir. 1978) — § 1209

U.S., Beckwith v.

U.S. v. Beech-Nut Nutrition Corp., 871 F.2d 1181 (2d Cir. 1989) — § 106

U.S. v. Beechum, 582 F.2d 898 (5th Cir. 1978) — § 1522; § 1523; § 1525; § 1805

U.S. v. Beeler, 587 F.2d 340 (6th Cir. 1978) — § 1514

U.S. v. Begun, 446 F.2d 32 (9th Cir. 1971) — § 912

U.S. v. Bejar-Matrecios, 618 F.2d 81 (9th Cir. 1980) — § 603

U.S. v. Belgrad, 894 F.2d 1092 (9th Cir. 1990) — § 1312

U.S. v. Bell, 335 F. Supp. 797 (E.D.N.Y. 1971) — § 1403

U.S. v. Bell, 457 F.2d 1231 (5th Cir. 1972) — § 207

U.S. v. Bell, 464 F.2d 667 (2d Cir. 1972) — § 241

U.S. v. Bell, 500 F.2d 1287 (2d Cir. 1974) — § 2140

U.S. v. Bell, 573 F.2d 1040 (8th Cir. 1978) — § 1252

U.S. v. Belleville, 505 F. Supp. 1083 (E.D. Mich. 1981) — § 1215

U.S., Bellis v.

U.S. v. Belt, 574 F.2d 1234 (5th Cir. 1978) — § 1274

U.S. v. Benchimol, 471 U.S. 453 (1985) — § 613

U.S. v. Benedetto, 571 F.2d 1246 (2d Cir. 1978) — § 1522; § 1807; § 1808; § 1813

U.S. v. Benfield, 593 F.2d 815 (8th Cir. 1979) — § 1603; § 2141; § 2147

U.S. v. Benjamin, 637 F.2d 1297 (7th Cir. 1981) — § 233

U.S. v. Bennett, 675 F.2d 596 (4th Cir. 1982) — § 318

U.S., Benson v.

U.S. v. Benson, 631 F.2d 1336 (8th Cir. 1980) — § 225

U.S., Bentley v.

U.S. v. Benveniste, 564 F.2d 335 (9th Cir. 1977) — § 2003; § 2145

U.S. v. Beran, 546 F.2d 1316 (8th Cir. 1976) — § 1301

U.S. v. Berardelli, 565 F.2d 24 (2d Cir. 1977) — § 420

U.S. v. Berardi, 675 F.2d 894 (7th Cir. 1982) — § 905

U.S. v. Berdick, 555 F.2d 1329 (5th Cir. 1977) — § 1819

U.S. v. Berenguer, 562 F.2d 206 (2d Cir. 1977) — § 226

U.S., Berger v.

U.S. v. Berger, 657 F.2d 88 (6th Cir. 1981) — § 419

U.S. v. Berkowitz, 429 F.2d 921 (1st Cir. 1970) — § 1502

U.S. v. Bermudez, 526 F.2d 89 (2d Cir. 1975) — § 2003

U.S. v. Bernard, 287 F.2d 715 (7th Cir. 1961) — § 1707

U.S. v. Bernard, 623 F.2d 551 (9th Cir. 1980) — § 803

U.S. v. Bernes, 602 F.2d 716 (5th Cir. 1979) — § 2102

U.S., Berra v.

U.S. v. Berrojo, 628 F.2d 368 (5th Cir. 1980) — § 1403

U.S. v. Bess, 593 F.2d 749 (6th Cir. 1979) — § 1102; § 1110; § 1111; § 1114

U.S. v. Bethea, 598 F.2d 331 (4th Cir. 1979) — § 245

U.S. v. Beusch, 596 F.2d 871 (9th Cir. 1979) — § 207

U.S., Beverly v.

U.S. v. Bey, 499 F.2d 194 (3d Cir. 1974) — § 601

U.S. v. Bianco, 534 F.2d 501 (2d Cir. 1976) — § 420

U.S. v. Bierey, 588 F.2d 620 (8th Cir. 1979) — § 318

U.S. v. Big Crow, 898 F.2d 1326 (8th Cir. 1990) — § 1326

U.S. v. Bigelow, 544 F.2d 904 (6th Cir. 1976) — § 1219

U.S. v. Bilir, 592 F.2d 735 (4th Cir. 1979) — § 229

U.S. v. Billingsley, 474 F.2d 63 (6th Cir. 1973) — § 1518

U.S. v. Bills, 555 F.2d 1250 (5th Cir. 1977) — § 247

U.S. v. Bilotti, 380 F.2d 649 (2d Cir. 1967) — § 1270

U.S. v. Bilsky, 664 F.2d 613 (6th Cir. 1981) — § 1238

U.S., Bins v.

U.S. v. Birdman, 602 F.2d 547 (3d Cir. 1979) — § 401

U.S. v. Birmley, 529 F.2d 103 (6th Cir. 1976) — § 701

U.S. v. Birnbaum, 337 F.2d 490 (2d Cir. 1976) — § 807

U.S., Bisno v.

U.S., Bittner v.

U.S. v. Bizzard, 674 F.2d 1382 (11th Cir. 1982) — § 1116; § 1207; § 1819

U.S. v. Blac, 472 F.2d 130 (6th Cir. 1972) — § 1905

U.S., Black v.

U.S. v. Black, 525 F.2d 668 (6th Cir. 1975) — § 1502

U.S. v. Black, 595 F.2d 1116 (5th Cir. 1979) — § 1522

U.S. v. Blackburn, 446 F.2d 1089 (5th Cir. 1971) — § 1918

U.S. v. Black Cloud, 590 F.2d 270 (8th Cir. 1979) — § 108; § 109

U.S. v. Blackwood, 456 F.2d 526 (2d Cir. 1972) — § 1817; § 1818

U.S., Blair v.

U.S. v. Blakemore, 489 F.2d 193 (6th Cir. 1973) — § 1514

U.S. v. Blakey, 607 F.2d 779 (7th Cir. 1979) — § 1602

U.S. v. Bland, 961 F.2d 123 (9th Cir. 1992) — § 2123

U.S. v. Blane, 375 F.2d 249 (6th Cir. 1967) — § 1264

U.S. v. Blanton, 697 F.2d 146 (6th Cir. 1983) — § 1304

U.S., Blare v.

U.S. v. Blasco, 581 F.2d 681 (7th Cir. 1978) — § 1010

U.S., Blau v.

U.S. v. Bleckner, 601 F.2d 382 (9th Cir. 1979) — § 1805

U.S. v. Blevins, 593 F.2d 646 (5th Cir. 1979) — § 1204; § 1239

U.S. v. Blewitt, 538 F.2d 1099 (5th Cir. 1976) — § 1526

U.S. v. Blitz, 533 F.2d 1329 (2d Cir. 1976) — § 1814

U.S. v. Block, 590 F.2d 535 (4th Cir. 1978) — § 245

U.S., Blockburger v.

U.S. v. Bloom, 538 F.2d 704 (5th Cir. 1976) — § 1526

U.S. v. Bloomfield, 594 F.2d 1200 (8th Cir. 1979) — § 236

U.S. v. Blouin, 666 F.2d 796 (2d Cir. 1981) — § 1248

U.S. v. Blue, 384 U.S. 251 (1966) — § 403

U.S. v. Blum, 614 F.2d 537 (6th Cir. 1980) — § 306

U.S., Blumenthal v.

U.S. v. Boatner, 478 F.2d 737 (2d Cir. 1973) — § 1817

U.S. v. Boberg, 565 F.2d 1059 (8th Cir. 1977) — § 404

U.S. v. Bobo, 477 F.2d 974 (4th Cir. 1973) — § 1905

U.S. v. Bobo, 586 F.2d 355 (5th Cir. 1978) — § 1009; § 1819

U.S. v. Bockius, 564 F.2d 1193 (5th Cir. 1977) — § 716

U.S. v. Bodey, 607 F.2d 265 (9th Cir. 1979) — § 1006

U.S. v. Boe, 491 F.2d 970 (8th Cir. 1974) — § 425

U.S. v. Bohle, 445 F.2d 54 (7th Cir. 1971) — § 109; § 1704; § 1921

U.S. v. Bohle, 475 F.2d 872 (2d Cir. 1973) — § 1502

U.S. v. Bolden, 461 F.2d 998 (8th Cir. 1972) — § 306

U.S., Bollenbach v.

U.S. v. Bolzer, 556 F.2d 948 (9th Cir. 1977) — § 1910

U.S. v. Bonanno, 430 F.2d 1060 (2d Cir. 1970) — § 1811

U.S. v. Bonanno, 487 F.2d 654 (2d Cir. 1973) — § 268; § 1602

U.S. v. Bonds, 422 F.2d 660 (8th Cir. 1970) — § 219

U.S. v. Boney, 572 F.2d 397 (2d Cir. 1978) — § 109

U.S. v. Boone, 869 F.2d 1089 (8th Cir. 1989) — § 618

U.S. v. Booth, 673 F.2d 27 (1st Cir. 1982) — § 1002; § 1005

U.S. v. Booz, 451 F.2d 719 (3d Cir. 1971) — § 1501

U.S. v. Borelli, 336 F.2d 376 (2d Cir. 1964) — § 807; § 1813

U.S. v. Borrero-Isaza, 887 F.2d 1349 (9th Cir. 1989) — § 1322

U.S. v. Bosby, 675 F.2d 1174 (11th Cir. 1982) — § 236; § 308; § 1246

U.S. v. Boscia, 573 F.2d 827 (3d Cir. 1978) — § 914; § 1249

U.S. v. Bostic, 206 F. Supp. 855 (D.D.C. 1962) — § 1919

U.S. v. Boston, 508 F.2d 1171 (2d Cir. 1974) — § 318

U.S. v. Botero, 589 F.2d 430 (9th Cir. 1979) — § 233

U.S. v. Bottone, 365 F.2d 389 (2d Cir. 1966) — § 306

U.S. v. Boulahanis, 677 F.2d 586 (7th Cir. 1982) — § 2147

U.S. v. Bourassa, 411 F.2d 69 (10th Cir. 1969) — § 904

U.S., Bourjaily v.

U.S. v. Bourque, 541 F.2d 290 (1st Cir. 1976) — § 1118

U.S. v. Bowers, 534 F.2d 186 (9th Cir. 1976) — § 2003

U.S. v. Bowers, 593 F.2d 376 (10th Cir. 1979) — § 708; § 1818; § 2123

U.S. v. Bowler, 585 F.2d 851 (7th Cir. 1978) — § 613

U.S., Bowles v.

U.S. v. Bowman, 602 F.2d 160 (8th Cir. 1979) — § 903; § 904

U.S. v. Bowman, 609 F.2d 12 (D.C. Cir. 1979) — § 2141

U.S., Bowman Dairy Co. v.

U.S. v. Boyce, 594 F.2d 1246 (9th Cir. 1979) — § 308; § 2144

U.S., Boyd v.

U.S. v. Boyd, 566 F.2d 929 (5th Cir. 1978) — § 1006; § 2104

U.S. v. Boyd, 595 F.2d 120 (3d Cir. 1978) — § 1522

U.S. v. Boyd, 610 F.2d 521 (8th Cir. 1979) — § 913; § 916; § 917

U.S. v. Boyer, 574 F.2d 951 (8th Cir. 1978) — § 304

U.S. v. Boyle, 675 F.2d 430 (1st Cir. 1982) — § 1528

U.S. v. Bozza, 234 F. Supp. 15 (E.D.N.Y. 1964) — § 701

U.S. v. Braasch, 505 F.2d 139 (7th Cir. 1974) — § 408

U.S. v. Bradley, 455 F.2d 1181 (1st Cir. 1972) — § 215

U.S. v. Bradwell, 388 F.2d 619 (2d Cir. 1968) — § 1532

U.S., Brady v.

U.S. v. Brady, 579 F.2d 1121 (9th Cir. 1978) — § 1516

U.S. v. Brady, 595 F.2d 359 (6th Cir. 1979) — § 1517

U.S. v. Brady, 895 F.2d 538 (9th Cir. 1990) — § 1312

U.S. v. Brady, 928 F.2d 844 (9th Cir. 1991) — § 1324

U.S. v. Branan, 457 F.2d 1062 (6th Cir. 1972) — § 108

U.S. v. Brandenfels, 522 F.2d 1259 (9th Cir. 1975) — § 2145

U.S. v. Brandon, 633 F.2d 773 (9th Cir. 1980) — § 1272; § 1502

U.S. v. Brannon, 546 F.2d 1242 (5th Cir. 1977) — § 1906

U.S. v. Brasco, 516 F.2d 816 (2d Cir. 1975) — § 2141

U.S., Brasfield v.

U.S. v. Brashier, 548 F.2d 1315 (9th Cir. 1976) — § 1530

U.S., Braswell v.

U.S. v. Braunstein, 474 F. Supp. 1 (D.N.J. 1979) — § 1801

U.S., Braverman v.

U.S., Braxton v.

U.S. v. Breedlove, 576 F.2d 57 (5th Cir. 1978) — § 1249

U.S. v. Brewer, 899 F.2d 503 (6th Cir. 1990) — § 1324; § 1326

U.S. v. Brickley, 426 F.2d 680 (8th Cir. 1970) — § 1605

U.S. v. Bridwell, 583 F.2d 1135 (10th Cir. 1978) — § 250; § 309; § 911

U.S. v. Briggs, 457 F.2d 908 (2d Cir. 1972) — § 1817

U.S. v. Bright, 588 F.2d 504 (5th Cir. 1979) — § 1261; § 1520

U.S. v. Bright, 630 F.2d 804 (5th Cir. 1980) — § 913

U.S. v. Brighton Building & Maintenance Co., 435 F. Supp. 222 (N.D. Ill. 1977) — § 718

U.S. v. Brighton Building & Maintenance Co., 598 F.2d 1101 (7th Cir. 1979) — § 1250

U.S. v. Brightwell, 563 F.2d 569 (3d Cir. 1977) — § 234

U.S. v. Brignoni-Ponce, 422 U.S 873 (1975) — § 228; § 229

U.S. v. Brim, 630 F.2d 1307 (8th Cir. 1980) — § 918; § 1223

U.S., Brinegar v.

U.S. v. Brittman, 872 F.2d 827 (8th Cir. 1989) — § 1312

U.S. v. Broadhead, 413 F.2d 1351 (7th Cir. 1969) — § 319

U.S. v. Broce, 488 U.S. 563 (1989) — § 603

U.S., Brock v.

U.S. v. Brock, 667 F.2d 1311 (9th Cir. 1982) — § 211

U.S. v. Bronco, 597 F.2d 1300 (9th Cir. 1979) — § 903; § 912

U.S., Brown v.

U.S. v. Brown, 349 F. Supp. 420 (N.D. Ill. 1972) — § 1917; § 1918

U.S. v. Brown, 411 F.2d 1134 (10th Cir. 1969) — § 1532

U.S. v. Brown, 456 F.2d 293 (2d Cir. 1972) — § 1502

U.S. v. Brown, 478 F.2d 1038 (7th Cir. 1973) — § 1917

U.S. v. Brown, 535 F.2d 424 (8th Cir. 1976) — § 313

U.S. v. Brown, 540 F.2d 1048 (10th Cir. 1976) — § 2001; § 2003

U.S. v. Brown, 541 F.2d 858 (10th Cir. 1976) — § 1116

U.S. v. Brown, 546 F.2d 166 (5th Cir. 1977) — § 1811

U.S. v. Brown, 547 F.2d 36 (3d Cir. 1976) — § 1819

U.S. v. Brown, 547 F.2d 438 (8th Cir. 1977) — § 1011; § 1817

U.S. v. Brown, 547 F.2d 1264 (5th Cir. 1977) — § 1516

U.S. v. Brown, 556 F.2d 304 (5th Cir. 1977) — § 215

U.S. v. Brown, 557 F.2d 541 (6th Cir. 1977) — § 301; § 313; § 2003

U.S. v. Brown, 562 F.2d 1144 (9th Cir. 1977) — § 713; § 719

U.S. v. Brown, 573 F.2d 1274 (5th Cir. 1978) — § 403

U.S. v. Brown, 582 F.2d 197 (2d Cir. 1978) — § 1261

U.S. v. Brown, 584 F.2d 252 (8th Cir. 1978) — § 208; § 1516

U.S. v. Brown, 587 F.2d 187 (5th Cir. 1979) — § 1272; § 1301

U.S. v. Brown, 600 F.2d 248 (10th Cir. 1979) — § 1207

U.S. v. Brown, 602 F.2d 1073 (2d Cir. 1979) — § 1272

U.S. v. Brown, 603 F.2d 1022 (1st Cir. 1979) — § 1801

U.S. v. Brown, 604 F.2d 557 (8th Cir. 1979) — § 1602

U.S. v. Brown, 617 F.2d 54 (4th Cir. 1980) — § 618

U.S. v. Brown, 671 F.2d 585 (D.C. Cir. 1982) — § 225

U.S. v. Brown, 742 F.2d 363 (7th Cir. 1984) — § 1304

U.S. v. Brown, 870 F.2d 1354 (7th Cir. 1989) — § 1339

U.S. v. Brown, 903 F.2d 540 (8th Cir. 1990) — § 1326

U.S. v. Brown, 961 F.2d 1039 (2d Cir. 1992) — § 245

U.S. v. Browne, 313 F.2d 197 (2d Cir. 1963) — § 1805

U.S., Brunelle v.

U.S. v. Bruner, 657 F.2d 1278 (D.C. Cir. 1981) — § 1703

U.S. v. Brunk, 615 F.2d 210 (5th Cir. 1980) — § 1002; § 1011

U.S., Bruno v.

U.S. v. Brunson, 549 F.2d 348 (5th Cir. 1977) — § 1522

U.S., Bruton v.

U.S. v. Bruzgo, 373 F.2d 383 (3d Cir. 1967) — § 404

U.S. v. Bryant, 439 F.2d 642 (D.C. Cir. 1971) — § 708

U.S. v. Bryant, 461 F.2d 912 (6th Cir. 1972) — § 1264; § 1801

U.S. v. Bryant, 563 F.2d 1227 (5th Cir. 1977) — § 1611

U.S. v. Bryant, 612 F.2d 799 (4th Cir. 1979) — § 1254

U.S. v. Bryant, 612 F.2d 806 (4th Cir. 1979) — § 1219; § 1221

U.S. v. Bryant, 640 F.2d 170 (8th Cir. 1981) — § 618

U.S. v. Bryant, 671 F.2d 450 (11th Cir. 1982) — § 1248

U.S. v. Bryza, 522 F.2d 414 (7th Cir. 1975) — § 1511

U.S. v. Buchanan, 585 F.2d 100 (5th Cir. 1978) — § 709

U.S. v. Buckley, 586 F.2d 498 (5th Cir. 1978) — § 708; § 712; § 1918

U.S. v. Buege, 578 F.2d 187 (7th Cir. 1978) — § 1252

U.S. v. Buenrostro, 868 F.2d 135 (5th Cir. 1989) — § 1346

U.S. v. Buettner-Jamusch, 646 F.2d 759 (2d Cir. 1981) — § 245

U.S. v. Bufalino, 576 F.2d 446 (2d Cir. 1978) — § 810; § 812

U.S. v. Bull, 565 F.2d 869 (4th Cir. 1977) — § 228

U.S. v. Bullock, 590 F.2d 117 (5th Cir. 1979) — § 243

U.S. v. Bunch, 730 F.2d 517 (7th Cir. 1984) — § 1316

U.S. v. Burch, 873 F.2d 765 (5th Cir. 1989) — § 1322; § 1339

U.S. v. Burgard, 551 F.2d 190 (8th Cir. 1977) — § 304

U.S. v. Burgos, 579 F.2d 749 (2d Cir. 1978) — § 304

U.S., Burke v.

U.S. v. Burkhalter, 583 F.2d 389 (8th Cir. 1978) — § 1204; § 1233

U.S. v. Burkley, 591 F.2d 903 (D.C. Cir. 1978) — § 904

U.S., Burks v.

U.S. v. Burks, 470 F.2d 432 (D.C. Cir. 1972) — § 1910; § 1911

U.S. v. Burnett, 476 F.2d 726 (5th Cir. 1973) — § 1512

U.S., Burney v.

U.S., Burns v.

U.S. v. Burns, 597 F.2d 939 (5th Cir. 1979) — § 1504

U.S. v. Burns, 668 F.2d 855 (5th Cir. 1982) — § 1116; § 1304

U.S. v. Burrell, 963 F.2d 976 (7th Cir. 1992) — § 1250; § 1328

U.S. v. Burse, 531 F.2d 1151 (2d Cir. 1976) — § 1501

U.S., Bursey v.

U.S., Busby v.

U.S. v. Busic, 592 F.2d 13 (2d Cir. 1978) — § 243

U.S. v. Bustamante-Gamez, 488 F.2d 4 (9th Cir. 1973) — § 215

U.S. v. Butcher, 557 F.2d 666 (9th Cir. 1977) — § 2001

U.S. v. Butera, 677 F.2d 1376 (11th Cir. 1982) — § 1819

U.S. v. Butler, 567 F.2d 885 (9th Cir. 1978) — § 719; § 722; § 1107; § 1303

U.S. v. Butler, 611 F.2d 1066 (5th Cir. 1980) — § 914

U.S. v. Buttorff, 572 F.2d 619 (8th Cir. 1978) — § 2113

U.S. v. Butts, 524 F.2d 975 (5th Cir. 1975) — § 1239

U.S. v. Bycer, 593 F.2d 549 (3d Cir. 1979) — § 1516

U.S. v. Bynum, 485 F.2d 490 (2d Cir. 1973) — § 264

U.S. v. Bynum, 513 F.2d 533 (2d Cir. 1975) — § 262

U.S. v. Cabral, 475 F.2d 715 (1st Cir. 1973) — § 1212

U.S., Cacy v.

U.S. v. Cafero, 473 F.2d 489 (3d Cir. 1973) — § 257; § 262; § 1905

U.S. v. Caggiano, 667 F.2d 1176 (5th Cir. 1982) — § 266; § 1246

U.S., Caha v.

U.S. v. Cain, 544 F.2d 1113 (1st Cir. 1976) — § 1906

U.S. v. Cain, 587 F.2d 678 (5th Cir. 1979) — § 2118

U.S. v. Calandra, 414 U.S. 338 (1974) — § 403; § 404; § 406

U.S. v. Calandrella, 605 F.2d 236 (6th Cir. 1979) — § 1110; § 1111

U.S. v. Caldera, 421 F.2d 152 (9th Cir. 1970) — § 224

U.S. v. Caldwell, 543 F.2d 1333 (D.C. Cir. 1974) — § 706; § 913

U.S. v. Calhoun, 542 F.2d 1094 (9th Cir. 1976) — § 244

U.S. v. Calhoun, 544 F.2d 291 (6th Cir. 1976) — § 2001

U.S., Callahan v.

U.S. v. Callahan, 551 F.2d 733 (6th Cir. 1977) — § 1531; § 1805

U.S. v. Callahan, 588 F.2d 1078 (5th Cir. 1979) — § 1518

U.S. v. Calvert, 498 F.2d 409 (6th Cir. 1974) — § 1103

U.S. v. Cammisano, 599 F.2d 851 (8th Cir. 1979) — § 609

U.S. v. Campagnuolo, 592 F.2d 852 (5th Cir. 1979) — § 717; § 718; § 723; § 801; § 804

U.S. v. Campanile, 516 F.2d 288 (2d Cir. 1975) — § 209

U.S., Campbell v.

U.S. v. Campbell, 426 F.2d 547 (2d Cir. 1970) — § 1811

U.S. v. Campbell, 575 F.2d 505 (5th Cir. 1978) — § 224

U.S. v. Campbell, 581 F.2d 22 (2d Cir. 1978) — § 233

U.S. v. Campisi, 583 F.2d 692 (3d Cir. 1978) — § 1320

U.S., Canaday v.

U.S. v. Canales, 572 F.2d 1182 (6th Cir. 1978) — § 220

U.S. v. Canales, 573 F.2d 908 (5th Cir. 1978) — § 1207

U.S., Cancino v.

U.S. v. Canniff, 521 F.2d 565 (2d Cir. 1975) — § 1520; § 1810; § 1818

U.S. v. Cannizzaro, 871 F.2d 809 (9th Cir. 1989) — § 1337

U.S. v. Cannone, 528 F.2d 296 (2d Cir. 1975) — § 712; § 713

U.S. v. Cantu, 555 F.2d 1327 (5th Cir. 1977) — § 1609

U.S. v. Capra, 501 F.2d 267 (2d Cir. 1974) — § 262

U.S. v. Cardello, 473 F.2d 325 (4th Cir. 1973) — § 521

U.S. v. Cardillo, 316 F.2d 606 (2d Cir. 1963) — § 807

U.S. v. Carey, 475 F.2d 1019 (9th Cir. 1973) — § 1265

U.S. v. Carey, 895 F.2d 318 (7th Cir. 1990) — § 1326

U.S. v. Carignan, 342 U.S. 36 (1951) — § 501

U.S. v. Carini, 562 F.2d 144 (2d Cir. 1977) — § 1225

U.S. v. Carleo, 576 F.2d 846 (10th Cir. 1978) — § 1115

U.S. v. Carlone, 666 F.2d 1112 (7th Cir. 1981) — § 1231

U.S. v. Carlson, 547 F.2d 1346 (8th Cir. 1976) — § 2140; § 2147

U.S. v. Carneglia, 468 F.2d 1084 (2d Cir. 1972) — § 1513; § 1923

U.S. v. Caro, 569 F.2d 411 (5th Cir. 1978) — § 2101; § 2116

U.S., Carpenter v.

U.S. v. Carranco, 551 F.2d 1197 (10th Cir. 1977) — § 2123

U.S. v. Carrasco, 537 F.2d 372 (9th Cir. 1976) — § 808; § 813

U.S. v. Carrasquillo, 667 F.2d 382 (3d Cir. 1981) — § 1213; § 1231

U.S. v. Carreon, 626 F.2d 528 (7th Cir. 1980) — § 1234

U.S. v. Carriger, 541 F.2d 545 (6th Cir. 1976) — § 221

U.S. v. Carriger, 592 F.2d 312 (6th Cir. 1979) — § 1701

U.S. v. Carrillo, 561 F.2d 1125 (5th Cir. 1977) — § 807; § 1526

U.S., Carroll v.

U.S. v. Carroll, 582 F.2d 942 (5th Cir. 1978) — § 1246

U.S. v. Carroll, 591 F.2d 1132 (5th Cir. 1979) — § 228

U.S. v. Carroll, 893 F.2d 1502 (6th Cir. 1990) — § 1323; § 1339

U.S. v. Carsello, 578 F.2d 199 (7th Cir. 1978) — § 248

U.S. v. Carson, 464 F.2d 424 (2d Cir. 1972) — § 905

U.S. v. Carter, 433 F.2d 874 (10th Cir. 1970) — § 1501

U.S. v. Carter, 566 F.2d 1265 (5th Cir. 1978) — § 215; § 233; § 1107

U.S. v. Carter, 603 F.2d 1204 (5th Cir. 1979) — § 1207

U.S. v. Carter, 619 F.2d 293 (3d Cir. 1980) — § 607

U.S. v. Carter, 621 F.2d 238 (6th Cir. 1980) — § 807

U.S. v. Carter, 662 F.2d 274 (4th Cir. 1981) — § 608

U.S. v. Carver, 671 F.2d 577 (D.C. Cir. 1982) — § 401

U.S. v. Case, 435 F.2d 766 (7th Cir. 1970) — § 215

U.S. v. Caserta, 199 F.2d 905 (3d Cir. 1952) — § 1803

U.S., Cash v.

U.S., Casias v.

U.S. v. Cassasa, 588 F.2d 282 (9th Cir. 1978) — § 1517

U.S. v. Castanon, 453 F.2d 932 (9th Cir. 1972) — § 1905

U.S. v. Castenada, 555 F.2d 605 (7th Cir. 1977) — § 1260

U.S. v. Castillo, 615 F.2d 878 (9th Cir. 1980) — § 615

U.S. v. Castro, 506 F.2d 674 (5th Cir. 1979) — § 222

U.S. v. Castro-Ayon, 537 F.2d 1055 (9th Cir. 1976) — § 2109

U.S., Catches v.

U.S. v. Cathey, 591 F.2d 268 (5th Cir. 1979) — § 1810

U.S., Cave v.

U.S. v. Cavender, 578 F.2d 528 (4th Cir. 1978) — § 1809; § 1810

U.S. v. Ceccolini, 435 U.S. 268 (1978) — § 248

U.S. v. Celaya-Garcia, 583 F.2d 210 (5th Cir. 1978) — § 112

U.S. v. Cella, 568 F.2d 1266 (9th Cir. 1977) — § 312

U.S. v. Cepeda Penes, 577 F.2d 754 (1st Cir. 1978) — § 304; § 1247; § 1610; § 2127

U.S. v. Chadwick, 433 U.S. 1 (1977) — § 222; § 225; § 235

U.S. v. Chaffen, 587 F.2d 920 (8th Cir. 1978) — § 220

U.S. v. Chagra, 669 F.2d 241 (5th Cir. 1982) — § 423; § 1002

U.S. v. Champion International Corp., 557 F.2d 1270 (9th Cir. 1977) — § 1814

U.S. v. Chanen, 540 F.2d 1306 (9th Cir. 1977) — § 402

U.S. v. Chapin, 515 F.2d 1274 (D.C. Cir. 1975) — § 111

U.S. v. Chaplinski, 579 F.2d 373 (5th Cir. 1978) — § 712

U.S., Chapman v.

U.S. v. Charleus, 871 F.2d 265 (2d Cir. 1989) — § 1311

U.S. v. Charlton, 565 F.2d 86 (6th Cir. 1977) — § 308; § 313

U.S., Chatman v.

U.S. v. Chatman, 573 F.2d 565 (9th Cir. 1977) — § 222; § 224

U.S. v. Chavez, 416 U.S. 562 (1974) — § 266

U.S. v. Cheape (Appeal of Klinefelter), 889 F.2d 477 (3d Cir. 1989) — § 1326

U.S., Chee v.

U.S., Cheek v.

U.S. v. Cheyenne, 558 F.2d 902 (8th Cir. 1977) — § 1802

U.S. v. Chiarizio, 525 F.2d 289 (2d Cir. 1975) — § 261; § 1602

U.S. v. Childs, 598 F.2d 169 (D.C. Cir. 1979) — § 1603

U.S. v. Chimurenga, 760 F.2d 400 (2d Cir. 1985) — § 512

U.S. v. Chisem, 667 F.2d 1192 (5th Cir. 1982) — § 1115

U.S. v. Chitwood, 457 F.2d 676 (6th Cir. 1972) — § 805; § 809

U.S. v. Choate, 276 F.2d 724 (5th Cir. 1960) — § 102; § 109

U.S. v. Chong, 544 F.2d 58 (2d Cir. 1976) — § 1103

U.S. v. Christian, 571 F.2d 64 (1st Cir. 1978) — § 305

U.S. v. Christman, 894 F.2d 339 (9th Cir. 1990) — § 1323

U.S., Christoffel v.

U.S., Chua Han Mow v.

U.S. v. Ciampaglia, 628 F.2d 632 (1st Cir. 1980) — § 913

U.S. v. Cifarelli, 401 F.2d 512 (2d Cir. 1968) — § 1532

U.S. v. Cioffi, 493 F.2d 1111 (2d Cir. 1974) — § 2001

U.S. v. Cirillo, 499 F.2d 872 (2d Cir. 1974) — § 262

U.S. v. Civella, 666 F.2d 1122 (8th Cir. 1981) — § 401

U.S. v. Clabaugh, 589 F.2d 1019 (9th Cir. 1979) — § 1246

U.S. v. Clancy, 276 F.2d 617 (7th Cir. 1960) — § 204

U.S. v. Clark, 407 F.2d 1336 (4th Cir. 1969) — § 601

U.S. v. Clark, 525 F.2d 314 (2d Cir. 1975) — § 306

U.S. v. Clark, 531 F.2d 928 (8th Cir. 1976) — § 247

U.S. v. Clark, 613 F.2d 391 (2d Cir. 1979) — § 1011

U.S. v. Clarkson, 567 F.2d 270 (4th Cir. 1977) — § 418

U.S. v. Clavey, 565 F.2d 111 (7th Cir. 1978) — § 415

U.S. v. Clements, 588 F.2d 1030 (5th Cir. 1979) — § 1605

U.S. v. Cleveland, 507 F.2d 731 (7th Cir. 1974) — § 807

U.S. v. Cleveland, 590 F.2d 24 (1st Cir. 1978) — § 314

U.S. v. Cleveland Trust Co., 474 F.2d 1234 (6th Cir. 1973) — § 1902

U.S. v. Cline, 570 F.2d 731 (8th Cir. 1978) — § 2104; § 2113

U.S. v. Cloud, 872 F.2d 846 (9th Cir. 1989) — § 1337

U.S. v. Clouston, 623 F.2d 485 (6th Cir. 1980) — § 213

U.S. v. Cluchette, 465 F.2d 749 (9th Cir. 1972) — § 304

U.S. v. Cluck, 544 F.2d 195 (5th Cir. 1976) — § 1809; § 1810

U.S. v. Coades, 549 F.2d 1303 (9th Cir. 1977) — § 302; § 318; § 1524

U.S., Cobb v.

U.S. v. Coe, 891 F.2d 405 (2d Cir. 1989) — § 1325

U.S. v. Coffey, 871 F.2d 39 (6th Cir. 1989) — § 1321

U.S., Cohen v.

U.S. v. Cohen, 388 F.2d 464 (9th Cir. 1967) — § 1902

U.S. v. Cohen, 444 F. Supp. 1314 (E.D. Pa. 1978) — § 404

U.S. v. Cohen, 518 F.2d 727 (2d Cir. 1975) — § 701

U.S. v. Coke, 339 F.2d 183 (2d Cir. 1964) — § 1923

U.S. v. Coker, 599 F.2d 950 (10th Cir. 1979) — § 219

U.S. v. Colasurdo, 453 F.2d 585 (2d Cir. 1971) — § 401

U.S. v. Colatriano, 624 F.2d 686 (5th Cir. 1980) — § 907

U.S. v. Colclough, 549 F.2d 937 (4th Cir. 1977) — § 318; § 1516

U.S. v. Cole, 449 F.2d 194 (8th Cir. 1971) — § 1805

U.S. v. Coleman, 340 F. Supp. 451 (E.D. Pa. 1972) — § 1816

U.S. v. Coleman, 631 F.2d 908 (D.C. Cir. 1980) — § 503

U.S. v. Coleman, 688 F.2d 663 (9th Cir. 1982) — § 1304

U.S. v. Colletti, 245 F.2d 781 (2d Cir. 1957) — § 1810

U.S. v. Collins, 478 F.2d 837 (5th Cir. 1973) — § 2140

U.S. v. Collins, 552 F.2d 243 (8th Cir. 1977) — § 1268

U.S. v. Collins, 596 F.2d 166 (6th Cir. 1979) — § 1605

U.S., Colton v.

U.S. v. Colyer, 571 F.2d 941 (5th Cir. 1978) — § 1904

U.S. v. Comissiong, 429 F.2d 834 (2d Cir. 1970) — § 1923

U.S., Communist Party v.

U.S. v. Comosona, 614 F.2d 695 (10th Cir. 1980) — § 1239

U.S. v. Comulada, 340 F.2d 449 (2d Cir. 1965) — § 1514

U.S. v. Concepcion Cueto, 515 F.2d 160 (1st Cir. 1975) — § 1303

U.S. v. Conley, 503 F.2d 520 (8th Cir. 1974) — § 1802

U.S. v. Conlin, 551 F.2d 534 (2d Cir. 1977) — § 1605

U.S. v. Conroy, 589 F.2d 1258 (5th Cir. 1979) — § 807; § 1246

U.S. v. Consolidated Laundries Corp., 291 F.2d 563 (2d Cir. 1961) — § 717

U.S. v. Consolidated Packaging, 575 F.2d 117 (7th Cir. 1978) — § 810

U.S. v. Constantine, 567 F.2d 266 (4th Cir. 1977) — § 228

U.S., Consumer Credit Insurance Agency, Inc. v.

U.S. v. Conti, 361 F.2d 153 (2d Cir. 1966) — § 213

U.S., Continental Oil Co. v.

U.S. v. Contreras, 667 F.2d 976 (11th Cir. 1982) — § 305

U.S. v. Cotroni, 527 F.2d 708 (2d Cir. 1975) — § 264; § 707; § 1914

U.S. v. Conzemius, 586 F.2d 97 (8th Cir. 1978) — § 1246

U.S. v. Conzemius, 611 F.2d 695 (8th Cir. 1979) — § 1301

U.S. v. Cook, 530 F.2d 145 (7th Cir. 1976) — § 712

U.S. v. Cook, 592 F.2d 877 (5th Cir. 1979) — § 112; § 1217; § 1523

U.S. v. Cook, 668 F.2d 317 (7th Cir. 1982) — § 613

U.S. v. Cook, 705 F.2d 350 (9th Cir. 1983) — § 1304

U.S., Cooper v.

U.S. v. Cooper, 567 F.2d 252 (3d Cir. 1977) — § 1516

U.S. v. Cooper, 577 F.2d 1079 (6th Cir. 1978) — § 701; § 1250; § 1522

U.S., Copeland v.

U.S. v. Coplen, 541 F.2d 211 (9th Cir. 1976) — § 236

U.S. v. Coppola, 281 F.2d 340 (2d Cir. 1960) — § 304

U.S. v. Coppola, 424 F.2d 991 (2d Cir. 1970) — § 1513

U.S. v. Corall-Martinez, 592 F.2d 263 (5th Cir. 1979) — § 907

U.S. v. Coran, 589 F.2d 70 (1st Cir. 1978) — § 2109

U.S., Corbett v.

U.S. v. Corbin, 590 F.2d 398 (1st Cir. 1979) — § 1246

U.S. v. Corbitt (Pulitzer Community Newspapers, Inc.), 879 F.2d 224 (7th Cir. 1989) — § 1318

U.S. v. Cordero, 668 F.2d 32 (1st Cir. 1981) — § 103

U.S. v. Corey, 566 F.2d 429 (2d Cir. 1977) — § 1522

U.S. v. Cornejo, 598 F.2d 554 (9th Cir. 1979) — § 245; § 306

U.S. v. Cornfield, 563 F.2d 967 (9th Cir. 1977) — § 1115; § 1116

U.S. v. Corona, 551 F.2d 1386 (5th Cir. 1977) — § 1116

U.S. v. Coronado, 554 F.2d 166 (5th Cir. 1977) — § 608

U.S. v. Corr, 543 F.2d 1042 (2d Cir. 1976) — § 2125

U.S. v. Corral-Martinez, 592 F.2d 263 (5th Cir. 1979) — § 304

U.S. v. Corrigan, 168 F.2d 641 (2d Cir. 1948) — § 1704

U.S. v. Cortellesso, 601 F.2d 28 (1st Cir. 1979) — § 211; § 245

U.S. v. Cortez, 449 U.S. 411 (1981) — § 228; § 229

U.S. v. Cortez, 595 F.2d 505 (9th Cir. 1979) — § 228

U.S. v. Cosby, 529 F.2d 143 (8th Cir. 1976) — § 1512

U.S., Coson v.

U.S. v. Costanza, 549 F.2d 1126 (8th Cir. 1977) — § 1204

U.S., Costello v.

U.S. v. Costello, 604 F.2d 589 (8th Cir. 1979) — § 222

U.S. v. Cotter, 60 F.2d 689 (2d Cir. 1932) — § 2001

U.S. v. Cotton, 567 F.2d 958 (10th Cir. 1977) — § 1911

U.S., Couch v.

U.S., Courtney v.

U.S. v. Courtney, 236 F.2d 921 (2d Cir. 1956) — § 1906

U.S. v. Covello, 410 F.2d 536 (2d Cir. 1969) — § 801; § 807; § 1707

U.S. v. Covington, 395 U.S. 57 (1969) — § 1905

U.S. v. Cowden, 545 F.2d 257 (1st Cir. 1976) — § 1513

U.S., Cox v.

U.S. v. Cox, 342 F.2d 167 (5th Cir. 1965) — § 401; § 427

U.S. v. Cox, 567 F.2d 930 (10th Cir. 1977) — § 259; § 261

U.S. v. Cox, 593 F.2d 46 (6th Cir. 1979) — § 1272

U.S. v. Cozzetti, 441 F.2d 344 (9th Cir. 1971) — § 513

U.S. v. Craig, 522 F.2d 29 (6th Cir. 1975) — § 1528

U.S. v. Craig, 573 F.2d 455 (7th Cir. 1977) — § 268; § 306; § 719; § 1111

U.S. v. Craig, 573 F.2d 513 (7th Cir. 1978) — § 106; § 306

U.S. v. Crane, 632 F.2d 663 (6th Cir. 1980) — § 1602

U.S. v. Cravero, 545 F.2d 406 (5th Cir. 1976) — § 401; § 2116

U.S. v. Crawford, 581 F.2d 489 (5th Cir. 1978) — § 913; § 916

U.S. v. Creamer, 555 F.2d 612 (7th Cir. 1977) — § 1114

U.S. v. Crews, 445 U.S. 463 (1980) — § 103; § 248; § 318

U.S. v. Crippen, 570 F.2d 535 (5th Cir. 1978) — § 1520

U.S. v. Crisona, 416 F.2d 107 (2d Cir. 1969) — § 706

U.S. v. Crocker, 568 F.2d 1049 (3d Cir. 1977) — § 405

U.S. v. Crockett, 534 F.2d 589 (5th Cir. 1976) — § 1910; § 1913; § 2114

U.S. v. Cromer, 598 F.2d 738 (2d Cir. 1979) — § 236

U.S. v. Cronic, 675 F.2d 1126 (10th Cir. 1982) — § 401

U.S. v. Crosby, 294 F.2d 928 (2d Cir. 1961) — § 1518

U.S. v. Crosby, 739 F.2d 1542 (11th Cir. 1984) — § 611

U.S., Cross v.

U.S. v. Crouch, 528 F.2d 625 (7th Cir. 1976) — § 1109

U.S. v. Croucher, 532 F.2d 1042 (5th Cir. 1976) — § 1805

U.S. v. Crouthers, 669 F.2d 635 (10th Cir. 1982) — § 245; § 1913

U.S. v. Crow Dog, 532 F.2d 1182 (8th Cir. 1976) — § 111; § 1237

U.S. v. Crowell, 586 F.2d 1020 (4th Cir. 1978) — § 722; § 812; § 813

U.S. v. Crozier, 674 F.2d 1293 (9th Cir. 1982) — § 211

U.S. v. Crumbley, 872 F.2d 975 (11th Cir. 1989) — § 618

U.S. v. Crumpler, 536 F.2d 1063 (5th Cir. 1976) — § 809

U.S. v. Cruz, 478 F.2d 408 (5th Cir. 1973) — § 403

U.S. v. Cruz, 568 F.2d 781 (1st Cir. 1978) — § 1003

U.S. v. Cruz, 581 F.2d 535 (5th Cir. 1978) — § 312

U.S. v. Cruz, 594 F.2d 268 (1st Cir. 1979) — § 264

U.S. v. Cuesta, 597 F.2d 903 (5th Cir. 1979) — § 805; § 809; § 917

U.S. v. Culver, 224 F. Supp. 419 (D. Md. 1963) — § 409

U.S. v. Cummings, 468 F.2d 274 (9th Cir. 1972) — § 1268

U.S. v. Cunningham, 446 F.2d 194 (2d Cir. 1971) — § 1813

U.S., Curcio v.

U.S. v. Curry, 358 F.2d 904 (2d Cir. 1965) — § 304

U.S. v. Curtis, 520 F.2d 1300 (1st Cir. 1975) — § 1607

U.S. v. Curtis, 568 F.2d 643 (9th Cir. 1978) — § 306

U.S. v. Cuthbertson, 630 F.2d 139 (3d Cir. 1980) — § 717; § 1922

U.S. v. Cylkouski, 556 F.2d 799 (6th Cir. 1977) — § 1518

U.S. v. Cyphers, 553 F.2d 1064 (7th Cir. 1977) — § 1523; § 2003

U.S. v. Czarnecki, 552 F.2d 698 (6th Cir. 1977) — § 1260; § 1522

U.S. v. Czeck, 671 F.2d 1195 (8th Cir. 1982) — § 1266

U.S., Daley v.

U.S. v. Daley, 564 F.2d 645 (2d Cir. 1977) — § 403

U.S. v. D'Alora, 585 F.2d 16 (1st Cir. 1978) — § 1102; § 1245

U.S. v. Daly, 535 F.2d 434 (8th Cir. 1976) — § 264

U.S. v. Dalzotto, 603 F.2d 642 (7th Cir. 1979) — § 913

U.S. v. Damiano, 579 F.2d 1001 (6th Cir. 1978) — § 1906

U.S. v. Damon, 676 F.2d 1060 (5th Cir. 1982) — § 210

U.S. v. D'Andrea, 585 F.2d 1351 (7th Cir. 1978) — § 1239

U.S., D'Angelo v.

U.S. v. Daniel, 667 F.2d 783 (9th Cir. 1982) — § 267

U.S. v. Daniels, 429 F.2d 1273 (6th Cir. 1970) — § 1403

U.S. v. Daniels, 528 F.2d 705 (6th Cir. 1976) — § 303

U.S. v. Daniels, 549 F.2d 665 (9th Cir. 1977) — § 1516

U.S. v. Daniels, 572 F.2d 535 (5th Cir. 1978) — § 1517; § 1522; 1524

U.S. v. Dansker, 537 F.2d 40 (3d Cir. 1976) — § 1805

U.S. v. Danzey, 594 F.2d 905 (2d Cir. 1979) — § 1525

U.S. v. D'Apice, 664 F.2d 75 (5th Cir. 1981) — § 423

U.S., D'Aquino v.

U.S., Darby v.

U.S. v. Dark, 597 F.2d 1097 (6th Cir. 1979) — § 712

U.S., Darland v.

U.S., Dauer v.

U.S. v. D'Auria, 672 F.2d 1085 (2d Cir. 1982) — § 405

U.S. v. Davidson, 477 F.2d 136 (6th Cir. 1973) — § 1243

U.S., Davis v.

U.S. v. Davis, 459 F.2d 167 (6th Cir. 1972) — § 304

U.S. v. Davis, 523 F.2d 1265 (5th Cir. 1975) — § 2003

U.S. v. Davis, 532 F.2d 22 (7th Cir. 1976) — § 304

U.S. v. Davis, 542 F.2d 743 (8th Cir. 1976) — § 2123

U.S. v. Davis, 544 F.2d 1056 (10th Cir. 1976) — § 609

U.S. v. Davis, 548 F.2d 840 (9th Cir. 1977) — § 1104

U.S. v. Davis, 551 F.2d 233 (8th Cir. 1977) — § 1802; § 1803; § 2104; § 2140; § 2141

U.S. v. Davis, 557 F.2d 1239 (8th Cir. 1977) — § 211

U.S. v. Davis, 562 F.2d 681 (D.C. Cir. 1977) — § 1516

U.S. v. Davis, 564 F.2d 840 (9th Cir. 1978) — § 1104; § 2005

U.S. v. Davis, 571 F.2d 1354 (5th Cir. 1978) — § 1702; § 2123; § 2136

U.S. v. Davis, 583 F.2d 190 (5th Cir. 1978) — § 1253; § 1254; § 1511

U.S. v. Davis, 589 F.2d 904 (5th Cir. 1979) — § 211; § 247

U.S. v. Davis, 597 F.2d 1237 (9th Cir. 1979) — § 1266

U.S. v. Davis, 617 F.2d 677 (D.C. Cir. 1979) — § 1906; § 1918

U.S. v. Davis, 623 F.2d 188 (1st Cir. 1980) — § 910; § 916

U.S. v. Davis, 636 F.2d 1028 (5th Cir. 1981) — § 1902

U.S. v. Davis, 900 F.2d 1524 (10th Cir. 1990) — § 603; § 614

U.S. v. Dawson, 576 F.2d 656 (5th Cir. 1978) — § 2116

U.S. v. Dayton, 604 F.2d 931 (5th Cir. 1979) — § 608; § 609; § 610

U.S. v. DeAlesandro, 361 F.2d 694 (2d Cir. 1966) — § 1110

U.S. v. Dean, 647 F.2d 779 (8th Cir. 1981) § 1002

U.S. v. Decker, 543 F.2d 1102 (5th Cir. 1976) — § 1810

U.S. v. DeFillipo, 590 F.2d 1228 (2d Cir. 1979) — § 1523; § 1817

U.S. v. Degand, 614 F.2d 176 (8th Cir. 1980) — § 609

U.S. v. DeGross, 960 F.2d 1433 (9th Cir. 1992) — § 1248

U.S. v. DeJean, 613 F.2d 1356 (5th Cir. 1980) — § 1272; § 1502

U.S. v. De La Fuente, 548 F.2d 528 (5th Cir. 1977) — § 252; § 253; § 259

U.S. v. De Larosa, 450 F.2d 1057 (3d Cir. 1971) — § 1903

U.S. v. Delay, 500 F.2d 1360 (8th Cir. 1974) — § 111

U.S. v. DeLeon, 498 F.2d 1327 (7th Cir. 1974) — § 1811

U.S. v. Delguyd, 542 F.2d 346 (6th Cir. 1976) — § 231

U.S. v. Del Soccorro Castro, 573 F.2d 213 (5th Cir. 1978) — § 306

U.S. v. Del Toro, 513 F.2d 656 (2d Cir. 1975) — § 404

U.S. v. Del Toro Soto, 676 F.2d 13 (1st Cir. 1982) — § 809; § 813

U.S., De Luna v.

U.S. v. De Luna-Trujillo, 868 F.2d 122 (5th Cir. 1989) — § 1323

U.S. v. Del Valle, 587 F.2d 699 (5th Cir. 1979) — § 807

U.S. v. DeMarchena, 330 F. Supp. 1223 (S.D. Cal. 1971) — § 504

U.S. v. Demchak, 545 F.2d 1029 (5th Cir. 1977) — § 1805

U.S., Dennis v.

U.S. v. Dennis, 183 F.2d 201 (2d Cir. 1950) — § 1704

U.S. v. Dennis, 625 F.2d 782 (8th Cir. 1980) — § 912; § 1215; § 1231

U.S. v. Denson, 588 F.2d 1112 (5th Cir. 1979) — § 1012

U.S. v. Denton, 556 F.2d 811 (6th Cir. 1977) — § 1254; § 1602

U.S. v. DePugh, 434 F.2d 548 (8th Cir. 1970) — § 521

U.S. v. DeRosa, 548 F.2d 464 (3d Cir. 1977) — § 1103

U.S. v. DeRosa, 670 F.2d 889 (9th Cir. 1982) — § 503; § 918

U.S. v. Derrich, 519 F.2d 1 (6th Cir. 1975) — § 1322

U.S. v. Derring, 592 F.2d 1003 (8th Cir. 1979) — § 316; § 1526

U.S., Desimone v.

U.S. v. De Sisto, 329 F.2d 929 (2d Cir. 1964) — § 1814

U.S. v. Desmond, 670 F.2d 414 (3d Cir. 1982) — § 1258

U.S. v. DeStafano, 429 F.2d 344 (2d Cir. 1970) — § 905

U.S. v. DeTienne, 468 F.2d 151 (7th Cir. 1972) — § 1212

U.S. v. Deutsch, 373 F. Supp. 289 (S.D.N.Y. 1974) — § 723

U.S. v. Deutsch, 451 F.2d 98 (2d Cir. 1971) — § 1514

U.S. v. Deutsch, 475 F.2d 55 (5th Cir. 1973) — § 719

U.S. v. DeVasto, 52 F.2d 26 (2d Cir. 1931) — § 1917

U.S. v. DeVaugn, 579 F.2d 225 (2d Cir. 1978) — § 2116

U.S., DeVincent v.

U.S. v. DeVincent, 546 F.2d 452 (1st Cir. 1976) — § 1270; § 1520

U.S. v. De Vincent, 632 F.2d 155 (1st Cir. 1980) — § 1003

U.S., De Vore v.

U.S. v. Diadone, 558 F.2d 775 (5th Cir. 1977) — § 259

U.S., Diaz v.

U.S. v. Diaz, 585 F.2d 116 (5th Cir. 1978) — § 1252; § 1810

U.S. v. Diaz, 655 F.2d 580 (5th Cir. 1981) — § 1923

U.S. v. Diaz-Alvarado, 587 F.2d 1002 (9th Cir. 1978) — § 1206

U.S. v. Diaz-Villafane, 874 F.2d 43 (1st Cir. 1989) — § 1324

U.S., DiBella v.

U.S., Di Carlo v.

U.S. v. DiCarlo, 575 F.2d 952 (1st Cir. 1978) — § 719; § 1108; § 1302

U.S. v. Didier, 542 F.2d 1182 (2d Cir. 1970) — § 1223

U.S. v. Diecidue, 603 F.2d 535 (5th Cir. 1979) — § 206; § 701

U.S. v. Diehl, 460 F. Supp. 1282 (S.D. Tex 1978) — § 2140

U.S. v. Diez, 515 F.2d 892 (5th Cir. 1975) — § 1605; § 2148

U.S. v. DiFrancesco, 449 U.S. 117 (1980) — § 1010; § 1012; § 1320; § 1346

U.S. v. DiFrancesco, 604 F.2d 769 (2d Cir. 1979) — § 1108; § 1207; § 1208

U.S. v. Diggs, 569 F.2d 1264 (3d Cir. 1977) — § 243

U.S. v. DiGiacomo, 579 F.2d 1211 (10th Cir. 1978) — § 241; § 305

U.S. v. DiGiovanni, 544 F.2d 642 (2d Cir. 1976) — § 719

U.S. v. DiGirlomo, 393 F. Supp. 997 (W.D. Mo. 1975) — § 401

U.S. v. DiGregorio, 605 F.2d 1184 (1st Cir. 1979) — § 1102

U.S., Dilia v.

U.S. v. Diltz, 622 F.2d 476 (10th Cir. 1980) — § 259

U.S. v. DiMauro, 441 F.2d 428 (8th Cir. 1971) — § 418; § 426

U.S. v. DiMuro, 540 F.2d 503 (1st Cir. 1976) — § 1602

U.S. v. Dinapoli, 557 F.2d 962 (2d Cir. 1977) — § 1810

U.S. v. Dingle, 546 F.2d 1378 (10th Cir. 1976) — § 722; § 805; § 1109

U.S. v. Dinitz, 424 U.S. 600 (1976) — § 1001; § 1008

U.S. v. Dinitz, 538 F.2d 1214 (5th Cir. 1976) — § 1103; § 1813

U.S. v. Dioguardi, 428 F.2d 1033 (2d Cir. 1970) — § 1610

U.S. v. Dionisio, 410 U.S. 1 (1973) — § 307; § 409; § 1901; § 1903

U.S. v. Di Re, 332 F.2d 581 (1948) — § 217; § 1514

U.S. v. Di Rodio, 565 F.2d 575 (9th Cir. 1977) — § 2116

U.S. v. Disston, 582 F.2d 1108 (7th Cir. 1978) — § 1108

U.S. v. Distler, 671 F.2d 954 (6th Cir. 1982) — § 2003; § 2109

U.S. v. Dixon, 547 F.2d 1079 (9th Cir. 1976) — § 1807

U.S. v. Dixon, 596 F.2d 178 (7th Cir. 1979) — § 1246

U.S., Dobbins v.

U.S., Doe v.

U.S. v. Doe, 361 F. Supp. 226 (E.D. Pa. 1973) — § 1903

U.S. v. Doe, 405 F.2d 436 (2d Cir. 1968) — § 1903

U.S. v. Doe, 457 F.2d 895 (2d Cir. 1972) — § 1903

U.S. v. Doe, 465 U.S. 605 (1984) — § 1902

U.S. v. Doe, 478 F.2d 194 (1st Cir. 1973) — § 404

U.S. v. Doe, 628 F.2d 694 (1st Cir. 1980) — § 1906

U.S., Doggett v.

U.S. v. Dohm, 597 F.2d 535 (5th Cir. 1979) — § 305; § 501

U.S. v. Dohm, 618 F.2d 1169 (5th Cir. 1980) — § 1906

U.S. v. Dolliole, 597 F.2d 102 (7th Cir. 1979) — § 1524

U.S. v. Domenech, 476 F.2d 1229 (2d Cir. 1973) — § 1903; § 1906

U.S. v. Dominguez, 783 F.2d 702 (7th Cir. 1986) — § 509

U.S. v. Donahue, 539 F.2d 1131 (8th Cir. 1976) — § 1010

U.S., Donaldson v.

U.S. v. Donaway, 447 F.2d 940 (9th Cir. 1971) — § 909

U.S., Donnelly v.

U.S. v. Donovan, 429 U.S. 413 (Cir. 1977) — § 259; § 262

U.S. v. Doremus, 414 F.2d 252 (6th Cir. 1969) — § 1609

U.S. v. Dorman, 496 F.2d 438 (4th Cir. 1974) — § 604

U.S. v. Dorn, 561 F.2d 1252 (7th Cir. 1977) — § 1250; § 1506; § 2116

U.S. v. Dornau, 359 F. Supp. 684 (S.D.N.Y. 1973) — § 419

U.S. v. Dorsett, 544 F.2d 687 (4th Cir. 1976) — § 312

U.S. v. Dorsey, 591 F.2d 922 (D.C. Cir. 1979) — § 209; § 1810

U.S. v. Dorsey, 641 F.2d 1213 (7th Cir. 1981) — § 227

U.S. v. Dorsey, 888 F.2d 79 (11th Cir. 1989) — § 1323

U.S., Doss v.

U.S. v. Doss, 563 F.2d 265 (6th Cir. 1977) — § 408; § 1403

U.S. v. Doto, 205 F.2d 416 (2d Cir. 1953) — § 1903

U.S. v. Dotson, 546 F.2d 1151 (5th Cir. 1977) — § 801; § 804

U.S. v. Douglas, 668 F.2d 459 (10th Cir. 1982) — § 1274; § 1502

U.S. v. Doulin, 538 F.2d 466 (2d Cir. 1976) — § 2116

U.S., Dow Chemical Co. v.

U.S. v. Dowdy, 479 F.2d 213 (4th Cir. 1973) — § 265

U.S., Dowling v.

U.S., Downum v.

U.S. v. Drake, 673 F.2d 15 (1st Cir. 1982) — § 204

U.S. v. Drebin, 557 F.2d 1316 (9th Cir. 1977) — § 209

U.S. v. Dreitzler, 577 F.2d 539 (9th Cir. 1978) — § 712; § 1207; § 1272; § 1274

U.S., Drew v.

U.S., Driscoll v.

U.S. v. Driscoll, 399 F.2d 135 (2d Cir. 1968) — § 1903; § 1921

U.S., Droback v.

U.S. v. Droms, 566 F.2d 361 (2d Cir. 1977) — § 905

U.S. v. Duarte, 901 F.2d 1498 (9th Cir. 1990) — § 1326

U.S. v. Dube, 520 F.2d 250 (1st Cir. 1975) — § 2003

U.S. v. Dubrofsky, 581 F.2d 208 (9th Cir. 1978) — § 241; § 1317

U.S. v. Dudek, 560 F.2d 1288 (6th Cir. 1977) — § 205; § 1524; § 1526

U.S. v. Duff, 551 F.2d 187 (7th Cir. 1977) — § 1111

U.S. v. Duffy, 454 F.2d 809 (5th Cir. 1972) — § 1706

U.S. v. Duggan, 743 F.2d 59 (2d Cir. 1984) — § 703

U.S. v. Duke, 527 F.2d 386 (5th Cir. 1976) — § 1204

U.S. v. Dukes, 727 F.2d 34 (2d Cir. 1984) — § 1304

U.S., Dunaway v.

U.S. v. Dunbar, 611 F.2d 985 (5th Cir. 1980) — § 1010

U.S. v. Duncan, 570 F.2d 292 (9th Cir. 1978) — § 248

U.S. v. Duncan, 598 F.2d 839 (4th Cir. 1979) — § 1246

U.S. v. Dunmore, 446 F.2d 1214 (8th Cir. 1971) — § 1264

U.S. v. Dunn, 480 U.S. 294 (1987) — § 238; § 240

U.S. v. Dunnings, 425 F.2d 836 (2d Cir. 1969) — § 212

U.S. v. Dupree, 553 F.2d 1189 (8th Cir. 1977) — § 316; § 812

U.S., Dupuy v.

U.S. v. Durham, 319 F.2d 590 (4th Cir. 1963) — § 1801

U.S. v. Durham, 587 F.2d 799 (5th Cir. 1979) — § 1248

U.S. v. Durland, 575 F.2d 1306 (10th Cir. 1978) — § 2116

U.S., Durns v.

U.S. v. Duvall, 537 F.2d 15 (2d Cir. 1976) — § 304

U.S. v. Duzac, 622 F.2d 911 (5th Cir. 1980) — § 903; § 914

U.S. v. Dye, 508 F.2d 1226 (6th Cir. 1974) — § 913; § 1266

U.S. v. Dykema, 666 F.2d 1096 (7th Cir. 1981) — § 1403

U.S. v. Dzialak, 441 F.2d 212 (2d Cir. 1971) — § 1512

U.S. v. Eades, 615 F.2d 617 (4th Cir. 1980) — § 902

U.S. v. Eagle, 586 F.2d 1193 (8th Cir. 1978) — § 111

U.S. v. Eagleston, 417 F.2d 11 (10th Cir. 1968) — § 905

U.S. v. E. A. Goodyear, Inc., 334 F. Supp. 1096 (S.D.N.Y. 1971) — § 1902

U.S. v. Eaton, 144 F.2d 677 (1892 Cir. 1892) — § 102

U.S. v. Echols, 577 F.2d 308 (5th Cir. 1979) — § 211; § 248

U.S. v. Eckmann, 656 F.2d 308 (8th Cir. 1981) — § 1517

U.S. v. Eddings, 478 F.2d 67 (6th Cir. 1973) — § 1923

U.S. v. Eddy, 549 F.2d 108 (9th Cir. 1976) — § 716

U.S. v. Eddy, 597 F.2d 430 (5th Cir. 1979) — § 2109

U.S. v. Eddy, 737 F.2d 564 (6th Cir. 1984) — § 1118

U.S. v. Edelman, 414 F.2d 539 (2d Cir. 1969) — § 1811

U.S. v. Edelson, 581 F.2d 1290 (7th Cir. 1978) — § 404; § 414

U.S. v. Edmons, 432 F.2d 577 (2d Cir. 1970) — § 316

U.S. v. Edwards, 415 U.S. 800 (1974) — § 220; § 222; § 245

U.S. v. Edwards, 469 F.2d 1362 (5th Cir. 1972) — § 1262

U.S. v. Edwards, 539 F.2d 689 (9th Cir. 1976) — § 304; § 2122

U.S. v. Edwards, 549 F.2d 362 (5th Cir. 1977) — § 1520

U.S. v. Edwards, 577 F.2d 883 (5th Cir. 1978) — § 1205

U.S. v. Edwards, 602 F.2d 458 (1st Cir. 1979) — § 231

U.S. v. Edwards, 627 F.2d 460 (D.C. Cir. 1980) — § 1231

U.S. v. Edwards, 644 F.2d 1 (5th Cir. 1981) — § 237; § 239

U.S. v. Ehrlichman, 546 F.2d 910 (D.C. Cir. 1976) — § 916; § 1511

U.S., Eisenberg v.

U.S. v. Eisenberg, 469 F.2d 156 (8th Cir. 1972) — § 1265

U.S., Elder v.

U.S. v. Eldred, 588 F.2d 746 (9th Cir. 1978) — § 1259; § 1512

U.S. v. Elemy, 656 F.2d 507 (9th Cir. 1981) — § 2111

U.S., Elkins v.

U.S. v. Elliott, 418 F.2d 219 (9th Cir. 1969) — § 904

U.S. v. Ellison, 557 F.2d 128 (7th Cir. 1977) — § 1805

U.S. v. Ellison, 684 F.2d 664 (10th Cir. 1982) — § 1010

U.S. v. Elsbery, 602 F.2d 1054 (2d Cir. 1979) — § 1204; § 1239

U.S. v. Empire Packing Co., 174 F.2d 16 (7th Cir. 1949) — § 1810

U.S., Emspak v.

U.S., Encinas-Sierras v.

U.S., England v.

U.S. v. Enright, 579 F.2d 980 (6th Cir. 1978) — § 1207; § 1208

U.S. v. Epperson, 454 F.2d 769 (4th Cir. 1972) — § 239

U.S., Epstein v.

U.S. v. Erb, 596 F.2d 412 (10th Cir. 1979) — § 231

U.S. v. Erwin, 507 F.2d 937 (5th Cir. 1975) — § 226

U.S. v. Eschweiler, 782 F.2d 1385 (7th Cir. 1986) — § 1317; § 1318

U.S. v. Escobar, 674 F.2d 469 (5th Cir. 1982) — § 806

U.S. v. Eskew, 469 F.2d 278 (9th Cir. 1972) — § 521

U.S. v. Espinosa-Cerpa, 630 F.2d 328 (5th Cir. 1980) — § 1011

U.S. v. Espinoza, 578 F.2d 224 (9th Cir. 1978) — § 1522

U.S. v. Esposito, 492 F.2d 6 (7th Cir. 1973) — § 1006

U.S. v. Estepa, 471 F.2d 1132 (2d Cir. 1972) — § 403

U.S. v. Estrella, 567 F.2d 1151 (1st Cir. 1977) — § 1923

U.S. v. Estremera, 531 F.2d 1103 (2d Cir. 1976) — § 317; § 710

U.S. v. Eubanks, 591 F.2d 513 (9th Cir. 1979) — § 2116

U.S., Evalt v.

U.S., Evans v.

U.S. v. Evans, 320 F.2d 482 (6th Cir. 1963) — § 302

U.S. v. Evans, 454 F.2d 813 (8th Cir. 1972) — § 1317

U.S. v. Evans, 569 F.2d 209 (4th Cir. 1978) — § 1520

U.S. v. Evans, 572 F.2d 455 (5th Cir. 1978) — § 250; § 303; § 1274; § 1502; § 2113; § 2136

U.S. v. Ewell, 383 U.S. 116 (1966) — § 1239

U.S., Fagan v.

U.S. v. Fahey, 510 F.2d 302 (2d Cir. 1974) — § 408

U.S. v. Fairchild, 505 F.2d 1378 (5th Cir. 1975) — § 1513

U.S. v. Falcone, 544 F.2d 607 (2d Cir. 1976) — § 1902

U.S. v. Falley, 489 F.2d 33 (2d Cir. 1973) — § 1902

U.S., Falter v.

U.S. v. Farnkoff, 535 F.2d 661 (1st Cir. 1976) — § 248; § 1114

U.S. v. Farris, 517 F.2d 226 (7th Cir. 1975) — § 1702; § 2127

U.S. v. Fatico, 441 F. Supp. 1285 (E.D.N.Y. 1977) — § 1403

U.S. v. Faudman, 640 F.2d 20 (6th Cir. 1981) — § 409

U.S. v. Faulkner, 538 F.2d 724 (6th Cir. 1976) — § 1254; § 1802

U.S. v. Fay, 668 F.2d 375 (8th Cir. 1981) — § 1317

U.S. v. Fayer, 573 F.2d 741 (2d Cir. 1978) — § 2001

U.S. v. Fearn, 589 F.2d 1316 (7th Cir. 1978) — § 303; § 712; § 1272; § 1275

U.S. v. Fearwell, 595 F.2d 771 (D.C. Cir. 1978) — § 1809

U.S. v. Feldman, 535 F.2d 1175 (9th Cir. 1976) — § 255; § 259

U.S. v. Feldman, 606 F.2d 673 (6th Cir. 1979) — § 250

U.S. v. Felix, 112 S. Ct. 1377 (1992) — § 1002

U.S. v. Felix-Jerez, 667 F.2d 1297 (9th Cir. 1982) — § 2122

U.S. v. Fels, 599 F.2d 142 (7th Cir. 1979) — § 607; § 609

U.S. v. Fench, 470 F.2d 1234 (D.C. Cir. 1972) — § 1816

U.S. v. Fernandez, 497 F.2d 730 (9th Cir. 1974) — § 1532

U.S. v. Fernandez-Angula, 897 F.2d 1514 (9th Cir. 1990) — § 1339; § 1318

U.S. v. Fernandez-Guzman, 577 F.2d 1093 (7th Cir. 1978) — § 217

U.S. v. Fielding, 645 F.2d 719 (9th Cir. 1981) — § 1228; § 1231

U.S., Fields v.

U.S. v. Figueroa, 618 F.2d 934 (2d Cir. 1980) — § 1522

U.S. v. Figueroa-Paz, 468 F.2d 1055 (9th Cir. 1972) — § 1913

U.S. v. Figurski, 545 F.2d 389 (4th Cir. 1976) — § 807; § 1113; § 1317

U.S. v. Finch, 557 F.2d 1234 (8th Cir. 1977) — § 308

U.S. v. Finefrock, 668 F.2d 1168 (10th Cir. 1982) — § 250

U.S. v. Finkelstein, 526 F.2d 517 (2d Cir. 1975) — § 914; § 1805

U.S. v. Finnegan, 568 F.2d 637 (9th Cir. 1977) — § 238

U.S. v. Fiore, 443 F.2d 112 (2d Cir. 1971) — § 2141; § 2147

U.S. v. Fischer, 531 F.2d 783 (5th Cir. 1976) — § 1264

U.S., Fisher v.

U.S. v. Fisher, 455 F.2d 1101 (2d Cir. 1972) — § 408

U.S. v. Fisher, 518 F.2d 836 (2d Cir. 1975) — § 1909; § 1913

U.S. v. Fitts, 576 F.2d 837 (10th Cir. 1978) — § 702

U.S. v. Fitzpatrick, 437 F.2d 19 (2d Cir. 1970) — § 1805

U.S. v. Flaherty, 668 F.2d 566 (1st Cir. 1981) — § 403; § 1104

U.S., Flavorland Industries, Inc. v.

U.S. v. Flecha, 539 F.2d 874 (2d Cir. 1976) — § 2114

U.S. v. Fleener, 900 F.2d 914 (6th Cir. 1990) — § 1323

U.S., Fleming v.

U.S. v. Fleming, 504 F.2d 1045 (7th Cir. 1974) — § 303

U.S. v. Fleming, 594 F.2d 598 (7th Cir. 1979) — § 1249

U.S. v. Flickinger, 573 F.2d 1349 (9th Cir. 1978) — § 233; § 235; § 318; § 1509

U.S. v. Flom, 558 F.2d 1179 (5th Cir. 1977) — § 701

U.S. v. Flores, 540 F.2d 432 (9th Cir. 1976) — § 719

U.S. v. Floyd, 496 F.2d 982 (2d Cir. 1974) — § 305

U.S. v. Floyd, 555 F.2d 45 (2d Cir. 1977) — § 2116

U.S. v. Foley, 598 F.2d 1323 (4th Cir. 1979) — § 809; § 810; § 1605

U.S., Fong Foo v.

U.S. v. Fontanez, 628 F.2d 687 (1st Cir. 1980) — § 1304

U.S., Ford v.

U.S. v. Ford, 553 F.2d 146 (D.C. Cir. 1977) — § 209

U.S. v. Ford, 563 F.2d 1366 (9th Cir. 1977) — § 308

U.S. v. Ford, 603 F.2d 1043 (2d Cir. 1979) — § 1002

U.S. v. Ford, 627 F.2d 807 (7th Cir. 1980) — § 113

U.S. v. Forrest, 623 F.2d 1107 (5th Cir. 1980) — § 901; § 903; § 912

U.S. v. Forsythe, 560 F.2d 1127 (3d Cir. 1977) — § 214; § 247

U.S. v. Forsythe, 594 F.2d 947 (3d Cir. 1979) — § 1810

U.S. v. Fortna, 769 F.2d 243 (5th Cir. 1985) — § 512

U.S. v. Fortune, 513 F.2d 883 (5th Cir. 1975) — § 2003

U.S. v. Foshee, 606 F.2d 111 (5th Cir. 1979) — § 1605

U.S. v. Fosher, 568 F.2d 207 (1st Cir. 1978) — § 319; § 1517

U.S. v. Fosher, 590 F.2d 381 (1st Cir. 1979) — § 2003

U.S. v. Fossler, 597 F.2d 478 (5th Cir. 1979) — § 236; § 1005

U.S. v. Foster, 580 F.2d 388 (10th Cir. 1978) — § 1403

U.S. v. Foutz, 540 F.2d 733 (4th Cir. 1976) — § 912

U.S. v. Fowler, 465 F.2d 664 (D.C. Cir. 1972) — § 1805; § 1815

U.S. v. Foxworth, 599 F.2d 1 (1st Cir. 1979) — § 1245

U.S. v. Frady, 102 S. Ct. 1584 (1982) — § 1254

U.S. v. Frady, 607 F.2d 383 (D.C. Cir. 1979) — § 1002

U.S. v. Francis, 646 F.2d 251 (6th Cir. 1981) — § 215

U.S. v. Francisco, 575 F.2d 815 (10th Cir. 1978) — § 1503

U.S. v. Francois, 889 F.2d 1341 (4th Cir. 1989) — § 1328

U.S. v. Franco-Torres, 869 F.2d 797 (5th Cir. 1989) — § 1323

U.S. v. Franicevich, 471 F.2d 427 (5th Cir. 1973) — § 1810

U.S., Frank v.

U.S. v. Frank, 864 F.2d 992 (3d Cir. 1988) — § 1312

U.S., Frankfeld v.

U.S., Frankfort Distilleries v.

U.S., Franklin v.

U.S. v. Franklin, 586 F.2d 560 (5th Cir. 1978) — § 2113

U.S. v. Franklin, 598 F.2d 954 (5th Cir. 1979) — § 1805

U.S. v. Franks, 511 F.2d 25 (6th Cir. 1975) — § 268; § 2003

U.S. v. Franz, 886 F.2d 973 (7th Cir. 1989) — § 1327

U.S. v. Franzese, 392 F.2d 954 (2d Cir. 1968) — § 1813; § 1817; § 1923

U.S. v. Frascone, 299 F.2d 824 (2d Cir. 1962) — § 1903; § 1904

U.S., Fraser v.

U.S., Frazier v.

U.S. v. Frazier, 385 F.2d 901 (6th Cir. 1967) — § 304

U.S. v. Frazier, 476 F.2d 891 (D.C. Cir. 1973) — § 1906

U.S. v. Frazier, 479 F.2d 983 (2d Cir. 1973) — § 805

U.S. v. Frazier, 560 F.2d 884 (8th Cir. 1977) — § 243

U.S. v. Frazier, 584 F.2d 790 (6th Cir. 1978) — § 910

U.S. v. Fredenburgh, 602 F.2d 1143 (3d Cir. 1979) — § 1012

U.S. v. Frederick, 583 F.2d 273 (6th Cir. 1978) — § 1005

U.S. v. Fredericks, 586 F.2d 470 (5th Cir. 1978) — § 248; § 2116

U.S. v. Frederickson, 581 F.2d 711 (8th Cir. 1978) — § 257

U.S. v. Fredia, 319 F.2d 853 (2d Cir. 1963) — § 1923

U.S. v. Free, 574 F.2d 1221 (5th Cir. 1978) — § 1523

U.S. v. Freed, 401 U.S. 601 (1971) — § 420; § 1905

U.S. v. Freeland, 562 F.2d 383 (6th Cir. 1977) — § 241; § 243

U.S. v. Freeman, 514 F.2d 1184 (10th Cir. 1975) — § 2001

U.S. v. Frezzo Bros., Inc., 602 F.2d 1123 (3d Cir. 1979) — § 1256

U.S. v. Fried, 486 F.2d 201 (2d Cir. 1973) — § 722

U.S. v. Fried, 576 F.2d 787 (9th Cir. 1978) — § 207

U.S. v. Friedman, 445 F.2d 1076 (9th Cir. 1971) — § 1918

U.S. v. Friedman, 593 F.2d 109 (9th Cir. 1979) — § 719; § 806; § 810; § 1903; § 2136

U.S., Frisone v.

U.S. v. Fritz, 580 F.2d 370 (10th Cir. 1978) — § 313

U.S. v. Frumento, 552 F.2d 534 (3d Cir. 1977) — § 420; § 1903

U.S., Frye v.

U.S. v. Fuel, 583 F.2d 978 (8th Cir. 1978) — § 917

U.S. v. Fuentes, 563 F.2d 527 (2d Cir. 1977) — § 713; § 1923

U.S. v. Fuiman, 546 F.2d 1155 (5th Cir. 1977) — § 1260

U.S., Fuller v.

U.S. v. Fullmer, 457 F.2d 447 (7th Cir. 1972) — § 1113

U.S. v. Fulton, 549 F.2d 1325 (9th Cir. 1977) — § 716; § 1111

U.S. v. Fultz, 602 F.2d 830 (8th Cir. 1979) — § 1003

U.S., Furlow v.

U.S. v. Furlow, 644 F.2d 764 (9th Cir. 1981) — § 1207

U.S. v. Gabriel, 597 F.2d 95 (7th Cir. 1979) — § 1112; § 1261

U.S. v. Gabriner, 571 F.2d 48 (1st Cir. 1978) — § 1516

U.S., Gagliardo v.

U.S. v. Gagnon, 470 U.S. 522 (1985) — § 1249

U.S. v. Gaines, 555 F.2d 618 (7th Cir. 1977) — § 304

U.S. v. Gainey, 380 U.S. 63 (1965) — § 1515

U.S. v. Galente, 547 F.2d 733 (2d Cir. 1976) — § 252

U.S. v. Gallagher, 557 F.2d 1041 (4th Cir. 1977) — § 229

U.S. v. Gallagher, 576 F.2d 1028 (3d Cir. 1978) — § 1114; § 1703

U.S. v. Gallagher, 602 F.2d 1139 (3d Cir. 1979) — § 1010

U.S. v. Gallo, 763 F.2d 1504 (6th Cir. 1985) — § 1215

U.S. v. Gallop, 606 F.2d 836 (9th Cir. 1979) — § 220

U.S., Galloway v.

U.S. v. Galvan-Garcia, 872 F.2d 638 (5th Cir. 1989) — § 1323

U.S. v. Galvin, 394 F.2d 228 (3d Cir. 1968) — § 2003

U.S. v. Gambino, 788 F.2d 938 (3d Cir. 1986) — § 1241

U.S., Gant v.

U.S. v. Garbett, 867 F.2d 1132 (8th Cir. 1989) — § 1339

U.S. v. Garcia, 377 F.2d 321 (2d Cir. 1967) — § 310

U.S. v. Garcia, 555 F.2d 708 (9th Cir. 1977) — § 1402

U.S. v. Garcia, 605 F.2d 349 (7th Cir. 1979) — § 225

U.S. v. Garcia, 672 F.2d 1349 (11th Cir. 1982) — § 229; § 1403

U.S. v. Garcia, 721 F.2d 721 (11th Cir. 1983) — § 1001

U.S. v. Gardin, 382 F.2d 601 (2d Cir. 1967) — § 805

U.S. v. Gardner, 516 F.2d 334 (7th Cir. 1975) — § 404

U.S. v. Gardner, 553 F.2d 946 (5th Cir. 1977) — § 233

U.S. v. Gardner, 611 F.2d 770 (9th Cir. 1980) — § 1605

U.S., Garner v.

U.S. v. Garner, 574 F.2d 1141 (4th Cir. 1978) — § 2147

U.S., Garrett v.

U.S. v. Garrett, 627 F.2d 14 (6th Cir. 1980) — § 219

U.S. v. Garza, 574 F.2d 298 (5th Cir. 1978) — § 1247; § 1811

U.S. v. Garza, 574 F.2d 908 (5th Cir. 1978) — § 1811

U.S. v. Garza, 608 F.2d 659 (5th Cir. 1979) — § 1114

U.S. v. Gaston, 608 F.2d 607 (5th Cir. 1979) — § 1108

U.S. v. Gates, 557 F.2d 1086 (5th Cir. 1977) — § 809; § 812

U.S. v. Gates, 680 F.2d 1117 (6th Cir. 1982) — § 317

U.S. v. Gaultney, 581 F.2d 1137 (5th Cir. 1978) — § 234

U.S. v. Gay, 567 F.2d 916 (9th Cir. 1978) — § 914

U.S. v. Gaynor, 472 F.2d 899 (2d Cir. 1973) — § 310

U.S. v. Geaney, 417 F.2d 1116 (2d Cir. 1969) — § 1252

U.S. v. Gebhard, 426 F.2d 965 (9th Cir. 1970) — § 424

U.S. v. Geders, 625 F.2d 31 (5th Cir. 1980) — § 1301

U.S., Gelbard v.

U.S. v. Genser, 582 F.2d 292 (3d Cir. 1978) — § 2004

U.S. v. Gentile, 495 F.2d 626 (5th Cir. 1974) — § 909

U.S. v. Gentile, 525 F.2d 252 (2d Cir. 1976) — § 306; § 1102

U.S. v. Gentile, 530 F.2d 461 (2d Cir. 1976) — § 317

U.S. v. George, 444 F.2d 310 (6th Cir. 1971) — § 401

U.S. v. George, 568 F.2d 1064 (4th Cir. 1978) — § 1516

U.S., Georgia-Pacific Corp. v.

U.S. v. Gerardi, 586 F.2d 896 (1st Cir. 1978) — § 261

U.S., Gerberding v.

U.S. v. Gerhart, 538 F.2d 807 (8th Cir. 1976) — § 1705; § 1707

U.S. v. German-American Vocational League, Inc., 153 F.2d 860 (3d Cir. 1946) — § 2003

U.S. v. Gernie, 252 F.2d 664 (2d Cir. 1958) — § 1256

U.S. v. Gerry, 515 F.2d 130 (2d Cir. 1975) — § 314; § 2148

U.S. v. Gervato, 474 F.2d 40 (3d Cir. 1973) — § 215

U.S. v. Giacalone, 588 F.2d 1158 (6th Cir. 1978) — § 1247; § 1249; § 1261

U.S. v. Giancola, 754 F.2d 898 (11th Cir. 1985) — § 517

U.S. v. Giangrosso, 763 F.2d 849 (7th Cir. 1985) — § 504

U.S. v. Gibbons, 607 F.2d 1320 (10th Cir. 1979) — § 408

U.S. v. Gibbs, 233 F. Supp. 934 (W.D. Pa. 1964) — § 1403

U.S. v. Gibson, 310 F.2d 79 (2d Cir. 1962) — § 905

U.S. v. Gibson, 444 F.2d 275 (5th Cir. 1971) — § 1903

U.S. v. Gibson, 536 F.2d 1110 (5th Cir. 1976) — § 1254

U.S. v. Gibson, 675 F.2d 825 (6th Cir. 1982) — § 1272; § 1502; § 1519; § 1819

U.S. v. Giese, 597 F.2d 1170 (9th Cir. 1979) — § 701; § 1246; § 2114

U.S., Giglio v.

U.S. v. Gilbert, 425 F.2d 490 (D.C. Cir. 1969) — § 513

656

U.S. v. Gilbert, 668 F.2d 94 (2d Cir. 1981) — § 1302

U.S. v. Gill, 490 F.2d 233 (7th Cir. 1973) — § 907

U.S. v. Gillen, 599 F.2d 541 (3d Cir. 1979) — § 1510

U.S. v. Gillings, 568 F.2d 1307 (9th Cir. 1978) — § 716

U.S. v. Gilliss, 645 F.2d 1269 (8th Cir. 1981) — § 1217; § 1232; § 1321

U.S. v. Gillock, 445 U.S. 360 (1980) — § 1908

U.S. v. Gimelstop, 475 F.2d 157 (3d Cir. 1973) — § 247

U.S. v. Giordano, 416 U.S. 505 (1974) — § 259; § 261

U.S. v. Gipe, 672 F.2d 777 (9th Cir. 1982) — § 101

U.S. v. Gladney, 563 F.2d 491 (1st Cir. 1977) — § 266; § 716

U.S. v. Glasby, 576 F.2d 734 (7th Cir. 1978) — § 233; § 243

U.S. v. Glasser, 443 F.2d 994 (2d Cir. 1971) — § 1906

U.S. v. Glassman, 562 F.2d 954 (5th Cir. 1977) — § 401

U.S. v. Glaziou, 402 F.2d 8 (2d Cir. 1968) — § 1816

U.S. v. Glen-Archila, 677 F.2d 809 (11th Cir. 1982) — § 306

U.S., Glickstein v.

U.S. v. Glover, 588 F.2d 876 (2d Cir. 1978) — § 1107; § 1815

U.S. v. Goble, 512 F.2d 458 (6th Cir. 1975) — § 917; § 1270

U.S. v. Godwin, 522 F.2d 1135 (4th Cir. 1975) — § 1802

U.S. v. Goichman, 547 F.2d 778 (3d Cir. 1976) — § 1701

U.S., Goings v.

U.S. v. Goins, 593 F.2d 88 (8th Cir. 1979) — § 2144

U.S. v. Gold, 470 F. Supp. 1336 (N.D. Ill. 1979) — § 401

U.S., Goldberg v.

U.S. v. Goldberg, 401 F.2d 644 (2d Cir. 1968) — § 1510

U.S. v. Goldberg, 582 F.2d 483 (9th Cir. 1978) — § 719; § 803; § 806; § 1108

U.S. v. Goldberg, 862 F.2d 101 (6th Cir. 1988) — § 610

U.S. v. Golden, 532 F.2d 1244 (9th Cir. 1976) — § 2004

U.S. v. Golden, 671 F.2d 369 (10th Cir. 1982) — § 2119

U.S. v. Goldfarb, 328 F.2d 280 (6th Cir. 1964) — § 1918

U.S., Goldman v.

U.S. v. Goldman, 563 F.2d 501 (1st Cir. 1977) — § 1115

U.S., Goldsby v.

U.S. v. Gomer, 764 F.2d 1221 (7th Cir. 1985) — § 1337

U.S., Gomez v.

U.S. v. Gomez, 553 F.2d 958 (5th Cir. 1977) — § 404

U.S. v. Gomez, 603 F.2d 147 (10th Cir. 1979) — § 2001

U.S. v. Gomez-Londono, 553 F.2d 805 (2d Cir. 1977) — § 306

U.S. v. Gonzales-Benitez, 537 F.2d 1051 (9th Cir. 1976) — § 1706

U.S. v. Gonzalez, 555 F.2d 308 (2d Cir. 1977) — § 713

U.S. v. Gonzalez, 559 F.2d 1271 (5th Cir. 1977) — § 2144; § 2147

U.S. v. Gonzalez, 671 F.2d 441 (11th Cir. 1982) — § 1213

U.S., Gooding v.

U.S. v. Goodman, 285 F.2d 378 (5th Cir. 1960) — § 905

U.S. v. Goodwin, 102 S. Ct. 2485 (1982) — § 1118

U.S. v. Goodwin, 612 F.2d 1103 (8th Cir. 1980) — § 1221

U.S. v. Goodwin, 625 F.2d 693 (5th Cir. 1980) — § 1904

U.S. v. Gopman, 531 F.2d 262 (5th Cir. 1976) — § 418

U.S., Gordon v.

U.S. v. Gordon, 580 F.2d 827 (5th Cir. 1978) — § 709

U.S. v. Gordon-Nikkar, 518 F.2d 972 (5th Cir. 1975) — § 1918

U.S. v. Gorham, 523 F.2d 1088 (D.C. Cir. 1975) — § 1403

U.S., Gorin v.

U.S. v. Gorman, 355 F.2d 151 (2d Cir. 1965) — § 304

U.S. v. Gosser, 339 F.2d 102 (6th Cir. 1964) — § 1264

U.S. v. Gottlieb, 493 F.2d 987 (2d Cir. 1974) — § 813

U.S. v. Gould, 536 F.2d 216 (8th Cir. 1976) — § 1401

U.S. v. Gouveia, 467 U.S. 180 (1984) — § 305

U.S. v. Grabiec, 563 F.2d 313 (7th Cir. 1977) — § 911; § 1112

U.S. v. Grabinski, 674 F.2d 677 (8th Cir. 1982) — § 1210; § 1238

U.S. v. Grady, 544 F.2d 598 (2d Cir. 1976) — § 2125

U.S., Grafton v.

U.S. v. Graham, 102 F.2d 436 (2d Cir. 1939) — § 1530

U.S. v. Graham, 538 F.2d 261 (9th Cir. 1976) — § 1209

U.S. v. Graham, 548 F.2d 1302 (8th Cir. 1977) — § 909

U.S., Granza v.

U.S. v. Grassi, 616 F.2d 1295 (5th Cir. 1980) — § 906; § 909

U.S., Graves v.

U.S. v. Gray, 448 F.2d 164 (9th Cir. 1971) — § 602

U.S. v. Gray, 507 F.2d 1013 (5th Cir. 1975) — § 2003

U.S. v. Gray, 565 F.2d 881 (5th Cir. 1978) — § 306

U.S. v. Gray, 584 F.2d 96 (5th Cir. 1978) — § 609

U.S. v. Gray, 611 F.2d 194 (7th Cir. 1979) — § 608

U.S. v. Grayson, 597 F.2d 1225 (9th Cir. 1979) — § 229

U.S., Green v.

U.S. v. Green, 499 F.2d 538 (D.C. Cir. 1974) — § 502

U.S. v. Green, 523 F.2d 229 (2d Cir. 1975) — § 1815; § 2003; § 2116

U.S. v. Green, 523 F.2d 968 (9th Cir. 1975) — § 245

U.S. v. Green, 548 F.2d 1261 (6th Cir. 1977) — § 706; § 2003; § 2116

U.S. v. Green, 600 F.2d 154 (8th Cir. 1979) — § 2116

U.S. v. Green, 670 F.2d 1148 (D.C. Cir. 1981) — § 219; § 253

U.S. v. Greene, 497 F.2d 1068 (7th Cir. 1974) — § 1110; § 2001

U.S. v. Greene, 578 F.2d 648 (5th Cir. 1978) — § 1208

U.S. v. Greer, 620 F.2d 1383 (10th Cir. 1980) — § 1209

U.S., Gregg v.

U.S. v. Gresham, 585 F.2d 103 (5th Cir. 1978) — § 303

U.S. v. Griffin, 579 F.2d 1104 (8th Cir. 1978) — § 1103

U.S. v. Griffin, 530 F.2d 739 (7th Cir. 1979) — § 243

U.S. v. Griffith, 537 F.2d 900 (7th Cir. 1976) — § 226

U.S., Grimaldi v.

U.S. v. Grismore, 564 F.2d 929 (10th Cir. 1977) — § 1207

U.S. v. Gross, 276 F.2d 816 (2d Cir. 1960) — § 1906

U.S. v. Gross, 329 F.2d 180 (4th Cir. 1964) — § 909

U.S. v. Gross, 961 F.2d 1097 (3rd Cir. 1992) — § 805; § 809

U.S., Grosso v.

U.S. v. Grosso, 358 F.2d 154 (3d Cir. 1966) — § 1264

U.S. v. Groves, 571 F.2d 450 (9th Cir. 1978) — § 1118

U.S., Gruleski v.

U.S., Grulkey v.

U.S., Grunewald v.

U.S. v. Gubelman, 571 F.2d 1252 (2d Cir. 1978) — § 1522; § 1524; § 1525

U.S. v. Guerra, 334 F.2d 138 (2d Cir. 1964) — § 1820

U.S. v. Guerrero, 650 F.2d 728 (5th Cir. 1981) — § 1517

U.S. v. Guerrero, 667 F.2d 862 (10th Cir. 1981) — § 1238

U.S. v. Guerrero, 863 F.2d 245 (2d Cir. 1988) — § 1323

U.S. v. Guevara, 598 F.2d 1094 (7th Cir. 1979) — § 2136

U.S. v. Guglielmini, 598 F.2d 1149 (9th Cir. 1979) — § 1261

U.S. v. Guillette, 547 F.2d 743 (2d Cir. 1976) — § 2145

U.S. v. Gulley, 374 F.2d 55 (6th Cir. 1967) — § 1515

U.S. v. Gullion, 575 F.2d 26 (1st Cir. 1978) — § 1247

U.S. v. Gumerlock, 590 F.2d 794 (9th Cir. 1979) — § 241

U.S. v. Gurney, 558 F.2d 1202 (5th Cir. 1977) — § 414

U.S. v. Gurtner, 474 F.2d 297 (9th Cir. 1973) — § 1917

U.S. v. Gurule, 437 F.2d 239 (10th Cir. 1970) — § 409

U.S. v. Guterma, 272 F.2d 344 (2d Cir. 1959) — § 1902

U.S. v. Haas, 583 F.2d 216 (5th Cir. 1978) — § 701

U.S. v. Hackett, 638 F.2d 1179 (9th Cir. 1980) — § 233

U.S. v. Haddad, 558 F.2d 968 (9th Cir. 1977) — § 312

U.S. v. Hadley, 671 F.2d 1112 (8th Cir. 1982) — § 318

U.S., Haggard v.

U.S., Haigler v.

U.S. v. Haines, 485 F.2d 564 (7th Cir. 1973) — § 1011

U.S. v. Hairrell, 521 F.2d 1264 (6th Cir. 1975) — § 905

U.S. v. Halbert, 436 F.2d 1226 (9th Cir. 1970) — § 304

U.S. v. Halbert, 668 F.2d 489 (10th Cir. 1982) — § 1810

U.S. v. Haldeman, 559 F.2d 31 (D.C. Cir. 1976) — § 111; § 717; § 916; § 1246; § 1403; § 1509; § 1523; § 2116

U.S. v. Hale, 422 U.S. 171 (1975) — § 2114

U.S. v. Haley, 500 F.2d 302 (8th Cir. 1974) — § 108

U.S. v. Hall, 348 F.2d 837 (2d Cir. 1965) — § 304

U.S. v. Hall, 536 F.2d 313 (10th Cir. 1976) — § 1266

U.S. v. Hall, 543 F.2d 1229 (9th Cir. 1976) — § 264

U.S. v. Hall, 559 F.2d 1160 (9th Cir. 1977) — § 1118

U.S. v. Hall, 565 F.2d 917 (5th Cir. 1978) — § 243; § 250

U.S. v. Hall, 565 F.2d 1052 (8th Cir. 1977) — § 1530

U.S. v. Hall, 588 F.2d 613 (8th Cir. 1978) — § 1246; § 1810

U.S. v. Hall, 653 F.2d 1002 (5th Cir. 1981) — § 1517

U.S. v. Haller, 543 F.2d 62 (9th Cir. 1976) — § 1518

U.S. v. Halper, 590 F.2d 422 (2d Cir. 1978) — § 904; § 1522

U.S., Hamer v.

U.S., Hamling v.

U.S. v. Hammack, 604 F.2d 437 (5th Cir. 1979) — § 228

U.S. v. Hammons, 566 F.2d 1301 (5th Cir. 1978) — § 1266

U.S. v. Hancock, 607 F.2d 337 (10th Cir. 1979) — § 618

U.S. v. Hand, 863 F.2d 1100 (3d Cir. 1988) — § 1337

U.S. v. Handler, 476 F.2d 709 (2d Cir. 1973) — § 425

U.S. v. Handly, 591 F.2d 1125 (5th Cir. 1979) — § 1103; § 1114

U.S. v. Handy, 454 F.2d 885 (9th Cir. 1971) — § 2003

U.S. v. Handy, 668 F.2d 407 (8th Cir. 1982) — § 2116

U.S. v. Handy, 753 F.2d 1487 (9th Cir. 1985) — § 517

U.S. v. Hankins, 565 F.2d 1344 (5th Cir. 1978) — § 1902

U.S. v. Hanna, 341 F.2d 906 (6th Cir. 1965) — § 1923

U.S., Hansen v.

U.S. v. Hansen, 583 F.2d 325 (7th Cir. 1978) — § 1115; § 2125

U.S., Hansford v.

U.S. v. Harary, 457 F.2d 471 (2d Cir. 1972) — § 1265

U.S. v. Harbin, 585 F.2d 904 (8th Cir. 1978) — § 1254

U.S. v. Harbin, 601 F.2d 773 (5th Cir. 1979) — § 303; § 1115; § 1116

U.S. v. Hare, 589 F.2d 242 (5th Cir. 1979) — § 250; § 1923

U.S. v. Hare, 589 F.2d 1291 (6th Cir. 1979) — § 213

U.S. v. Harmon, 339 F.2d 354 (6th Cir. 1964) — § 1904

U.S., Harney v.

U.S. v. Haro, 573 F.2d 661 (10th Cir. 1978) — § 1815

U.S. v. Haro-Espinosa, 619 F.2d 789 (9th Cir. 1979) — § 914; § 1108

U.S. v. Harper, 450 F.2d 1032 (5th Cir. 1971) — § 1921

U.S. v. Harper, 579 F.2d 1235 (10th Cir. 1978) — § 1516

U.S. v. Harrington, 490 F.2d 487 (2d Cir. 1973) — § 318; § 403

U.S. v. Harrington, 543 F.2d 1151 (5th Cir. 1976) — § 1209

U.S., Harris v.

U.S. v. Harris, 403 U.S. 573 (1971) — § 207; § 2144

U.S. v. Harris, 635 F.2d 526 (6th Cir. 1980) — § 612; § 903; § 912

U.S. v. Harris, 551 F.2d 621 (5th Cir. 1977) — § 1702; § 2127

U.S. v. Harris, 543 F.2d 1247 (9th Cir. 1976) — § 812

U.S. v. Harris, 542 F.2d 1283 (7th Cir. 1976) — § 712; § 804; § 806; § 809; § 810; § 812; § 1811; § 1904

U.S. v. Harris, 530 F.2d 576 (4th Cir. 1976) — § 1403

U.S. v. Harris, 462 F.2d 1033 (10th Cir. 1972) — § 722; § 1811

U.S. v. Harris, 409 F.2d 77 (4th Cir. 1969) — § 1802

U.S. v. Harris, 321 F.2d 739 (6th Cir. 1963) — § 221

U.S. v. Harris, 368 F. Supp. 697 (E.D. Pa. 1973) — § 806

U.S. v. Harrison, 524 F.2d 421 (D.C. Cir. 1975) — § 812; § 813

U.S. v. Hart, 526 F.2d 344 (5th Cir. 1976) — § 503

U.S. v. Hart, 565 F.2d 360 (5th Cir. 1978) — § 1811

U.S. v. Hart, 566 F.2d 977 (5th Cir. 1978) — § 608

U.S. v. Hart, 779 F.2d 575 (10th Cir. 1985) — § 519

U.S. v. Harvey, 526 F.2d 529 (2d Cir. 1975) — § 1805; § 2104

U.S. v. Harvey, 547 F.2d 720 (2d Cir. 1976) — § 1813

U.S. v. Harvey, 961 F.2d 1361 (8th Cir. 1992) — § 206

U.S., Hass v.

U.S. v. Hastings, 461 U.S. 499 (1983) — § 1115; § 1515; § 1907

U.S. v. Hastings, 847 F.2d 920 (1st Cir. 1988) — § 1234

U.S. v. Hathorn, 451 F.2d 1337 (5th Cir. 1971) — § 304

U.S. v. Hatrak, 588 F.2d 414 (3d Cir. 1978) — § 1011

U.S., Haupt v.

U.S. v. Havens, 446 U.S. 620 (1980) — § 1818

U.S., Hawkins v.

U.S. v. Hawkins, 501 F.2d 1029 (9th Cir. 1974) — § 424; § 425

U.S. v. Hawkins, 566 F.2d 1006 (5th Cir. 1978) — § 1245

U.S. v. Hawkins, 595 F.2d 751 (D.C. Cir. 1979) — § 1111

U.S. v. Hawkins, 901 F.2d 863 (10th Cir. 1990) — § 1325

U.S. v. Hawley, 554 F.2d 50 (2d Cir. 1977) — § 1810

U.S., Hayes v.

U.S. v. Hayes, 535 F.2d 479 (8th Cir. 1976) — § 2140

U.S. v. Hayes, 553 F.2d 824 (2d Cir. 1977) — § 225; § 1260; § 1809; § 1810

U.S. v. Hayes, 676 F.2d 1359 (11th Cir. 1982) — § 1012

U.S. v. Haygood, 502 F.2d 166 (7th Cir. 1974) — § 904

U.S., Haynes v.

U.S. v. Haynes, 398 F.2d 980 (2d Cir. 1968) — § 306

U.S. v. Hazeem, 679 F.2d 770 (9th Cir. 1982) — § 1304

U.S. v. Hazel, 928 F.2d 420 (D.C. Cir. 1991) — § 1346

U.S. v. Hazime, 762 F.2d 34 (6th Cir. 1985) — § 512

U.S. v. H. B. Gregory Co., 502 F.2d 700 (7th Cir. 1974) — § 1403

U.S. v. Head, 586 F.2d 508 (5th Cir. 1978) — § 403

U.S. v. Hearst, 563 F.2d 1331 (9th Cir. 1977) — § 1108; § 1904; § 1906

U.S. v. Heath, 528 F.2d 191 (9th Cir. 1975) — § 1815

U.S. v. Heath, 580 F.2d 1011 (10th Cir. 1978) — § 806; § 813

U.S. v. Hecht, 638 F.2d 651 (3d Cir. 1981) — § 610

U.S. v. Heck, 499 F.2d 778 (9th Cir. 1974) — § 907; § 909

U.S. v. Hedgeman, 564 F.2d 763 (7th Cir. 1977) — § 719

U.S. v. Heinze, 361 F. Supp. 46 (D. Del. 1973) — § 415

U.S. v. Helberg, 565 F.2d 993 (8th Cir. 1977) — § 1703

U.S. v. Heldt, 668 F.2d 1238 (D.C. Cir. 1981) — § 423; § 1903

U.S. v. Helgesen, 669 F.2d 69 (2d Cir. 1982) — § 1243

U.S. v. Helina, 549 F.2d 713 (9th Cir. 1977) — § 1115; § 1902

U.S. v. Helstoski, 576 F.2d 511 (3d Cir. 1978) — § 1512

U.S. v. Henciar, 568 F.2d 489 (6th Cir. 1977) — § 1524

U.S. v. Henderson, 434 F.2d 84 (6th Cir. 1970) — § 1503

U.S. v. Henderson, 471 F.2d 204 (7th Cir. 1972) — § 914

U.S. v. Henderson, 489 F.2d 802 (5th Cir. 1973) — § 317

U.S. v. Hendrix, 595 F.2d 883 (D.C. Cir. 1979) — § 232; § 243; § 245

U.S., Henry v.

U.S. v. Henry, 560 F.2d 963 (9th Cir. 1977) — § 1519

U.S. v. Henry, 604 F.2d 908 (5th Cir. 1979) — § 306

U.S. v. Henry, 447 U.S. 264 (1980) — § 310

U.S. v. Henry, 615 F.2d 1223 (9th Cir. 1980) — § 1207; § 1209

U.S. v. Henry, 883 F.2d 1010 (11th Cir. 1989) — § 1323

U.S. v. Hensel, 672 F.2d 578 (6th Cir. 1982) — § 255

U.S. v. Hensler, 625 F.2d 1141 (4th Cir. 1980) — § 235

U.S. v. Hensley, 469 U.S. 221 (1985) — § 228

U.S. v. Herbst, 565 F.2d 638 (10th Cir. 1977) — § 113

U.S. v. Herman, 576 F.2d 1139 (5th Cir. 1978) — § 1207

U.S. v. Herman, 589 F.2d 1191 (3d Cir. 1978) — § 423; § 1520

U.S. v. Herman, 614 F.2d 369 (3d Cir. 1980) — § 1302

U.S. v. Hernandez, 574 F.2d 1362 (5th Cir. 1978) — § 304; § 308; § 313

U.S. v. Hernandez, 588 F.2d 346 (2d Cir. 1978) — § 1517

U.S. v. Hernandez-Berceda, 572 F.2d 680 (9th Cir. 1978) — § 713

U.S. v. Herrera, 640 F.2d 958 (9th Cir. 1981) — § 611

U.S. v. Herring, 582 F.2d 535 (10th Cir. 1978) — § 318

U.S. v. Herring, 602 F.2d 1220 (5th Cir. 1979) — § 911; § 916

U.S. v. Herrold, 635 F.2d 213 (3d Cir. 1980) — § 609

U.S., Hester v.

U.S., Hibdon v.

U.S. v. Hickey, 596 F.2d 1082 (1st Cir. 1979) — § 2116

U.S. v. Hickok, 481 F.2d 377 (9th Cir. 1973) — § 403

U.S., Hicks v.

U.S. v. Hiett, 581 F.2d 1199 (5th Cir. 1978) — § 1112

U.S., Hilderbrand v.

U.S., Hill v.

U.S. v. Hill, 417 F.2d 279 (5th Cir. 1969) — § 1264

U.S. v. Hill, 589 F.2d 1344 (8th Cir. 1979) — § 701; § 717

U.S. v. Hill, 622 F.2d 900 (5th Cir. 1980) — § 1237

U.S. v. Hill, 655 F.2d 512 (3d Cir. 1981) — § 2003

U.S. v. Hillegas, 578 F.2d 453 (2d Cir. 1978) — § 1215

U.S. v. Hilliard, 569 F.2d 143 (D.C. Cir. 1977) — § 1103

U.S. v. Hillyard, 677 F.2d 1336 (9th Cir. 1982) — § 2011

U.S. v. Hilton, 521 F.2d 164 (2d Cir. 1975) — § 813

U.S. v. Hilton, 534 F.2d 556 (3d Cir. 1976) — § 409

U.S., Himmelfarb v.

U.S. v. Hinckley, 672 F.2d 115 (D.C. Cir. 1982) — § 308

U.S. v. Hinderman, 625 F.2d 994 (10th Cir. 1980) — § 108

U.S. v. Hindmarsh, 389 F.2d 137 (6th Cir. 1968) — § 304

U.S., Hinds v.

U.S. v. Hines, 455 F.2d 1317 (D.C. Cir. 1971) — § 318

U.S. v. Hines, 564 F.2d 925 (10th Cir. 1977) — § 2123

U.S. v. Hinton, 219 F.2d 324 (7th Cir. 1955) — § 211

U.S. v. Hirst, 668 F.2d 1180 (11th Cir. 1982) — § 1302

U.S. v. Hiscott, 586 F.2d 1271 (8th Cir. 1978) — § 1264

U.S. v. Hittle, 575 F.2d 799 (10th Cir. 1978) — § 207

U.S., Ho v.

U.S., Hobby v.

U.S. v. Hockenberry, 474 F.2d 247 (3d Cir. 1973) — § 420

U.S. v. Hodge, 496 F.2d 87 (5th Cir. 1974) — § 403

U.S. v. Hodge, 539 F.2d 898 (6th Cir. 1976) — § 268

U.S. v. Hodge, 594 F.2d 1163 (7th Cir. 1979) — § 1602

U.S. v. Hodges, 556 F.2d 366 (5th Cir. 1977) — § 810

U.S., Hoffa v.

U.S. v. Hoffa, 349 F.2d 20 (6th Cir. 1965) — § 913; § 1112; § 1908; § 1918

U.S. v. Hoffa, 247 F. Supp. 692 (E.D. Tenn. 1965) — § 1302

U.S., Hoffman v.

U.S., Holder v.

U.S. v. Holder, 399 F. Supp. 220 (D.S.D. 1975) — § 111

U.S., Holland v.

U.S. v. Holleman, 575 F.2d 139 (7th Cir. 1978) — § 314; § 1249

U.S. v. Hollinger, 553 F.2d 535 (7th Cir. 1977) — § 1113

U.S., Hollingsworth v.

U.S. v. Holloway, 781 F.2d 124 (8th Cir. 1986) — § 509

U.S. v. Hollywood Motor Car Co., 102 S. Ct. 3081 (1982) — § 1118

U.S. v. Holmes, 414 F. Supp. 831 (D. Md. 1976) — § 1403

U.S. v. Holmes, 594 F.2d 1167 (8th Cir. 1979) — § 1818; § 1819

U.S., Holt v.

U.S. v. Homburg, 546 F.2d 1350 (9th Cir. 1976) — § 241

U.S. v. Homer, 545 F.2d 864 (3d Cir. 1976) — § 1111

U.S. v. Honea, 556 F.2d 906 (8th Cir. 1977) — § 1605

U.S. v. Honneus, 508 F.2d 566 (1st Cir. 1974) — § 1815; § 2001

U.S. v. Hood, 593 F.2d 293 (8th Cir. 1979) — § 1249; § 1906

U.S. v. Hooker, 541 F.2d 300 (1st Cir. 1976) — § 1115

U.S. v. Hooker, 607 F.2d 286 (9th Cir. 1979) — § 1207

U.S. v. Hooper, 576 F.2d 1382 (9th Cir. 1978) — § 1008

U.S. v. Hooper, 596 F.2d 219 (7th Cir. 1979) — § 1239

U.S. v. Hoosier, 542 F.2d 687 (6th Cir. 1976) — § 2114

U.S., Horsley v.

U.S. v. Horton, 526 F.2d 884 (5th Cir. 1976) — § 1802

U.S. v. Horton, 601 F.2d 319 (7th Cir. 1979) — § 268

U.S. v. Hospital Monteflores, Inc., 575 F.2d 332 (1st Cir. 1978) — § 1006

U.S. v. Houle, 603 F.2d 1297 (8th Cir. 1979) — § 232

U.S. v. Houltin, 566 F.2d 1027 (5th Cir. 1978) — § 248

U.S. v. Housand, 550 F.2d 818 (2d Cir. 1977) — § 420

U.S. v. House, 551 F.2d 756 (8th Cir. 1977) — § 1502

U.S. v. House, 604 F.2d 1135 (8th Cir. 1979) — § 210

U.S. v. Howard, 590 F.2d 564 (4th Cir. 1979) — § 1005

U.S. v. Howze, 668 F.2d 322 (7th Cir. 1982) — § 1528

U.S. v. Hoyos, 573 F.2d 1111 (9th Cir. 1978) — § 2144; § 2145; § 2147

U.S. v. Huang, 960 F.2d 1128 (2d Cir. 1992) — § 1008

U.S. v. Huber, 603 F.2d 387 (2d Cir. 1979) — § 1257

U.S., Huddleston v.

U.S. v. Hudson, 564 F.2d 1377 (9th Cir. 1977) — § 319; § 2111

U.S. v. Hudson, 566 F.2d 889 (4th Cir. 1977) — § 703

U.S. v. Huerta, 878 F.2d 89 (2d Cir. 1989) — § 1328

U.S. v. Huff, 873 F.2d 709 (3d Cir. 1989) — § 1323

U.S. v. Huffman, 595 F.2d 551 (10th Cir. 1979) — § 1011

U.S., Hughes v.

U.S. v. Hughes, 542 F.2d 246 (5th Cir. 1976) — § 1403

U.S., Hughey v.

U.S. v. Hulphers, 421 F.2d 1291 (9th Cir. 1969) — § 1512

U.S. v. Humer, 542 F.2d 254 (5th Cir. 1976) — § 1103

U.S. v. Hunley, 567 F.2d 822 (8th Cir. 1977) — § 207

U.S. v. Hunt, 661 F.2d 72 (6th Cir. 1981) — § 1240

U.S. v. Hunter, 672 F.2d 815 (10th Cir. 1982) — § 112; § 1522

U.S. v. Hurtado, 779 F.2d 1467 (11th Cir. 1985) — § 509; § 512

U.S. v. Hutchings, 757 F.2d 11 (2d Cir. 1984) — § 1322

U.S. v. Hutchinson, 488 F.2d 484 (8th Cir. 1973) — § 215

U.S. v. Hutul, 416 F.2d 607 (7th Cir. 1969) — § 909; § 916

U.S. v. Hyatt, 565 F.2d 229 (2d Cir. 1977) — § 1923

U.S., Hyde v.

U.S. v. Hykel, 461 F.2d 721 (3d Cir. 1972) — § 1810; § 1817

U.S. v. Iaconetti, 540 F.2d 574 (2d Cir. 1976) — § 2136

U.S. v. Iaquinta, 674 F.2d 260 (4th Cir. 1982) — § 1212

U.S. v. Ibarra, 112 S. Ct. 4 (1991) — § 256

U.S., IBM v.

U.S. v. Imperial Chemical Industries, Ltd., 100 F. Supp. 504 (S.D.N.Y. 1951) — § 1703

U.S. v. Inadi, 475 U.S. 387 (1986) — § 2116; § 2139

U.S. v. Incrovato, 611 F.2d 5 (1st Cir. 1979) — § 611

U.S. v. Indian Boy X, 565 F.2d 585 (9th Cir. 1977) — § 304

U.S. v. Industrial Laboratories Co., 456 F.2d 908 (10th Cir. 1972) — § 1502

U.S., In re

U.S. v. Interstate Dress Carriers, Inc., 280 F.2d 52 (2d Cir. 1960) — § 411

U.S. v. Iozia, 13 F.R.D. 335 (S.D.N.Y. 1952) — § 717

U.S. v. Ireland, 456 F.2d 74 (10th Cir. 1972) — § 304

U.S. v. Irizarry, 673 F.2d 554 (1st Cir. 1982) — § 255

U.S. v. Irwin, 593 F.2d 138 (1st Cir. 1979) — § 1261

U.S. v. Isaacs, 493 F.2d 1124 (7th Cir. 1974) — § 102

U.S. v. Ismail, 756 F.2d 1253 (6th Cir. 1985) — § 1924

U.S. v. Isom, 588 F.2d 858 (2d Cir. 1978) — § 245; § 304

U.S. v. Izzi, 427 F.2d 293 (2d Cir. 1970) — § 1903

U.S. v. Jabara, 644 F.2d 574 (6th Cir. 1981) — § 1001

U.S., Jaben v.

U.S., Jackson v.

U.S. v. Jackson, 425 F.2d 574 (D.C. Cir. 1970) — § 2003

U.S. v. Jackson, 451 F.2d 259 (5th Cir. 1971) — § 1802

U.S. v. Jackson, 508 F.2d 1001 (7th Cir. 1975) — § 716

U.S. v. Jackson, 542 F.2d 403 (7th Cir. 1976) — § 1258

U.S. v. Jackson, 562 F.2d 789 (D.C. Cir. 1977) — § 906; § 907

U.S. v. Jackson, 569 F.2d 1003 (7th Cir. 1978) — § 2001

U.S. v. Jackson, 576 F.2d 46 (5th Cir. 1978) — § 1805; § 1815

U.S. v. Jackson, 576 F.2d 749 (8th Cir. 1978) — § 226

U.S. v. Jackson, 578 F.2d 1162 (5th Cir. 1978) — § 306

U.S. v. Jackson, 579 F.2d 553 (10th Cir. 1978) — § 719; § 1108

U.S. v. Jackson, 585 F.2d 653 (4th Cir. 1978) — § 215

U.S. v. Jackson, 588 F.2d 1046 (5th Cir. 1979) — § 1518

U.S. v. Jackson, 627 F.2d 883 (8th Cir. 1980) — § 609

U.S. v. Jackson, 659 F.2d 73 (5th Cir. 1981) — § 603; § 614

U.S. v. Jacobs, 322 F. Supp. 1299 (C.D. Cal. 1971) — § 1919

U.S. v. Jacobs, 547 F.2d 772 (2nd Cir. 1976) — § 405

U.S. v. Jacobsen, 466 U.S. 109 (1984) — § 202

U.S., Jacobson v.

U.S. v. Jacobson, 536 F.2d 793 (8th Cir. 1976) — § 303; § 1513; § 2104

U.S. v. Jalbert, 504 F.2d 892 (1st Cir. 1974) — § 1605

U.S. v. Jamar, 561 F.2d 1103 (4th Cir. 1977) — § 912

U.S., James v.

U.S. v. James, 493 F.2d 323 (2d Cir. 1974) — § 305; § 312

U.S. v. James, 495 F.2d 434 (5th Cir. 1974) — § 706

U.S. v. James, 555 F.2d 992 (D.C. Cir. 1977) — § 233; § 1522

U.S. v. James, 576 F.2d 1121 (5th Cir. 1978) — § 1528

U.S. v. James, 590 F.2d 575 (5th Cir. 1979) — § 2116

U.S. v. James, 674 F.2d 886 (11th Cir. 1982) — § 504

U.S. v. Jamison, 505 F.2d 407 (D.C. Cir. 1974) — § 1118

U.S. v. Janis, 428 U.S. 433 (1976) — § 248

U.S. v. Jannotti, 673 F.2d 578 (3d Cir. 1982) — § 1501

U.S. v. Janovich, 688 F.2d 1227 (9th Cir. 1982) — § 1304

U.S. v. Jardan, 552 F.2d 216 (8th Cir. 1977) — § 1102

U.S., Jarrett v.

U.S., Jeffers v.

U.S. v. Jefferson, 650 F.2d 854 (6th Cir. 1981) — § 228

U.S., Jencks v.

U.S., Jenkins v.

U.S. v. Jenkins, 420 U.S. 358 (1975) — § 1006

U.S. v. Jenkins, 496 F.2d 57 (2d Cir. 1974) — § 222

U.S. v. Jenkins, 510 F.2d 495 (2d Cir. 1975) — § 108; § 1805

U.S. v. Jenkins, 544 F.2d 180 (4th Cir. 1976) — § 1115

U.S. v. Jennewein, 590 F.2d 191 (6th Cir. 1978) — § 1513

U.S., Jennings v.

U.S. v. Jensen, 561 F.2d 1297 (8th Cir. 1977) — § 304

U.S. v. Jensen, 608 F.2d 1349 (10th Cir. 1979) — § 706

U.S. v. Jessup, 757 F.2d 378 (1st Cir. 1985) — § 507

U.S. v. Jimenez, 602 F.2d 139 (7th Cir. 1979) — § 306

U.S. v. Jimenez, 613 F.2d 1373 (5th Cir. 1980) — § 1802

U.S. v. Jimenez-Lopez, 873 F.2d 769 (5th Cir. 1989) — § 1322

U.S. v. Jodoin, 672 F.2d 232 (1st Cir. 1982) — § 1223

U.S. v. John, 587 F.2d 683 (5th Cir. 1979) — § 1003

U.S. v. John Bernard Industries, Inc., 589 F.2d 1353 (8th Cir. 1979) — § 108; § 712

U.S. v. John Doe, Inc., I, 107 S. Ct. 1656 (1987) — § 412; § 416

U.S. v. Johns, 469 U.S. 478 (1985) — § 237

U.S., Johnson v.

U.S. v. Johnson, 319 U.S. 503 (1943) — § 1605; § 2005

U.S. v. Johnson, 371 F.2d 800 (3d Cir. 1967) — § 1270

U.S. v. Johnson, 463 F.2d 216 (9th Cir. 1972) — § 2116

U.S. v. Johnson, 476 F.2d 1251 (5th Cir. 1973) — § 1269

U.S. v. Johnson, 495 F.2d 1097 (5th Cir. 1974) — § 1801

U.S. v. Johnson, 506 F.2d 674 (8th Cir. 1974) — § 238

U.S. v. Johnson, 525 F.2d 999 (2d Cir. 1975) — § 706; § 716; § 1818

U.S. v. Johnson, 529 F.2d 581 (8th Cir. 1976) — § 302

U.S. v. Johnson, 539 F.2d 181 (D.C. Cir. 1976) — § 261

U.S. v. Johnson, 561 F.23d 832 (D.C. Cir. 1977) — § 232

U.S. v. Johnson, 562 F.2d 515 (8th Cir. 1977) — § 706; § 1514; § 1524

U.S. v. Johnson, 569 F.2d 269 (5th Cir. 1978) — § 1252

U.S. v. Johnson, 575 F.2d 1347 (5th Cir. 1978) — § 2003

U.S. v. Johnson, 577 F.2d 1304 (5th Cir. 1978) — § 2127

U.S. v. Johnson, 579 F.2d 122 (5th Cir. 1978) — § 1209

U.S. v. Johnson, 584 F.2d 148 (6th Cir. 1978) — § 1246; § 1250

U.S. v. Johnson, 585 F.2d 119 (5th Cir. 1978) — § 1517

U.S. v. Johnson, 588 F.2d 961 (5th Cir. 1979) — § 1810

U.S. v. Johnson, 594 F.2d 1253 (9th Cir. 1980) — § 1605

U.S. v. Johnson, 713 F.2d 654 (11th Cir. 1983) — § 1302

U.S. v. Johnston, 543 F.2d 55 (8th Cir. 1976) — § 719

U.S., Jones v.

U.S. v. Jones, 392 F.2d 567 (4th Cir. 1968) — § 1705

U.S. v. Jones, 438 F.2d 461 (7th Cir. 1971) — § 2116

U.S. v. Jones, 466 F.2d 1364 (5th Cir. 1972) — § 215

U.S. v. Jones, 524 F.2d 834 (D.C. Cir. 1975) — § 1239

U.S. v. Jones, 527 F.2d 817 (D.C. Cir. 1975) — § 1004

U.S. v. Jones, 542 F.2d 661 (6th Cir. 1976) — § 268

U.S. v. Jones, 543 F.2d 1171 (5th Cir. 1976) — § 1239

U.S. v. Jones, 554 F.2d 251 (5th Cir. 1977) — § 2123

U.S. v. Jones, 557 F.2d 1237 (8th Cir. 1977) — § 1810

U.S. v. Jones, 580 F.2d 219 (6th Cir. 1978) — § 1010; § 1402

U.S. v. Jones, 580 F.2d 785 (5th Cir. 1978) — § 245

U.S. v. Jones, 592 F.2d 1038 (9th Cir. 1979) — § 1103; § 1116

U.S. v. Jones, 597 F.2d 485 (5th Cir. 1979) — § 1302

U.S. v. Jones, 612 F.2d 453 (9th Cir. 1979) — § 1270

U.S. v. Jones, 669 F.2d 559 (8th Cir. 1982) — § 1304

U.S. v. Jones, 676 F.2d 327 (8th Cir. 1982) — § 1212

U.S. v. Jordan, 399 F.2d 610 (2d Cir. 1968) — § 708

U.S. v. Jordan, 570 F.2d 635 (6th Cir. 1978) — § 313

U.S. v. Jordan, 602 F.2d 171 (8th Cir. 1979) — § 903

U.S. v. Jorn, 400 U.S. 470 (1971) — § 1007; § 1008

U.S. v. Joseph, 278 F.2d 504 (3d Cir. 1960) — § 214

U.S. v. Joseph, 533 F.2d 282 (5th Cir. 1976) — § 722

U.S. v. Joyce, 499 F.2d 9 (7th Cir. 1974) — § 1204; § 1503

U.S. v. Joyner, 547 F.2d 1199 (4th Cir. 1977) — § 1813

U.S. v. Juarez, 549 F.2d 1113 (7th Cir. 1977) — § 1517

U.S. v. Juarez, 561 F.2d 65 (7th Cir. 1977) — § 1522

U.S. v. Juarez, 566 F.2d 511 (5th Cir. 1978) — § 1111

U.S. v. Juarez, 573 F.2d 267 (5th Cir. 1978) — § 243; § 268; § 1819; § 1919

U.S., Juarez-Casares v.

U.S. v. Judon, 567 F.2d 1289 (5th Cir. 1978) — § 2122

U.S. v. Judson, 322 F.2d 460 (9th Cir. 1963) — § 1902

U.S. v. Julian, 469 F.2d 371 (10th Cir. 1972) — § 1921

U.S. v. Kahan, 415 U.S. 239 (1974) — § 1906

U.S. v. Kahaner, 317 F.2d 459 (2d Cir. 1963) — § 1813

U.S. v. Kahaner, 203 F. Supp. 78 (S.D.N.Y. 1963) — § 701

U.S. v. Kahl, 583 F.2d 1351 (5th Cir. 1978) — § 103

U.S. v. Kahn, 251 F. Supp. 702 (S.D.N.Y. 1966) — § 1918; § 1919

U.S. v. Kahn, 381 F.2d 824 (7th Cir. 1967) — § 914

U.S. v. Kahn, 415 U.S. 143 (1974) — § 261

U.S. v. Kahn, 471 F.2d 191 (7th Cir. 1972) — § 1914

U.S. v. Kahn, 472 F.2d 272 (2d Cir. 1973) — § 1809

U.S. v. Kaibney, 155 F.2d 795 (2d Cir. 1946) — § 1707

U.S. v. Kail, 612 F.2d 443 (9th Cir. 1980) — § 1239

U.S. v. Kampbell, 574 F.2d 962 (8th Cir. 1978) — § 244

U.S. v. Kaplan, 510 F.2d 606 (2d Cir. 1974) — § 2116

U.S. v. Kaplan, 554 F.2d 958 (9th Cir. 1977) — § 403; § 918

U.S. v. Kaplan, 554 F.2d 577 (3d Cir. 1977) — § 716

U.S. v. Karo, 468 U.S. 705 (1984) — § 201

U.S., Kastigar v.

U.S., Katz v.

U.S., Kaufman v.

U.S. v. Kaufman, 429 F.2d 240 (2d Cir. 1970) — § 1902

U.S. v. Kaylor, 491 F.2d 1127 (2d Cir. 1973) — § 317

U.S. v. Kearney, 420 F.2d 170 (D.C. Cir. 1969) — § 1815

U.S., Keeble v.

U.S. v. Keeble, 459 F.2d 757 (8th Cir. 1972) — § 304

U.S., Keel v.

U.S. v. Keiswetter, 866 F.2d 1301 (10th Cir. 1989) — § 610

U.S. v. Kellerman, 432 F.2d 371 (10th Cir. 1970) — § 912

U.S. v. Kelly, 349 F.2d 720 (2d Cir. 1965) — § 1403

U.S. v. Kelly, 551 F.2d 760 (8th Cir. 1977) — § 245

U.S. v. Kelly, 569 F.2d 928 (5th Cir. 1978) — § 716

U.S. v. Kelton, 446 F.2d 669 (8th Cir. 1971) — § 1502

U.S. v. Kendrick, 331 F.2d 110 (4th Cir. 1964) — § 1918

U.S. v. Kendricks, 623 F.2d 1165 (6th Cir. 1980) — § 916

U.S. v. Kennedy, 573 F.2d 657 (9th Cir. 1978) — § 306

U.S., Kenney v.

U.S. v. Kenney, 601 F.2d 211 (5th Cir. 1979) — § 229

U.S. v. Kenny, 462 F.2d 1205 (3d Cir. 1972) — § 1818

U.S. v. Kenny, 645 F.2d 1323 (9th Cir. 1981) — § 1301

U.S. v. Keuylian, 602 F.2d 1033 (2d Cir. 1979) — § 112; § 241

U.S., Kercheval v.

U.S. v. Kerrigan, 514 F.2d 35 (9th Cir. 1975) — § 261

U.S. v. Key, 717 F.2d 1206 (8th Cir. 1983) — § 1810

U.S. v. Kiamie, 258 F.2d 924 (2d Cir. 1958) — § 1605

U.S. v. Kibler, 667 F.2d 452 (4th Cir. 1982) — § 105

U.S. v. Kiendra, 663 F.2d 349 (1st Cir. 1981) — § 1810

U.S. v. Kilbourne, 559 F.2d 1263 (4th Cir. 1977) — § 2114

U.S., Kilgore v.

U.S. v. Killebrew, 594 F.2d 1103 (6th Cir. 1979) — § 253

U.S. v. Killian, 524 F.2d 1268 (5th Cir. 1975) — § 1815

U.S. v. Kilrain, 566 F.2d 979 (5th Cir. 1978) — § 701; § 813

U.S. v. Kim, 577 F.2d 473 (9th Cir. 1978) — § 317; § 414

U.S. v. Kim, 595 F.2d 755 (D.C. Cir. 1979) — § 912; § 2123; § 2136

U.S., Kincade v.

U.S., King v.

U.S. v. King, 472 F.2d 1 (9th Cir. 1973) — § 1703

U.S. v. King, 521 F.2d 61 (10th Cir. 1975) — § 1264

U.S. v. King, 560 F.2d 122 (2d Cir. 1977) — § 1532

U.S. v. King, 563 F.2d 559 (2d Cir. 1977) — § 105; § 109

U.S. v. King, 587 F.2d 956 (9th Cir. 1978) — § 1602

U.S. v. King, 590 F.2d 253 (8th Cir. 1978) — § 2125

U.S. v. King, 618 F.2d 550 (9th Cir. 1980) — § 618

U.S. v. Kinnard, 465 F.2d 566 (D.C. Cir. 1972) — § 1817

U.S. v. Kirk, 584 F.2d 773 (6th Cir. 1978) — § 1516

U.S. v. Klein, 522 F.2d 296 (1st Cir. 1975) — § 224

U.S. v. Klein, 592 F.2d 909 (5th Cir. 1979) — § 305

U.S. v. Kleinschmidt, 596 F.2d 133 (5th Cir. 1979) — § 229

U.S., Knapp v.

U.S. v. Knife, 592 F.2d 472 (8th Cir. 1979) — § 911; § 1516; § 2119

U.S. v. Knight, 509 F.2d 354 (D.C. Cir. 1974) — § 1805

U.S. v. Knight, 905 F.2d 189 (8th Cir. 1990) — § 1323

U.S. v. Knohl, 379 F.2d 427 (2d Cir. 1967) — § 1707

U.S. v. Knotts, 460 U.S. 276 (1983) — § 201

U.S. v. Knowles, 594 F.2d 753 (9th Cir. 1979) — § 813

U.S. v. Knox, 396 U.S. 77 (1969) — § 1902; § 1905

U.S. v. Knuckles, 581 F.2d 305 (2d Cir. 1978) — § 314; § 2116

U.S., Kolod v.

U.S. v. Kopel, 552 F.2d 1265 (7th Cir. 1977) — § 1204; § 1239

U.S. v. Korman, 614 F.2d 541 (6th Cir. 1980) — § 233

U.S. v. Kossa, 562 F.2d 959 (5th Cir. 1977) — § 2001

U.S., Kotteakos v.

U.S. v. Kovaleski, 406 F. Supp. 267 (E.D. Mich. 1976) — § 408

U.S. v. Kovel, 296 F.2d 918 (2d Cir. 1961) — § 1917; § 1918; § 1921

U.S. v. Krasny, 607 F.2d 840 (9th Cir. 1979) — § 1302

U.S. v. Kravitz, 281 F.2d 581 (3d Cir. 1960) — § 1906

U.S. v. Kriz, 586 F.2d 1178 (8th Cir. 1978) — § 610

U.S. v. Krohn, 558 F.2d 390 (8th Cir. 1977) — § 716

U.S. v. Krohn, 573 F.2d 1382 (10th Cir. 1978) — § 2104

U.S., Krulewitch v.

U.S. v. Kushner, 135 F.2d 668 (2d Cir. 1943) — § 1706

U.S., Kyle v.

U.S. v. Laca, 499 F.2d 922 (5th Cir. 1974) — § 907

U.S. v. Lace, 669 F.2d 46 (2d Cir. 1982) — § 207

U.S. v. Lacob, 416 F.2d 756 (7th Cir. 1969) — § 1605

U.S. v. La Guardia, 902 F.2d 1010 (1st Cir. 1990) — § 1328

U.S. v. L'Hoste, 609 F.2d 796 (5th Cir. 1980) — § 1246

U.S. v. Lamar, 545 F.2d 488 (5th Cir. 1977) — § 202

U.S. v. Lamb, 575 F.2d 1310 (10th Cir. 1978) — § 111; § 1526; § 1810; § 1906

U.S., Lambert v.

U.S. v. Lambert, 580 F.2d 740 (5th Cir. 1978) — § 716

U.S. v. Lambert, 603 F.2d 808 (10th Cir. 1979) — § 1301

U.S. v. Lam Lek Chong, 544 F.2d 58 (2d Cir. 1976) — § 2116

U.S. v. Landof, 591 F.2d 36 (9th Cir. 1978) — § 1802

U.S. v. Lane, 106 S. Ct. 725 (1986) — § 911; § 919

U.S. v. Lane, 561 F.2d 1075 (2d Cir. 1977) — § 1207

U.S. v. Lane, 584 F.2d 60 (5th Cir. 1978) — § 909

U.S. v. Lang, 589 F.2d 92 (2d Cir. 1978) — § 2144; § 2148

U.S. v. Lang, 644 F.2d 1232 (7th Cir. 1981) — § 401

U.S. v. Langston, 576 F.2d 1138 (5th Cir. 1978) — § 1810

U.S. v. Lanier, 578 F.2d 1246 (8th Cir. 1978) — § 2124

U.S. v. Lanza, 260 U.S. 377 (1922) — § 1004

U.S. v. Lara, 905 F.2d 599 (2d Cir. 1990) — § 1326

U.S. v. Largent, 545 F.2d 1039 (6th Cir. 1976) — § 701; § 1204; § 1522

U.S. v. LaRiche, 549 F.2d 1088 (6th Cir. 1977) — § 1805

U.S. v. Larios, 640 F.2d 938 (9th Cir. 1981) — § 1322

U.S. v. Larkin, 605 F.2d 1360 (5th Cir. 1979) — § 1003; § 1010

U.S. v. Larry, 536 F.2d 1149 (6th Cir. 1976) — § 1906

U.S. v. Larson, 555 F.2d 673 (8th Cir. 1977) — § 712; § 809

U.S. v. Lartey, 716 F.2d 955 (2d Cir. 1983) — § 413

U.S. v. LaSalle Nat'l Bank, 437 U.S. 297 (1978) — § 401

U.S. v. Lasater, 535 F.2d 1041 (8th Cir. 1976) — § 1006

U.S. v. Lasky, 600 F.2d 765 (9th Cir. 1979) — § 1011

U.S., Latham v.

U.S., Latona v.

U.S. v. LaVallee, 436 F. Supp. 946 (S.D. Tex. 1977) — § 502

U.S. v. Lavallie, 666 F.2d 1217 (8th Cir. 1981) — § 1805

U.S. v. Lawhon, 499 F.2d 352 (5th Cir. 1974) — § 105

U.S., Lawn v.

U.S. v. Lawson, 507 F.2d 433 (7th Cir. 1974) — § 106

U.S. v. Lawson, 608 F.2d 1129 (6th Cir. 1979) — § 2149

U.S. v. Lawson, 653 F.2d 299 (7th Cir. 1981) — § 2001

U.S. v. Lawson, 670 F.2d 923 (10th Cir. 1982) — § 104; § 1245; § 1320

U.S. v. Leach, 613 F.2d 1295 (5th Cir. 1980) — § 906; § 909

U.S., Leary v.

U.S. v. Lechoco, 542 F.2d 84 (D.C. Cir. 1976) — § 1518; § 1918; § 2149

U.S., Lee v.

U.S. v. Lee, 274 U.S. 559 (1927) — § 238

U.S. v. Lee, 542 F.2d 353 (6th Cir. 1976) — § 261

U.S. v. Lee, 581 F.2d 1173 (6th Cir. 1978) — § 213; § 247

U.S. v. Lee, 589 F.2d 980 (9th Cir. 1979) — § 1702; § 2127

U.S. v. Lee, 818 F.2d 1052 (2d Cir. 1987) — § 1339

U.S. v. Leftwich, 461 F.2d 586 (3d Cir. 1972) — § 1819

U.S. v. Leighton, 265 F. Supp. 27 (S.D.N.Y. 1967) — § 1904

U.S. v. Leja, 568 F.2d 493 (6th Cir. 1977) — § 1517

U.S., Lelles v.

U.S. v. Lemon, 550 F.2d 467 (9th Cir. 1977) — § 243

U.S. v. Lenz, 616 F.2d 960 (6th Cir. 1980) — § 419; § 423

U.S. v. Leon, 468 U.S. 897 (1984) — § 248

U.S. v. Leon, 534 F.2d 667 (6th Cir. 1976) — § 1113

U.S. v. Leonard, 445 F.2d 234 (D.C. Cir. 1971) — § 903

U.S. v. Leonard, 494 F.2d 955 (D.C. Cir. 1974) — § 1815

U.S. v. Leonard, 589 F.2d 470 (9th Cir. 1970) — § 1318

U.S. v. Leonard, 609 F.2d 1163 (5th Cir. 1980) — § 703

U.S. v. Leonard, 639 F.2d 101 (2d Cir. 1981) — § 1212

U.S. v. Leonelli, 428 F. Supp. 880 (S.D.N.Y. 1977) — § 701

U.S., Lepera v.

U.S. v. Le Pera, 443 F.2d 810 (9th Cir. 1971) — § 1902

U.S. v. Leppo, 634 F.2d 101 (3d Cir. 1980) — § 1010

U.S. v. Leslie, 542 F.2d 285 (5th Cir. 1976) — § 2136

U.S. v. Lester, 248 F.2d 329 (2d Cir. 1957) — § 1817

U.S. v. Leverage Funding Sys., Inc., 637 F.2d 645 (9th Cir. 1980) — § 401

U.S. v. Levine, 546 F.2d 658 (5th Cir. 1977) — § 1703

U.S. v. Levy, 578 F.2d 896 (2d Cir. 1978) — § 315

U.S. v. Lewin, 467 F.2d 1132 (7th Cir. 1972) — § 1518

U.S., Lewis v.

U.S. v. Lewis, 362 F.2d 759 (2d Cir. 1966) — § 219

U.S. v. Lewis, 406 F.2d 486 (7th Cir. 1969) — § 1801

U.S. v. Lewis, 433 F.2d 1146 (D.C. Cir. 1970) — § 1911

U.S. v. Lewis, 447 F.2d 134 (2d Cir. 1971) — § 1805

U.S. v. Lewis, 475 F.2d 571 (5th Cir. 1972) — § 1905

U.S. v. Lewis, 482 F.2d 632 (D.C. Cir. 1973) — § 1518; § 1519; § 1520

U.S. v. Lewis, 511 F.2d 798 (D.C. Cir. 1975) — § 706

U.S. v. Lewis, 547 F.2d 1030 (8th Cir. 1976) — § 912

U.S. v. Lewis, 556 F.2d 446 (6th Cir. 1977) — § 306

U.S. v. Lewis, 565 F.2d 1248 (2d Cir. 1977) — § 319; § 1270; § 2111

U.S. v. Lewis, 592 F.2d 1282 (5th Cir. 1979) — § 1266

U.S. v. Lewis, 626 F.2d 940 (D.C. Cir. 1980) — § 903; § 912

U.S. v. Lewis, 671 F.2d 1025 (7th Cir. 1982) — § 713; § 1923

U.S. v. Lewis, 676 F.2d 508 (11th Cir. 1982) — § 106

U.S. v. Librach, 536 F.2d 1228 (8th Cir. 1976) — § 1116

U.S. v. Licavoli, 604 F.2d 613 (9th Cir. 1979) — § 210; § 263; § 266; § 1906

U.S. v. Lieberman, 608 F.2d 889 (1st Cir. 1979) — § 1239

U.S. v. Lieblich, 246 F.2d 890 (2d Cir. 1957) — § 1816

U.S. v. Liles, 670 F.2d 989 (11th Cir. 1982) — § 107

U.S. v. Lilley, 581 F.2d 182 (8th Cir. 1978) — § 1909; § 1913; § 2140; § 2144

U.S. v. Lilly, 576 F.2d 1240 (5th Cir. 1978) — § 242; § 312

U.S. v. Lind, 542 F.2d 598 (2d Cir. 1976) — § 1810

U.S. v. Lindstrom, 698 F.2d 1154 (11th Cir. 1982) — § 1924

U.S. v. Ling, 581 F.2d 1118 (4th Cir. 1978) — § 1810

U.S., Lipscomb v.

U.S. v. Lipton, 467 F.2d 1161 (2d Cir. 1972) — § 1906

U.S. v. Little, 567 F.2d 346 (8th Cir. 1977) — § 1810

U.S. v. Little, 562 F.2d 578 (8th Cir. 1978) — § 712

U.S. v. Littlewind, 551 F.2d 244 (8th Cir. 1977) — § 1801

U.S. v. Litton Sys., Inc., 573 F.2d 195 (4th Cir. 1978) — § 1118

U.S. v. Llinas, 603 F.2d 506 (5th Cir. 1979) — § 1602

U.S., Lloyd v.

U.S. v. Lloyd, 400 F.2d 414 (6th Cir. 1968) — § 1923

U.S. v. Lochan, 674 F.2d 960 (1st Cir. 1982) — § 255

U.S., Locken v.

U.S. v. Lockett, 674 F.2d 843 (11th Cir. 1982) — § 206

U.S. v. Lombardi, 550 F.2d 827 (2d Cir. 1977) — § 1264; § 2110

U.S. v. Long, 524 F.2d 660 (9th Cir. 1976) — § 245

U.S. v. Long, 533 F.2d 505 (9th Cir. 1976) — § 1514

U.S. v. Long, 574 F.2d 761 (3d Cir. 1978) — § 1517; § 1522

U.S. v. Long Elk, 565 F.2d 1032 (8th Cir. 1977) — § 1246

U.S. v. Long Soldier, 562 F.2d 601 (9th Cir. 1977) — § 1801; § 1807; § 1813

U.S., Lopez v.

U.S. v. Lopez, 475 F.2d 537 (7th Cir. 1973) — § 1611

U.S. v. Lopez, 542 F.2d 283 (5th Cir. 1976) — § 103

U.S. v. Lopez, 581 F.2d 1338 (9th Cir. 1978) — § 243; § 1242

U.S. v. Lopez, 625 F.2d 889 (9th Cir. 1980) — § 1272

U.S. v. Lopez-Espindola, 632 F.2d 107 (9th Cir. 1980) — § 1219; § 1221; § 1228

U.S. v. Lord, 565 F.2d 831 (2d Cir. 1977) — § 1530

U.S. v. LoRusso, 695 F.2d 45 (2d Cir. 1982) — § 1318

U.S. v. Losing, 539 F.2d 1174 (8th Cir. 1976) — § 266

U.S., Lott v.

U.S. v. Louderman, 576 F.2d 1383 (9th Cir. 1978) — § 314

U.S. v. Loud Hawk, 106 S. Ct. 648 (1986) — § 1204; § 1205; § 1207

U.S. v. Lovasco, 431 U.S. 783 (1977) — § 1204; § 1239

U.S. v. Lovato, 520 F.2d 1270 (9th Cir. 1975) — § 103

U.S. v. Love, 482 F.2d 213 (5th Cir. 1973) — § 1903

U.S. v. Love, 592 F.2d 1022 (8th Cir. 1979) — § 2144; § 2147

U.S. v. Love, 597 F.2d 81 (6th Cir. 1979) — § 1008; § 1262

U.S. v. Lowe, 575 F.2d 1193 (6th Cir. 1978) — § 206; 229

U.S. v. Lucas, 6 F.2d 327 (W.D. Wash. 1925) — § 1403

U.S. v. Lucchetti, 553 F.2d 28 (2d Cir. 1976) — § 1403

U.S., Luce v.

U.S. v. Luman, 622 F.2d 490 (10th Cir. 1980) — § 1271

U.S., Lumetta v.

U.S. v. Lustig, 555 F.2d 737 (9th Cir. 1977) — § 214; § 1253; § 1909; § 1910; § 1911; § 1912

U.S., Lutwak v.

U.S. v. Lutz, 420 F.2d 414 (3d Cir. 1970) — § 2003

U.S. v. Lyles, 593 F.2d 182 (2d Cir. 1979) — § 913

U.S. v. Lynch, 598 F.2d 132 (D.C. Cir. 1978) — § 1008

U.S. v. Lynn, 608 F.2d 132 (5th Cir. 1979) — § 1102

U.S. v. Lyon, 567 F.2d 777 (8th Cir. 1977) — § 210; § 1212; § 2140; § 2147

U.S. v. Lyon, 588 F.2d 581 (8th Cir. 1978) — § 1217; § 1221; § 1528

U.S. v. MacDonald, 435 U.S. 850 (1978) — § 1238

U.S. v. MacDonald, 102 S. Ct. 1497 (1982) — § 1204; § 1239

U.S. v. MacDonald, 585 F.2d 1211 (4th Cir. 1978) — § 1011

U.S. v. Macino, 486 F.2d 750 (7th Cir. 1973) — § 1204

U.S., Mack v.

U.S. v. Mackey, 571 F.2d 376 (7th Cir. 1978) — § 719; § 807; § 1112; § 2116

U.S. v. Mackin, 561 F.2d 958 (D.C. Cir. 1977) — § 2144

U.S. v. Macklin, 573 F.2d 1046 (8th Cir. 1978) — § 2116

U.S. v. Maclean, 578 F.2d 64 (3d Cir. 1978) — § 1250

U.S. v. Madden, 525 F.2d 972 (5th Cir. 1976) — § 1265

U.S. v. Maddox, 444 F.2d 148 (2d Cir. 1971) — § 2148

U.S. v. Madrid, 673 F.2d 1114 (10th Cir. 1982) — § 1903

U.S. v. Maestas, 546 F.2d 1177 (5th Cir. 1977) — § 1525

U.S., Mafie v.

U.S. v. Mahler, 442 F.2d 1172 (9th Cir. 1971) — § 207

U.S. v. Mahler, 579 F.2d 730 (2d Cir. 1978) — § 1810

U.S. v. Mahone, 537 F.2d 922 (7th Cir. 1976) — § 1103; § 1514; § 1810

U.S. v. Mahoney, 508 F. Supp. 263 (E.D. Pa. 1980) — § 403

U.S. v. Mahoney, 859 F.2d 47 (7th Cir. 1988) — § 1337

U.S. v. Main, 598 F.2d 1086 (7th Cir. 1979) — § 245

U.S. v. Mainello, 345 F. Supp. 863 (E.D.N.Y. 1972) — § 1923

U.S. v. Makris, 535 F.2d 899 (5th Cir. 1976) — § 2003

U.S., Malatkofski v.

U.S., Mallory v.

U.S. v. Malmay, 671 F.2d 869 (5th Cir. 1982) — § 104

U.S. v. Maloney, 262 F.2d 535 (2d Cir. 1959) — § 1109

U.S. v. Mandel, 591 F.2d 1347 (4th Cir. 1979) — § 913; § 1010; § 1808; § 2101; § 2115; § 2136

U.S. v. Mandujano, 425 U.S. 564 (1976) — § 306; § 401; § 404; § 405

U.S. v. Manetta, 551 F.2d 1352 (5th Cir. 1977) — § 706; § 716; § 1204

U.S. v. Manfredi, 488 F.2d 588 (2d Cir. 1973) — § 262; § 264

U.S. v. Manfredonia, 341 F. Supp. 790 (S.D.N.Y. 1972) — § 1903

U.S. v. Mangan, 575 F.2d 32 (2d Cir. 1978) — § 2006; § 2132; § 2140

U.S., Manley v.

U.S. v. Mann, 590 F.2d 361 (1st Cir. 1978) — § 2140

U.S. v. Manning, 448 F.2d 992 (2d Cir. 1971) — § 215; § 219

U.S. v. Mapp, 476 F.2d 67 (2d Cir. 1973) — § 215

U.S. v. Mapp, 561 F.2d 685 (7th Cir. 1977) — § 306

U.S. v. Mara, 410 U.S. 19 (1973) — § 409

U.S. v. Marcantoni, 590 F.2d 1324 (5th Cir. 1979) — § 1707

U.S., Marcello v.

U.S. v. March, 700 F.2d 1322 (10th Cir. 1983) — § 1304

U.S. v. Marchand, 564 F.2d 983 (2d Cir. 1977) — § 319; § 2111

U.S., Marchetti v.

U.S. v. Marchisio, 344 F.2d 653 (2d Cir. 1965) — § 717

U.S., Maresca v.

U.S. v. Marin, 669 F.2d 73 (2d Cir. 1982) — § 219

U.S. v. Marino, 658 F.2d 1120 (6th Cir. 1981) — § 1524

U.S. v. Marion, 404 U.S. 307 (1971) — § 1204; § 1237; § 1239

U.S. v. Marks, 585 F.2d 164 (6th Cir. 1978) — § 2141; § 2147

U.S. v. Marks, 603 F.2d 582 (5th Cir. 1979) — § 306

U.S. v. Marques, 600 F.2d 742 (9th Cir. 1979) — § 812; § 813; § 1111

U.S. v. Marra, 482 F.2d 1196 (2d Cir. 1973) — § 424

U.S. v. Marrero, 450 F.2d 373 (2d Cir. 1971) — § 304

U.S., Marron v.

U.S., Marshall v.

U.S. v. Marshall, 431 F.2d 944 (5th Cir. 1970) — § 1269

U.S. v. Marshall, 532 F.2d 1279 (9th Cir. 1976) — § 708

U.S. v. Marshall, 557 F.2d 527 (5th Cir. 1977) — § 1516

U.S. v. Marson, 408 F.2d 644 (4th Cir. 1968) — § 215

U.S., Martin v.

U.S. v. Martin, 459 F.2d 1009 (9th Cir. 1972) — § 2003

U.S. v. Martin, 562 F.2d 673 (D.C. Cir. 1977) — § 232

U.S. v. Martin, 565 F.2d 362 (5th Cir. 1978) — § 812

U.S. v. Martin, 587 F.2d 31 (9th Cir. 1978) — § 1208; § 1226

U.S. v. Martin, 599 F.2d 880 (9th Cir. 1979) — § 261

U.S. v. Martin, 600 F.2d 1175 (5th Cir. 1979) — § 213

U.S. v. Martin, 782 F.2d 1141 (2d Cir. 1986) — § 509

U.S. v. Martin-Trigona, 767 F.2d 35 (2d Cir. 1985) — § 511

U.S. v. Martinello, 556 F.2d 1215 (5th Cir. 1977) — § 1318

U.S. v. Martinez, 479 F.2d 824 (1st Cir. 1973) — § 907

U.S. v. Martinez, 536 F.2d 886 (9th Cir. 1976) — § 2142

U.S. v. Martinez, 555 F.2d 1273 (5th Cir. 1977) — § 1810

U.S. v. Martinez, 577 F.2d 960 (5th Cir. 1978) — § 309

U.S. v. Martinez, 588 F.2d 1227 (9th Cir. 1978) — § 261

U.S. v. Martinez, 588 F.2d 495 (5th Cir. 1979) — § 306

U.S. v. Martinez, 616 F.2d 185 (5th Cir. 1980) — § 1252

U.S. v. Martinez-Fuerte, 428 U.S. 543 (1976) — § 228; § 229

U.S. v. Martin Linen Supply Co., 430 U.S. 564 (1977) — § 1001; § 1006

U.S. v. Martino, 648 F.2d 367 (5th Cir. 1981) — § 809

U.S. v. Martorano, 557 F.2d 1 (1st Cir. 1977) — § 2116

U.S. v. Marvin, 720 F.2d 12 (8th Cir. 1983) — § 1302

U.S. v. Marzano, 537 F.2d 257 (7th Cir. 1976) — § 1270; § 1813

U.S. v. Marzgliano, 588 F.2d 395 (3d Cir. 1978) — § 606

U.S. v. Masciarelli, 558 F.2d 1064 (2d Cir. 1977) — § 261

U.S. v. Mase, 556 F.2d 671 (2d Cir. 1977) — § 503; § 812

U.S. v. Maselli, 534 F.2d 1197 (6th Cir. 1976) — § 1270

U.S. v. Maskeny, 609 F.2d 183 (5th Cir. 1980) — § 1245

U.S., Mason v.

U.S. v. Massaro, 544 F.2d 547 (1st Cir. 1976) — § 318

U.S. v. Massey, 594 F.2d 676 (8th Cir. 1979) — § 1116

U.S., Massiah v.

U.S. v. Masson, 582 F.2d 961 (5th Cir. 1978) — § 2005

U.S. v. Mastberg, 503 F.2d 465 (9th Cir. 1974) — § 224; § 2001

U.S. v. Mastrangelo, 662 F.2d 946 (2d Cir. 1981) — § 1008

U.S. v. Mathis, 535 F.2d 1303 (D.C. Cir. 1976) — § 1262

U.S. v. Mathis, 550 F.2d 180 (4th Cir. 1976) — § 2140; § 2141

U.S. v. Mathis, 559 F.2d 294 (5th Cir. 1977) — § 2136; § 2140

U.S. v. Matlock, 415 U.S. 164 (1974) — § 245; § 248; § 252; § 253

U.S. v. Matlock, 558 F.2d 1328 (8th Cir. 1977) — § 1524

U.S. v. Matlock, 675 F.2d 981 (8th Cir. 1982) — § 701

U.S. v. Matos, 409 F.2d 1245 (2d Cir. 1969) — § 2003

U.S. v. Matthews, 603 F.2d 48 (8th Cir. 1979) — § 218; § 225; § 243

U.S., Mattox v.

U.S. v. Mattucci, 502 F.2d 883 (6th Cir. 1974) — § 1111

U.S. v. Matya, 541 F.2d 741 (8th Cir. 1976) — § 261

U.S. v. Mauchlin, 670 F.2d 746 (7th Cir. 1982) — § 1703

U.S. v. Maull, 773 F.2d 1479 (8th Cir. 1985) — § 512

U.S. v. Mauro, 436 U.S. 340 (1978) — § 1233

U.S. v. Mauro, 501 F.2d 45 (2d Cir. 1974) — § 1403

U.S., May v.

U.S. v. Mayes, 512 F.2d 637 (6th Cir. 1975) — § 917

U.S. v. Mayes, 552 F.2d 729 (6th Cir. 1977) — § 244; § 304

U.S. v. Mayes, 670 F.2d 126 (9th Cir. 1982) — § 232

U.S. v. Mays, 738 F.2d 1188 (11th Cir. 1984) — § 1118

U.S. v. McCain, 556 F.2d 253 (5th Cir. 1979) — § 306

U.S. v. McCain, 677 F.2d 657 (8th Cir. 1982) — § 211

U.S. v. McCaleb, 552 F.2d 717 (6th Cir. 1977) — § 243

U.S. v. McCallie, 554 F.2d 770 (6th Cir. 1977) — § 812

U.S. v. McCambridge, 551 F.2d 865 (1st Cir. 1977) — § 1919

U.S., McCarthy v.

U.S. v. McCarthy, 473 F.2d 300 (2d Cir. 1972) — § 1903

U.S. v. McCauley, 601 F.2d 336 (8th Cir. 1979) — § 2005

U.S., McClain v.

U.S. v. McClain, 469 F.2d 68 (3d Cir. 1972) — § 1819

U.S. v. McClellan, 868 F.2d 210 (7th Cir. 1989) — § 1337

U.S., McClendon v.

U.S. v. McClintic, 570 F.2d 685 (8th Cir. 1978) — § 911; § 1107; § 2001

U.S. v. McConahy, 505 F.2d 770 (7th Cir. 1974) — § 1207

U.S., McCowan v.

U.S. v. McCoy, 539 F.2d 1050 (5th Cir. 1976) — § 259; § 261; § 1270; § 2005

U.S. v. McCracken, 581 F.2d 719 (8th Cir. 1978) — § 1509

U.S. v. McCrane, 547 F.2d 204 (3d Cir. 1976) — § 719

U.S. v. McCrary, 569 F.2d 429 (6th Cir. 1978) — § 1219

U.S. v. McCray, 458 F.2d 389 (9th Cir. 1972) — § 502

U.S., McCroskey v.

U.S. v. McCulley, 673 F.2d 346 (11th Cir. 1982) — § 913

U.S. v. McCurdy, 450 F.2d 282 (9th Cir. 1971) — § 1243

U.S. v. McDaniel, 482 F.2d 305 (8th Cir. 1973) — § 420

U.S. v. McDaniel, 538 F.2d 408 (D.C. Cir. 1976) — § 909

U.S. v. McDaniel, 428 F. Supp. 1226 (W.D. Okla. 1977) — § 719

U.S., McDonald v.

U.S. v. McDonald, 435 U.S. 850 (1978) — § 1203

U.S. v. McDonald, 576 F.2d 1350 (9th Cir. 1978) — § 111; § 911

U.S. v. McDonnel, 550 F.2d 1010 (5th Cir. 1977) — § 2104

U.S. v. McDowell, 539 F.2d 435 (5th Cir. 1976) — § 1115

U.S. v. McEachern, 675 F.2d 618 (4th Cir. 1982) — § 225

U.S. v. McEachin, 670 F.2d 1139 (D.C. Cir. 1981) — § 207; § 216; § 232

U.S. v. McFayden-Snider, 552 F.2d 1178 (6th Cir. 1977) — § 1107

U.S., McFee v.

U.S. v. McGlynn, 671 F.2d 1140 (8th Cir. 1982) — § 207; § 256

U.S. v. McGovern, 499 F.2d 1140 (1st Cir. 1974) — § 1801

U.S. v. McGrath, 613 F.2d 361 (2d Cir. 1979) — § 1230; § 1231; § 1235

U.S. v. McGrath, 622 F.2d 36 (2d Cir. 1980) — § 1222; § 1223

U.S. v. McGuire, 608 F.2d 1028 (5th Cir. 1979) — § 917

U.S. v. McKeever, 271 F.2d 669 (2d Cir. 1959) — § 1802

U.S. v. McKenley, 895 F.2d 184 (4th Cir. 1990) — § 1325

U.S. v. McKenzie, 678 F.2d 629 (5th Cir. 1982) — § 403

U.S. v. McKinney, 379 F.2d 259 (6th Cir. 1967) — § 916

U.S. v. McKoy, 591 F.2d 218 (3d Cir. 1979) — § 1008

U.S. v. McManus, 535 F.2d 460 (8th Cir. 1976) — § 112

U.S. v. McManus, 560 F.2d 747 (6th Cir. 1977) — § 713; § 1923

U.S. v. McMillan, 508 F.2d 101 (8th Cir. 1974) — § 268; § 1602

U.S. v. McMillen, 489 F.2d 229 (7th Cir. 1972) — § 804

U.S., McNabb v.

U.S. v. McNally, 485 F.2d 398 (8th Cir. 1973) — § 111

U.S. v. McPartlin, 595 F.2d 1321 (7th Cir. 1979) — § 913; § 916; § 1108; § 1111; § 1522; § 2123

U.S. v. McRae, 593 F.2d 700 (5th Cir. 1979) — § 1111

U.S. v. McRary, 616 F.2d 181 (5th Cir. 1980) — § 104; § 107

U.S. v. Mechanik, 106 S. Ct. 938 (1986) — § 401

U.S. v. Medel, 592 F.2d 1305 (5th Cir. 1979) — § 805; § 807; § 810; § 1104

U.S. v. Medical Therapy Sciences, Inc., 583 F.2d 36 (2d Cir. 1978) — § 1809

U.S. v. Medico, 557 F.2d 309 (2d Cir. 1977) — § 2118; § 2147

U.S. v. Medina-Herrera, 606 F.2d 770 (7th Cir. 1979) — § 1603

U.S., Medley v.

U.S. v. Mehrmanesh, 652 F.2d 766 (7th Cir. 1981) — § 1210; § 1238

U.S. v. Mejias, 552 F.2d 435 (2d Cir. 1977) — § 1004; § 1204; § 1212

U.S. v. Melchor Moreno, 536 F.2d 1042 (5th Cir. 1976) — § 1904

U.S., Melickian v.

U.S. v. Melville, 309 F. Supp. 822 (S.D.N.Y. 1970) — § 504

U.S. v. Melvin, 596 F.2d 492 (1st Cir. 1979) — § 206; § 312

U.S. v. Mendell, 447 F.2d 639 (7th Cir. 1971) — § 108

U.S. v. Mendell, 538 F.2d 1238 (6th Cir. 1976) — § 1813

U.S. v. Mendenhall, 446 U.S. 544 (1980) — § 228; § 243

U.S. v. Mendoza, 473 F.2d 697 (5th Cir. 1973) — § 501

U.S. v. Mendoza, 581 F.2d 89 (5th Cir. 1978) — § 1317

U.S. v. Menendez, 612 F.2d 51 (2d Cir. 1979) — § 109

U.S. v. Merlino, 595 F.2d 1016 (5th Cir. 1979) — § 806; § 808

U.S. v. Merrell, 303 F. Supp. 490 (N.D.N.Y. 1969) — § 1918

U.S., Merrill v.

U.S. v. Mespoulede, 597 F.2d 329 (2d Cir. 1979) — § 1011

U.S. v. Messina, 507 F.2d 73 (2d Cir. 1974) — § 308

U.S. v. Metz, 608 F.2d 147 (5th Cir. 1979) — § 1209; § 2144

U.S., Meyer v.

U.S., Meyers v.

U.S. v. Meyers, 646 F.2d 1142 (6th Cir. 1981) — § 1321

U.S. v. Michel, 588 F.2d 986 (5th Cir. 1979) — § 910

U.S., Michelson v.

U.S. v. Micieli, 594 F.2d 102 (5th Cir. 1979) — § 303; § 306

U.S. v. Middleton, 344 F.2d 78 (2d Cir. 1965) — § 304

U.S. v. Middleton, 599 F.2d 1349 (5th Cir. 1979) — § 208

U.S., Midland Asphalt v.

U.S. v. Mierzwicki, 500 F. Supp. 1331 (D. Md. 1980) — § 1919

U.S. v. Migely, 596 F.2d 511 (1st Cir. 1979) — § 414

U.S. v. Mikka, 586 F.2d 152 (9th Cir. 1978) — § 1110

U.S., Mikus v.

U.S. v. Miley, 513 F.2d 1191 (2d Cir. 1975) — § 244

U.S. v. Milhollan, 599 F.2d 518 (3d Cir. 1979) — § 318

U.S., Miller v.

U.S. v. Miller, 411 F.2d 825 (2d Cir. 1969) — § 722; § 1303

U.S. v. Miller, 449 F.2d 974 (D.C. Cir. 1970) — § 903

U.S. v. Miller, 478 F.2d 1315 (2d Cir. 1973) — § 1105

U.S. v. Miller, 529 F.2d 1125 (9th Cir. 1976) — § 1270

U.S. v. Miller, 546 F.2d 320 (9th Cir. 1976) — § 1252

U.S. v. Miller, 573 F.2d 388 (7th Cir. 1978) — § 1522; § 1524

U.S. v. Miller, 589 F.2d 1117 (1st Cir. 1978) — § 232; § 235; § 239; § 243; § 244

U.S. v. Miller, 600 F.2d 498 (5th Cir. 1979) — § 1605; § 1919; § 2005

U.S. v. Miller, 664 F.2d 94 (5th Cir. 1981) — § 1807

U.S. v. Miller, 676 F.2d 359 (9th Cir. 1982) — § 311

U.S. v. Miller, 772 F.2d 562 (9th Cir. 1983) — § 611

U.S. v. Miller, 753 F.2d 19 (3d Cir. 1985) — § 517

U.S. v. Miller, 871 F.2d 488 (4th Cir. 1989) — § 1339

U.S. v. Milton, 555 F.2d 1198 (5th Cir. 1977) — § 2005

U.S., Mims v.

U.S. v. Minicone, 960 F.2d 1099 (2d Cir. 1992) — § 1326

U.S., Minor v.

U.S. v. Minor, 459 F.2d 103 (5th Cir. 1972) — § 2001

U.S., Miranda v.

U.S. v. Miranda, 510 F.2d 385 (9th Cir. 1975) — § 1805

U.S. v. Miranda, 593 F.2d 590 (5th Cir. 1979) — § 1116

U.S. v. Miranti, 253 F.2d 135 (2d Cir. 1958) — § 1906

U.S. v. Missio, 597 F.2d 60 (5th Cir. 1979) — § 1318

U.S. v. Missler, 414 F.2d 1293 (4th Cir. 1969) — § 310

U.S., Mistretta v.

U.S., Mitchell v.

U.S. v. Mitchell, 137 F.2d 1006 (2d Cir. 1943) — § 1911; § 1913

U.S. v. Mitchell, 322 U.S. 65 (1944) — § 304

U.S. v. Mitchell, 540 F.2d 1163 (3d Cir. 1976) — § 712

U.S. v. Mitchell, 556 F.2d 371 (6th Cir. 1977) — § 314; § 1247

U.S. v. Mitchell, 590 F.2d 816 (6th Cir. 1979) — § 1249

U.S. v. Mitchell, 666 F.2d 1385 (11th Cir. 1982) — § 1522

U.S. v. Mitchell, 778 F.2d 1271 (7th Cir. 1985) — § 1005

U.S. v. Mock, 604 F.2d 341 (5th Cir. 1979) — § 1011

U.S. v. Modica, 663 F.2d 1173 (2d Cir. 1981) — § 1114; § 1117

U.S. v. Mohney, 476 F. Supp. 421 (D. Hawaii 1979) — § 109

U.S. v. Molt, 631 F.2d 258 (3d Cir. 1980) — § 1223; § 1226; § 1231

U.S. v. Montalvo-Murillo, 493 U.S. 807 (1990) — § 509

U.S. v. Montamedi, 767 F.2d 1403 (9th Cir. 1985) — § 512

U.S. v. Montano, 613 F.2d 147 (6th Cir. 1980) — § 233

U.S. v. Montes-Zarate, 552 F.2d 1330 (9th Cir. 1977) — § 304

U.S., Montgomery v.

U.S. v. Montgomery, 126 F.2d 151 (3d Cir. 1942) — § 1801

U.S. v. Montgomery, 582 F.2d 514 (10th Cir. 1978) — § 2116

U.S. v. Monti, 100 F. Supp. 209 (E.D.N.Y. 1951) — § 1919

U.S. v. Montiell, 526 F.2d 1008 (2d Cir. 1975) — § 233

U.S. v. Montoya, 676 F.2d 428 (10th Cir. 1982) — § 1923

U.S. v. Montoya de Hernandez, 105 S. Ct. 3304 (1985) — § 229

U.S. v. Moody, 339 F.2d 161 (6th Cir. 1964) — § 1605

U.S., Moore v.

U.S. v. Moore, 522 F.2d 1068 (9th Cir. 1975) — § 2114

U.S. v. Moore, 556 F.2d 479 (10th Cir. 1977) — § 1810

U.S. v. Moore, 562 F.2d 106 (1st Cir. 1977) — § 248

U.S. v. Moore, 571 F.2d 76 (2d Cir. 1978) — § 2111

U.S. v. Moore, 616 F.2d 1030 (7th Cir. 1980) — § 1304

U.S. v. Morales, 566 F.2d 402 (2d Cir. 1977) — § 424

U.S. v. Morell, 524 F.2d 550 (2d Cir. 1975) — § 719

U.S. v. Moreno, 569 F.2d 1049 (9th Cir. 1978) — § 225; § 235

U.S. v. Moreno, 588 F.2d 490 (5th Cir. 1978) — § 713; § 1923

U.S. v. Moreno-Nunez, 595 F.2d 1186 (9th Cir. 1979) — § 1260; § 1524

U.S., Morgan v.

U.S. v. Morgan, 554 F.2d 31 (2d Cir. 1977) — § 1520

U.S. v. Morgan, 555 F.2d 238 (9th Cir. 1977) — § 1705; § 2109

U.S. v. Morgan, 581 F.2d 933 (D.C. Cir. 1978) — § 2114

U.S. v. Morin, 665 F.2d 765 (5th Cir. 1982) — § 220

U.S., Morissette v.

U.S. v. Morlang, 531 F.2d 183 (4th Cir. 1975) — § 1802

U.S. v. Morris, 568 F.2d 396 (5th Cir. 1978) — § 1923

U.S. v. Morris, 612 F.2d 483 (10th Cir. 1979) — § 1262

U.S., Morrison v.

U.S. v. Morrison, 531 F.2d 1089 (1st Cir. 1976) — § 2004

U.S. v. Morrow, 541 F.2d 1229 (7th Cir. 1976) — § 1103

U.S. v. Mortimer, 118 F.2d 266 (2d Cir. 1941) — § 1605

U.S. v. Moscahlaidis, 868 F.2d 1357 (3rd Cir. 1989) — § 613

U.S. v. Moskowitz, 581 F.2d 14 (2d Cir. 1978) — § 319; § 2111

U.S. v. Mosley, 555 F.2d 191 (8th Cir. 1977) — § 2109

U.S. v. Moss, 591 F.2d 428 (8th Cir. 1979) — § 1246

U.S. v. Mota, 598 F.2d 995 (5th Cir. 1979) — § 1703; § 2003

U.S. v. Moten, 564 F.2d 620 (2d Cir. 1977) — § 1815; § 2003

U.S. v. Moten, 582 F.2d 654 (2d Cir. 1978) — § 1249

U.S. v. Muckenthaler, 584 F.2d 240 (8th Cir. 1978) — § 211

U.S. v. Mullens, 583 F.2d 134 (5th Cir. 1978) — § 911

U.S. v. Mullings, 364 F.2d 173 (2d Cir. 1966) — § 1921

U.S. v. Munoz-Flores, 110 S. Ct. 1964 (1990) — § 1336

U.S. v. Murphy, 569 F.2d 771 (3d Cir. 1978) — § 801; § 803; § 804

U.S., Murray v.

U.S. v. Murray, 297 F.2d 812 (2d Cir. 1962) — § 717

U.S. v. Muscarella, 585 F.2d 242 (7th Cir. 1978) — § 1115

U.S. v. Musgrave, 444 F.2d 755 (5th Cir. 1971) — § 1264

U.S. v. Mustin, 369 F.2d 626 (7th Cir. 1966) — § 2003

U.S. v. Mutchler, 559 F.2d 955 (5th Cir. 1977) — § 1246

U.S., Myers v.

U.S. v. Myers, 451 F.2d 402 (9th Cir. 1972) — § 609

U.S. v. Myers, 550 F.2d 1036 (5th Cir. 1977) — § 702; § 1522; § 1528

U.S. v. Nace, 561 F.2d 763 (9th Cir. 1977) — § 1813

U.S. v. Nadolney, 601 F.2d 940 (7th Cir. 1979) — § 105

U.S., Namet v.

U.S. v. Nance, 666 F.2d 353 (9th Cir. 1982) — § 1231

U.S. v. Narciso, 446 F. Supp. 252 (E.D. Mich. 1977) — § 2121

U.S., Nardone v.

U.S. v. Natale, 526 F.2d 1160 (2d Cir. 1975) — § 1703

U.S. v. Nathan, 476 F.2d 456 (2d Cir. 1973) — § 1818

U.S. v. Navarro-Flores, 628 F.2d 1178 (9th Cir. 1980) — § 1321

U.S. v. Nazzaro, 472 F.2d 302 (2d Cir. 1973) — § 1303

U.S. v. Neal, 532 F. Supp. 942 (D. Colo. 1982) — § 1911

U.S. v. Nebbia, 357 F.2d 303 (2d Cir. 1966) — § 504

U.S. v. Nedd, 582 F.2d 965 (5th Cir. 1978) — § 247

U.S. v. Neidelman, 356 F. Supp. 979 (S.D.N.Y. 1973) — § 404

U.S., Neidinger v.

U.S. v. Nelson, 599 F.2d 714 (5th Cir. 1979) — § 1008

U.S. v. Nemes, 555 F.2d 51 (2d Cir. 1977) — § 420

U.S. v. Netterville, 553 F.2d 903 (5th Cir. 1977) — § 1209

U.S. v. Nettles, 570 F.2d 547 (5th Cir. 1978) — § 909

U.S. v. Neumann, 585 F.2d 355 (8th Cir. 1978) — § 226

U.S. v. New Buffalo Amusement Corp., 600 F.2d 368 (2d Cir. 1979) — § 1207; § 1209; § 1223; § 1231

U.S. v. Newcomb, 488 F.2d 190 (5th Cir. 1974) — § 403

U.S. v. Newman, 481 F.2d 222 (2d Cir. 1973) — § 1817

U.S. v. Newton, 510 F.2d 1149 (7th Cir. 1975) — § 202

U.S. v. Nicholas, 319 F.2d 697 (2d Cir. 1963) — § 215

U.S. v. Nichols, 534 F.2d 202 (9th Cir. 1976) — § 1524

U.S., Nick v.

U.S. v. Nick, 604 F.2d 1199 (9th Cir. 1979) — § 2119

U.S. v. Nickell, 552 F.2d 684 (6th Cir. 1977) — § 801; § 805; § 807

U.S. v. Nickerson, 669 F.2d 1016 (5th Cir. 1982) — § 1116

U.S., Nicola v.

U.S. v. Niederberger, 580 F.2d 63 (3d Cir. 1978) — § 812; § 813; § 911

U.S., Niro v.

U.S. v. Nix, 601 F.2d 214 (5th Cir. 1979) — § 1239

U.S. v. Nixon, 418 U.S. 683 (1974) — § 404; § 717; § 1922

U.S. v. Noah, 475 F.2d 688 (9th Cir. 1973) — § 1245

U.S. v. Noble, 155 F.2d 315 (3d Cir. 1946) — § 1264

U.S. v. Nobles, 422 U.S. 225 (1975) — § 814; § 1803; § 1920

U.S. v. Nolan, 416 F.2d 588 (10th Cir. 1969) — § 1604

U.S. v. Nolan, 551 F.2d 266 (10th Cir. 1977) — § 1522; § 1524

U.S. v. Noll, 600 F.2d 1123 (5th Cir. 1979) — § 1207; § 1209

U.S. v. Norris, 281 U.S. 619 (1930) — § 604

U.S., Nova Scotia v.

U.S. v. Novelli, 544 F.2d 800 (5th Cir. 1977) — § 1237

U.S. v. Null, 415 F.2d 1178 (4th Cir. 1969) — § 1520

U.S. v. Nunley, 873 F.2d 182 (8th Cir. 1989) — § 1323

U.S. v. Nussen, 531 F.2d 15 (2d Cir. 1976) — § 1818

U.S., Nutt v.

U.S. v. Oakes, 565 F.2d 170 (1st Cir. 1977) — § 1810

U.S. v. Oates, 560 F.2d 45 (2d Cir. 1977) — § 228; § 2123; § 2125

U.S. v. Oaxaca, 569 F.2d 518 (9th Cir. 1978) — § 222; § 234; § 2111

U.S. v. O'Brien, 601 F.2d 1067 (9th Cir. 1979) — § 1252; § 1605

U.S. v. O'Brien, 618 F.2d 1234 (7th Cir. 1980) — § 615

U.S. v. Ocanas, 628 F.2d 353 (5th Cir. 1980) — § 613

U.S. v. Ochoa-Sanchez, 676 F.2d 1283 (9th Cir. 1982) — § 1818

U.S. v. Ochs, 595 F.2d 1247 (2d Cir. 1979) — § 1530

U.S. v. Ochs, 461 F. Supp. 1 (S.D.N.Y. 1978) — § 252; § 253

U.S. v. O'Conner, 580 F.2d 38 (2d Cir. 1978) — § 1526

U.S. v. Odom, 526 F.2d 339 (5th Cir. 1976) — § 304

U.S. v. O'Donnell, 510 F.2d 1190 (6th Cir. 1975) — § 105

U.S. v. Ogden, 572 F.2d 501 (5th Cir. 1978) — § 313

U.S. v. Ogull, 149 F. Supp. 272, 276 (S.D.N.Y. 1957) — § 1256

U.S. v. O'Henry's Film Works, Inc., 598 F.2d 313 (2d Cir. 1979) — § 1902; § 1906

U.S. v. Ojala, 544 F.2d 940 (8th Cir. 1976) — § 2114; § 2115

U.S. v. Olander, 584 F.2d 876 (9th Cir. 1978) — § 908

U.S., Olender v.

U.S. v. Olivares-Vega, 495 F.2d 827 (2d Cir. 1974) — § 305

U.S., Oliver v.

U.S. v. Oliver, 570 F.2d 397 (1st Cir. 1978) — § 1923

U.S. v. Oliver, 683 F.2d 224 (7th Cir. 1982) — § 1301

U.S. v. Oliveras, 905 F.2d 623 (2d Cir. 1990) — § 1323

U.S. v. O'Looney, 544 F.2d 385 (9th Cir. 1976) — § 304; § 1256

U.S. v. Olson, 576 F.2d 1267 (8th Cir. 1978) — § 703

U.S. v. Olwares, 786 F.2d 659 (5th Cir. 1986) — § 1002

U.S. v. One 1972 Chevrolet Nova, 560 F.2d 464 (1st Cir. 1977) — § 236

U.S. v. One Assortment of 89 Firearms, 465 U.S. 354 (1984) — § 1011

U.S., One Lot Emerald Cut Stones and One Ring v.

U.S., O'Neill v.

U.S. v. O'Neill, 767 F.2d 780 (11th Cir. 1985) — § 1318

U.S. v. Ong, 541 F.2d 331 (2d Cir. 1976) — § 1111; § 1805

U.S. v. Onori, 535 F.2d 938 (5th Cir. 1976) — § 1602

U.S. v. Opager, 589 F.2d 799 (5th Cir. 1979) — § 710; § 713; § 1810; § 1923

U.S., Opper v.

U.S., O'Quinn v.

U.S. v. Oropeza, 564 F.2d 316 (9th Cir. 1977) — § 2144

U.S. v. Orozco, 590 F.2d 789 (9th Cir. 1979) — § 1610; § 2125

U.S., Orr v.

U.S. v. Orta, 760 F.2d 887 (8th Cir. 1985) — § 506; § 509

U.S. v. Ortega, 471 F.2d 1350 (2d Cir. 1972) — § 304; § 1923

U.S. v. Ortega, 561 F.2d 803 (9th Cir. 1977) — § 1809

U.S. v. Ortiz, 422 U.S. 891 (1975) — § 229

U.S. v. Ortiz, 488 F.2d 175 (9th Cir. 1973) — § 2003

U.S. v. Ortiz, 507 F.2d 1224 (6th Cir. 1974) — § 1513

U.S. v. Ortiz, 603 F.2d 76 (9th Cir. 1979) — § 907

U.S. v. Orzechowski, 547 F.2d 978 (7th Cir. 1977) — § 709

U.S., Ottomano v.

U.S. v. Outpost Development Co., 552 F.2d 868 (9th Cir. 1977) — § 905

U.S., Overton v.

U.S. v. Owens, 484 U.S. 554 (1988) — § 319; § 2111

U.S., Owensby v.

U.S. v. Pacelli, 491 F.2d 1108 (2d Cir. 1974) — § 807; § 2101

U.S. v. Pacelli, 521 F.2d 135 (2d Cir. 1975) — § 1805

U.S. v. Pachay, 711 F.2d 488 (2d Cir. 1983) — § 1242

U.S. v. Pacheco, 489 F.2d 554 (5th Cir. 1974) — § 809

U.S. v. Pacheco-Ruiz, 549 F.2d 1204 (9th Cir. 1976) — § 232

U.S. v. Padgent, 432 F.2d 701 (2d Cir. 1970) — § 1811

U.S. v. Padro, 508 F. Supp. 184 (D. Del. 1981) — § 1212

U.S. v. Pagano, 207 F.2d 884 (2d Cir. 1953) — § 1611

U.S. v. Page, 544 F.2d 982 (8th Cir. 1976) — § 2123

U.S. v. Palacios, 556 F.2d 1359 (5th Cir. 1977) — § 2109

U.S., Palermo v.

U.S. v. Palmer, 536 F.2d 1278 (9th Cir. 1976) — § 1805; § 1906

U.S. v. Palmer, 603 F.2d 1286 (8th Cir. 1979) — § 228

U.S. v. Palmer, 667 F.2d 1118 (4th Cir. 1981) — § 211

U.S. v. Palumbo, 401 F.2d 270 (2d Cir. 1968) — § 1810

U.S., Pandelli v.

U.S. v. Panebianco, 543 F.2d 447 (2d Cir. 1976) — § 1510

U.S. v. Panetta, 436 F. Supp. 114 (E.D. Pa. 1977) — § 1809

U.S. v. Papaleo, 853 F.2d 16 (1st Cir. 1988) — § 613

U.S. v. Papia, 560 F.2d 827 (7th Cir. 1977) — § 1530; § 1809; § 1817

U.S. v. Pappadio, 346 F.2d 5 (2d Cir. 1965) — § 1918

U.S. v. Pappas, 602 F.2d 131 (7th Cir. 1979) — § 1302

U.S., Paradiso v.

U.S. v. Pardone, 406 F.2d 560 (2d Cir. 1969) — § 716

U.S. v. Parhms, 424 F.2d 152 (9th Cir. 1970) — § 1604

U.S. v. Park, 531 F.2d 754 (5th Cir. 1976) — § 903; § 906

U.S., Parker v.

U.S. v. Parker, 491 F.2d 517 (8th Cir. 1973) — § 1705

U.S. v. Parker, 549 F.2d 1217 (9th Cir. 1977) — § 1115; § 1532

U.S. v. Parker, 586 F.2d 422 (5th Cir. 1978) — § 719; § 1108; § 1206; § 1239

U.S. v. Parker, 622 F.2d 298 (8th Cir. 1980) — § 101

U.S. v. Parnell, 581 F.2d 1374 (10th Cir. 1978) — 1510; § 1516

U.S. v. Parness, 503 F.2d 430 (2d Cir. 1974) — § 1529

U.S. v. Parr-Pla, 549 F.2d 660 (9th Cir. 1977) — § 1113; § 1805

U.S. v. Parry, 649 F.2d 292 (5th Cir. 1981) — § 2110

U.S. v. Partida-Parra, 859 F.2d 629 (9th Cir. 1988) — § 611

U.S. v. Partin, 493 F.2d 750 (5th Cir. 1974) — § 1270

U.S. v. Partin, 552 F.2d 621 (5th Cir. 1977) — § 1270

U.S., Paschen v.

U.S. v. Pascual, 606 F.2d 561 (5th Cir. 1979) — § 706

U.S. v. Passodelis, 615 F.2d 975 (3rd Cir. 1980) — § 108

U.S. v. Pastor, 557 F.2d 930 (2d Cir. 1977) — § 1246

U.S. v. Patacchia, 602 F.2d 218 (9th Cir. 1979) — § 243

U.S. v. Pate, 543 F.2d 1148 (5th Cir. 1976) — § 2104

U.S. v. Patterson, 446 F.2d 1358 (5th Cir. 1971) — § 1707

U.S. v. Patterson, 554 F.2d 852 (8th Cir. 1977) — § 245

U.S., Patton v.

U.S. v. Paul, 614 F.2d 115 (6th Cir. 1980) — § 242

U.S. v. Payden, 759 F.2d 202 (2d Cir. 1985) — § 509

U.S., Payne v.

U.S. v. Payner, 447 U.S. 727 (1980) — § 255

U.S. v. Payner, 572 F.2d 144 (6th Cir. 1978) — § 250

U.S. v. Peacock, 654 F.2d 339 (5th Cir. 1981) — § 2118

U.S. v. Peden, 556 F.2d 278 (5th Cir. 1977) — § 2123

U.S., Pegram v.

U.S. v. Pelley, 572 F.2d 264 (10th Cir. 1978) — § 228; § 1923

U.S. v. Peltier, 585 F.2d 314 (8th Cir. 1978) — § 1528

U.S. v. Pelton, 578 F.2d 701 (8th Cir. 1978) — § 706; § 713; § 1516

U.S. v. Pena, 527 F.2d 1356 (5th Cir. 1976) — § 2144

678

U.S. v. Penn, 647 F.2d 876 (9th Cir. 1980) — § 215

U.S. v. Pensinger, 549 F.2d 1150 (8th Cir. 1977) — § 1911

U.S. v. Pepe, 367 F. Supp. 1365 (D. Conn. 1973) — § 404

U.S. v. Percevault, 490 F.2d 126 (2d Cir. 1974) — § 712; § 801; § 2116

U.S. v. Perea, 413 F.2d 65 (10th Cir. 1969) — § 1817

U.S., Pereira v.

U.S., Peretz v.

U.S. v. Perez, 22 U.S. 579 (1824) — § 1008

U.S. v. Perez, 565 F.2d 1227 (2d Cir. 1977) — § 1001

U.S. v. Perez, 648 F.2d 219 (5th Cir. 1981) — § 1250

U.S. v. Perez-Franco, 873 F.2d 455 (1st Cir. 1989) — § 1323

U.S. v. Perkins, 433 F.2d 1182 (D.C. Cir. 1970) — § 502

U.S. v. Perkins, 748 F.2d 1519 (11th Cir. 1984) — § 1303

U.S. v. Perno, 605 F.2d 432 (9th Cir. 1979) — § 1302

U.S. v. Perri, 513 F.2d 572 (9th Cir. 1975) — § 1318

U.S. v. Perry, 550 F.2d 524 (9th Cir. 1977) — § 1813

U.S. v. Perry, 788 F.2d 100 (3d Cir. 1986) — § 504; § 509

U.S. v. Persico, 349 F.2d 6 (2d Cir. 1965) — § 1270

U.S. v. Peter, 479 F.2d 147 (6th Cir. 1973) — § 1902

U.S. v. Peters, 587 F.2d 1267 (D.C. Cir. 1978) — § 1215

U.S. v. Petersen, 611 F.2d 1313 (10th Cir. 1979) — § 106; § 909; § 913

U.S. v. Peterson, 524 F.2d 167 (4th Cir. 1975) — § 809

U.S. v. Peterson, 548 F.2d 279 (9th Cir. 1977) — § 1250

U.S. v. Peterson, 549 F.2d 654 (9th Cir. 1977) — § 1109; § 1261

U.S., Petite v.

U.S. v. Petito, 671 F.2d 68 (2d Cir. 1982) — § 426; § 803

U.S. v. Petsas, 592 F.2d 525 (9th Cir. 1979) — § 1808

U.S., Pettibone v.

U.S. v. Petty, 601 F.2d 883 (5th Cir. 1979) — § 243

U.S., Pettyjohn v.

U.S. v. Pfeiffer, 539 F.2d 668 (8th Cir. 1976) — § 1811; § 2123

U.S. v. Pfingst, 490 F.2d 262 (2d Cir. 1973) — § 722

U.S. v. Pheaster, 544 F.2d 353 (9th Cir. 1976) — § 318; § 2120

U.S. v. Phillips 476 F.2d 538 (D.C. Cir. 1973) — § 1111

U.S. v. Phillips, 497 F.2d 1131 (9th Cir. 1974) — § 215

U.S. v. Phillips, 540 F.2d 319 (8th Cir. 1976) — § 252

U.S. v. Phillips, 569 F.2d 1315 (5th Cir. 1978) — § 1212

U.S. v. Phillips, 577 F.2d 495 (9th Cir. 1978) — § 807

U.S. v. Phillips, 593 F.2d 553 (4th Cir. 1978) — § 2001

U.S. v. Phillips, 607 F.2d 808 (8th Cir. 1979) — § 913

U.S. v. Phillips, 625 F.2d 543 (5th Cir. 1980) — § 521

U.S. v. Phillips, 515 F. Supp. 758 (E.D. Ky. 1981) — § 1819

U.S. v. Phillips Petroleum Co., 435 F. Supp. 610 (N.D. Okla. 1977) — § 401

U.S. v. Phipps, 543 F.2d 576 (5th Cir. 1976) — § 1275

U.S. v. Piatt, 576 F.2d 659 (5th Cir. 1978) — § 236

U.S., Picciurro v.

U.S. v. Pickney, 551 F.2d 1241 (D.C. Cir. 1976) — § 1268

U.S. v. Pierce, 593 F.2d 415 (1st Cir. 1979) — § 1008

U.S. v. Pierson, 503 F.2d 173 (D.C. Cir. 1974) — § 2001

U.S. v. Pilla, 550 F.2d 1085 (8th Cir. 1977) — § 1237

U.S. v. Pilnick, 267 F. Supp. 791 (S.D.N.Y. 1967) — § 1904

U.S., Pinkerton v.

U.S. v. Pinkney, 551 F.2d 1241 (D.C. Cir. 1976) — § 1268

U.S. v. Pinna, 229 F.2d 216 (7th Cir. 1956) — § 1611

U.S. v. Pinto, 875 F.2d 143 (7th Cir. 1989) — § 1312

U.S. v. Pipkins, 528 F.2d 559 (5th Cir. 1976) — § 1918

U.S. v. Pirolli, 673 F.2d 1200 (11th Cir. 1982) — § 239

U.S. v. Pitts, 569 F.2d 343 (5th cir. 1978) — § 1209

U.S. v. Place, 462 U.S. 696 (1983) — § 228

U.S. v. Ploof, 464 F.2d 116 (2d Cir. 1972) — § 1514

U.S. v. Plum, 558 F.2d 568 (10th Cir. 1977) — § 2109; § 2123

U.S. v. Poeta, 455 F.2d 117 (2d Cir. 1972) — § 261; § 262

U.S., Pointer v.

U.S., Poliafico v.

U.S. v. Polin, 323 F.2d 549 (3d Cir. 1963) — § 109

U.S. v. Pollack, 534 F.2d 964 (D.C. Cir. 1976) — § 723; § 1239

U.S., Pollard v.

U.S. v. Pollard, 788 F.2d 1177 (6th Cir. 1985) — § 517

U.S., Pollock v.

U.S. v. Polsinelli, 649 F.2d 793 (10th Cir. 1981) — § 1520

U.S., Pon v.

U.S. v. Ponder, 475 F.2d 37 (5th Cir. 1973) — § 1904; § 1918

U.S., Pool v.

U.S. v. Pope, 529 F.2d 112 (9th Cir. 1976) — § 1107

U.S. v. Pope, 574 F.2d 320 (6th Cir. 1978) — § 812; § 813

U.S. v. Pordum, 451 F.2d 1015 (2d Cir. 1971) — § 1302

U.S. v. Portac, Inc., 869 F.2d 1288 (9th Cir. 1989) — § 1262

U.S. v. Porter, 544 F.2d 936 (8th Cir. 1976) — § 2113

U.S. v. Portes, 786 F.2d 758 (7th Cir. 1985) — § 504; § 509; § 512

U.S., Portomene v.

U.S. v. Posey, 611 F.2d 1389 (5th Cir. 1980) — § 615

U.S. v. Postal, 589 F.2d 862 (5th Cir. 1979) — § 306

U.S. v. Poulack, 556 F.2d 83 (1st Cir. 1977) — § 1811

U.S. v. Powe, 591 F.2d 833 (D.C. Cir. 1978) — § 313; § 1903

U.S., Powell v.

U.S. v. Powell, 469 U.S. 57 (1984) — § 1011

U.S. v. Powell, 498 F.2d 890 (9th Cir. 1974) — § 109

U.S. v. Powell, 587 F.2d 443 (9th Cir. 1978) — § 1522; § 1525

U.S. v. Powell, 761 F.2d 1277 (8th Cir. 1985) — § 517

U.S. v. Powell, 788 F.2d 1227 (8th Cir. 1985) — § 518

U.S. v. Powers, 572 F.2d 146 (8th Cir. 1978) — § 2123

U.S. v. Pozzy, 902 F.2d 133 (1st Cir. 1990) — § 1326

U.S. v. Prada, 451 F.2d 1319 (2d Cir. 1971) — § 1923

U.S. v. Pratter, 465 F.2d 227 (7th Cir. 1972) — § 215

U.S. v. Pressley, 602 F.2d 709 (5th Cir. 1979) — § 618

U.S. v. Prevatt, 526 F.2d 400 (5th Cir. 1976) — § 1706; § 2123; § 2133

U.S. v. Prewitt, 553 F.2d 1082 (7th Cir. 1977) — § 306

U.S. v. Price, 345 F.2d 256 (2d Cir. 1964) — § 304

U.S. v. Price, 573 F.2d 356 (5th Cir. 1978) — § 1246

U.S. v. Price, 599 F.2d 494 (2d Cir. 1979) — § 243

U.S. v. Prichard, 645 F.2d 854 (10th Cir. 1981) — § 228

U.S. v. Prince, 515 F.2d 564 (5th Cir. 1975) — § 1104

U.S. v. Prior, 546 F.2d 1254 (5th Cir. 1977) — § 719

U.S. v. Proctor and Gamble Co., 356 U.S. 677 (1958) — § 414

U.S. v. Provoo, 215 F.2d 531 (2d Cir. 1954) — § 1809

U.S. v. Pruitt, 341 F.2d 700 (4th Cir. 1965) — § 1320

U.S. v. Pry, 625 F.2d 689 (5th Cir. 1980) — § 112; § 1524

U.S. v. Pryba, 502 F.2d 391 (D.C. Cir. 1974) — § 202

U.S. v. Puco, 476 F.2d 1099 (2d Cir. 1973) — § 2112

U.S. v. Purin, 486 F.2d 1363 (2d Cir. 1973) — § 306; § 717

U.S. v. Qamar, 671 F.2d 732 (2d Cir. 1982) — § 1522; § 1525

U.S., Quercia v.

U.S. v. Quinn, 445 F.2d 940 (2d Cir. 1971) — § 719

U.S. v. Quinn, 543 F.2d 640 (8th Cir. 1976) — § 1109

U.S. v. Quinones, 516 F.2d 1309 (1st Cir. 1975) — § 1403

U.S. v. Quinto, 582 F.2d 224 (2d Cir. 1978) — § 2110

U.S. v. Rabbitt, 583 F.2d 1014 (8th Cir. 1978) — § 903

U.S. v. Raddatz, 447 U.S. 667 (1980) — § 254

U.S. v. Radetsky, 535 F.2d 556 (10th Cir. 1976) — § 415

U.S. v. Radmall, 591 F.2d 548 (10th Cir. 1978) — § 1239

U.S., Raffel v.

U.S. v. Ragghianti, 560 F.2d 1376 (9th Cir. 1977) — § 2109

U.S. v. Raineri, 670 F.2d 702 (7th Cir. 1982) — § 903; § 1245

U.S. v. Rajewski, 526 F.2d 149 (7th Cir. 1975) — § 1529

U.S., Ramer v.

U.S. v. Ramirez, 608 F.2d 1261 (9th Cir. 1979) — § 1108

U.S. v. Ramos, 586 F.2d 1078 (5th Cir. 1978) — § 1204; § 1239

U.S. v. Ramos Algarin, 584 F.2d 562 (1st Cir. 1978) — § 1239

U.S., Ramsey v.

U.S. v. Ramsey, 431 U.S. 606 (1977) — § 229

U.S. v. Rangel, 585 F.2d 344 (8th Cir. 1978) — § 1705

U.S. v. Ranta, 482 F.2d 1344 (8th Cir. 1973) — § 2001

U.S. v. Rapoport, 545 F.2d 802 (2d Cir. 1976) — § 1111

U.S. v. Rappy, 157 F.2d 964 (2d Cir. 1946) — § 1802; § 1803

U.S. v. Rasmussen, 642 F.2d 165 (5th Cir. 1981) — § 618

U.S. v. Rasor, 599 F.2d 1330 (5th Cir. 1979) — § 207

U.S. v. Rastelli, 870 F.2d 822 (2d Cir. 1989) — § 1262

U.S. v. Rath, 406 F.2d 757 (6th Cir. 1969) — § 2003

U.S. v. Rauscher, 119 U.S. 407 (1886) — § 1403

U.S., Reagan v.

U.S. v. Reamer, 589 F.2d 769 (4th Cir. 1978) — § 1530

U.S. v. Reason, 549 F.2d 309 (4th Cir. 1977) — § 2003

U.S. v. Redmond, 546 F.2d 1386 (10th Cir. 1977) — § 1247

U.S. v. Reece, 547 F.2d 432 (8th Cir. 1977) — § 2003; § 2004

U.S. v. Reed, 631 F.2d 87 (6th Cir. 1980) — § 306

U.S. v. Reed, 647 F.2d 678 (6th Cir. 1980) — § 405

U.S. v. Reed, 670 F.2d 622 (5th Cir. 1982) — § 1524

U.S. v. Reese, 561 F.2d 894 (D.C. Cir. 1977) — § 1904; 2123

U.S. v. Reese, 568 F.2d 1246 (6th Cir. 1977) — § 1520; § 1524; § 2123

U.S. v. Reeves, 594 F.2d 536 (6th Cir. 1979) — § 245; § 1268

U.S. v. Reeves, 674 F.2d 739 (8th Cir. 1982) — § 913

U.S. v. Regan, 525 F.2d 1151 (8th Cir. 1975) — § 226

U.S. v. Regilio, 669 F.2d 1169 (7th Cir. 1981) — § 1223; § 1268

U.S. v. Regner, 677 F.2d 754 (9th Cir. 1982) — § 1252

U.S. v. Reifsteck, 535 F.2d 1030 (8th Cir. 1976) — § 1921; § 2003

U.S., Remmer v.

U.S. v. Renaldi, 301 F.2d 576 (2d Cir. 1962) — § 1303

U.S. v. Renfro, 620 F.2d 568 (6th Cir. 1980) — § 1005

U.S., Reno v.

U.S. v. Rentaria, 625 F.2d 1279 (5th Cir. 1980) — § 1524

U.S. v. R. Enterprises, Inc., 111 S. Ct. 722 (1991) — § 400; § 404; § 409

U.S. v. Restrepo, 896 F.2d 1228 (9th Cir. 1990) — § 1323

U.S. v. Rettig, 589 F.2d 418 (9th Cir. 1978) — § 247

U.S. v. Rewald, 835 F.2d 215 (9th Cir. 1988) — § 1311

U.S., Reyes v.

U.S. v. Reyes-Padron, 538 F.2d 33 (2d Cir. 1976) — § 719

U.S. v. Reynolds, 345 U.S. 1 (1958) — § 1904

U.S. v. Reynolds, 781 F.2d 135 (8th Cir. 1986) — § 1215

U.S. v. Rhodes, 556 F.2d 599 (1st Cir. 1977) — § 1303

U.S. v. Rhodes, 569 F.2d 384 (5th Cir. 1978) — § 721

U.S. v. Ribero, 532 F.2d 450 (5th Cir. 1976) — § 807

U.S. v. Riccardi, 174 F.2d 883 (3d Cir. 1949) — § 1802

U.S. v. Ricciardi, 357 F.2d 91 (2d Cir. 1966) — § 1401; § 1403

U.S. v. Ricco, 549 F.2d 264 (2d Cir. 1977) — § 1112; § 1239

U.S. v. Riccobene, 451 F.2d 586 (3d Cir. 1971) — § 404

U.S., Rice v.

U.S. v. Rich, 589 F.2d 1025 (10th Cir. 1978) — § 1008

U.S. v. Richards, 500 F.2d 1025 (9th Cir. 1974) — § 220

U.S. v. Richards, 638 F.2d 765 (5th Cir. 1981) — § 229; § 1516

U.S., Richardson v.

U.S. v. Richardson, 562 F.2d 476 (7th Cir. 1977) — § 1703

U.S. v. Richardson, 582 F.2d 968 (5th Cir. 1978) — § 1247

U.S. v. Richardson, 651 F.2d 1251 (8th Cir. 1981) — § 1522

U.S. v. Richman, 600 F.2d 286 (1st Cir. 1979) — § 1207; § 1602

U.S. v. Ricketson, 498 F.2d 367 (7th Cir. 1974) — § 1204; § 2140

U.S. v. Rickey, 457 F.2d 1027 (3d Cir. 1972) — § 907

U.S. v. Rickus, 351 F. Supp. 1386 (E.D. Pa. 1972) — § 1245

U.S. v. Rico, 594 F.2d 320 (2d Cir. 1979) — § 228

U.S. v. Ridling, 350 F. Supp. 90 (E.D. Mich. 1972) — § 1518

U.S. v. Riker, 670 F.2d 987 (11th Cir. 1982) — § 101

U.S. v. Riley, 550 F.2d 233 (5th Cir. 1977) — § 1531

U.S. v. Riley, 554 F.2d 1282 (4th Cir. 1977) — § 243

U.S., Rinaldi v.

U.S. v. Rinaldi, 393 F.2d 97 (2d Cir. 1968) — § 2116

U.S. v. Rinn, 586 F.2d 113 (9th Cir. 1978) — § 1108; § 1602; § 2110

U.S. v. Rios, 495 U.S. 257 (1990) — § 265; § 266

U.S. v. Rippy, 606 F.2d 1150 (D.C. Cir. 1979) — § 813; § 1239

U.S. v. Ritch, 583 F.2d 1179 (1st Cir. 1978) — § 903; § 911; § 912

U.S. v. Ritz, 548 F.2d 510 (5th Cir. 1977) — § 1109

U.S. v. Rivera, 513 F.2d 519 (2d Cir. 1975) — § 1813; § 1814

U.S. v. Rivero, 532 F.2d 450 (5th Cir. 1976) — § 805; § 1402

U.S. v. Rivero-Nunez, 605 F.2d 152 (5th Cir. 1979) — § 502

U.S. v. Rizzo, 491 F.2d 215 (2d Cir. 1974) — § 264

U.S. v. Rizzo, 492 F.2d 443 (2d Cir. 1974) — § 262; § 264

U.S. v. Rizzo, 583 F.2d 907 (7th Cir. 1978) — § 247

U.S. v. R.J. Reynolds Tobacco Co., 416 F. Supp. 313 (D.N.J. 1976) — § 2003; § 2007

U.S. v. R.L.C., 112 S. Ct. 1329 (1992) — § 1341

U.S. v. RMI Co., 599 F.2d 1183 (3d Cir. 1979) — § 411

U.S. v. Roach, 590 F.2d 181 (5th Cir. 1979) — § 306; § 1815

U.S., Robbins v.

U.S. v. Robbins, 579 F.2d 1151 (9th Cir. 1978) — § 1819

U.S., Roberts v.

U.S. v. Roberts, 466 F.2d 193 (7th Cir. 1972) — § 1512

U.S. v. Roberts, 481 F.2d 892 (5th Cir. 1973) — § 1903

U.S. v. Roberts, 515 F.2d 642 (2d Cir. 1975) — § 1225

U.S. v. Roberts, 548 F.2d 665 (6th Cir. 1977) — § 1207; § 1526

U.S. v. Roberts, 618 F.2d 530 (9th Cir. 1980) — § 1111

U.S. v. Roberts, 644 F.2d 683 (8th Cir. 1980) — § 202

U.S. v. Roberts, 676 F.2d 1185 (8th Cir. 1982) — § 2105

U.S. v. Robertson, 588 F.2d 575 (8th Cir. 1978) — § 1239

U.S. v. Robinson, 432 F.2d 1348 (D.C. Cir. 1970) — § 916

U.S. v. Robinson, 414 U.S. 218 (1973) — § 218; § 224

U.S. v. Robinson, 485 U.S. 25 (1988) — § 1112; § 1907

U.S. v. Robinson, 530 F.2d 1076 (D.C. Cir. 1976) — § 712; § 817; § 1923

U.S. v. Robinson, 544 F.2d 110 (2d Cir. 1976) — § 2127

U.S. v. Robinson, 546 F.2d 309 (9th Cir. 1976) — § 812

U.S. v. Robinson, 560 F.2d 507 (2d Cir. 1977) — § 1517

U.S. v. Robinson, 585 F.2d 274 (7th Cir. 1979) — § 801; § 805

U.S. v. Robinson, 953 F.2d 433 (8th Cir. 1992) — § 1261

U.S. v. Robson, 477 F.2d 13 (9th Cir. 1973) — § 244

U.S. v. Roby, 592 F.2d 406 (8th Cir. 1979) — § 1243

U.S. v. Rochan, 563 F.2d 1246 (5th Cir. 1977) — § 1703

U.S. v. Rodarte, 596 F.2d 141 (5th Cir. 1979) — § 1114; § 1522

U.S. v. Rodriguez, 556 F.2d 638 (2d Cir. 1977) — § 1115

U.S. v. Rodriguez, 585 F.2d 1234 (5th Cir. 1978) — § 1114

U.S. v. Rodriguez, 592 F.2d 553 (9th Cir. 1979) — § 224

U.S. v. Rodriguez, 596 F.2d 169 (6th Cir. 1979) — § 241; § 245

U.S. v. Rodriguez-Sandoval, 475 F.2d 542 (1st Cir. 1973) — § 1269

U.S. v. Roe, 670 F.2d 956 (11th Cir. 1982) — § 1248; § 1522; § 2116

U.S., Rogers v.

U.S. v. Rogers, 469 F.2d 1317 (5th Cir. 1972) — § 601

U.S. v. Rogers, 475 F.2d 821 (7th Cir. 1973) — § 1906

U.S. v. Rogers, 549 F.2d 490 (8th Cir. 1976) — § 1813; § 2144

U.S. v. Rogers, 899 F.2d 917 (10th Cir. 1990) — § 1223

U.S. v. Rojas, 574 F.2d 476 (9th Cir. 1978) — § 1301

U.S. v. Rojas, 671 F.2d 159 (5th Cir. 1982) — § 243

U.S. v. Rojas-Contreras, 106 S. Ct. 555 (1985) — § 1215

U.S. v. Rollins, 522 F.2d 160 (2d Cir. 1975) — § 205; § 250; § 1819

U.S. v. Romero, 249 F.2d 371 (2d Cir. 1957) — § 1904

U.S. v. Romero, 585 F.2d 391 (9th Cir. 1978) — § 1204; § 1209

U.S. v. Romero, 640 F.2d 1014 (9th Cir. 1981) — § 601

U.S. v. Romo, 669 F.2d 285 (5th Cir. 1982) — § 235; § 1810

U.S. v. Rone, 598 F.2d 564 (9th Cir. 1979) — § 1275

U.S. v. Rone, 743 F.2d 1169 (7th Cir. 1984) — § 1320

U.S. v. Rooks, 577 F.2d 33 (8th Cir. 1978) — § 311

U.S. v. Roper, 676 F.2d 841 (D.C. Cir. 1982) — § 1805

U.S., Rosales-Lopez v.

U.S. v. Rosales-Lopez, 617 F.2d 1349 (9th Cir. 1980) — § 1246

U.S. v. Rosario, 677 F.2d 614 (7th Cir. 1982) — § 1118

U.S. v. Rose, 562 F.2d 409 (7th Cir. 1977) — § 2123

U.S. v. Rose, 590 F.2d 232 (7th Cir. 1978) — § 1705

U.S. v. Rosenfeld, 545 F.2d 98 (10th Cir. 1976) — § 1113

U.S. v. Rosenstein, 474 F.2d 705 (2d Cir. 1973) — § 1703; § 1902; § 1917

U.S. v. Rosner, 485 F.2d 1213 (2d Cir. 1973) — § 1322

U.S. v. Rosner, 516 F.2d 269 (2d Cir. 1975) — § 721

U.S. v. Ross, 456 U.S. 798 (1982) — § 237

U.S. v. Ross, 321 F.2d 61 (2d Cir. 1963) — § 1707; § 2101

U.S. v. Ross, 464 F.2d 1278 (9th Cir. 1972) — § 907

U.S. v. Ross, 511 F.2d 757 (5th Cir. 1975) — § 708

U.S. v. Rosse, 418 F.2d 38 (2d Cir. 1969) — § 219

U.S. v. Rotchford, 575 F.2d 166 (8th Cir. 1978) — § 261

U.S. v. Roth, 430 F.2d 1137 (2d Cir. 1970) — § 317

U.S. v. Rothman, 463 F.2d 488 (2d Cir. 1972) — § 1809

U.S., Rotolo v.

U.S. v. Roundtree, 420 F.2d 845 (5th Cir. 1969) — § 1904

U.S., Roviaro v.

U.S. v. Rowell, 612 F.2d 1176 (7th Cir. 1980) — § 1239

U.S. v. Rubalcava-Montoya, 597 F.2d 140 (9th Cir. 1978) — § 248

U.S. v. Rubin, 591 F.2d 278 (5th Cir. 1979) — § 2105

U.S. v. Rucker, 557 F.2d 1046 (4th Cir. 1977) — § 1246

U.S. v. Rucker, 586 F.2d 899 (2d Cir. 1978) — § 911; § 913; § 1237

U.S. v. Rudolph, 403 F.2d 805 (6th Cir. 1968) — § 1805

U.S. v. Ruffin, 575 F.2d 346 (2d Cir. 1978) — § 1610; § 2125; § 2136

U.S. v. Ruiz-Estrella, 481 F.2d 723 (2d Cir. 1973) — § 239

U.S., Rumely v.

U.S. v. Runck, 601 F.2d 968 (8th Cir. 1979) — § 611

U.S. v. Runge, 593 F.2d 66 (8th Cir. 1979) — § 1107; § 1235

U.S. v. Russ, 362 F.2d 843 (2d Cir. 1966) — § 1923

U.S., Ryan v.

U.S. v. Ryan, 402 U.S. 530 (1971) — § 409

U.S. v. Ryan, 548 F.2d 782 (9th Cir. 1976) — § 268

U.S. v. Ryan, 866 F.2d 604 (3d Cir. 1989) — § 1324

U.S. v. Rylander, 460 U.S. 572 (1983) — § 1902

U.S. v. Sabatka, 623 F.2d 764 (2d Cir. 1980) — § 414

U.S., Sabbath v.

U.S. v. Sacasas, 381 F.2d 451 (2d Cir. 1967) — § 803

U.S. v. Sacco, 563 F.2d 552 (2d Cir. 1977) — § 252

U.S. v. Sackett, 598 F.2d 739 (2d Cir. 1979) — § 1532; § 2123

U.S. v. St. Pierre, 132 F.2d 837 (2d Cir. 1942) — § 1906

U.S. v. Saks & Co., 426 F. Supp. 812 (S.D.N.Y. 1976) — § 411

U.S. v. Salazar, 485 F.2d 1272 (2d Cir. 1973) — § 701

U.S. v. Salerno, 107 S. Ct. 2095 (1987) — § 504; § 506

U.S. v. Salerno, 112 S. Ct. 2503 (1992) — § 2141

U.S., Salinger v.

U.S. v. Salliey, 360 F.2d 699 (4th Cir. 1966) — § 1264

U.S. v. Salsedo, 607 F.2d 318 (9th Cir. 1979) — § 1820

U.S. v. Salva, 894 F.2d 225 (7th Cir. 1990) — § 609; § 1323

U.S. v. Salvucci, 448 U.S. 83 (1980) — § 255

U.S. v. Salzmann, 417 F. Supp. 1139 (E.D.N.Y. 1976) — § 1402; § 1403

U.S., Sanabria v.

U.S. v. Sanchez, 422 F.2d 1198 (2d Cir. 1970) — § 316; § 317

U.S. v. Sanchez, 459 F.2d 100 (2d Cir. 1972) — § 1904

U.S. v. Sanchez, 509 F.2d 886 (6th Cir. 1975) — § 213

U.S. v. Sanchez-Meza, 547 F.2d 461 (9th Cir. 1976) — § 1240

U.S., Sanders v.

U.S. v. Sanderson, 595 F.2d 1021 (5th Cir. 1979) — § 606

U.S. v. Sandler, 644 F.2d 1163 (5th Cir. 1981) — § 229

U.S. v. Sanfilippo, 565 F.2d 176 (5th Cir. 1977) — § 1107

U.S. v. Sanfilippo, 581 F.2d 1152 (5th Cir. 1978) — § 1260

U.S. v. Sanford, 673 F.2d 1070 (9th Cir. 1982) — § 256

U.S. v. Sangrey, 586 F.2d 1312 (9th Cir. 1978) — § 1252

U.S. v. Saniti, 604 F.2d 603 (9th Cir. 1979) — § 1608

U.S. v. San Juan, 545 F.2d 314 (2d Cir. 1976) — § 1511

U.S., Sansone v.

U.S. v. Santana, 427 U.S. 38 (1976) — § 234

U.S. v. Santarpio, 560 F.2d 448 (1st Cir. 1977) — § 2144

U.S. v. Santillo, 507 F.2d 629 (3d Cir. 1975) — § 268

U.S. v. Santoni, 585 F.2d 667 (4th Cir. 1978) — § 907

U.S. v. Santos, 588 F.2d 1300 (9th Cir. 1979) — § 1245

U.S. v. Santucci, 674 F.2d 624 (7th Cir. 1982) — § 409

U.S. v. Sargent Elec. Co., 785 F.2d 1123 (3d Cir. 1986) — § 1001

U.S. v. Satterfield, 558 F.2d 655 (2d Cir. 1976) — § 310

U.S. v. Satterfield, 548 F.2d 1341 (9th Cir. 1977) — § 901; § 905; § 907

U.S. v. Satterfield, 572 F.2d 687 (9th Cir. 1978) — § 2145

U.S. v. Sauls, 520 F.2d 568 (5th Cir. 1975) — § 1270

U.S. v. Savage, 470 F.2d 948 (3d Cir. 1972) — § 317

U.S. v. Savage, 482 F.2d 1371 (9th Cir. 1973) — § 1707

U.S. v. Savage, 564 F.2d 728 (5th Cir. 1977) — § 226; § 239

U.S. v. Sawyer, 607 F.2d 1190 (7th Cir. 1979) — § 2125

U.S. v. Scafidi, 564 F.2d 633 (2d Cir. 1977) — § 263; § 264; § 909

U.S. v. Scaglione, 446 F.2d 182 (5th Cir. 1971) — § 809

U.S., Scales v.

U.S. v. Scales, 594 F.2d 558 (6th Cir. 1979) — § 1250; § 1270; § 1605; § 1706; § 2003; § 2124

U.S. v. Scalzitti, 578 F.2d 507 (3d Cir. 1978) — § 1242

U.S. v. Scalzo, 716 F.2d 463 (7th Cir. 1983) — § 1317

U.S. v. Scavo, 593 F.2d 837 (8th Cir. 1979) — § 113; § 248; § 2003; § 2005; § 2116

U.S. v. Schackelford, 677 F.2d 422 (5th Cir. 1982) — § 1110

U.S., Schaffer v.

U.S. v. Scharf, 558 F.2d 498 (8th Cir. 1977) — § 1811

U.S., Schebergen v.

U.S. v. Scheer, 600 F.2d 5 (3d Cir. 1979) — § 229

U.S. v. Scheffer, 463 F.2d 567 (5th Cir. 1972) — § 1320

U.S. v. Schennault, 429 F.2d 852 (7th Cir. 1970) — § 1817

U.S. v. Scherer, 673 F.2d 176 (7th Cir. 1982) — § 1302

U.S. v. Schiff, 612 F.2d 73 (2d Cir. 1979) — § 1603

U.S. v. Schipani, 435 F.2d 26 (2d Cir. 1970) — § 1818

U.S. v. Schleis, 582 F.2d 1166 (8th Cir. 1978) — § 225

U.S. v. Schmidt, 573 F.2d 1057 (9th Cir. 1978) — § 312

U.S. v. Schmoker, 564 F.2d 289 (9th Cir. 1977) — § 306

U.S., Schmuck v.

U.S. v. Schoendorf, 454 F.2d 349 (7th Cir. 1971) — § 1902

U.S. v. Scholle, 553 F.2d 1109 (8th Cir. 1977) — § 1517; § 1522; § 2123

U.S. v. Schor, 418 F.2d 26 (2d Cir. 1969) — § 1264

U.S. v. Schwanke, 598 F.2d 575 (10th Cir. 1979) — § 2116

U.S. v. Schwarck, 961 F.2d 121 (8th Cir. 1992) — § 1337

U.S. v. Schwartz, 372 F.2d 678 (4th Cir. 1967) — § 502

U.S. v. Schwartzbaum, 527 F.2d 249 (2d Cir. 1975) — § 1802

U.S. v. Scios, 590 F.2d 956 (D.C. Cir. 1978) — § 226; § 248; § 311

U.S. v. Scijo, 537 F.2d 694 (2d Cir. 1976) — § 1003

U.S. v. Sclamo, 578 F.2d 888 (1st Cir. 1978) — § 207; § 712

U.S., Scott v.

U.S. v. Scott, 437 U.S. 82 (1978) — § 1006; § 1010

U.S. v. Scott, 520 F.2d 697 (9th Cir. 1975) — § 234

U.S. v. Scott, 547 F.2d 334 (6th Cir. 1977) — § 1261

U.S. v. Scott, 578 F.2d 1186 (6th Cir. 1978) — § 243

U.S. v. Scott, 583 F.2d 362 (7th Cir. 1978) — § 1243

U.S. v. Scott, 590 F.2d 531 (3d Cir. 1979) — § 243

U.S. v. Scott, 592 F.2d 1139 (10th Cir. 1979) — § 309; § 1818

U.S. v. Scott, 625 F.2d 623 (5th Cir. 1980) — § 609

U.S., Screws v.

U.S. v. Scruggs, 583 F.2d 238 (5th Cir. 1978) — § 708; § 1261

U.S. v. Scully, 546 F.2d 255 (9th Cir. 1976) — § 259

U.S. v. Seamster, 568 F.2d 188 (10th Cir. 1978) — § 1809

U.S. v. Searp, 586 F.2d 1117 (6th Cir. 1978) — § 214

U.S. v. Sears, 663 F.2d 896 (9th Cir. 1981) — § 2114

U.S. v. Sears Roebuck & Co., 518 F. Supp. 179 (C.D. Cal. 1981) — § 1117

U.S. v. Seastrunk, 580 F.2d 800 (5th Cir. 1978) — § 1532

U.S. v. Seavers, 472 F.2d 607 (6th Cir. 1973) — § 1902

U.S. v. Seawald, 450 F.2d 1159 (2d Cir. 1971) — § 1902; § 1903

U.S. v. Seawell, 550 F.2d 1159 (9th Cir. 1977) — § 1261

U.S. v. Seawell, 583 F.2d 416 (9th Cir. 1978) — § 1261

U.S. v. Sebastian, 497 F.2d 1267 (2d Cir. 1974) — § 801

U.S. v. Sebastian, 428 F. Supp. 967 (W.D.N.Y. 1977) — § 1215

U.S. v. Secondino, 347 F.2d 725 (2d Cir. 1965) — § 1518

U.S. v. Sedillo, 496 F.2d 151 (9th Cir. 1974) — § 1518

U.S. v. Segna, 555 F.2d 226 (9th Cir. 1977) — § 1113; § 1116

U.S., Segura v.

U.S. v. Seijo, 514 F.2d 1357 (2d Cir. 1975) — § 722

U.S. v. Seijo, 537 F.2d 694 (2d Cir. 1976) — § 1265

U.S. v. Seijo, 595 F.2d 116 (2d Cir. 1979) — § 2140

U.S. v. Sellers, 566 F.2d 884 (4th Cir. 1977) — § 2003

U.S. v. Sellers, 603 F.2d 53 (8th Cir. 1979) — § 1118

U.S. v. Sellers, 667 F.2d 1123 (4th Cir. 1981) — § 913

U.S. v. Sells Engineering, Inc., 463 U.S. 418 (1983) — § 412; § 414; § 416

U.S. v. Seluk, 873 F.2d 15 (1st Cir. 1989) — § 1312

U.S. v. Sentovich, 677 F.2d 834 (11th Cir. 1982) — § 206

U.S. v. Seohnlein, 423 F.2d 1051 (4th Cir. 1970) — § 304

U.S., Serfass v.

U.S. v. Serlin, 538 F.2d 737 (7th Cir. 1976) — § 1526

U.S. v. Serubo, 604 F.2d 807 (3d Cir. 1979) — § 404

U.S. v. Seta, 669 F.2d 400 (6th Cir. 1982) — § 208; § 1818

U.S. v. Seymour, 576 F.2d 1345 (9th Cir. 1978) — § 712

U.S. v. Shafer, 445 F.2d 579 (7th Cir. 1971) — § 1503

U.S. v. Shannahan, 605 F.2d 539 (10th Cir. 1979) — § 809

U.S., Shapiro v.

U.S. v. Shapiro, 565 F.2d 479 (7th Cir. 1977) — § 1810

U.S. v. Shapiro, 669 F.2d 593 (9th Cir. 1982) — § 1249

U.S. v. Sharp, 920 F.2d 1167 (4th Cir. 1990) — § 1903

U.S. v. Sharpe, 469 U.S. 809 (1985) — § 228

U.S. v. Shaw, 555 F.2d 1295 (5th Cir. 1977) — § 307

U.S. v. Shearer, 606 F.2d 819 (8th Cir. 1979) — § 903; § 910

U.S. v. Sheehan, 583 F.2d 30 (1st Cir. 1978) — § 317

U.S. v. Sheiner, 410 F.2d 337 (2d Cir. 1969) — § 2003

U.S. v. Shelton, 588 F.2d 1242 (9th Cir. 1978) — § 719; § 1108; § 1256

U.S., Shendal v.

U.S., Shepard v.

U.S. v. Shepard, 515 F.2d 1324 (D.C. Cir. 1975) — § 1003

U.S. v. Shephard, 538 F.2d 107 (6th Cir. 1976) — § 2003

U.S. v. Shepherd, 576 F.2d 719 (7th Cir. 1978) — § 1262

U.S. v. Sherman, 576 F.2d 292 (10th Cir. 1978) — § 713; § 1923

U.S. v. Sherod, 960 F.2d 1075 (D.C. Cir. 1992) — § 1275

U.S. v. Sherrif, 546 F.2d 604 (5th Cir. 1977) — § 1112

U.S. v. Sherwin, 572 F.2d 196 (9th Cir. 1977) — § 205

U.S. v. Sherwood, 435 F.2d 867 (10th Cir. 1970) — § 1319

U.S. v. Shields, 573 F.2d 18 (10th Cir. 1978) — § 241; § 2004

U.S. v. Shields, 675 F.2d 1152 (11th Cir. 1982) — § 265

U.S., Shillitani v.

U.S. v. Shima, 545 F.2d 1026 (5th Cir. 1977) — § 231

U.S. v. Shoemaker, 542 F.2d 561 (10th Cir. 1976) — § 301; § 304; § 1517

U.S. v. Short, 493 F.2d 1170 (9th Cir. 1974) — § 403

U.S. v. Short, 671 F.2d 178 (6th Cir. 1982) — § 414

U.S. v. Shorteeth, 887 F.2d 253 (10th Cir. 1989) — § 1322

U.S. v. Shorter, 600 F.2d 585 (6th Cir. 1979) — § 214

U.S. v. Shoulberg, 895 F.2d 882 (2d Cir. 1990) — § 1323

U.S. v. Shoupe, 548 F.2d 636 (6th Cir. 1977) — § 1801; § 1802; § 1807; § 1813

U.S. v. Shuford, 454 F.2d 772 (4th Cir. 1971) — § 913

U.S. v. Siegel, 587 F.2d 721 (5th Cir. 1979) — § 1274

U.S. v. Sigal, 572 F.2d 1320 (9th Cir. 1978) — § 1524

U.S. v. Signer, 482 F.2d 394 (6th Cir. 1973) — § 1103

U.S. v. Sihler, 562 F.2d 349 (5th Cir. 1977) — § 243

U.S. v. Silkman, 543 F.2d 1218 (8th Cir. 1976) — § 1903

U.S. v. Silva, 580 F.2d 144 (5th Cir. 1978) — § 712; § 1923

U.S. v. Silverman, 430 F.2d 106 (2d Cir. 1970) — § 1918

U.S. v. Silverman, 449 F.2d 1341 (2d Cir. 1971) — § 1245; § 1902

U.S. v. Silverstein, 314 F.2d 789 (2d Cir. 1963) — § 1902

U.S., Silverthorne Lumber Co. v.

U.S. v. Silvestain, 668 F.2d 1161 (10th Cir. 1982) — § 1902

U.S., Simmons v.

U.S. v. Simmons, 536 F.2d 827 (9th Cir. 1976) — § 1237

U.S. v. Simmons, 567 F.2d 314 (7th Cir. 1977) — § 226

U.S. v. Simon, 425 F.2d 796 (2d Cir. 1969) — § 1532

U.S. v. Simonetti, 326 F.2d 614 (2d Cir. 1964) — § 1923

U.S. v. Simpkins, 953 F.2d 443 (8th Cir. 1992) — § 1005; § 1819

U.S., Simpson v.

U.S., Sims v.

U.S. v. Sims, 514 F.2d 147 (9th Cir. 1975) — § 2004

U.S. v. Sims, 588 F.2d 1145 (6th Cir. 1978) — § 1810

U.S. v. Sinclair, 444 F.2d 888 (D.C. Cir. 1971) — § 1265

U.S., Sincox v.

U.S., Singer v.

U.S. v. Sing Kee, 250 F.2d 236 (2d Cir. 1957) — § 1906

U.S. v. Singleton, 439 F.2d 381 (3d Cir. 1971) — § 215

U.S. v. Singleton, 447 F. Supp. 852 (S.D.N.Y. 1978) — § 1265

U.S. v. Sink, 586 F.2d 1041 (5th Cir. 1978) — § 809; § 1516

U.S. v. Sircovich, 555 F.2d 1301 (5th Cir. 1977) — § 1514

U.S. v. Sisson, 339 U.S. 267 (1970) — § 1305

U.S. v. Sisto, 534 F.2d 616 (5th Cir. 1976) — § 1252

U.S. v. Skalicky, 615 F.2d 1117 (5th Cir. 1980) — § 1605

U.S. v. Skinner, 667 F.2d 1306 (9th Cir. 1982) — § 1265

U.S. v. Skipper, 633 F.2d 1177 (5th Cir. 1981) — § 504

U.S. v. Sklaroff, 323 F. Supp. 296 (S.D. Fla. 1971) — § 262

U.S. v. Sklaroff, 552 F.2d 1156 (5th Cir. 1977) — § 401

U.S. v. Sledge, 546 F.2d 1120 (4th Cir. 1977) — § 305

U.S. v. Slutsky, 352 F. Supp. 1105 (S.D.N.Y. 1972) — § 1902

U.S. v. Slutsky, 487 F.2d 832 (2d Cir. 1973) — § 105

U.S. v. Smaldone, 544 F.2d 456 (10th Cir. 1976) — § 801; § 807

U.S. v. Smallwood, 473 F.2d 98 (D.C. Cir. 1972) — § 316

U.S. v. Smedes, 760 F.2d 109 (6th Cir. 1985) — § 1242

U.S., Smith v.

U.S. v. Smith, 433 F.2d 1266 (5th Cir. 1970) — § 806

U.S. v. Smith, 437 F.2d 538 (6th Cir. 1970) — § 2003

U.S. v. Smith, 444 F.2d 61 (8th Cir. 1971) — § 504

U.S. v. Smith, 515 F.2d 1028 (5th Cir. 1975) — § 113

U.S. v. Smith, 521 F.2d 957 (D.C. Cir. 1975) — § 1802; § 1803

U.S. v. Smith, 524 F.2d 1288 (D.C. Cir. 1975) — § 1803

U.S. v. Smith, 533 F.2d 1077 (8th Cir. 1976) — § 1909; § 1911

U.S. v. Smith, 537 F.2d 862 (6th Cir. 1976) — § 1602

U.S. v. Smith, 551 F.2d 348 (D.C. Cir. 1976) — § 1810

U.S. v. Smith, 550 F.2d 277 (5th Cir. 1977) — § 2001

U.S. v. Smith, 552 F.2d 257 (8th Cir. 1977) — § 404; § 1524

U.S. v. Smith, 557 F.2d 1206 (5th Cir. 1977) — § 306; § 716

U.S. v. Smith, 562 F.2d 619 (10th Cir. 1977) — § 1262

U.S. v. Smith, 565 F.2d 292 (4th Cir. 1977) — § 224

U.S. v. Smith, 574 F.2d 707 (2d Cir. 1978) — § 313

U.S. v. Smith, 574 F.2d 882 (6th Cir. 1978) — § 228

U.S. v. Smith, 584 F.2d 759 (6th Cir. 1978) — § 1602

U.S. v. Smith, 588 F.2d 737 (9th Cir. 1978) — § 210

U.S. v. Smith, 595 F.2d 1176 (9th Cir. 1979) — § 233

U.S. v. Smith, 596 F.2d 319 (8th Cir. 1979) — § 2116

U.S. v. Smith, 602 F.2d 834 (8th Cir. 1979) — § 318

U.S. v. Smith, 929 F.2d 1453 (10th Cir. 1991) — § 1012

U.S. v. Smith, 962 F.2d 923 (9th Cir. 1992) — § 1114

U.S. v. Smolar, 557 F.2d 13 (1st Cir. 1977) — § 914; § 917; § 1811

U.S. v. Smyth, 556 F.2d 1179 (5th Cir. 1977) — § 1111; § 1605; § 1610

U.S. v. Snell, 592 F.2d 1083 (9th Cir. 1979) — § 1005

U.S. v. Snelling, 961 F.2d 93 (6th Cir. 1991) — § 1328

U.S. v. Snow, 537 F.2d 1166 (4th Cir. 1976) — § 807; § 813

U.S. v. Snow, 552 F.2d 165 (6th Cir. 1977) — § 1115

U.S. v. Snyder, 668 F.2d 686 (2d Cir. 1982) — § 1239

U.S. v. Sobell, 314 F.2d 314 (2d Cir. 1963) — § 1906

U.S. v. Socony Vacuum Oil Co., 310 U.S. 150 (1940) — § 1802

U.S. v. Sokolow, 109 S. Ct. 1581 (1989) — § 228

U.S. v. Solano, 605 F.2d 1141 (9th Cir. 1979) — § 1002; § 1004; § 1005

U.S. v. Soles, 482 F.2d 105 (2d Cir. 1973) — § 1810; § 1923

U.S. v. Sonderup, 639 F.2d 294 (5th Cir. 1981) — § 1316

U.S. v. Sorenson, 504 F.2d 406 (7th Cir. 1974) — § 1402

U.S. v. Sor-Lokken, 557 F.2d 755 (10th Cir. 1977) — § 248

U.S. v. Sorzano, 602 F.2d 1201 (5th Cir. 1979) — § 1115

U.S. v. Sotoj-Lopez, 603 F.2d 789 (9th Cir. 1979) — § 304

U.S. v. Southland Corp., 760 F.2d 1366 (2d Cir. 1985) — § 417

U.S. v. Spagnolo, 546 F.2d 1117 (4th Cir. 1976) — § 1260

U.S. v. Spain, 536 F.2d 170 (7th Cir. 1976) — § 1110

U.S. v. Sparks, 560 F.2d 1173 (4th Cir. 1977) — § 1524

U.S. v. Sparrow, 673 F.2d 862 (5th Cir. 1982) — § 1321

U.S. v. Spaulding, 588 F.2d 669 (9th Cir. 1978) — § 1208

U.S. v. Sperling, 506 F.2d 1323 (2d Cir. 1974) — § 806; § 807

U.S. v. Spiegel, 604 F.2d 961 (5th Cir. 1979) — § 1217

U.S., Spinelli v.

U.S. v. Splain, 545 F.2d 1131 (8th Cir. 1976) — § 1104; § 1111; § 1254

U.S. v. Spraggins, 868 F.2d 1541 (11th Cir. 1989) — § 1323

U.S. v. Spruille, 544 F.2d 303 (7th Cir. 1976) — § 313

U.S. v. Stacey, 571 F.2d 440 (8th Cir. 1978) — § 1118

U.S. v. Staller, 616 F.2d 1284 (5th Cir. 1980) — § 236; § 911; § 1252

U.S. v. Stanchich, 550 F.2d 1294 (2d Cir. 1977) — § 2116

U.S. v. Standard Oil Co., 316 F.2d 884 (7th Cir. 1963) — § 1264

U.S., Standefer v.

U.S. v. Standing Soldier, 538 F.2d 196 (8th Cir. 1976) — § 304; § 1707

U.S. v. Stanford, 589 F.2d 285 (7th Cir. 1978) — § 411; § 414

U.S. v. Stanley, 597 F.2d 866 (4th Cir. 1979) — § 243; § 247; § 306; § 905

U.S. v. Starks, 515 F.2d 112 (3d Cir. 1975) — § 905

U.S. v. Starr, 584 F.2d 235 (8th Cir. 1978) — § 911

U.S. v. Starusko, 729 F.2d 256 (3d Cir. 1984) — § 714

U.S. v. Stassi, 544 F.2d 579 (2d Cir. 1976) — § 1112

U.S. v. Stavros, 597 F.2d 108 (7th Cir. 1979) — § 1003

U.S., Steagald v.

U.S. v. Stearns, 550 F.2d 1167 (9th Cir. 1977) — § 1604; § 1703

U.S. v. Steed, 646 F.2d 136 (4th Cir. 1981) — § 1010

U.S., Steele v.

U.S. v. Steinberg, 525 F.2d 1126 (2d Cir. 1975) — § 261; § 266

U.S. v. Steinkoetter, 592 F.2d 747 (6th Cir. 1979) — § 1103

U.S. v. Steinkoetter, 633 F.2d 719 (6th Cir. 1980) — § 1111

U.S. v. Sten, 342 F.2d 491 (2d Cir. 1965) — § 805

U.S. v. Stephen, 569 F.2d 860 (5th Cir. 1978) — § 1532

U.S. v. Stephens, 492 F.2d 1367 (6th Cir. 1974) — § 1805

U.S., Stern v.

U.S. v. Stern, 511 F.2d 1364 (2d Cir. 1975) — § 1917

U.S. v. Sternman, 415 F.2d 1165 (6th Cir. 1969) — § 426

U.S. v. Stevens, 510 F.2d 1101 (5th Cir. 1975) — § 407

U.S. v. Stevie, 582 F.2d 1175 (8th Cir. 1978) — § 223

U.S., Stewart v.

U.S. v. Stewart, 445 F.2d 897 (8th Cir. 1971) — § 1903

U.S. v. Stewart, 513 F.2d 957 (2d Cir. 1975) — § 718

U.S. v. Stewart, 579 F.2d 356 (5th Cir. 1978) — § 314

U.S. v. Stewart, 585 F.2d 799 (5th Cir. 1979) — § 305

U.S. v. Stifel, 433 F.2d 431 (6th Cir. 1970) — § 2003

U.S., Stillman v.

U.S. v. Stinson, 957 F.2d 813 (11th Cir. 1992) — § 1308

U.S. v. Stinson, 594 F.2d 982 (4th Cir. 1979) — § 1239; § 1308

U.S. v. Stirling, 571 F.2d 708 (2d Cir. 1978) — § 315; § 1503; § 1902

U.S. v. Stirone, 168 F. Supp. 490 (W.D. Pa. 1957) — § 1801

U.S. v. Stober, 604 F.2d 1274 (10th Cir. 1979) — § 603

U.S. v. Stocks, 594 F.2d 113 (5th Cir. 1979) — § 236

U.S. v. Stofsky, 527 F.2d 237 (2d Cir. 1975) — § 1514

U.S., Stokes v.

U.S., Stone v.

U.S. v. Stone, 471 F.2d 170 (7th Cir. 1973) — § 720

U.S. v. Story, 891 F.2d 988 (2d Cir. 1990) — § 1311

U.S., Stout v.

U.S. v. Stout, 599 F.2d 866 (8th Cir. 1979) — § 2105

U.S. v. Stover, 565 F.2d 1010 (8th Cir. 1977) — § 1523

U.S. v. Strahan, 674 F.2d 96 (1st Cir. 1982) — § 236

U.S. v. Strahl, 590 F.2d 10 (1st Cir. 1978) — § 809

U.S. v. Strand, 566 F.2d 530 (5th Cir. 1978) — § 1230

U.S. v. Stratton, 649 F.2d 1066 (5th Cir. 1981) — § 104

U.S. v. Stratton, 779 F.2d 820 (2d Cir. 1985) — § 1241

U.S., Strauss v.

U.S. v. Street, 570 F.2d 1 (1st Cir. 1977) — § 1302

U.S. v. Stricklin, 591 F.2d 1112 (5th Cir. 1979) — § 1001; § 1002

U.S. v. Strissel, 920 F.2d 1162 (4th Cir. 1990) — § 1605

U.S. v. Stroman, 667 F.2d 416 (2d Cir. 1981) — § 1003

U.S. v. Strong, 775 F.2d 504 (3d Cir. 1985) — § 515

U.S. v. Stulga, 584 F.2d 142 (6th Cir. 1978) — § 812; § 1114; § 1223; § 1514

U.S. v. Stull, 521 F.2d 687 (6th Cir. 1975) — § 2003

U.S. v. Sturgeon, 501 F.2d 1270 (8th Cir. 1974) — § 212

U.S. v. Sturgis, 578 F.2d 1296 (9th Cir. 1978) — § 2003

U.S., Suarez v.

U.S. v. Suarez, 582 F.2d 1007 (5th Cir. 1978) — § 712

U.S. v. Suchy, 540 F.2d 254 (6th Cir. 1976) — § 2116

U.S., Sullivan v.

U.S. v. Sullivan, 274 U.S. 259 (1927) — § 1905

U.S. v. Sullivan, 625 F.2d 9 (4th Cir. 1980) — § 204

U.S. v. Sumlin, 567 F.2d 684 (6th Cir. 1977) — § 243; § 245

U.S. v. Summers, 598 F.2d 450 (5th Cir. 1979) — § 2115

U.S. v. Sumpter, 669 F.2d 1215 (8th Cir. 1982) — § 207; § 208

U.S., Sutton v.

U.S. v. Sutton, 426 F.2d 1202 (D.C. Cir. 1969) — § 1703

U.S. v. Sutton, 542 F.2d 1239 (4th Cir. 1976) — § 719

U.S. v. Swainson, 548 F.2d 657 (6th Cir. 1977) — § 1239

U.S. v. Sweet, 548 F.2d 198 (7th Cir. 1977) — § 722

U.S. v. Sweig, 441 F.2d 114 (2d Cir. 1971) — § 909

U.S. v. Swihart, 554 F.2d 264 (6th Cir. 1977) — § 207

U.S. v. Syal, 963 F.2d 900 (6th Cir. 1992) — § 608

U.S. v. Syler, 430 F.2d 68 (7th Cir. 1970) — § 215

U.S. v. Taborda, 635 F.2d 131 (2d Cir. 1980) — § 201

U.S. v. Tager, 638 F.2d 167 (10th Cir. 1980) — § 414

U.S. v. Taglione, 546 F.2d 194 (5th Cir. 1977) — § 1522; § 1524; § 2120

U.S. v. Talavera, 668 F.2d 625 (1st Cir. 1982) — § 916

U.S., Tallent v.

U.S., Tallo v.

U.S. v. Tanner, 471 F.2d 128 (7th Cir. 1972) — § 905

U.S. v. Tanu, 589 F.2d 82 (2d Cir. 1978) — § 1204; § 1212

U.S. v. Tarlowski, 305 F. Supp. 112 (E.D.N.Y. 1969) — § 1917

U.S. v. Tarnowski, 583 F.2d 903 (6th Cir. 1978) — § 814; § 1245

U.S. v. Tasto, 586 F.2d 1068 (5th Cir. 1978) — § 206

U.S. v. Taxe, 540 F.2d 961 (9th Cir. 1976) — § 1111; § 2125

U.S., Taylor v.

U.S. v. Taylor, 303 F.2d 165 (4th Cir. 1962) — § 606

U.S. v. Taylor, 507 F.2d 166 (5th Cir. 1975) — § 1262

U.S. v. Taylor, 530 F.2d 639 (5th Cir. 1976) — § 317; § 318; § 1604

U.S. v. Taylor, 562 F.2d 1345 (2d Cir. 1977) — § 2005

U.S. v. Taylor, 569 F.2d 448 (7th Cir. 1978) — § 1213

U.S. v. Taylor, 599 F.2d 832 (8th Cir. 1979) — § 204

U.S. v. Taylor, 603 F.2d 732 (8th Cir. 1979) — § 1239

U.S. v. Taylor, 612 F.2d 1272 (10th Cir. 1980) — § 1603

U.S. v. Taylor, 487 U.S. 326 (1988) — § 1234

U.S. v. Tedesco, 635 F.2d 902 (1st Cir. 1980) — § 105

U.S. v. Tempesta, 587 F.2d 931 (8th Cir. 1978) — § 1239

U.S. v. Tenorio-Angel, 756 F.2d 1505 (11th Cir. 1985) — § 1235

U.S. v. Tercero, 580 F.2d 312 (8th Cir. 1978) — § 1001

U.S. v. Tercero, 640 F.2d 190 (9th Cir. 1980) — § 1235

U.S. v. Termini, 267 F.2d 18 (2d Cir. 1959) — § 1911

U.S., Test v.

U.S. v. Testa, 458 F.2d 847 (9th Cir. 1977) — § 110

U.S. v. Thetford, 676 F.2d 170 (5th Cir. 1982) — § 1266

U.S. v. Thevis, 665 F.2d 616 (5th Cir. 1982) — § 2147

U.S. v. Thirty-seven Photographs, 402 U.S. 363 (1971) — § 229

U.S. v. Thomann, 609 F.2d 560 (1st Cir. 1979) — § 911

U.S., Thomas v.

U.S. v. Thomas, 299 F. Supp. 494 (E.D. Mo. 1968) — § 111

U.S. v. Thomas, 453 F.2d 141 (9th Cir. 1971) — § 1516

U.S. v. Thomas, 551 F.2d 347 (D.C. Cir. 1976) — § 238

U.S. v. Thomas, 571 F.2d 285 (5th Cir. 1978) — § 2140; § 2144; § 2145

U.S. v. Thomas, 586 F.2d 123 (9th Cir. 1978) — § 317

U.S. v. Thomas, 593 F.2d 615 (5th Cir. 1979) — § 1118

U.S. v. Thomas, 610 F.2d 1166 (3d Cir. 1979) — § 910; § 912

U.S. v. Thomas, 676 F.2d 239 (7th Cir. 1980) — § 911

U.S. v. Thomas, 676 F.2d 531 (11th Cir. 1982) — § 1518; § 1808; § 2003

U.S. v. Thomas, 870 F.2d 174 (5th Cir. 1989) — § 1323

U.S., Thompson v.

U.S. v. Thompson, 251 U.S. 407 (1920) — § 409

U.S. v. Thompson, 261 F.2d 809 (2d Cir. 1958) — § 1528

U.S. v. Thompson, 490 F.2d 1218 (8th Cir. 1974) — § 1265

U.S. v. Thompson, 493 F.2d 305 (9th Cir. 1974) — § 709

U.S. v. Thompson, 558 F.2d 522 (9th Cir. 1977) — § 250

U.S., Thor v.

U.S. v. Thorne, 547 F.2d 56 (8th Cir. 1976) — § 1810

U.S. v. Thurmond, 541 F.2d 744 (8th Cir. 1976) — § 1115

U.S. v. Tillman, 470 F.2d 142 (3d Cir. 1972) — § 903

U.S. v. Timmreck, 441 U.S. 780 (1979) — § 609; § 616

U.S. v. Timpani, 665 F.2d 1 (1st Cir. 1981) — § 230

U.S. v. Tingle, 658 F.2d 1332 (9th Cir. 1981) — § 313

U.S., Tinker v.

U.S. v. Tobin, 576 F.2d 687 (5th Cir. 1978) — § 243

U.S. v. Tokoph, 514 F.2d 597 (10th Cir. 1975) — § 111

U.S. v. Tolias, 548 F.2d 277 (9th Cir. 1977) — § 243

U.S. v. Tomaiolo, 249 F.2d 683 (2d Cir. 1957) — § 1906; § 1913

U.S. v. Toney, 599 F.2d 787 (6th Cir. 1979) — § 2140; § 2144; § 2145

U.S. v. Torbert, 496 F.2d 154 (9th Cir. 1974) — § 1819

U.S. v. Torres, 503 F.2d 1120 (2d Cir. 1974) — § 1813

U.S. v. Torres, 663 F.2d 1019 (10th Cir. 1981) — § 304

U.S. v. Tortorello, 480 F.2d 764 (2d Cir. 1973) — § 261; § 1905

U.S. v. Toscanino, 500 F.2d 267 (2d Cir. 1974) — § 267

U.S., Tot v.

U.S., Trammel v.

U.S. v. Tramunti, 500 F.2d 1334 (2d Cir. 1974) — § 420

U.S. v. Tranowski, 659 F.2d 750 (7th Cir. 1981) — § 2003

U.S., Travis v.

U.S. v. Traylor, 578 F.2d 108 (5th Cir. 1978) — § 1209

U.S. v. Trejo-Zambrano, 582 F.2d 460 (9th Cir. 1978) — § 713; § 2144

U.S. v. Trenary, 473 F.2d 680 (9th Cir. 1973) — § 108

U.S. v. Trenton Potteries, Co., 273 U.S. 392 (1927) — § 2001

U.S. v. Trevino, 556 F.2d 1265 (5th Cir. 1977) — § 806

U.S. v. Tropeano, 476 F.2d 586 (1st Cir. 1973) — § 1104

U.S. v. Tropiano, 418 F.2d 1069 (2d Cir. 1969) — § 1518

U.S. v. Trotter, 538 F.2d 217 (8th Cir. 1976) — § 303; § 1702

U.S. v. Troxler Hosiery Co., 681 F.2d 934 (4th Cir. 1982) — § 1240

U.S. v. Truesdale, 400 F.2d 620 (2d Cir. 1968) — § 1923

U.S. v. Truong Dihn Hung, 667 F.2d 1105 (4th Cir. 1981) — § 805

U.S. v. Tsanas, 572 F.2d 340 (2d Cir. 1978) — § 1265

U.S. v. Tucker, 380 F.2d 1206 (2d Cir. 1967) — § 1403

U.S. v. Tucker, 404 U.S. 443 (1972) — § 1322; § 1810

U.S. v. Tucker, 526 F.2d 279 (5th Cir. 1976) — § 407; § 414

U.S. v. Tucker, 552 F.2d 202 (7th Cir. 1977) — § 1923

U.S. v. Turbide, 558 F.2d 1053 (2d Cir. 1977) — § 713; § 1923

U.S. v. Turcotte, 515 F.2d 145 (2d Cir. 1975) — § 1805

U.S. v. Turk, 526 F.2d 654 (5th Cir. 1976) — § 268

U.S. v. Turner, 480 F.2d 272 (7th Cir. 1973) — § 1902

U.S. v. Turner, 586 F.2d 395 (5th Cir. 1978) — § 108

U.S. v. Turner, 741 F.2d 696 (5th Cir. 1984) — § 1321

U.S. v. Turquitt, 557 F.2d 464 (5th Cir. 1977) — § 1805

U.S. v. Tussell, 441 F. Supp. 1092 (M.D. Pa. 1977) — § 253

U.S. v. Tutt, 704 F.2d 1567 (11th Cir. 1983) — § 1303

U.S. v. Tweel, 550 F.2d 297 (5th Cir. 1977) — § 244

U.S. v. Tyler, 592 F.2d 261 (5th Cir. 1979) — § 317

U.S. v. UCO Oil Co., 546 F.2d 833 (9th Cir. 1976) — § 1503

U.S. v. Udziela, 671 F.2d 995 (7th Cir. 1982) — § 403

U.S., Ullmann v.

U.S. v. Umbower, 602 F.2d 754 (5th Cir. 1979) — § 1213

U.S. v. Umentum, 401 F. Supp. 746 (E.D. Wis. 1975) — § 1403

U.S. v. Underwood, 577 F.2d 157 (1st Cir. 1978) — § 1603

U.S. v. Union Nacional De Trabajadores, 576 F.2d 388 (1st Cir. 1978) — § 2125

U.S., United Brotherhood of Carpenters and Joiners of America v.

U.S. v. U.S. Coin & Currency, 401 U.S. 715 (1971) — § 1905

U.S. v. U.S. Currency, 626 F.2d 11 (6th Cir. 1980) — § 1906

U.S. v. U.S. District Court, 238 F.2d 713 (4th Cir. 1956) — § 402

U.S. v. U.S. District Court, 407 U.S. 297 (1972) — § 257

U.S. v. U.S. Gypsum Co., 438 U.S. 422 (1978) — § 1249; § 1269; § 1505; § 1510

U.S. v. U.S. Machinery Corp., 89 F. Supp. 357 (D. Mass. 1950) — § 1915

U.S. v. Universal C.I.T. Credit Corp., 344 U.S. 218 (1952) — § 905

U.S., Universal Manufacturing Co. v.

U.S. v. Universal Manufacturing Co., 525 F.2d 808 (8th Cir. 1975) — § 409

U.S., Upjohn Co. v.

U.S. v. Urbanis, 490 F.2d 384 (9th Cir. 1974) — § 2003

U.S. v. Valdes, 545 F.2d 957 (5th Cir. 1977) — § 1109

U.S. v. Valenzuela, 584 F.2d 374 (10th Cir. 1978) — § 1005

U.S. v. Valenzuela, 596 F.2d 824 (9th Cir. 1979) — § 208; § 215; § 909; § 1239

U.S. v. Valera-Elyonda, 761 F.2d 1020 (5th Cir. 1985) — § 516

U.S. v. Vancier, 515 F.2d 1378 (2d Cir. 1975) — § 419

U.S. v. Van Cleave, 599 F.2d 954 (10th Cir. 1979) — § 1239

U.S. v. Vandivere, 579 F.2d 1240 (10th Cir. 1978) — § 503

U.S. v. Van Drunen, 501 F.2d 1393 (7th Cir. 1974) — § 1911; § 1914

U.S. v. Van Dyke, 605 F.2d 220 (6th Cir. 1979) — § 1209

U.S. v. Van Dyke, 895 F.2d 984 (4th Cir. 1990) — § 1326

U.S. v. Vannelli, 595 F.2d 402 (8th Cir. 1979) — § 1809

U.S. v. Van Orsdell, 521 F.2d 1323 (2d Cir. 1975) — § 1923

U.S. v. Vargas, 558 F.2d 631 (1st Cir. 1977) — § 1114

U.S. v. Vargas, 583 F.2d 380 (7th Cir. 1978) — § 1111

U.S. v. Vasilios, 598 F.2d 387 (5th Cir. 1979) — § 1805

U.S. v. Vasquez, 534 F.2d 1142 (5th Cir. 1976) — § 304

U.S. v. Vasquez, 597 F.2d 192 (9th Cir. 1979) — § 1250

U.S. v. Vasquez-Santiago, 602 F.2d 1069 (2d Cir. 1979) — § 243

U.S. v. Vasser, 648 F.2d 507 (9th Cir. 1980) — § 206

U.S. v. Vaughan, 565 F.2d 283 (4th Cir. 1977) — § 1118

U.S. v. Veatch, 674 F.2d 1217 (9th Cir. 1981) — § 703

U.S. v. Vega, 589 F.2d 1147 (2d Cir. 1978) — § 1818

U.S. v. Vela, 673 F.2d 86 (5th Cir. 1982) — § 702; § 2123

U.S. v. Velasquez-Mercado, 872 F.2d 632 (5th Cir. 1989) — § 1323; § 1327

U.S. v. Vento, 533 F.2d 838 (3d Cir. 1976) — § 261

U.S. v. Ventresca, 380 U.S. 102 (1965) — § 208; § 209

U.S. v. Verdoon, 528 F.2d 103 (8th Cir. 1976) — § 1811

U.S., Verdugo v.

U.S. v. Verdugo-Urquidez, 110 S. Ct. 1056 (1990) — § 203

U.S. v. Viale, 312 F.2d 595 (2d Cir. 1963) — § 219

U.S. v. Viggiano, 433 F.2d 716 (2d Cir. 1970) — § 207

U.S. v. Vigil, 561 F.2d 1316 (9th Cir. 1977) — § 914

U.S. v. Viglia, 549 F.2d 335 (5th Cir. 1977) — § 2003

U.S. v. Vigo, 487 F.2d 295 (2d Cir. 1973) — § 306

U.S. v. Vila, 599 F.2d 21 (2d Cir. 1979) — § 1207

U.S. v. Villa, 470 F. Supp. 315 (N.D.N.Y. 1979) — § 1213

U.S. v. Villamonte-Marquez, 462 U.S. 579 (1983) — § 228

U.S. v. Villano, 529 F.2d 1046 (10th Cir. 1976) — § 246

U.S., Villarreal v.

U.S. v. Vinson, 606 F.2d 149 (6th Cir. 1979) — § 916; § 1252; § 2116

U.S. v. Viserto, 596 F.2d 531 (2d Cir. 1979) — § 705; § 1260; § 2134

U.S. v. Vispi, 545 F.2d 328 (2d Cir. 1976) — § 1204

U.S. v. Vita, 294 F.2d 524 (2d Cir. 1961) — § 304

U.S. v. Vortis, 785 F.2d 327 (D.C. Cir. 1986) — § 509

U.S., Wade v.

U.S. v. Wade, 388 U.S. 218 (1967) — § 307; § 317; § 319; § 1903

U.S. v. Wainwright, 413 F.2d 796 (10th Cir. 1969) — § 1917

U.S. v. Walden, 590 F.2d 85 (3d Cir. 1979) — § 812; § 813

U.S., Walder v.

U.S. v. Waldron, 568 F.2d 185 (10th Cir. 1977) — § 1525

U.S., Walker v.

U.S. v. Walker, 313 F.2d 236 (6th Cir. 1963) — § 1808; § 1906

U.S. v. Walker, 538 F.2d 266 (9th Cir. 1976) — § 706

U.S. v. Walker, 552 F.2d 566 (4th Cir. 1977) — § 101

U.S. v. Walker, 557 F.2d 741 (10th Cir. 1977) — § 1249

U.S. v. Walker, 559 F.2d 365 (5th Cir. 1977) — § 112

U.S. v. Walker, 575 F.2d 209 (9th Cir. 1978) — § 1260

U.S. v. Walker, 601 F.2d 1051 (9th Cir. 1979) — § 1239

U.S. v. Walker, 652 F.2d 708 (7th Cir. 1981) — § 1704

U.S. v. Walking Crow, 560 F.2d 386 (8th Cir. 1977) — § 1003

U.S. v. Wallace, 468 F.2d 571 (4th Cir. 1972) — § 1816

U.S. v. Wallace, 528 F.2d 863 (4th Cir. 1976) — § 414

U.S. v. Wallace, 578 F.2d 735 (8th Cir. 1978) — § 1005

U.S. v. Waller, 607 F.2d 49 (3d Cir. 1979) — § 1115

U.S. v. Waloke, 962 F.2d 824 (8th Cir. 1992) — § 306

U.S., Walters v.

U.S. v. Walter, 591 F.2d 1195 (5th Cir. 1979) — § 1206

U.S., Walton v.

U.S. v. Walton, 552 F.2d 1354 (10th Cir. 1977) — § 1502

U.S. v. Ward, 522 F.2d 1080 (5th Cir. 1977) — § 2147

U.S. v. Ward, 448 U.S. 242 (1980) — § 1905

U.S. v. Warden, 545 F.2d 32 (7th Cir. 1976) — § 807

U.S. v. Warner, 428 F.2d 730 (8th Cir. 1970) — § 905

U.S. v. Warren, 453 F.2d 738 (2d Cir. 1972) — § 1516; § 1902

U.S. v. Warren, 578 F.2d 1058 (5th Cir. 1978) — § 309

U.S. v. Warren, 594 F.2d 1046 (5th Cir. 1979) — § 229; § 1262

U.S. v. Washabaugh, 442 F.2d 1127 (9th Cir. 1971) — § 801

U.S. v. Washington, 341 F.2d 277 (3d Cir. 1965) — § 609

U.S. v. Washington, 431 U.S. 181 (1977) — § 405; § 1906

U.S. v. Washington, 586 F.2d 1147 (7th Cir. 1978) — § 1252

U.S. v. Washington, 677 F.2d 394 (4th Cir. 1982) — § 239

U.S., Wasman v.

U.S. v. Watchmaker, 761 F.2d 1459 (11th Cir. 1985) — § 1002

U.S., Watkins v.

U.S. v. Watkins, 505 F.2d 545 (7th Cir. 1974) — § 421

U.S. v. Watkins, 600 F.2d 201 (9th Cir. 1979) — § 1103

U.S. v. Watson, 423 U.S. 411 (1976) — § 243; § 247

U.S. v. Watson, 587 F.2d 365 (7th Cir. 1978) — § 319; § 1520; § 2003

U.S. v. Watson, 591 F.2d 1058 (5th Cir. 1979) — § 304

U.S. v. Watson, 594 F.2d 1330 (10th Cir. 1979) — § 1602

U.S. v. Watson, 599 F.2d 1149 (2d Cir. 1979) — § 1239

U.S. v. Watson, 669 F.2d 1374 (11th Cir. 1982) — § 1250; § 1808

U.S. v. Watson, 868 F.2d 157 (5th Cir. 1989) — § 1344

U.S. v. Weaklem, 517 F.2d 70 (9th Cir. 1975) — § 226

U.S. v. Weatherspoon, 581 F.2d 595 (7th Cir. 1978) — § 716; § 1610

U.S., Weaver v.

U.S. v. Weber, 668 F.2d 552 (1st Cir. 1981) — § 227

U.S. v. Webster, 960 F.2d 1301 (5th Cir. 1992) — § 1301

U.S. v. Wehling, 676 F.2d 1053 (5th Cir. 1982) — § 1239

U.S. v. Weidman, 572 F.2d 1199 (7th Cir. 1978) — § 806; § 1108; § 1524; § 1526

U.S. v. Weil, 561 F.2d 1109 (4th Cir. 1977) — § 2110

U.S. v. Weinberg, 439 F.2d 743 (9th Cir. 1971) — § 404

U.S. v. Weinrich, 586 F.2d 481 (5th Cir. 1978) — § 233; § 314; § 2113

U.S. v. Weinstein, 452 F.2d 704 (2d Cir. 1971) — § 1272

U.S. v. Weir, 575 F.2d 668 (8th Cir. 1978) — § 713; § 1517

U.S. v. Weir, 861 F.2d 542 (9th Cir. 1988) — § 1338

U.S. v. Weisman, 624 F.2d 1118 (2d Cir. 1980) — § 907

U.S. v. Well, 572 F.2d 1383 (9th Cir. 1978) — § 810; § 812

U.S., Welsh v.

U.S. v. Wentland, 582 F.2d 1022 (5th Cir. 1978) — § 1510

U.S. v. Werbrouck, 589 F.2d 273 (7th Cir. 1978) — § 1245; § 1809; § 1810

U.S. v. Werner, 620 F.2d 922 (2d Cir. 1980) — § 903; § 910; § 911

U.S. v. Wertis, 505 F.2d 683 (5th Cir. 1974) — § 1815

U.S. v. West, 549 F.2d 545 (8th Cir. 1977) — § 1512

U.S. v. West, 574 F.2d 1131 (4th Cir. 1978) — § 2147

U.S. v. West, 607 F.2d 300 (9th Cir. 1979) — § 1112; § 1210; § 1518

U.S. v. West, 670 F.2d 675 (7th Cir. 1982) — § 1112; § 1116; § 1518; § 2110

U.S. v. Westbo, 576 F.2d 285 (10th Cir. 1978) — § 1266

U.S. v. Wetterlin, 583 F.2d 346 (7th Cir. 1978) — § 608

U.S., Whalen v.

U.S., Whaley v.

U.S. v. Wharton, 433 F.2d 451 (D.C. Cir. 1970) — § 1269

U.S. v. Wheeler, 435 U.S. 313 (1978) — § 1004

U.S. v. Whetzel, 589 F.2d 707 (D.C. Cir. 1978) — § 1524

U.S., White v.

U.S. v. White, 322 U.S. 694 (1944) — § 1902

U.S. v. White, 324 F.2d 814 (2d Cir. 1963) — § 1923

U.S. v. White, 377 F.2d 908 (4th Cir. 1967) — § 2106

U.S. v. White, 401 U.S. 745 (1971) — § 268; § 1602

U.S. v. White, 477 F.2d 757 (5th Cir. 1973) — § 1902

U.S. v. White, 553 F.2d 310 (2d Cir. 1977) — § 2144

U.S. v. White, 583 F.2d 819 (6th Cir. 1978) — § 611

U.S. v. White, 583 F.2d 899 (6th Cir. 1978) — § 702

U.S. v. White, 589 F.2d 1283 (5th Cir. 1979) — § 1254; § 1906

U.S. v. White, 611 F.2d 531 (5th Cir. 1980) — § 108

U.S. v. White, 671 F.2d 1126 (8th Cir. 1982) — § 1266

U.S. v. White, 869 F.2d 822 (5th Cir. 1989) — § 1312

U.S. v. White, 893 F.2d 276 (10th Cir. 1990) — § 1324

U.S. v. White Bear, 668 F.2d 409 (8th Cir. 1982) — § 1902

U.S. v. Whitehead, 424 F.2d 446 (6th Cir. 1970) — § 1905

U.S. v. Whitehead, 539 F.2d 1023 (4th Cir. 1976) — § 907

U.S. v. Whitehead, 618 F.2d 523 (4th Cir. 1980) — § 916; § 1115

U.S. v. Whitmire, 595 F.2d 1303 (5th Cir. 1979) — § 227

U.S. v. Whitson, 587 F.2d 948 (9th Cir. 1978) — § 1113; § 1818

U.S., Wilcoxon v.

U.S. v. Widgery, 674 F.2d 710 (8th Cir. 1982) — § 1302

U.S. v. Wiebold, 507 F.2d 932 (8th Cir. 1974) — § 1261

U.S. v. Wigerman, 549 F.2d 1192 (8th Cir. 1977) — § 2123

U.S. v. Wiggins, 566 F.2d 944 (5th Cir. 1978) — § 1209; § 1810

U.S. v. Wiley

U.S. v. Wiley, 278 F.2d 500 (7th Cir. 1960) — § 1322

U.S. v. Wiley, 524 F.2d 659 (6th Cir. 1976) — § 1111

U.S. v. Wilkins, 385 F.2d 465 (4th Cir. 1967) — § 1530

U.S. v. Wilkinson, 513 F.2d 227 (7th Cir. 1975) — § 1270

U.S. v. Wilkinson, 601 F.2d 791 (5th Cir. 1979) — § 1010

U.S. v. Wilks, 629 F.2d 669 (10th Cir. 1980) — § 1212

U.S., Williams v.

U.S. v. Williams, 112 S. Ct. 1735 (1992) — § 402; § 403

U.S. v. Williams, 523 F.2d 407 (2d Cir. 1975) — § 1906

U.S. v. Williams, 523 F.2d 1203 (5th Cir. 1975) — § 111

U.S. v. Williams, 545 F.2d 47 (8th Cir. 1976) — § 1517

U.S. v. Williams, 571 F.2d 344 (6th Cir. 1978) — § 2122

U.S. v. Williams, 573 F.2d 284 (5th Cir. 1978) — § 2110; § 2136

U.S. v. Williams, 583 F.2d 1194 (2d Cir. 1978) — § 1114; § 2003

U.S. v. Williams, 587 F.2d 1 (6th Cir. 1978) — § 1810

U.S. v. Williams, 594 F.2d 86 (5th Cir. 1979) — § 206

U.S. v. Williams, 603 F.2d 1168 (5th Cir. 1979) — § 206

U.S. v. Williams, 604 F.2d 1102 (8th Cir. 1979) — § 252; § 913; § 1514

U.S. v. Williams, 605 F.2d 495 (10th Cir. 1979) — § 207; § 208

U.S. v. Williams, 613 F.2d 573 (5th Cir. 1980) — § 1301; § 1302

U.S. v. Williams, 623 F.2d 535 (8th Cir. 1980) — § 232

U.S. v. Williams, 668 F.2d 1064 (9th Cir. 1981) — § 1318

U.S. v. Williams, 753 F.2d 329 (4th Cir. 1985) — § 512

U.S. v. Williams, 891 F.2d 212 (1st Cir. 1989) — § 1326

U.S. v. Williams, 952 F.2d 1504 (6th Cir. 1991) — § 1605

U.S. v. Williamsburg Check Cashing Corp., 905 F.2d 25 (2d Cir. 1990) — § 613

U.S. v. Willis, 473 F.2d 450 (6th Cir. 1973) — § 1923

U.S. v. Willis, 583 F.2d 203 (5th Cir. 1978) — § 1239

U.S. v. Willoz, 449 F.2d 1321 (5th Cir. 1971) — § 1902

U.S., Wilson v.

U.S. v. Wilson, 420 U.S. 332 (1975) — § 1010

U.S. v. Wilson, 451 F.2d 209 (5th Cir. 1971) — § 2003

U.S. v. Wilson, 529 F.2d 913 (10th Cir. 1976) — § 303

U.S. v. Wilson, 534 F.2d 375 (D.C. Cir. 1976) — § 1514

U.S. v. Wilson, 536 F.2d 883 (9th Cir. 1976) — § 245

U.S. v. Wilson, 569 F.2d 392 (5th Cir. 1978) — § 248

U.S. v. Wilson, 629 F.2d 439 (6th Cir. 1980) — § 1258; § 1303

U.S. v. Wilson, 666 F.2d 1241 (9th Cir. 1982) — § 1212

U.S. v. Wilson, 669 F.2d 922 (4th Cir. 1982) — § 613

U.S. v. Wilson, 896 F.2d 856 (4th Cir. 1990) — § 1328

U.S. v. Wilson, 900 F.2d 1350 (9th Cir. 1990) — § 1339

U.S. v. Wingate, 520 F.2d 309 (2d Cir. 1975) — § 314; § 2141

U.S. v. Wingender, 711 F.2d 869 (9th Cir. 1983) — § 1012

U.S. v. Winkle, 587 F.2d 705 (5th Cir. 1979) — § 1512; § 1705; § 1707

U.S. v. Winn, 577 F.2d 86 (9th Cir. 1978) — § 703

U.S., Withers v.

U.S. v. Wolf, 535 F.2d 476 (8th Cir. 1976) — § 303

U.S. v. Wolfish, 525 F.2d 457 (2d Cir. 1975) — § 1703

U.S., Wolfle v.

U.S., Wolford v.

U.S. v. Wolfson, 437 F.2d 862 (2d Cir. 1970) — § 1805; § 1811

U.S. v. Wolfson, 573 F.2d 216 (5th Cir. 1978) — § 1805

U.S. v. Wolfson, 634 F.2d 1217 (9th Cir. 1980) — § 1322

U.S. v. Wolk, 398 F. Supp. 405 (E.D. Pa. 1975) — § 2003

U.S. v. Wong, 431 U.S. 174 (1977) — § 405; § 1903

U.S., Wong Sun v.

U.S., Wong Tai v.

U.S., Wood v.

U.S. v. Wood, 550 F.2d 435 (9th Cir. 1976) — § 248; § 1810; § 2140

U.S. v. Woodard, 671 F.2d 1097 (8th Cir. 1982) — § 702

U.S. v. Woodring, 444 F.2d 749 (9th Cir. 1971) — § 215

U.S. v. Woods, 544 F.2d 242 (6th Cir. 1976) — § 221; § 317; § 408

U.S., Woodward v.

U.S., Woody v.

U.S. v. Woolridge, 572 F.2d 1027 (5th Cir. 1978) — § 909

U.S. v. Wright, 365 F.2d 135 (7th Cir. 1966) — § 1268

U.S. v. Wright, 483 F.2d 1068 (4th Cir. 1973) — § 504

U.S. v. Wright, 491 F.2d 942 (6th Cir. 1974) — § 1243; § 2116

U.S. v. Wright, 524 F.2d 1100 (2d Cir. 1975) — § 266

U.S. v. Wright, 564 F.2d 785 (8th Cir. 1977) — § 245

U.S. v. Wright, 573 F.2d 681 (1st Cir. 1978) — § 268

U.S. v. Wright, 577 F.2d 378 (6th Cir. 1978) — § 226

U.S. v. Wright, 593 F.2d 105 (9th Cir. 1979) — § 1266

U.S. v. Wright, 667 F.2d 793 (9th Cir. 1982) — § 211; § 403

U.S. v. Wright, 873 F.2d 437 (1st Cir. 1989) — § 1346

U.S. v. Wyant, 576 F.2d 1312 (5th Cir. 1978) — § 1502

U.S., Wyatt v.

U.S. v. Wyatt, 561 F.2d 1388 (4th Cir. 1977) — § 222

U.S. v. Wyder, 674 F.2d 224 (4th Cir. 1982) — § 259

U.S. v. Wylie, 462 F.2d 1178 (D.C. Cir. 1972) — § 215

U.S. v. Wylie, 569 F.2d 62 (D.C. Cir. 1977) — § 228

U.S. v. Wynn, 544 F.2d 786 (5th Cir. 1977) — § 248

U.S., Xydas v.

U.S. v. Yanagita, 552 F.2d 940 (2d Cir. 1977) — § 1903

U.S., Yates v.

U.S. v. Yates, 553 F.2d 518 (6th Cir. 1977) — § 2123

U.S. v. Yazbeck, 524 F.2d 641 (1st Cir. 1975) — § 609

U.S. v. Yee Soon Shin, 953 F.2d 559 (9th Cir. 1992) — § 1820

U.S., Yeloushan v.

U.S. v. Yeo, 739 F.2d 385 (8th Cir. 1984) — § 1810

U.S., Yoder v.

U.S. v. Yopp, 577 F.2d 362 (6th Cir. 1978) — § 1522

U.S. v. Young, 470 U.S. 1 (1985) — § 1104; § 1112

U.S. v. Young, 464 F.2d 160 (5th Cir. 1972) — § 1266

U.S. v. Young, 527 F.2d 1334 (5th Cir. 1976) — § 304

U.S. v. Young, 553 F.2d 1132 (8th Cir. 1977) — § 233

U.S. v. Young, 570 F.2d 152 (6th Cir. 1978) — § 1245

U.S. v. Young, 573 F.2d 1137 (9th Cir. 1978) — § 1522

U.S. v. Young Buffalo, 591 F.2d 506 (9th Cir. 1979) — § 2001

U.S. v. Yurasovich, 580 F.2d 1212 (3d Cir. 1978) — § 1906

U.S. v. Zammiello, 432 F.2d 72 (9th Cir. 1970) — § 103

U.S. v. Zarattini, 552 F.2d 753 (7th Cir. 1977) — § 706

U.S. v. Zeidman, 540 F.2d 314 (7th Cir. 1976) — § 2124

U.S. v. Zicree, 605 F.2d 1381 (5th Cir. 1979) — § 907

U.S. v. Zimeri-Safie, 585 F.2d 1318 (5th Cir. 1978) — § 1268

U.S. v. Ziperstein, 601 F.2d 281 (7th Cir. 1979) — § 916; § 2116

U.S. v. Zirpolo, 288 F. Supp. 993 (D.N.J. 1968) — § 717

U.S. v. Zolin, 109 S. Ct. 2619 (1989) — § 1918

U.S. v. Zurita, 369 F.2d 474 (7th Cir. 1966) — § 810

U.S. Coin & Currency, U.S. v.

U.S. Currency, U.S. v.

U.S. Dep't of Air Force, Mead Data Central, Inc. v.

U.S. Dep't of Justice v. Julian, 486 U.S. 1 (1988) — § 1318

U.S. District Court, U.S. v.

U.S. District Court, U.S. Industries, Inc. v.

U.S. ex rel. Anthony v. Sielaff, 552 F.2d 588 (7th Cir. 1977) — § 1261

U.S. ex rel. Baldwin v. Yeager, 428 F.2d 182 (3d Cir. 1970) — § 310

U.S. ex rel. Barksdale v. Blackburn, 610 F.2d 253 (5th Cir. 1980) — § 1245

U.S. ex rel. Barksdale v. Sielaff, 585 F.2d 288 (7th Cir. 1978) — § 1208

U.S. ex rel. Clark v. Fine, 538 F.2d 750 (7th Cir. 1976) — § 1819

U.S. ex rel. Clark v. Maroney, 339 F.2d 710 (3d Cir. 1965) — § 220

U.S. ex rel. Cummings v. Zelker, 455 F.2d 714 (2d Cir. 1972) — § 317

U.S. ex rel. Fong Foo v. Shaughnessy, 234 F.2d 715 (2d Cir. 1955) — § 1401

U.S. ex rel. Gentry v. Circuit Court, etc., 586 F.2d 1142 (7th Cir. 1978) — § 1243

U.S. ex rel. Glinton v. Denno, 309 F.2d 543 (2d Cir. 1962) — § 304

U.S. ex rel. Goldberg v. Warden, 622 F.2d 60 (3d Cir. 1980) — § 613

U.S. ex rel. Guy v. McCauley, 385 F. Supp. 193 (E.D. Wis. 1974) — § 224

U.S. ex rel. LaBelle v. LaVallee, 517 F.2d 750 (2d Cir. 1975) — § 219

U.S. ex rel. Lucas v. Regan, 503 F.2d 1 (2d Cir. 1974) — § 723

U.S. ex rel. Marino v. Holton, 227 F.2d 886 (7th Cir. 1955) — § 1820

U.S. ex rel. Meers v. Wilkins, 326 F.2d 135 (2d Cir. 1964) — § 721

U.S. ex rel. Milani v. Pate, 425 F.2d 6 (7th Cir. 1970) — § 310

U.S. ex rel. Miller v. Follette, 397 F.2d 363 (2d Cir. 1968) — § 1515

U.S. ex rel. Moore v. Illinois, 577 F.2d 411 (7th Cir. 1978) — § 318

U.S. ex rel. Nickens v. LaVallee, 391 F.2d 123 (2d Cir. 1968) — § 222

U.S. ex rel. Ormento v. Warden, 216 F. Supp. 609 (D. Kan. 1963) — § 1403

U.S. ex rel. Richardson v. McMann, 408 F.2d 48 (2d Cir. 1969) — § 1919

U.S. ex rel. Riley v. Franzen, 653 F.2d 1153 (7th Cir. 1981) — § 308

U.S. ex rel. Robinson v. Zelker, 468 F.2d 159 (2d Cir. 1972) — § 317

U.S. ex rel. Sanney v. Montanye, 500 F.2d 411 (2d Cir. 1974) — § 306

U.S. ex rel. Walker v. Follette, 443 F.2d 167 (2d Cir. 1971) — § 1810; § 1818

U.S. Gypsum Co., Fanelli v.

U.S. Gypsum Co., U.S. v.

U.S. Hoffman Can Corp., In re

U.S. Industries, Inc. v. U.S. District Court, 345 F.2d 18 (9th Cir. 1965) — § 411; § 414

U.S. Machinery Corp., U.S. v.

U.S. Rubber Co., Underwater Storage, Inc. v.

U.S. Steel Corp., Texas v.

U.S. v. Webster, 960 F.2d 1301 (5th Cir. 1992) — § 2005

United Telecommunications, Inc. v. American Television & Communications Corp., 536 F.2d 1310 (10th Cir. 1976) — § 2005

Universal C.I.T. Credit Corp., U.S. v.

Universal Manufacturing Co., U.S. v.

Universal Manufacturing Co. v. U.S., 508 F.2d 684 (8th Cir. 1975) — § 425

Upjohn Co., Nichols v.

Upjohn Co. v. U.S., 449 U.S. 383 (1981) — § 1916

Upton, Massachusetts v.

Urbanis, U.S. v.

Utah, Thiede v.

## V

Valdes, U.S. v.

Valenzuela, U.S. v.

Valera-Elyonda, U.S. v.

Van Arsdall, Delaware v.

Vancier, U.S. v.

Van Cleave, U.S. v.

Vandivere, U.S. v.

Van Drunen, U.S. v.

Van Dyke, U.S. v.

Van Ermen v. Burke, 398 F.2d 329 (7th Cir. 1968) — § 304

Vannelli, U.S. v.

Van Orsdell, U.S. v.

Vargas, U.S. v.

Vasilios, U.S. v.

Vasquez v. Hillery, 474 U.S. 254 (1986) — § 400; § 401

Vasquez, U.S. v.

Vasquez-Santiago, U.S. v.

Vasser, U.S. v.

Vaughan, U.S. v.

Veatch, U.S. v.

Vega, U.S. v.

Vela, U.S. v.

Velasquez-Mercado, U.S. v.

Vento, U.S. v.

Ventresca, U.S. v.

Verdoon, U.S. v.

Verdugo v. U.S., 402 F.2d 599 (9th Cir. 1968) — § 1322

Verdugo-Urquidez, U.S. v.

Verzosa v. Merrill Lynch, Pierce, Fenner, and Smith, Inc., 589 F.2d 974 (9th Cir. 1978) — § 2001

Viale, U.S. v.

Viggiano, U.S. v.

Vigil, U.S. v.

Viglia, U.S. v.

Vigo, U.S. v.

Vigorito, In re

Vila, U.S. v.

Villa, U.S. v.

Villamonte-Marquez, U.S. v.

Villarreal v. U.S., 508 F.2d 1132 (9th Cir. 1974) — § 609

Vinson, U.S. v.

Vinzant, Steinsvik v.

Virginia, Jackson v.

Virginia, Mu'min v.

Virgin Islands v. Bedford, 671 F.2d 758 (3d Cir. 1982) — § 1810

Virgin Islands v. Berry, 631 F.2d 214 (3d Cir. 1980) — § 618

Virgin Islands v. Carr, 451 F.2d 652 (3d Cir. 1971) — § 1276

Virgin Islands v. Christensen, 673 F.2d 713 (3d Cir. 1982) — § 1010

Virgin Islands v. Felix, 569 F.2d 1274 (3d Cir. 1978) — § 1247

Virgin Islands v. Gereau, 502 F.2d 914 (3d Cir. 1974) — § 247

Virgin Islands v. Gereau, 523 F.2d 140 (3d Cir. 1975) — § 1400; § 1402

Virgin Islands, Gonzales v.

Virgin Islands v. Lovell, 410 F.2d 307 (3d Cir. 1969) — § 809

Virgin Islands v. Smith, 558 F.2d 691 (3d Cir. 1977) — § 1003

Virgin Islands v. Taylor, 375 F.2d 771 (3d Cir. 1967) — § 1611

Virgin Islands v. Testamark, 528 F.2d 742 (3d Cir. 1976) — § 1403

Virgin Islands v. Toto, 529 F.2d 278 (3d Cir. 1976) — § 1809

Virgin Islands v. Turner, 409 F.2d 102 (3d Cir. 1968) — § 1102

Viserto, U.S. v.

Visitor, In re

Vispi, U.S. v.

Vita, U.S. v.

Vitale, Illinois v.

Volianitis v. Immigration & Naturalization Service, 352 F.2d 766 (9th Cir. 1965) — § 1911

Volkswagen of America, Inc., Perkins v.

Von Cleef v. New Jersey, 395 U.S. 814 (1969) — § 222

Vortis, U.S. v.

## W

Wabash R.R., Rucker v.

Wade v. Hunter, 336 U.S. 684 (1949) — § 1007

Wade, Roe v.

Wade, U.S. v.

Wade v. U.S., 112 S. Ct. 1840 (1992) — § 1328

Wagner v. International Harvester Co., 611 F.2d 224 (8th Cir. 1979) — § 1603

Wainwright, Alvarez v.

Wainwright, Bishop v.

Wainwright, Blackmon v.

Wainwright, Braswell v.

Wainwright, Byrd v.

Wainwright, Galtieri v.

Wainwright, Gideon v.

Wainwright, Gissendanner v.

Wainwright v. Greenfield, 474 U.S. 284 (1986) — § 309

Wainwright, Hall v.

Wainwright, Jackson v.

Wainwright, Nettles v.

Wainwright, Reed v.

Wainwright, Stanley v.

Wainwright, U.S. v.

Wainwright, Williams v.

Walden, U.S. v.

Walder v. U.S., 347 U.S. 62 (1954) — § 1818

Waldron, U.S. v.

Waley v. Johnston, 316 U.S. 101 (1942) — § 606

Walker, Brown v.

Walker v. Butterworth, 599 F.2d 1074 (1st Cir. 1979) — § 1903

Walker, Cervantes v.

Walker, Jackson v.

Walker, U.S. v.

Walker v. U.S., 418 F.2d 1116 (D.C. Cir. 1969) — § 1265

Walker v. U.S., 636 F.2d 1138 (6th Cir. 1980) — § 1322

Walking Crow, U.S. v.

Wallace, Scholz Homes, Inc. v.

Wallace, U.S. v.

Waller v. Florida, 397 U.S. 387 (1970) — § 1004

Waller v. Georgia, 467 U.S. 39 (1984) — § 254

Waller, U.S. v.

Waloke, U.S. v.

Walsh v. Wisconsin, 466 U.S. 740 (1984) — § 234

Walter v. U.S., 447 U.S. 649 (1980) — § 202

Walters, U.S. v.

Walton, U.S. v.

Walton v. U.S., 334 F.2d 343 (10th Cir. 1964) — § 304

Ward, U.S. v.

Warden v. Hayden, 387 U.S. 294 (1967) — § 234; § 247

Warden, U.S. v.

Warden, U.S. ex rel. Goldberg v.

Warden, U.S. ex rel. Ormento v.

Warden, Maryland Penitentiary, Barbee v.

Warnaco Inc., Hirsch-Weis Div., Randall v.

Warner, U.S. v.

Warren, U.S. v.

Washabaugh, U.S. v.

Washington, Arizona v.

Washington v. Chrisman, 455 U.S. 1 (1982) — § 238

Washington, Garland v.

Washington, Haynes v.

Washington, U.S. v.

Wasman v. U.S., 468 U.S. 559 (1984) — § 1012; § 1118

Watchmaker, U.S. v.

Waterfront Commission, Murphy v.

Waters-Pierce Oil Co. v. Deselms, 212 U.S. 159 (1909) — § 1403

Watkins, Modern Woodmen v.

Watkins v. Sowders, 449 U.S. 341 (1981) — § 318

Watkins, U.S. v.

Watkins v. U.S., 287 F.2d 932 (1st Cir. 1961) — § 1605

Watkins v. U.S., 564 F.2d 201 (6th Cir. 1977) — § 226

Watson, U.S. v.

Weaklem, U.S. v.

Weatherford v. Bursey, 429 U.S. 545 (1977) — § 611; § 722; § 801

Weatherspoon, U.S. v.

Weaver v. U.S., 111 F.2d 603 (8th Cir. 1940) — § 1815

Weber, U.S. v.

Webster, U.S. v.

Wehling, U.S. v.

Weidman, U.S. v.

Weil, U.S. v.

Weinberg, U.S. v.

Weinrich, U.S. v.

Weinstein, U.S. v.

Weintraub, Commodity Futures Trading Comm'n v.

Weir, Fletcher v.

Weir, In re

Weir, U.S. v.

Weisman, U.S. v.

Well, U.S. v.

Wells, Florida v.

Welsh v. U.S., 348 F.2d 885 (6th Cir. 1965) — § 1320

Welsh v. Wisconsin, 466 U.S. 740 (1984) — § 219

Wentland, U.S. v.

Werbrouck, U.S. v.

Werk v. Parker, 249 U.S. 130 (1919) — § 1401

Werner, U.S. v.

Wertis, U.S. v.

West, U.S. v.

Westbo, U.S. v.

Westcott, Massachusetts v.

Western Waterproofing Co., Inc., Marshall v.

Westinghouse Electric Co., City of Philadelphia v.

Wetterlin, U.S. v.

Whalen v. U.S., 445 U.S. 684 (1980) — § 1002; § 1003

Whaley v. U.S., 394 F.2d 399 (10th Cir. 1968) — § 1320

Wharton, U.S. v.

Wheeler, U.S. v.

Whelan, Robbins v.

Whetzel, U.S. v.

White, Alabama v.

White v. Finkbeiner, 570 F.2d 194 (7th Cir. 1978) — § 308

White v. Henderson, 467 F. Supp. 96 (S.D.N.Y. 1979) — § 1320

White v. Illinois, 112 S. Ct. 736 (1992) — § 2100; § 2119; § 2121; § 2139

White v. Maryland, 373 U.S. 59 (1963) — § 503

White, Massachusetts v.

White, Texas v.

White, U.S. v.

White v. U.S., 399 F.2d 813 (8th Cir. 1968) — § 2003

White Bear, U.S. v.

Whitehead, U.S. v.

Whitmire, U.S. v.

Whitson, U.S. v.

W.H.O. Alfalfa Milling Co., Allen v.

Whorton, Kentucky v.

Widgery, U.S. v.

Wiebold, U.S. v.

Wigerman, U.S. v.

Wiggins, U.S. v.

Wilbur, Mullaney v.

Wilbur v. Mullaney, 496 F.2d 1303 (1st Cir. 1974) — § 1501

Wilcoxon v. U.S., 231 F.2d 384 (10th Cir. 1956) — § 1820

Wild Canid Survival & Research Center, Inc., Mahlandt v.

Wiley, U.S. v.

Wiley v. U.S., 257 F.2d 900 (8th Cir. 1958) — § 1707; § 2001

Wilkins, U.S. v.

Wilkins, U.S. ex rel. Meers v.

Wilkinson, U.S. v.

Wilks, U.S. v.

William, Mabry v.

William C. Ellis & Sons, Iron Works, Inc., Johnson v.

Williams, Adams v.

Williams, Brewer v.

Williams, Carey v.

Williams, Estelle v.

Williams v. Florida, 399 U.S. 78 (1970) — § 702; § 1241

Williams v. McKenzie, 576 F.2d 566 (4th Cir. 1978) — § 318

Williams v. Missouri, 640 F.2d 140 (8th Cir. 1981) — § 606; § 609

Williams, Nix v.

Williams, U.S. v.

Williams v. U.S., 218 F.2d 473 (5th Cir. 1955) — § 1400

Williams v. U.S., 323 F.2d 90 (10th Cir. 1963) — § 222

Williams v. U.S., 416 F.2d 1064 (8th Cir. 1969) — § 906

Williams v. U.S., 112 S. Ct. 1112 (1992) — § 1308; § 1324; § 1325; § 1326; § 1327; § 1346

Williams v. Wainwright, 673 F.2d 1182 (11th Cir. 1982) — § 1115

Williamsburg Check Cashing Corp., U.S. v.

Willis, U.S. v.

Willoz, U.S. v.

Wilson, Kuhlmann v.

Wilson v. Shaw, 204 U.S. 24 (1907) — § 1400

Wilson, U.S. v.

Wilson v. U.S., 221 U.S. 361 (1911) — § 1902

Wilson v. U.S., 232 U.S. 563 (1914) — § 1815

Wilson v. U.S., 369 F.2d 198 (D.C. Cir. 1966) — § 1512

Wilson v. U.S., 554 F.2d 893 (8th Cir. 1977) — § 803

Wingate, U.S. v.

Wingender, U.S. v.

Wingo, Barker v.

Wingo, Stone v.

Winkle, U.S. v.

Winn, U.S. v.

Winship, In re

Winston v. Lee, 470 U.S. 753 (1985) — § 201

Wisconsin, Griffin v.

Wisconsin, McNeil v.

Wisconsin, Walsh v.

Wisconsin, Welsh v.

Witham v. Mabry, 596 F.2d 293 (8th Cir. 1979) — § 2140; § 2144

Withers v. U.S., 602 F.2d 124 (6th Cir. 1979) — § 1111

Witherspoon v. Illinois, 391 U.S. 510 (1968) — § 1247

Wolf, U.S. v.

Wolfel v. Sanborn, 555 F.2d 583 (6th Cir. 1977) — § 245

Wolff, Hall v.

Wolfinbarger, Garner v.

Wolfish, Bell v.

Wolfish, U.S. v.

Wolfle v. U.S., 291 U.S. 7 (1934) — § 1911

Wolford v. U.S., 401 F.2d 331 (10th Cir. 1968) — § 2003

Wolfson, U.S. v.

Wolk, U.S. v.

Wong, U.S. v.

Wong Sun v. U.S., 371 U.S. 471 (1963) — § 215; § 219; § 248; § 303; § 312; § 2116

Wong Tai v. U.S., 273 U.S. 77 (1927) — § 701

Wood, U.S. v.

Wood v. U.S., 357 F.2d 425 (10th Cir. 1966) — § 2003

Woodard, U.S. v.

Woodring, U.S. v.

Woods, U.S. v.

Woodward v. U.S., 426 F.2d 959 (3d Cir. 1970) — § 608

Woody v. U.S., 3790 U.S. 130 (D.C. Cir. 1967) — § 1906

Woolridge, U.S. v.

Worden v. Tri State Ins. Co., 347 F.2d 336 (10th Cir. 1965) — § 1704

Wright, Idaho v.

Wright, U.S. v.

Wursthorn, Public Ser. Ry. v.

Wyant, U.S. v.

Wyatt, U.S. v.

Wyatt v. U.S., 362 U.S. 525 (1960) — § 1913; § 1914

Wyatt v. U.S., 591 F.2d 260 (4th Cir. 1979) — § 1243

Wyder, U.S. v.

Wylie, U.S. v.

Wynn, U.S. v.

Wyrick, Camillo v.

Wyrick v. Fields, 459 U.S. 42 (1982) — § 308

Wyrick, Hill v.

Wyrick, Phillips v.

Wyrick, Starkey v.

Wyrick, Toler v.

# X

Xydas v. U.S., 445 F.2d 660 (D.C. Cir. 1971) — § 714

# Y

Yanagita, U.S. v.

Yanes v. Romero, 619 F.2d 851 (10th Cir. 1980) — § 1903

Yates v. Evatt, 111 S. Ct. 1884 (1991) — § 1505; § 1509

Yates, U.S. v.

Yates v. U.S., 355 U.S. 66 (1957) — § 424

Yazbeck, U.S. v.

Ybarra v. Illinois, 444 U.S. 85 (1979) — § 228

Yeager, U.S. ex rel. Baldwin v.

Yee Soon Shin, U.S. v.

Yeloushan v. U.S., 339 F.2d 533 (5th Cir. 1964) — § 109; § 112; § 113

Yeo, U.S. v.

Yiu Fong Cheung v. Immigration & Naturalization Service, 418 F.2d 460 (D.C. Cir. 1969) — § 1903

Yoder v. U.S., 80 F.2d 665 (10th Cir. 1935) — § 1911

Yopp, U.S. v.

Young, Harris v.

Young v. Taylor, 466 F.2d 1329 (10th Cir. 1972) — § 1917; § 1918

Young, U.S. v.

Youngblood, Arizona v.

Young Buffalo, U.S. v.

Yurasovich, U.S. v.

## Z

Zahradnick, Gibson v.

Zammiello, U.S. v.

Zarattini, U.S. v.

Zeidman, U.S. v.

Zelker, U.S. ex rel. Cummings v.

Zelker, U.S. ex rel. Robinson v.

Zerbst, Johnson v.

Zerelli v. Bell, 458 F. Supp. 26 (D.D.C. 1978) — § 1922

Zicarelli v. New Jersey Investigation Commission, 406 U.S. 472 (1972) — § 1903

Zicree, U.S. v.

Zilka v. Estelle, 529 F.2d 388 (5th Cir. 1976) — § 1810

Zimeri-Safie, U.S. v.

Ziperstein, U.S. v.

Zirpolo, U.S. v.

Zletz, Natta v.

Zolin, U.S. v.

Zuniga, In re

Zurcher v. Stanford Daily, 436 U.S. 547 (1978) — § 206

Zurita, U.S. v.

# TABLE OF STATUTES AND RULES

## STATUTES

1 U.S.C. § 3500 ...................... § 403
5 U.S.C. § 552 ...................... §§ 414;
712
8 U.S.C. § 1357 ...................... § 219
§ 1357(a)(3) ...................... § 229
12 U.S.C. § 3415 ...................... § 409
15 U.S.C. § 15f(b) ...................... § 414
§§ 375-378 ...................... § 1902
16 U.S.C. § 559 ...................... § 219
18 U.S.C. § 1(3) ...................... § 1240
§ 7 ...................... § 101
§ 13 ...................... § 101
§ 18 ...................... §§ 1307;
1340
§ 20 ...................... §§ 703;
1501; 1508
§ 235(a)(1) ...................... § 1311
§ 373 ...................... § 1501
§ 401 ...................... §§ 424; 426
§ 495 ...................... § 1323
§ 924(c) ...................... § 1012
§ 1462 ...................... § 403
§ 1963(a) ...................... § 1257
§ 2320 ...................... § 1501
§§ 2510-2520 ...................... §§ 257;
407; 1818; 1905
§ 2510(9) ...................... § 261
§ 2511(2)(c) ...................... § 268
§ 2511(2)(d) ...................... § 268
§ 2515 ...................... § 257
§ 2516(1)(a)-(g) ...................... § 259
§ 2516(1) ...................... § 259
§ 2518(1) ...................... § 261
§ 2518(3) ...................... § 261
§ 2518(3)(a) ...................... § 261
§ 2518(4) ...................... § 262
§ 2518(5) ...................... §§ 262;
264
§ 2518(8)(a) ...................... §§ 265;
266
§ 2518(8)(b) ...................... §§ 265;
266
§ 2518(8)(d) ...................... § 264
§ 2518(9) ...................... § 706

§ 2518(10)(a) ...................... § 266
§ 2518(10)(b) ...................... §§ 266;
1222
§ 3013 ...................... § 1336
§ 3050 ...................... § 219
§ 3052 ...................... § 219
§ 3053 ...................... § 219
§ 3056 ...................... § 219
§ 3060 ...................... § 503
§ 3060(e) ...................... § 503
§ 3061 ...................... § 219
§ 3105 ...................... § 213
§ 3109 ...................... §§ 215;
219
§§ 3141-3150 ...................... § 504
§ 3142 ...................... § 506
§ 3142(b) ...................... § 508
§ 3142(c) ...................... § 507
§ 3142(c)(2)(j) ...................... § 511
§ 3142(e) ...................... § 509
§ 3142(f) ...................... §§ 509;
511
§ 3142(g) ...................... §§ 510;
511
§ 3142(h) ...................... § 511
§ 3142(i) ...................... § 511
§ 3143(a) ...................... § 515
§ 3143(b) ...................... § 516
§ 3143(b)(2) ...................... § 517
§ 3144 ...................... § 520
§ 3145 ...................... § 512
§ 3146 ...................... § 521
§ 3146(b) ...................... § 521
§ 3146(c) ...................... § 521
§ 3147 ...................... § 522
§ 3148 ...................... § 425
§§ 3161-3174 ...................... §§ 1202;
1210
§ 3161(b) ...................... §§ 1210;
1212; 1215
§ 3161(c)(1) ...................... §§ 1210;
1213; 1215
§ 3161(c)(2) ...................... §§ 1210;
1215

§ 3161(d)(1) ..................... § 1215
§ 3161(d)(2) ..................... § 1216
§ 3161(d)(3) ..................... § 1217
§ 3161(e) ..................... § 1217
§ 3161(h) ..................... §§ 1210;
1217;
1236
§ 3161(h)(1)-(7) ................. § 1218
§ 3161(h)(1)(B) ................. § 1220
§ 3161(h)(1)(C) ................. § 1220
§ 3161(h)(1)(E) ................. § 1222
§ 3161(h)(1)(F) ............... §§ 1223;
1224
§ 3161(h)(1)(G) ................. § 1224
§ 3161(h)(1)(H) ............... §§ 1219;
1220; 1224
§ 3161(h)(1)(I) ................. § 1225
§ 3161(h)(1)(J) ............... §§ 1219;
1220; 1223;
1224; 1226
§ 3161(h)(2) ..................... § 1227
§ 3161(h)(3) ..................... § 1228
§ 3161(h)(3)(A) ................. § 1228
§ 3161(h)(3)(B) ................. § 1228
§ 3161(h)(4) ..................... § 1229
§ 3161(h)(5) ..................... § 1220
§ 3161(h)(6) ..................... § 1215
§ 3161(h)(7) ..................... § 1230
§ 3161(h)(8) ................. §§ 1218;
1231; 1232
§ 3161(h)(8)(A) ................. § 1231
§ 3161(h)(8)(B) ............... §§ 1223;
1231
§ 3161(h)(8)(C) ................. § 1231
§ 3161(i) ..................... § 1232
§ 3161(j) ..................... § 1233
§ 3162 ..................... §§ 1210;
1217
§ 3162(a)(1) ................. §§ 1234;
1235
§ 3162(a)(2) ................. §§ 1228;
1234; 1235
§ 3162(b) ..................... § 1236
§ 3164(a)(2) ................. §§ 1234
1238;
§ 3164(b) ..................... § 1236
§ 3172 ..................... § 1211
§ 3173 ..................... § 1211
§ 3174(b) ..................... § 1222
§ 3231 ..................... § 101

§ 3236 ..................... § 101
§ 3237(a) ..................... § 106
§ 3238 ..................... §§ 101;
107
§ 3241 ..................... § 101
§ 3290 ..................... § 107
§§ 3331-3334 ..................... § 401
§ 3331(a) ..................... § 401
§ 3333 ..................... § 426
§ 3333(e) ..................... § 401
§ 3432 ..................... § 712
§ 3481 ..................... §§ 916;
1515; 1907
§§ 3491-3496 ..................... § 1702
§ 3500 ..................... §§ 253;
403; 414; 711;
801; 1802; 1803;
1920
§ 3500(a) ..................... § 804
§ 3500(b) ..................... §§ 803;
806; 807
§ 3500(c) ..................... §§ 805; 807
§ 3500(d) ..................... § 811
§ 3500(e)(2) ..................... § 810
§ 3501(c) ..................... § 304
§ 3552(b) ..................... § 1318
§ 3552(d) ..................... § 1318
§ 3553(a) ..................... § 1333
§ 3553(b) ..................... §§ 1307; 1315;
1324
§ 3553(c) ..................... §§ 1307; 1328
§ 3553(c)(2) ..................... § 1324
§ 3553(e) ..................... §§ 1328; 1344
§ 3555 ..................... § 1338
§ 3557 ..................... § 1337
§ 3559(a)(1) ..................... § 1329
§ 3561 ..................... § 1329
§ 3563 ..................... § 1329
§ 3565 ..................... § 1329
§ 3571 ..................... §§ 1307; 1332;
1340
§ 3572(a) ..................... § 1333
§ 3572(b) ..................... § 1337
§ 3572(d) ..................... § 1333
§ 3572(e) ..................... § 1333
§ 3572(f) ..................... § 1333
§ 3573 ..................... § 1334
§ 3573(a)(1) ..................... § 1334
§ 3573(a)(2) ..................... §§ 1333;
1334

§ 3582(c) .......................... § 1344
§ 3582(c)(1)(A) .................. § 1344
§ 3582(c)(1)(B) .................. § 1344
§ 3582(c)(2) ....................... § 1344
§ 3583 ............................. § 1331
§ 3584 ............................. § 1330
§ 3624 ............................. § 1307
§ 3624(b) .......................... § 1307
§ 3653 ............................... § 219
§ 3661 ............................. § 1339
§ 3663 ............................. § 1337
§ 3663(e)(1) ....................... § 1337
§ 3664 ............................. § 1337
§ 3664(a) ........................... § 1337
§ 3664(d) ............... §§ 1337; 1339
§ 3731 ....................... §§ 250;
                     256; 409; 1010;
                          1222; 1301
§ 3742 ..................§§ 1307; 1315;
                          1343; 1346
§ 3742(a) ......................... § 1327
§ 3742(b) ......................... § 1327
§ 3742(b)(4) ..................... § 1346
§ 3742(d) ......................... § 1327
§ 3742(e) ......................... § 1346
§ 3742(e)(2) ..................... § 1324
§ 3742(f)(2) ...................... § 1327
§ 4205(c) ......................... § 1320
§ 4244 ........................... §§ 1219;
                          1903; 1921
§§ 5031-5042 ................... § 1211
§ 5033 ............................. § 304
§ 5036 ............................. § 1211
§ 5037(c)(1)(B) ................. § 1341
§§ 6001-6005 ................... § 419
§ 6002 ....................§§ 418; 419;
                               1903
§ 6003(b) .......................... § 419
19 U.S.C. § 1581 ..................... § 219
§ 1581(a) .......................... § 228
§ 1581(b) .......................... § 219
21 U.S.C. §§ 801-904 ............... § 1905
§ 848(a)(2) ...................... § 1257
§ 878(2) ........................... § 219
§ 878(3) ........................... § 219
§ 879 .............................. § 212
§ 955(a) ........................... § 101
22 U.S.C. § 2667 ..................... § 219
26 U.S.C. § 7607 ..................... § 219

§ 7608 ............................. § 219
28 U.S.C. § 753(b) ................... § 1702
§ 841 .............................. § 211
§ 846 .............................. § 211
§§ 991 ............................. § 1307
§§ 991(b)(1)(B) ................. § 1307
§§ 992 ............................. § 1312
§§ 994 ............................. § 1344
§§ 994(a) ......................... § 1308
§§ 994(a)(2)(E) ................. § 1313
§ 994(b) .......................... § 1307
§ 994(d)(11) ..................... § 1322
§§ 994(e) ......................... § 1322
§ 994(k) .......................... § 1307
§ 994(n) .......................... § 1328
§ 1292 ............................. § 1222
§§ 1442-1443 ..................... § 101
§ 1651 ............................. § 427
§ 1651(a) .......................... § 402
§ 1731 ............................. § 2001
§ 1732 ............................. § 1705
§ 1736 ............................. § 1702
§ 1738 ............................. § 1702
§ 1739 ............................. § 1702
§ 1740 ............................. § 1702
§ 1741 ............................. § 1702
§ 1826 ............................. § 424
§ 1826(a)(2) ..................... § 425
§ 1826(b) .......................... § 425
§§ 1862-1871 ................... § 1244
§§ 1862-1875 ................... § 400
§ 1861 ..................§§ 400; 1244;
                               1245
§ 1862 ............................. § 1244
§ 1863(a) .......................... § 1244
§ 1865 ............................. § 1247
§ 1865(a) .......................... § 1244
§ 1865(b) .......................... § 1244
§ 1866(c)(1) ..................... § 1247
§ 1866(c)(5) ..................... § 1247
§ 1867 ............................. § 1245
§ 1867(a) .......................... § 1245
§ 1867(f) .......................... § 1245
§ 2255 ........................... §§ 617;
                          619; 1320
§ 2902 ............................. § 1220
42 U.S.C. § 3505 ................... § 1702
44 U.S.C. § 1507 ................... § 1403

# FEDERAL RULES OF APPELLATE PROCEDURE

Rule 4(b) ............................ §§ 256;    Rule 8 ................................ § 425
                 1304; 1346    Rule 9(b) ............................. § 519

# FEDERAL RULES OF CIVIL PROCEDURE

Rule 26(b)(3) .......................... § 1920    44(b) .............................. § 1702
Rule 32(a)(3) .......................... § 2140    Rule 44.1 ........................... § 1403
Rule 44 ............................... § 1702    Rule 62 ............................. § 425

# FEDERAL RULES OF CRIMINAL PROCEDURE

Rule 5 ................................ § 502    8(b) ......................... §§ 901; 902;
   5(a) ............................ §§ 219;                      906; 907;
              304; 501                      908
   5(c) ........................... §§ 501; 503    Rule 9(b)(1) .......................... § 504
Rule 5.1 .............................. § 502    Rule 10 .............................. § 601
   5.1(a) ............................ § 503    Rule 11 ......................... §§ 113; 602;
   5.1(b) ............................ § 503                      606; 607;
   5.1(c)(1) .......................... § 503                      608; 609;
   5.1(c)(2) .......................... § 503                      616
Rule 6 ................................ § 401    11(a) .............................. § 602
   6(b)(1) ........................... § 1245    11(a)(2) ..................... §§ 602; 614
   6(b)(2) ........................... § 1245    11(b) .............................. § 604
   6(c) .............................. § 401    11(c) .............................. § 607
   6(e) ......................... §§ 410; 415    11(c)(1) ........................... § 609
   6(e)(1) ........................... § 401    11(c)(2) ........................... § 602
   6(e)(2) ........................... §§ 410;    11(d) ....................... §§ 606; 611
                     415    11(e) ............................. §§ 611;
   6(e)(3) ........................... § 411                      1313; 1314
   6(e)(3)(A)(i) ...................... § 412    11(e)(1) ........................... §§ 611;
   6(e)(3)(A)(ii) ..................... § 413                      612
   6(e)(3)(B) ........................ § 413    11(e)(1)(A) ....................... §§ 611;
   6(e)(3)(C)(i) ..................... § 414                      1315
Rule 6(e)(3)(D) ....................... § 414    11(e)(1)(B) ....................... §§ 611;
Rule 6(e)(4) .......................... § 417                      1346
Rule 6(e)(5) .......................... § 410    11(e)(1)(C) ....................... §§ 611;
Rule 6(e)(6) .......................... § 410                      1315; 1346
   6(f) .............................. § 401    11(e)(2) ........................... § 611
Rule 6(g) ............................. § 401    11(e)(3) ........................... § 611
Rule 7(c) ............................. §§ 401;    11(e)(4) ........................... §§ 611;
                     1257                      1315
   7(c)(1) ........................... § 905    11(e)(6) ........................... §§ 315;
   7(e)(2) ........................... § 1257                      615; 2113
   7(f) .............................. §§ 700; 701    11(e)(6)(B) ....................... § 604
Rule 8 ................................ §§ 901; 910    11(f) ............................. §§ 604;
   8(a) ............................. §§ 902; 903;                      610
                     904

| | | | |
|---|---|---|---|
| 11(g) | §§ 602; 616 | Rule 16(b)(1) | § 710 |
| 11(h) | § 610 | Rule 16(b)(1)(B) | § 710 |
| Rule 12(b) | §§ 250; 705 | Rule 16(b)(2) | § 712 |
| | | Rule 16(c) | §§ 706; 708 |
| 12(b)(1) | § 1001 | Rule 16(d)(1) | §§ 706; 712; 715 |
| 12(b)(2) | §§ 102; 403 | Rule 16(d)(2) | § 716 |
| 12(b)(5) | § 918 | Rule 17(c) | §§ 409; 717 |
| 12(c) | §§ 248; 705 | Rule 17(g) | § 424 |
| | | Rule 17.1 | § 2145 |
| 12(d)(1) | § 250 | Rule 18 | §§ 104; 903 |
| 12(e) | §§ 250; 254 | Rule 20 | §§ 109; 110; 113; 502; 1224; 1323 |
| 12(f) | §§ 250; 918; 712; 801 | Rule 20(b) | § 113 |
| Rule 12.1 | §§ 700; 702 | Rule 20(c) | § 113 |
| | | Rule 21 | §§ 109; 110; 1224 |
| 12.1(a) through (d) | § 702 | Rule 21(a) | § 111 |
| 12.1(f) | § 702 | Rule 21(b) | § 112 |
| 12.2 | §§ 700; 703; 1219 | Rule 22 | § 110 |
| | | Rule 23 | § 1240 |
| Rule 12.2(b) | § 703 | Rule 23(a) | § 1243 |
| Rule 12.2(c) | §§ 703; 1219; 1903 | Rule 23(b) | §§ 1241; 1242; 1243 |
| Rule 12.3 | §§ 700; 704 | Rule 23(c) | § 1258 |
| | | Rule 24(a) | § 1246 |
| Rule 13 | §§ 904; 908 | Rule 24(b) | § 1248 |
| Rule 14 | §§ 910; 912; 918 | Rule 24(c) | §§ 1241; 1248 |
| | | Rule 25(b) | § 1301 |
| Rule 15 | § 2141 | Rule 26 | § 1908 |
| Rule 15(a) | § 520 | Rule 26.1 | § 1403 |
| Rule 15(e) | § 2140 | Rule 26.2 | §§ 712; 801; 814 |
| Rule 16 | §§ 411; 700; 705; 706; 712; 714; 716; 717; 1605 | Rule 26.2(e) | § 814 |
| | | Rule 27 | § 1702 |
| | | Rule 28 | § 1820 |
| Rule 16(a) | § 2116 | Rule 29 | § 1273 |
| Rule 16(a)(1)(A) | §§ 706; 707; 712; 716 | Rule 29(a) | §§ 1271; 1272; 1502 |
| Rule 16(a)(1)(B) | §§ 707; 709 | Rule 29(b) | § 1275 |
| Rule 16(a)(1)(C) | §§ 708; 708; 709; 710 | Rule 29(c) | § 1276 |
| Rule 16(a)(1)(D) | §§ 710; 709 | Rule 30 | §§ 1253; 1254; 1264 |
| Rule 16(a)(2) | § 712 | Rule 31(a) | § 1242 |
| Rule 16(a)(3) | § 712 | Rule 31(c) | § 1265 |
| | | Rule 31(d) | § 1262 |
| | | Rule 31(e) | § 1257 |
| | | Rule 32 | § 1324 |
| | | Rule 32(a) | § 1320 |

Rule 32(a)(1) ..................§§ 1320; 1321
Rule 32(a)(1)(B) ......................§ 1321
Rule 32(a)(1)(C) ......................§ 1321
Rule 32(a)(2) ..........................§ 1345
Rule 32(b)(1) ..........................§ 1342
Rule Rule 32(b)(2) ...................§ 1342
Rule 32(c) ............................. § 807
Rule 32(c)(1) ..........................§ 1316
Rule 32(c)(2) .................§§ 1317; 1318
Rule 32(c)(2)(D) ..............§§ 1317; 1337
Rule 32(c)(3) ..........................§ 1318
Rule 32(c)(3)(A) ..............§§ 1318; 1339
Rule 32(c)(3)(B) ......................§ 1318
Rule 32(c)(3)(C) ......................§ 1318
Rule 32(c)(3)(D) ..............§§ 1318; 1339
Rule 32(c)(3)(E) ......................§ 1318
Rule 32(d) ........................... §§ 617;
                              619; 1320
Rule 33 ................................§ 1272
Rule 34 ................................ § 603
Rule 35(a) ............................§ 1343
Rule 35(b) ....................§§ 1343; 1344
Rule 35(c) ............................§ 1343
Rule 40 ............................. §§ 502;
                              1224
Rule 40 ............................... § 502
Rule 40(a) ............................ § 502
Rule 40(b) ............................ § 502
Rule 40(d) ............................ § 502
Rule 40(e) ............................ § 502
Rule 40(f) ............................ § 502
Rule 41 ............................... § 204
Rule 41(a) ............................ § 205
Rule 41(a)(1) ......................... § 205
Rule 41(a)(2) ......................... § 205

Rule 41(b) ............................ § 247
Rule 41(b)(4) ......................... § 247
Rule 41(c) ........................... §§ 213;
                         206; 213; 214
Rule 41(c)(1) ......................... § 207
Rule 41(c)(2) ......................... § 216
Rule 41(h) ............................ § 214
Rule 42 ............................... § 424
Rule 42(a) ............................ § 426
Rule 42(b) ............................ § 426
Rule 43 ............................. §§ 1249;
                              1611
Rule 43(a) ....................§§ 601; 602;
                              1246
Rule 43(c)(1) ........................ §§ 103;
                              602
Rule 43(c)(2) ......................... § 601
Rule 44(a) ........................... §§ 501;
                              503
Rule 45(a) ............................ § 401
Rule 45(b) ........................... §§ 1276;
                              1304
Rule 46 ............................. §§ 426;
                              504
Rule 46(b) ............................ § 513
Rule 46(e) ............................ § 521
Rule 46(g) ............................ § 520
Rule 48(a) ............................ § 111
Rule 48(b) ........................... §§ 1202;
                              1237
Rule 52(b) ........................... §§ 402;
                              1254
Rule 50(b) ............................ § 1237
Rule 54(c) ............................ § 412
Rule 62 ............................... § 425

## FEDERAL RULES OF EVIDENCE

Rule 104 ............................. § 253
Rule 104(a) .................§§ 1522; 2101;
                              2145
Rule 104(b) .......................... § 1701
Rule 105 ........................... §§ 1222;
                              1517
Rule 106 ........................... §§ 1517;
                         1704; 1708
Rule 201(a) .......................... § 1401
Rule 201(b) .......................... § 1401
Rule 201(d) .......................... § 1402

Rule 201(e) .......................... § 1402
Rule 201(f) .......................... § 1402
Rule 201(g) .......................... § 1402
Rule 401 ........................... §§ 1517;
                              1609
Rule 402 ........................... §§ 1517;
                              1701
Rule 403 ........................... §§ 1517;
                         1520; 1522;
                              1608;
                              1609;

1701; 1810;
2001; 2005; 2144
Rule 404 ............................§§ 1520;
2133
Rule 404(a) ........................§§ 1518;
1808
Rule 404(a)(1) .....................§§ 1518;
1801
Rule 404(a)(2) ........................§ 1518
Rule 404(a)(3) ........................§ 1518
Rule 404(b) ........................§§ 1011;
1252; 1518;
1521; 1522;
1523; 1524
Rule 405 ...........................§§ 1519;
1520; 2100
Rule 405(a) ........................§§ 2133;
1520
Rule 405(b) ...................§§ 1518; 1519
Rule 406 ..............................§ 1531
Rule 410 ............................§§ 315;
615; 2113
Rule 412 ..............................§ 1518
Rule 501 ................§§ 404; 503; 1908;
1921; 1922;
1924
Rule 602 ...........................§§ 2137;
2144
Rule 604 ..............................§ 1820
Rule 606(b) ..........................§ 1259
Rule 607 ...........................§§ 1801;
1807; 1820
Rule 608 ...........................§§ 1520;
2133
Rule 608(a) ........................§§ 1518;
1808
Rule 608(b) ........................§§ 1809;
1810; 1906
Rule 609 ...........................§§ 1520;
1809
Rule 609(a) ..........................§ 1809
Rule 609(a)(1) .......................§ 1810
Rule 609(a)(2) .......................§ 1810
Rule 609(b) ..........................§ 1810
Rule 609(c) ..........................§ 1810
Rule 609(d) ........................§§ 1520;
1810
Rule 609(e) ..........................§ 1810
Rule 611(b) ..........................§ 1805
Rule 611(c) ..........................§ 1801

Rule 612 ...........................§§ 1801;
1802;
1803; 2122
Rule 612(2) ..........................§ 1803
Rule 613 ..............................§ 1813
Rule 613(b) ..........................§ 1813
Rule 615 ..............................§ 1819
Rule 701 ...........................§§ 2001;
2003
Rule 701(a) ..........................§ 2001
Rule 701(b) ..........................§ 2001
Rule 702 ...........................§§ 2001;
2003
Rule 703 ..............................§ 2004
Rule 704 ...........................§§ 2001;
2005
Rule 704(b) ........................§§ 2003;
2005
Rule 705 ..............................§ 2006
Rule 706 ..............................§ 2007
Rule 706(a) ..........................§ 2007
Rule 706(b) ..........................§ 2007
Rule 706(c) ..........................§ 2007
Rule 801 ................§§ 319; 2101
Rule 801(a) ..........................§ 2100
Rule 801(a)(1) .......................§ 2101
Rule 801(a)(2) .......................§ 2101
Rule 801(c) ..........................§ 2100
Rule 801(d) ..........................§ 2100
Rule 801(d)(1) .....................§§ 2108;
2109
Rule 801(d)(1)(A) ..................§§ 1814;
2109
Rule 801(d)(1)(B) ....................§ 2110
Rule 801(d)(1)(C) ..................§§ 319
319; 2111
Rule 801(d)(2) .....................§§ 302;
2112
Rule 801(d)(2)(A) ....................§ 2113
Rule 801(d)(2)(B) ....................§ 2114
Rule 801(d)(2)(C) ....................§ 2115
Rule 801(d)(2)(D) ....................§ 2115
Rule 801(d)(2)(E) ..................§§ 2116;
2139
Rule 802 ..............................§ 2100
Rule 803 ...........................§§ 2100;
2117; 2137; 2136
Rule 803(1) ..........................§ 2118
Rule 803(2) ..........................§ 2119
Rule 803(3) ..........................§ 2120

Rule 803(4) ........................... § 2121
Rule 803(5) .......................... §§ 1801; 2122; 2125
Rule 803(6) .......................... §§ 2123; 2124
Rule 803(7) .......................... §§ 2124; 2127
Rule 803(8) .......................... §§ 1610; 2123; 2125; 2128
Rule 803(8)(B) ...................... §§ 2125; 2127
Rule 803(8)(C) ...................... §§ 2125; 2127
Rule 803(9) ........................... § 2126
Rule 803(10) ........................ §§ 1702; 2127
Rule 803(11) .......................... § 2128
Rule 803(12) .......................... § 2128
Rule 803(13) .......................... § 2128
Rule 803(14) .......................... § 2129
Rule 803(15) .......................... § 2129
Rule 803(17) .......................... § 2131
Rule 803(18) .......................... § 2132
Rule 803(19) ........................ §§ 2133; 2135
Rule 803(20) ........................ §§ 2133; 2135
Rule 803(21) .......................... § 2133
Rule 803(22) ........................ §§ 2134; 2135
Rule 803(23) .......................... § 2135
Rule 803(24) ........................ §§ 2147; 2136
Rule 804 ........................... §§ 2100; 2117; 2137
    804(a) ........................ §§ 2140; 2141
Rule 804(b)(1) ..................... §§ 2141; 2144; 2147

804(b)(2) ........................... § 2142
804(b)(3) ........................ §§ 2143; 2145
804(b)(4) ........................... § 2146
804(b)(5) ........................... § 2147
Rule 805 ........................... § 2148
Rule 806 ...................... §§ 2100; 2149
Rule 901 ........................... §§ 319; 1701
    901(a) ........................ §§ 1701; 1702
    901(b) ........................... § 1701
    901(b)(1) ........................ § 1703
    901(b)(2) ........................ § 2001
    901(b)(3) ........................ §§ 1703; 2001
    901(b)(7) ........................ § 1702
    901(b)(8) ........................ § 2130
Rule 902(1) through (5) ............. § 1702
Rule 902 ........................... §§ 1701; 1702; 2127
    902(1) ........................... § 1702
    902(2) ........................... § 1702
    902(3) ........................... § 1702
Rule 1001(3) ........................ § 1705
Rule 1001(4) ........................ § 1705
Rule 1002 ........................... § 1705
Rule 1003 ........................ §§ 1705; 1707
Rule 1004 ........................... § 1707
Rule 1006 ........................... § 1605
Rule 1008 ........................... § 1707
Rule 1008(c) ........................ § 1605
Rule 1101(c) ........................ § 404
Rule 1101(d) ........................ § 404
Rule 1101(d)(1) ..................... § 251
Rule 1101(d)(2) ..................... § 403
    1101(d)(3) ............... §§ 503; 1339

## SENTENCING GUIDELINES
### (United States Sentencing Guidelines)

§ U.S.S.G. 1A2 ...................... § 1307
§ 1A3 ............................... § 1309
§ 1A4(3) ............................ § 1310
§ 1A.4(a) ........................... § 1310
§ 1A.4(d) ........................... § 1326

§ 1B1.1 ............................. § 1323
§ 1B1.2(a) .......................... § 1323
§ 1B1.3(a)(2) ....................... § 1323
§ 1B1.4 ............................. § 1339
§ 1B1.7 ............................. § 1308

TABLE OF STATUTES AND RULES

§ 1B1.8(a) ............................. § 1322
§ 1B1.9 ............................... § 1307
§ 2 ................................... § 1323
§ 2D1.1 .............................. § 1323
§ 2F1.1(a) ............................ § 1323
§ 3 ................................... § 1323
§ 3A-D ............................... § 1323
§ 3B1.2 .............................. § 1323
§ 3C1.1 .............................. § 1323
§ 3E1.1 .............................. § 1323
§ 4(2) ................................ § 1310
§ 4A .................................. § 1323
§ 4A1.2(a)(2) ......................... § 1323
§ 4A1.3 ............................... § 1323
§ 4B .................................. § 1323
§ 4B1.1 ............................... § 1323
§ 5A-K ................................ § 1323
§§ 5B1.1 — 5B1.4 .................... § 1329
§§ 5D3.1 — 5D3.3 ................... § 1331
§ 5E1.1(c) ............................ § 1337
§ 5E1.2 ............................... § 1332
§ 5E1.2(f) ............................. § 1332
§ 5E1.2(i) ............................. § 1332
§ 5E1.3 ............................... § 1336
§§ 5H1.1 — 5H1.10 ................. § 1322
§ 5K1.1 ......................§§ 1328; 1344
§ 5K1.2 ............................... § 1322
§§ 5K2.1 — 5K2.14 ................. § 1325
§ 6A1.1 ............................... § 1314
§ 6A1.1(a) ............................ § 1316
§ 6A1.1(b) ............................ § 1318
§ 6A1.2 ............................... § 1318
§ 6A1.3 ............................... § 1339
§ 6B .................................. § 1313
§ 6B1.2 ............................... § 1315
§ 6B1.2(b)(c) ......................... § 1315
§ 6B1.3 ............................... § 1315
§ 6B1.4 ............................... § 1315
§ 8 ................................... § 1340
§ 8A1.1 ............................... § 1340
Appendix A ........................... § 1323

# Index

## A

**ABANDONED PROPERTY.**
Search of premises and seizure of objects, §239.

**ABDUCTION.**
Defendant brought into jurisdiction by, §103.

**ABSENCE OF DEFENDANT OR WITNESS.**
Speedy trial act excludes delays, §1228.

**ABUSE OF PROCESS.**
Grand jury calling defendant after indictment returned, §408.

**ACCOMPLICES.**
Joinder of defendants.
See JOINDER OF DEFENDANTS.
Jury instructions on testimony of, §1270.
Severance of defendants.
See SEVERANCE.

**ACCOUNTANT-CLIENT PRIVILEGE,** §1924.

**ACQUITTAL.**
Jeopardy protection, §1006.
Motion for acquittal, §§1271 to 1276.
Burden of proof, §1502.
Close of all evidence, §1275.
Close of government's case, §1274.
Discharge of jury, §1276.
Generally, §1271.
Grounds, §1272.
Time for making generally, §1273.

**ADJUDICATIVE FACTS.**
Judicial notice, §1401.

**ADMISSIONS,** §§2112 to 2116.
Coconspirator declarations, §2116.
Confessions generally, §§301 to 315.
See CONFESSIONS.

**ADMISSIONS—Cont'd**
Defendant's admissions, §2113.
Defendant's adoptive admissions, §2114.
Generally, §2112.
Guilty plea, §603.
Nolo contendere plea, §604.
Representative admissions, §2115.
Statements against interest.
Hearsay exceptions, declarant unavailable.
Generally, §2144.
Penal interest offered to exculpate, §2145.
Vicarious admissions, §2115.

**ADULTS WITH COMMUNICATION PROBLEMS.**
Leading questions permitted, §1801.

**ADVERSE PUBLICITY.**
Transfer of venue because of prejudice, §111.

**ADVERSE TESTIMONY PRIVILEGE.**
Marital communications privilege, §1910.

**AFFIDAVITS.**
Search warrants, §206.
False statements, §210.

**AFFIRMATIVE DEFENSES.**
Burden of proof, §1501.
Insanity, §1508.

**AGENTS.**
Hearsay exception, availability of declarant immaterial.
Statements in documents, §2130.
Vicarious and representative admissions, §2115.

**AGGRAVATING CIRCUMSTANCES.**
Departure from sentencing guidelines, §1324.

**AIDER AND ABETTER INSTRUCTIONS,** §1270.

**AIR PIRACY.**
Anti-skyjacking searches, §241.

**ALIBI.**
Notice, §702.

**ALIENS.**
Confessions made during unnecessary delay in initial appearance.
Applicability to deportation proceedings, §304.
Foreign searches of, §203.
Miranda rights.
When rights attach, §306.

**ALLEN CHARGE,** §1261.

**ALLOCUTION,** §1321.

**AMENDMENTS TO CONSTITUTION OF THE UNITED STATES,**
Appendix A.

**AMOUNT OR QUANTITY OF ITEM CHARGED.**
Burden of proof, §1503.

**ANCESTRAL RECORDS.**
Hearsay exception, availability of declarant immaterial.
Records of religious organizations, §2128.

**ANTICIPATORY SEARCH WARRANTS,** §205.

**ANTI-SKYJACKING SEARCHES,** §241.

**APPEALS,** §1010.
Civil contempt proceedings, §425.
Conditional pleas to preserve issue for appellate review, §614.
Double jeopardy motions, §1010.
Notice to defendant of right of appeal, §1345.
Pretrial release or detention order, §512.
Prosecutorial misconduct.
Standard for review, §1116.
Release pending appeal, §§516 to 519.
Appeal of denial, §519.
Generally, §516.
Likely to result in reversal or new trial, §518.

**APPEALS—Cont'd**
Release pending appeal—Cont'd
Substantial question, §517.
Right to appeal.
Notice to defendant, §1345.
Sentencing.
Departure from guidelines, §1327.
Review of sentences generally, §1346.
Speedy trial act, §1238.
Charges reinstated on appeal, §1216.
Interlocutory appeals delays excluded, §1222.
Suppression hearing, §256.

**APPEARANCE.**
Failure to appear, §521.
Initial appearance, §501.
Confession after arrest but before appearance, §304.

**AREAS WITHIN ARRESTEE'S IMMEDIATE CONTROL.**
Search incident to lawful arrest, §226.

**ARGUMENTATIVE AND INFLAMMATORY COMMENTS.**
Closing argument errors by prosecutors, §1111.
Opening statement errors by prosecutor, §1105.

**ARGUMENT OF COUNSEL.**
Closing argument.
Prosecutorial misconduct, §§1110 to 1115.
See CLOSING ARGUMENT.
Opening statement.
Prosecutorial misconduct, §§1102 to 1105.
See OPENING STATEMENT.

**ARRAIGNMENT,** §601.
Confessions after arraignment, §310.
Pleas generally, §§602 to 619.
See PLEAS.

**ARREST.**
Confession after arrest but before initial appearance, §304.

**ARREST**—Cont'd
Conflict of laws.
  Validity of arrest for federal offense
    without warrant.
      State law governs in absence of
        federal statute, §219.
Exclusionary rule.
  Illegal arrest, §248.
Federal statutes authorizing federal
  officers to make arrest, §219.
Illegal arrest.
  Exclusionary rule, §248.
  Jurisdiction over person of defendant,
    §103.
Probable cause, §219.
Search incident to valid arrest, §§218 to
  226.
  Areas within arrestee's immediate
    control, §226.
  Arrest in good faith and not pretext to
    justify search, §221.
  Articles carried by arrestee, §225.
  Generally, §218.
  Scope of searches generally, §223.
  Search contemporaneous with arrest,
    §222.
  Search of person, §224.
  Validity of arrest generally, §219.
  When person under arrest, §220.
Stop and frisk, §228.
Validity of arrest, §219.
When person under arrest, §220.

**ARREST OF JUDGMENT.**
Motion for, §1305.

**ARTICLES CARRIED BY**
  **ARRESTEE.**
Search incident to lawful arrest, §225.

**ASSIMILATIVE CRIMES ACT,** §101.

**ASSOCIATIONS.**
Sentencing of organizations, §1340.

**ATTORNEY-CLIENT PRIVILEGE,**
  §§1915 to 1919.
Communications about crime or fraud to
  be committed in future, §1918.
Communications by client for legal
  services, §1918.

**ATTORNEY-CLIENT PRIVILEGE**
  —Cont'd
Communications in presentence of third
  parties necessary to provide legal
  service, §1918.
Communications with lawyer.
  Prerequisite to assertion, §1917.
Consultation with lawyer as lawyer,
  §1917.
Corporations.
  Clients for purposes of privilege,
    §1916.
Generally, §1915.
Holder of privilege must be client,
  §1916.
Waiver, §1919.

**ATTORNEY FOR GOVERNMENT.**
Disclosures to in grand jury proceedings,
  §412.
Prosecutorial misconduct generally,
  §§1101 to 1117.
  See PROSECUTORIAL
    MISCONDUCT.
Prosecutorial vindictiveness, §1118.

**ATTORNEY GENERAL.**
Wiretap authorizations, §259.

**ATTORNEYS.**
Attorney-client privilege, §§1915 to
  1919.
  See ATTORNEY-CLIENT
    PRIVILEGE.
Civil contempt proceedings.
  Right to counsel, §425.
Confessions.
  Rights to silence and counsel
    generally, §§305 to 311.
  See CONFESSIONS.
Custodial interrogations.
  Right to counsel, §301.
Identifications before trial.
  Right to counsel, §317.
Initial appearance.
  Right to counsel, §501.
Multiple representation of witnesses in
  grand jury proceedings, §418.
Pleas.
  Right to counsel, §602.

**ATTORNEYS**—Cont'd
Preliminary examination.
Right to counsel, §503.
Self-incrimination privilege.
Attorney asserting client's privilege, §1902.
When right to counsel attaches, §305.
Work product, §1920.

**AUDIO RECORDINGS.**
Admissibility, §1602.

**AUTOMOBILE SEARCHES.**
See MOTOR VEHICLE SEARCHES.

**B**

**BAIL,** §504.
Failure to appear.
Penalties, §521.
Offenses committed while on release, §522.
Pretrial release or detention, §§506 to 512.
Appeal, §512.
Detention generally, §509.
Factors to be considered, §510.
Generally, §506.
Lease on conditions, §507.
Order, §511.
Temporary detention, §508.
Purposes, §504.
Release during trial, §513.
Release of material witness, §520.
Release or detention after conviction, §§515 to 519.
Pending appeal, §516.
Likely to result in reversal or new trial, §518.
Substantial question, §517.
Pending sentencing, §515.
Procedures and appeal of denial, §519.

**BAIL REFORM ACT OF 1984.**
Release and detention generally, §§506 to 522.
See BAIL.

**BARKER-WINGO BALANCING TEST.**
Speedy trial protection, §1205 to 1209.
Generally, §1205.

**BARKER-WINGO BALANCING TEST**—Cont'd
Speedy trial protection—Cont'd
Length of delays, §1206.
Prejudice to defendant caused by delay, §1209.
Reasons for delay, §1207.
Timely assertion of right, §1208.

**BEST EVIDENCE RULE,** §§1705 to 1707.
Exceptions, §1706.
Generally, §1705.
Secondary evidence, §1707.

**BEYOND REASONABLE DOUBT.**
Criminal contempt proceedings.
Require, §426.
Jury instructions on, §1268.
Proving venue, §108.

**BIAS.**
Challenges of jurors for cause, §1247.
Leading questions permitted bias witness, §1801.
Prior misconduct and other crimes.
Evidence showing witness bias, §1811.
Rebuttal evidence.
Admissible to refute witness bias, §1817.
Voir dire questions.
Racial bias, §1247.

**BIBLES.**
Hearsay exception, availability of declarant immaterial.
Statements of fact concerning personal or family history, §2128.

**BILL OF PARTICULARS,** §701.

**BIRTH RECORDS.**
Hearsay exception, availability of declarant immaterial.
Records of religious organizations, §2128.

**BODY CAVITY SEARCHES.**
Prison searches generally, §242.
Search of person incident to lawful arrest, §224.

**BORDER SEARCHES,** §229.
Custodial interrogations.
Routine stops do not amount to, §306.

**BOUNDARIES.**
Hearsay exceptions, availability of
    declarant immaterial.
    Judgments as to, §2135.
    Reputation, §2133.

**BRADY DOCTRINE,** §§718 to 724.
Categories requiring disclosures
    generally, §§719, 720.
Exculpatory material, §721.
Impeachment material, §722.
Material that must be disclosed, §§719,
    720.
Required disclosures, §§719, 720.
Reservation of evidence, §724.
Rule generally, §718.
Time for disclosure, §723.

**BREACH OF PLEA AGREEMENT,**
    §613.

**BUGGING.**
Wiretapping and other electronic
    surveillance generally, §§257 to 268.
    See WIRETAPPING AND
        ELECTRONIC SURVEILLANCE.

**BURDEN OF PROOF,** §1501.
Affirmative defenses, §1501.
Assimilative crimes act.
    Status of site of offenses, §101.
Audio recordings.
    Admissibility, §1602.
Civil contempt proceedings, §425.
Confessions.
    Voluntariness, §301.
Consent searches.
    Voluntariness of consent, §243.
Conspiracies.
    Withdrawal, §1510.
Defenses, §1501.
Discriminatory jury selection, §1245.
Double jeopardy.
    Claims, §1001.
False statements in affidavit supporting
    search warrant, §210.
Insanity defense, §§703, 1501, 1508.
Jury instructions on reasonable doubt,
    §1268.
Motion for acquittal, §1502.
Motions to suppress, §252.

**BURDEN OF PROOF**—Cont'd
Presumptions generally.
    See PRESUMPTIONS.
Pretrial detention, §509.
Specific items generally, §1503.
Venue, §108.
    Transfer because of prejudice to
        defendant, §111.
Warrantless searches, §217.

**BUSINESS RECORDS.**
Records of regularly conducted activity,
    §2123.
    Absence of entries in records kept in
        regularly conducted activity,
        §2124.

C

**CAREER OFFENDERS.**
Sentencing.
    Application of guidelines, §1323.

**CAUSE OF DEATH.**
Expert testimony, §2003.

**CAUTIONARY INSTRUCTIONS,**
    §1252.

**CHALLENGE OF ARRAY.**
Jury selection, §1245.

**CHALLENGES FOR CAUSE.**
Jury selection, §1247.

**CHANGE OF VENUE.**
Convenience, §112.
Prejudice to defendant, §111.
Transfer for plea and sentence
    generally, §113.
Transfer of venue generally, §110.

**CHARACTER EVIDENCE,** §§1518 to
    1520.
Cross-examination of witnesses, §1520.
Generally, §1518.
Hearsay exceptions, availability of
    declarant immaterial.
    Reputation, §2133.
Methods of proving, §1519.
Rebuttal of witnesses, §1520.
Used for impeachment, §1808.

**CHARGE OFFENSE SENTENCING,**
    §1310.

**CHARGES TO JURY.**
Jury instructions generally.
　See JURY INSTRUCTIONS.

**CHARTS.**
Admissibility of summary charts, §1605.
Hearsay exception, availability of
　declarant immaterial.
　Statements of fact concerning personal
　　or family history, §2128.

**CIRCUMSTANTIAL EVIDENCE,**
　§1516.
Proving venue, §108.

**CIVIL ACTIONS BY**
　**GOVERNMENT.**
Disclosure of grand jury material for use
　in, §416.

**CIVIL CONTEMPT PROCEEDINGS.**
Enforcement of grand jury subpoenas
　and orders compelling testimony,
　§425.

**CLEAR AND CONVINCING**
　**EVIDENCE.**
Audio recordings.
　Admissibility, §1602.
Insanity defense, §§703, 1508.

**CLOSE OF EVIDENCE.**
Motion for acquittal, §1275.

**CLOSE OF GOVERNMENT'S CASE.**
Motion for acquittal, §1274.

**CLOSING ARGUMENT.**
Prosecutorial misconduct, §§1110 to
　1115.
Defense.
　Provocation response, §1112.
Inflammatory comments, §1111.
Invading province of court, §1113.
Personal opinion statement, §1114.
Reasonable inferences, §1111.
Silence post-arrest and in-trial
　comment on, §1115.
Statement of the law, §1113.

**COCONSPIRATORS'**
　**DECLARATIONS,** §2116.

**CODEFENDANTS.**
Joinder of defendants generally.
　See JOINDER OF DEFENDANTS.

**CODEFENDANTS**—Cont'd
Severance of defendants generally.
　See SEVERANCE.

**COERCION.**
Confessions, §313.
Use to secure consent to search, §244.

**COLLATERAL ESTOPPEL,** §1011.

**COMMERCIAL PUBLICATIONS.**
Hearsay exceptions, availability of
　declarant immaterial, §2131.

**COMMON KNOWLEDGE.**
Judicial notice, §1403.

**COMMUNICATIONS WITH JURORS**
　**DURING TRIAL,** §1249.

**COMMUNIST PARTY TEACHINGS**
　**AND PURPOSES.**
Expert testimony, §2003.

**COMPLETENESS RULE.**
Use of entire writing or recorded
　statement, §1708.

**COMPUTER RECORDS.**
Admissibility, §1610.

**CONCEALMENT OF IDENTITY.**
Evidence admissible to prove
　consciousness of guilt, §1528.

**CONCLUSIVE PRESUMPTIONS.**
Constitutionality, §1505.

**CONCURRENT SENTENCES,** §1330.

**CONDITIONAL PLEAS,** §§256, 614.

**CONDITIONS ON PRETRIAL**
　**RELEASE,** §507.

**CONDUCT.**
Methods of proving character.
　Testimony as to specific instances of
　　conduct, §1519.

**CONDUCT OF BUSINESS.**
Lay witness testimony, §2001.

**CONFESSIONS,** §§301 to 315.
Burden of proof.
　Voluntariness, §301.
Coerced confessions, §313.
Corroboration, §303.

**CONFESSIONS**—Cont'd
Discovery.
    Statements of defendants generally,
        §706.
Form, §302.
Fruit of poisonous tree, §312.
Generally, §301.
Hearsay.
    Admissibility for purposes of
        corroborating, §303.
    Statements reduced to writing by one
        other than accused precludes
        hearsay objection, §302.
Initial appearance.
    Confession after arrest but before
        appearance, §304.
Instructions on voluntariness, §1270.
Joint trial use, §314.
Miranda rights.
    Rights to silence and counsel, §§305 to
        311.
Motions to suppress.
    Generally, §§250 to 256.
        See MOTIONS TO SUPPRESS.
    Hearings conducted out of hearing of
        jury, §253.
Offers of pleas.
    Inadmissibility of statements
        relating to, §315.
Pleas.
    Inadmissibility of statements relating
        to, §315.
Rights to silence and counsel, §§305 to
    311.
    Confessions obtained after indictment,
        §310.
    Generally, §305.
    Impeachments.
        When statements taken in violation
            of fifth and sixth amendments,
            §311.
    Scope of Miranda, §307.
    Silence of defendants, §309.
    Termination of questioning, §308.
    When Miranda rights attach, §306.
Searches and seizures.
    Improper search tainting valid
        confessions, §312.

**CONFESSIONS**—Cont'd
Severance of defendants.
    Admitting codefendant's confession,
        §915.
Unnecessary delay in initial appearance,
    §304.
Venue.
    Established solely by confession, §303.
Voluntariness.
    Ultimate test of admissibility, §301.

**CONFIDENTIAL
COMMUNICATIONS
PRIVILEGE.**
Marital communications privilege,
    §1911.

**CONFLICT OF LAWS.**
Arrest.
    Validity of arrest for federal offense
        without warrant.
        State law governs in absence of
            federal statute, §219.

**CONFLICTS OF INTEREST.**
Multiple representation of witnesses in
    grand jury proceedings, §418.

**CONFRONTATION CLAUSE.**
Hearsay exceptions, declarant
    unavailable.
    Sixth amendment limitations, §2139.

**CONJUNCTIVE CHARGES.**
Burden of proof, §1503.

**CONSCIOUSNESS OF GUILT.**
False exculpatory statements to prove,
    §1529.
Flight and concealment of identity to
    prove, §1528.
Suppression, destruction or fabrication
    of evidence, §1530.

**CONSECUTIVE SENTENCES,** §1330.

**CONSENT OF PARTY TO
INTERCEPT
COMMUNICATION,** §268.

**CONSENT SEARCHES,** §§243 to 245.
Generally, §243.
Third-party consent, §245.
Use of deceit to secure consent, §244.

**CONSISTENT PRIOR STATEMENTS.**
Non-hearsay by definition, §2110.

**CONSOLIDATION FOR TRIAL.**
Joinder of defendants, §908.
  Generally.
    See JOINDER OF DEFENDANTS.
Joinder of offenses generally.
  See JOINDER OF OFFENSES.
Severance of defendants and offenses
    generally.
  See SEVERANCE.

**CONSPIRACIES.**
Burden of proof.
  Withdrawal, §1510.
Coconspirators' declarations, §2116.
Confessions used at joint trials, §314.
Continuance.
  Presumptions, §1510.
Declarations of coconspirators, §2116.
Double jeopardy, §1002.
Joinder of defendants, §909.
Jury instructions on joint venture,
    common scheme charge, §1270.
Presumption as to continuance, §1510.
Severance of defendant, §917.
Venue, §106.
Withdrawal.
  Burden, §1510.

**CONSTITUTION OF THE UNITED STATES.**
Amendments to, Appendix A.
Judicial notice, §1403.

**CONSTITUTIONS OF STATES.**
Judicial notice, §1403.

**CONTAINERS.**
Searches of containers found in vehicles,
    §237.

**CONTEMPORANEOUS DECLARATIONS,** §2106.
Excited utterances, §2119.
Present sense impression, §2118.

**CONTEMPT.**
Grand jury procedures for enforcement
    of subpoenas and orders.
  Civil contempt proceedings, §425.
  Criminal contempt proceedings, §426.

**CONTEMPT—Cont'd**
Grand jury procedures for enforcement
    of subpoenas and orders—Cont'd
  Generally, §424.
Prosecutorial misconduct sanctions,
    §1117.

**CONTINUANCES.**
Sanctions for failure to provide
    discovery, §716.
Speedy trial act.
  Excludable delays, §1231.

**CONTRABAND.**
Exigent circumstances justify
    warrantless search.
  Threatened destruction or removal,
      §233.
Property that may be seized during
    search, §247.

**CONVENIENCE OF PARTIES AND WITNESSES.**
Transfer of venue, §112.

**CORPORATIONS.**
Attorney-client privilege.
  Clients for purposes of privilege,
      §1916.
Entry of appearance, §103.
Self-incrimination privilege.
  Production of books of organization,
      §1902.
Sentencing of organizations, §1340.

**CORRECTION OF SENTENCE,** §1343.

**CORROBORATION.**
Confessions, §303.

**COUNSEL.**
Attorney-client privilege, §§1915 to
    1919.
  See ATTORNEY-CLIENT
      PRIVILEGE.
Generally.
  See ATTORNEYS.

**COURT-APPOINTED EXPERTS,** §2007.

**COURT ORDERS.**
Interception of oral or wire
    communications pursuant to
    generally, §§258 to 267.
  See WIRETAPPING AND
      ELECTRONIC SURVEILLANCE.
Pretrial release or detention, §§511, 512.
Protective orders.
  Discovery, §715.

**COURT RECORDS AND FILES.**
Judicial notice, §1403.

**CREDIBILITY OF WITNESSES.**
Impeachment generally.
  See IMPEACHMENT OF
    WITNESSES.
Jury instructions on, §1270.

**CRIMINAL CONTEMPT
    PROCEEDINGS.**
Enforcement of grand jury subpoenas
  and orders compelling testimony,
  §426.

**CRIMINAL FORFEITURE.**
Judgment of forfeiture, §1342.
Special verdicts, §1257.

**CRIMINAL LIVELIHOOD.**
Sentencing.
  Application of guidelines, §1323.

**CRIMINAL PROCEDURE RULES,**
    Appendix B.

**CRIMINAL RECORDS.**
Discovery of defendants prior records,
  §707.

**CROSS-EXAMINATION OF
    WITNESSES,** §1805.
Character witnesses, §1520.
Impeachment generally.
  See IMPEACHMENT OF
    WITNESSES.
Prior inconsistent statements, §§1813,
  1814.
Purposes, §1805.
Refreshing recollection used on, §1804.
Scope, §1805.
Silence of accused after Miranda
  warnings given, §309.

**CURTILAGE OF RESIDENCE.**
Fourth amendment protection of area,
  §240.

**CUSTODIAL INTERROGATION.**
Confessions generally, §§301 to 315.
  See CONFESSIONS.
Right to counsel at, §301.

**CUSTOM,** §1531.

**CUSTOM SEARCHES,** §229.
Custodial interrogations.
  Routine inspections do not amount to,
    §306.

### D

**DAYTIME EXECUTION OF
    SEARCH WARRANTS,** §214.

**DEADLOCKED JURIES.**
Allen charge, §1261.

**DEAF OR HEARING IMPAIRED
    PERSONS.**
Use of interpreters during examination,
  §1820.

**DEATH IMPENDING.**
Hearsay exceptions, declarant
  unavailable.
  Statement under belief of, §2142.

**DEATH PENALTY.**
Challenges of jurors for cause.
  Conscientious scruples against capital
    punishment, §1247.
Guilty plea.
  Entered to avoid, §609.

**DEATH RECORDS.**
Hearsay exception, availability of
  declarant immaterial.
  Records of religious organizations,
    §2128.

**DECEIT.**
Use to secure consent to search, §244.

**DECEPTIVE PRACTICES.**
Notice to victims by defendants, §1338.

**DECLARATIONS OF
    COCONSPIRATORS,** §2116.

**DEEDS.**
Hearsay exception, availability of
  declarant immaterial.
  Documents and statements affecting
    interest in property, §2129.

**DEFENSES.**
Alibi.
  Notice, §702.
Burden of proof, §1501.
Conflicting defenses.
  Severance of defendant, §916.
Double jeopardy.
  Generally, §§1001 to 1006.
    See JEOPARDY.
Insanity defense.
  See INSANITY DEFENSE.
Jury instructions on defense theories,
  §1266.
Public authority.
  Notice of defense based upon, §704.
Severance of defendants.
  Conflicting defenses, §916.
Theory of defense.
  Jury instructions, §1266.

**DEFERRAL OF PROSECUTIONS.**
Speedy trial act excludes delays, §1220.

**DELAYS.**
Imposition of sentence, §1320.
Initial appearance, §501.
  Confessions, §304.
Pre-accusation delays generally, §1239.
Speedy trial.
  Generally, §§1202 to 1239.
    See SPEEDY TRIAL.

**DEMONSTRATIVE EVIDENCE,**
  §§1600 to 1611.
Audio recordings, §1602.
Computer records, §1610.
Experiments, §1609.
Introduction, §1600.
Jury view of premises, §1611.
Models, §1607.
Overlays, §1608.
Photographs, §1604.
Summary charts, §1605.
Video recordings, §1603.

**DEPORTATION PROCEEDINGS.**
Confessions by aliens during
  unnecessary delay in initial
  proceeding, §304.

**DEPOSITIONS.**
Videotaped depositions, §1603.

**DERIVATIVE USE IMMUNITY
  CONCEPT.**
Immunity of witnesses generally, §§419
  to 423.
  See IMMUNITY OF WITNESSES.

**DESCRIPTION.**
Search warrants.
  Particularity, §211.

**DESIGN.**
Proof of other crimes, §1526.

**DESTRUCTION OF EVIDENCE.**
Admissibility, §1530.

**DETAINERS.**
Interstate agreement on detainers.
  Speedy trial act, §1233.

**DISCHARGE OF JURY.**
Motion for acquittal, §1276.

**DISCLOSURE.**
Alibi.
  Notice, §702.
Bill of particulars, §701.
Brady doctrine generally, §§718 to 724.
  See BRADY DOCTRINE.
Defendants evidence, §710.
Discovery generally.
  See DISCOVERY.
Exculpatory evidence, §714.
  Brady doctrine generally, §§718 to
    724.
    See BRADY DOCTRINE.
Jencks Act and Rule 26.2.
  Generally, §§801 to 814.
    See JENCKS ACT AND RULE
      26.2.
Prosecutorial misconduct, §1108.
Favorable evidence to defendant.
  Brady doctrine generally, §§718 to
    724.
    See BRADY DOCTRINE.
Informants identities, §713.

**DISCLOSURE**—Cont'd
Insanity defense or defense based upon
    mental condition.
    Notice, §703.
Introduction, §700.
Presentence report and investigation,
    §1318.
Prior statements.
    Trial discvovery generally, §§801 to
        814.
        See JENCKS ACT AND RULE
            26.2.
Prosecutorial misconduct.
    Undisclosed favorable defense
        evidence, §1108.
Public authority.
    Notice of defense based upon, §704.
Purposes, §700.
Work-product, §1920.

**DISCOVERY.**
Alibi.
    Notice, §702.
Brady doctrine, §§718 to 724.
    See BRADY DOCTRINE.
Confessions.
    Statements of defendants.
        Generally, §706.
Criminal record of defendants, §707.
Defendant's evidence, §710.
Defendant's prior record, §707.
Defendant's statements, §706.
Documents and tangible objects, §708.
    Subpoena for production, §717.
Examinations and test reports, §709.
Exculpatory evidence, §714.
    Brady doctrine generally, §§718 to
        724.
        See BRADY DOCTRINE.
    Jencks Act and Rule 26.2.
        Generally, §§801 to 814.
            See JENCKS ACT AND RULE
                26.2.
    Prosecutorial misconduct, §1108.
Failure to provide, §716.
Favorable evidence to defendant.
    Brady doctrine generally, §§718 to
        724.
        See BRADY DOCTRINE.
Generally, §705.

**DISCOVERY**—Cont'd
Government discovery request, §710
Grand jury testimony of defendants,
    §706.
Identities of witnesses, §712.
Informants identities, §713.
Insanity defense or defense based upon
    mental condition.
    Notice, §703.
Introduction, §700.
Names of witnesses, §712.
Prior statements.
    Trial discovery generally, §§801 to
        814.
        See JENCKS ACT AND RULE
            26.2.
Prosecutorial misconduct.
    Undiscovered favorable defense
        evidence, §1108.
Protective orders, §715.
Public authority.
    Notice of defense based upon, §704.
Purposes of rules concerning, §700.
Recorded statements of defendants,
    §706.
Sanctions for failure to provide, §716.
Subpoenas duces tecum, §717.
Videotaped depositions, §1603.
Wiretapping and electronic
    surveillance.
    Recorded statements of defendants,
        §706.
Witness statements and identities, §712.
Work product, §§712, 1920.
Written statements of defendants, §706.

**DISCOVERY AT TRIAL OF PRIOR
    STATEMENTS.**
Generally, §§801 to 814.
    See JENCKS ACT AND RULE 26.2.

**DISCRIMINATORY JURY
    SELECTION.**
Challenge of array, §1245.

**DISMISSALS.**
Jeopardy.
    Does not attach when defense motion
        granted, §1006.
Speedy trial act.
    Dismissals generally, §1237.

**DISMISSALS—Cont'd**
Speedy trial act—Cont'd
Reinstitution of dismissed charges,
§1215.
Sanctions, §1234.

**DISPUTED SENTENCING FACT
RESOLUTION,** §1339.

**DISTINCTIVE COMMUNITY
GROUPS.**
Challenge of array for systematic
exclusion from jury, §1245.

**DISTRICT COURTS.**
Concurrent jurisdiction, §101.
Grand jury supervisory powers, §402.
Original jurisdiction, §101.

**DIVORCE RECORDS.**
Hearsay exception, availability of
declarant immaterial.
Records of religious organizations,
§2128.

**DOCUMENTARY EVIDENCE,** §§1701
to 1708.
Admissibility generally, §1701.
Authentication generally, §1701.
Best evidence rule, §§1705 to 1707.
Exceptions, §1706.
Generally, §1705.
Secondary evidence, §1707.
Documents containing inadmissible
materials, §1704.
Entire writing or recorded statement.
Use of, §1708.
Inadmissible material contained in
documents, §1704.
Official documents, §1702.
Private or nonofficial documents, §1703.
Subpoena for production, §717.

**DOCUMENTS AND TANGIBLE
OBJECTS.**
Disclosure of evidence by defendants,
§710.
Discovery, §708.
Jencks Act and Rule 26.2.
Generally, §§801 to 814.
See JENCKS ACT AND RULE
26.2.

**DOCUMENTS AND TANGIBLE
OBJECTS—Cont'd**
Self-incrimination privilege.
Compulsory production, §1902.
Subpoena for production, §717.

**DOGS.**
Use to sniff luggage for drugs, §206.

**DOUBLE JEOPARDY.**
Generally, §§1001 to 1006.
See JEOPARDY.

**DRUG ADDICTION AS GROUNDS
FOR IMPEACHMENT,** §1815.

**DRUG-INFLUENCED GUILTY
PLEA,** §606.

**DRUG SNIFFING DOGS.**
Probable cause for search, §206.

**DRUG VIOLATIONS ON HIGH
SEAS.**
Venue, §107.

**DUE PROCESS.**
Identifications before trial.
Fifth amendment due process rights,
§318.

**DUPLICITY.**
Joining single count of two or more
distinct and separate offenses, §905.

**E**

**EIGHTH AMENDMENT
PROTECTIONS.**
Excessive bail, §504.

**ELECTRONIC SURVEILLANCE.**
Generally, §§257 to 268.
See WIRETAPPING AND
ELECTRONIC SURVEILLANCE.

**EMANCIPATED CHILD-PARENT
PRIVILEGE,** §1924.

**EMERGENCIES.**
Exigent circumstances to justify
warrantless search.
Officers responding to, §232.

726

**EMOTIONAL CONDITION.**
Hearsay exception, availability of
declarant immaterial.
Then existing condition, §2120.

**ENTRY TO SEARCH.**
Manner of, §215.

**EQUAL PROTECTION.**
Peremptory challenges, §1248.

**ESCAPE.**
Exigent circumstances to justify
warrantless search.
Likely escape of suspect, §233.

**EVIDENCE.**
Admissions.
See ADMISSIONS.
Authentication.
Documentary evidence generally,
§§1701 to 1704.
See DOCUMENTARY EVIDENCE.
Best evidence rule, §§1705 to 1707.
Brady doctrine generally, §§718 to 724.
See BRADY DOCTRINE.
Burden of proof generally.
See BURDEN OF PROOF.
Cautionary instructions, §1252.
Character of defendant, §§1518 to 1520.
Cross-examination and rebuttal of
witnesses, §1520.
Generally, §1518.
Methods of proving character, §1519.
Circumstantial evidence, §1516.
Proving venue, §108.
Comment on by judges, §1264.
Concealment of identity, §1528.
Confessions.
Generally, §§301 to 315.
See CONFESSIONS.
Demonstrative evidence.
Generally, §§1600 to 1611.
See DEMONSTRATIVE
EVIDENCE.
Destruction of evidence, §1530.
Disclosure generally.
See DISCLOSURE.
Discovery generally.
See DISCOVERY.

**EVIDENCE**—Cont'd
Documentary evidence generally, §§1701
to 1708.
See DOCUMENTARY EVIDENCE.
Examination of witnesses.
Generally, §§1801 to 1820.
See EXAMINATION OF
WITNESSES.
Exclusionary rule, §248.
Confessions.
Illegal search and seizure or invalid
arrest, §312.
Obtained during unnecessary delay
in initial appearance, §304.
Cross-examination of defendant's
witness or rebuttal.
Admissibility, §1818.
Grand jury proceedings, §406.
Exculpatory evidence.
Brady doctrine generally, §§718 to
724.
See BRADY DOCTRINE.
Duty to disclose, §714.
False exculpatory statements.
Admissible to prove consciousness of
guilt, §1529.
Jencks Act and Rule 26.2.
Generally, §§801 to 814.
See JENCKS ACT AND RULE
26.2.
Prosecutorial misconduct, §1108.
Exigent circumstances to justify
warrantless search.
Threatened destruction or removal,
§233.
Expert testimony.
See EXPERT TESTIMONY.
Fabrication of evidence, §1530.
False exculpatory statements, §1529.
False testimony.
Prosecutorial misconduct.
Obtaining conviction with aid of,
§1107.
Favorable evidence to defendant.
Brady doctrine generally, §§718 to
724.
See BRADY DOCTRINE.
Flight, §1528.

**EVIDENCE**—Cont'd
Grand jury.
Calling and questioning of witnesses,
§§404 to 408.
Evidence before generally, §403.
Subpoenas duces tecum, §409.
Habit and custom, §1531.
Hearsay exceptions, availability of
declarant immaterial, §§2117 to
2136.
See HEARSAY EXCEPTIONS,
AVAILABILITY OF
DECLARANT IMMATERIAL.
Hearsay exceptions, declarant
unavailable, §§2137 to 2147.
See HEARSAY EXCEPTIONS,
DECLARANT UNAVAILABLE.
Hearsay generally.
See HEARSAY.
Identifications before trial generally,
§§316 to 319.
See IDENTIFICATIONS BEFORE
TRIAL.
Illegally obtained evidence.
Exclusionary rule, §248.
Insufficiency.
Motion for acquittal.
Generally, §§1271 to 1276.
See MOTION FOR ACQUITTAL.
Judicial notice, §§1400 to 1403.
See JUDICIAL NOTICE.
Limiting instructions, §1252.
Misleading evidence.
Prosecutorial misconduct.
Obtaining conviction with aid of,
§1107.
Motion for acquittal.
Generally, §§1271 to 1276.
See MOTION FOR ACQUITTAL.
Motions to suppress, §§250 to 256.
See MOTIONS TO SUPPRESS.
Motive, §1532.
Newly discovered evidence.
Motion for new trial, §1302.
Opinion evidence.
See OPINION EVIDENCE.
Plain view evidence.
See PLAIN VIEW EVIDENCE.

**EVIDENCE**—Cont'd
Pleas and plea discussions.
Inadmissibility, §615.
Presumptions generally.
See PRESUMPTIONS.
Pretrial identification of defendants
generally, §§316 to 319.
See IDENTIFICATIONS BEFORE
TRIAL.
Prior statements.
Generally.
See PRIOR STATEMENTS.
Jencks Act and Rule 26.2.
Generally, §§801 to 814.
See JENCKS ACT AND RULE
26.2.
Privileges.
Generally.
See PRIVILEGES.
Self-incrimination.
See SELF-INCRIMINATION.
Proof of other crimes, §§1521 to 1526.
See PROOF OF OTHER CRIMES.
Prosecutorial misconduct.
Reference to inadmissible evidence in
opening statement, §1103.
Rebuttal evidence.
See REBUTTAL EVIDENCE.
Relevancy generally, §1517.
Res gestae, §2106.
Rules of evidence, Appendix C.
Same evidence test.
Subsequent prosecution for offenses
with identical statutory elements,
§1002.
Searches and seizures.
Evidence affected by search and
seizure generally, §§246 to 256.
See SEARCHES AND SEIZURES.
Search without warrant justified.
Threatened destruction or removal,
§233.
Self-incrimination.
See SELF-INCRIMINATION.
Subpoenas duces tecum, §409.
Grand jury powers, §409.
Suppression motions, §§250 to 256.
See MOTIONS TO SUPPRESS.
Suppression of evidence, §1530.

**EVIDENCE**—Cont'd
Wiretapping and electronic surveillance.
  Generally, §§257 to 268.
    See WIRETAPPING AND
      ELECTRONIC
      SURVEILLANCE.

**EXAMINATION OF WITNESSES,**
    §§1801 to 1820.
Character witnesses.
  Cross-examination, §1520.
Cross-examination, §1805.
  Character witnesses, §1520.
  Prior inconsistent statements, §§1813,
    1814.
  Refreshing recollection used on, §1804.
Exclusion of witnesses, §1819.
Grand jury calling and questioning.
  After indictment returned, §408.
  Electronic surveillance, questions
    based on illegal surveillance,
    §407.
  Exclusionary rule, §406.
  Generally, §404.
  Miranda warnings, §405.
Guilty plea.
  Effect, §603.
Impeachment.
  Character evidence, §1808.
  Exclusionary rule evidence.
    Admissibility, §1818.
  Hearsay declarants, §2149.
  Insanity, §1815.
  Narcotics addiction, §1815.
  Own witness, §1807.
  Prior inconsistent statements, §1813.
  Prior misconduct and other crimes,
    §1809.
    Evidence showing witness bias,
      §1811.
    Probative value versus prejudicial
      effect, §1810.
  Silence used to impeach credibility,
    §1818.
Interpreters.
  Use, §1820.
Leading questions, §1801.
Motions to suppress, §253.
Prior inconsistent statements.
  Affirmative evidence, §1814.
  For impeachment, §1813.

**EXAMINATION OF WITNESSES**
    —Cont'd
Privileges.
  Generally.
    See PRIVILEGES.
  Self-incrimination.
    See SELF-INCRIMINATION.
Rebuttal, §§1816 to 1818.
  Character witnesses, §1520.
  Exclusionary rule of evidence, §1818.
  Generally, §1816.
  Scope, §1817.
Refreshing recollection, §1802.
  Inspection of exhibit, §1803.
  Use on cross-examination, §1804.
Self-incrimination.
  See SELF-INCRIMINATION.
Separation of witnesses, §1819.

**EXAMINATIONS.**
Discovery of reports, §709.
Speedy trial act excludes delays
  resulting from, §1220.

**EXCITED UTTERANCES.**
Hearsay exceptions, availability of
  declarant immaterial, §2119.

**EXCLUSIONARY RULE,** §248.
Confessions.
  Illegal search and seizure or invalid
    arrest, §312.
  Obtained during period of unnecessary
    delay in initial appearance,
    §304.
Cross-examination of defendant's
  witness or rebuttal.
  Admissibility, §1818.
Grand jury proceedings, §406.

**EXCLUSION OF WITNESSES,** §1819.

**EXCULPATING STATEMENTS.**
Statements against penal interest
  offered to exculpate, §2145.

**EXCULPATORY EVIDENCE.**
Brady doctrine generally, §§718 to 724.
  See BRADY DOCTRINE.
Duty to disclose, §714.
False exculpatory statements.
  Admissibility to prove consciousness of
    guilt, §1529.

**EXCULPATORY EVIDENCE**—Cont'd
Jencks Act and Rule 26.2.
  Generally, §§801 to 814.
    See JENCKS ACT AND RULE
      26.2.
Prosecutorial misconduct.
  Undiscovered and undisclosed
    favorable defense evidence, §1108.

**EXECUTION OF SEARCH
  WARRANTS.**
Manner of entry, §215.
When executed, §214.
Who may execute, §213.

**EXECUTIVE ORDERS AND
  PROCLAMATIONS.**
Judicial notice, §1403.

**EXHIBITS.**
Demonstrative evidence generally,
  §§1600 to 1611.
  See DEMONSTRATIVE EVIDENCE.
Refreshing presentence recollection of
  past events, §1803.

**EXIGENT CIRCUMSTANCES.**
Entry to search, §215.
Warrantless searches justified, §§231 to
  234.
  Generally, §231.
  Hot pursuit, §234.
  Officers responding to emergencies,
    §232.
  Threatened destruction or removal of
    contraband, §233.

**EXPERIMENTAL EVIDENCE.**
Admissibility, §1609.

**EXPERT TESTIMONY, §§2003 to
  2007.**
Basis of opinion testimony, §2004.
Court-appointed experts, §2007.
Factors considered in admitting, §2003.
Hypothetical questions, §2006.
Mental disease bearing upon issue of
  guilt.
  Notice of intent to rely on, §703.
Prejudicial impact, §2003.
Principle upon which opinion based,
  §2003.
Qualifications, §2003.

**EXPERT TESTIMONY**—Cont'd
Scientific, technical or specialized
  knowledge, §2003.
Ultimate issue rule, §2005.

**EXTRADITION.**
Improper extradition.
  Jurisdiction over person of defendant,
    §103.

**EXTRAJUDICIAL
  IDENTIFICATION, §319.**

**F**

**FABRICATION OF EVIDENCE.**
Admissibility, §1530.

**FAILURE OF DEFENDANT TO
  TESTIFY.**
Inference or presumption, §1515.

**FAILURE TO APPEAR.**
Penalties for, §521.

**FAILURE TO CALL WITNESS.**
Inference, §1514.

**FAIR AND JUST STANDARD.**
Withdrawal of plea, §618.

**FALSE EXCULPATORY
  STATEMENTS.**
Admissible to prove consciousness of
  guilt, §1529.

**FALSE TESTIMONY.**
Prosecutorial misconduct.
  Obtaining conviction with aid of,
    §1107.

**FAMILY HISTORY.**
Hearsay exceptions, availability of
  declarant immaterial.
  Judgment as to, §2135.
  Records of, §2128.
  Reputation, §2133.
Hearsay exceptions, declarant
  unavailable.
  Statements of, §2146.

**FAVORABLE EVIDENCE TO
  DEFENDANT.**
Brady doctrine generally, §§718 to 724.
  See BRADY DOCTRINE.

**FAVORABLE EVIDENCE TO DEFENDANT**—Cont'd
Prosecutorial misconduct.
Undiscovered and undisclosed favorable defense evidence, §1108.

**FEDERAL AGENTS.**
Execution of search warrants, §213.

**FEDERAL MAGISTRATES.**
Search warrants.
Issuance, §205.
Neutrality in probable cause determinations, §209.

**FEDERAL RULES OF CRIMINAL PROCEDURE,** Appendix B.

**FEDERAL RULES OF EVIDENCE,** Appendix C.

**FEES.**
Arraignment, §601.

**FIFTH AMENDMENT PROTECTIONS.**
Confessions.
Generally, §§301 to 315.
See CONFESSIONS.
Identifications before trial, §316.
Jeopardy.
Generally, §§1001 to 1006.
See JEOPARDY.
Self-incrimination.
See SELF-INCRIMINATION.

**FINES,** §§1332 to 1334.
Factors considered in imposing, §1333.
Imposition generally, §1333.
Modification or remission, §1334.

**FIREARMS AND BALLISTICS.**
Expert testimony, §2003.

**FLIGHT.**
Evidence admissible to prove consciousness of guilt, §1528.

**FORCED ENTRY.**
Entry to search, §215.

**FOREIGN SEARCHES OF ALIENS,** §203.

**FORFEITURE.**
Criminal forfeiture special verdicts, §1257.
Judgment of forfeiture, §1342.

**FORMER TESTIMONY.**
Hearsay exceptions, declarant unavailable, §2141.

**FORUM NON CONVENIENS.**
Transfer of venue for convenience of parties and witnesses, §112.

**FOURTH AMENDMENT PROTECTIONS.**
Searches and seizures generally, §§201 to 256.
See SEARCHES AND SEIZURES.
Wiretapping and other electronic surveillance, §§257 to 268.
See WIRETAPPING AND ELECTRONIC SURVEILLANCE.

**FRAUD.**
Notice to victims by defendants, §1338.

**FREEDOM OF INFORMATION ACT.**
Disclosure of presentence report and investigation, §1318.

**FRUIT OF THE POISONOUS TREE.**
Confessions, §312.
Exclusionary rule, §248.

**FRUITS OF CRIME.**
Permissible inference as to recent possession, §1513.
Property that may be seized during search, §247.

**G**

**GENDER.**
Peremptory challenges used to exclude on basis of, §1248.

**GENEALOGIES.**
Hearsay exception, availability of declarant immaterial.
Statements of fact concerning personal or family history, §2128.

**GENERAL SEARCH WARRANTS.**
Prohibited, §211.

**GOVERNMENT CIVIL ACTIONS.**
Disclosure of grand jury material for use in, §416.

**GOVERNMENT PERSONNEL.**
Disclosure of grand jury materials to, §413.

**GOVERNMENT PRIVILEGE.**
Identities of informants, §1923.

**GRAND JURY,** §§400 to 427.
Abuse of process to call defendant after indictment returned, §408.
Attorneys.
  Multiple representation of witnesses, §418.
Calling and questioning of witnesses, §§404 to 408.
  After indictment returned, §408.
  Electronic surveillance, questions based on illegal surveillance, §407.
  Exclusionary rule, §406.
  Generally, §404.
  Miranda warnings, §405.
Conflicts of interest.
  Multiple representation of witnesses, §418.
Contempt to enforce orders compelling testimony, §§424 to 426.
  Civil contempt, §425.
  Criminal contempt, §426.
  Generally, §424.
Disclosure exceptions to secrecy requirement, §§410 to 417.
  Attorney for government.
    Disclosures to, §412.
  Disclosures by or to witnesses, §415.
  Matters occuring before grand jury, §411.
  Other government personnel.
    Disclosures to, §413.
  Preliminary to or in connection with judicial proceedings, §414.
  Sealed indictments, §417.
  Secrecy of proceedings generally, §410.
  Use in government civil actions, §416.
Discovery of testimony of defendants before, §706.
District court supervisory powers, §402.
Electronic surveillance.
  Questions based on illegal surveillance, §407.

**GRAND JURY**—Cont'd
Evidence before.
  Calling and questioning of witnesses and warnings, §§404 to 408.
  Exclusionary rule not extended to proceeding, §406.
  Generally, §403.
  Subpoenas duces tecum, §409.
Immunity, §§419 to 423.
  Civil proceeding use, §422.
  Defense witnesses, §423.
  Generally, §419.
  Other sovereigns.
    Immunity grants, §421.
  Perjury prosecution, §420.
Introduction, §400.
Jury selection generally.
  See JURY TRIAL.
Miranda warnings to witnesses, §405.
Multiple representation of witnesses, §418.
Presumptions.
  Regularity of proceedings, §403.
Procedures generally, §401.
Reports, §427.
Sealed indictments, §417.
Secrecy of proceedings, §§410 to 417.
  Attorney for government.
    Disclosures to, §412.
  Civil actions.
    Disclosures for use in government civil actions, §416.
  Disclosures by or to witnesses, §415.
  Generally, §410.
  Matters occuring before, §411.
  Other government personnel.
    Disclosures to, §413.
  Preliminary to or in connection with judicial proceedings.
    Disclosures, §314.
  Sealed indictments, §417.
Subpoenas.
  Calling and questioning of witnesses, §404.
  Contempt to enforce subpoenas, §§424 to 426.
Subpoenas duces tecum, §409.

**GRAND JURY**—Cont'd
Wiretapping and electronic surveillance.
  Questions based on illegal
    surveillance, §407.

**GUILTY MIND EVIDENCE,** §§1528 to
  1530.
False exculpatory statements, §1529.
Flight and concealment of identity,
  §1528.
Suppression, destruction or fabrication
  of evidence, §1530.

**GUILTY PLEAS.**
Admissions by defendant, §2113.
Advice to defendant before accepting,
  §607.
Conditional pleas to preserve issue for
  appellate review, §614.
Factual basis for plea, §610.
Nature of charge.
  Understanding, §608.
Penalty.
  Understanding, §609.
Plea agreements, §§611 to 613.
  Breach of agreement, §613.
  Generally, §611.
  Judge participation, §612.
Technical violations of Rule 11, §616.
Voluntariness, §606.
Withdrawal, §§617 to 619.
  After sentence, §619.
  Before sentence, §618.
  Generally, §617.
  Speedy trial act excludes delays,
    §1232.

**H**

**HABIT,** §1531.

**HANDWRITING.**
Expert testimony, §2003.
Lay witness testimony, §2001.

**HARMLESS ERROR.**
Jencks Act and Rule 26.2, §813.
Misjoinder, §919.

**HEARINGS.**
Civil contempt proceedings, §425.
Criminal contempt proceedings, §426.

**HEARINGS**—Cont'd
Grand jury proceedings.
  Closure, §410.
Judicial notice.
  Propriety of taking, §1402.
Motions to suppress.
  Appeals, §256.
  Burden of proof, §252.
  Evidentiary rules, §253.
  Right to hearing, §254.
Preliminary examination, §503.
Pretrial detention, §509.
Removal hearings, §502.

**HEARSAY.**
Admissions, §§2112 to 2116.
  Coconspirators' declarations, §2116.
  Defendant's admission, §2113.
  Defendant's adoptive admission,
    §2114.
  Generally, §2112.
  Vicarious and representative
    admission, §2115.
Attacking credibility of declarant,
  §2149.
Conduct of listeners.
  Statements to show effect on, §2105.
Confessions.
  Admissibility for purposes of
    corroborating, §303.
  Statements reduced to writing by one
    other than accused precludes
    hearsay objection, §302.
Credibility of declarant.
  Attacking and supporting, §2149.
Exceptions.
  Availability of declarant immaterial,
    §§2117 to 2136.
  See HEARSAY EXCEPTIONS,
    AVAILABILITY OF
    DECLARANT IMMATERIAL.
  Declarant unavailable, §§2137 to
    2147.
  See HEARSAY EXCEPTIONS,
    DECLARANT UNAVAILABLE.
Extrajudicial identification, §319.
Hearsay within hearsay, §2148.
Introduction, §2100.
Motions to suppress.
  Admissibility, §253.

733

**HEARSAY**—Cont'd
Non-hearsay by definition.
  Admissions, §§2112 to 2116.
    Coconspirators' declarations, §2116.
    Defendant's admissions, §2113.
    Defendant's adoptive admissions,
      §2114.
    Generally, §2112.
    Vicarious and representative
      admissions, §2115.
  Prior statement of witness, §§2108 to
    2111.
    Consistent statements, §2110.
    Generally, §2108.
    Inconsistent statements, §2109.
    Prior identification, §2111.
Non-hearsay by use, §§2104 to 2106.
  Effect on listener's conduct, §2105.
  Proof statement made, §2104.
  Res gestae, §2106.
Non-hearsay generally, §2102.
Out-of-court statements, §2101.
Preliminary examination.
  Finding of probable cause based upon,
    §503.
Prior statements of witness, §§2108 to
  2111.
  Consistent statements, §2110.
  Generally, §2108.
  Inconsistent statements, §2109.
  Pretrial identification, §2111.
Probable cause supporting search
  warrant.
  Established by, §207.
Proof that statement made, §2104.
Res gestae, §2106.
Rules states, §2100.
Search warrants.
  Probable cause established by, §207.
Supporting credibility of declarant,
  §2149.

**HEARSAY EXCEPTIONS,**
  **AVAILABILITY OF**
  **DECLARANT IMMATERIAL,**
  §§2117 to 2136.
Agent documents.
  Statements in, §2130.
Boundaries.
  Judgments as to, §2135.

**HEARSAY EXCEPTIONS,**
  **AVAILABILITY OF**
  **DECLARANT IMMATERIAL**
  —Cont'd
Boundaries—Cont'd
  Reputation, §2133.
Character.
  Reputation, §2133.
Commercial publications, §2131.
Excited utterances, §2119.
Family history.
  Judgment as to, §2135.
  Records of, §2128.
  Reputation, §2133.
General history, §2133.
  Judgment as to, §2135.
Generally, §2117.
Interest in property.
  Records of documents and statements
    in documents affecting, §2129.
Judgment of previous conviction, §2134.
Learned treatises, §2132.
Market reports, §2131.
Medical diagnosis or treatment.
  Statements for purposes of, §2121.
Mental, emotional or physical condition.
  Then existing condition, §2120.
Other exceptions, §2136.
Personal history.
  Judgment as to, §2135.
  Reputation, §2133.
Present sense impression, §2118.
Previous convictions.
  Judgment, §2134.
Public records and reports, §2125.
  Absence of public record or entry,
    §2127.
  Vital statistics records, §2126.
Recorded recollection, §2122.
Records of regularly conducted activity,
  §2123.
  Absence of entries in records, §2124.
Religious organization records.
  Marriage, baptismal and similar
    certificates, §2128.
Reputation.
  Personal or family history, boundaries
    or general history or character,
    §2133.

**HEARSAY EXCEPTIONS, AVAILABILITY OF DECLARANT IMMATERIAL**
—Cont'd
Vital statistics records, §2126.

**HEARSAY EXCEPTIONS, DECLARANT UNAVAILABLE,**
§§2137 to 2147.
Absence from hearing, §2140.
Confrontation clause of sixth amendment.
Limitations, §2139.
Death impending.
Statement under belief of, §2142.
Death of declarant, §2140.
Family history.
Statements of, §2146.
Former testimony, §2141.
Homicide.
Statements under belief of impending death, §2142.
Impending death.
Statement under belief of, §2142.
Lack of memory.
Unavailability sufficient to qualify, §2140.
Mental illness or physical infirmity, §2140.
Other exceptions, §2147.
Personal history.
Statements of, §2146.
Privileges.
Unavailability sufficient to qualify under rule, §2140.
Qualification under rule.
Unavailability sufficient to qualify, §2140.
Refusal to testify.
Unavailability sufficient to qualify, §2140.
Sixth amendment protections.
Confrontation clause limitations, §2139.
Statements against interest.
Generally, §2144.
Penal interest offered to exculpate, §2145.
Unavailability sufficient to qualify under rule, §2140.

**HEARSAY WITHIN HEARSAY,**
§2148.

**HIGH RISK DESIGNEES AND DETAINEES.**
Speedy trial act, §1236.

**HIGH SEAS OFFENSES.**
Venue, §107.

**HIGHWAY SOBRIETY CHECKPOINTS.**
Constitutionality, §228.

**HISTORY.**
Hearsay exceptions, availability of declarant immaterial.
General history, §2133.
Judgment as to, §2135.
Medical history.
Statements for purposes of medical diagnosis or treatment, §2121.
Personal or family history.
Family records, §2128.
Judgments as to, §2135.
Reputation, §2133.
Hearsay exceptions, declarant unavailable.
Family history, §2146.
Personal history, §2146.

**HOBBS ACT PROSECUTIONS.**
Venue, §106.

**HOME SEARCHES.**
Curtilage and open fields doctrine, §240.
Detention of occupants while home searched pursuant to warrant, §230.
Search incident to lawful arrest.
Areas within arrestee's immediate control, §226.

**HOMICIDE.**
Hearsay exceptions, declarant unavailable.
Statements under belief of impending death, §2142.

**HOSTILE WITNESSES.**
Leading questions permitted, §1801.

**HOT PURSUIT, §234.**

**HUNG JURIES.**
Allen charge, §1261.

**HUSBAND-WIFE PRIVILEGE.**
Generally, §§1909 to 1914.
  See MARITAL COMMUNICATIONS
    PRIVILEGE.

**HYPOTHETICAL QUESTIONS.**
Experts, §2006.


**I**


**IDENTIFICATION OF
   INFORMANTS, §713.**
Government privilege, §1923.

**IDENTIFICATIONS BEFORE
   TRIAL, §§316 to 319.**
Extrajudicial identification, §319.
Fifth amendment due process rights,
  §318.
Generally, §316.
Imperissively suggestive, §318.
Non-hearsay by definition, §2111.
Sixth amendment rights, §317.

**IDENTITIES OF WITNESSES.**
Discovery, §712.

**IDENTITY OF DEFENDANT.**
Concealment.
  Evidence admissible to prove
    consciousness of guilt, §1528.
Proof of other crimes to established,
  §1525.

**ILLEGAL ARREST.**
Jurisdiction over person of defendant,
  §103.

**ILLEGALLY OBTAINED
   EVIDENCE.**
Exclusionary rule, §248.

**IMMIGRATION AND
   NATIONALITY ACT.**
Border searches, §229.

**IMMUNITY OF WITNESSES, §§419
  to 423.**
Act reflects use and derivative use
  immunity, §419.
Civil proceeding use, §422.
Contempt to force orders compelling
  testimony, §§424 to 426.
Defense witnesses immunity, §423.
Generally, §419.

**IMMUNITY OF WITNESSES—Cont'd**
Jury instructions on immunized
  witnesses, §1270.
Limited grant of immunity compelled
  under threat of imprisonment, §419.
Notice and hearing on immunity
  request.
  Witnesses not entitled, §419.
Other sovereigns.
  Grant of immunity.
    Recognition requirements, §421.
Perjury prosecutions.
  Use of compelled testimony in, §420.
Use immunity statutes application to
  past offenses, §420.

**IMPEACHMENT OF VERDICT.**
Post-verdict juror interrogation, §1259.

**IMPEACHMENT OF WITNESSES.**
Brady doctrine.
  Disclosure of impeachment material,
    §722.
  Generally, §§718 to 724.
  See BRADY DOCTRINE.
Character evidence, §1808.
Exclusionary rule evidence, §1818.
Hearsay declarants.
  Attacking generally, §2149.
Insanity, §1815.
Narcotics addiction, §1815.
Own witness, §1807.
Prior inconsistent statements, §1813.
Prior misconduct and other crimes,
  §1809.
  Evidence showing witness bias, §1811.
  Probative value versus prejudicial
    effect, §1810.
Silence used to impeach credibility,
  §1818.
Statements taken in violation of fifth
  and sixth amendments, §311.

**IMPENDING DEATH.**
Hearsay exceptions, declarant
  unavailable.
  Statement under belief of, §2142.

**IMPOUNDED AUTOMOBILES.**
Inventory searches, §236.

**IMPRISONMENT.**
Sentencing generally, §§1306 to 1346.
    See SENTENCING.

**INCOMPETENCY.**
Speedy trial act.
    Exclusion of delay caused by physical
        or mental incompetency, §1229.

**INDICTMENTS.**
Confessions obtained after, §310.
Duplicity, §905.
Grand jury generally, §§400 to 427.
    See GRAND JURY.
Multiple counts.
    Joinder of offenses, §903.
Multiple indictments.
    Joinder of offenses, §904.
Multiplicity, §905.
Sealed indictments, §417.

**INFERENCES.**
Failure of defendant to testify, §1515.
Failure to call witness, §1514.
Lay witness testimony, §2001.
Presumptions generally.
    See PRESUMPTIONS.
Recent possession of fruits of crime,
    §1513.
Self-incrimination privilege, §1907.

**INFLAMMATORY COMMENTS.**
Closing argument errors by prosecutors,
    §1111.
Opening statement errors by
    prosecutors, §1105.

**INFORMANTS.**
Disclosure of identities of informants,
    §713.
    Government privilege, §1923.
Probable cause for search warrant.
    Establishing, §207.

**INITIAL APPEARANCE,** §501.
Confessions.
    Confession after arrest but before
        appearance, §304.

**IN-LAW PRIVILEGE,** §1924.

**INNOCENCE.**
Jury instructions on presumption of,
    §1269.
Presumptions, §1507.

**INSANITY AS GROUNDS FOR
    IMPEACHMENT,** §1815.

**INSANITY DEFENSE.**
Burden of proof, §§1501, 1508.
Notice, §703.

**INSANITY PRESUMPTION,** §1508.

**INSPECTION.**
Discovery generally.
    See DISCOVERY.

**INSTRUCTIONS TO JURY.**
See JURY INSTRUCTIONS.

**INSUFFICIENCY OF EVIDENCE.**
Motion for acquittal.
    Generally, §§1271 to 1276.
        See MOTION FOR ACQUITTAL.

**INTENT.**
Presumptions, §1509.
Proof of other crimes to established,
    §1524.

**INTERCEPTION OF ORAL OR
    WIRE COMMUNICATIONS.**
Wiretapping and other electronic
    surveillance generally, §§257 to 268.
See WIRETAPPING AND
    ELECTRONIC SURVEILLANCE.

**INTEREST IN PROPERTY.**
Hearsay exception, availability of
    declarant immaterial.
    Records of documents and statements
        in documents affecting, §2129.

**INTERNATIONAL LAWS.**
Judicial notice of principles and
    traditions, §1403.

**INTERPRETERS.**
Use during examination of witnesses,
    §1820.

**INTERROGATION OF JUROR.**
Post-verdict, §1259.

**INTERROGATORIES.**
Special interrogatories to jury, §1258.

**INTERSTATE AGREEMENT ON
    DETAINERS.**
Speedy trial act, §1233.

**INTERSTATE COMMERCE.**
Offenses.
  Venue, §106.

**INVADING PROVINCE OF COURT.**
Closing argument errors by prosecutors.
  Statement of law, §1113.

**INVENTORY SEARCHES OF VEHICLE,** §236.

**INVESTIGATIONS AND PRESENTENCE REPORTS,** §§1316 to 1318.

**INVESTIGATIVE DETENTION.**
Occupants while home searched
  pursuant to warrant, §230.
Stop and frisk, §228.

**INVITED RESPONSE RULE.**
Prosecutorial response to defense
  provocations, §1112.

**J**

**JENCKS ACT AND RULE 26.2,** §§801 to 814.
Court's obligation, §805.
Defense witnesses rule, §814.
Destruction of statements or notes, §812.
Documents subject to production
  generally, §808.
Generally, §801.
Harmless error rule, §813.
Material of defense witness, §814.
Motion by defense counsel, §803.
Motions to suppress.
  Disclosure of materials, §253.
Obligation of trial court, §805.
Possession of United States, §806.
Purposes of act and rule, §801.
Refusal to produce generally, §811.
Relation to witness' direct testimony,
  §807.
Request by defense counsel, §803.
Substantially verbatim and
  contemporaneously made
  documents, §810.
Time for production, §804.
Written, signed, adopted or approved
  documents by witnesses, §809.

**JEOPARDY,** §§1001 to 1006.
Acquittals, §1006.
Appeals.
  Denial of pretrial motions, §1010.
  Re-prosecution after successful appeal
    by defendant, §1010.
Burden of proof, §1001.
Collateral estoppel, §1011.
Dismissals, §1006.
Dual sovereigns, §1004.
Generally, §1001.
Lesser included offenses, §1003.
Mistrial, §1007.
  Manifest necessity, §1008.
  Prosecutorial manipulation to abort
    trial, §1009.
Petite policy, §1005.
Probation revocation, §1012.
Re-prosecution after successful appeal by
  defendant, §1010.
Same offense, §1002.
Sentencing imposed harsher on retrial
  conviction, §1012.
Suspension of sentence revoked, §1012.
Waiver, §1001.
When jeopardy attaches, §1001.

**JOINDER OF DEFENDANTS.**
Consolidation for trial, §906.
Conspiracy, §909.
Generally, §§901, 906.
Misjoinder, §919.
Same indictments, §907.
Severance as relief from prejudicial
  joinder.
  See SEVERANCE.
Speedy trial act excludes delay caused
  by, §1230.

**JOINDER OF OFFENSES.**
Duplicity, §905.
Generally, §§901, 902.
Misjoinder, §919.
Multiple counts, §903.
Multiple indictments, §904.
Multiplicity, §905.
Severance as relief from prejudicial
  joinder.
  See SEVERANCE.

**JOINT STOCK COMPANIES.**
Sentencing of organizations, §1340.

**JOINT TRIALS.**
Confessions used at, §314.
Joinder of defendants.
  See JOINDER OF DEFENDANTS.

**JUDGES OF STATE COURTS.**
Search warrants.
  Issuance by, §205.

**JUDGMENT OF CONVICTION,**
  §1342.

**JUDGMENT OF FORFEITURE,**
  §1324.

**JUDICIAL ADMISSIONS, §2113.**

**JUDICIAL NOTICE, §§1400 to 1403.**
Adjudicative facts, §1401.
Introduction, §1400.
Matters to be noticed, §1403.
Procedure, §1402.
Venue determination, §108.

**JURISDICTION.**
Defined, §101.
Generally, §101.
Person of the defendant, §103.
Subject matter jurisdiction, §102.

**JURY INSTRUCTIONS.**
Accuracy, §1264.
Allen charge, §1261.
Cautionary instructions, §1252.
Circumstantial evidence, §1516.
Instructions on law, §§1264 to 1270.
  Contents of charge generally, §1264.
  Credibility issues, §1270.
  Defense theories, §1266.
  Lesser included offenses, §1265.
  Presumptions, §1269.
  Reasonable doubt, §1268.
Layman's language request.
  Supplemental charges, §1260.
Limiting instructions, §1252.
Missing witness inference, §1514.
New trial for incorrect charge to jury,
  §1303.
Objections, §1254.
Presumption jurors properly followed,
  §1512.
Repetition, §1264.

**JURY INSTRUCTIONS—Cont'd**
Requests for, §1253.
Summary chart nature and use, §1605.
Supplemental instructions, §1260.
Venue.
  Burden of proof, §108.
Waiver of objections, §1254.

**JURY QUESTIONS.**
Venue, §108.

**JURY SELECTION AND SERVICE**
  **ACT.**
Jury selection generally, §§1244 to 1250.
  See JURY TRIAL.

**JURY TRIAL.**
Communications with jurors during
  trial, §1249.
Discharge of jury.
  Motion for acquittal after, §1276.
Instructions to jurors.
  See JURY INSTRUCTIONS.
Interrogation of juror.
  Post-verdict, §1259.
Materials in jury room, §1250.
Polling jurors, §1262.
Right to trial by jury, §1240.
Selection of jury, §§1244 to 1250.
  Challenge of array, §1245.
  Challenges for cause, §1247.
  Contamination by trial participants,
    §1249.
  Generally, §1244.
  Materials in jury room, §1250.
  Peremptory challenges, §1248.
  Voir dire, §1246.
Size of jury, §1241.
Special interrogatories, §1258.
Verdict.
  Polling jurors, §1262.
  Post-verdict juror interrogation, §1259.
  Special interrogatories to, §1258.
  Special verdicts, §1256.
    Criminal forfeiture special verdicts,
      §1257.
  Unanimous jury verdict, §1242.
Waiver, §1243.

**JURY VIEW OF PREMISES, §1611.**

**JUVENILE DELINQUENCY ACT.**
Confessions made during unnecessary delay in initial appearance, §304.

**JUVENILE OFFENDERS.**
Sentencing, §1341.

**K**

**KER-FRISBIE DOCTRINE.**
Personal jurisdiction of defendant gives court complete jurisdiction, §103.

**KIDNAPPING ON HIGH SEAS.**
Venue, §107.

**KNOCK AND ANNOUNCE REQUIREMENTS.**
Manner of entry to search, §215.

**KNOWLEDGE.**
Proof of other crimes to established, §1524.

**KNOWLEDGE OF LAW.**
Presumptions, §1511.

**L**

**LAY WITNESS TESTIMONY, §2001.**

**LEADING QUESTIONS, §1801.**

**LEARNED TREATISES.**
Hearsay exceptions, availability of declarant immaterial, §2132.

**LEGITIMACY ON THE PREMISES EXCEPTION.**
Standing to challenge evidence obtained in illegal search and seizure, §255.

**LEGITIMACY RECORDS.**
Hearsay exception, availability of declarant immaterial.
Records of religious organizations, §2128.

**LESSER INCLUDED OFFENSES.**
Double jeopardy, §1003.
Jury instructions on, §1265.

**LETTERS WRITTEN BY DEFENDANTS.**
Discovery of statements of defendants, §706.

**LIMITING INSTRUCTIONS, §1252.**

**LINEUPS.**
Identifications before trial generally, §§316 to 319.
See IDENTIFICATIONS BEFORE TRIAL.

**LOITERING STATUTES.**
Unconstitutionally vague statute, §228.

**M**

**MAGISTRATES.**
Search warrants.
Issuance by, §205.
Neutrality in probable cause determinations, §209.

**MAIL.**
Venue of offenses involving use of, §106.

**MALLORY RULE.**
Confessions made during unnecessary delay in initial appearance, §304.

**MANDATORY PRESUMPTIONS.**
Constitutionality, §1505.

**MANSLAUGHTER.**
Place offense deemed to have been committed, §101.

**MARITAL COMMUNICATIONS PRIVILEGE, §§1909 to 1914.**
Adverse testimony privilege, §1910.
Confidential communications privilege, §1911.
Exceptions, §1914.
Existence of marriage required, §1912.
Generally, §1909.
Objections, §1913.
Waivers, §1913.

**MARITIME JURISDICTION, §101.**

**MARKET REPORTS.**
Hearsay exceptions, availability of declarant immaterial, §2131.

**MARRIAGE RECORDS.**
Hearsay exception, availability of declarant immaterial.
Records of religious organizations, §2128.

**MATERIAL WITNESSES.**
Release, §520.

**MEDICAL DIAGNOSIS OR TREATMENT.**
Hearsay exceptions, availability of declarant immaterial.
Statements for purposes of, §2121.

**MEDICAL HISTORY.**
Statements for purposes of medical diagnosis or treatment.
Hearsay exception, availability of declarant immaterial, §2121.

**MENTAL CAPACITY.**
Expert testimony, §2003.
Lay witness testimony, §2001.

**MENTAL CONDITION.**
Hearsay exception, availability of declarant immaterial.
Then existing mental condition, §2120.
Notice of defense based upon, §703.

**MENTAL DISEASE OR DEFECT.**
Insanity defense generally.
See INSANITY DEFENSE.

**MENTAL EXAMINATIONS.**
Discovery of reports of examinations and tests, §709.
Motion by government to order defendant to submit to psychiatric or psychological examination, §703.

**MENTAL ILLNESS AS GROUNDS FOR IMPEACHMENT**, §1815.

**MILITARY TRIBUNALS.**
In applicability of speedy trial act, §1211.

**MINORITY GROUPS.**
Peremptory challenges used to exclude, §1248.

**MIRANDA WARNINGS.**
Confessions and rights to silence and counsel, §§305 to 311.
Confessions obtained after indictment, §310.
Generally, §305.

**MIRANDA WARNINGS**—Cont'd
Confessions and rights to silence and counsel—Cont'd
Impeachment with statements taken in violation of fifth and sixth amendments, §311.
Right to terminate questioning, §308.
Scope of Miranda, §307.
Silence of defendant, §309.
When rights attach, §306.
Consent to search.
Voluntariness, §243.
Grand jury witnesses, §405.
Silence of defendant, §309.
Statement of warnings, §305.
Volunteered statements, §306.
When rights attach, §306.

**MISCONDUCT OF PROSECUTOR.**
Generally, §§1101 to 1117.
See PROSECUTORIAL MISCONDUCT.

**MISJOINDER**, §919.

**MISLEADING TESTIMONY.**
Prosecutorial misconduct.
Obtaining conviction with aid of, §1107.

**MISREPRESENTATION.**
Use to secure consent to search, §244.

**MISSING WITNESS INFERENCE**, §1514.

**MISTRIAL**, §1007.
Manifest necessity, §1008.
Prosecutorial manipulation to abort trial, §1009.

**MITIGATING CIRCUMSTANCES.**
Departure from sentencing guidelines, §1324.

**MODELS.**
Admissibility, §1607.

**MODIFICATION OF SENTENCE AFTER IMPOSITION**, §1344.

**MOTION FOR ARREST OF JUDGMENT**, §1305.

**MOTION FOR BILL OF PARTICULARS**, §701.

**MOTION FOR NEW TRIAL,** §§1301 to 1304.
Generally, §1301.
Newly discovered evidence, §1302.
Other grounds, §1303.
Time for, §1304.

**MOTION FOR TRANSFER OF VENUE,** §110.

**MOTION OF ACQUITTAL,** §§1271 to 1276.
Burden of proof, §1502.
Ground, §1272.
Time for making, §1273.
   Close of all evidence, §1275.
   Close of government's case, §1274.
   Discharge of jury, §1276.

**MOTION PICTURES.**
Admissibility, §1603.

**MOTIONS PRETRIAL.**
Speedy trial act excludes delays caused by, §1223.

**MOTIONS TO SUPPRESS,** §§250 to 256.
Appeals, §256.
Burden of proof, §252.
Electronic surveillance fruits, §266.
Evidentiary rules, §253.
Right to hearing, §254.
Standing, §255.
Timing, §250.

**MOTION TO WITHDRAW GUILTY PLEA OR NOLO CONTENDERE,** §617.

**MOTIVE,** 1532.
Proof of other crimes to established, §1523.

**MOTOR VEHICLE SEARCHES.**
Areas within arrestee's immediate control, §226.
Containers found in vehicle, §237.
Inventory searches, §236.
Stop and frisk principles, §228.
Vehicle searches generally, §235.

**MUGSHOTS,** §319.
Identifications before trial generally, §§316 to 319.
  See IDENTIFICATIONS BEFORE TRIAL.

**MULTIPLE COUNTS.**
Joinder, §903.

**MULTIPLE INDICTMENTS.**
Joinder of offenses, §904.

**MULTIPLICITY.**
Charging single offense in separate counts, §905.

**MULTISPECIFICATION COUNTS.**
Burden of proof, §1503.

**MURDER.**
Place offense deemed to have been committed, §101.

### N

**NAMES OF WITNESSES.**
Discovery, §712.

**NARCOTICS ADDICTION AS GROUNDS FOR IMPEACHMENT,** §1815.

**NARCOTICS ADDICTION REHABILITATION ACT.**
Speedy trial act excludes delays resulting from proceedings, §1220.

**NATURAL AND PROBABLE CONSEQUENCES OF ACTS.**
Presumptions, §1509.

**NATURE OF CHARGE.**
Understanding as requirement for accepting guilty plea or nolo contendere, §608.

**NEWLY DISCOVERED EVIDENCE.**
Motion for new trial, §1302.

**NEWS MEDIA.**
Reporter-source privilege, §1922.

**NEW TRIAL.**
Motion, §§1301 to 1304.
  Generally, §1301.
  Newly discovered evidence, §1302.
  Other grounds, §1303.

**NEW TRIAL**—Cont'd
Motion—Cont'd
Time for motion, §1304.
Release pending appeal, §518.

**NIGHTTIME SEARCHES.**
When warrants to be executed, §214.

**NO KNOCK RULE.**
Exigent circumstances in executing
    search warrant, §215.

**NOLO CONTENDERE,** §604.
Advice to defendant generally, §607.
Conditional pleas to preserve issue for
    appellate review, §614.
Factual basis for plea, §610.
Nature of charge.
    Understanding, §608.
Penalty.
    Understanding, §609.
Plea agreements, §611 to 613.
    Breach of agreements, §613.
    Generally, §611.
    Judge participation, §612.
Voluntariness, §606.
Withdrawal, §§617 to 619.
    After sentence, §619.
    Before sentence, §618.
    Generally, §617.
    Speedy trial act excludes delays,
        §1232.

**NON-PROFIT ORGANIZATIONS.**
Sentencing, §1340.

**NOTICE.**
Alibi, §702.
Appeals.
    Defendant right to appeal, §1345.
Civil contempt proceedings, §425.
Criminal contempt proceedings, §426.
Insanity defense or defense based upon
    mental condition, §703.
Judicial notice, §§1400 to 1403.
    See JUDICIAL NOTICE.
Public authority.
    Defense based upon, §704.
Victims notice.
    Defendants found guilty of offenses
        involving fraud or deceptive
        practices, §1338.

**O**

**OBJECTIONS TO INSTRUCTIONS,**
    §1254.

**OBSTRUCTION OF JUSTICE.**
Venue, §105.

**OFFENSES COMMITTED IN MORE
    THAN ONE DISTRICT.**
Venue, §106.

**OFFENSES COMMITTED WHILE
    ON RELEASE.**
Penalty for, §522.

**OFFENSES NOT COMMITTED IN
    ANY DISTRICT.**
Venue, §107.

**OFFICIAL DOCUMENTS.**
Authentication and admissibility
    generally, §1702.

**OMNIBUS CRIME AND CONTROL
    AND SAFE STREETS ACT OF
    1968.**
Title III.
    Wiretapping and other electronic
        surveillance generally, §§257 to
        268.
        See WIRETAPPING AND
            ELECTRONIC
            SURVEILLANCE.

**ON-THE-SCENE
    IDENTIFICATIONS.**
Identifications before trial generally,
    §§316 to 319.
    See IDENTIFICATIONS BEFORE
        TRIAL.

**OPEN-ENDED SEARCH
    WARRANTS.**
Prohibited, §211.

**OPEN FIELDS DOCTRINE,** §240.

**OPENING STATEMENT.**
Prosecutorial misconduct, §§1102 to
    1105.
    Argumentative and inflammatory
        comments, §1105.
    Generally, §1102.
    Inadmissible evidence references,
        §1103.

**OPENING STATEMENT**—Cont'd
Prosecutorial misconduct—Cont'd
Personal opinion statements, §1104.

**OPINION EVIDENCE.**
Expert witness testimony, §§2003 to
 2007.
 Basis of opinion, §2004.
 Court-appointed experts, §2007.
 Hypothetical questions, §2006.
 Scientific, technical or specialized
  knowledge, §2003.
 Ultimate issue rule, §2005.
Impeachment of witness.
 Use of character evidence, §1808.
Lay witness testimony, §2001.
Methods of proving character, §1519.

**ORDERS OF COURT.**
Interception of communications pursuant
 to court order, §§258 to 267.
 See WIRETAPPING AND
  ELECTRONIC SURVEILLANCE.
Pretrial release or detention order,
 §511.
 Appeal, §512.
Protective orders.
 Discovery, §715.

**ORGANIZATIONS.**
Self-incrimination privilege.
 Production of books of organization,
  §1902.
Sentencing of, §1340.

**ORGANIZED CRIME CONTROL
 ACT OF 1970.**
Immunity of witnesses generally, §§419
 to 423.
 See IMMUNITY OF WITNESSES.

**OTHER CRIMES.**
Impeachment of witnesses.
 Prior misconduct and other crimes,
  §1809.
  Evidence showing witness bias,
   §1811.
  Probative value versus prejudicial
   effect, §1810.
Proof, §§1521 to 1526.
 See PROOF OF OTHER CRIMES.

**OVERLAYS.**
Admissibility, §1608.

**P**

**PAROLE.**
Accepting guilty pleas or nolo
 contendere.
 Informing defendant as to special
  parole, §609.

**PARTIES.**
Transfer of venue for convenience of,
 §112.

**PARTNERSHIPS.**
Self-incrimination privilege.
 Production of books of organization,
  §1902.
Sentencing of organizations, §1340.

**PAST RECOLLECTION
 RECORDED,** §2122.

**PENAL INTEREST.**
Statements against offered to exculpate,
 §2145.

**PEN REGISTERS.**
Not wiretaps, §267.

**PENSION FUNDS.**
Sentencing of organizations, §1340.

**PEREMPTORY CHALLENGES.**
Jury selection, §1248.

**PERJURY.**
Immunity of witnesses.
 Use of compelled testimony in, §420.
Prosecutorial misconduct.
 Obtaining conviction with aid of false
  or misleading testimony, §1107.
Self-incrimination.
 Privilege not used as license to lie,
  §1903.

**PERMISSIVE PRESUMPTIONS.**
Constitutionality, §1505.

**PERSONAL HISTORY.**
Hearsay exceptions, availability of
 declarant immaterial.
 Judgment as to, §2135.
 Reputation, §2133.
Hearsay exceptions, declarant
 unavailable.
 Statements of, §2146.

**PERSONAL JURISDICTION,** §103.

**PERSONAL OPINION OF PROSECUTOR.**
Closing argument errors, §1114.
Opening statement errors, §1104.

**PETITE POLICY,** §1005.

**PETIT JURY.**
Jury selection generally.
See JURY TRIAL.

**PETTY OFFENSES.**
Exempted from constitutional dictates of jury trial, §1240.
In applicability of speedy trial act, §1211.

**PHOTO ARRAYS.**
Identifications before trial generally, §§316 to 319.
See IDENTIFICATIONS BEFORE TRIAL.

**PHOTOGRAPHS.**
Admissibility, §1604.
Expert testimony, §2003.
Lay witness testimony as to identification of person in, §2001.
Overlays.
Admissibility, §1608.

**PHYSICAL CONDITION.**
Hearsay exception, availability of declarant immaterial.
Then existing condition, §2120.
Lay witness testimony, §2001.

**PHYSICAL EXAMINATIONS.**
Discovery of reports of examinations and tests, §709.

**PHYSICAL INCOMPETENCY.**
Speedy trial act excludes delay caused by, §1229.

**PHYSICIAN-PATIENT PRIVILEGE,** §1921.

**PLAIN ERROR RULE.**
Exception to rule requiring objection to preserve record, §1254.

**PLAIN VIEW EVIDENCE.**
Abandoned property.
Searches and seizures, §239.
Curtilage and open fields doctrine, §240.

**PLAIN VIEW EVIDENCE—Cont'd**
Offices responding to emergency.
Seizure of evidence in plain view, §232.
Warrantless searches generally, §238.

**PLAN.**
Proof of other crimes, §1526.

**PLEA BARGAINING.**
Breach of agreement, §613.
Generally, §611.
Inadmissibility of pleas and plea discussions, §615.
Judge participation, §612.
Sentencing reform act plea agreements, §§1313 to 1315.
Generally, §1313.
Procedure, §1314.
Standards for acceptance, §1315.
Speedy trial act excludes delays caused by plea agreement, §1225.
Statements relating to offers of pleas.
Inadmissibility, §315.

**PLEAS,** §§602 to 619.
Allowed pleas, §602.
Conditional pleas, §§256, 614.
Confession.
Inadmissibility of statements relating to, §315.
Generally, §602.
Guilty pleas.
Admissions by defendant, §2113.
Effect, §603.
Technical violations of Rule 11, §616.
Inadmissibility of pleas and plea discussions, §615.
Nolo contendere, §604.
Plea agreements, §§611 to 613.
Breach of agreement, §613.
Generally, §611.
Judge participation, §612.
Requirements for accepting guilty pleas or nolo contendere, §§605 to 610.
Advice to defendant generally, §607.
Factual basis for plea, §610.
Understanding nature of charge, §608.
Understanding penalties, §609.
Voluntariness of plea, §606.
Right to counsel, §602.

**PLEAS**—Cont'd
Technical violations of Rule 11, §616.
Venue transfer for plea and sentence, §113.
Withdrawal of guilty plea or nolo contendere.
  Generally, §617.
  Speedy trial act excludes delays, §1232.
  Withdrawal after sentencing, §619.
  Withdrawal before sentencing, §618.

**POLITICAL SUBDIVISIONS.**
Sentencing, §1340.

**POLLING JURORS,** §1262.

**POSSESSION OF FRUITS OF CRIME.**
Permissible inference as to recent possession, §1513.

**POST-INDICTMENT CONFESSIONS,** §310.

**POST-VERDICT JUROR INTERROGATION,** §1259.

**PRE-ACCUSATION DELAYS.**
Unreasonable delays, §1239.

**PREJUDICE.**
Expert testimony, §2003.
Prior misconduct and other crimes used to impeach, §1810.
Severance as relief from prejudicial joinder generally.
  See SEVERANCE.
Speedy trial protection.
  Prejudice caused by delay, §1209.
Transfer of venue, §111.

**PRELIMINARY EXAMINATION,** §503.
Removal hearings, §502.

**PRELIMINARY PROCEEDINGS.**
Arraignment, §601.
Bail, §504.
Failure to appear, §521.
Initial appearance, §501.
Offenses committed while on release, §522.
Preliminary examination, §503.

**PRELIMINARY PROCEEDINGS**
  —Cont'd
Pretrial release or retention, §§506 to 512.
Release during trial, §513.
Release of material witnesses, §520.
Release or detention after conviction, §§515 to 519.
Removal hearings, §502.

**PREPONDERANCE OF EVIDENCE.**
False statements in affidavit for search warrants, §210.
Proving venue, §108.
Warrantless searches.
  Search within exception to warrant requirement, §217.

**PRESENCE OF DEFENDANT.**
Arraignment, §601.
Voir dire, §1246.

**PRESENTENCE INVESTIGATION AND REPORT,** §§1316 to 1318.
Contents, §1317.
Disclosure, §1318.
Disputed sentencing fact resolution, §1339.
Generally, §1316.
Victim impact statements part of, §1337.

**PRESENT RECOLLECTION REVIVED,** §2122.

**PRESENT SENSE IMPRESSION.**
Hearsay exceptions, availability of declarant immaterial, §2118.

**PRESUMPTIONS.**
Affidavits supporting search warrants.
  Validity, §210.
Conclusive presumptions.
  Constitutionality, §1505.
Conspiracy continuance, §1510.
Constitutionality, §1505.
Defined, §1504.
Failure of defendant to testify, §1515.
Failure to call witness, §1514.
Generally, §1504.
Grand jury.
  Regularity of proceedings, §403.
Innocence, §1507.
  Jury instructions on, §1269.

**PRESUMPTIONS—Cont'd**
Intent, §1509.
Juror contacts during trial, §1249.
Jury instructions, §1269.
Knowledge of law, §1511.
Mandatory presumptions.
　Constitutionality, §1505.
Natural and probable consequences of
　acts, §1509.
Permissive presumptions.
　Constitutionality, §1505.
Pretrial detention, §509.
Regularity of proceedings, §1512.
Sanity, §1508.
Search warrants.
　Validity of affidavits supporting, §210.

**PRETRIAL DISCLOSURE.**
See DISCLOSURE.

**PRETRIAL DISCOVERY.**
See DISCOVERY.

**PRETRIAL DIVERSION.**
Speedy trial act excludes delays, §1227.

**PRETRIAL IDENTIFICATION, §§316
　to 319.**
See IDENTIFICATIONS BEFORE
　TRIAL.

**PRETRIAL PUBLICITY.**
Transfer of venue because of prejudice,
　§111.

**PRETRIAL RELEASE OR
　DETENTION.**
Generally, §§506 to 512.
　See BAIL.

**PREVIOUS CONVICTIONS.**
Hearsay exceptions, availability of
　declarant immaterial.
　Judgment, §2134.

**PRIOR CONSISTENT
　STATEMENTS.**
Non-hearsay by definition, §2110.

**PRIOR INCONSISTENT
　STATEMENTS.**
Affirmative evidence, §1814.
Impeachment, §1813.
Non-hearsay by definition, §2109.

**PRIOR MISCONDUCT AND OTHER
　CRIMES.**
Impeachment of witnesses, §1809.
Proof of other crimes.
　See PROOF OF OTHER CRIMES.

**PRIOR STATEMENTS.**
Inconsistent statements.
　Affirmative evidence, §1814.
　Impeachment, §1813.
　Non-hearsay by definition, §2109.
Non-hearsay by definition, §§2108 to
　2111.
　Consistent statements, §2110.
　Generally, §2108.
　Inconsistent statements, §2109.
　Pretrial identification, §2111.
Trial discovery generally, §§801 to 814.
　See JENCKS ACT AND RULE 26.2.

**PRISON SEARCHES, §242.**

**PRIVACY RIGHT PROTECTIONS.**
Searches and seizures generally, §§201
　to 256.
　See SEARCHES AND SEIZURES.
Wiretapping and other electronic
　surveillance generally, §§257 to 268.
　See WIRETAPPING AND
　　ELECTRONIC SURVEILLANCE.

**PRIVATE OR NONOFFICIAL
　DOCUMENTS.**
Authentication or admissibility, §1703.

**PRIVATE SEARCHES, §202.**

**PRIVATE SECURITY GUARDS.**
Miranda warnings need not be given by,
　§306.

**PRIVILEGE AGAINST SELF-
　INCRIMINATION.**
See SELF-INCRIMINATION.

**PRIVILEGED COMMUNICATIONS.**
Generally, §§1908 to 1922.
　See PRIVILEGES.

**PRIVILEGES.**
Accountant-client privilege, §1924.
Attorney-client privilege, §§1915 to
　1919.
　Communication by client for legal
　　services, §1918.

**PRIVILEGES**—Cont'd
Attorney-client privilege—Cont'd
　Communication with lawyer, §1917.
　Generally, §1915.
　Privilege holder must be client, §1916.
　Waiver, §1919.
Emancipated child-parent privilege,
　§1924.
Hearsay exceptions, declarant
　unavailable.
　Unavailability sufficient to qualify
　　under rule, §2140.
Informants identities.
　Government privilege, §1923.
In-law privilege, §1924.
Marital communications privilege,
　§§1909 to 1914.
　Adverse testimony.
　　Privilege, §1910.
　Confidential communications, §1911.
　Exceptions, §1914.
　Existence of marriage, §1912.
　Generally, §1909.
　Objection and waiver, §1913.
Other privileges generally, §1924.
Physician-patient privilege, §1921.
Privileged communications generally,
　§1908.
Prosecutorial misconduct.
　Forcing claim of, §1109.
Psychotherapist-patient privilege, §1924.
Reporter-source privilege, §1922.
Scholar's privilege, §1924.
Self-incrimination.
　See SELF-INCRIMINATION.
Sibling privilege, §1924.
Work-product doctrine, §1920.

**PROBABLE CAUSE.**
Arrest, §219.
Preliminary examination, §503.
Search warrants, §206.
　Established by hearsay, §207.
　False statements in affidavit, §210.
　Neutrality of magistrate, §209.
　Sufficiency determination, §208.
Seizures without probable cause, §§227
　to 230.
Wiretap authorization.
　Application for, §261.

**PROBATION,** §1329.
Double jeopardy not bar to revocation,
　§1012.

**PROBATIVE VALUE.**
Prior misconduct and other crimes used
　to impeach, §1810.

**PROCEEDINGS UNDER
ADVISEMENT.**
Speedy trial act excludes delays caused
　by, §1226.

**PRODUCTION OF DOCUMENTS
AND TANGIBLE OBJECTS,**
　§708.
Disclosure of evidence by defendants,
　§710.
Jencks Act and Rule 26.2.
　Generally, §§801 to 814.
　　See JENCKS ACT AND RULE
　　26.2.
Self-incrimination privilege, §1902.
Subpoenas, §717.

**PROOF OF OTHER CRIMES,** §§1521
　to 1526.
Identity of defendant, §1525.
Impeachment of witnesses.
　Prior misconduct and other crimes,
　　§1809.
　Evidence showing witness bias,
　　§1811.
　Probative value versus prejudicial
　　effect, §1810.
Intent and knowledge, §1524.
Motive, §1523.
Plan, scheme or design, §1526.
Prerequisites, §1522.
Rule of evidence stated, §1521.

**PROPAGANDA THEMES.**
Expert testimony, §2003.

**PROSECUTORIAL MISCONDUCT,**
　§§1102 to 1117.
Appeals.
　Standard for review, §1116.
Closing argument errors, §§1110 to
　1115.
　Defense provocation responses, §1112.
　Generally, §1110.
　Inflammatory comments, §1111.

**PROSECUTORIAL MISCONDUCT**
—Cont'd
Closing argument errors—Cont'd
Invading province of court, §1113.
Invited response by defense
provocations, §1112.
Personal opinion statement, §1114.
Purposes, §1110.
Reasonable inferences, §1111.
Silence post-arrest and in-trial
comments on, §1115.
Statement of law, §1113.
Double jeopardy.
Prosecutorial manipulation to abort
trial, §1009.
False or misleading testimony, §1107.
Favorable defense evidence undiscovered
and undisclosed, §1108.
Introduction, §1100.
Mistrial.
Prosecutorial manipulation to abort
trial, §1009.
New trial.
Grounds for motion, §1303.
Opening statement errors, §§1102 to
1105.
Argumentative and inflammatory
comments, §1105.
Generally, §1102.
Inadmissible evidence references,
§1103.
Personal opinion statements, §1104.
Purposes of opening statement, §1102.
Privilege.
Forcing claim of, §1109.
Review standards, §1116.
Sanctions, §1117.

**PROSECUTORIAL
VINDICTIVENESS,** §1118.
Introduction, §1100.

**PROTECTIVE ORDERS.**
Discovery, §715.

**PSYCHIATRIC OR
PSYCHOLOGICAL
EXAMINATIONS.**
Discovery of reports of examinations and
tests, §709.

**PSYCHIATRIC OR
PSYCHOLOGICAL
EXAMINATIONS**—Cont'd
Motion by government to order
defendant to submit to, §703.

**PSYCHOLOGICAL PRESSURES.**
Confessions based on, §313.

**PSYCHOTHERAPIST-PATIENT
PRIVILEGE,** §1924.

**PUBLIC AUTHORITY.**
Notice of defense based upon, §704.

**PUBLICITY.**
Transfer of venue because of prejudice,
§111.

**PUBLIC RECORDS AND
DOCUMENTS.**
Authentication and admissibility of
official documents generally, §1702.
Hearsay exception, availability of
declarant immaterial.
Absence of record or entry, §2127.
Generally, §2125.
Vital statistics, §2126.

**PUBLIC SCHOOL OFFICIALS.**
Searches conducted by, §217.

**R**

**RACIAL BIAS.**
Voir dire questioning, §1246.

**REAL OFFENSE SENTENCING,**
§1310.

**REASONABLE DOUBT.**
Criminal contempt proceedings, §426.
Jury instructions, §1268.
Proof beyond reasonable doubt, §426.
Proving venue, §108.

**REBUTTAL EVIDENCE.**
Character witnesses, §1520.
Exclusionary rule of evidence, §1818.
Generally, §1816.
Scope, §1817.

**RECALCITRANT WITNESSES.**
Civil contempt proceedings, §425.
Criminal contempt proceedings, §426.

**RECENT POSSESSION OF FRUITS OF CRIME.**
Permissible inference, §1513.

**RECESS OF TRIAL.**
Sanctions for failure to provide discovery, §716.

**RECORDED RECOLLECTION.**
Hearsay exceptions, availability of declarant immaterial, §2122.

**RECORDINGS.**
Audio recordings.
Admissibility, §1602.
Video recordings.
Admissibility, §1603.

**RECORDS AND REPORTS.**
Best evidence rule, §§1705 to 1707.
See BEST EVIDENCE RULE.
Demonstrative evidence generally, §§1600 to 1611.
See DEMONSTRATIVE EVIDENCE.
Discovery of defendants prior criminal records, §707.
Discovery of examinations and test reports, §709.
Documentary evidence.
Generally, §§1701 to 1708.
See DOCUMENTARY EVIDENCE.
Family records.
Hearsay exception, availability of declarant immaterial, §2128.
Grand jury report, §427.
Interest in property.
Hearsay exception, availability of declarant immaterial.
Documents and statements affecting, §2129.
Judicial notice of records and matters in court files, §1403.
Official documents.
Authentication and admissibility generally, §1702.
Presentence investigation and reports, §§1316 to 1318.
Private or nonofficial documents.
Authentication and admissibility, §1703.

**RECORDS AND REPORTS**—Cont'd
Public records and reports.
Authentication and admissibility, §1702.
Hearsay exception, availability of declarant immaterial.
Absence of record or entry, §2127.
Generally, §2125.
Vital statistics, §2126.
Regularly conducted activity.
Hearsay exception, availability of declarant immaterial, §2123.
Absence of entries in records, §2124.
Religious organizations.
Hearsay exception, availability of declarant immaterial, §2128.
Self-incrimination.
Reporting provisions, §1905.
State records.
Immune from grand jury process, §409.

**REDACTION.**
Deleting reference to non-confessing defendant, §314.

**REFRESHING RECOLLECTION,** §1802.
Inspection of exhibit, §1803.
Use on cross-examination, §1804.

**REGISTRATION.**
Self-incrimination.
Registration provisions, §1905.

**REGULARITY OF PROCEEDINGS.**
Presumptions, §1512.

**RELEASE OR DETENTION.**
Generally, §§506 to 522.
See BAIL.

**RELEVANT EVIDENCE.**
Generally, §1517.

**RELIEF FROM PREJUDICIAL JOINDER.**
Severance generally.
See SEVERANCE.

**RELIGIOUS ORGANIZATION RECORDS.**
Hearsay exceptions, availability of declarant immaterial.
Marriage, baptismal and similar certificates, §2128.

**REMOVAL.**
Hearings, §502.
Speedy trial act excludes delay caused by removal of defendant, §1224.

**REPORTER-SOURCE PRIVILEGE,** §1922.

**REPORTS.**
See RECORDS AND REPORTS.

**REPRESENTATIVE ADMISSIONS,** §2115.

**REPRIMAND.**
Prosecutorial misconduct sanctions, §1117.

**REPUTATION.**
Hearsay exceptions, availability of declarant immaterial.
Personal or family history, boundaries or general history or character, §2133.
Impeachment.
Use of character evidence, §1808.
Methods of proving character, §1519.

**RESERVATION OF EVIDENCE.**
Brady doctrine, §724.

**RES GESTAE,** §2106.

**RESTITUTION.**
Victims assistance, §1337.

**RETALIATION AGAINST ACCUSED.**
Prosecutorial vindictiveness, §1118.

**RETRIAL.**
Defendant successfully appealing conviction, §1010.
Speedy trial act, §1217.

**REVERSAL ON APPEAL.**
Release pending appeal, §518.

**RIGHT TO APPEAL.**
Notice to defendant, §1345.

**RIGHT TO COUNSEL.**
Civil contempt proceeding, §425.
Confessions and rights to silence and counsel generally, §§305 to 311.
See MIRANDA WARNINGS.
Custodial interrogations, §301.
Identifications before trial, §317.
Initial appearance, §501.
Pleas, §602.
Preliminary examination, §503.
When right attaches, §305.

**RIGHT TO SILENCE.**
Confessions and rights to silence and counsel generally, §§305 to 311.
See MIRANDA WARNINGS.

**RIGHT TO SPEEDY TRIAL,** §1202.
Speedy trial generally, §§1201 to 1239.
See SPEEDY TRIAL.

**RIGHT TO TRIAL BY JURY,** §1240.
Jury trial generally.
See JURY TRIAL.

**ROADBLOCKS.**
Sobriety checkpoints.
Constitutionality, §228.

**ROADSIDE QUESTIONING.**
Miranda warnings not required, §305.

**RULE OF COMPLETENESS.**
Use of entire writing or recorded statement, §1708.

**RULES AND REGULATIONS.**
Judicial notice, §1403.

**RULES OF CRIMINAL PROCEDURE,** Appendix B.

**RULES OF EVIDENCE,** Appendix C.

**S**

**SAME EVIDENCE TEST.**
Subsequent prosecution for offenses with identical statutory elements, §1002.

**SANCTIONS FOR FAILURE TO OBSERVE SPEEDY TRIAL ACT,** §1234.

**SANCTIONS FOR FAILURE TO PROVIDE DISCOVERY,** §716.

**SANCTIONS FOR PROSECUTORIAL MISCONDUCT,** §1117.

**SANITIZATION.**
Deleting reference to non-confessing defendant, §314.

**SANITY.**
Presumptions, §1508.

**SCALE MODELS.**
Admissibility, §1607.

**SCHEME.**
Proof of other crimes, §1526.

**SCHOLAR'S PRIVILEGE,** §1924.

**SCIENTIFIC KNOWLEDGE.**
Testimony of experts, §2003.

**SCIENTIFIC TESTS.**
Admissibility, §1609.

**SEALED INDICTMENTS,** §417.

**SEARCHES AND SEIZURES,** §§201 to 256.
Abandoned property, §239.
Anti-skyjacking searches, §241.
Arrest.
  Search incident to valid arrest, §§218 to 226.
    Areas within arrestee's immediate control, §226.
    Arrest in good faith and not pretext to search, §221.
    Articles carried by arrestee, §225.
    Generally, §218.
    Scope of search generally, §223.
    Search contemporaneous with arrest, §222.
    Search of person, §224.
    Validity of arrest, §219.
    When person under arrest, §220.
Body cavity searches.
  Search of person incident to lawful arrest, §224.
Border searches, §229.
Confessions.
  Improper search tainting valid confessions, §312.
Consent searches, §§243 to 245.
  Generally, §243.

**SEARCHES AND SEIZURES**—Cont'd
Consent searches—Cont'd
  Third-party consent, §245.
  Use of deceit to secure consent, §244.
Contraband.
  Destruction or removal, §233.
Customs searches, §229.
Electronic surveillance generally, §§257 to 268.
  See WIRETAPPING AND ELECTRONIC SURVEILLANCE.
Emergencies.
  Officers responding to, §232.
Escape of suspect likely, §233.
Evidence affected by search and seizure, §§247 to 256.
  Exclusionary rule, §248.
  Motions to suppress.
    Appeals, §256.
    Burden of proof, §252.
    Evidentiary rules, §253.
    Right to hearing, §254.
    Standing, §255.
    Timing of motions, §250.
  Property that may be seized, §247.
Exclusionary rule, §248.
Exigent circumstances to justify warrantless search, §§231 to 234.
  Generally, §231.
  Hot pursuit, §234.
  Officers responding to emergencies, §232.
  Threatened destruction or removal of contraband or likely escape, §235.
Foreign searches of aliens, §203.
Fourth amendment protections generally, §201.
Hot pursuit, §234.
Motions to suppress, §§250 to 256.
  Appeals, §256.
  Burden of proof, §252.
  Exclusionary rules during hearing, §253.
  Right to hearing, §254.
  Standing, §255.
  Timing, §250.
Open fields doctrine, §240.
Plain view evidence, §§238 to 240.
  Abandoned property, §239.

**SEARCHES AND SEIZURES**—Cont'd
Plain view evidence—Cont'd
Curtilage and open fields doctrine,
§240.
Generally, §238.
Prison searches, §242.
Privacy expectation test, §201.
Private searches, §202.
Probable cause.
Seizures without probable cause,
§§227 to 230.
Property that may be seized, §247.
Seizures without probable cause, §§227
to 230.
Border and custom searches, §229.
Detention of occupants while home
searched pursuant to warrant,
§230.
Generally, §227.
Stop and frisk, §228.
Stop and frisk, §228.
Strip searches.
Search of person incident to lawful
arrest, §224.
Suppression motions, §§250 to 256.
Vehicle seizures, §§235 to 237.
Containers found in vehicle, §237.
Generally, §235.
Inventory searches, §236.
Warrantless searches.
Anti-skyjacking searches, §241.
Consent searches, §243.
Third-party consent, §245.
Use of deceit to secure consent,
§244.
Exigent circumstances to justifying
search, §231.
Hot pursuit, §234.
Officers responding to emergencies,
§232.
Threatened destruction or removal
of contraband or likely escape,
§233.
Generally, §217.
Incident to valid arrest, §218.
Areas within arrestee's immediate
control, §226.
Arrest in good faith not pretext to
search, §221.

**SEARCHES AND SEIZURES**—Cont'd
Warrantless searches—Cont'd
Incident to valid arrest—Cont'd
Articles carried by arrestee, §225.
Scope of searches, §223.
Search contemporaneous with
arrest, §222.
Search of person, §224.
Validity of arrest, §219.
When person under arrest, §220.
Plain view evidence, §238.
Abandoned property, §239.
Curtilage and open fields doctrine,
§240.
Prison searches, §242.
Seizures without probable cause,
§227.
Border and custom searches, §229.
Detention of occupants while home
searched pursuant to warrant,
§230.
Stop and frisk, §228.
Vehicle searches, §235.
Containers found, §237.
Inventory searches, §236.
Warrants.
Affidavit, §206.
False statements, §210.
Presumption of validity, §210.
Anticipatory warrants, §205.
Description.
Particularity, §211.
Execution.
Manner of entry, §215.
When executed, §214.
Who may execute, §213.
Generally, §204.
General warrants prohibited, §211.
Hearsay.
Establishing probable cause, §207.
Informants.
Establishing probable cause, §207.
Items to be seized particularized, §211.
Open-ended warrants prohibited, §211.
Particularity of description, §211.
Probable cause, §206.
Established by hearsay, §207.
False statements in affidavit, §210.
Neutrality of magistrate, §209.

**SEARCHES AND SEIZURES**—Cont'd
Warrants—Cont'd
Probable cause—Cont'd
Sufficiency determination, §208.
Who may issue, §205.
Telephone search warrants, §216.
Wiretapping and other electronic
surveillance, §§257 to 268.
See WIRETAPPING AND
ELECTRONIC SURVEILLANCE.

**SECONDARY EVIDENCE.**
Admissibility under best evidence rule,
§1707.

**SECRECY OF GRAND JURY
PROCEEDINGS,** §§410 to 417.
See GRAND JURY.

**SELF-INCRIMINATION.**
Advising person in custody of
constitutional rights, §1906.
Applicability of privilege, §1902.
Assertion on behalf of another, §1902.
Attorney asserting client's privilege,
§1902.
Comment on failure to testify, §1907.
Confessions generally, §§301 to 315.
See CONFESSIONS.
Exercise of privilege, §1904.
Generally, §1901.
Guilty plea.
Effect, §603.
Immunity of witnesses generally, §§419
to 423.
See IMMUNITY OF WITNESSES.
Natural persons.
Privilege applies only to, §1902.
Perjury.
Privilege not used as license to lie,
§1903.
Production of documents incriminating
in nature, §1902.
Prosecutorial misconduct.
Forcing claim of privilege, §1109.
Registration provisions, §1905.
Reporting provisions, §1905.
Scope of privilege, §1903.
Silence used to impeach testimony at
trial, §1906.

**SELF-INCRIMINATION**—Cont'd
Testimonial or communicative evidence
protected, §1903.
Waiver of privilege, §1906.

**SENTENCING,** §§1306 to 1346.
Acceptance of responsibility.
Application of guidelines, §1323.
Aggravating circumstances.
Departure from guidelines, §1324.
Allocution, §1321.
Appeals.
Departure from guidelines, §1327.
Review of sentences generally, §1346.
Application of guidelines, §1323.
Career offenders.
Application of guidelines, §1323.
Charge offense sentencing, §1310.
Civil contempt proceedings, §425.
Commission.
Duties, §1307.
Comprehensive crime control act.
Sentencing commission established,
§1307.
Concurrent sentences, §1330.
Consecutive sentences, §1330.
Constitutionality of sentencing reform
act, §1312.
Correction of sentence, §1343.
Credit for good behavior, §1307.
Criminal contempt proceedings, §426.
Criminal history of defendant.
Application of guidelines, §1323.
Criminal livelihood.
Application of guidelines, §1323.
Delays.
Imposition of sentence, §1320.
Departure from guidelines, §§1324 to
1328.
Appeal, §1327.
Generally, §1324.
Increase sentence, §1325.
Reduce sentence, §1326.
Substantial assistance to authorities,
§1328.
Disputed sentencing facts.
Resolving, §1339.
Double jeopardy, §1012.
Effective date of sentencing reform act,
§1311.

**SENTENCING**—Cont'd
Factors considered in imposition, §1322.
Fines, §§1332 to 1334.
    Factors considered in imposing, §1333.
    Imposition generally, §1332.
    Modification or remission, §1334.
Guidelines.
    Application, §1323.
    Constitutional challenges, §1312.
    Departure from, §§1324 to 1328.
        Appeal, §1327.
        Generally, §1324.
        Increase sentence, §1325.
        Reduce sentence, §1326.
        Substantial assistance to
            authorities, §1328.
    Duties of sentencing commission,
        §1307.
    Factors considered, §1322.
    Generally, §1308.
    Plea agreements, §§1313 to 1315.
        Generally, §1313.
        Procedure, §1314.
        Standards for acceptance, §1315.
    Policy considerations, §1309.
Guilty pleas or nolo contendere.
    Withdrawal after sentence, §619.
    Withdrawal before sentence, §618.
Harsher sentence imposed upon
    conviction on retrial, §1012.
Increase sentence.
    Departure from guidelines, §1325.
Introduction, §1307.
Judgment of conviction, §1342.
Juvenile offenders, §1341.
Mitigating circumstances.
    Departure from guidelines, §1324.
Modification after imposition, §1344.
Organizations, §1340.
Plea agreements under sentencing
    reform act, §§1313 to 1315.
    Agreements not to undermine act,
        §611.
    Generally, §1313.
    Plea bargaining generally.
        See PLEA BARGAINING.
    Procedure, §1314.
    Standards for acceptance, §1315.
Policy consideration, §1309.

**SENTENCING**—Cont'd
Policy statements.
    Generally, §1308.
Presentence investigation and reports,
    §§1316 to 1318.
    Contents, §1317.
    Disclosure, §1318.
    Disputed sentencing fact resolution,
        §1339.
    Generally, §1316.
    Victim impact statements part of,
        §1337.
Probation, §1329.
Real offense system, §1310.
Reduced sentence.
    Departure from guidelines, §1326.
    Modification after imposition, §1344.
Release pending sentencing, §515.
Review of sentences, §1346.
Substantial assistance to authorities.
    Departure from guidelines, §1328.
Supervisory release after imprisonment,
    §1331.
Suspension of sentence.
    Double jeopardy not bar to revocation,
        §1012.
Time for imposition, §1320.
Unnecessary delays.
    Imposition of sentence, §1320.
Venue transfer for plea and sentence,
    §113.
Victims assistance, §§1336 to 1338.
    Notice to victims, §1338.
    Restitution, §1337.
    Special assessments, §1336.
Withdrawal of guilty plea or nolo
    contendere.
    After sentence, §619.
    Before sentence, §618.

**SENTENCING REFORM ACT.**
Constitutionality, §1312.
Effective date, §1311.
Plea agreements may not be used to
    undermine, §611.
Sentencing generally, §§1306 to 1346.
    See SENTENCING.

**SEPARATION OF WITNESSES,**
    §1819.

**SEVERANCE,** §§910 to 918.
Defendants, §§913 to 917.
  Confession of codefendants, §915.
  Conflicting defenses, §916.
  Conspiracy, §917.
  Generally, §913.
  Need for codefendant's testimony,
    §914.
Discretion of court, §911.
Generally, §910.
Offenses, §912.
Speedy trial act excludes delay caused
  by, §1230.
Waiver, §918.

**SHOWUPS.**
Identifications before trial generally,
  §§316 to 319.
  See IDENTIFICATIONS BEFORE
    TRIAL.

**SIBLING PRIVILEGE,** §1924.

**SILENCE.**
Confessions and rights to silence and
  counsel generally, §§305 to 311.
  See MIRANDA WARNINGS.
Defendant's adoptive admission, §2114.
Impeachment of defendant's credibility,
  §1818.
Prosecutorial misconduct.
  Closing argument comment on post-
    arrest and in-trial silence, §1115.

**SIXTH AMENDMENT
  PROTECTIONS.**
Hearsay exceptions, declarant
  unavailable.
  Confrontation clause limitations,
    §2139.
Identifications before trial, §317.
Miranda warnings.
  See MIRANDA WARNINGS.
Right to counsel.
  See RIGHT TO COUNSEL.
Right to trial by jury, §1240.
Speedy trial, §§1201 to 1239.
  See SPEEDY TRIAL.

**SKYJACKING.**
Anti-skyjacking searches, §241.

**SOBRIETY CHECKPOINTS.**
Constitutionality, §228.

**SPECIAL ASSESSMENTS.**
Victims assistance, §1336.

**SPECIALIZED KNOWLEDGE.**
Testimony of experts, §2003.

**SPECIAL VERDICTS,** §1256.
Criminal forfeiture, §1257.

**SPEECH IMPAIRED PERSONS.**
Use of interpreters during examination,
  §1820.

**SPEED OF MOVING OBJECTS OR
  VEHICLES.**
Lay witness testimony, §2001.

**SPEEDY TRIAL,** §§1201 to 1239.
Constitutional speedy trial protection,
  §§1203 to 1209.
  Balancing test, §1205.
  Generally, §1203.
  Length of delay, §1206.
  Prejudice to defendant caused by
    delay, §1209.
  Reasons for delay, §1207.
  Timely assertion of right, §1208.
  When right attaches, §1204.
Pre-accusation delay, §1239.
Right to, §1202.
Speedy trial act, §§1210 to 1238.
  Appeal, §1238.
  Applicability, §1211.
  Dismissal by court, §1237.
  Excludable time, §1218.
    Absence or unavailability of
      defendant or witness, §1228.
    Continuance which furthers ends of
      justice, §1231.
    Examination, deferral and
      treatment, §1220.
    Interlocutory appeals, §1222.
    Joinder and severance, §1230.
    Other proceedings, §1219.
    Physical or mental incapacity,
      §1229.
    Plea agreements, §1225.
    Pretrial diversions, §1227.
    Pretrial motions, §1223.

**SPEEDY TRIAL**—Cont'd
Speedy trial act—Cont'd
　Excludable time—Cont'd
　　Proceedings under advisement,
　　　§1226.
　　Removal of defendant or transfer of
　　　case, §1224.
　　Trial of defendant on other charges,
　　　§1221.
　　First interval, §1212.
　　Generally, §1210.
　　High risk designees and detainees,
　　　§1236.
　　Incarcerated defendant, §1233.
　　Reinstitution.
　　　Appeals, §1216.
　　　Dismissed charges, §1215.
　　　Retrial, §1217.
　　Sanctions, §1234.
　　Second interval, §1213.
　　Waiver, §1235.
　　Withdrawn pleas, §1232.

**SPEEDY TRIAL ACT.**
Generally, §§1210 to 1238.
　See SPEEDY TRIAL.

**SPOKEN WORDS.**
Lay witness testimony as to meaning,
　§2001.

**SPONTANEOUS DECLARATIONS,**
　§2106.
Excited utterances, §2119.

**SPOUSAL PRIVILEGE.**
Generally, §§1909 to 1914.
　See MARITAL COMMUNICATIONS
　　PRIVILEGE.

**STANDING.**
Motions to suppress, §255.
　Electronic surveillance, §266.

**STATE LAWS.**
Judicial notice, §1403.

**STATEMENTS AGAINST
　INTEREST.**
Hearsay exceptions, declarant
　unavailable.
　Generally, §2144.
　Penal interest offered to exculpate,
　　§2145.

**STATE OF MIND.**
Lay witness testimony, §2001.

**STATE RECORDS.**
Immune from grand jury process, §409.

**STIPULATIONS.**
Admissions by defendant, §2113.

**STOP AND FRISK, §228.**
Anti-skyjacking profile, §241.

**STRIP SEARCHES.**
Prison searches generally, §242.
Search of person incident to lawful
　arrest, §224.

**SUBJECT MATTER
　JURISDICTION, §102.**

**SUBPOENAS.**
Grand jury.
　Calling and questioning of witnesses,
　　§404.
　Contempt to enforce subpoenas, §§424
　　to 426.
Production of documentary evidence and
　objects, §717.

**SUBPOENAS DUCES TECUM.**
Grand jury, §409.
Production of documentary evidence and
　objects, §717.

**SUBSTANTIAL ASSISTANCE TO
　AUTHORITIES.**
Departure from sentencing guidelines,
　§1328.

**SUBSTANTIAL QUESTION.**
Release pending appeal, §517.

**SUFFICIENCY OF EVIDENCE.**
Motion for acquittal generally, §§1271 to
　1276.
　See MOTION FOR ACQUITTAL.

**SUGGESTIVE IDENTIFICATION
　PROCEDURES.**
Fifth amendment due process rights,
　§318.

**SUMMARY CHARTS.**
Admissibility, §1605.

**SUMMARY CONTEMPT.**
Criminal contempt proceedings, §426.

**SUPERVISORY RELEASE AFTER IMPRISONMENT,** §1331.

**SUPPLEMENTAL JUROR INSTRUCTIONS,** §1260.

**SUPPRESSION MOTIONS,** §§250 to 256.
See MOTIONS TO SUPPRESS.

**SUPPRESSION OF EVIDENCE.**
Admissibility, §1530.

**SURREPTITIOUS ENTRY.**
Wiretapping authorization, §263.

**SUSPENSION OF SENTENCE.**
Double jeopardy not bar to revocation, §1012.

**T**

**TAPE RECORDINGS.**
Admissibility of audio recordings, §1602.
Admissibility of video recordings, §1603.
Discovery of statements of defendants, §706.

**TAX CASES.**
Venue, §105.

**TECHNICAL KNOWLEDGE.**
Testimony of experts, §2003.

**TELEPHONE SEARCH WARRANTS,** §216.

**TERRITORIAL JURISDICTION,** §101.

**TESTS.**
Discovery of reports, §709.

**THEORY OF DEFENSE.**
Jury instructions, §1266.

**THIRD-PARTY CONSENT TO SEARCH,** §245.

**THREATS.**
Confessions, §313.
Guilty plea induced by threats, §606.
Use to secure consent to search, §244.

**TIME FOR DISCLOSURE UNDER BRADY DOCTRINE,** §723.

**TIME FOR MOTION FOR ARREST OF JUDGMENT,** §1305.

**TIME FOR MOTION FOR NEW TRIAL,** §1304.

**TIME FOR MOTION OF ACQUITTAL,** §§1273 to 1276.

**TIMELY ASSERTION OF SPEEDY TRIAL RIGHTS,** §1208.

**TIME OR DATE OF OFFENSE.**
Burden of proof, §1503.

**TIME SEARCH WARRANT TO BE EXECUTED,** §214.

**TIMING OF MOTIONS TO SUPPRESS,** §250.

**TITLE III OF OMNIBUS CRIME CONTROL AND SAFE STREETS ACT OF 1968.**
Wiretapping and other electronic surveillance generally, §§257 to 268.
See WIRETAPPING AND ELECTRONIC SURVEILLANCE.

**TOMBSTONES.**
Hearsay exception, availability of declarant immaterial.
Statements of fact concerning personal or family history, §2128.

**TRANSCRIPTS OF TAPE RECORDED CONVERSATIONS.**
Admissibility, §1602.

**TRANSFER OF CASES.**
Speedy trial act excludes delay caused by, §1224.

**TRANSFER OF VENUE,** §110.
Convenience, §112.
For plea and sentence, §113.
Prejudiced to defendant, §111.

**TRANSPORTATION IN INTERSTATE COMMERCE.**
Venue of offenses, §106.

**TREATIES.**
Judicial notice, §1403.

**TREATISES.**
Hearsay exception, availability of declarant immaterial.
Learned treatises, §2132.

**TREATMENT.**
Medical diagnosis or treatment.
  Hearsay exception, availability of
    declarant immaterial, §2121.
Speedy trial act excludes delays
    resulting from, §1220.

**TRIAL BY JURY.**
Generally.
  See JURY TRIAL.

**TRIAL DISCOVERY OF PRIOR
  STATEMENTS.**
Generally, §§801 to 814.
  See JENCKS ACT AND RULE 26.2.

**TRICKERY.**
Use to secure consent to search, §244.

**TRUSTS.**
Sentencing of organizations, §1340.


**U**

**ULTIMATE ISSUE RULE.**
Expert testimony, §2005.
Lay witness testimony, §2001.

**UNAVAILABLILITY OF
  DEFENDANT OR WITNESS.**
Speedy trial act excludes delays, §1228.

**UNINCORPORATED
  ASSOCIATIONS OR
  ORGANIZATIONS.**
Self-incrimination privilege.
  Production of books of organization,
    §1902.
Sentencing, §1340.

**UNIONS.**
Self-incrimination privilege.
  Production of books of organization,
    §1902.
Sentencing of organizations, §1340.

**UNNECESSARY DELAYS.**
Imposition of sentence, §1320.
Initial appearance, §501.
  Confessions, §304.
Pre-accusation delays, §1239.
Speedy trial generally, §§1201 to 1239.
  See SPEEDY TRIAL.

**USE IMMUNITY CONCEPT.**
Immunity of witnesses generally, §§419
    to 423.
  See IMMUNITY OF WITNESSES.


**V**

**VALUE OF PROPERTY.**
Expert testimony, §2003.
Lay witness testimony, §2001.

**VEHICLE SEARCHES.**
Containers found in, §237.
Generally, §235.
Inventory searches, §236.
Stop and frisk principles, §228.

**VENUE,** §104.
Burden of proof, §108.
Confessions.
  Established solely by confession, §303.
Defined, §§101, 104.
Generally, §§101, 104.
Multiple counts, §903.
Proof, §108.
State and district of crime.
  Generally, §105.
  Offenses committed in more than one
    district, §106.
  Offenses not committed in any
    district, §107.
Transfer, §110.
  Convenience, §112.
  For plea and sentence, §113.
  Prejudice to defendant, §111.
Waiver, §109.

**VERDICT.**
Impeachment.
  Post-verdict juror interrogation, §1259.
Interrogation of jury.
  Post-verdict, §1259.
Polling jurors, §1262.
Post-verdict juror interrogation, §1259.
Special interrogatories to jury, §1258.
Special verdicts, §1256.
  Criminal forfeiture special verdicts,
    §1257.
Unanimous jury verdict, §1242.

**VICARIOUS ADMISSIONS,** §2115.

**VICTIM IMPACT STATEMENTS.**
Part of presentence investigation, §1337.

**VICTIMS ASSISTANCE, §§1336 to 1338.**
Notice to victims, §1338.
Restitution, §1337.
Special assessments, §1336.

**VIDEO RECORDINGS.**
Admissibility, §1603.

**VINDICTIVENESS OF PROSECUTOR, §1118.**
Introductions, §1100.

**VITAL STATISTICS.**
Hearsay exception, availability of declarant immaterial, §2126.

**VOICEPRINTS OR SPECTOGRAMS.**
Expert testimony, §2003.

**VOIR DIRE, §1246.**

**VOLUNTARINESS OF GUILTY PLEAS OR NOLO CONTENDERE, §606.**

**VOLUNTEERED STATEMENTS.**
Miranda rights do not attach to, §306.

**W**

**WAIVER OF ATTORNEY-CLIENT PRIVILEGE, §1919.**

**WAIVER OF DOUBLE JEOPARDY DEFENSE, §1001.**

**WAIVER OF JURY TRIAL, §1243.**

**WAIVER OF MARITAL COMMUNICATIONS PRIVILEGE, §1913.**

**WAIVER OF OBJECTIONS TO JURY INSTRUCTIONS, §1254.**

**WAIVER OF PERSONAL JURISDICTION, §103.**

**WAIVER OF SELF-INCRIMINATION PRIVILEGE, §1906.**

**WAIVER OF SEVERANCE OF CHARGES OR DEFENDANTS, §918.**

**WAIVER OF SPEEDY TRIAL ACT, §1235.**

**WAIVER OF SUBJECT MATTER JURISDICTION, §102.**

**WAIVER OF VENUE, §109.**

**WAIVER OF WORK-PRODUCT DOCTRINE, §1920.**

**WARRANTLESS SEARCHES, §§217 to 245.**
See SEARCHES AND SEIZURES.

**WARRANTS.**
Search warrants generally.
See SEARCHES AND SEIZURES.

**WIRETAPPING AND ELECTRONIC SURVEILLANCE, §§257 to 268.**
Audio recordings.
Admissibility, §1602.
Consent of one party, §268.
Court order, interception pursuant to, §§258 to 267.
Application, §261.
Authorization, §259.
Generally, §258.
Minimization of interception, §264.
Motion to suppress, §266.
Order, §262.
Scope of statute, §267.
Sealing of applications, orders, etc., §265.
Surreptitious entry, §263.
Discovery.
Recorded statements of defendants, §706.
Generally, §257.
Grand jury questions based on illegal surveillance, §407.
Video recordings.
Admissibility, §1603.

**WITHDRAWAL OF GUILTY PLEAS OR NOLO CONTENDERE, §§617 to 619.**
After sentence, §619.
Before sentence, §618.
Generally, §617.
Speedy trial act excludes delays, §1232.

**WITNESSES.**

Absence or unavailability.
  Speedy trial act excludes delays, §1228.
Compelling testimony.
  Immunity generally, §§419 to 423.
    See IMMUNITY OF WITNESSES.
Contempt to enforce grand jury subpoenas and orders compelling testimony, §§424 to 426.
Credibility.
  Jury instructions on, §1270.
Discovery of witness statements and identities, §712.
Examination of witnesses generally, §§1801 to 1820.
  See EXAMINATION OF WITNESSES.
Failure to call.
  Inference, §1514.
Grand jury proceedings.
  Calling and questioning of witnesses, §§404 to 408.
    See GRAND JURY.
  Disclosures by or to witnesses, §415.

**WITNESSES**—Cont'd

Immunity of witnesses, §§419 to 423.
  See IMMUNITY OF WITNESSES.
Impeachment.
  Statements taken in violation of fifth and sixth amendments, §311.
Inference resulting from failure to call, §1514.
Material witnesses.
  Release, §520.
Missing witness inference, §1514.
Prior statements.
  Trial discovery generally, §§801 to 814.
    See JENCKS ACT AND RULE 26.2.
Separation of witnesses, §1819.
Transfer of venue for convenience of, §112.

**WORDS SPOKEN.**

Lay witness testimony as to meaning, §2001.

**WORK-PRODUCT**, §1920.
Discovery, §712.